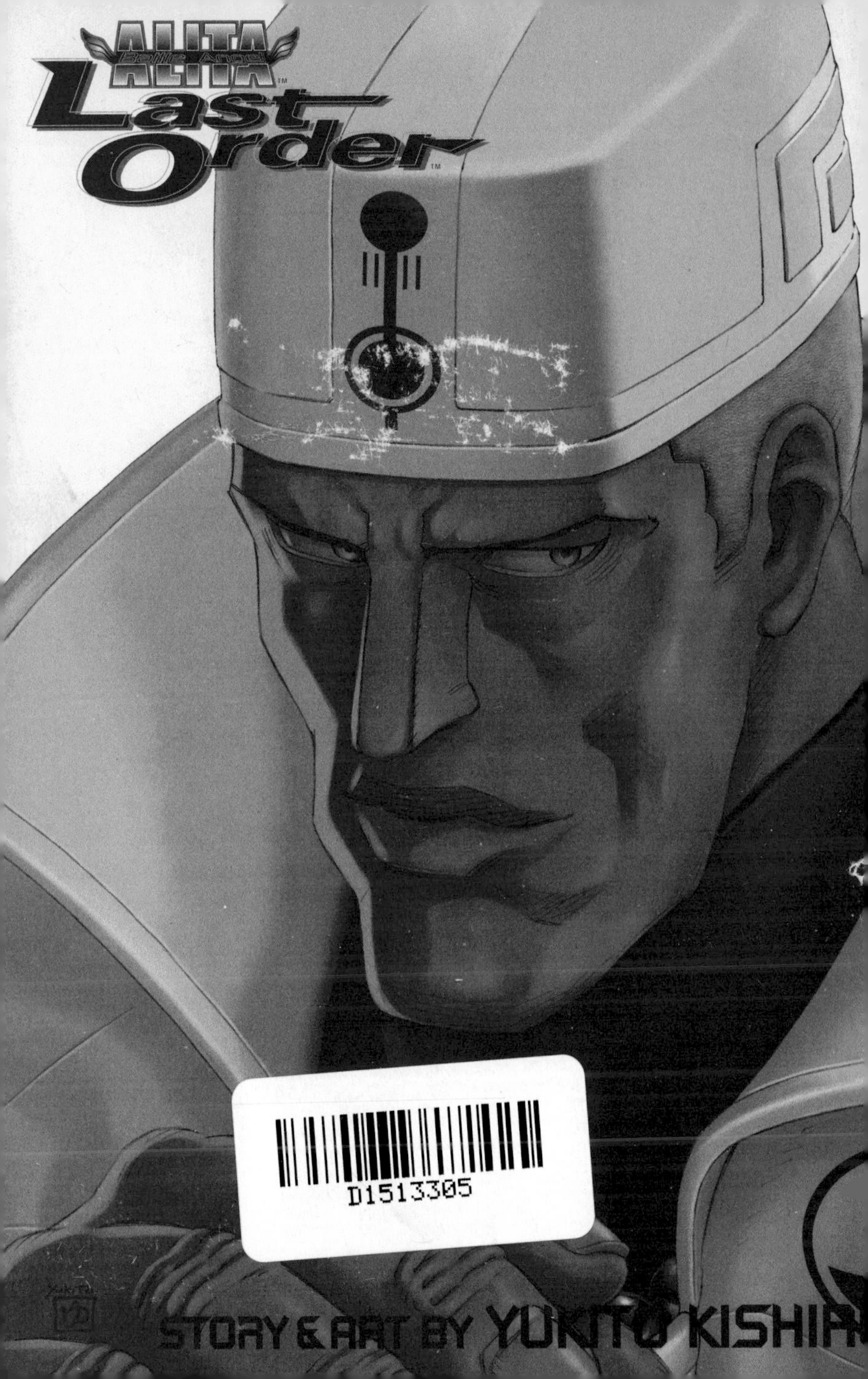
ALITA
Battle Angel
ALITA™
Last Order™
STORY & ART BY YUKITO KISHIR

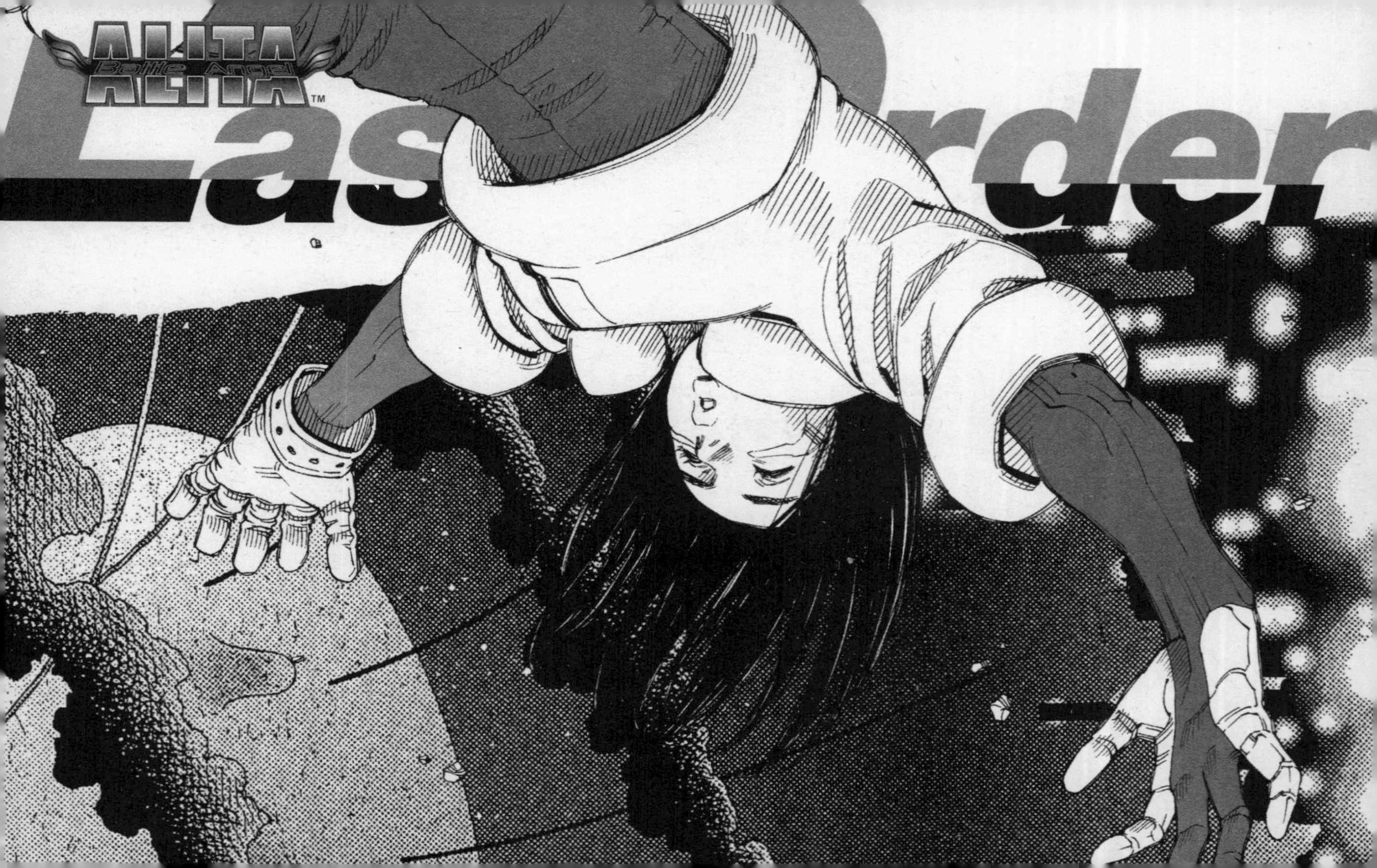

ALITA Battle Angel™
Last Order

OUTLINE

The Future. The development of cyborg technology cheapened human life. The sky city Tiphares dominated life on the surface, and directly beneath it, built on the trash it threw away, was a unique community called the Scrapyard. Amid a tumultuous city full of crime, people struggled to survive.

It was there that Ido, a cybernetic doctor in the Scrapyard, found the head of a cyborg several hundred years old in a pile of rubble. Miraculously resurrected, the girl was named Alita. She had lost her memory, but her flesh remembered the legendary martial art Panzer Kunst. With Ido by her side, she became a bounty hunter and started down the path to self-discovery.

But an incident caused by the genius Tipharean scientist known as Nova led to Ido's death. Alita herself was arrested as a criminal by the Tipharean organization G.I.B. She was then forced to become a TUNED, an agent of Tiphares, and began to hunt down Nova, who held the key to Ido's resurrection.

After a series of battles, Alita cornered and defeated Nova, but he revealed a shocking truth: The brains of the people of Tiphares had been replaced with microchips. Even they were nothing more than experimental guinea pigs.

Are Tiphareans human or machine? The secret revealed by Nova turns Tiphares upside down, and leads Alita into new battles...

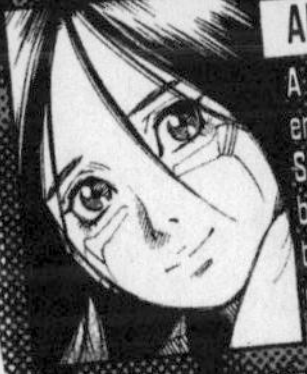

Alita (Yoko): A cyborg girl discovered in a pile of trash. She lost her memory, but her body knows the legendary art of Panzer Kunst.

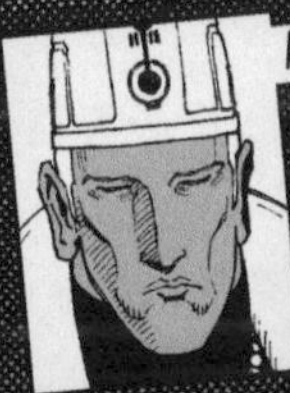

Aga Mbadi: A hero who saved humanity from a crisis, he is the de facto head of LADDER. His alias is Trinidad.

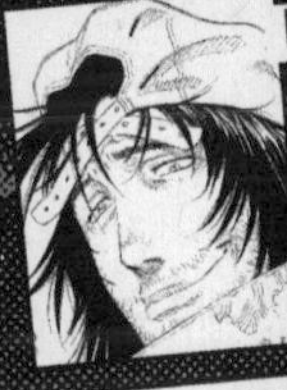

Ping Wu: A genius hacker, who once plotted against LADDER. Since being defeated by Mbadi, he's lived in the shadows in Ketheres.

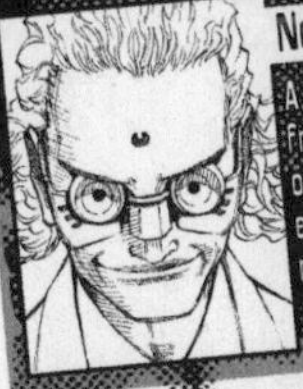

Nova: A scientific genius from Tiphares. An obsessive and extremely dangerous man, he feels bound by no social norms.

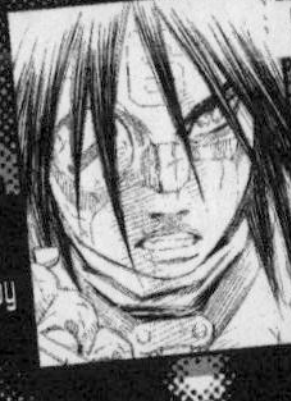

Sechs: An AR series robot, she wants to defeat Alita to prove herself. She has a massive gun in her right arm.

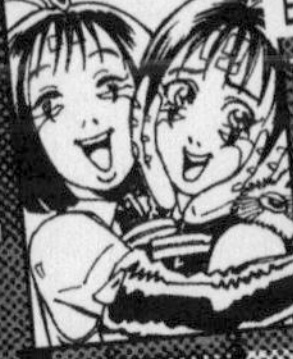

Elf & Zwölf: Two of the surviving AR series robots, built as replicas of Alita. Serving as Nova's bodyguards.

CONTENTS

PHASE 19
What Makes a Warrior

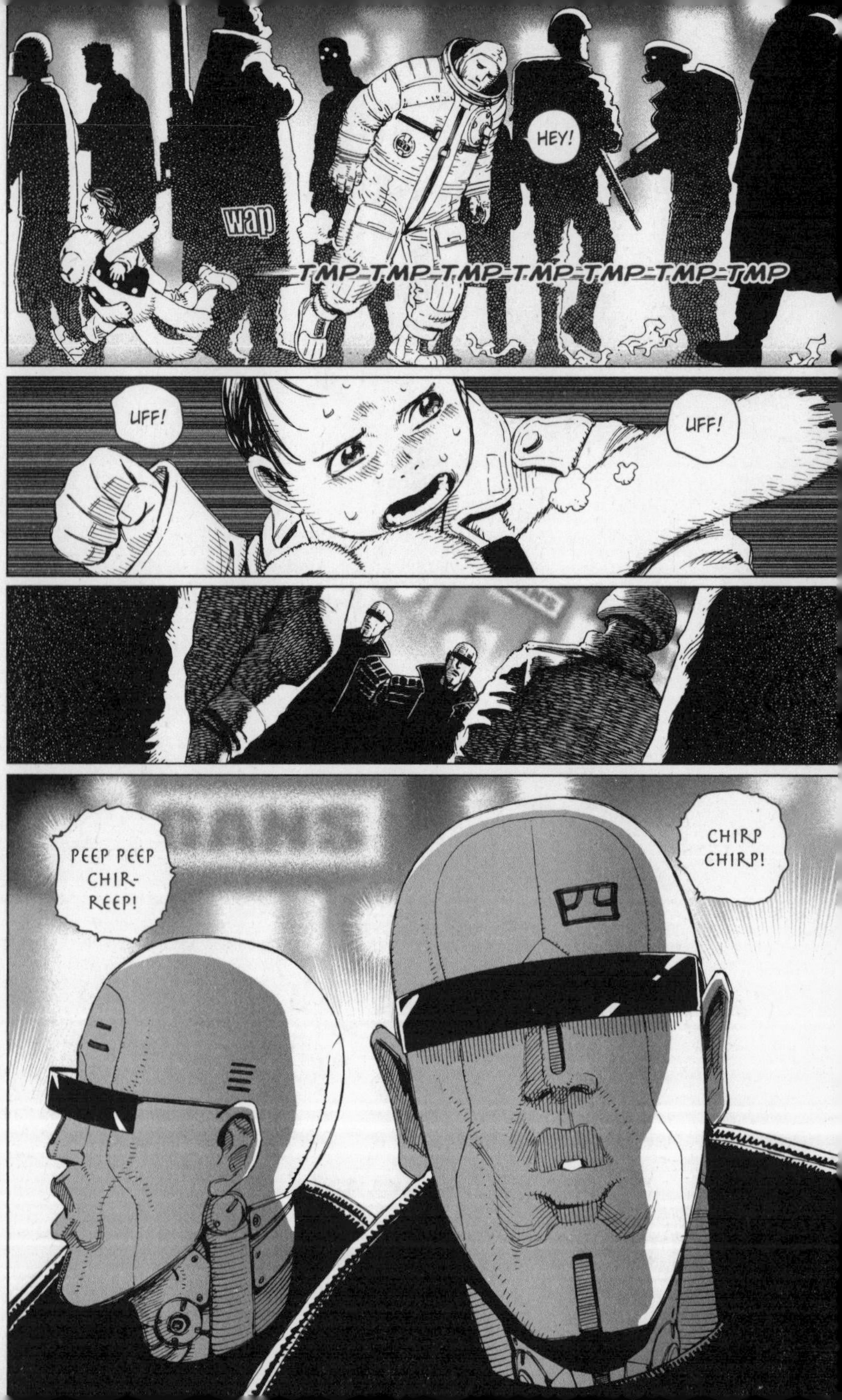
HEY!
wap
TMP TMP TMP TMP TMP TMP TMP
UFF!
UFF!
CHIRP CHIRP!
PEEP PEEP CHIR-REEP!

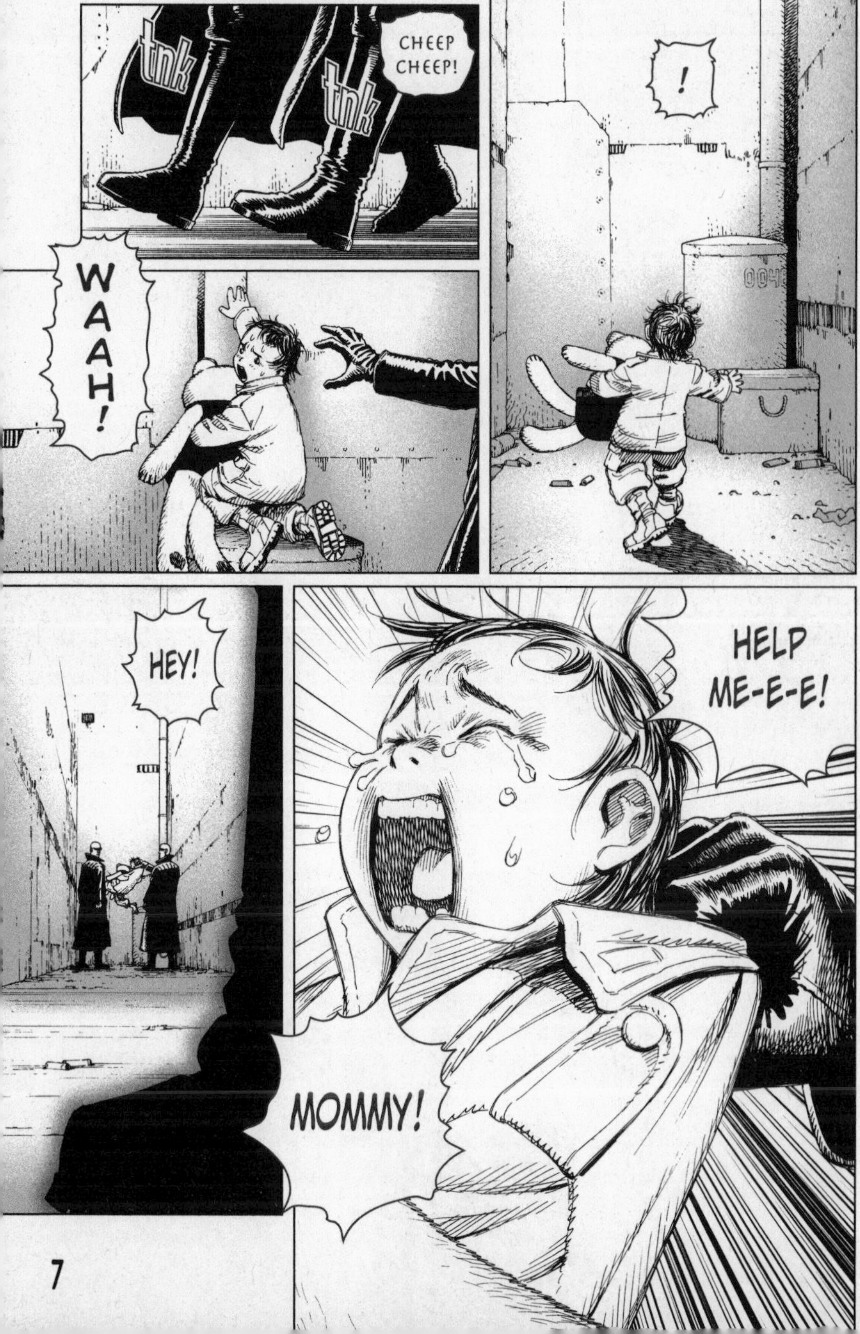
!
CHEEP CHEEP!
tnk
tnk
WAAH!
HELP ME-E-E!
MOMMY!
HEY!

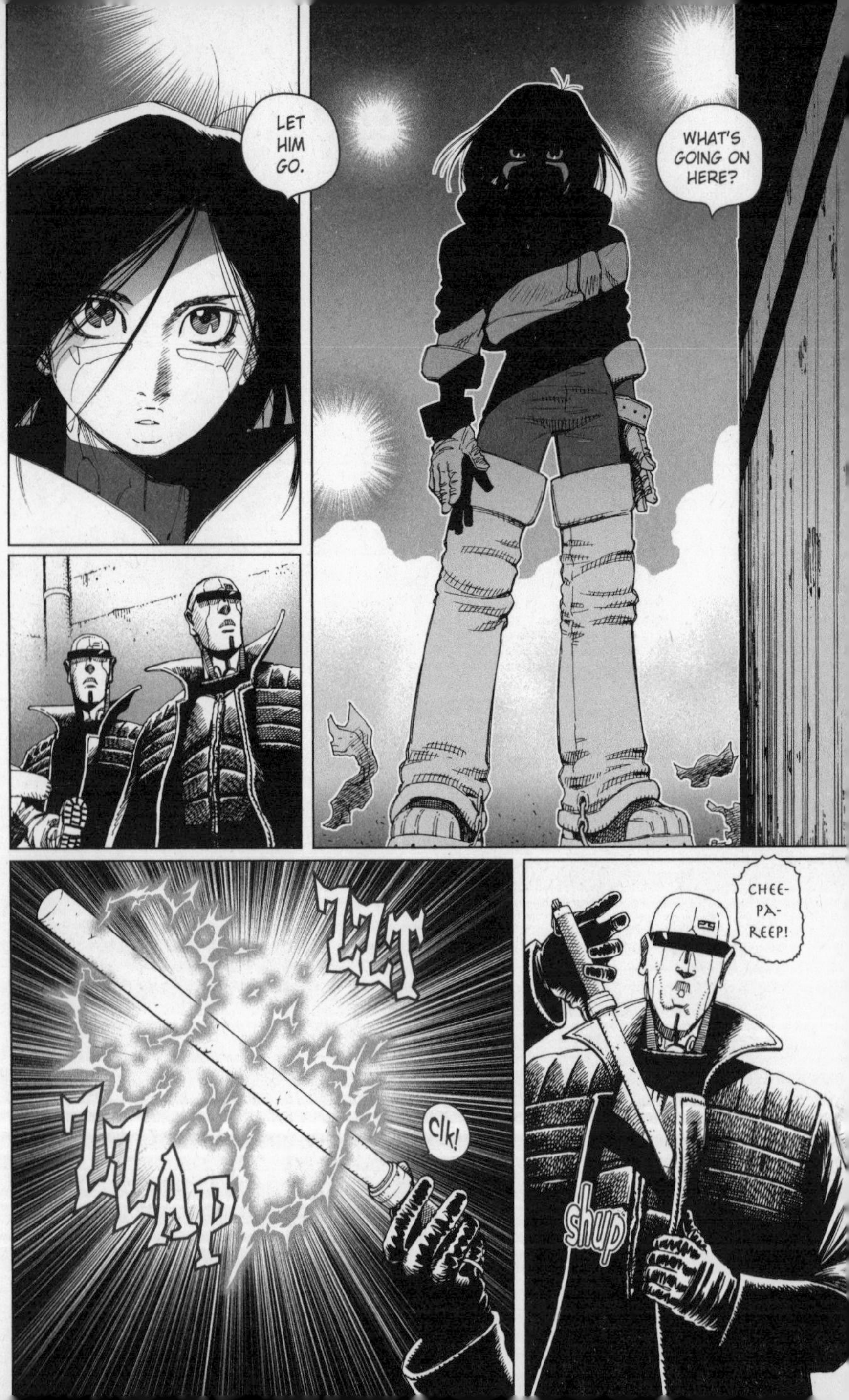
WHAT'S GOING ON HERE?
LET HIM GO.
CHEE-PA-REEP!
shup
ZZT
ZZAP
clk!

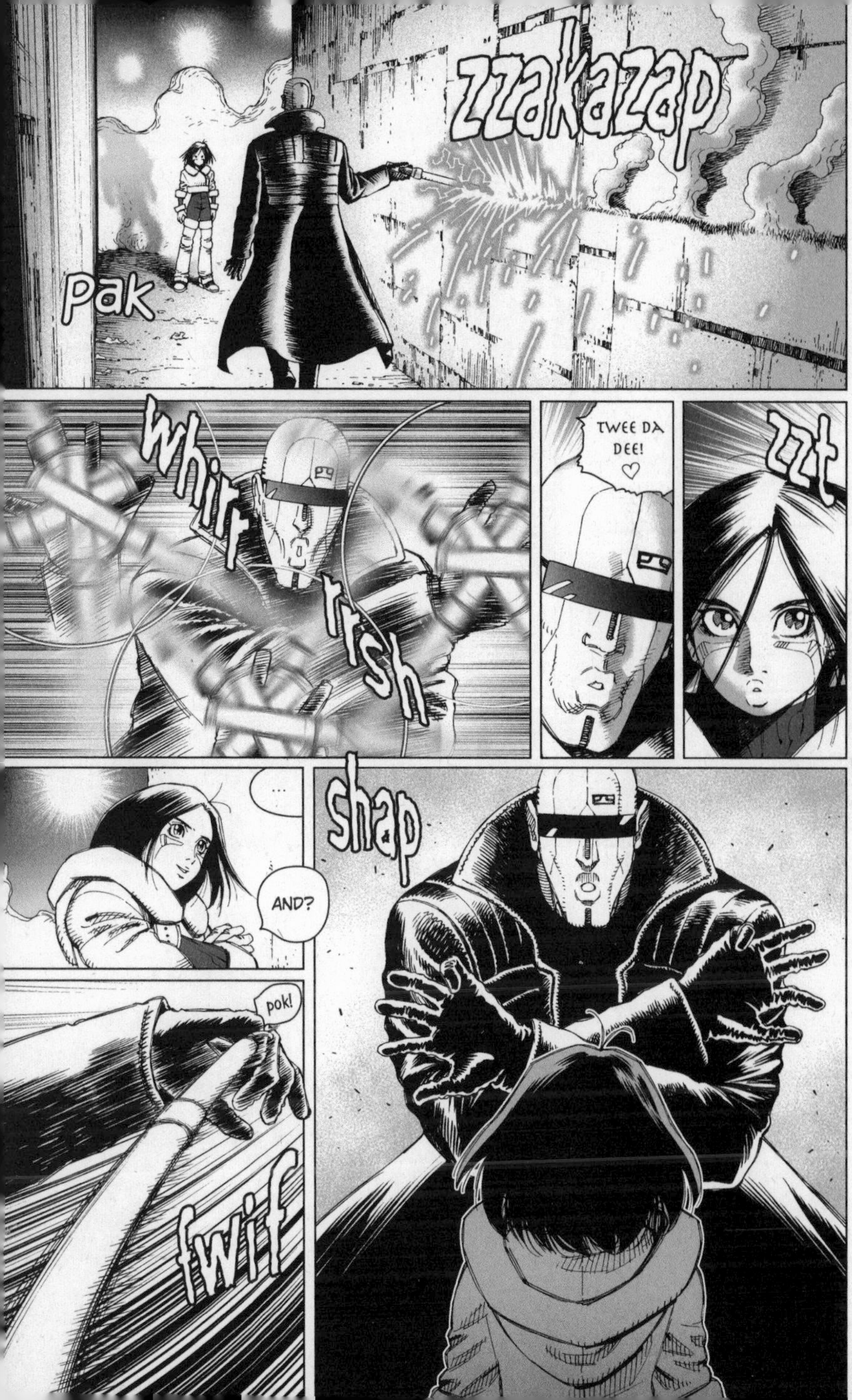
zzakazap
pak
zzt
TWEE DA DEE! ♡
whirr
rrsh
shap
...
AND?
pok!
fwif

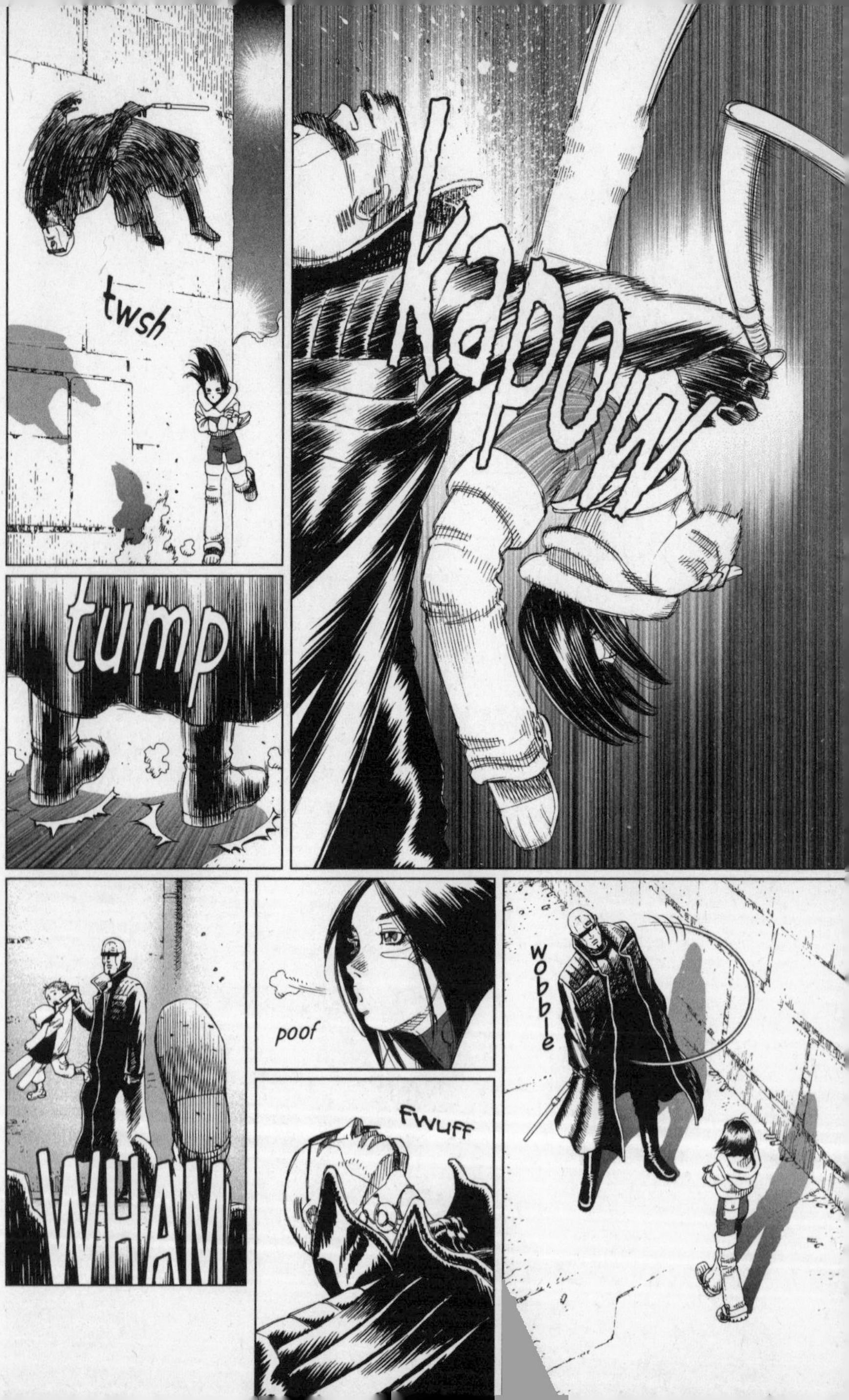
kapow
twsh
tump
wobble
poof
fwuff
WHAM

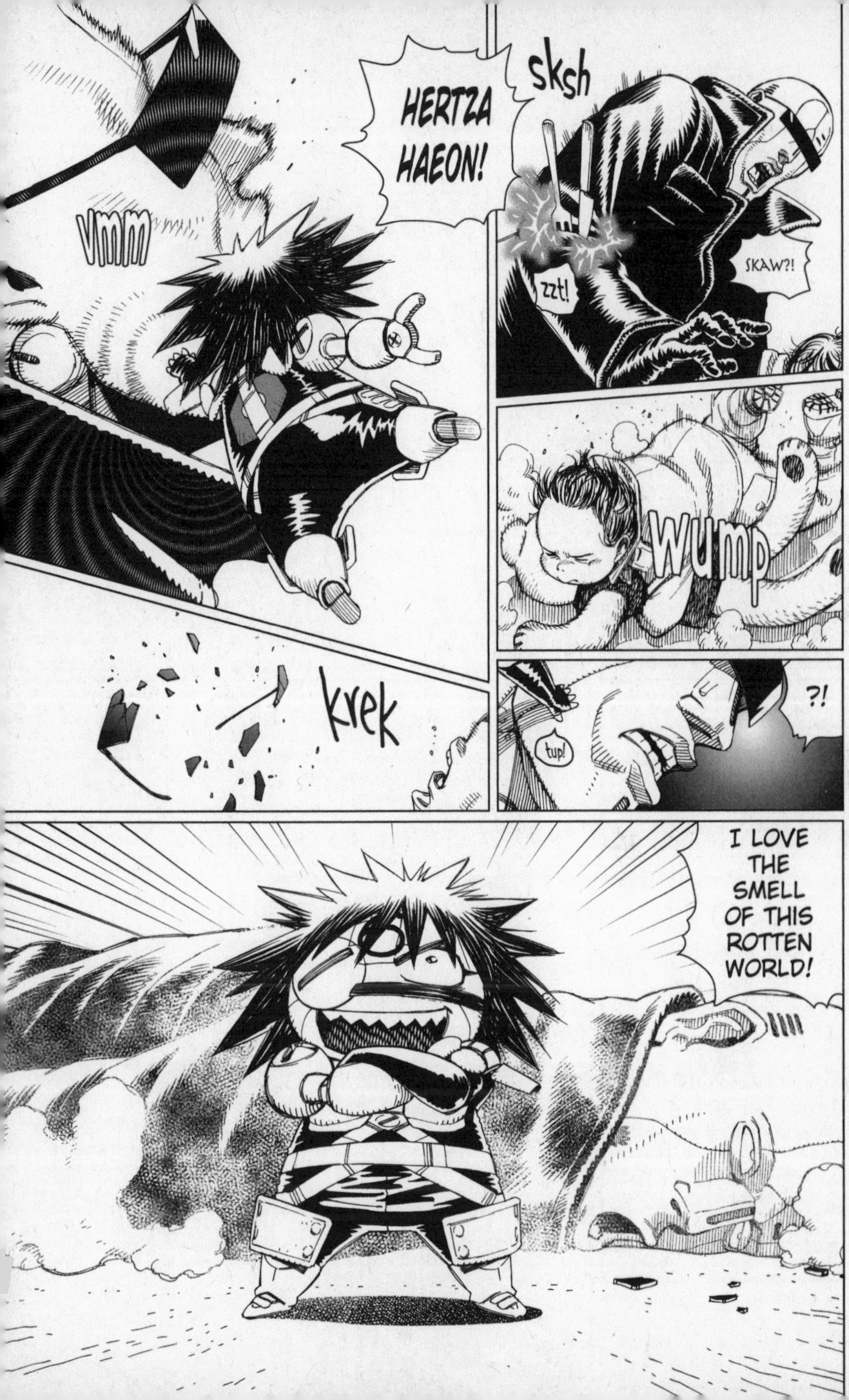
sksh
zzt!
SKAW?!
wump
?!
tup!
HERTZA HAEON!
vmm
krek
I LOVE THE SMELL OF THIS ROTTEN WORLD!

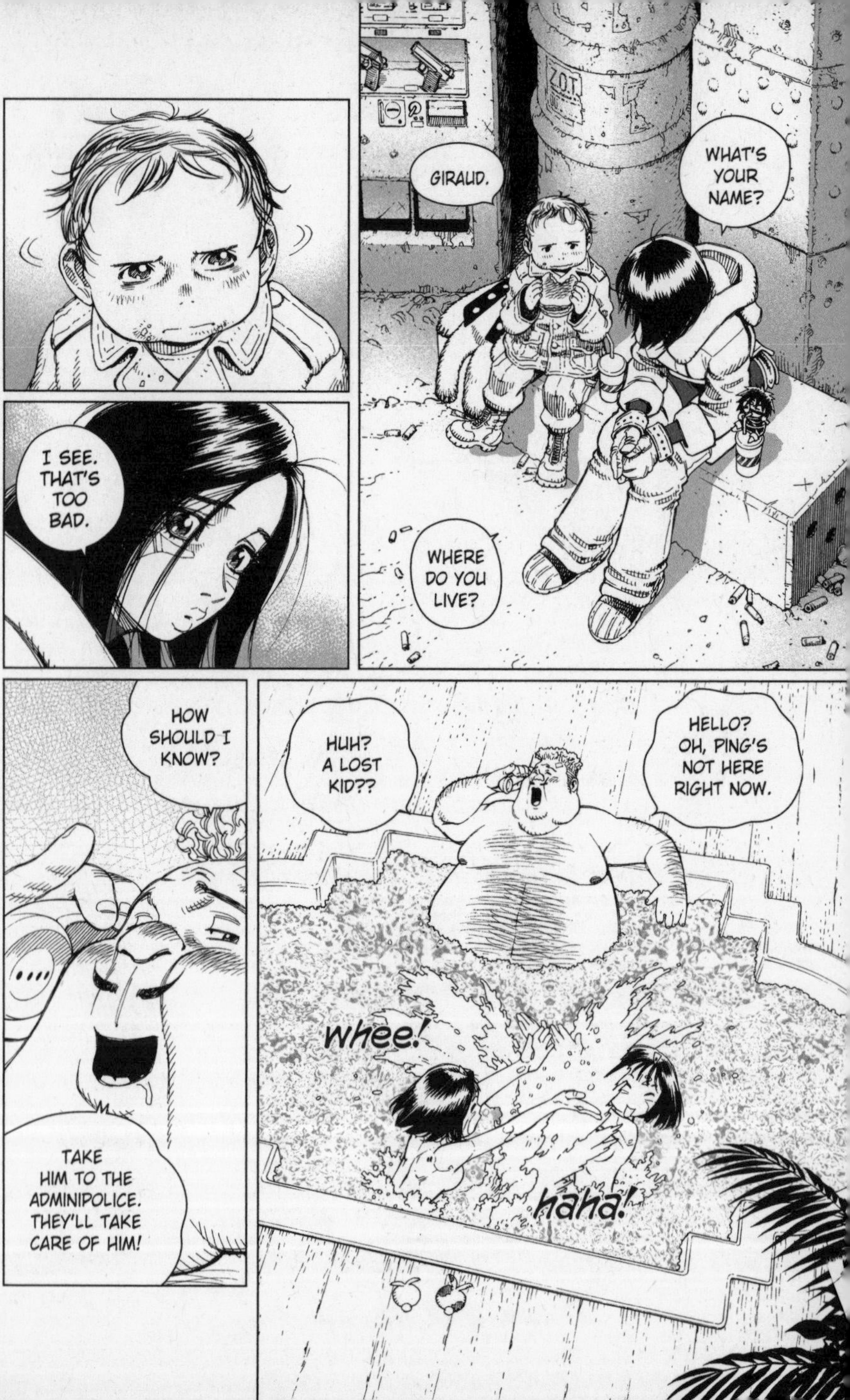
WHAT'S YOUR NAME?
GIRAUD.
WHERE DO YOU LIVE?
I SEE. THAT'S TOO BAD.
HELLO? OH, PING'S NOT HERE RIGHT NOW.
HUH? A LOST KID??
whee!
haha!
HOW SHOULD I KNOW?
....
TAKE HIM TO THE ADMINIPOLICE. THEY'LL TAKE CARE OF HIM!

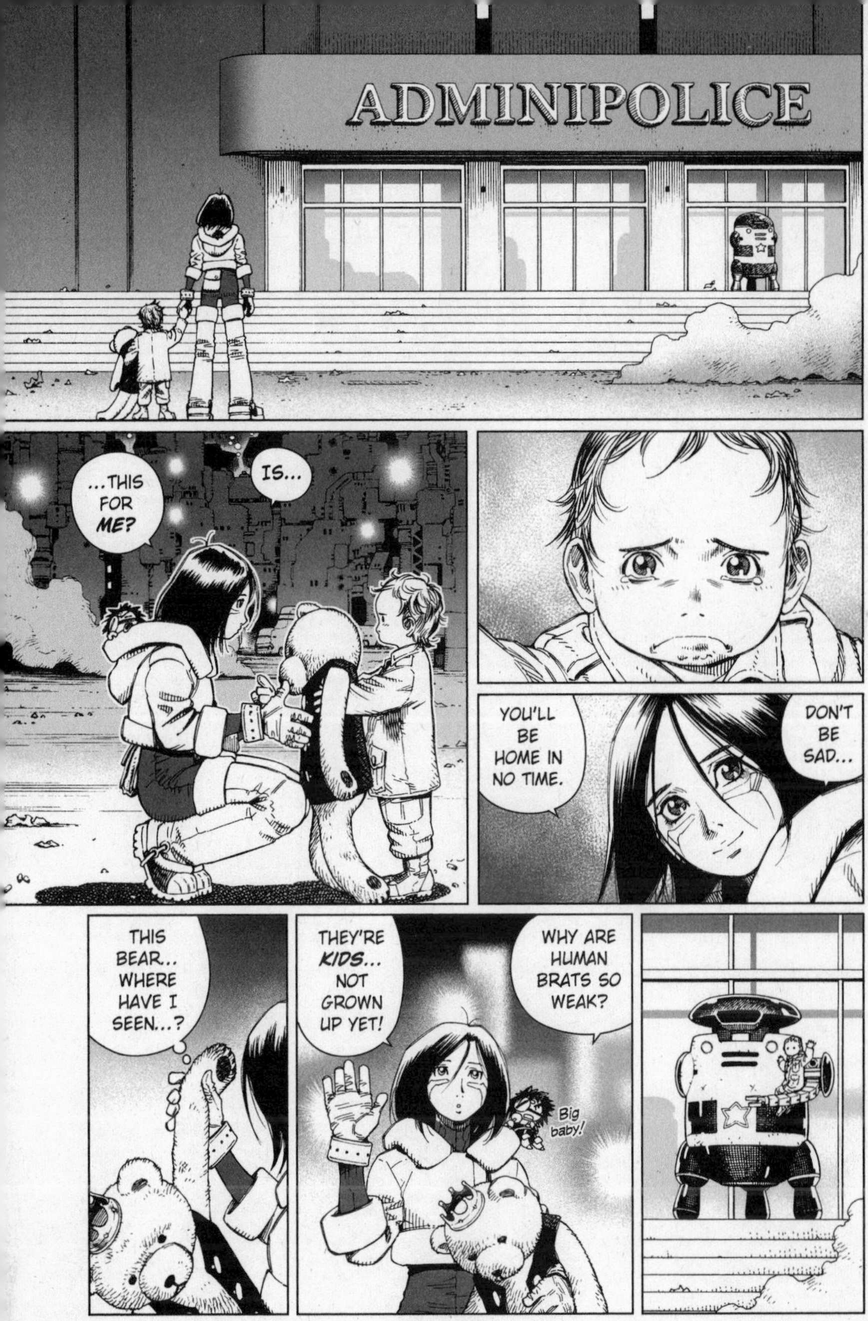
ADMINIPOLICE
DON'T BE SAD...
YOU'LL BE HOME IN NO TIME.
IS...
...THIS FOR ME?
WHY ARE HUMAN BRATS SO WEAK?
THEY'RE KIDS... NOT GROWN UP YET!
Big baby!
THIS BEAR... WHERE HAVE I SEEN...?

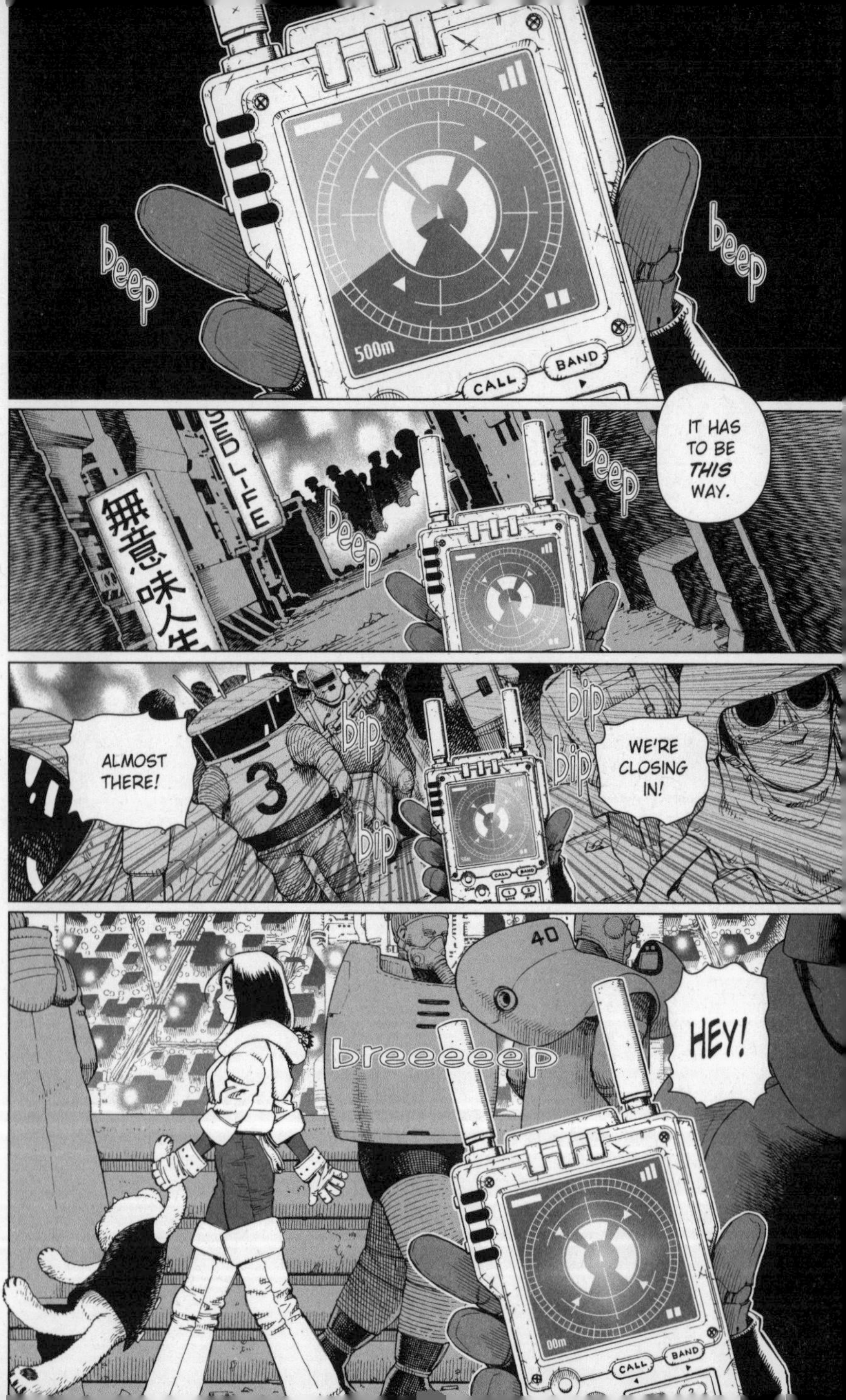
beep
beep
500m
CALL
BAND
IT HAS TO BE *THIS* WAY.
beep
beep
ED LIFE
無意味人
bip
bip
WE'RE CLOSING IN!
bip
bip
ALMOST THERE!
HEY!
40
breeeeeep
CALL
BAND

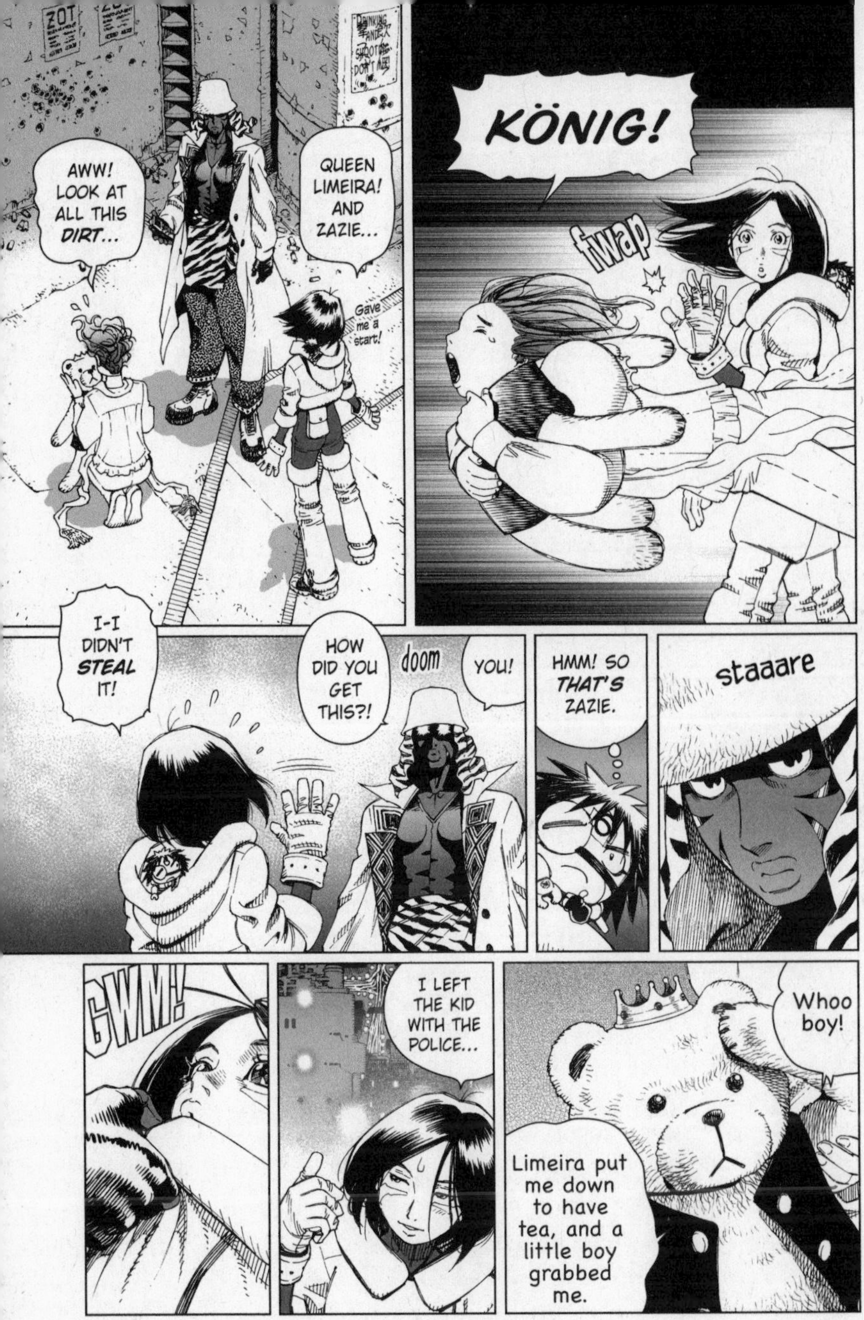
KÖNIG!
fwap
QUEEN LIMEIRA! AND ZAZIE...
AWW! LOOK AT ALL THIS DIRT...
Gave me a start!
staaare
HMM! SO THAT'S ZAZIE.
YOU!
doom
HOW DID YOU GET THIS?!
I-I DIDN'T STEAL IT!
Whoo boy!
Limeira put me down to have tea, and a little boy grabbed me.
I LEFT THE KID WITH THE POLICE...
GWM!

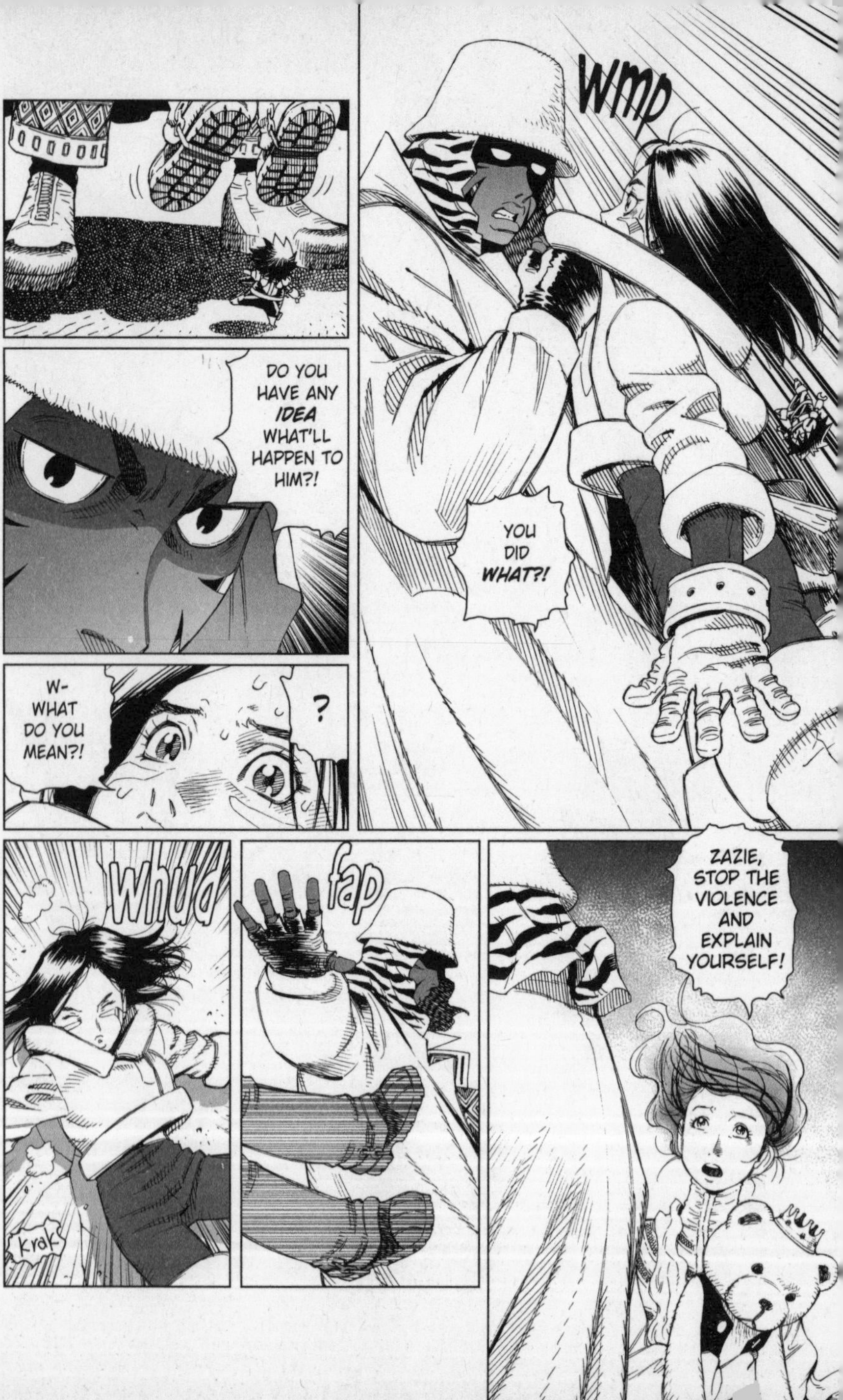

WMP
YOU DID WHAT?!
DO YOU HAVE ANY IDEA WHAT'LL HAPPEN TO HIM?!
W- WHAT DO YOU MEAN?!
?
ZAZIE, STOP THE VIOLENCE AND EXPLAIN YOURSELF!
fap
whud
krak

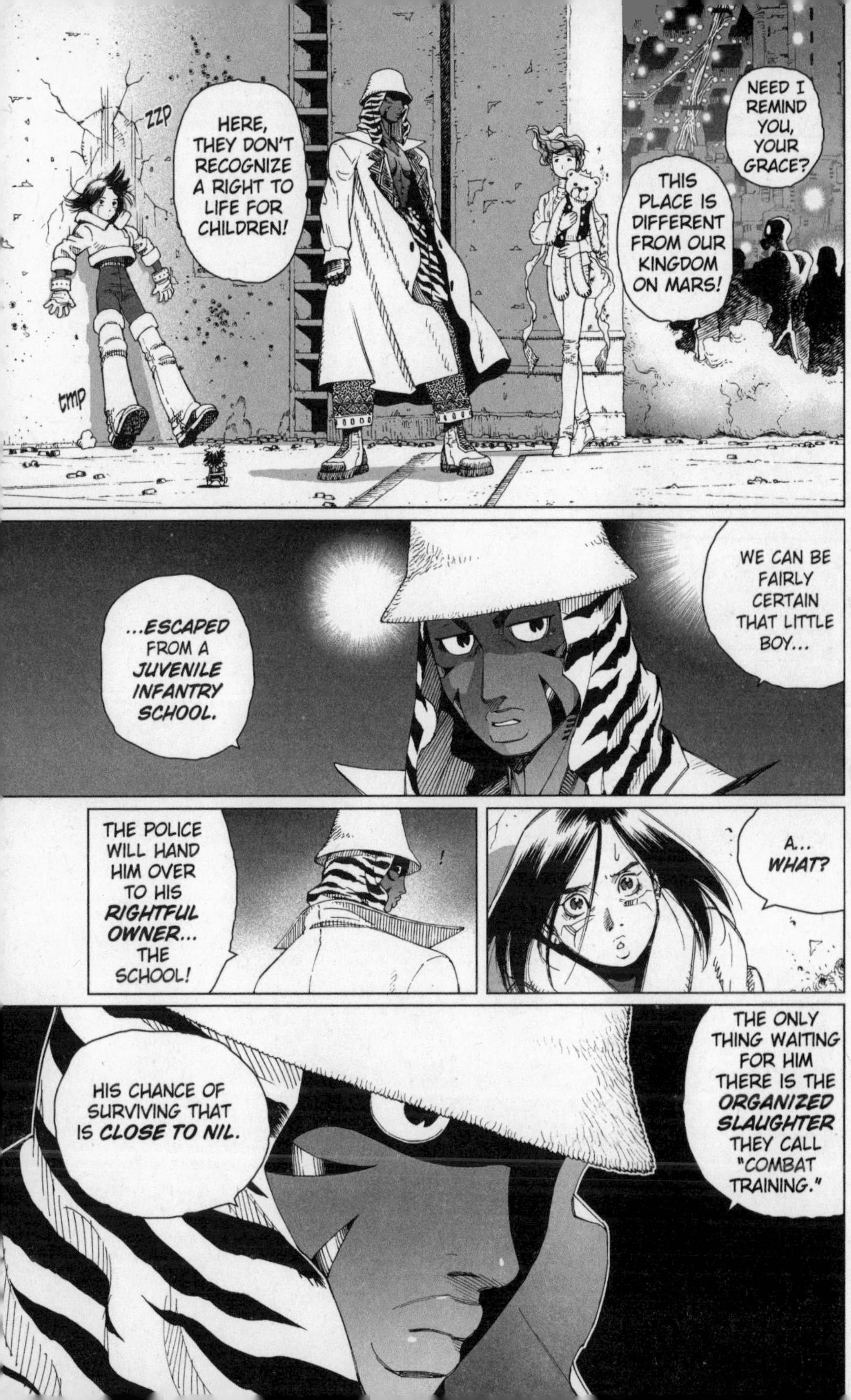
NEED I REMIND YOU, YOUR GRACE?
THIS PLACE IS DIFFERENT FROM OUR KINGDOM ON MARS!
HERE, THEY DON'T RECOGNIZE A RIGHT TO LIFE FOR CHILDREN!
ZZP
tmp
WE CAN BE FAIRLY CERTAIN THAT LITTLE BOY...
...ESCAPED FROM A JUVENILE INFANTRY SCHOOL.
A... WHAT?
THE POLICE WILL HAND HIM OVER TO HIS RIGHTFUL OWNER... THE SCHOOL!
THE ONLY THING WAITING FOR HIM THERE IS THE ORGANIZED SLAUGHTER THEY CALL "COMBAT TRAINING."
HIS CHANCE OF SURVIVING THAT IS CLOSE TO NIL.

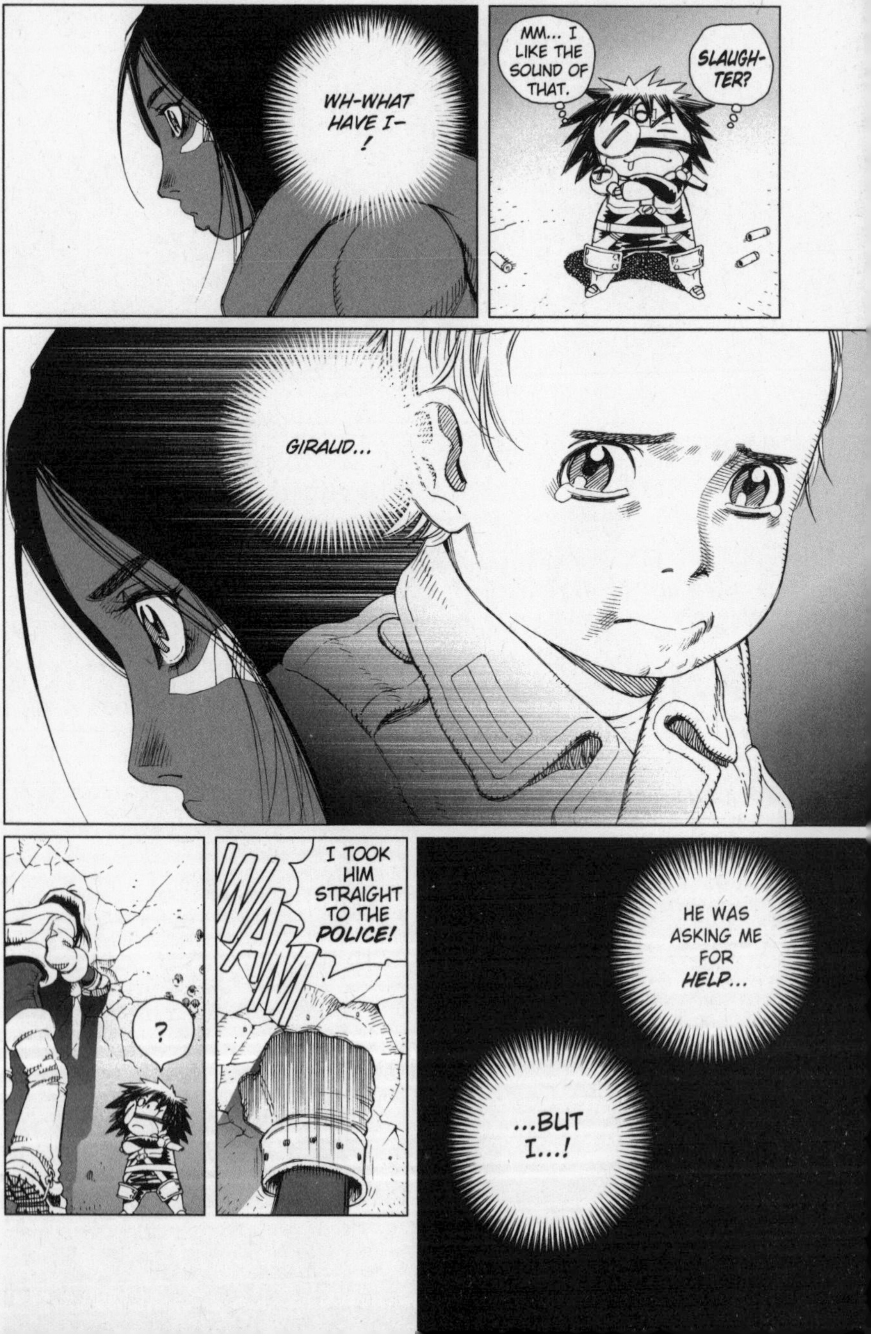
SLAUGH-TER?
MM... I LIKE THE SOUND OF THAT.
WH-WHAT HAVE I-!
GIRAUD...
HE WAS ASKING ME FOR HELP...
...BUT I...!
I TOOK HIM STRAIGHT TO THE **POLICE!**
WAM
?

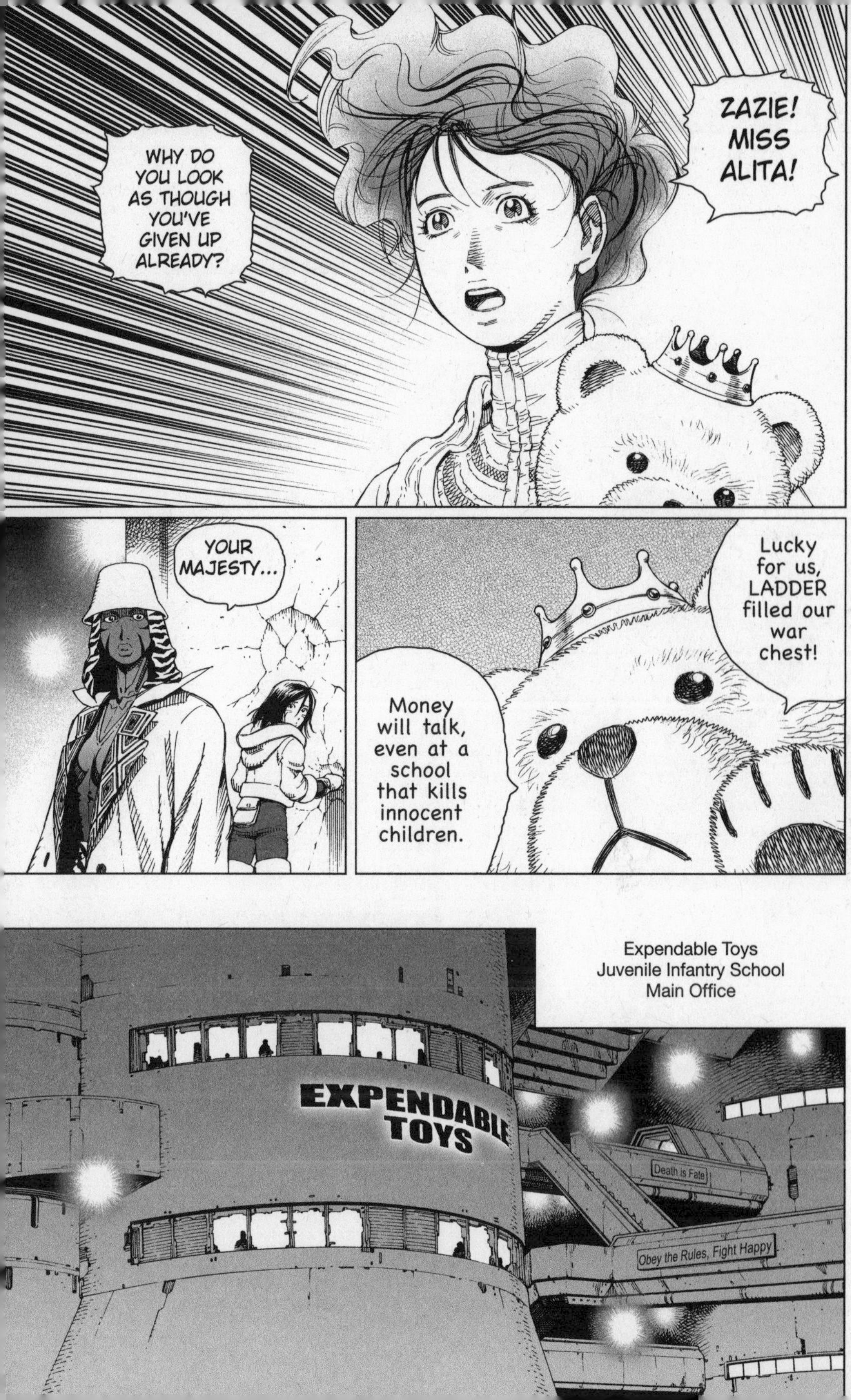
ZAZIE! MISS ALITA!
WHY DO YOU LOOK AS THOUGH YOU'VE GIVEN UP ALREADY?
Lucky for us, LADDER filled our war chest!
Money will talk, even at a school that kills innocent children.
YOUR MAJESTY...
Expendable Toys
Juvenile Infantry School
Main Office
EXPENDABLE TOYS
Death is Fate
Obey the Rules, Fight Happy

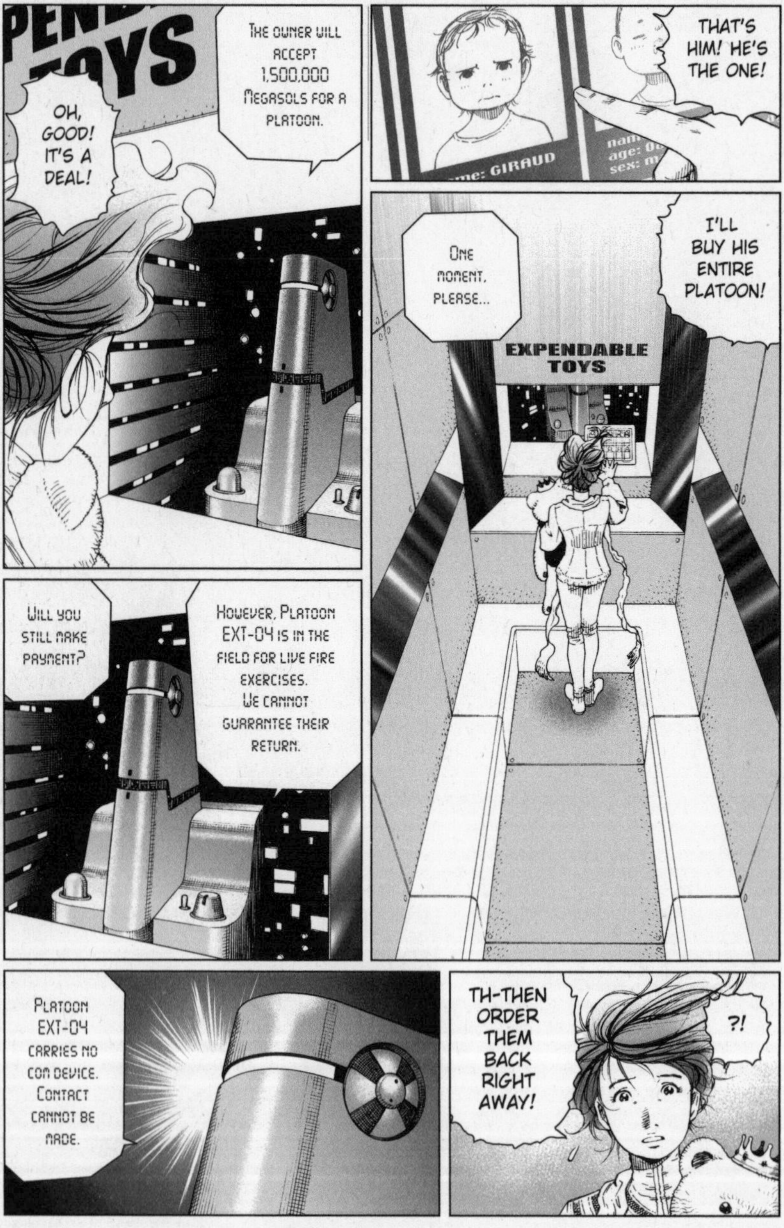
THAT'S HIM! HE'S THE ONE!
I'LL BUY HIS ENTIRE PLATOON!
One moment, please...
EXPENDABLE TOYS
The owner will accept 1,500,000 Megasols for a platoon.
OH, GOOD! IT'S A DEAL!
However, Platoon EXT-04 is in the field for live fire exercises. We cannot guarantee their return.
Will you still make payment?
TH-THEN ORDER THEM BACK RIGHT AWAY!
?!
Platoon EXT-04 carries no com device. Contact cannot be made.

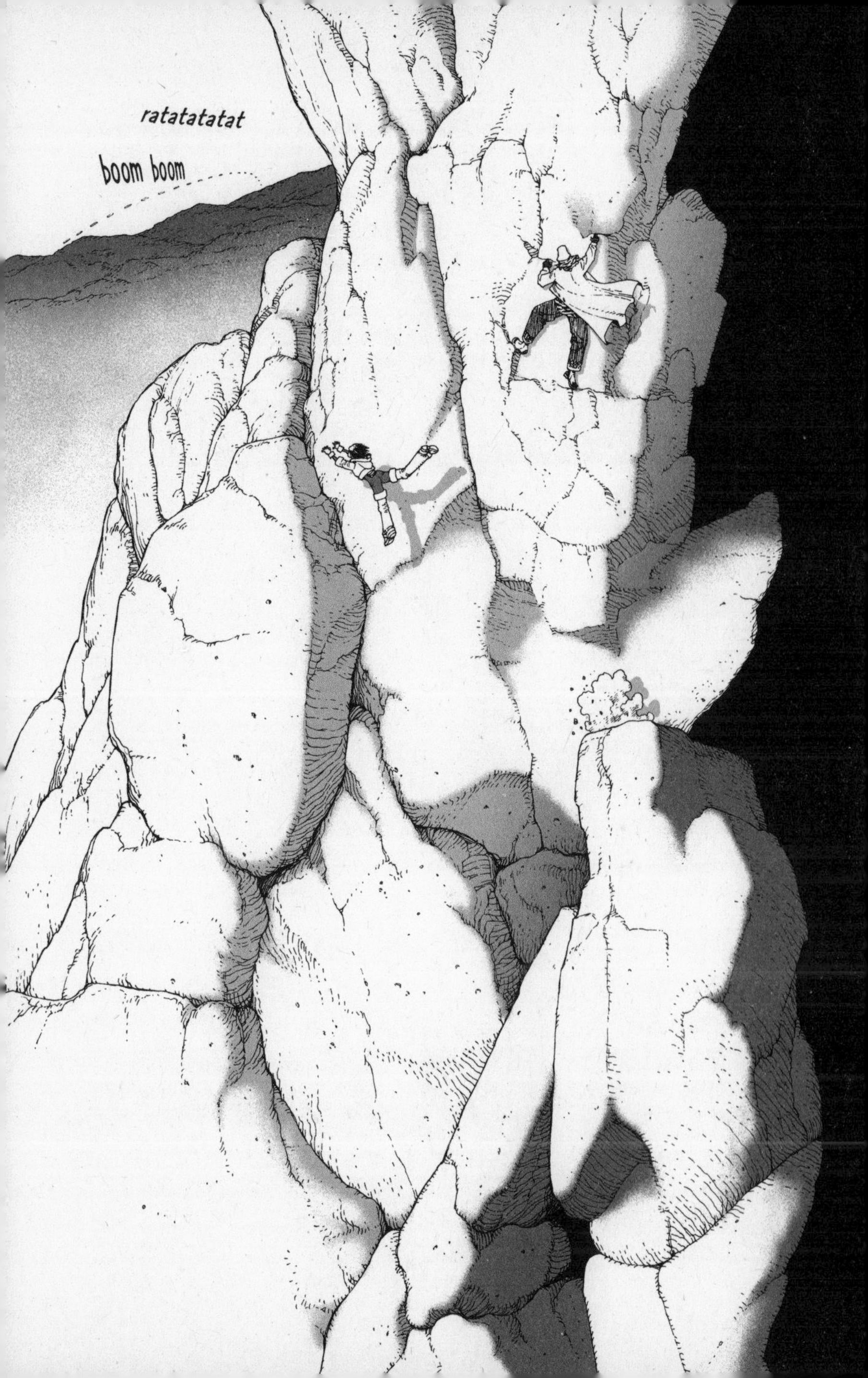
ratatatatat
boom boom

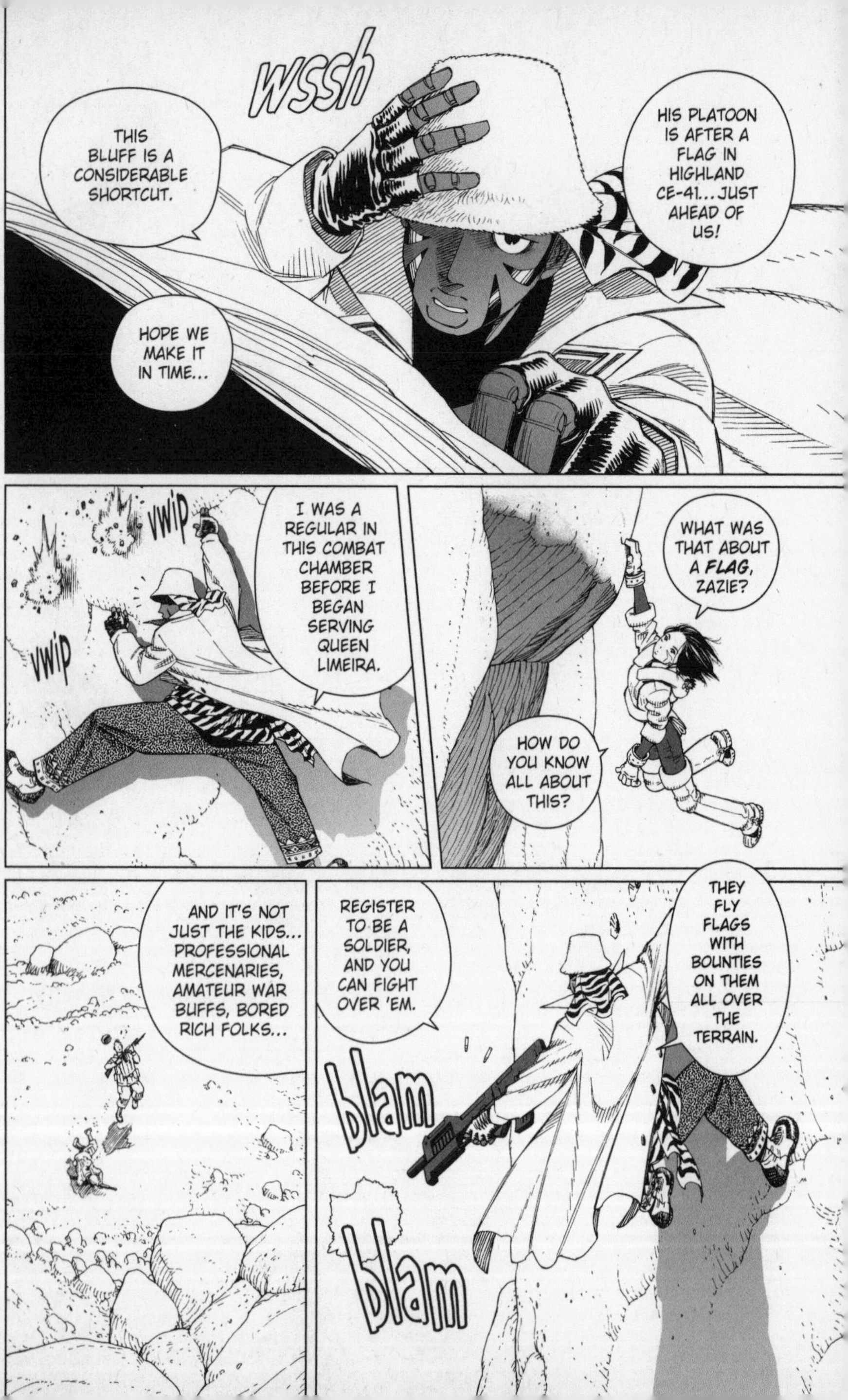
HIS PLATOON IS AFTER A FLAG IN HIGHLAND CE-41... JUST AHEAD OF US!
wssh
THIS BLUFF IS A CONSIDERABLE SHORTCUT.
HOPE WE MAKE IT IN TIME...
WHAT WAS THAT ABOUT A FLAG, ZAZIE?
HOW DO YOU KNOW ALL ABOUT THIS?
I WAS A REGULAR IN THIS COMBAT CHAMBER BEFORE I BEGAN SERVING QUEEN LIMEIRA.
vwip
vwip
THEY FLY FLAGS WITH BOUNTIES ON THEM ALL OVER THE TERRAIN.
REGISTER TO BE A SOLDIER, AND YOU CAN FIGHT OVER 'EM.
blam
blam
AND IT'S NOT JUST THE KIDS... PROFESSIONAL MERCENARIES, AMATEUR WAR BUFFS, BORED RICH FOLKS...

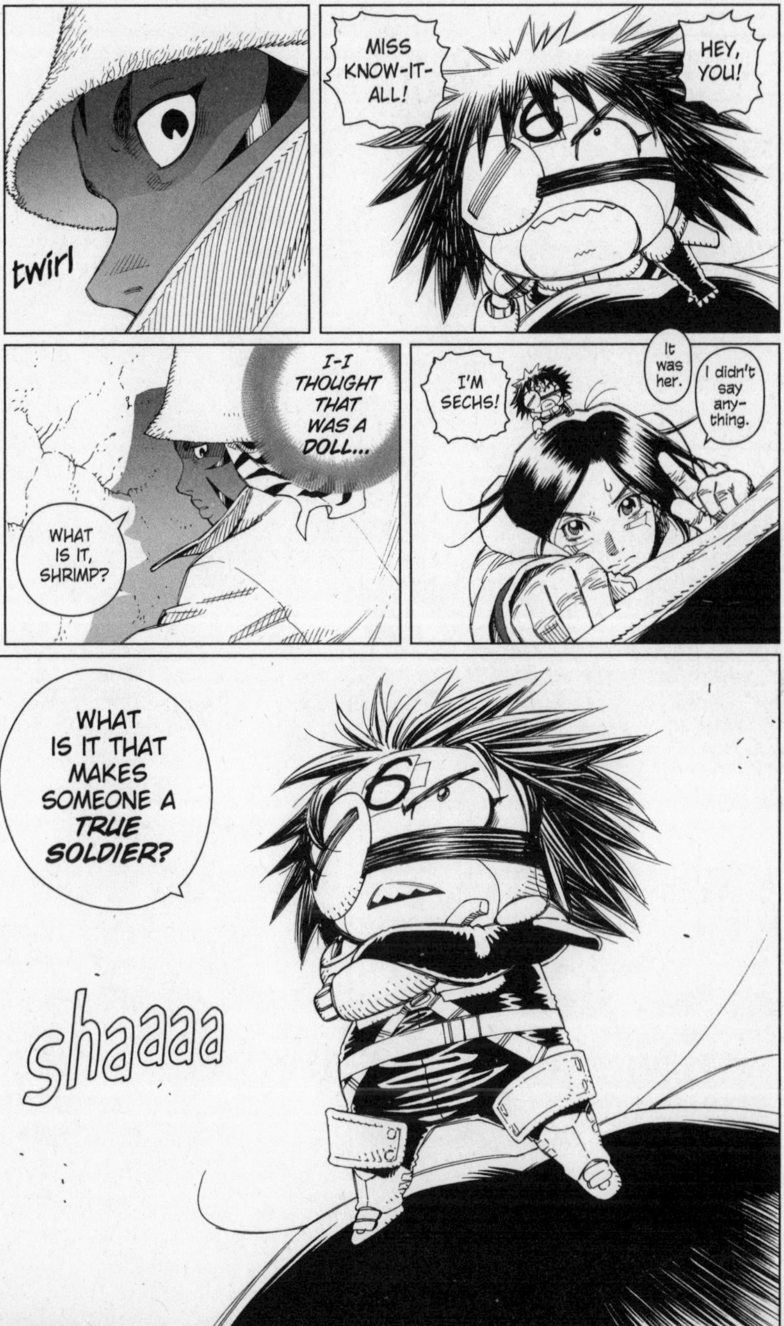
HEY, YOU!
MISS KNOW-IT-ALL!
twirl
It was her.
I didn't say any-thing.
I'M SECHS!
I-I THOUGHT THAT WAS A DOLL...
WHAT IS IT, SHRIMP?
WHAT IS IT THAT MAKES SOMEONE A TRUE SOLDIER?
shaaaa

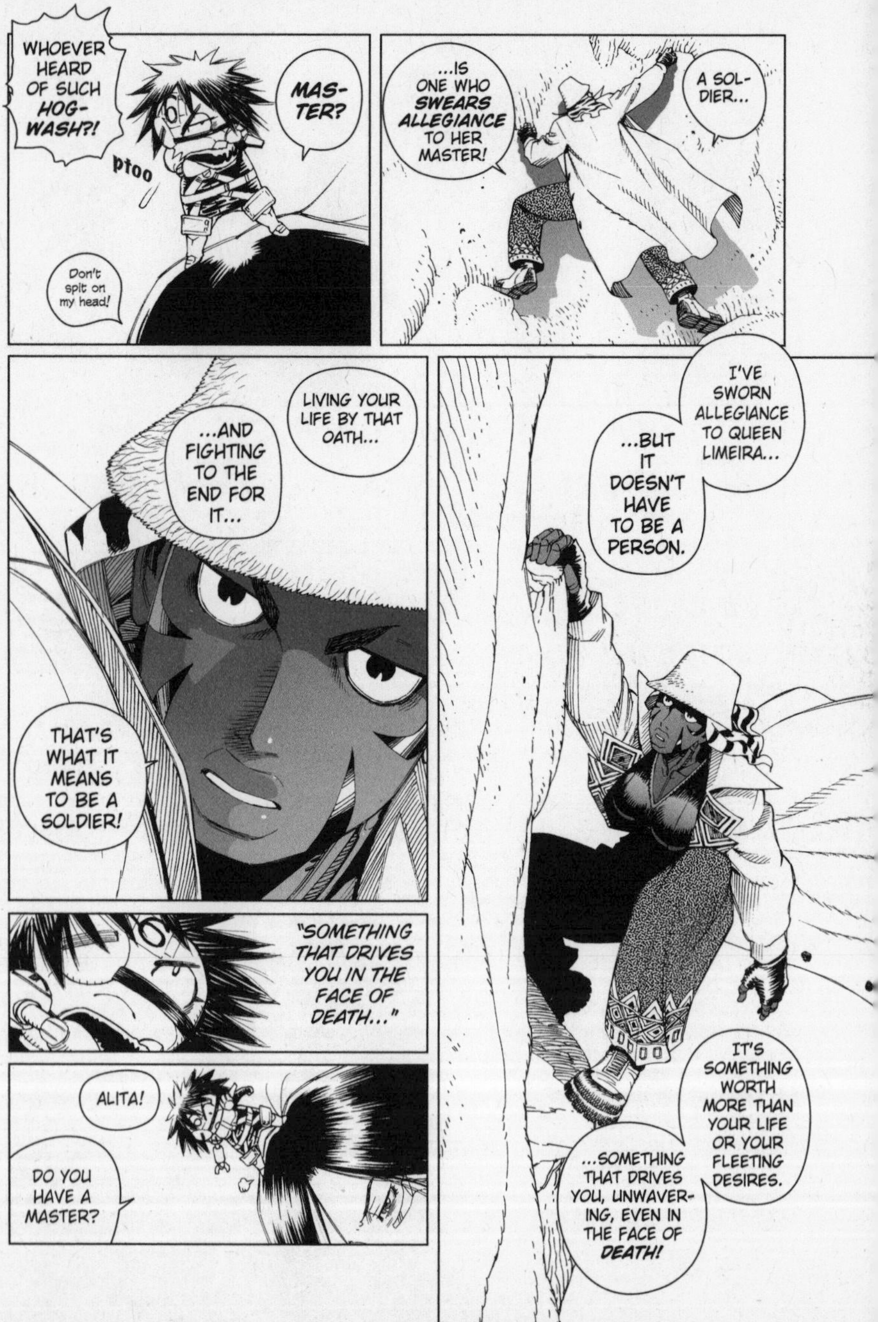
A SOL-DIER...
...IS ONE WHO SWEARS ALLEGIANCE TO HER MASTER!
MAS-TER?
WHOEVER HEARD OF SUCH HOG-WASH?!
ptoo
Don't spit on my head!
I'VE SWORN ALLEGIANCE TO QUEEN LIMEIRA...
...BUT IT DOESN'T HAVE TO BE A PERSON.
IT'S SOMETHING WORTH MORE THAN YOUR LIFE OR YOUR FLEETING DESIRES.
...SOMETHING THAT DRIVES YOU, UNWAVER-ING, EVEN IN THE FACE OF DEATH!
LIVING YOUR LIFE BY THAT OATH...
...AND FIGHTING TO THE END FOR IT...
THAT'S WHAT IT MEANS TO BE A SOLDIER!
"SOMETHING THAT DRIVES YOU IN THE FACE OF DEATH..."
ALITA!
DO YOU HAVE A MASTER?

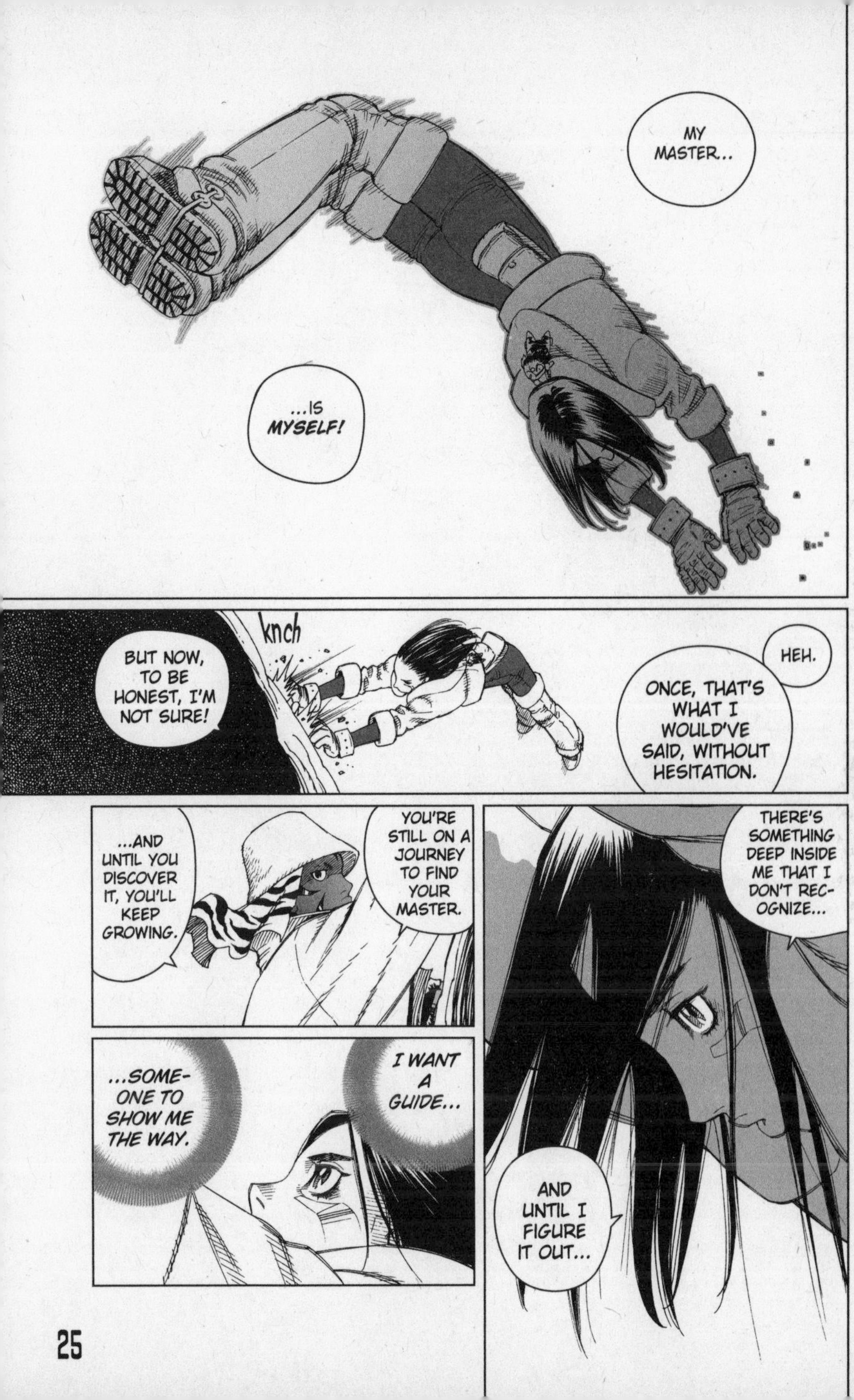
MY MASTER...
...IS MYSELF!
HEH.
ONCE, THAT'S WHAT I WOULD'VE SAID, WITHOUT HESITATION.
knch
BUT NOW, TO BE HONEST, I'M NOT SURE!
THERE'S SOMETHING DEEP INSIDE ME THAT I DON'T RECOGNIZE...
AND UNTIL I FIGURE IT OUT...
YOU'RE STILL ON A JOURNEY TO FIND YOUR MASTER.
...AND UNTIL YOU DISCOVER IT, YOU'LL KEEP GROWING.
I WANT A GUIDE...
...SOMEONE TO SHOW ME THE WAY.

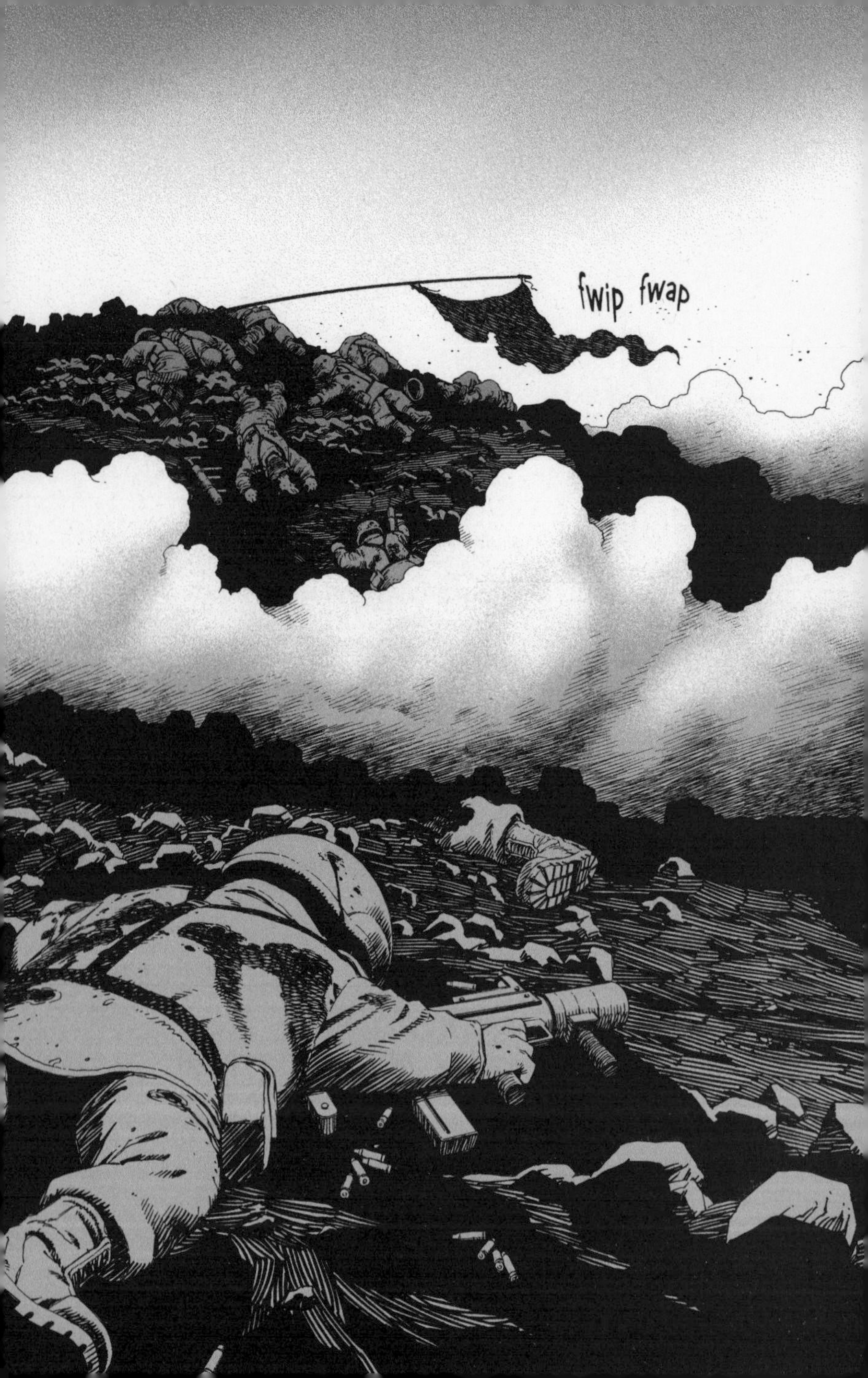
fwip fwap

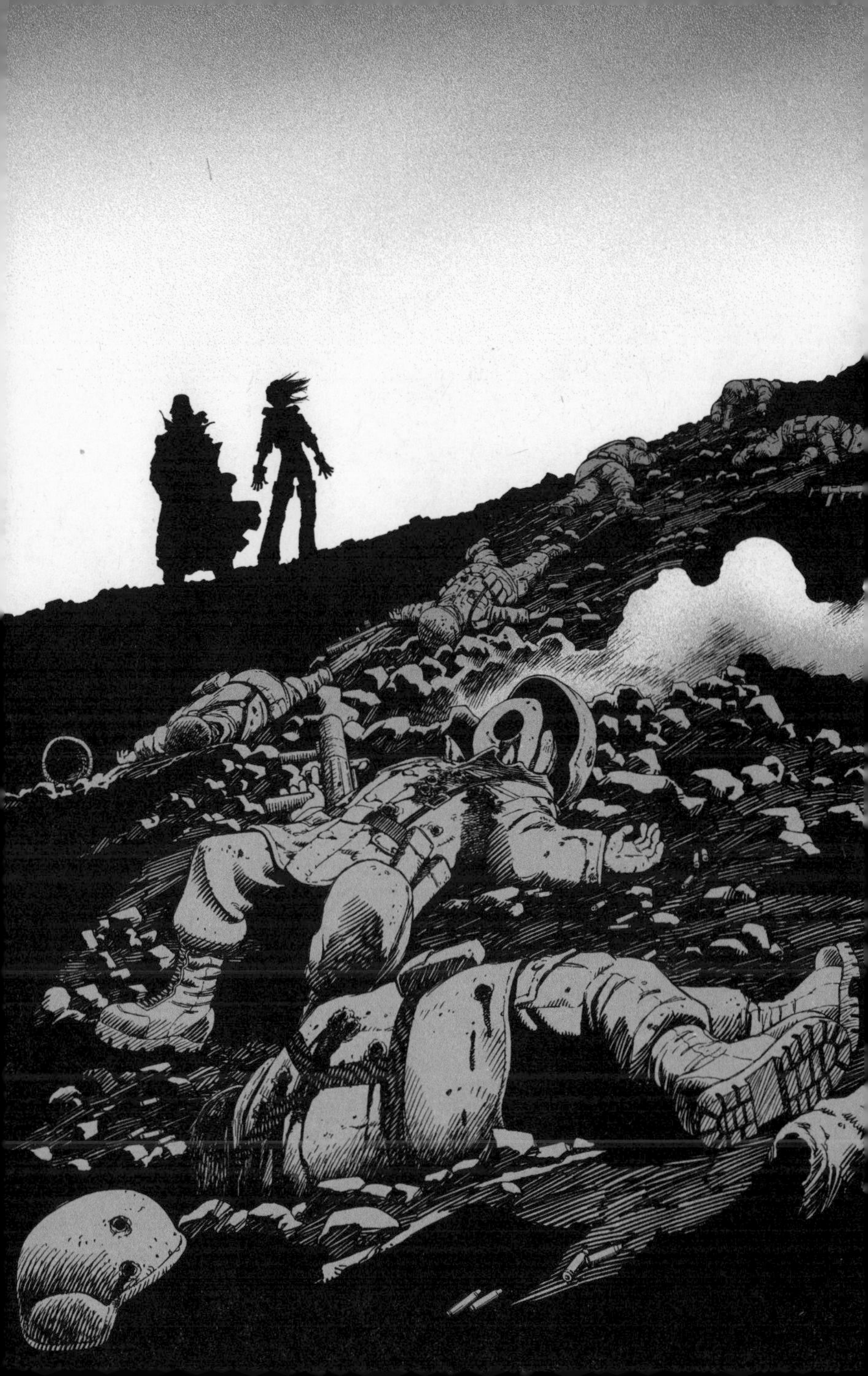

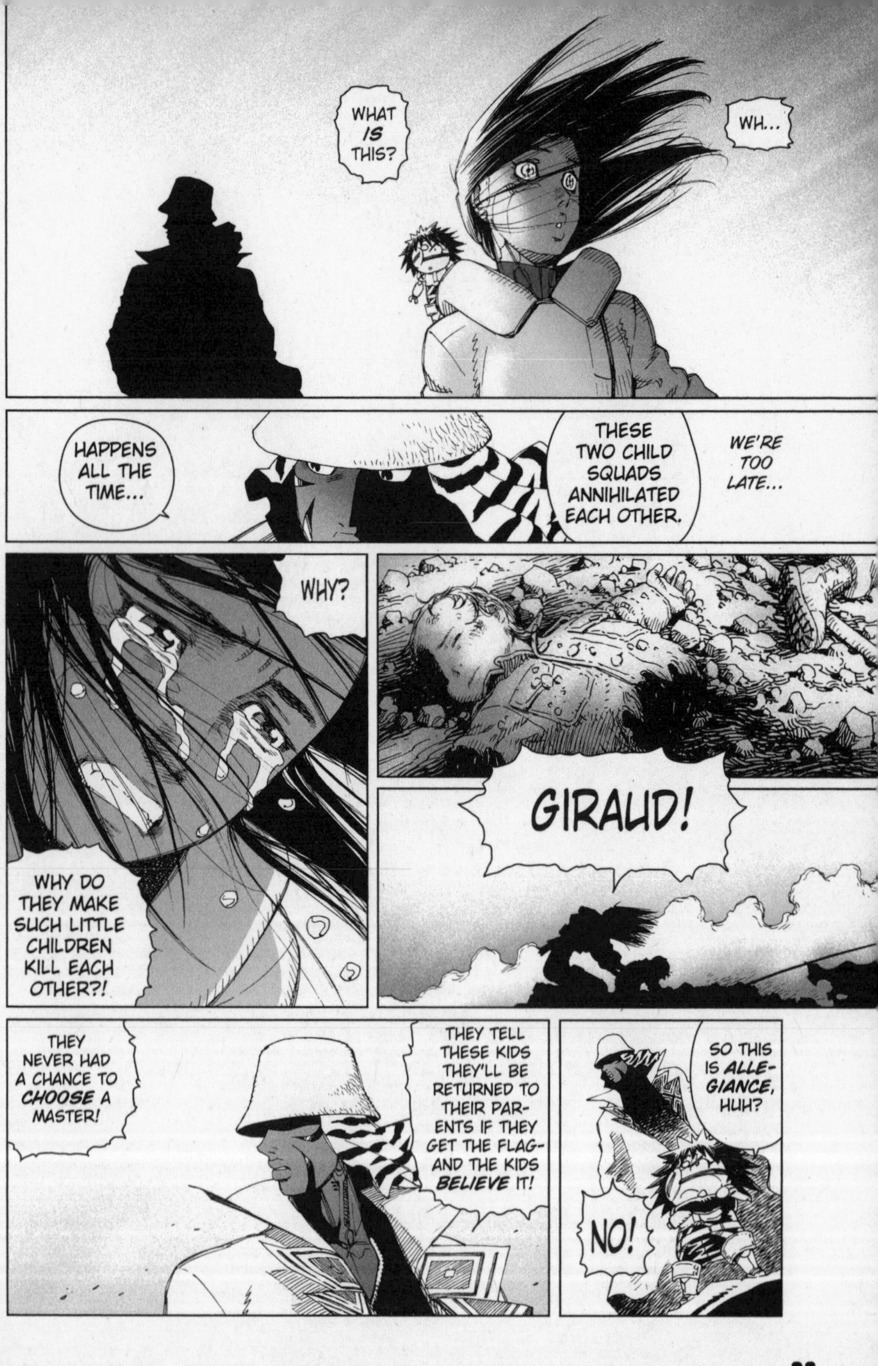
WH...
WHAT IS THIS?
WE'RE TOO LATE...
THESE TWO CHILD SQUADS ANNIHILATED EACH OTHER.
HAPPENS ALL THE TIME...
GIRAUD!
WHY?
WHY DO THEY MAKE SUCH LITTLE CHILDREN KILL EACH OTHER?!
SO THIS IS ALLE-GIANCE, HUH?
NO!
THEY TELL THESE KIDS THEY'LL BE RETURNED TO THEIR PAR-ENTS IF THEY GET THE FLAG-AND THE KIDS BELIEVE IT!
THEY NEVER HAD A CHANCE TO CHOOSE A MASTER!

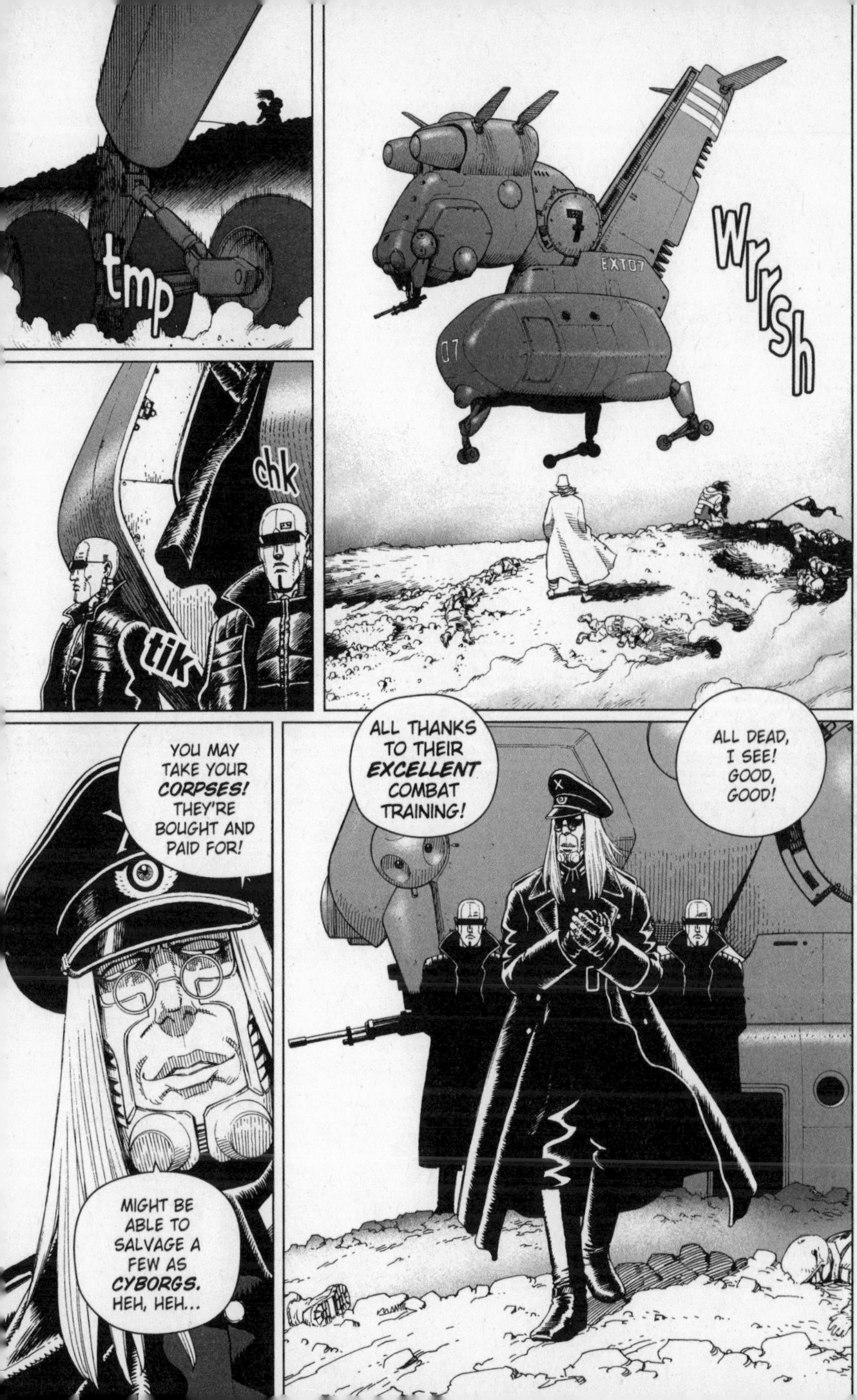
Wrrrsh
tmp
chk
tik
ALL DEAD, I SEE! GOOD, GOOD!
ALL THANKS TO THEIR *EXCELLENT* COMBAT TRAINING!
YOU MAY TAKE YOUR *CORPSES!* THEY'RE BOUGHT AND PAID FOR!
MIGHT BE ABLE TO SALVAGE A FEW AS *CYBORGS.* HEH, HEH...

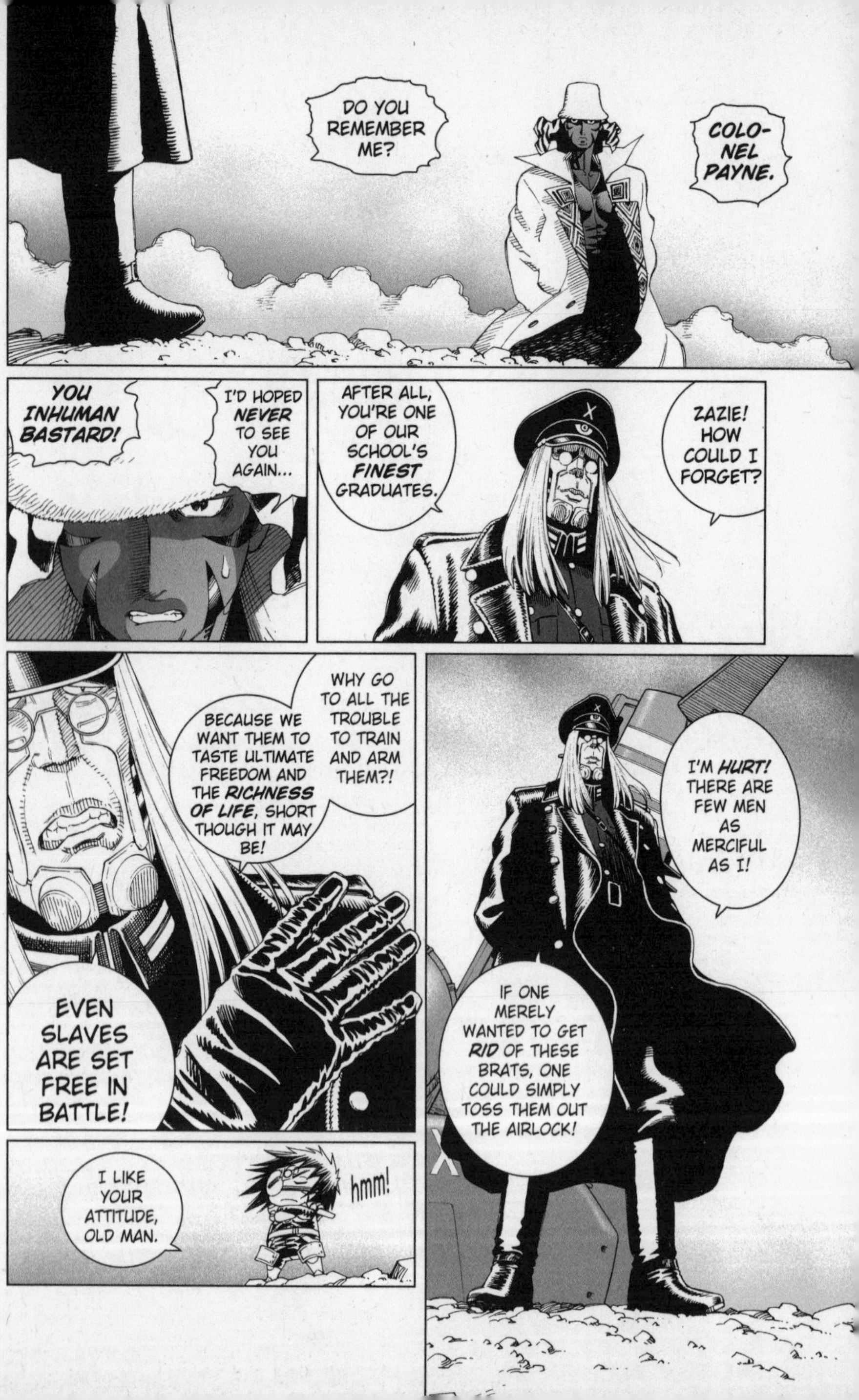
COLO-NEL PAYNE.
DO YOU REMEMBER ME?
ZAZIE! HOW COULD I FORGET?
AFTER ALL, YOU'RE ONE OF OUR SCHOOL'S FINEST GRADUATES.
I'D HOPED NEVER TO SEE YOU AGAIN...
YOU INHUMAN BASTARD!
I'M HURT! THERE ARE FEW MEN AS MERCIFUL AS I!
IF ONE MERELY WANTED TO GET RID OF THESE BRATS, ONE COULD SIMPLY TOSS THEM OUT THE AIRLOCK!
WHY GO TO ALL THE TROUBLE TO TRAIN AND ARM THEM?!
BECAUSE WE WANT THEM TO TASTE ULTIMATE FREEDOM AND THE RICHNESS OF LIFE, SHORT THOUGH IT MAY BE!
EVEN SLAVES ARE SET FREE IN BATTLE!
hmm!
I LIKE YOUR ATTITUDE, OLD MAN.

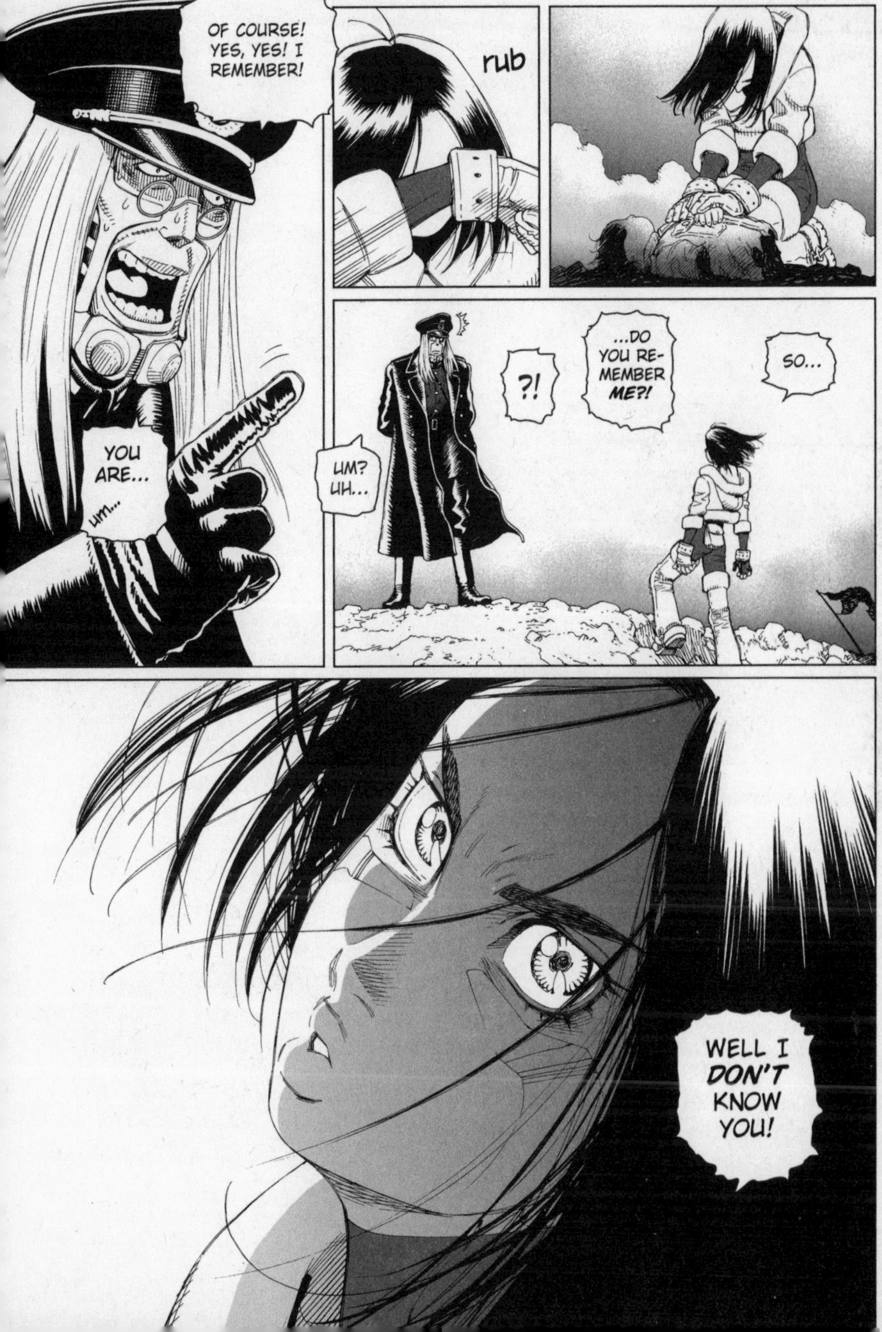
rub
SO...
...DO YOU REMEMBER ME?!
?!
UM? UH...
OF COURSE! YES, YES! I REMEMBER!
YOU ARE... um...
WELL I DON'T KNOW YOU!

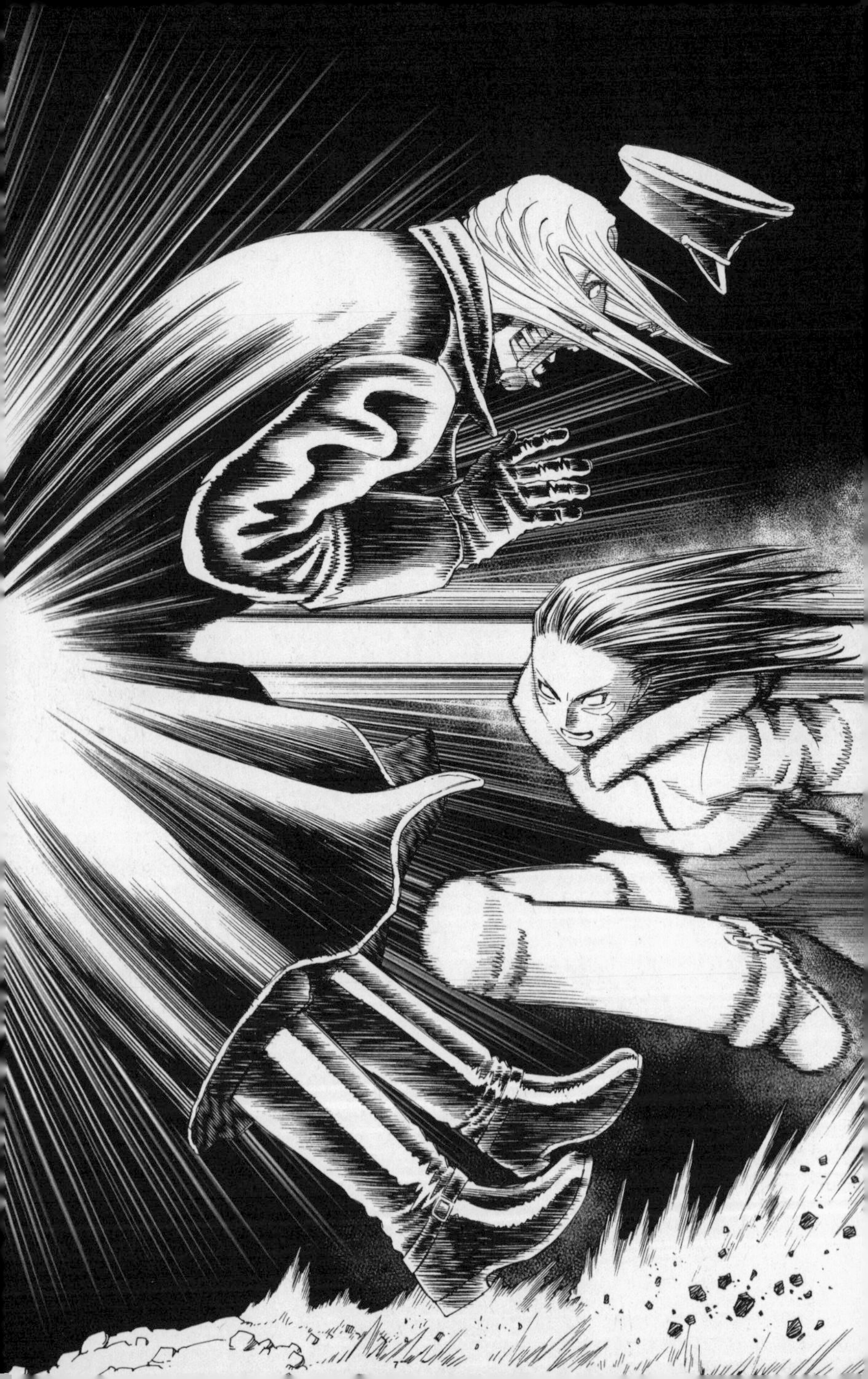

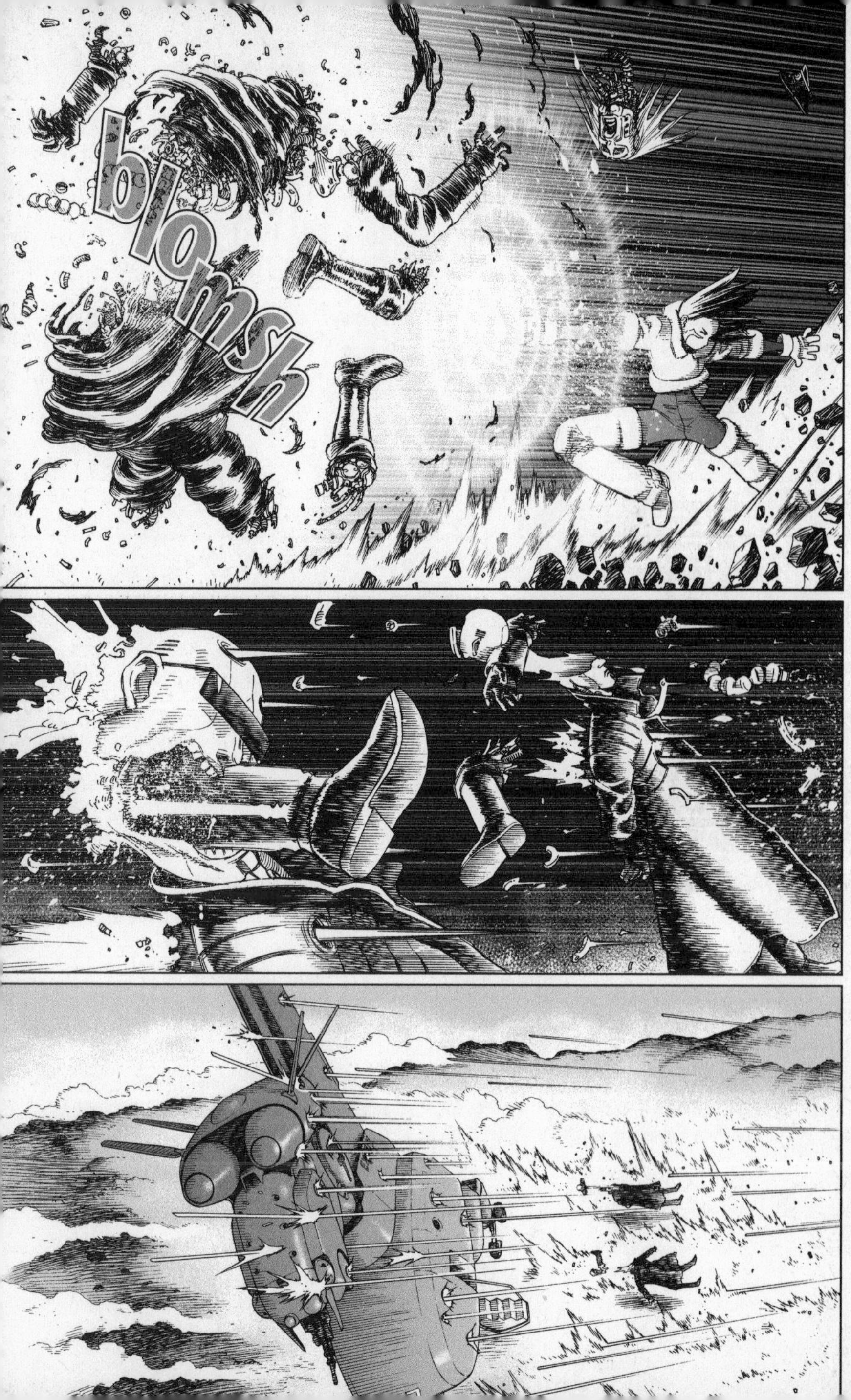
blomsh

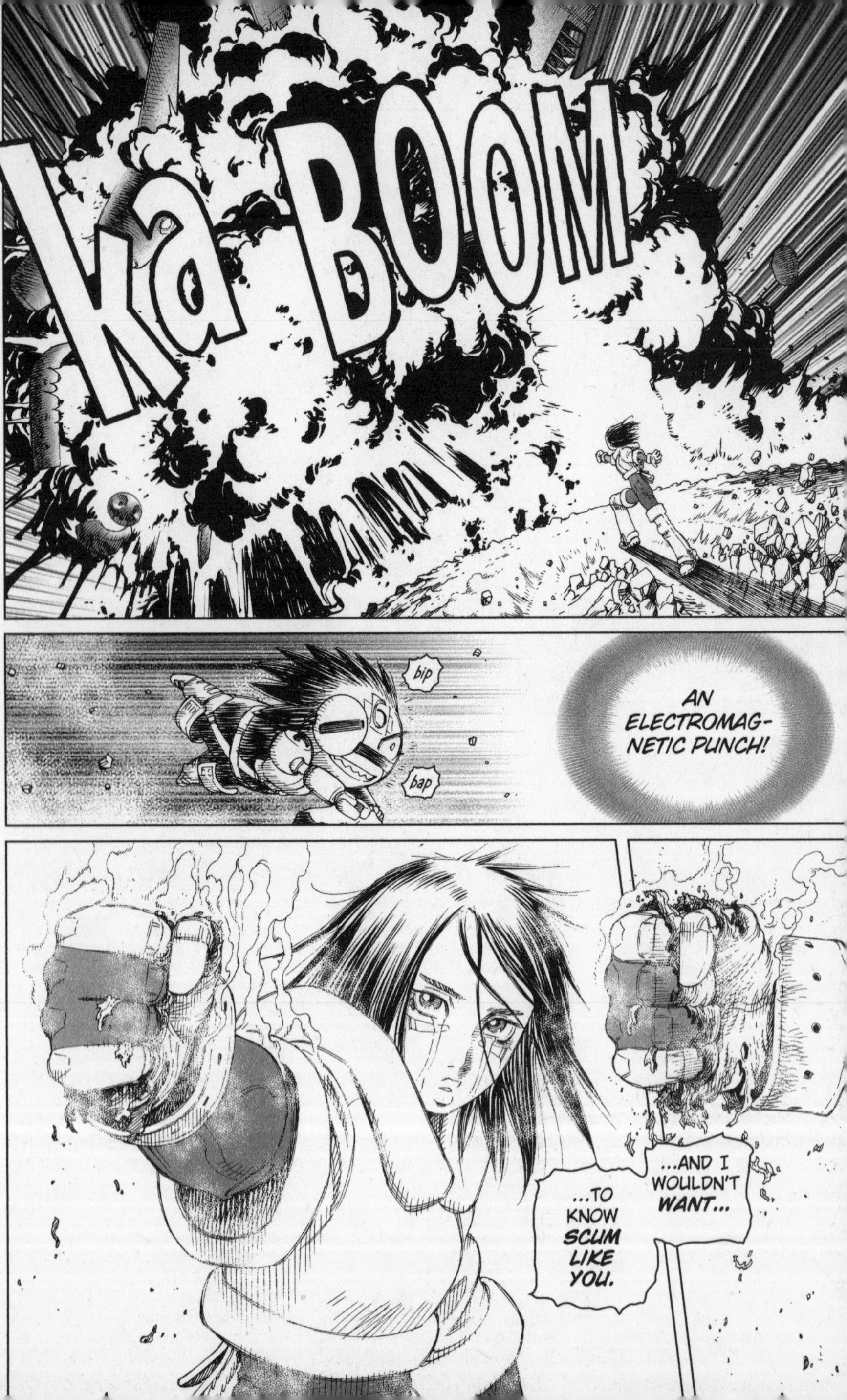
KA-BOOM
AN ELECTROMAGNETIC PUNCH!
bip
bap
...AND I WOULDN'T WANT...
...TO KNOW SCUM LIKE YOU.

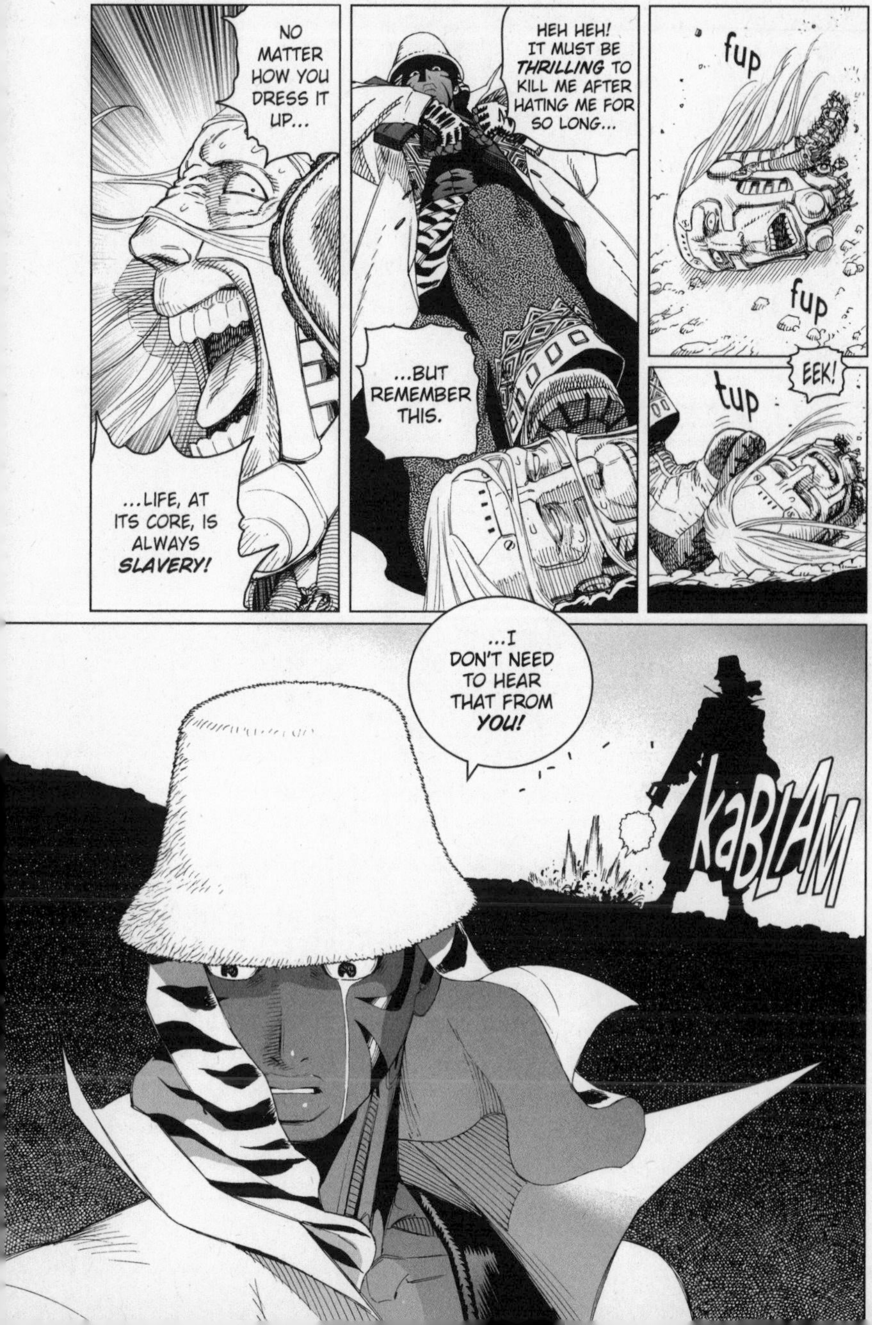
fup
fup
EEK!
tup
HEH HEH! IT MUST BE THRILLING TO KILL ME AFTER HATING ME FOR SO LONG...
...BUT REMEMBER THIS.
NO MATTER HOW YOU DRESS IT UP...
...LIFE, AT ITS CORE, IS ALWAYS SLAVERY!
...I DON'T NEED TO HEAR THAT FROM YOU!
KaBLAM

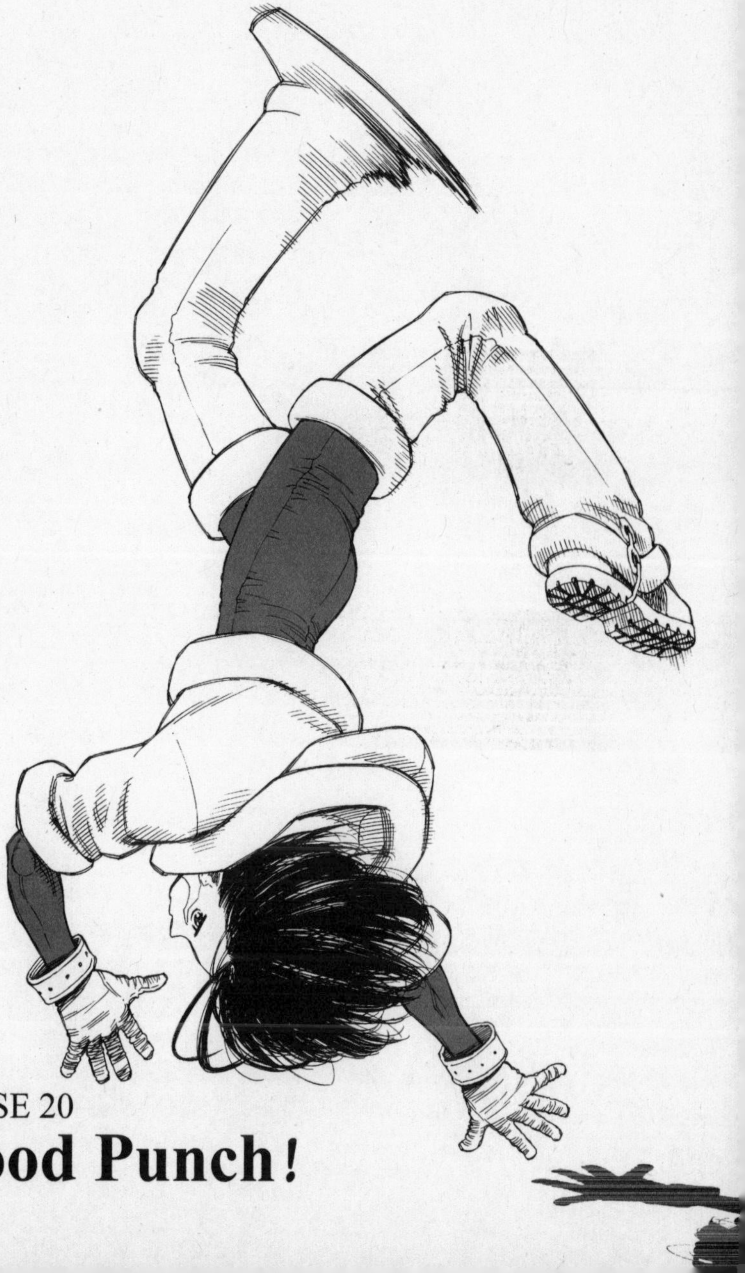

PHASE 20

Good Punch!

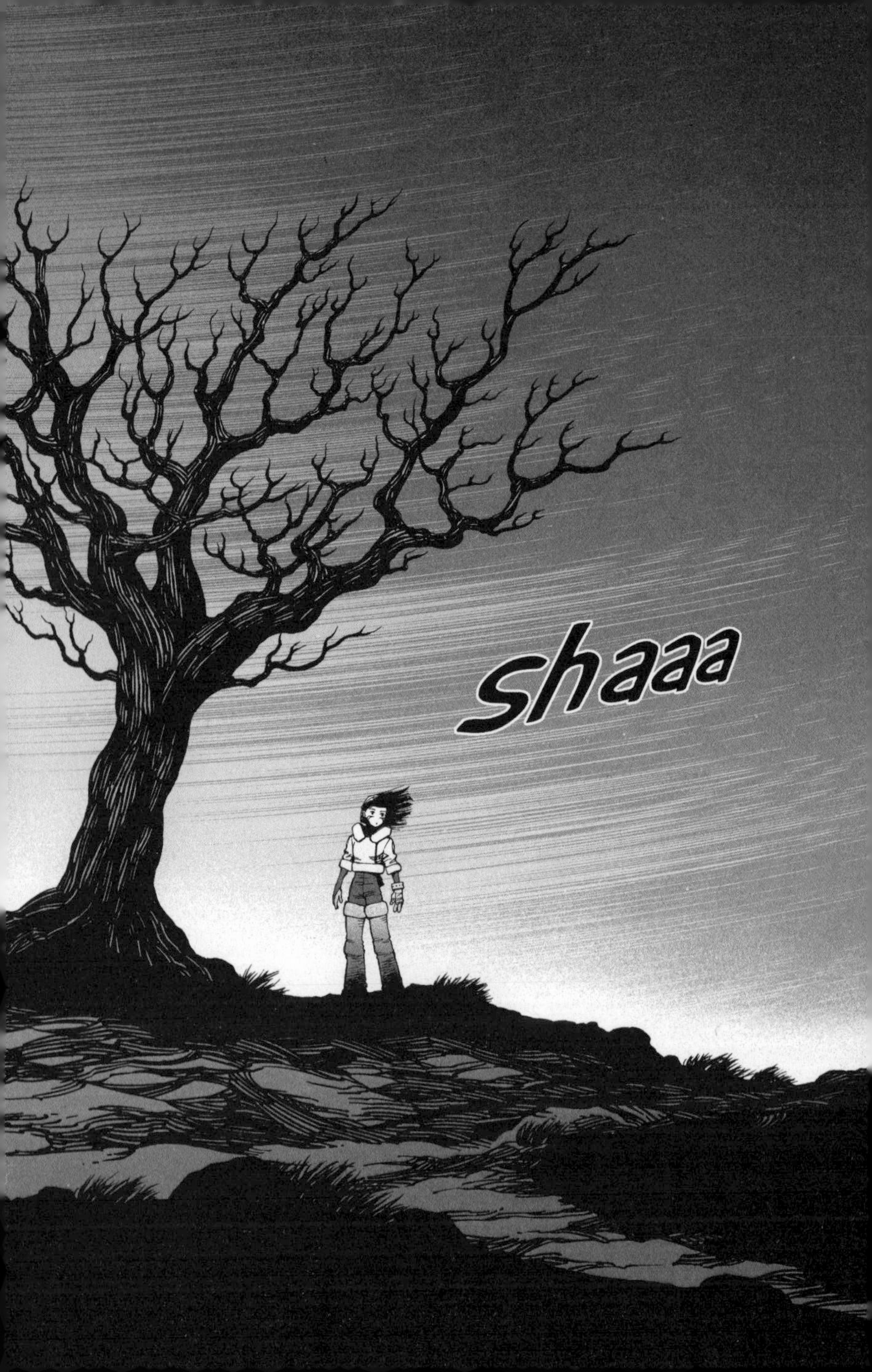
shaaa

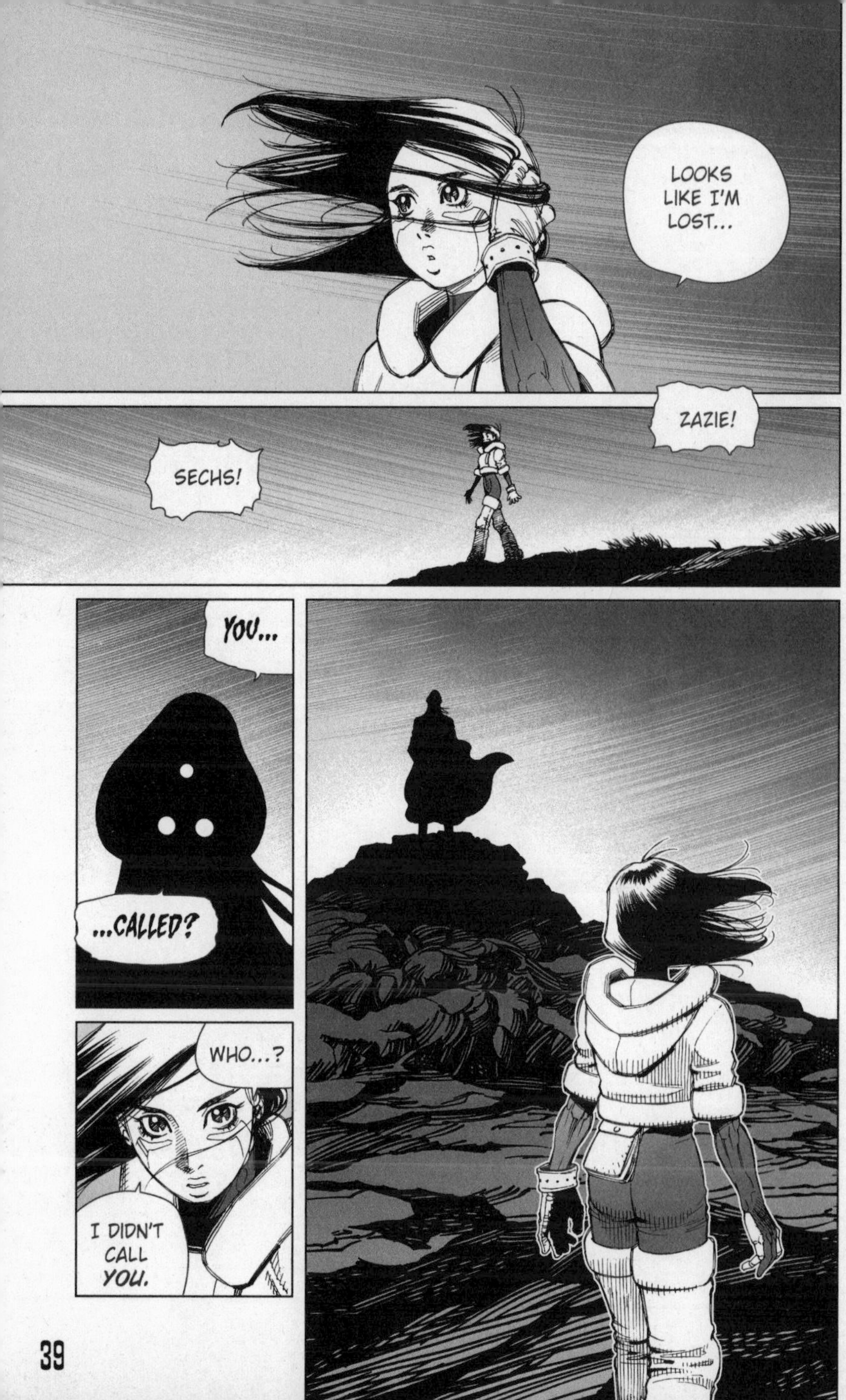
LOOKS LIKE I'M LOST...
ZAZIE!
SECHS!
YOU...
...CALLED?
WHO...?
I DIDN'T CALL YOU.

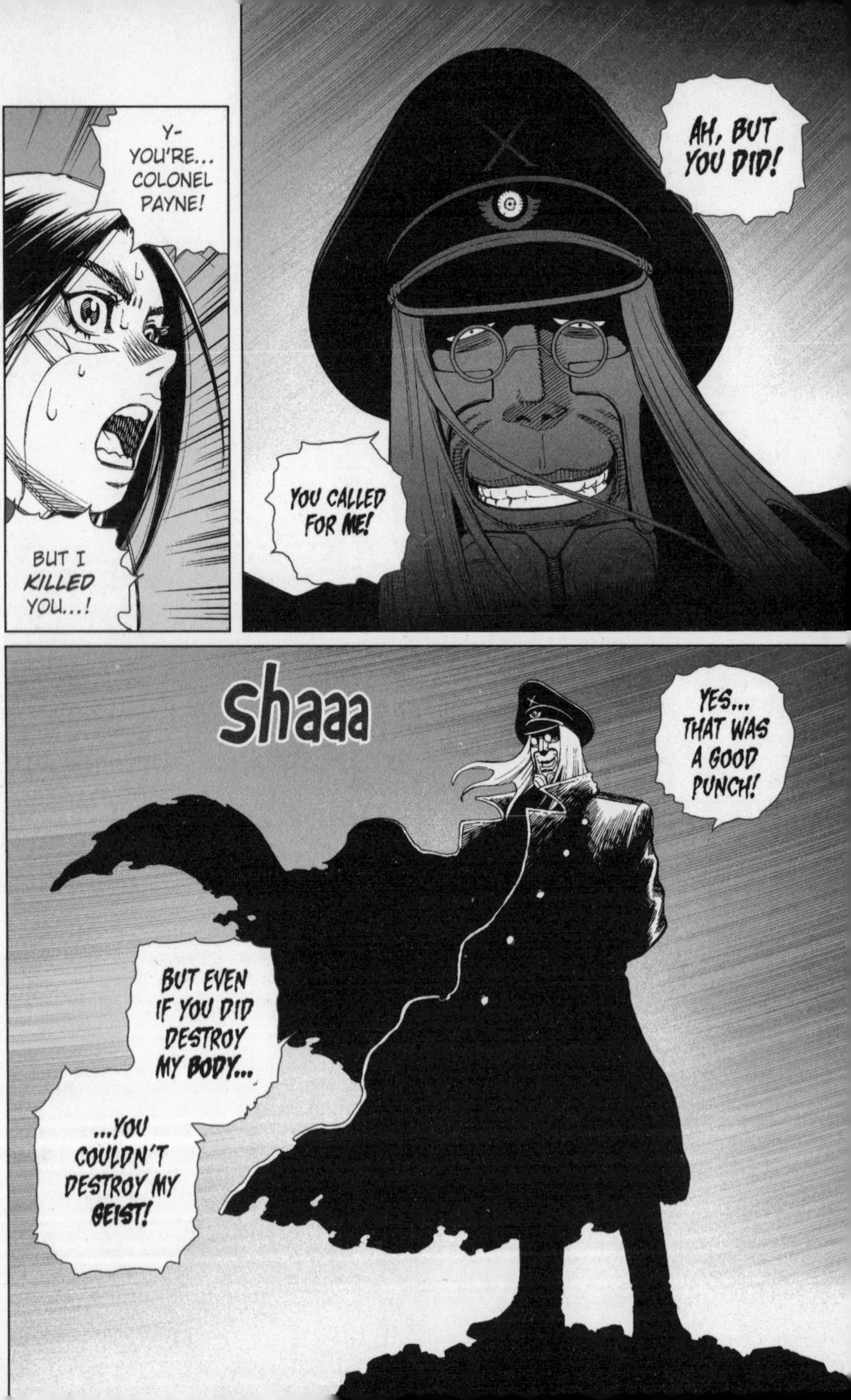
AH, BUT YOU DID!
YOU CALLED FOR ME!
Y- YOU'RE... COLONEL PAYNE!
BUT I *KILLED* YOU...!
YES... THAT WAS A GOOD PUNCH!
shaaa
BUT EVEN IF YOU DID DESTROY MY BODY...
...YOU COULDN'T DESTROY MY GEIST!

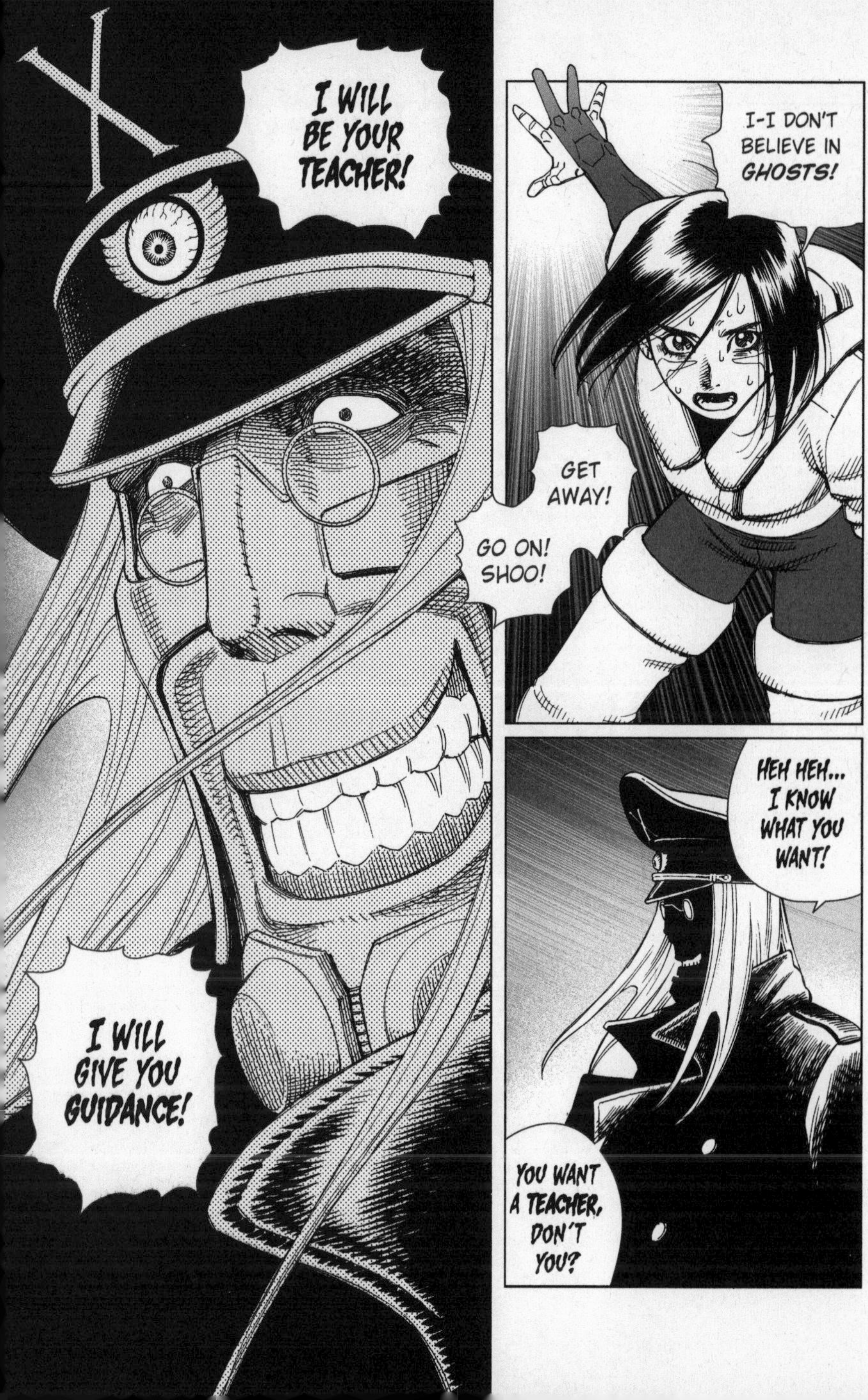
I-I DON'T BELIEVE IN GHOSTS!
GET AWAY!
GO ON! SHOO!
HEH HEH... I KNOW WHAT YOU WANT!
YOU WANT A TEACHER, DON'T YOU?
I WILL BE YOUR TEACHER!
I WILL GIVE YOU GUIDANCE!

WHO'D WANT YOU AS A TEACHER?!

WOOO

tmp

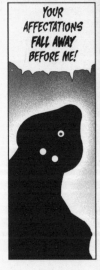

YOUR AFFECTATIONS FALL AWAY BEFORE ME!

?!

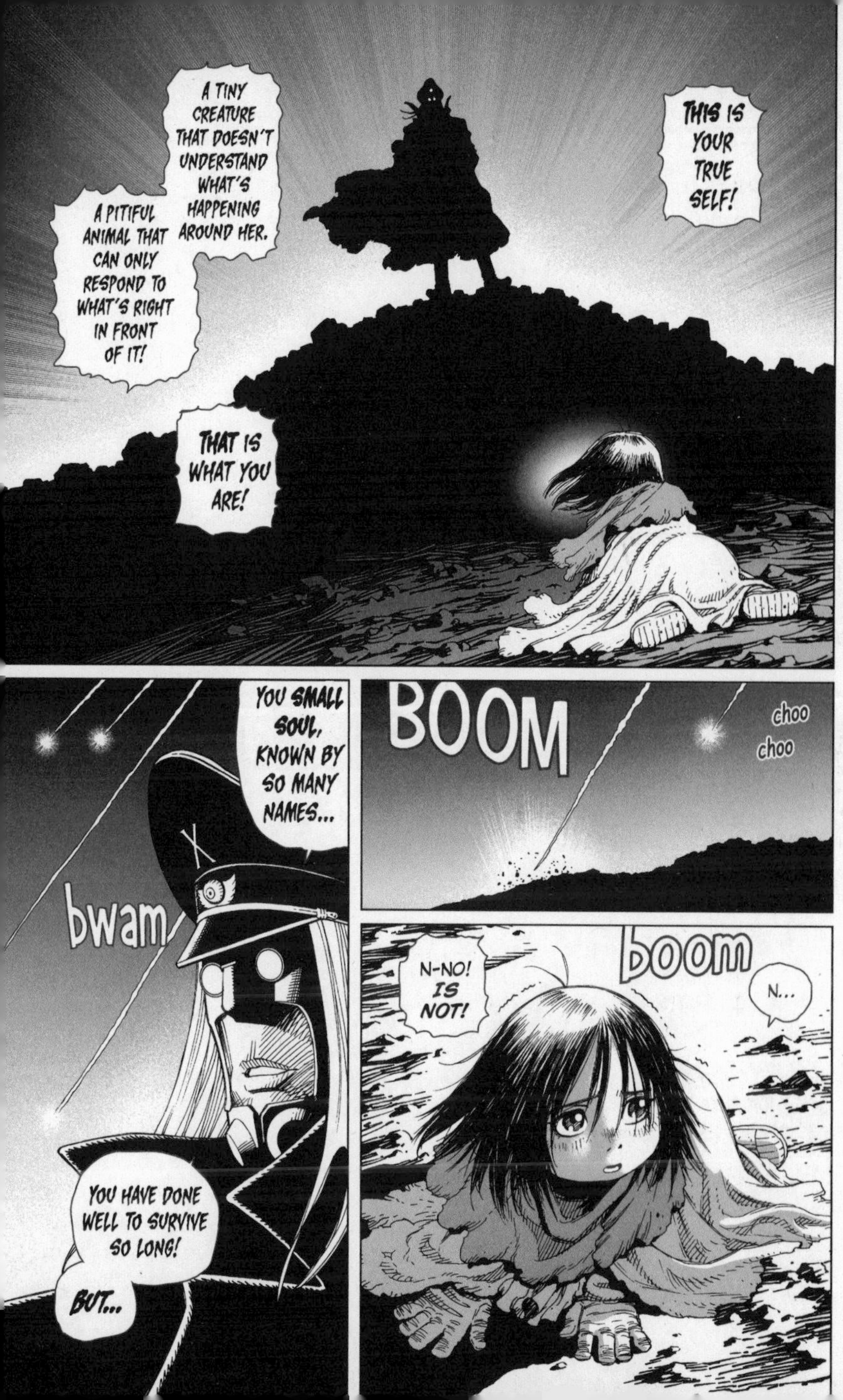
THIS IS YOUR TRUE SELF!
A TINY CREATURE THAT DOESN'T UNDERSTAND WHAT'S HAPPENING AROUND HER.
A PITIFUL ANIMAL THAT CAN ONLY RESPOND TO WHAT'S RIGHT IN FRONT OF IT!
THAT IS WHAT YOU ARE!
BOOM
choo
choo
boom
N...
N-NO! IS NOT!
YOU SMALL SOUL, KNOWN BY SO MANY NAMES...
bwam
YOU HAVE DONE WELL TO SURVIVE SO LONG!
BUT...

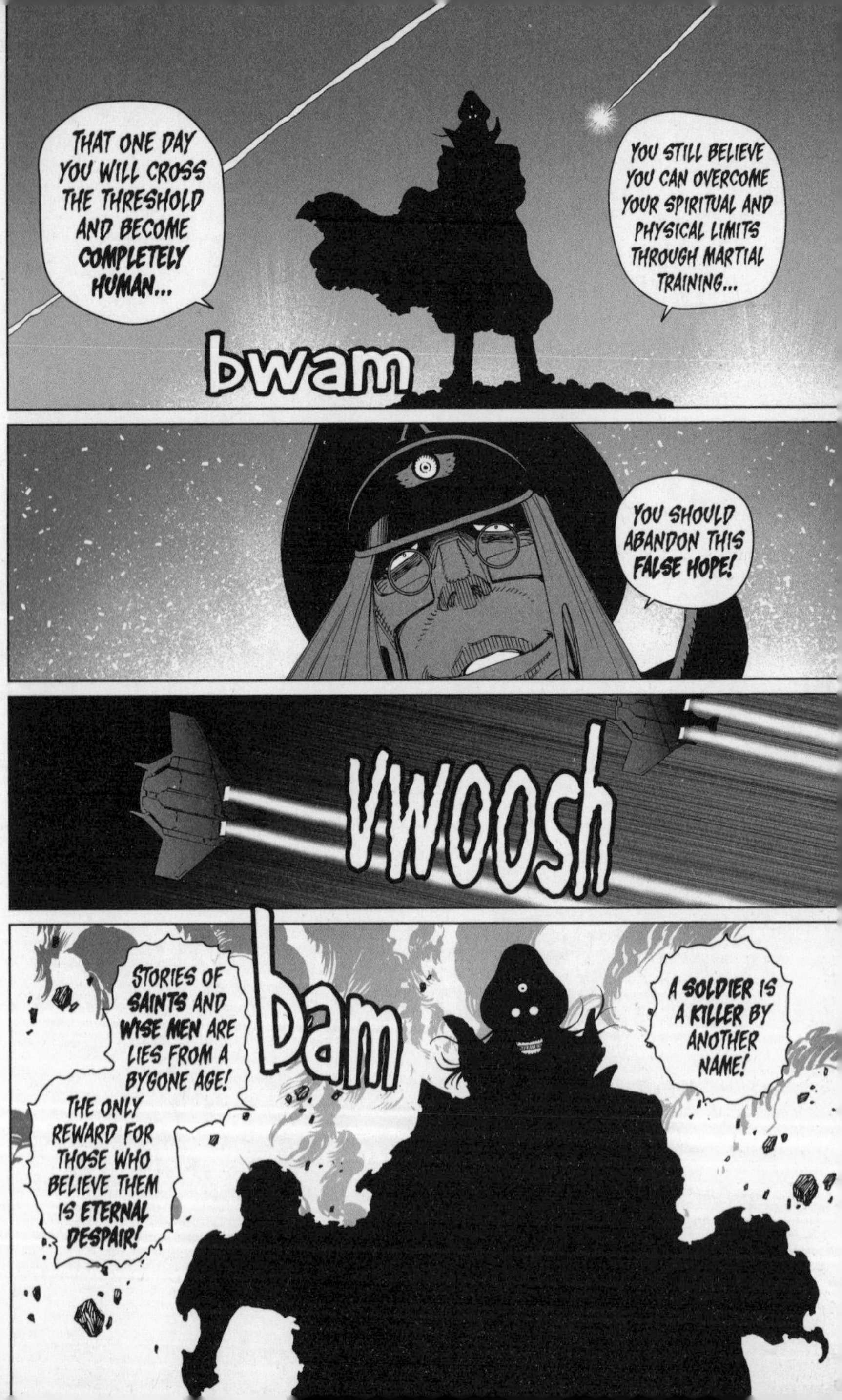
YOU STILL BELIEVE YOU CAN OVERCOME YOUR SPIRITUAL AND PHYSICAL LIMITS THROUGH MARTIAL TRAINING...
THAT ONE DAY YOU WILL CROSS THE THRESHOLD AND BECOME COMPLETELY HUMAN...
bwam
YOU SHOULD ABANDON THIS FALSE HOPE!
vwoosh
A SOLDIER IS A KILLER BY ANOTHER NAME!
bam
STORIES OF SAINTS AND WISE MEN ARE LIES FROM A BYGONE AGE!
THE ONLY REWARD FOR THOSE WHO BELIEVE THEM IS ETERNAL DESPAIR!

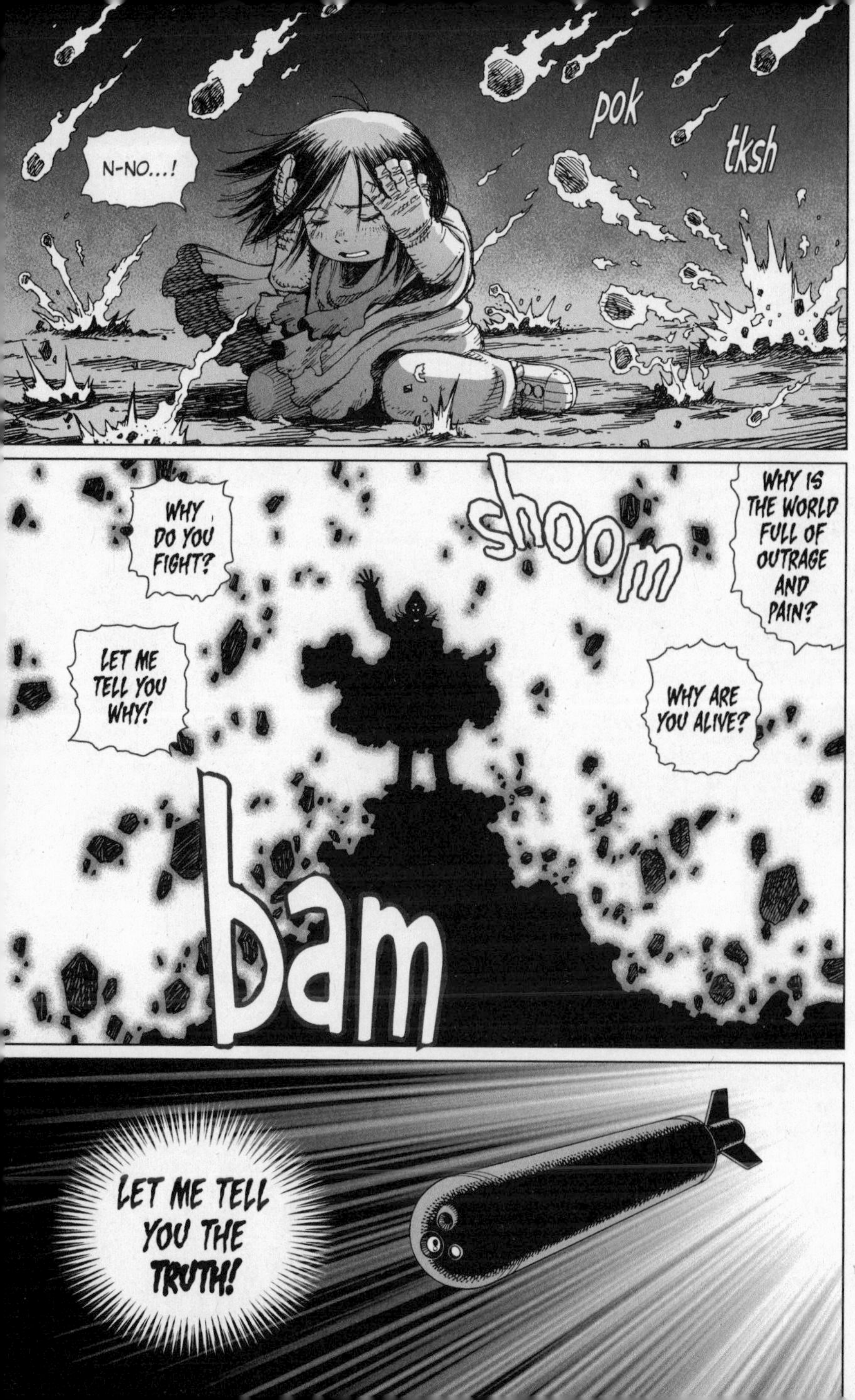
pok
tksh
N-NO...!
WHY IS THE WORLD FULL OF OUTRAGE AND PAIN?
shoom
WHY DO YOU FIGHT?
WHY ARE YOU ALIVE?
LET ME TELL YOU WHY!
bam
LET ME TELL YOU THE TRUTH!

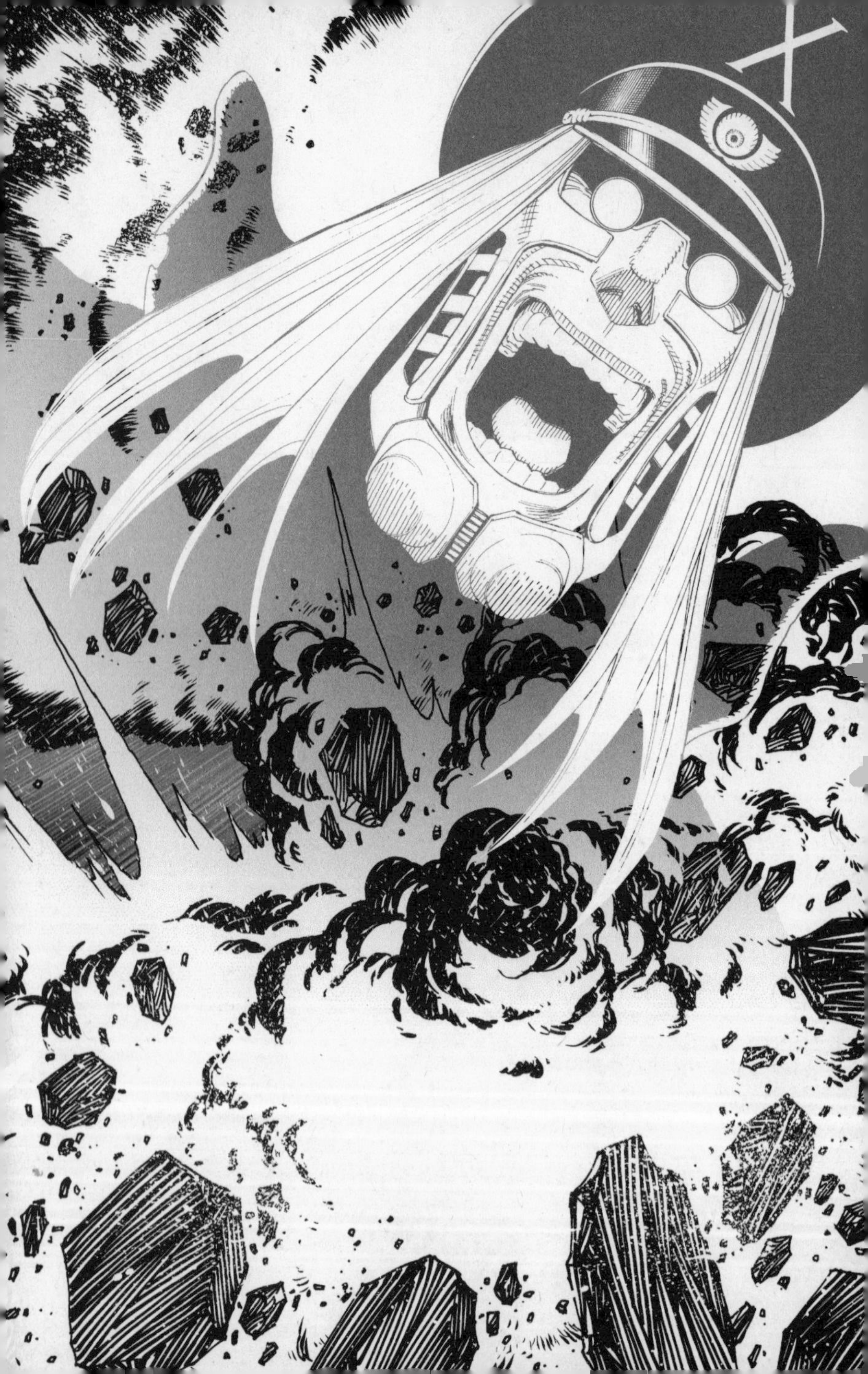

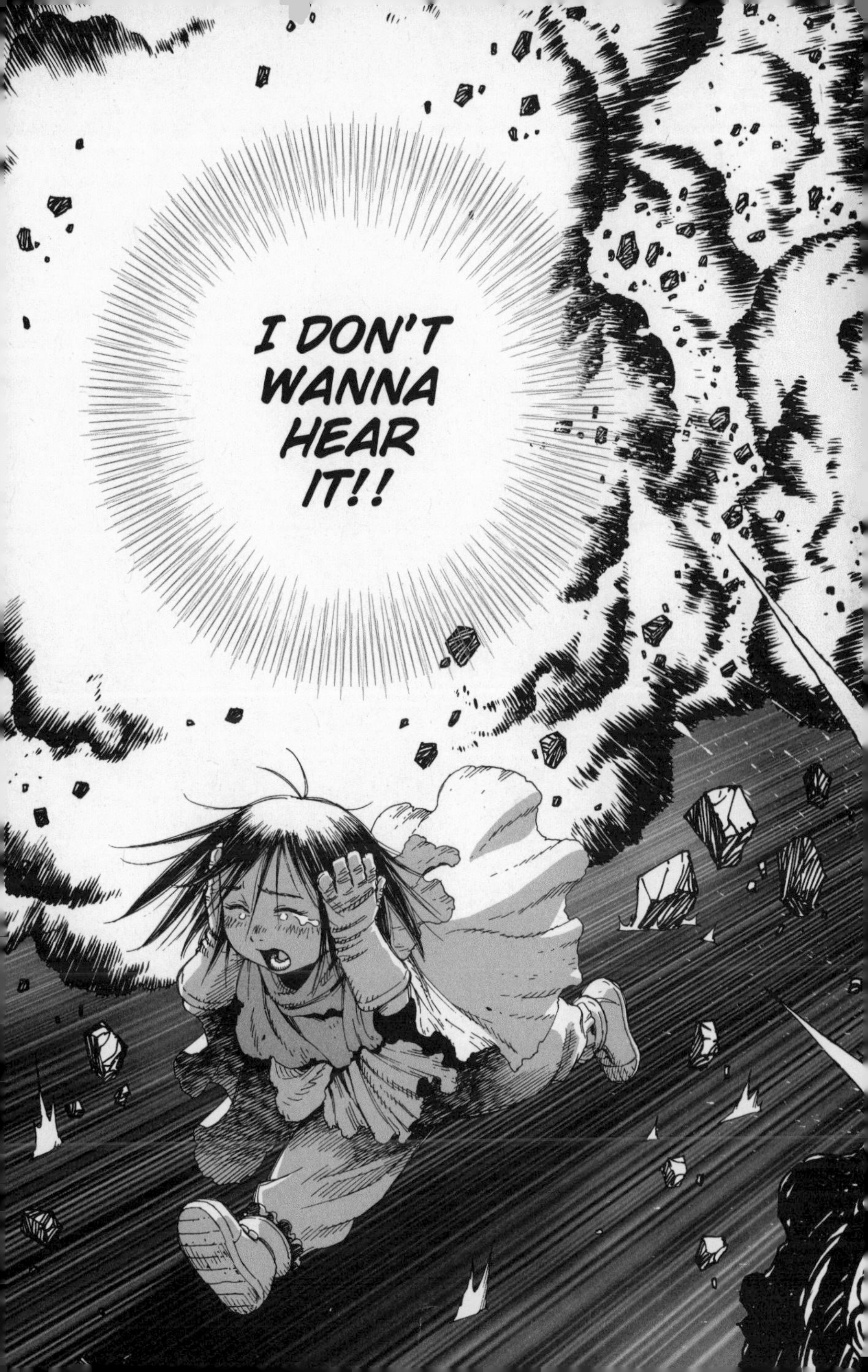
I DON'T WANNA HEAR IT!!

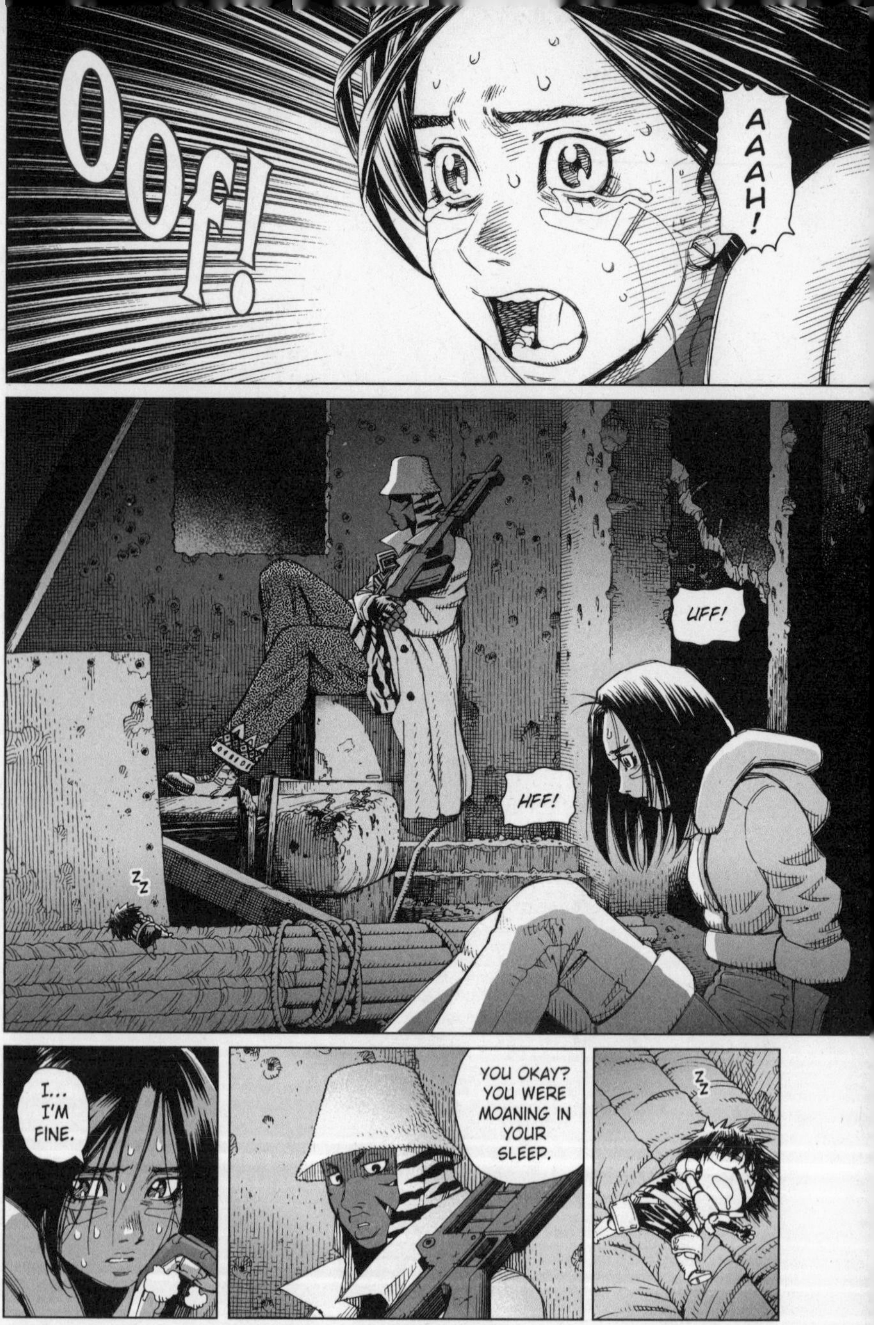
AAAH!
OOF!
UFF!
HFF!
ZZ
ZZ
YOU OKAY? YOU WERE MOANING IN YOUR SLEEP.
I... I'M FINE.

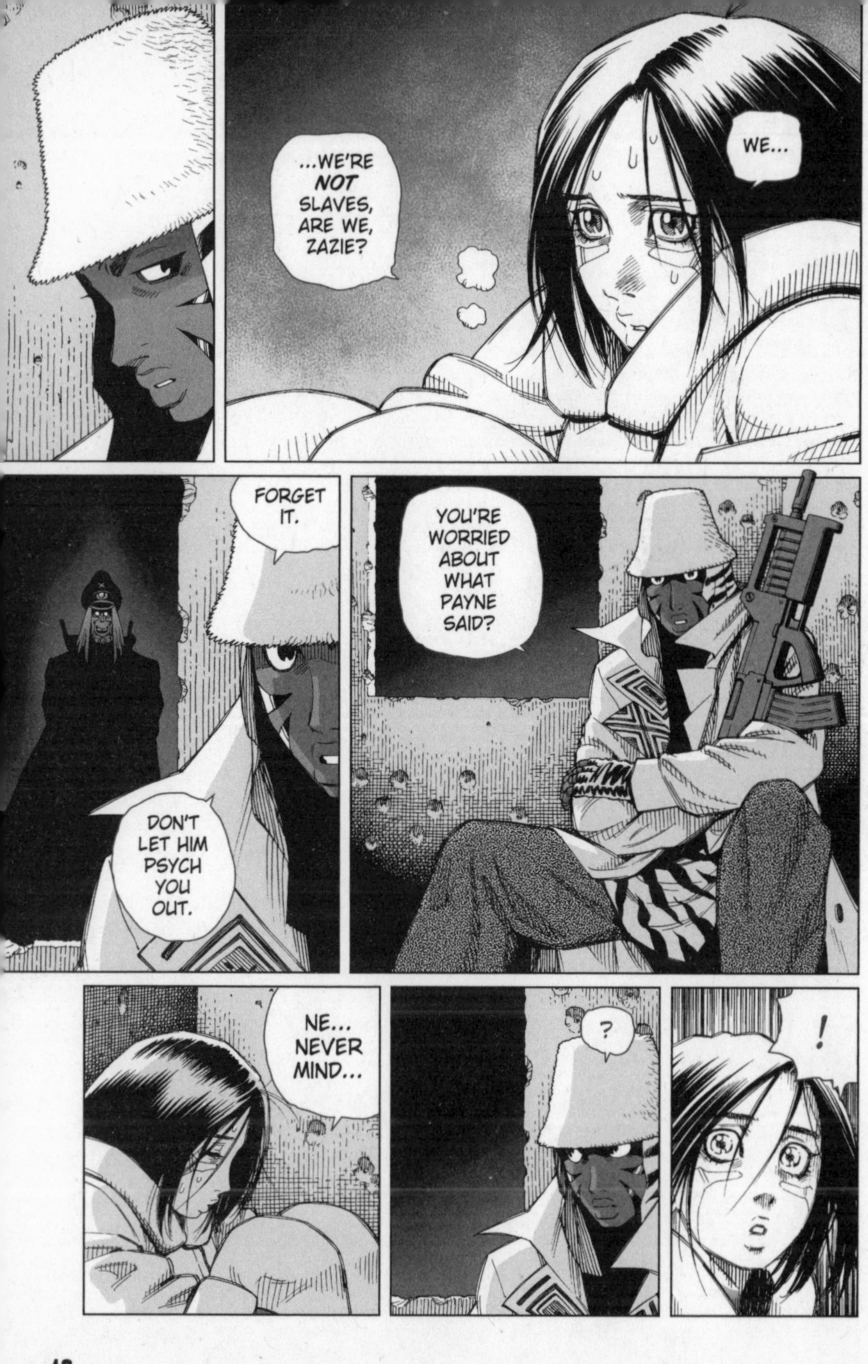
WE...
...WE'RE NOT SLAVES, ARE WE, ZAZIE?
YOU'RE WORRIED ABOUT WHAT PAYNE SAID?
FORGET IT.
DON'T LET HIM PSYCH YOU OUT.
!
?
NE... NEVER MIND...

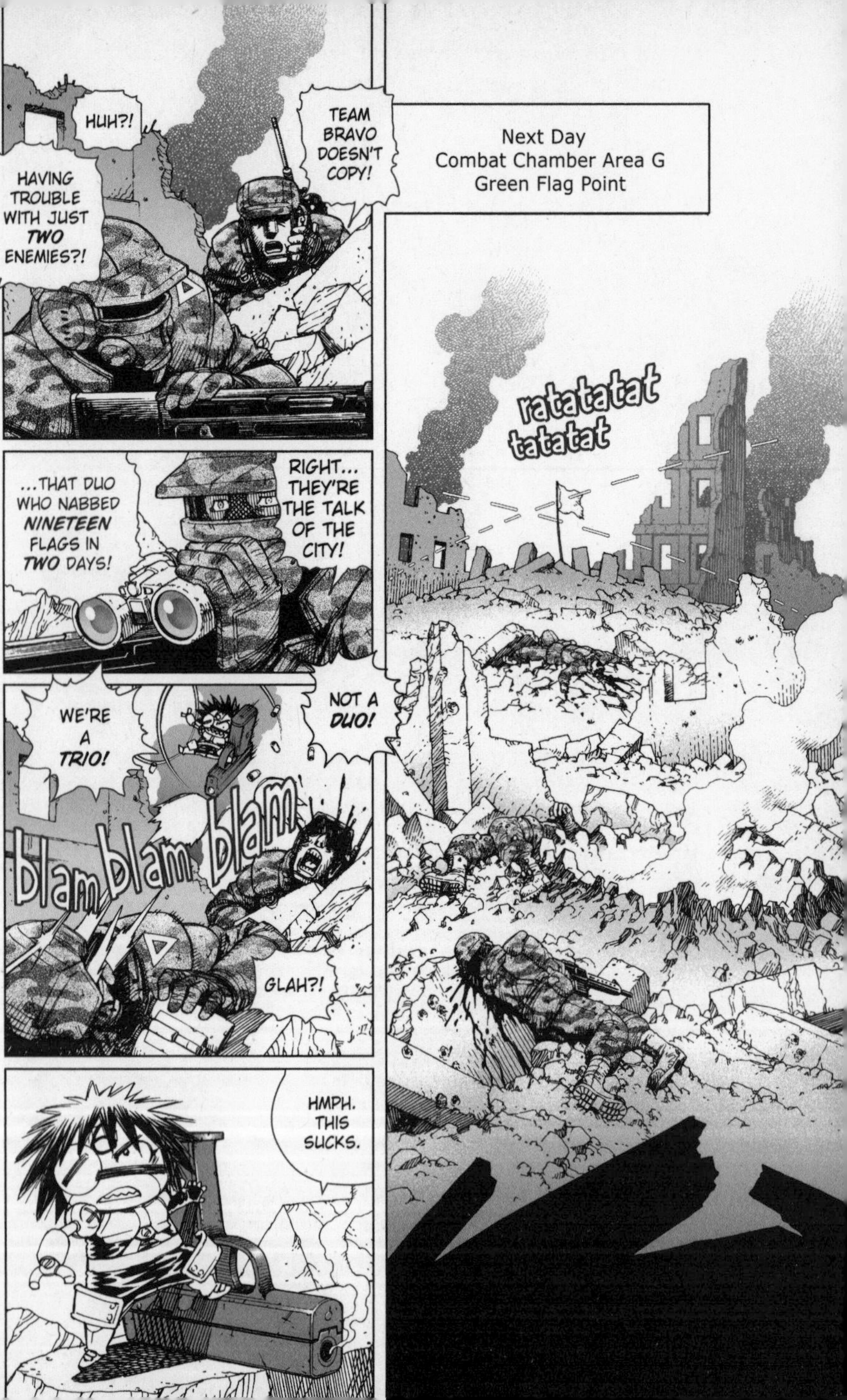
Next Day
Combat Chamber Area G
Green Flag Point
ratatatat tatatat
TEAM BRAVO DOESN'T COPY!
HUH?!
HAVING TROUBLE WITH JUST TWO ENEMIES?!
RIGHT... THEY'RE THE TALK OF THE CITY!
...THAT DUO WHO NABBED NINETEEN FLAGS IN TWO DAYS!
NOT A DUO!
WE'RE A TRIO!
blam blam blam
GLAH?!
HMPH. THIS SUCKS.

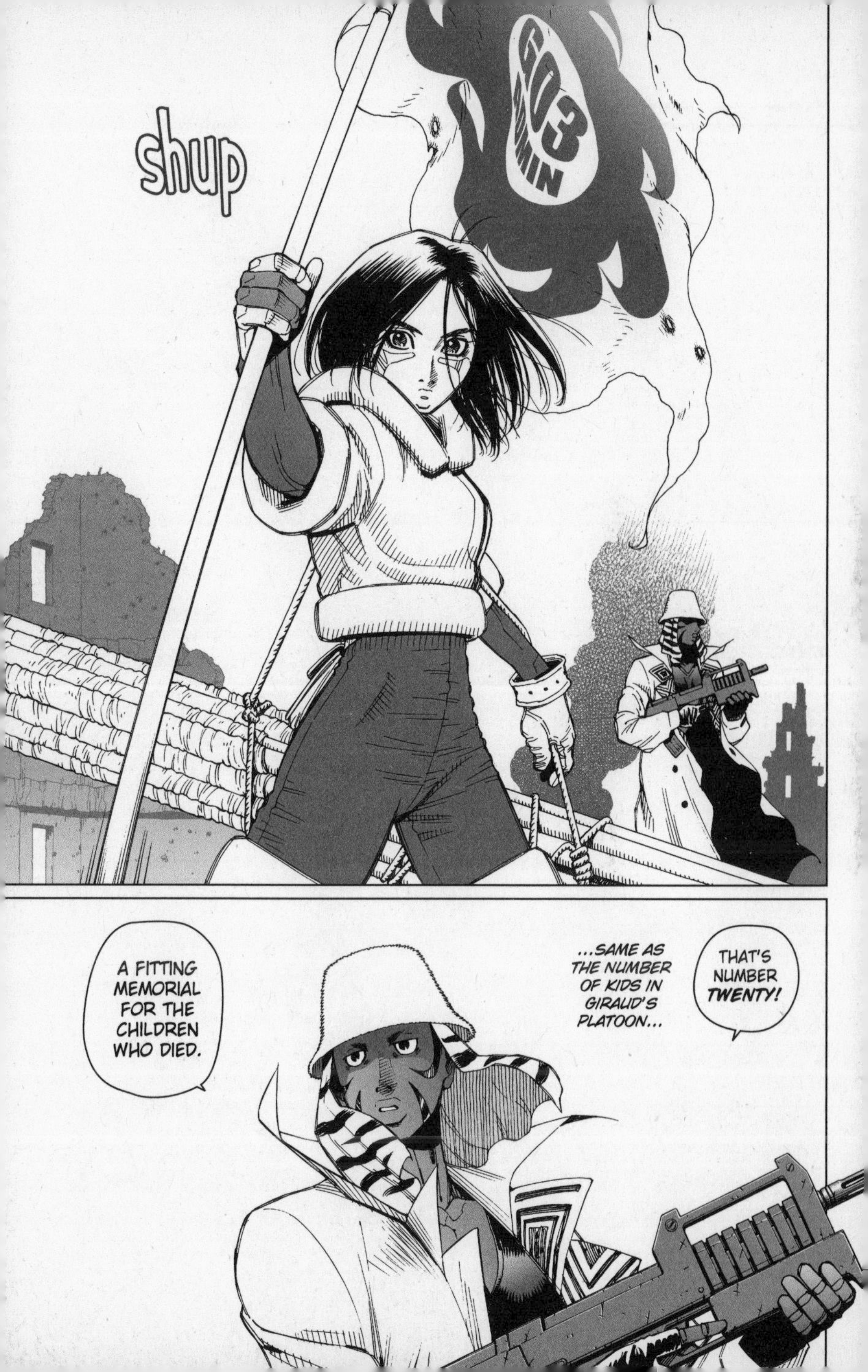
shup
GO3
THAT'S NUMBER *TWENTY!*
...SAME AS THE NUMBER OF KIDS IN GIRAUD'S PLATOON...
A FITTING MEMORIAL FOR THE CHILDREN WHO DIED.

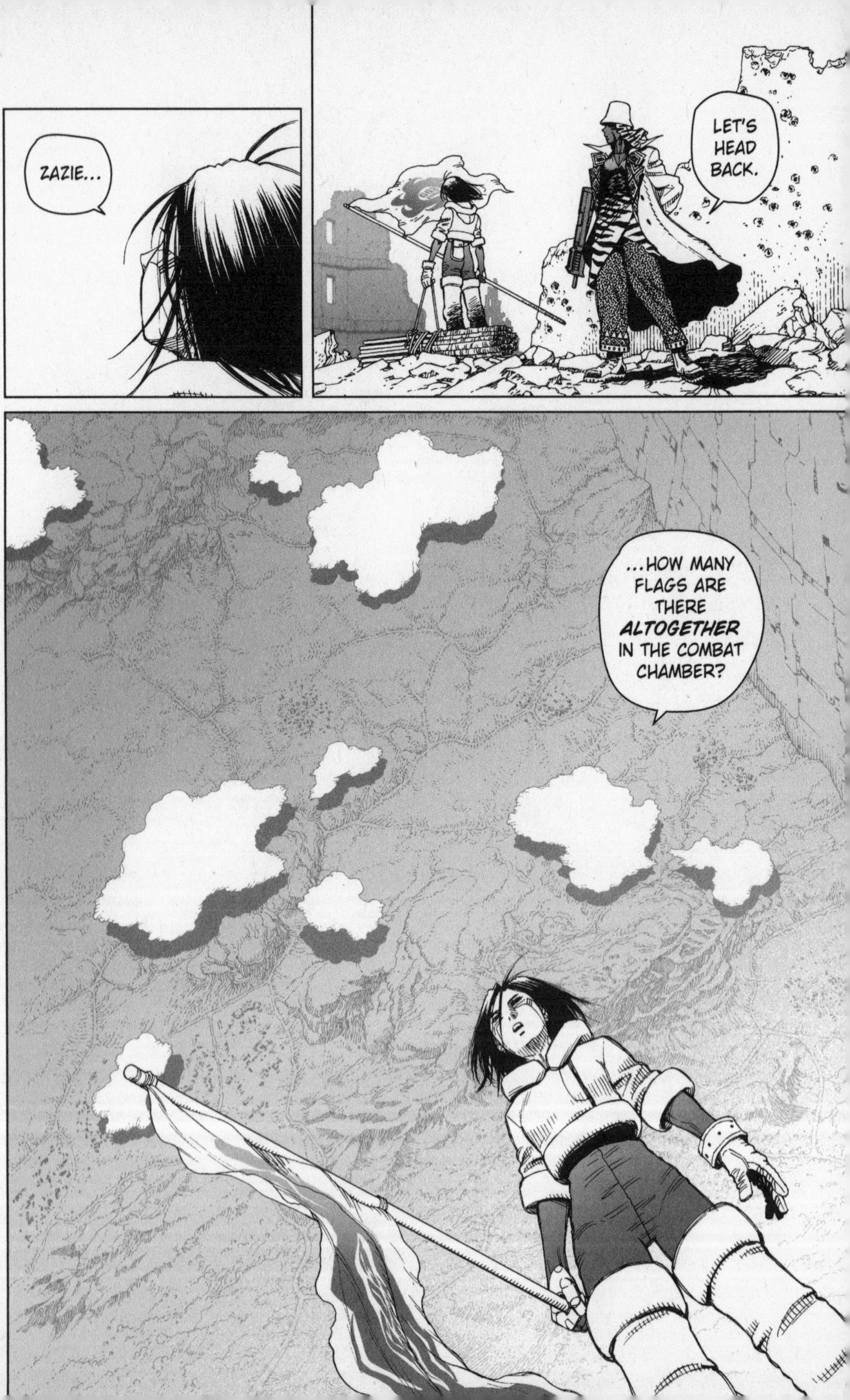
LET'S HEAD BACK.
ZAZIE...
...HOW MANY FLAGS ARE THERE **ALTOGETHER** IN THE COMBAT CHAMBER?

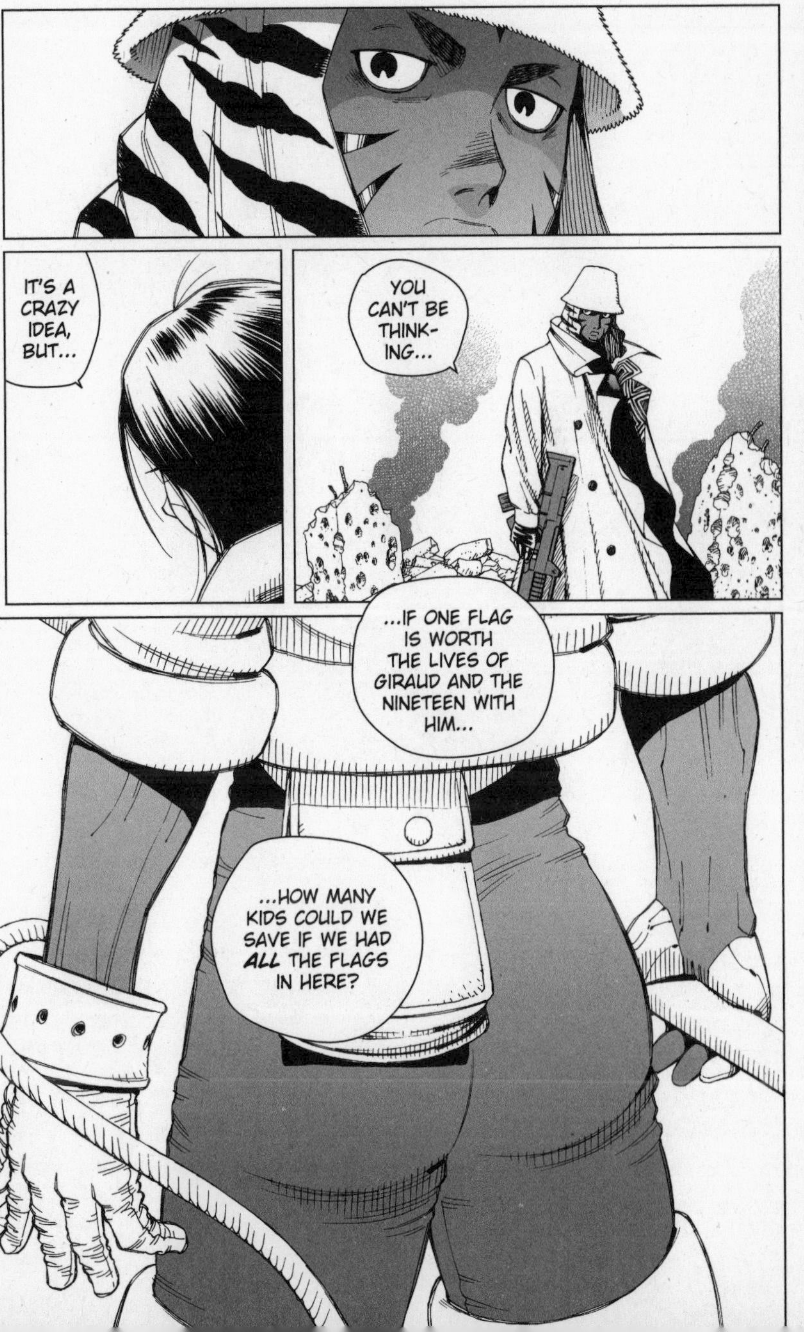
YOU CAN'T BE THINK-ING...
IT'S A CRAZY IDEA, BUT...
...IF ONE FLAG IS WORTH THE LIVES OF GIRAUD AND THE NINETEEN WITH HIM...
...HOW MANY KIDS COULD WE SAVE IF WE HAD ALL THE FLAGS IN HERE?

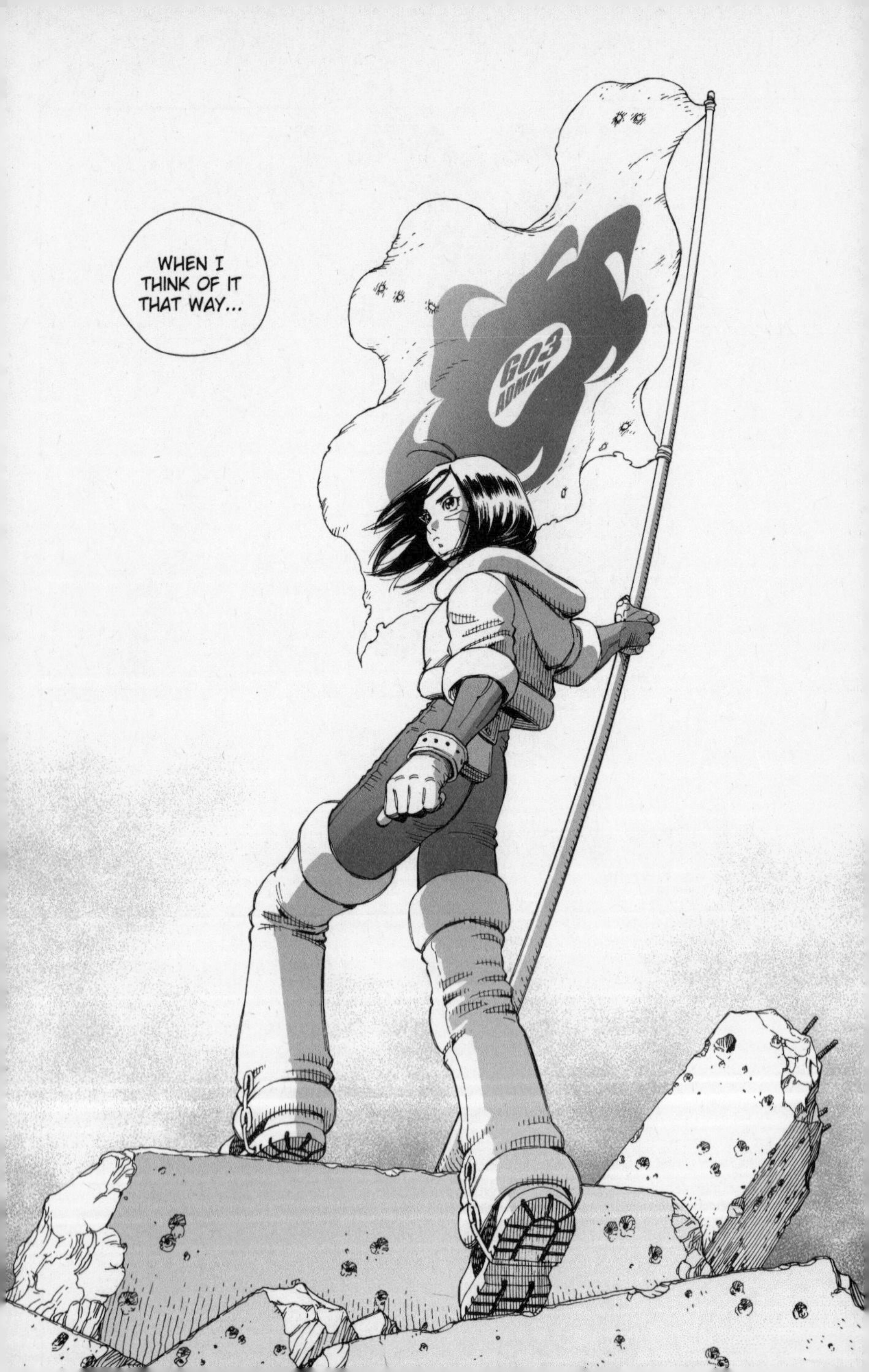
WHEN I THINK OF IT THAT WAY...

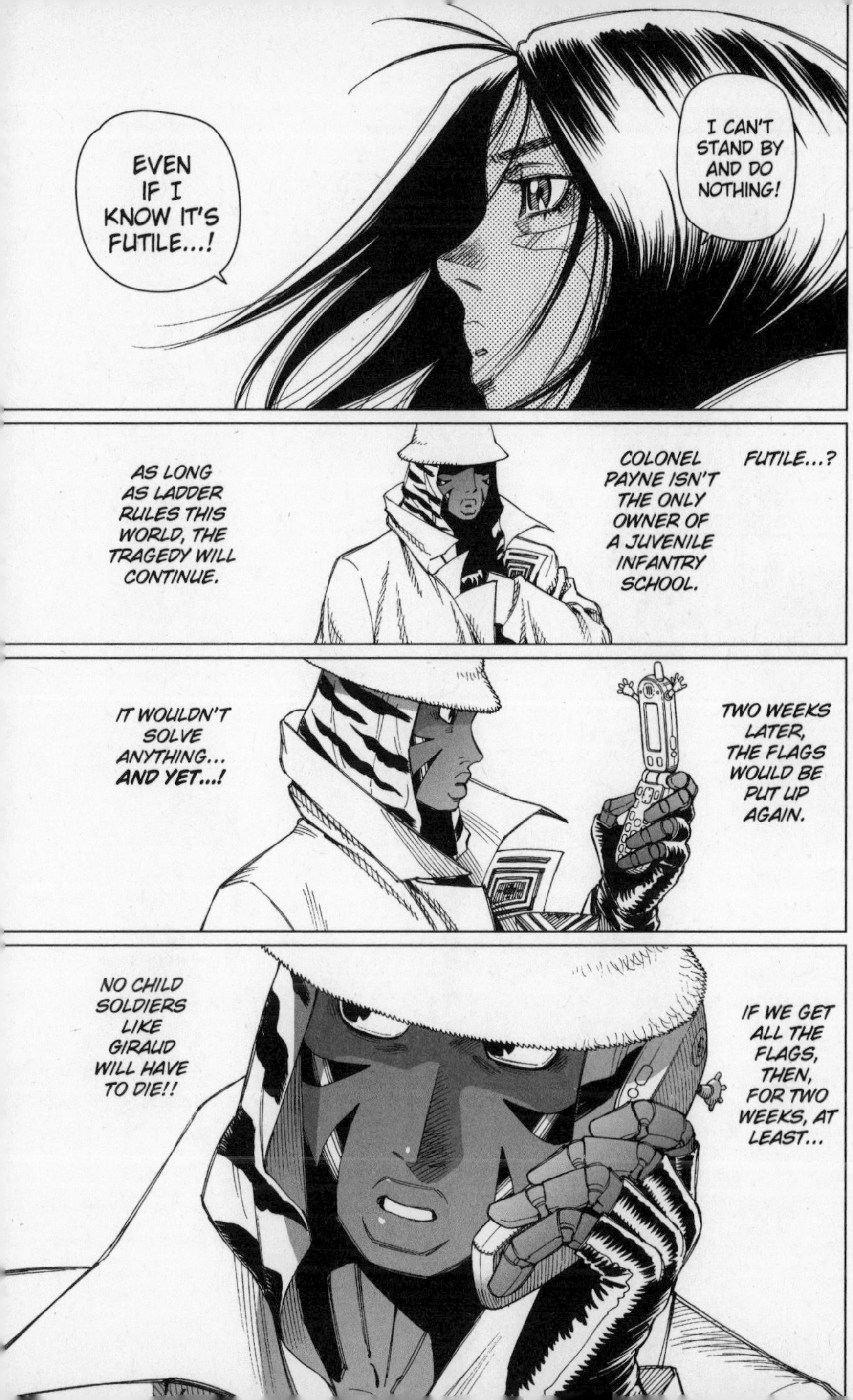
I CAN'T STAND BY AND DO NOTHING!
EVEN IF I KNOW IT'S FUTILE...!
FUTILE...?
COLONEL PAYNE ISN'T THE ONLY OWNER OF A JUVENILE INFANTRY SCHOOL.
AS LONG AS LADDER RULES THIS WORLD, THE TRAGEDY WILL CONTINUE.
TWO WEEKS LATER, THE FLAGS WOULD BE PUT UP AGAIN.
IT WOULDN'T SOLVE ANYTHING... AND YET...!
IF WE GET ALL THE FLAGS, THEN, FOR TWO WEEKS, AT LEAST...
NO CHILD SOLDIERS LIKE GIRAUD WILL HAVE TO DIE!!

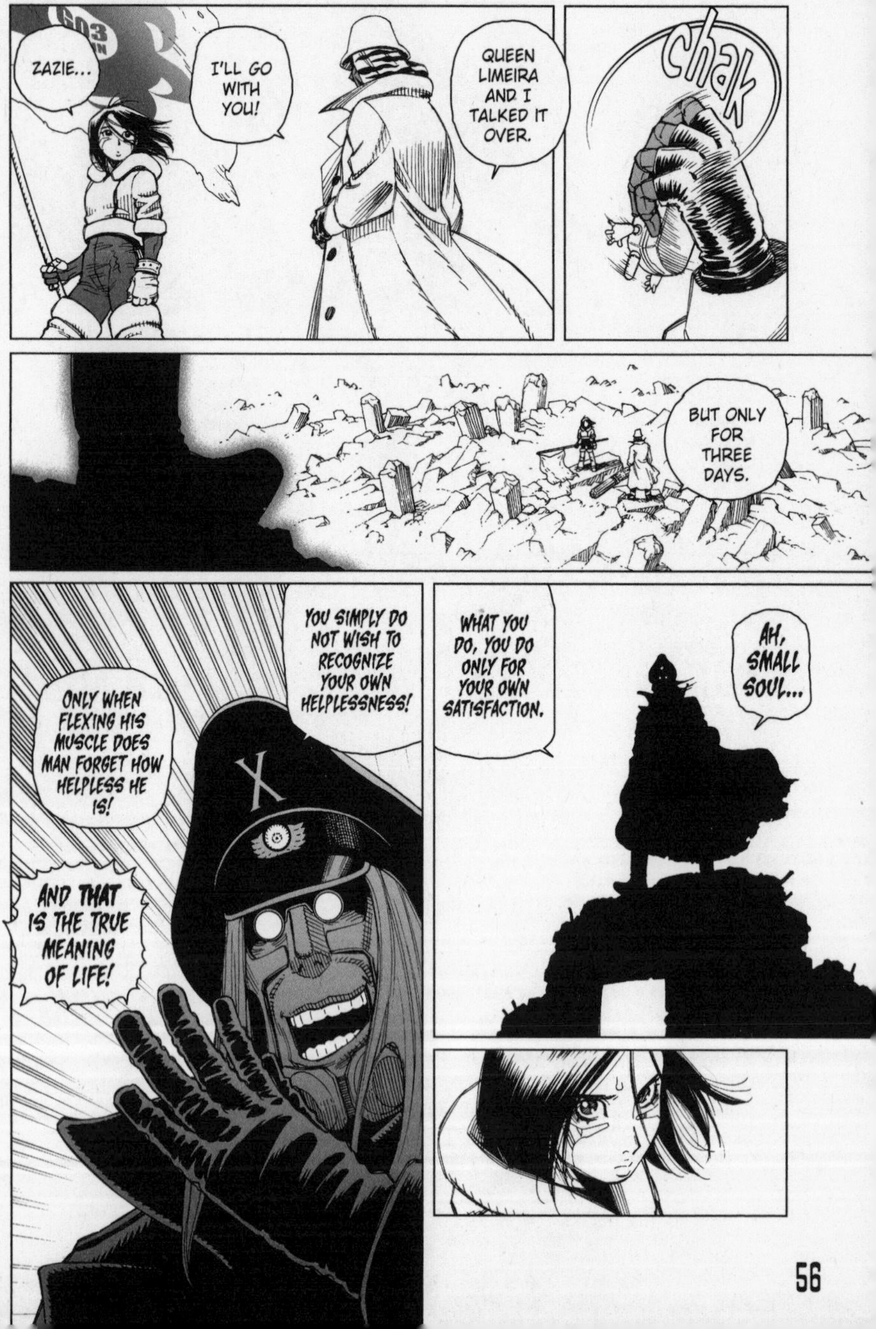
chak
QUEEN LIMEIRA AND I TALKED IT OVER.
I'LL GO WITH YOU!
ZAZIE...
BUT ONLY FOR THREE DAYS.
AH, SMALL SOUL...
WHAT YOU DO, YOU DO ONLY FOR YOUR OWN SATISFACTION.
YOU SIMPLY DO NOT WISH TO RECOGNIZE YOUR OWN HELPLESSNESS!
ONLY WHEN FLEXING HIS MUSCLE DOES MAN FORGET HOW HELPLESS HE IS!
AND THAT IS THE TRUE MEANING OF LIFE!

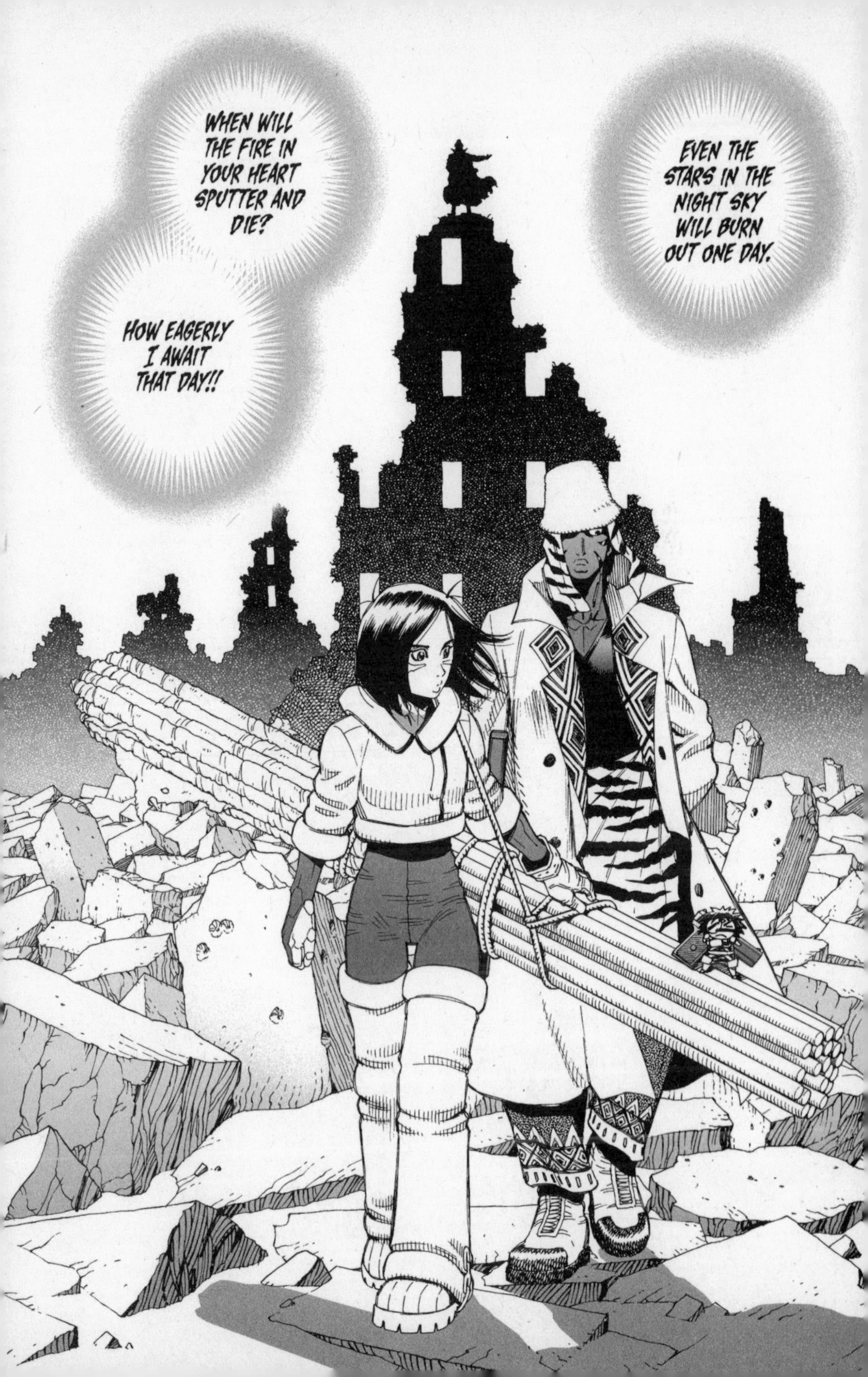
EVEN THE STARS IN THE NIGHT SKY WILL BURN OUT ONE DAY.
WHEN WILL THE FIRE IN YOUR HEART SPUTTER AND DIE?
HOW EAGERLY I AWAIT THAT DAY!!

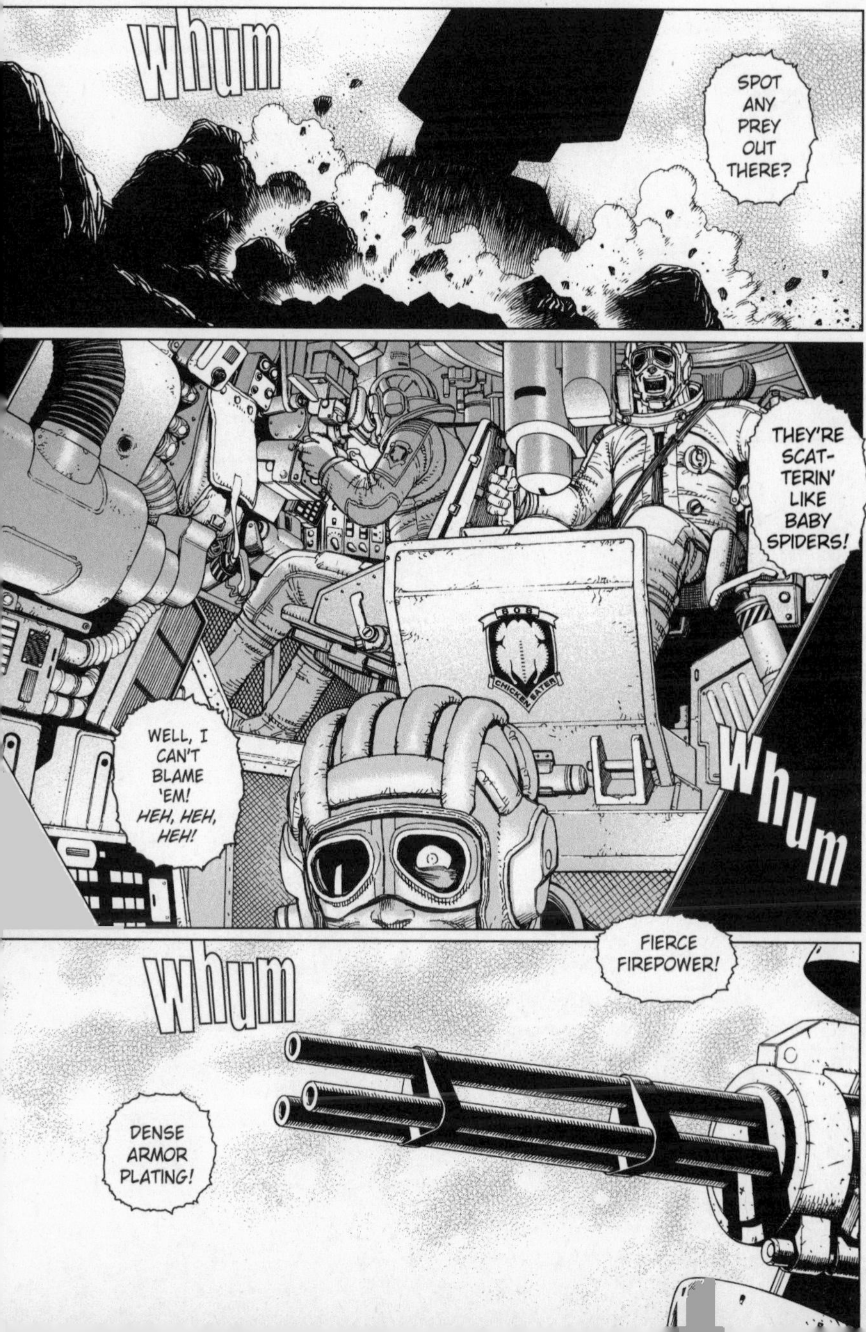
SPOT ANY PREY OUT THERE?
whum
THEY'RE SCAT-TERIN' LIKE BABY SPIDERS!
SOS
CHICKEN EATER
Whum
WELL, I CAN'T BLAME 'EM! HEH, HEH, HEH!
FIERCE FIREPOWER!
whum
DENSE ARMOR PLATING!

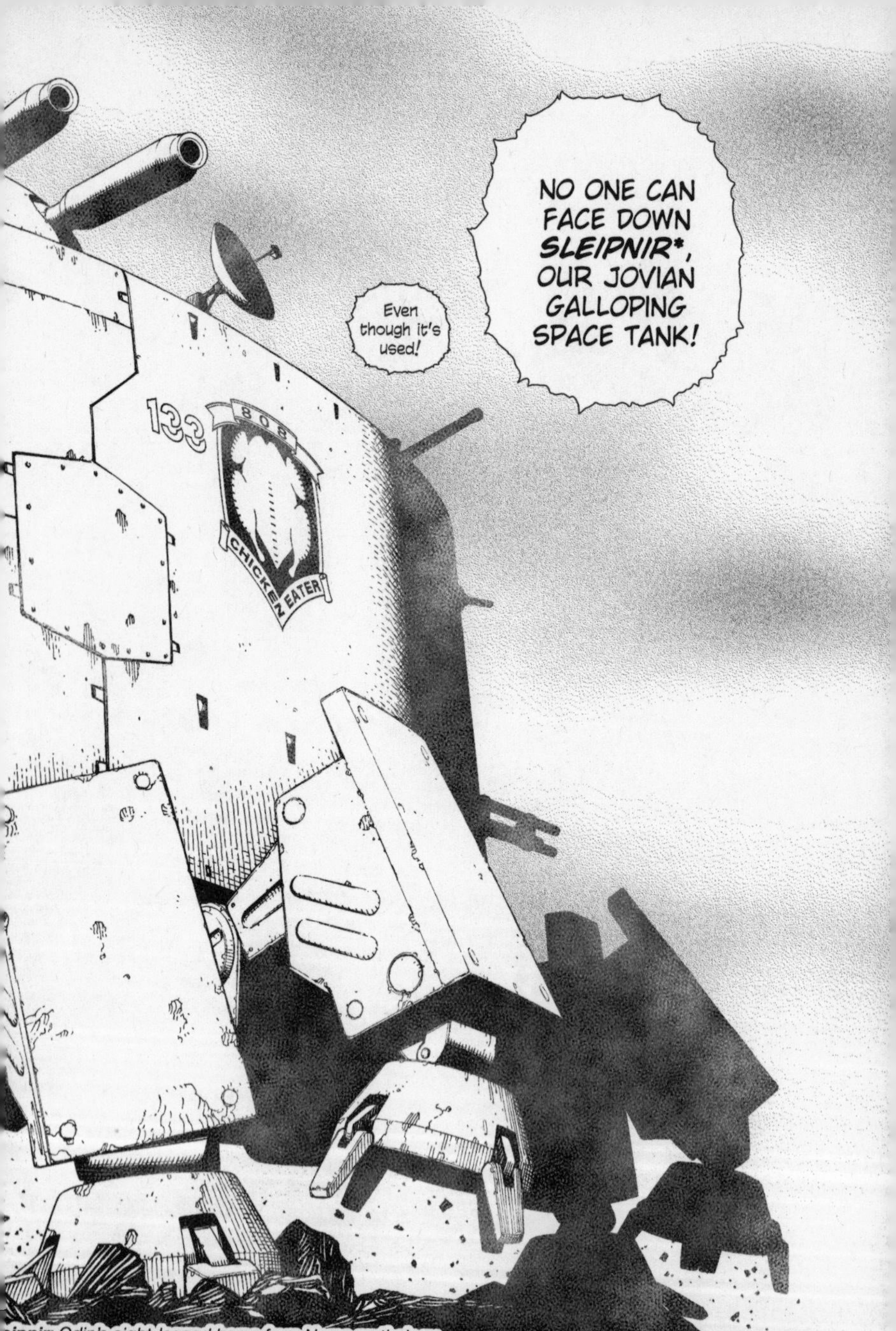
NO ONE CAN FACE DOWN *SLEIPNIR**, OUR JOVIAN GALLOPING SPACE TANK!
Even though it's used!
133
808
CHICKEN EATER

***eipnir:** Odin's eight-legged horse from Norse mythology.*

PHASE 21
Let Me Give You Some Advice

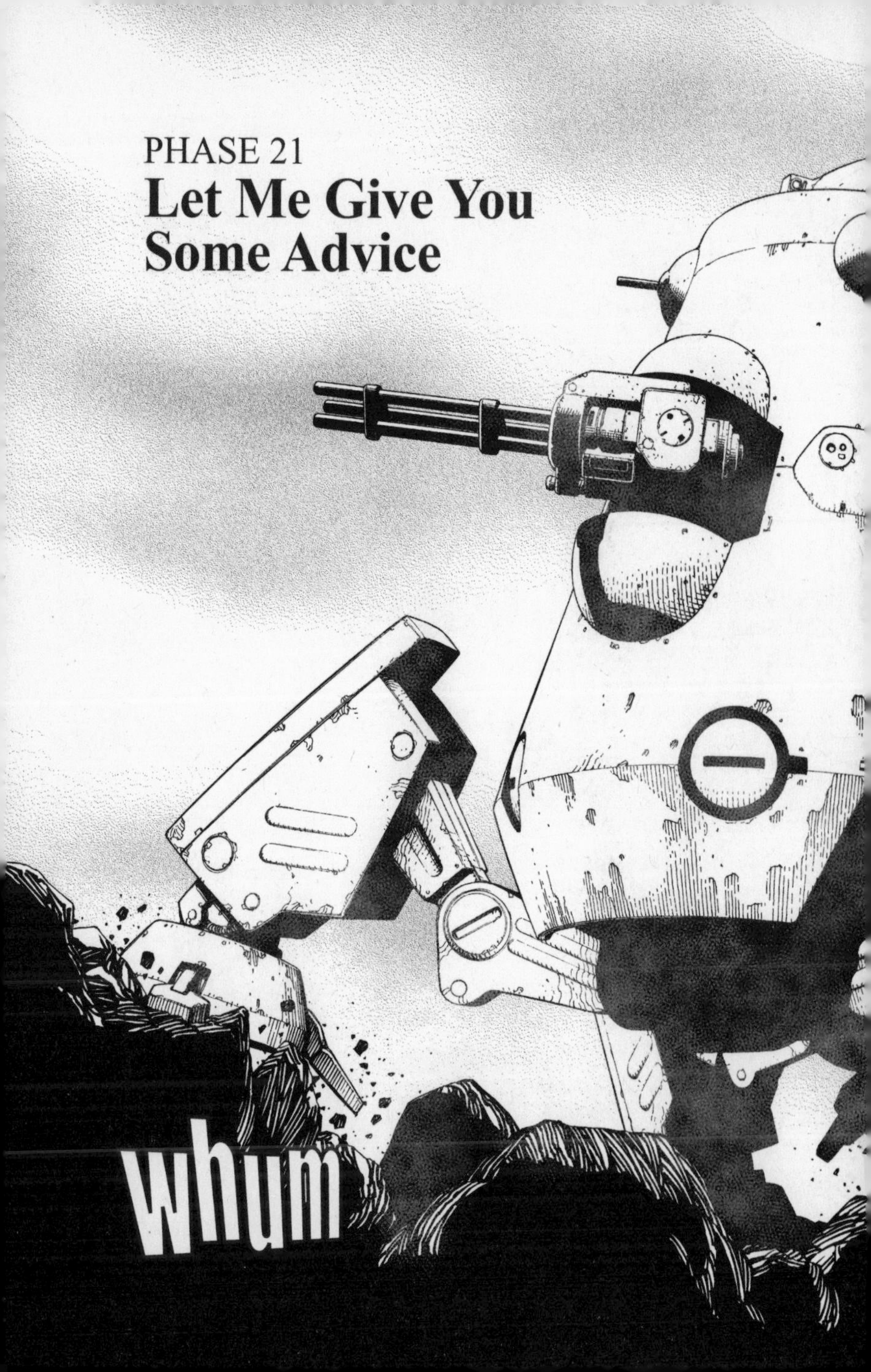
whum

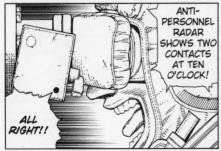

ANTI-PERSONNEL RADAR SHOWS TWO CONTACTS AT TEN O'CLOCK!

ALL RIGHT!!

FLAG Z-03 IN SIGHT! DISTANCE EIGHT HUNDRED METERS!

SERVE 'EM UP HOT!!

brrraaat

whrrr

DEEE-LICIOUS!

ratatat tat

HUH?

foom

tnk

wooom

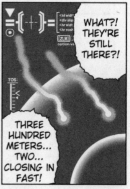
WHAT?! THEY'RE STILL THERE?!

THREE HUNDRED METERS... TWO... CLOSING IN FAST!

tnk

tnk

twnk

tnk

tnk

pip

DID YOU SEE *THAT*?!

HEY! WHY'DJA STOP FIRING?!

I *AM* FIRING! THE GUN MUST BE JAMMED!

OOM

!

THEY'RE RIGHT ON TOP OF US!

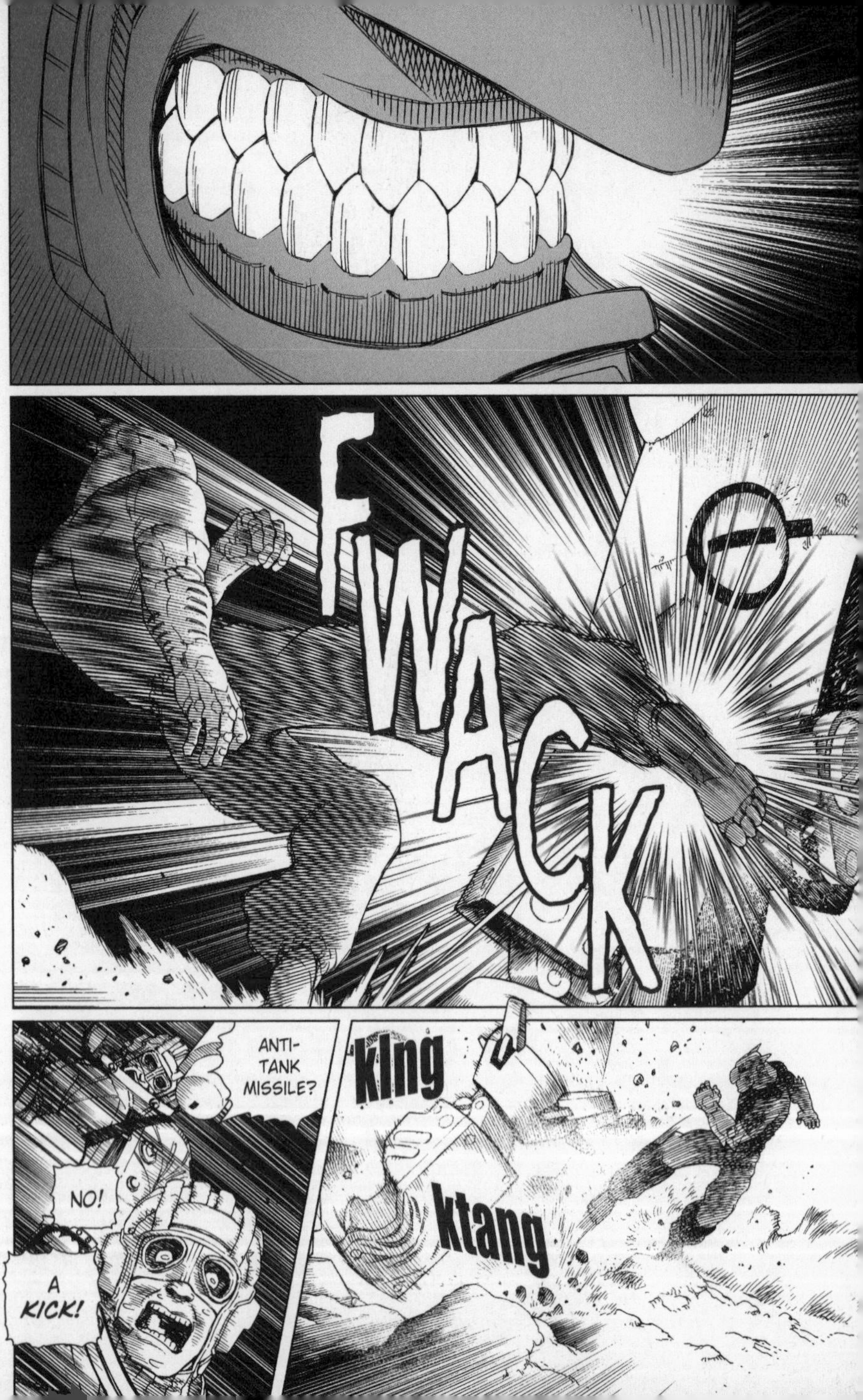
FWACK
kling
ktang
ANTI-TANK MISSILE?
NO!
A KICK!

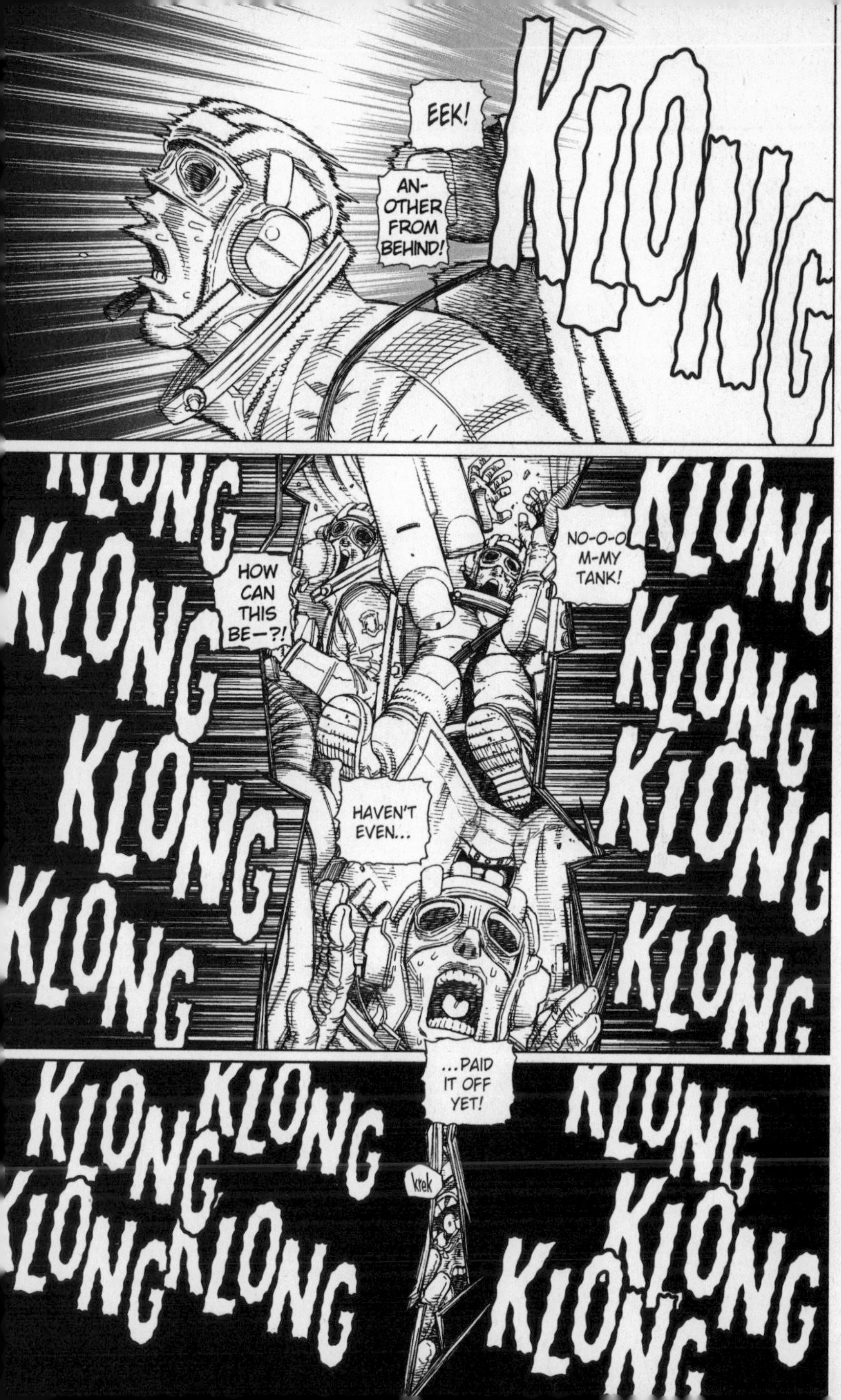
KLONG
EEK!
AN-OTHER FROM BEHIND!
KLONG
KLONG
KLONG
KLONG
KLONG
NO-O-O M-MY TANK!
HOW CAN THIS BE—?!
HAVEN'T EVEN...
KLONG
KLONG
KLONG
KLONG
KLONG
...PAID IT OFF YET!
KLONG
KLONG
KLONG
KLONG
krek
KLONG
KLONG
KLONG
KLONG
KLONG

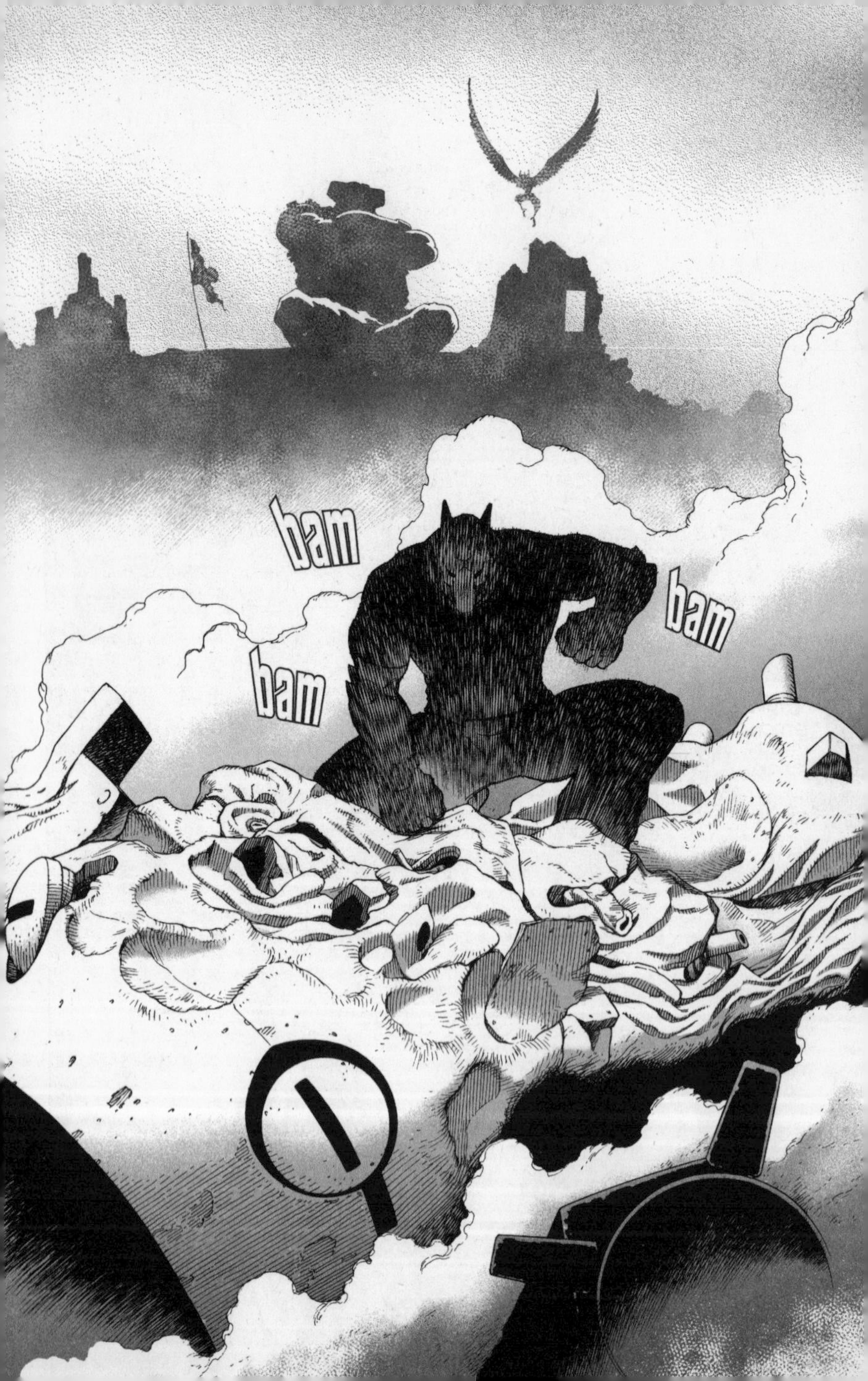
bam
bam
bam

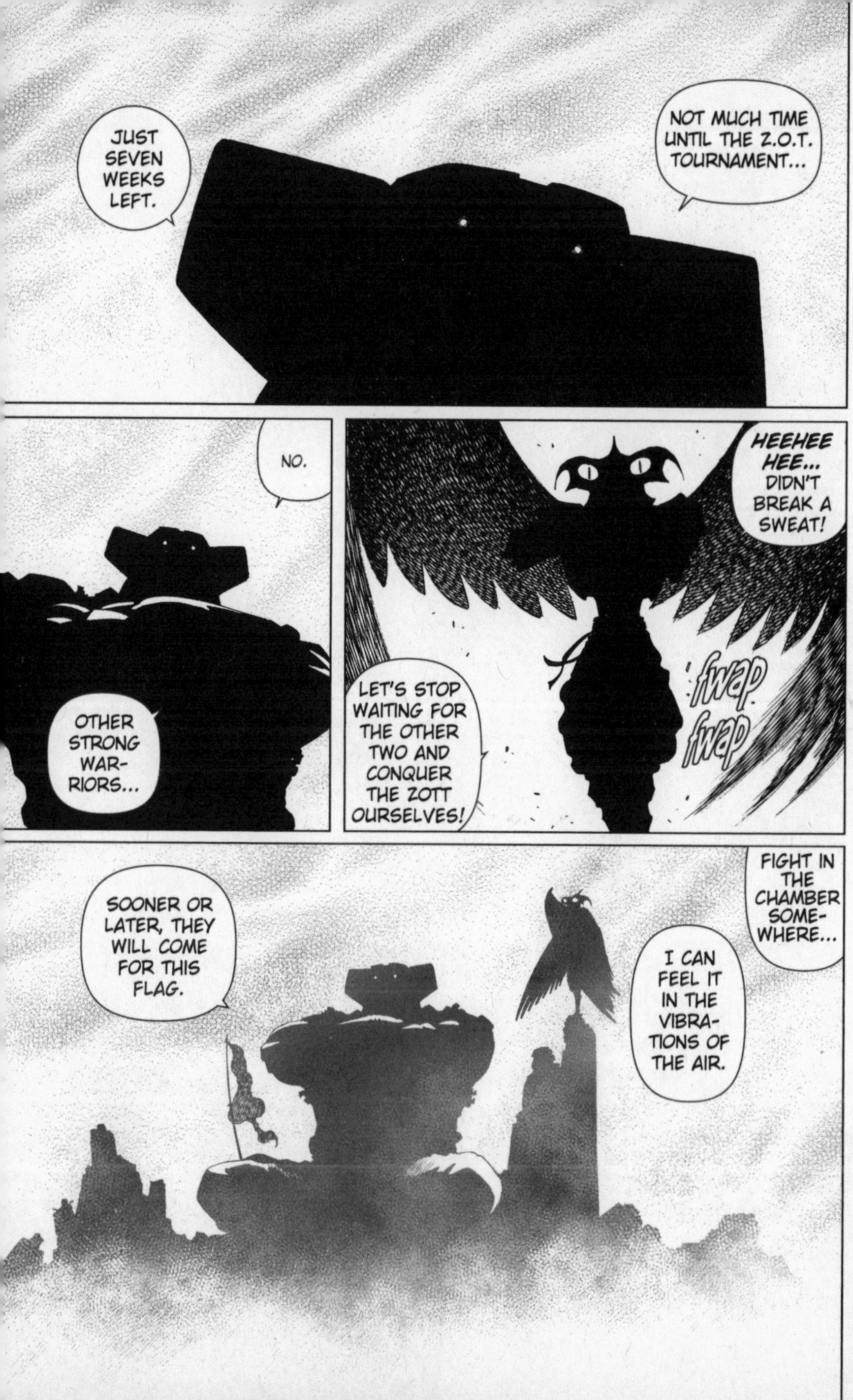
NOT MUCH TIME UNTIL THE Z.O.T. TOURNAMENT...
JUST SEVEN WEEKS LEFT.
HEEHEE HEE... DIDN'T BREAK A SWEAT!
fwap fwap
LET'S STOP WAITING FOR THE OTHER TWO AND CONQUER THE ZOTT OURSELVES!
NO.
OTHER STRONG WAR-RIORS...
FIGHT IN THE CHAMBER SOME-WHERE...
I CAN FEEL IT IN THE VIBRA-TIONS OF THE AIR.
SOONER OR LATER, THEY WILL COME FOR THIS FLAG.

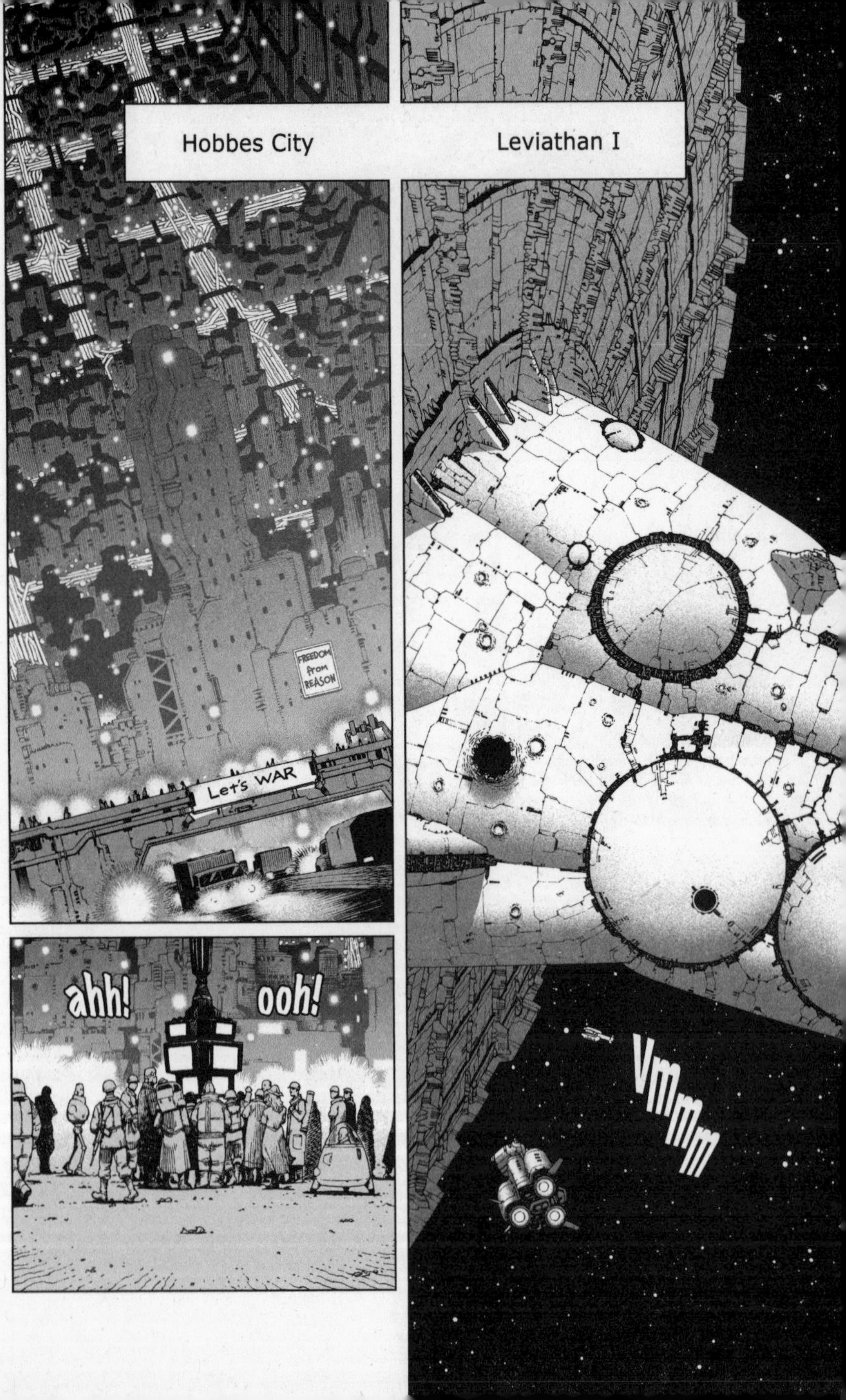

Leviathan I
Vmmm
Hobbes City
FREEDOM from REASON
Let's WAR
ooh!
ahh!

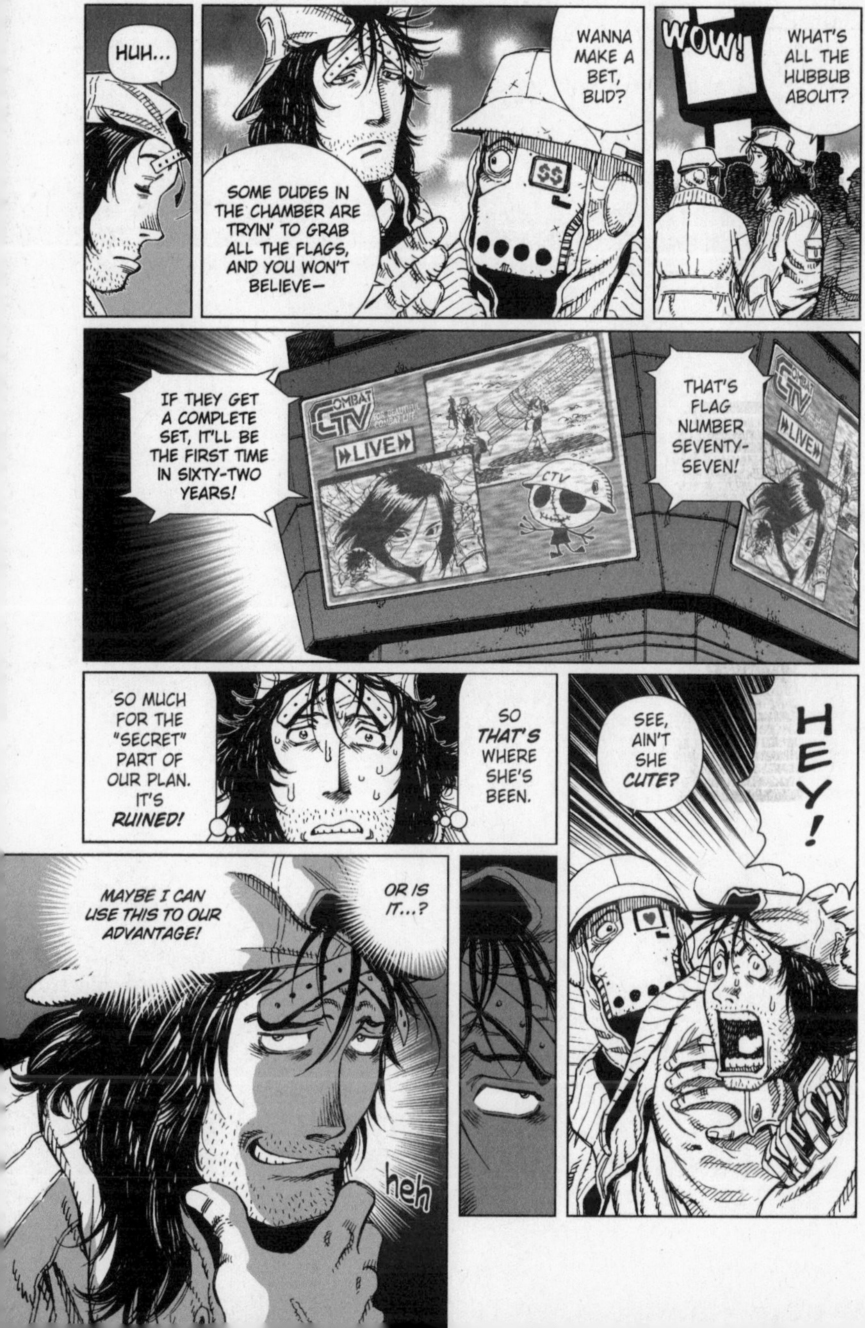
WOW!
WHAT'S ALL THE HUBBUB ABOUT?
WANNA MAKE A BET, BUD?
SOME DUDES IN THE CHAMBER ARE TRYIN' TO GRAB ALL THE FLAGS, AND YOU WON'T BELIEVE—
HUH...
COMBAT CTV
LIVE
THAT'S FLAG NUMBER SEVENTY-SEVEN!
CTV
IF THEY GET A COMPLETE SET, IT'LL BE THE FIRST TIME IN SIXTY-TWO YEARS!
HEY!
SEE, AIN'T SHE *CUTE?*
SO *THAT'S* WHERE SHE'S BEEN.
SO MUCH FOR THE "SECRET" PART OF OUR PLAN. IT'S ***RUINED!***
OR IS IT...?
MAYBE I CAN USE THIS TO OUR ADVANTAGE!
heh

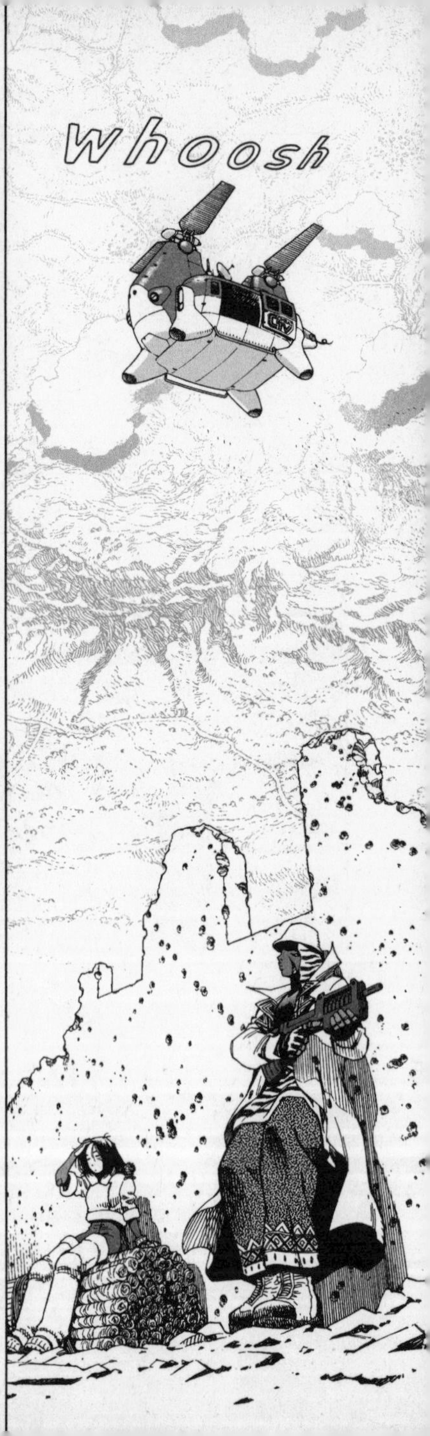
whoosh

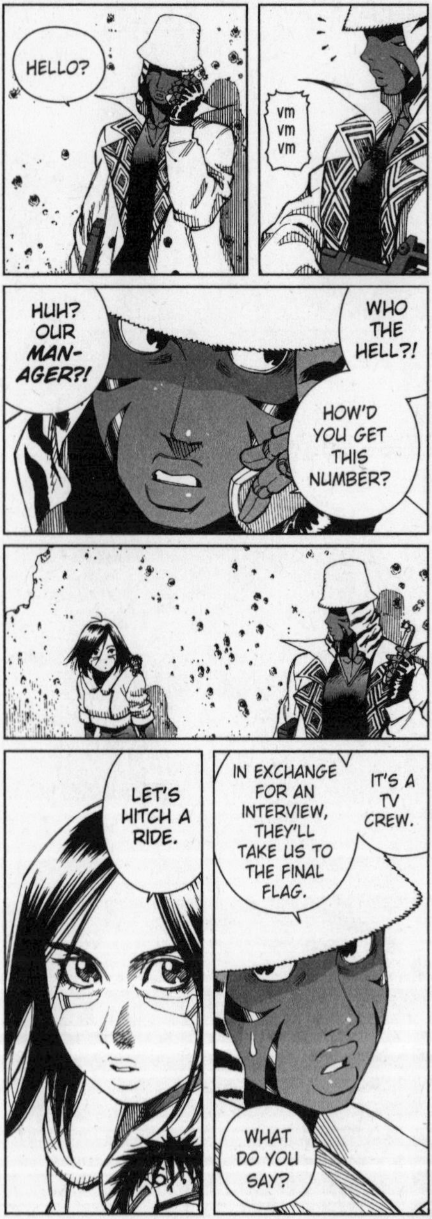
vm
vm
vm
HELLO?
WHO THE HELL?!
HUH? OUR MANAGER?!
HOW'D YOU GET THIS NUMBER?
IT'S A TV CREW.
IN EXCHANGE FOR AN INTERVIEW, THEY'LL TAKE US TO THE FINAL FLAG.
WHAT DO YOU SAY?
LET'S HITCH A RIDE.

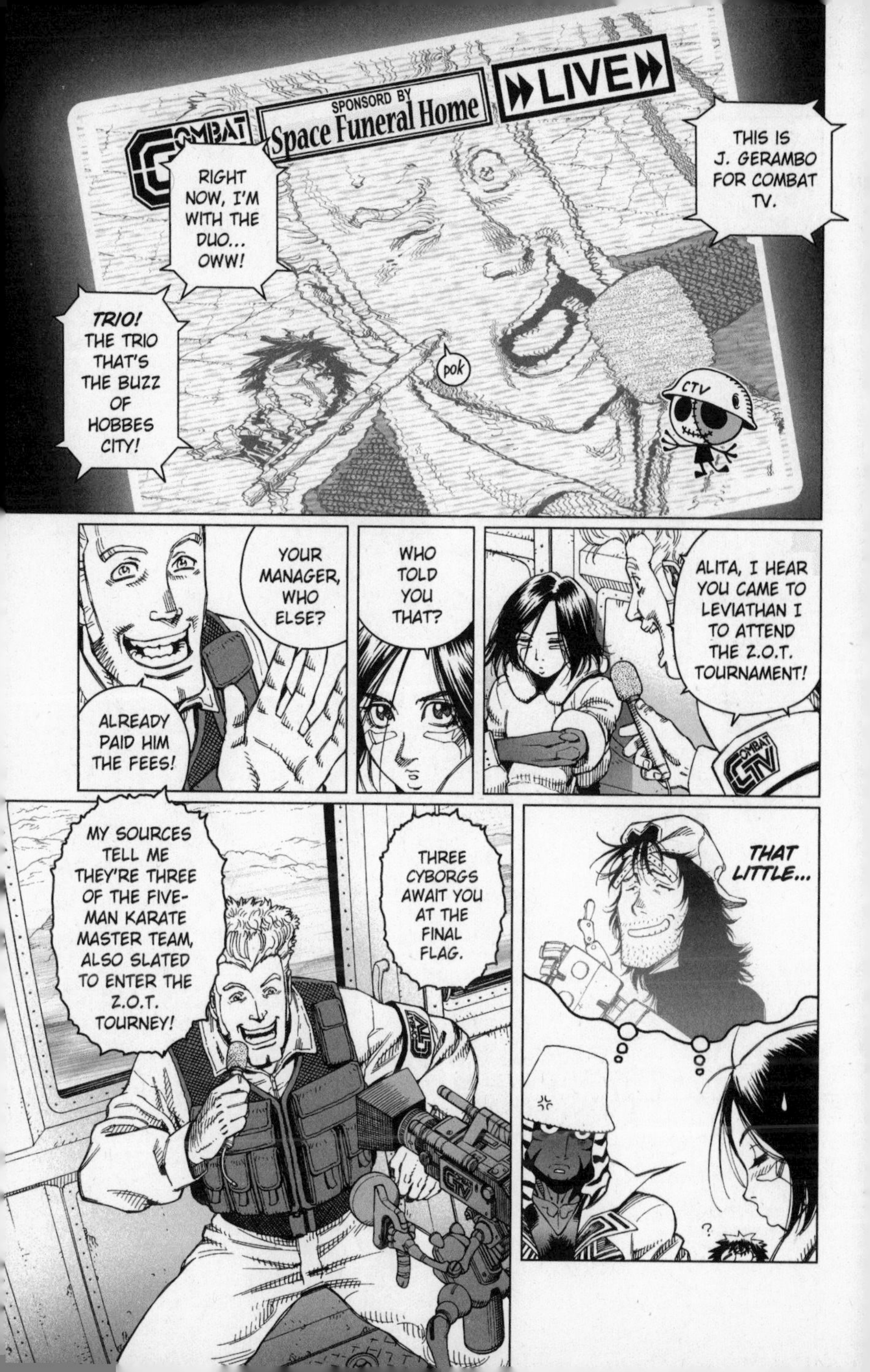
COMBAT
SPONSORD BY Space Funeral Home
LIVE
THIS IS J. GERAMBO FOR COMBAT TV.
RIGHT NOW, I'M WITH THE DUO... OWW!
pok
TRIO! THE TRIO THAT'S THE BUZZ OF HOBBES CITY!
CTV
ALITA, I HEAR YOU CAME TO LEVIATHAN I TO ATTEND THE Z.O.T. TOURNAMENT!
WHO TOLD YOU THAT?
YOUR MANAGER, WHO ELSE?
ALREADY PAID HIM THE FEES!
THAT LITTLE...
?
THREE CYBORGS AWAIT YOU AT THE FINAL FLAG.
MY SOURCES TELL ME THEY'RE THREE OF THE FIVE-MAN KARATE MASTER TEAM, ALSO SLATED TO ENTER THE Z.O.T. TOURNEY!

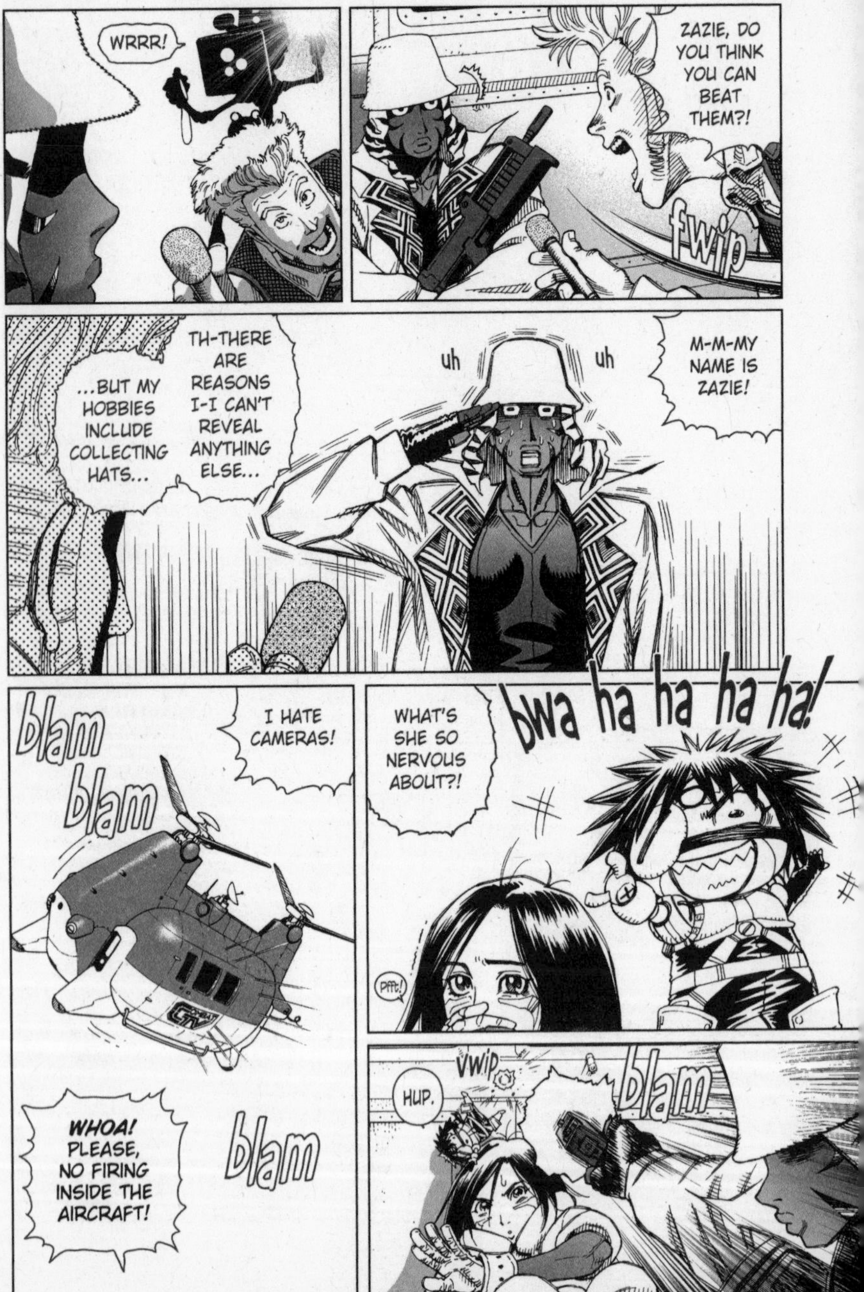
ZAZIE, DO YOU THINK YOU CAN BEAT THEM?!
fwip
WRRR!
M-M-MY NAME IS ZAZIE!
uh
uh
TH-THERE ARE REASONS I-I CAN'T REVEAL ANYTHING ELSE...
...BUT MY HOBBIES INCLUDE COLLECTING HATS...
bwa ha ha ha ha!
WHAT'S SHE SO NERVOUS ABOUT?!
Pfft!
blam
VWIP
HUP.
I HATE CAMERAS!
blam
blam
WHOA! PLEASE, NO FIRING INSIDE THE AIRCRAFT!
blam

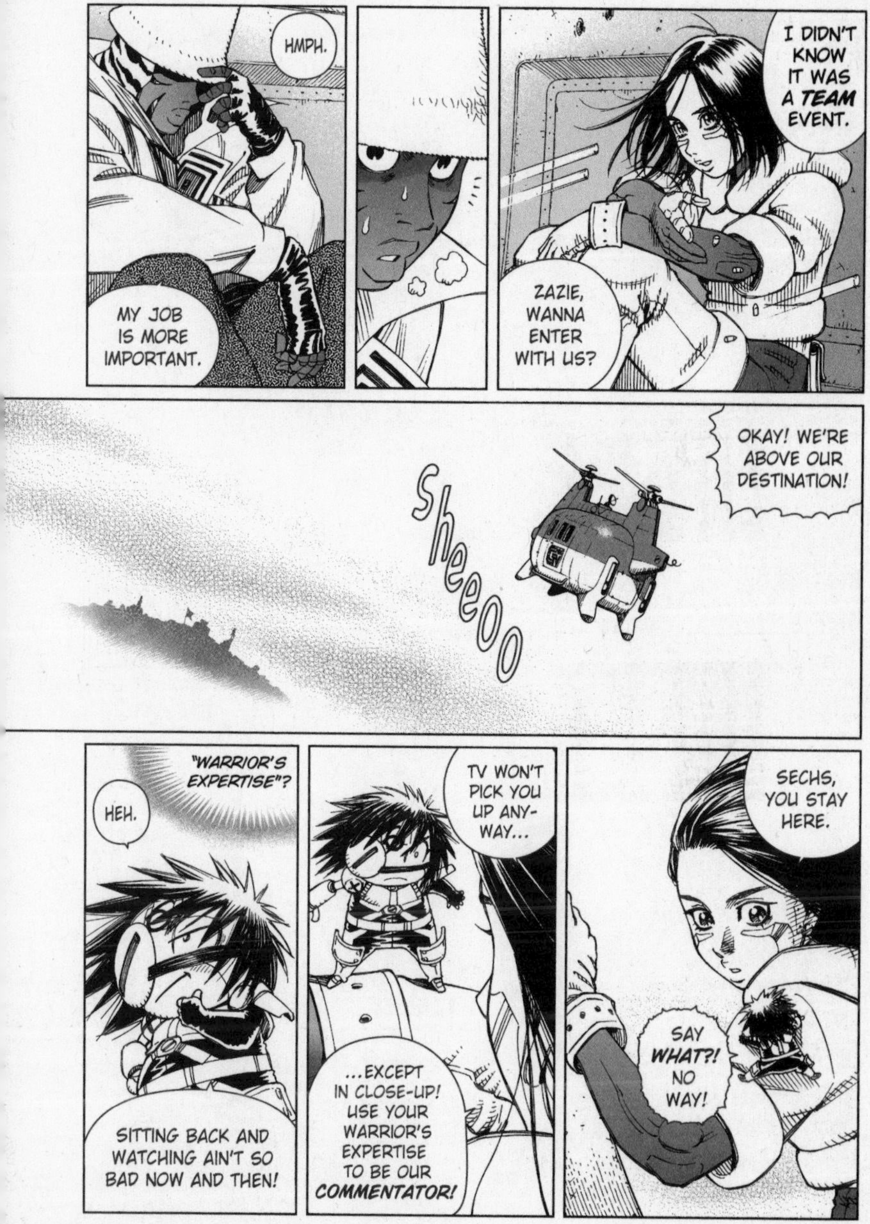
I DIDN'T KNOW IT WAS A TEAM EVENT.
ZAZIE, WANNA ENTER WITH US?
HMPH.
MY JOB IS MORE IMPORTANT.
OKAY! WE'RE ABOVE OUR DESTINATION!
Sheeoo
SECHS, YOU STAY HERE.
SAY WHAT?! NO WAY!
TV WON'T PICK YOU UP ANY-WAY...
...EXCEPT IN CLOSE-UP! USE YOUR WARRIOR'S EXPERTISE TO BE OUR COMMENTATOR!
"WARRIOR'S EXPERTISE"?
HEH.
SITTING BACK AND WATCHING AIN'T SO BAD NOW AND THEN!

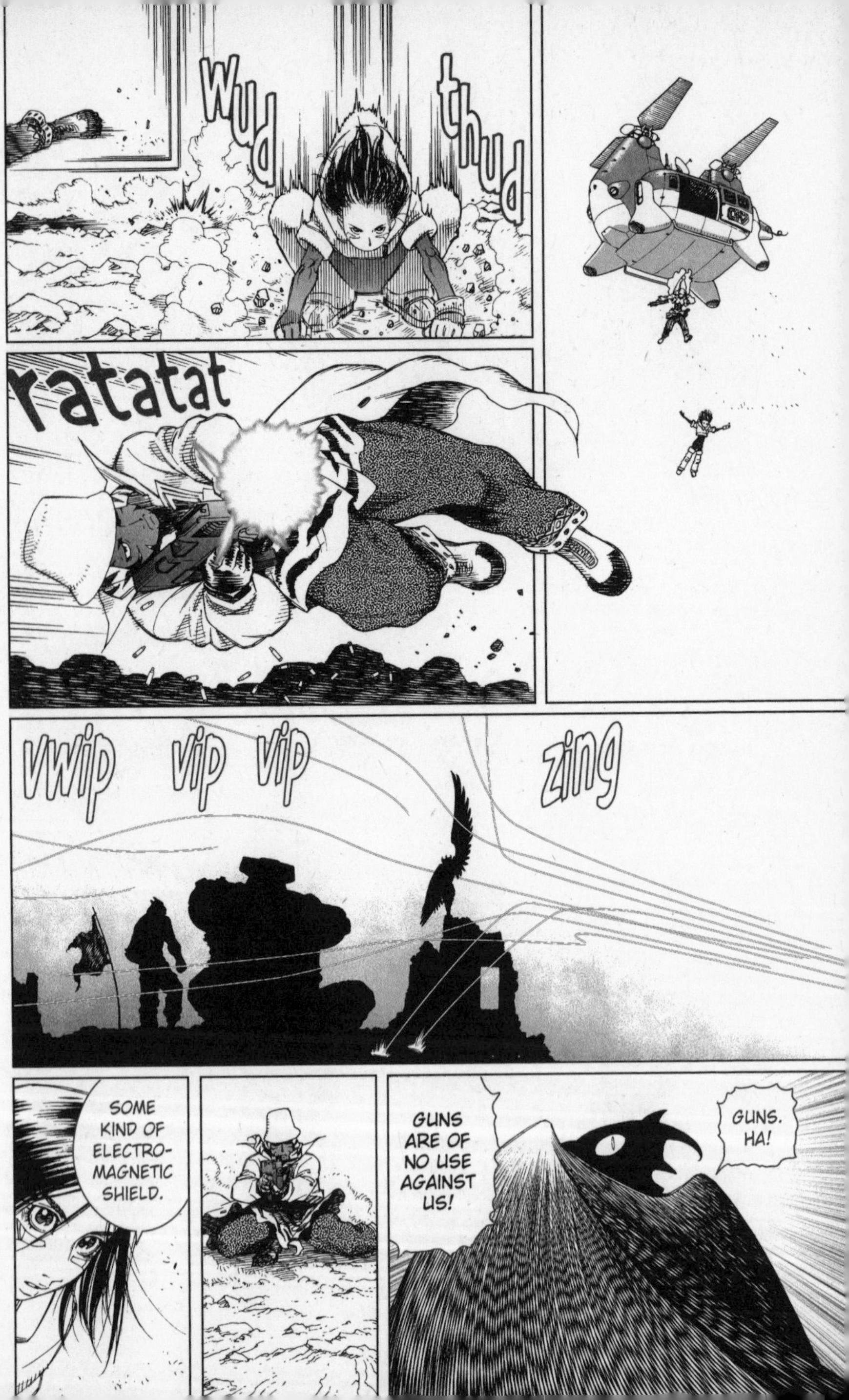
thud
wud
ratatat
zing
vip
vip
vwip
GUNS. HA!
GUNS ARE OF NO USE AGAINST US!
SOME KIND OF ELECTRO-MAGNETIC SHIELD.

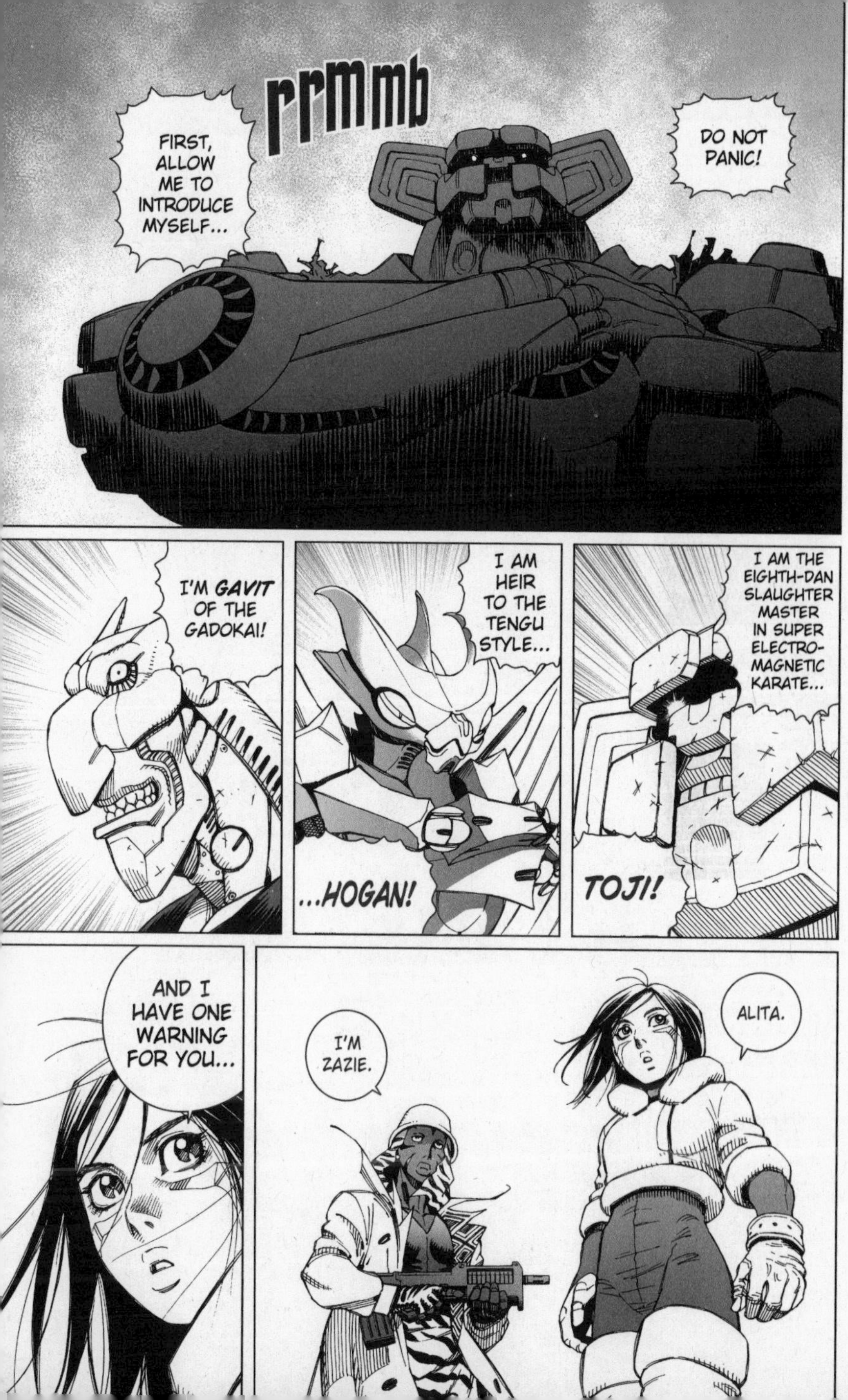
DO NOT PANIC!
rrmmb
FIRST, ALLOW ME TO INTRODUCE MYSELF...
I AM THE EIGHTH-DAN SLAUGHTER MASTER IN SUPER ELECTRO-MAGNETIC KARATE...
TOJI!
I AM HEIR TO THE TENGU STYLE...
...HOGAN!
I'M GAVIT OF THE GADOKAI!
ALITA.
I'M ZAZIE.
AND I HAVE ONE WARNING FOR YOU...

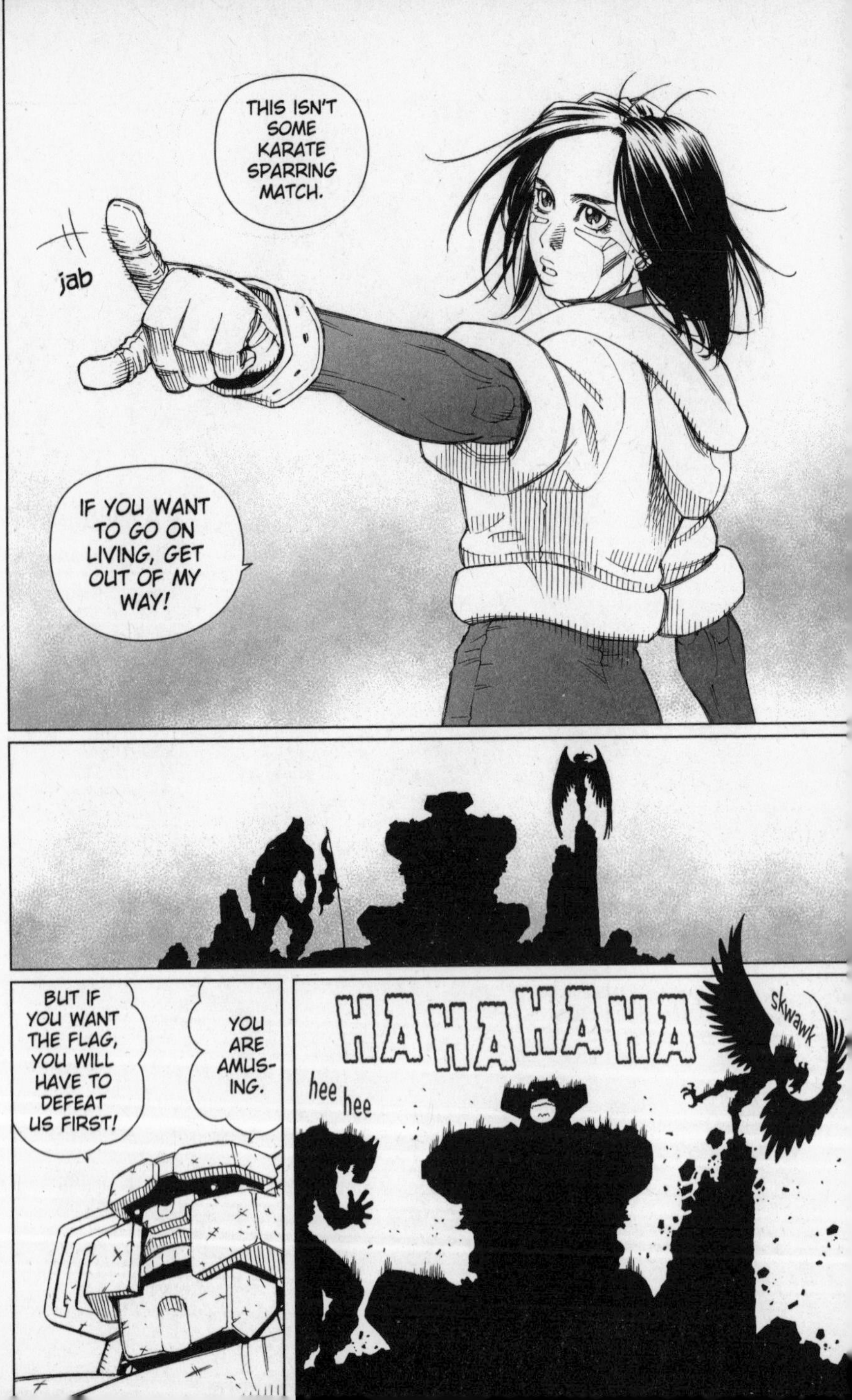
THIS ISN'T SOME KARATE SPARRING MATCH.
jab
IF YOU WANT TO GO ON LIVING, GET OUT OF MY WAY!
HAHAHAHA
skwawk
hee hee
YOU ARE AMUS-ING.
BUT IF YOU WANT THE FLAG, YOU WILL HAVE TO DEFEAT US FIRST!

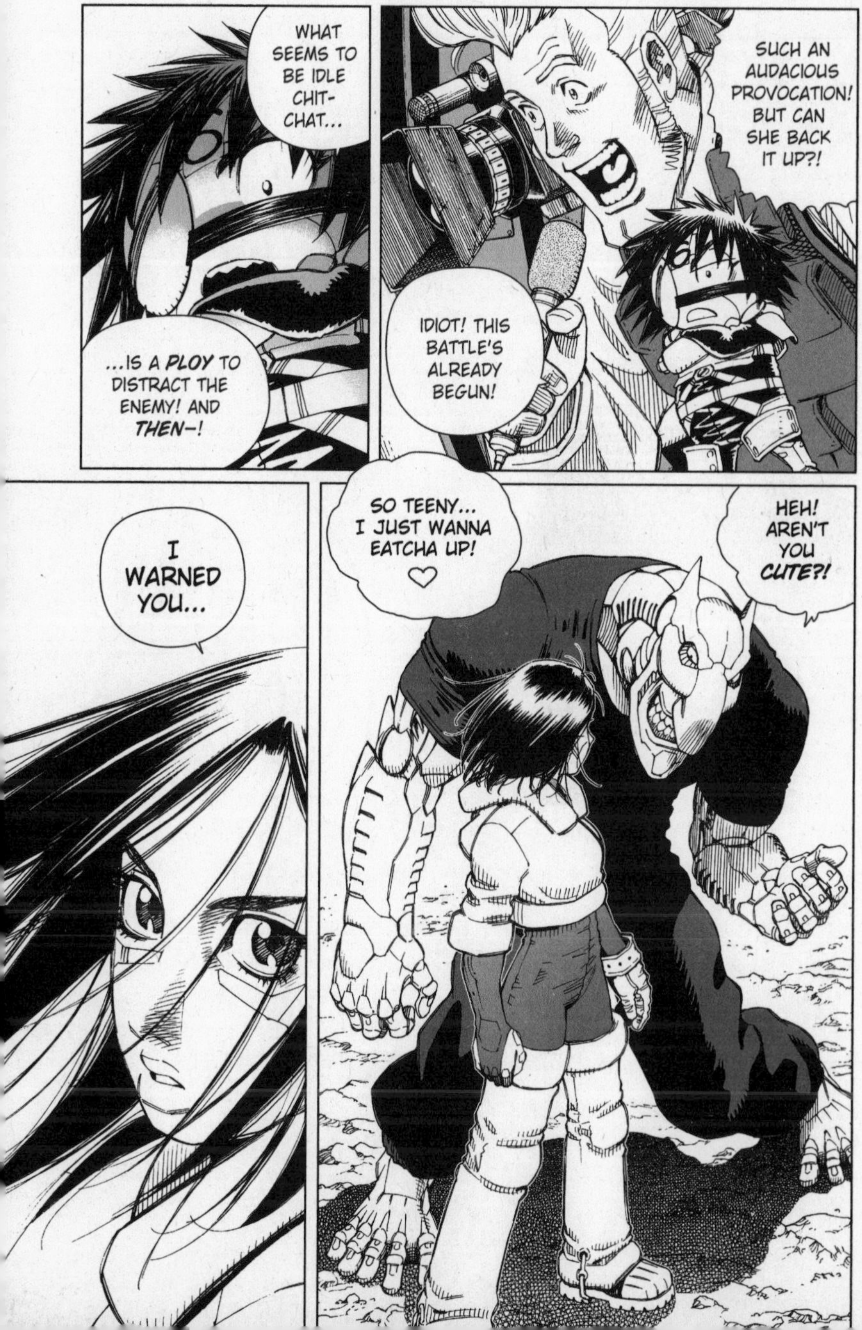
SUCH AN AUDACIOUS PROVOCATION! BUT CAN SHE BACK IT UP?!
IDIOT! THIS BATTLE'S ALREADY BEGUN!
WHAT SEEMS TO BE IDLE CHIT-CHAT...
...IS A *PLOY* TO DISTRACT THE ENEMY! AND *THEN*–!
HEH! AREN'T YOU *CUTE*?!
SO TEENY... I JUST WANNA EATCHA UP! ♡
I WARNED YOU...

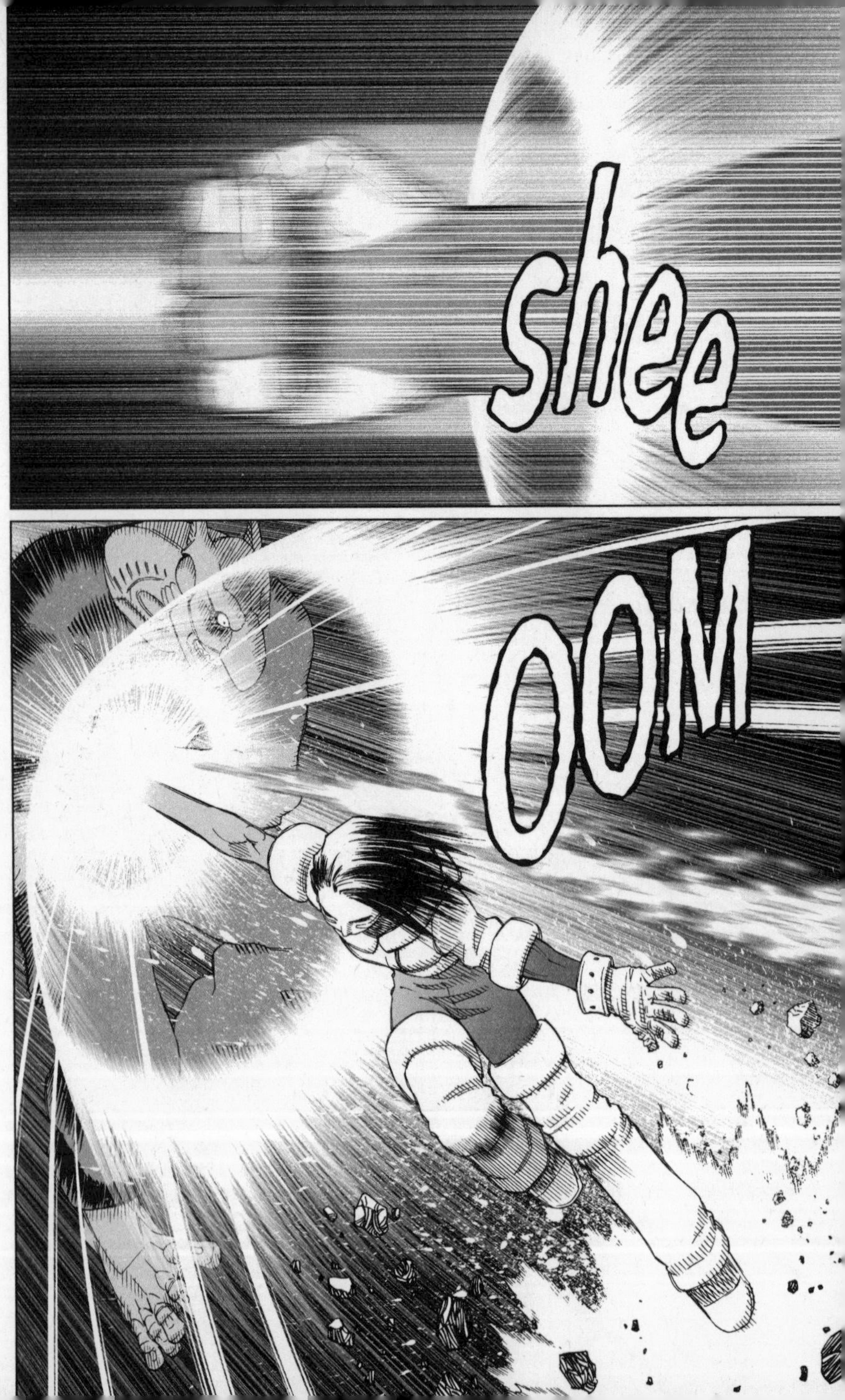
shee
OOM

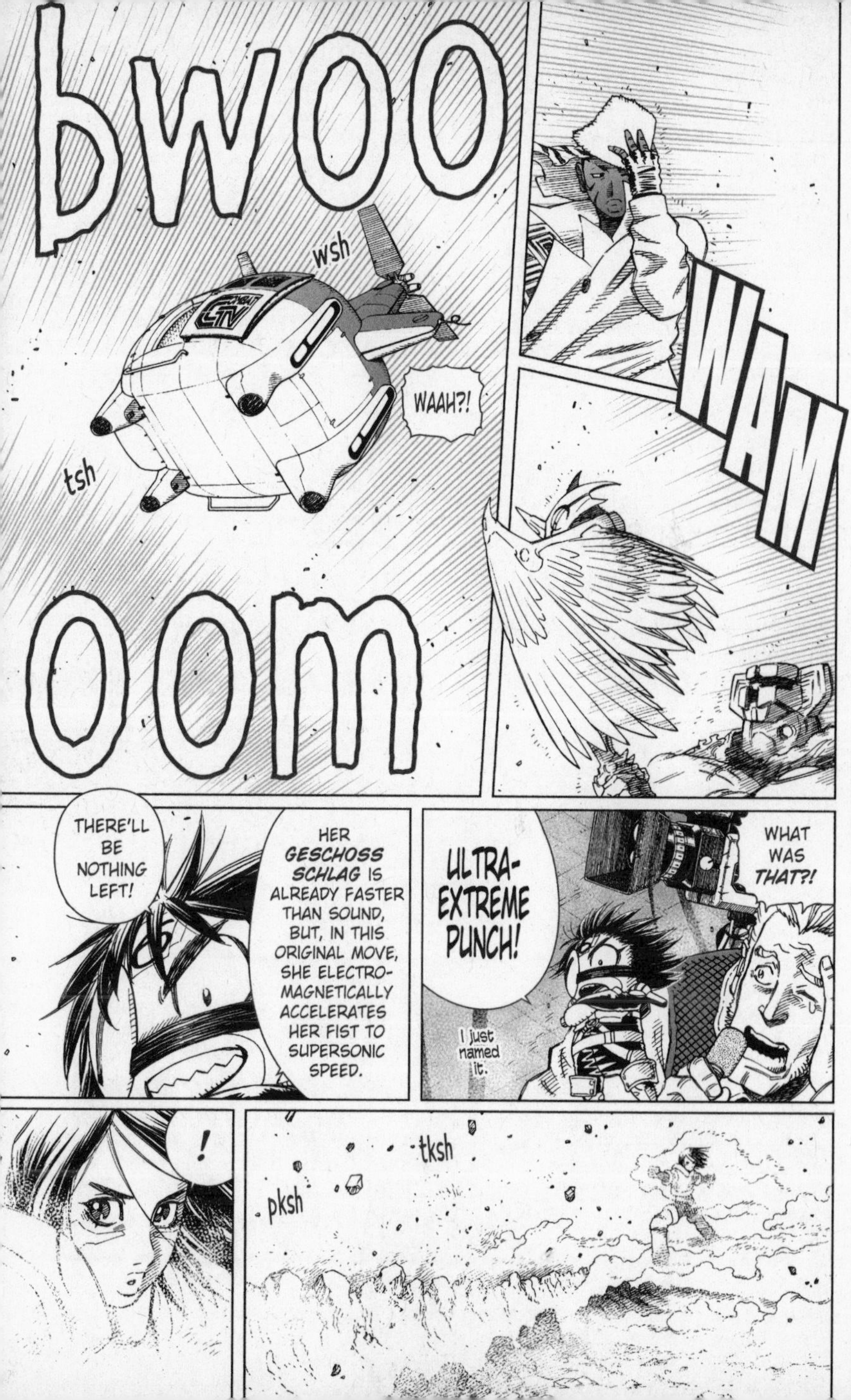
WAM
bwoooom
wsh
WAAH?!
tsh
WHAT WAS THAT?!
ULTRA-EXTREME PUNCH!
I just named it.
HER GESCHOSS SCHLAG IS ALREADY FASTER THAN SOUND, BUT, IN THIS ORIGINAL MOVE, SHE ELECTRO-MAGNETICALLY ACCELERATES HER FIST TO SUPERSONIC SPEED.
THERE'LL BE NOTHING LEFT!
tksh
pksh
!

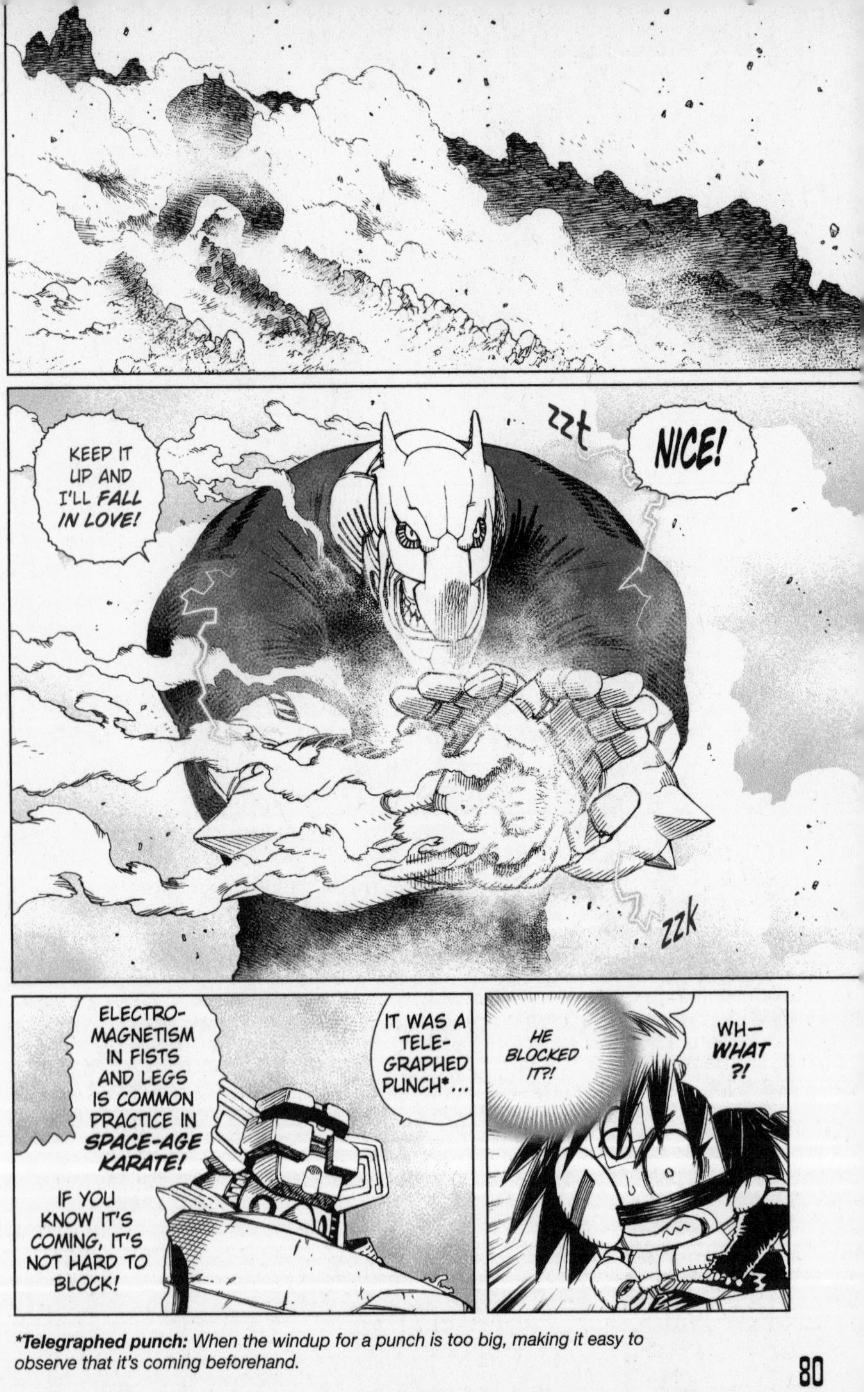
NICE!
zzt
KEEP IT UP AND I'LL FALL IN LOVE!
zzk
WH— WHAT?!
HE BLOCKED IT?!
IT WAS A TELE-GRAPHED PUNCH*...
ELECTRO-MAGNETISM IN FISTS AND LEGS IS COMMON PRACTICE IN SPACE-AGE KARATE!
IF YOU KNOW IT'S COMING, IT'S NOT HARD TO BLOCK!

***Telegraphed punch:** *When the windup for a punch is too big, making it easy to observe that it's coming beforehand.*

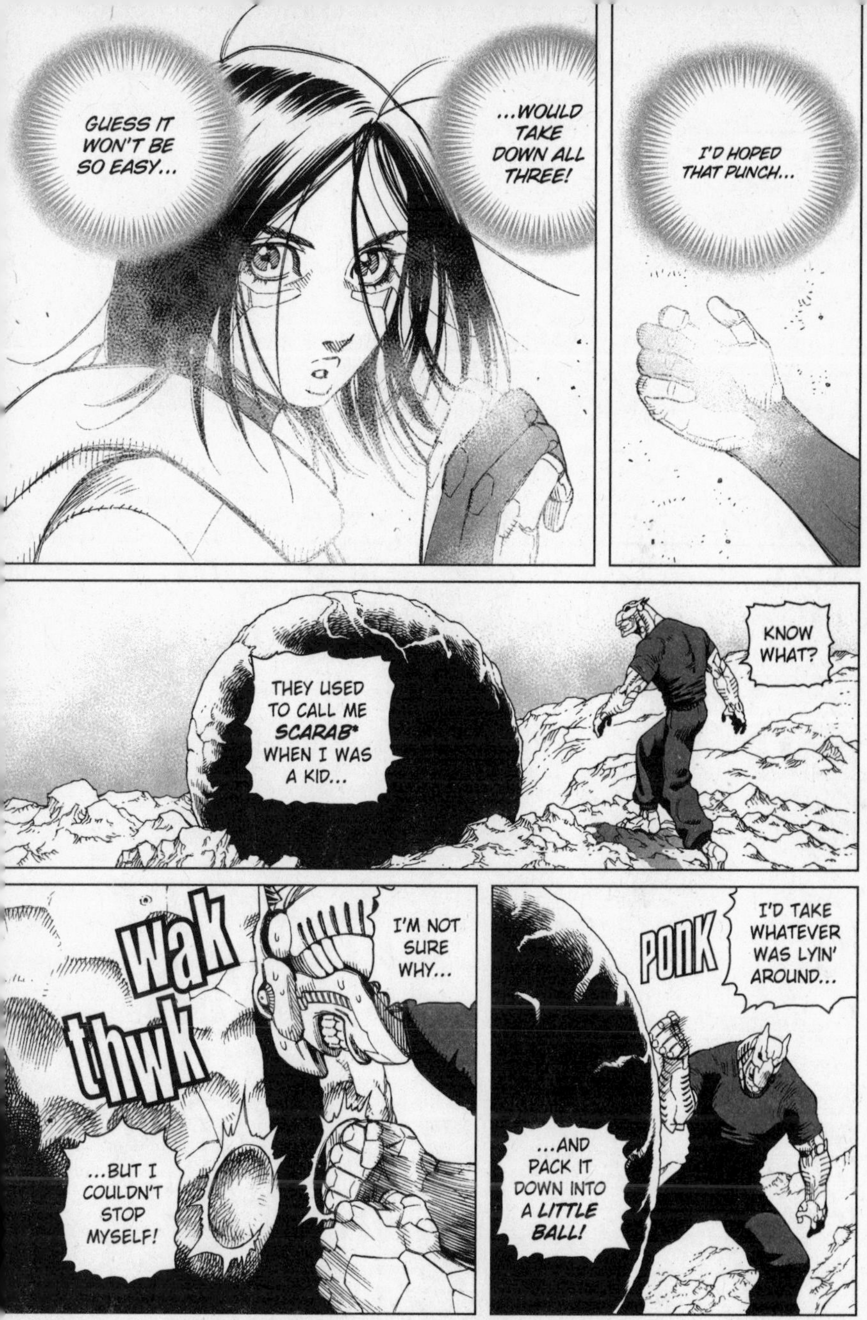
I'D HOPED THAT PUNCH...
...WOULD TAKE DOWN ALL THREE!
GUESS IT WON'T BE SO EASY...
KNOW WHAT?
THEY USED TO CALL ME SCARAB* WHEN I WAS A KID...
PONK
I'D TAKE WHATEVER WAS LYIN' AROUND...
...AND PACK IT DOWN INTO A LITTLE BALL!
I'M NOT SURE WHY...
wak
thwk
...BUT I COULDN'T STOP MYSELF!

***Scarab:** *A type of beetle known for rolling around balls of animal dung. Known by the name* funkorogashi *("dung-roller") in Japanese.*

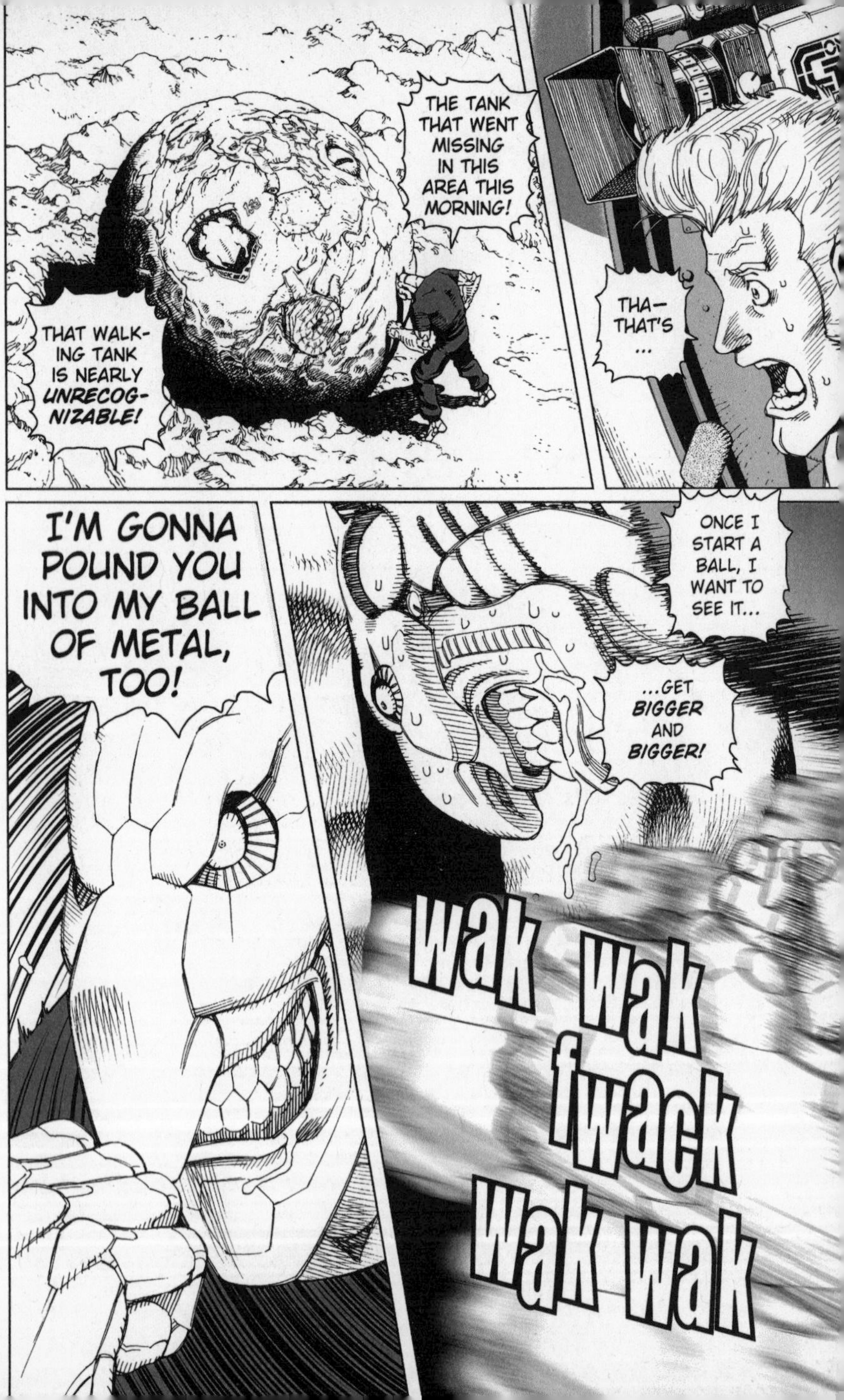
THA— THAT'S ...
THE TANK THAT WENT MISSING IN THIS AREA THIS MORNING!
THAT WALKING TANK IS NEARLY *UNRECOGNIZABLE!*
ONCE I START A BALL, I WANT TO SEE IT...
...GET *BIGGER* AND *BIGGER!*
wak wak fwack wak wak
I'M GONNA POUND YOU INTO MY BALL OF METAL, TOO!

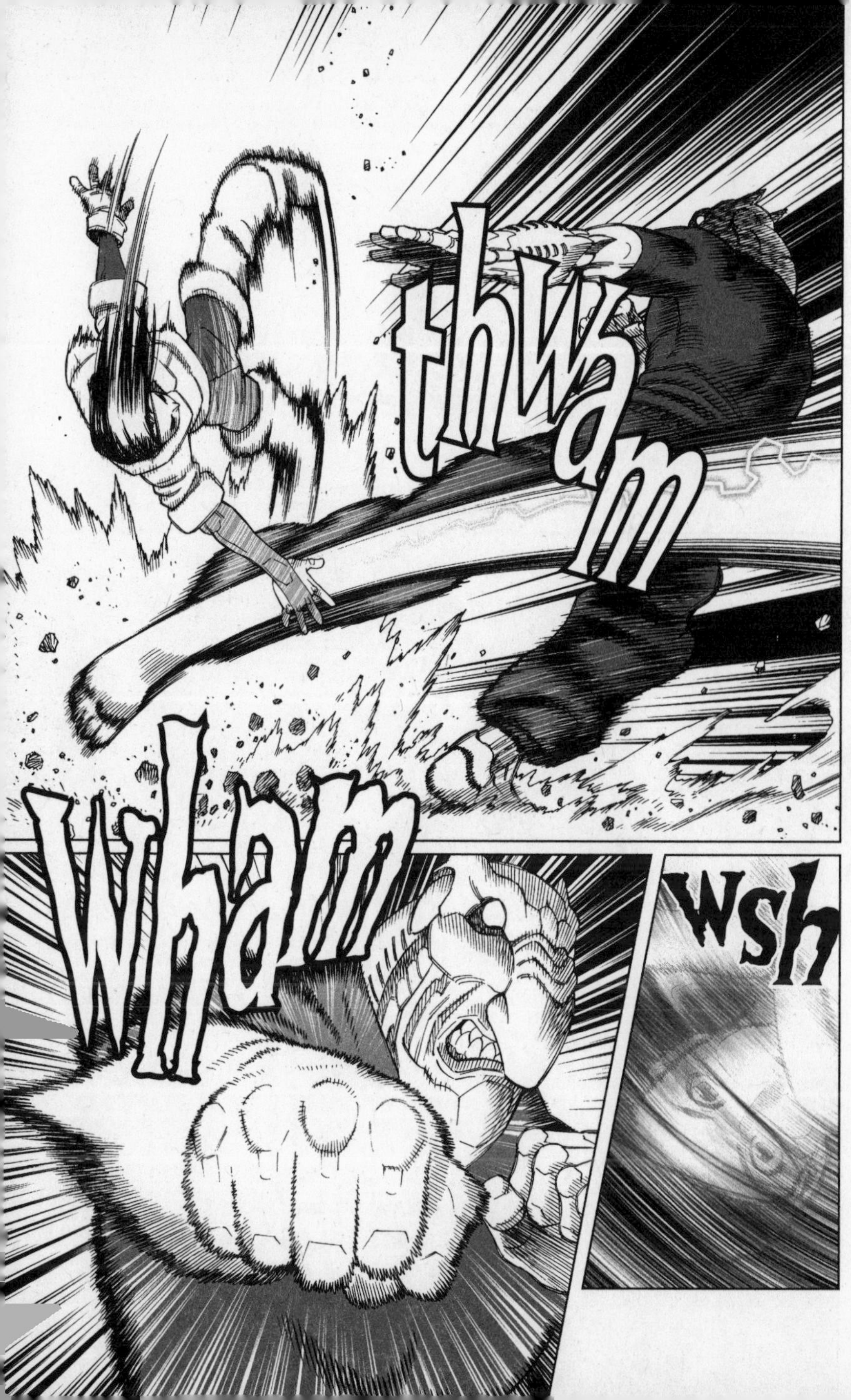
thwam
wsh
wham

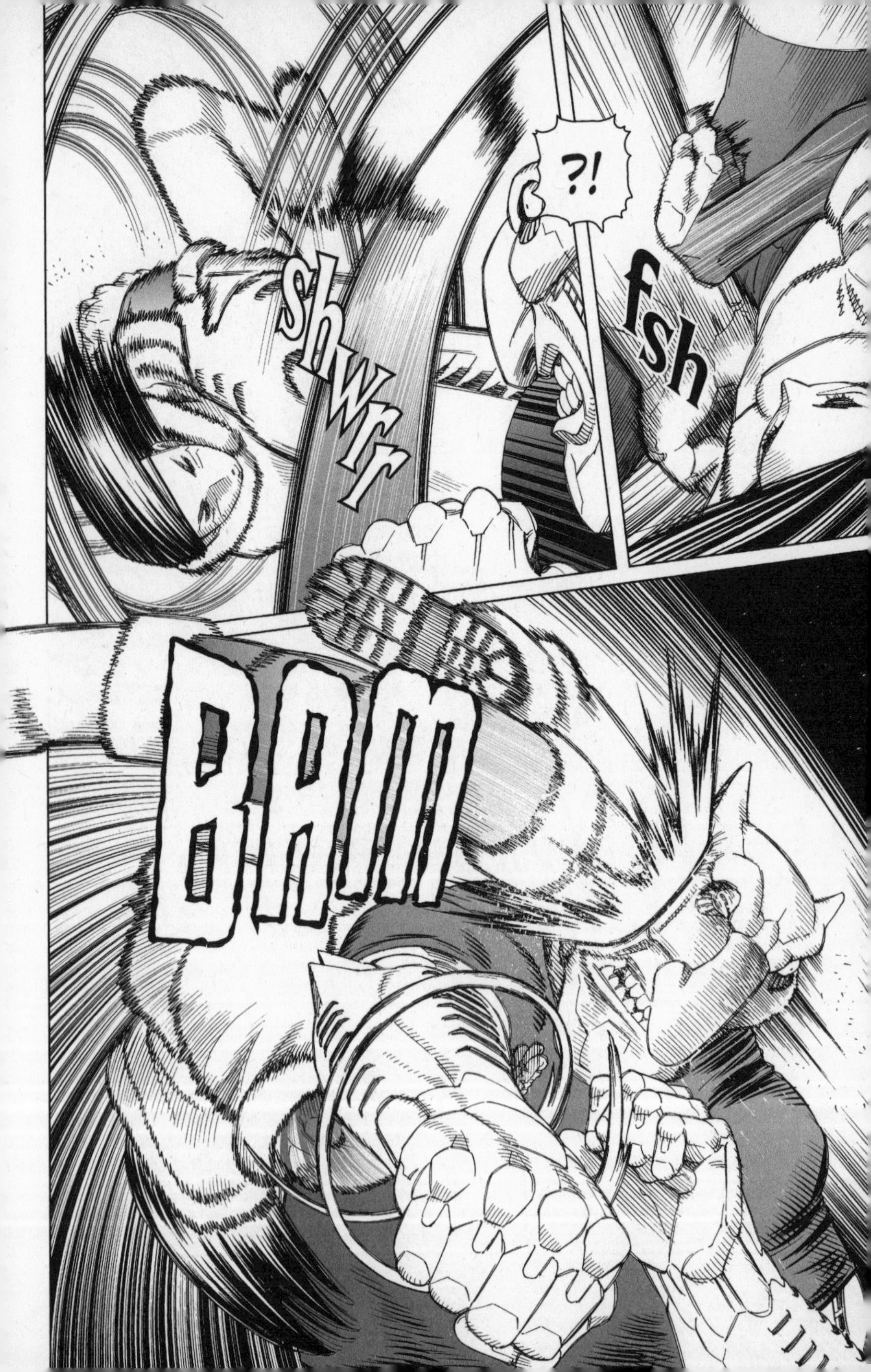
?!
fsh
Shwrr
BAM

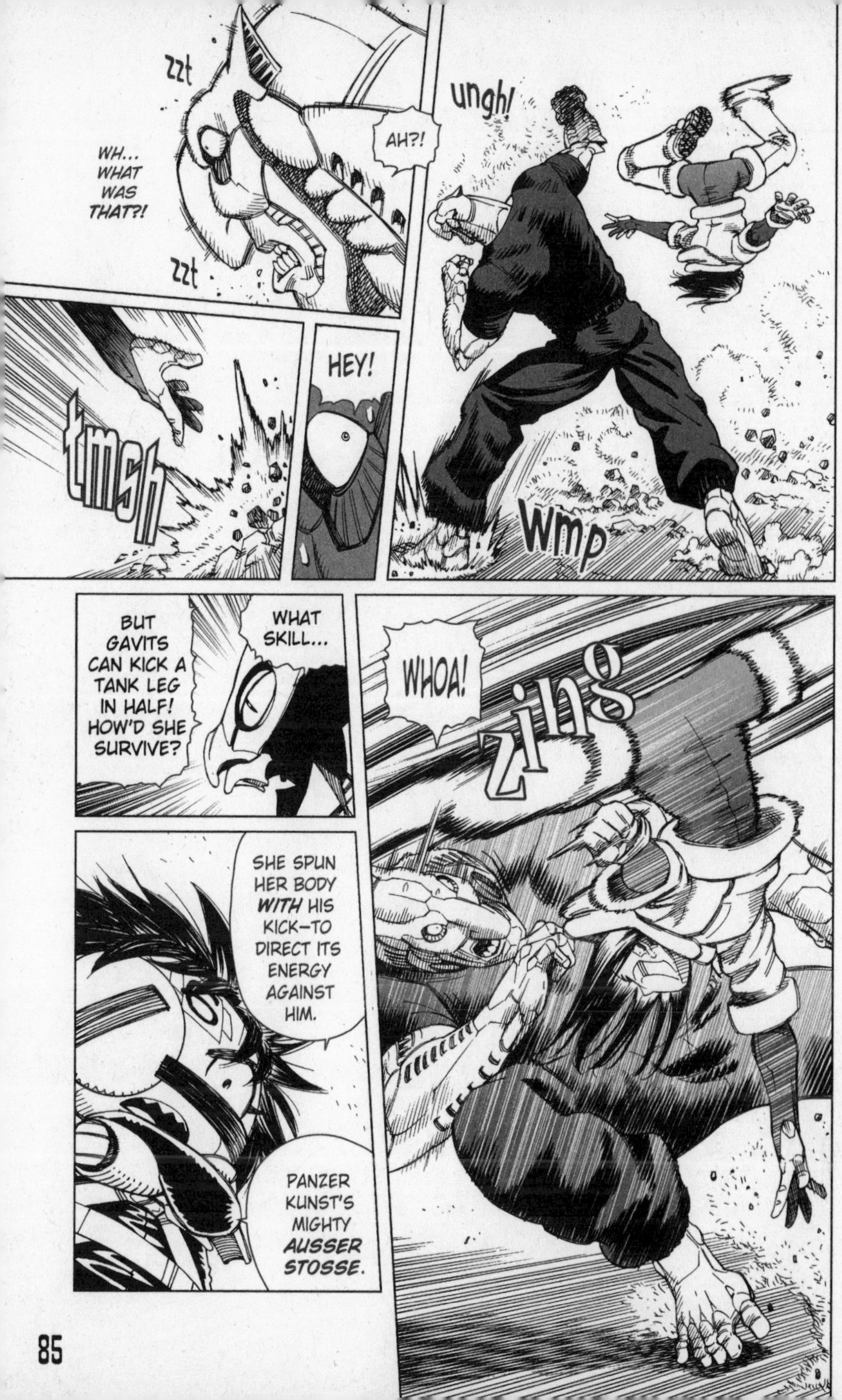

ungh!
AH?!
wmp
zzt
WH... WHAT WAS THAT?!
zzt
HEY!
tmsh
WHOA!
zing
WHAT SKILL...
BUT GAVITS CAN KICK A TANK LEG IN HALF! HOW'D SHE SURVIVE?
SHE SPUN HER BODY *WITH* HIS KICK—TO DIRECT ITS ENERGY AGAINST HIM.
PANZER KUNST'S MIGHTY *AUSSER STOSSE*.

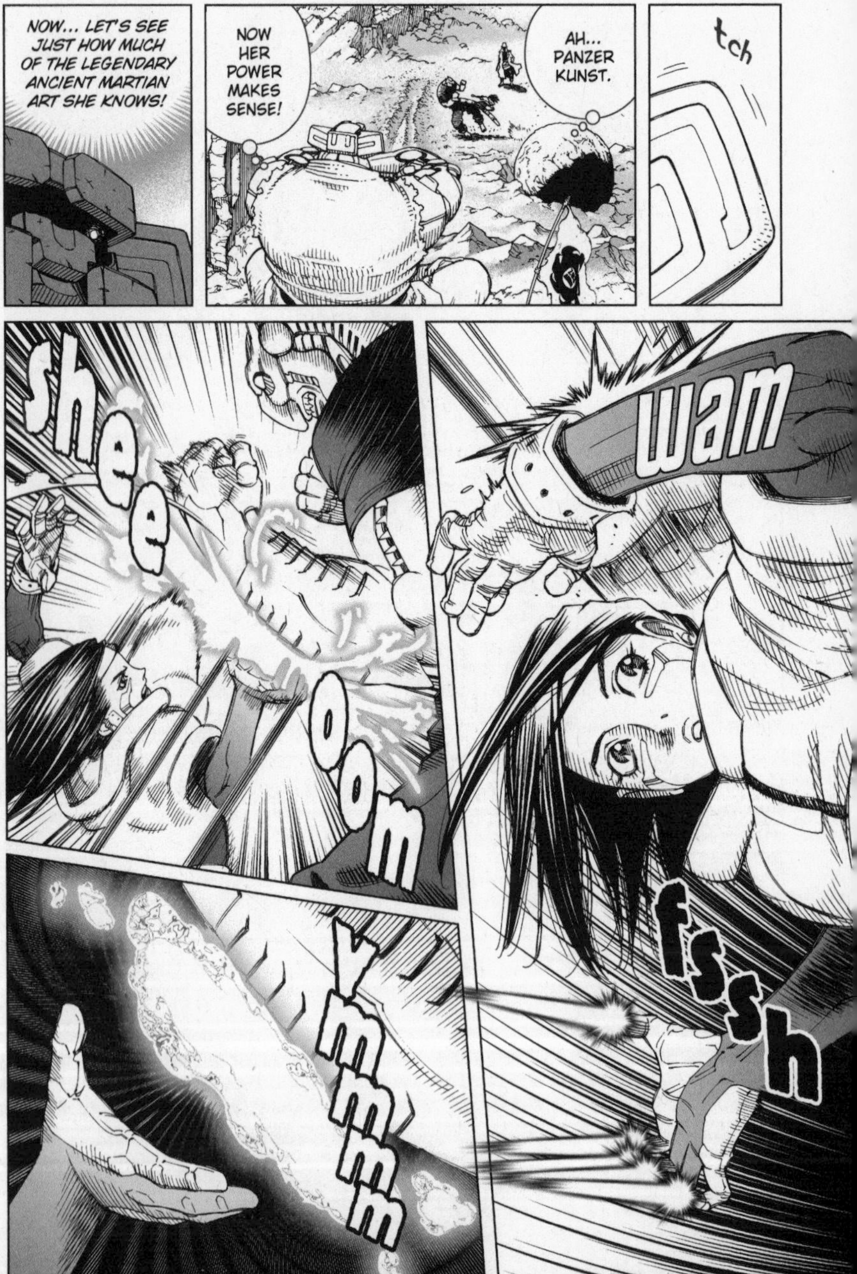
tch
AH... PANZER KUNST.
NOW HER POWER MAKES SENSE!
NOW... LET'S SEE JUST HOW MUCH OF THE LEGENDARY ANCIENT MARTIAN ART SHE KNOWS!
wam
sheeoom
fssh
vmmmm

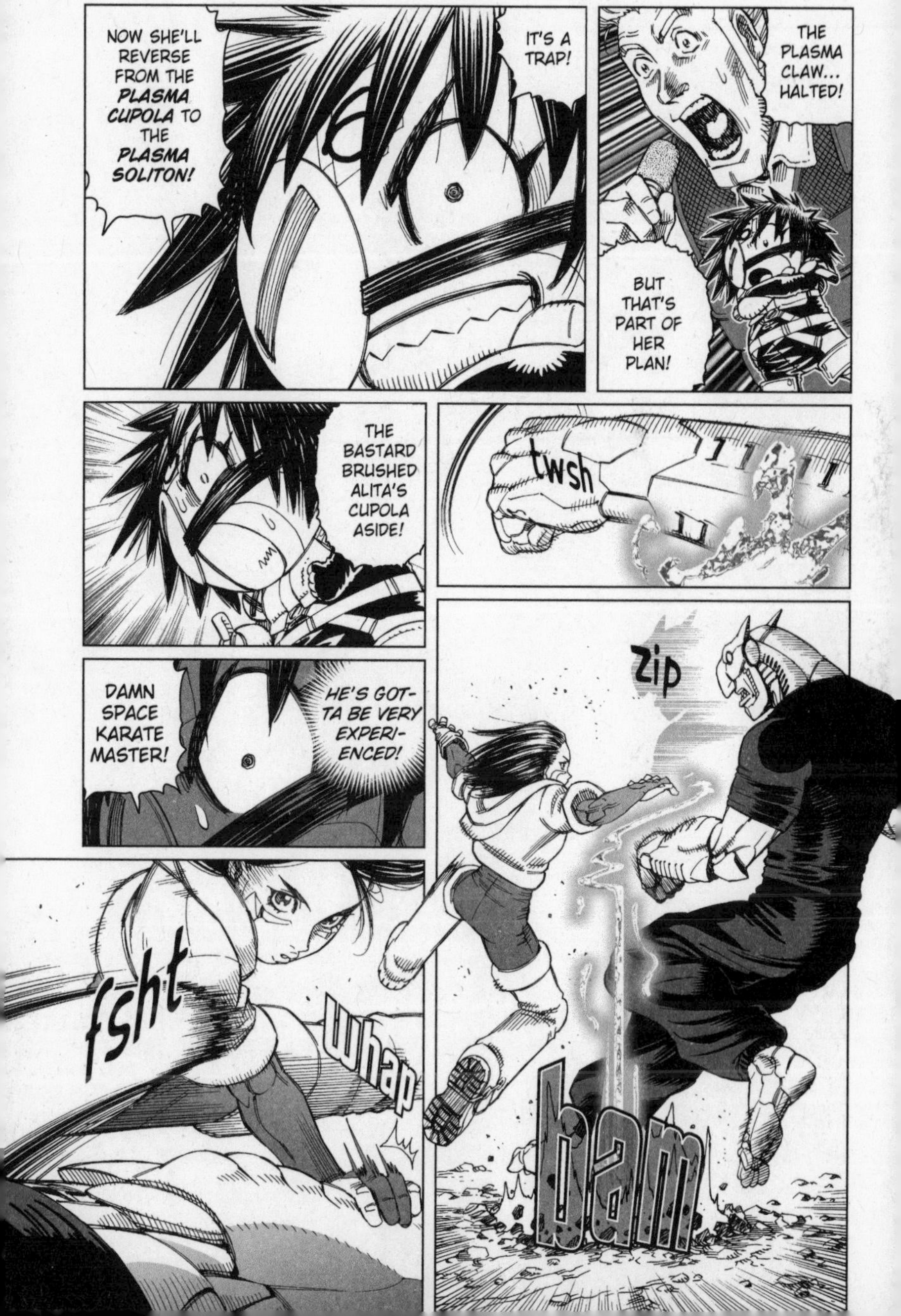
THE PLASMA CLAW... HALTED!
BUT THAT'S PART OF HER PLAN!
IT'S A TRAP!
NOW SHE'LL REVERSE FROM THE PLASMA CUPOLA TO THE PLASMA SOLITON!
twsh
THE BASTARD BRUSHED ALITA'S CUPOLA ASIDE!
HE'S GOT-TA BE VERY EXPERI-ENCED!
DAMN SPACE KARATE MASTER!
zip
bam
fsht
whap

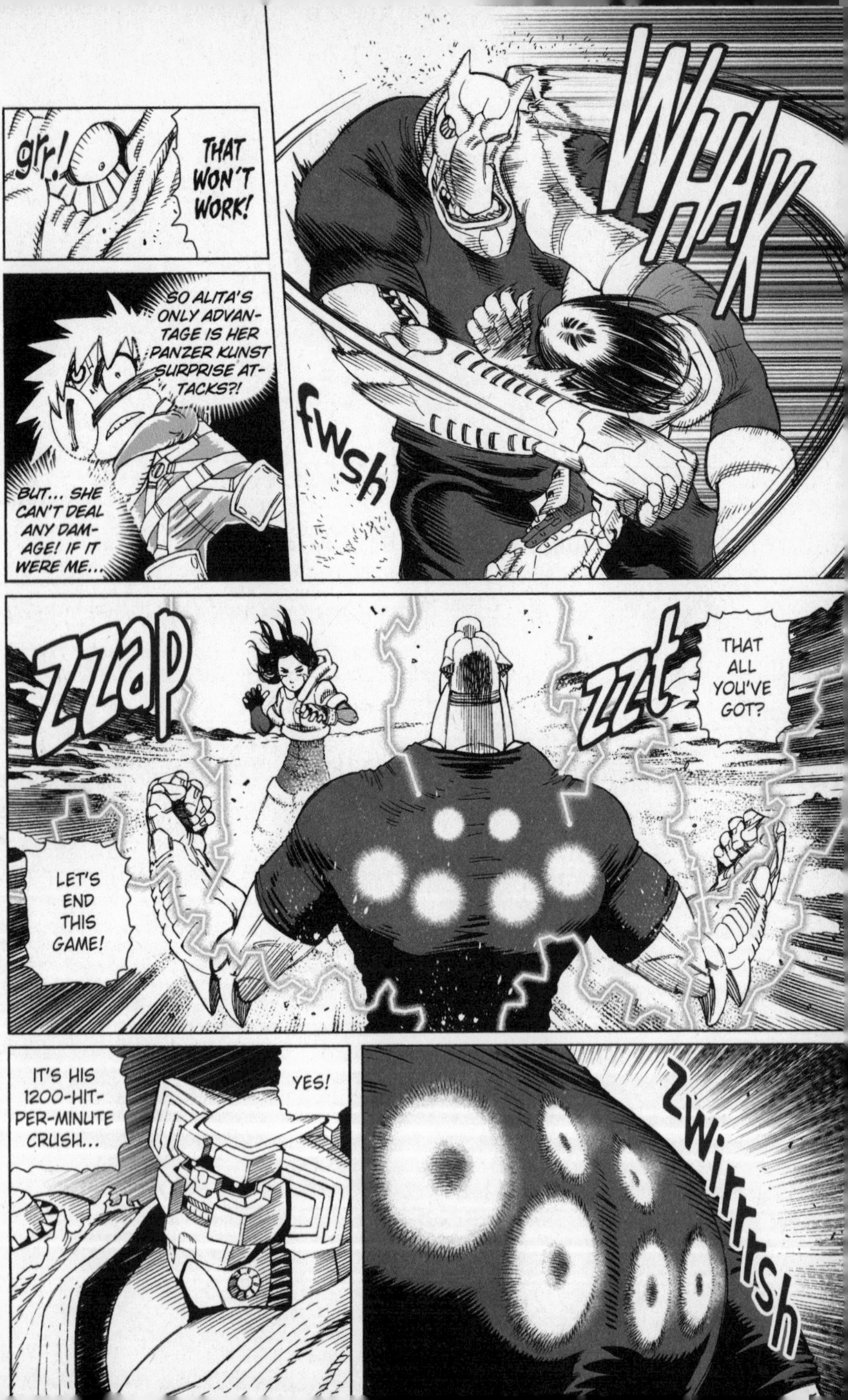
WHAK
fwsh
grr!
THAT WON'T WORK!
SO ALITA'S ONLY ADVANTAGE IS HER PANZER KUNST SURPRISE ATTACKS?!
BUT... SHE CAN'T DEAL ANY DAMAGE! IF IT WERE ME...
THAT ALL YOU'VE GOT?
zzzt
zzap
LET'S END THIS GAME!
Zwirrrsh
IT'S HIS 1200-HIT-PER-MINUTE CRUSH...
YES!

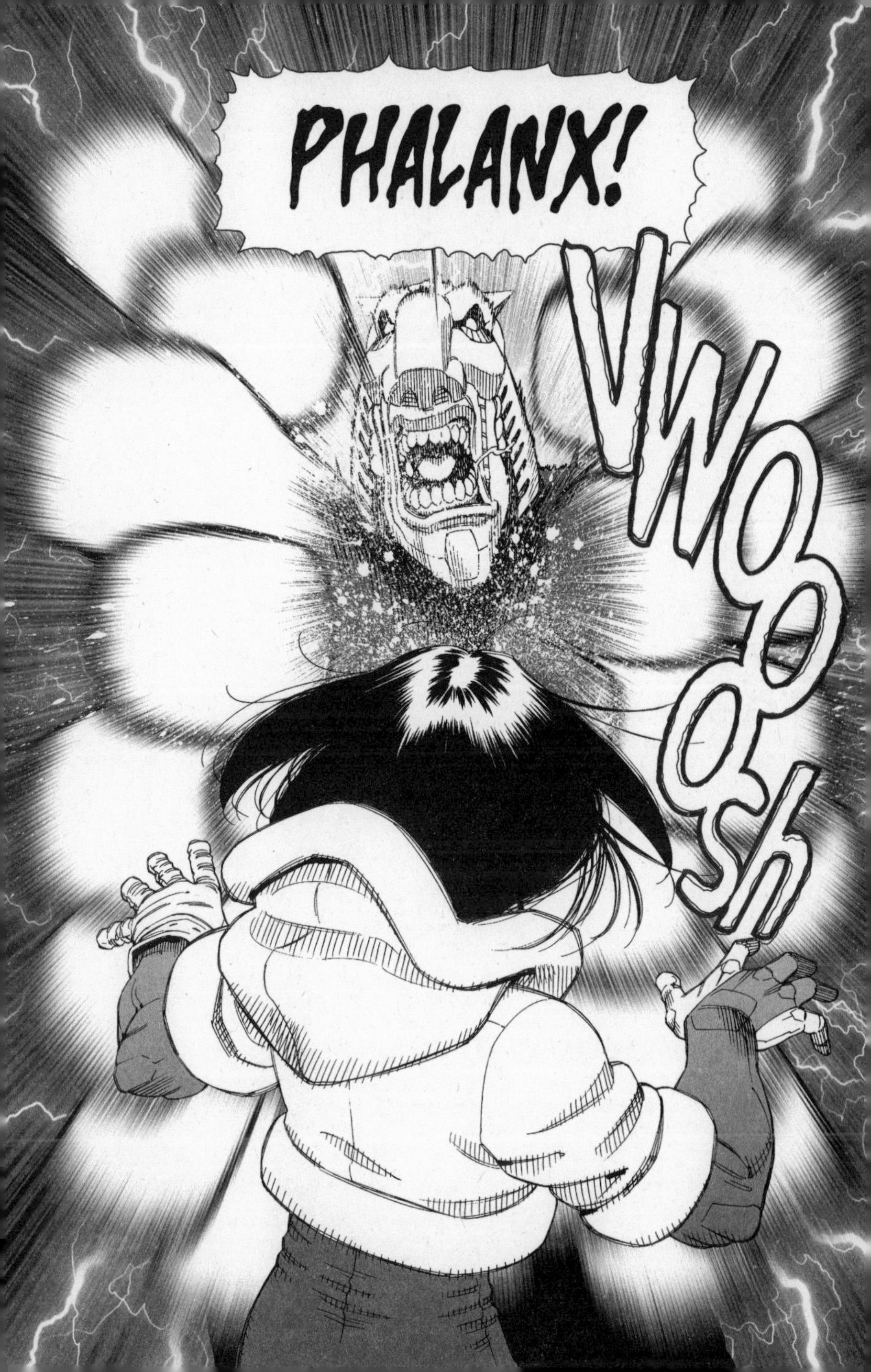
PHALANX!
VWOOOOSH

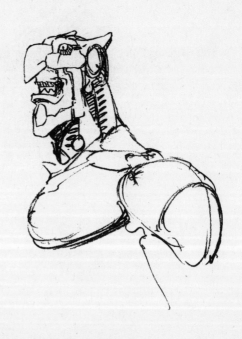

PHASE 22
Did You See That?!

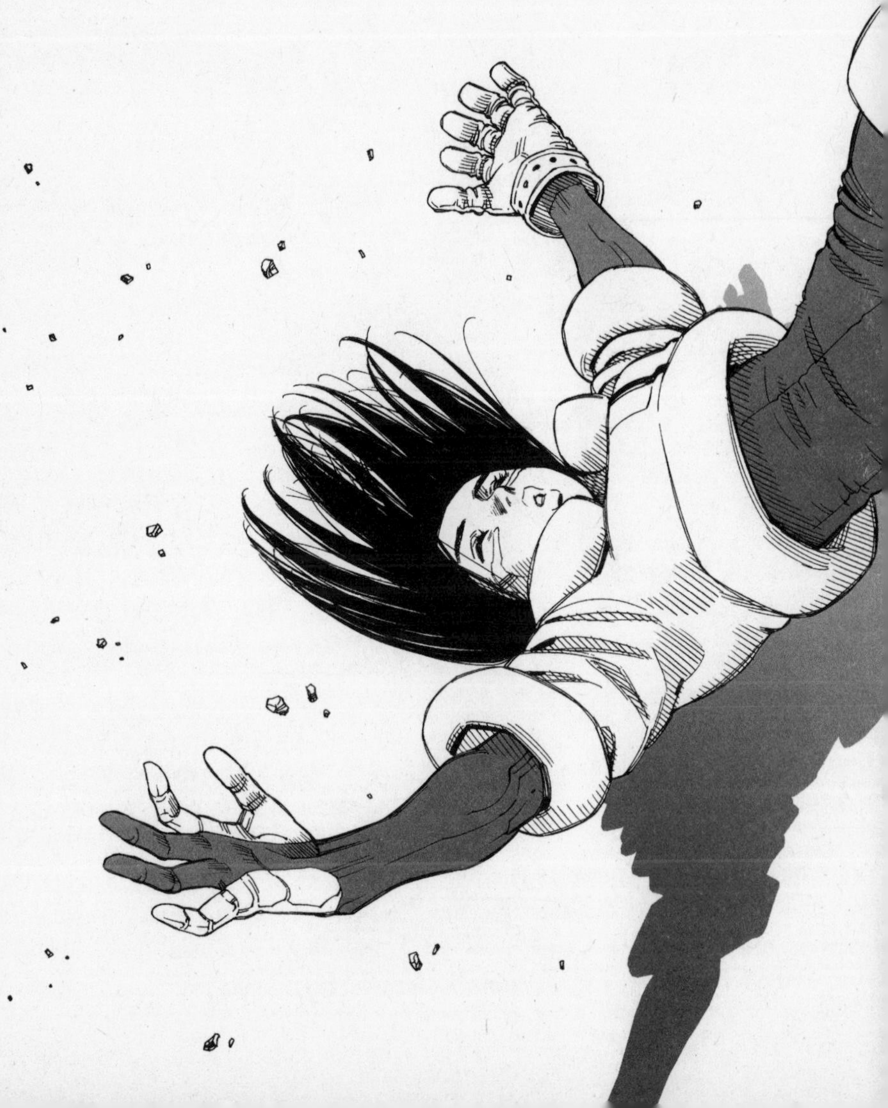

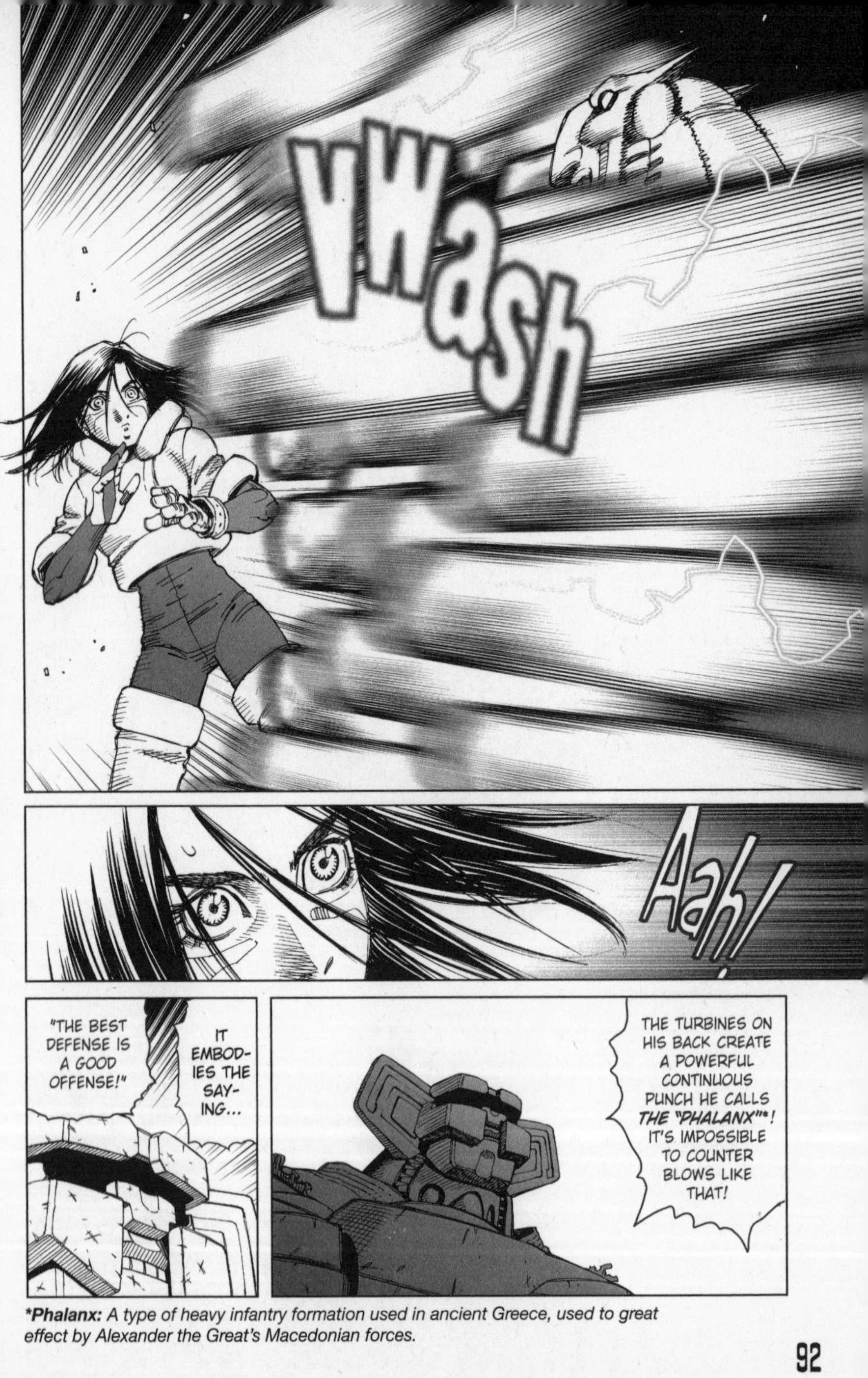
VWASH
Aah!
THE TURBINES ON HIS BACK CREATE A POWERFUL CONTINUOUS PUNCH HE CALLS THE "PHALANX"*! IT'S IMPOSSIBLE TO COUNTER BLOWS LIKE THAT!
IT EMBODIES THE SAYING...
"THE BEST DEFENSE IS A GOOD OFFENSE!"

***Phalanx:** A type of heavy infantry formation used in ancient Greece, used to great effect by Alexander the Great's Macedonian forces.*

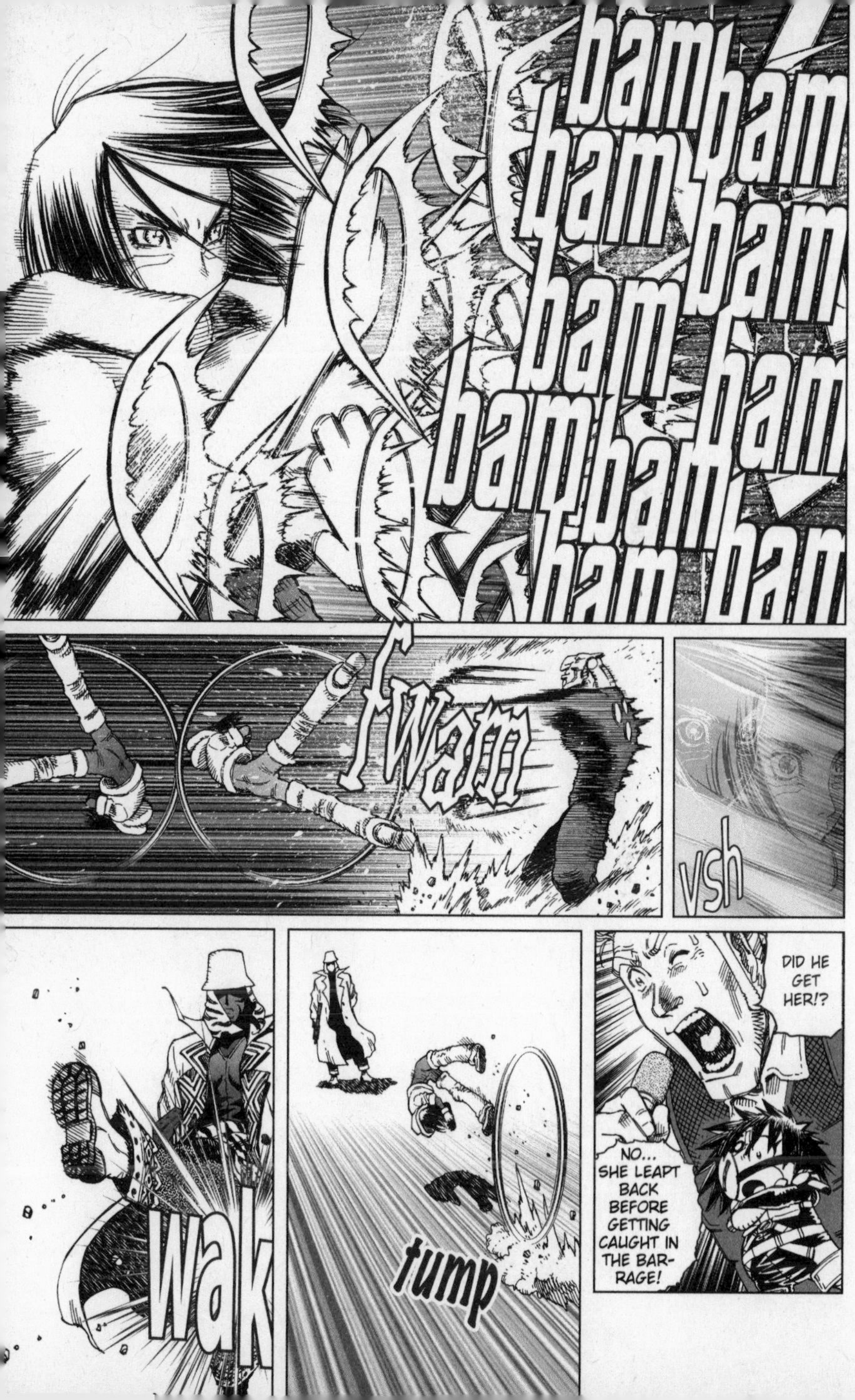
bam bam
bam bam
bam bam
bam bam
bam bam
bam bam
vsh
fwam
DID HE GET HER!?
NO... SHE LEAPT BACK BEFORE GETTING CAUGHT IN THE BAR-RAGE!
tump
wak

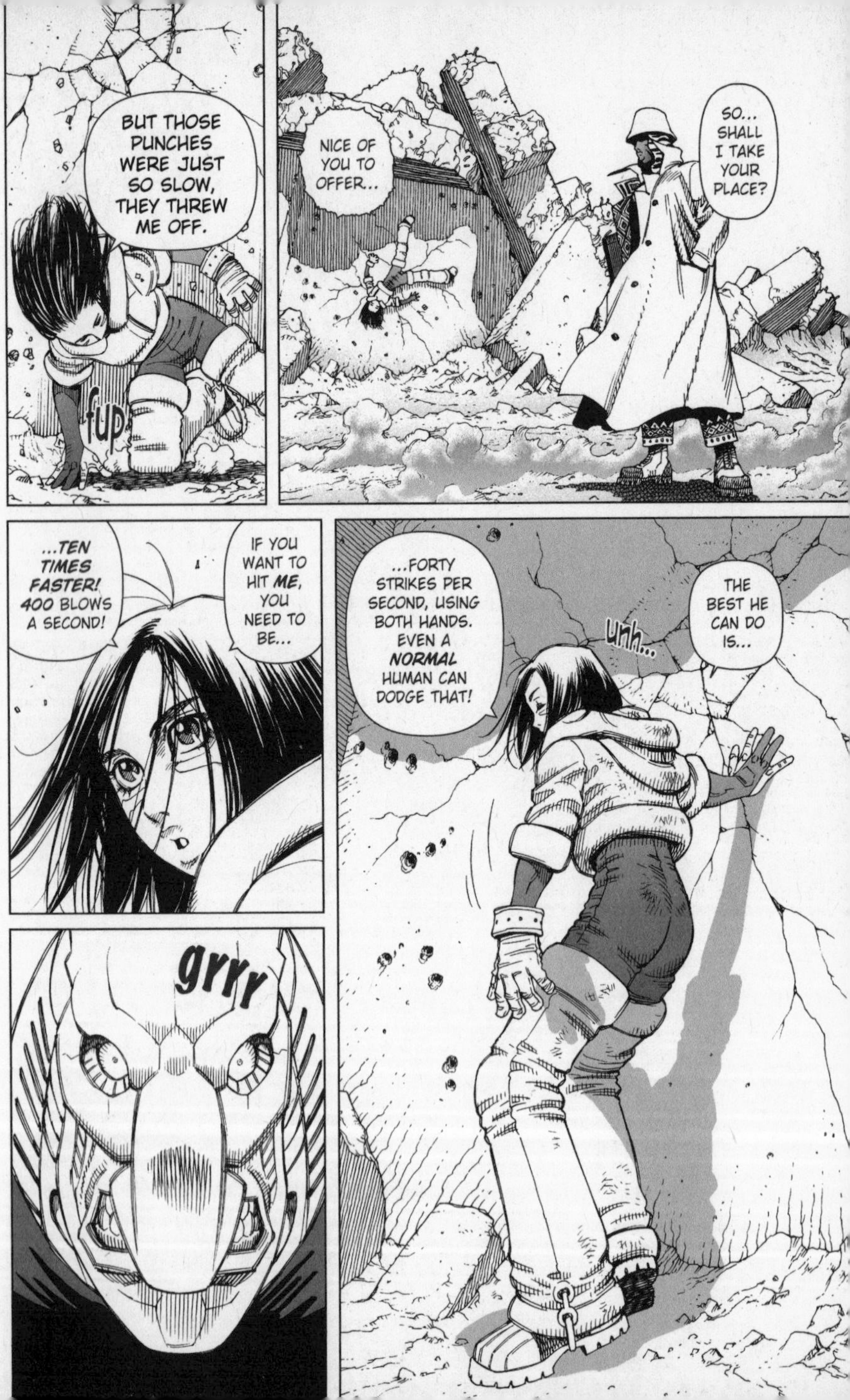
SO... SHALL I TAKE YOUR PLACE?
NICE OF YOU TO OFFER...
BUT THOSE PUNCHES WERE JUST SO SLOW, THEY THREW ME OFF.
fup
THE BEST HE CAN DO IS...
unh...
...FORTY STRIKES PER SECOND, USING BOTH HANDS. EVEN A *NORMAL* HUMAN CAN DODGE THAT!
IF YOU WANT TO HIT *ME*, YOU NEED TO BE...
...TEN TIMES FASTER! 400 BLOWS A SECOND!
grrr

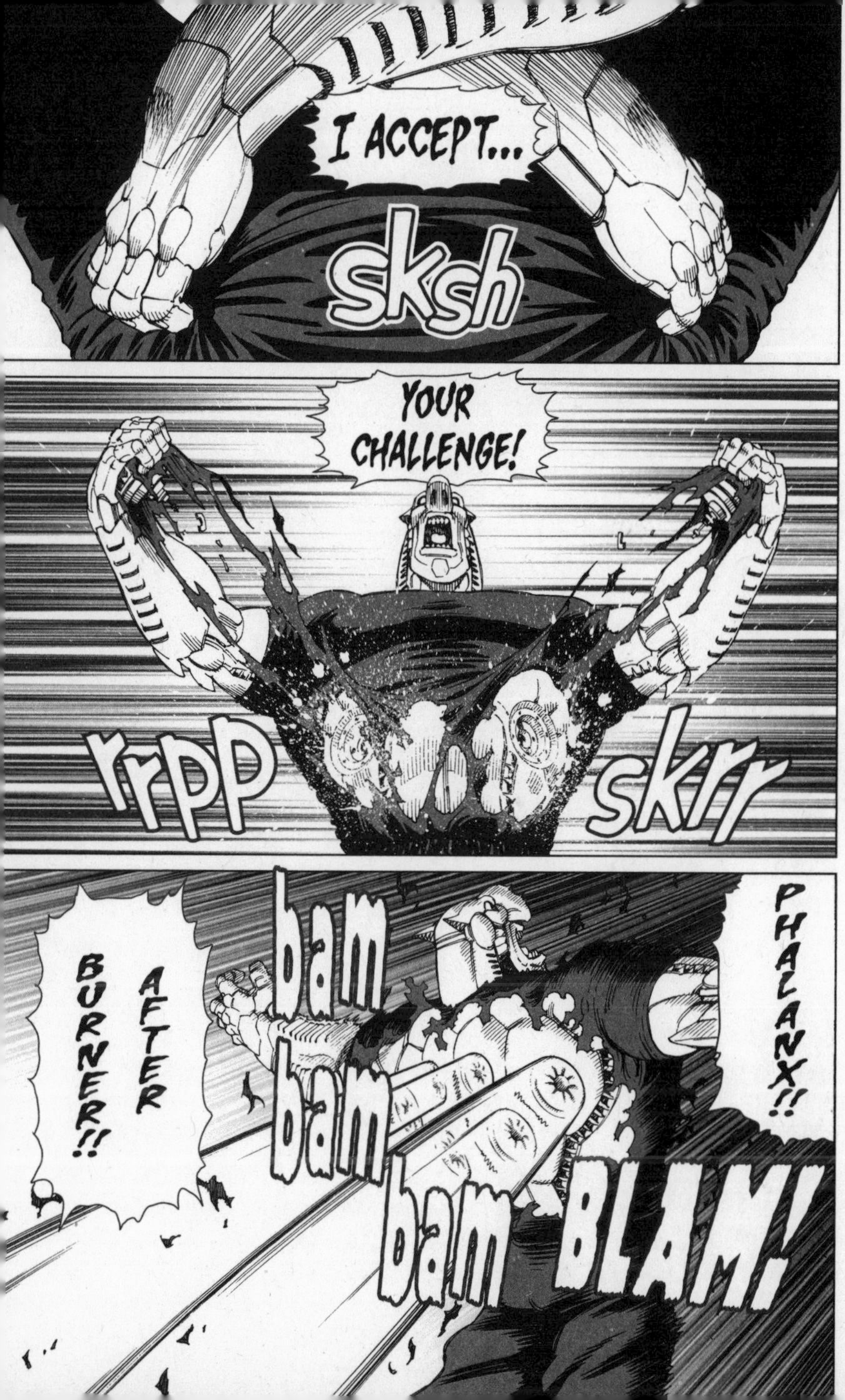
I ACCEPT...
sksh
YOUR CHALLENGE!
skrr
rrpp
PHALANX!!
bam
bam
bam
bam
BLAM!
AFTER BURNER!!

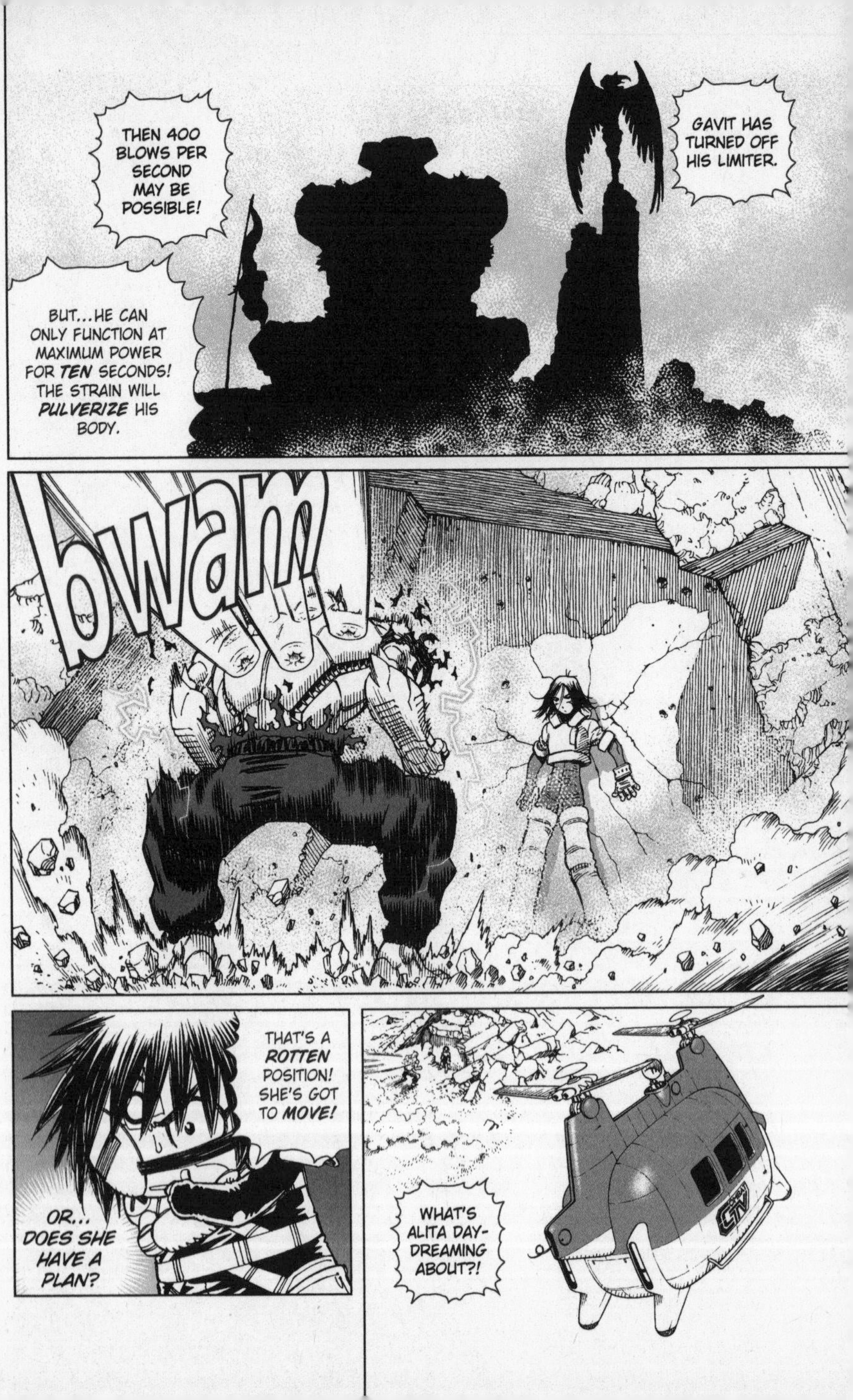
GAVIT HAS TURNED OFF HIS LIMITER.
THEN 400 BLOWS PER SECOND MAY BE POSSIBLE!
BUT...HE CAN ONLY FUNCTION AT MAXIMUM POWER FOR TEN SECONDS! THE STRAIN WILL PULVERIZE HIS BODY.
bwam
WHAT'S ALITA DAY-DREAMING ABOUT?!
THAT'S A ROTTEN POSITION! SHE'S GOT TO MOVE!
OR... DOES SHE HAVE A PLAN?

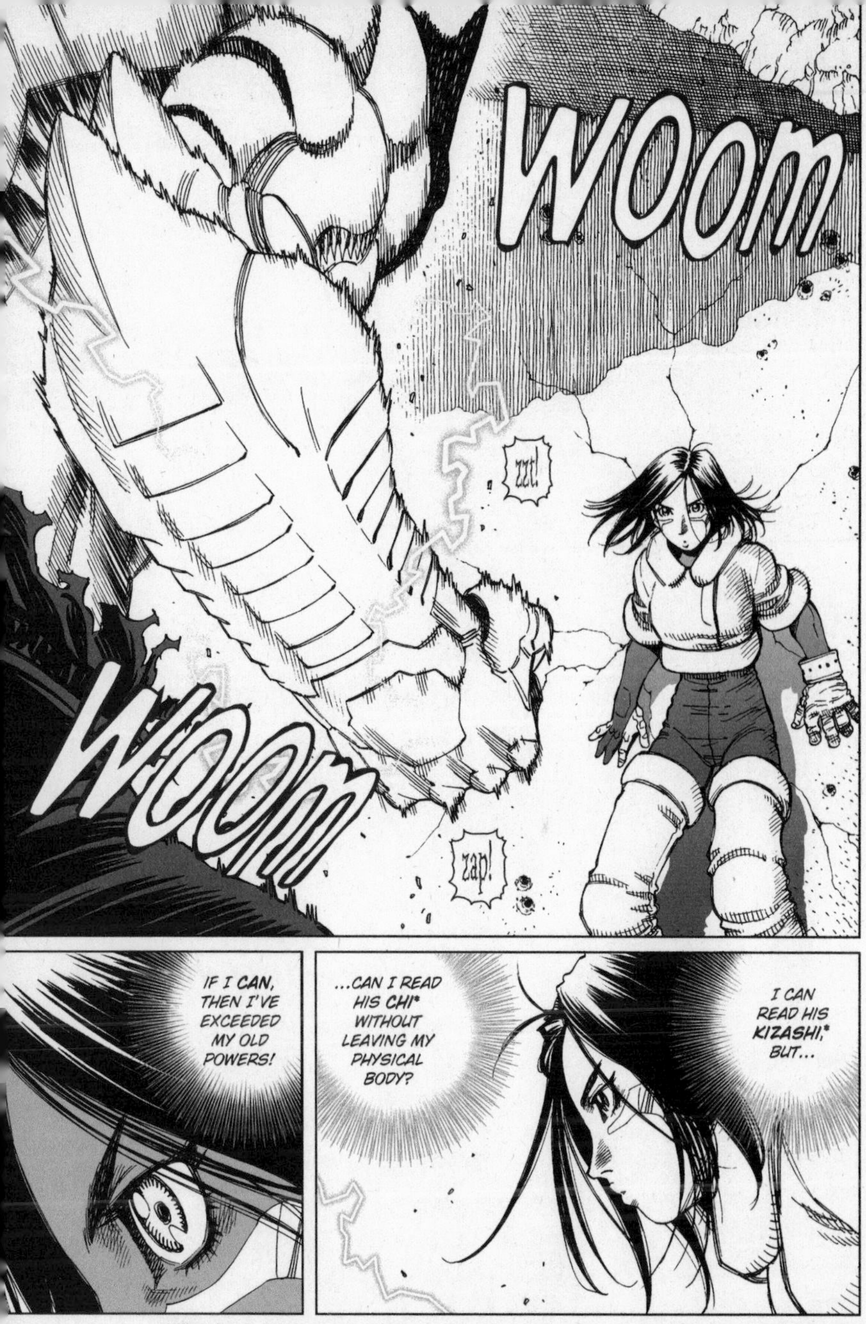
WOOM
zzt!
WOOM
zap!
I CAN READ HIS KIZASHI,* BUT...
...CAN I READ HIS CHI* WITHOUT LEAVING MY PHYSICAL BODY?
IF I CAN, THEN I'VE EXCEEDED MY OLD POWERS!

***Kizashi:** *Subtle mental and physical predictors that occur just before intended actions.*

***Chi:** *Source of timing and concentration in any body. See Battle Angel Alita, chapter 16.*

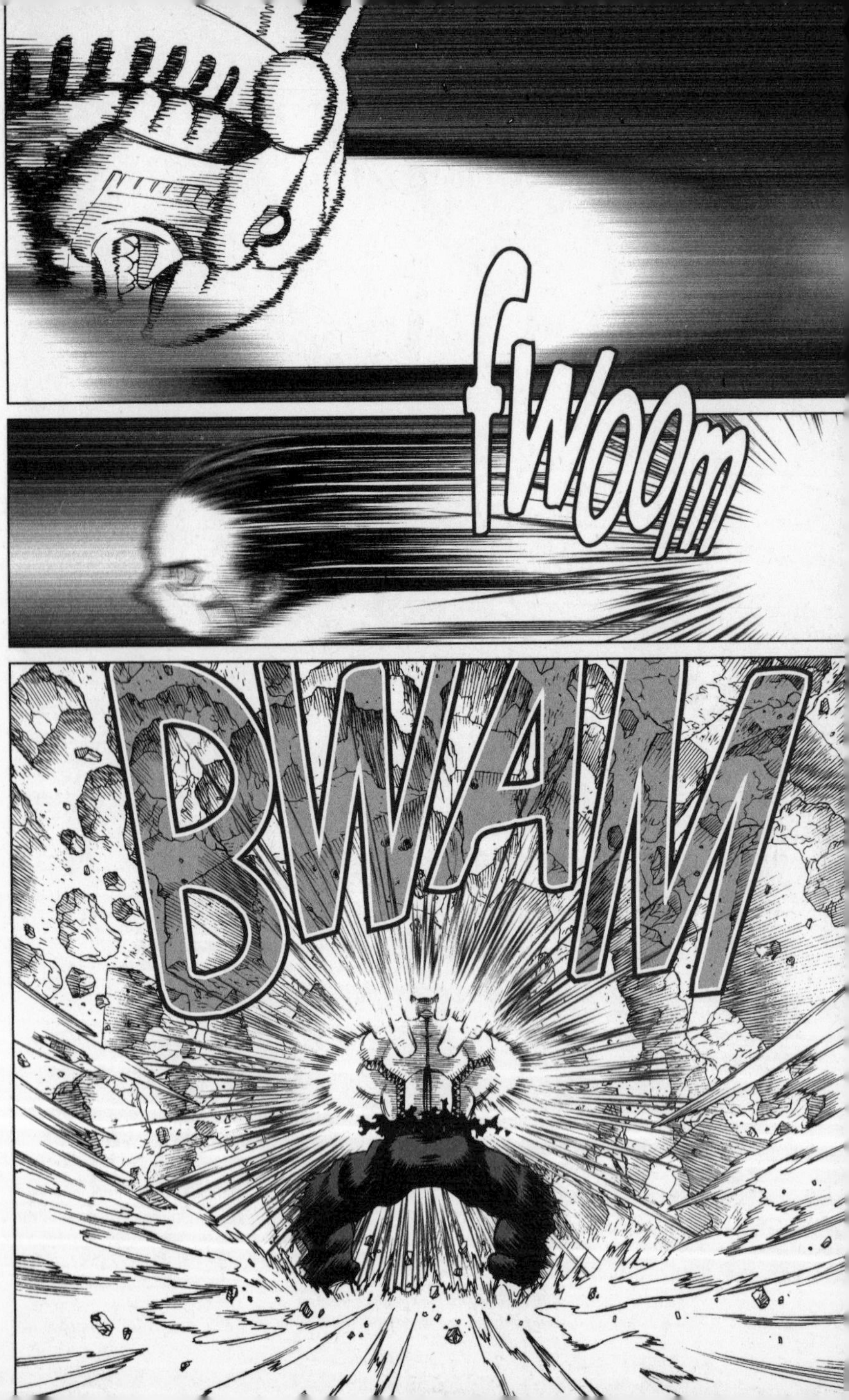
fwoom
BWAM

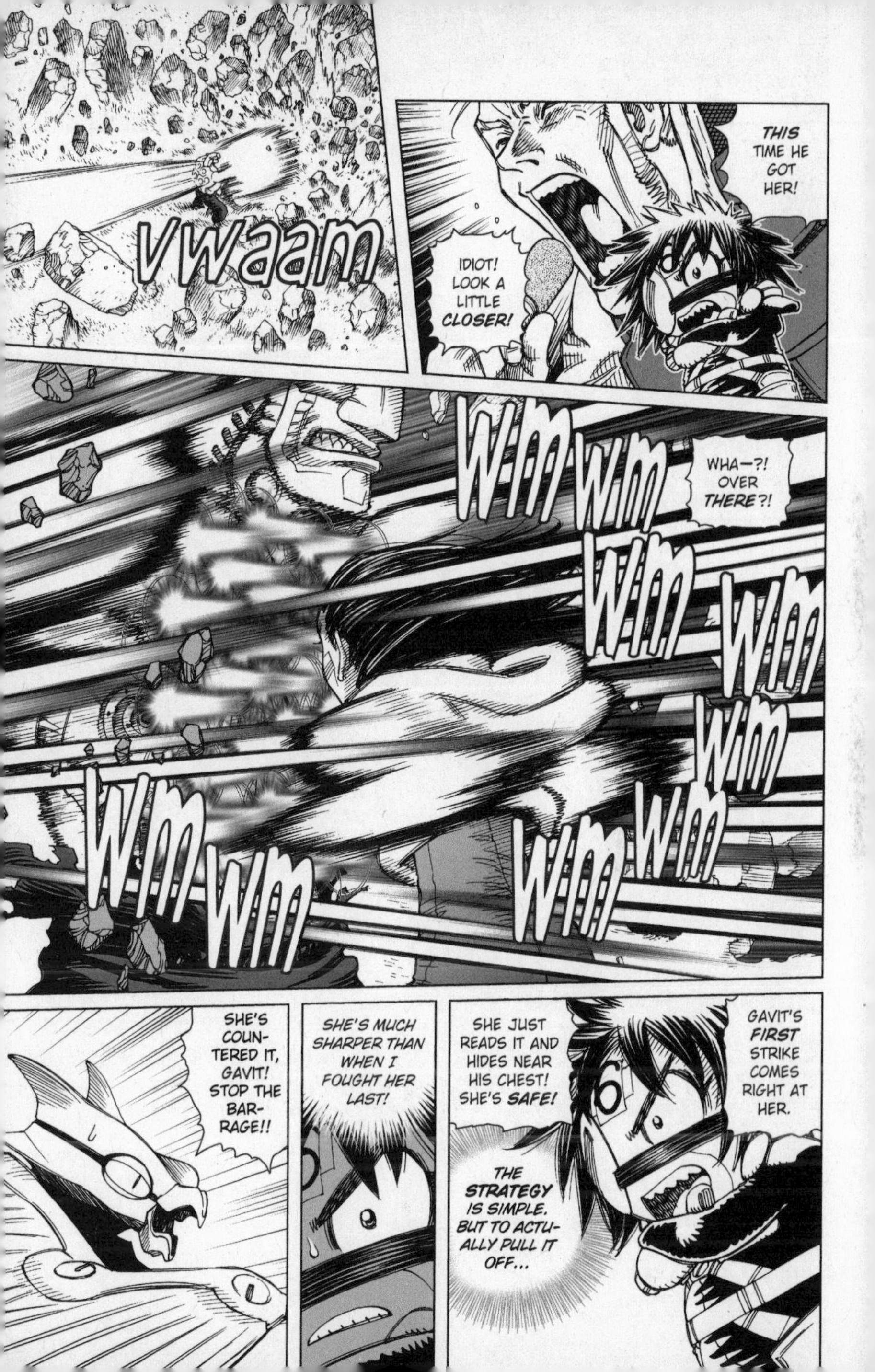
THIS TIME HE GOT HER!
IDIOT! LOOK A LITTLE CLOSER!
vwaam
WHA—?! OVER THERE?!
wm wm
wm
wm
wm
wm wm
wm wm
GAVIT'S FIRST STRIKE COMES RIGHT AT HER.
SHE JUST READS IT AND HIDES NEAR HIS CHEST! SHE'S SAFE!
THE STRATEGY IS SIMPLE. BUT TO ACTU-ALLY PULL IT OFF...
SHE'S MUCH SHARPER THAN WHEN I FOUGHT HER LAST!
SHE'S COUN-TERED IT, GAVIT! STOP THE BAR-RAGE!!

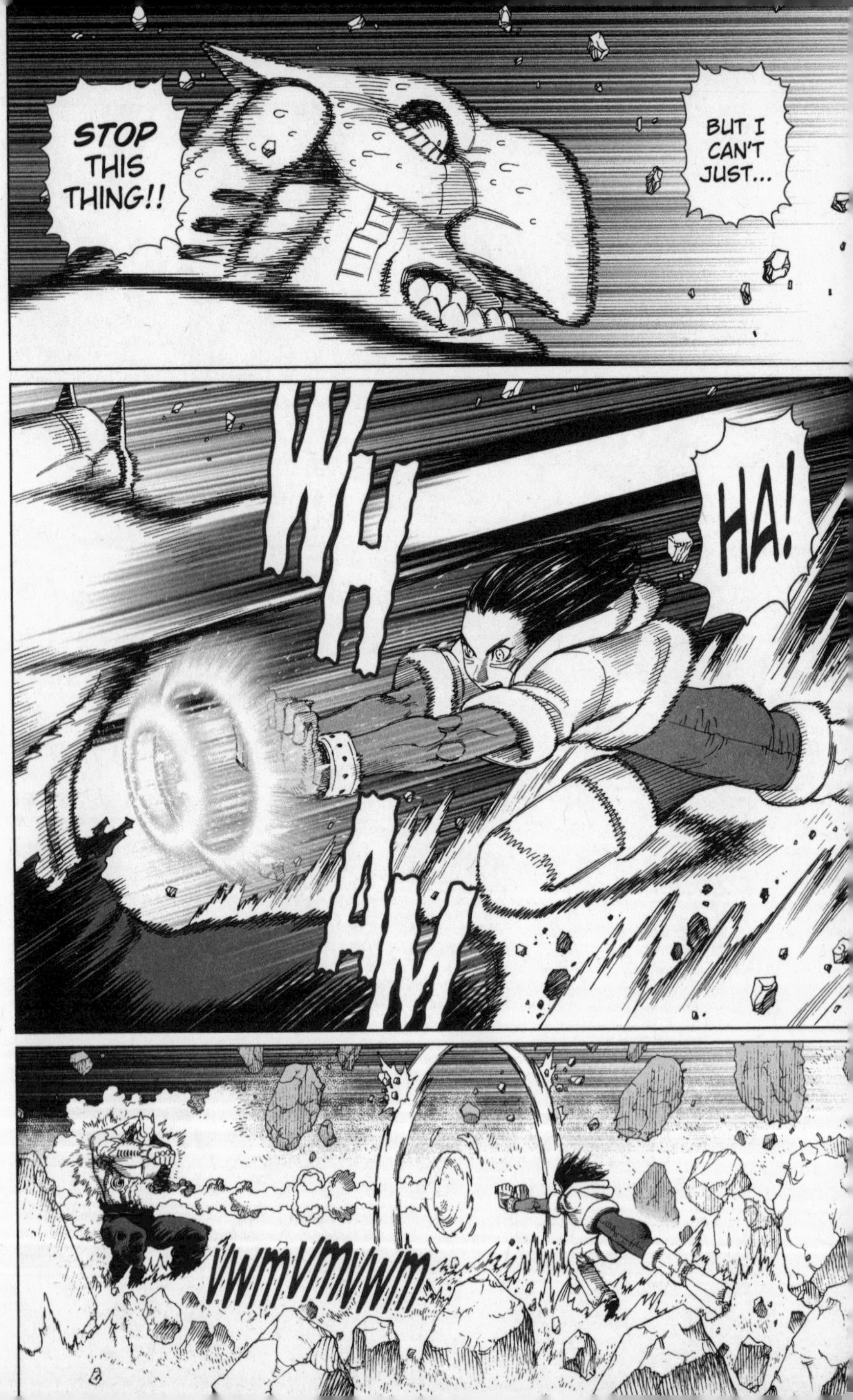
BUT I CAN'T JUST...
STOP THIS THING!!
HA!
WHAM
VWMVMVWM

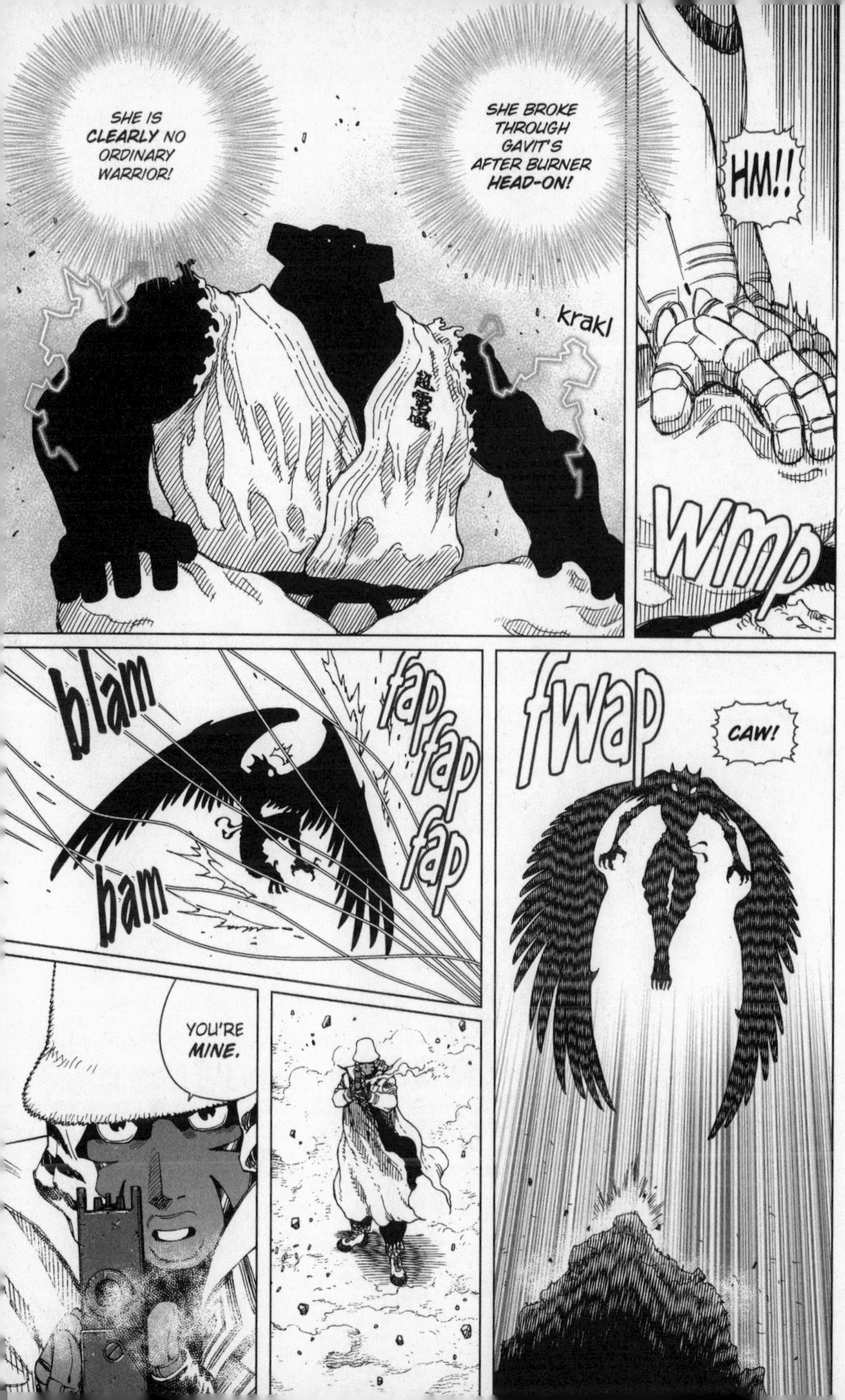
HM!!
WMP
SHE BROKE THROUGH GAVIT'S AFTER BURNER HEAD-ON!
SHE IS CLEARLY NO ORDINARY WARRIOR!
krakl
fwap
CAW!
fap fap fap
blam
bam
YOU'RE MINE.

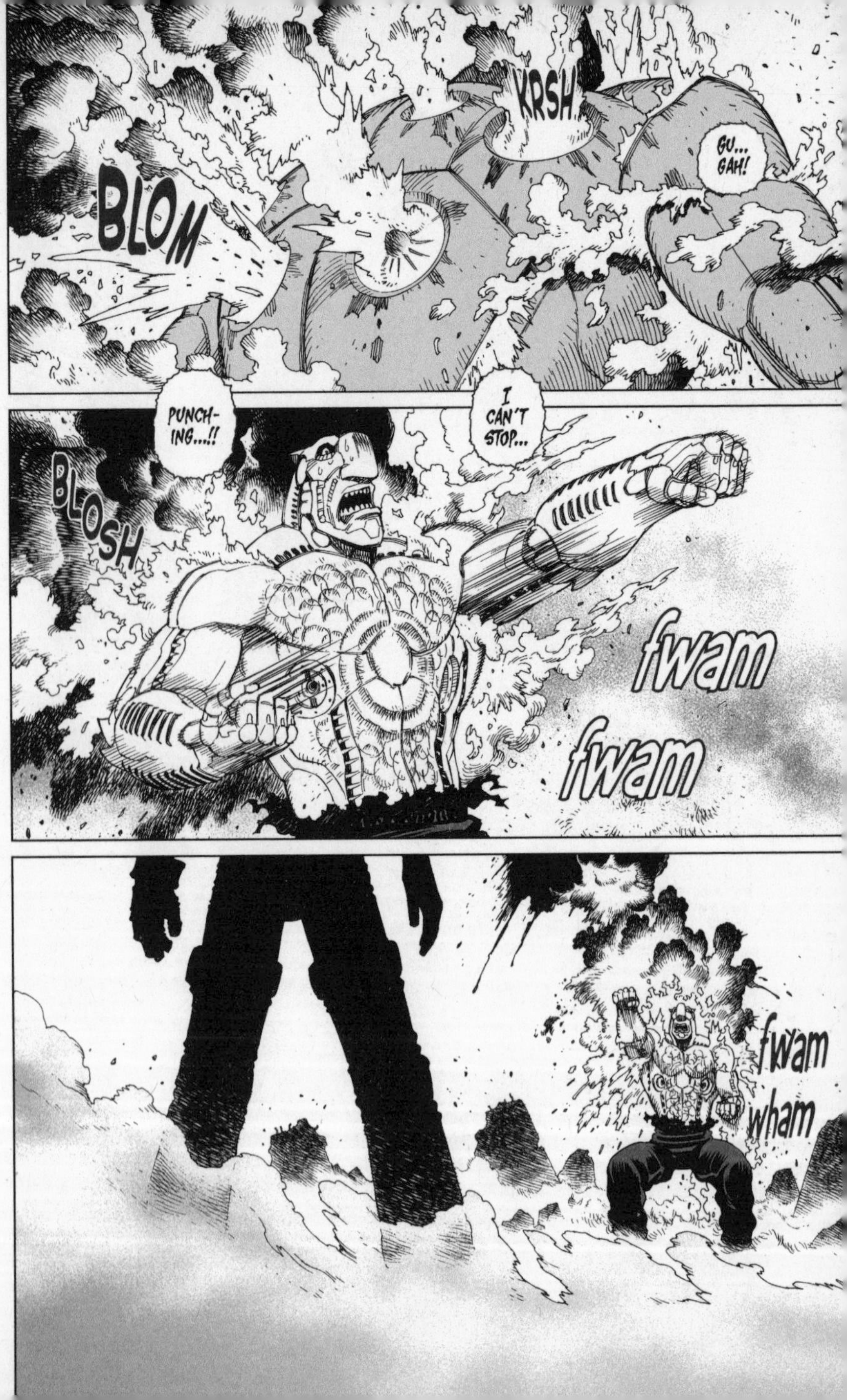
GU... GAH!
KRSH
BLOM
I CAN'T STOP...
PUNCH-ING...!!
BLOSH
fwam
fwam
fwam
wham

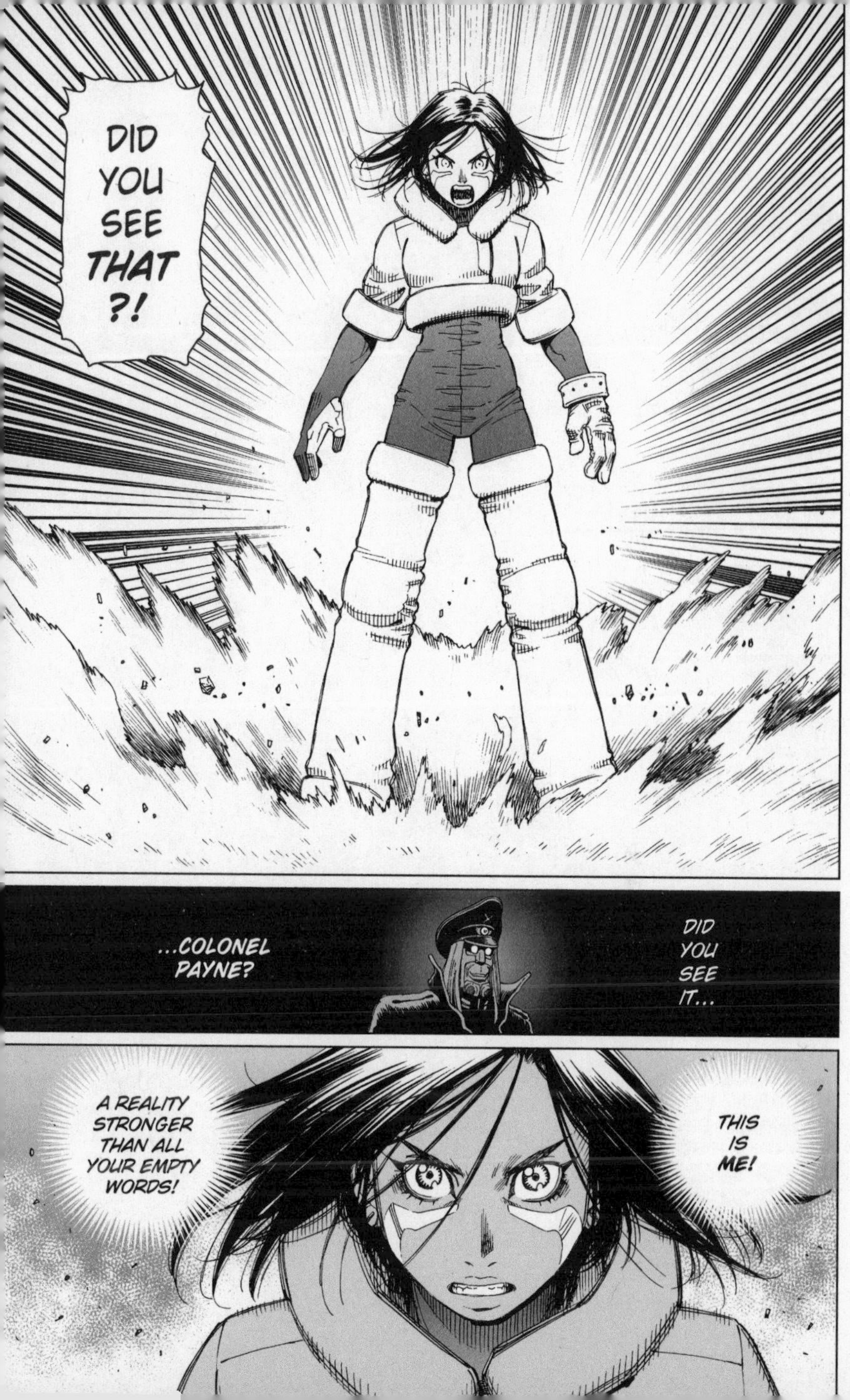
DID YOU SEE THAT?!
DID YOU SEE IT...
...COLONEL PAYNE?
THIS IS ME!
A REALITY STRONGER THAN ALL YOUR EMPTY WORDS!

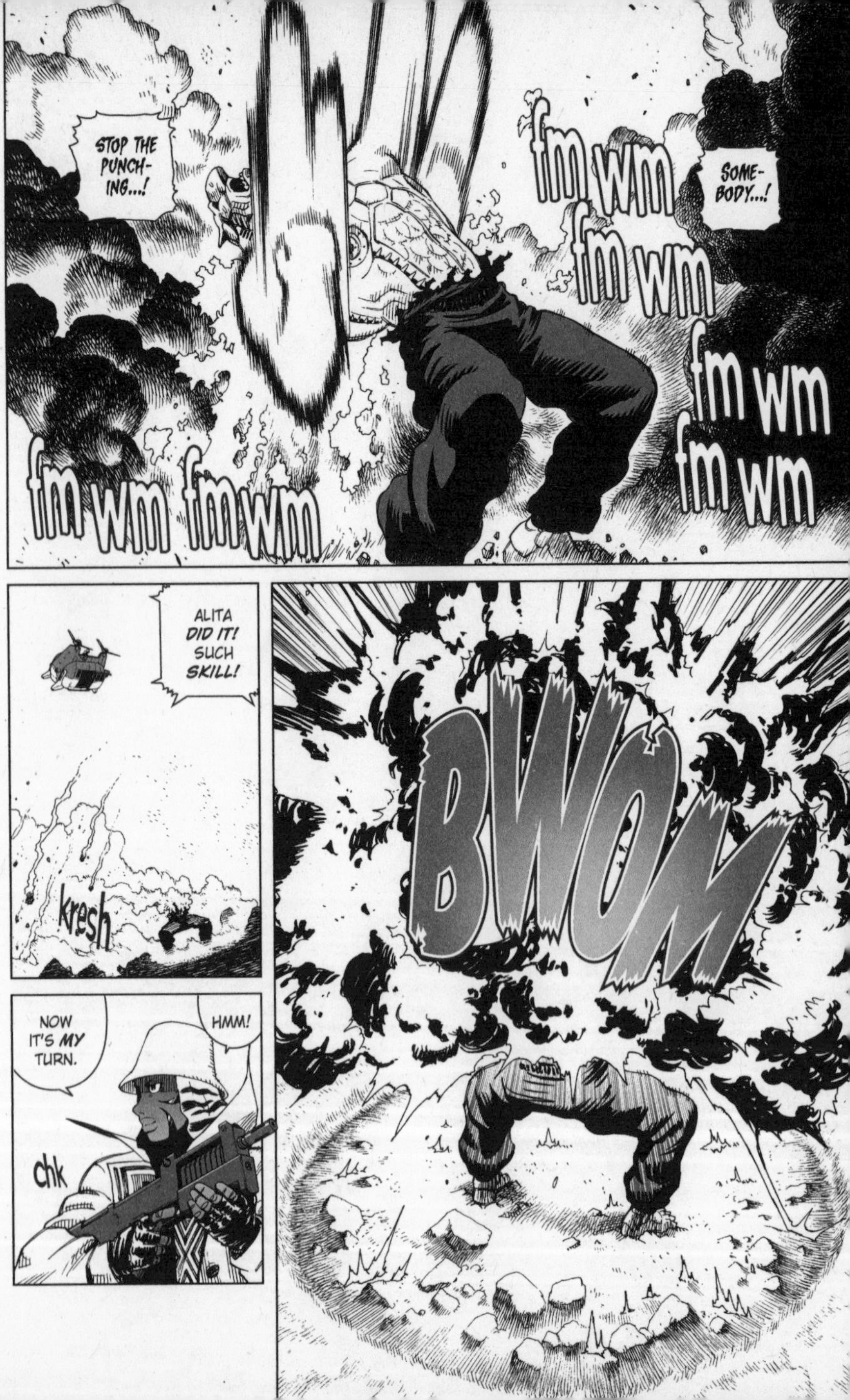
fm wm fm wm
SOME-BODY...!
STOP THE PUNCH-ING...!
fm wm fm wm
fm wm fm wm
BWOM
ALITA DID IT! SUCH SKILL!
kresh
HMM!
NOW IT'S MY TURN.
chk

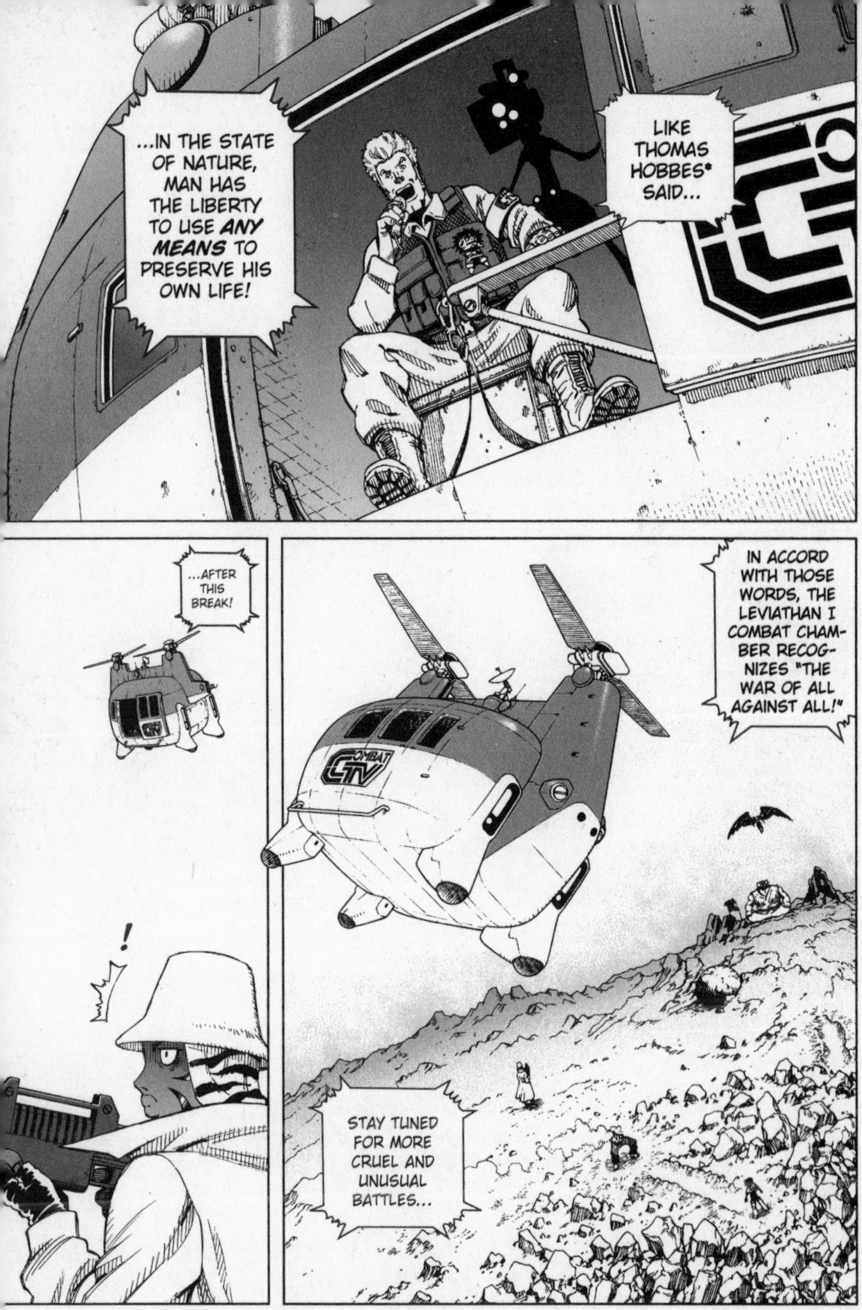
LIKE THOMAS HOBBES* SAID...
...IN THE STATE OF NATURE, MAN HAS THE LIBERTY TO USE ANY MEANS TO PRESERVE HIS OWN LIFE!
IN ACCORD WITH THOSE WORDS, THE LEVIATHAN I COMBAT CHAMBER RECOGNIZES "THE WAR OF ALL AGAINST ALL!"
COMBAT CTV
STAY TUNED FOR MORE CRUEL AND UNUSUAL BATTLES...
...AFTER THIS BREAK!
!

***Thomas Hobbes (1588-1679):** *A British political philosopher. His best-known work is "Leviathan" (1651).*

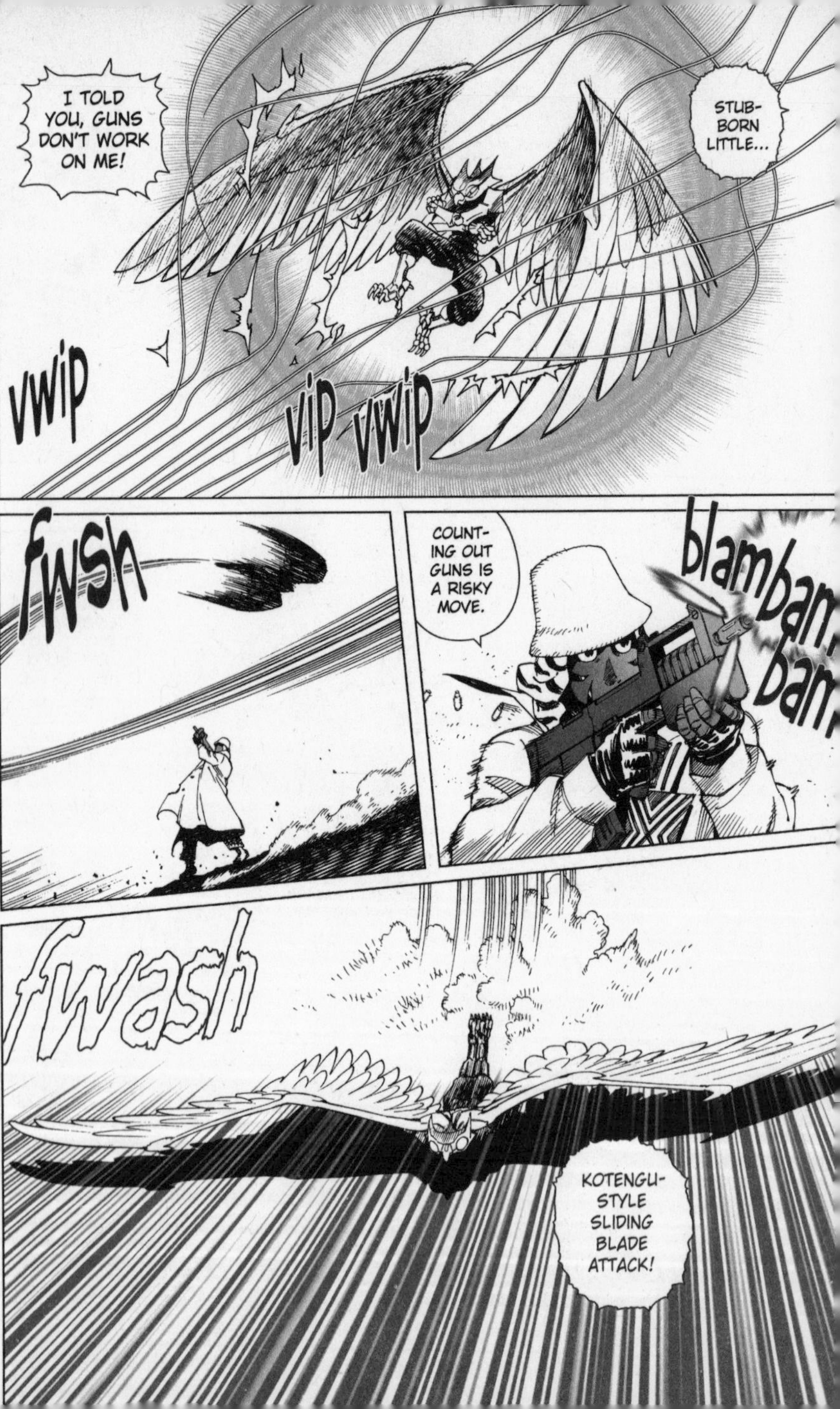
STUBBORN LITTLE...
I TOLD YOU, GUNS DON'T WORK ON ME!
vip vwip
vwip
blambam bam
COUNTING OUT GUNS IS A RISKY MOVE.
fwsh
fwash
KOTENGU-STYLE SLIDING BLADE ATTACK!

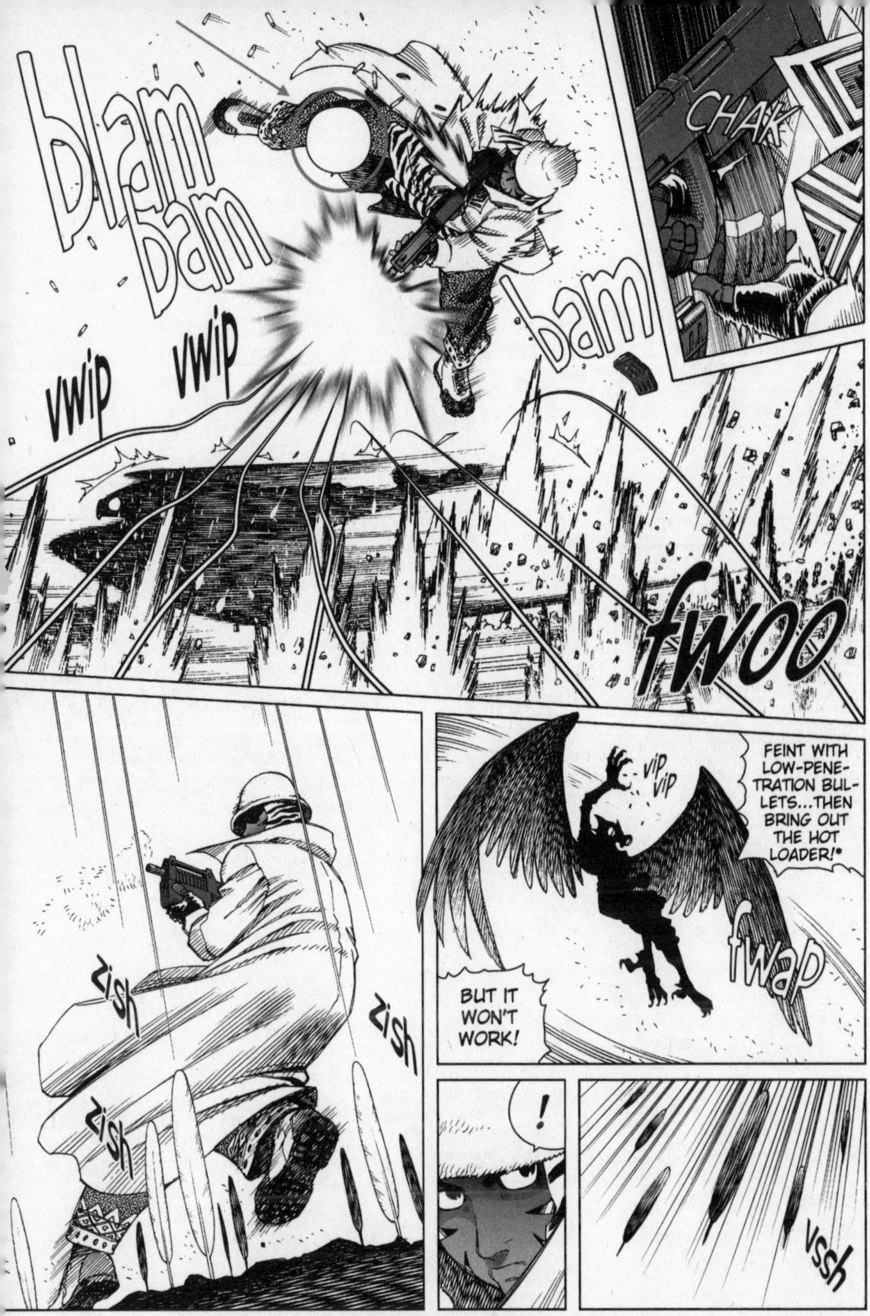
CHAK
blam
bam
bam
vwip
vwip
fwoo
FEINT WITH LOW-PENETRATION BULLETS...THEN BRING OUT THE HOT LOADER!*
vip vip
fwap
BUT IT WON'T WORK!
vssh
!
zish
zish
zish

***Hot loader:** A modded cartridge using explosive powder that's stronger than specs allow. It places great strain on the gun itself, which makes long-term use dangerous.*

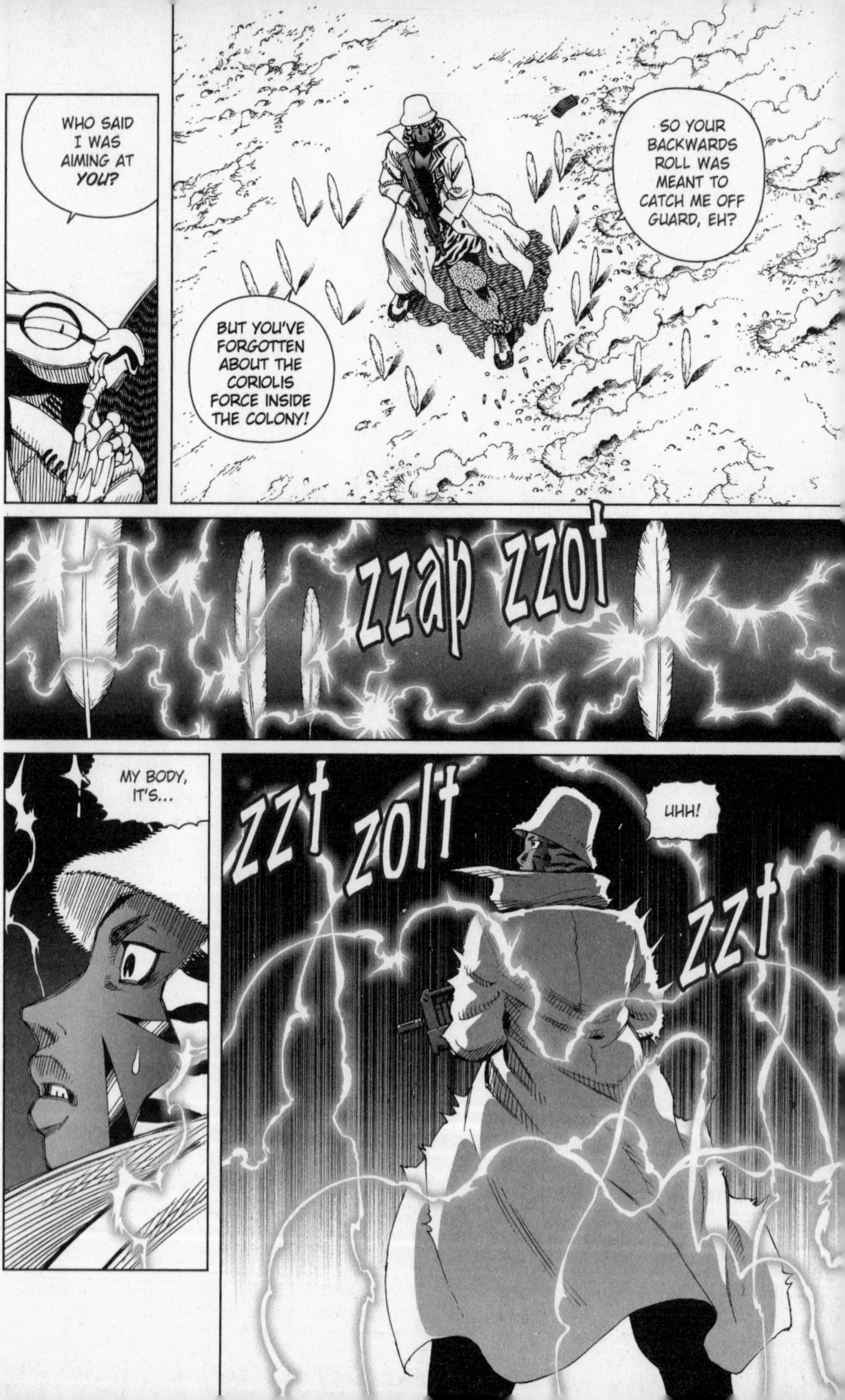
SO YOUR BACKWARDS ROLL WAS MEANT TO CATCH ME OFF GUARD, EH?
BUT YOU'VE FORGOTTEN ABOUT THE CORIOLIS FORCE INSIDE THE COLONY!
WHO SAID I WAS AIMING AT *YOU?*
ZZAP ZZOT
UHH!
ZZT ZOLT
ZZT
MY BODY, IT'S...

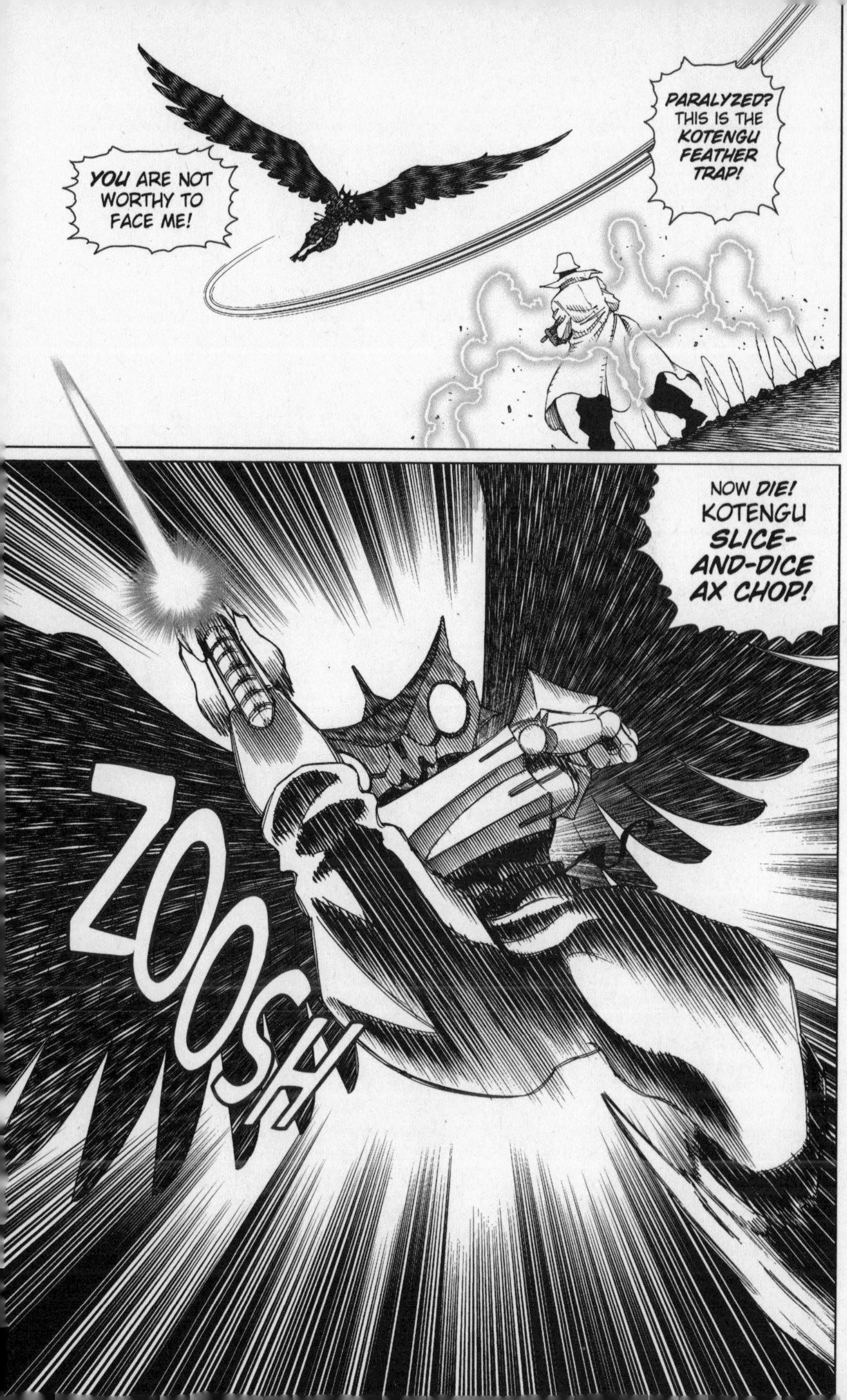
PARALYZED? THIS IS THE KOTENGU FEATHER TRAP!
YOU ARE NOT WORTHY TO FACE ME!
NOW DIE! KOTENGU SLICE-AND-DICE AX CHOP!
ZOOSH

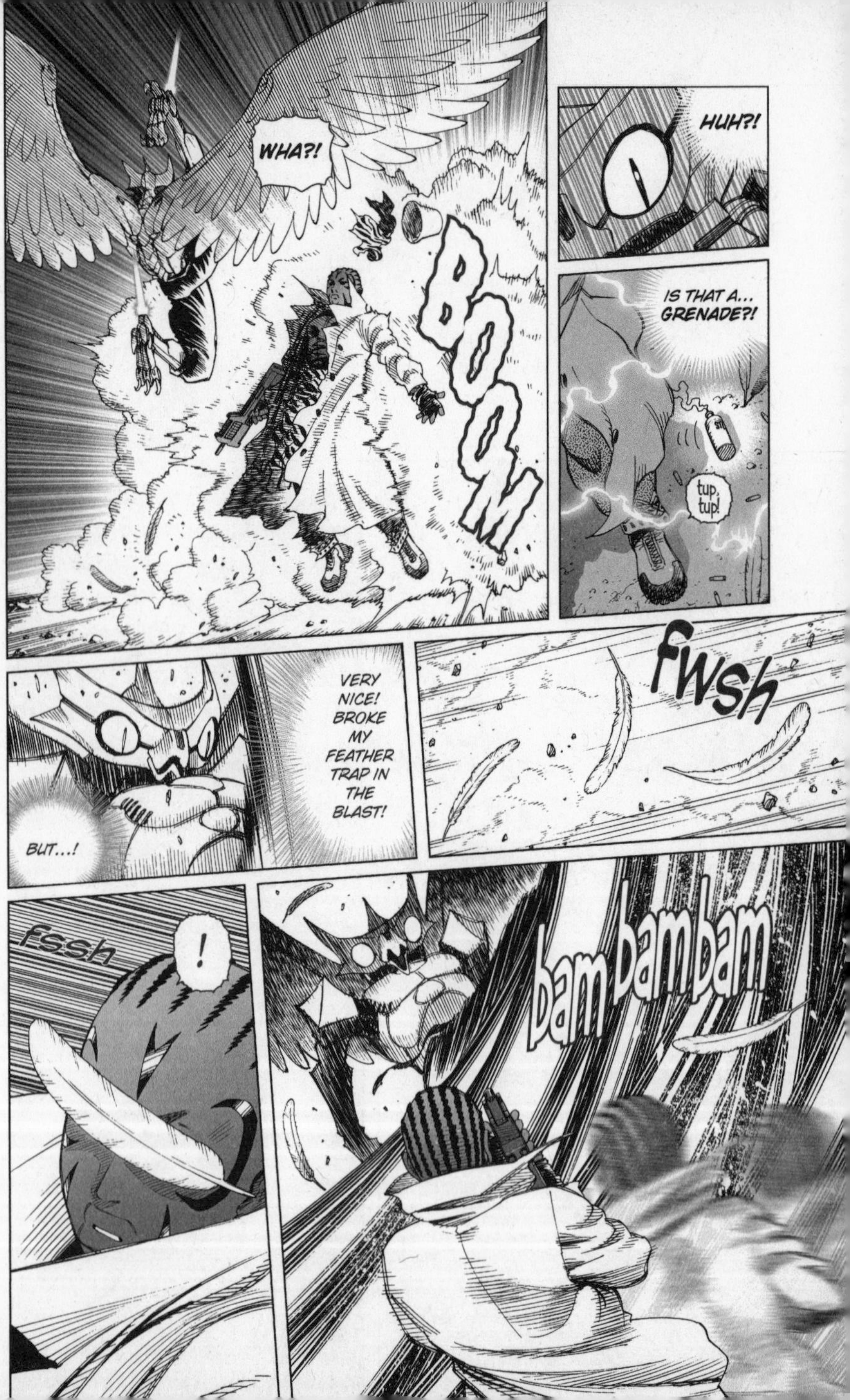
HUH?!
IS THAT A... GRENADE?!
tup, tup!
WHA?!
BOOM
fwsh
VERY NICE! BROKE MY FEATHER TRAP IN THE BLAST!
BUT...!
bam bam bam
fssh
!

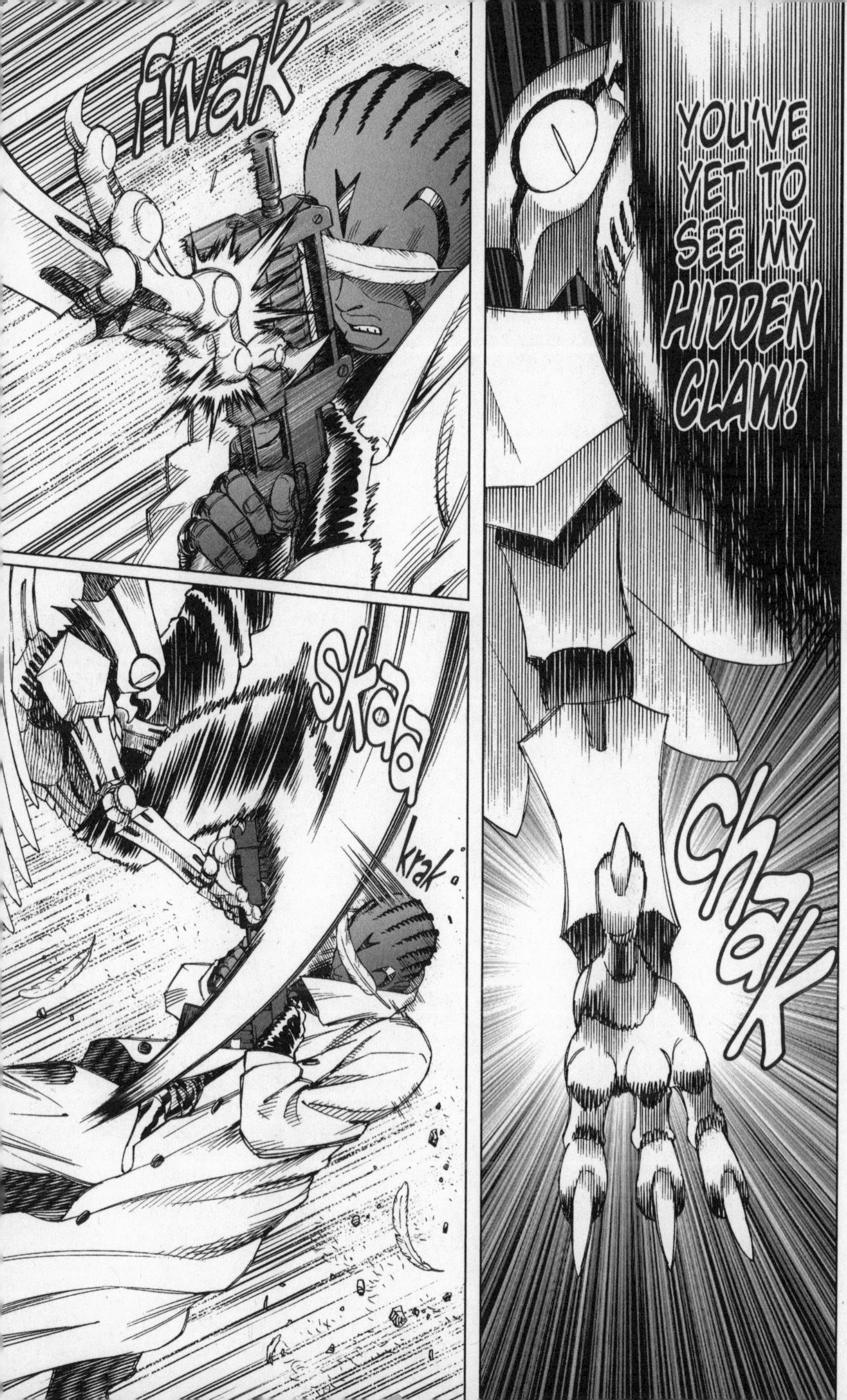
YOU'VE YET TO SEE MY HIDDEN CLAW!
Chak
fwak
skaa
krak

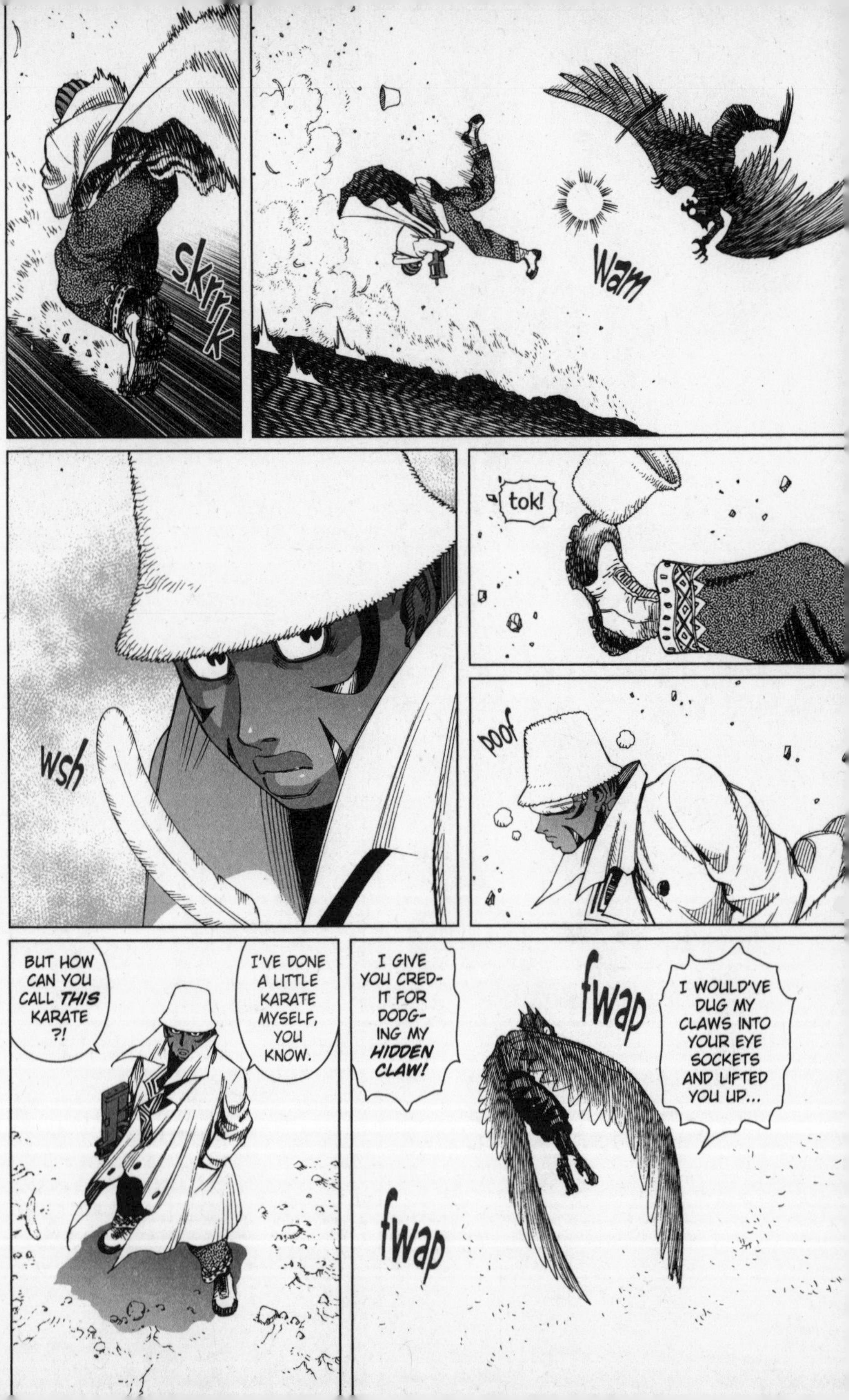
Wam
skrrk
tok!
poof
wsh
I WOULD'VE DUG MY CLAWS INTO YOUR EYE SOCKETS AND LIFTED YOU UP...
fwap
I GIVE YOU CRED-IT FOR DODG-ING MY *HIDDEN CLAW!*
fwap
I'VE DONE A LITTLE KARATE MYSELF, YOU KNOW.
BUT HOW CAN YOU CALL *THIS* KARATE ?!

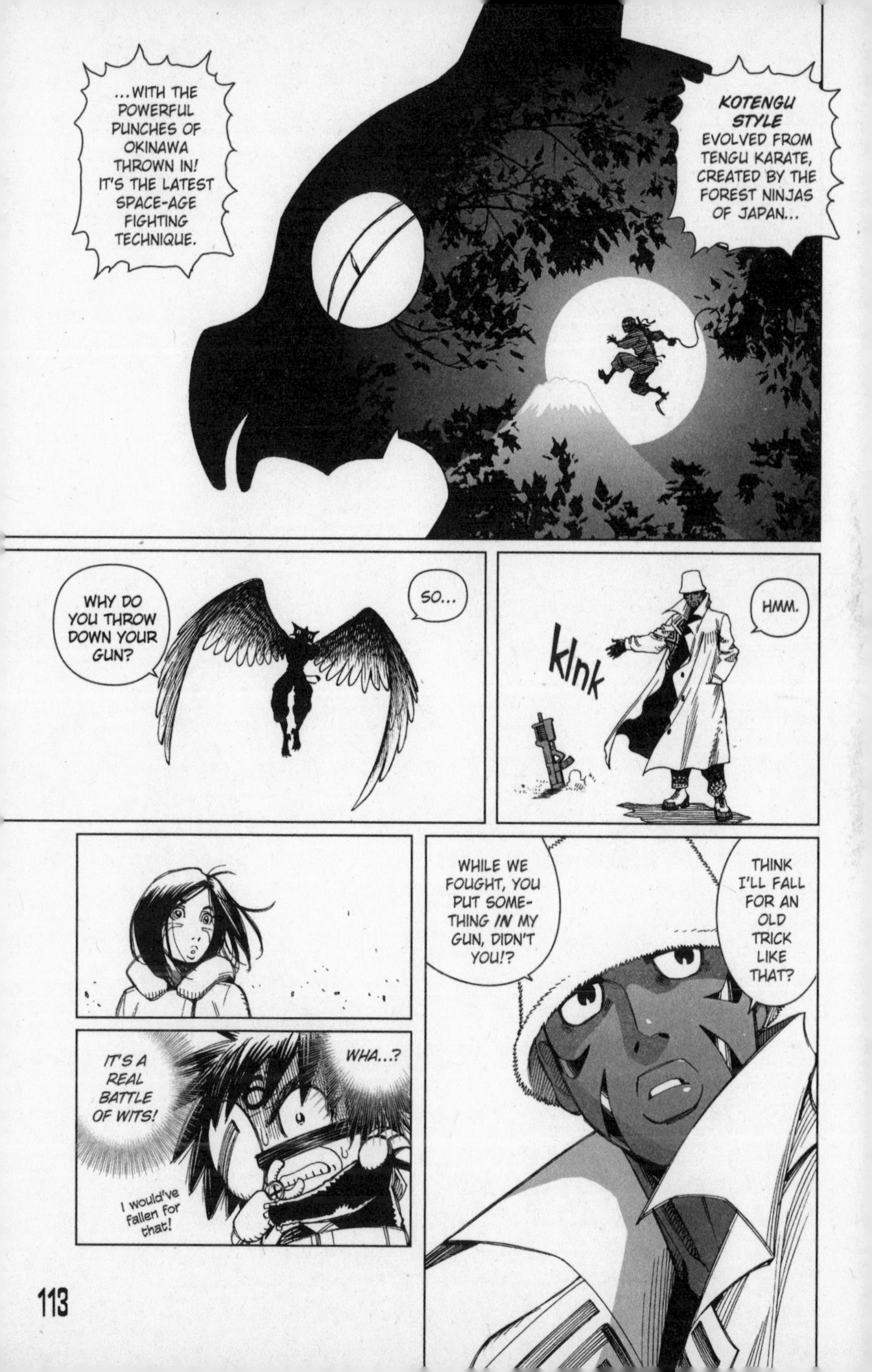
KOTENGU STYLE EVOLVED FROM TENGU KARATE, CREATED BY THE FOREST NINJAS OF JAPAN...
...WITH THE POWERFUL PUNCHES OF OKINAWA THROWN IN! IT'S THE LATEST SPACE-AGE FIGHTING TECHNIQUE.
HMM.
klnk
SO...
WHY DO YOU THROW DOWN YOUR GUN?
THINK I'LL FALL FOR AN OLD TRICK LIKE THAT?
WHILE WE FOUGHT, YOU PUT SOME-THING *IN* MY GUN, DIDN'T YOU!?
WHA...?
IT'S A REAL BATTLE OF WITS!
I would've fallen for that!

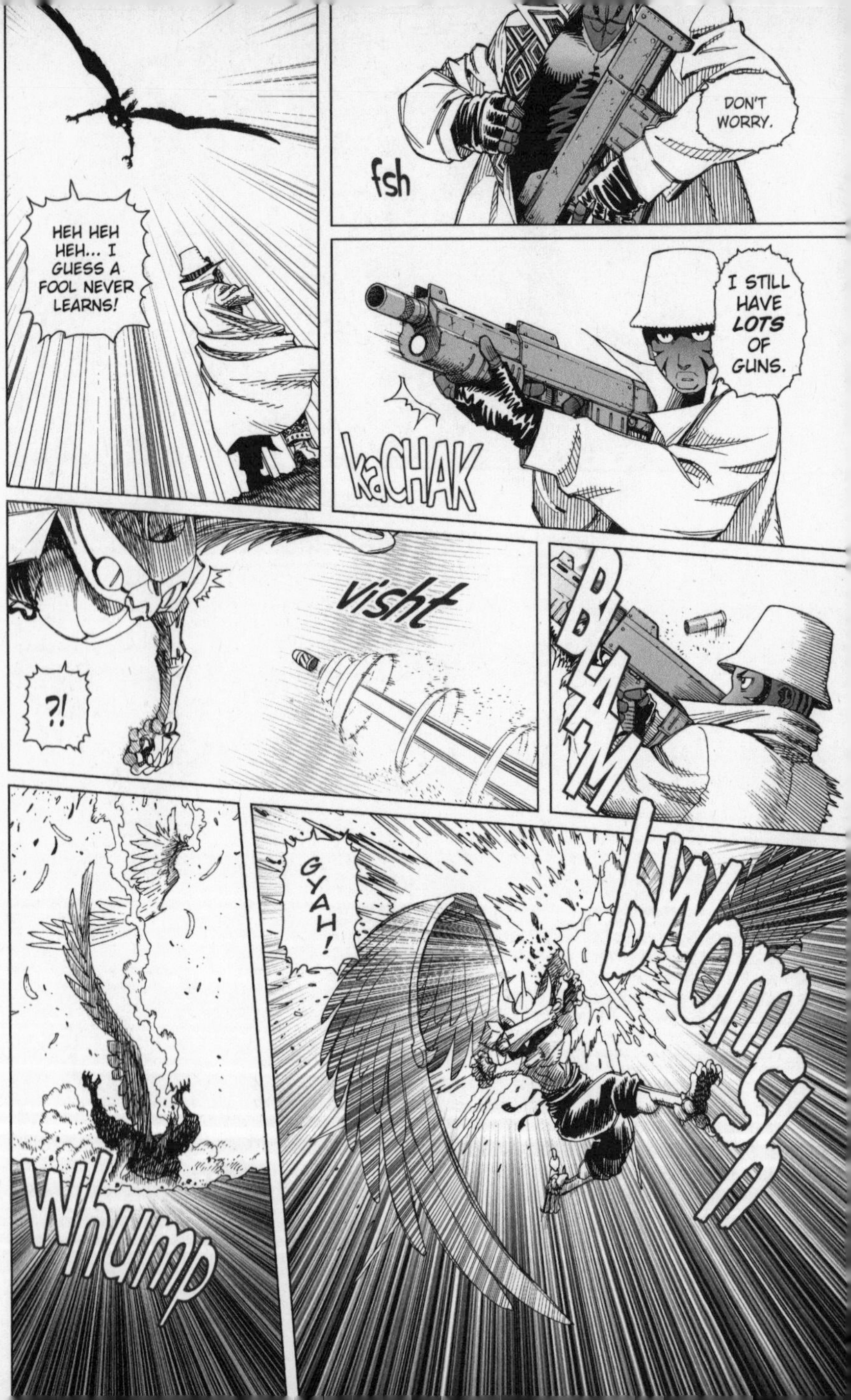
DON'T WORRY.
fsh
I STILL HAVE LOTS OF GUNS.
kaCHAK
HEH HEH HEH... I GUESS A FOOL NEVER LEARNS!
BLAM
visht
?!
GYAH!
bwomsh
whump

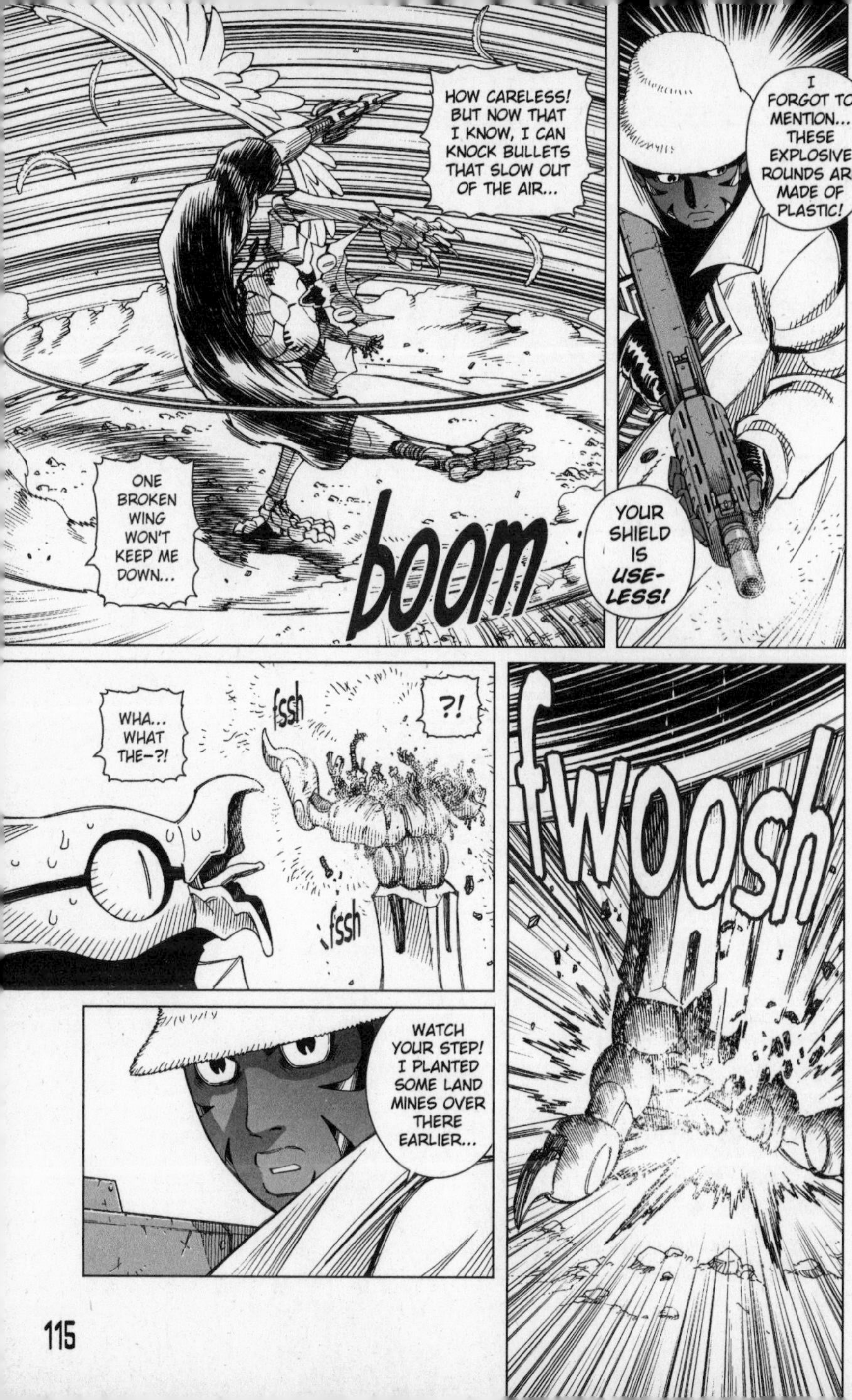
I FORGOT TO MENTION... THESE EXPLOSIVE ROUNDS ARE MADE OF PLASTIC!
YOUR SHIELD IS USE-LESS!
HOW CARELESS! BUT NOW THAT I KNOW, I CAN KNOCK BULLETS THAT SLOW OUT OF THE AIR...
ONE BROKEN WING WON'T KEEP ME DOWN...
boom
fwoosh
?!
fssh
WHA... WHAT THE-?!
fssh
WATCH YOUR STEP! I PLANTED SOME LAND MINES OVER THERE EARLIER...

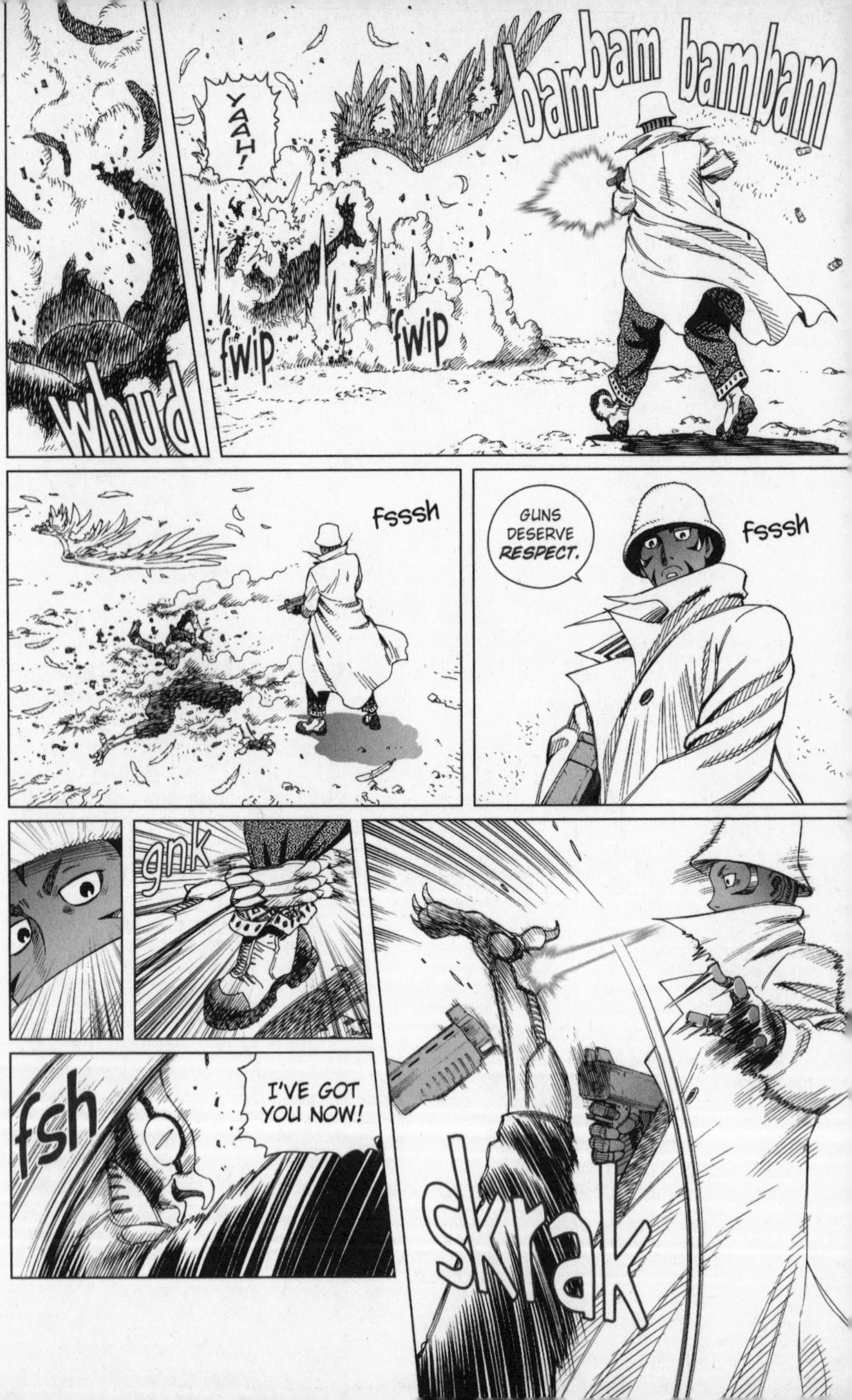
bambam
bambam
YAAH!
fwip
fwip
whud
GUNS DESERVE RESPECT.
fsssh
fsssh
skrak
gnk
I'VE GOT YOU NOW!
fsh

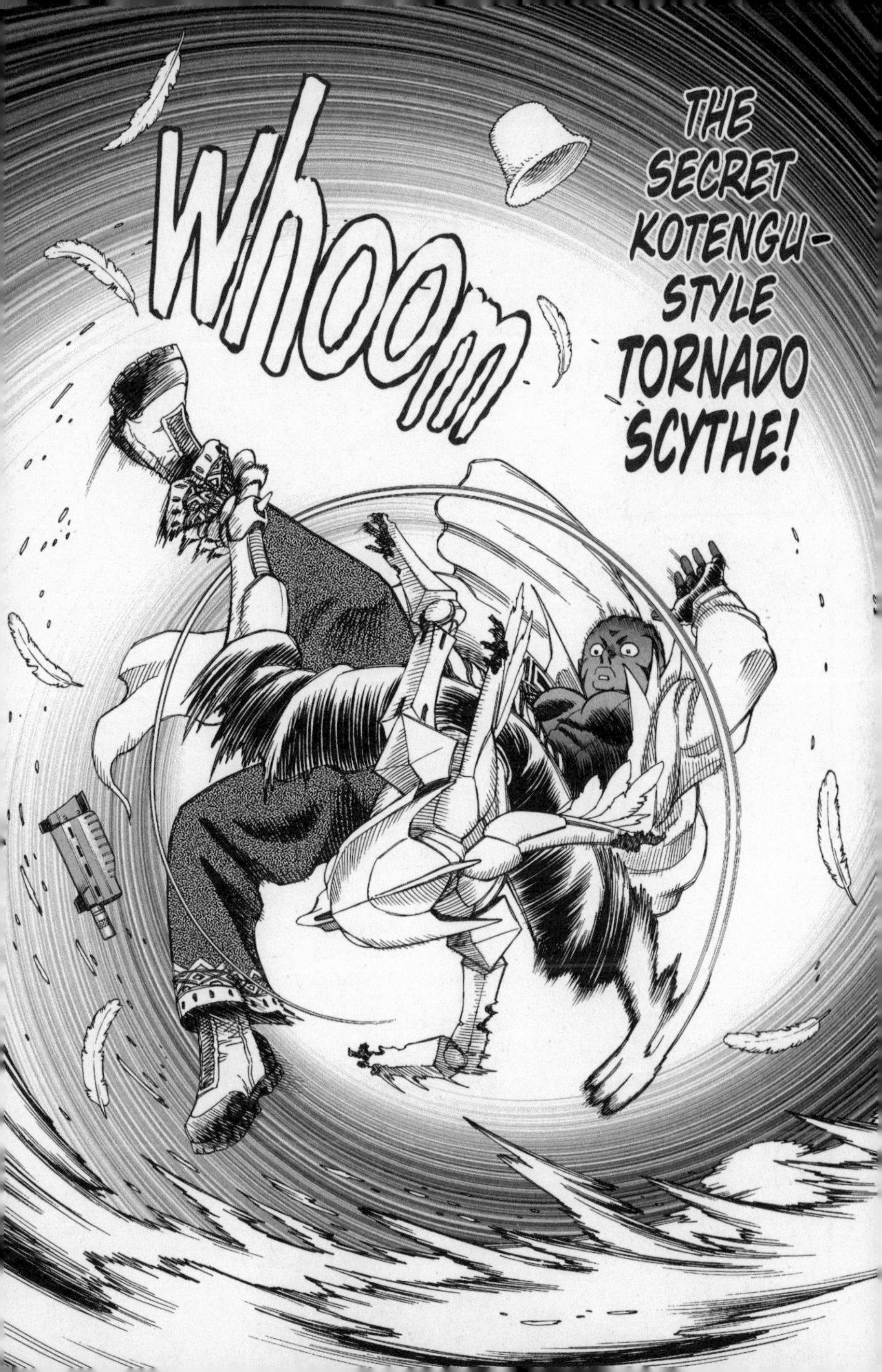
THE SECRET KOTENGU-STYLE TORNADO SCYTHE!
WHOOM

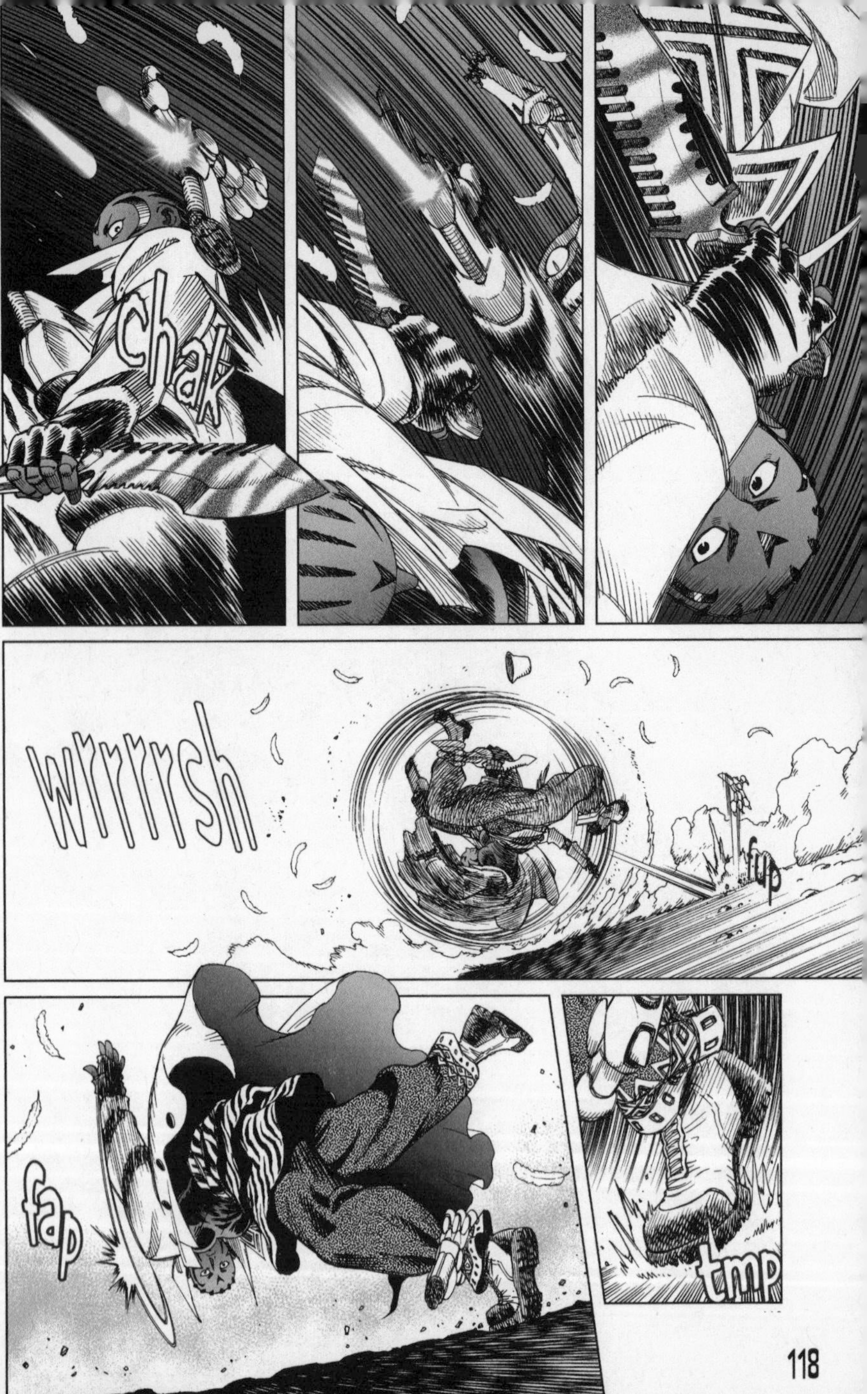
Chak
fup
wrrrrsh
tmp
fap

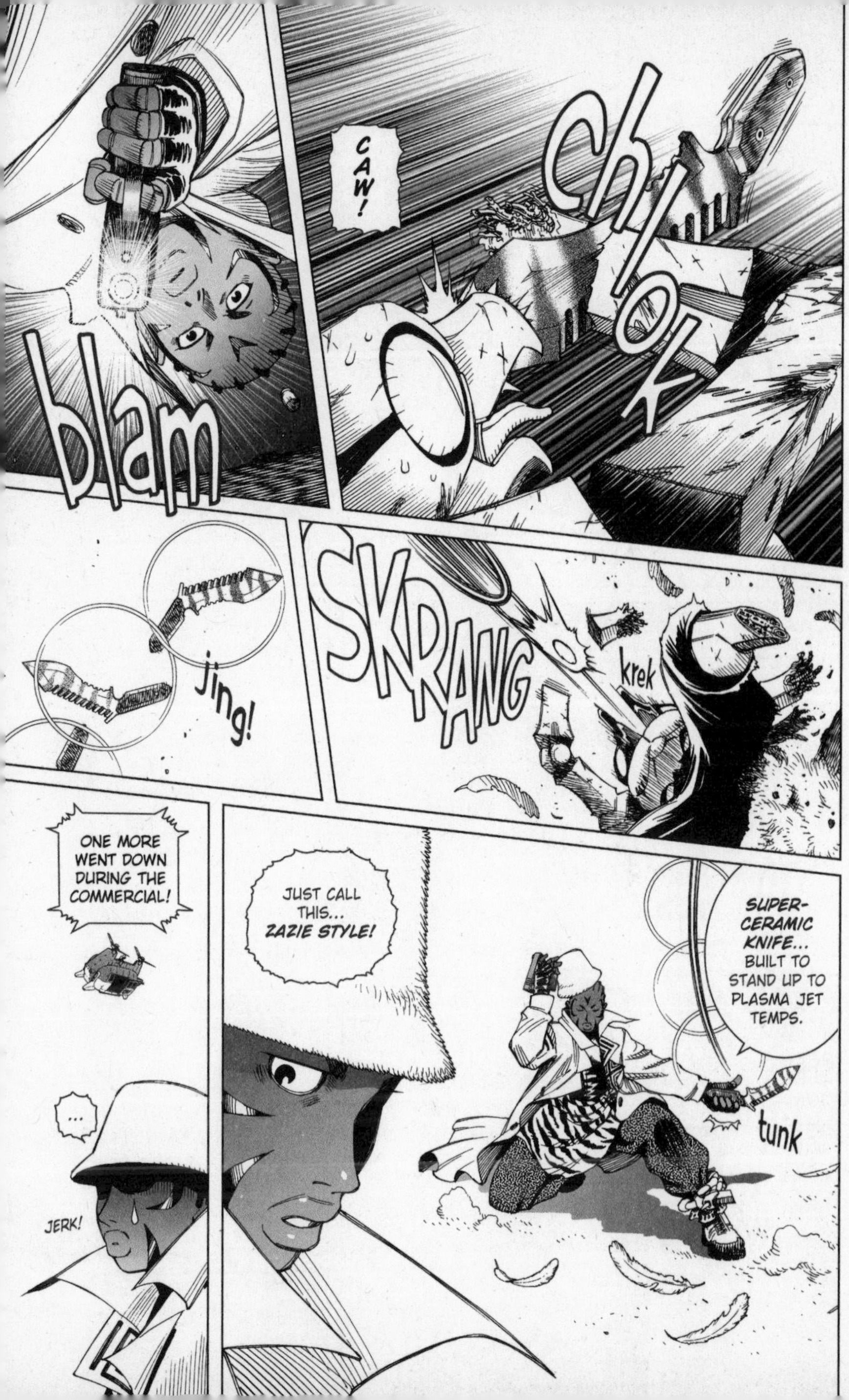
CAW!
chiok
blam
SKRANG
krek
jing!
SUPER-CERAMIC KNIFE... BUILT TO STAND UP TO PLASMA JET TEMPS.
JUST CALL THIS... ZAZIE STYLE!
tunk
ONE MORE WENT DOWN DURING THE COMMERCIAL!
...
JERK!

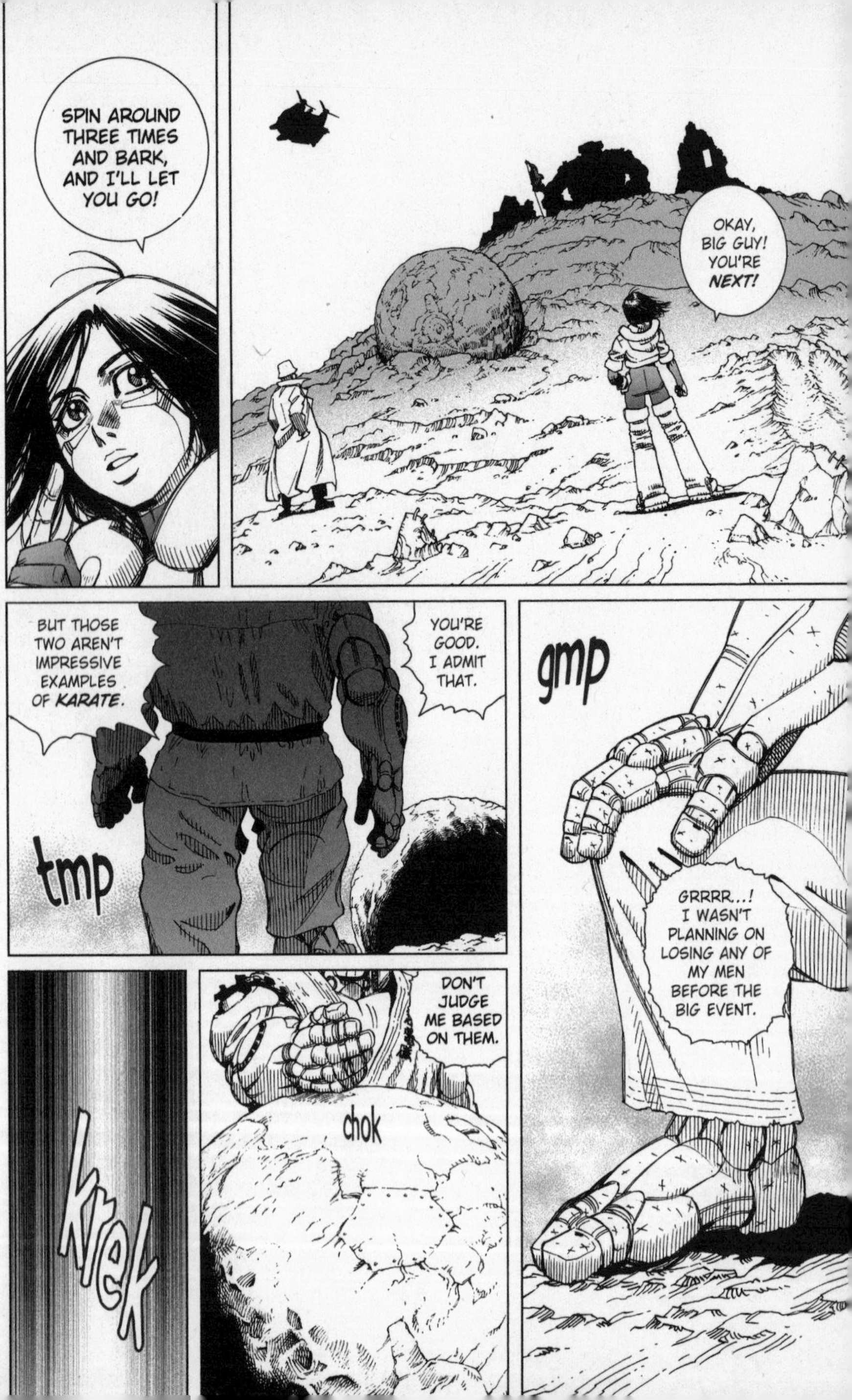
OKAY, BIG GUY! YOU'RE *NEXT!*
SPIN AROUND THREE TIMES AND BARK, AND I'LL LET YOU GO!
gmp
GRRRR...! I WASN'T PLANNING ON LOSING ANY OF MY MEN BEFORE THE BIG EVENT.
YOU'RE GOOD. I ADMIT THAT.
BUT THOSE TWO AREN'T IMPRESSIVE EXAMPLES OF *KARATE*.
tmp
DON'T JUDGE ME BASED ON THEM.
chok
krek

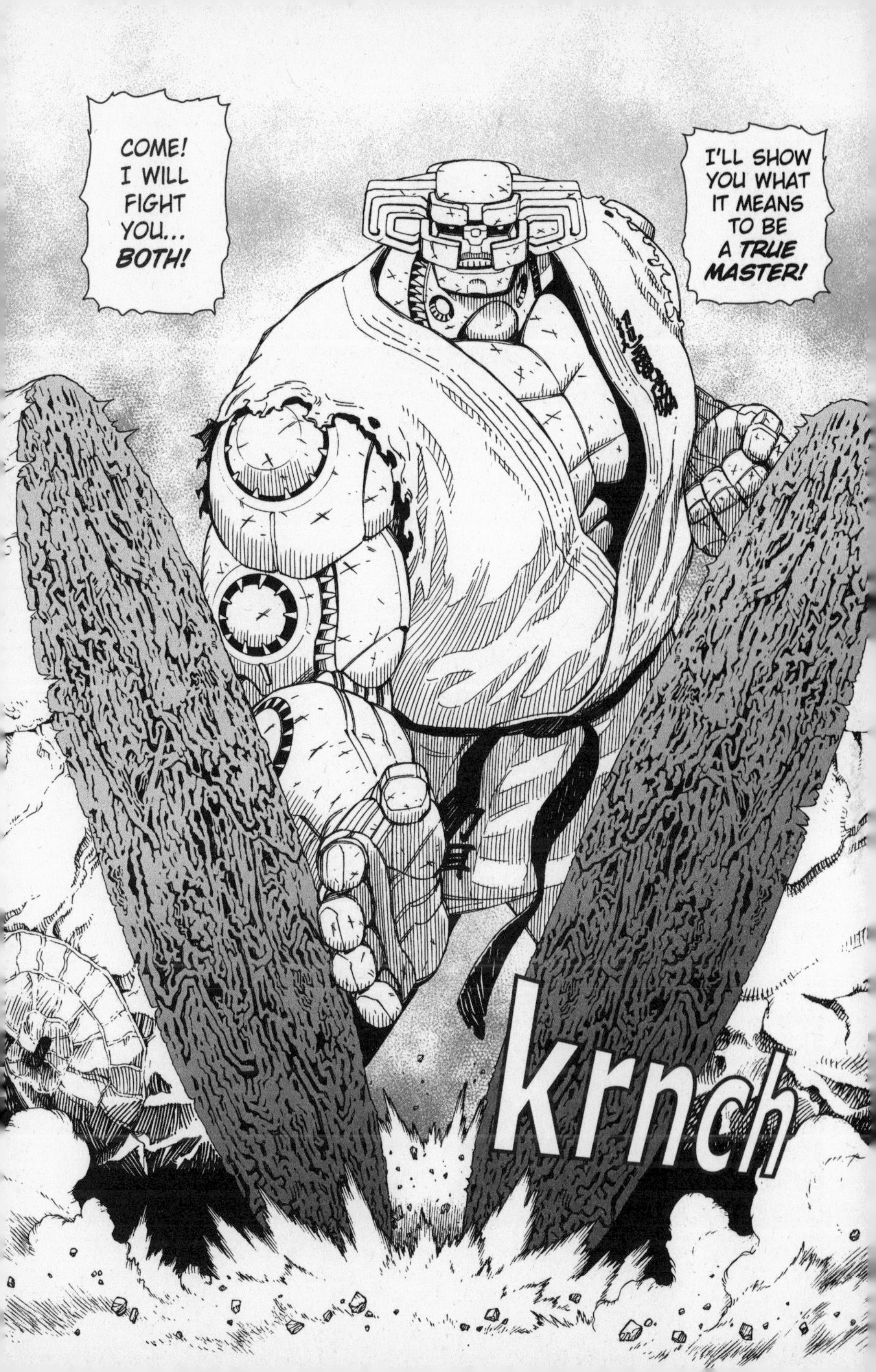
I'LL SHOW YOU WHAT IT MEANS TO BE A *TRUE MASTER!*
COME! I WILL FIGHT YOU... *BOTH!*
krnch

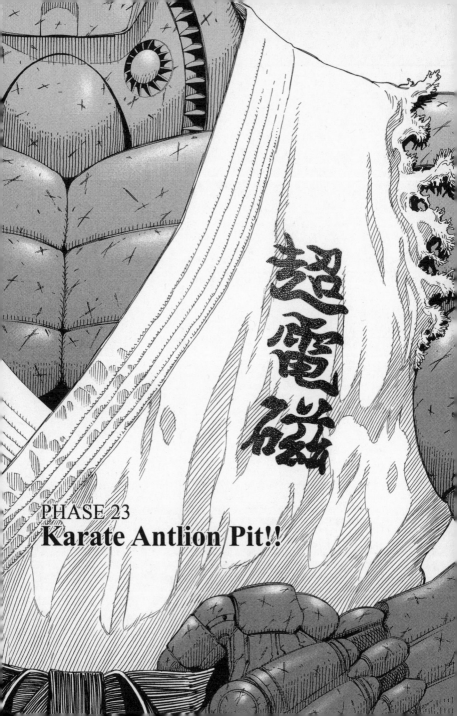

超電磁

PHASE 23
Karate Antlion Pit!!

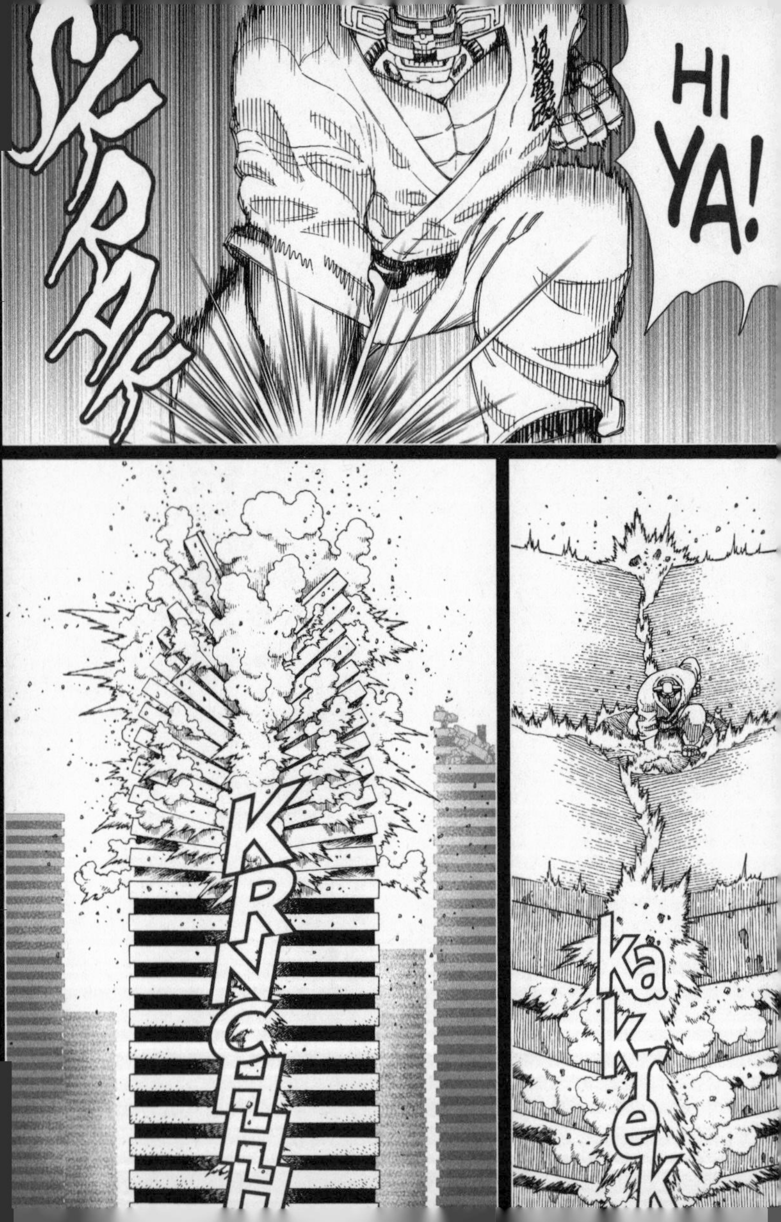
HI YA!
SKRAK
kakrek
KRNCHHH

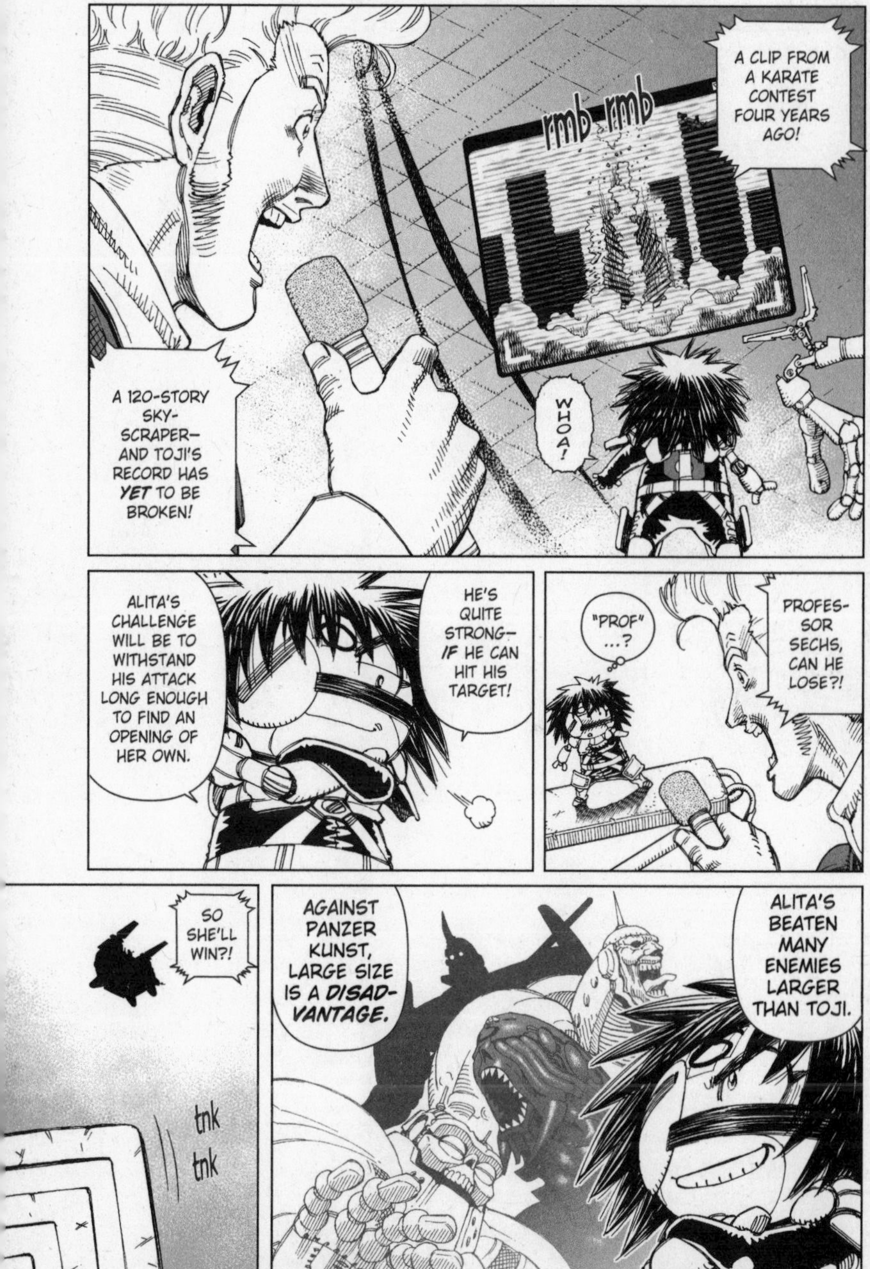
A CLIP FROM A KARATE CONTEST FOUR YEARS AGO!
rmb rmb
A 120-STORY SKY-SCRAPER— AND TOJI'S RECORD HAS *YET* TO BE BROKEN!
WHOA!
PROFES-SOR SECHS, CAN HE LOSE?!
"PROF" ...?
HE'S QUITE STRONG— *IF* HE CAN HIT HIS TARGET!
ALITA'S CHALLENGE WILL BE TO WITHSTAND HIS ATTACK LONG ENOUGH TO FIND AN OPENING OF HER OWN.
ALITA'S BEATEN *MANY* ENEMIES LARGER THAN TOJI.
AGAINST PANZER KUNST, LARGE SIZE IS A ***DISAD-VANTAGE.***
SO SHE'LL WIN?!
tnk tnk

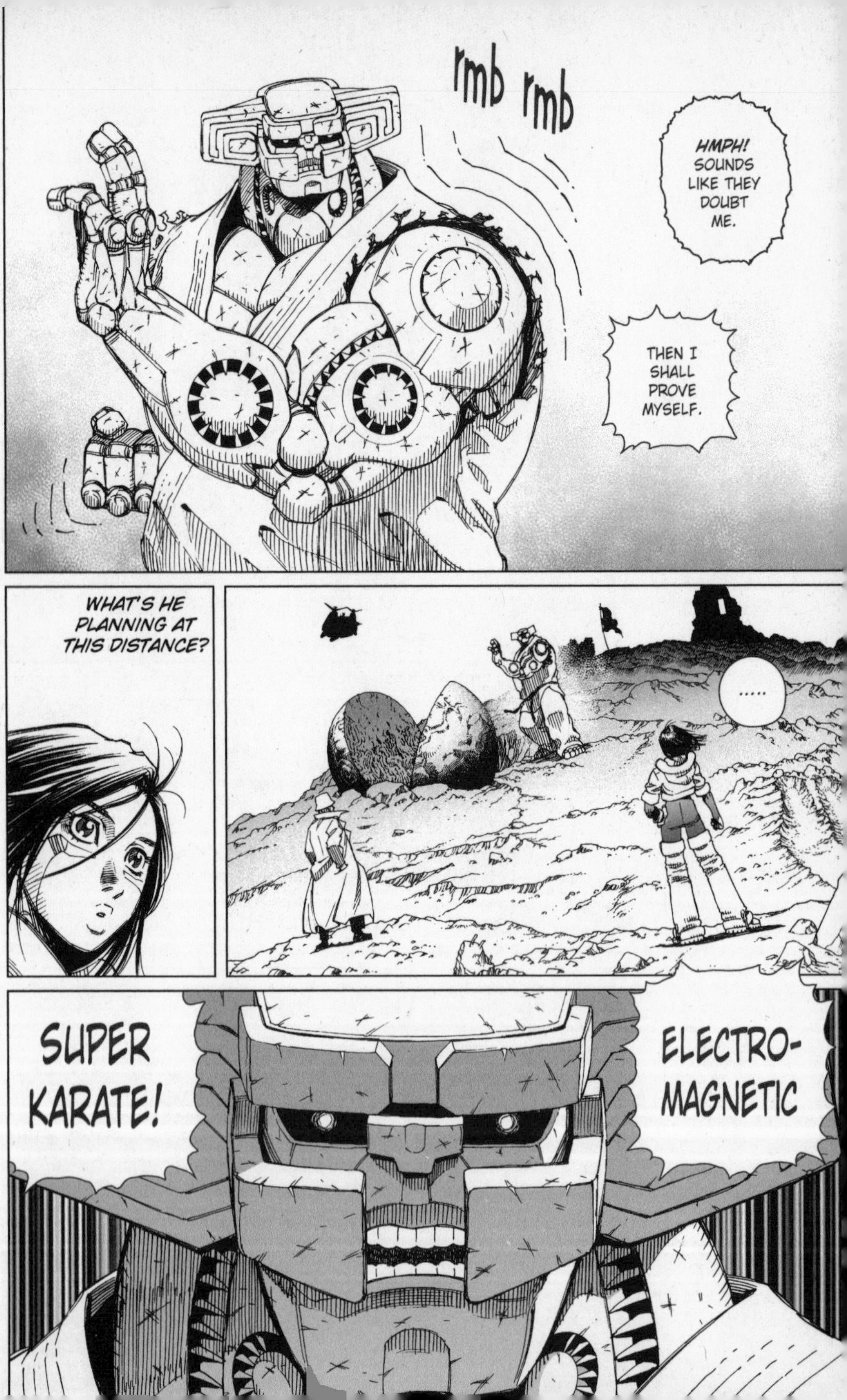
rmb rmb
HMPH! SOUNDS LIKE THEY DOUBT ME.
THEN I SHALL PROVE MYSELF.
......
WHAT'S HE PLANNING AT THIS DISTANCE?
ELECTRO-MAGNETIC
SUPER KARATE!

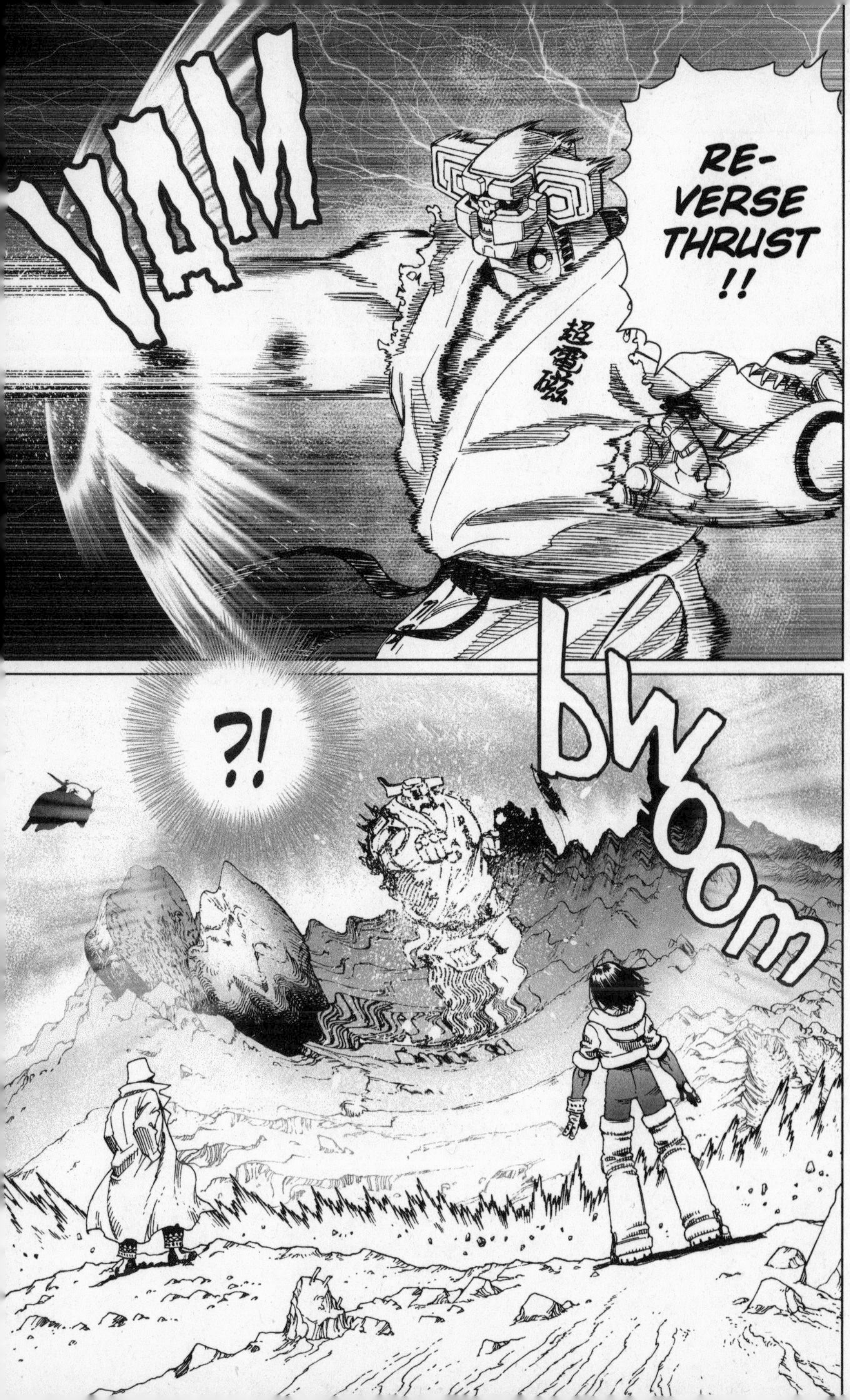
RE-
VERSE
THRUST
!!
超電磁
VAM
bwoom
?!

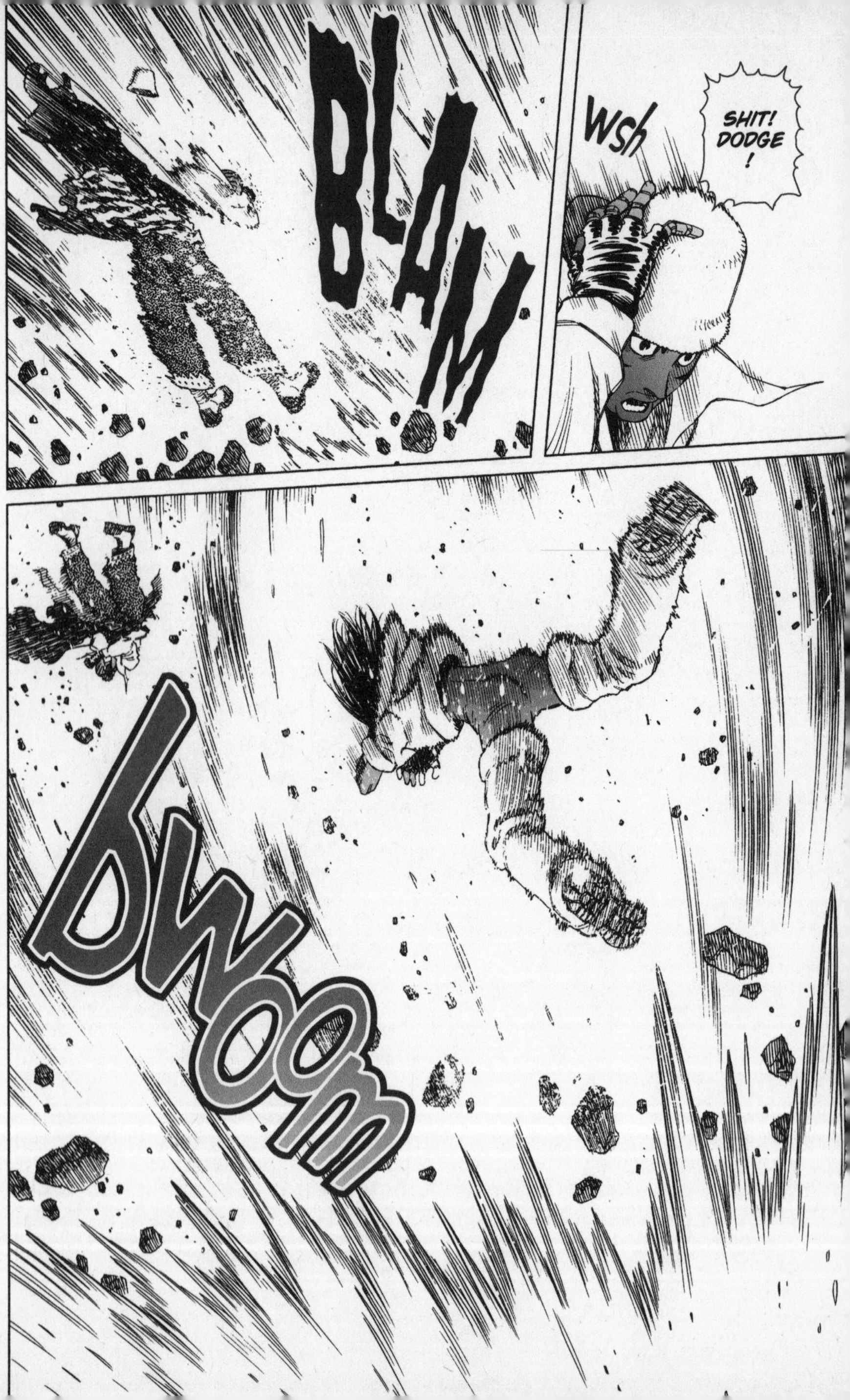
WSH
SHIT! DODGE!
BLAM
BWOOM

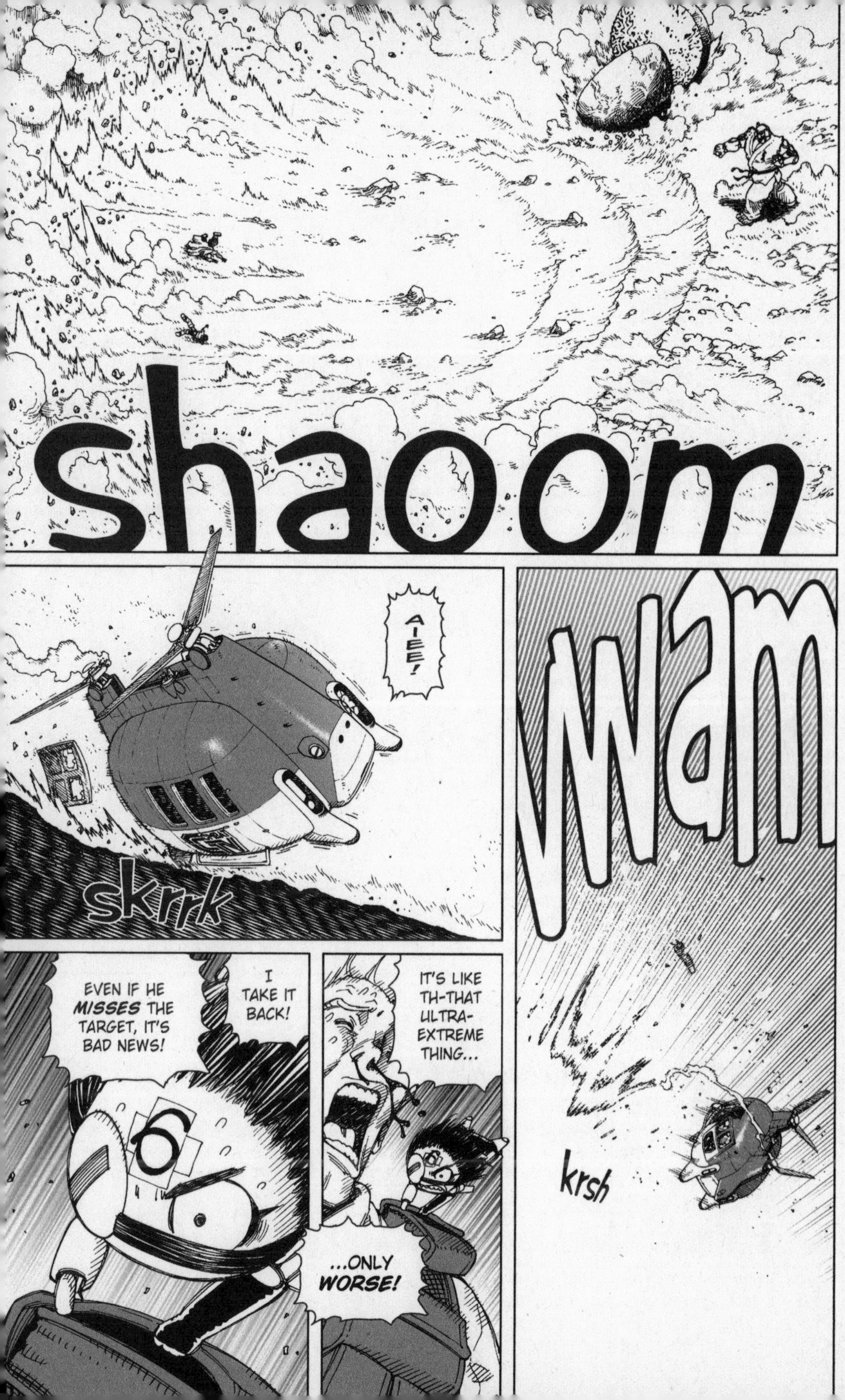
shaoom
wam
krsh
AIEE!
skrrk
IT'S LIKE TH-THAT ULTRA-EXTREME THING...
...ONLY WORSE!
I TAKE IT BACK!
EVEN IF HE MISSES THE TARGET, IT'S BAD NEWS!

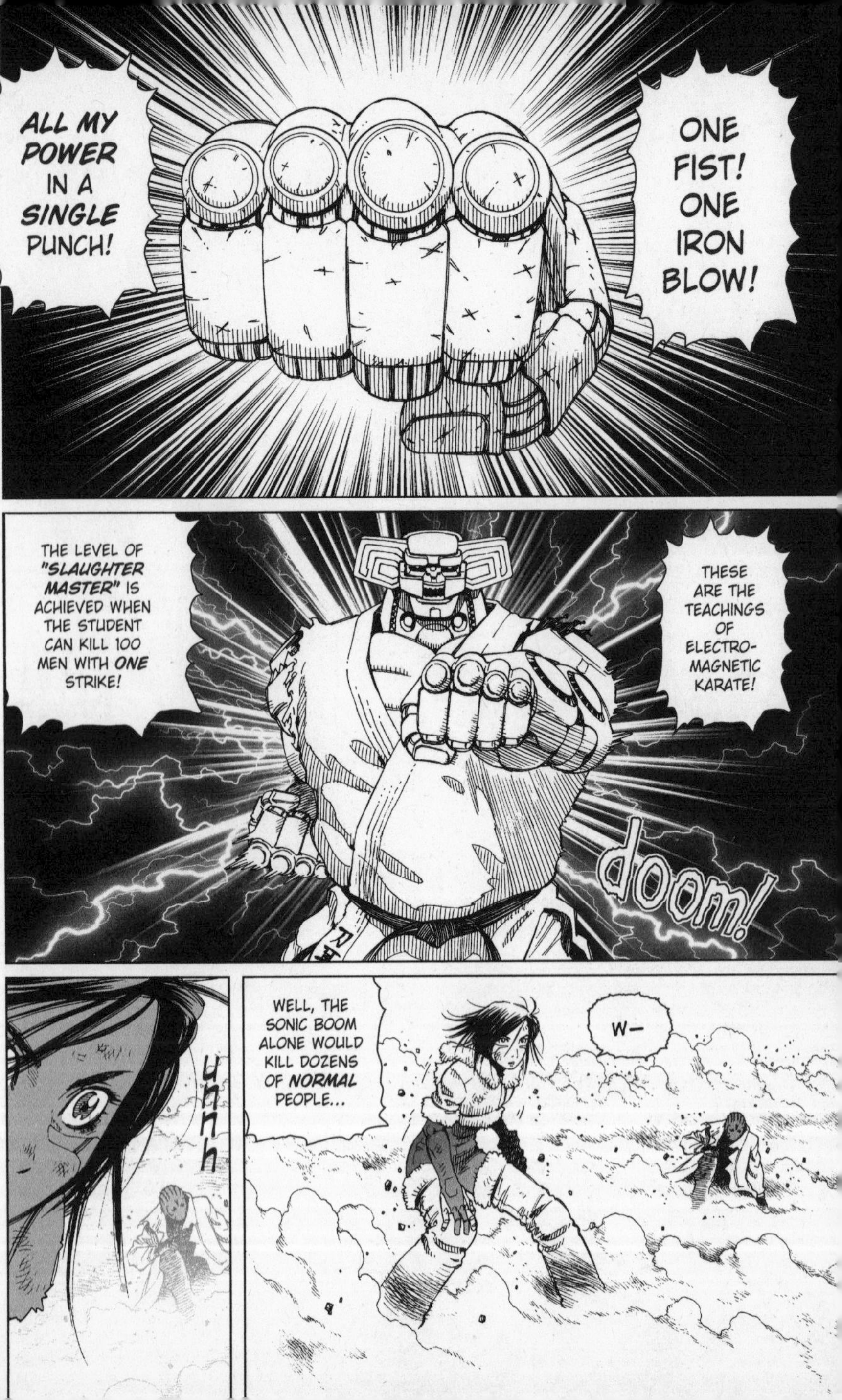
ONE FIST! ONE IRON BLOW!
ALL MY POWER IN A SINGLE PUNCH!
THESE ARE THE TEACHINGS OF ELECTRO-MAGNETIC KARATE!
THE LEVEL OF "SLAUGHTER MASTER" IS ACHIEVED WHEN THE STUDENT CAN KILL 100 MEN WITH ONE STRIKE!
doom!
W—
WELL, THE SONIC BOOM ALONE WOULD KILL DOZENS OF NORMAL PEOPLE...
unnh

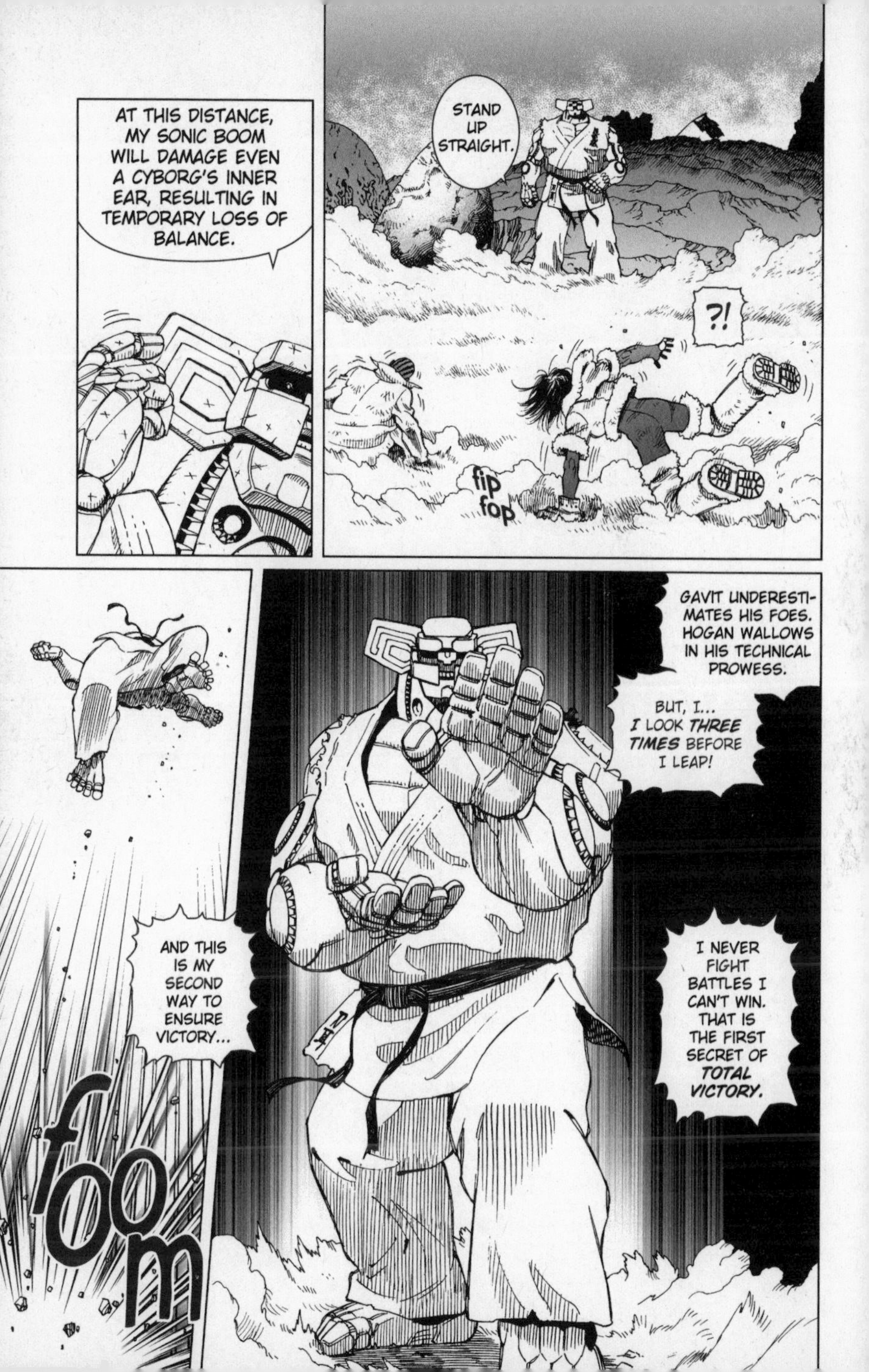
STAND UP STRAIGHT.
?!
fip fop
AT THIS DISTANCE, MY SONIC BOOM WILL DAMAGE EVEN A CYBORG'S INNER EAR, RESULTING IN TEMPORARY LOSS OF BALANCE.
GAVIT UNDERESTIMATES HIS FOES. HOGAN WALLOWS IN HIS TECHNICAL PROWESS.
BUT, I... I LOOK *THREE TIMES* BEFORE I LEAP!
I NEVER FIGHT BATTLES I CAN'T WIN. THAT IS THE FIRST SECRET OF *TOTAL VICTORY*.
AND THIS IS MY SECOND WAY TO ENSURE VICTORY...
foom

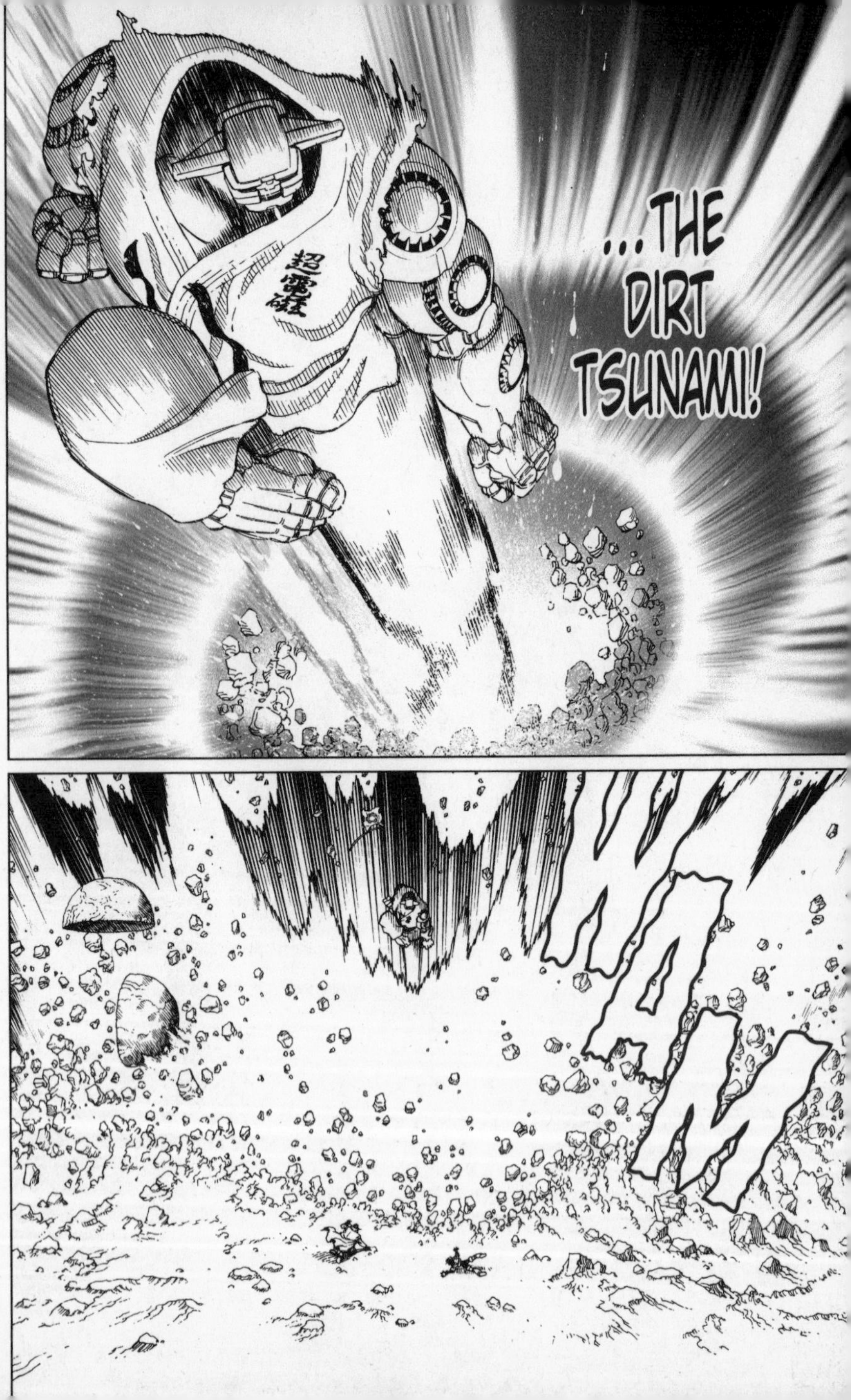
超電磁
...THE DIRT TSUNAMI!

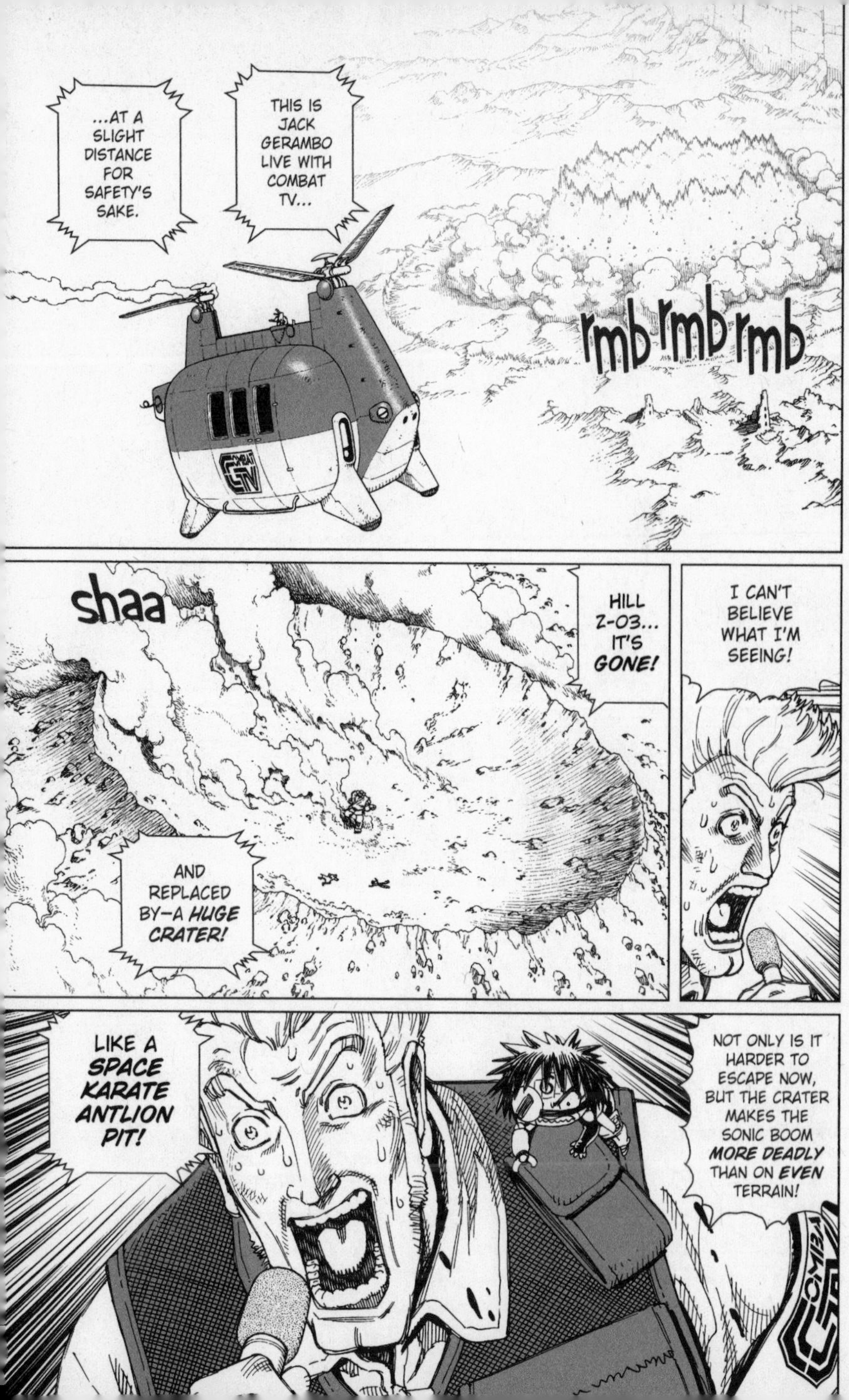
THIS IS JACK GERAMBO LIVE WITH COMBAT TV...
...AT A SLIGHT DISTANCE FOR SAFETY'S SAKE.
rmb rmb rmb
I CAN'T BELIEVE WHAT I'M SEEING!
HILL Z-03... IT'S *GONE!*
shaa
AND REPLACED BY—A *HUGE CRATER!*
NOT ONLY IS IT HARDER TO ESCAPE NOW, BUT THE CRATER MAKES THE SONIC BOOM *MORE DEADLY* THAN ON *EVEN* TERRAIN!
LIKE A *SPACE KARATE ANTLION PIT!*

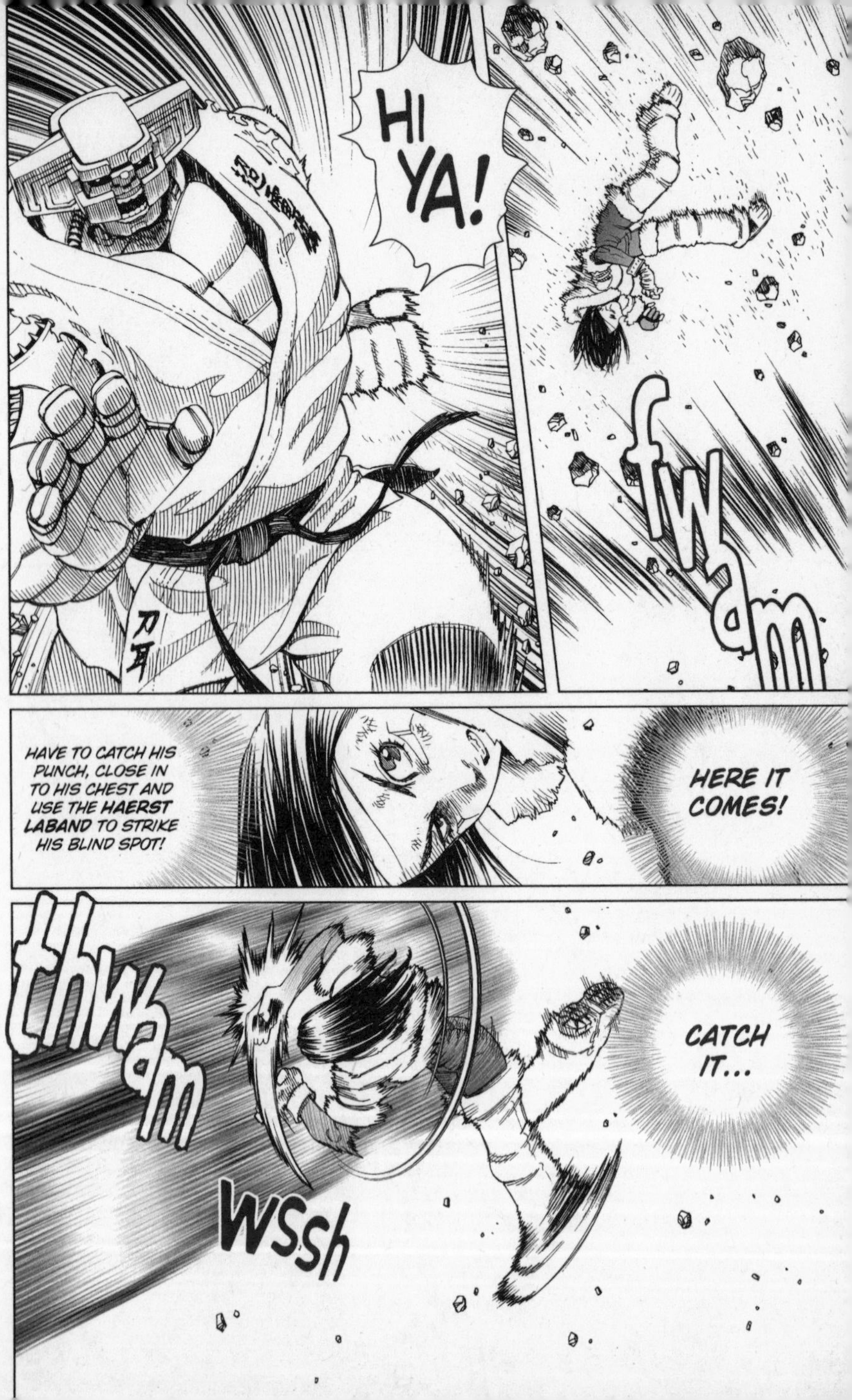
fwam
HI YA!
HERE IT COMES!
HAVE TO CATCH HIS PUNCH, CLOSE IN TO HIS CHEST AND USE THE HAERST LABAND TO STRIKE HIS BLIND SPOT!
CATCH IT...
thwam
wssh

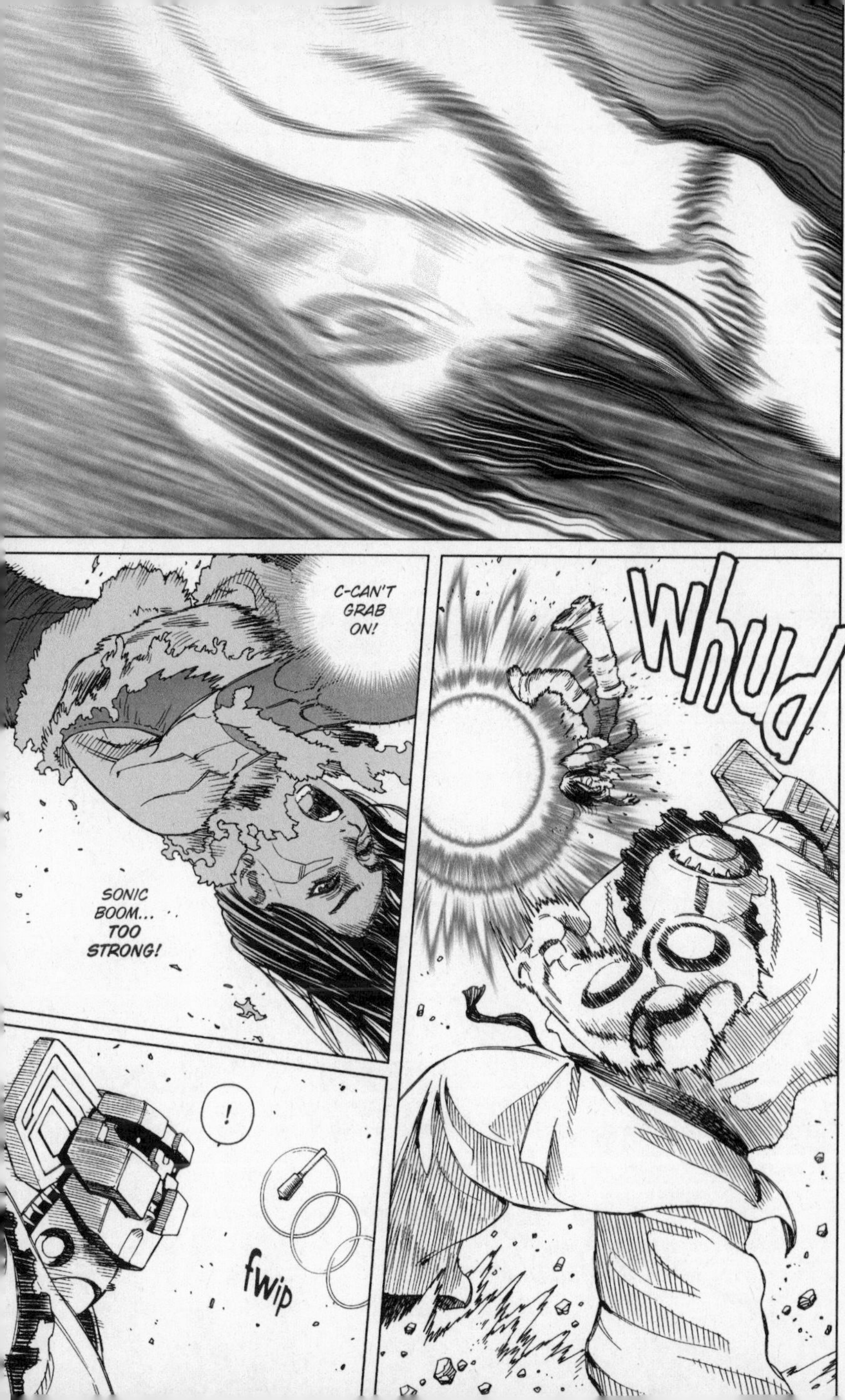
whud
C-CAN'T GRAB ON!
SONIC BOOM... TOO STRONG!
!
fwip

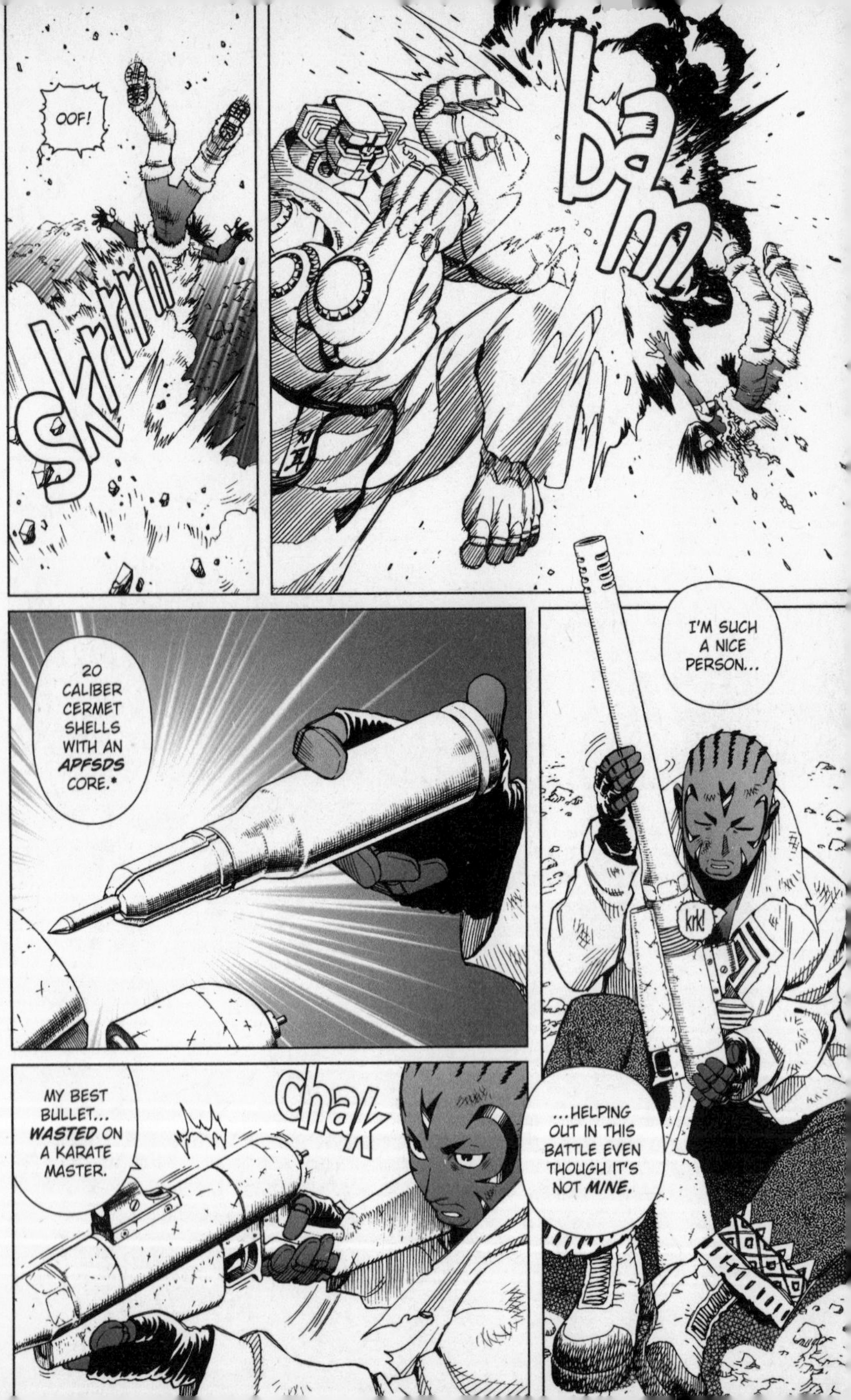
bam
OOF!
skrrn
I'M SUCH A NICE PERSON...
krk!
...HELPING OUT IN THIS BATTLE EVEN THOUGH IT'S NOT **MINE.**
20 CALIBER CERMET SHELLS WITH AN ***APFSDS*** CORE.*
chak
MY BEST BULLET... ***WASTED*** ON A KARATE MASTER.

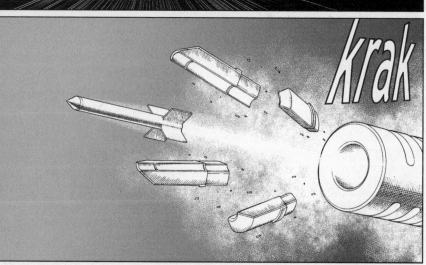

Cermet: Material synthesized from metal and ceramic. Resistant to high temperatures and ballistic shock.
APFSDS (Armor-piercing fin-stabilized discarding sabot): An anti-tank round with stabilizing wings and loading cylinder. After firing, the loading cylinder falls away and the round flies at high speed. Highly penetrating due to kinetic energy focused in the round.

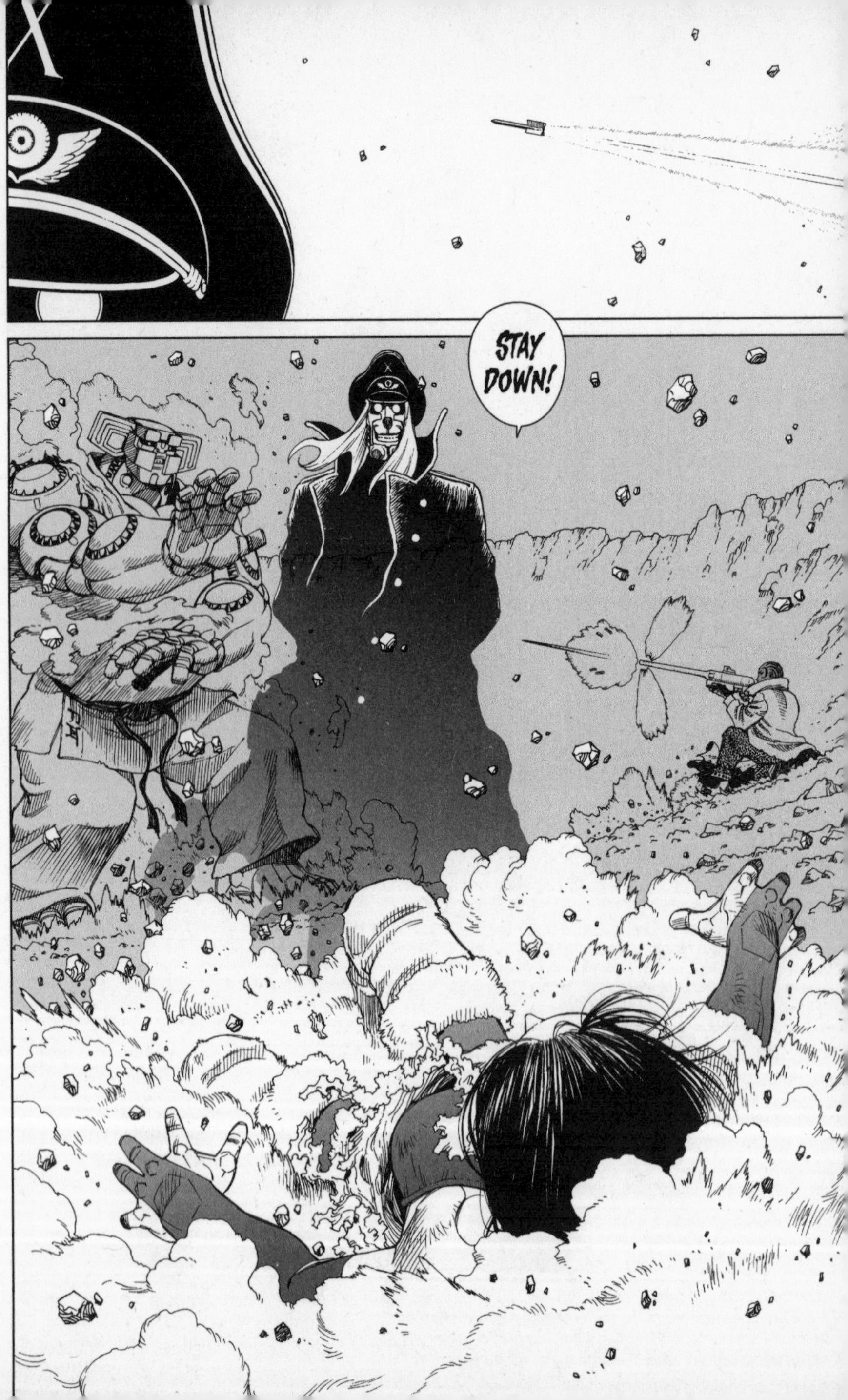
STAY DOWN!

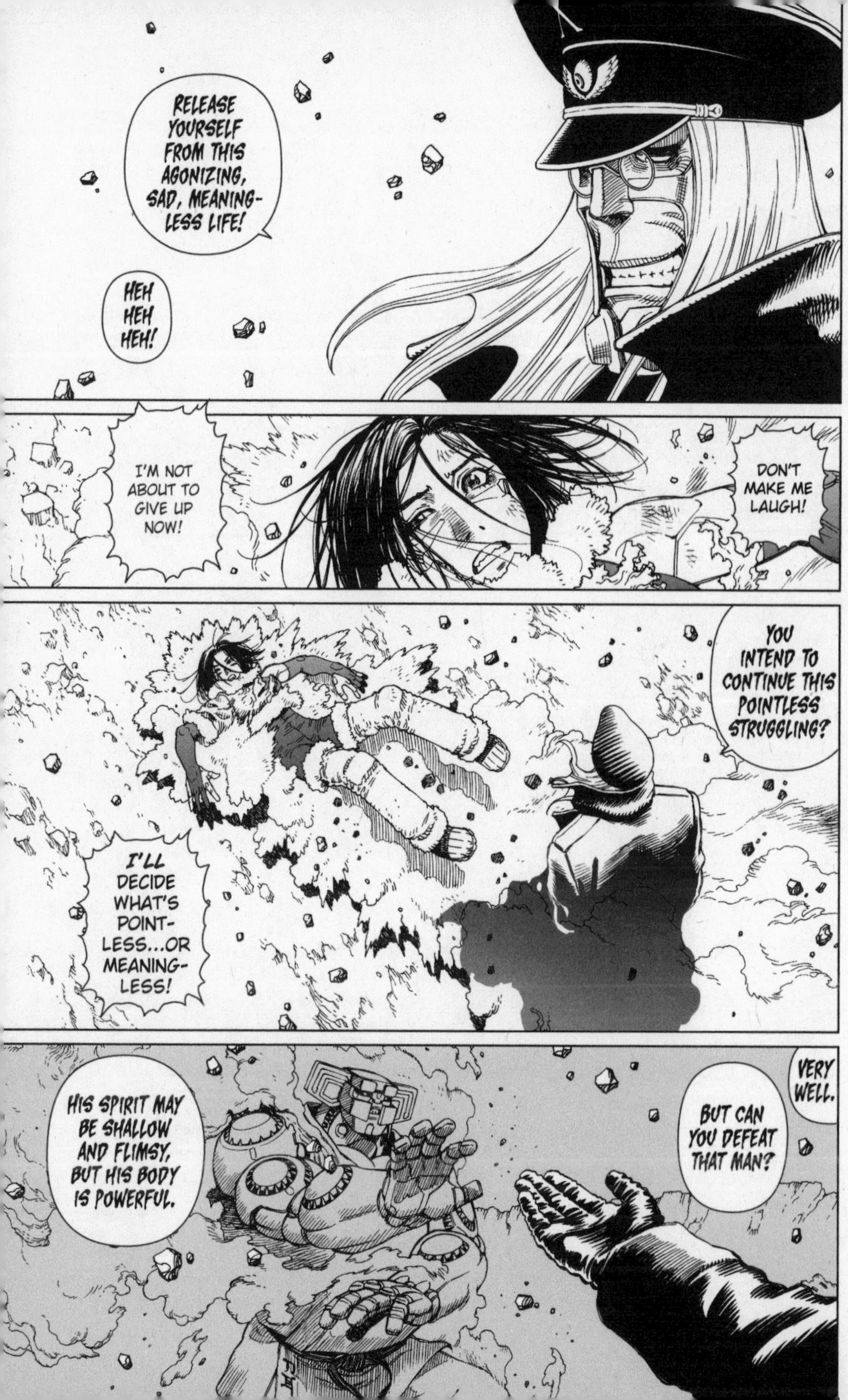
RELEASE YOURSELF FROM THIS AGONIZING, SAD, MEANINGLESS LIFE!
HEH HEH HEH!
DON'T MAKE ME LAUGH!
I'M NOT ABOUT TO GIVE UP NOW!
YOU INTEND TO CONTINUE THIS POINTLESS STRUGGLING?
I'LL DECIDE WHAT'S POINTLESS...OR MEANINGLESS!
VERY WELL.
BUT CAN YOU DEFEAT THAT MAN?
HIS SPIRIT MAY BE SHALLOW AND FLIMSY, BUT HIS BODY IS POWERFUL.

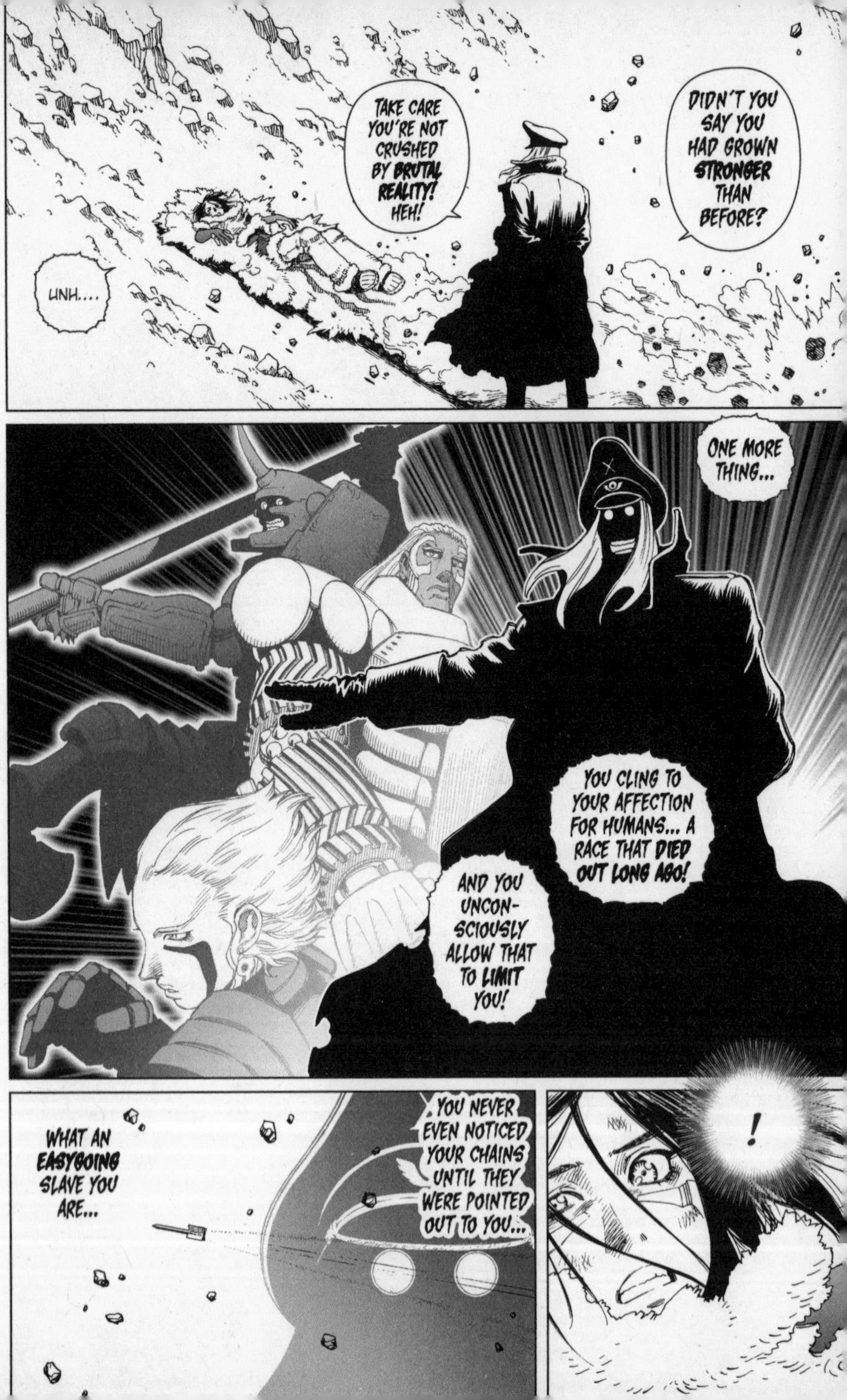
DIDN'T YOU SAY YOU HAD GROWN STRONGER THAN BEFORE?
TAKE CARE YOU'RE NOT CRUSHED BY BRUTAL REALITY! HEH!
UNH....
ONE MORE THING...
YOU CLING TO YOUR AFFECTION FOR HUMANS... A RACE THAT DIED OUT LONG AGO!
AND YOU UNCON-SCIOUSLY ALLOW THAT TO LIMIT YOU!
!
YOU NEVER EVEN NOTICED YOUR CHAINS UNTIL THEY WERE POINTED OUT TO YOU...
WHAT AN EASYGOING SLAVE YOU ARE...

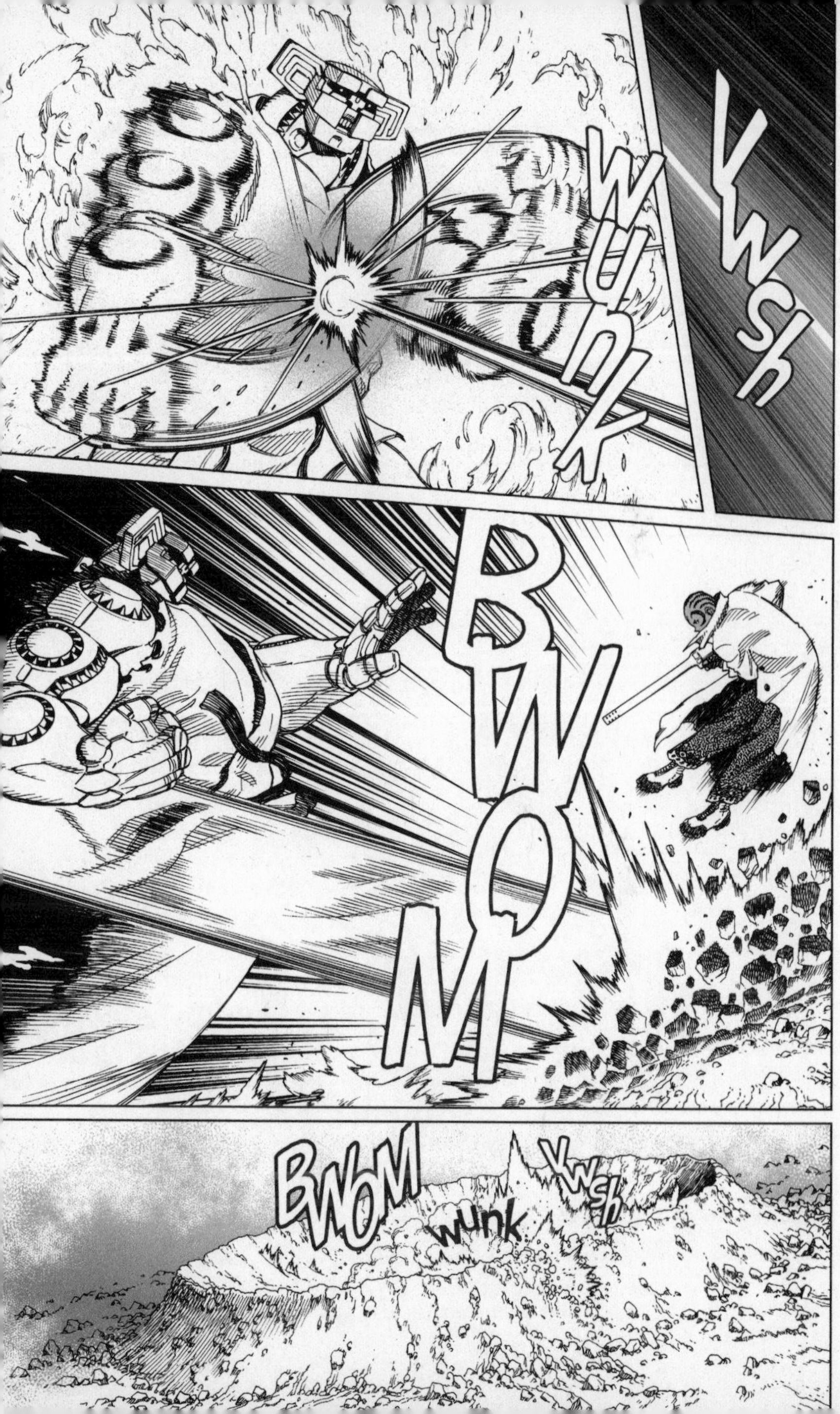
VWSH
WUNK
BWOOM
VWSH
WUNK
BWOOM

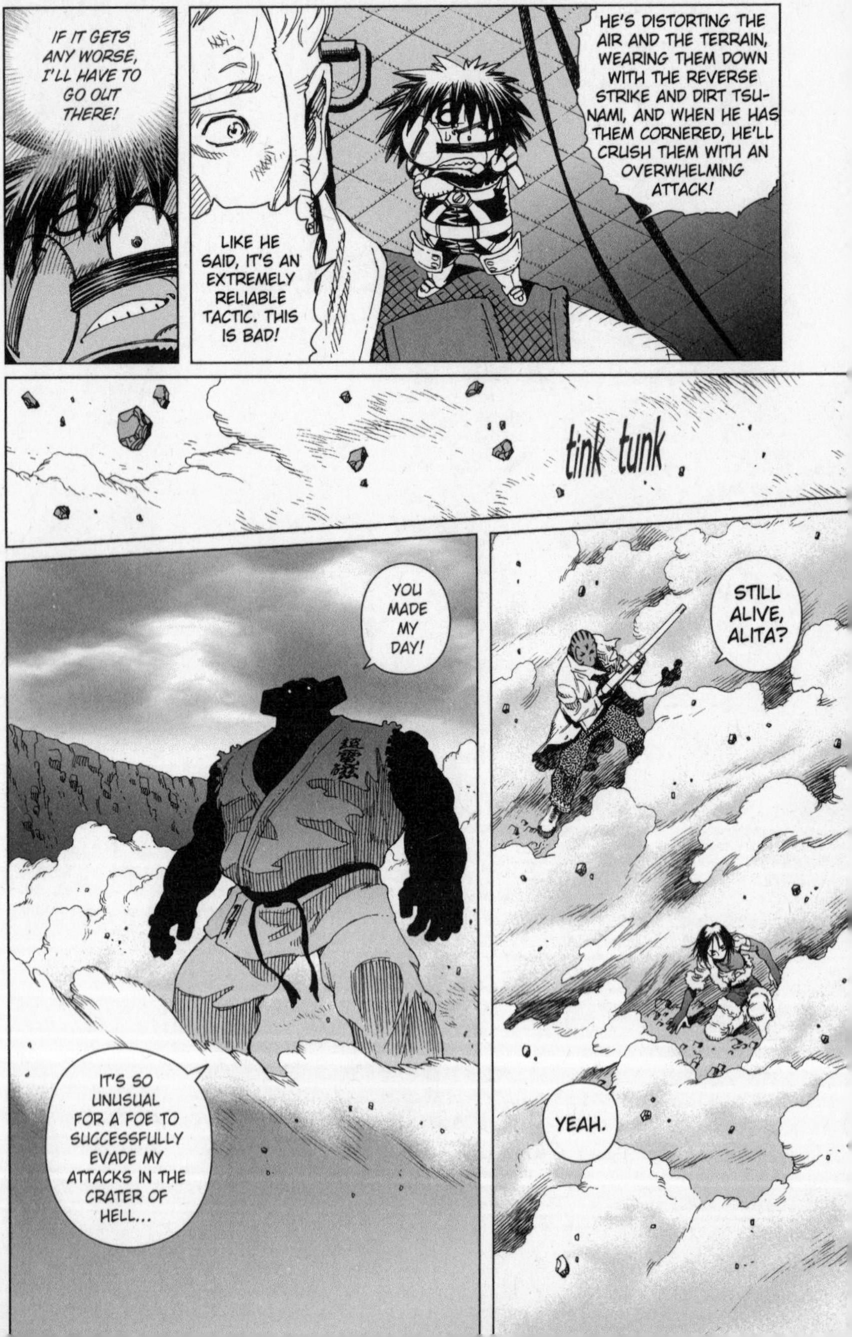
HE'S DISTORTING THE AIR AND THE TERRAIN, WEARING THEM DOWN WITH THE REVERSE STRIKE AND DIRT TSU-NAMI, AND WHEN HE HAS THEM CORNERED, HE'LL CRUSH THEM WITH AN OVERWHELMING ATTACK!
LIKE HE SAID, IT'S AN EXTREMELY RELIABLE TACTIC. THIS IS BAD!
IF IT GETS ANY WORSE, I'LL HAVE TO GO OUT THERE!
tink tunk
STILL ALIVE, ALITA?
YEAH.
YOU MADE MY DAY!
IT'S SO UNUSUAL FOR A FOE TO SUCCESSFULLY EVADE MY ATTACKS IN THE CRATER OF HELL...

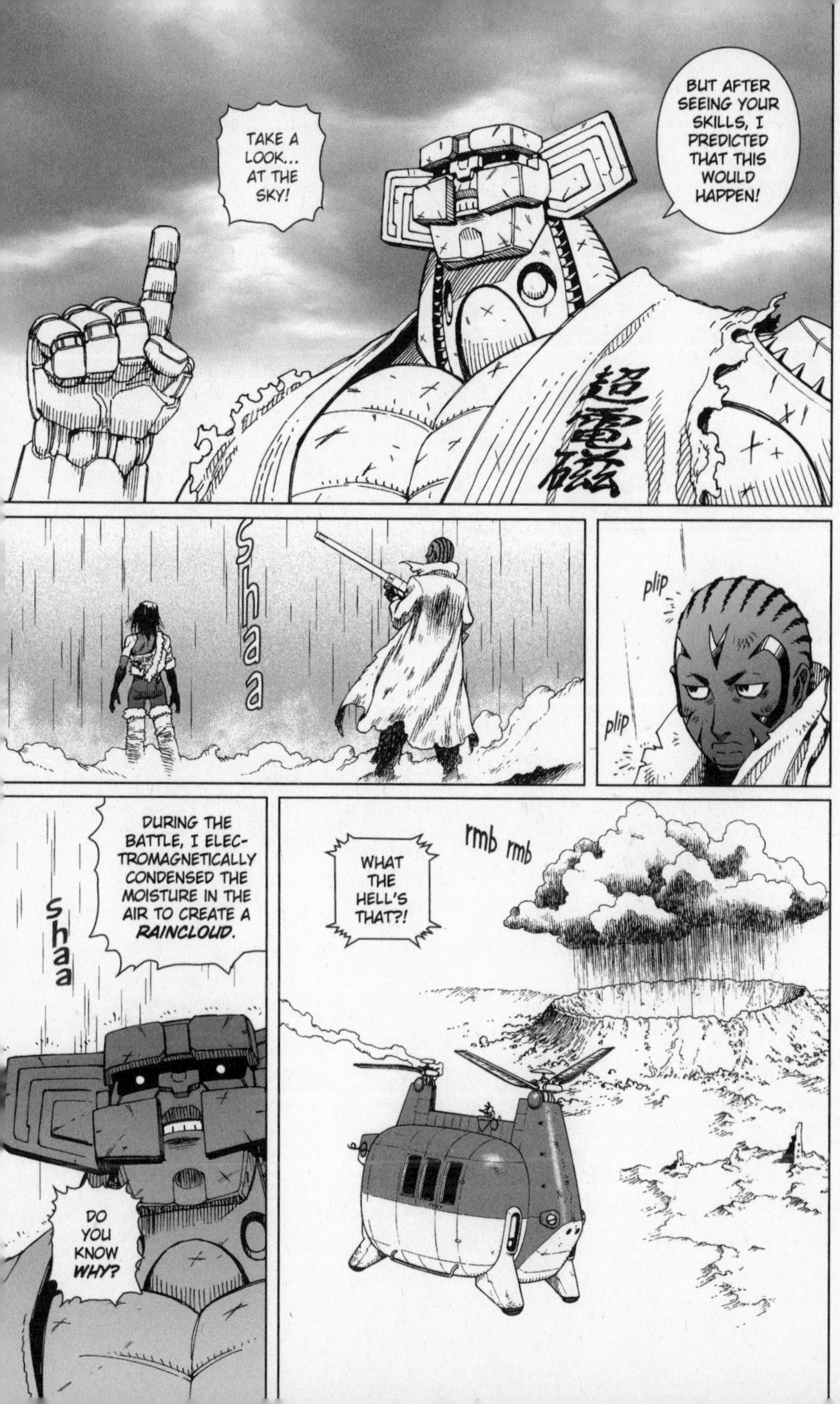
BUT AFTER SEEING YOUR SKILLS, I PREDICTED THAT THIS WOULD HAPPEN!
TAKE A LOOK... AT THE SKY!
超電磁
plip
plip
Shaa
rmb rmb
WHAT THE HELL'S THAT?!
DURING THE BATTLE, I ELECTROMAGNETICALLY CONDENSED THE MOISTURE IN THE AIR TO CREATE A *RAINCLOUD*.
Shaa
DO YOU KNOW *WHY?*

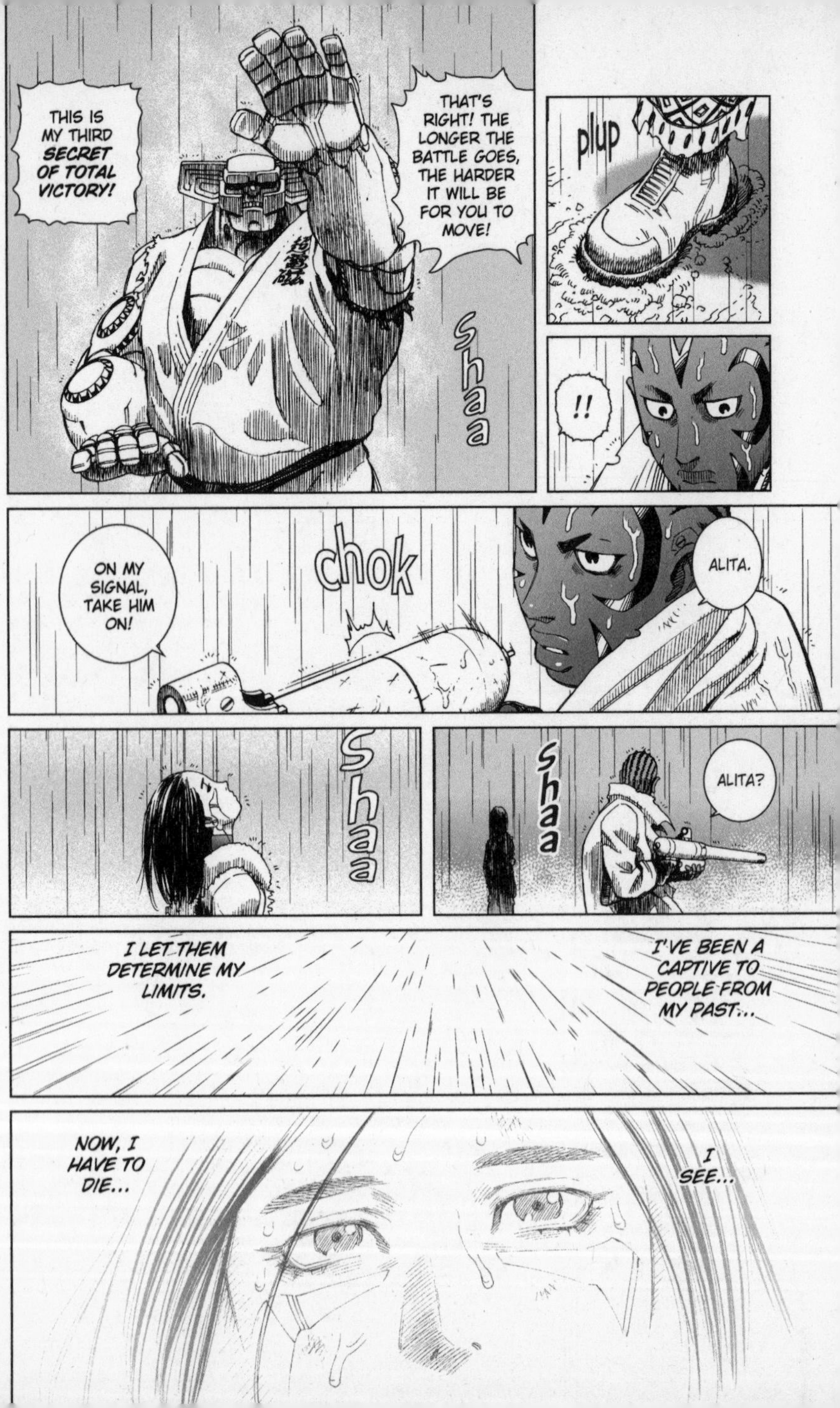
plup
!!
THAT'S RIGHT! THE LONGER THE BATTLE GOES, THE HARDER IT WILL BE FOR YOU TO MOVE!
THIS IS MY THIRD SECRET OF TOTAL VICTORY!
Shaa
ALITA.
chok
ON MY SIGNAL, TAKE HIM ON!
ALITA?
Shaa
Shaa
I'VE BEEN A CAPTIVE TO PEOPLE FROM MY PAST...
I LET THEM DETERMINE MY LIMITS.
I SEE...
NOW, I HAVE TO DIE...

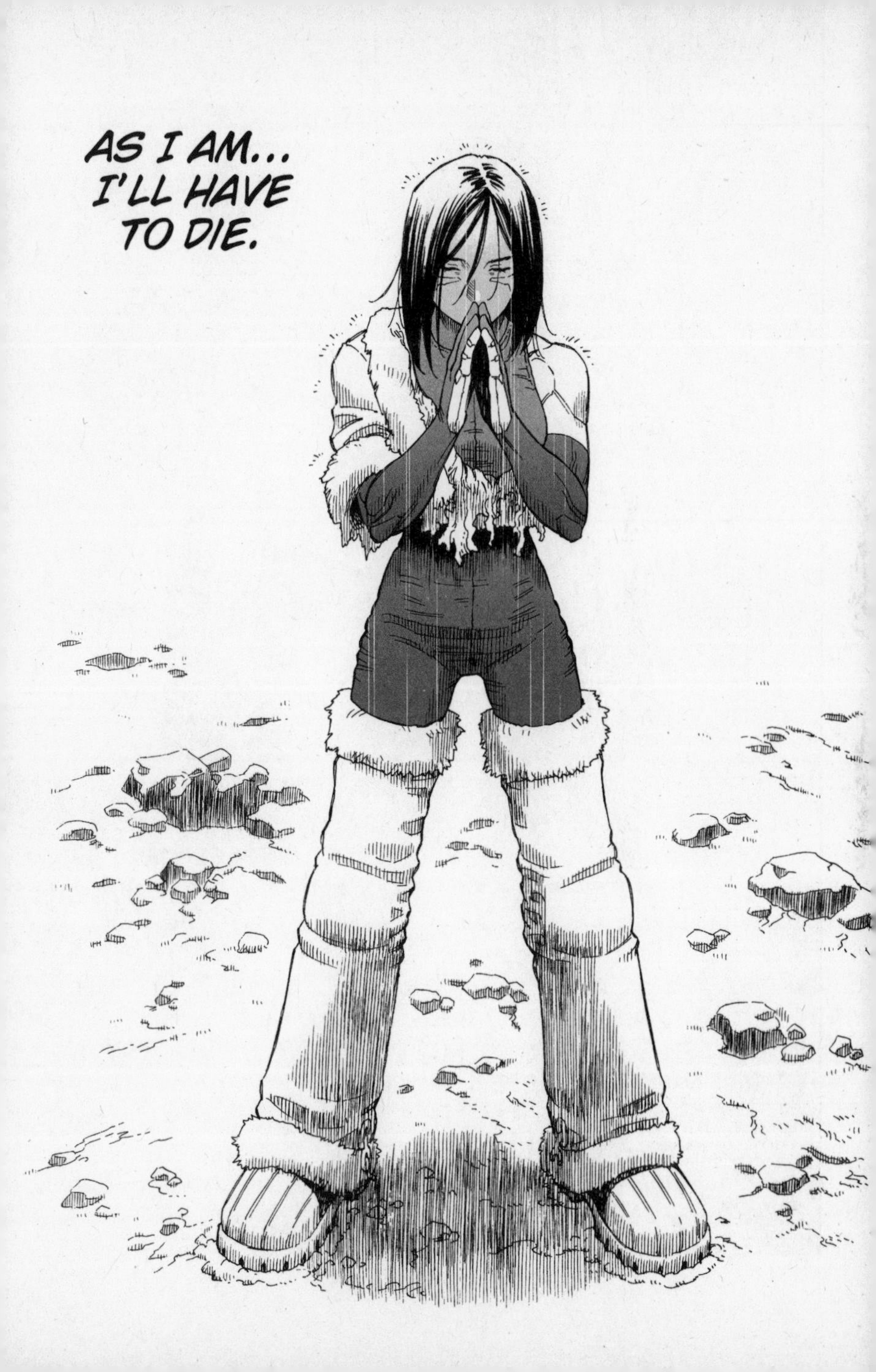
AS I AM...
I'LL HAVE
TO DIE.

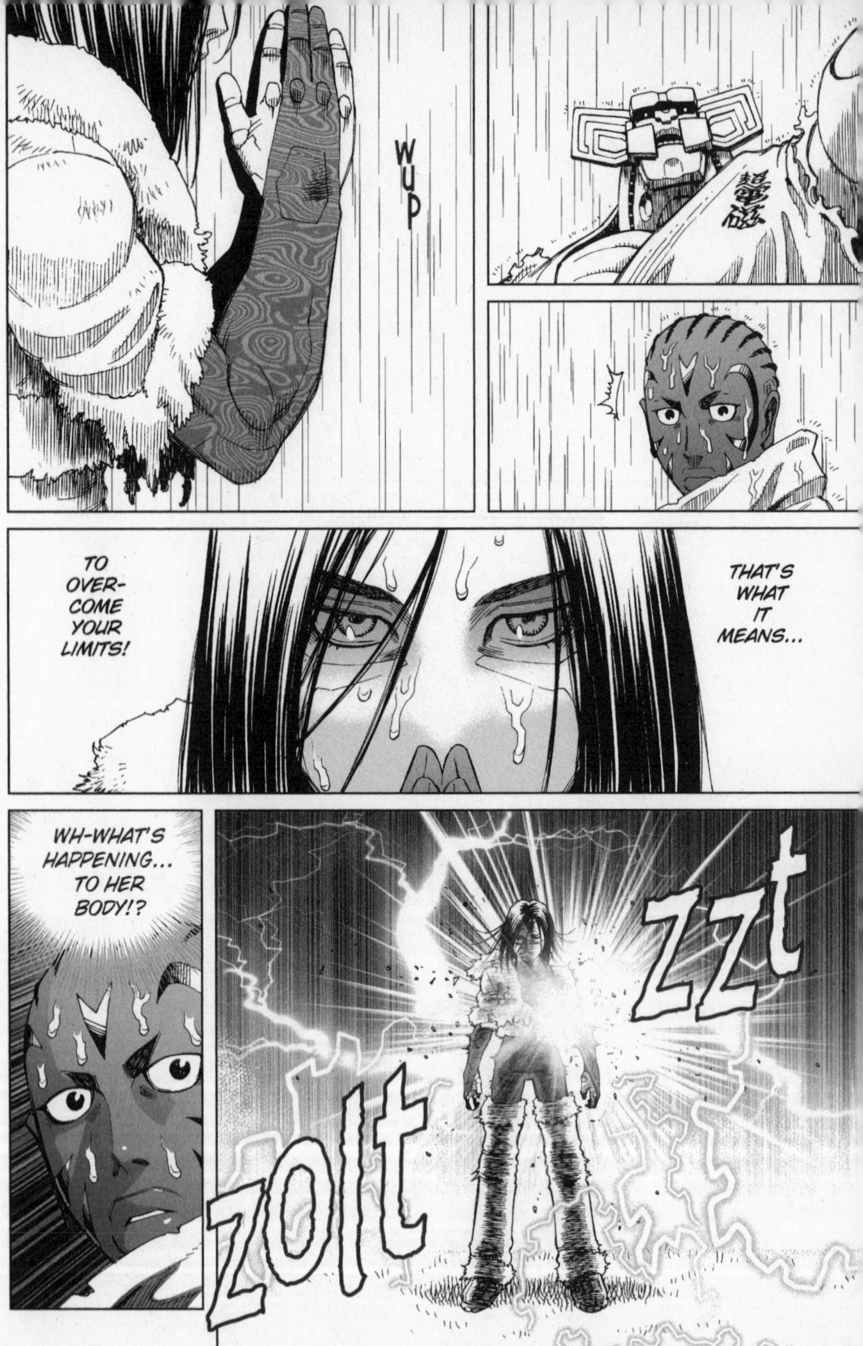
WUP
THAT'S WHAT IT MEANS...
TO OVER-COME YOUR LIMITS!
zzt
zolt
WH-WHAT'S HAPPENING... TO HER BODY!?

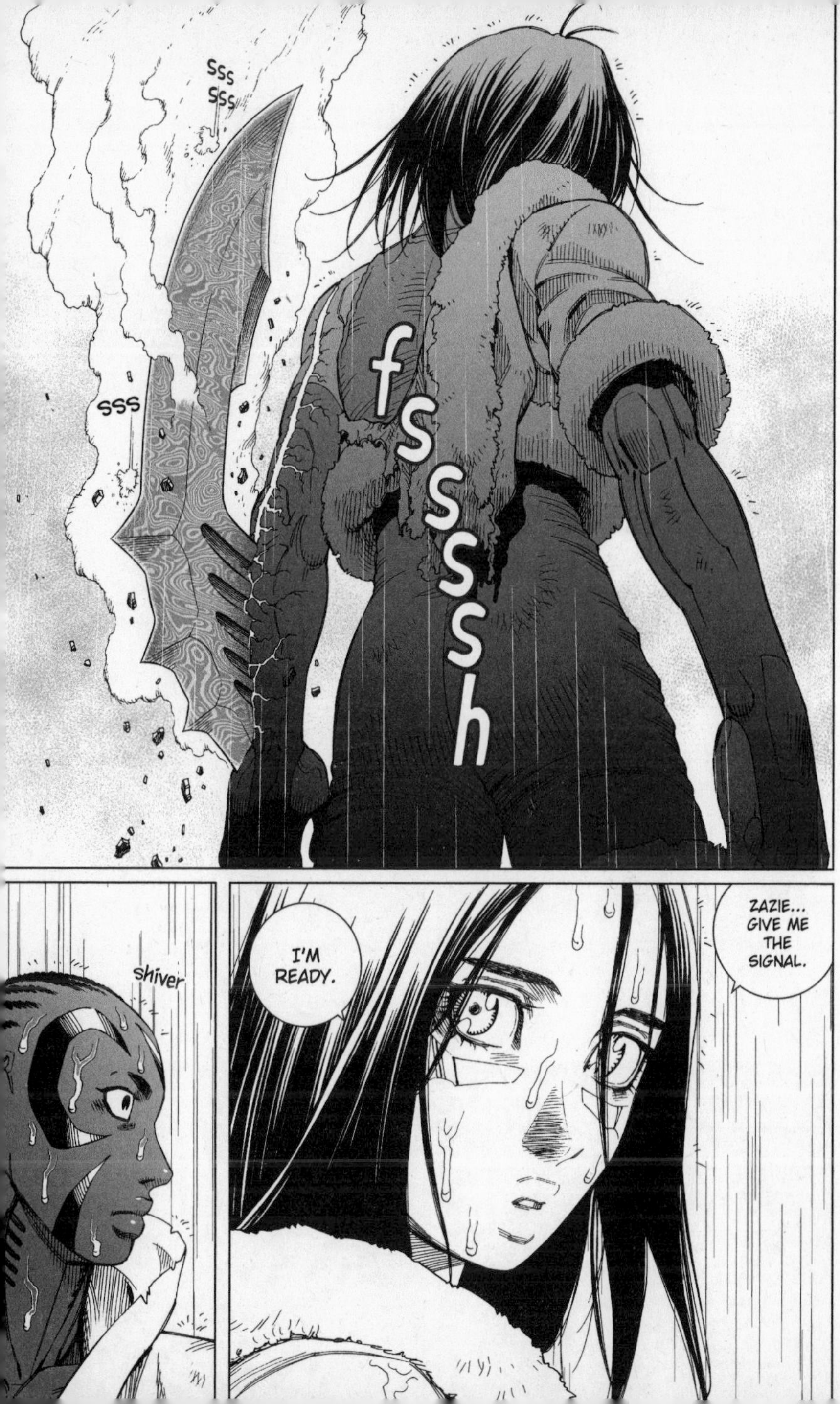
SSS
SSS
fsssh
SSS
ZAZIE... GIVE ME THE SIGNAL.
I'M READY.
shiver

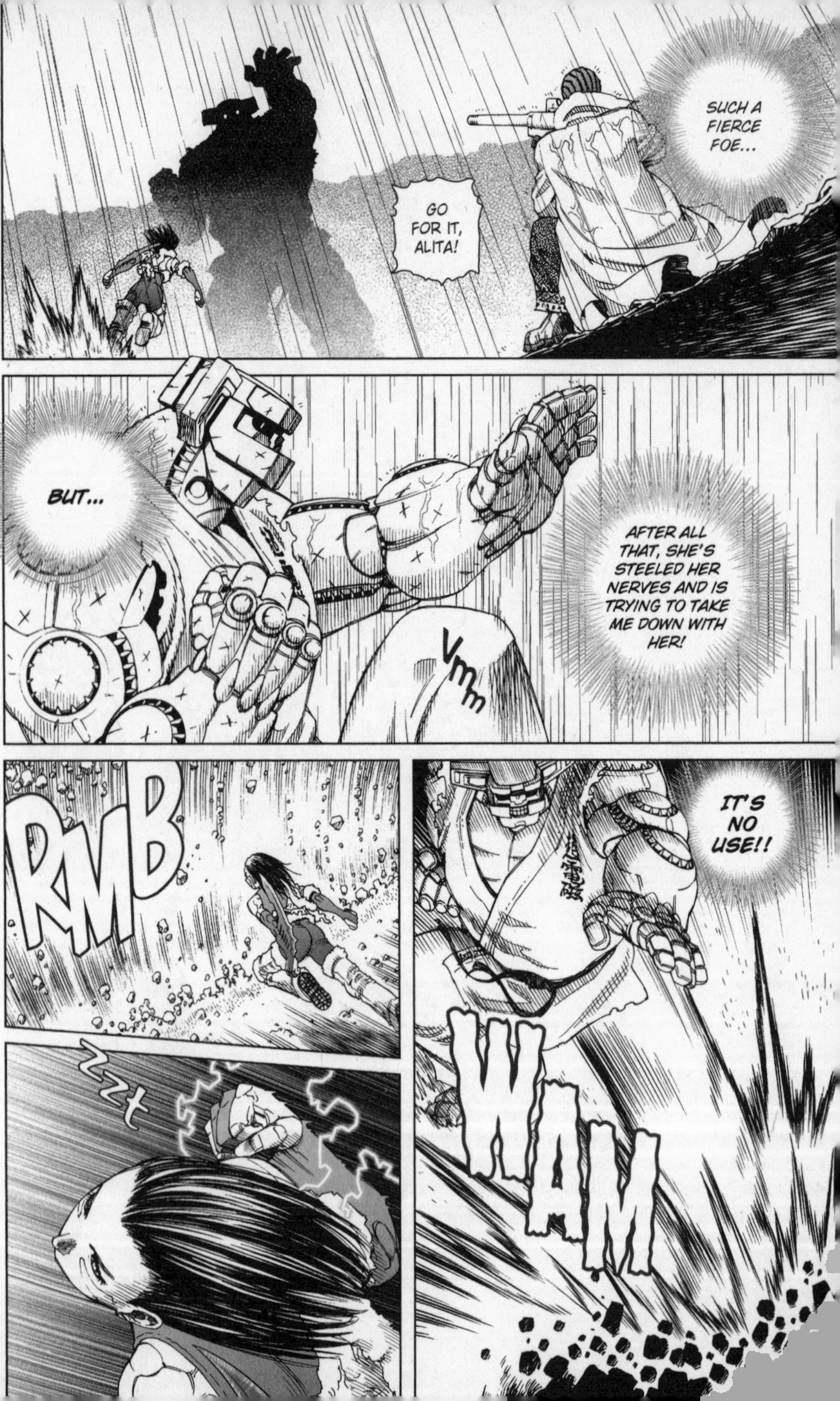
SUCH A FIERCE FOE...
GO FOR IT, ALITA!
BUT...
AFTER ALL THAT, SHE'S STEELED HER NERVES AND IS TRYING TO TAKE ME DOWN WITH HER!
Vmm
IT'S NO USE!!
WAM
RMB
ZZzt

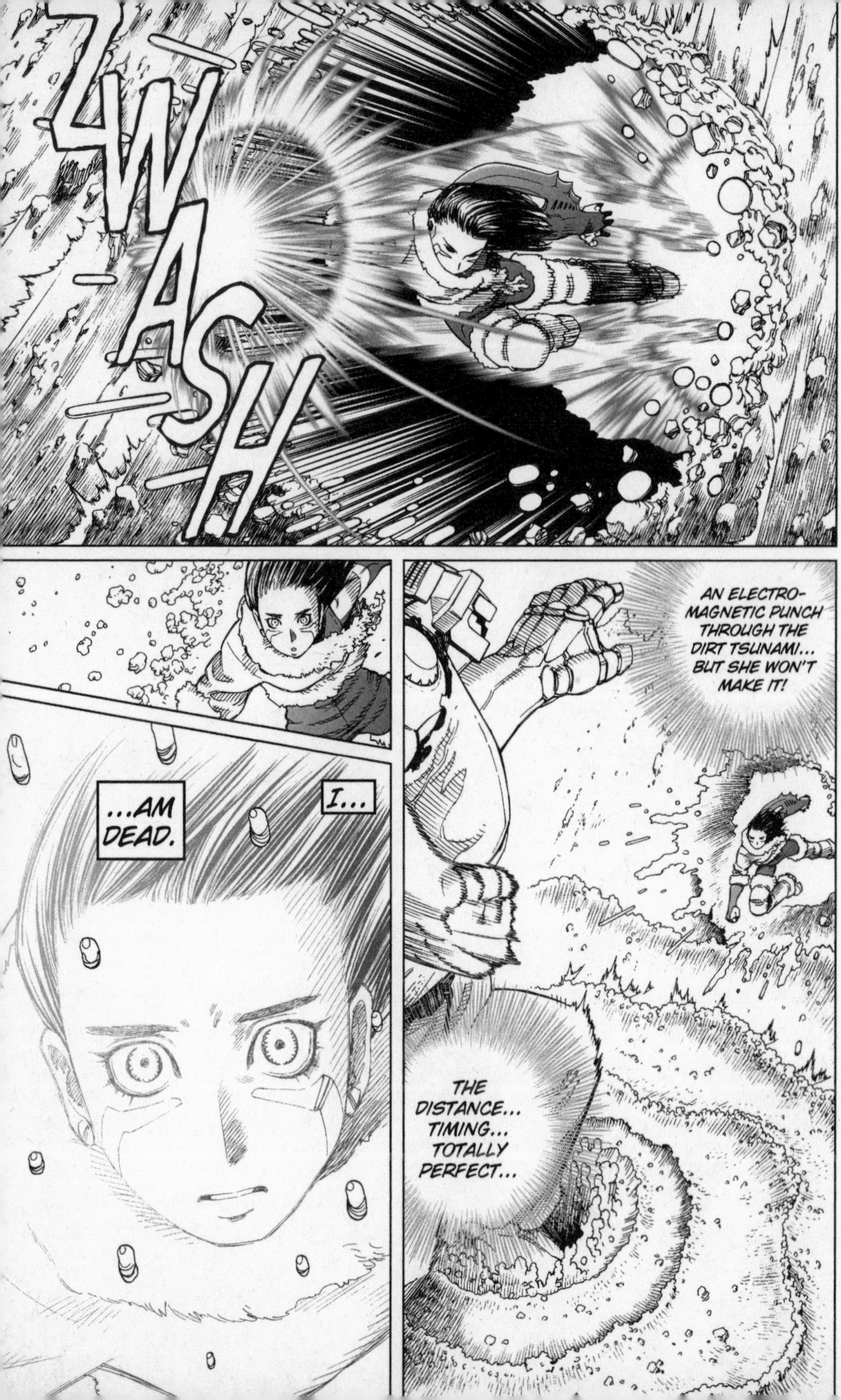
ZWASH
AN ELECTRO-MAGNETIC PUNCH THROUGH THE DIRT TSUNAMI... BUT SHE WON'T MAKE IT!
THE DISTANCE... TIMING... TOTALLY PERFECT...
I...
...AM DEAD.

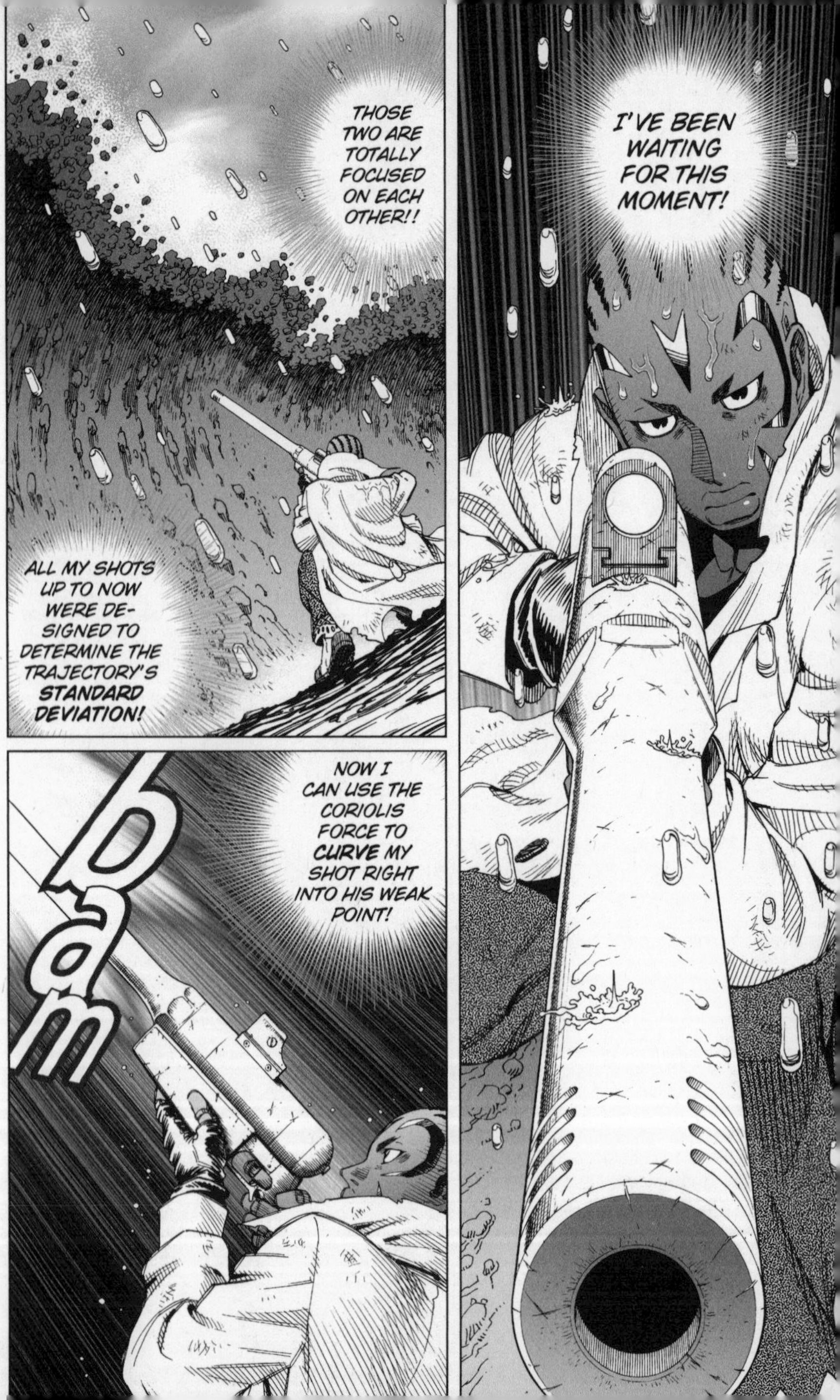
I'VE BEEN WAITING FOR THIS MOMENT!
THOSE TWO ARE TOTALLY FOCUSED ON EACH OTHER!!
ALL MY SHOTS UP TO NOW WERE DE-SIGNED TO DETERMINE THE TRAJECTORY'S **STANDARD DEVIATION!**
NOW I CAN USE THE CORIOLIS FORCE TO **CURVE** MY SHOT RIGHT INTO HIS WEAK POINT!
bam

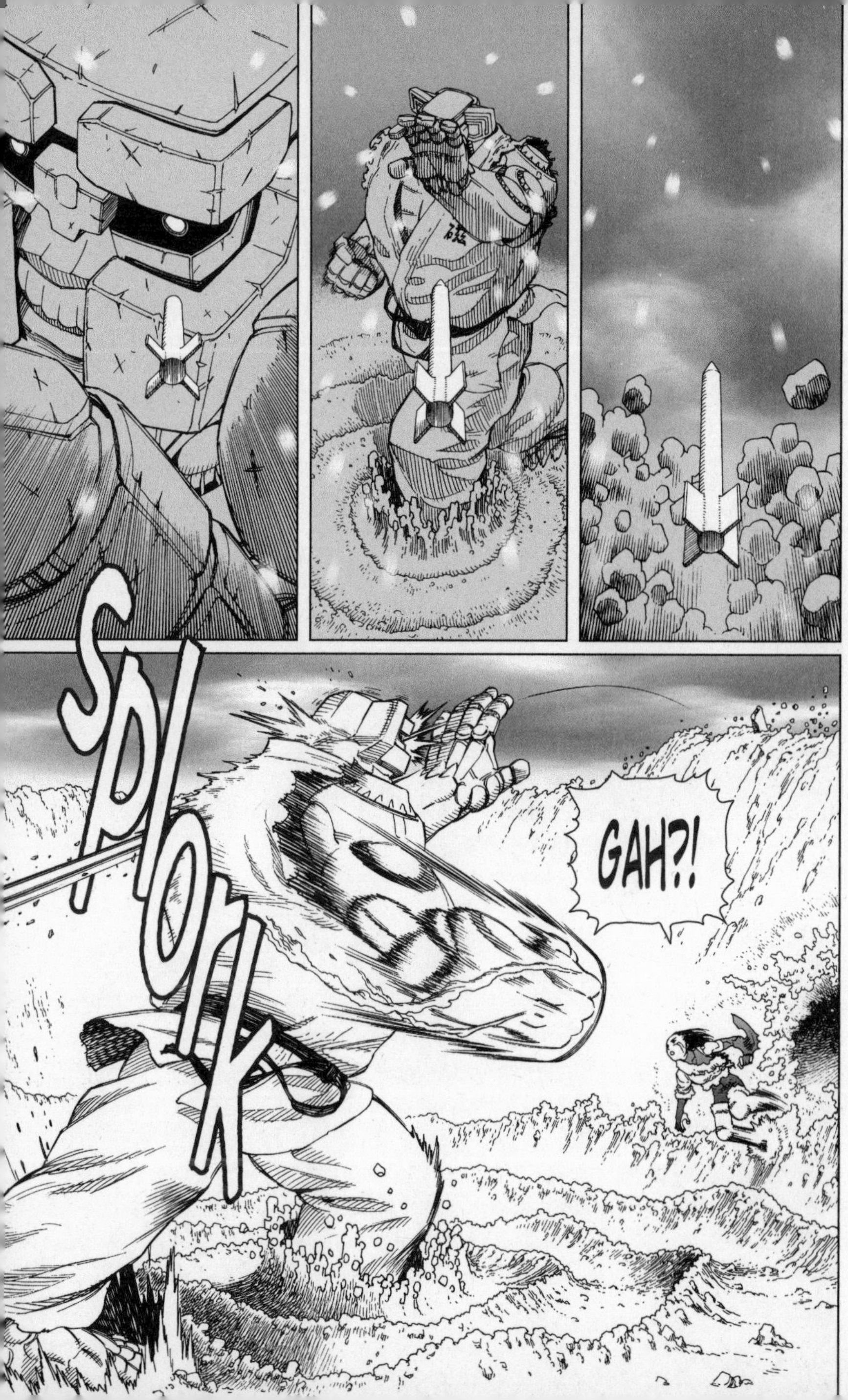
SPLONK
GAH?!

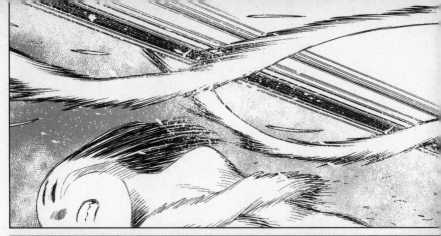

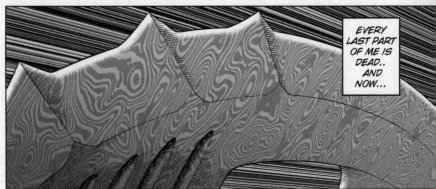

EVERY LAST PART OF ME IS DEAD.. AND NOW...

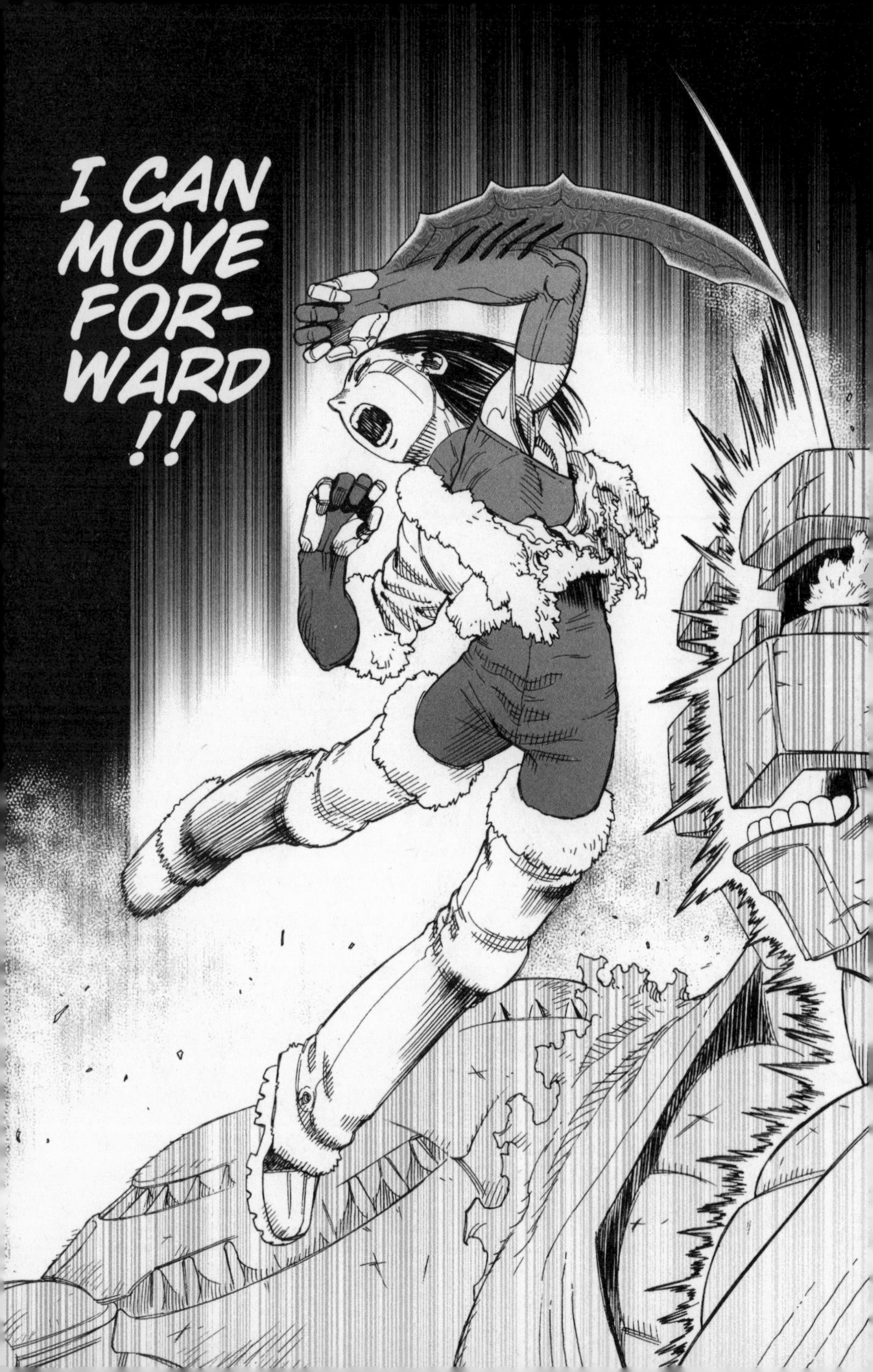
I CAN MOVE FOR-WARD!!

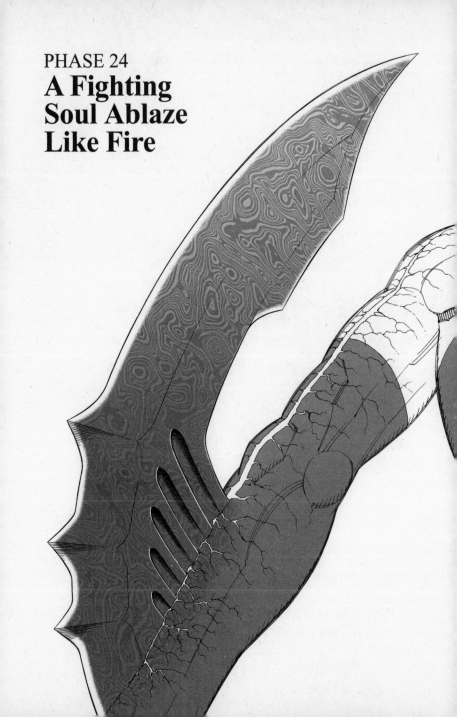

PHASE 24
A Fighting Soul Ablaze Like Fire

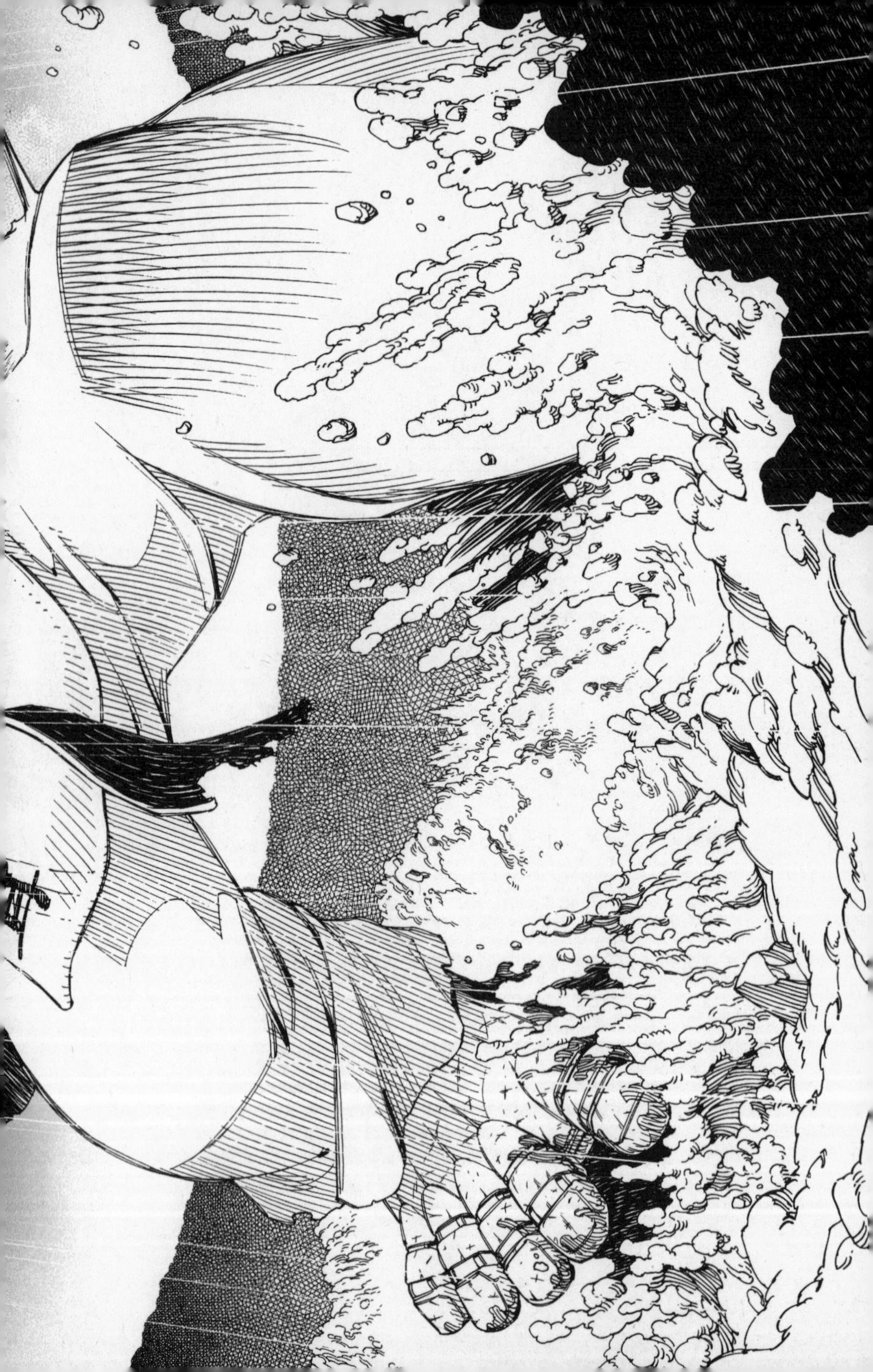

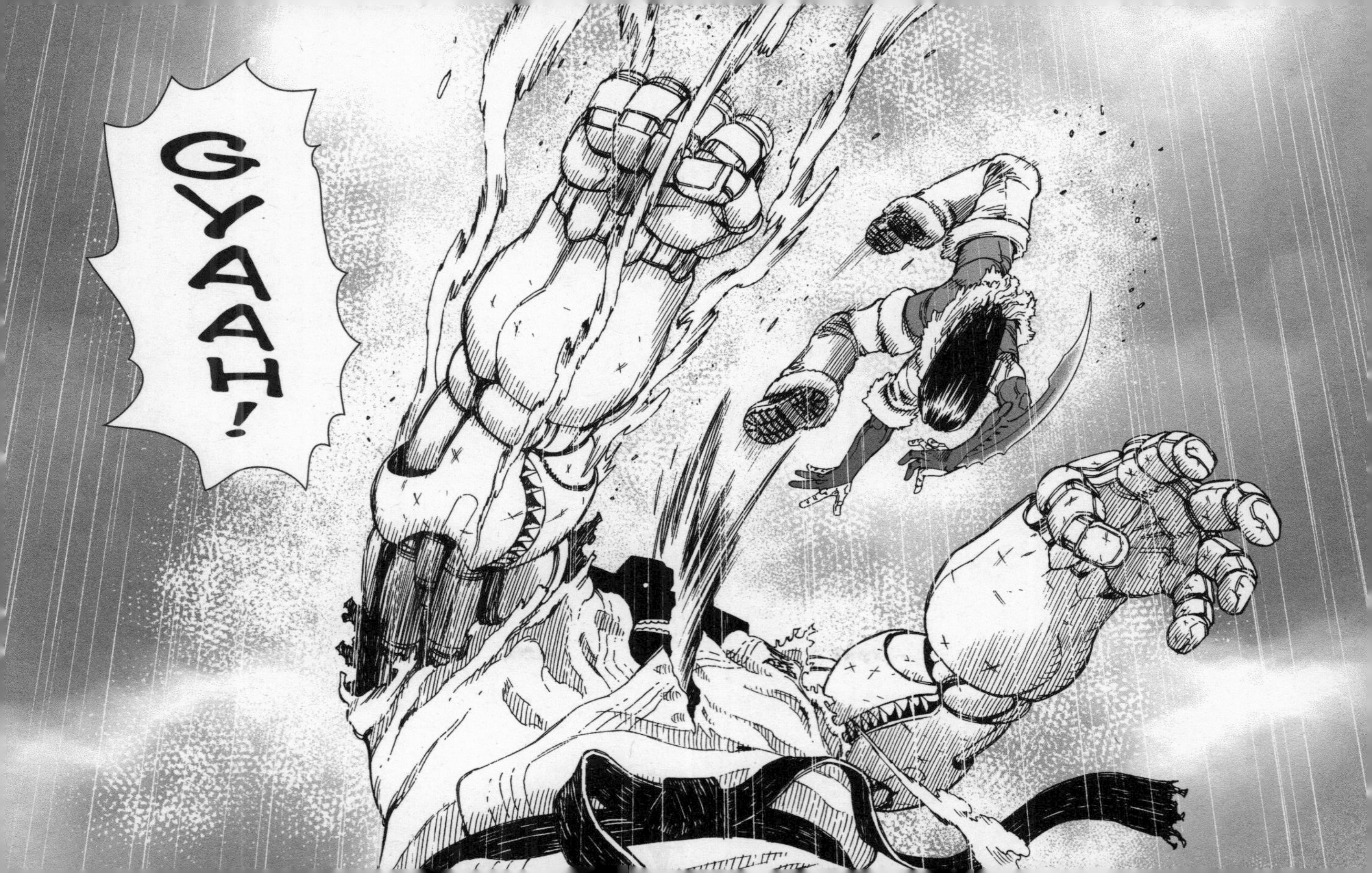
GYAAH!

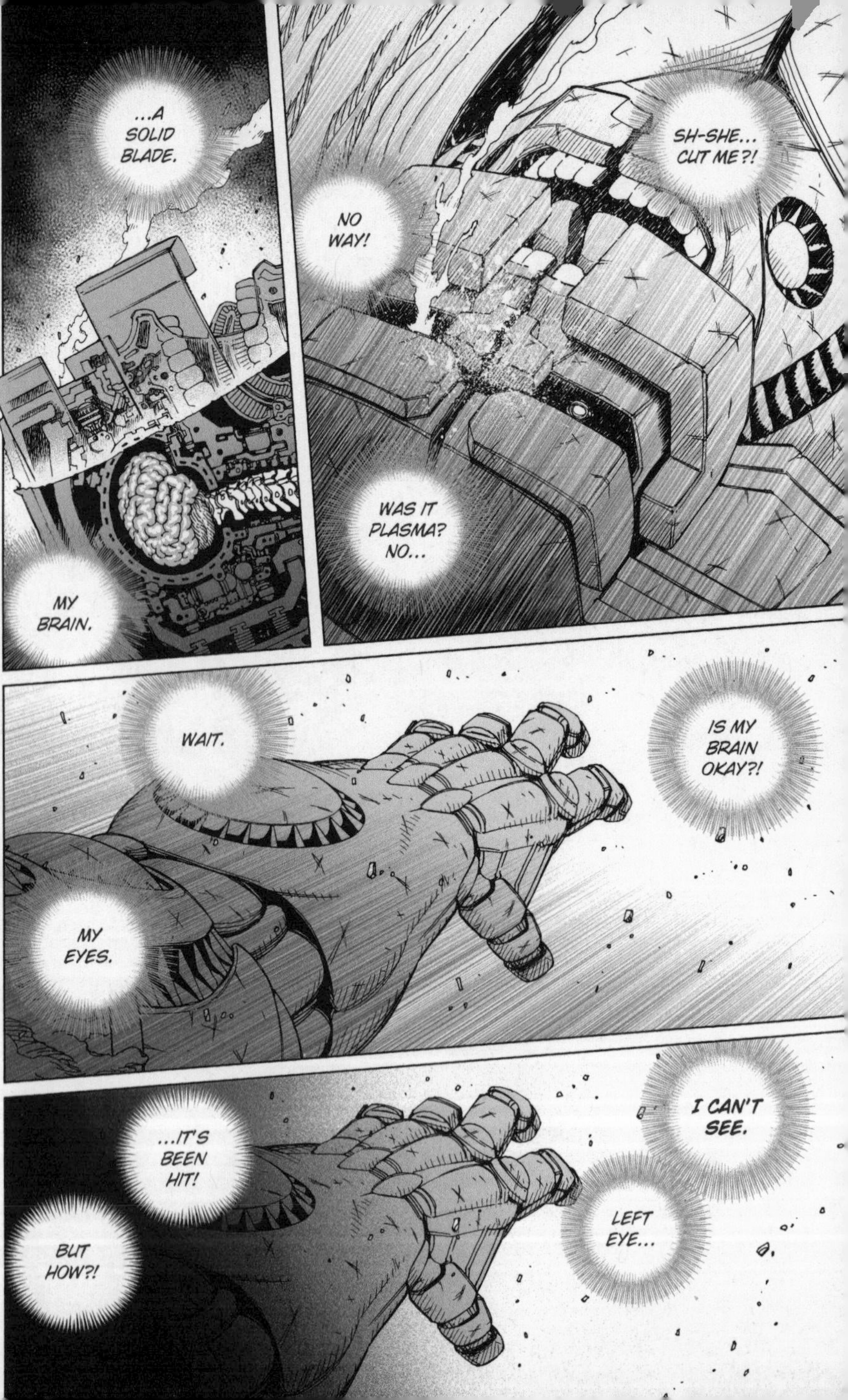
SH-SHE... CUT ME?!
NO WAY!
WAS IT PLASMA? NO...
...A SOLID BLADE.
MY BRAIN.
IS MY BRAIN OKAY?!
WAIT.
MY EYES.
I CAN'T SEE.
LEFT EYE...
...IT'S BEEN HIT!
BUT HOW?!

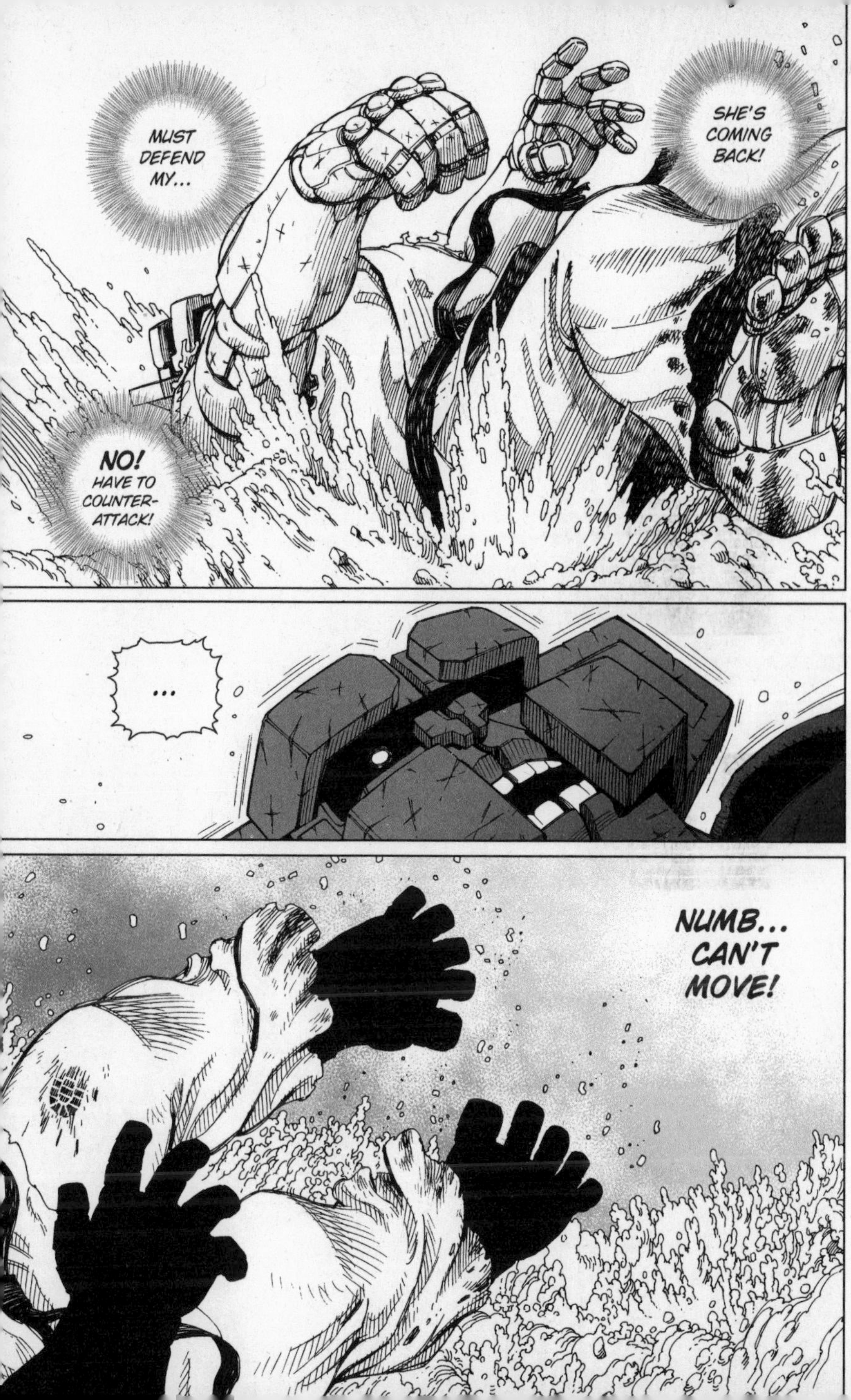
SHE'S COMING BACK!
MUST DEFEND MY...
NO! HAVE TO COUNTER-ATTACK!
...
NUMB... CAN'T MOVE!

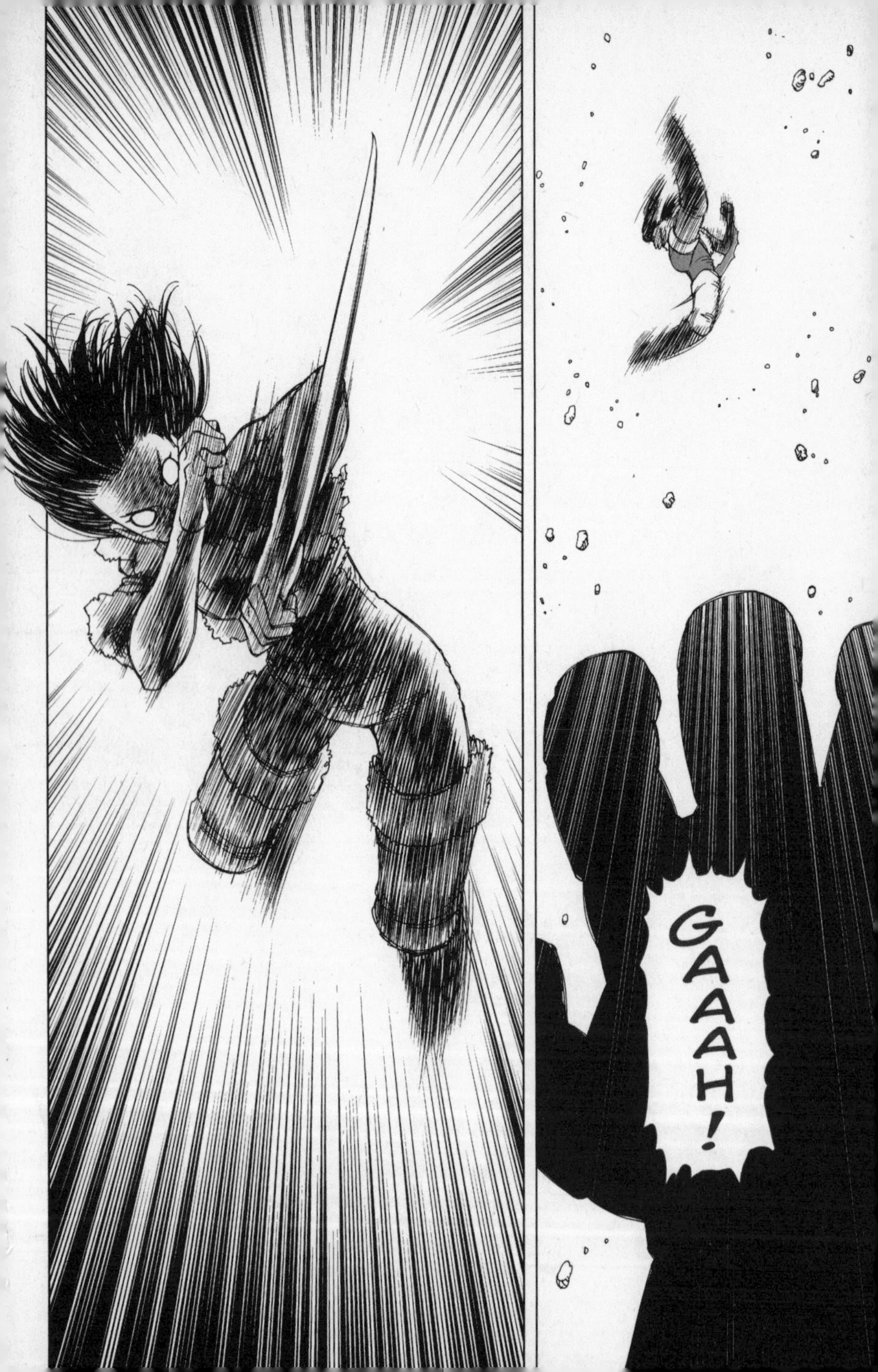
GAAAH!

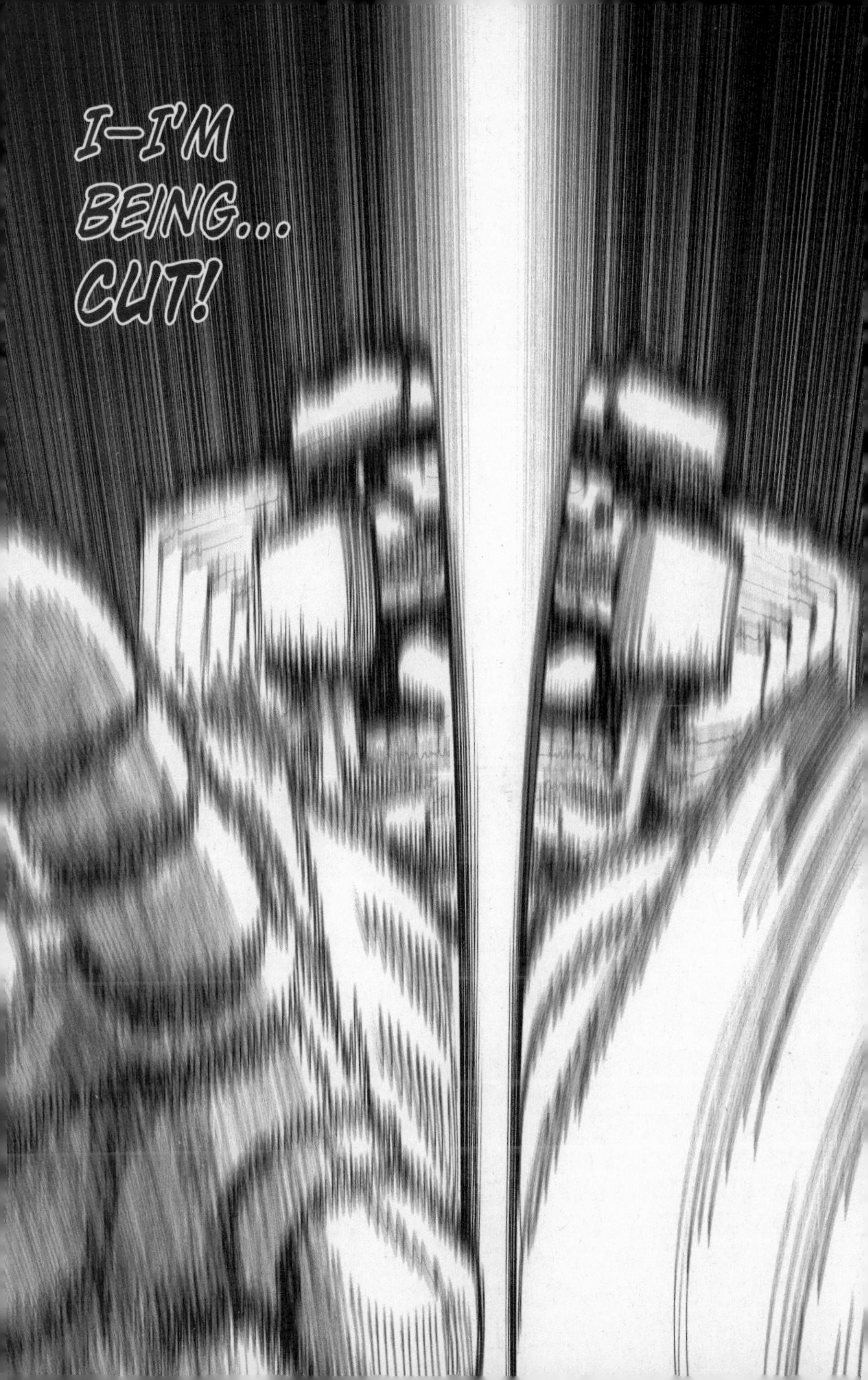
I-I'M BEING... CUT!

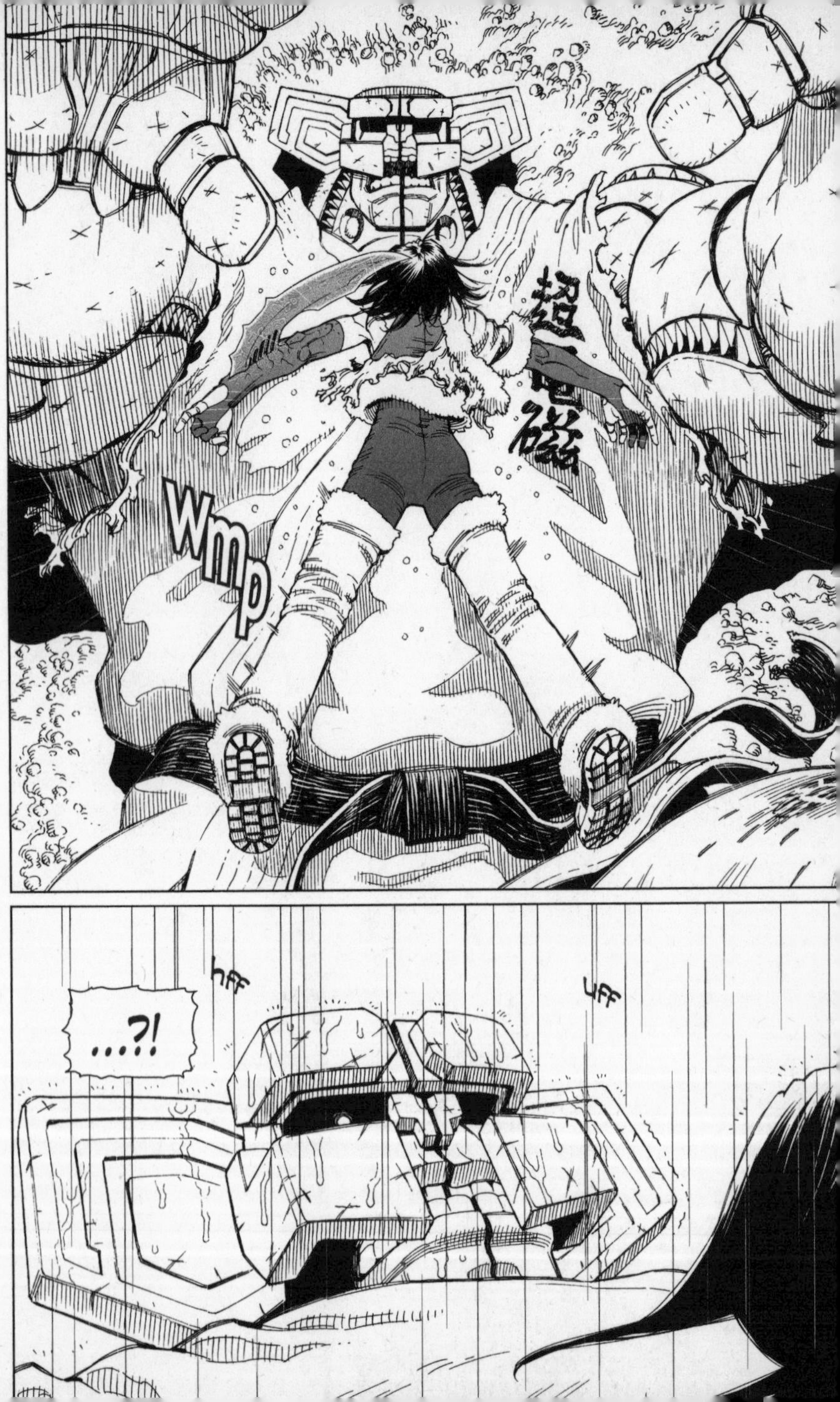
超電磁
Wmp
uff
hff
...?!

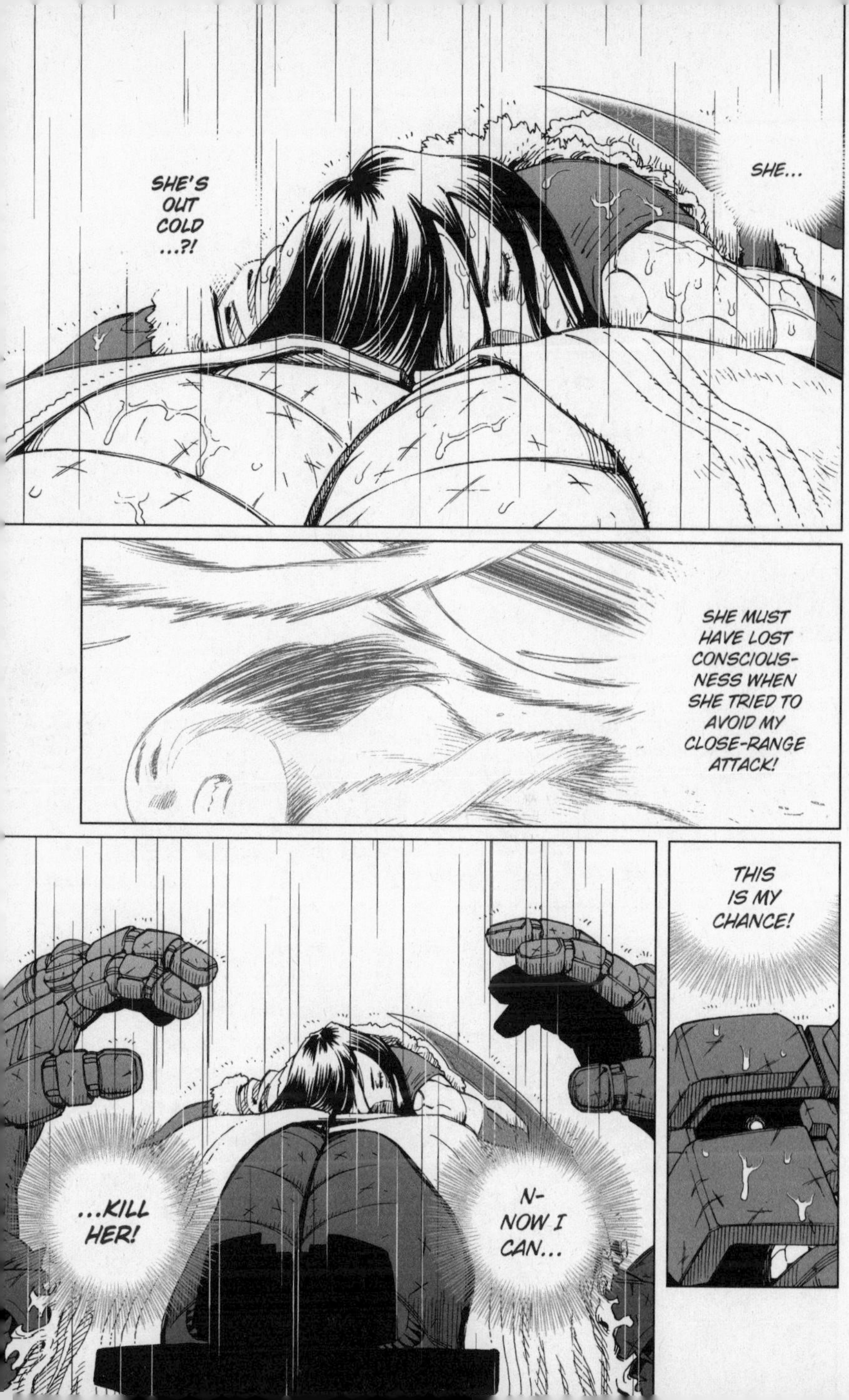
SHE...
SHE'S OUT COLD ...?!
SHE MUST HAVE LOST CONSCIOUS-NESS WHEN SHE TRIED TO AVOID MY CLOSE-RANGE ATTACK!
THIS IS MY CHANCE!
N- NOW I CAN...
...KILL HER!

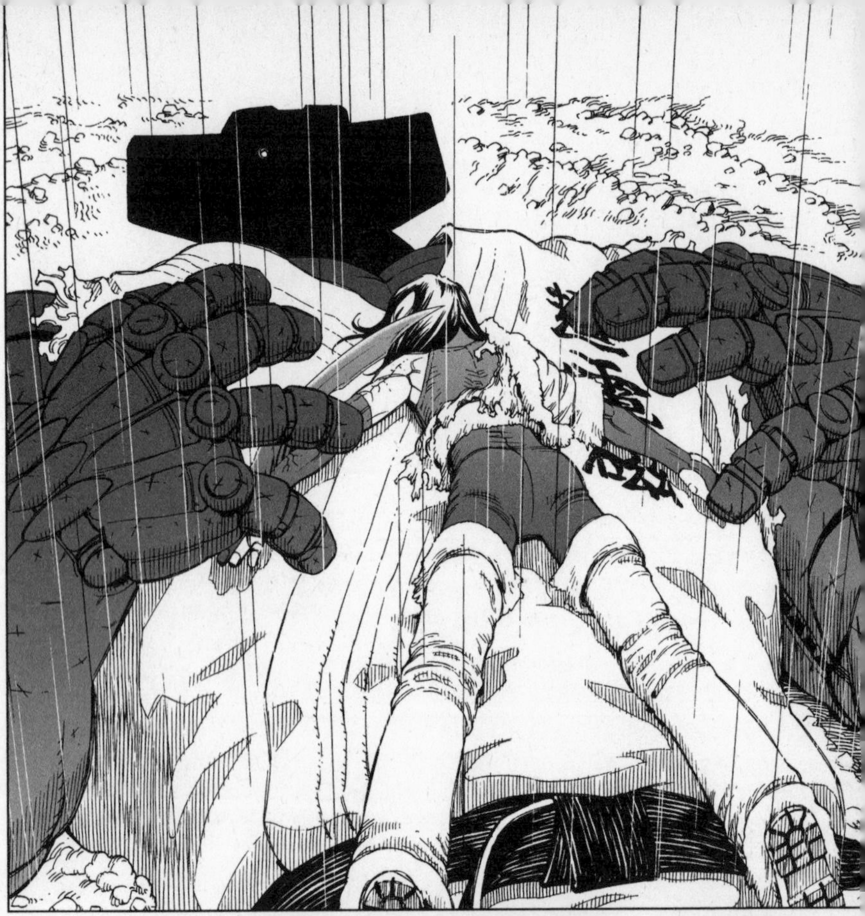
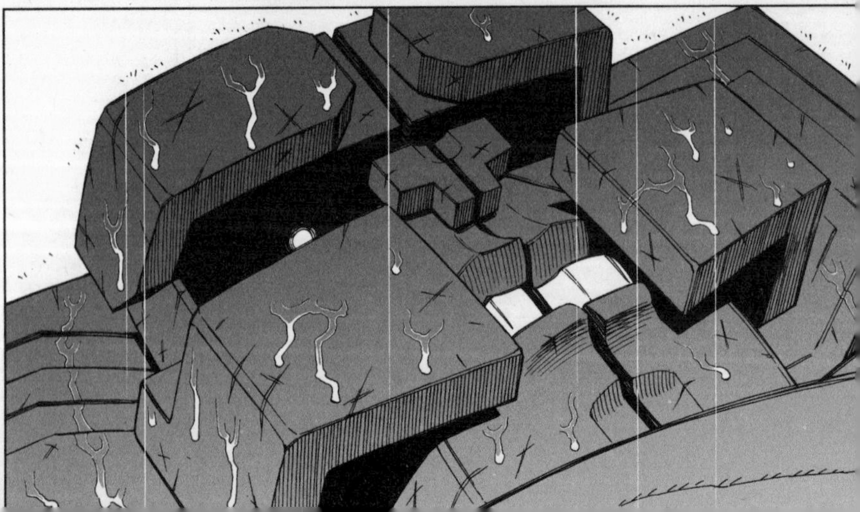

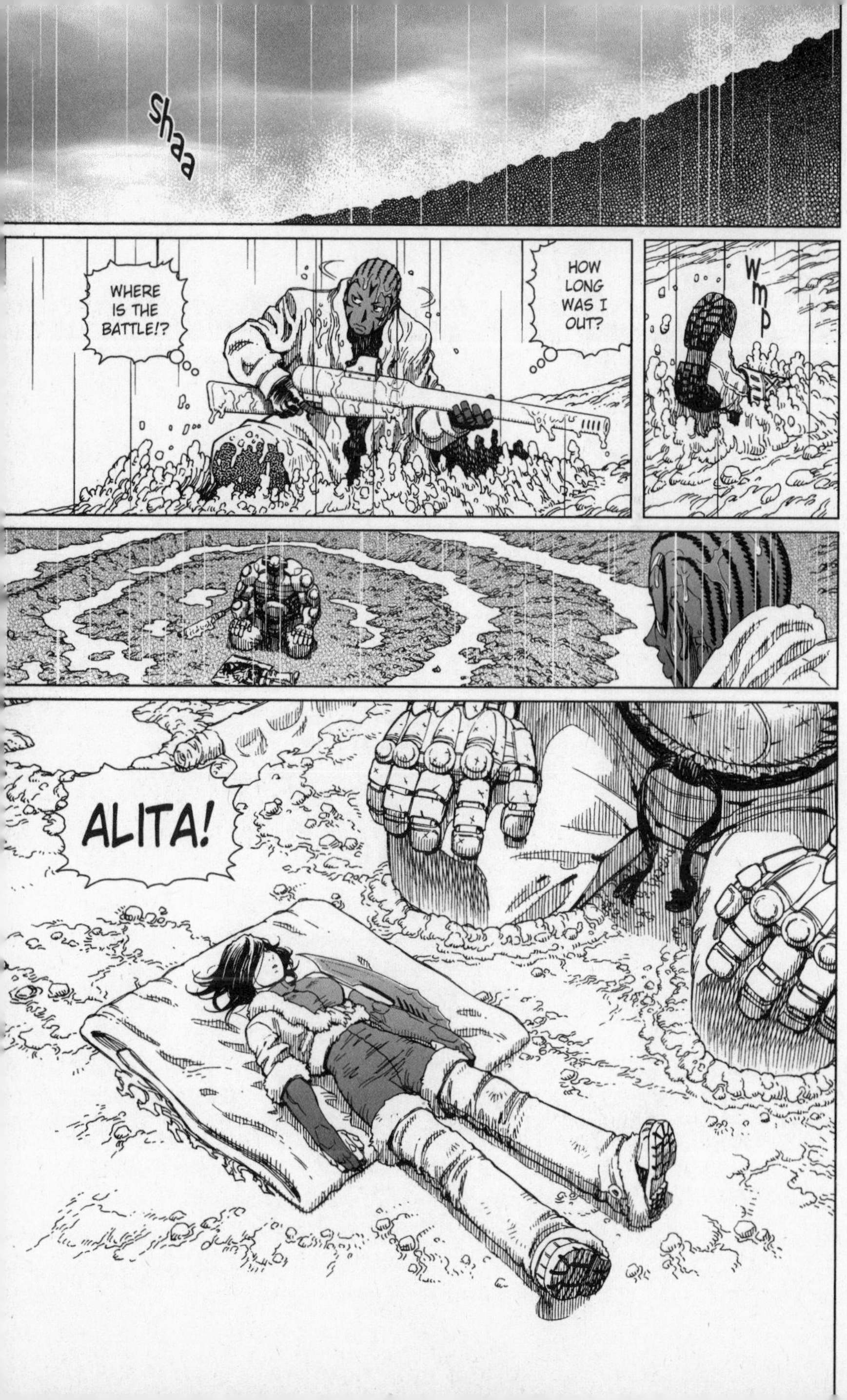
shaa
Wmp
HOW LONG WAS I OUT?
WHERE IS THE BATTLE!?
ALITA!

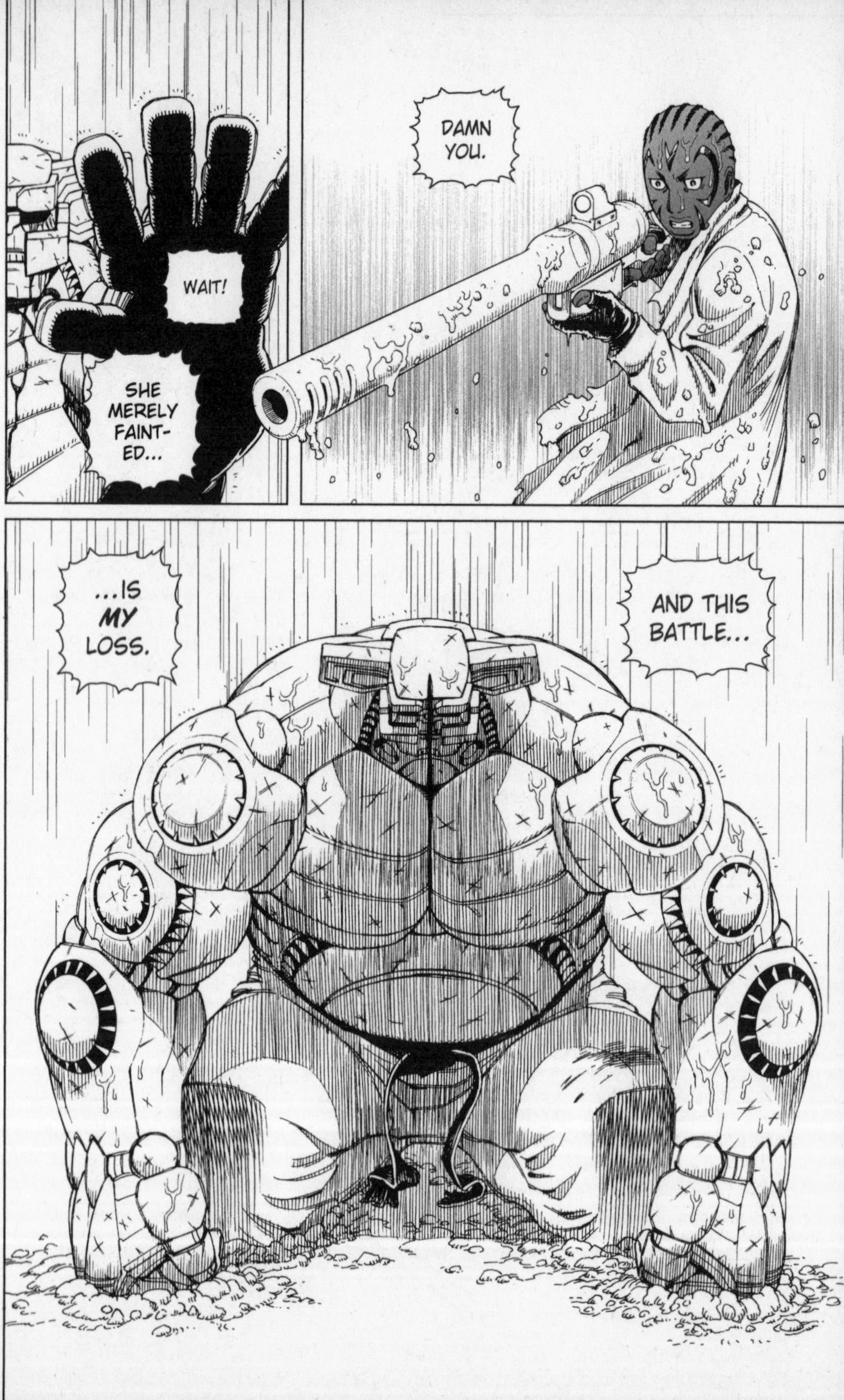
DAMN YOU.
WAIT!
SHE MERELY FAINT-ED...
AND THIS BATTLE...
...IS MY LOSS.

SHE'S DOWN... WHY NOT FINISH HER OFF?

...
...

A MERCENERY LIKE YOU MAY NOT UNDERSTAND, BUT...

KILLING AN OPPONENT IN THIS STATE CANNOT BE CALLED KARATE.

SHE IS TRULY FEARSOME.

THOUGH YOUR SHOOTING WAS ALSO SUPERB...

SHE CUT ME DOWN WHILE ALREADY UNCONSCIOUS, USING ONLY HER WARRIOR'S INSTANCTS!

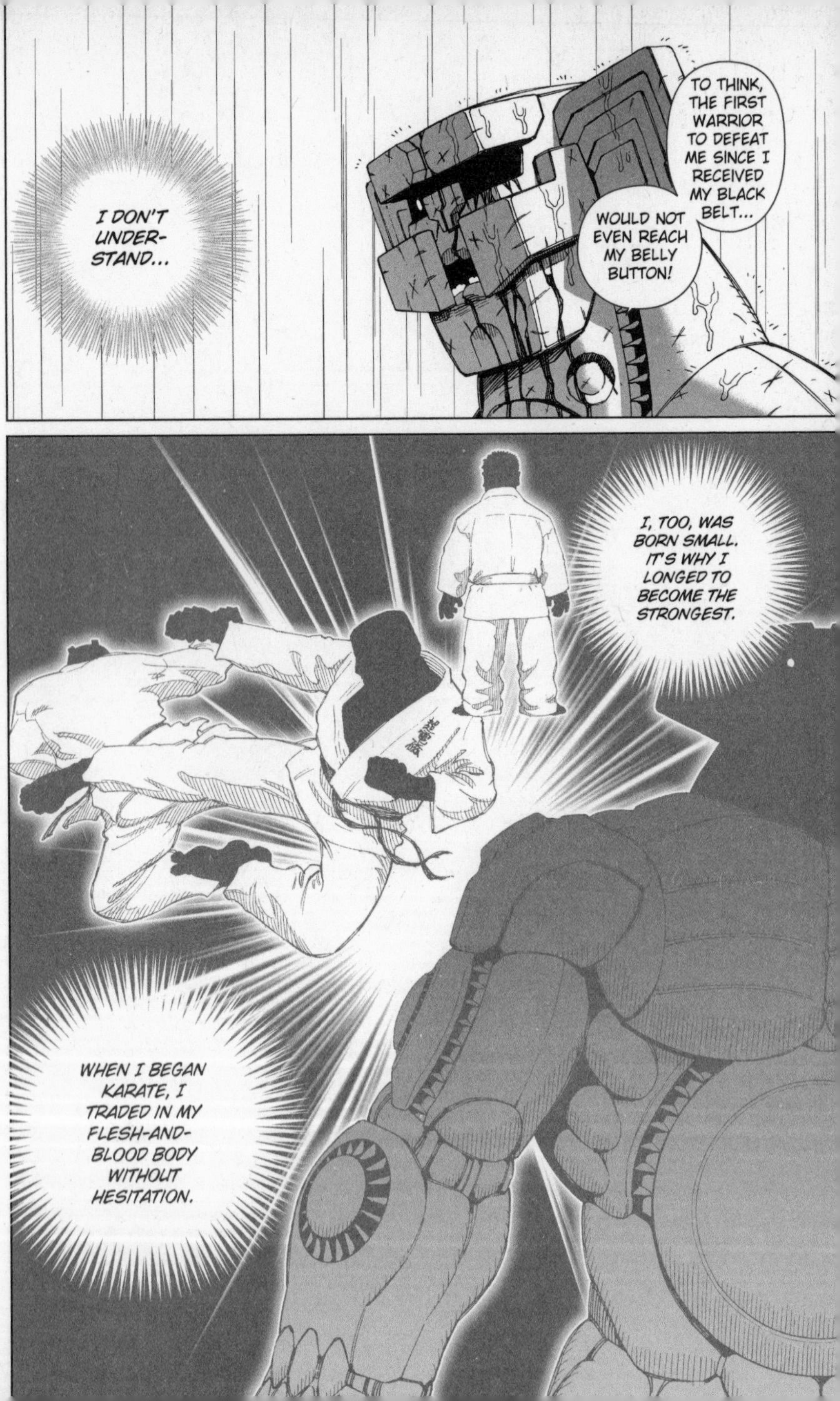
TO THINK, THE FIRST WARRIOR TO DEFEAT ME SINCE I RECEIVED MY BLACK BELT...
WOULD NOT EVEN REACH MY BELLY BUTTON!
I DON'T UNDER-STAND...
I, TOO, WAS BORN SMALL. IT'S WHY I LONGED TO BECOME THE STRONGEST.
WHEN I BEGAN KARATE, I TRADED IN MY FLESH-AND-BLOOD BODY WITHOUT HESITATION.

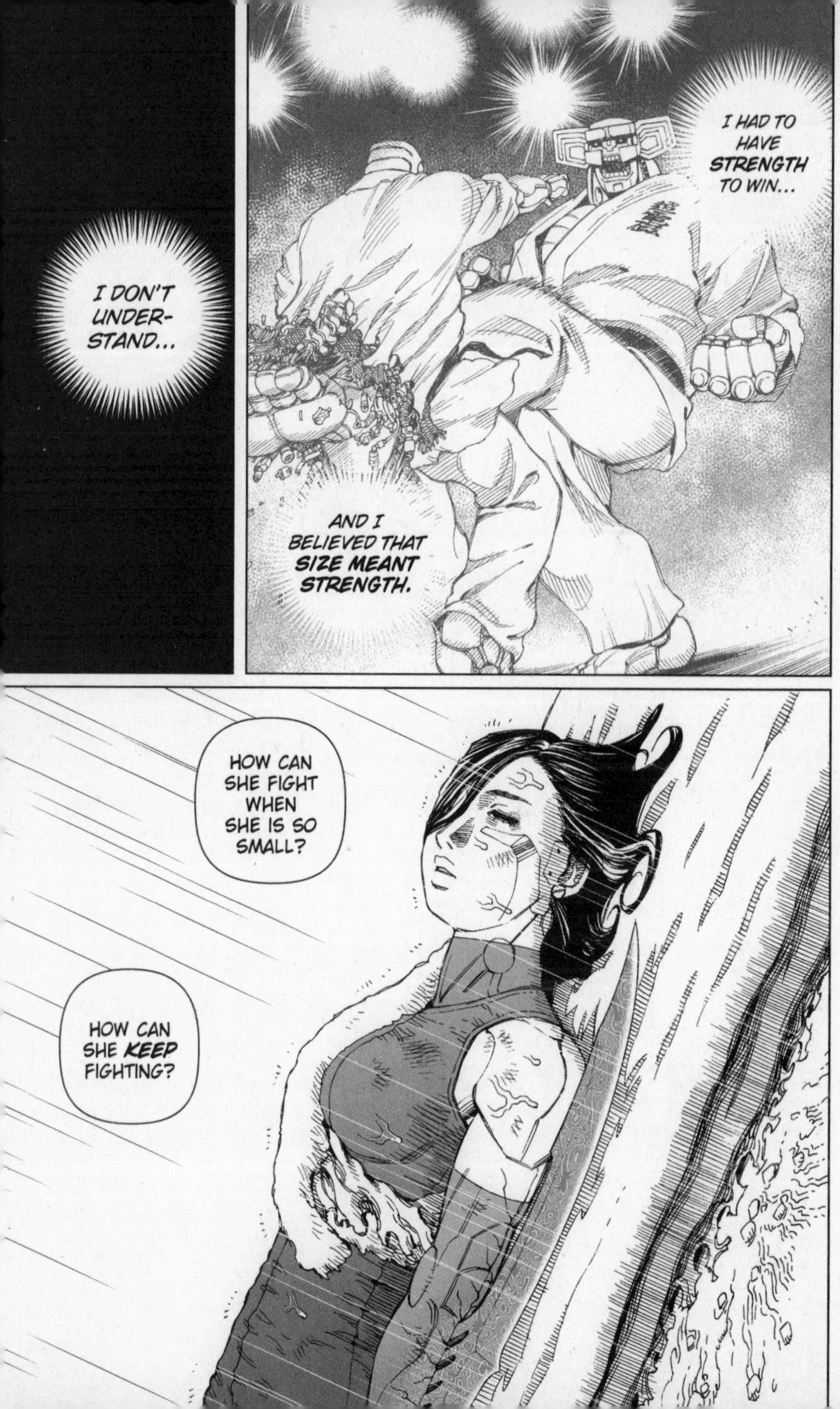
I HAD TO HAVE **STRENGTH** TO WIN...
AND I BELIEVED THAT **SIZE MEANT STRENGTH.**
I DON'T UNDER-STAND...
HOW CAN SHE FIGHT WHEN SHE IS SO SMALL?
HOW CAN SHE ***KEEP*** FIGHTING?

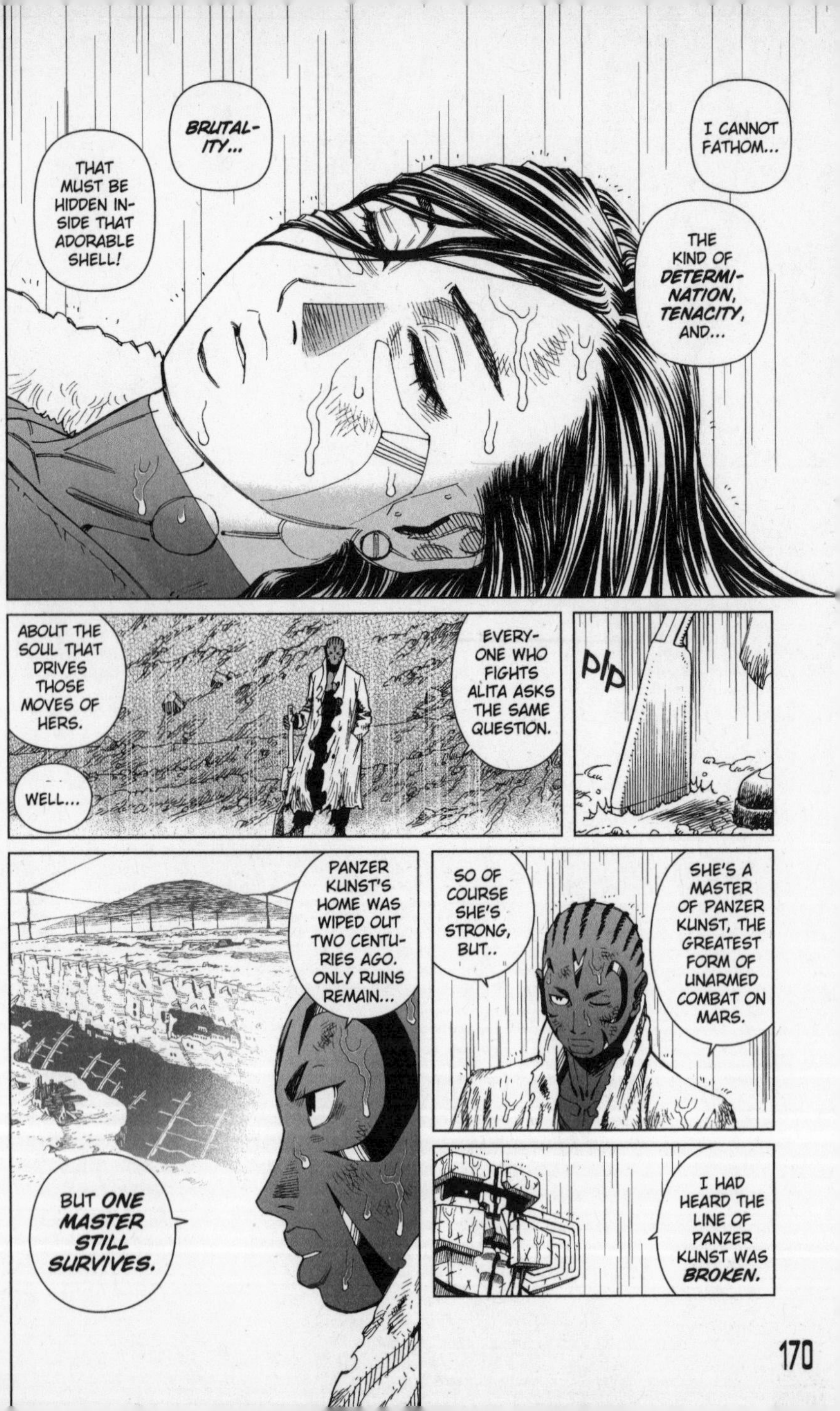
I CANNOT FATHOM...
THE KIND OF DETERMINATION, TENACITY, AND...
BRUTALITY...
THAT MUST BE HIDDEN INSIDE THAT ADORABLE SHELL!
P/P
EVERYONE WHO FIGHTS ALITA ASKS THE SAME QUESTION.
ABOUT THE SOUL THAT DRIVES THOSE MOVES OF HERS.
WELL...
SHE'S A MASTER OF PANZER KUNST, THE GREATEST FORM OF UNARMED COMBAT ON MARS.
SO OF COURSE SHE'S STRONG, BUT..
I HAD HEARD THE LINE OF PANZER KUNST WAS BROKEN.
PANZER KUNST'S HOME WAS WIPED OUT TWO CENTURIES AGO. ONLY RUINS REMAIN...
BUT ONE MASTER STILL SURVIVES.

ONE WITH A FIGHT-ING SOUL ABLAZE LIKE FIRE.
THE COPTER IS COMING.
PLEASE TAKE THE FLAG.
I WILL TAKE PART IN THE TOURNEY AS PLANNED... WITH AN EVEN STRONGER BODY!
AND I WILL BE VICTORIOUS.
IF WE FACE EACH OTHER AGAIN, I WILL NOT BE BEATEN!
I'LL PASS ON THE MESSAGE TO HER.

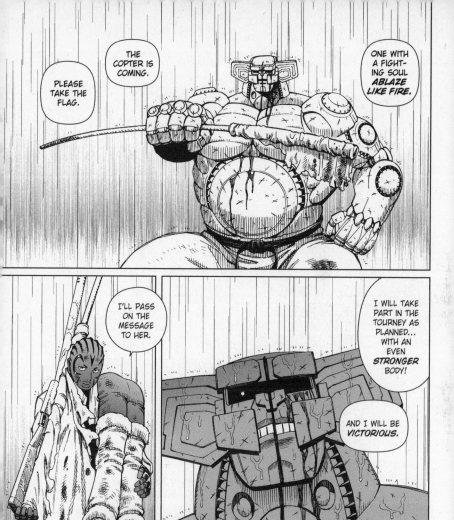

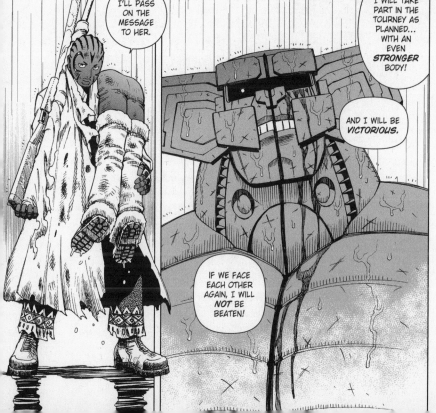

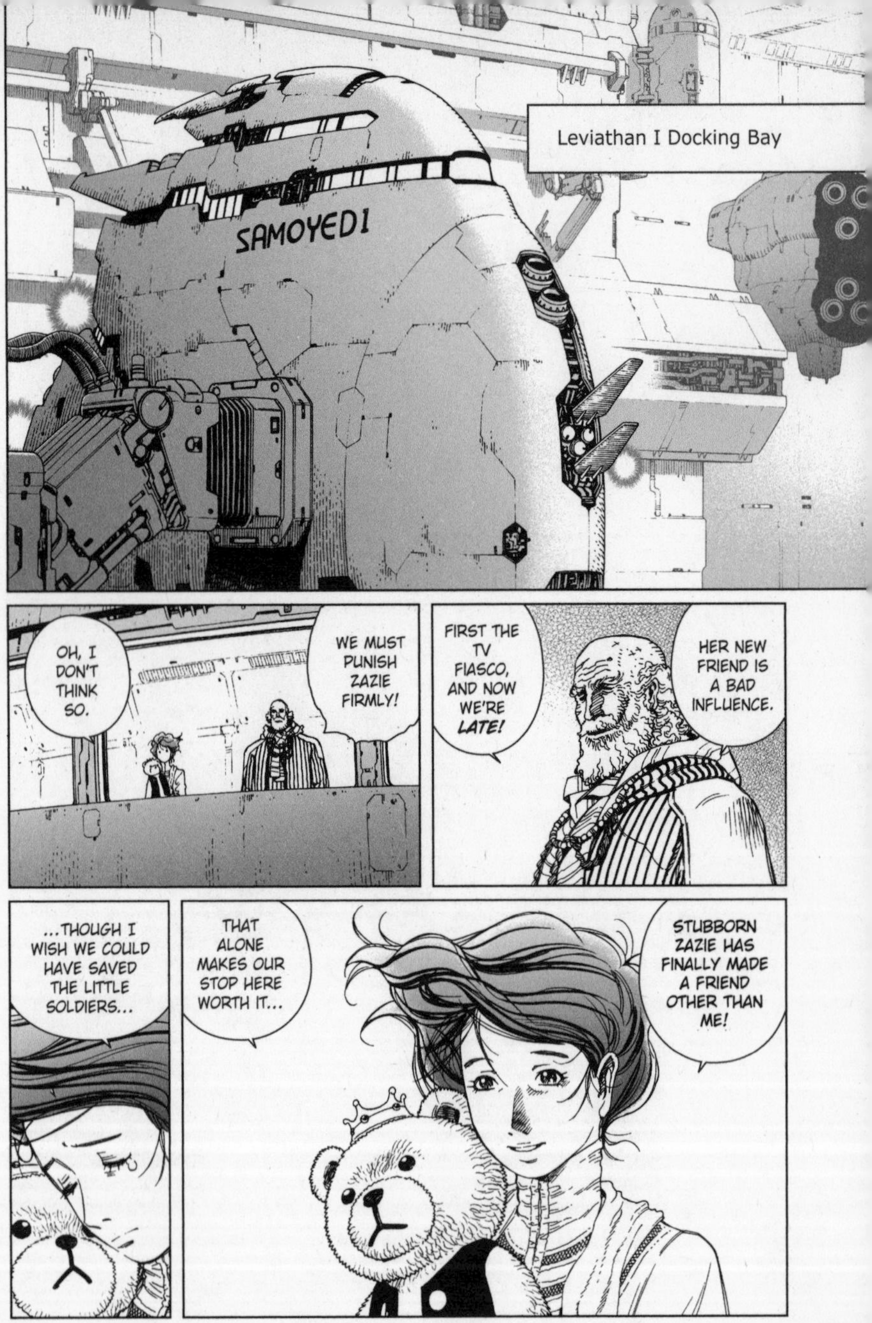
Leviathan I Docking Bay
SAMOYED1
HER NEW FRIEND IS A BAD INFLUENCE.
FIRST THE TV FIASCO, AND NOW WE'RE *LATE!*
WE MUST PUNISH ZAZIE FIRMLY!
OH, I DON'T THINK SO.
STUBBORN ZAZIE HAS FINALLY MADE A FRIEND OTHER THAN ME!
THAT ALONE MAKES OUR STOP HERE WORTH IT...
...THOUGH I WISH WE COULD HAVE SAVED THE LITTLE SOLDIERS...

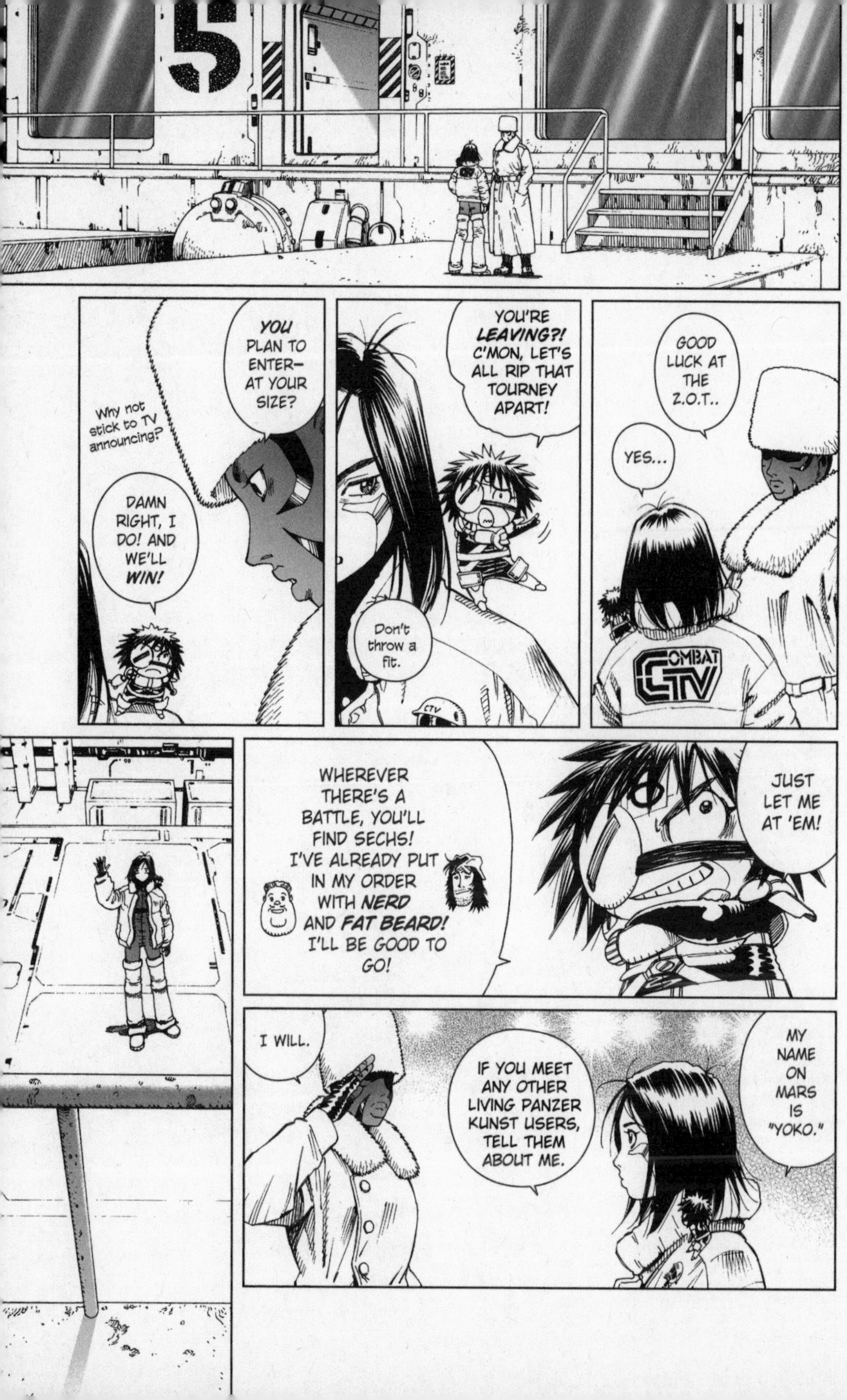
GOOD LUCK AT THE Z.O.T..
YES...
COMBAT CTV
YOU'RE LEAVING?! C'MON, LET'S ALL RIP THAT TOURNEY APART!
Don't throw a fit.
YOU PLAN TO ENTER– AT YOUR SIZE?
Why not stick to TV announcing?
DAMN RIGHT, I DO! AND WE'LL WIN!
JUST LET ME AT 'EM!
WHEREVER THERE'S A BATTLE, YOU'LL FIND SECHS! I'VE ALREADY PUT IN MY ORDER WITH NERD AND FAT BEARD! I'LL BE GOOD TO GO!
MY NAME ON MARS IS "YOKO."
IF YOU MEET ANY OTHER LIVING PANZER KUNST USERS, TELL THEM ABOUT ME.
I WILL.

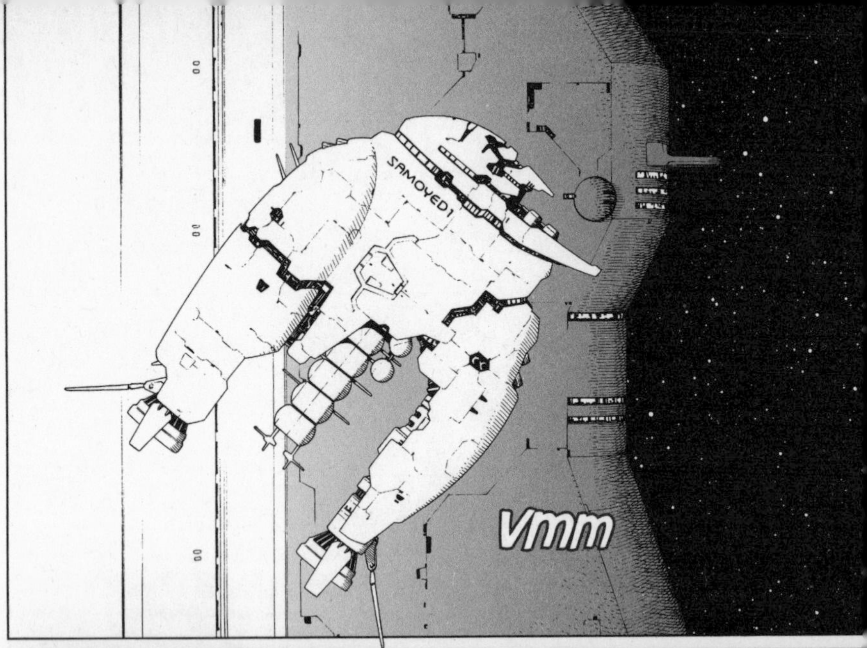
SAMOYED1
Vmm
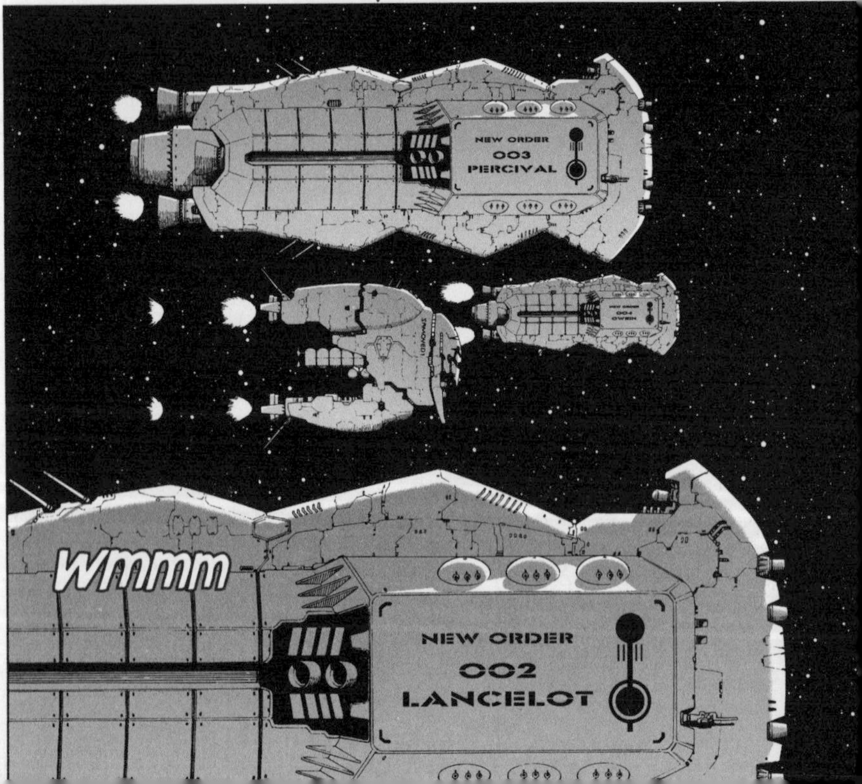
NEW ORDER
003
PERCIVAL
Wmmm
NEW ORDER
002
LANCELOT

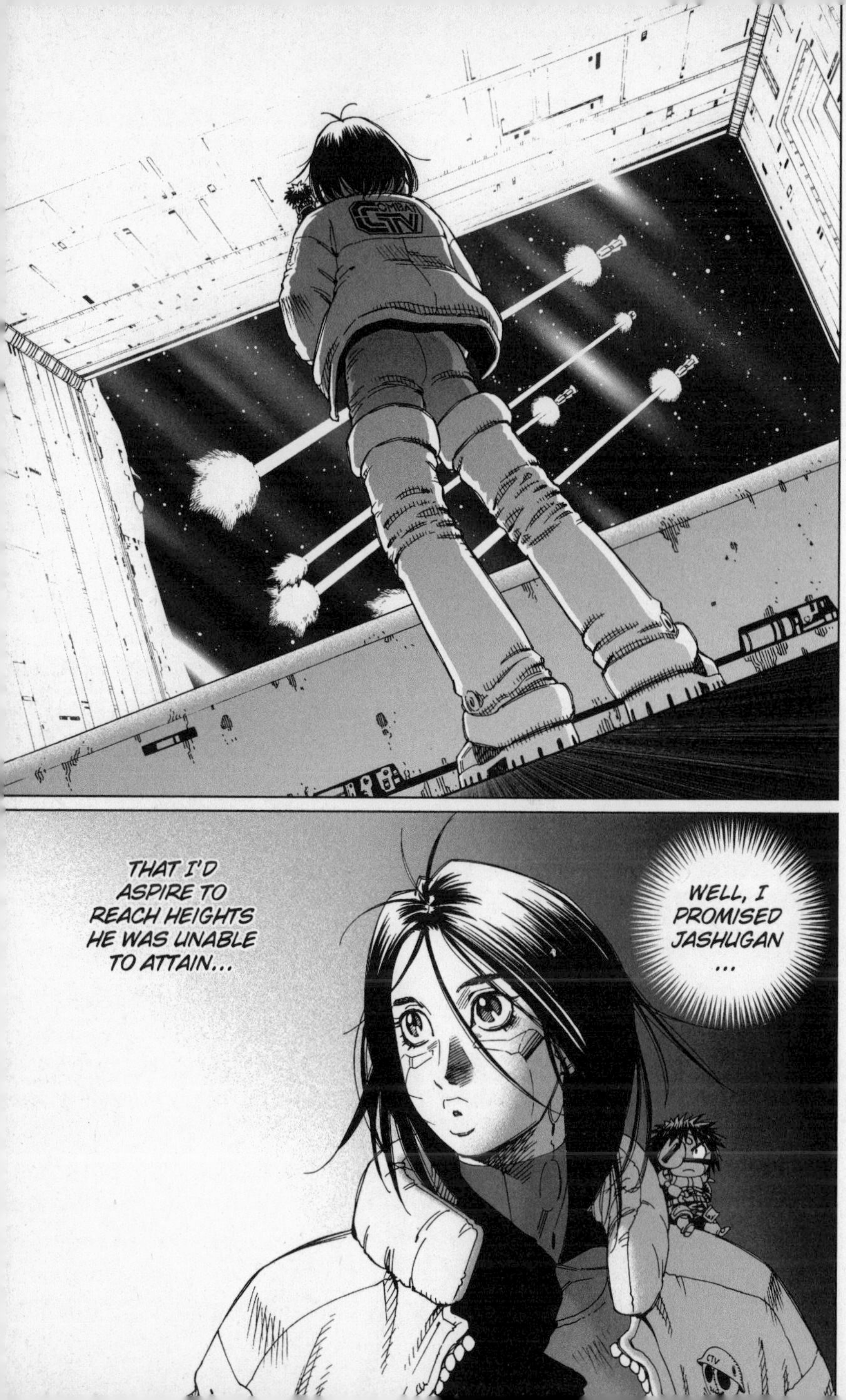
COMBAT CTV
WELL, I PROMISED JASHUGAN ...
THAT I'D ASPIRE TO REACH HEIGHTS HE WAS UNABLE TO ATTAIN...

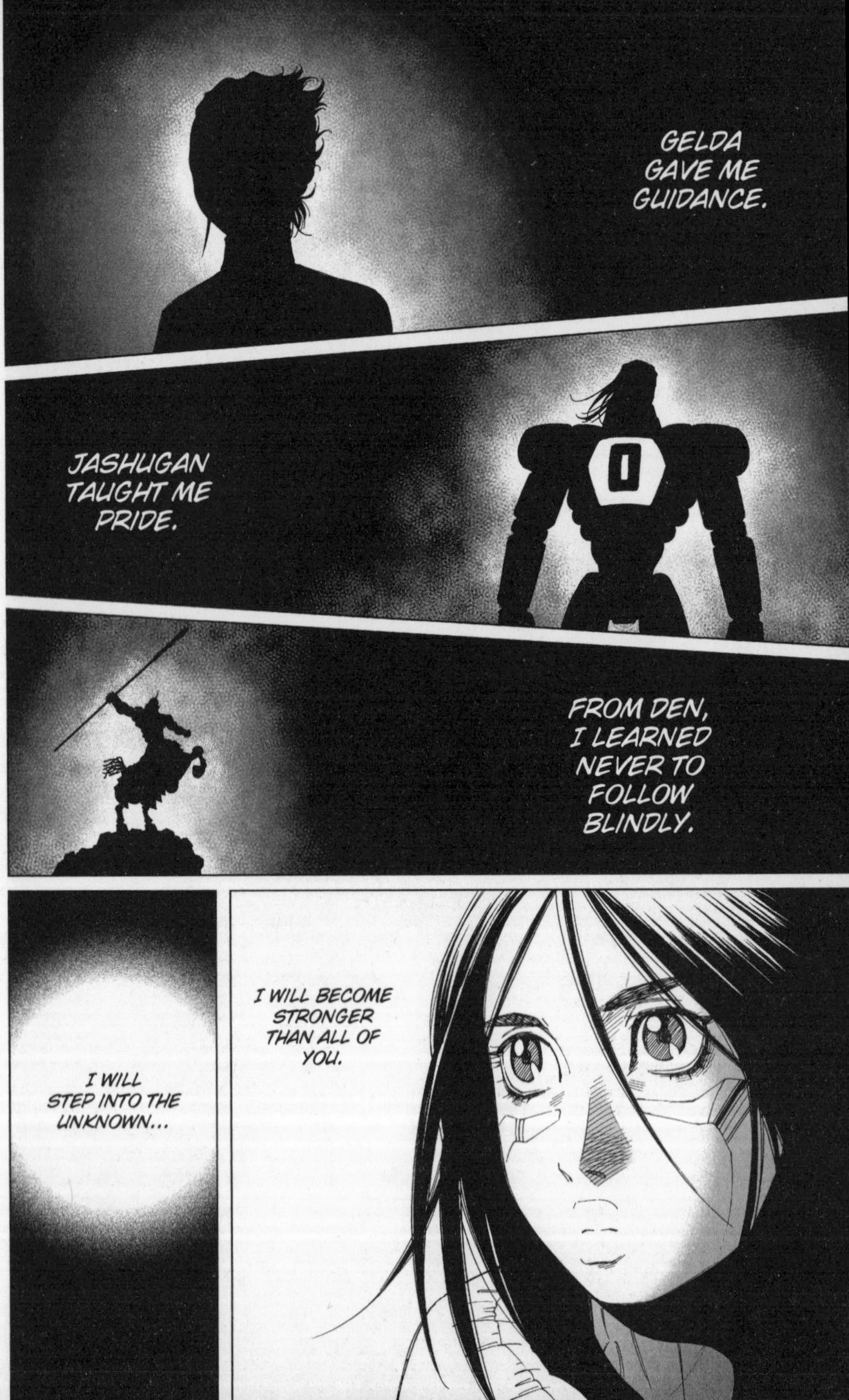
GELDA GAVE ME GUIDANCE.
JASHUGAN TAUGHT ME PRIDE.
FROM DEN, I LEARNED NEVER TO FOLLOW BLINDLY.
I WILL BECOME STRONGER THAN ALL OF YOU.
I WILL STEP INTO THE UNKNOWN...

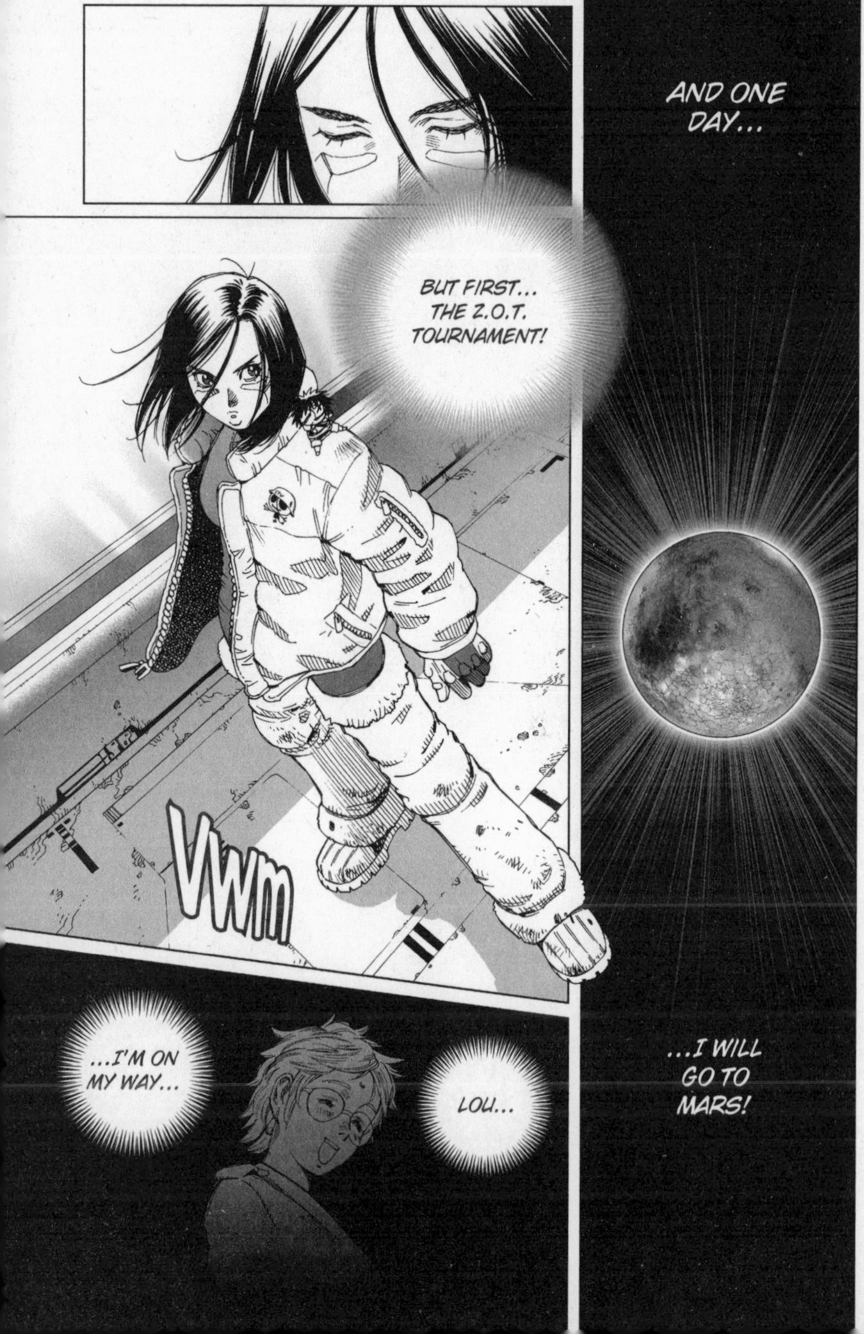
AND ONE DAY...
...I WILL GO TO MARS!
BUT FIRST... THE Z.O.T. TOURNAMENT!
VWM
...I'M ON MY WAY...
LOU...

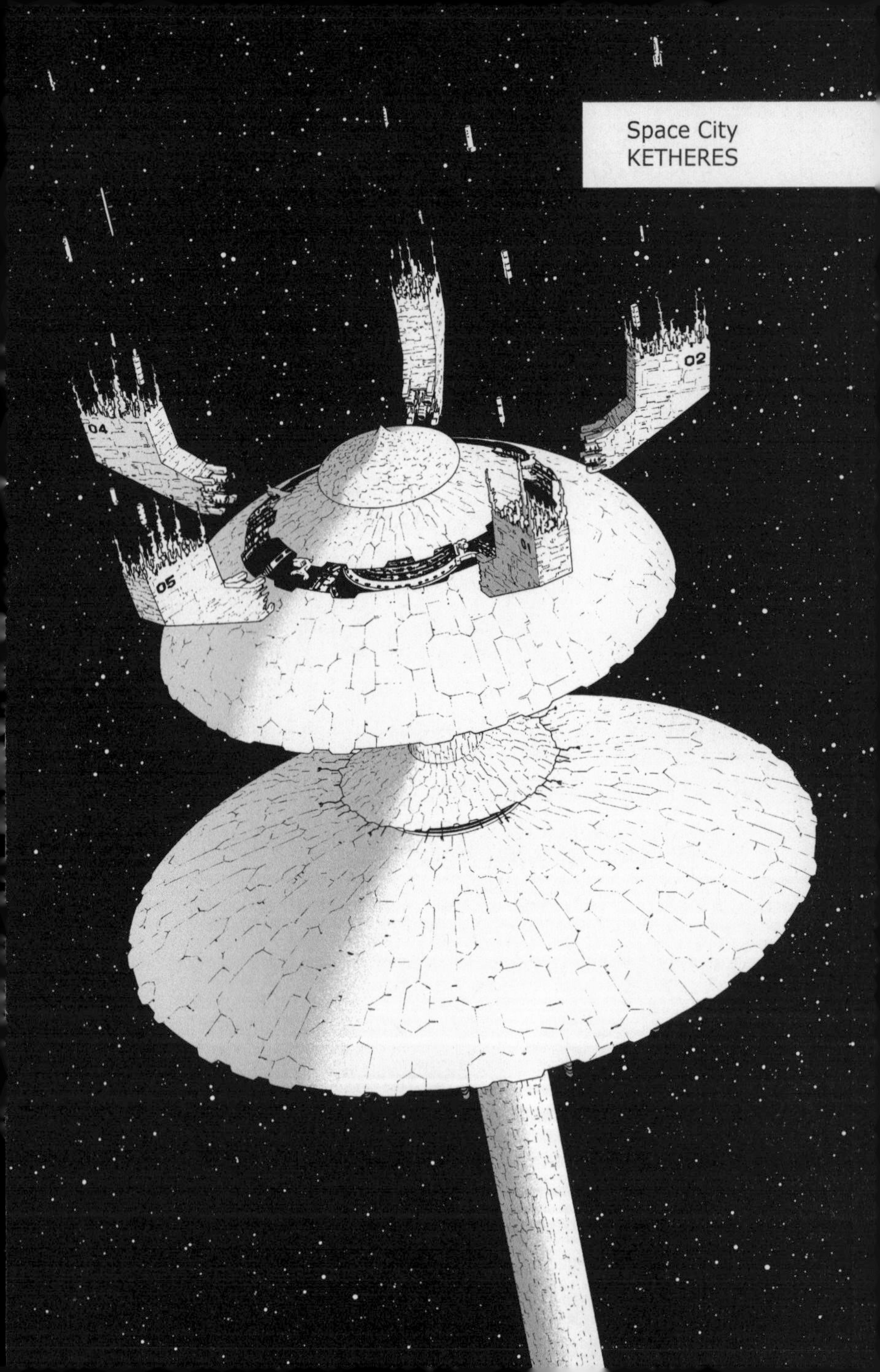
Space City
KETHERES
02
04
01
05

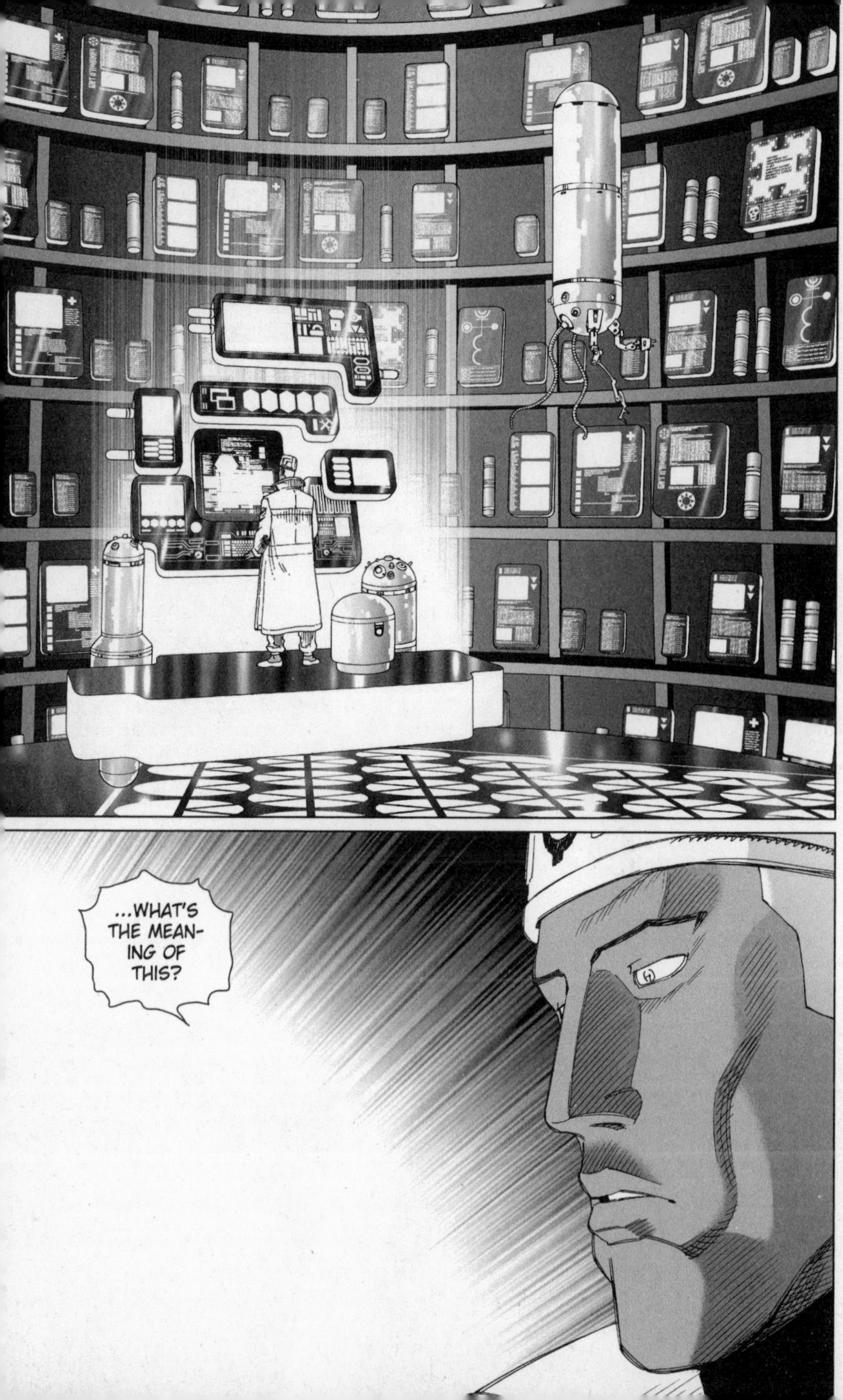
...WHAT'S THE MEAN-ING OF THIS?

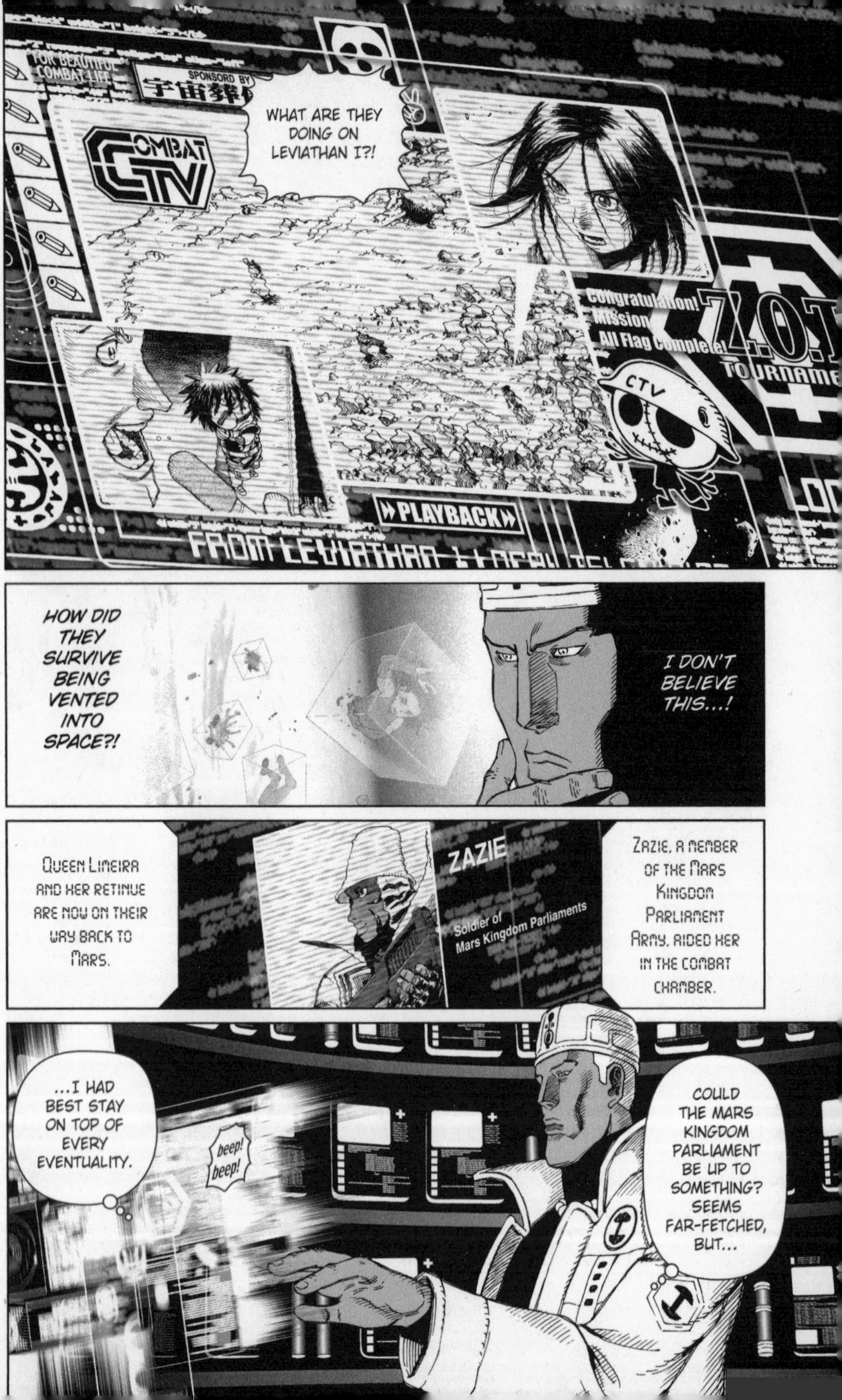

SPONSORED BY
FOR BEAUTIFUL COMBAT LIFE
WHAT ARE THEY DOING ON LEVIATHAN I?!
COMBAT CTV
Congratulation! Mission All Flag Complete!
TOURNAME
CTV
PLAYBACK
I DON'T BELIEVE THIS...!
HOW DID THEY SURVIVE BEING VENTED INTO SPACE?!
Zazie, a member of the Mars Kingdom Parliament Army, aided her in the combat chamber.
ZAZIE
Soldier of Mars Kingdom Parliaments
Queen Limeira and her retinue are now on their way back to Mars.
COULD THE MARS KINGDOM PARLIAMENT BE UP TO SOMETHING? SEEMS FAR-FETCHED, BUT...
beep! beep!
...I HAD BEST STAY ON TOP OF EVERY EVENTUALITY.

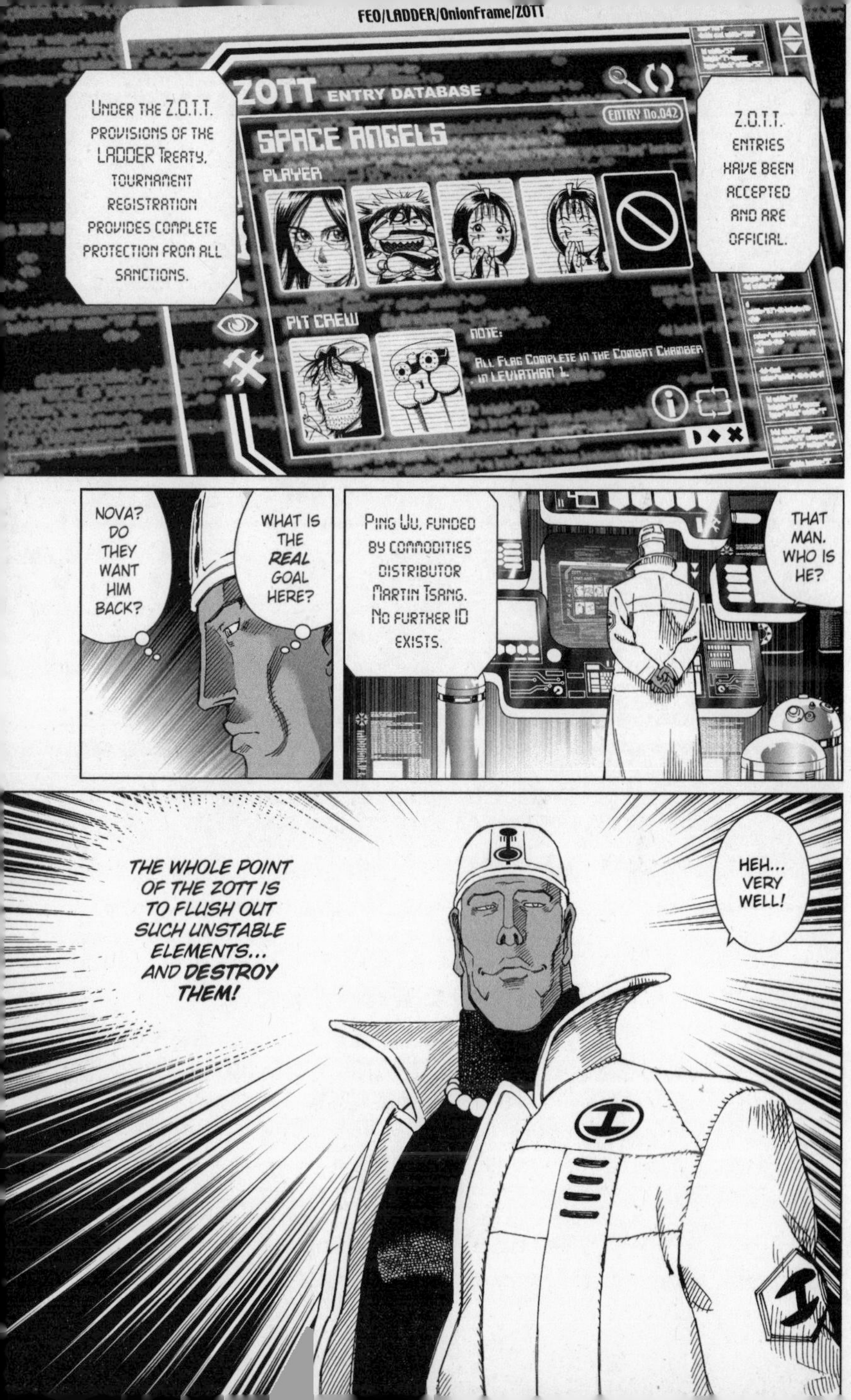
FEO/LADDER/OnionFrame/ZOTT
Z.O.T.T. entries have been accepted and are official.
Under the Z.O.T.T. provisions of the LADDER Treaty, tournament registration provides complete protection from all sanctions.
ZOTT ENTRY DATABASE
ENTRY No.042
SPACE ANGELS
PLAYER
PIT CREW
NOTE:
All Flag Complete in the Combat Chamber in LEVIATHAN 1.
That man. Who is he?
Ping Wu, funded by commodities distributor Martin Tsang. No further ID exists.
What is the real goal here?
Nova? Do they want him back?
Heh... very well!
The whole point of the ZOTT is to flush out such unstable elements... and destroy them!

Zenith of Things

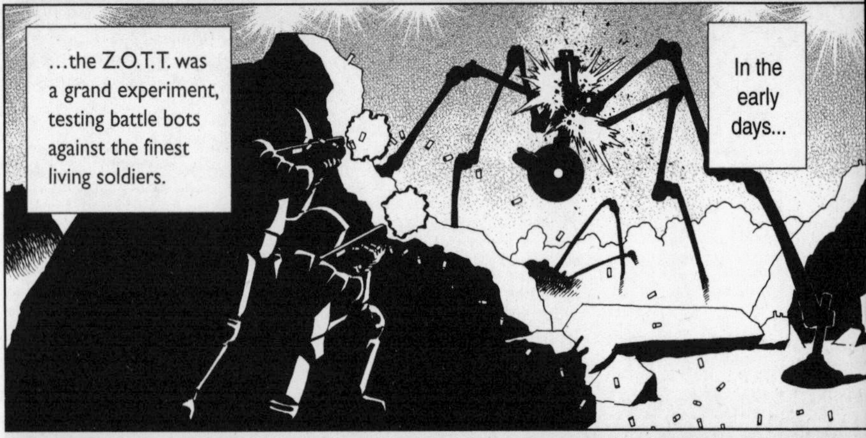
In the early days...
...the Z.O.T.T. was a grand experiment, testing battle bots against the finest living soldiers.

Year ES 491
The first open Z.O.T. Tournament is held, at the suggestion of Aga Mbadi.

Z.O.T. Tournament Rules

- Five players per team. All players may fight simultaneously.
- No limit to the number of weapons.
- Gunpowder allotment = 5% of the total weight of all players on a team.
- Player height range: 5 centimeters to 50 meters. Weight limit: 500 tons.
- Players must be fully autonomous robots, cyborgs, or humans. Remote control from outside the battlefield is not permitted.
- Battle time = 60 minutes. The battle is over when all members of a team are incapacitated, dead, or forfeit.
- As long as they obey the rules above, no player will be punished for any act in a match, even in case of the death of a player.

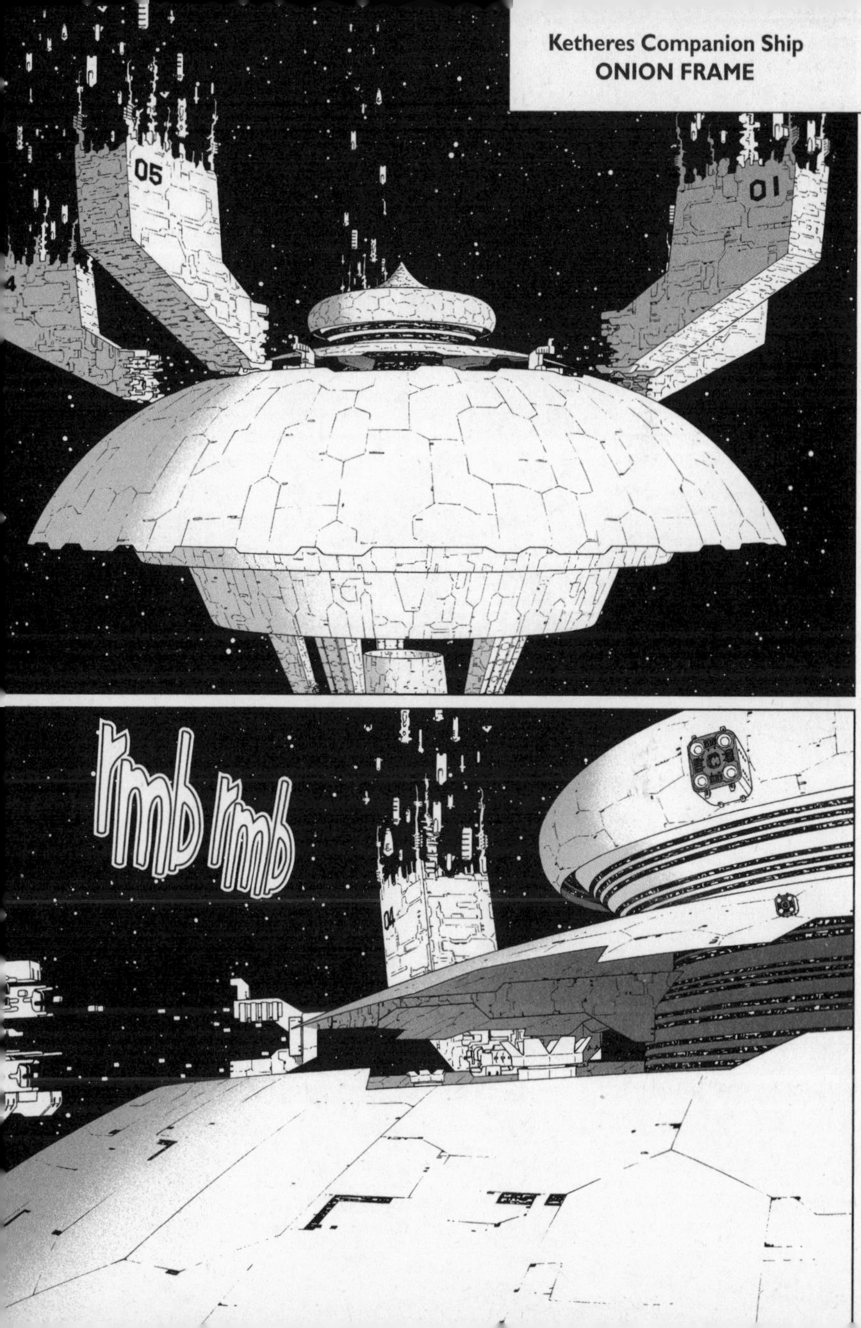
Ketheres Companion Ship
ONION FRAME
05
01
rmb rmb
04

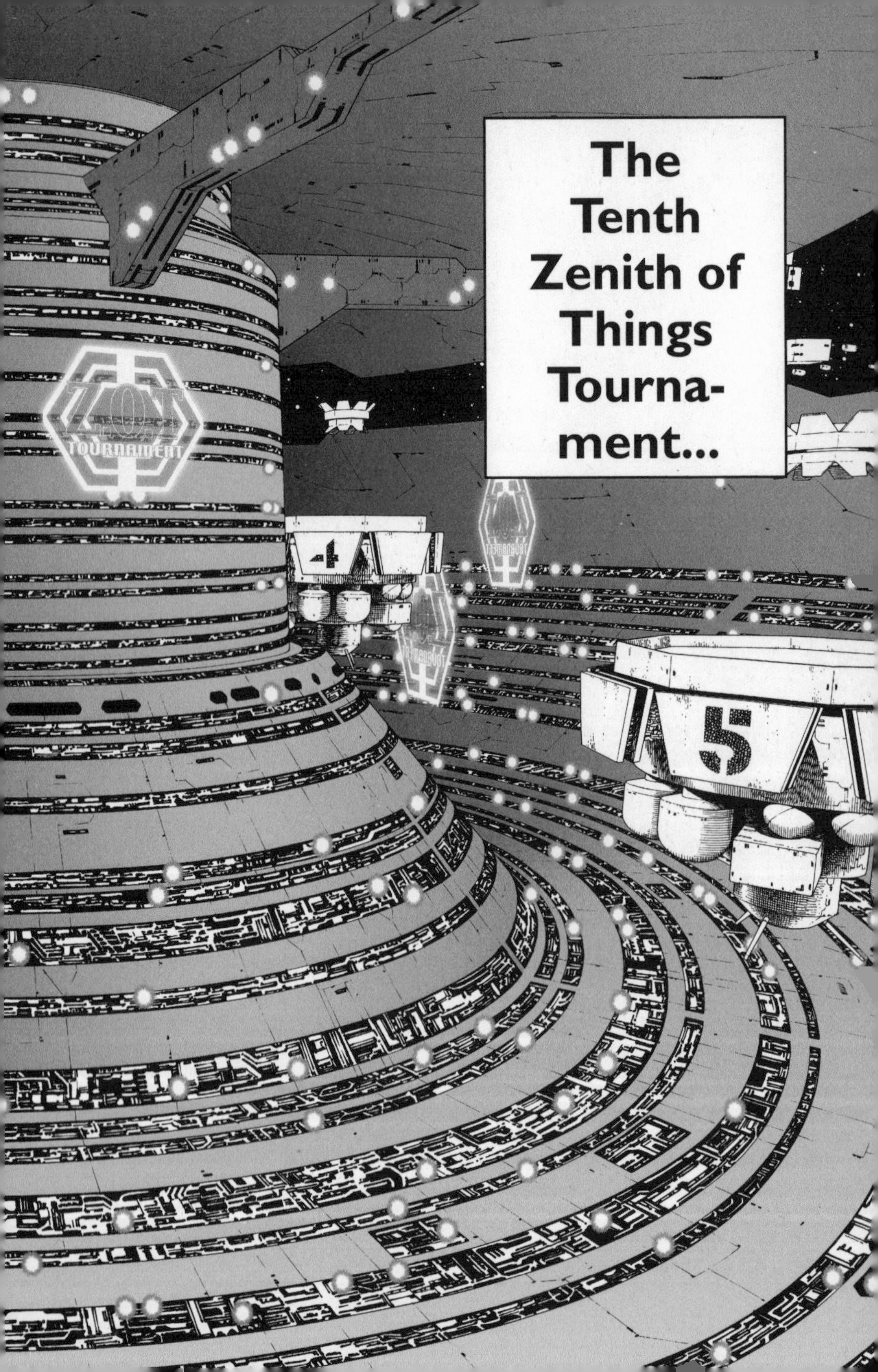
The Tenth Zenith of Things Tournament...
TOURNAMENT
4
5

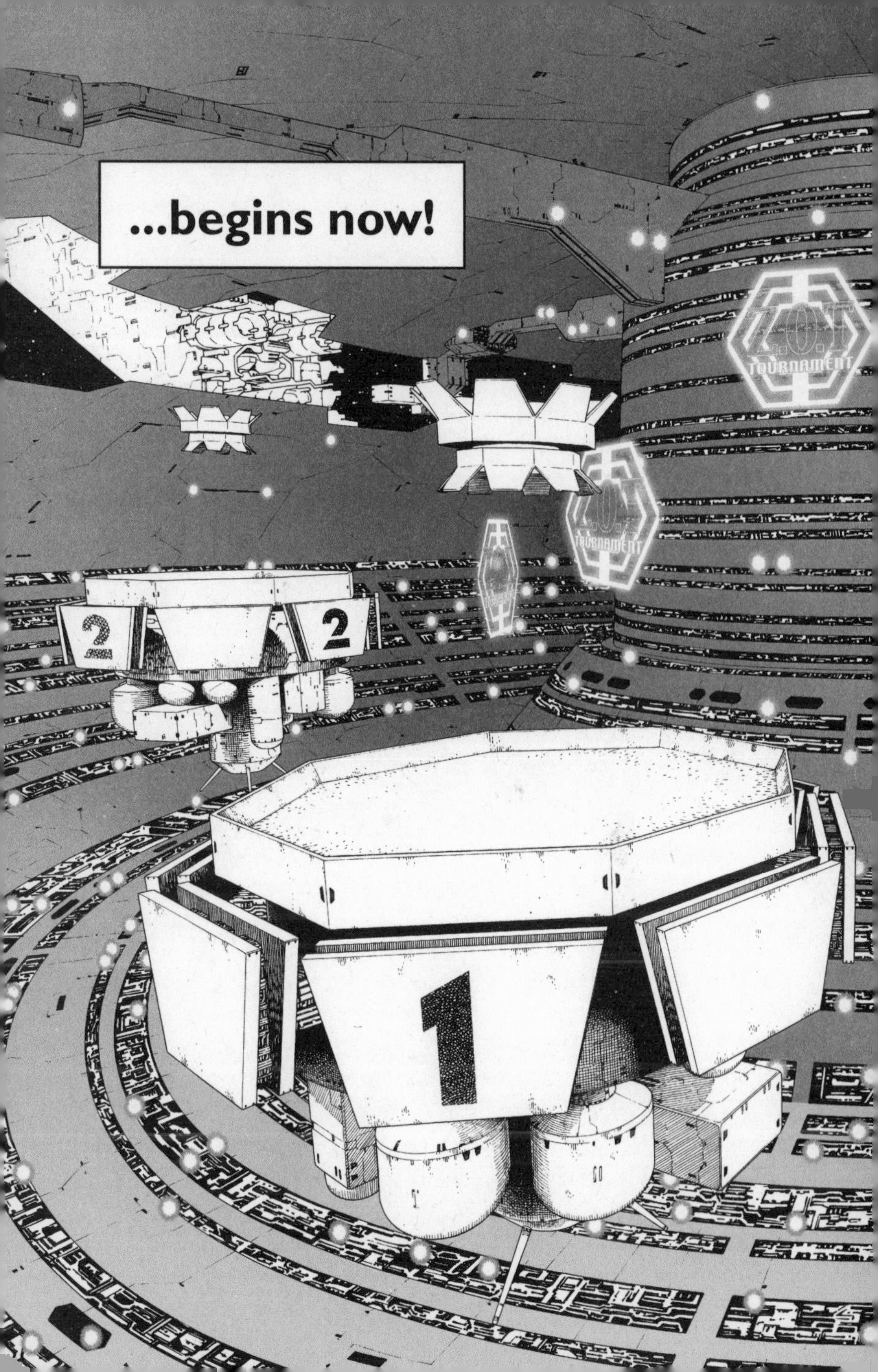
...begins now!
Z.O.I. TOURNAMENT
Z.O.I. TOURNAMENT
2
2
1

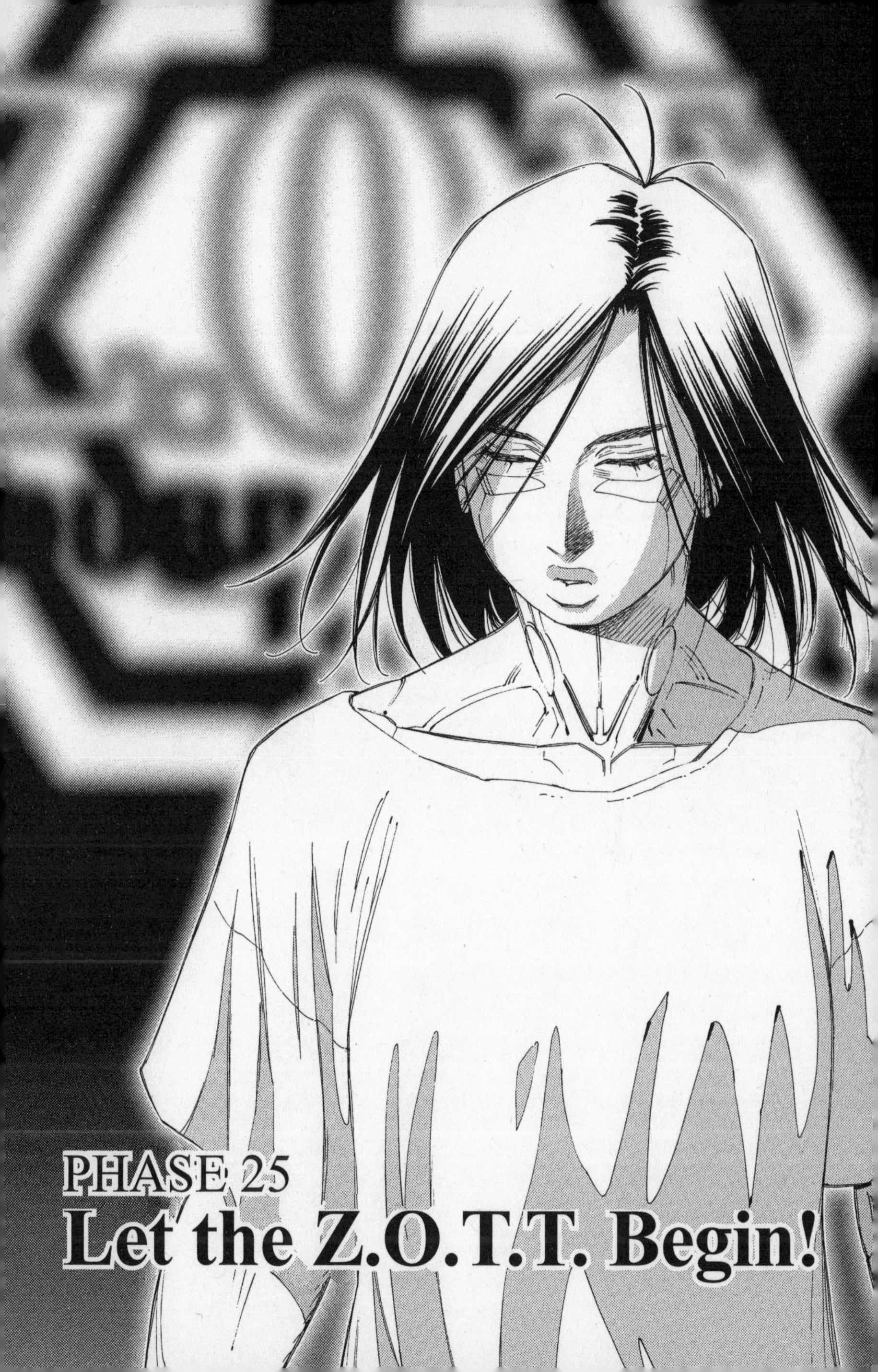
PHASE 25
Let the Z.O.T.T. Begin!

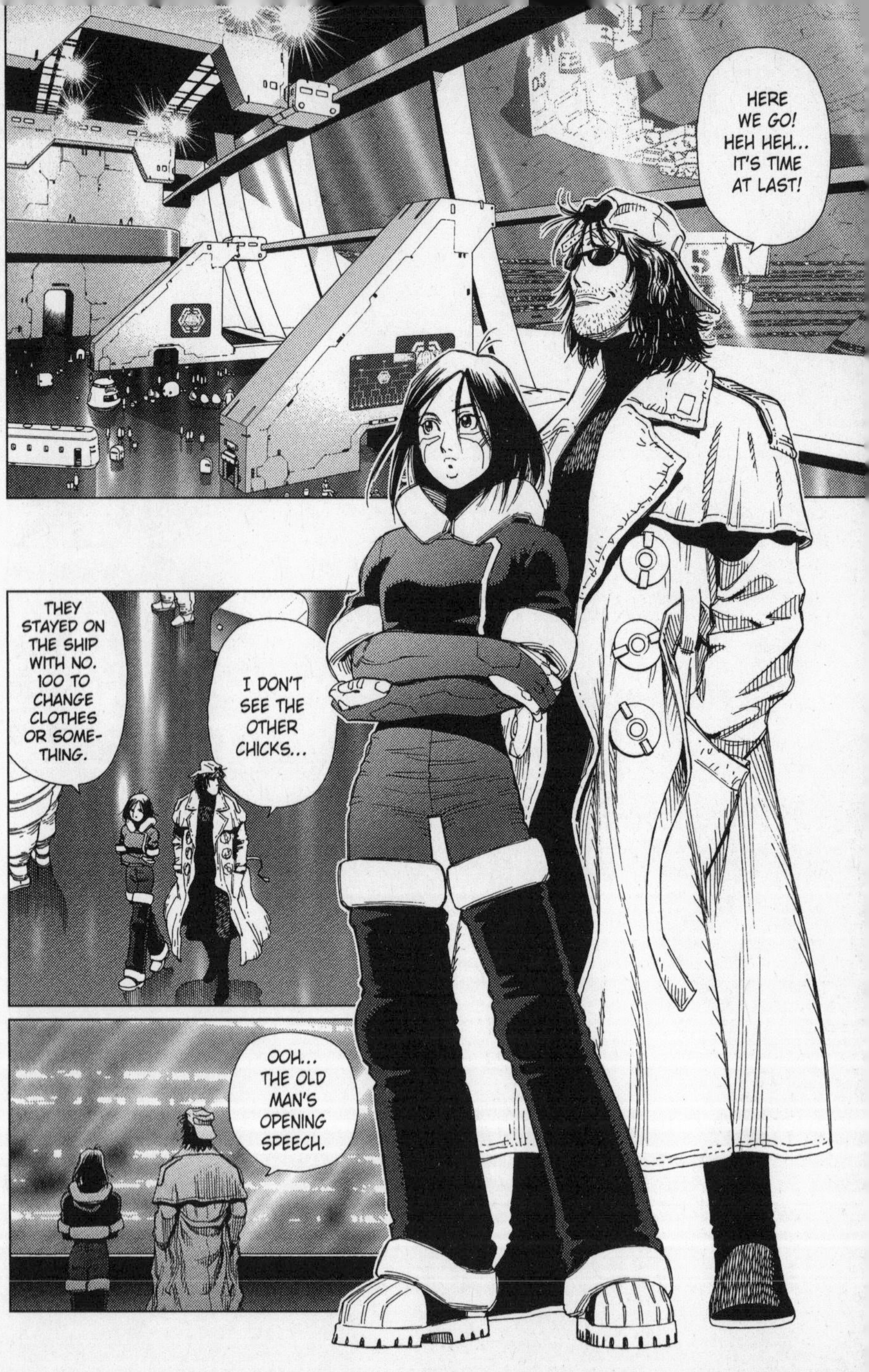
HERE WE GO! HEH HEH... IT'S TIME AT LAST!
I DON'T SEE THE OTHER CHICKS...
THEY STAYED ON THE SHIP WITH NO. 100 TO CHANGE CLOTHES OR SOME-THING.
OOH... THE OLD MAN'S OPENING SPEECH.

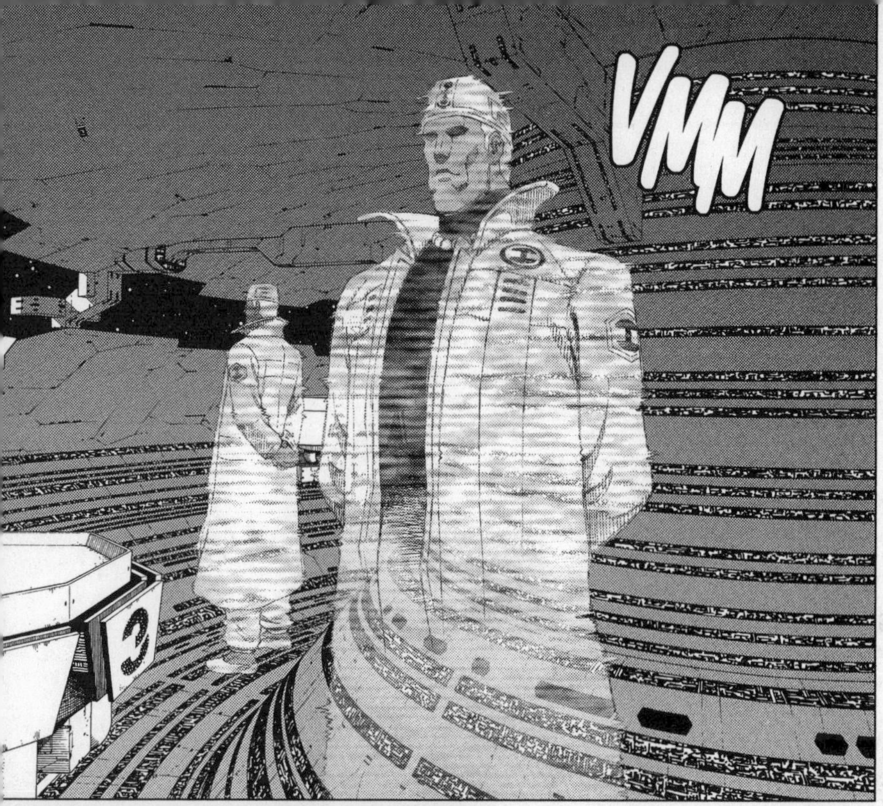
VMM
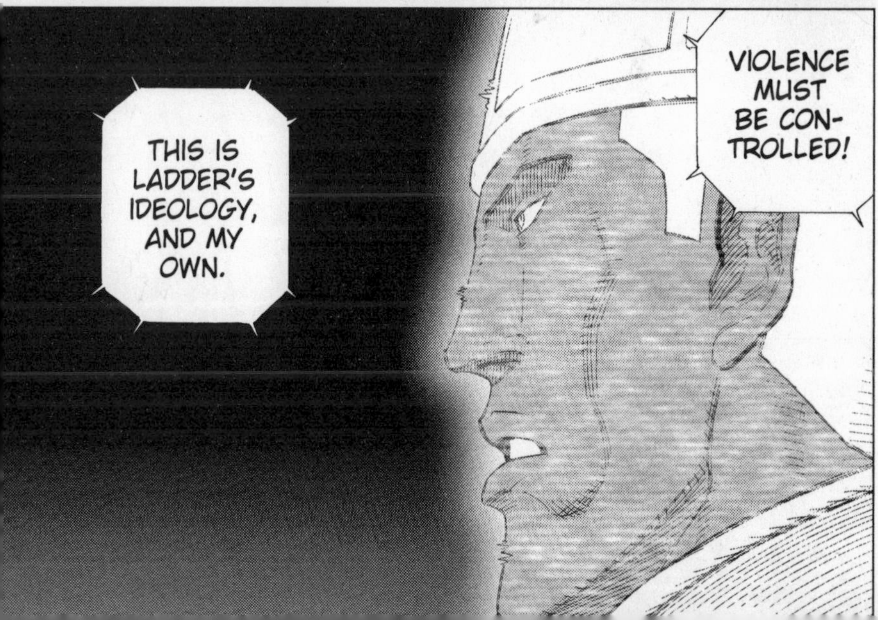
VIOLENCE MUST BE CON- TROLLED!
THIS IS LADDER'S IDEOLOGY, AND MY OWN.

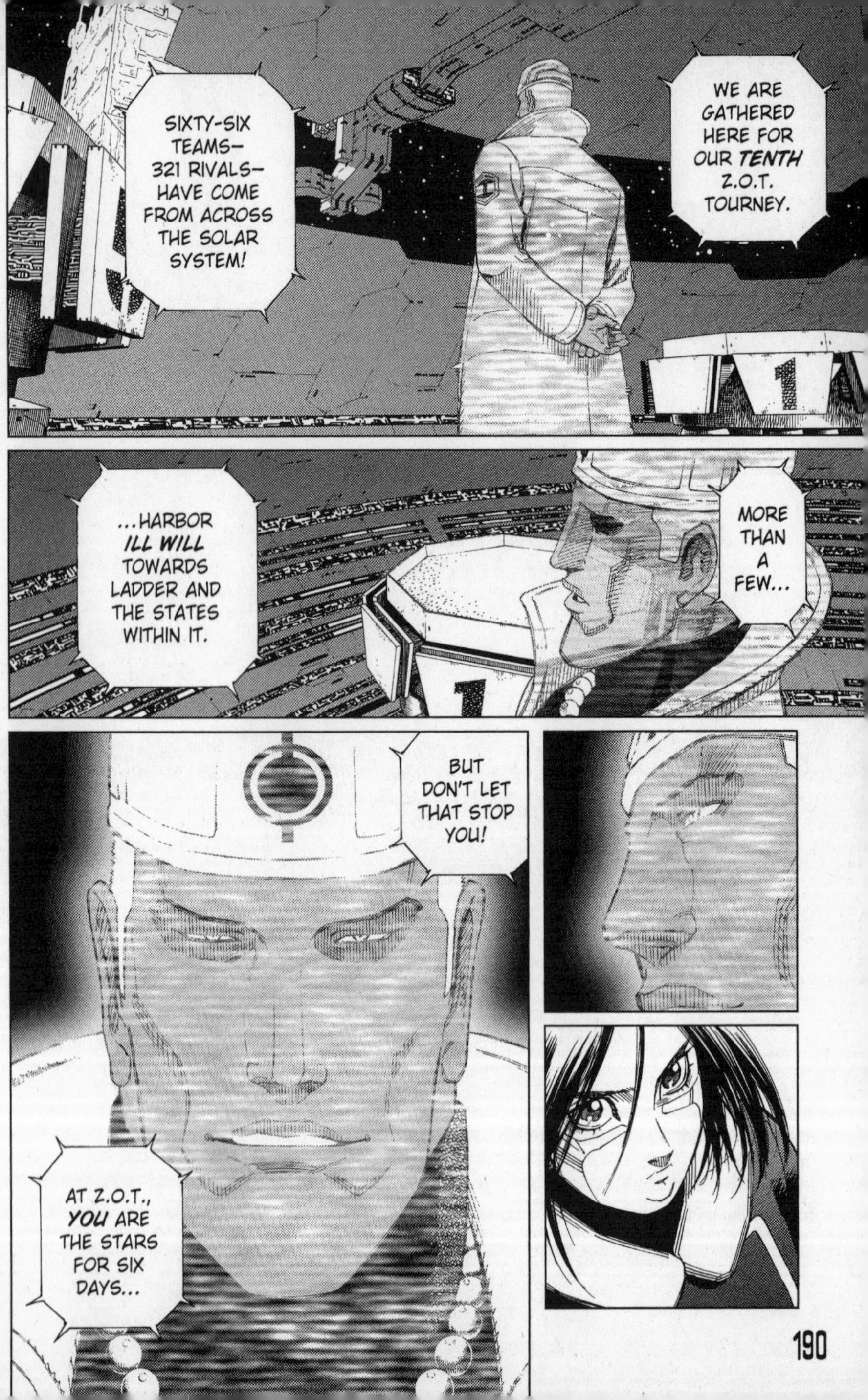
WE ARE GATHERED HERE FOR OUR *TENTH* Z.O.T. TOURNEY.
SIXTY-SIX TEAMS—321 RIVALS—HAVE COME FROM ACROSS THE SOLAR SYSTEM!
MORE THAN A FEW...
...HARBOR *ILL WILL* TOWARDS LADDER AND THE STATES WITHIN IT.
BUT DON'T LET THAT STOP YOU!
AT Z.O.T., *YOU* ARE THE STARS FOR SIX DAYS...

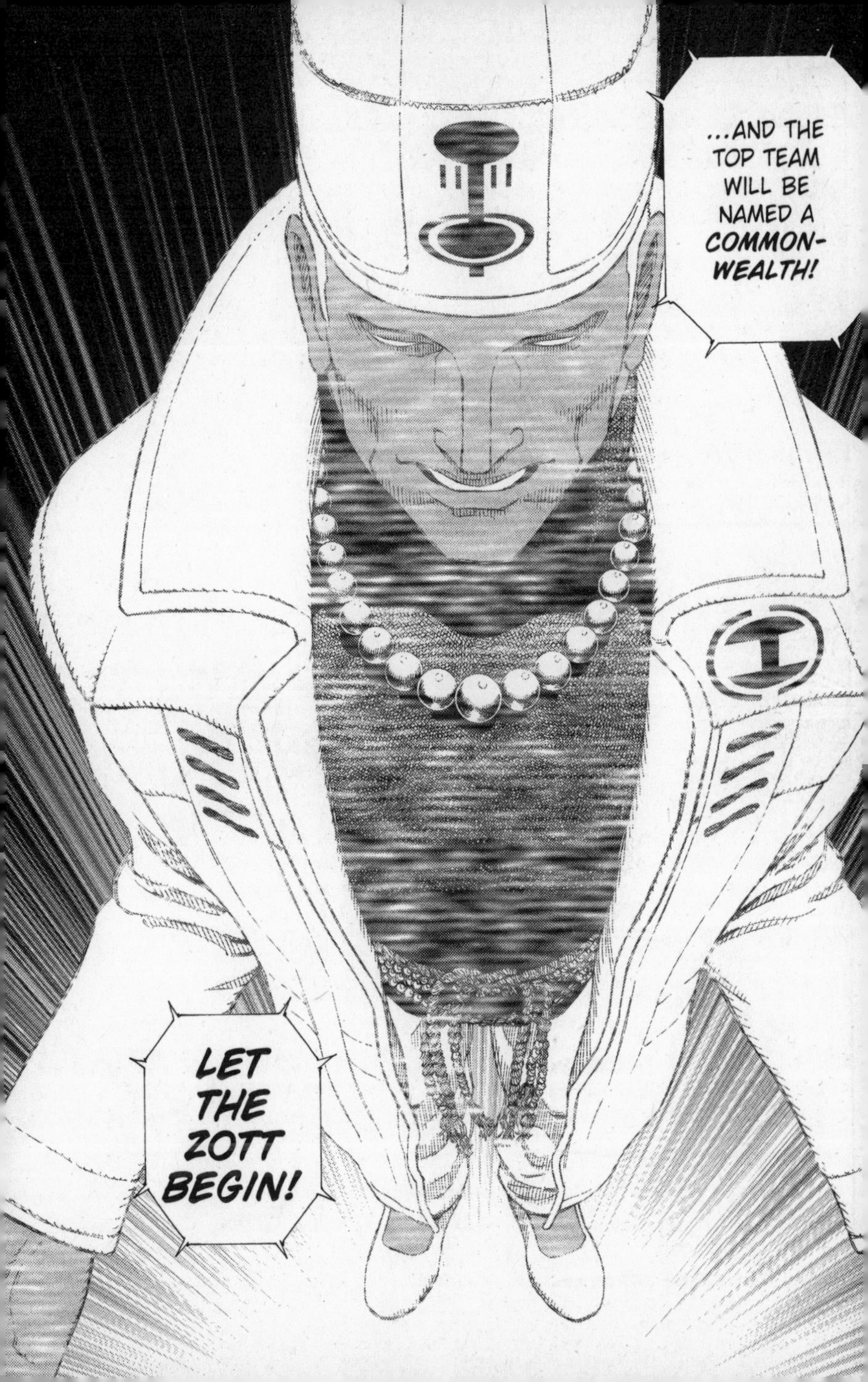
...AND THE TOP TEAM WILL BE NAMED A COMMON-WEALTH!
LET THE ZOTT BEGIN!

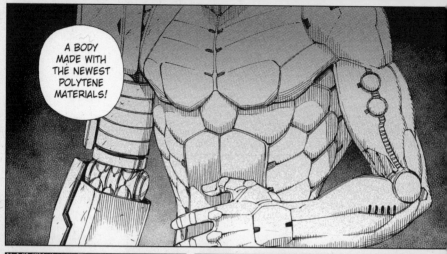

A BODY MADE WITH THE NEWEST POLYTENE MATERIALS!

ka-chk

I LIKE IT!

kl ek

heh!

THIS'LL EQUAL EVEN ALITA'S *IMAGINOS* BODY!

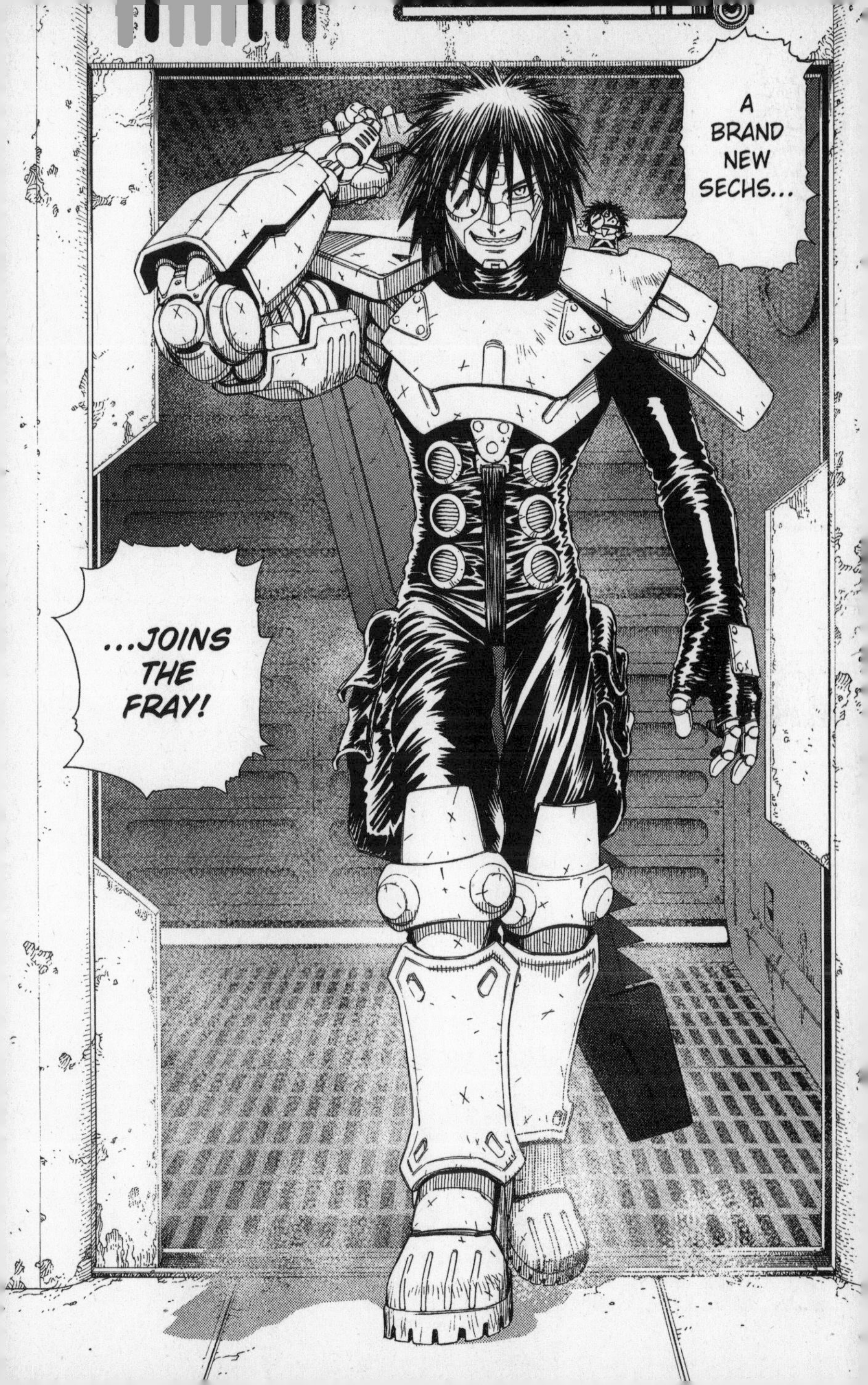
A BRAND NEW SECHS...
...JOINS THE FRAY!

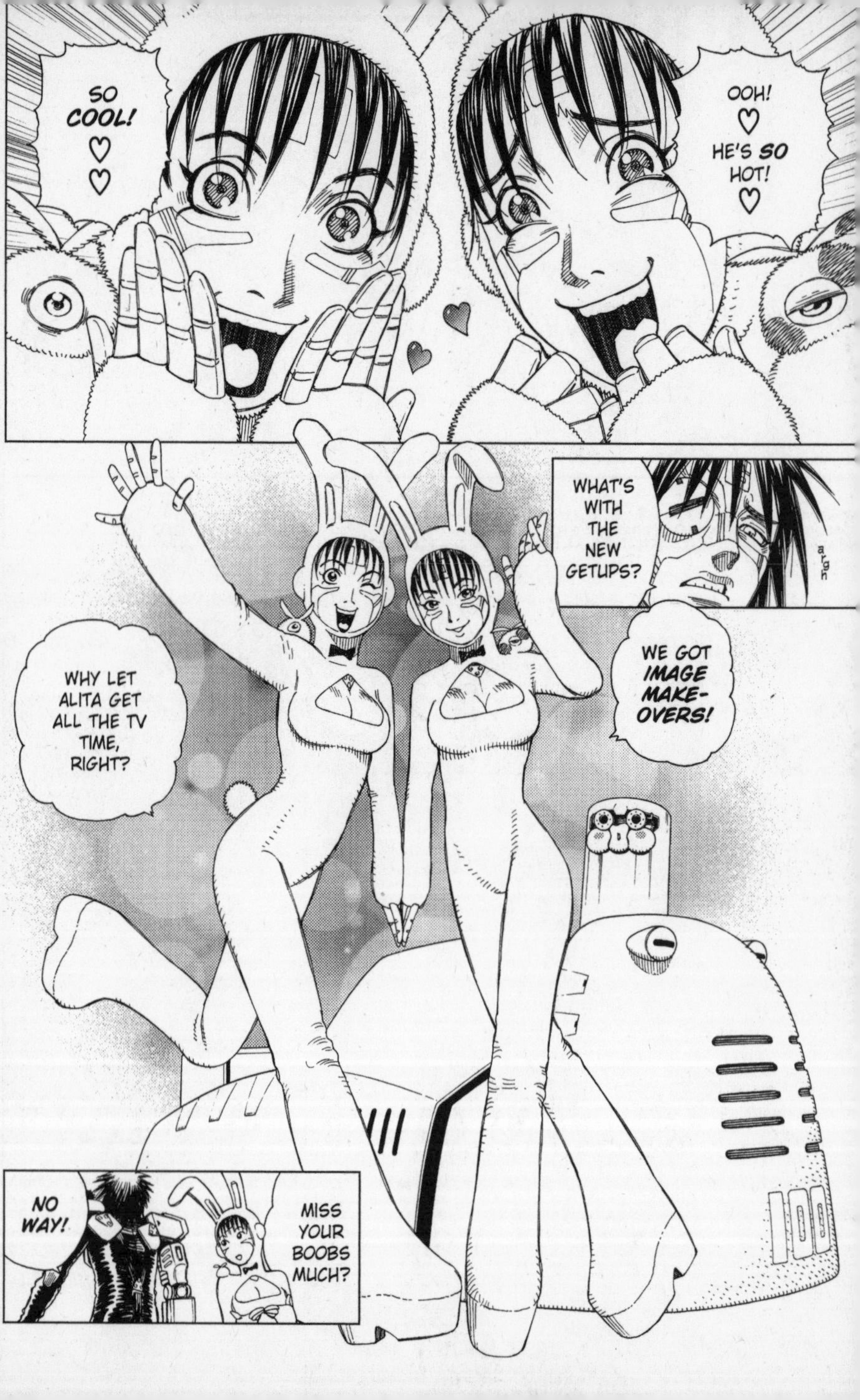
OOH! ♡ HE'S SO HOT! ♡
SO COOL! ♡ ♡
WHAT'S WITH THE NEW GETUPS?
WE GOT IMAGE MAKE-OVERS!
WHY LET ALITA GET ALL THE TV TIME, RIGHT?
MISS YOUR BOOBS MUCH?
NO WAY!

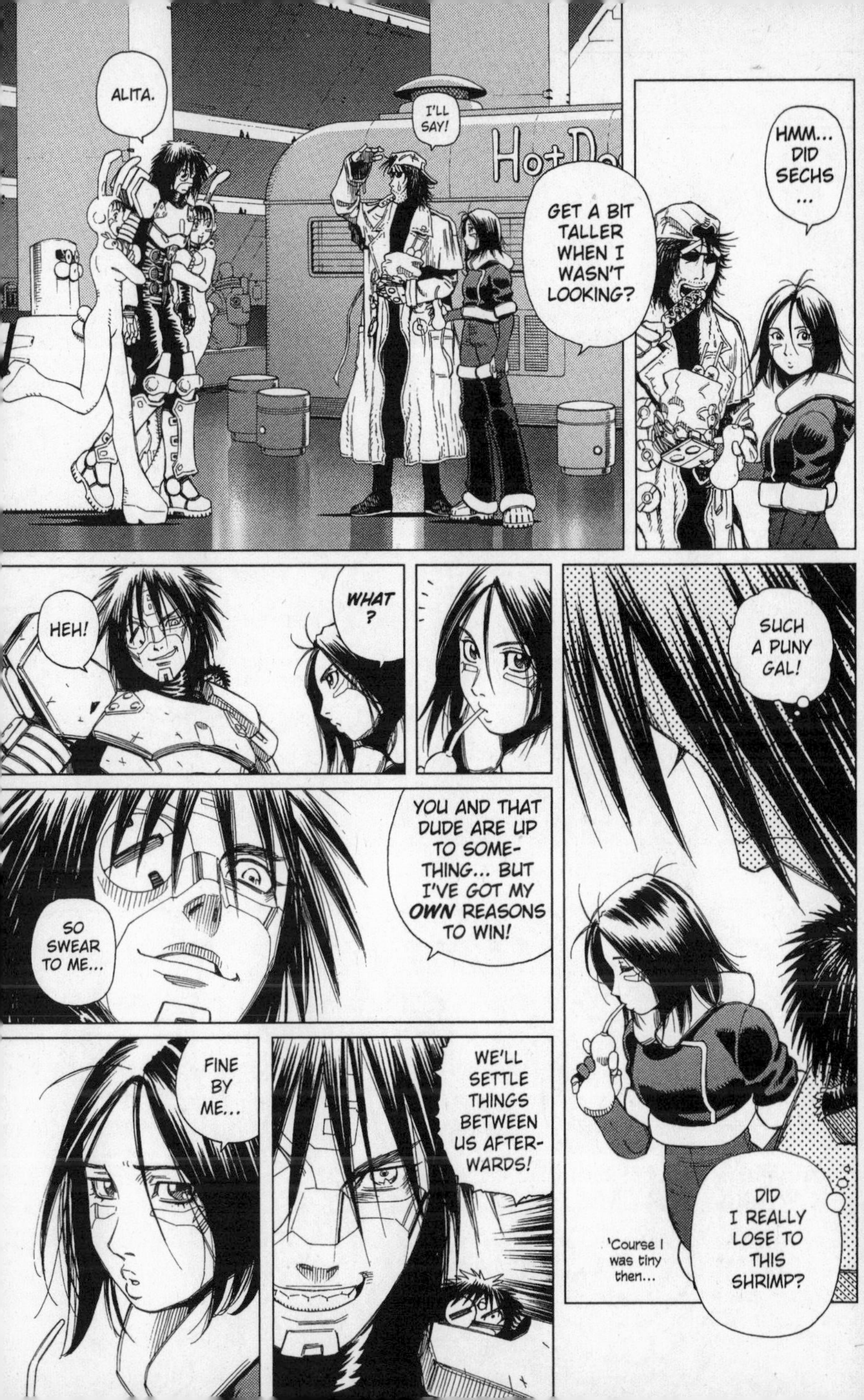
HMM... DID SECHS ...
GET A BIT TALLER WHEN I WASN'T LOOKING?
I'LL SAY!
ALITA.
SUCH A PUNY GAL!
DID I REALLY LOSE TO THIS SHRIMP?
'Course I was tiny then...
WHAT ?
HEH!
YOU AND THAT DUDE ARE UP TO SOME-THING... BUT I'VE GOT MY OWN REASONS TO WIN!
SO SWEAR TO ME...
WE'LL SETTLE THINGS BETWEEN US AFTER-WARDS!
FINE BY ME...

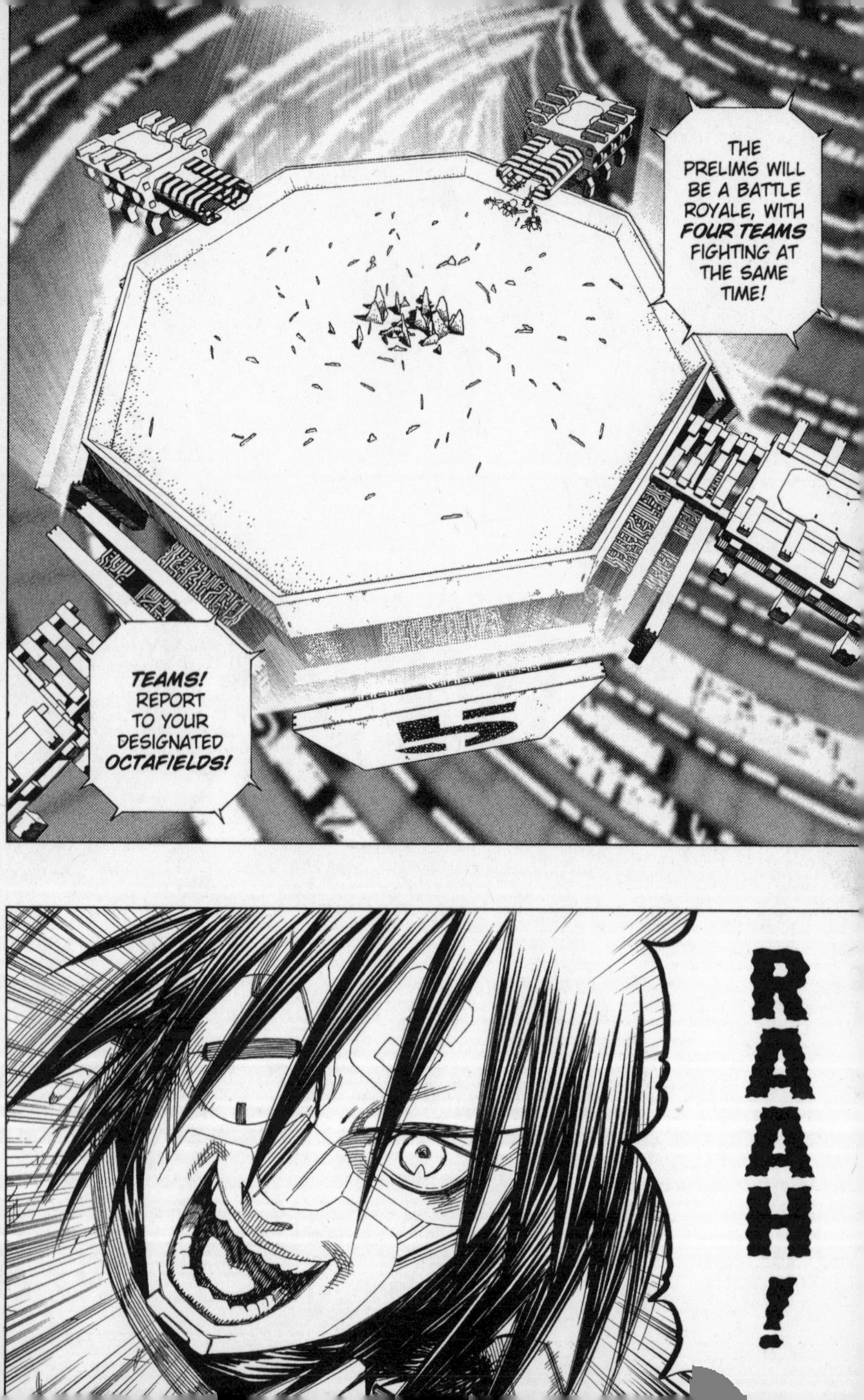
THE PRELIMS WILL BE A BATTLE ROYALE, WITH *FOUR TEAMS* FIGHTING AT THE SAME TIME!
TEAMS! REPORT TO YOUR DESIGNATED *OCTAFIELDS!*
RAAH!

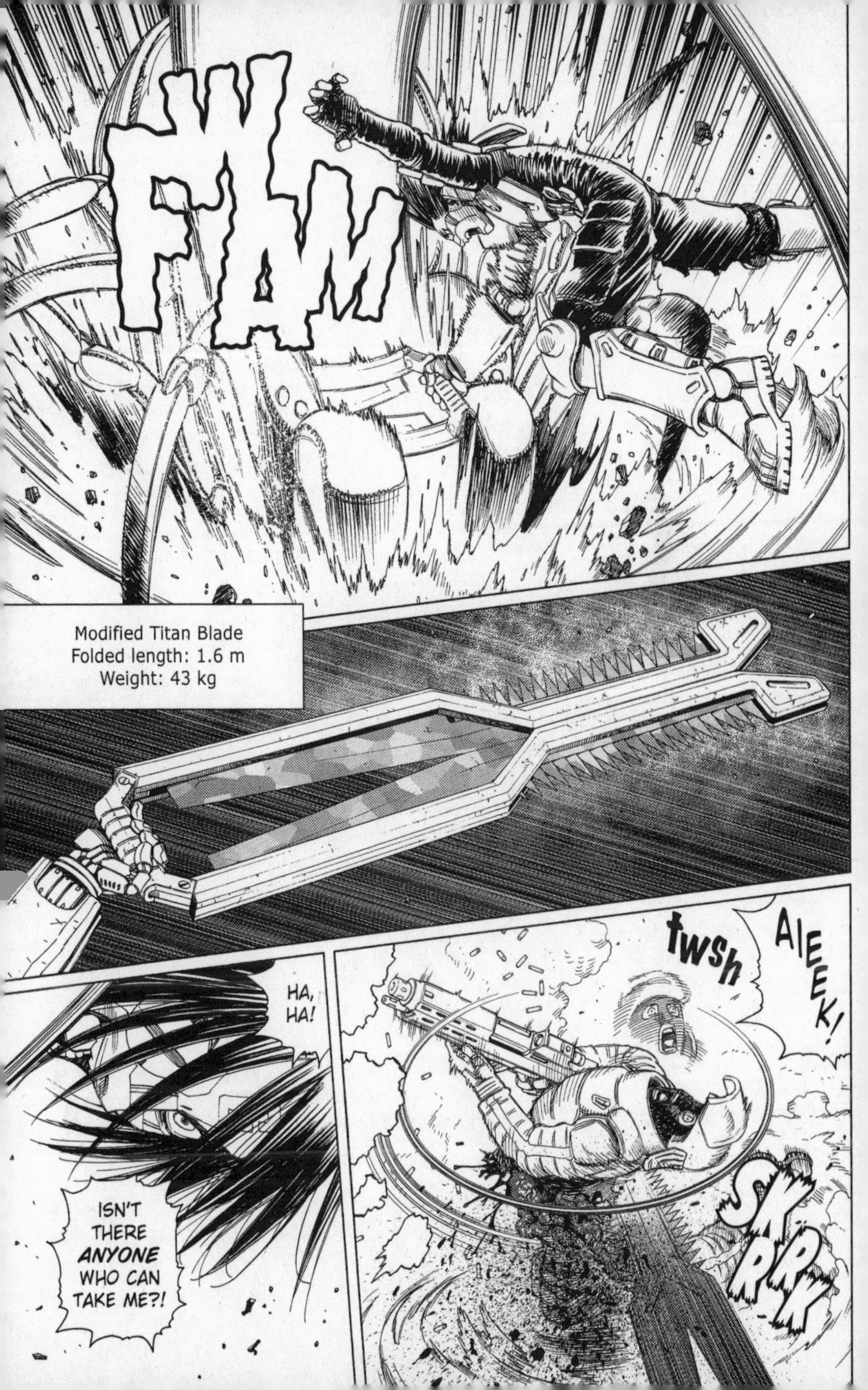
FWAM
Modified Titan Blade
Folded length: 1.6 m
Weight: 43 kg
twsh
AIEEK!
SKRRK
HA, HA!
ISN'T THERE ANYONE WHO CAN TAKE ME?!

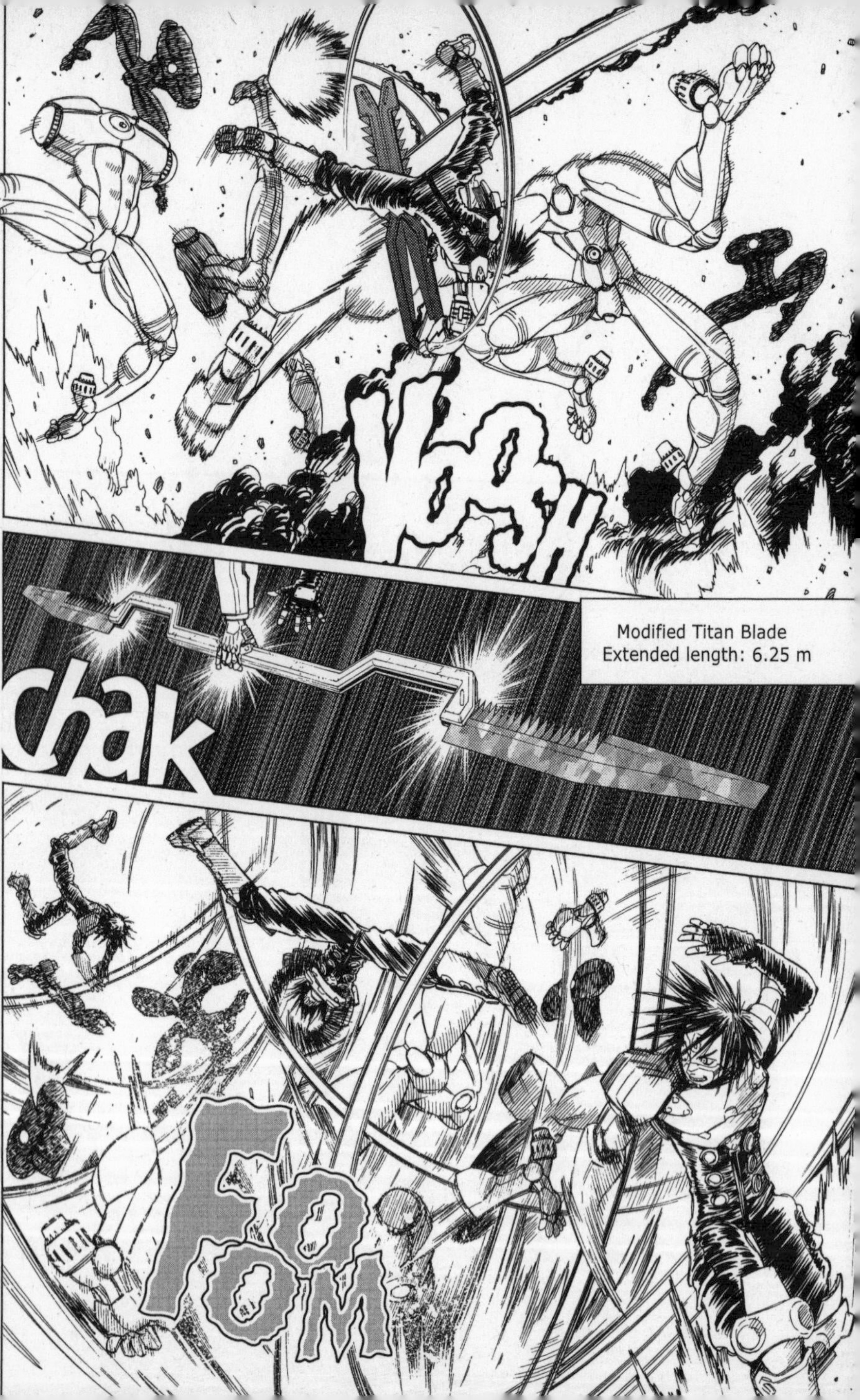
VOOSH
Modified Titan Blade
Extended length: 6.25 m
Chak
FOOM

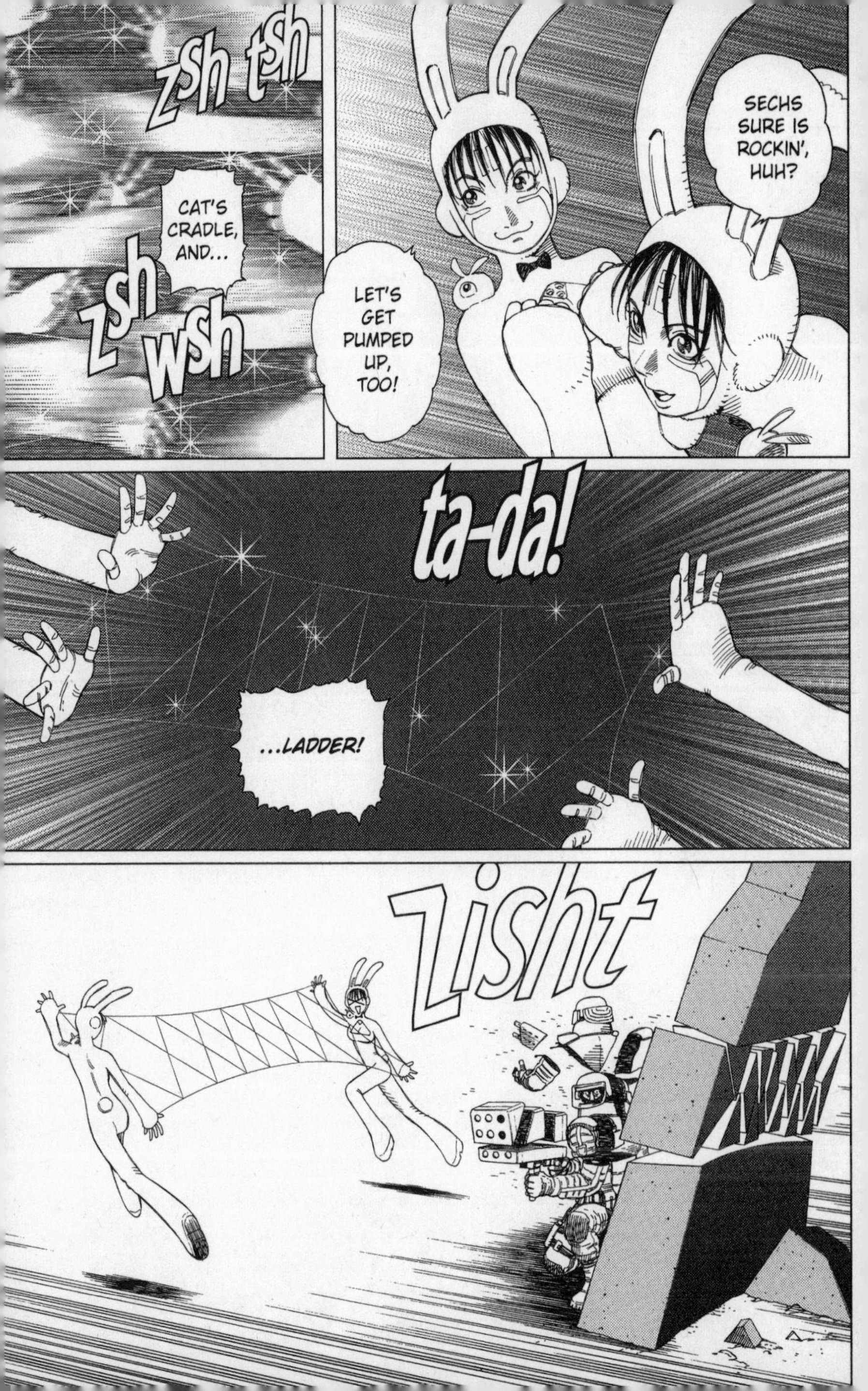
SECHS SURE IS ROCKIN', HUH?
LET'S GET PUMPED UP, TOO!
zsh tsh
CAT'S CRADLE, AND...
zsh wsh
ta-da!
...LADDER!
zisht

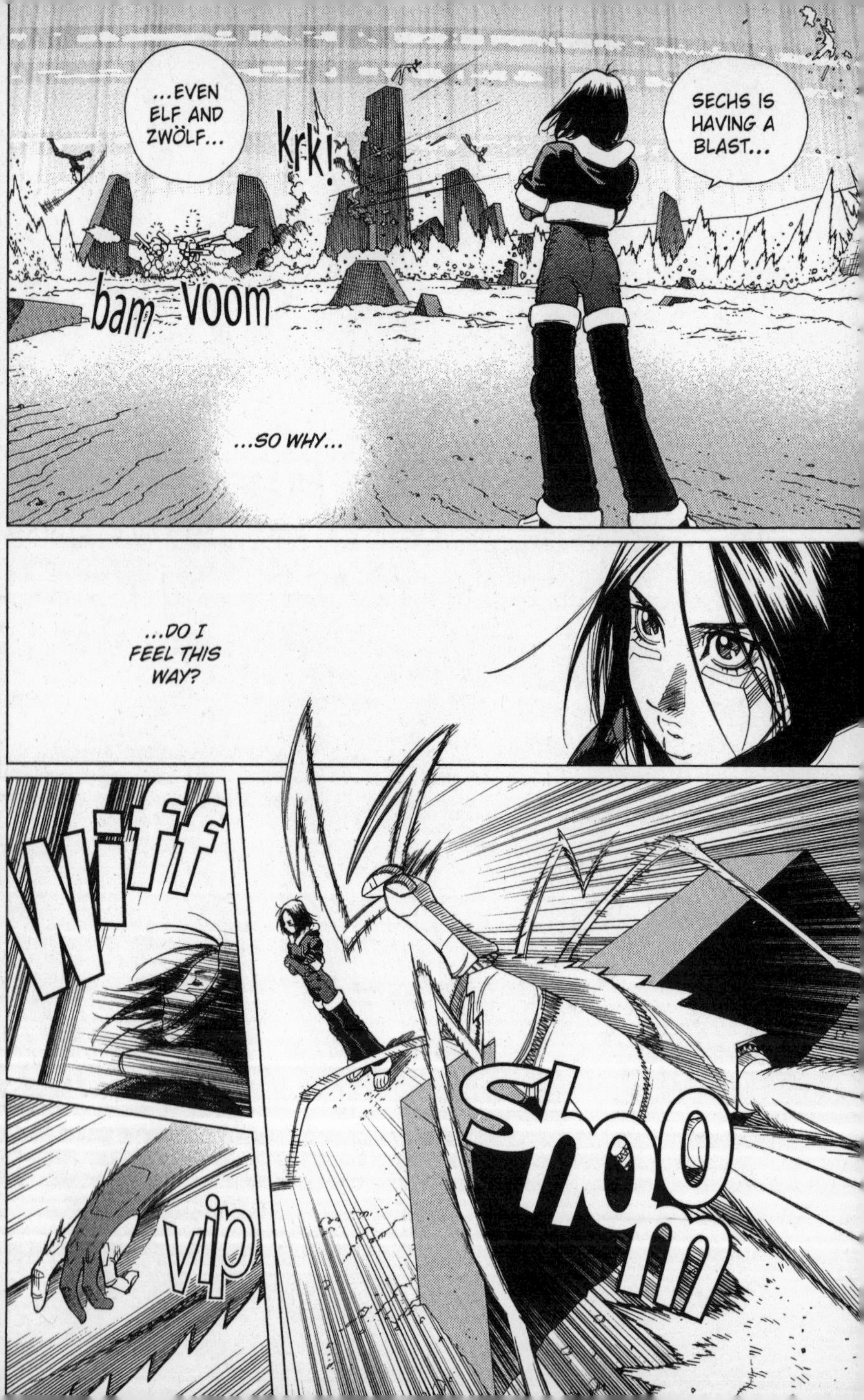
SECHS IS HAVING A BLAST...
...EVEN ELF AND ZWÖLF...
krk!
bam
voom
...SO WHY...
...DO I FEEL THIS WAY?
shoom
Wiff
vip

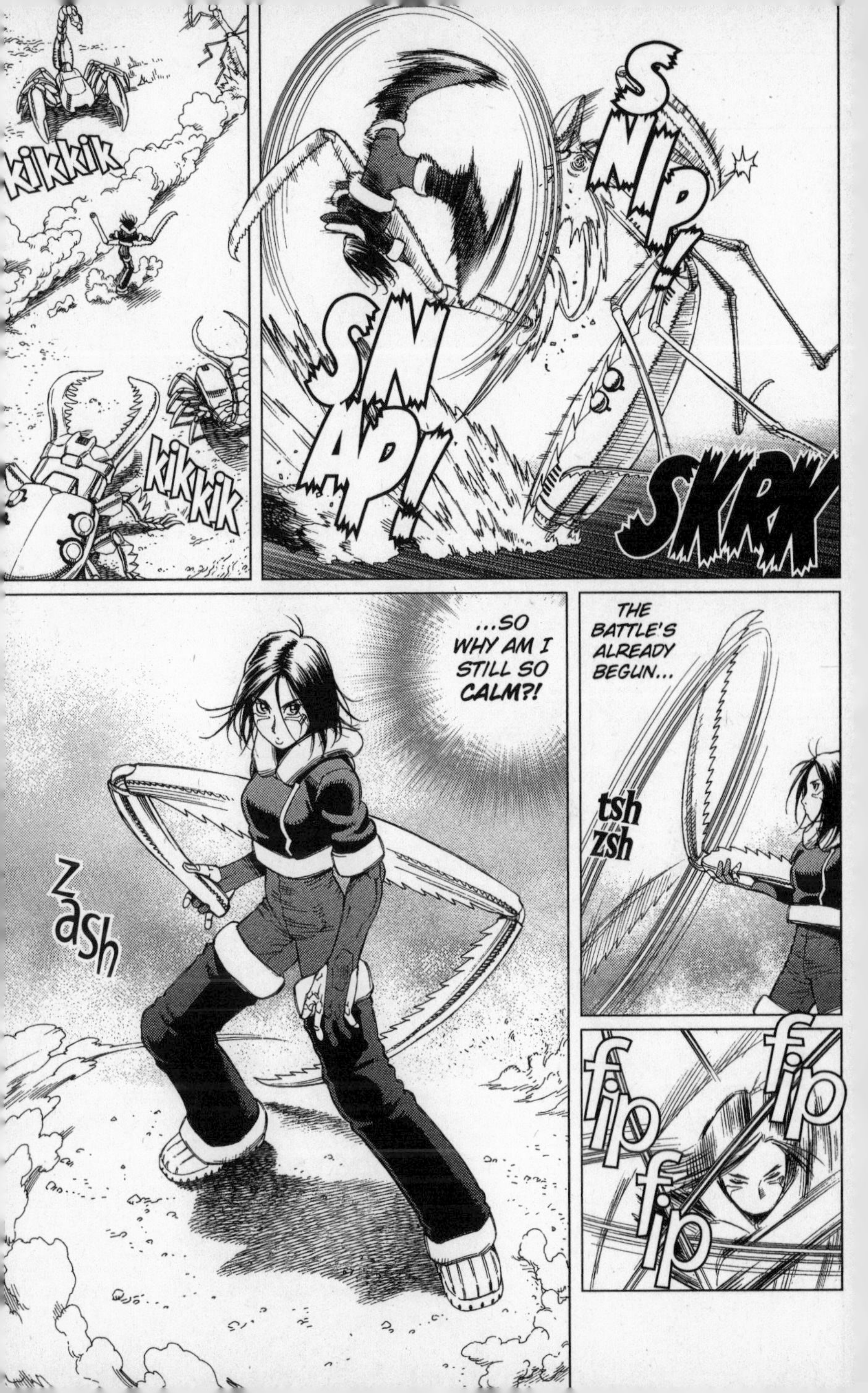
SNIP!
SNAP!
SKRAK
kikkik
kikkik
THE BATTLE'S ALREADY BEGUN...
tsh zsh
fip fip
fip fip
...SO WHY AM I STILL SO CALM?!
zash

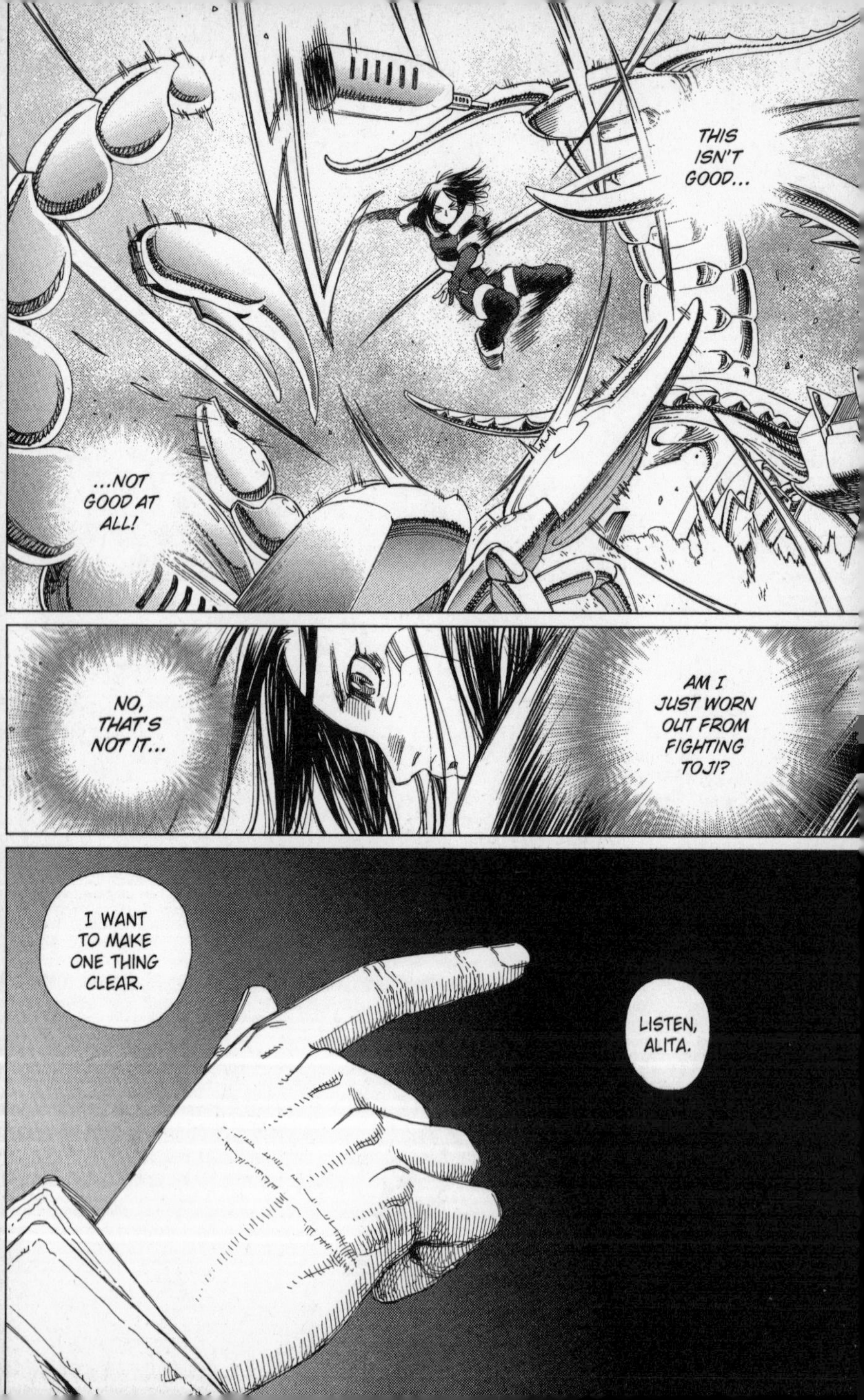
THIS ISN'T GOOD...
...NOT GOOD AT ALL!
AM I JUST WORN OUT FROM FIGHTING TOJI?
NO, THAT'S NOT IT...
LISTEN, ALITA.
I WANT TO MAKE ONE THING CLEAR.

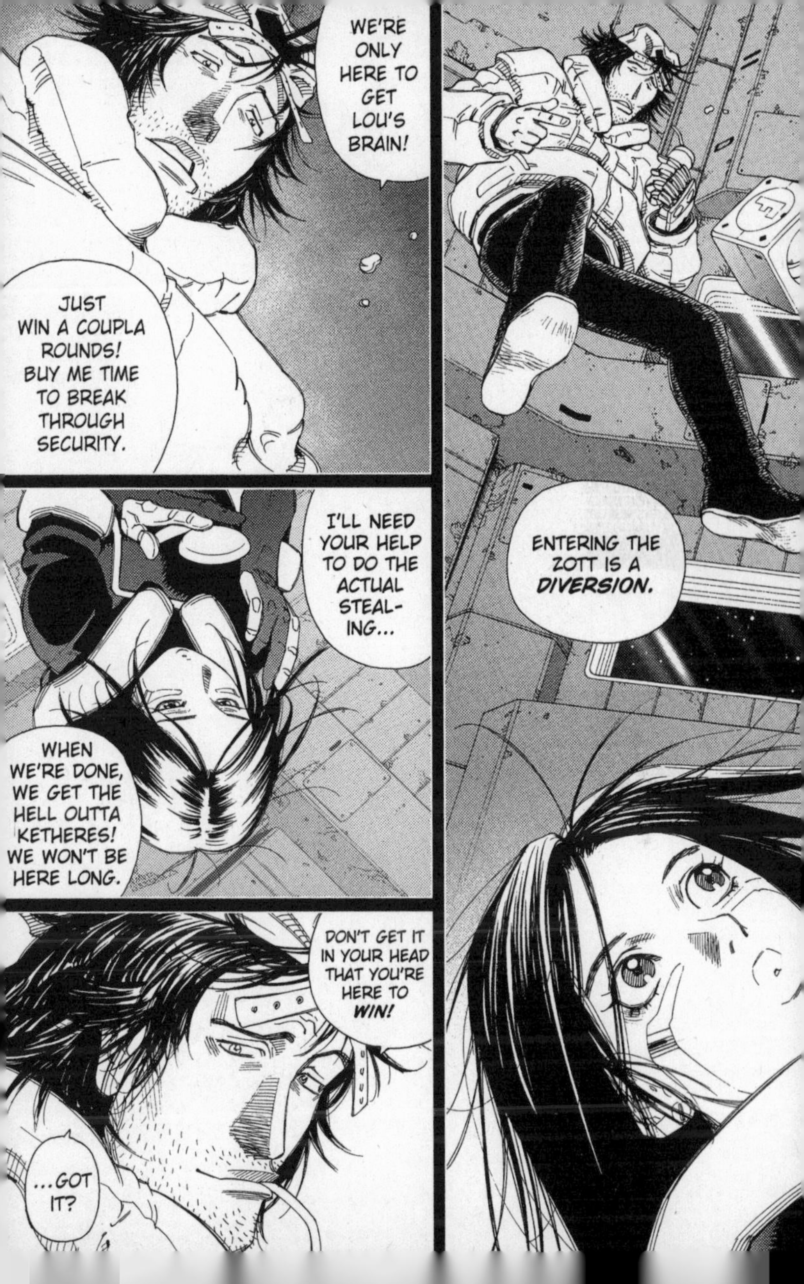
ENTERING THE ZOTT IS A *DIVERSION.*
WE'RE ONLY HERE TO GET LOU'S BRAIN!
JUST WIN A COUPLA ROUNDS! BUY ME TIME TO BREAK THROUGH SECURITY.
I'LL NEED YOUR HELP TO DO THE ACTUAL STEAL-ING...
WHEN WE'RE DONE, WE GET THE HELL OUTTA KETHERES! WE WON'T BE HERE LONG.
DON'T GET IT IN YOUR HEAD THAT YOU'RE HERE TO *WIN!*
...GOT IT?

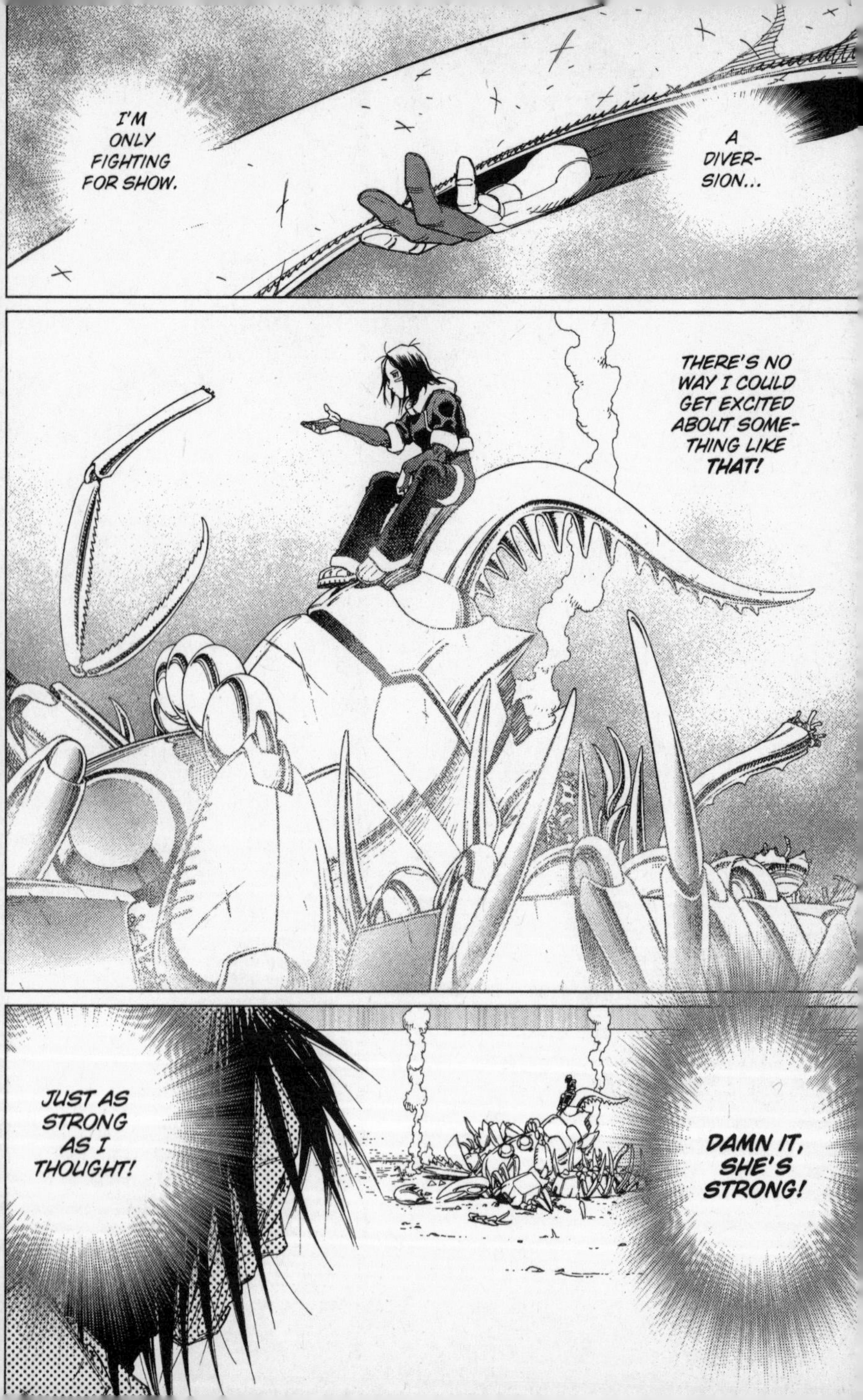
A DIVERSION...
I'M ONLY FIGHTING FOR SHOW.
THERE'S NO WAY I COULD GET EXCITED ABOUT SOMETHING LIKE THAT!
DAMN IT, SHE'S STRONG!
JUST AS STRONG AS I THOUGHT!

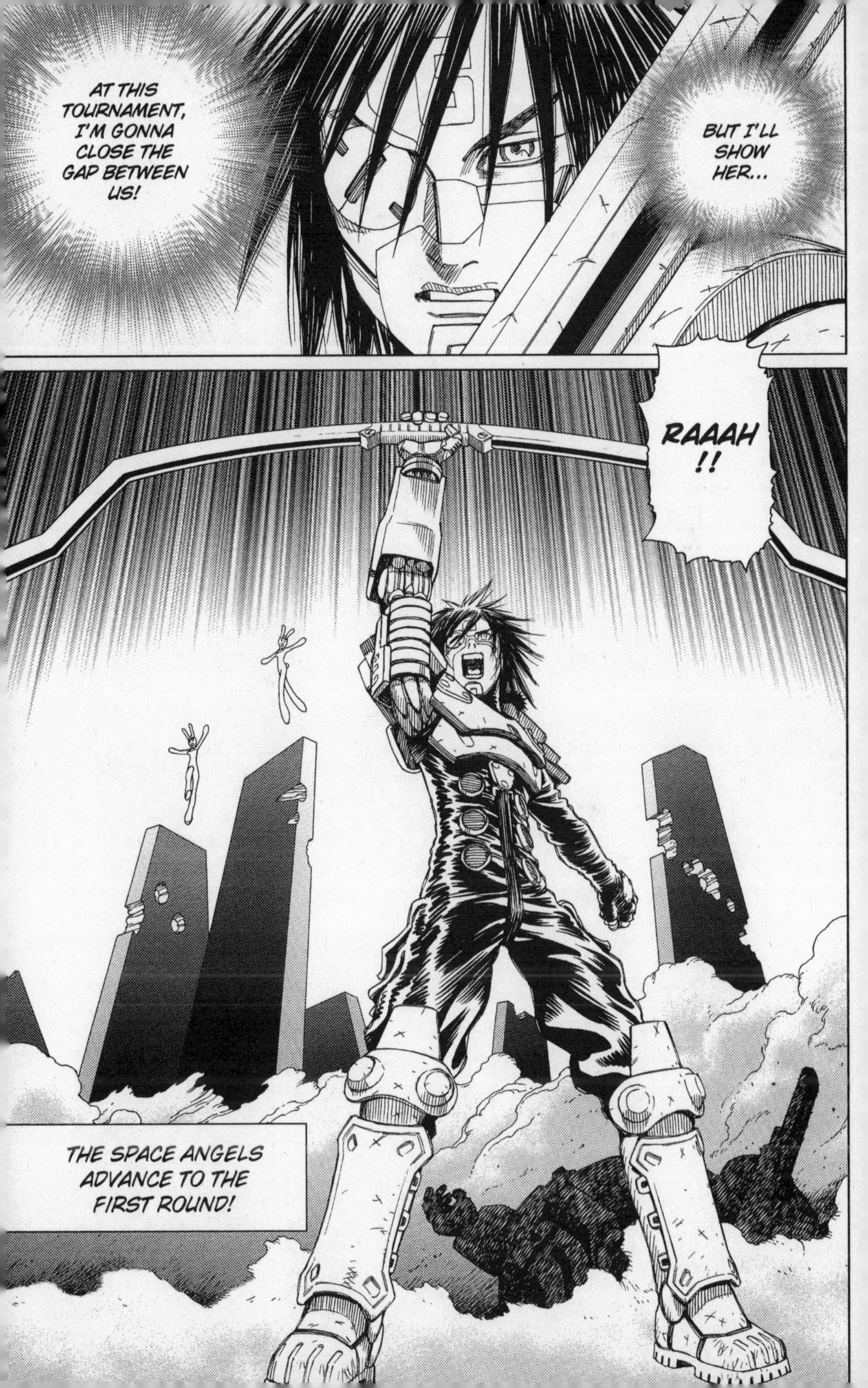
BUT I'LL SHOW HER...
AT THIS TOURNAMENT, I'M GONNA CLOSE THE GAP BETWEEN US!
RAAAH !!
THE SPACE ANGELS ADVANCE TO THE FIRST ROUND!

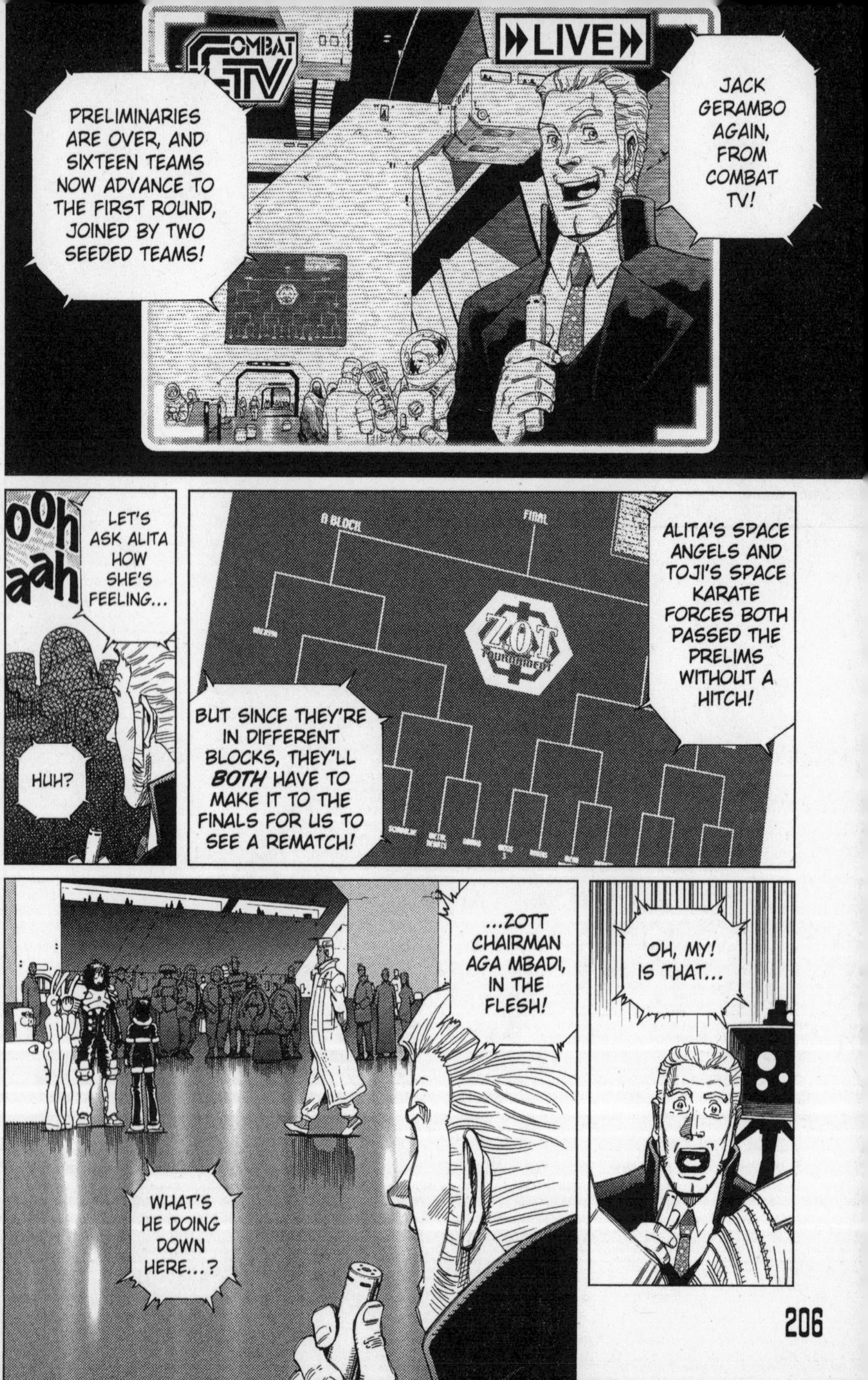
COMBAT TV
LIVE
JACK GERAMBO AGAIN, FROM COMBAT TV!
PRELIMINARIES ARE OVER, AND SIXTEEN TEAMS NOW ADVANCE TO THE FIRST ROUND, JOINED BY TWO SEEDED TEAMS!
A BLOCK
FINAL
Z.O.T
ALITA'S SPACE ANGELS AND TOJI'S SPACE KARATE FORCES BOTH PASSED THE PRELIMS WITHOUT A HITCH!
BUT SINCE THEY'RE IN DIFFERENT BLOCKS, THEY'LL ***BOTH*** HAVE TO MAKE IT TO THE FINALS FOR US TO SEE A REMATCH!
ooh
aah
LET'S ASK ALITA HOW SHE'S FEELING...
HUH?
OH, MY! IS THAT...
...ZOTT CHAIRMAN AGA MBADI, IN THE FLESH!
WHAT'S HE DOING DOWN HERE...?

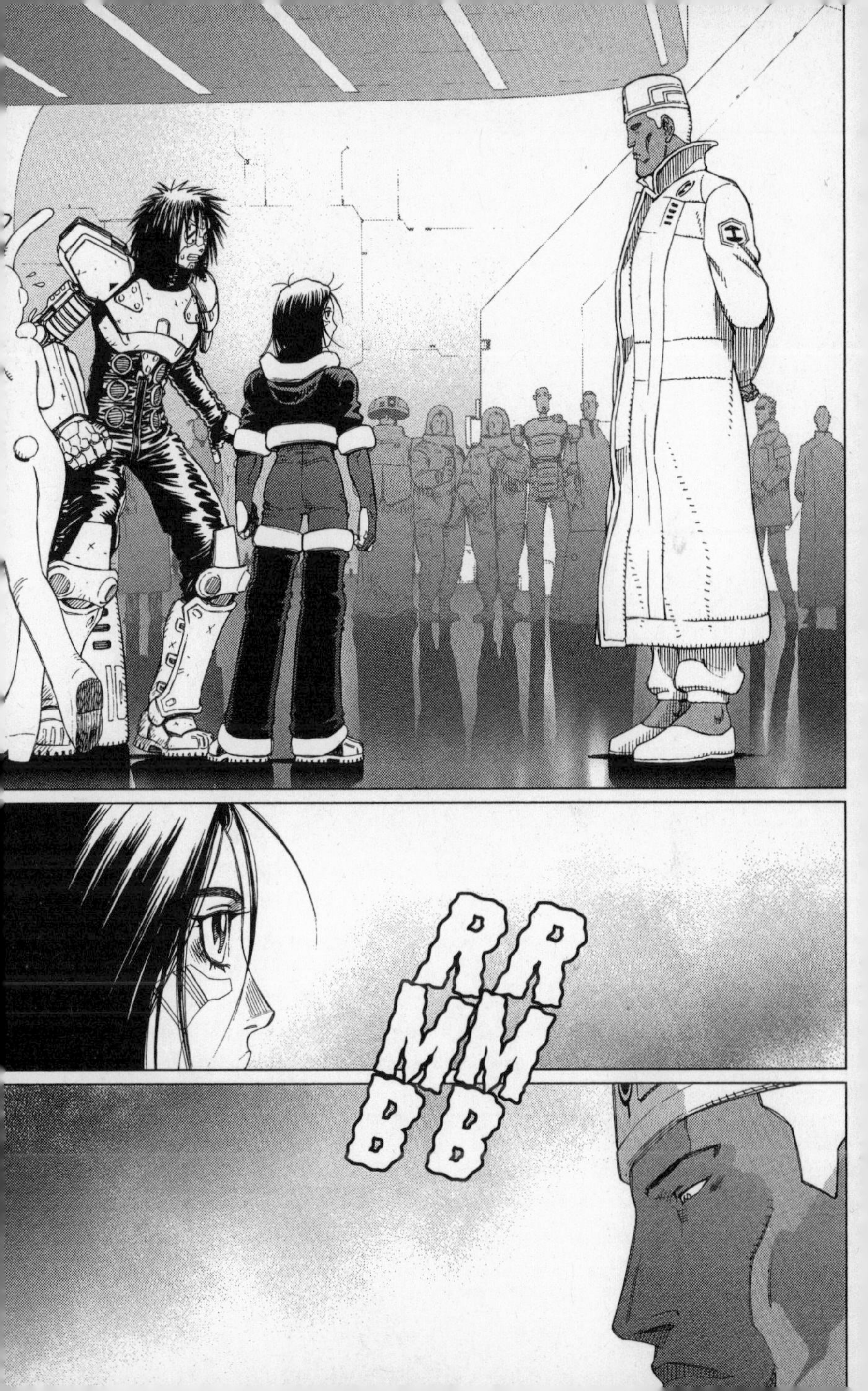
RRMMBB

YOU
PASSED
THE
PRELIMI-
NARIES.

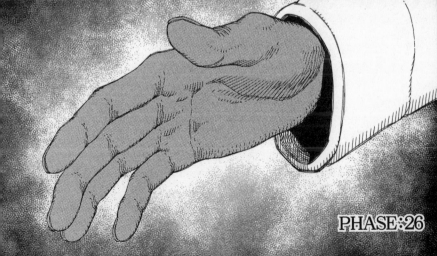

PHASE:26

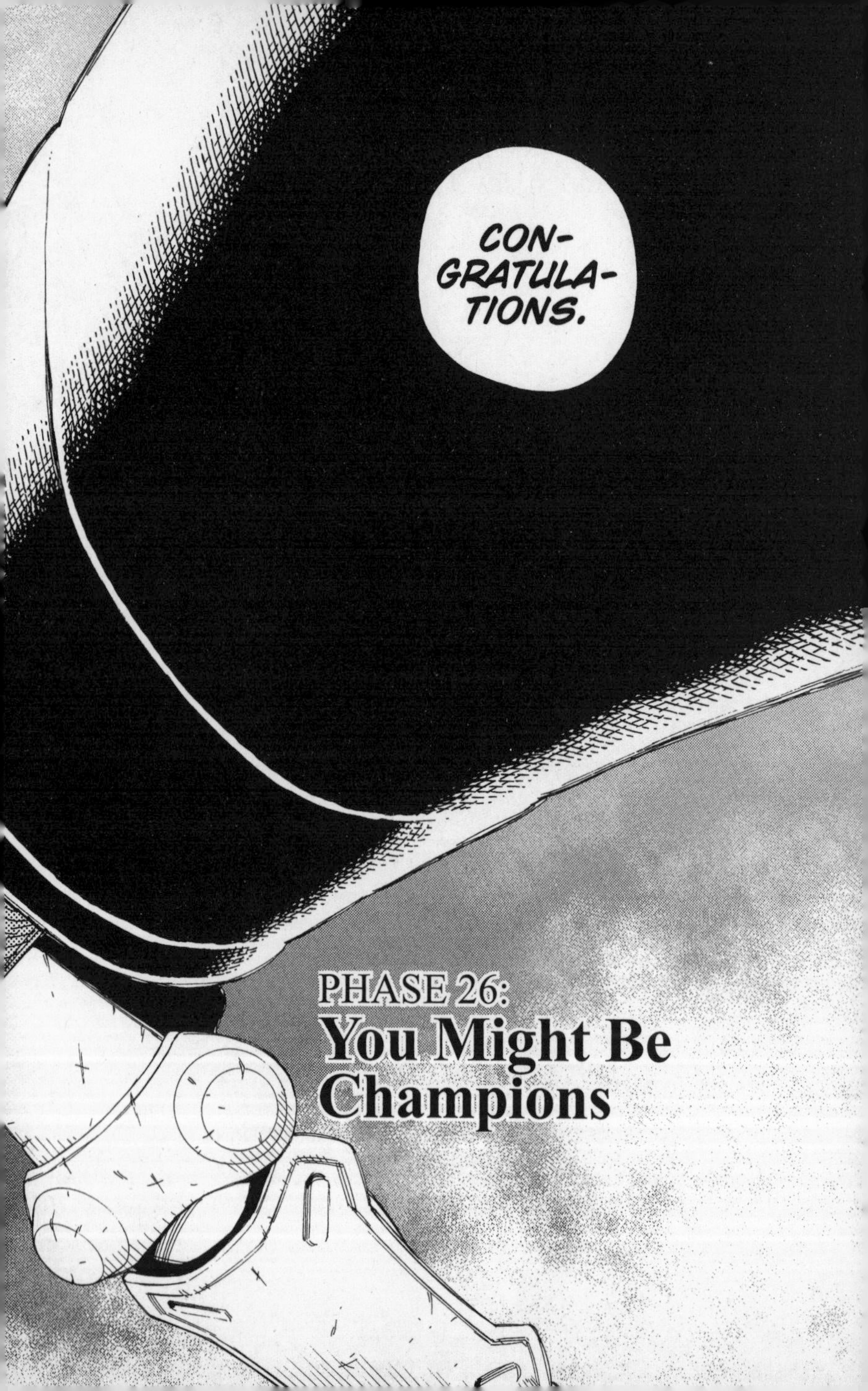
CON-GRATULA-TIONS.
PHASE 26:
You Might Be Champions

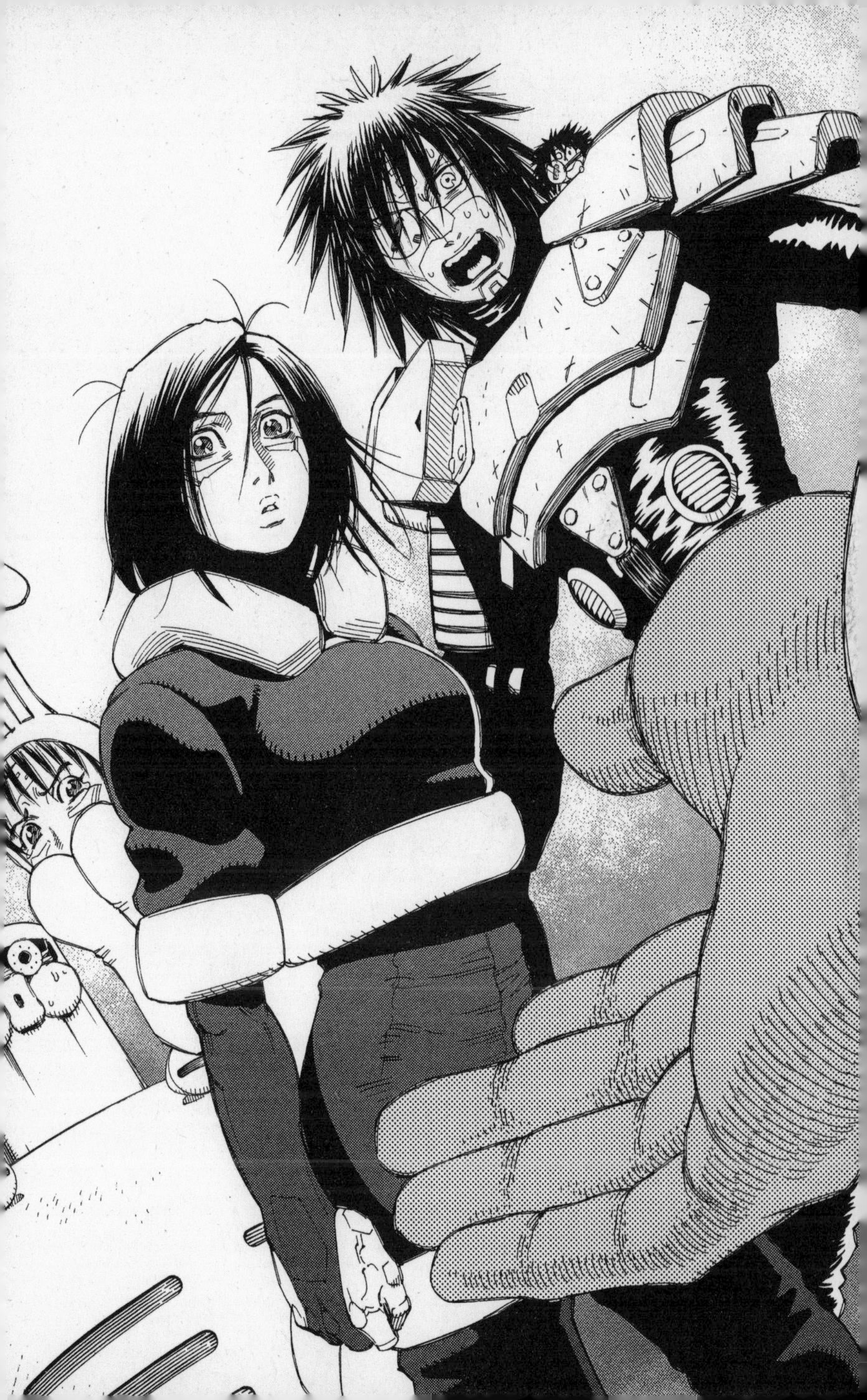

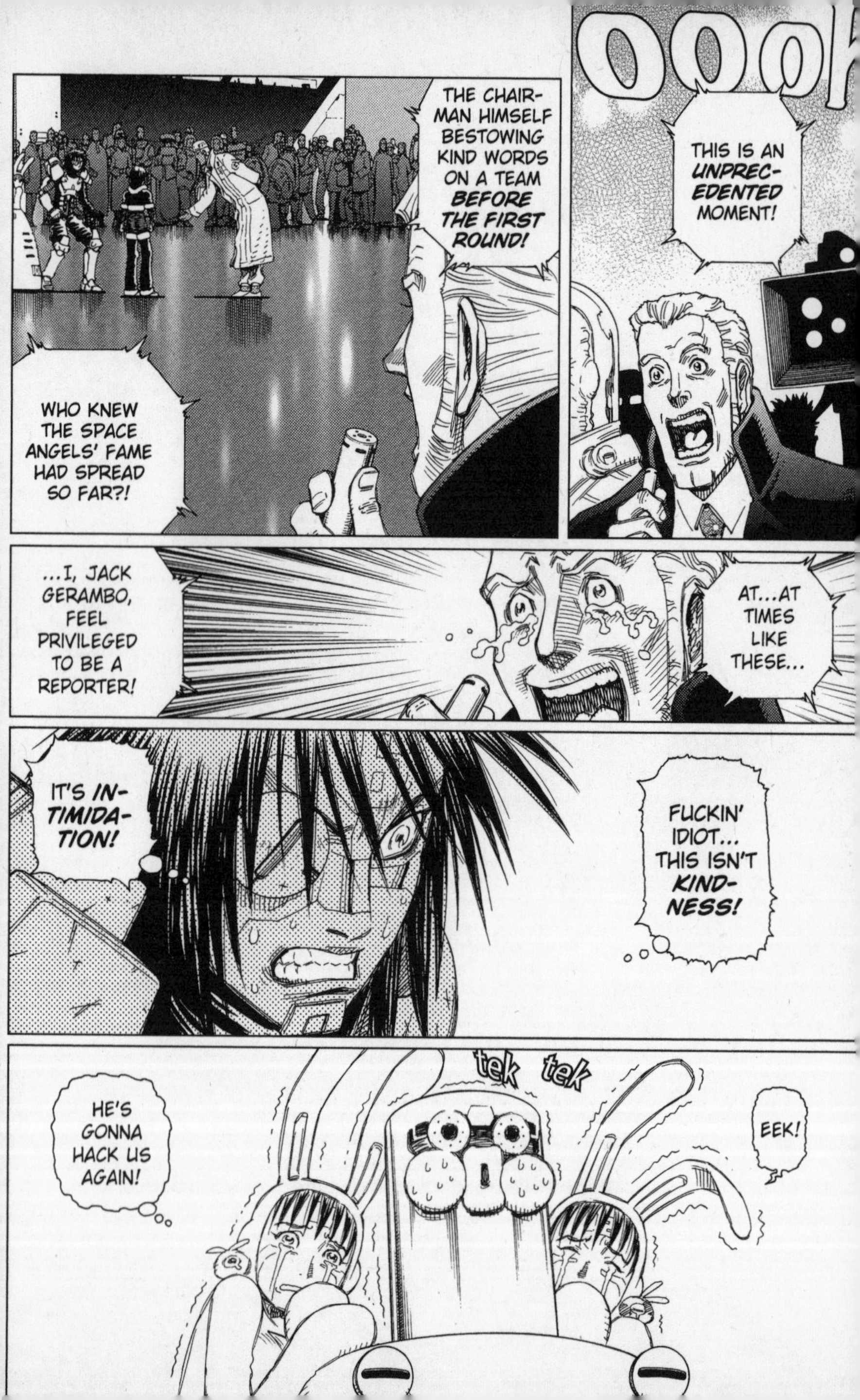
OOO
THIS IS AN UNPRECEDENTED MOMENT!
THE CHAIRMAN HIMSELF BESTOWING KIND WORDS ON A TEAM BEFORE THE FIRST ROUND!
WHO KNEW THE SPACE ANGELS' FAME HAD SPREAD SO FAR?!
AT...AT TIMES LIKE THESE...
...I, JACK GERAMBO, FEEL PRIVILEGED TO BE A REPORTER!
FUCKIN' IDIOT... THIS ISN'T KINDNESS!
IT'S INTIMIDATION!
tek tek
EEK!
HE'S GONNA HACK US AGAIN!

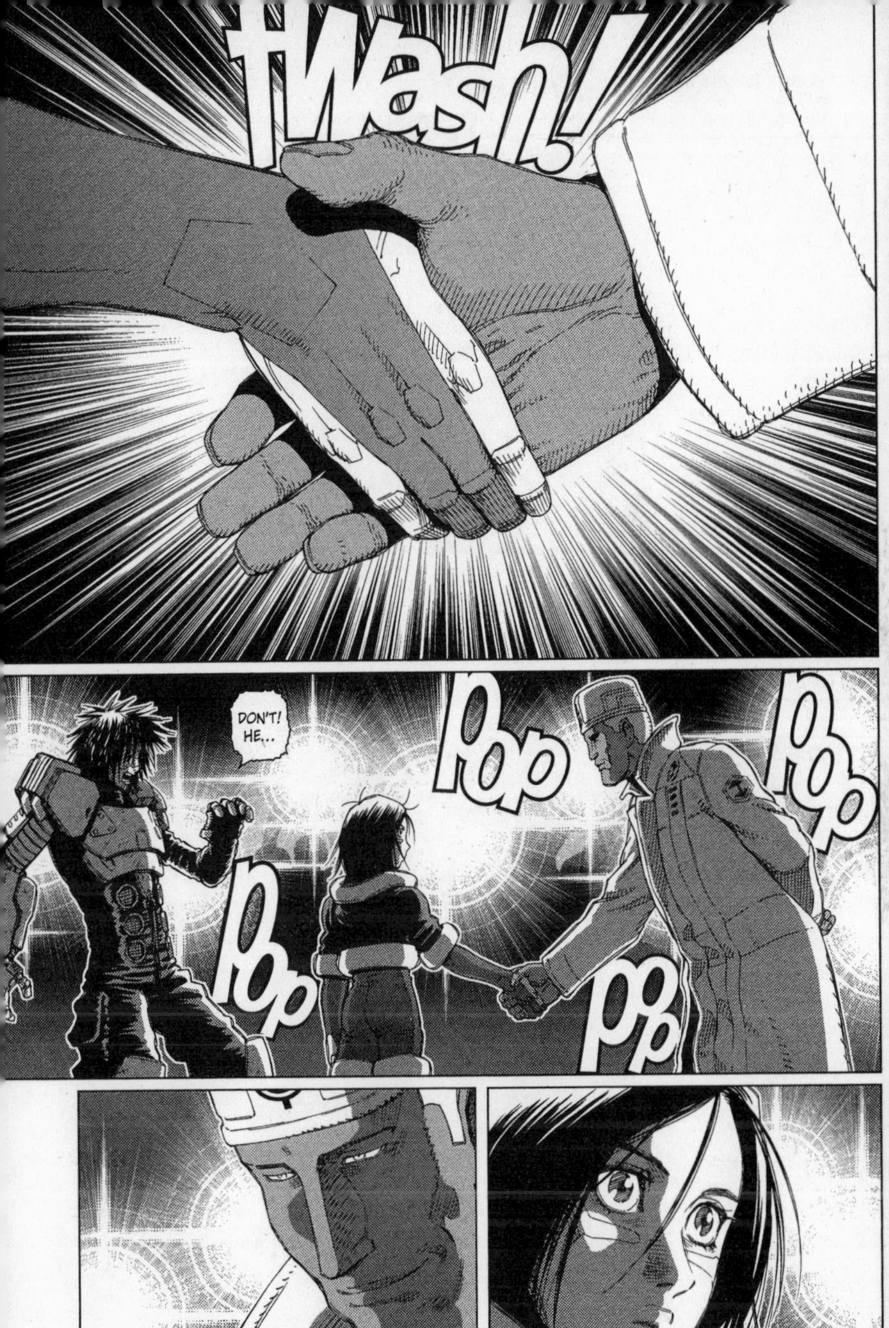
fwash!
pop
pop
DON'T! HE...
pop
pp

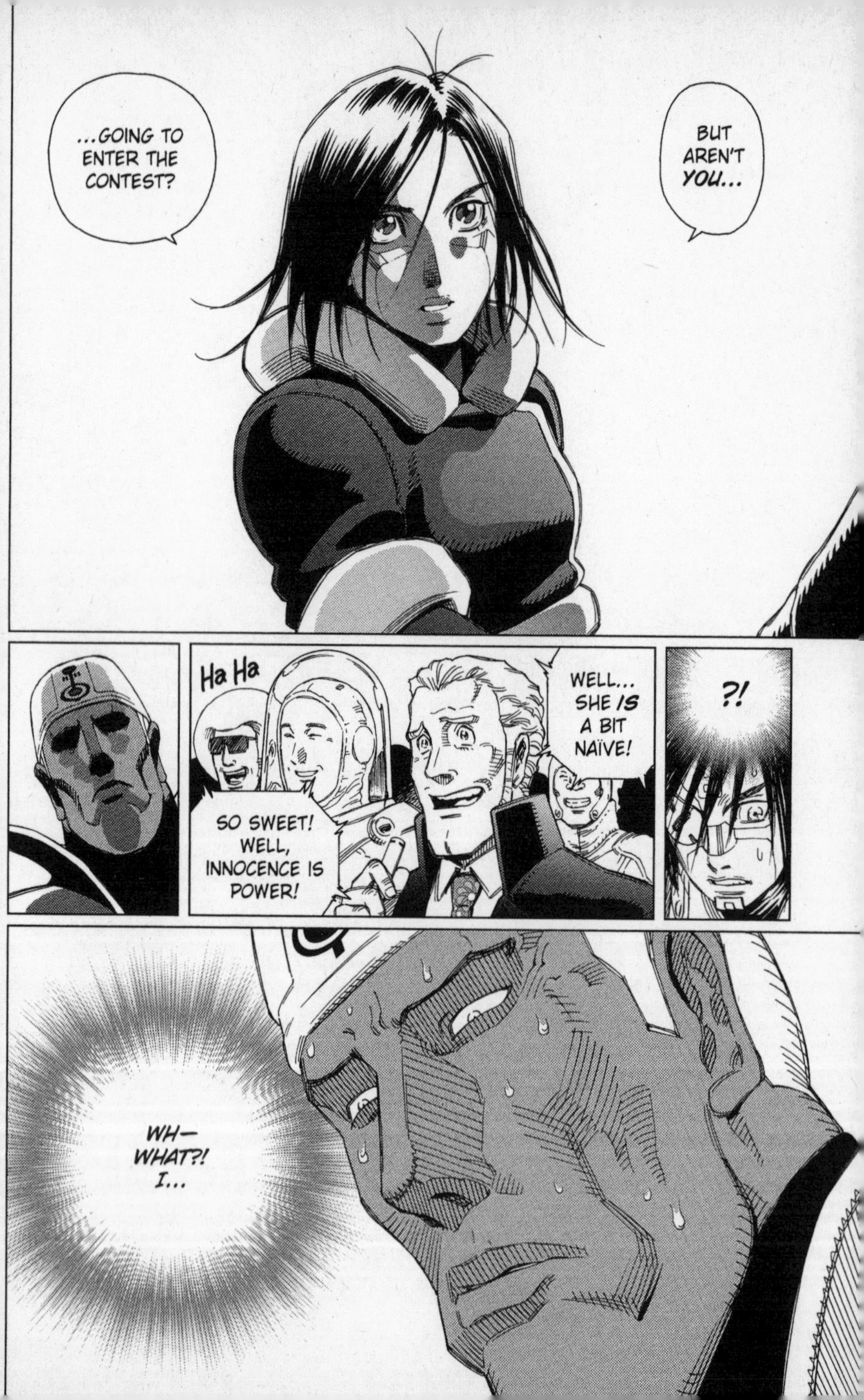
BUT AREN'T *YOU...*
...GOING TO ENTER THE CONTEST?
?!
WELL... SHE *IS* A BIT NAÏVE!
Ha Ha
SO SWEET! WELL, INNOCENCE IS POWER!
WH— WHAT?! I...

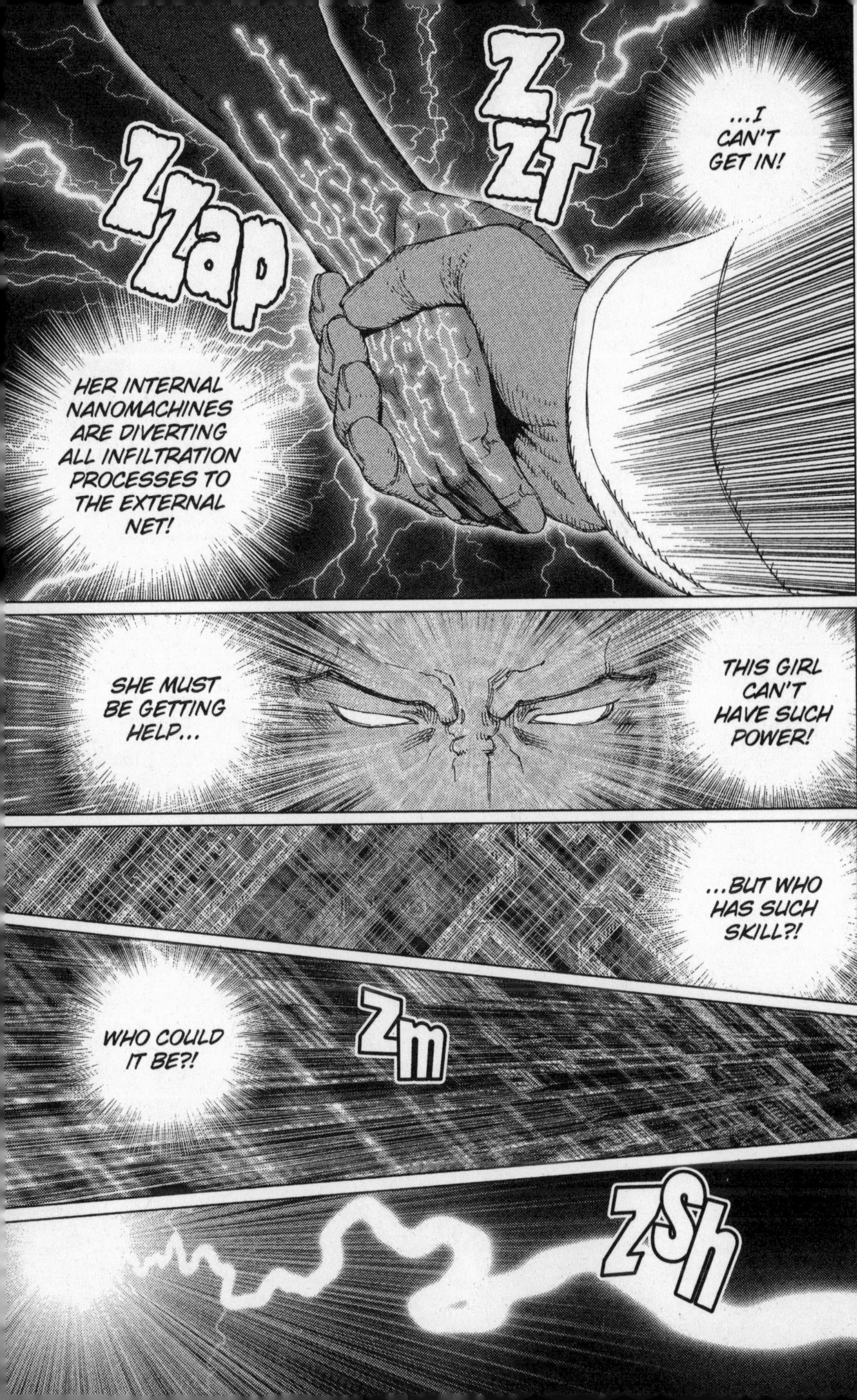
ZZt
...I CAN'T GET IN!
ZZap
HER INTERNAL NANOMACHINES ARE DIVERTING ALL INFILTRATION PROCESSES TO THE EXTERNAL NET!
THIS GIRL CAN'T HAVE SUCH POWER!
SHE MUST BE GETTING HELP...
...BUT WHO HAS SUCH SKILL?!
Zm
WHO COULD IT BE?!
ZSh

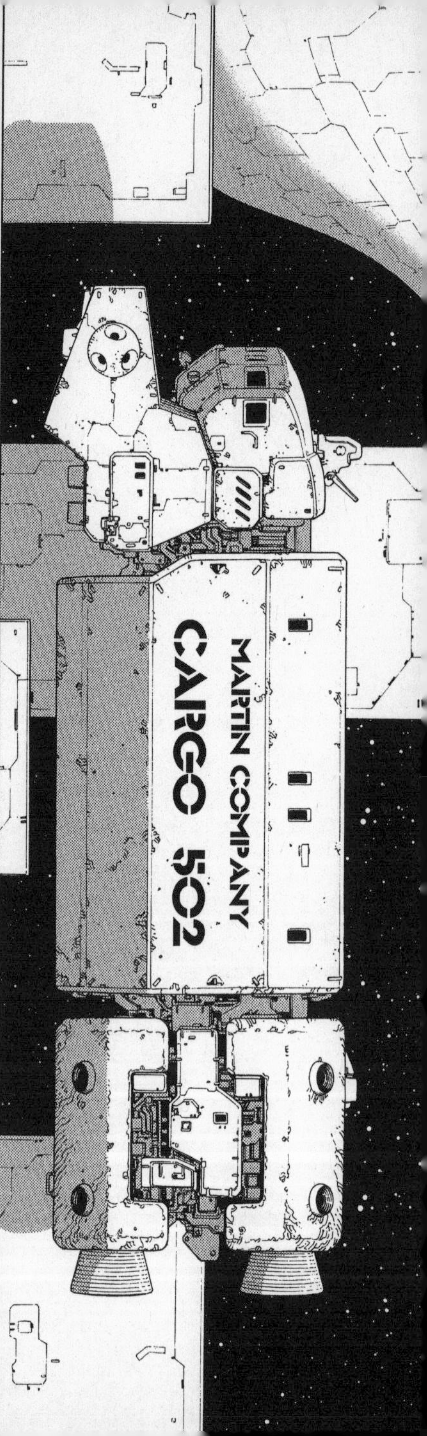
MARTIN COMPANY
CARGO 502

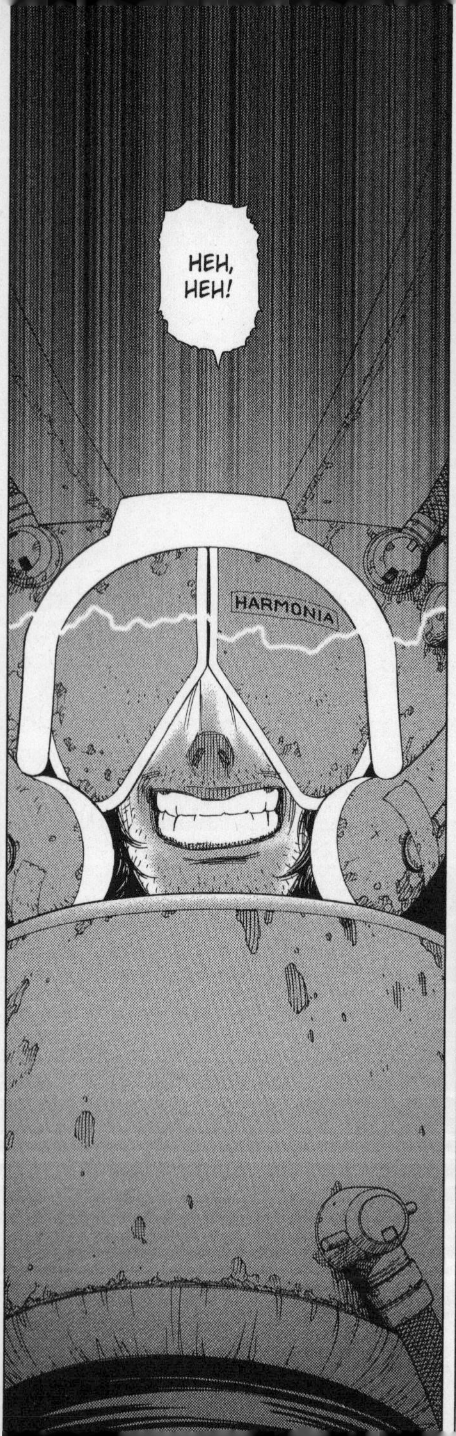
HEH, HEH!
HARMONIA

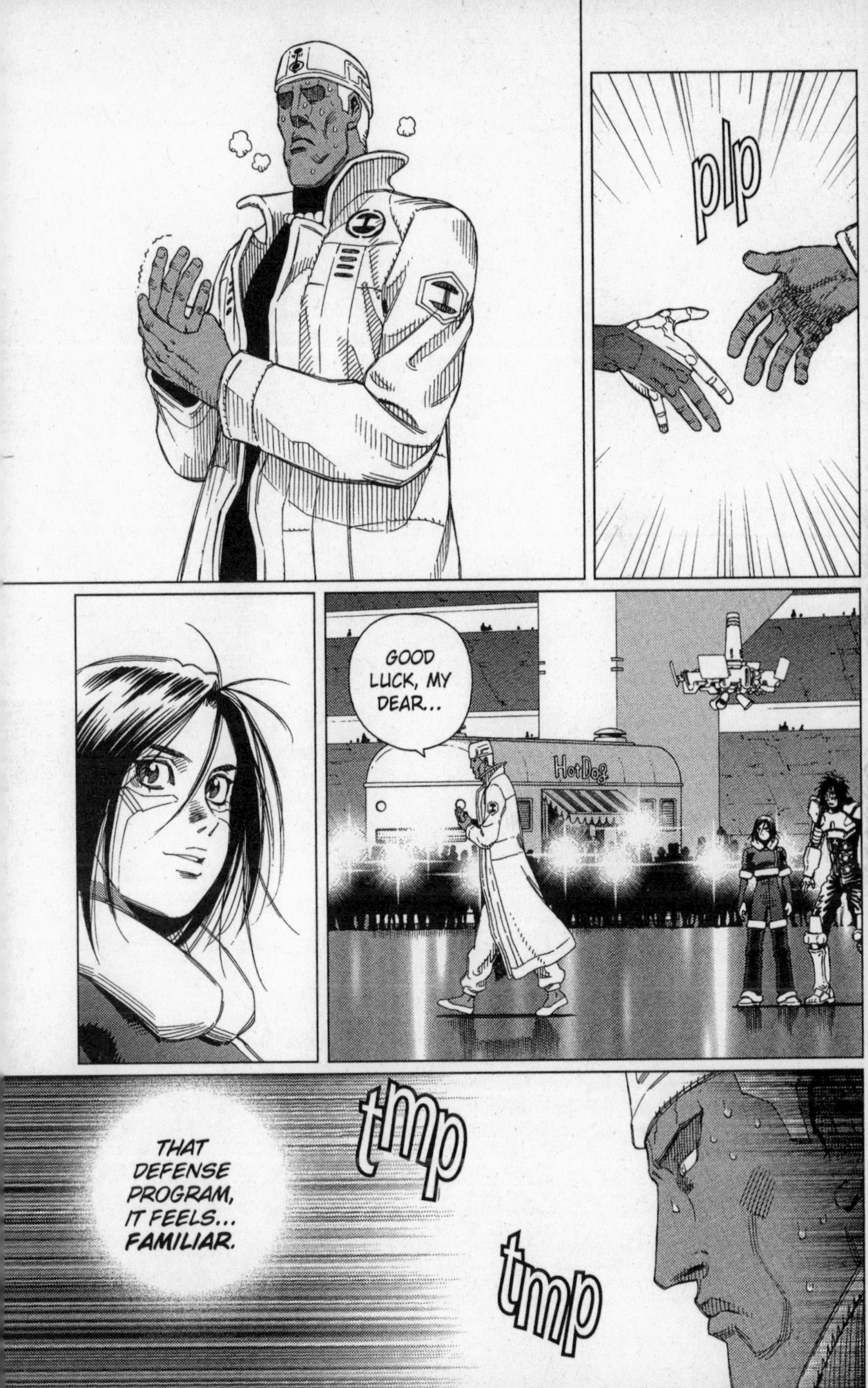
plp
GOOD LUCK, MY DEAR...
Hot Dog
tmp
THAT DEFENSE PROGRAM, IT FEELS... FAMILIAR.
tmp

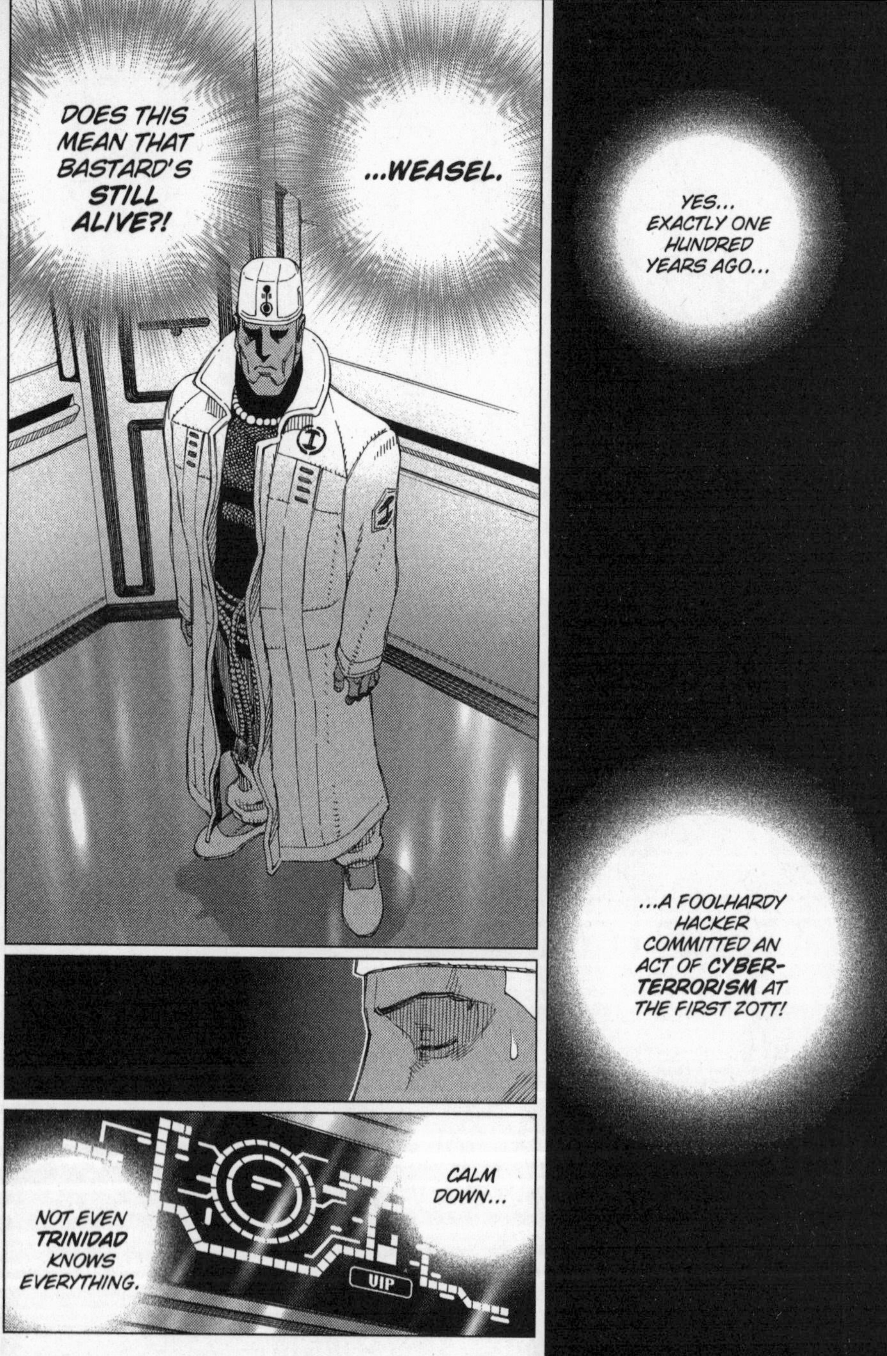
YES... EXACTLY ONE HUNDRED YEARS AGO...
...A FOOLHARDY HACKER COMMITTED AN ACT OF CYBER-TERRORISM AT THE FIRST ZOTT!
...WEASEL.
DOES THIS MEAN THAT BASTARD'S STILL ALIVE?!
CALM DOWN...
VIP
NOT EVEN TRINIDAD KNOWS EVERYTHING.

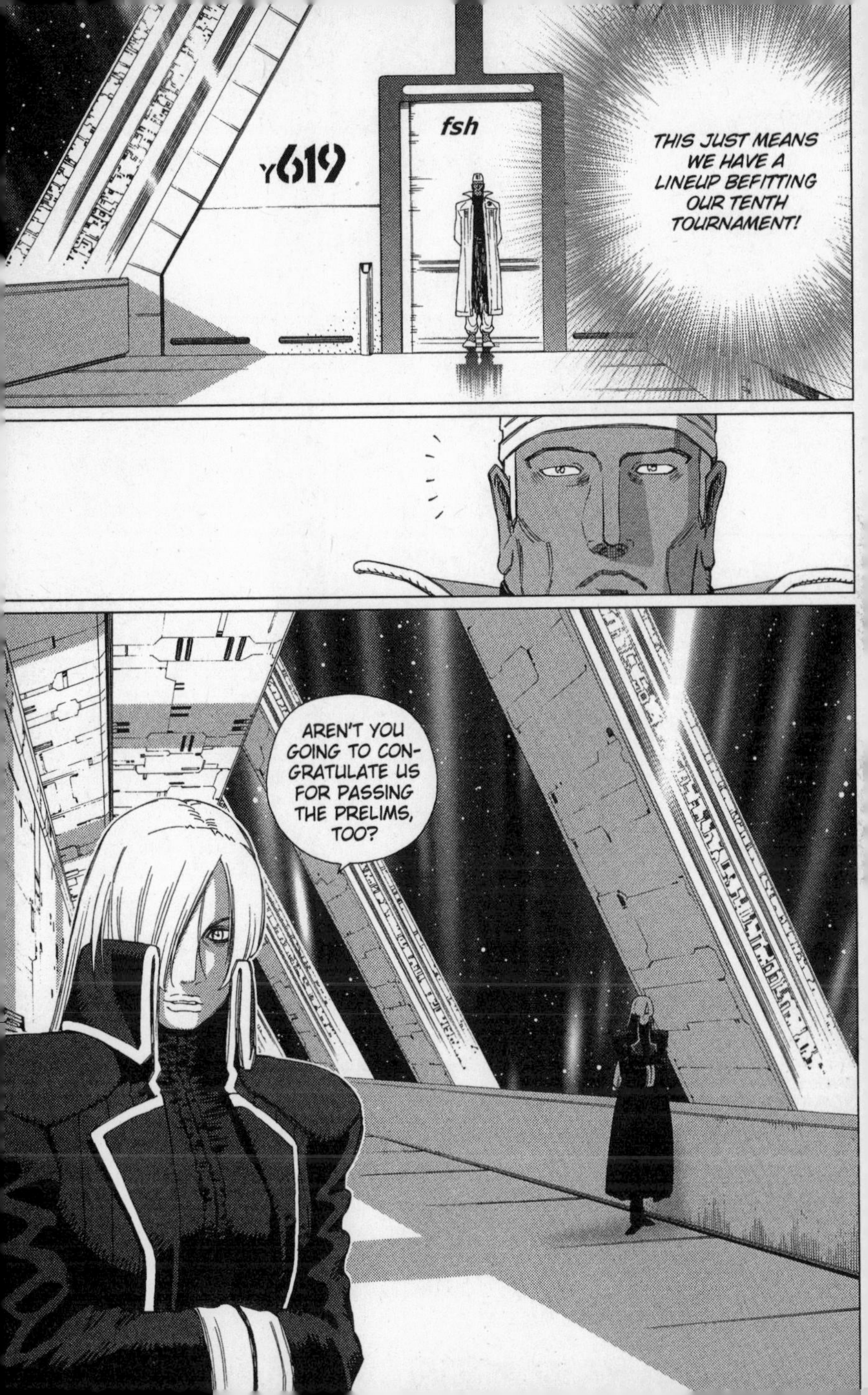
fsh
y619
THIS JUST MEANS WE HAVE A LINEUP BEFITTING OUR TENTH TOURNAMENT!
AREN'T YOU GOING TO CON-GRATULATE US FOR PASSING THE PRELIMS, TOO?

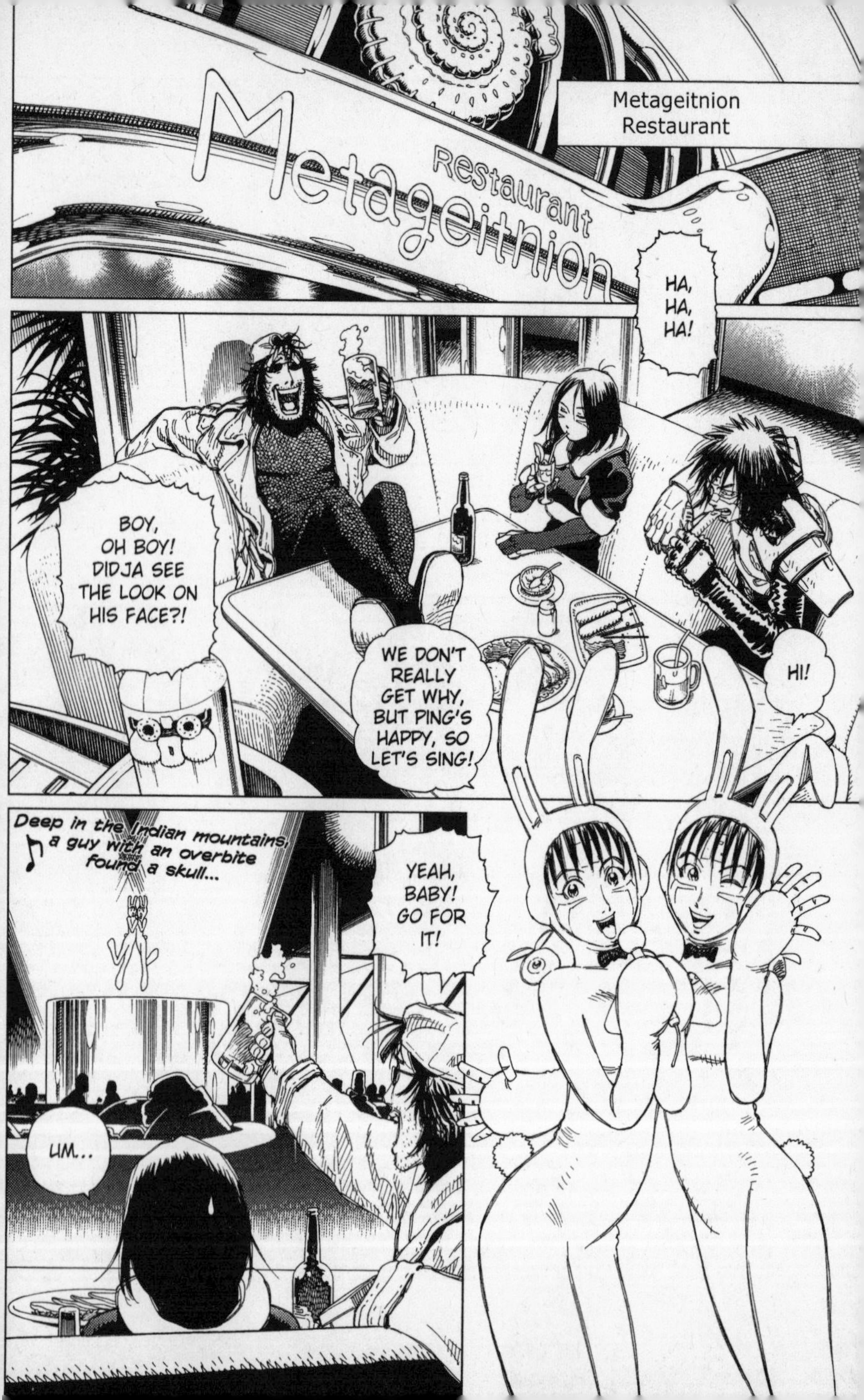
Metageitnion Restaurant
Metageitnion
Restaurant
HA, HA, HA!
HI!
BOY, OH BOY! DIDJA SEE THE LOOK ON HIS FACE?!
WE DON'T REALLY GET WHY, BUT PING'S HAPPY, SO LET'S SING!
♪ Deep in the Indian mountains, a guy with an overbite found a skull...
YEAH, BABY! GO FOR IT!
UM...

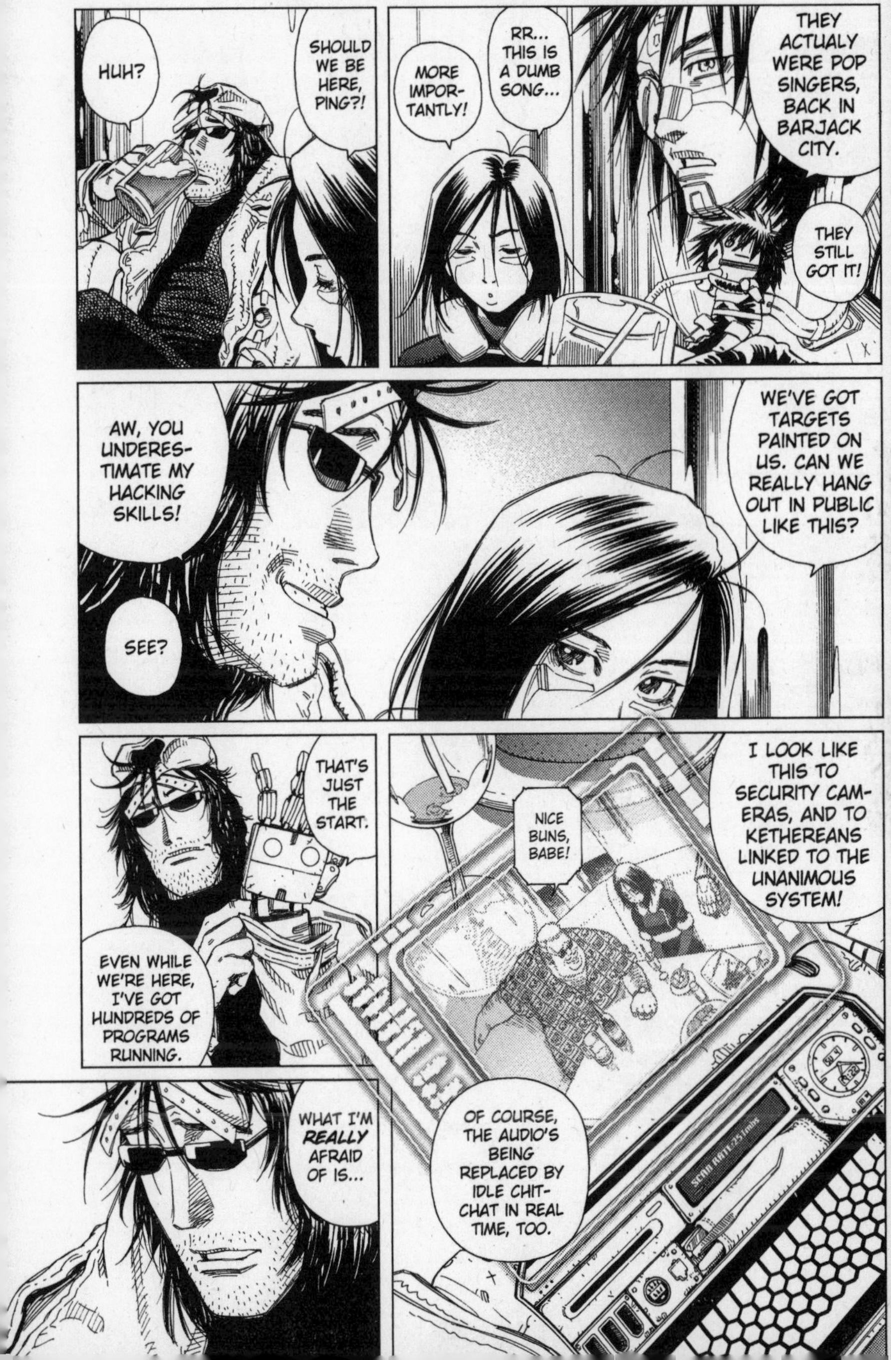

THEY ACTUALY WERE POP SINGERS, BACK IN BARJACK CITY.
RR... THIS IS A DUMB SONG...
MORE IMPOR-TANTLY!
THEY STILL GOT IT!
SHOULD WE BE HERE, PING?!
HUH?
WE'VE GOT TARGETS PAINTED ON US. CAN WE REALLY HANG OUT IN PUBLIC LIKE THIS?
AW, YOU UNDERES-TIMATE MY HACKING SKILLS!
SEE?
I LOOK LIKE THIS TO SECURITY CAM-ERAS, AND TO KETHEREANS LINKED TO THE UNANIMOUS SYSTEM!
NICE BUNS, BABE!
OF COURSE, THE AUDIO'S BEING REPLACED BY IDLE CHIT-CHAT IN REAL TIME, TOO.
THAT'S JUST THE START.
EVEN WHILE WE'RE HERE, I'VE GOT HUNDREDS OF PROGRAMS RUNNING.
WHAT I'M *REALLY* AFRAID OF IS...

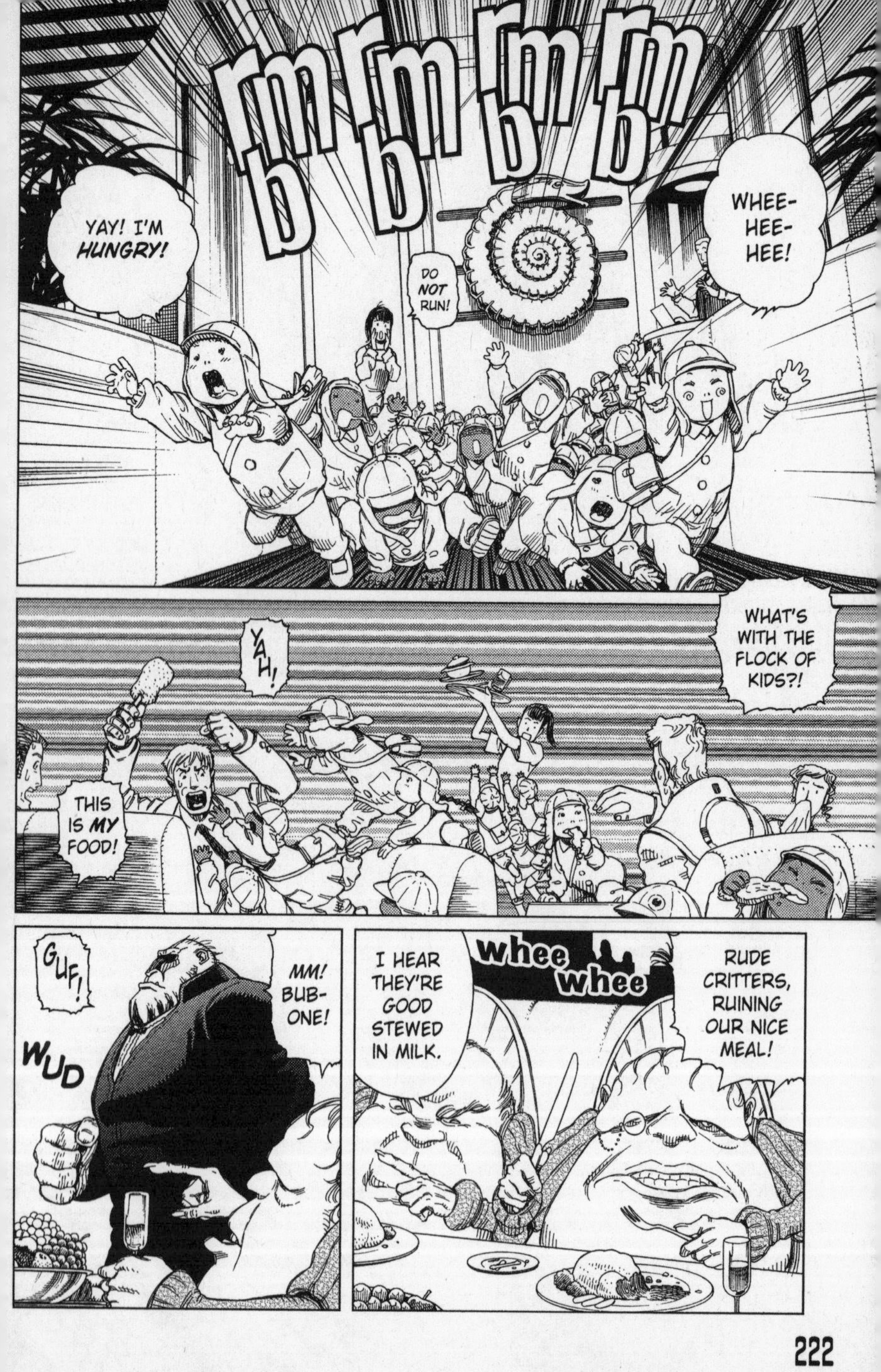
WHEE-HEE-HEE!
rmb rmb rmb rmb
DO NOT RUN!
YAY! I'M HUNGRY!
WHAT'S WITH THE FLOCK OF KIDS?!
YAH!
THIS IS MY FOOD!
RUDE CRITTERS, RUINING OUR NICE MEAL!
whee whee
I HEAR THEY'RE GOOD STEWED IN MILK.
MM! BUB-ONE!
GUF!
WUD

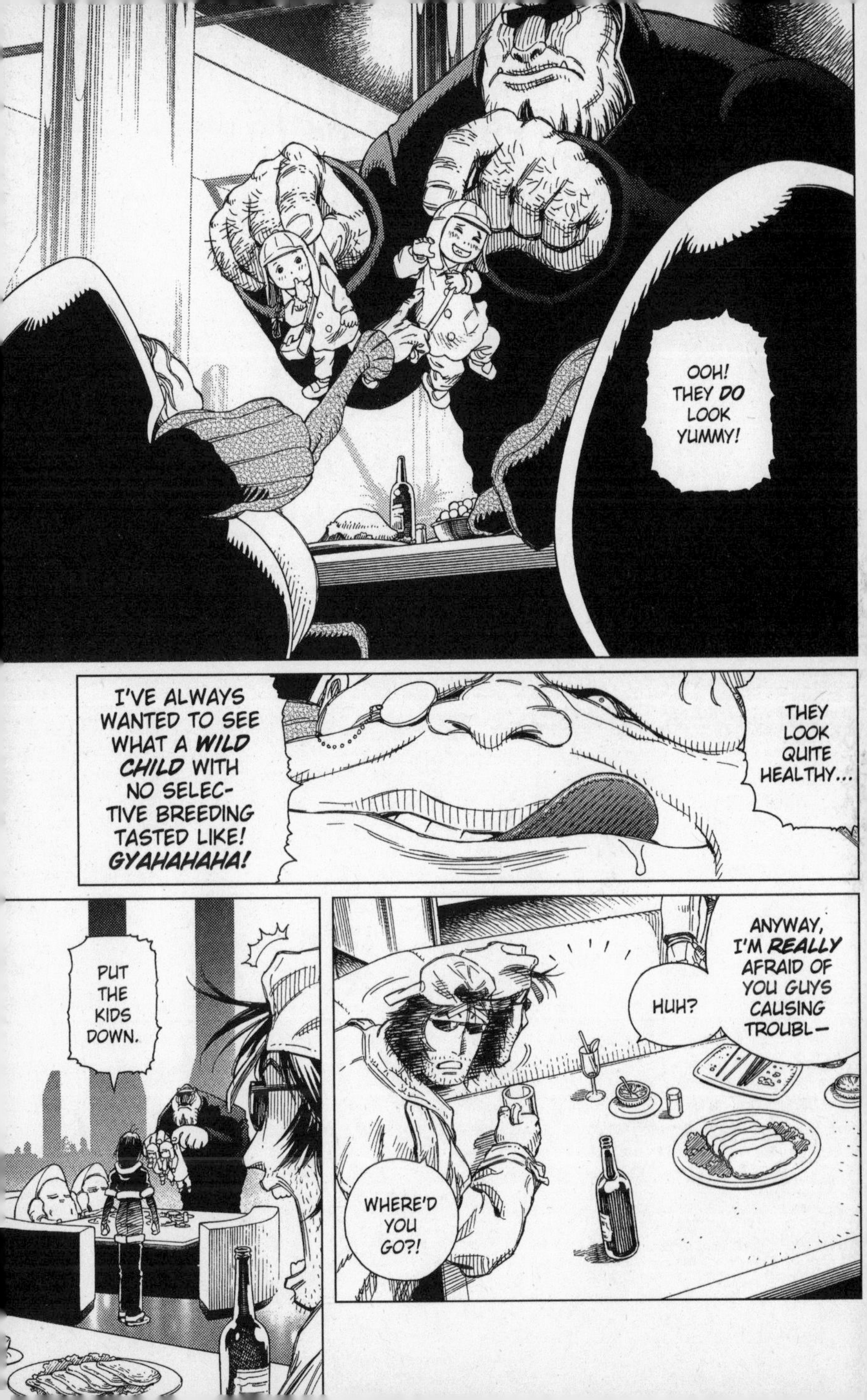
OOH! THEY *DO* LOOK YUMMY!
THEY LOOK QUITE HEALTHY...
I'VE ALWAYS WANTED TO SEE WHAT A ***WILD CHILD*** WITH NO SELEC-TIVE BREEDING TASTED LIKE! ***GYAHAHAHA!***
ANYWAY, I'M ***REALLY*** AFRAID OF YOU GUYS CAUSING TROUBL—
HUH?
WHERE'D YOU GO?!
PUT THE KIDS DOWN.

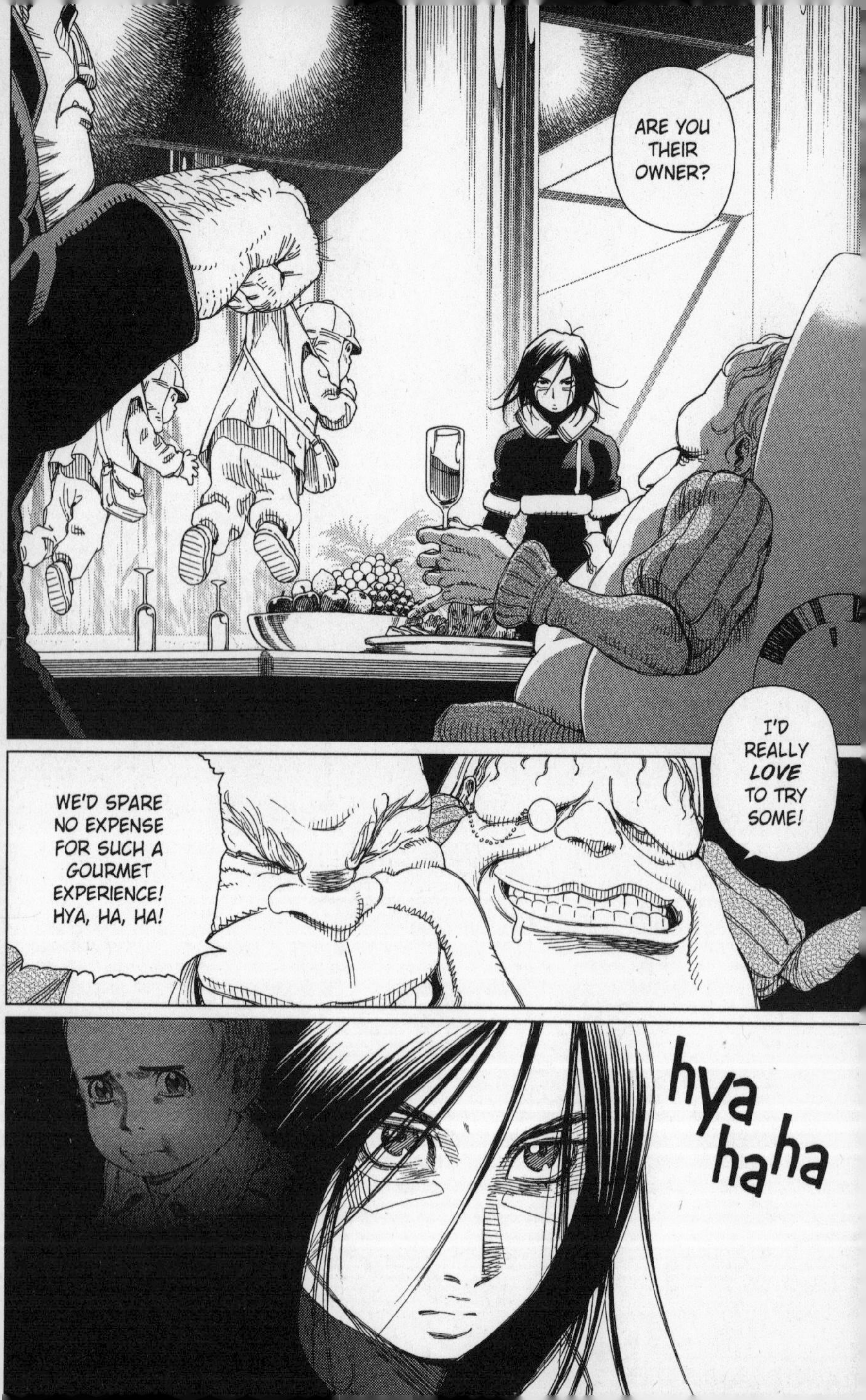
ARE YOU THEIR OWNER?
I'D REALLY *LOVE* TO TRY SOME!
WE'D SPARE NO EXPENSE FOR SUCH A GOURMET EXPERIENCE! HYA, HA, HA!
hya haha

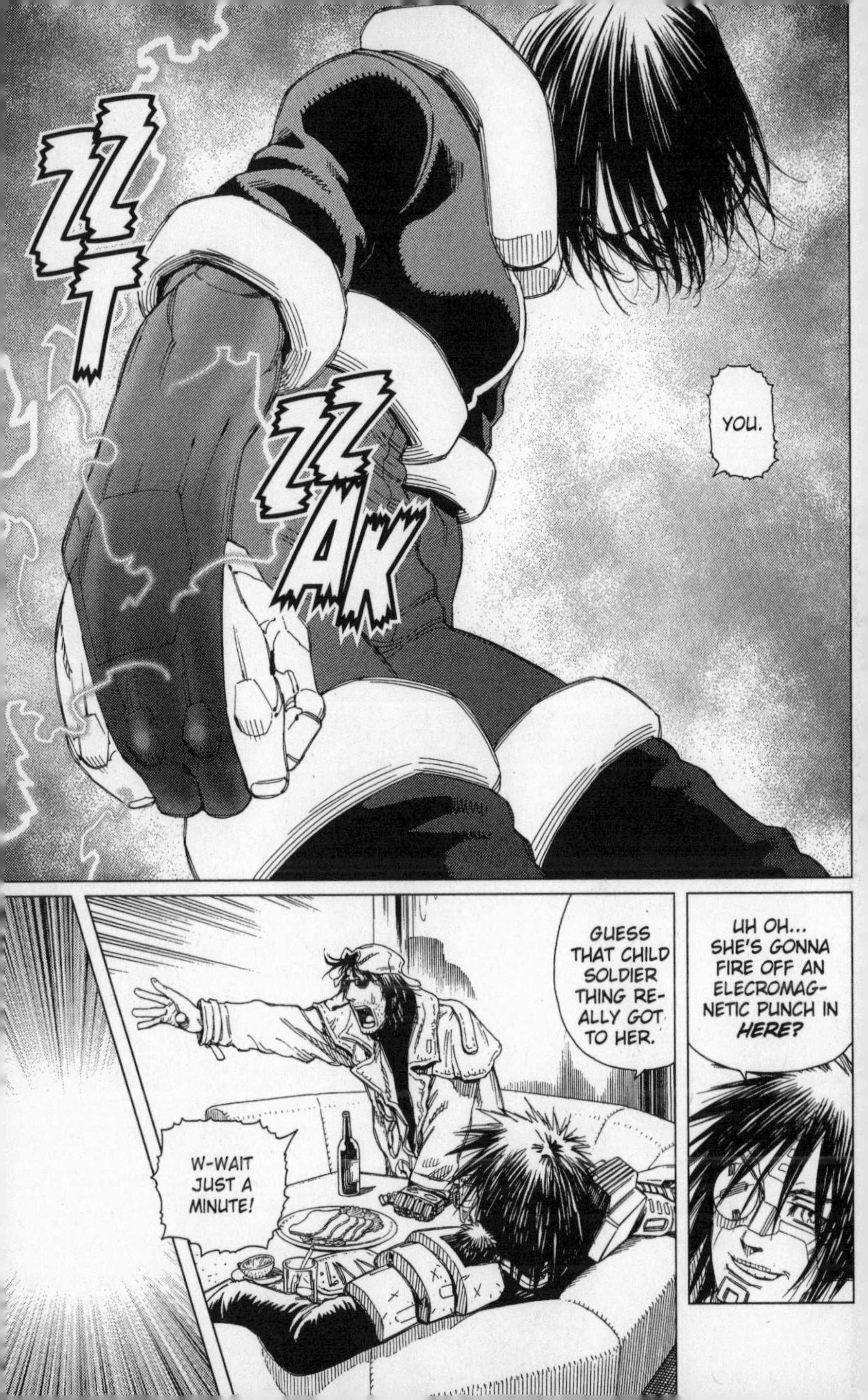
ZZT
ZZAK
YOU.
UH OH... SHE'S GONNA FIRE OFF AN ELECROMAG-NETIC PUNCH IN *HERE?*
GUESS THAT CHILD SOLDIER THING RE-ALLY GOT TO HER.
W-WAIT JUST A MINUTE!

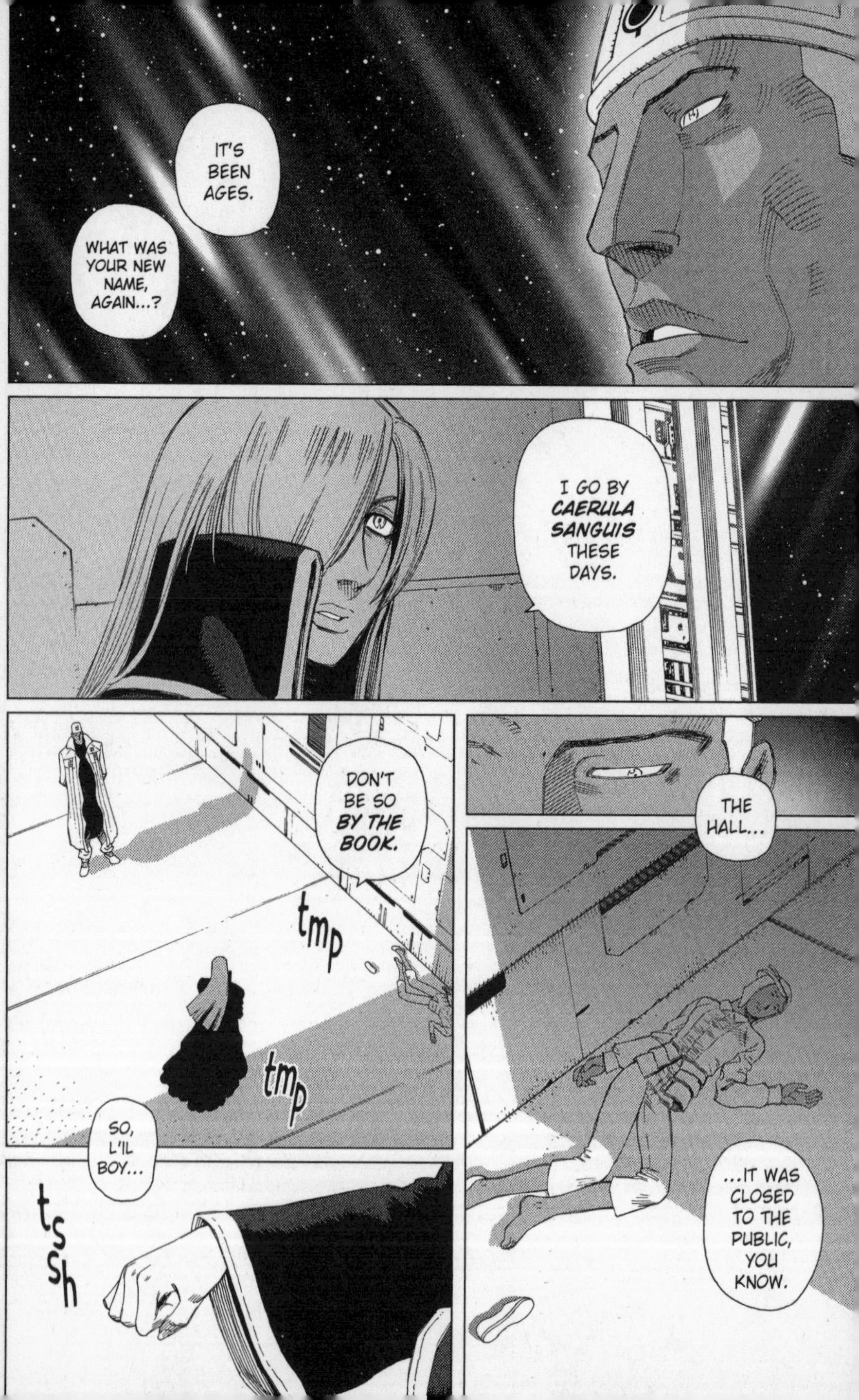
IT'S BEEN AGES.
WHAT WAS YOUR NEW NAME, AGAIN...?
I GO BY ***CAERULA SANGUIS*** THESE DAYS.
THE HALL...
...IT WAS CLOSED TO THE PUBLIC, YOU KNOW.
DON'T BE SO ***BY THE BOOK.***
tmp
tmp
SO, L'IL BOY...
tssh

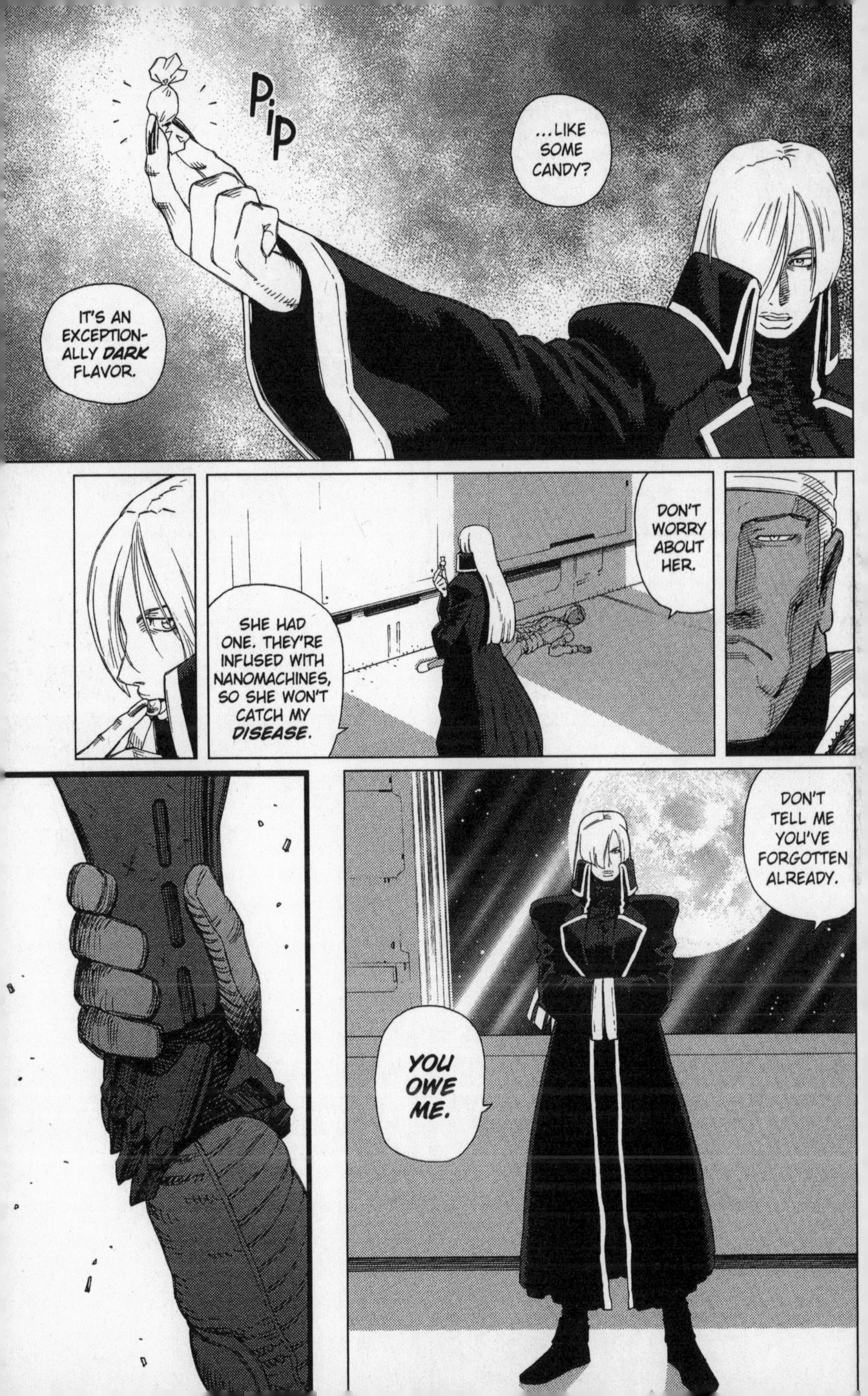
...LIKE SOME CANDY?
PIP
IT'S AN EXCEPTIONALLY *DARK* FLAVOR.
DON'T WORRY ABOUT HER.
SHE HAD ONE. THEY'RE INFUSED WITH NANOMACHINES, SO SHE WON'T CATCH MY *DISEASE*.
DON'T TELL ME YOU'VE FORGOTTEN ALREADY.
YOU OWE ME.

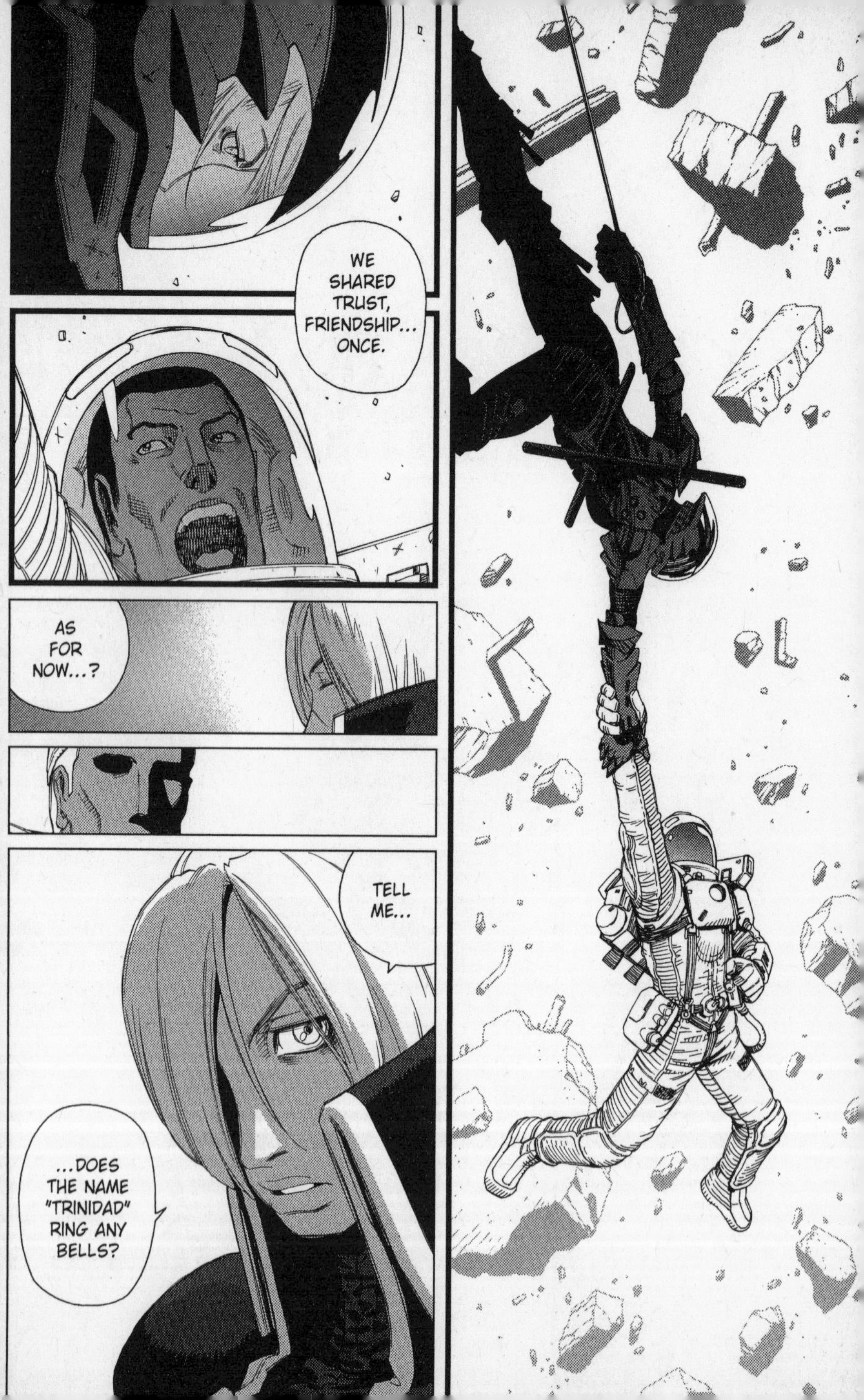
WE SHARED TRUST, FRIENDSHIP... ONCE.
AS FOR NOW...?
TELL ME...
...DOES THE NAME "TRINIDAD" RING ANY BELLS?

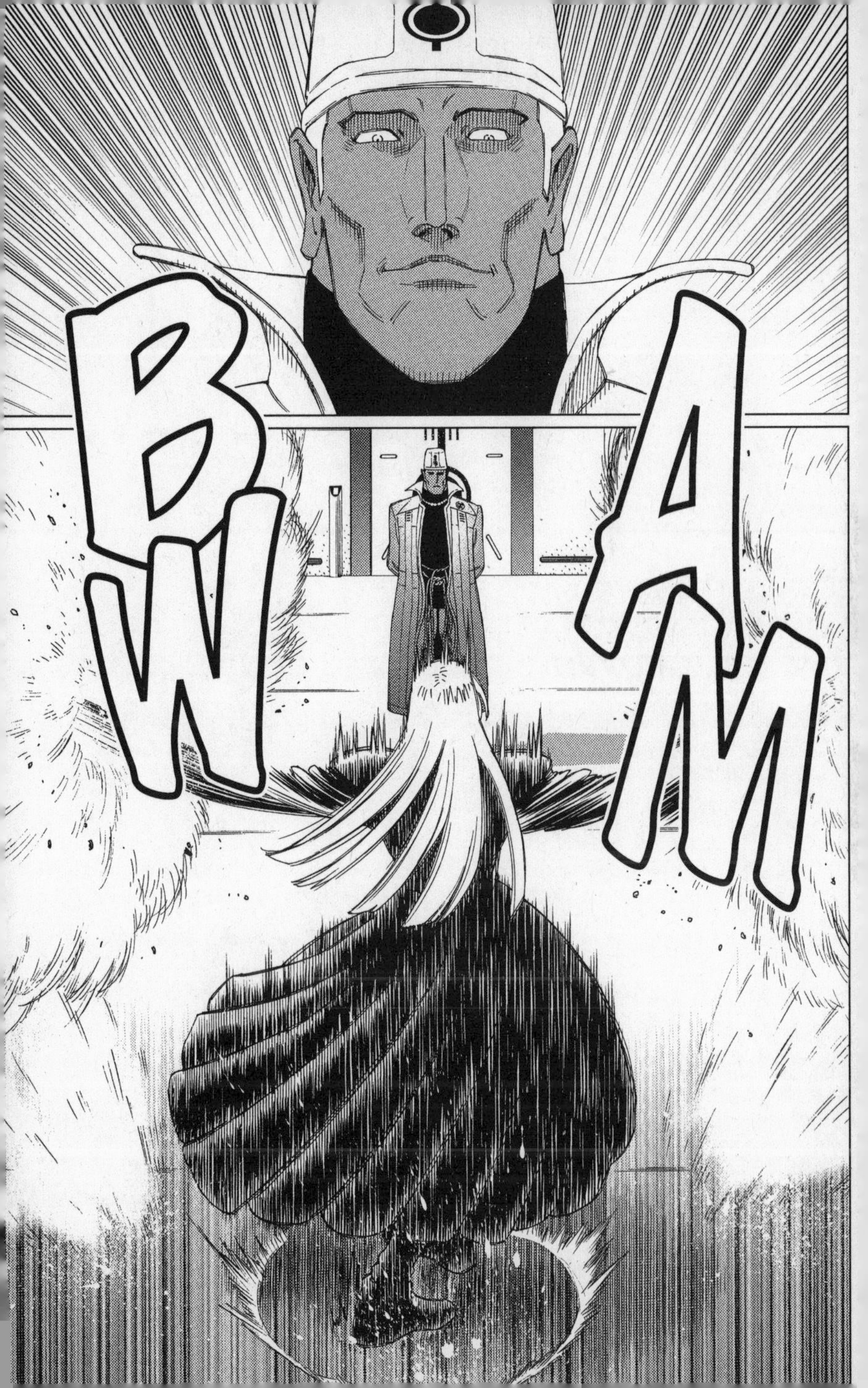
BWAM

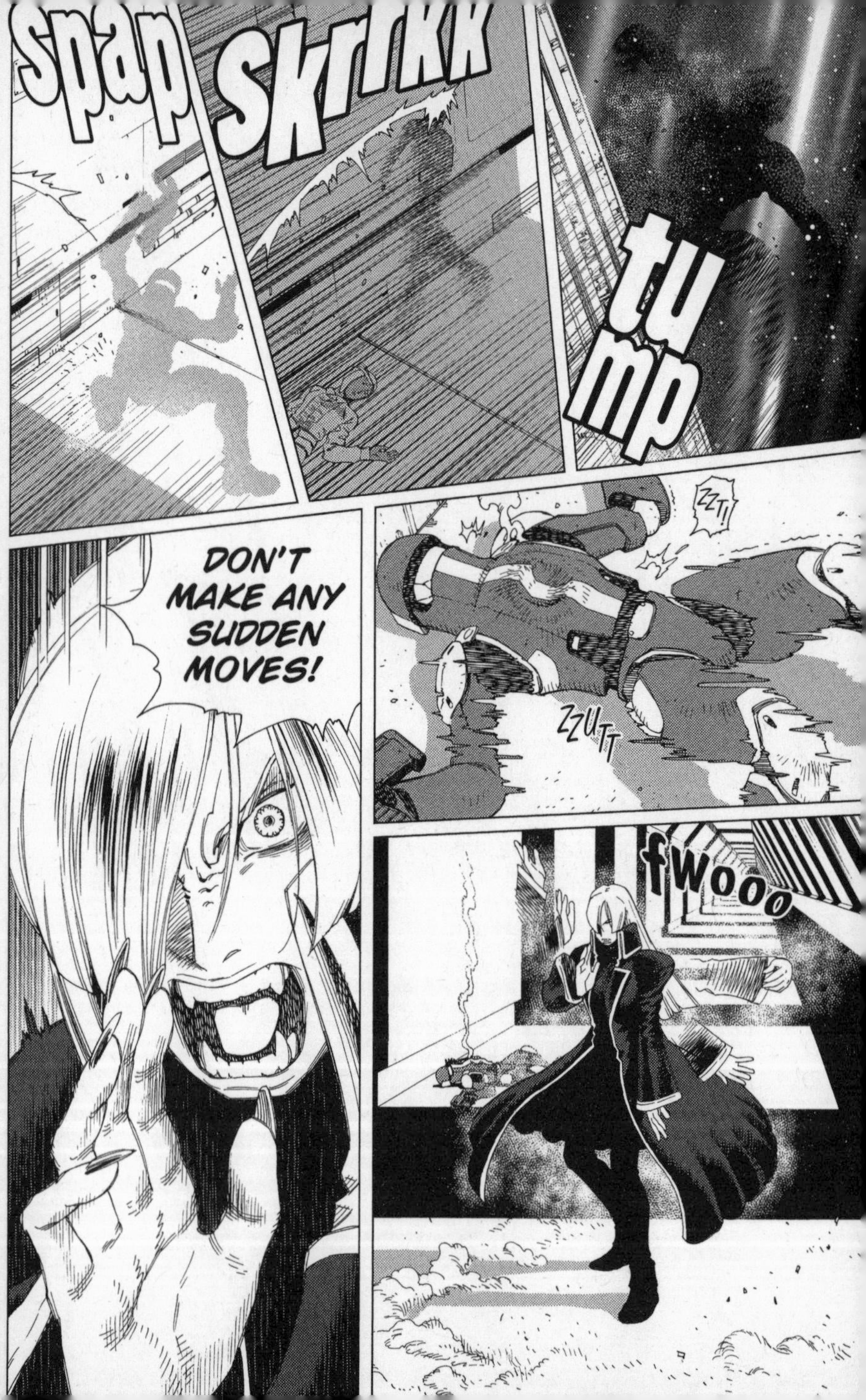
tump
SKRRKK
spap
ZZT!
ZZUTT
fwooo
DON'T MAKE ANY SUDDEN MOVES!

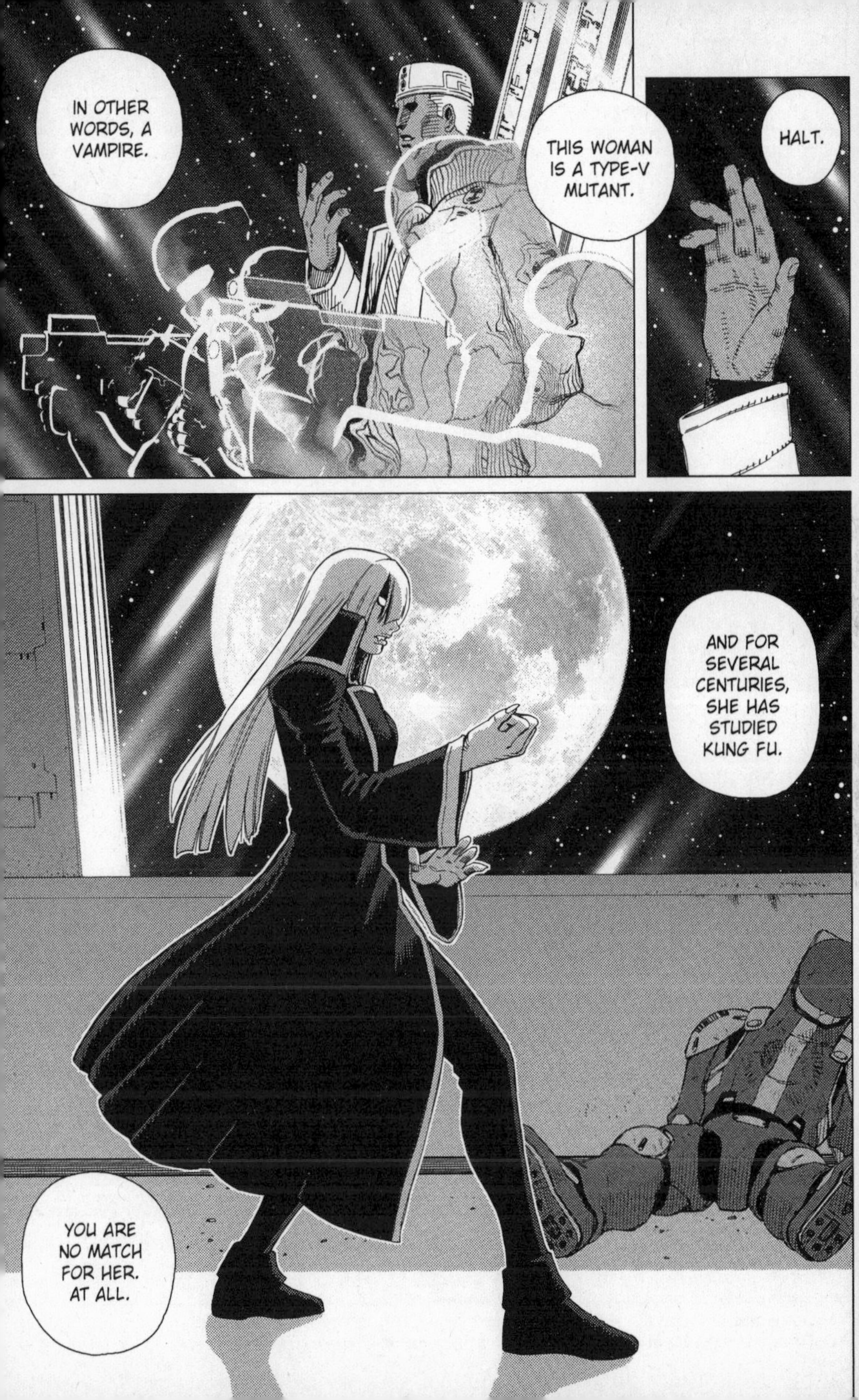
HALT.
THIS WOMAN IS A TYPE-V MUTANT.
IN OTHER WORDS, A VAMPIRE.
AND FOR SEVERAL CENTURIES, SHE HAS STUDIED KUNG FU.
YOU ARE NO MATCH FOR HER. AT ALL.

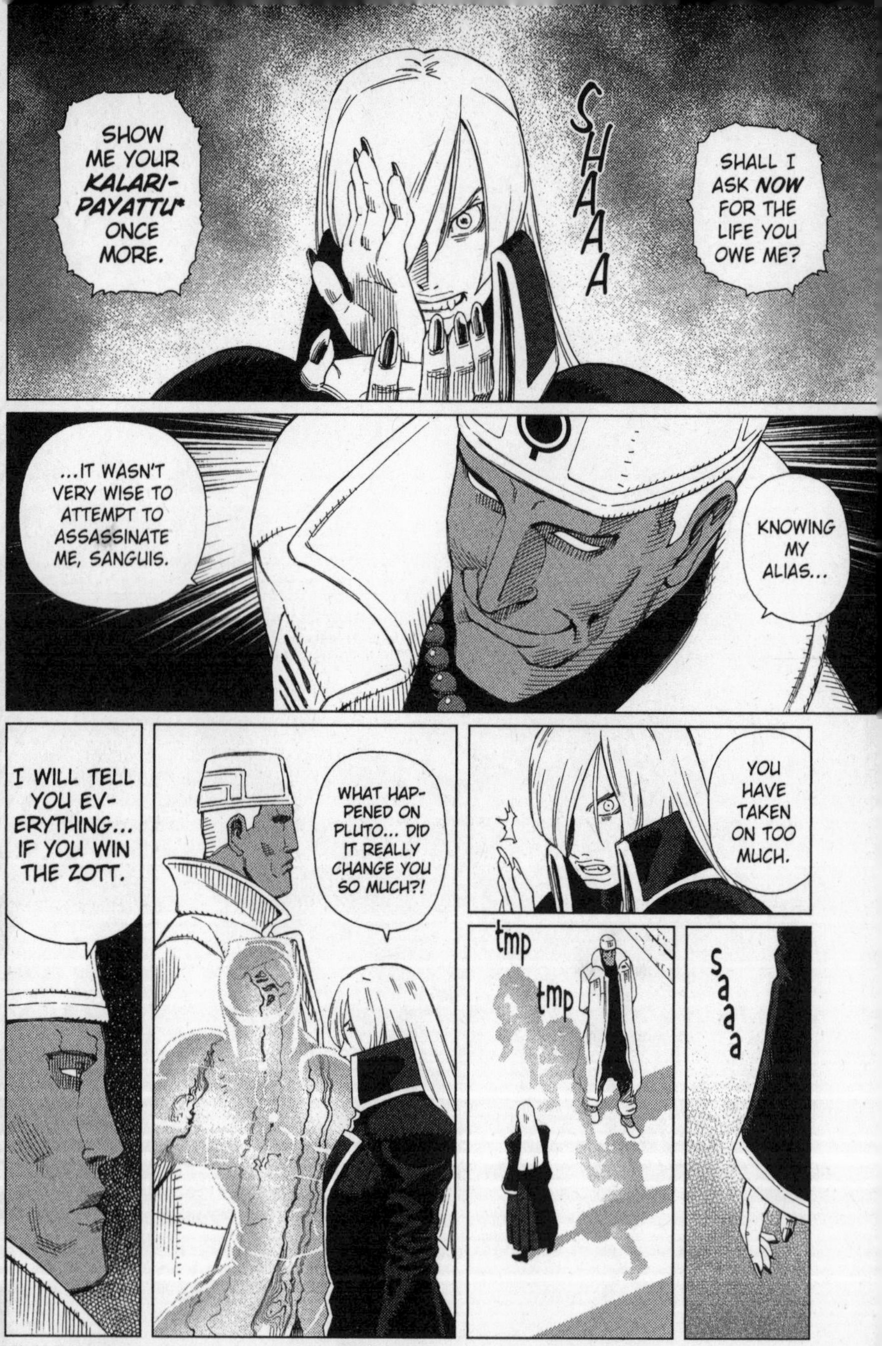
SHALL I ASK **NOW** FOR THE LIFE YOU OWE ME?
SHAAAA
SHOW ME YOUR ***KALARIPAYATTU**** ONCE MORE.
KNOWING MY ALIAS...
...IT WASN'T VERY WISE TO ATTEMPT TO ASSASSINATE ME, SANGUIS.
YOU HAVE TAKEN ON TOO MUCH.
saaaa
tmp
tmp
WHAT HAPPENED ON PLUTO... DID IT REALLY CHANGE YOU SO MUCH?!
I WILL TELL YOU EVERYTHING... IF YOU WIN THE ZOTT.

***Kalaripayattu:** An Indian martial art. According to legend, Shakyamuni, the founder of Buddhism, was a master of kalaripayattu. It was a precursor to Chinese kung fu.*

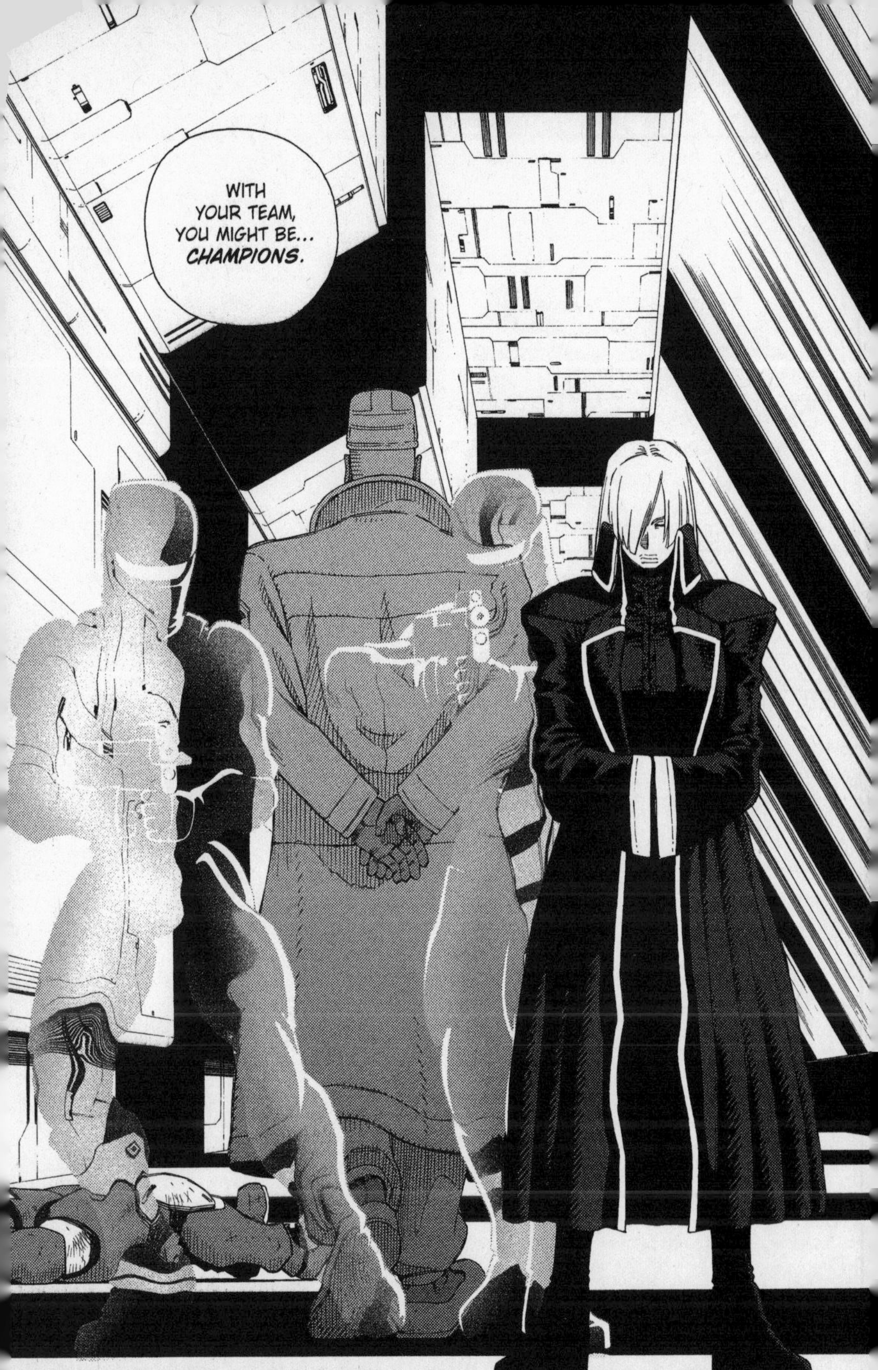
WITH YOUR TEAM, YOU MIGHT BE... CHAMPIONS.

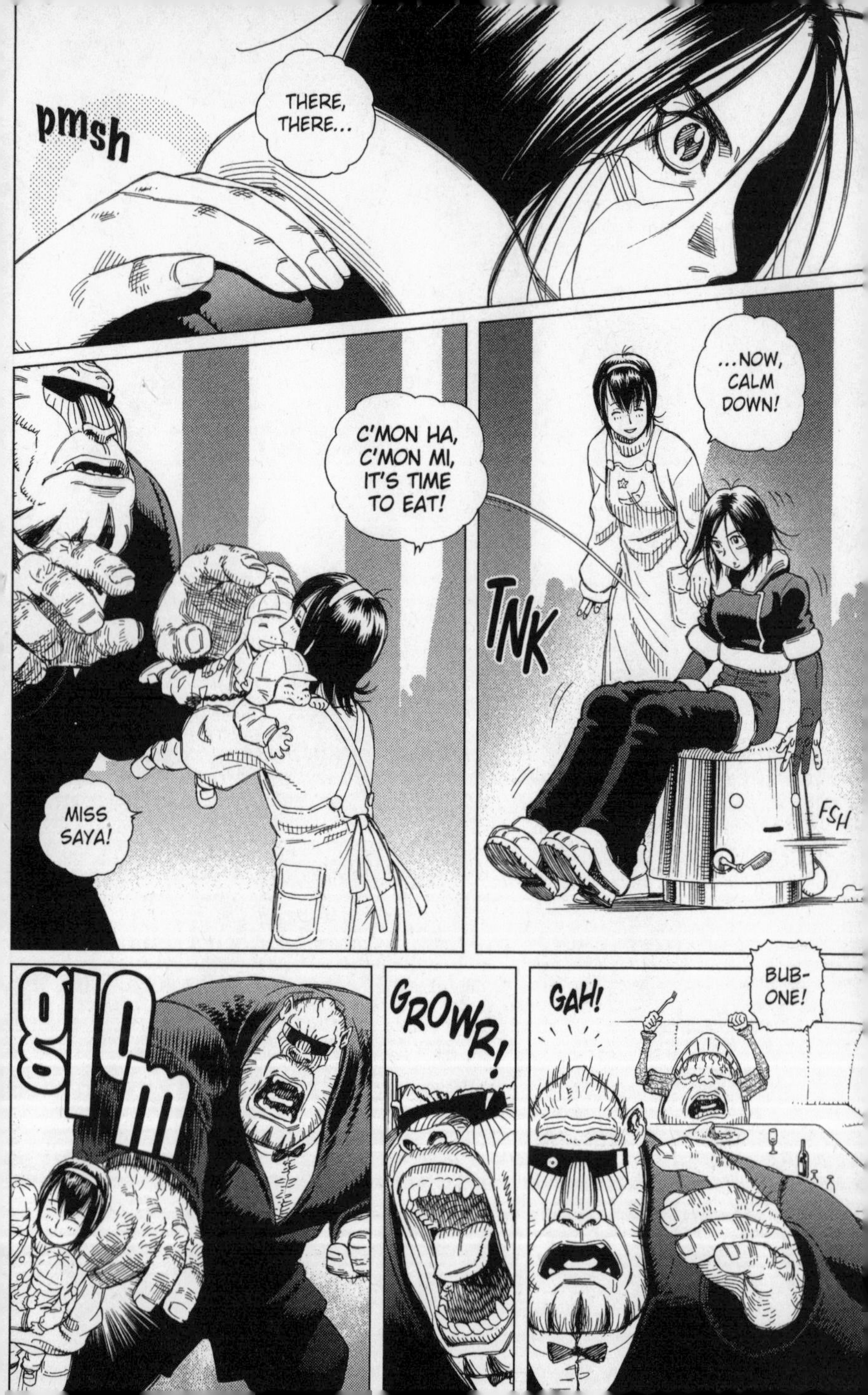
THERE, THERE...
pmsh
...NOW, CALM DOWN!
TNK
FSH
C'MON HA, C'MON MI, IT'S TIME TO EAT!
MISS SAYA!
BUB-ONE!
GAH!
GROWR!
glom

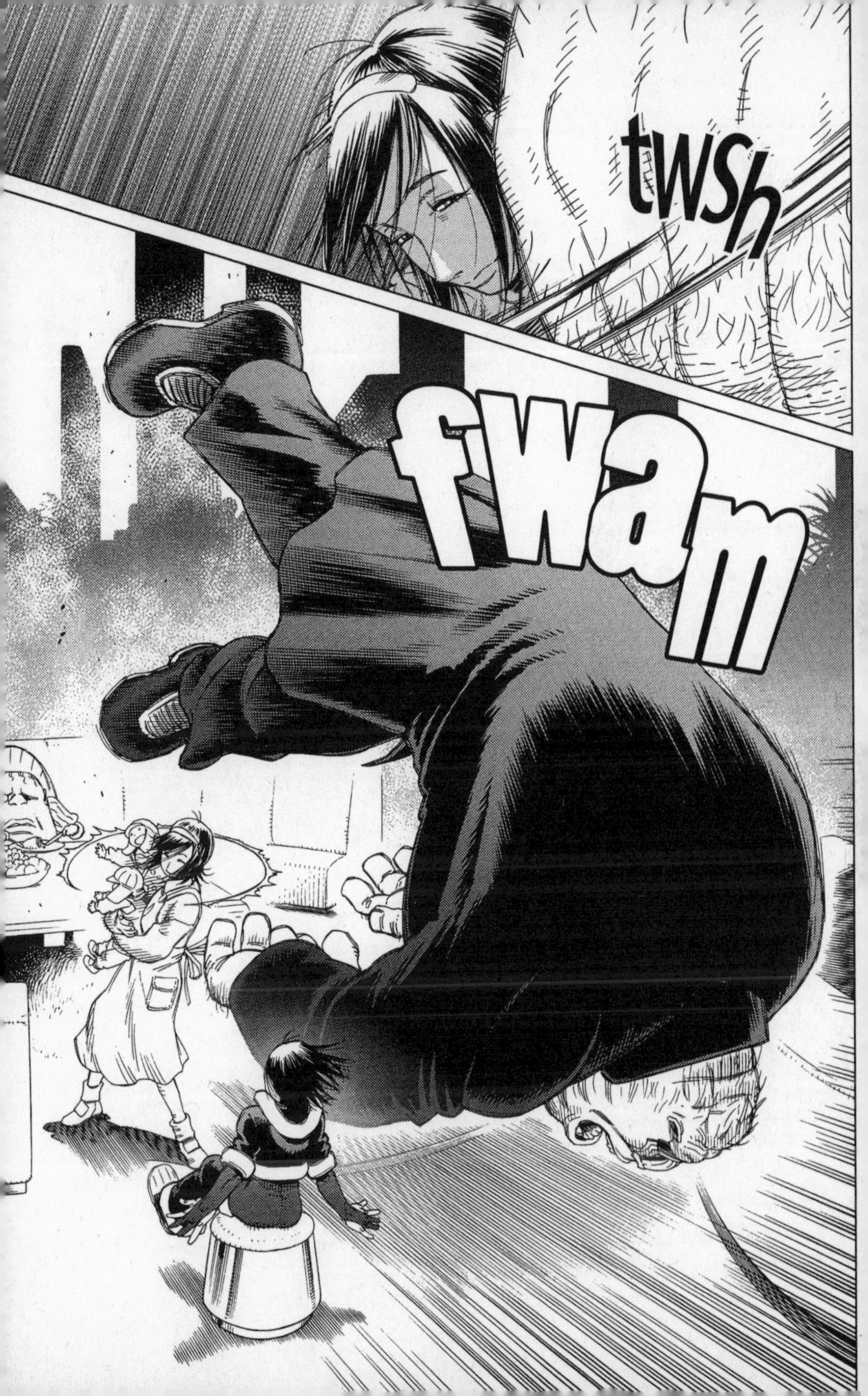
twsh
fwam

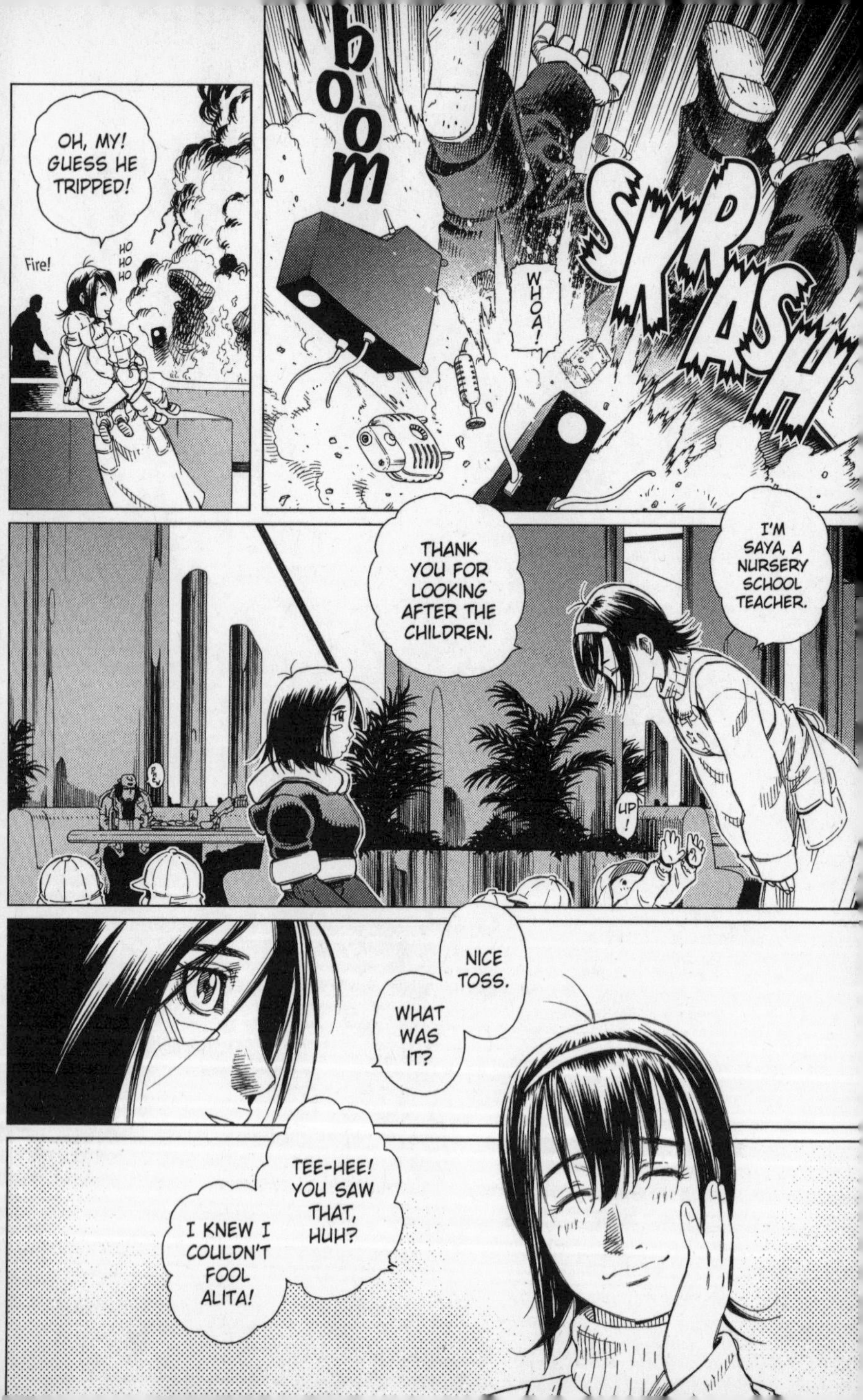
SKRASH
boom
WHOA!
OH, MY! GUESS HE TRIPPED!
HO HO HO
Fire!
I'M SAYA, A NURSERY SCHOOL TEACHER.
THANK YOU FOR LOOKING AFTER THE CHILDREN.
UP!
NICE TOSS.
WHAT WAS IT?
TEE-HEE! YOU SAW THAT, HUH?
I KNEW I COULDN'T FOOL ALITA!

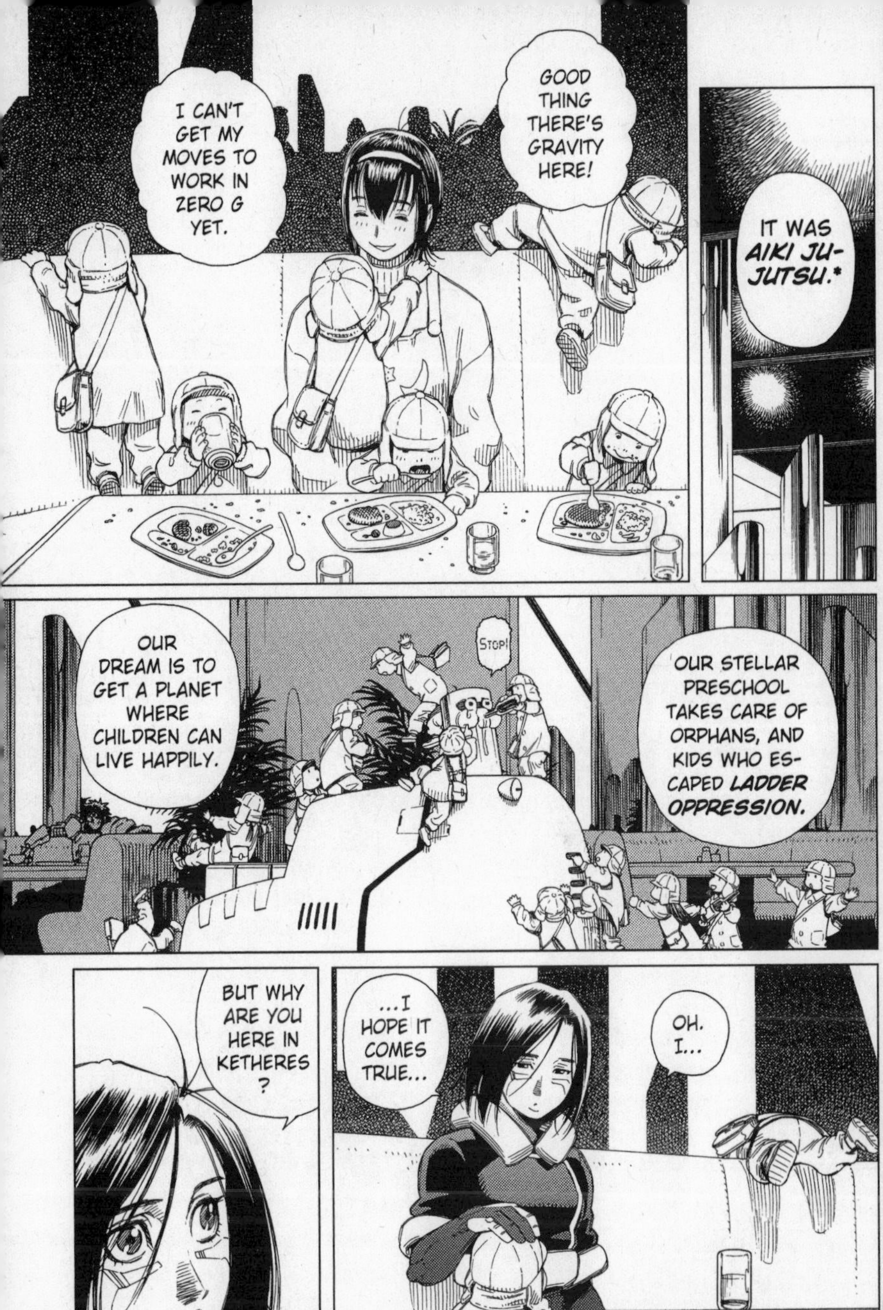
IT WAS AIKI JUJUTSU.*
GOOD THING THERE'S GRAVITY HERE!
I CAN'T GET MY MOVES TO WORK IN ZERO G YET.
OUR STELLAR PRESCHOOL TAKES CARE OF ORPHANS, AND KIDS WHO ES-CAPED LADDER OPPRESSION.
STOP!
OUR DREAM IS TO GET A PLANET WHERE CHILDREN CAN LIVE HAPPILY.
OH. I...
...I HOPE IT COMES TRUE...
BUT WHY ARE YOU HERE IN KETHERES?

Aiki jujutsu: *A hand-to-hand martial art that was the forefather of classic Japanese jujutsu. According to legend, the "baritsu" techniques that Sherlock Holmes used to throw Prof. Moriarty over the waterfall were actually this martial art.*

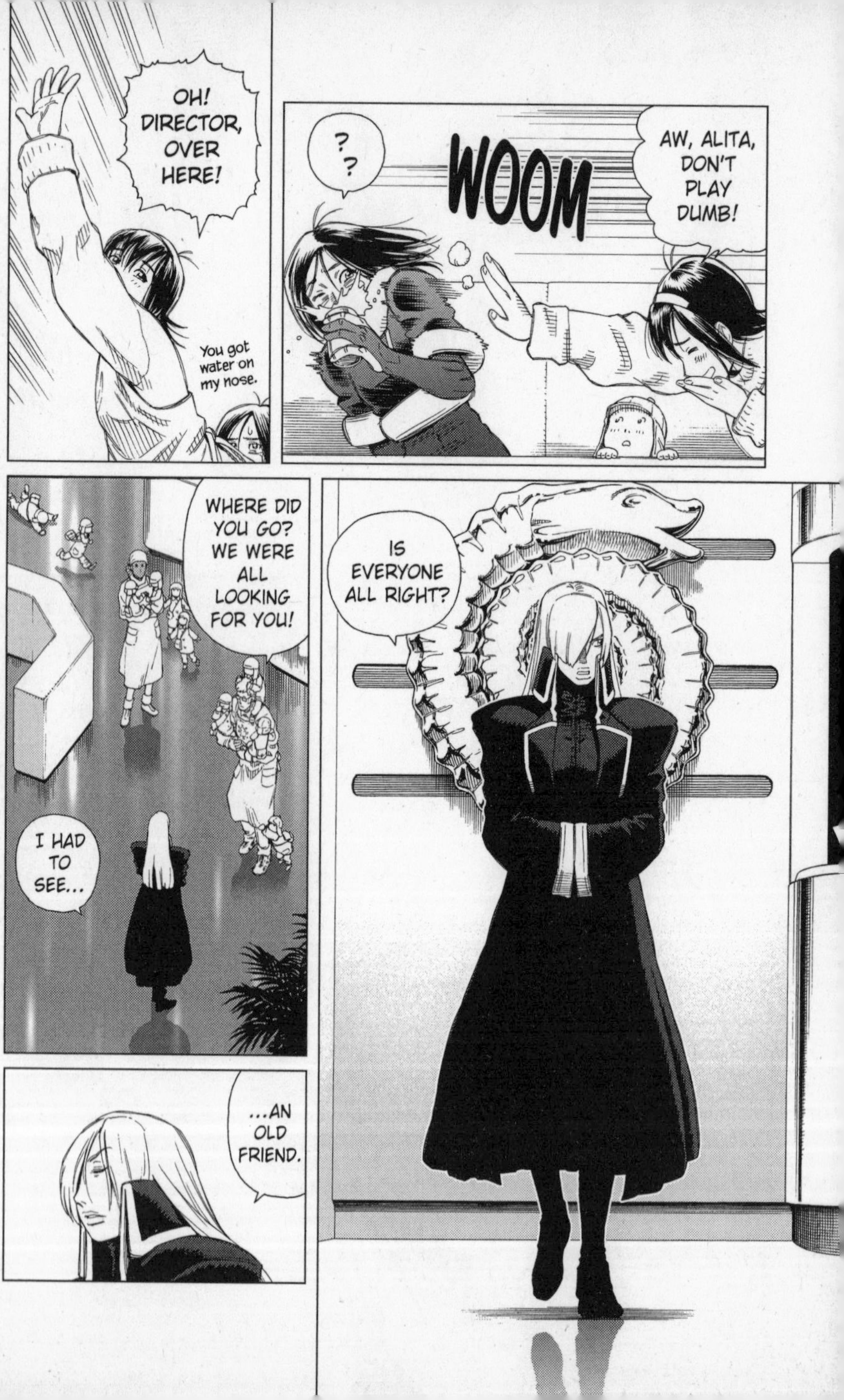
AW, ALITA, DON'T PLAY DUMB!
WOOM
??
OH! DIRECTOR, OVER HERE!
You got water on my nose.
IS EVERYONE ALL RIGHT?
WHERE DID YOU GO? WE WERE ALL LOOKING FOR YOU!
I HAD TO SEE...
...AN OLD FRIEND.

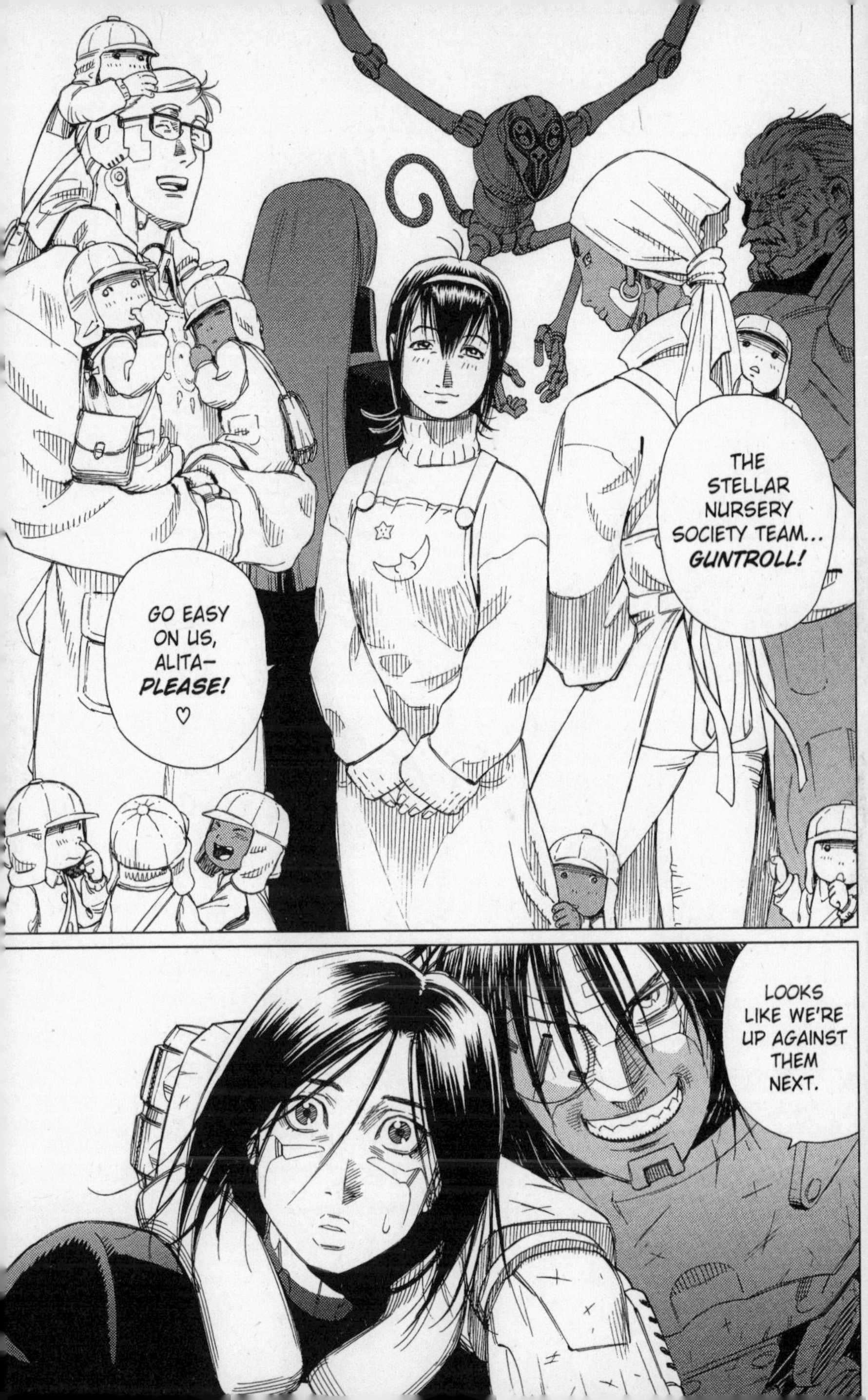
THE STELLAR NURSERY SOCIETY TEAM... *GUNTROLL!*
GO EASY ON US, ALITA— *PLEASE!* ♡
LOOKS LIKE WE'RE UP AGAINST THEM NEXT.

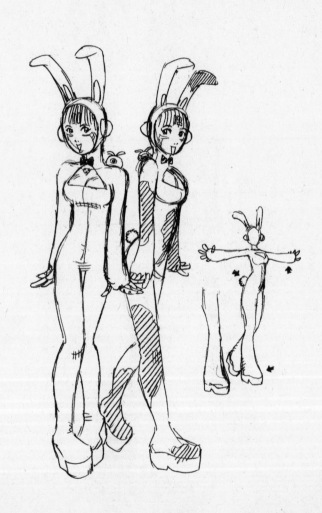

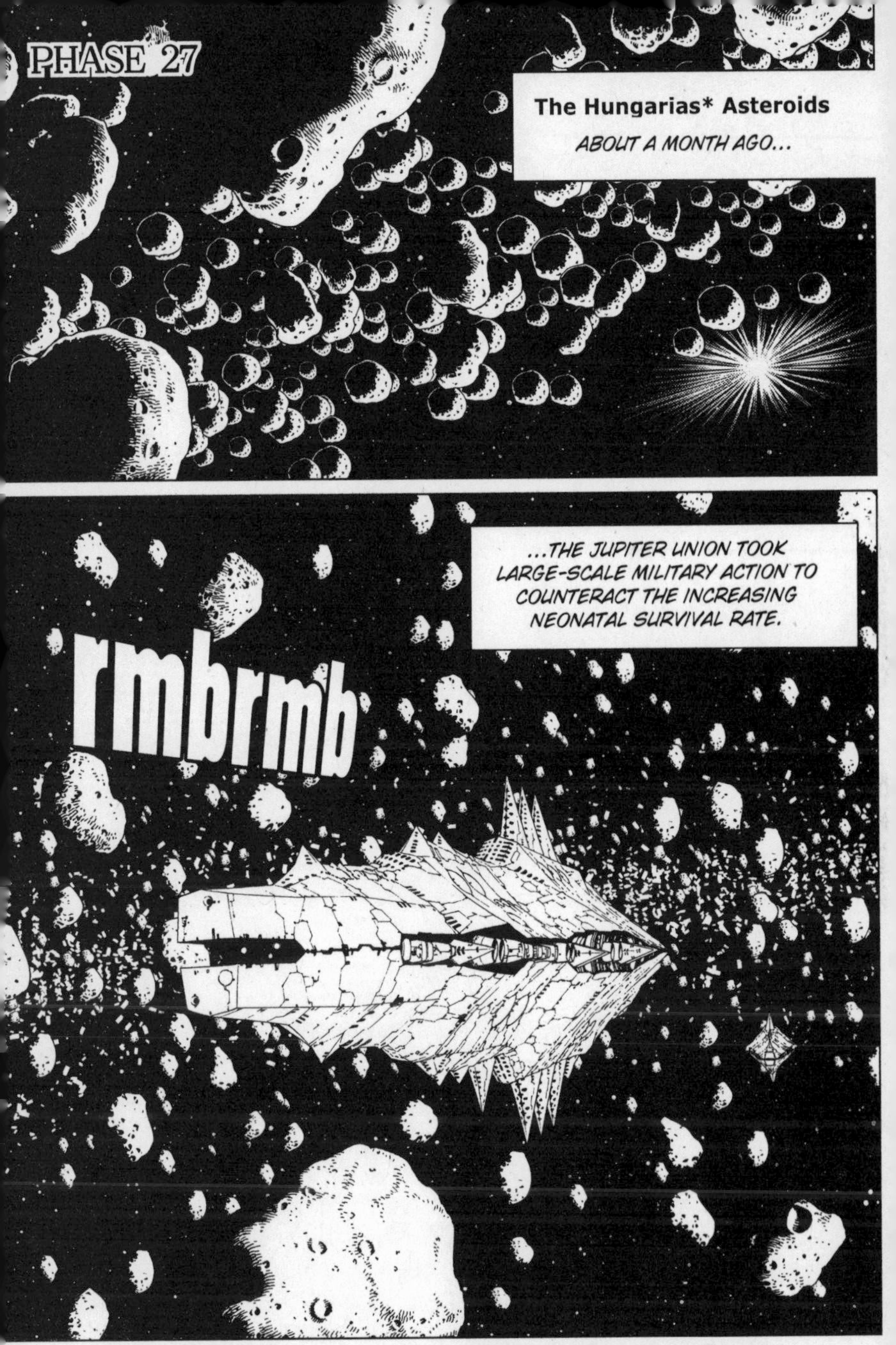
PHASE 27
The Hungarias* Asteroids
ABOUT A MONTH AGO...
...THE JUPITER UNION TOOK LARGE-SCALE MILITARY ACTION TO COUNTERACT THE INCREASING NEONATAL SURVIVAL RATE.
rmbrmb

***Hungarias:** *Asteroids in the asteroid belt are subdivided by orbit into groups. These groups are called "families," and were identified in 1918 by Kiyotsugu Hirayama of Japan. Other asteroid families include the Floras, Phocaea, Koronis, Eos, Themis, Cybeles, and Hildas.*

Operation Lawnmower

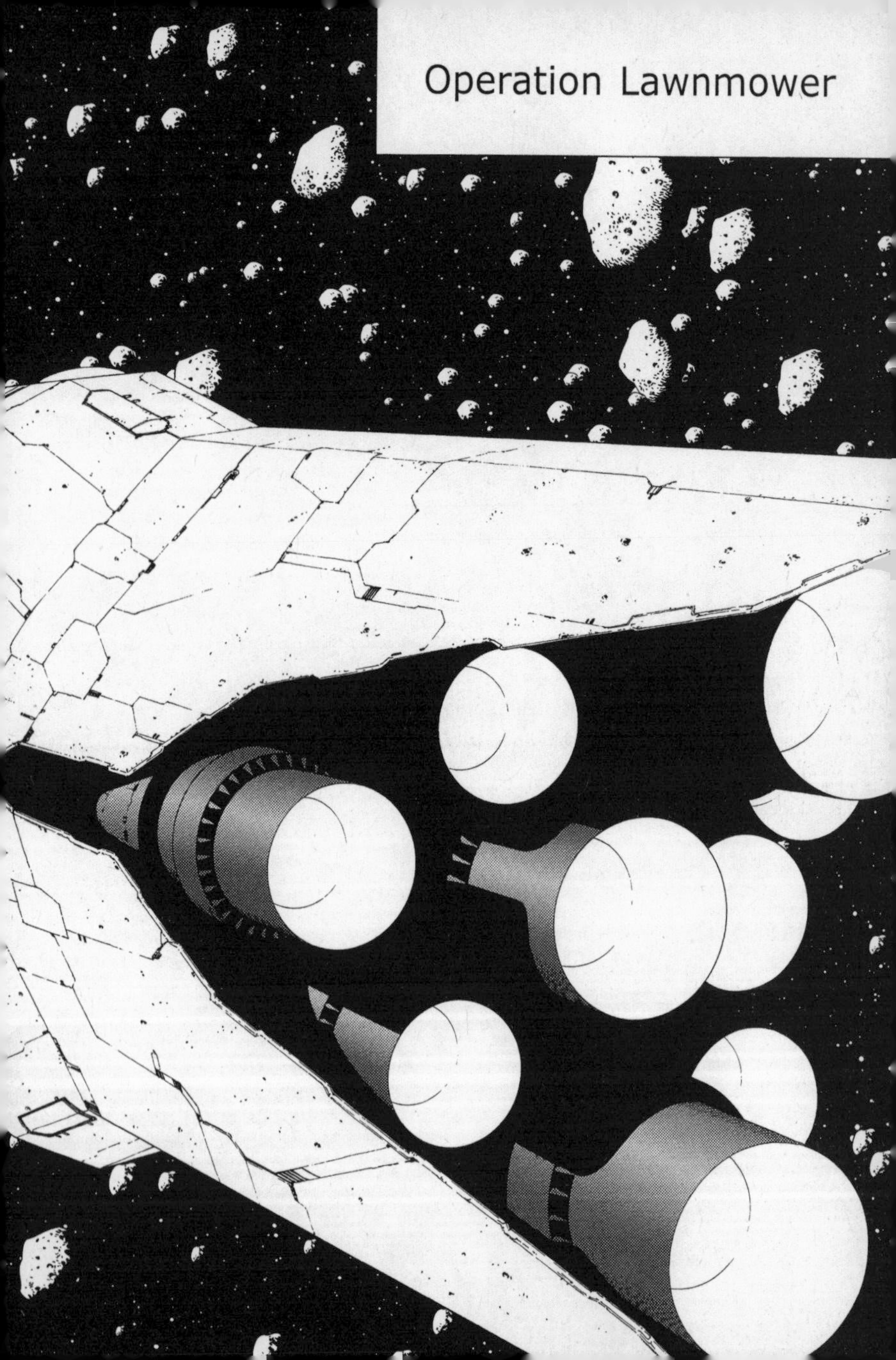

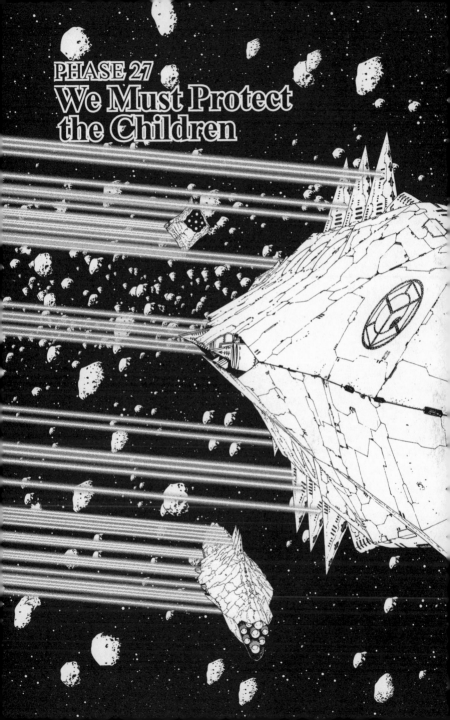

PHASE 27
We Must Protect the Children

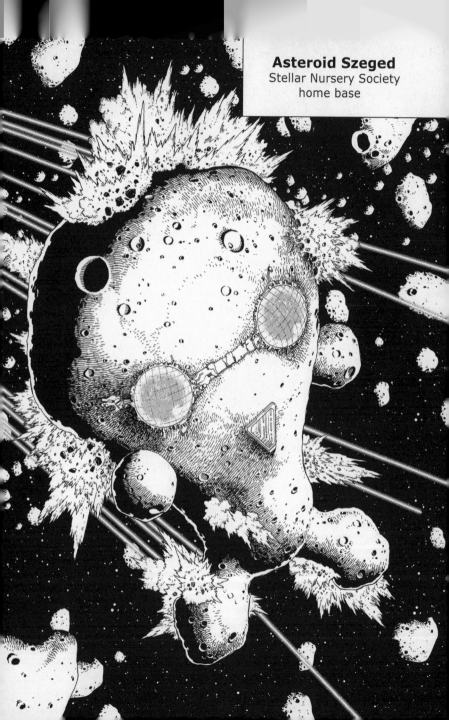

Asteroid Szeged
Stellar Nursery Society
home base

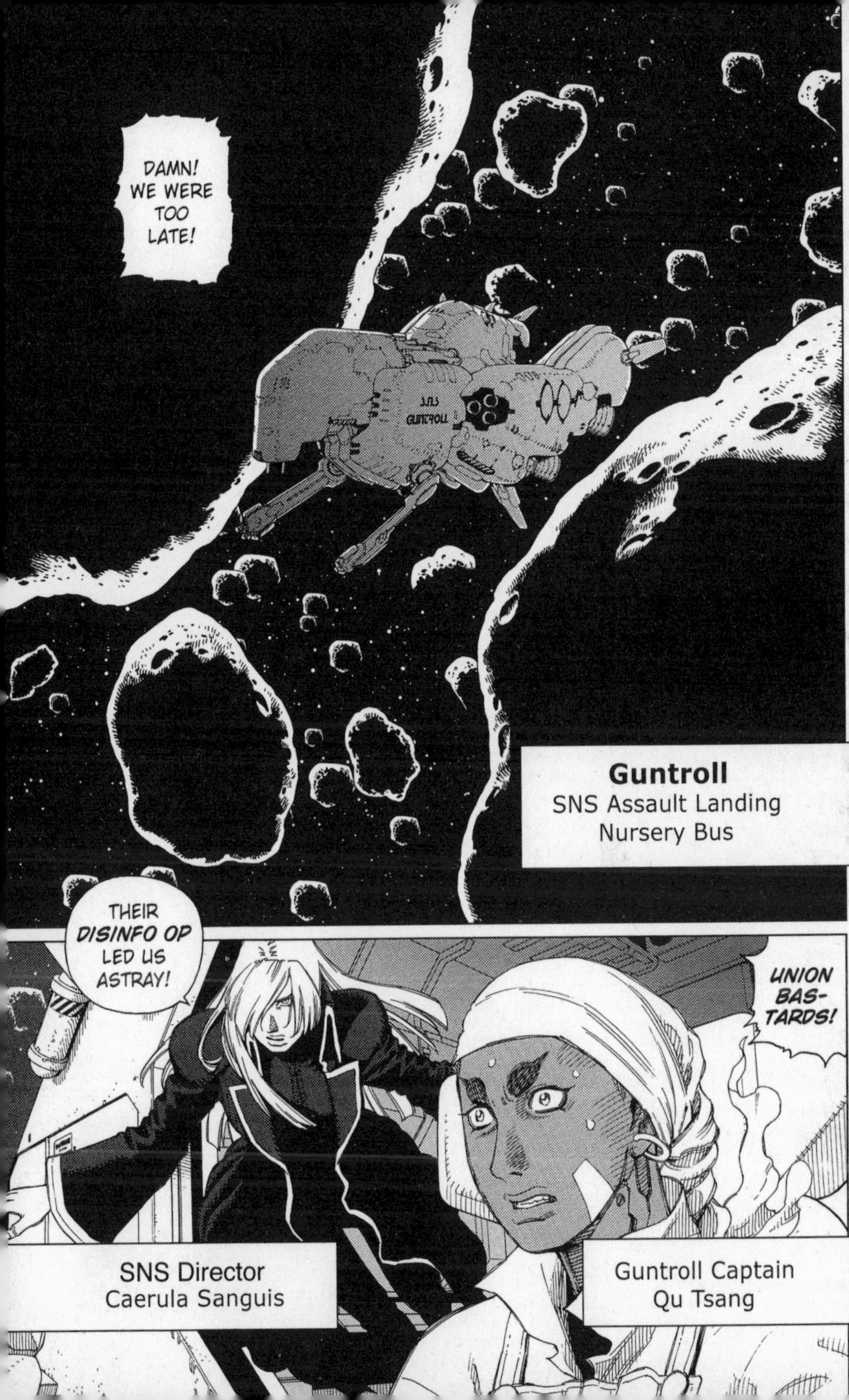
DAMN! WE WERE TOO LATE!
Guntroll
SNS Assault Landing Nursery Bus
UNION BASTARDS!
THEIR DISINFO OP LED US ASTRAY!
Guntroll Captain
Qu Tsang
SNS Director
Caerula Sanguis

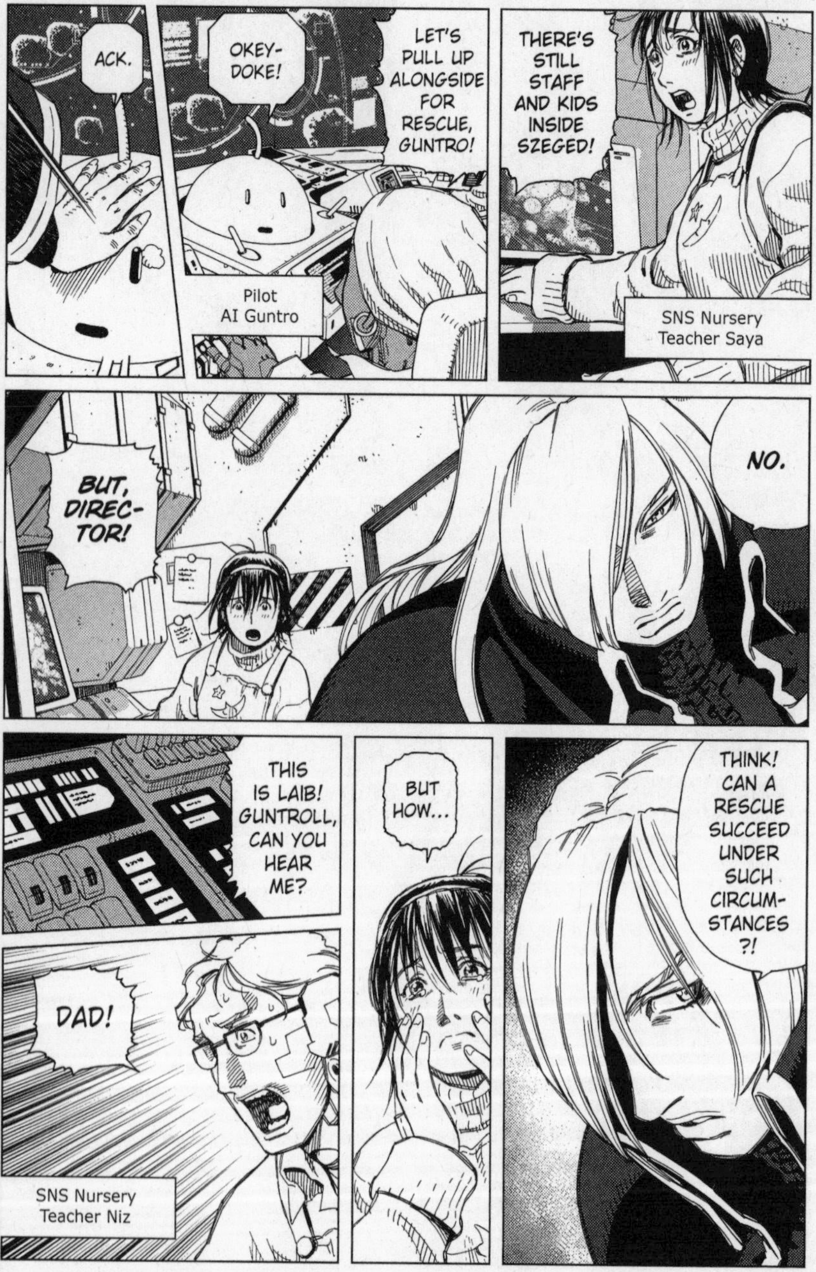
THERE'S STILL STAFF AND KIDS INSIDE SZEGED!
SNS Nursery Teacher Saya
LET'S PULL UP ALONGSIDE FOR RESCUE, GUNTRO!
OKEY-DOKE!
Pilot AI Guntro
ACK.
NO.
BUT, DIREC-TOR!
THINK! CAN A RESCUE SUCCEED UNDER SUCH CIRCUM-STANCES ?!
BUT HOW...
THIS IS LAIB! GUNTROLL, CAN YOU HEAR ME?
DAD!
SNS Nursery Teacher Niz

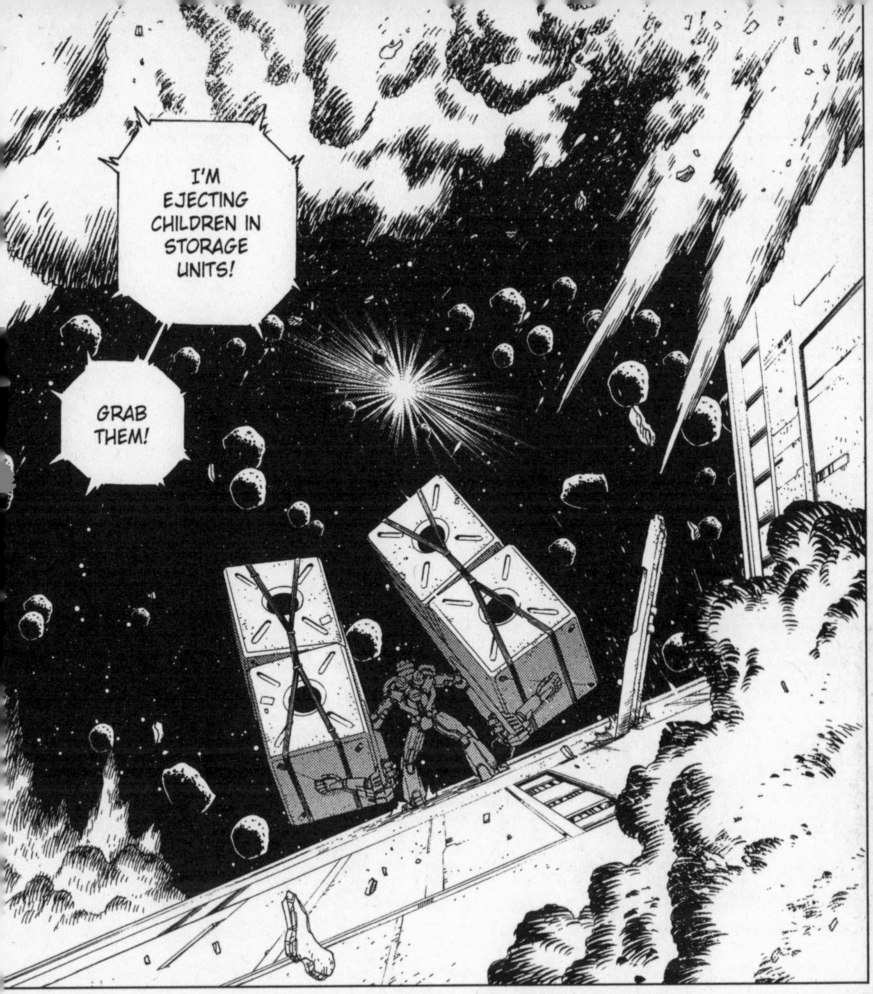
I'M EJECTING CHILDREN IN STORAGE UNITS!
GRAB THEM!
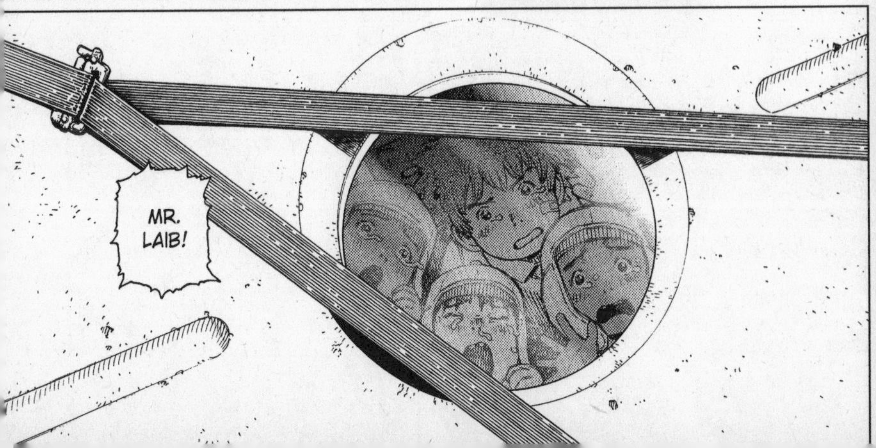
MR. LAIB!

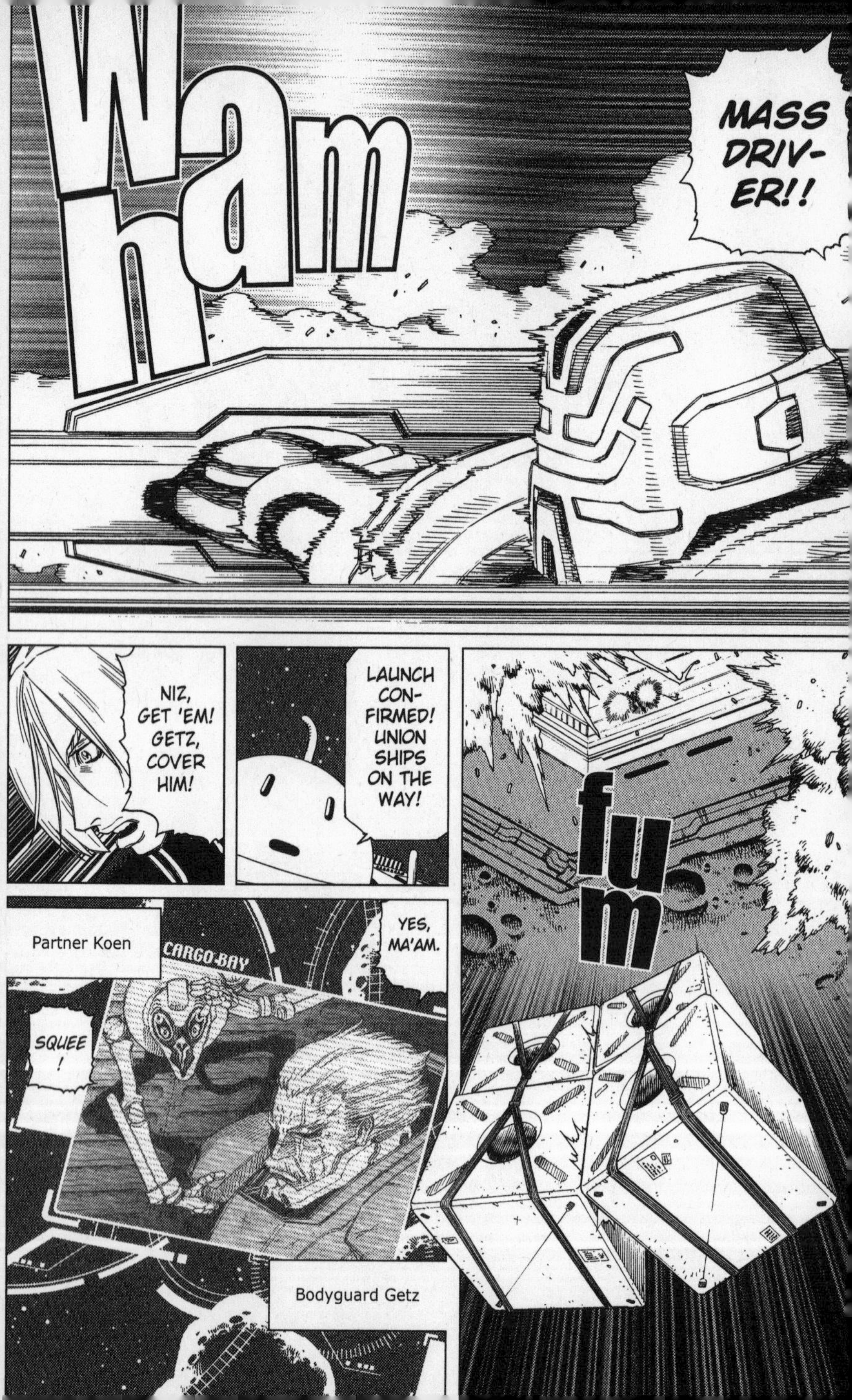
MASS DRIVER!!
Wham
fum
LAUNCH CONFIRMED! UNION SHIPS ON THE WAY!
NIZ, GET 'EM! GETZ, COVER HIM!
YES, MA'AM.
Partner Koen
CARGO BAY
SQUEE!
Bodyguard Getz

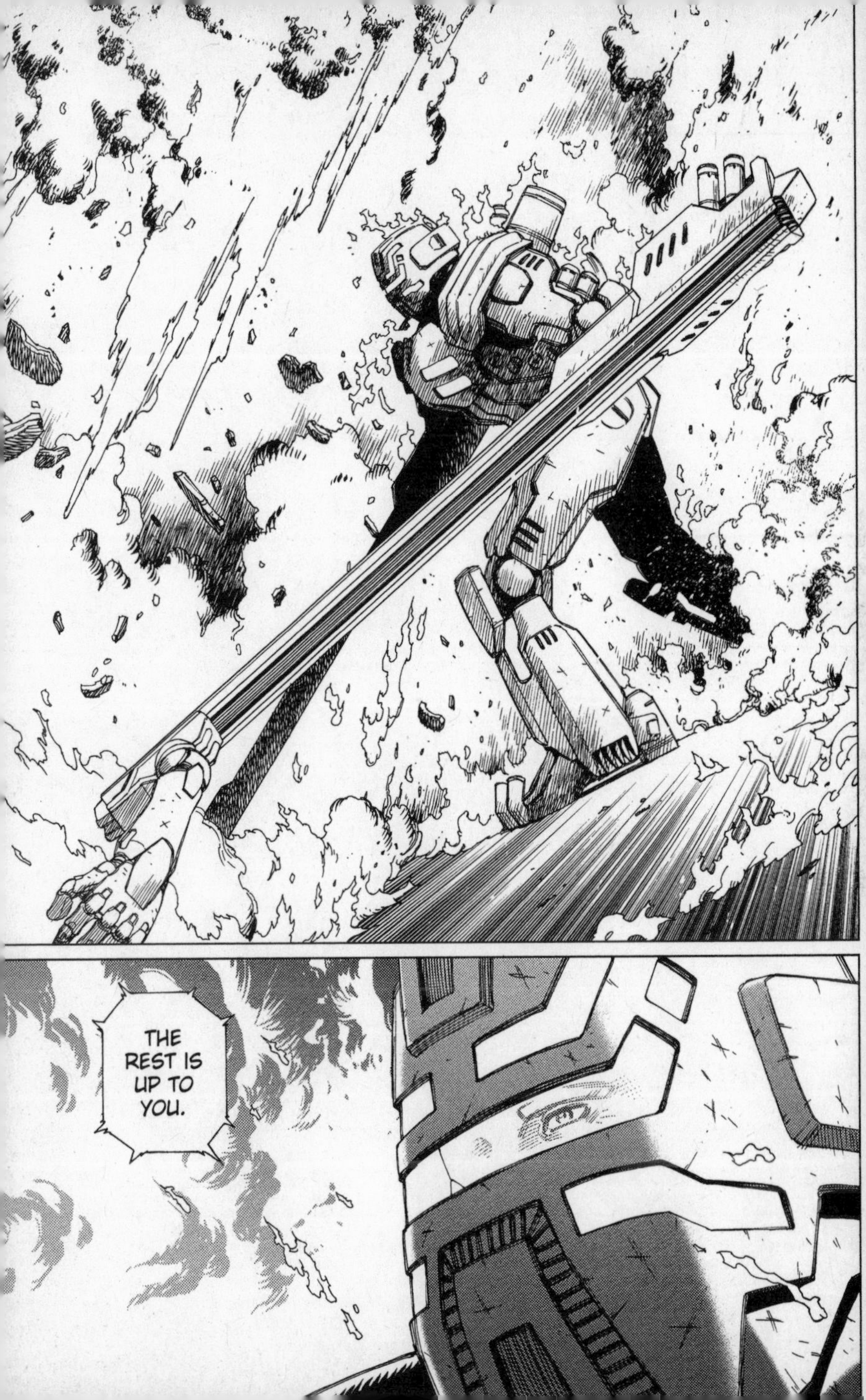
THE REST IS UP TO YOU.

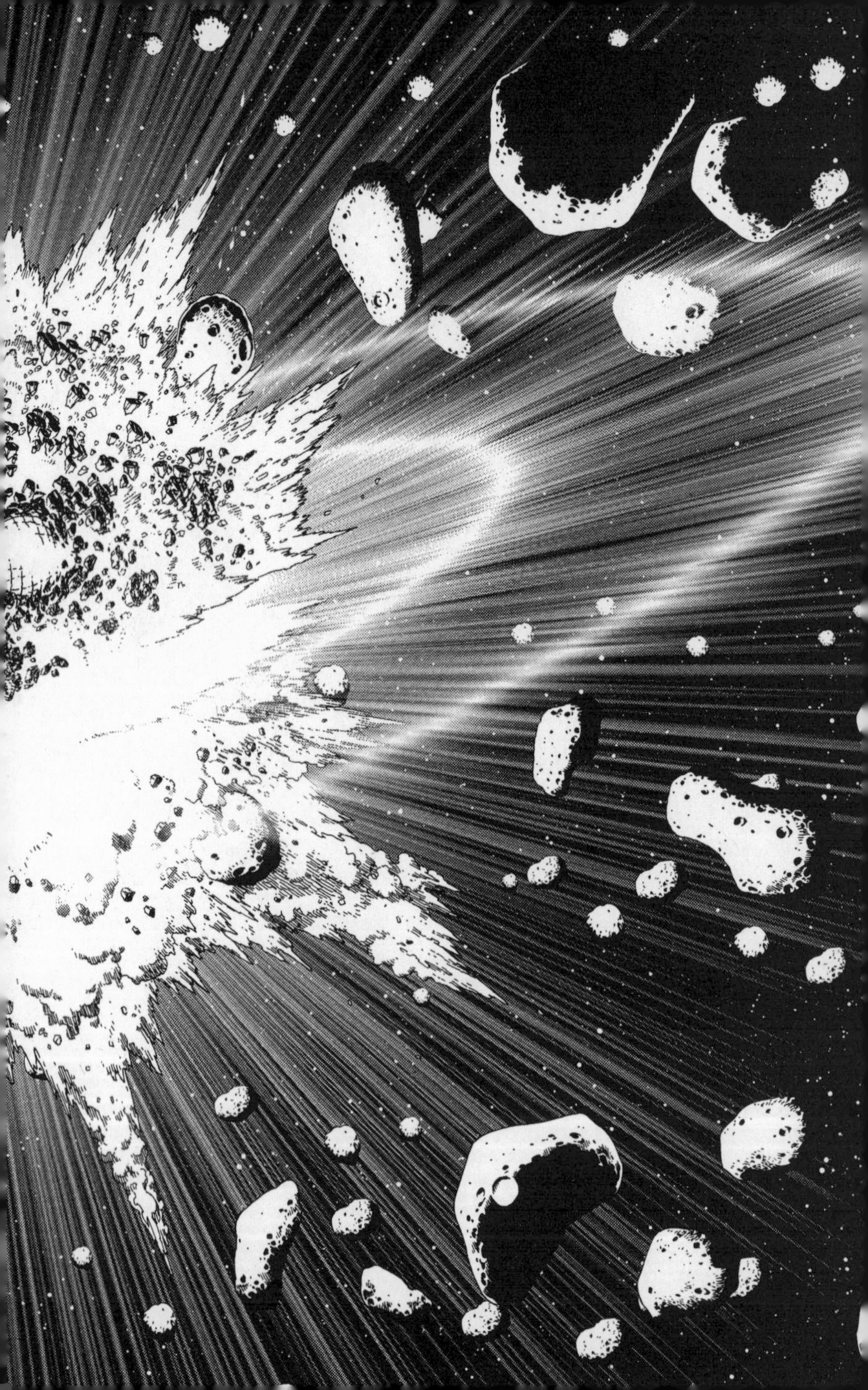

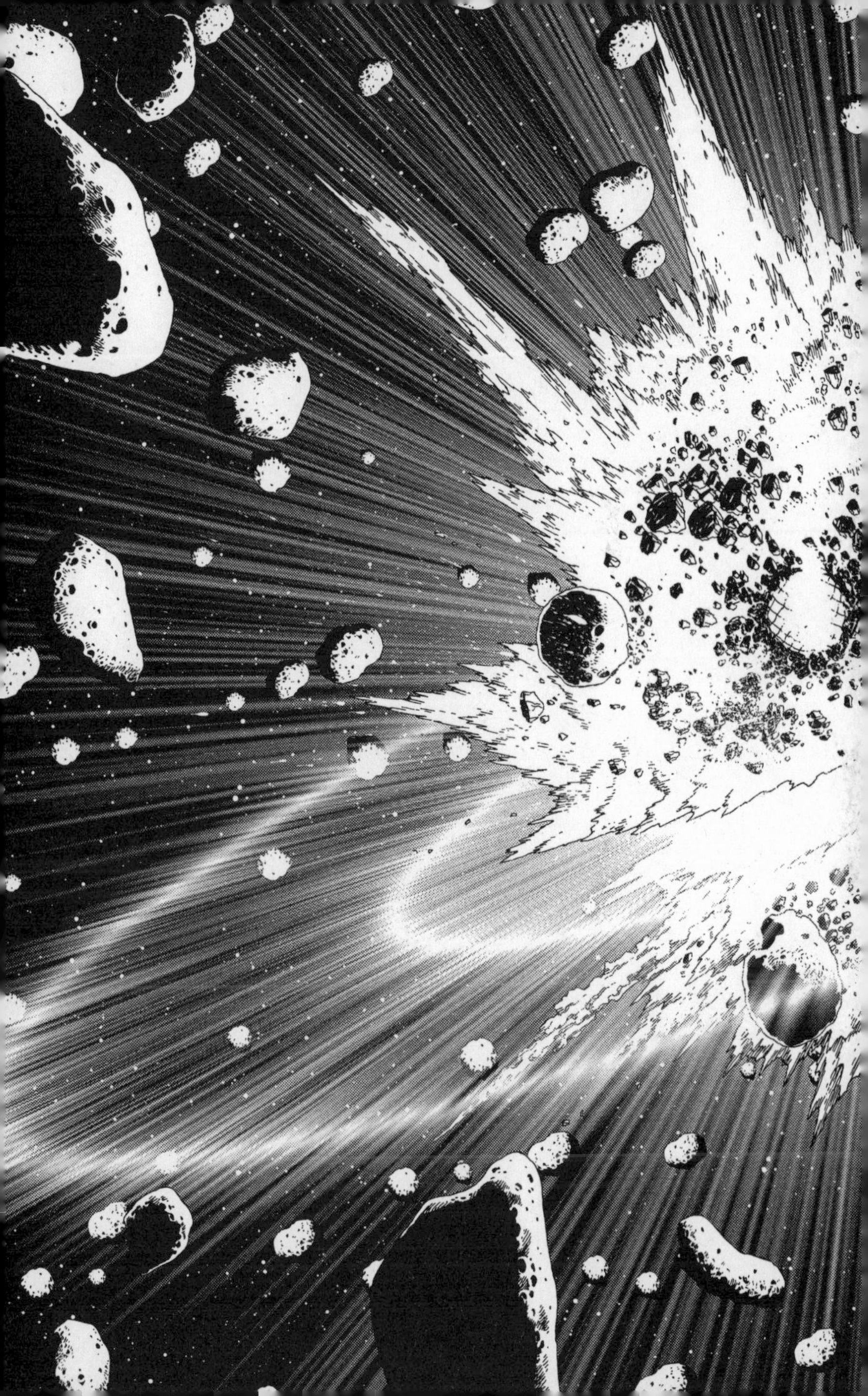

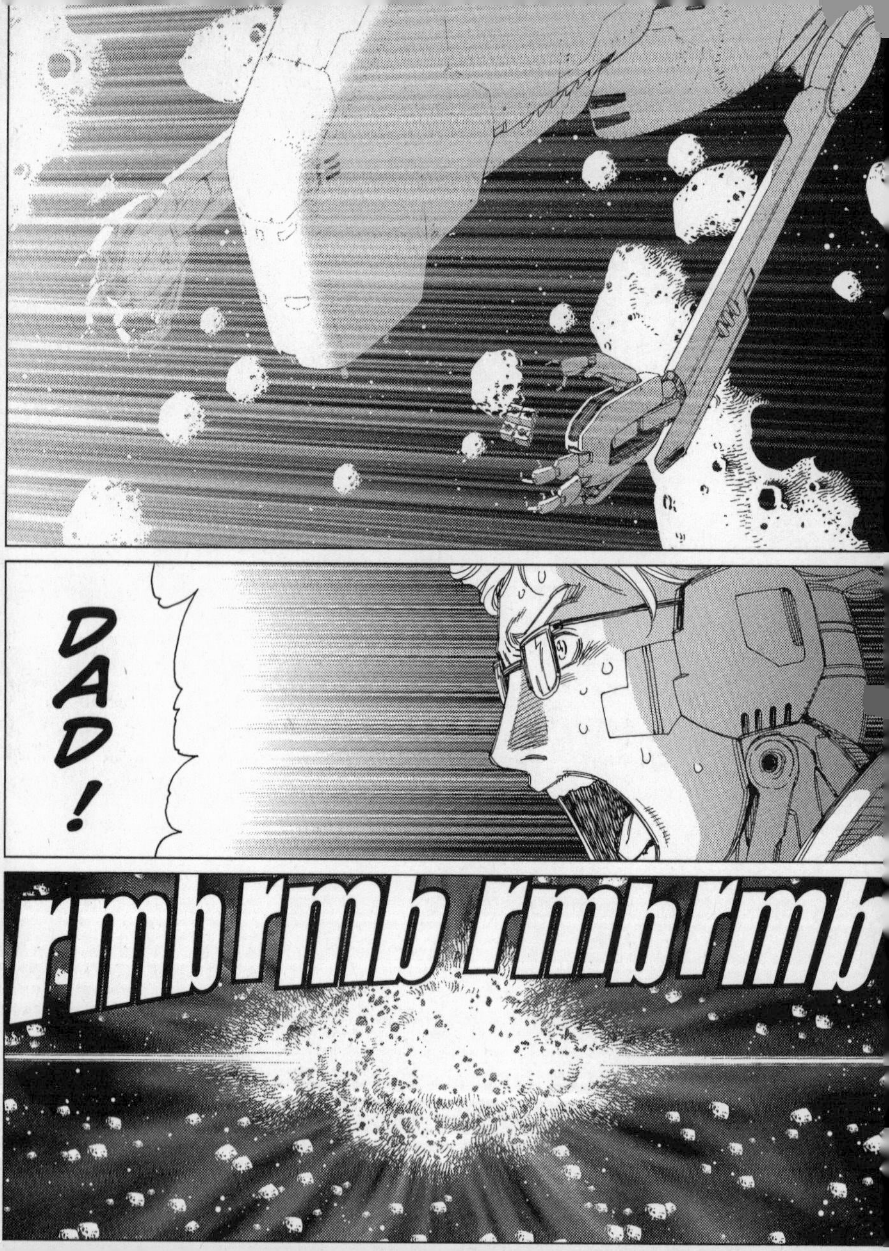
DAD!
rmb rmb rmb rmb

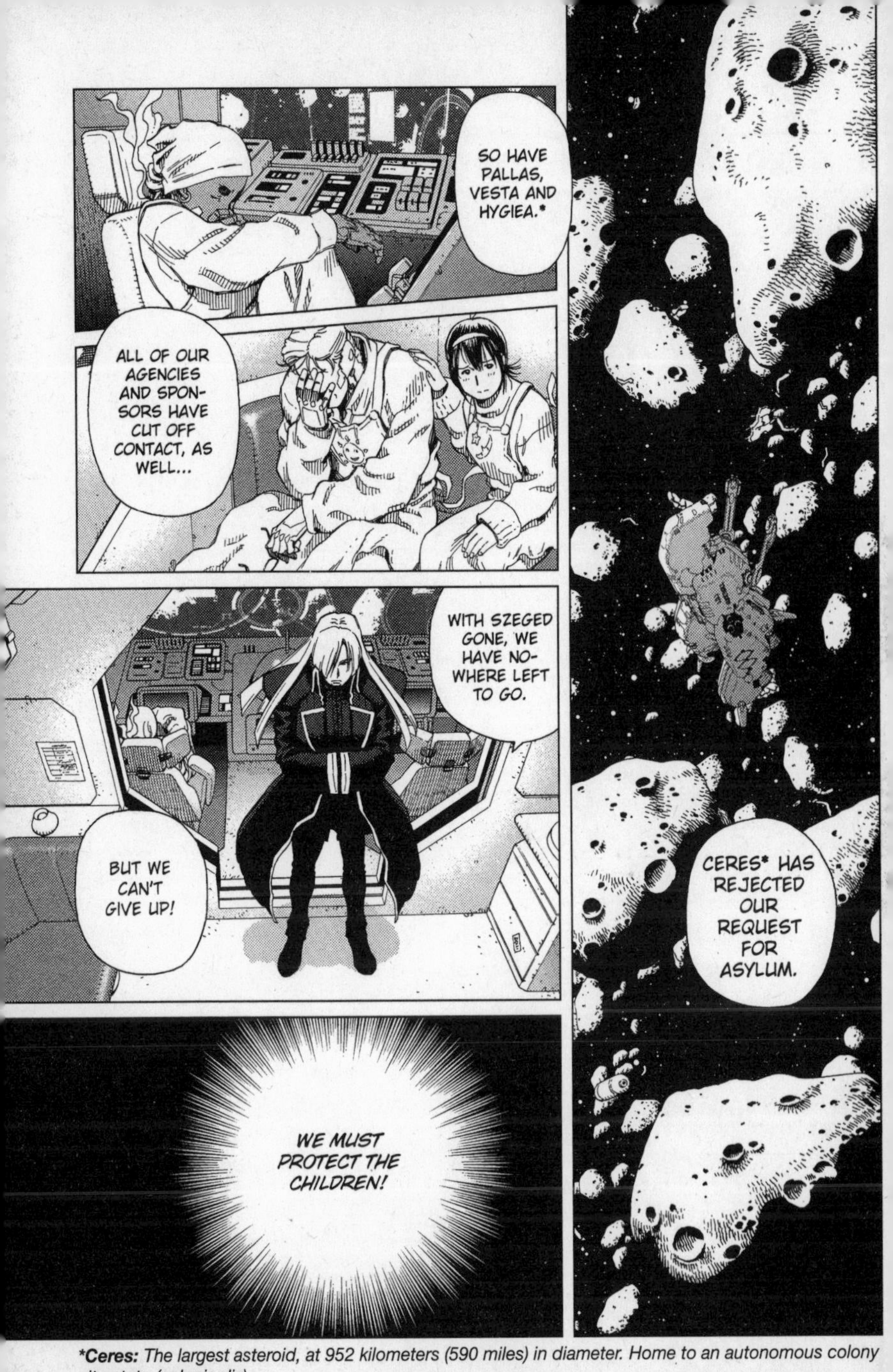
CERES* HAS REJECTED OUR REQUEST FOR ASYLUM.
SO HAVE PALLAS, VESTA AND HYGIEA.*
ALL OF OUR AGENCIES AND SPONSORS HAVE CUT OFF CONTACT, AS WELL...
WITH SZEGED GONE, WE HAVE NOWHERE LEFT TO GO.
BUT WE CAN'T GIVE UP!
WE MUST PROTECT THE CHILDREN!

***Ceres:** The largest asteroid, at 952 kilometers (590 miles) in diameter. Home to an autonomous colony city-state (colonipolis).*

***Pallas, Vesta, Hygiea**: The second, third, and fourth-largest asteroids. Each has a colonipolis.*

ZOTT Day 2: Round One, First Match

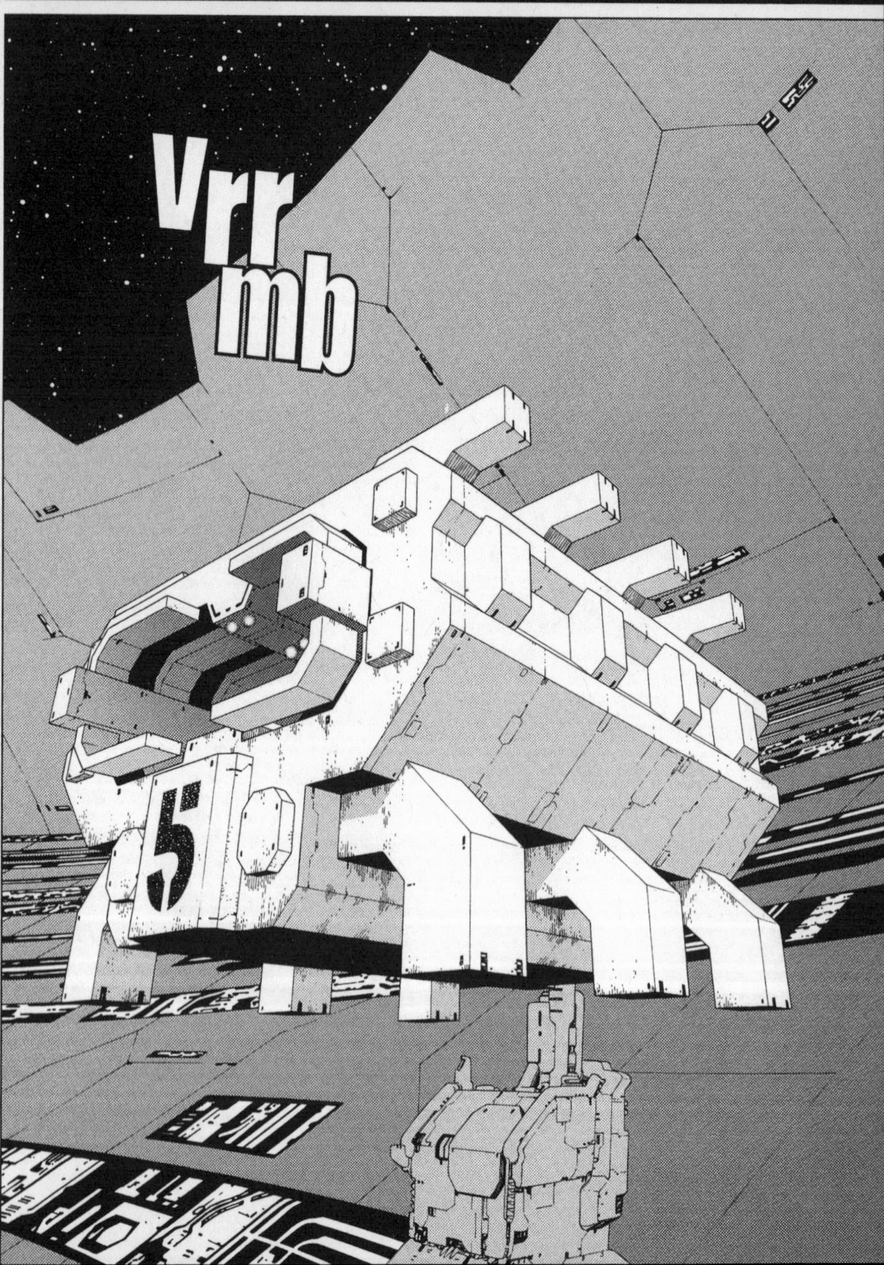
Vrr
mb

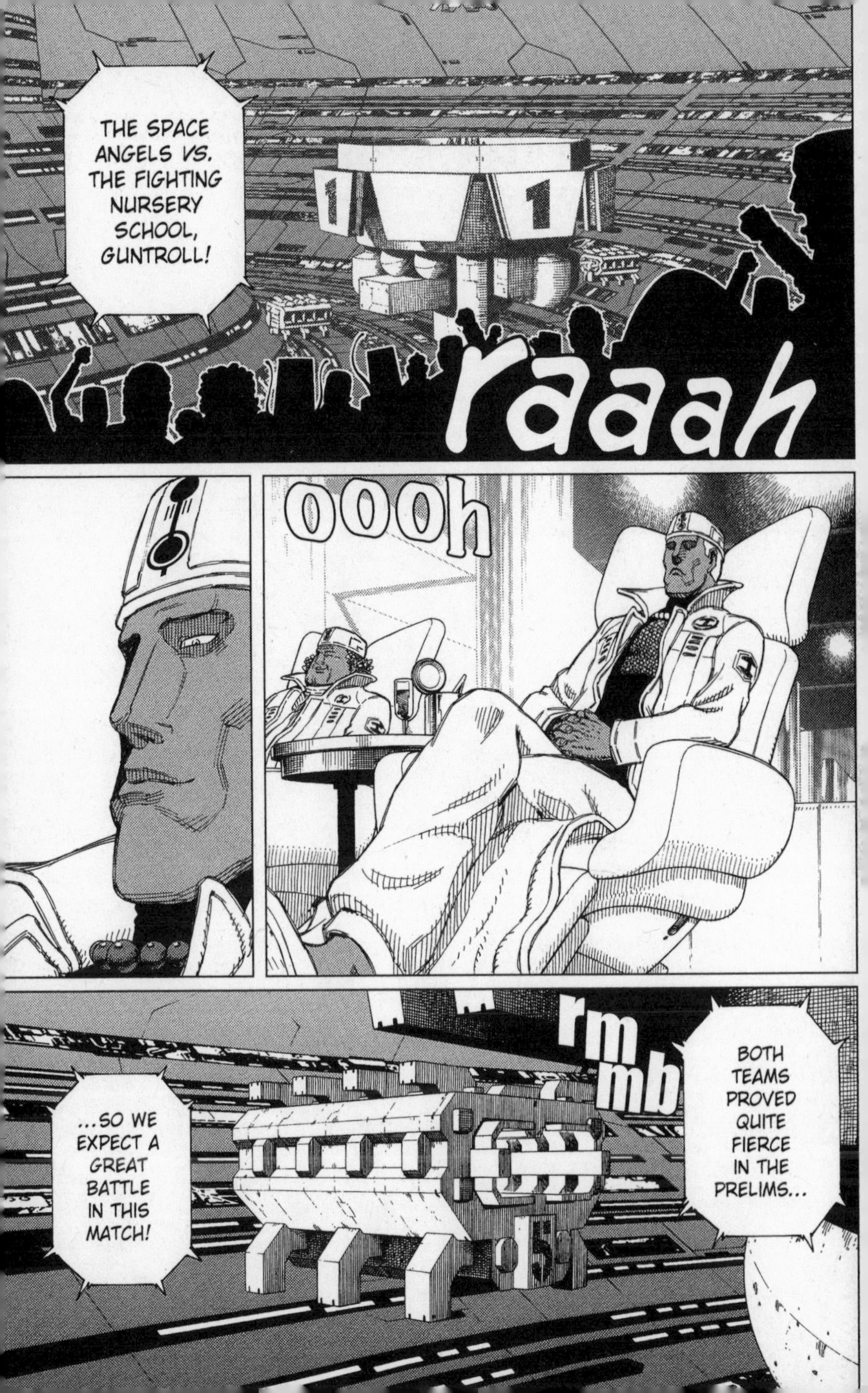
THE SPACE ANGELS VS. THE FIGHTING NURSERY SCHOOL, GUNTROLL!
raaah
oooh
rm mb
BOTH TEAMS PROVED QUITE FIERCE IN THE PRELIMS...
...SO WE EXPECT A GREAT BATTLE IN THIS MATCH!

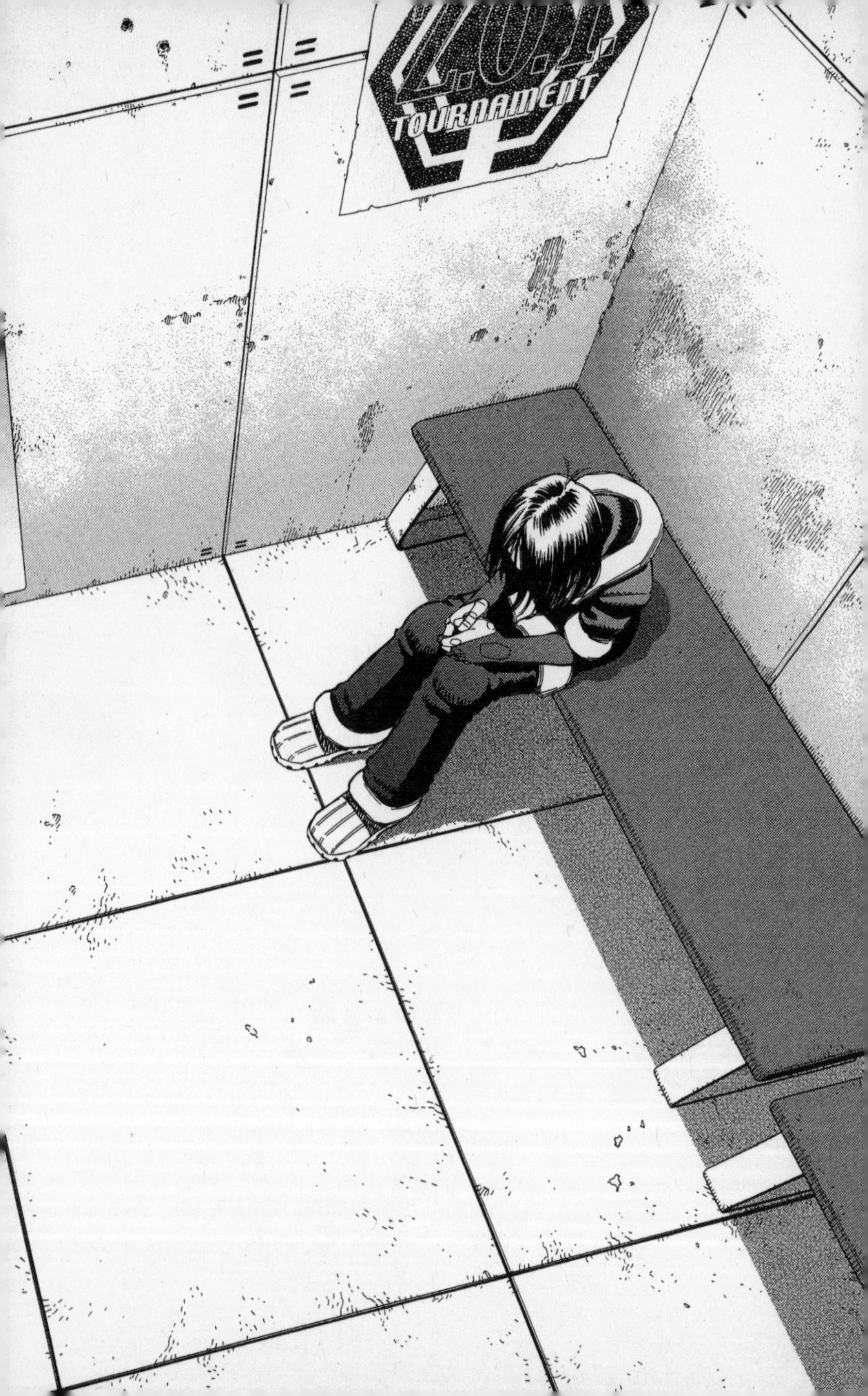
TOURNAMENT

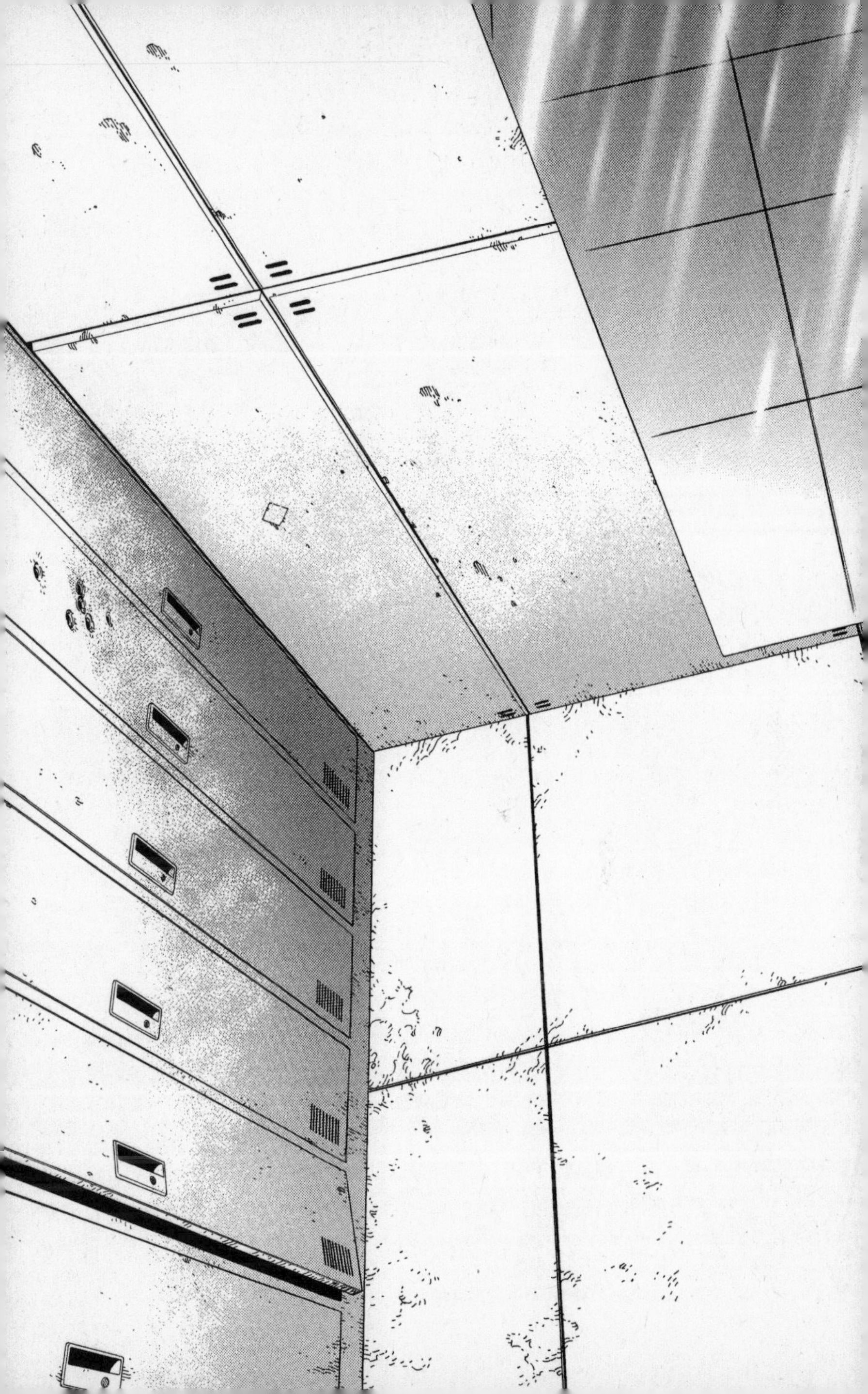

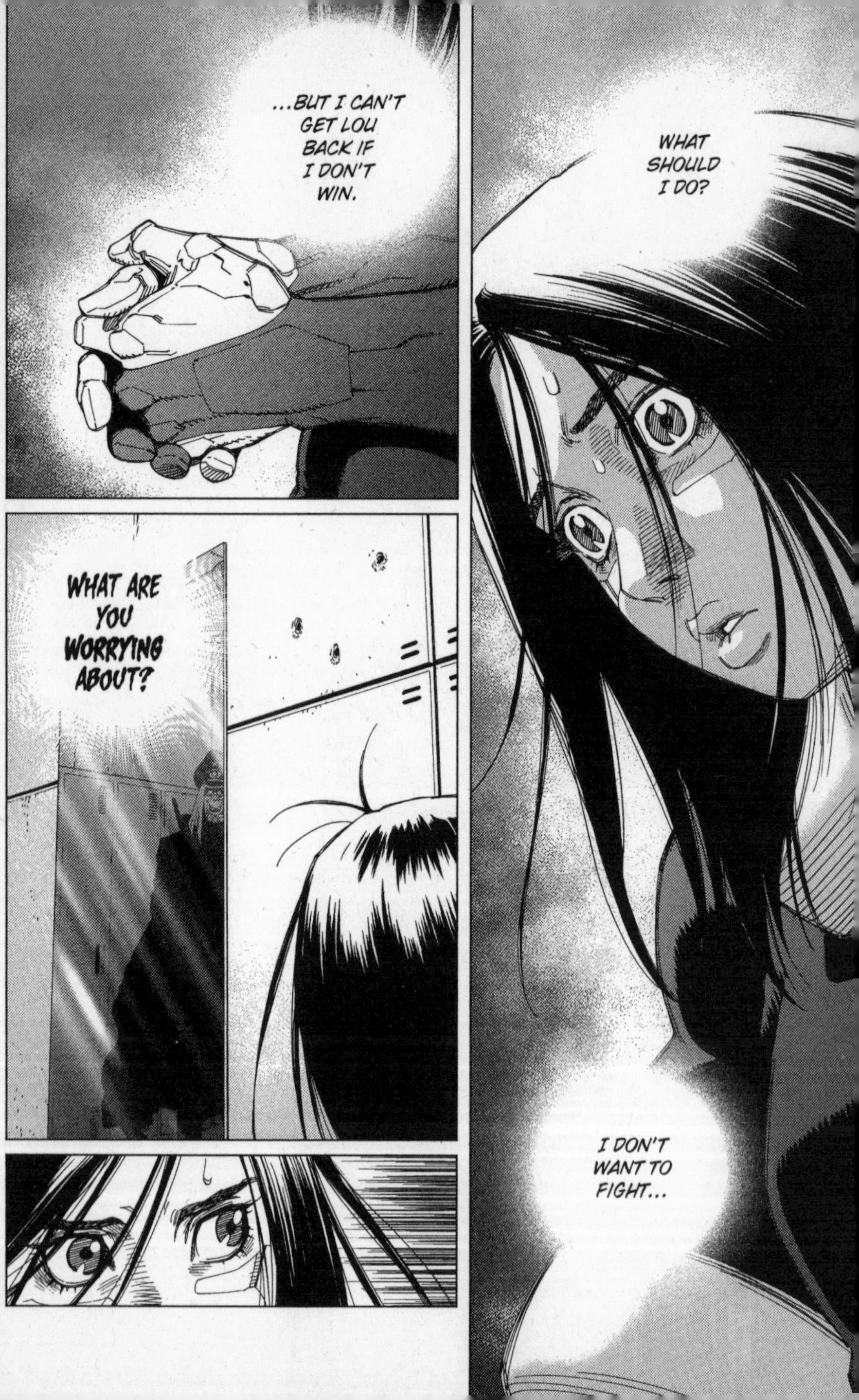
WHAT SHOULD I DO?
I DON'T WANT TO FIGHT...
...BUT I CAN'T GET LOU BACK IF I DON'T WIN.
WHAT ARE YOU WORRYING ABOUT?

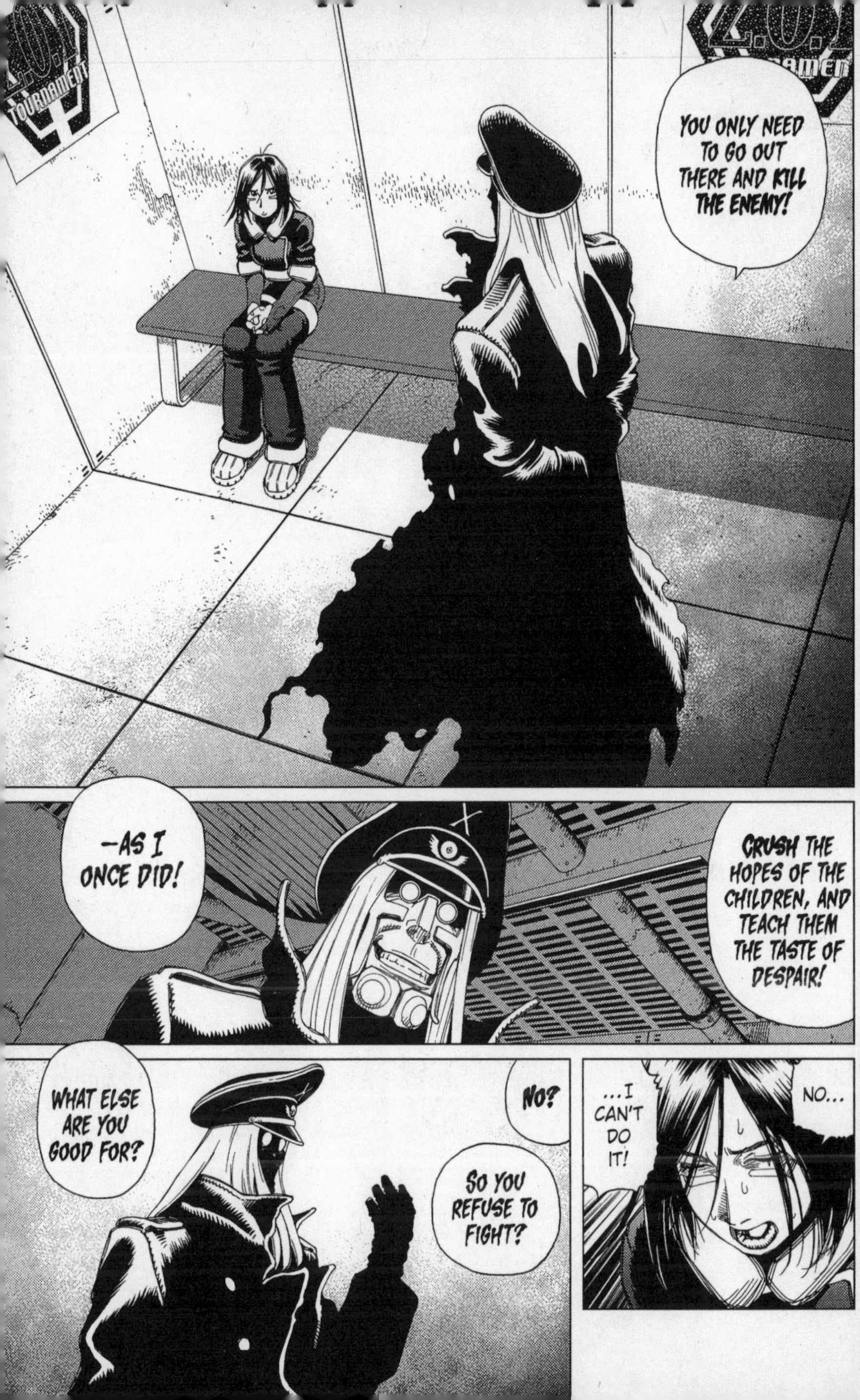
TOURNAMENT
YOU ONLY NEED TO GO OUT THERE AND KILL THE ENEMY!
CRUSH THE HOPES OF THE CHILDREN, AND TEACH THEM THE TASTE OF DESPAIR!
—AS I ONCE DID!
NO...
...I CAN'T DO IT!
NO?
SO YOU REFUSE TO FIGHT?
WHAT ELSE ARE YOU GOOD FOR?

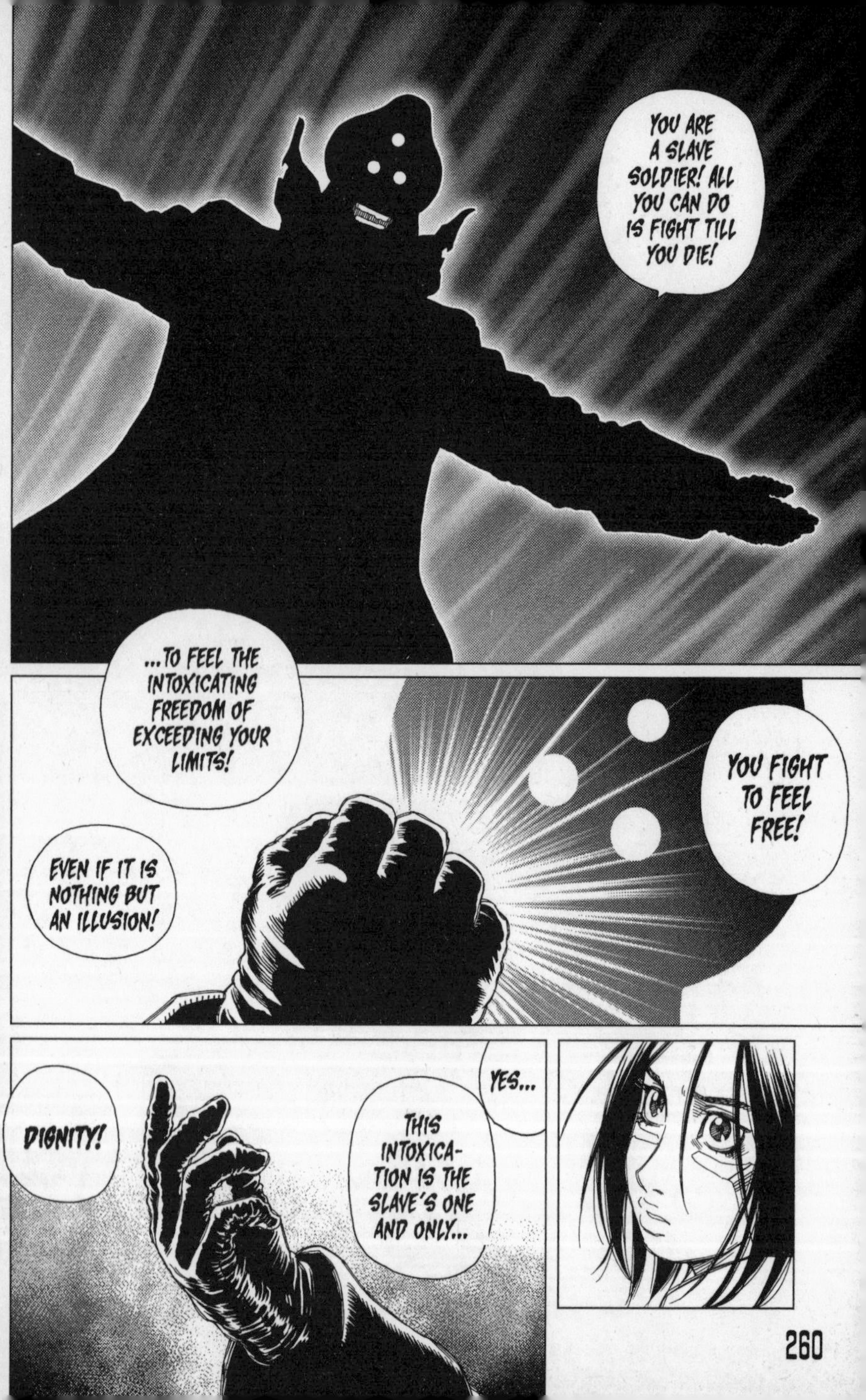
YOU ARE A SLAVE SOLDIER! ALL YOU CAN DO IS FIGHT TILL YOU DIE!
YOU FIGHT TO FEEL FREE!
...TO FEEL THE INTOXICATING FREEDOM OF EXCEEDING YOUR LIMITS!
EVEN IF IT IS NOTHING BUT AN ILLUSION!
YES...
THIS INTOXICATION IS THE SLAVE'S ONE AND ONLY...
DIGNITY!

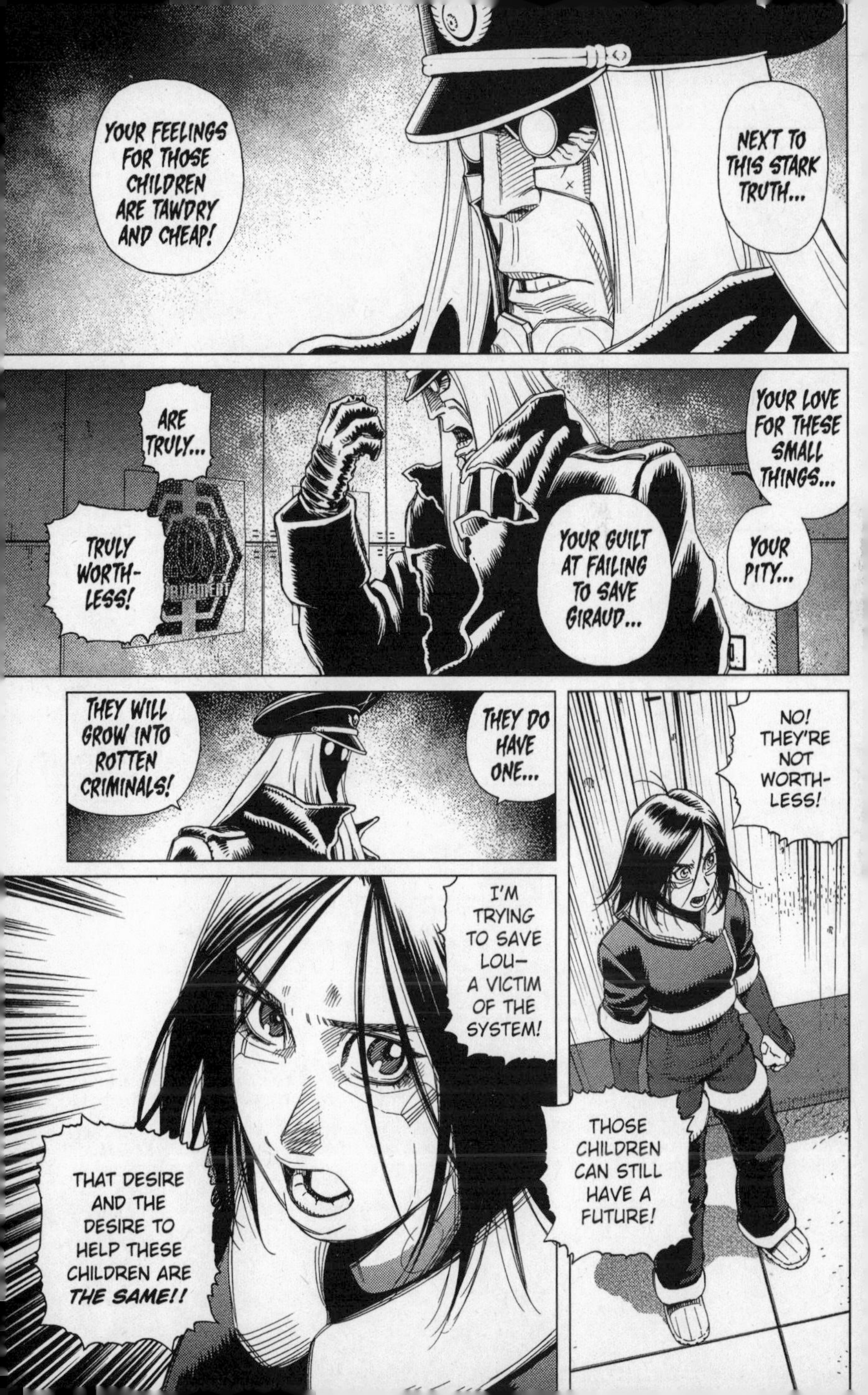
NEXT TO THIS STARK TRUTH...
YOUR FEELINGS FOR THOSE CHILDREN ARE TAWDRY AND CHEAP!
YOUR LOVE FOR THESE SMALL THINGS...
YOUR PITY...
YOUR GUILT AT FAILING TO SAVE GIRAUD...
ARE TRULY...
TRULY WORTH-LESS!
NO! THEY'RE NOT WORTH-LESS!
THOSE CHILDREN CAN STILL HAVE A FUTURE!
THEY DO HAVE ONE...
THEY WILL GROW INTO ROTTEN CRIMINALS!
I'M TRYING TO SAVE LOU— A VICTIM OF THE SYSTEM!
THAT DESIRE AND THE DESIRE TO HELP THESE CHILDREN ARE *THE SAME!!*

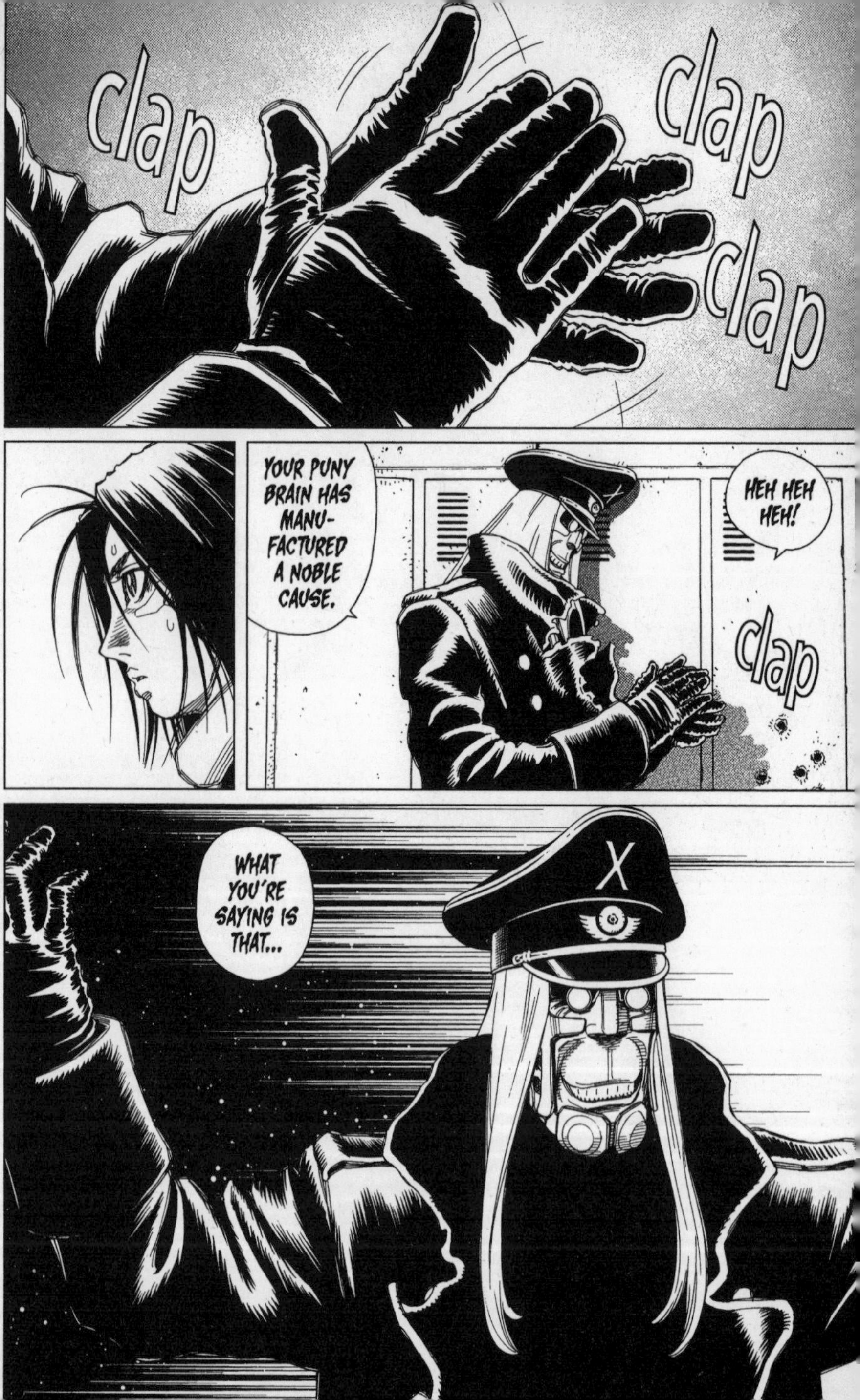
clap
clap
clap
HEH HEH HEH!
YOUR PUNY BRAIN HAS MANU-FACTURED A NOBLE CAUSE.
clap
WHAT YOU'RE SAYING IS THAT...

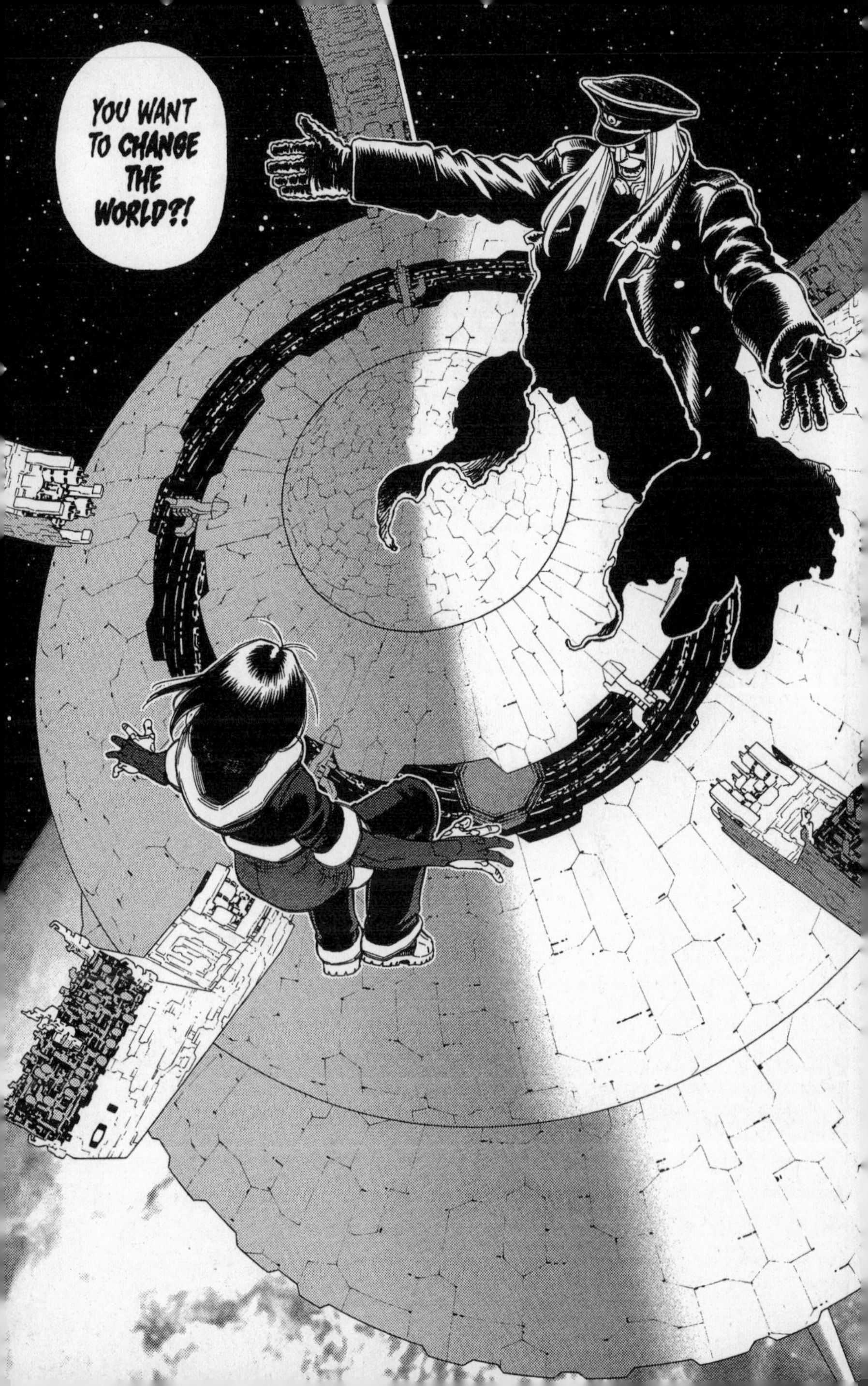
YOU WANT TO CHANGE THE WORLD?!

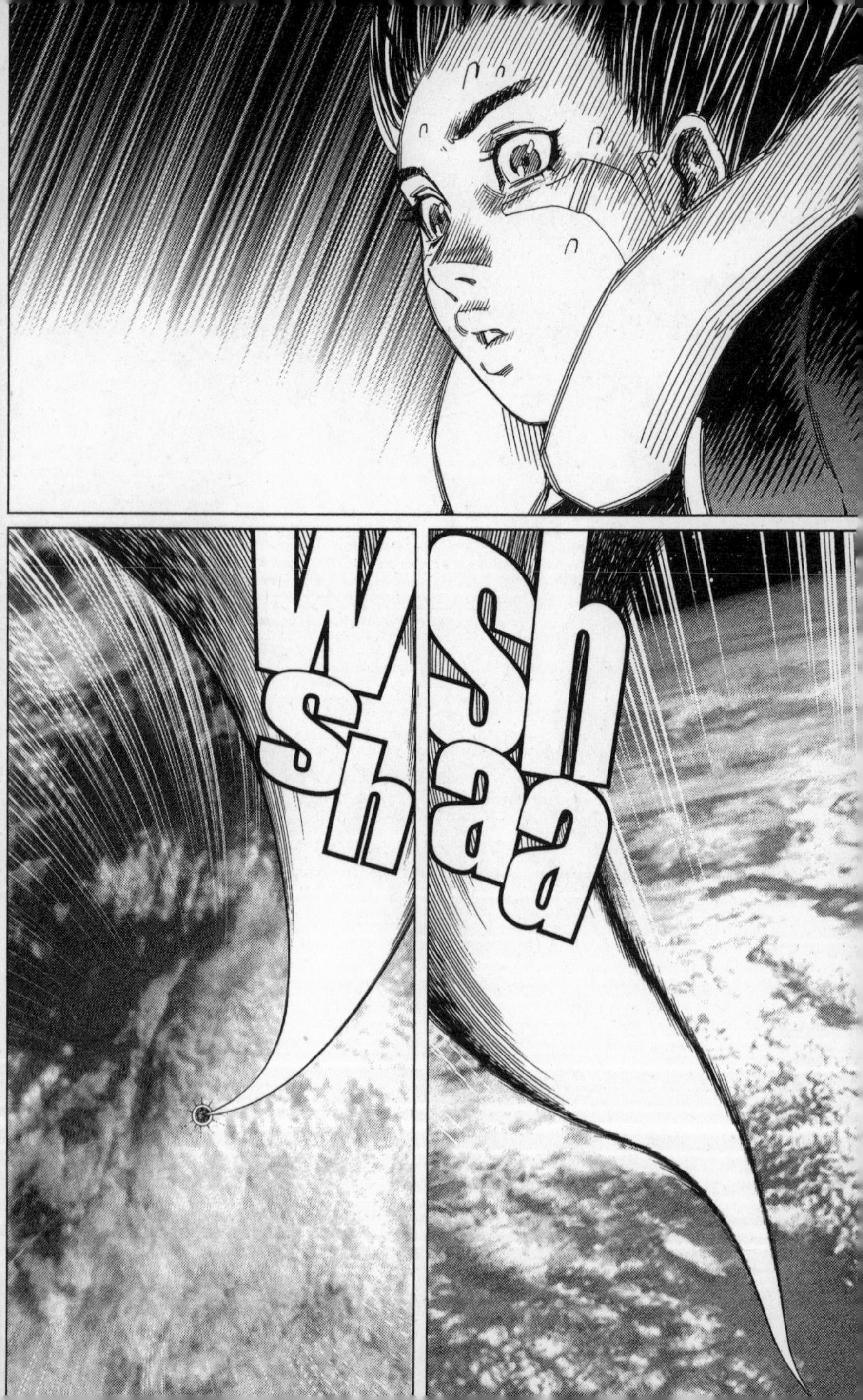
WSh
Shaa

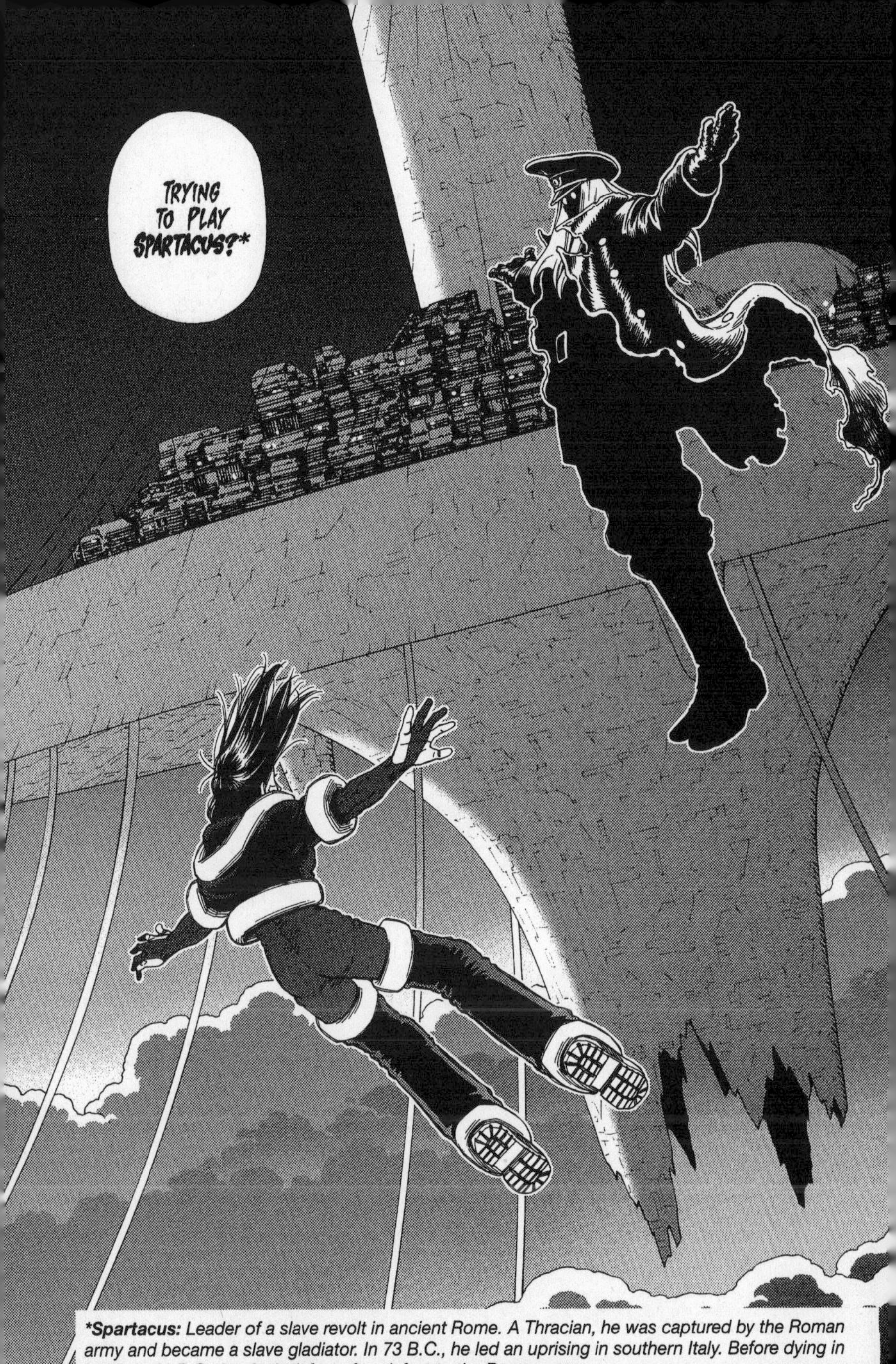
TRYING TO PLAY SPARTACUS?*

***Spartacus:** Leader of a slave revolt in ancient Rome. A Thracian, he was captured by the Roman army and became a slave gladiator. In 73 B.C., he led an uprising in southern Italy. Before dying in battle in 71 B.C., he dealt defeat after defeat to the Roman army.*

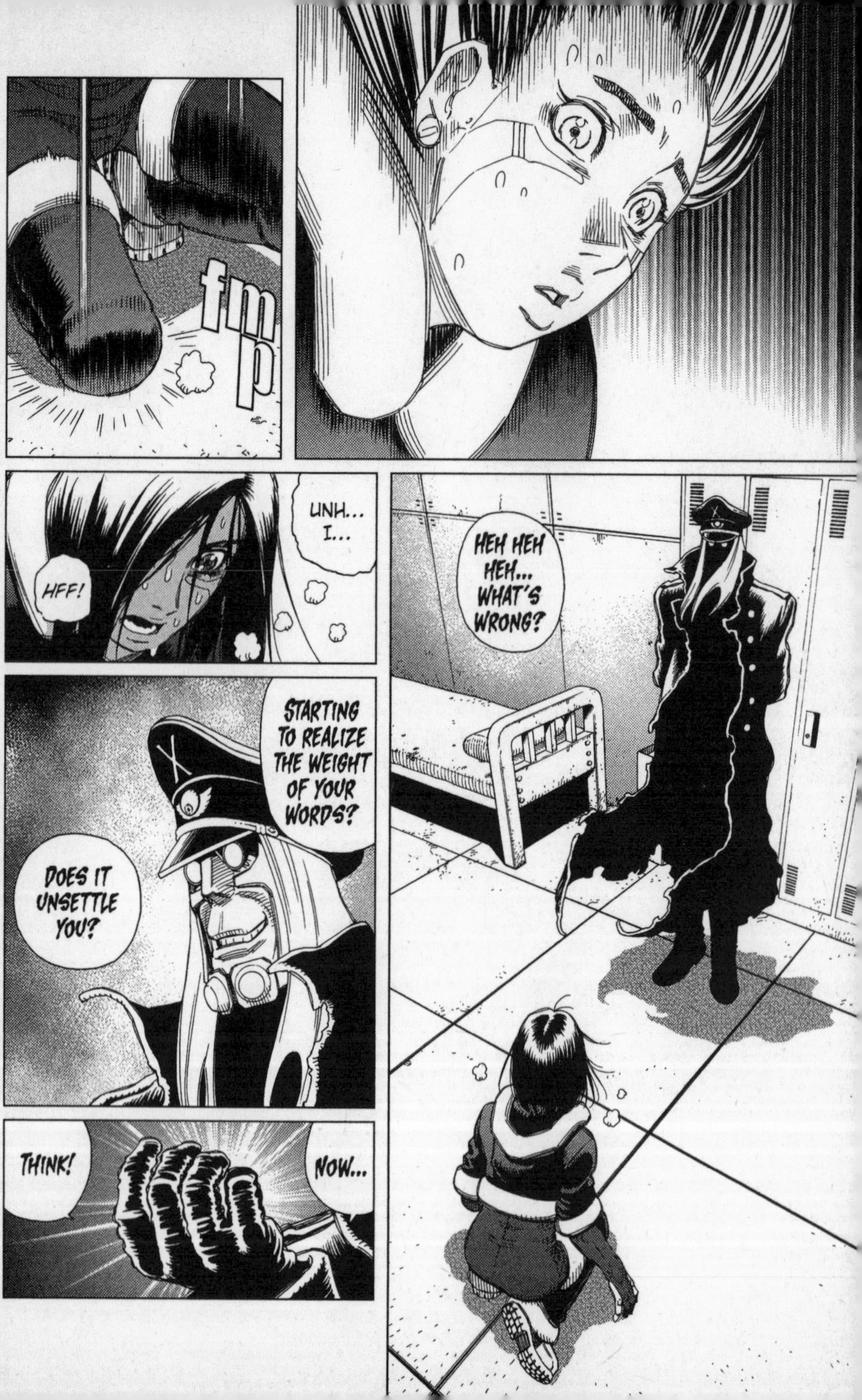
fmp
HEH HEH HEH... WHAT'S WRONG?
UNH... I...
HFF!
STARTING TO REALIZE THE WEIGHT OF YOUR WORDS?
DOES IT UNSETTLE YOU?
NOW...
THINK!

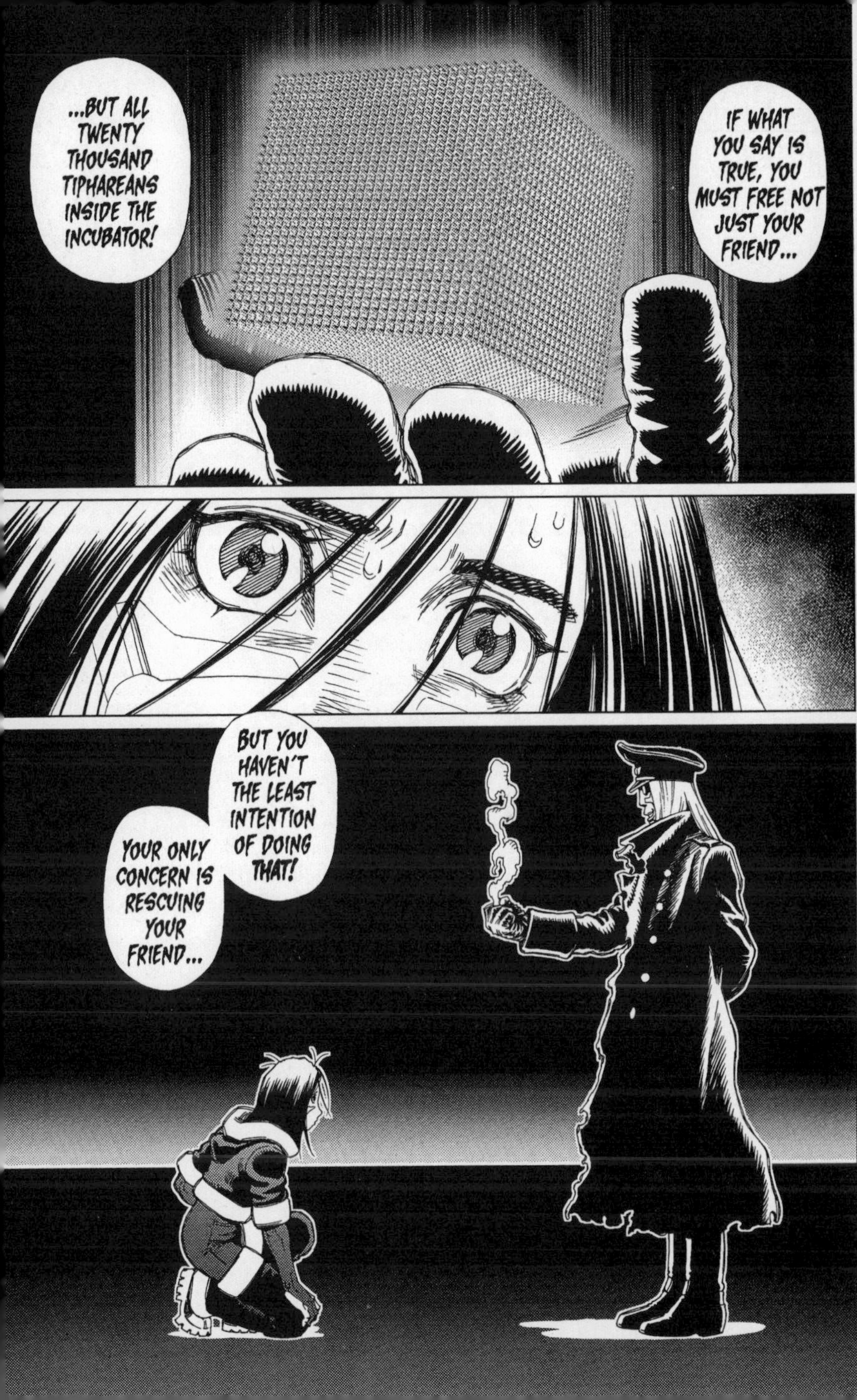
IF WHAT YOU SAY IS TRUE, YOU MUST FREE NOT JUST YOUR FRIEND...
...BUT ALL TWENTY THOUSAND TIPHAREANS INSIDE THE INCUBATOR!
BUT YOU HAVEN'T THE LEAST INTENTION OF DOING THAT!
YOUR ONLY CONCERN IS RESCUING YOUR FRIEND...

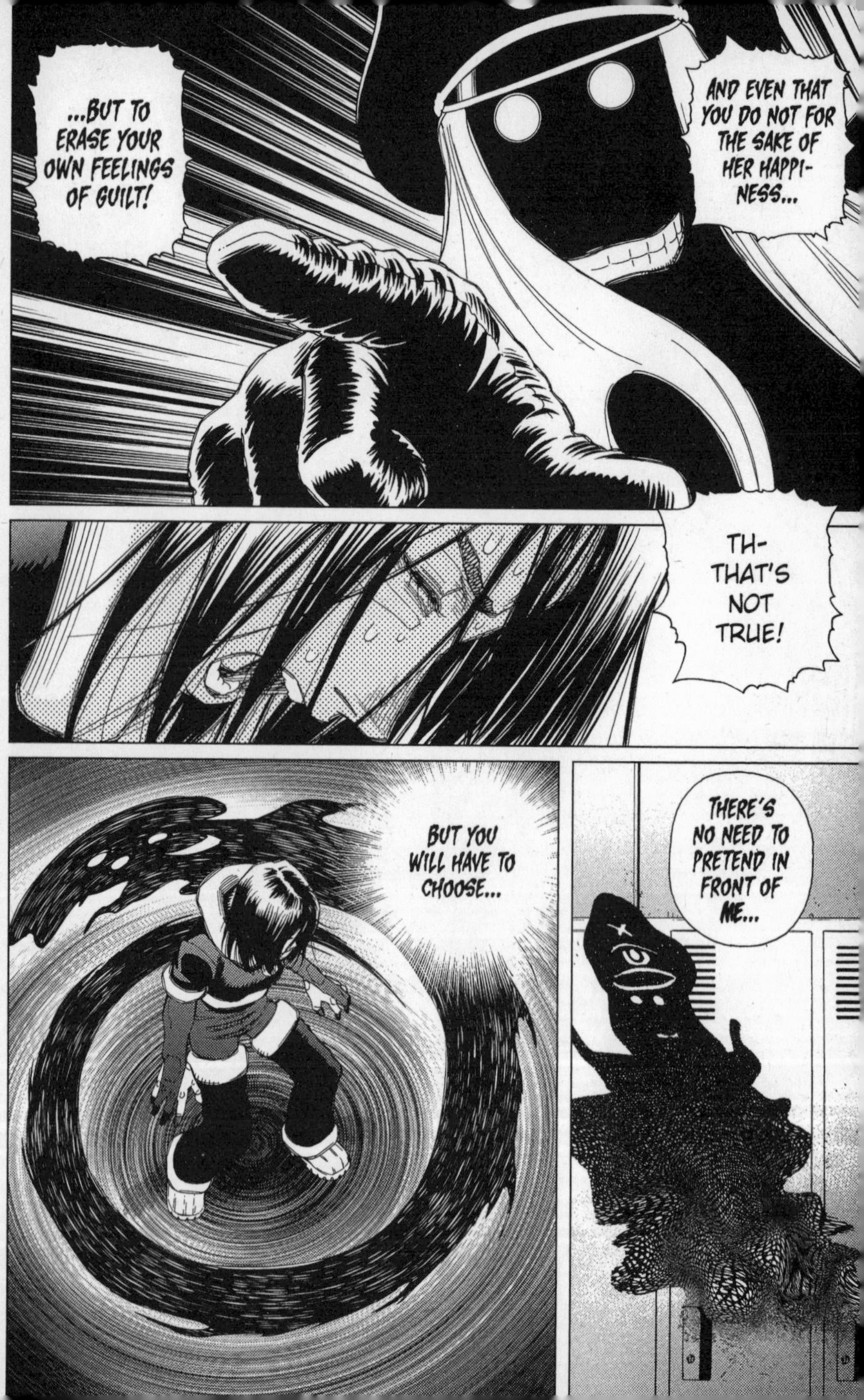
AND EVEN THAT YOU DO NOT FOR THE SAKE OF HER HAPPINESS...
...BUT TO ERASE YOUR OWN FEELINGS OF GUILT!
TH-THAT'S NOT TRUE!
THERE'S NO NEED TO PRETEND IN FRONT OF ME...
BUT YOU WILL HAVE TO CHOOSE...

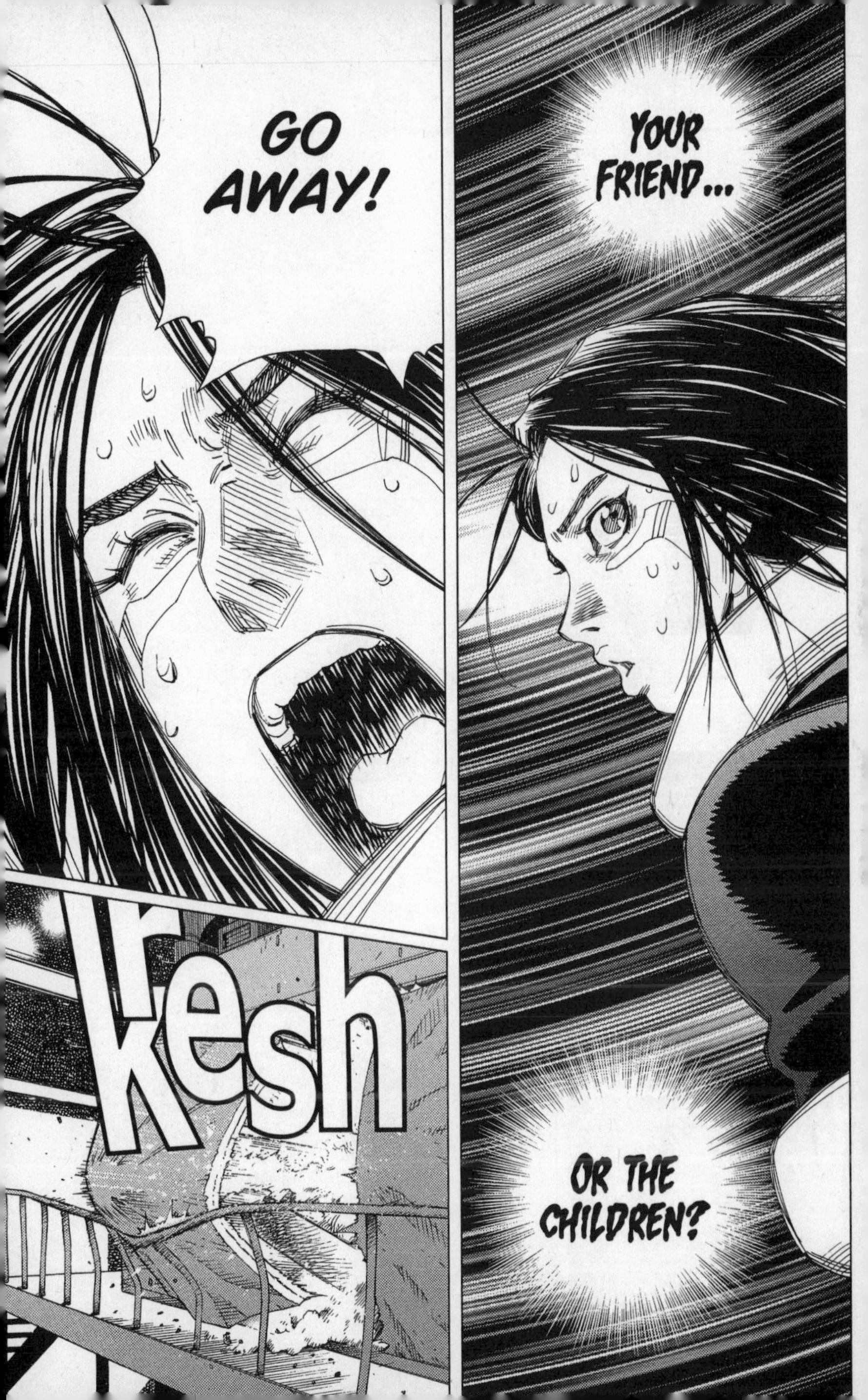
YOUR FRIEND...
OR THE CHILDREN?
GO AWAY!
Kesh

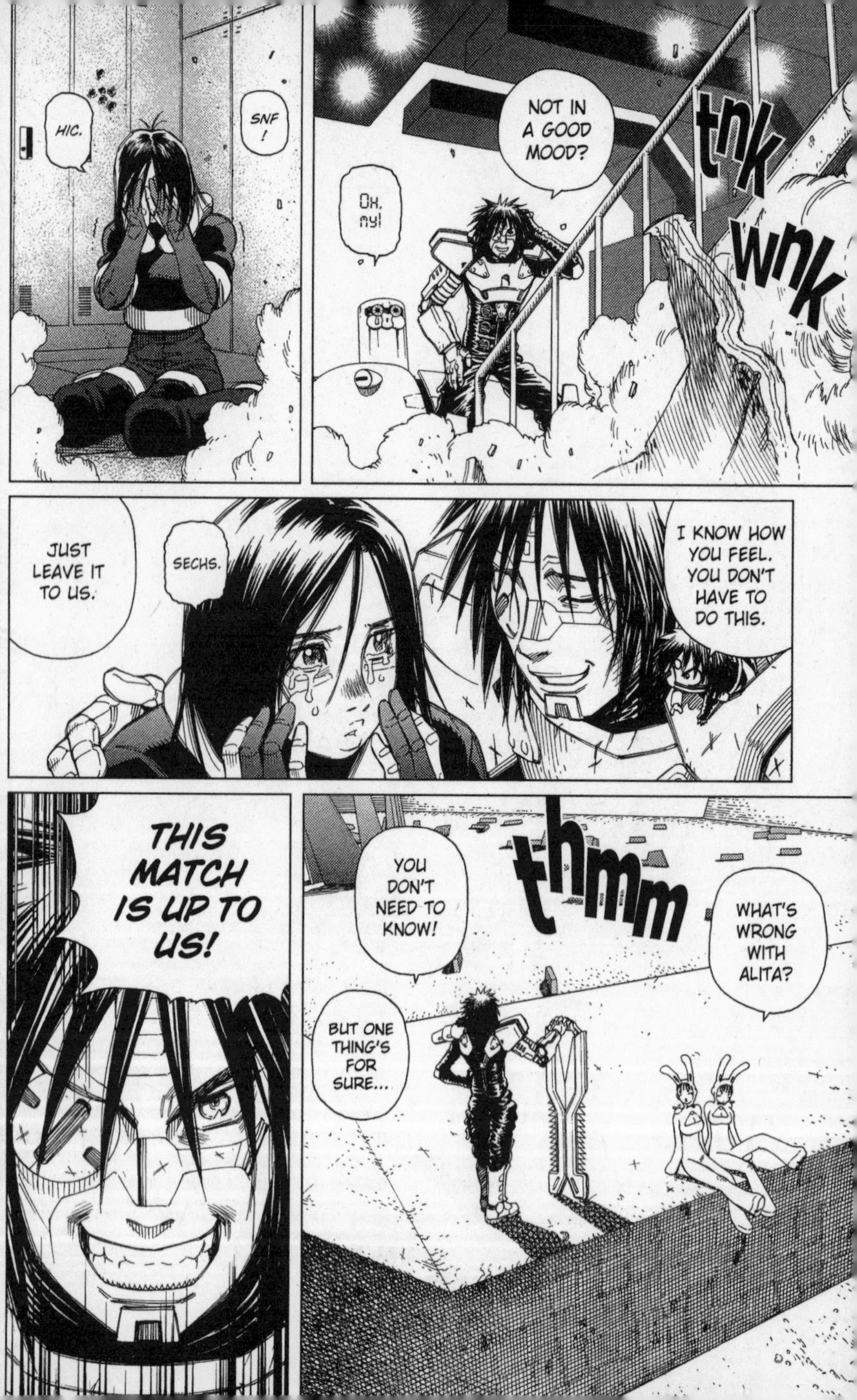
tnk
wnk
NOT IN A GOOD MOOD?
OH, MY!
SNF!
HIC.
I KNOW HOW YOU FEEL. YOU DON'T HAVE TO DO THIS.
SECHS.
JUST LEAVE IT TO US.
thmm
WHAT'S WRONG WITH ALITA?
YOU DON'T NEED TO KNOW!
BUT ONE THING'S FOR SURE...
THIS MATCH IS UP TO US!

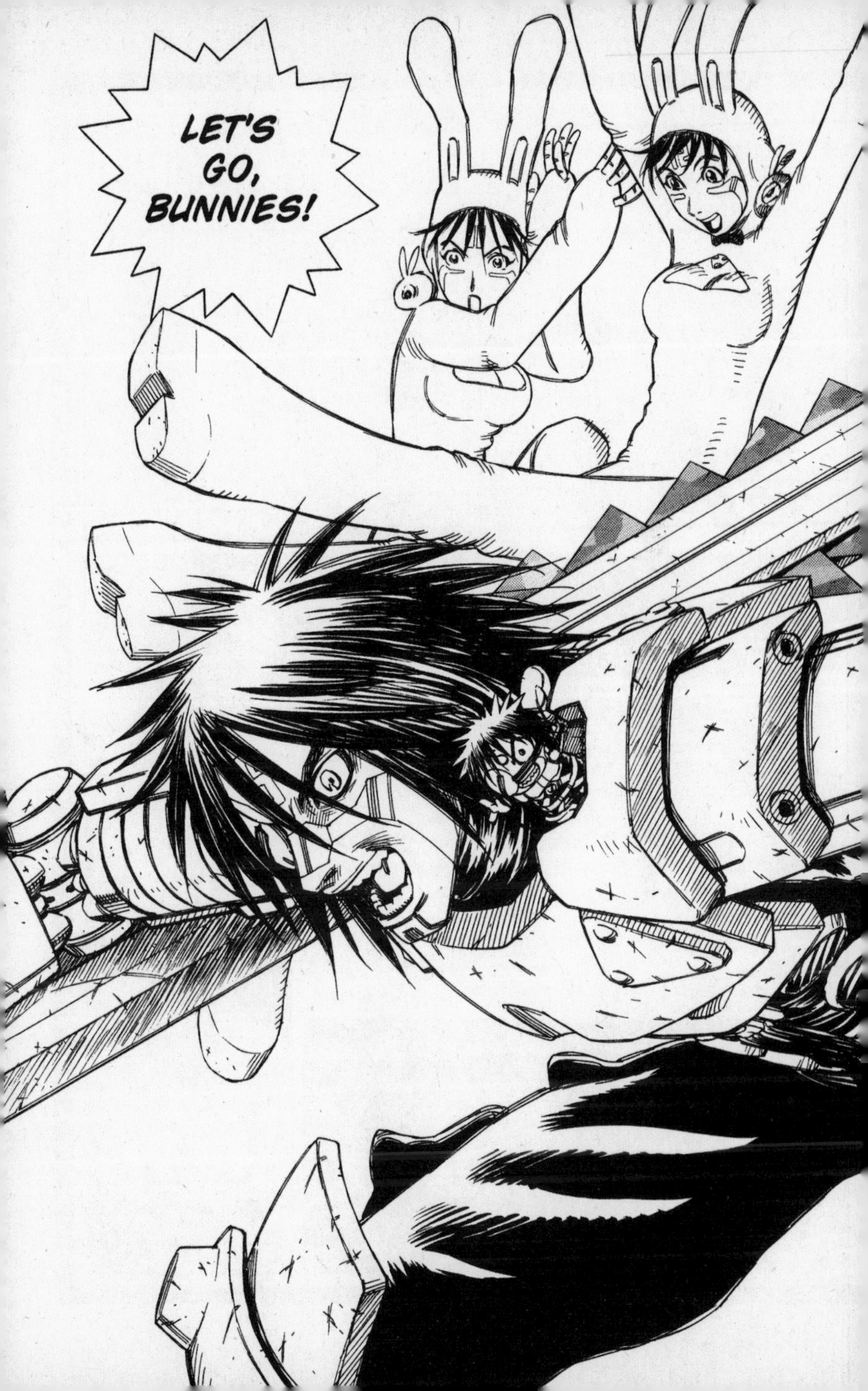
LET'S GO, BUNNIES!

This is a true story that occurred during a meeting regarding Phase 23 of *Last Order*.

No Good World!

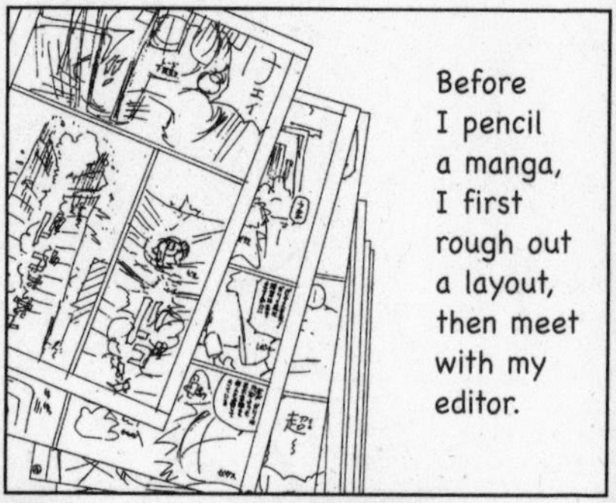
Before I pencil a manga, I first rough out a layout, then meet with my editor.

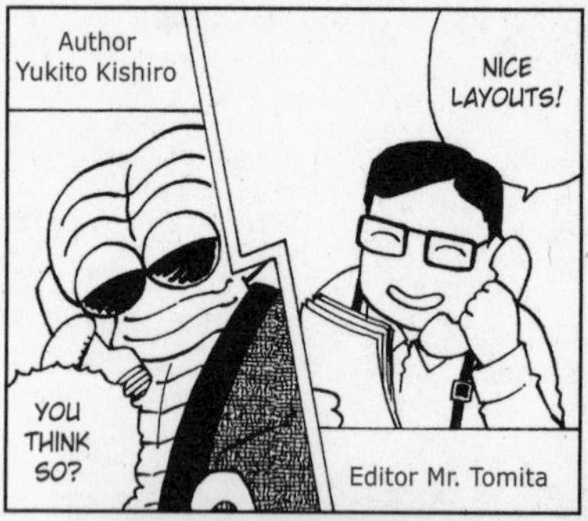
Author Yukito Kishiro
NICE LAYOUTS!
Editor Mr. Tomita
YOU THINK SO?

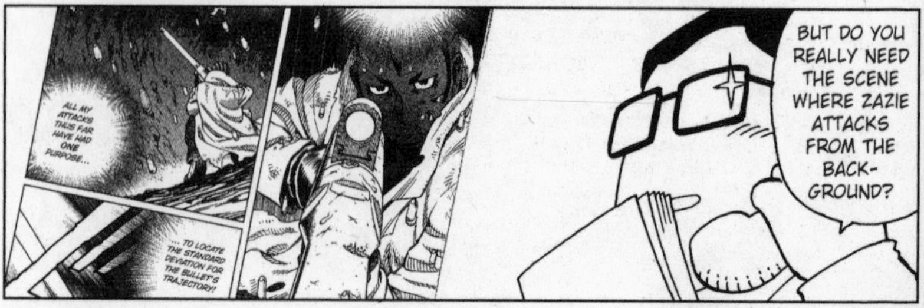
BUT DO YOU REALLY NEED THE SCENE WHERE ZAZIE ATTACKS FROM THE BACK-GROUND?
ALL MY ATTACKS THUS FAR HAVE HAD ONE PURPOSE...
...TO LOCATE THE STANDARD DEVIATION FOR THE BULLET'S TRAJECTORY!

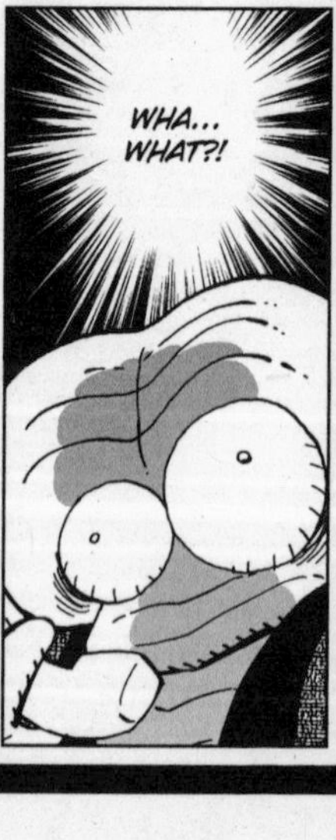
WHA... WHAT?!

Mr. Tomita felt that Zazie's actions lessened the impact of Alita's climactic attack.

Sometimes the author gets so into his story that he can't see the forest for the trees. At those times, the editor's opinion is very important.

Here's what I saw!

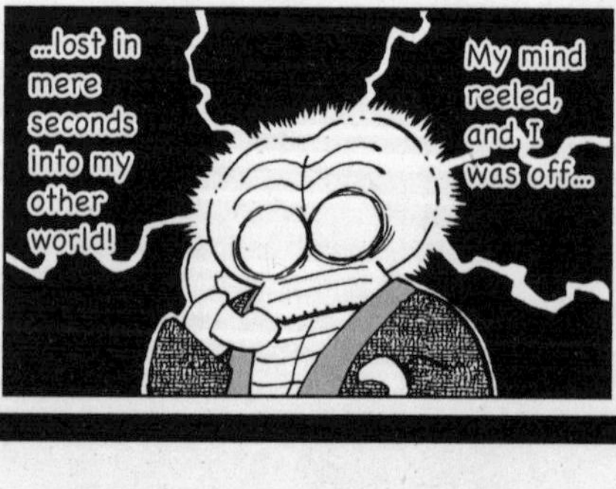
My mind reeled, and I was off...
...lost in mere seconds into my other world!

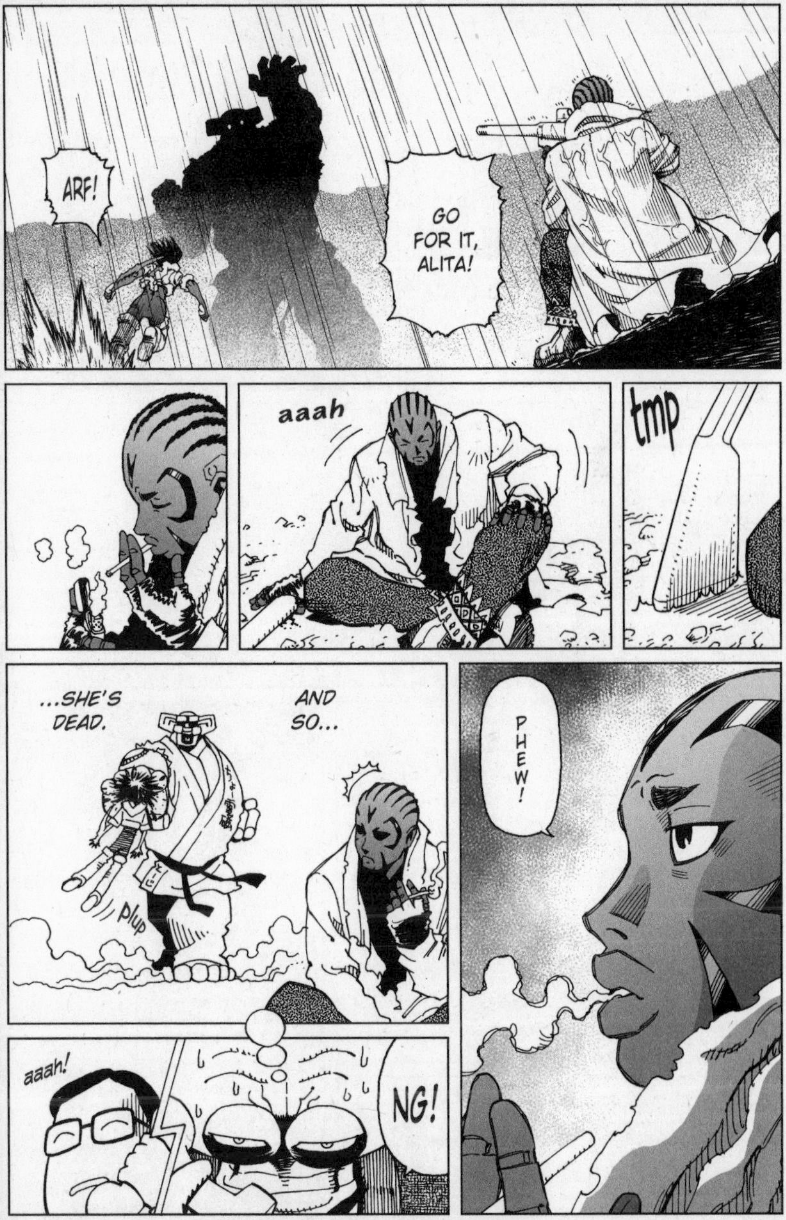
GO FOR IT, ALITA!
ARF!
tmp
aaah
PHEW!
AND SO...
...SHE'S DEAD.
plup
NG!
aaah!

Value your life!

A local legend...

No Good Punch!

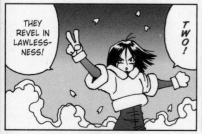

ONE!
THEY SUCK THE SPIRITS OF MEN!
TWO!
THEY REVEL IN LAWLESS-NESS!
NOW FOR THE HARD PART!
WHAT IS THE THIRD ELEMENT?
HUH!?
WHAT'S HARD ABOUT THAT?!
THREE!
STRONGER THAN ALL!
BZZZT! SAME CONCEPT, BUT WRONG SHOW!
Besides, that was covered under Number One!
AW, THAT'S NOT FAIR!
POW!
YOU WON'T GET IT...
Sorry for the '70s flashback! The correct answer is: "Three! All the ugly ogres of the world—Momotaro will vanquish them all!" That's the catch phrase from the show "Momotaro Samurai." Payne was trying to sing the song from the anime "Inakappe Taisho."

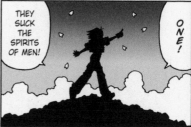

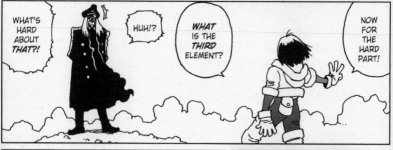

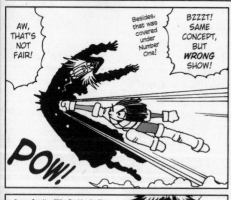

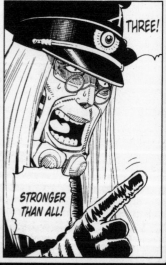

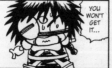

ALITA Last Order™

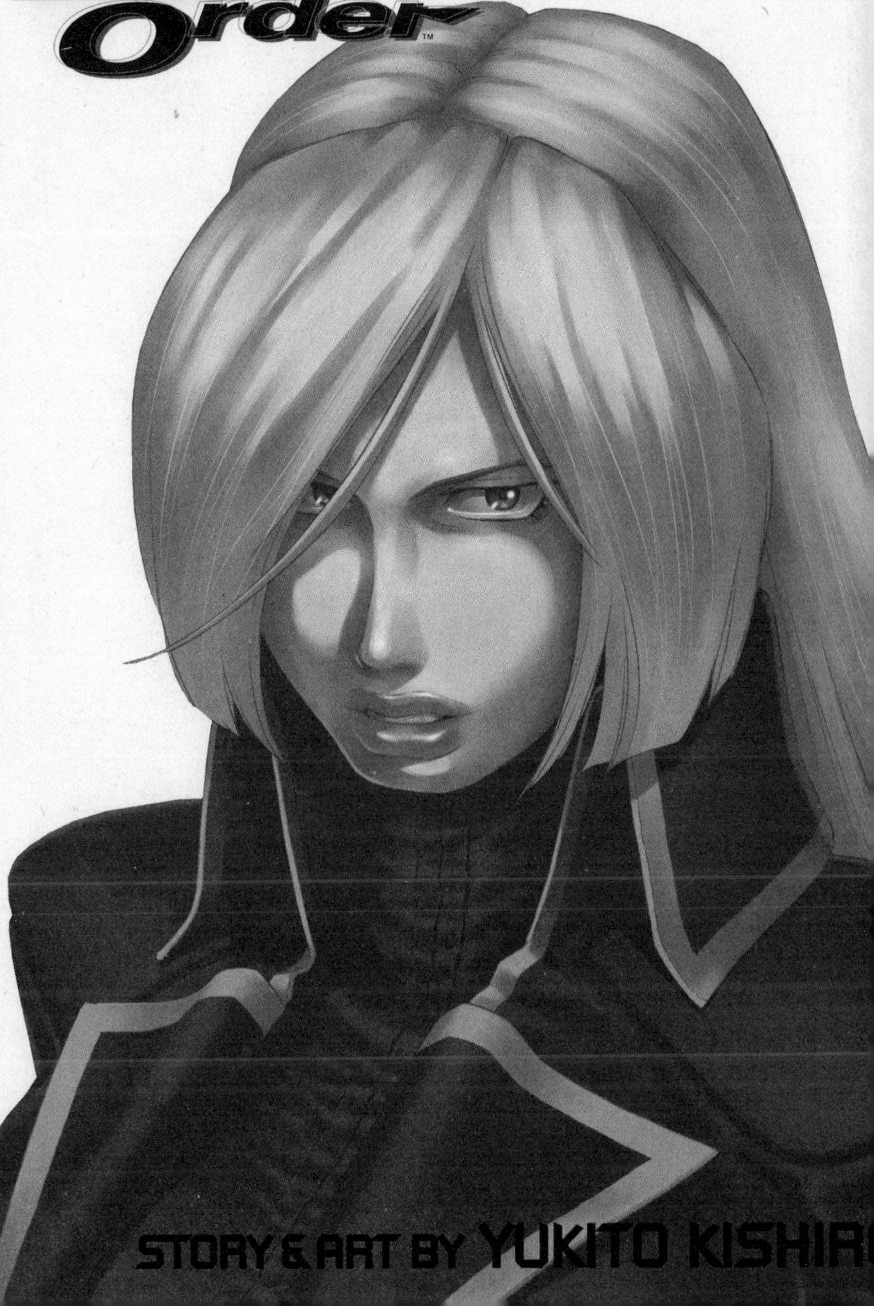

STORY & ART BY YUKITO KISHIRO

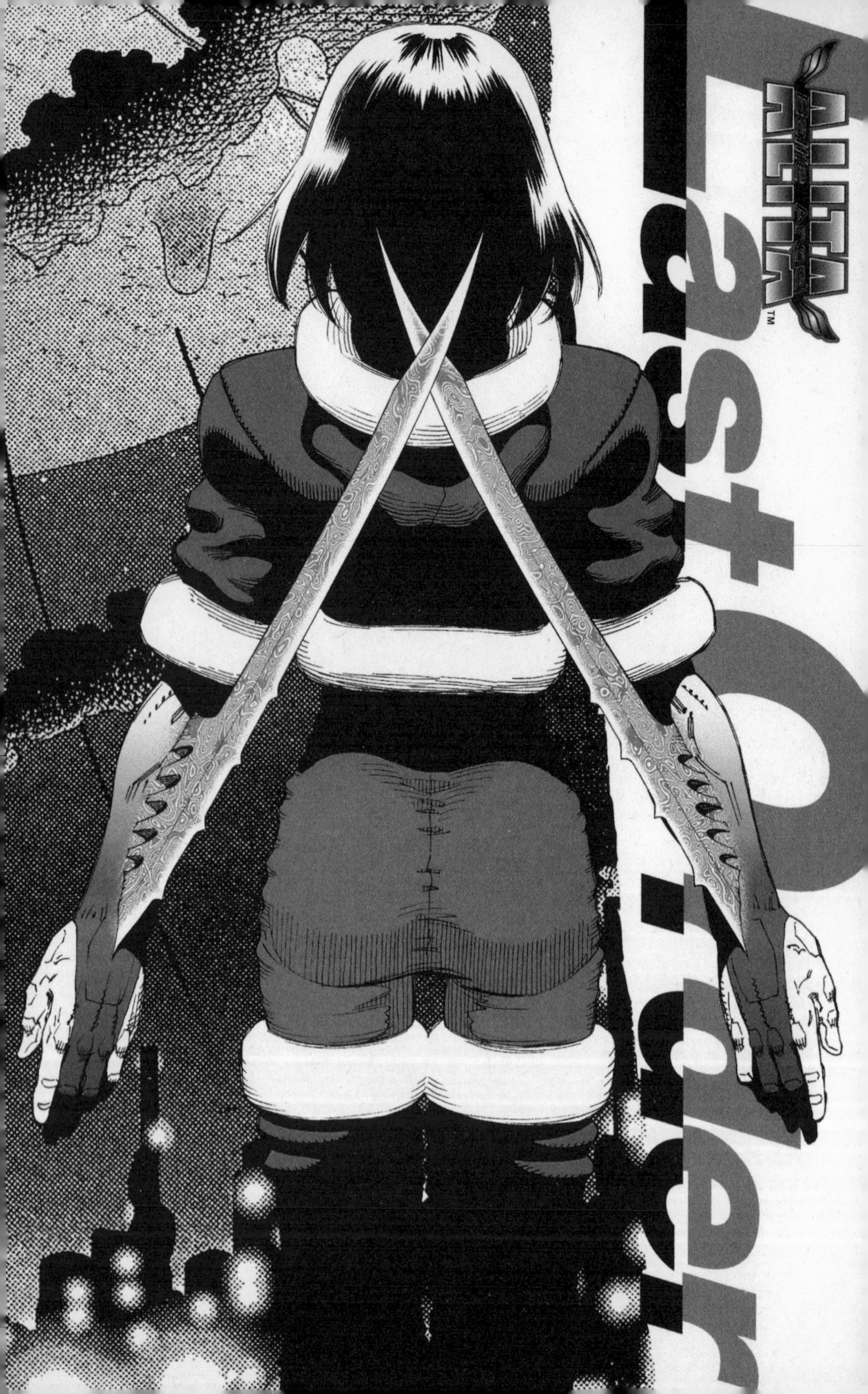
Last Order

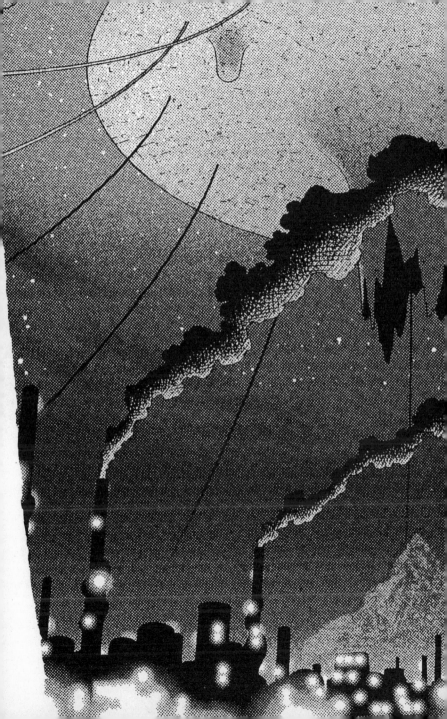

GUNTROLL

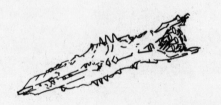

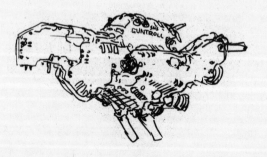

PHASE 28

Want to Hear My Song?

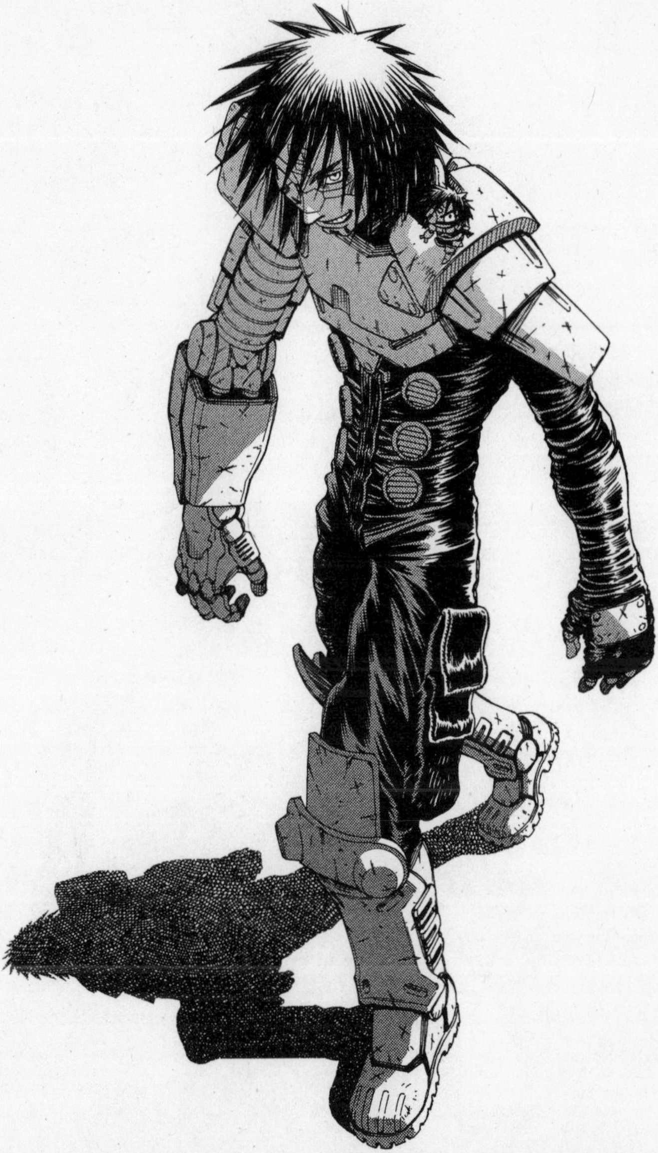

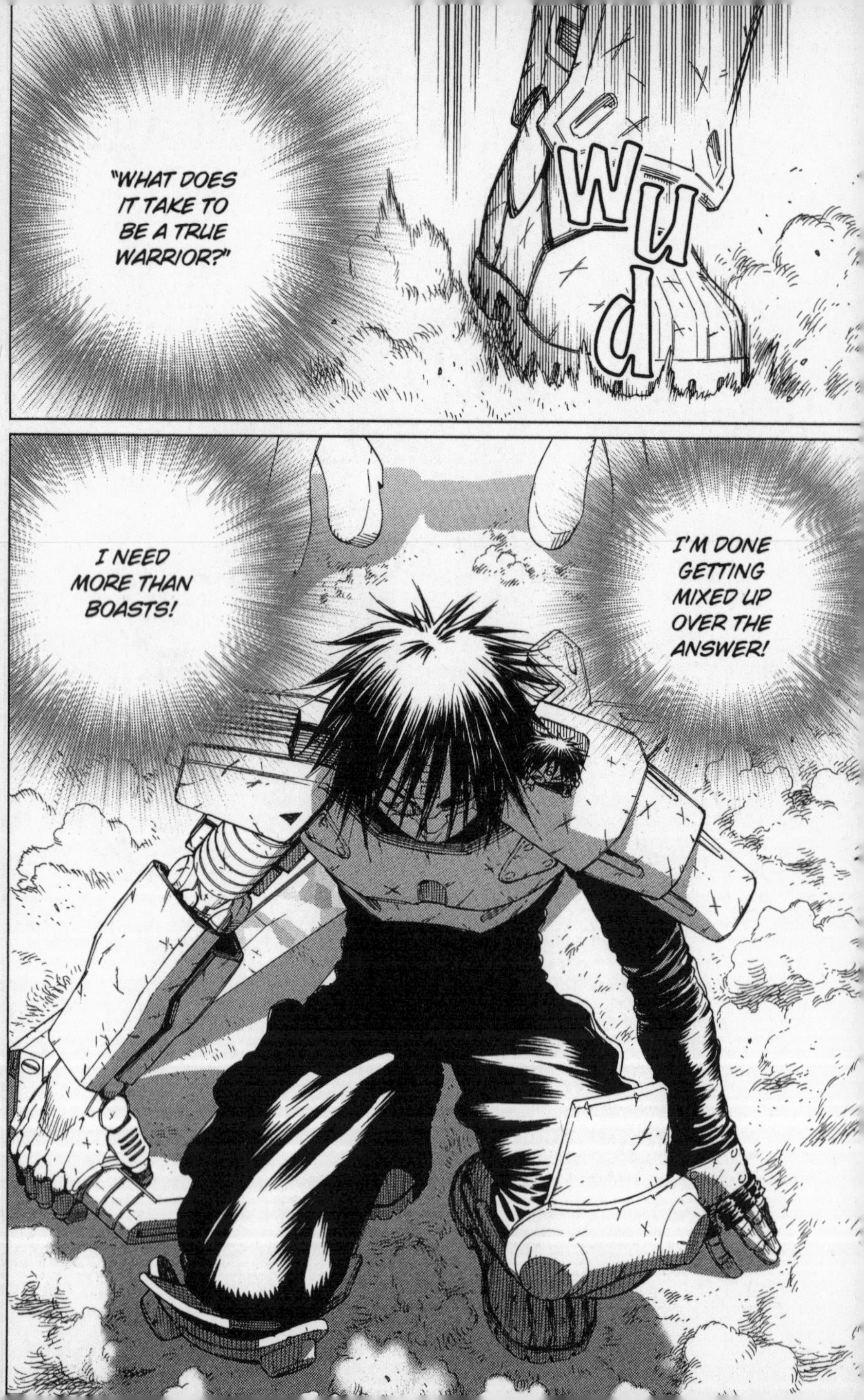
Wud
"WHAT DOES IT TAKE TO BE A TRUE WARRIOR?"
I'M DONE GETTING MIXED UP OVER THE ANSWER!
I NEED MORE THAN BOASTS!

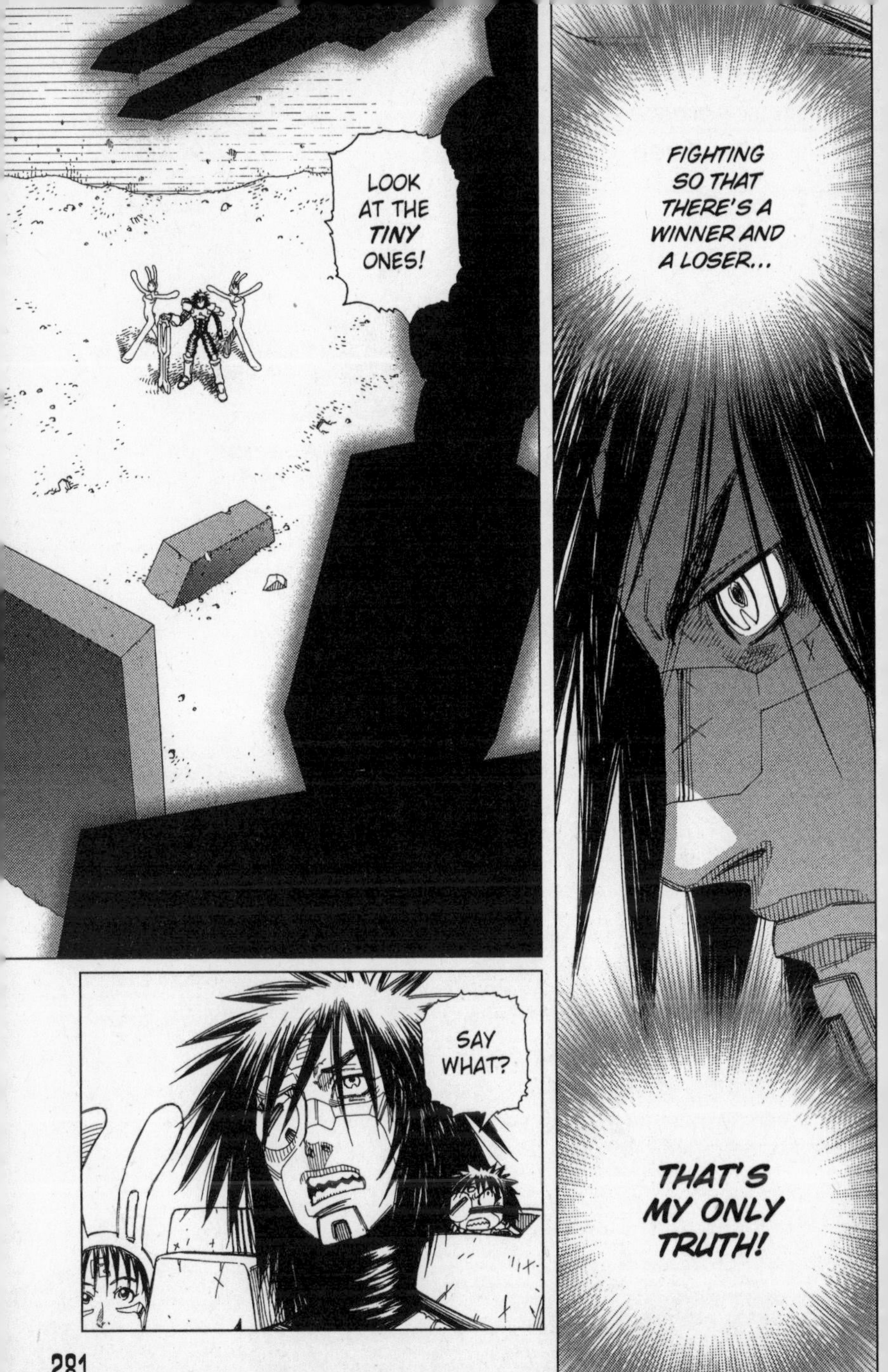
FIGHTING SO THAT THERE'S A WINNER AND A LOSER...
THAT'S MY ONLY TRUTH!
LOOK AT THE *TINY* ONES!
SAY WHAT?

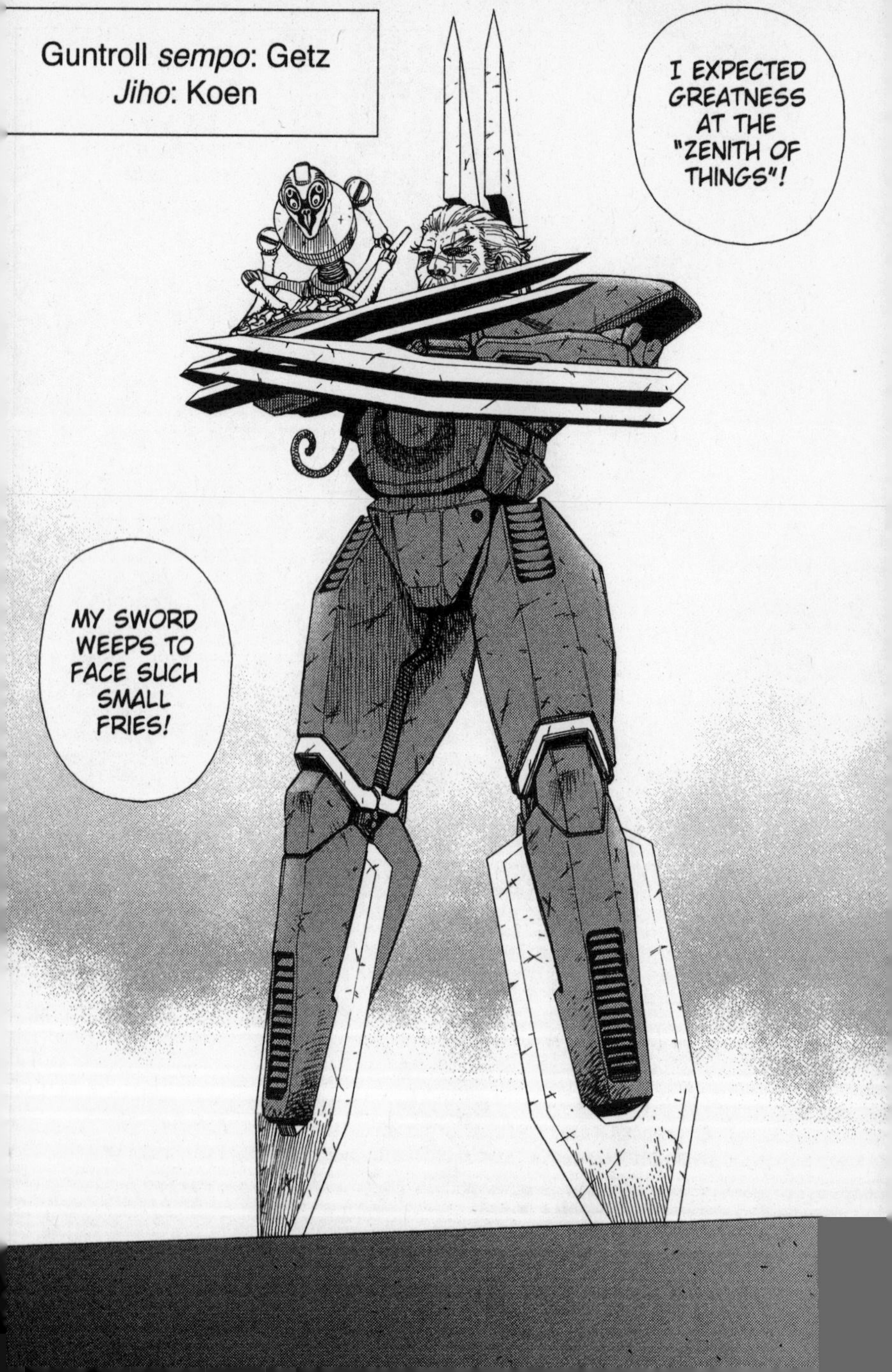
Guntroll *sempo*: Getz
Jiho: Koen
I EXPECTED GREATNESS AT THE "ZENITH OF THINGS"!
MY SWORD WEEPS TO FACE SUCH SMALL FRIES!

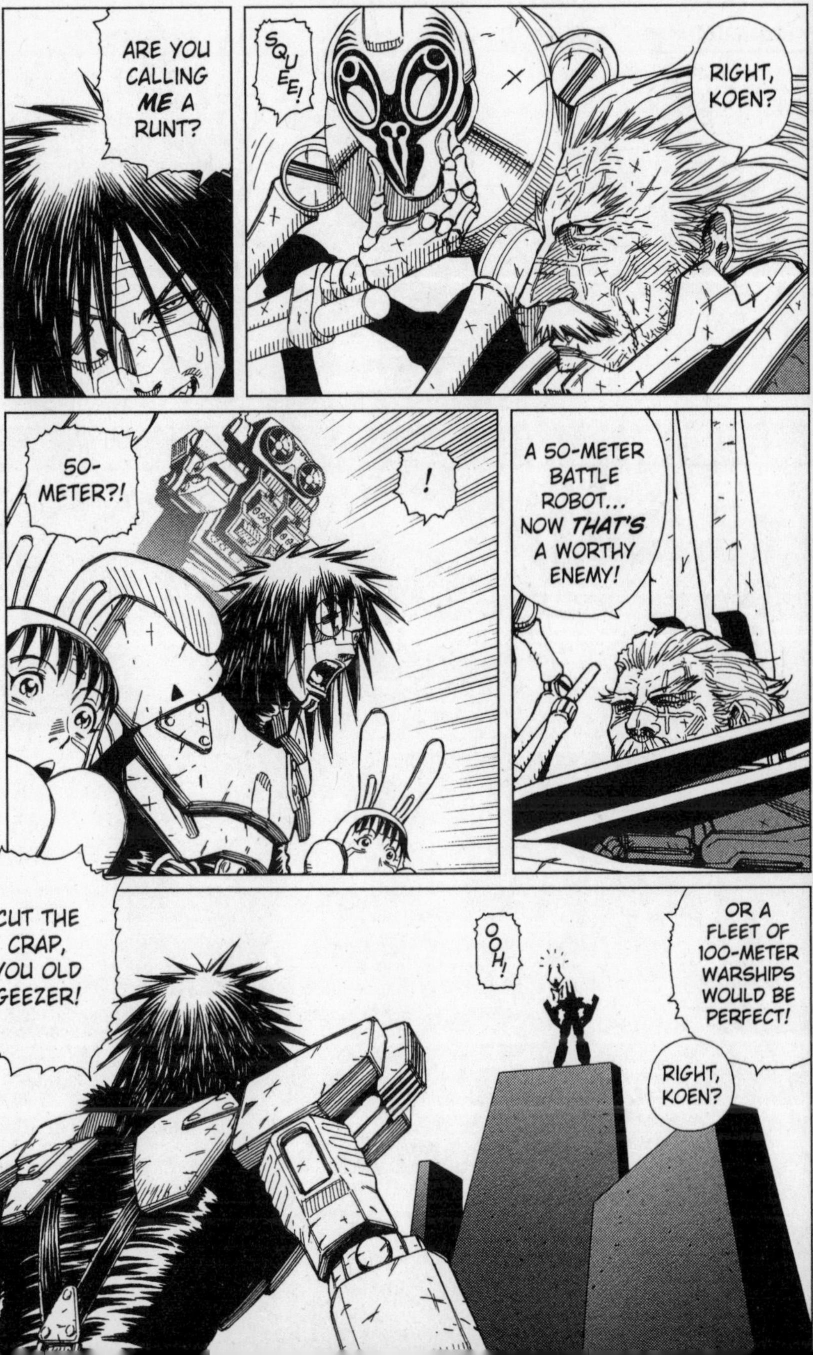
RIGHT, KOEN?
SQUEEE!
ARE YOU CALLING ME A RUNT?
A 50-METER BATTLE ROBOT... NOW THAT'S A WORTHY ENEMY!
!
50-METER?!
OR A FLEET OF 100-METER WARSHIPS WOULD BE PERFECT!
RIGHT, KOEN?
OOH!
CUT THE CRAP, YOU OLD GEEZER!

KEE, KEE, KEE!

LET'S DO IT, KOEN!

HATE TO SWAT A FLY WITH A BILLY CLUB...

BUT I MUST! FORGIVE ME!

ch ak

SNI KT

KA CH IK

S W AK

WSH

THE DEADLY *SPINNING SWALLOW MOON!*

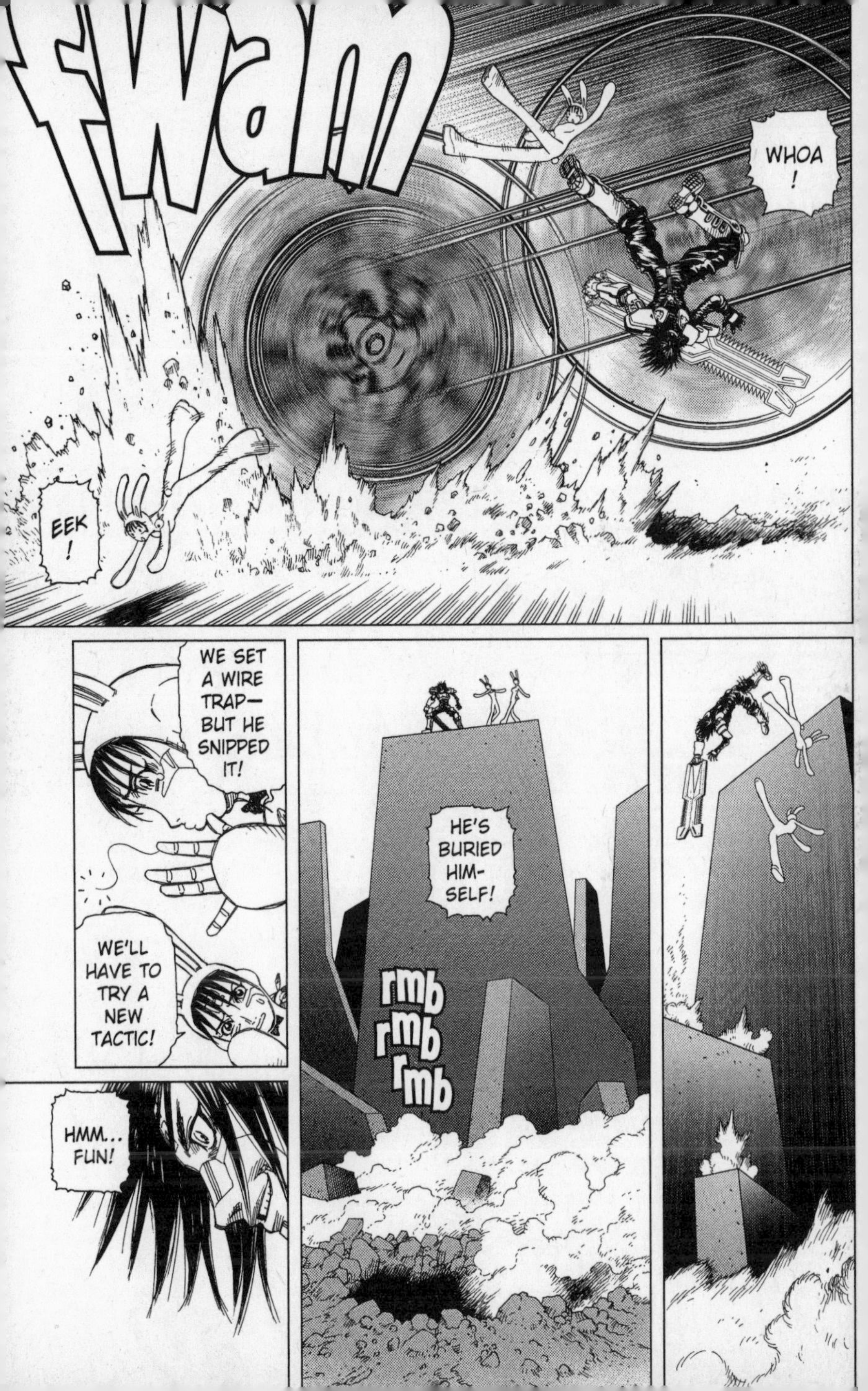
WHOA!
fwam
EEK!
HE'S BURIED HIM-SELF!
rmb rmb rmb
WE SET A WIRE TRAP—BUT HE SNIPPED IT!
WE'LL HAVE TO TRY A NEW TACTIC!
HMM... FUN!

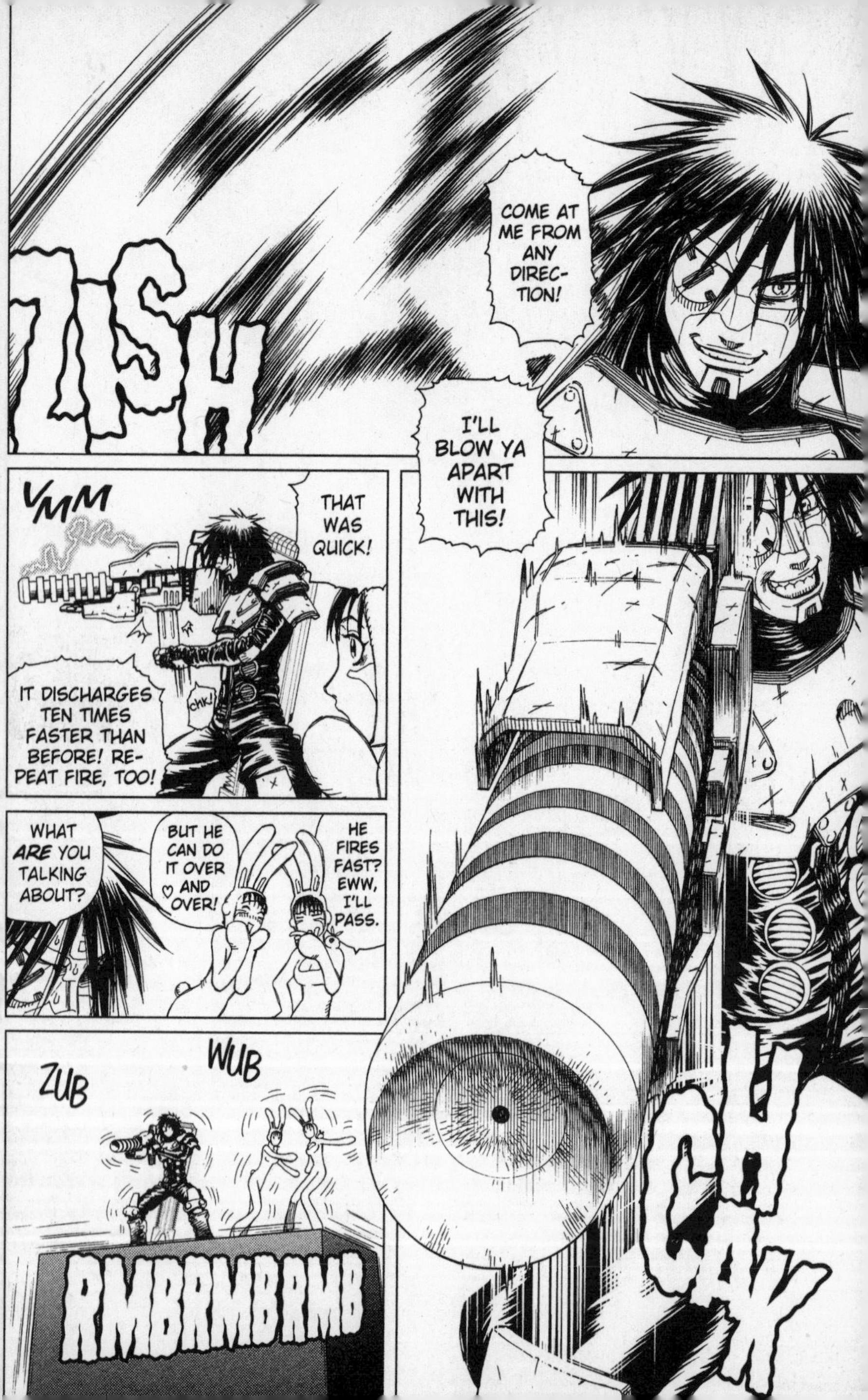
COME AT ME FROM ANY DIRECTION!
TISH
I'LL BLOW YA APART WITH THIS!
CHAK
THAT WAS QUICK!
VMM
IT DISCHARGES TEN TIMES FASTER THAN BEFORE! RE-PEAT FIRE, TOO!
CHK!
HE FIRES FAST? EWW, I'LL PASS.
BUT HE CAN DO IT OVER ♡ AND OVER!
WHAT *ARE* YOU TALKING ABOUT?
WUB
ZUB
RMBRMBRMB

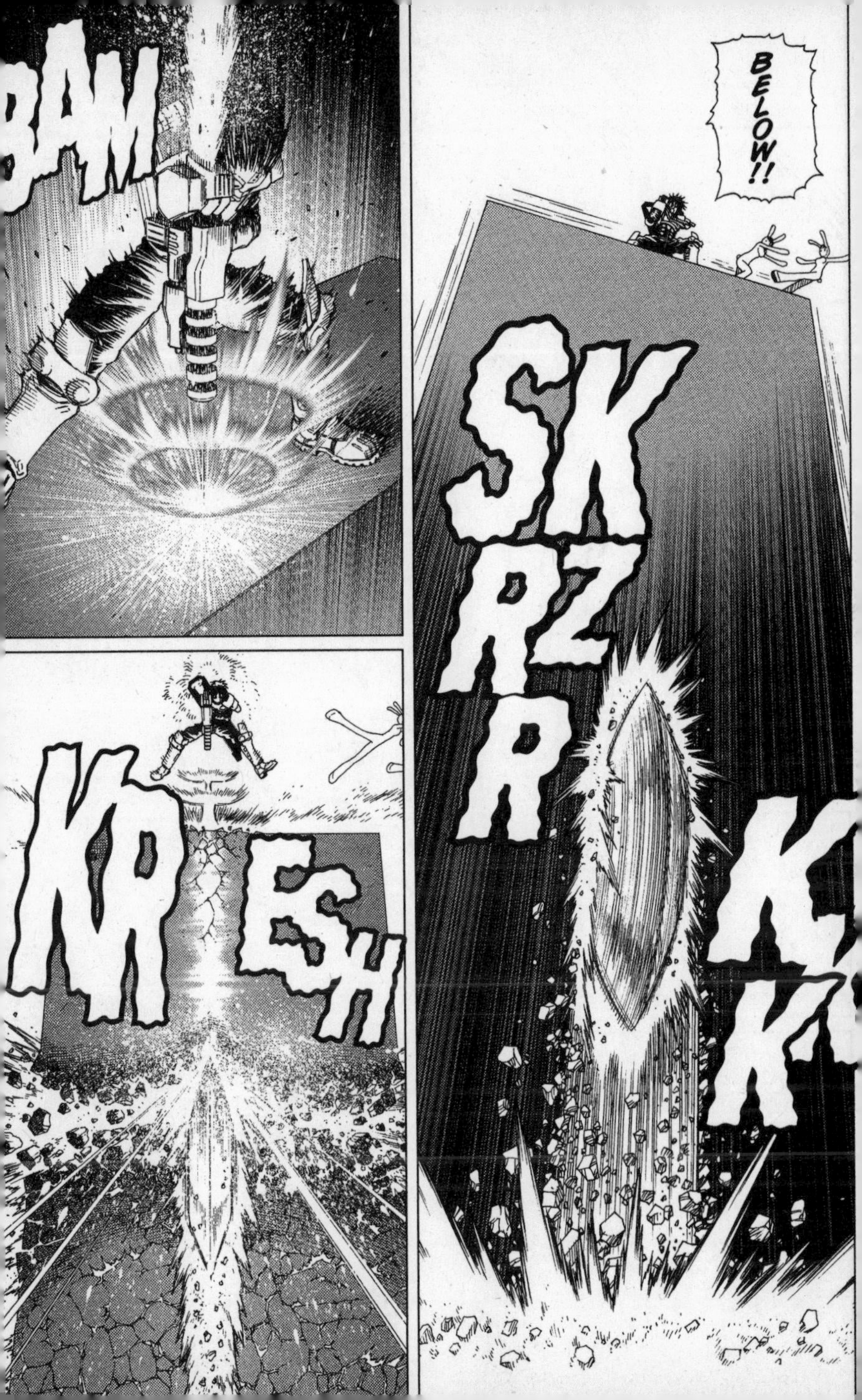
BELOW!!
SKRZR
BAM
KRESH

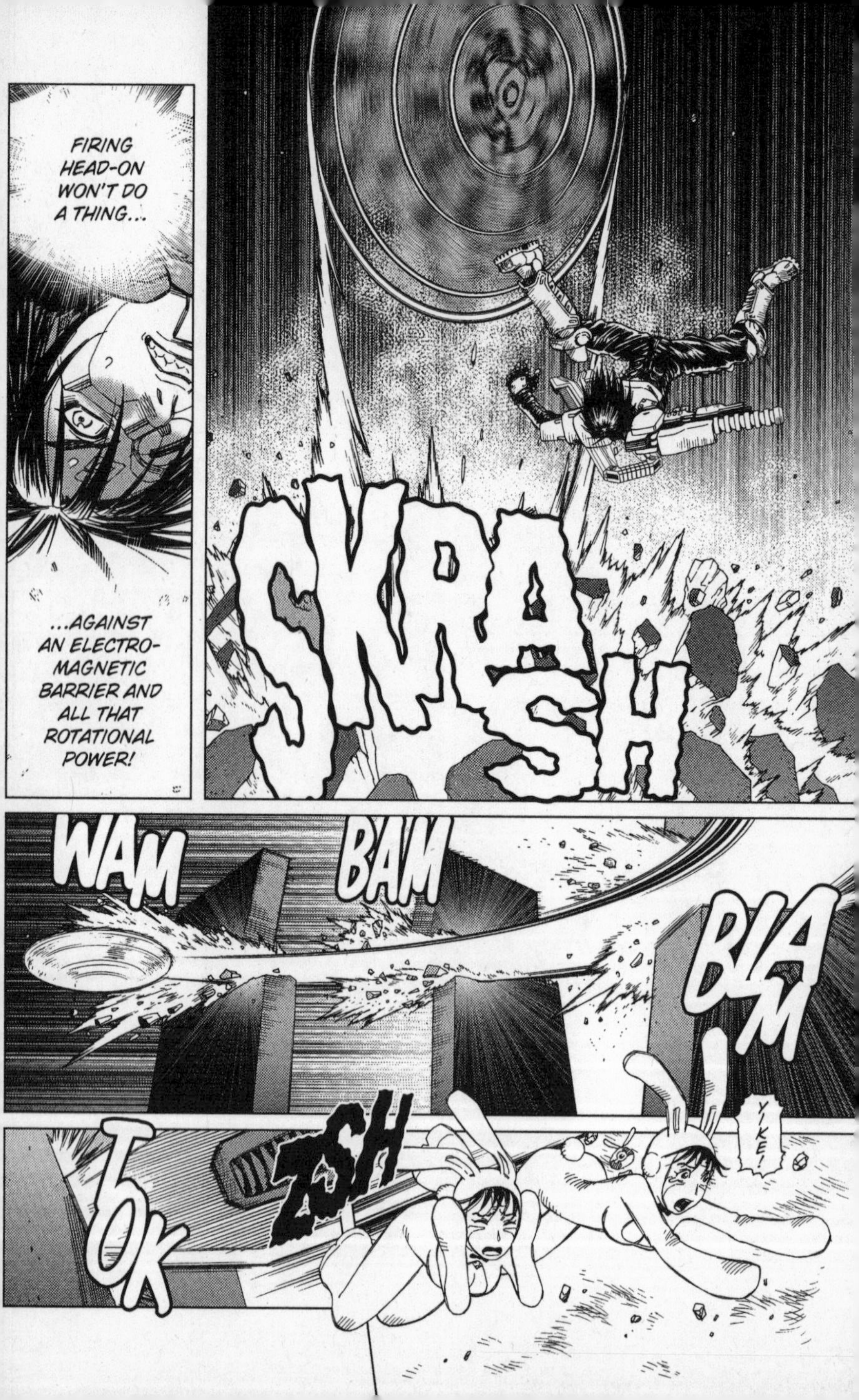
SKRASH
FIRING HEAD-ON WON'T DO A THING...
...AGAINST AN ELECTRO-MAGNETIC BARRIER AND ALL THAT ROTATIONAL POWER!
BLAM
BAM
WAM
YIKE!
ZSH
TOK

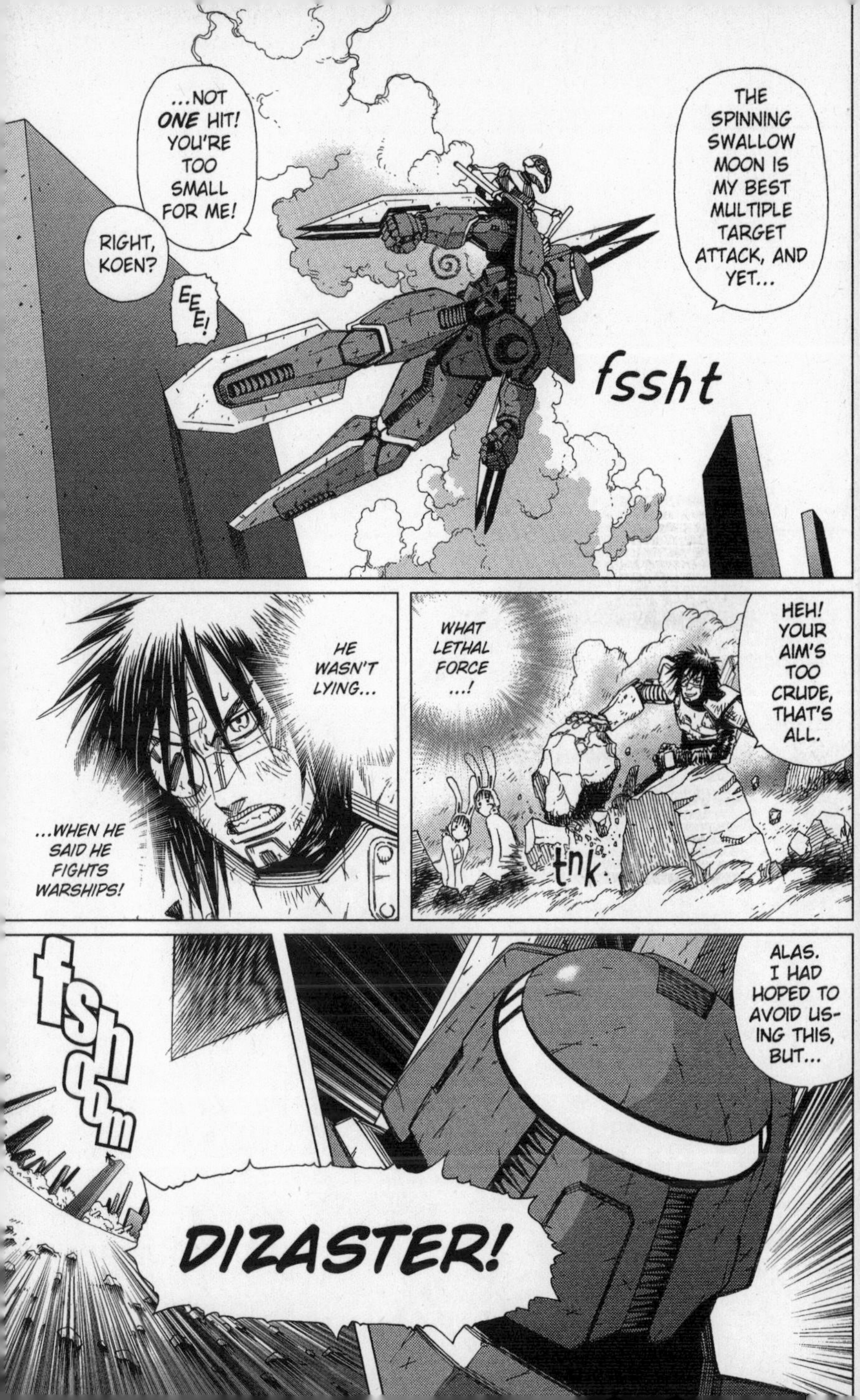
THE SPINNING SWALLOW MOON IS MY BEST MULTIPLE TARGET ATTACK, AND YET...
...NOT ***ONE*** HIT! YOU'RE TOO SMALL FOR ME!
RIGHT, KOEN?
EEE!
fssht
HEH! YOUR AIM'S TOO CRUDE, THAT'S ALL.
WHAT LETHAL FORCE...!
tnk
HE WASN'T LYING...
...WHEN HE SAID HE FIGHTS WARSHIPS!
ALAS. I HAD HOPED TO AVOID US-ING THIS, BUT...
fshooom
DIZASTER!

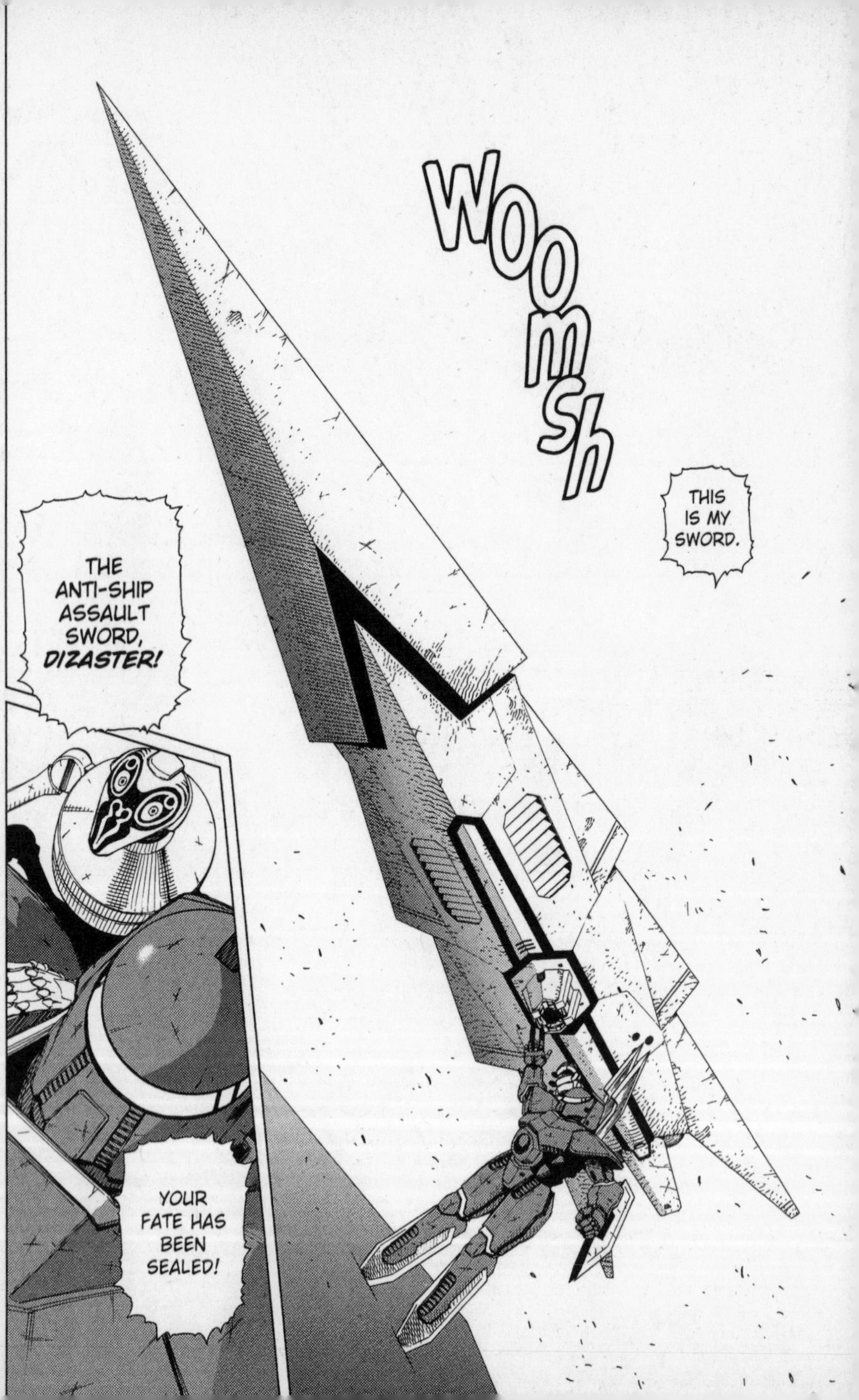
WOOMSH
THIS IS MY SWORD.
THE ANTI-SHIP ASSAULT SWORD, DIZASTER!
YOUR FATE HAS BEEN SEALED!

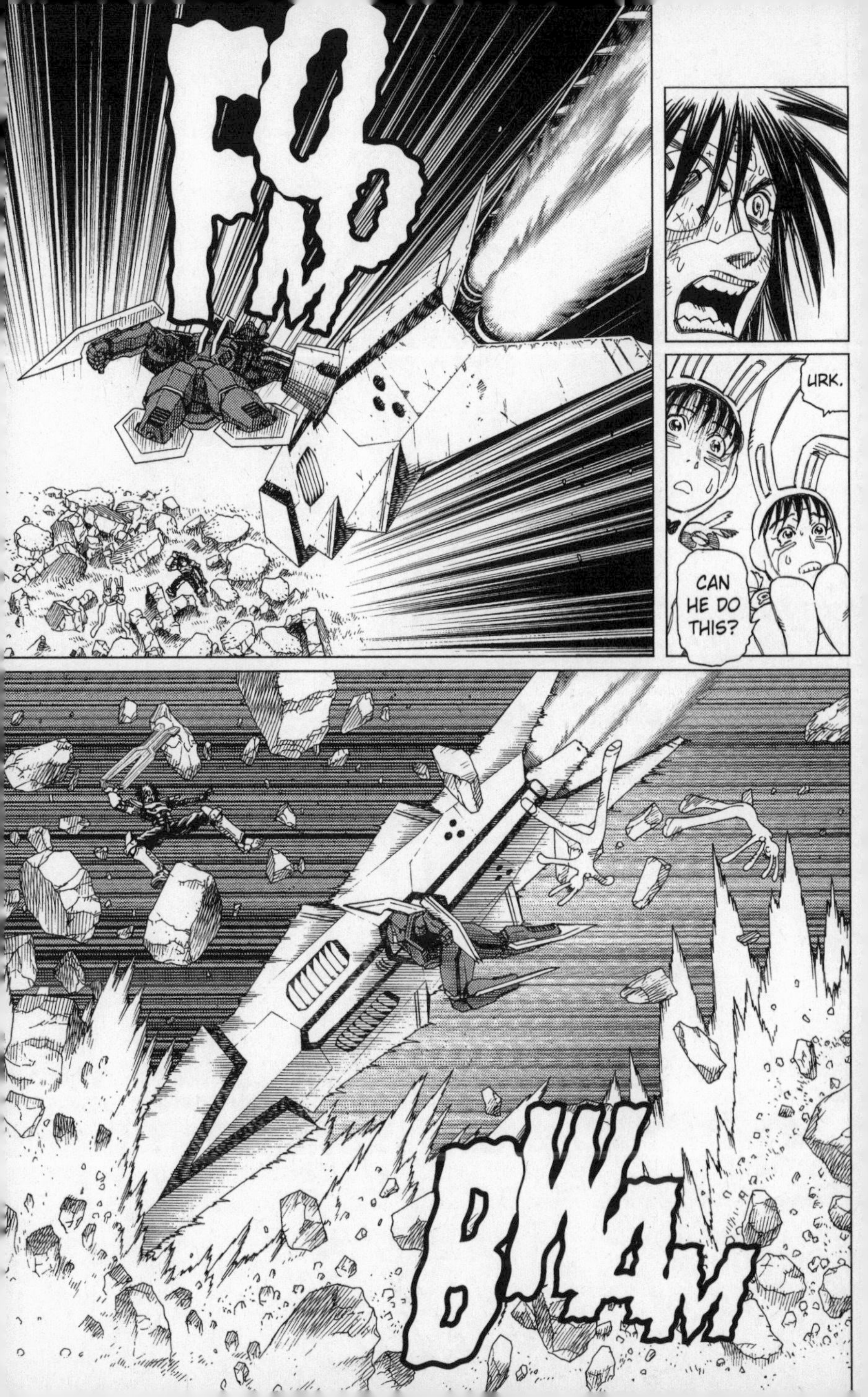
FOOM
URK.
CAN HE DO THIS?
BWAM

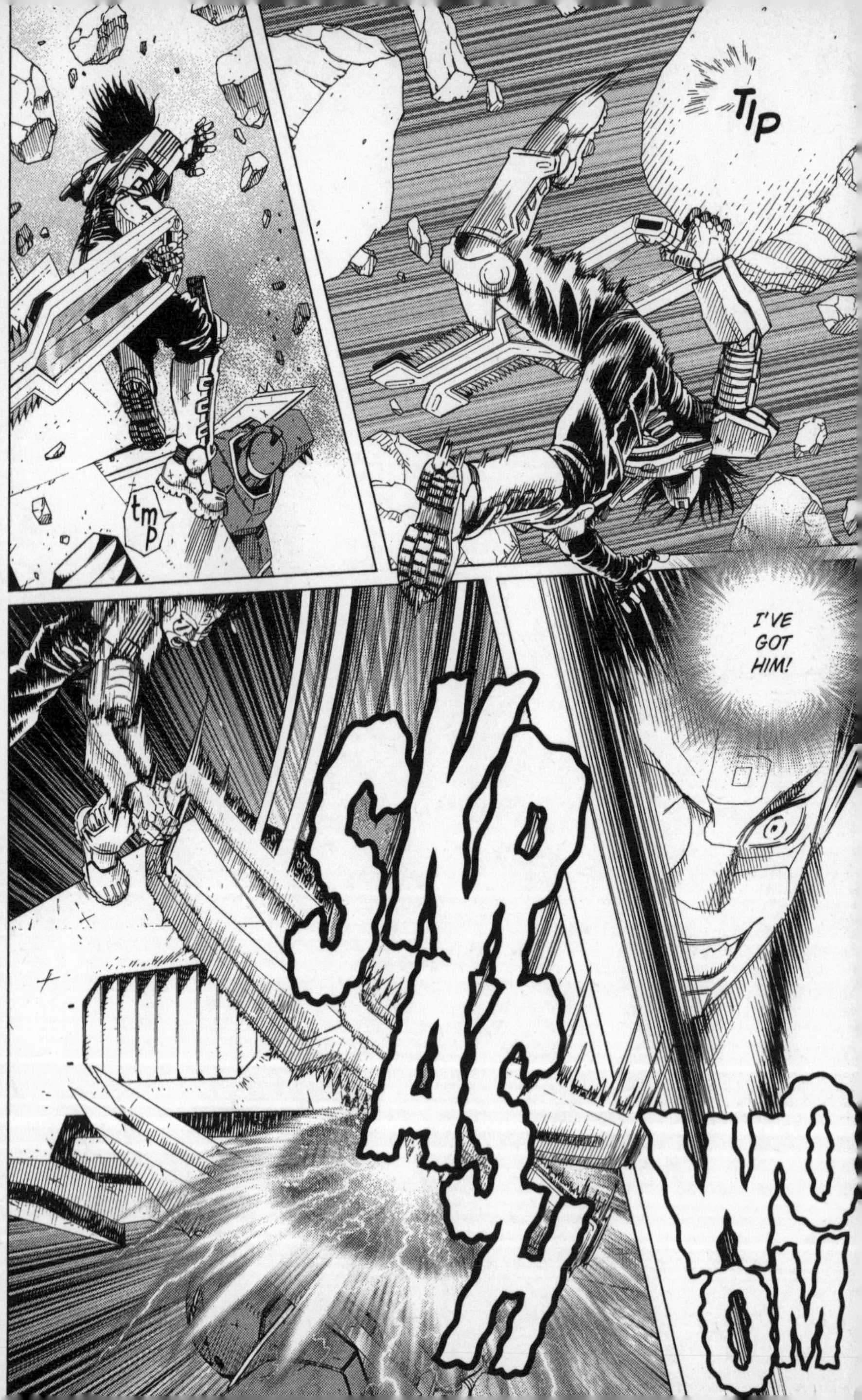
TIP
tmp
I'VE GOT HIM!
WOOM
SKRASH

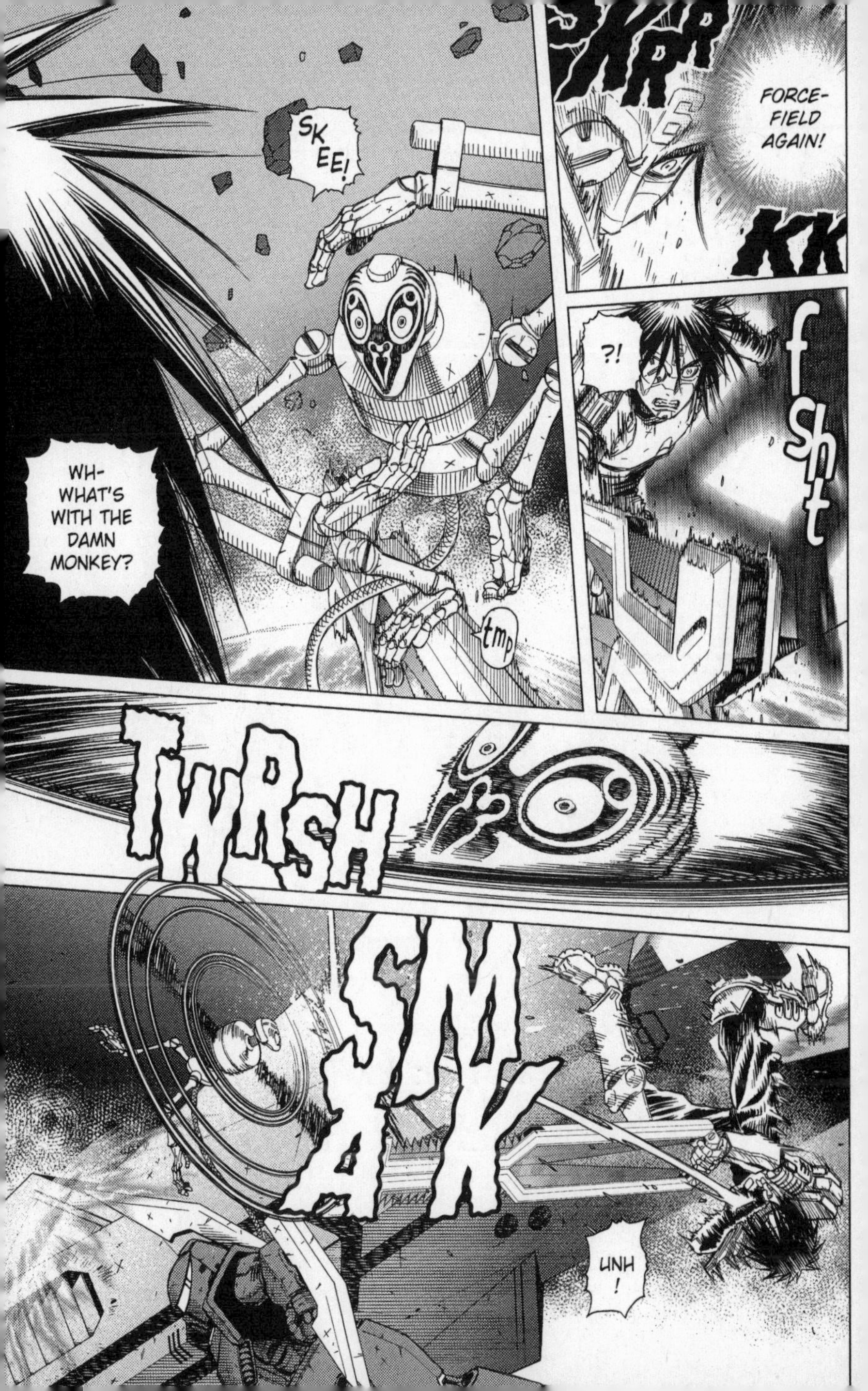
FORCE-FIELD AGAIN!
KK
?!
fsht
SKEE!
WH- WHAT'S WITH THE DAMN MONKEY?
tmp
TWRSH
SMAK
UNH!

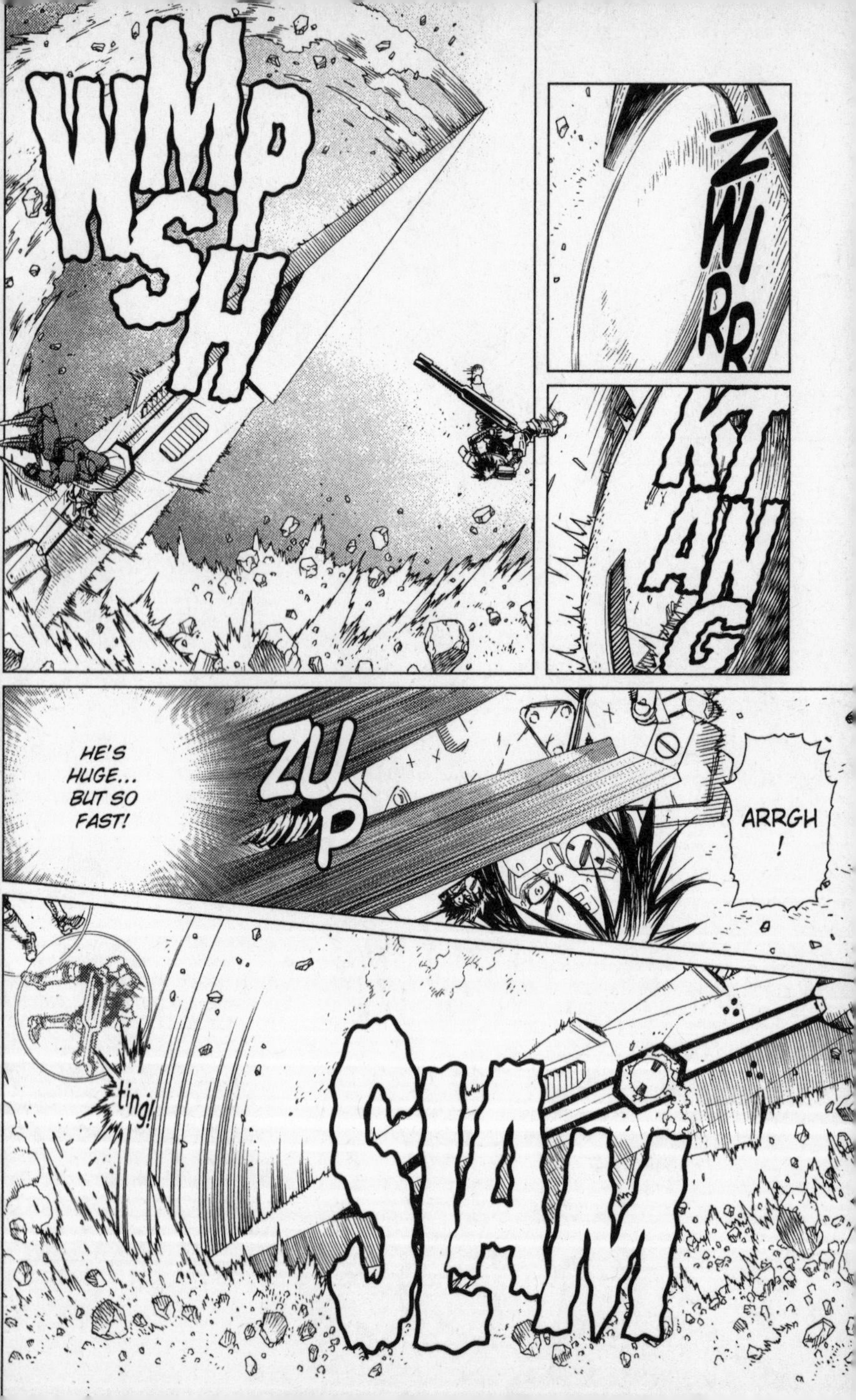
ZWIRRR
KTANG
WMPSH
ARRGH!
HE'S HUGE... BUT SO FAST!
ZUP
SLAM
tingi!

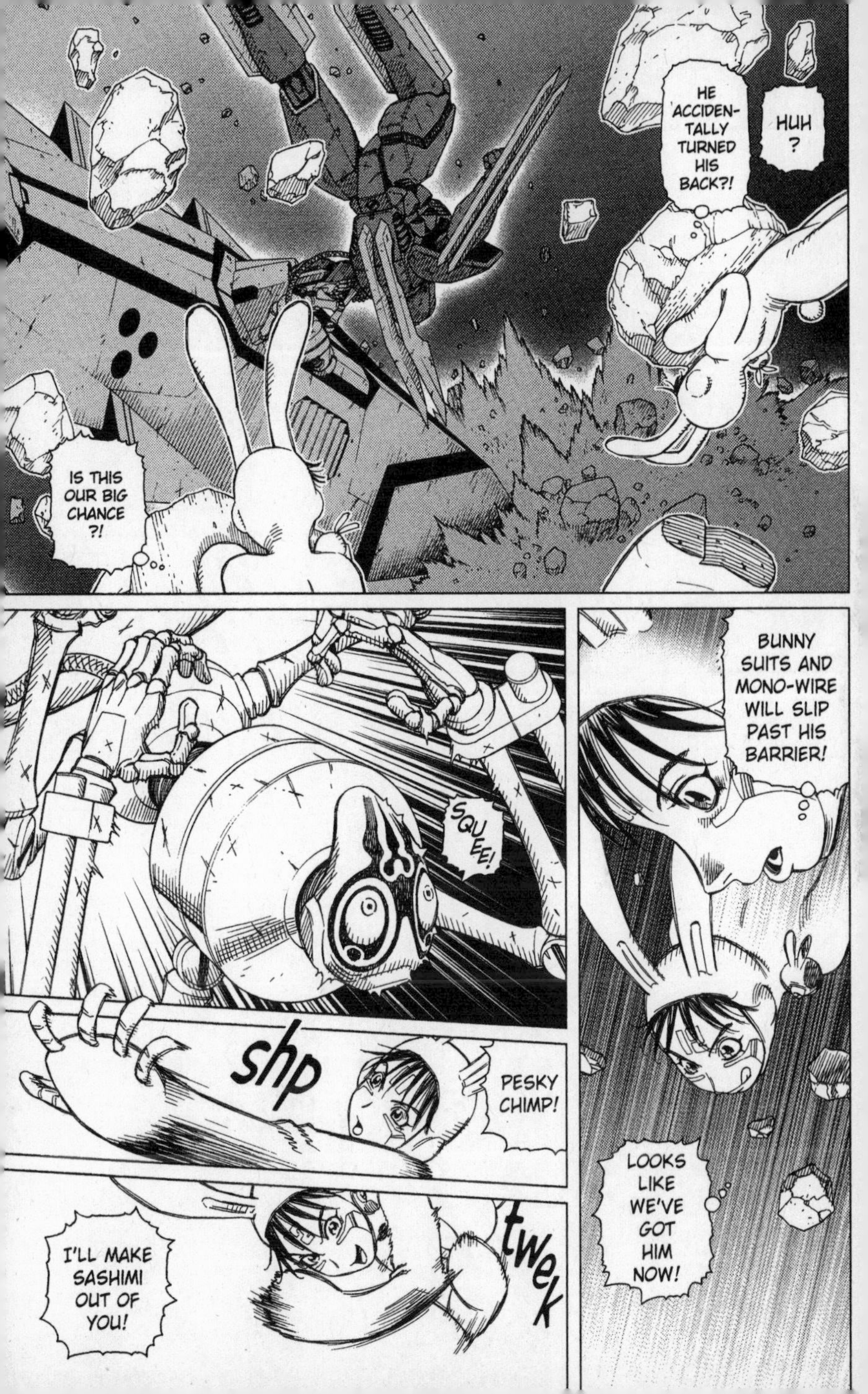
HUH?
HE ACCIDENTALLY TURNED HIS BACK?!
IS THIS OUR BIG CHANCE?!
BUNNY SUITS AND MONO-WIRE WILL SLIP PAST HIS BARRIER!
LOOKS LIKE WE'VE GOT HIM NOW!
SQUEE!
PESKY CHIMP!
shp
tweek
I'LL MAKE SASHIMI OUT OF YOU!

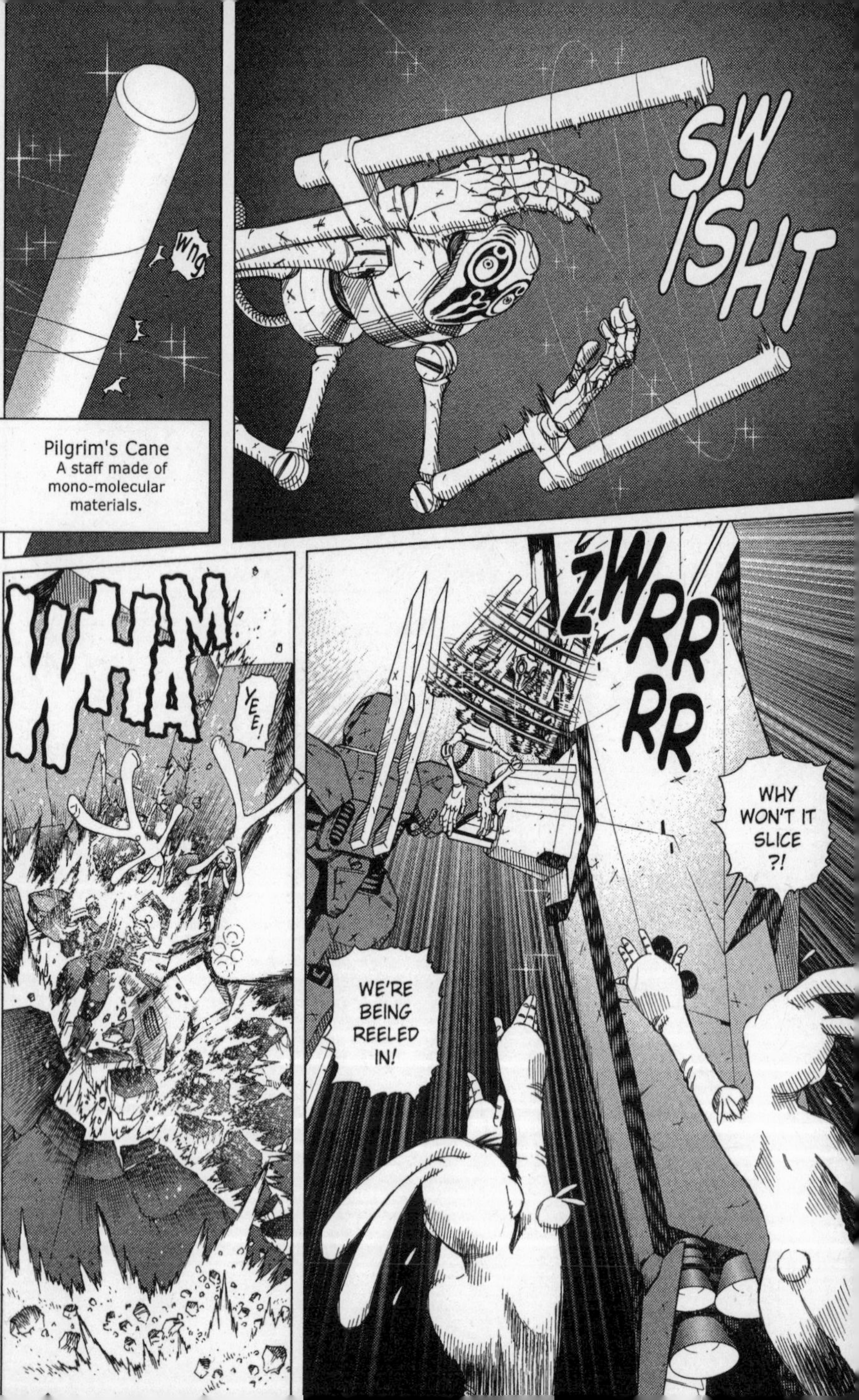
SWISHT
wng
Pilgrim's Cane
A staff made of mono-molecular materials.
ZWRRRR
WHY WON'T IT SLICE ?!
WE'RE BEING REELED IN!
WHAM
YEE!

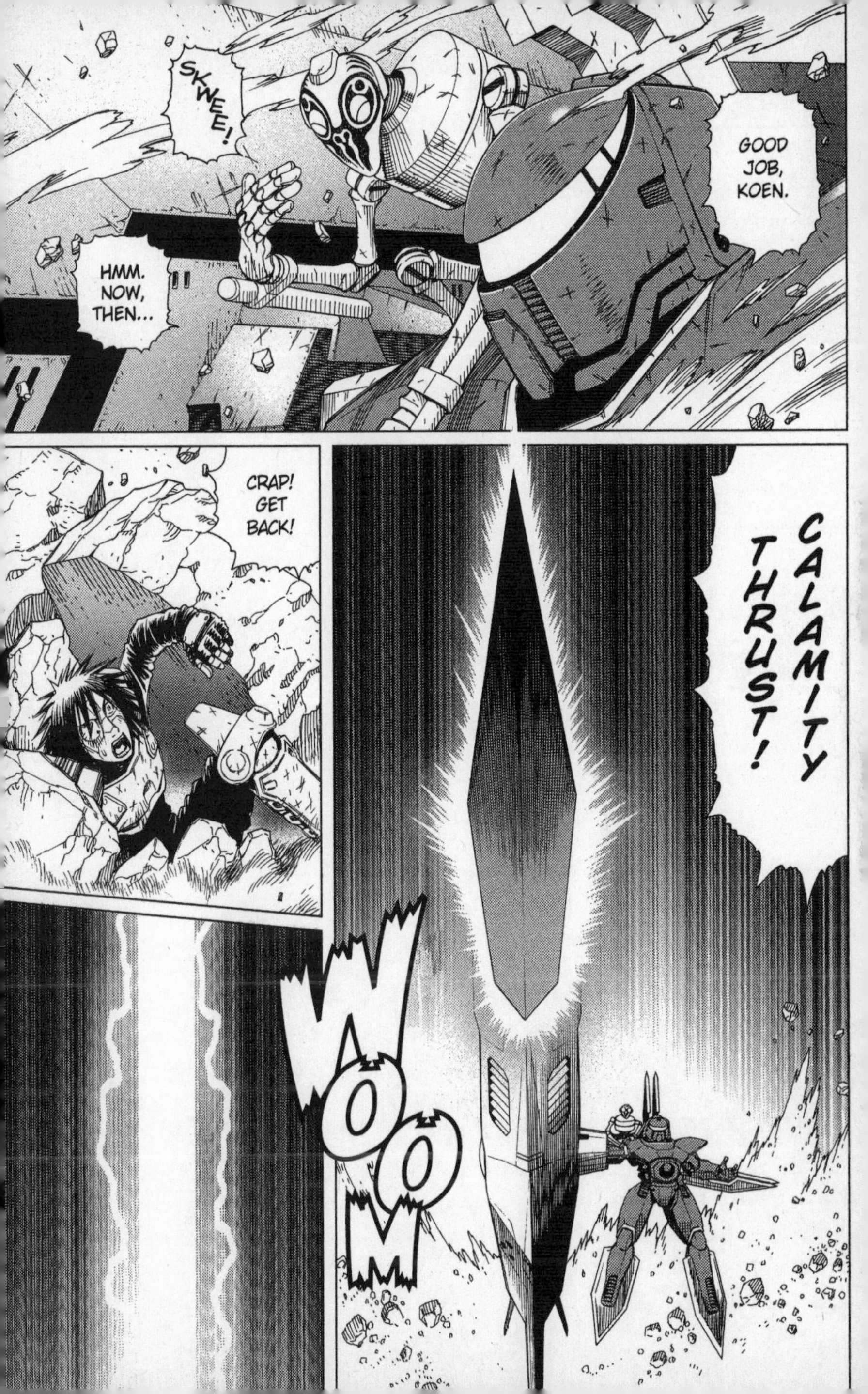
GOOD JOB, KOEN.
SKWEE!
HMM. NOW, THEN...
CALAMITY THRUST!
WOOOM
CRAP! GET BACK!

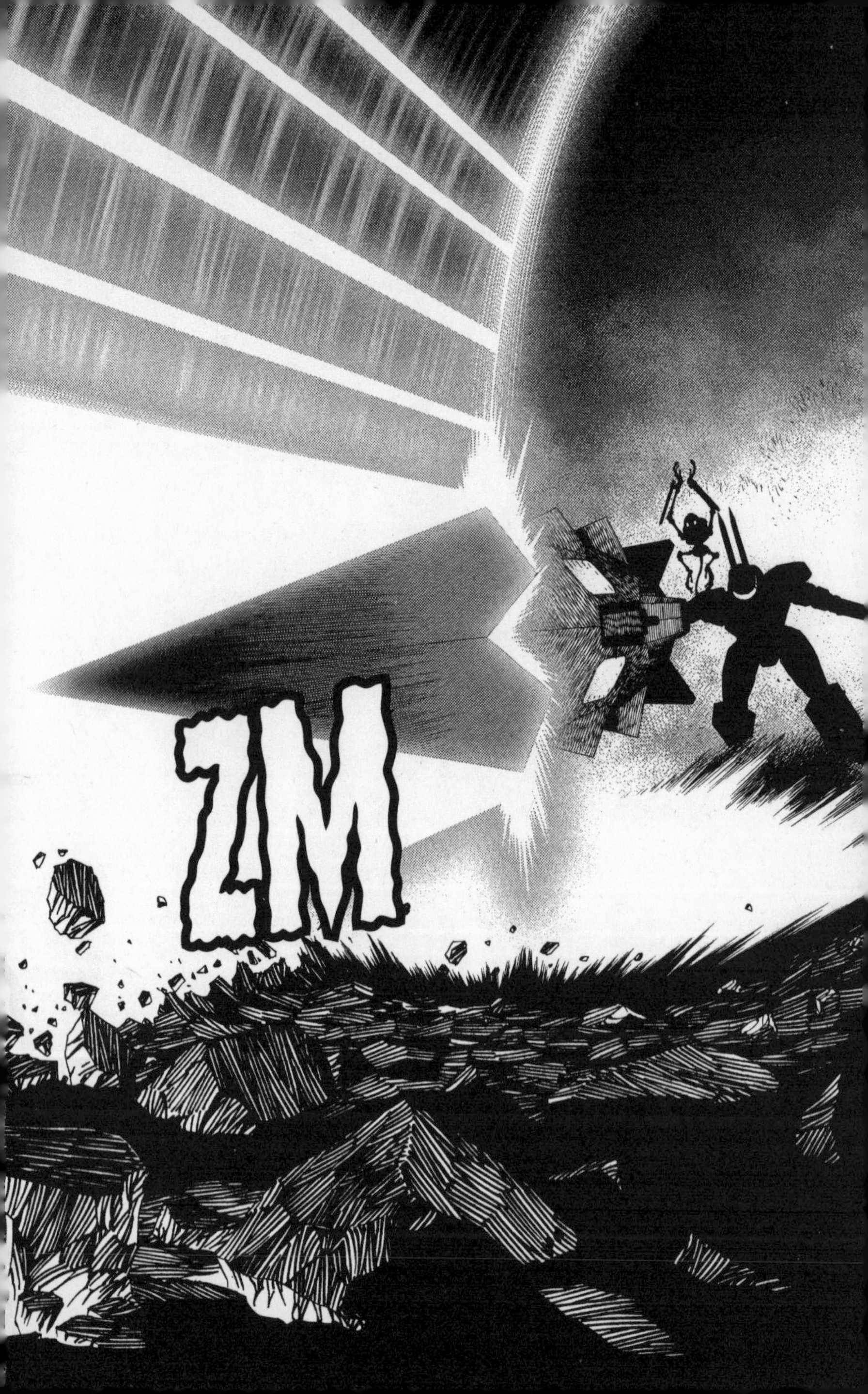
ZM

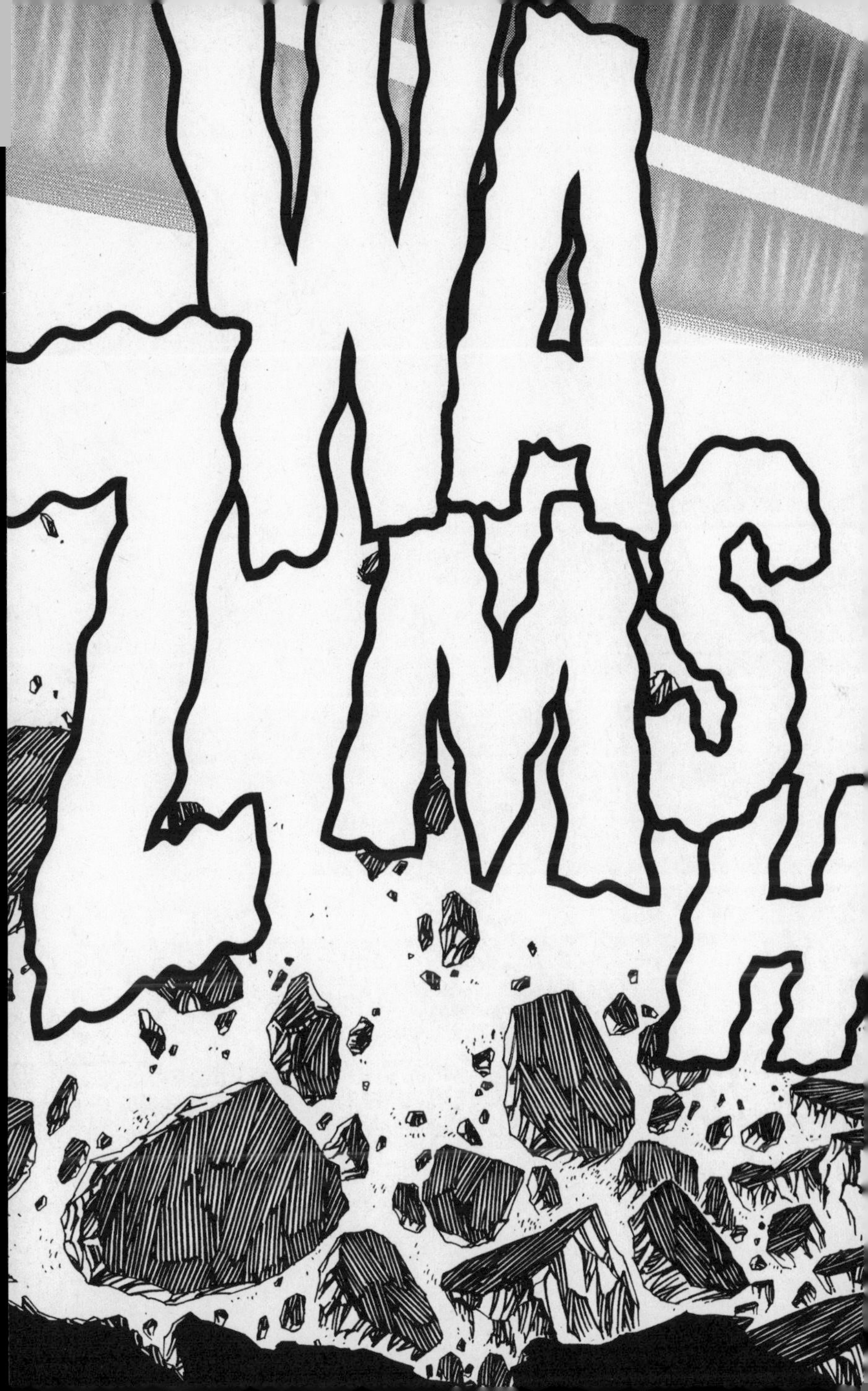

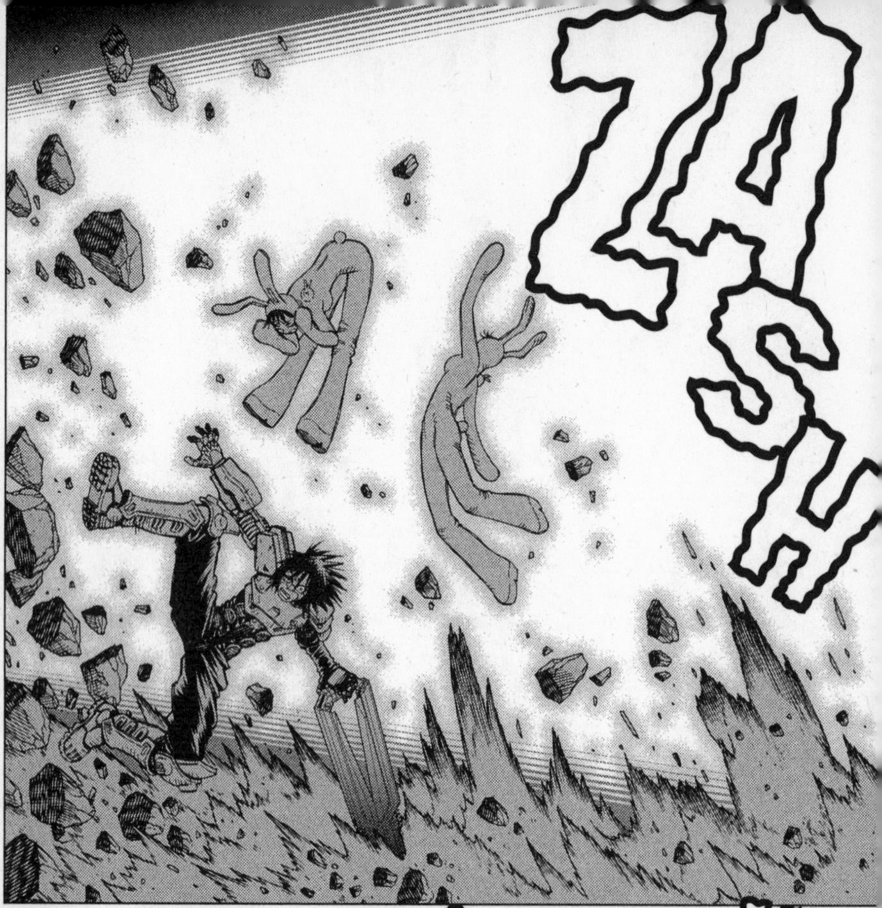
ZASH

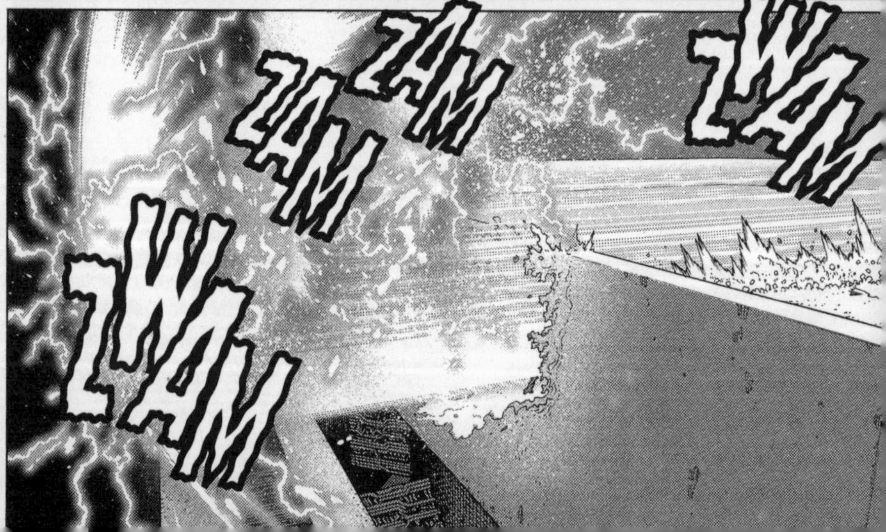
ZWAM
ZAM
ZAM
ZWAM

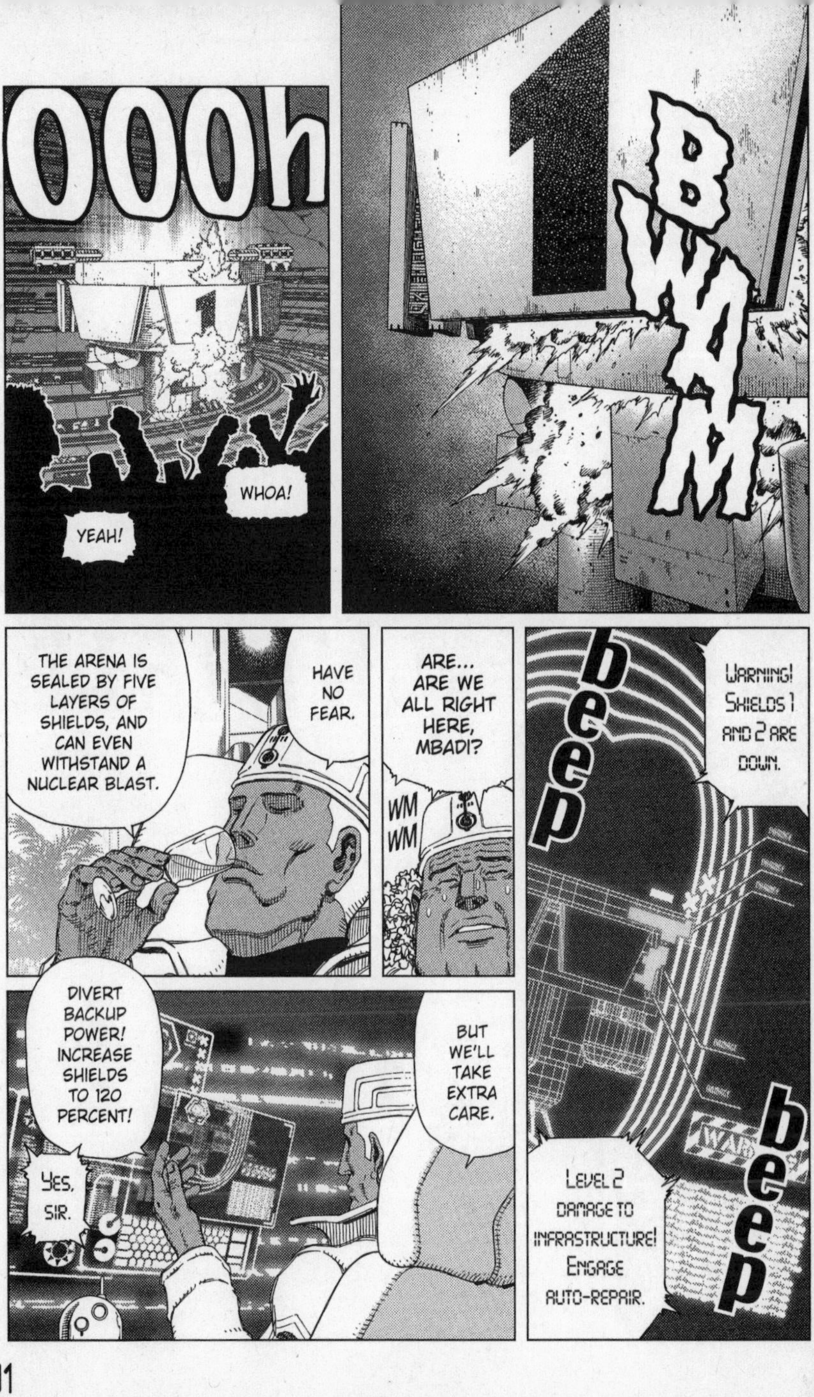
BWAM
OOOh
WHOA!
YEAH!
beep beep
WARNING! SHIELDS 1 AND 2 ARE DOWN.
LEVEL 2 DAMAGE TO INFRASTRUCTURE! ENGAGE AUTO-REPAIR.
beep beep
ARE... ARE WE ALL RIGHT HERE, MBADI?
WM WM
HAVE NO FEAR.
THE ARENA IS SEALED BY FIVE LAYERS OF SHIELDS, AND CAN EVEN WITHSTAND A NUCLEAR BLAST.
BUT WE'LL TAKE EXTRA CARE.
DIVERT BACKUP POWER! INCREASE SHIELDS TO 120 PERCENT!
YES, SIR.

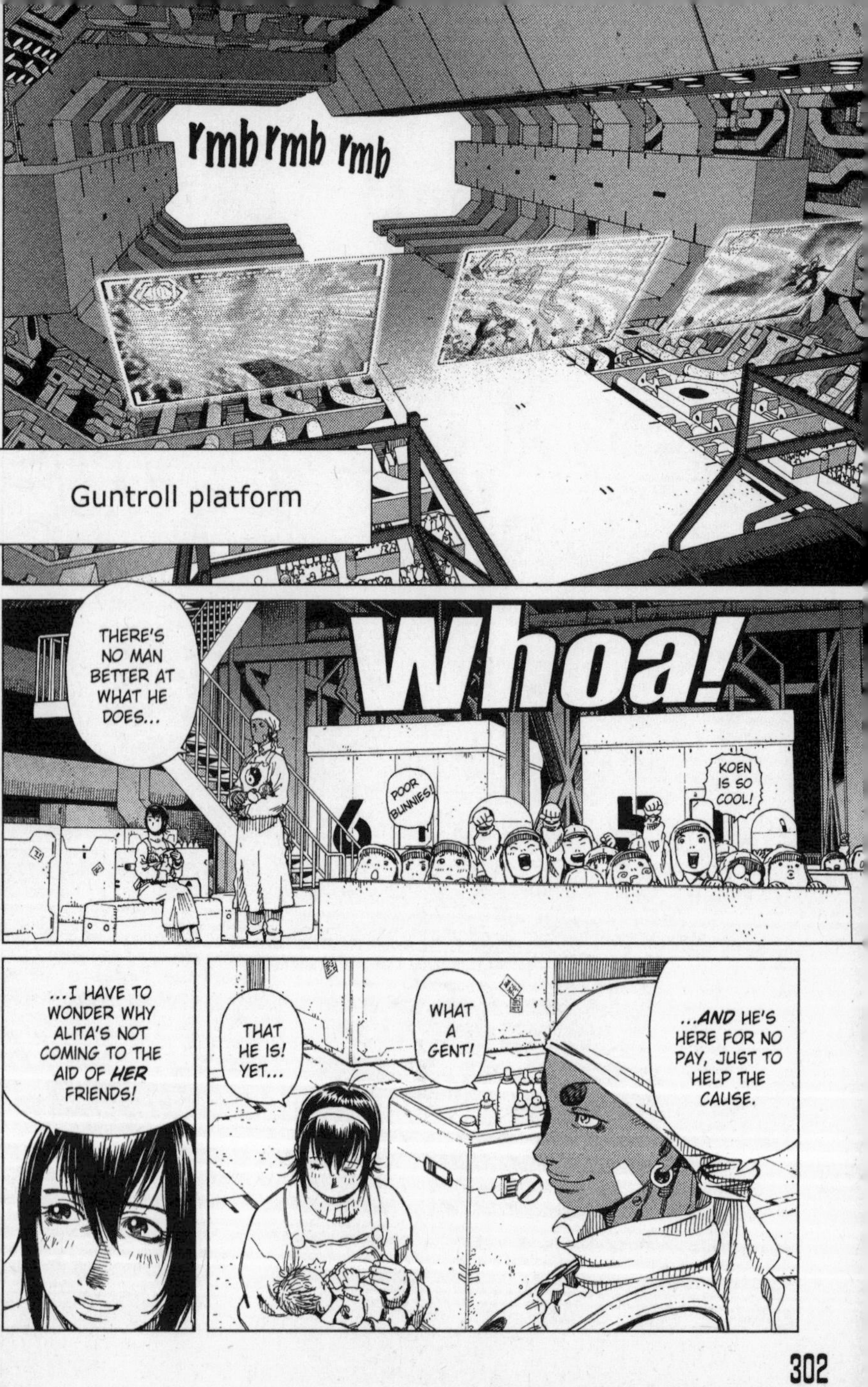
rmb rmb rmb
Guntroll platform
KOEN IS SO COOL!
Whoa!
POOR BUNNIES!
THERE'S NO MAN BETTER AT WHAT HE DOES...
...*AND* HE'S HERE FOR NO PAY, JUST TO HELP THE CAUSE.
WHAT A GENT!
THAT HE IS! YET...
...I HAVE TO WONDER WHY ALITA'S NOT COMING TO THE AID OF *HER* FRIENDS!

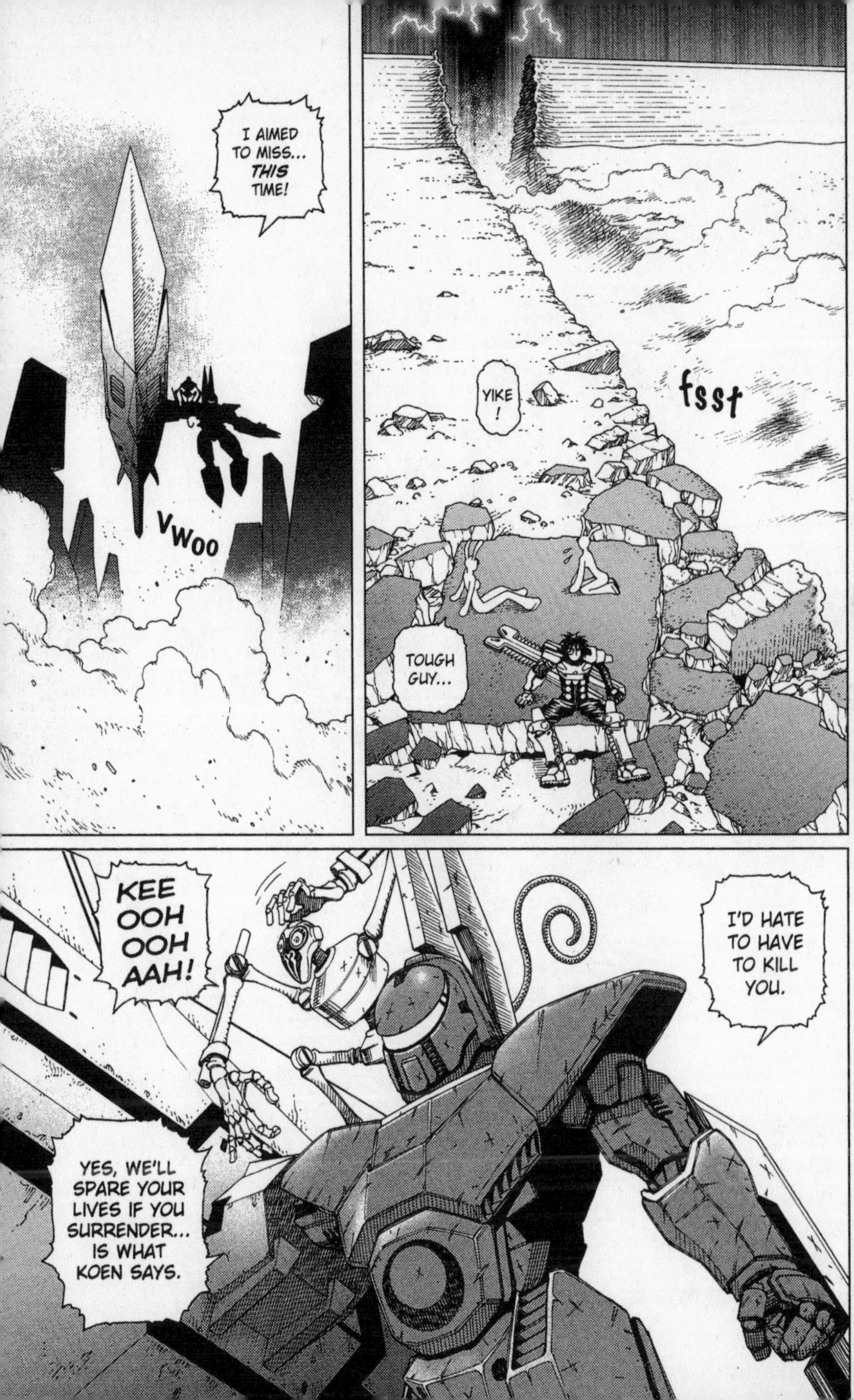
YIKE!
fsst
TOUGH GUY...
I AIMED TO MISS... THIS TIME!
VWOO
I'D HATE TO HAVE TO KILL YOU.
KEE OOH OOH AAH!
YES, WE'LL SPARE YOUR LIVES IF YOU SURRENDER... IS WHAT KOEN SAYS.

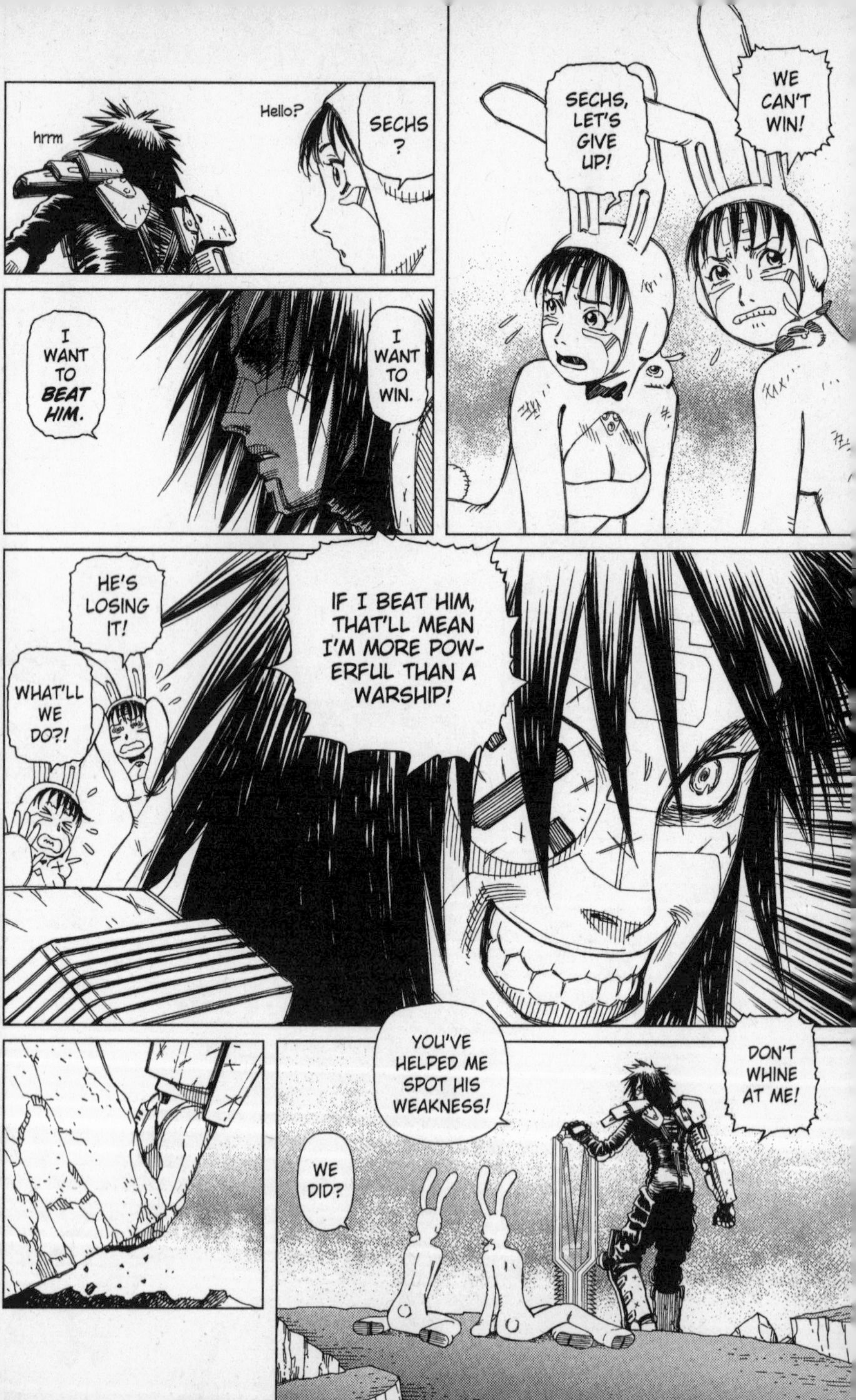
WE CAN'T WIN!
SECHS, LET'S GIVE UP!
SECHS ?
Hello?
hrrm
I WANT TO WIN.
I WANT TO BEAT HIM.
IF I BEAT HIM, THAT'LL MEAN I'M MORE POW-ERFUL THAN A WARSHIP!
HE'S LOSING IT!
WHAT'LL WE DO?!
DON'T WHINE AT ME!
YOU'VE HELPED ME SPOT HIS WEAKNESS!
WE DID?

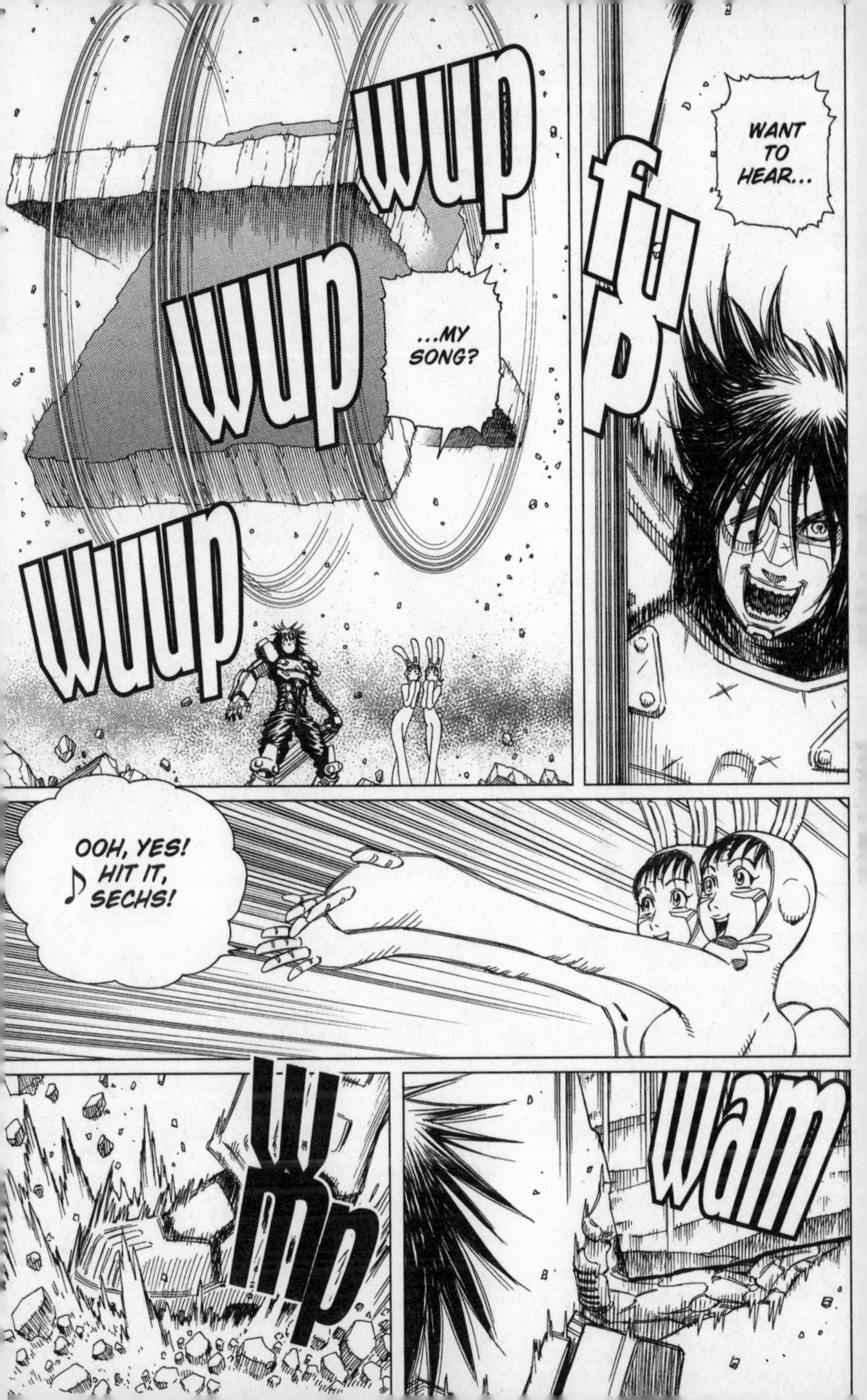
WANT TO HEAR...
wup
wup
...MY SONG?
wuup
OOH, YES! ♪ HIT IT, SECHS!
wam

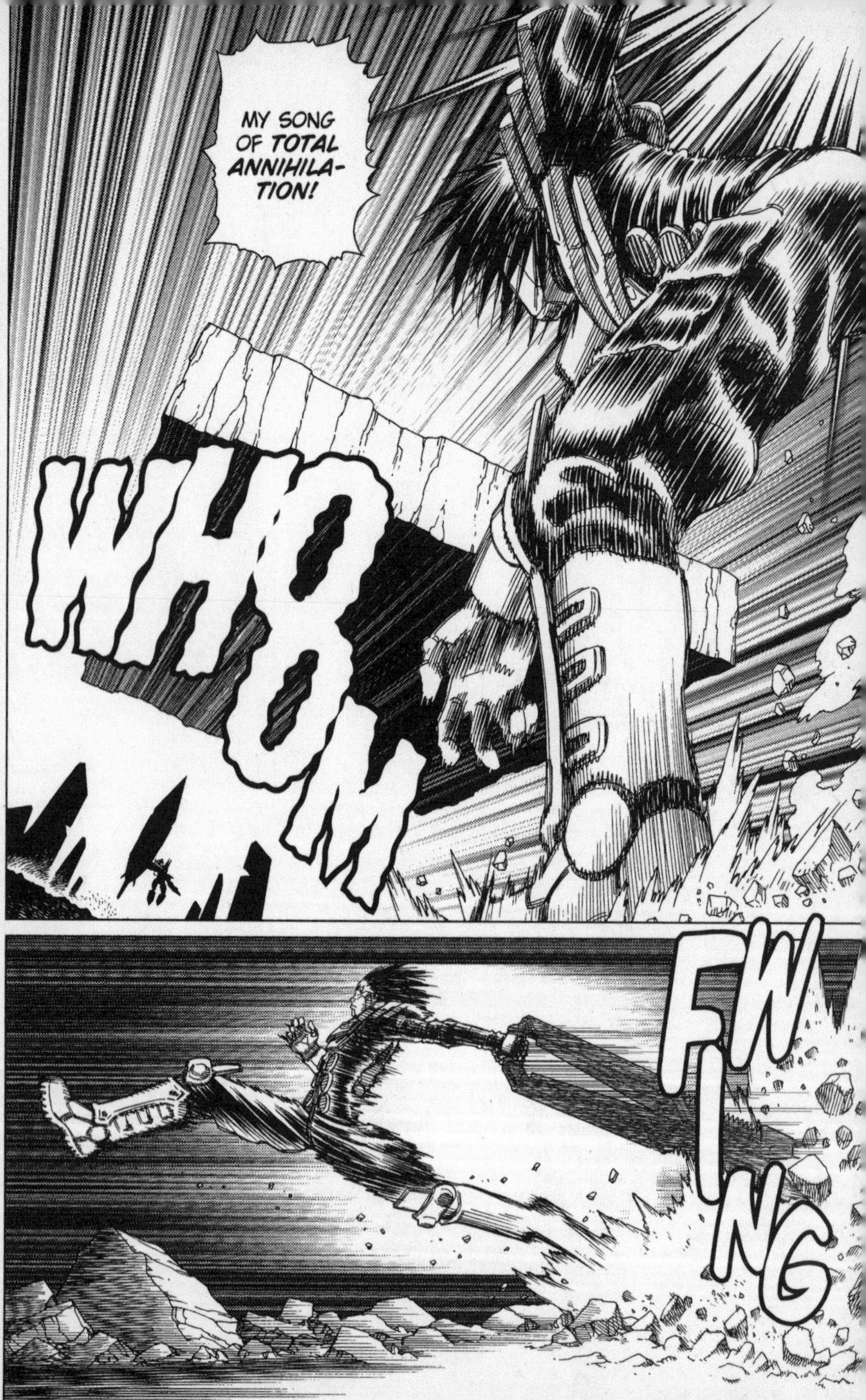
MY SONG OF *TOTAL* ANNIHILATION!
WHOOM
FWING

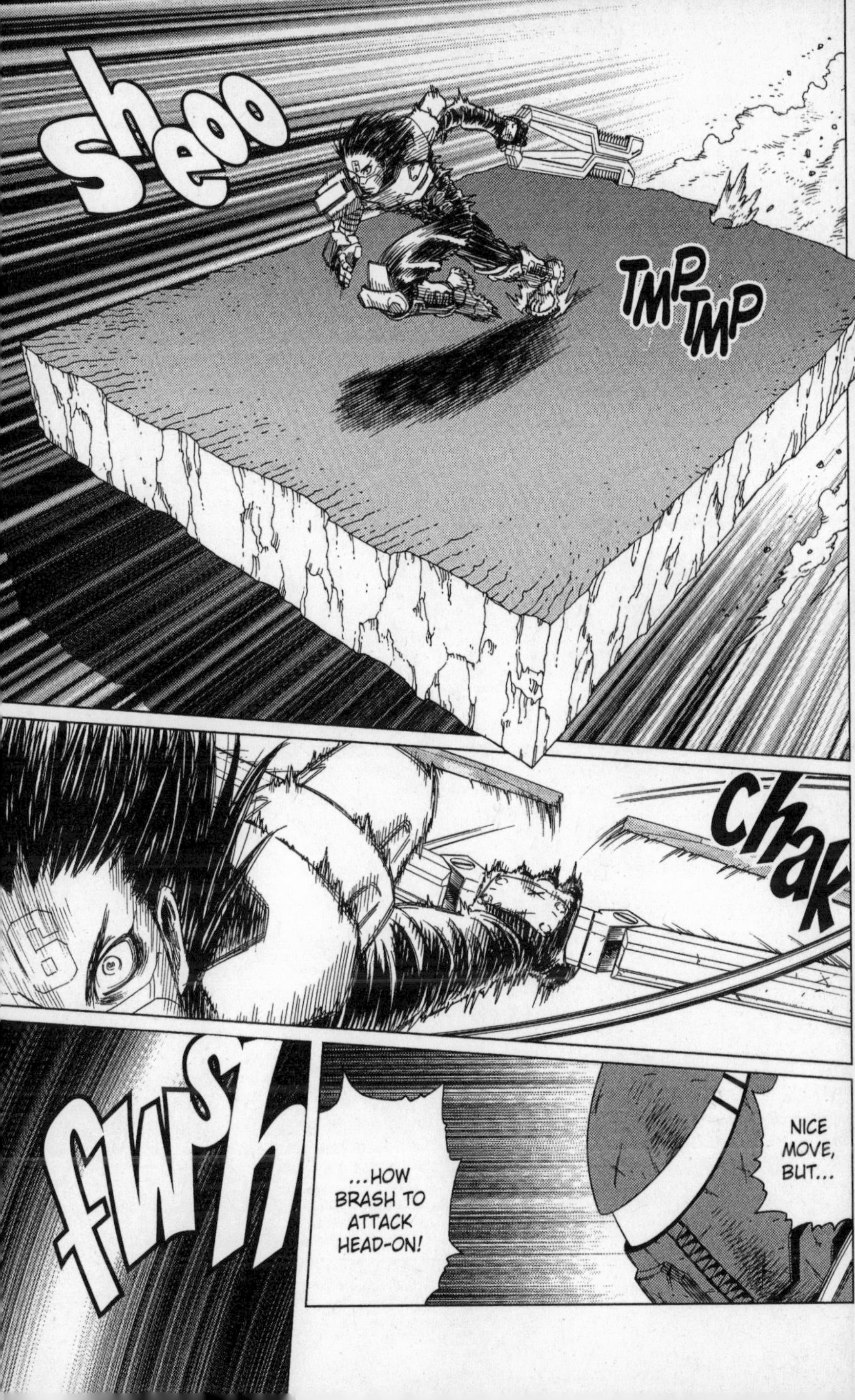
sheoo
TMP TMP
chak
NICE MOVE, BUT...
...HOW BRASH TO ATTACK HEAD-ON!
fwsh

HMM
?!

WHERE
ARE THE
RABBIT-
GIRLS?

KA
BAM

THEY'RE
BEHIND
THE WALL!

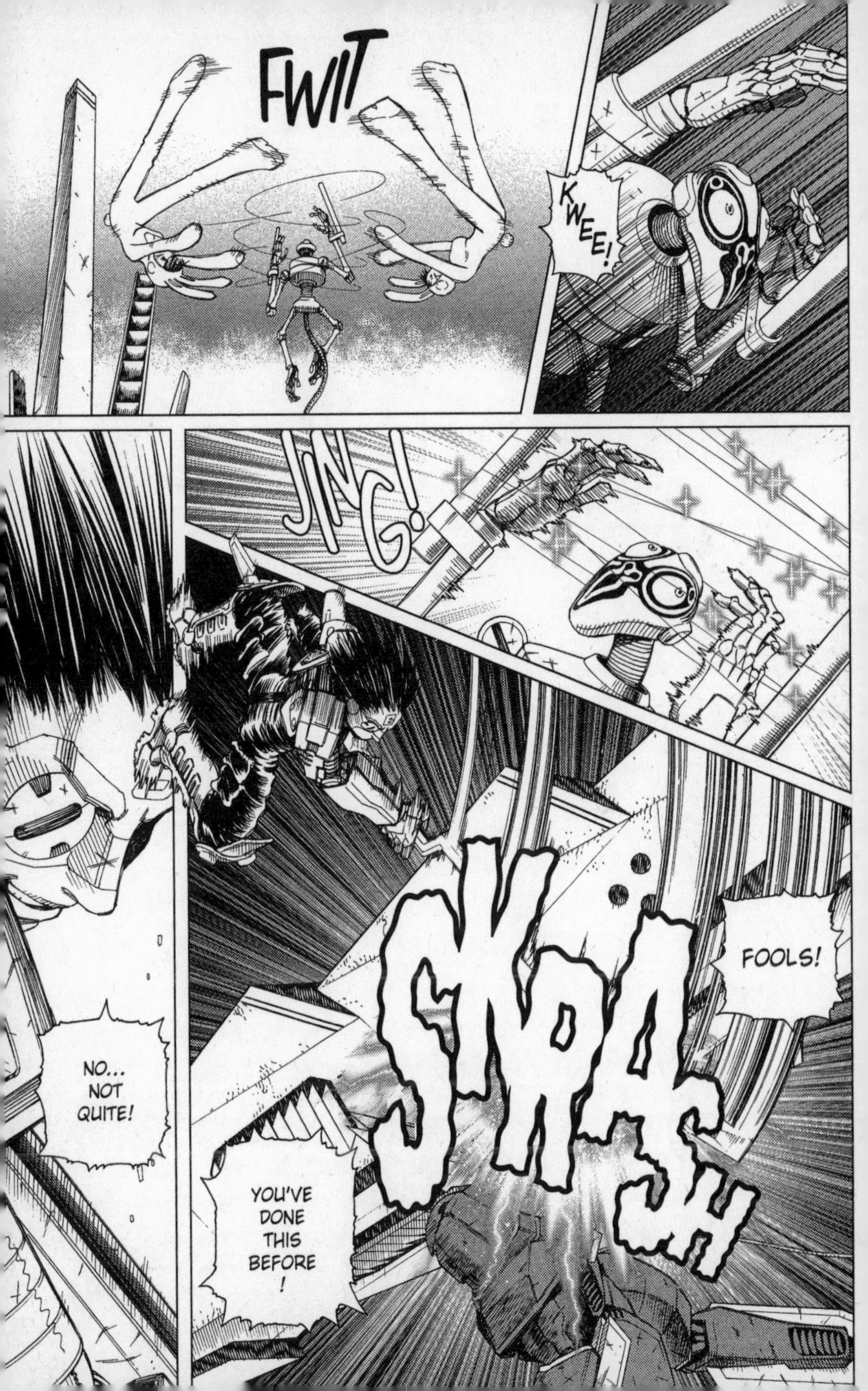
KWEEE!
FWIT
JING!
FOOLS!
SMASH
YOU'VE DONE THIS BEFORE!
NO... NOT QUITE!

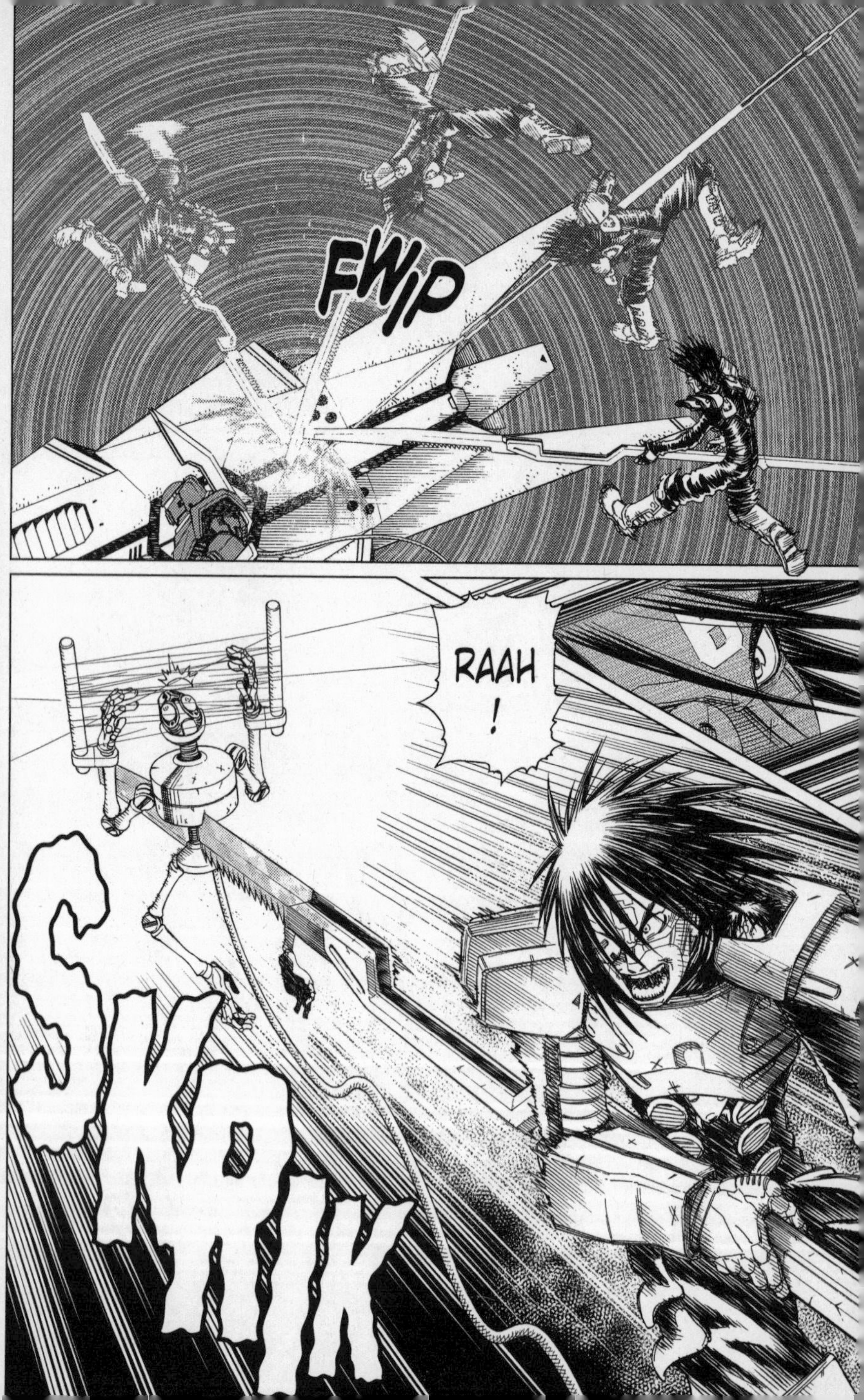
FWIP
RAAH!
SKRIK

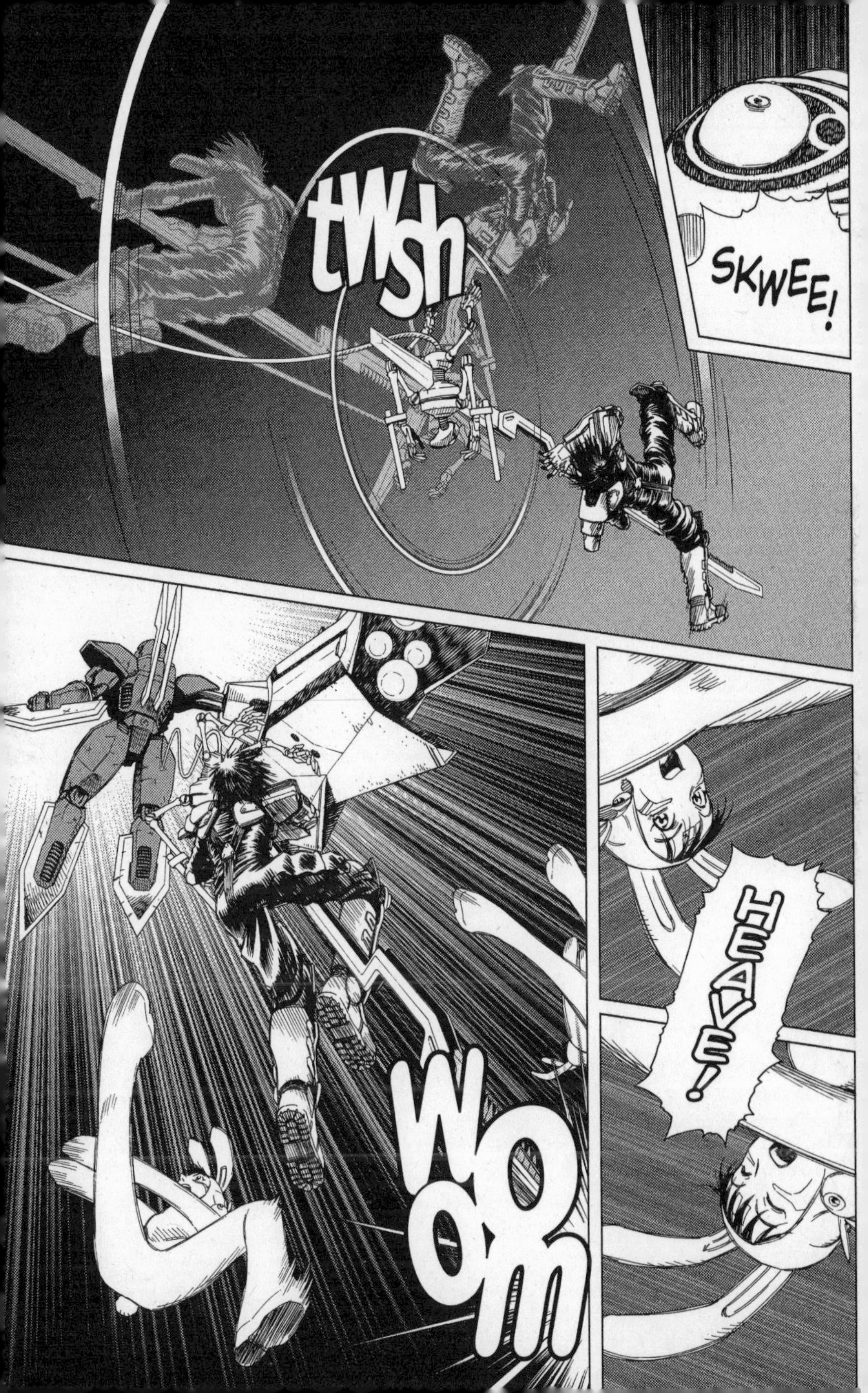
SKWEE!
tWsh
HEAVE!
WOOM

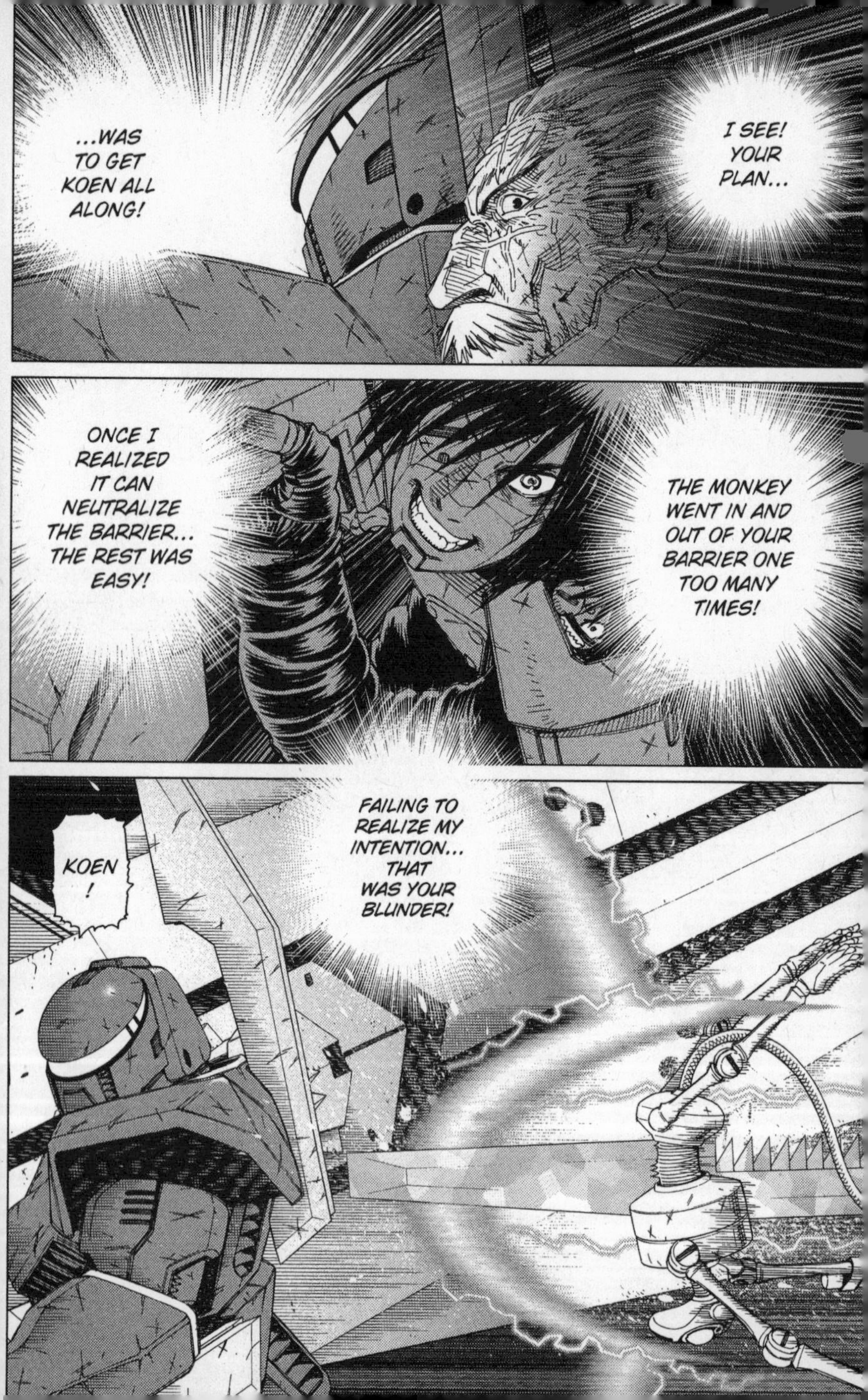
I SEE! YOUR PLAN...
...WAS TO GET KOEN ALL ALONG!
THE MONKEY WENT IN AND OUT OF YOUR BARRIER ONE TOO MANY TIMES!
ONCE I REALIZED IT CAN NEUTRALIZE THE BARRIER... THE REST WAS EASY!
FAILING TO REALIZE MY INTENTION... THAT WAS YOUR BLUNDER!
KOEN!

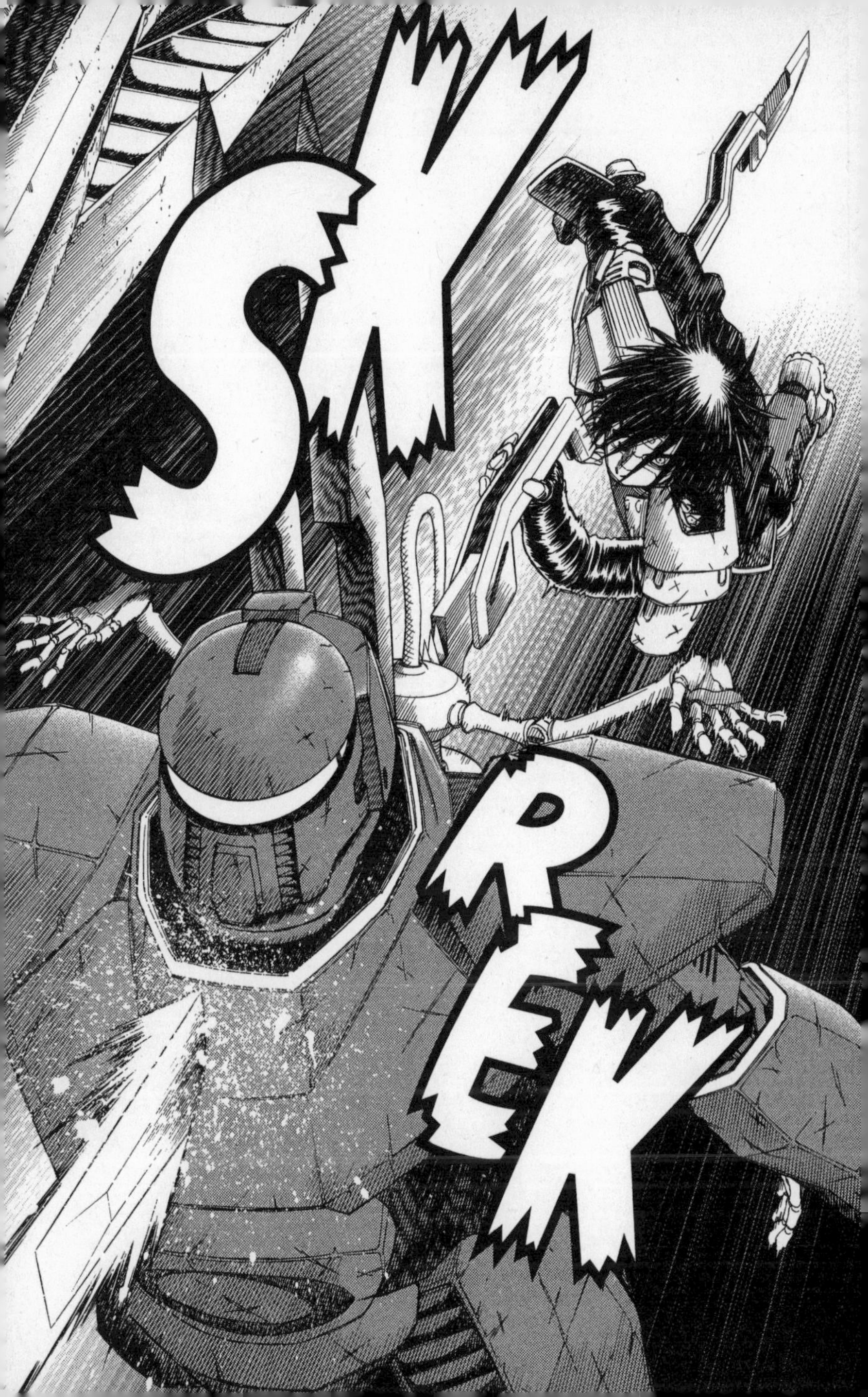
SKREEK

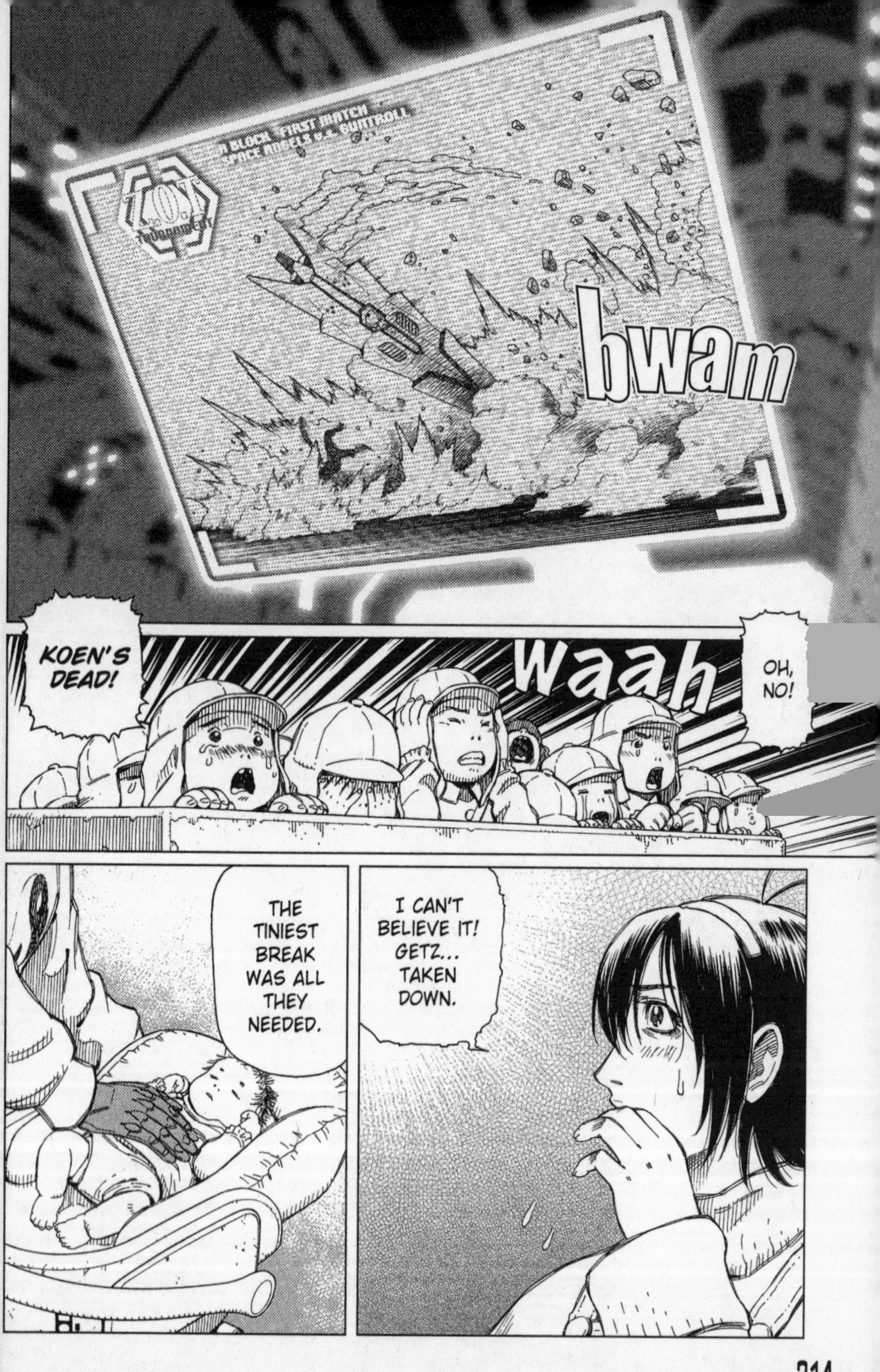

A BLOCK FIRST MATCH
bwam
OH, NO!
waah
KOEN'S DEAD!
I CAN'T BELIEVE IT! GETZ... TAKEN DOWN.
THE TINIEST BREAK WAS ALL THEY NEEDED.

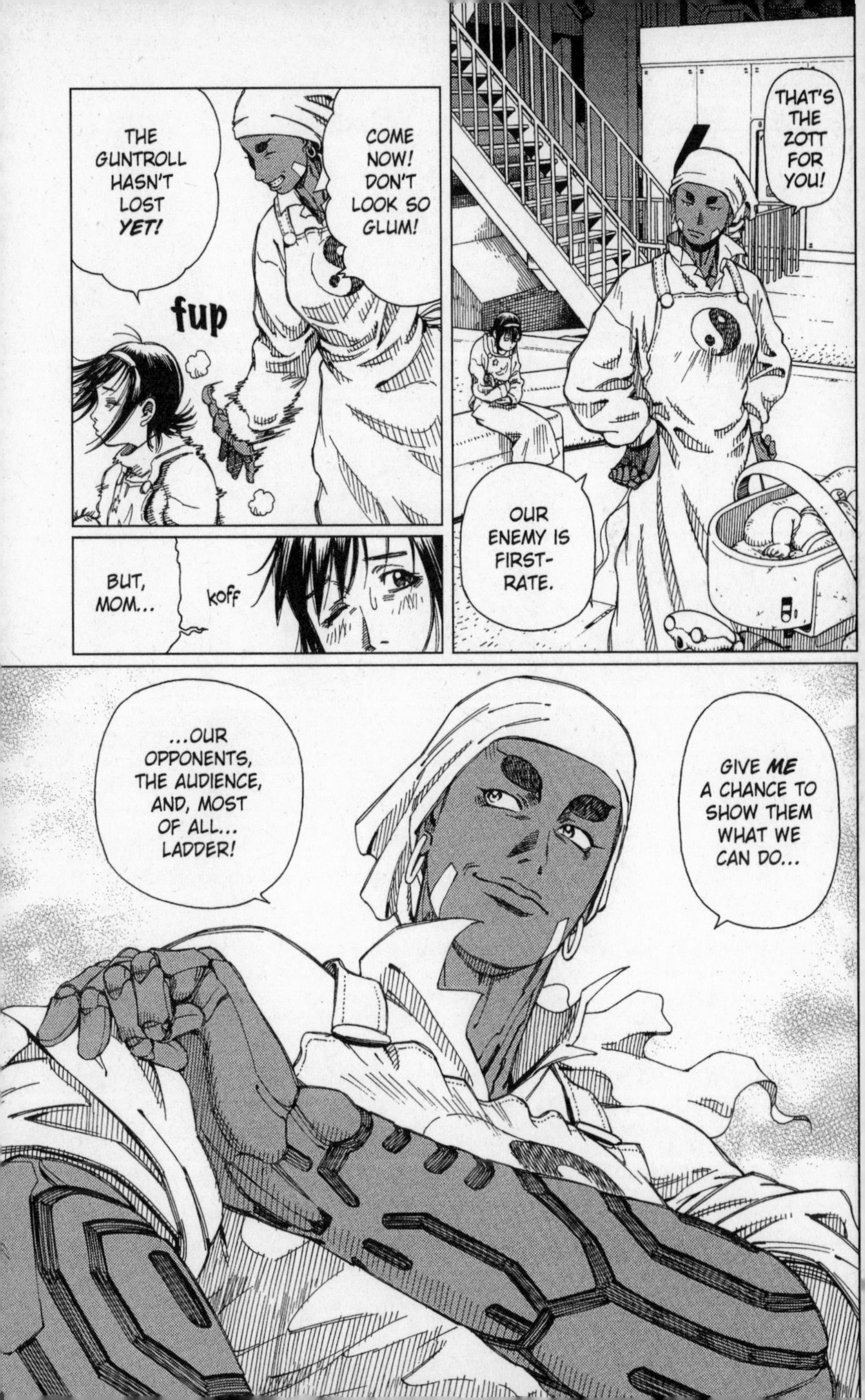
THAT'S THE ZOTT FOR YOU!
OUR ENEMY IS FIRST-RATE.
COME NOW! DON'T LOOK SO GLUM!
THE GUNTROLL HASN'T LOST *YET!*
fup
koff
BUT, MOM...
GIVE *ME* A CHANCE TO SHOW THEM WHAT WE CAN DO...
...OUR OPPONENTS, THE AUDIENCE, AND, MOST OF ALL... LADDER!

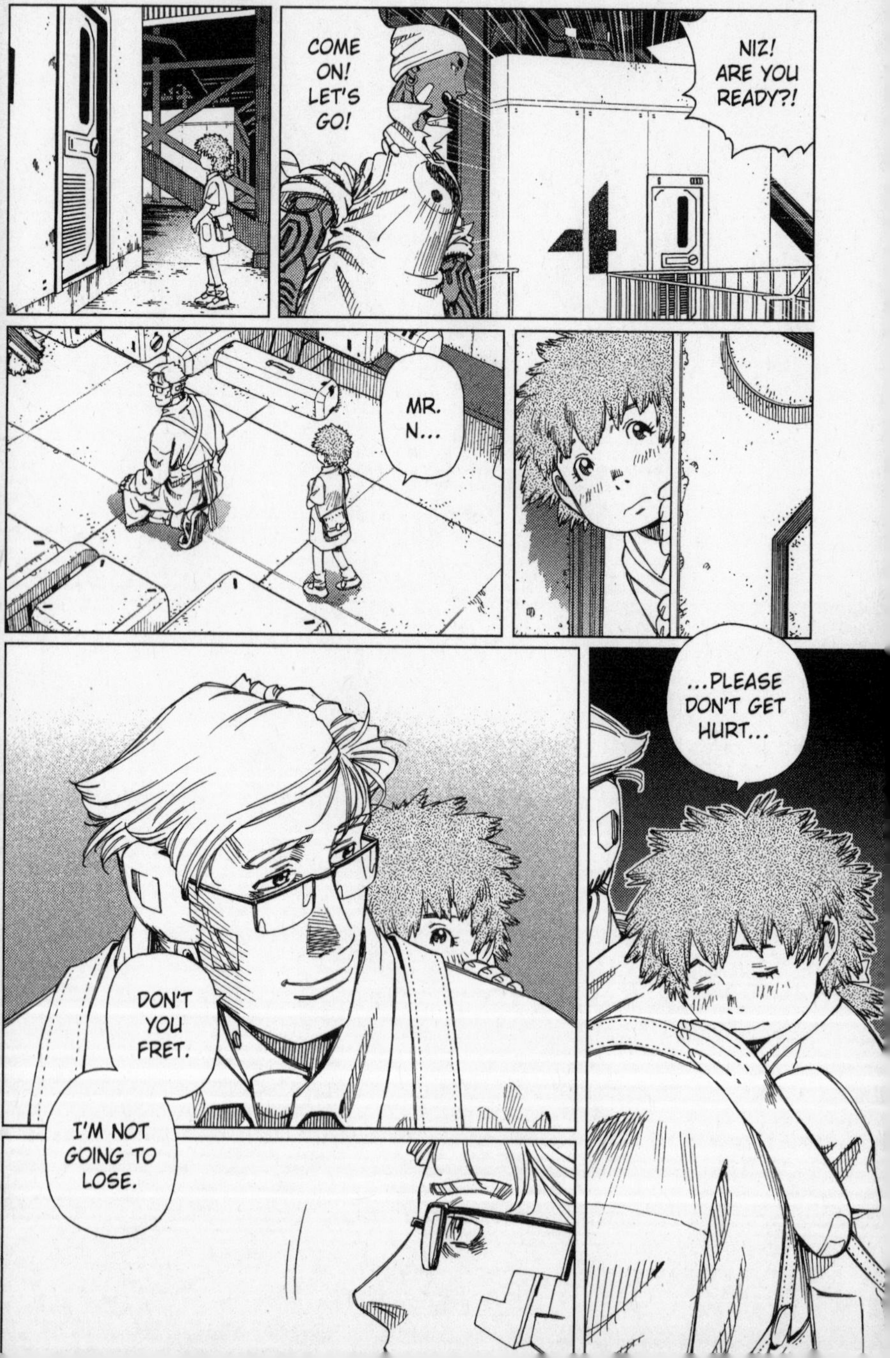
NIZ! ARE YOU READY?!
COME ON! LET'S GO!
MR. N...
...PLEASE DON'T GET HURT...
DON'T YOU FRET.
I'M NOT GOING TO LOSE.

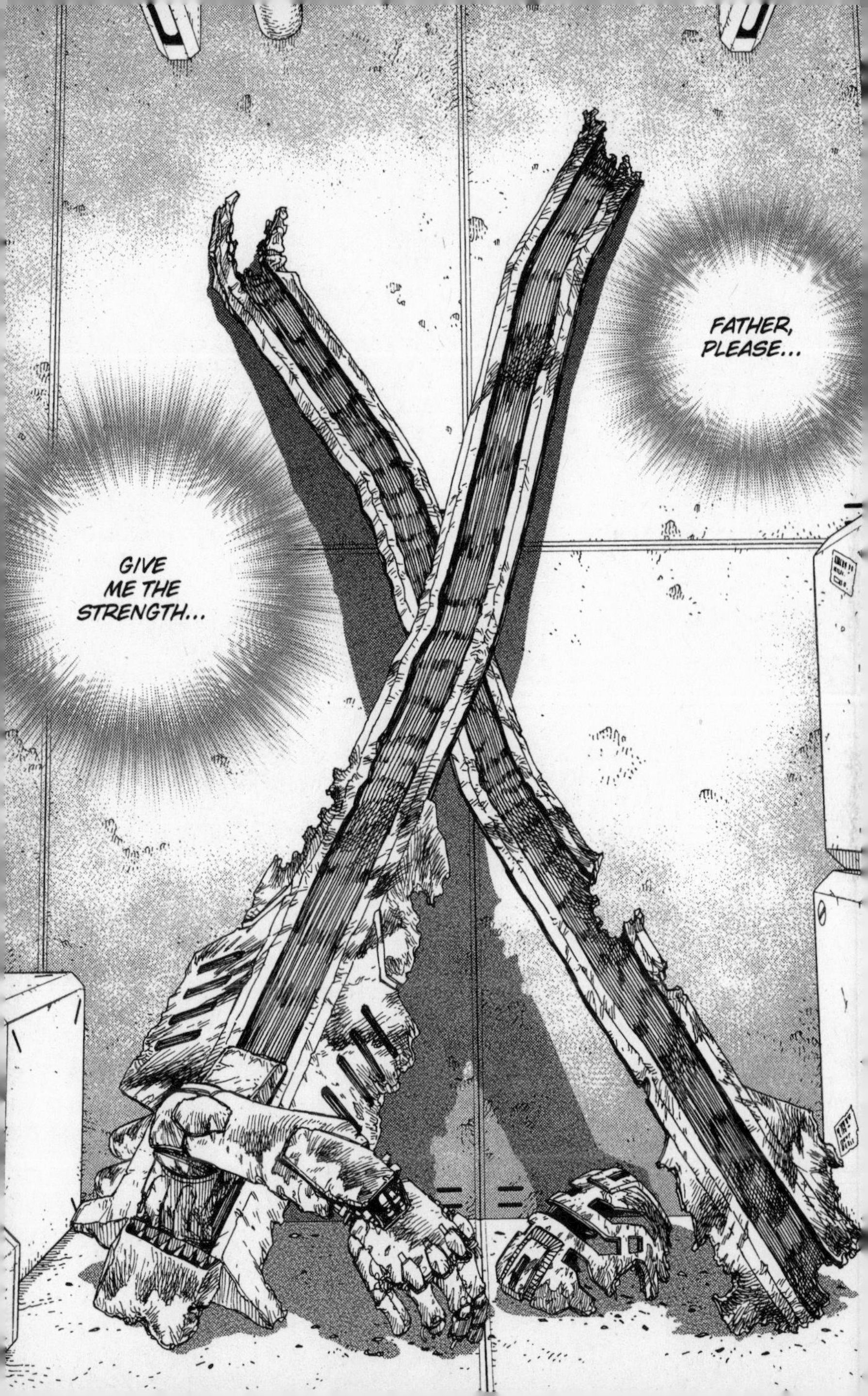
FATHER, PLEASE...
GIVE ME THE STRENGTH...

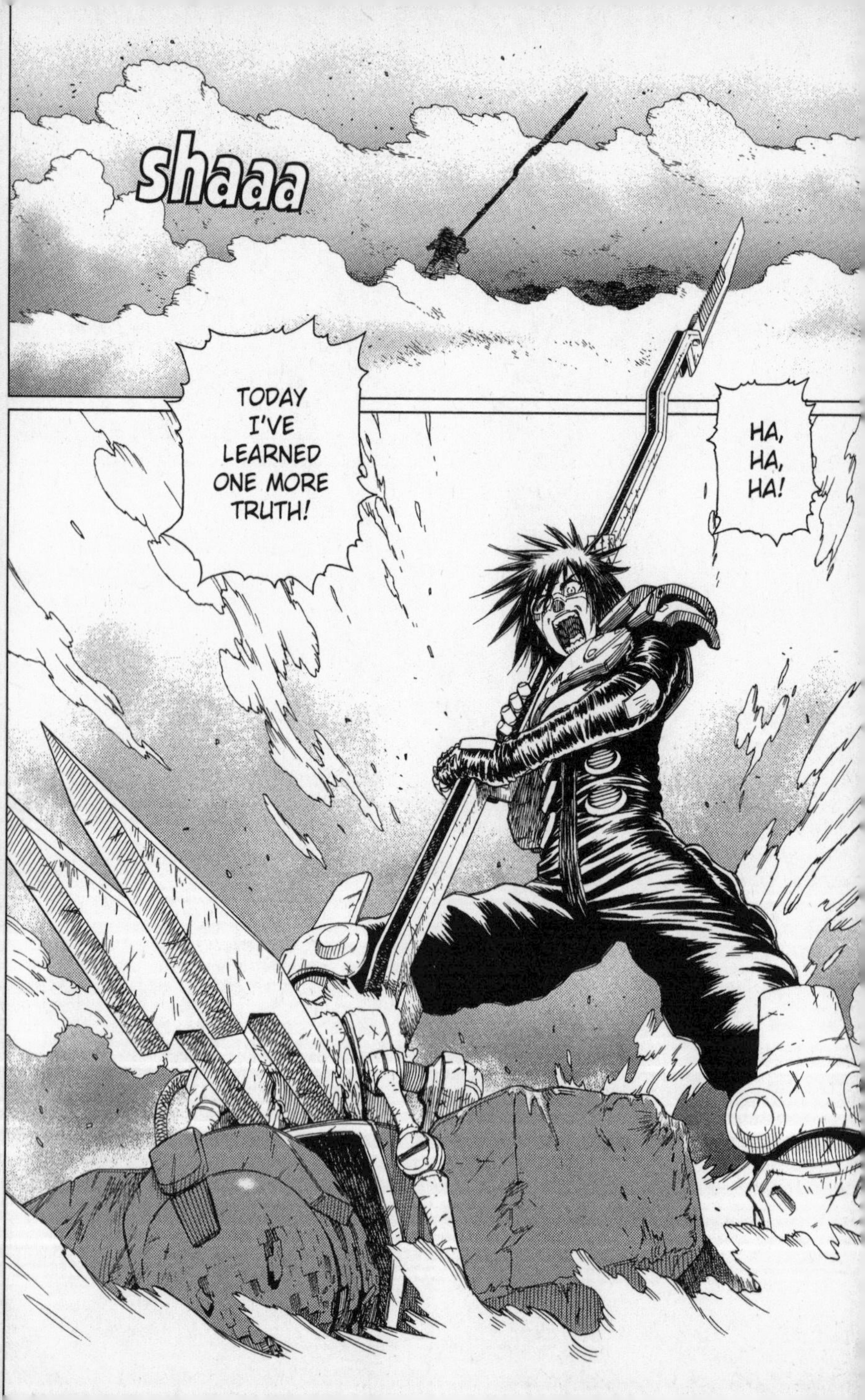
shaaa
TODAY I'VE LEARNED ONE MORE TRUTH!
HA, HA, HA!

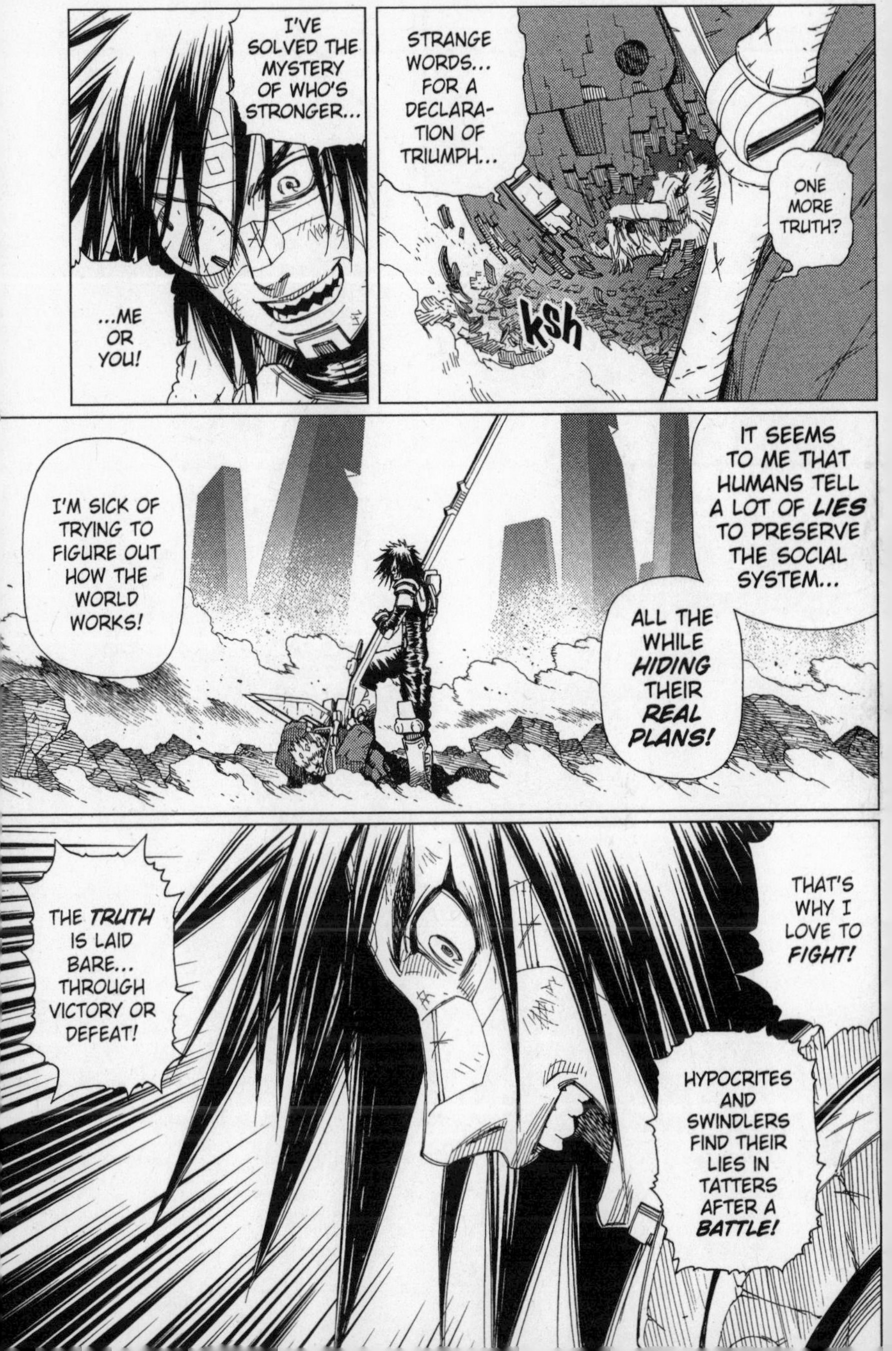
STRANGE WORDS... FOR A DECLARATION OF TRIUMPH...
ONE MORE TRUTH?
ksh
I'VE SOLVED THE MYSTERY OF WHO'S STRONGER...
...ME OR YOU!
IT SEEMS TO ME THAT HUMANS TELL A LOT OF *LIES* TO PRESERVE THE SOCIAL SYSTEM...
ALL THE WHILE *HIDING* THEIR *REAL PLANS!*
I'M SICK OF TRYING TO FIGURE OUT HOW THE WORLD WORKS!
THAT'S WHY I LOVE TO *FIGHT!*
HYPOCRITES AND SWINDLERS FIND THEIR LIES IN TATTERS AFTER A *BATTLE!*
THE *TRUTH* IS LAID BARE... THROUGH VICTORY OR DEFEAT!

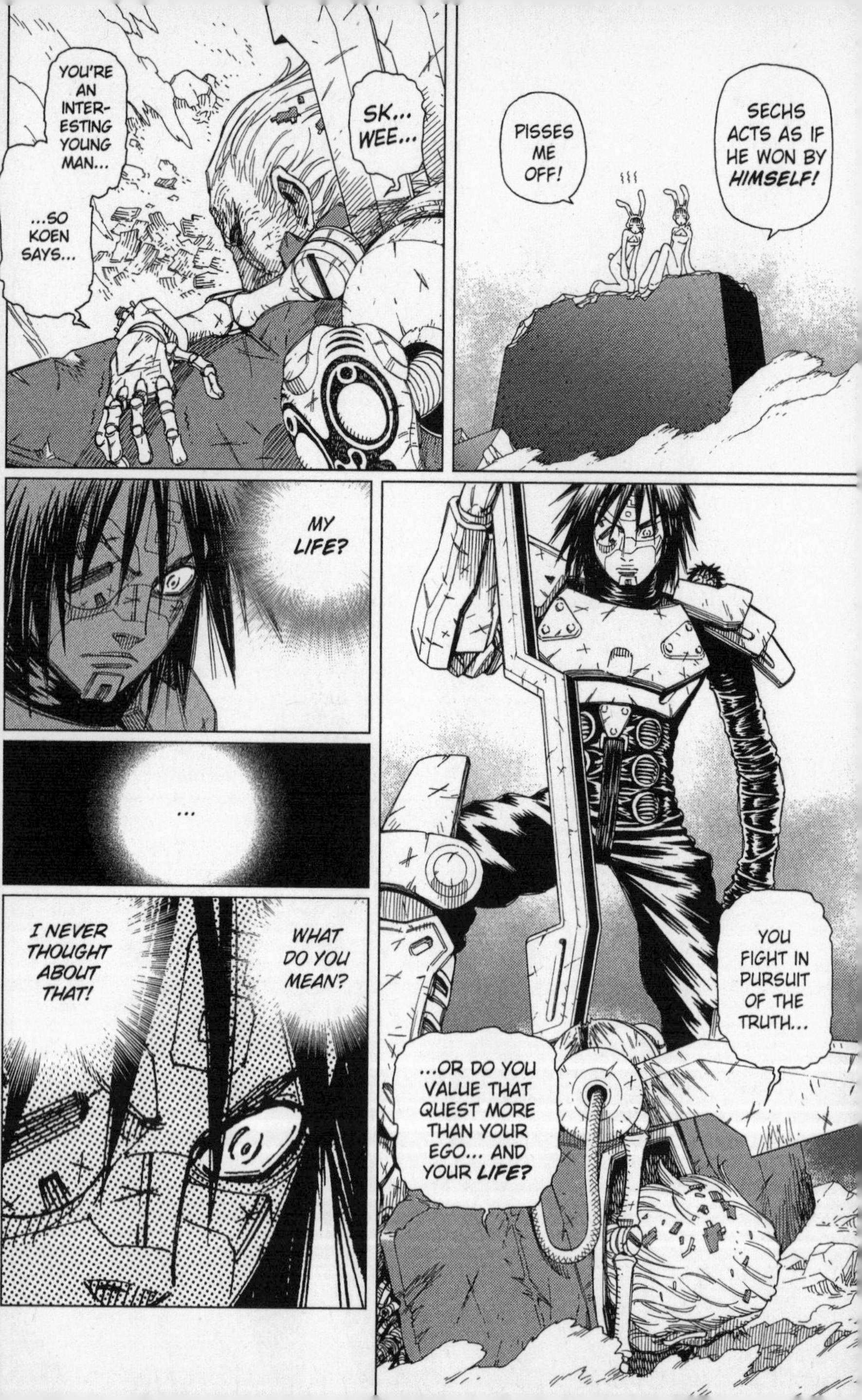
SECHS ACTS AS IF HE WON BY *HIMSELF!*
PISSES ME OFF!
SK... WEE...
YOU'RE AN INTER-ESTING YOUNG MAN...
...SO KOEN SAYS...
YOU FIGHT IN PURSUIT OF THE TRUTH...
...OR DO YOU VALUE THAT QUEST MORE THAN YOUR EGO... AND YOUR *LIFE?*
MY *LIFE?*
...
WHAT DO YOU MEAN?
I NEVER THOUGHT ABOUT THAT!

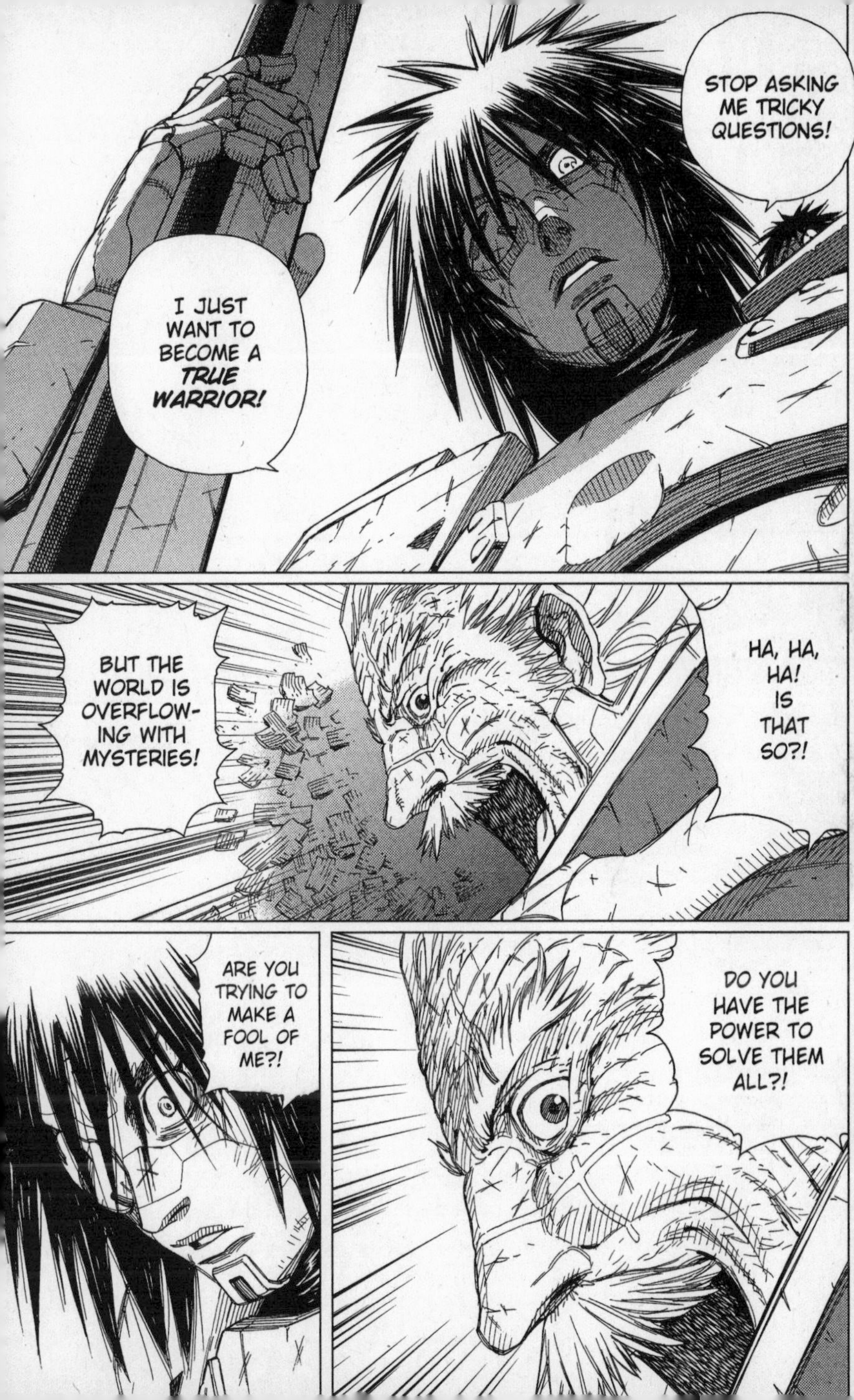
STOP ASKING ME TRICKY QUESTIONS!
I JUST WANT TO BECOME A *TRUE WARRIOR!*
HA, HA, HA! IS THAT SO?!
BUT THE WORLD IS OVERFLOW-ING WITH MYSTERIES!
DO YOU HAVE THE POWER TO SOLVE THEM ALL?!
ARE YOU TRYING TO MAKE A FOOL OF ME?!

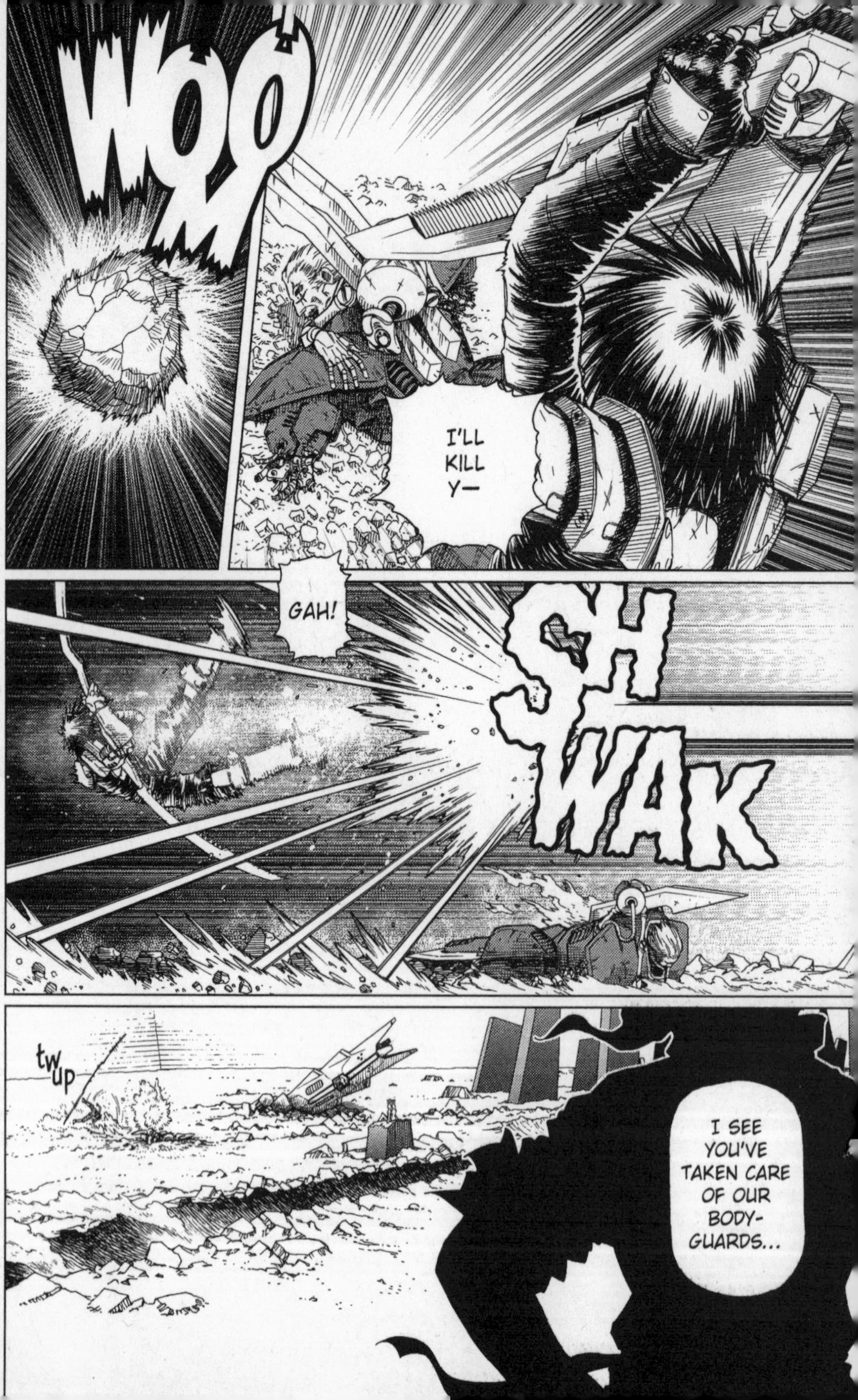
I'LL KILL Y—
WOO
GAH!
SHWAK
I SEE YOU'VE TAKEN CARE OF OUR BODY-GUARDS...
twup

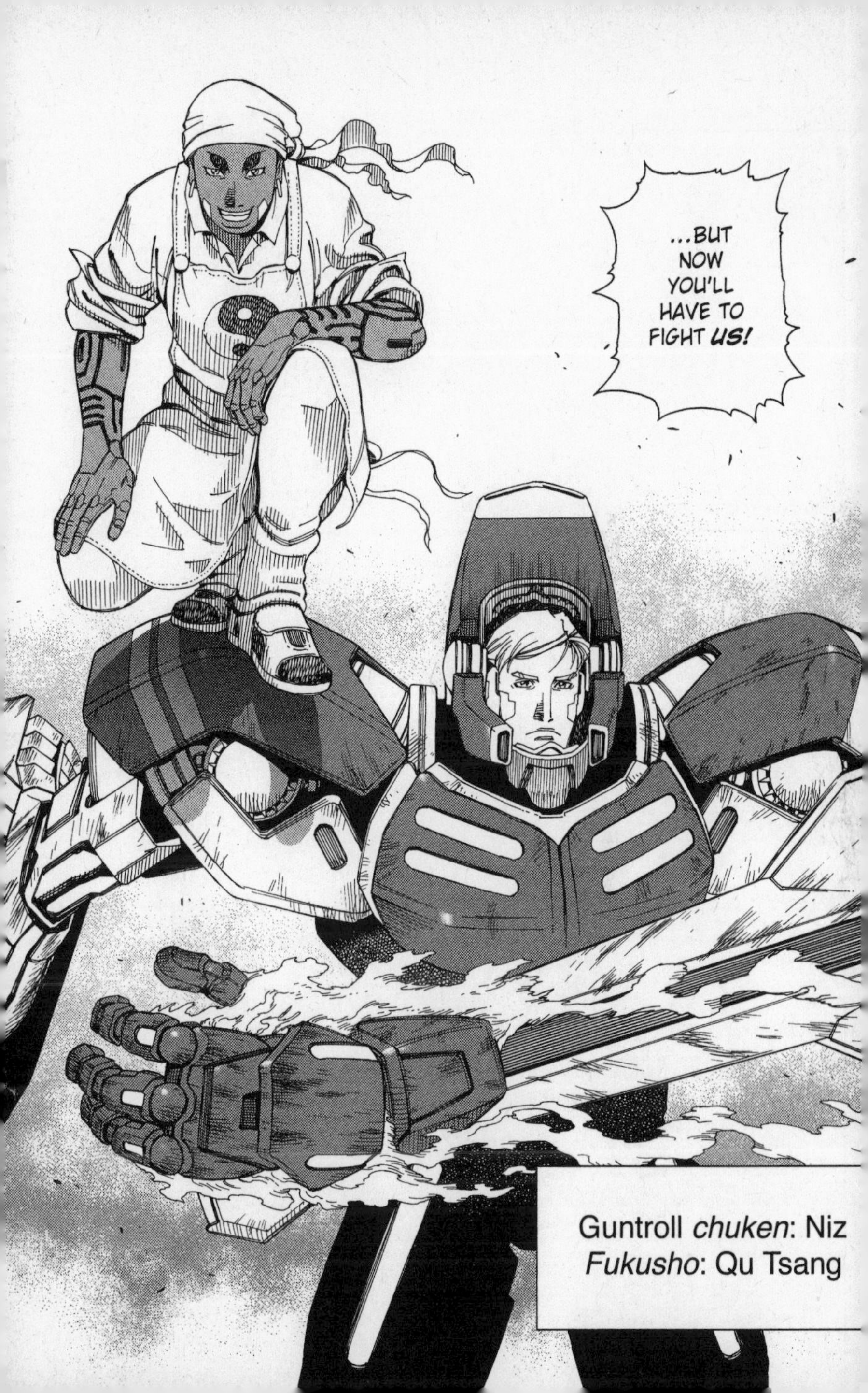
...BUT NOW YOU'LL HAVE TO FIGHT *US!*
Guntroll *chuken*: Niz
Fukusho: Qu Tsang

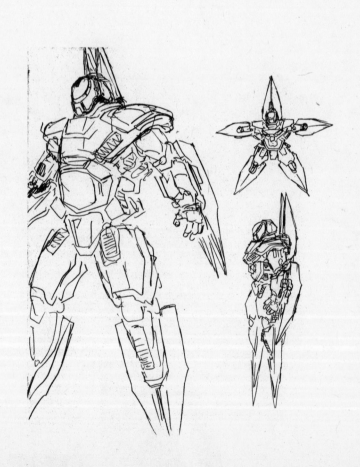

PHASE 29

This Is Sooo Good!

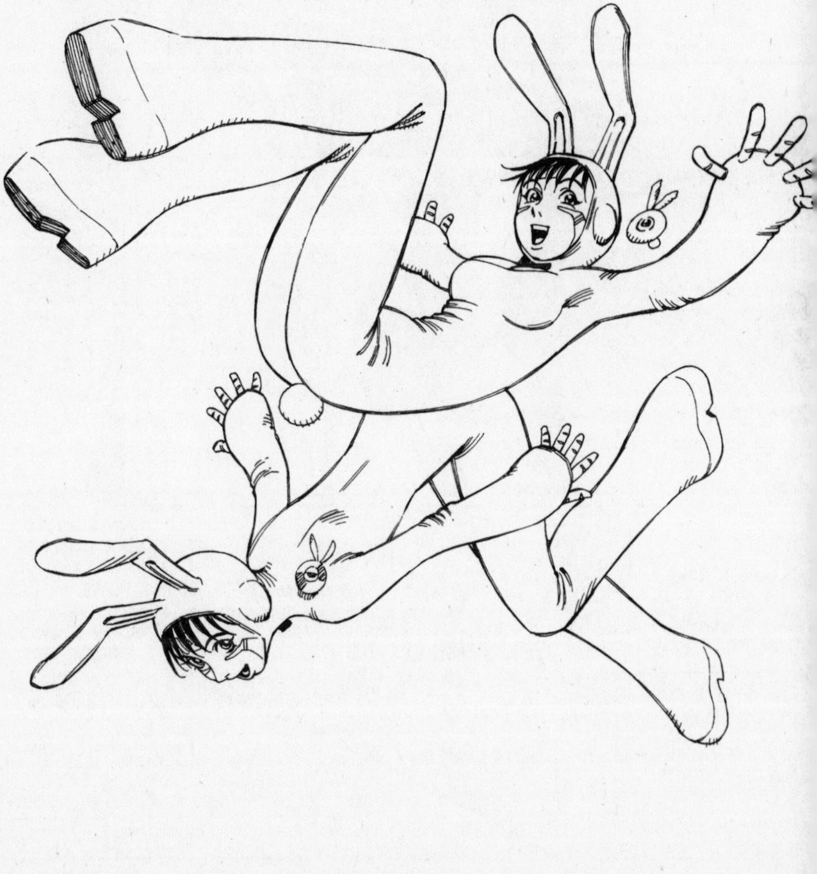

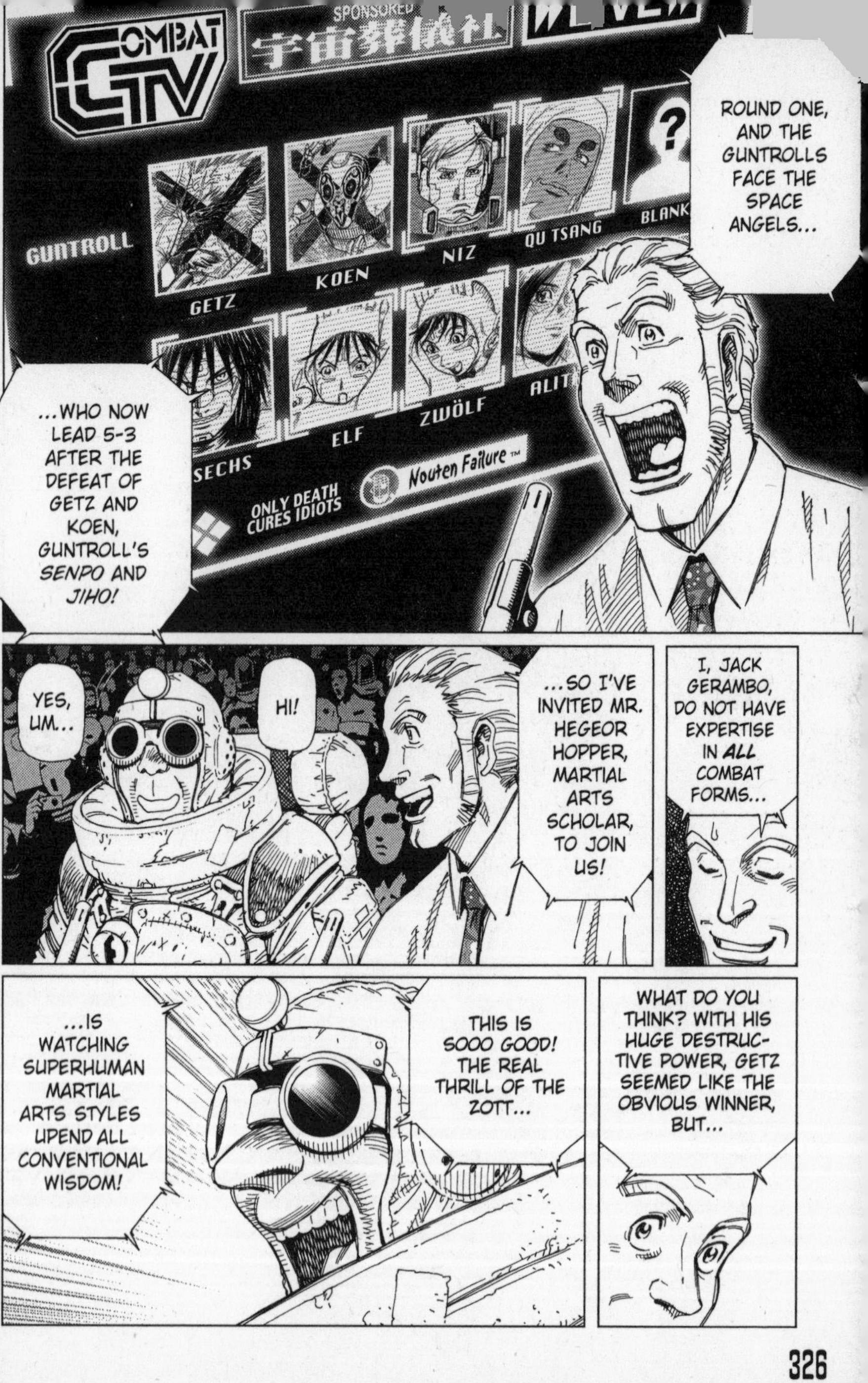

COMBAT TV
SPONSORED
宇宙葬儀社
GUNTROLL
GETZ
KOEN
NIZ
QU TSANG
?
BLANK
SECHS
ELF
ZWÖLF
ALIT
ONLY DEATH CURES IDIOTS
Nouten Failure™
ROUND ONE, AND THE GUNTROLLS FACE THE SPACE ANGELS...
...WHO NOW LEAD 5-3 AFTER THE DEFEAT OF GETZ AND KOEN, GUNTROLL'S *SENPO* AND *JIHO*!
I, JACK GERAMBO, DO NOT HAVE EXPERTISE IN ***ALL*** COMBAT FORMS...
...SO I'VE INVITED MR. HEGEOR HOPPER, MARTIAL ARTS SCHOLAR, TO JOIN US!
HI!
YES, UM...
WHAT DO YOU THINK? WITH HIS HUGE DESTRUCTIVE POWER, GETZ SEEMED LIKE THE OBVIOUS WINNER, BUT...
THIS IS SOOO GOOD! THE REAL THRILL OF THE ZOTT...
...IS WATCHING SUPERHUMAN MARTIAL ARTS STYLES UPEND ALL CONVENTIONAL WISDOM!

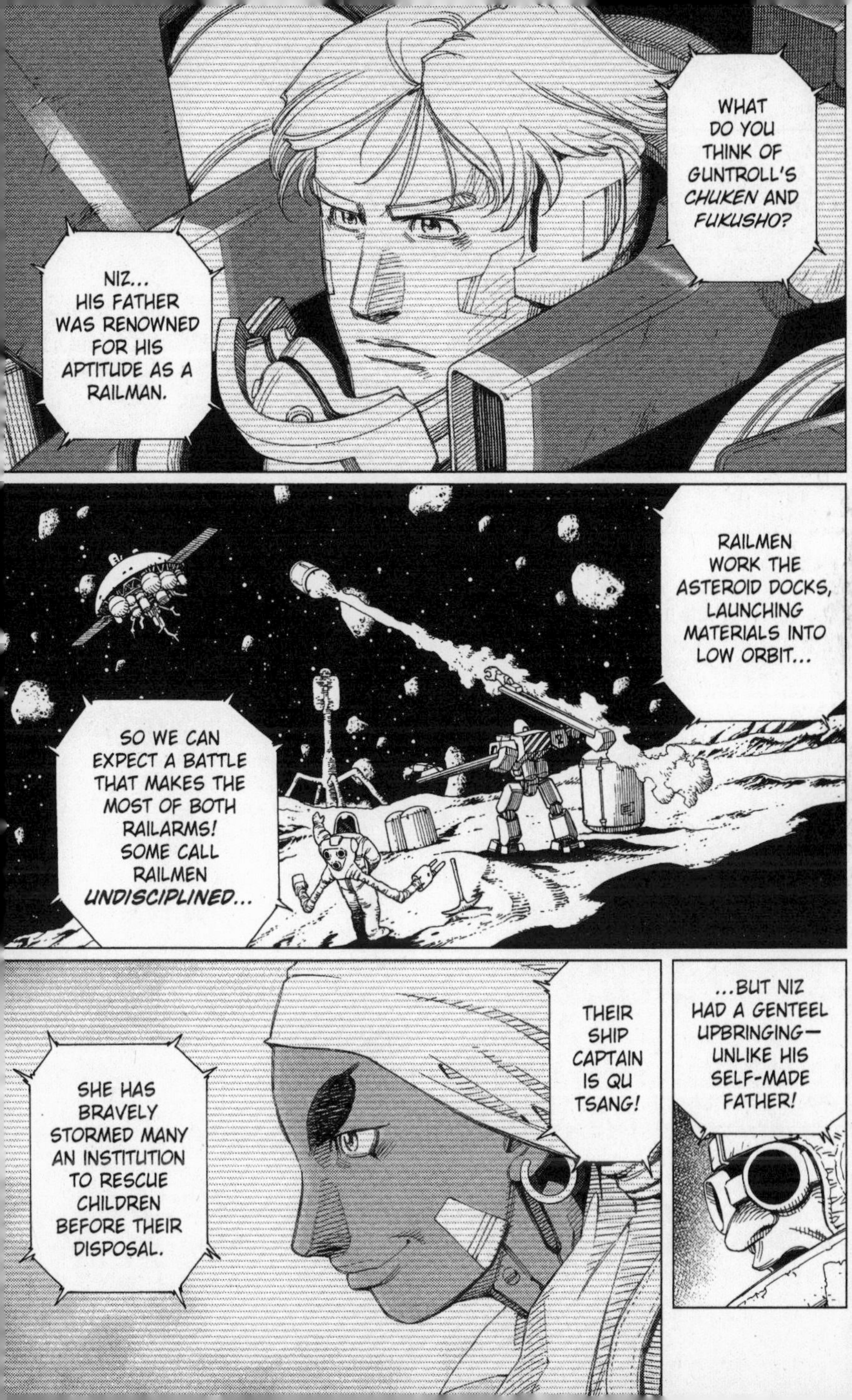
WHAT DO YOU THINK OF GUNTROLL'S *CHUKEN* AND *FUKUSHO?*
NIZ... HIS FATHER WAS RENOWNED FOR HIS APTITUDE AS A RAILMAN.
RAILMEN WORK THE ASTEROID DOCKS, LAUNCHING MATERIALS INTO LOW ORBIT...
SO WE CAN EXPECT A BATTLE THAT MAKES THE MOST OF BOTH RAILARMS! SOME CALL RAILMEN *UNDISCIPLINED...*
...BUT NIZ HAD A GENTEEL UPBRINGING— UNLIKE HIS SELF-MADE FATHER!
THEIR SHIP CAPTAIN IS QU TSANG!
SHE HAS BRAVELY STORMED MANY AN INSTITUTION TO RESCUE CHILDREN BEFORE THEIR DISPOSAL.

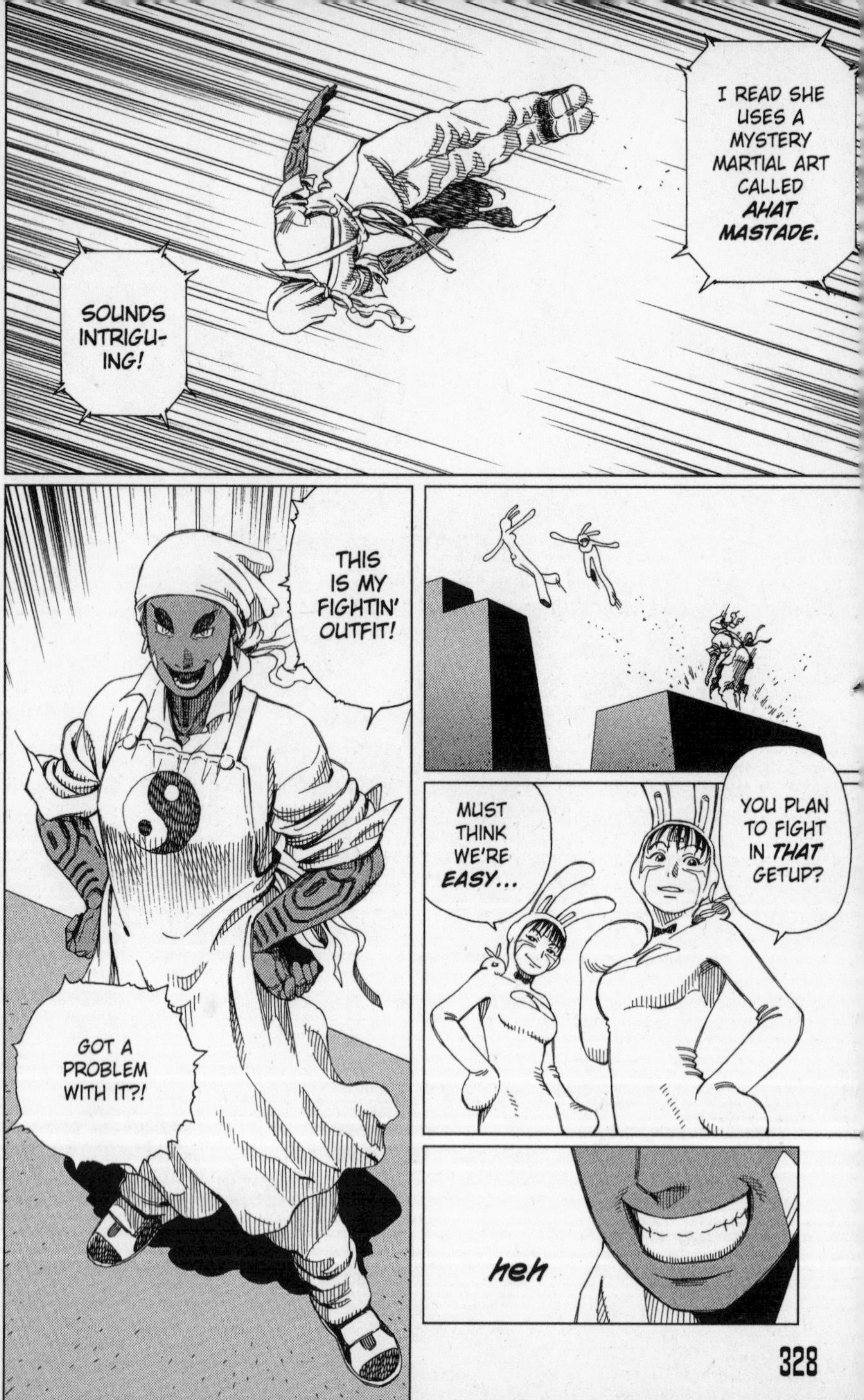
I READ SHE USES A MYSTERY MARTIAL ART CALLED AHAT MASTADE.
SOUNDS INTRIGU-ING!
YOU PLAN TO FIGHT IN THAT GETUP?
MUST THINK WE'RE EASY...
heh
THIS IS MY FIGHTIN' OUTFIT!
GOT A PROBLEM WITH IT?!

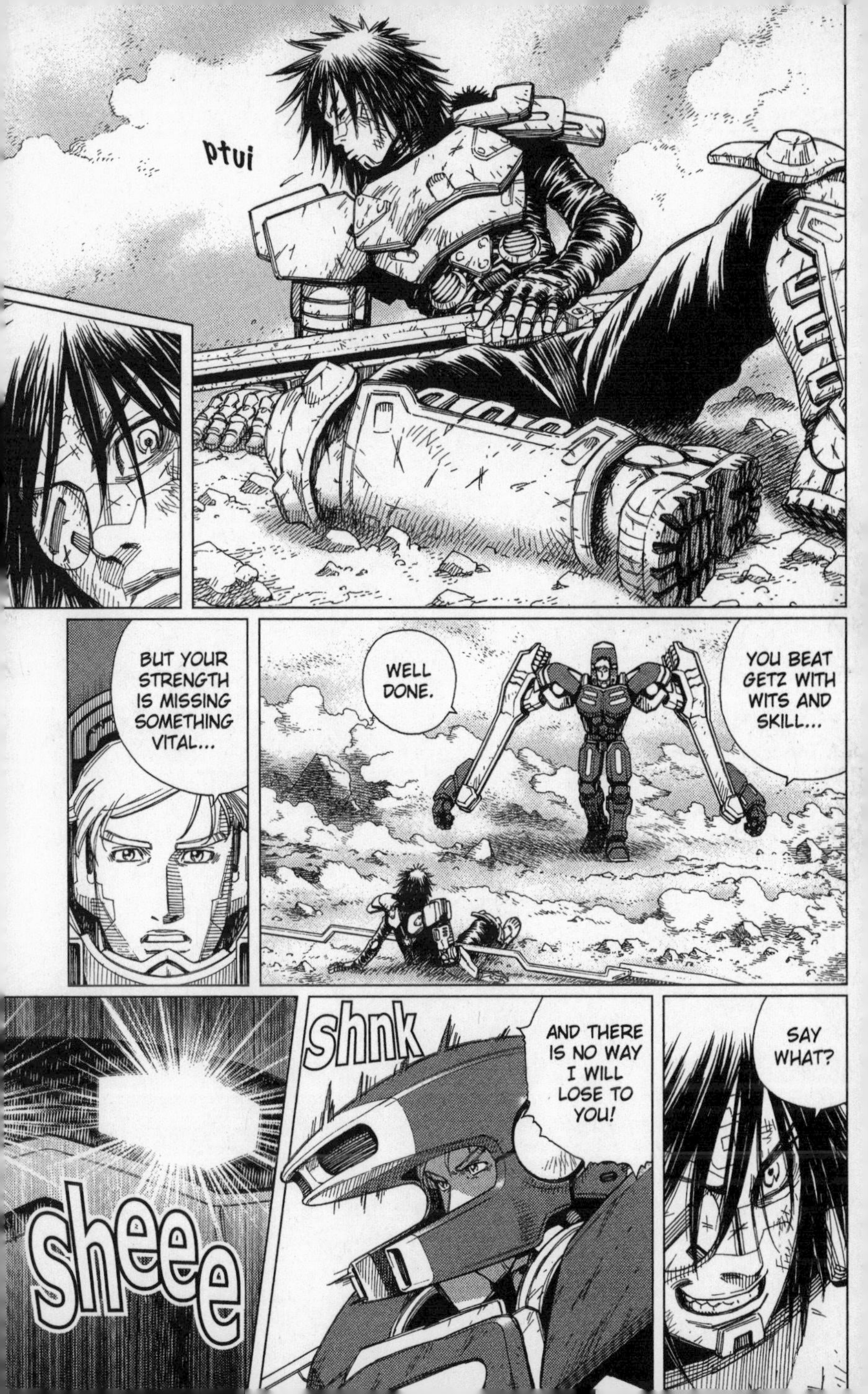
ptui
YOU BEAT GETZ WITH WITS AND SKILL...
WELL DONE.
BUT YOUR STRENGTH IS MISSING SOMETHING VITAL...
SAY WHAT?
AND THERE IS NO WAY I WILL LOSE TO YOU!
shnk
sheee

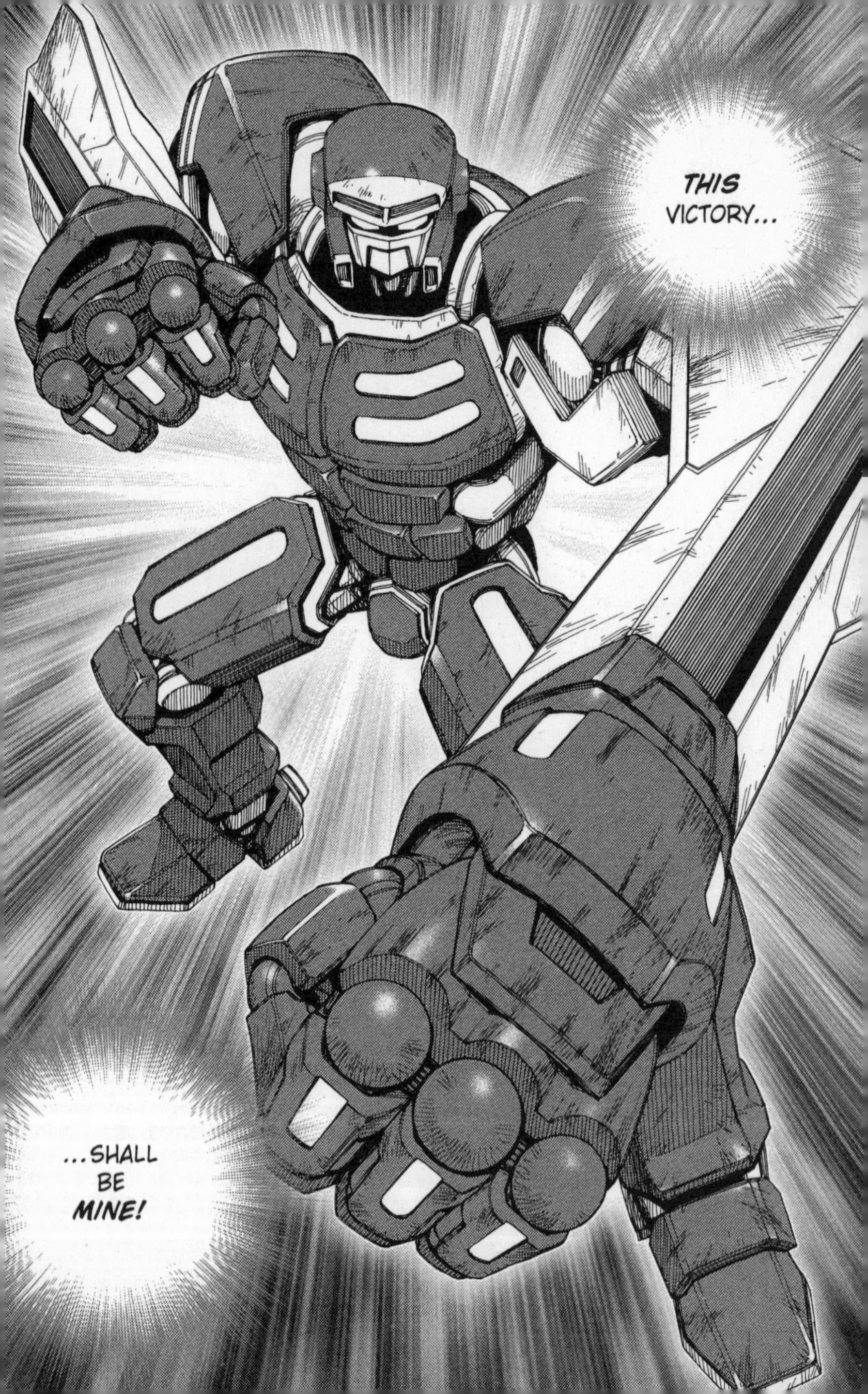
THIS VICTORY...
...SHALL BE MINE!

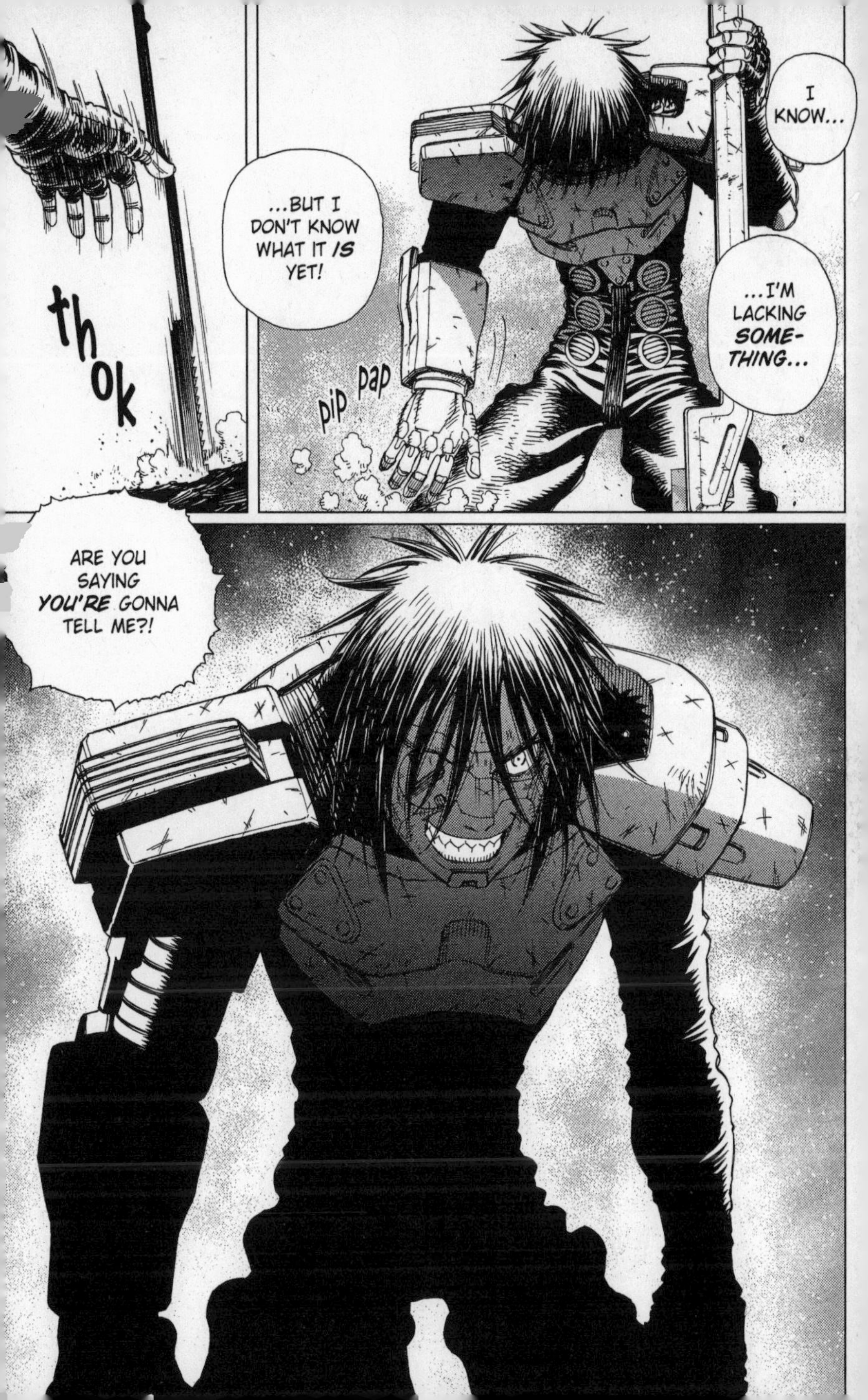
I KNOW...
...I'M LACKING *SOME-THING*...
...BUT I DON'T KNOW WHAT IT *IS* YET!
pip pap
thok
ARE YOU SAYING *YOU'RE* GONNA TELL ME?!

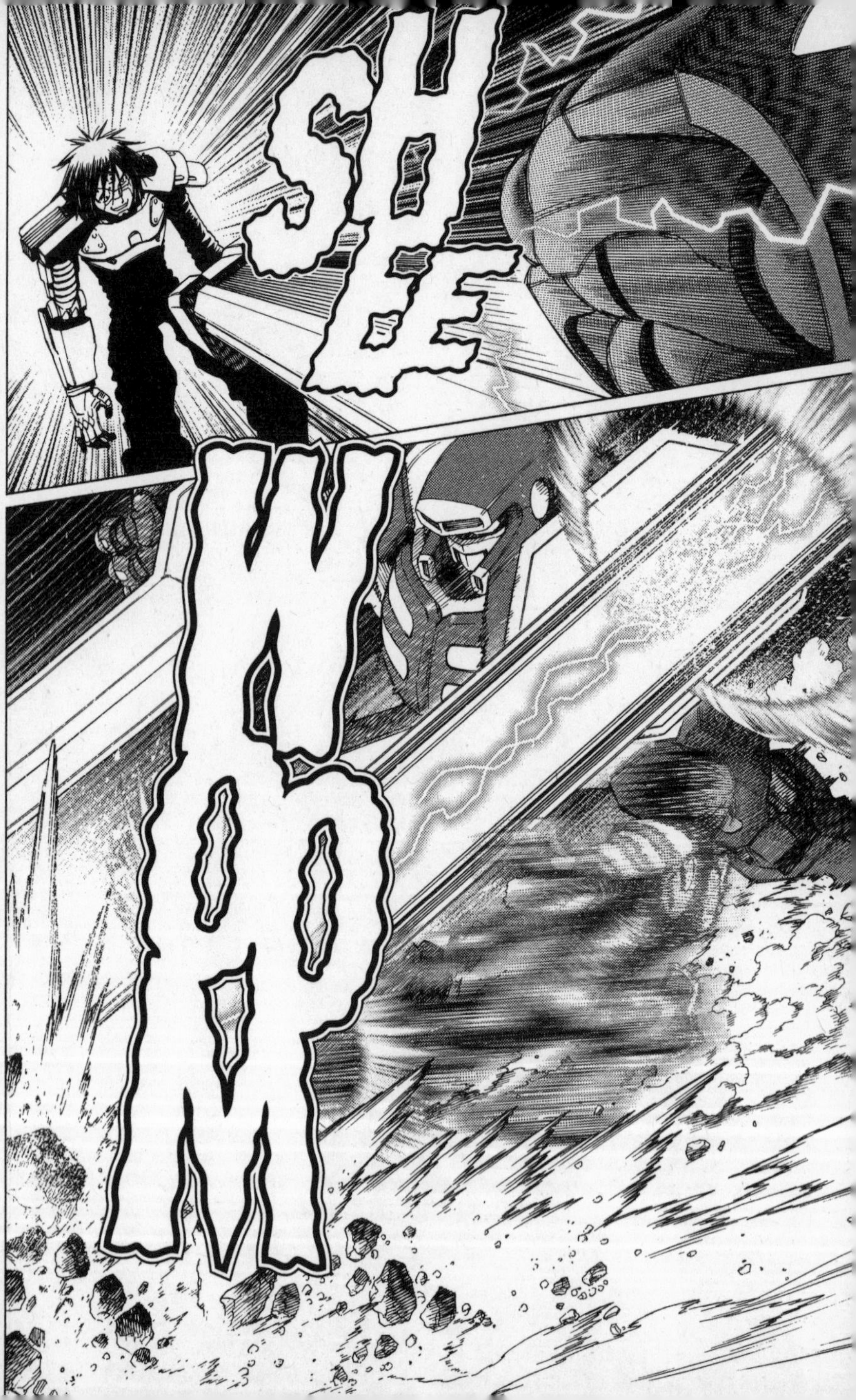

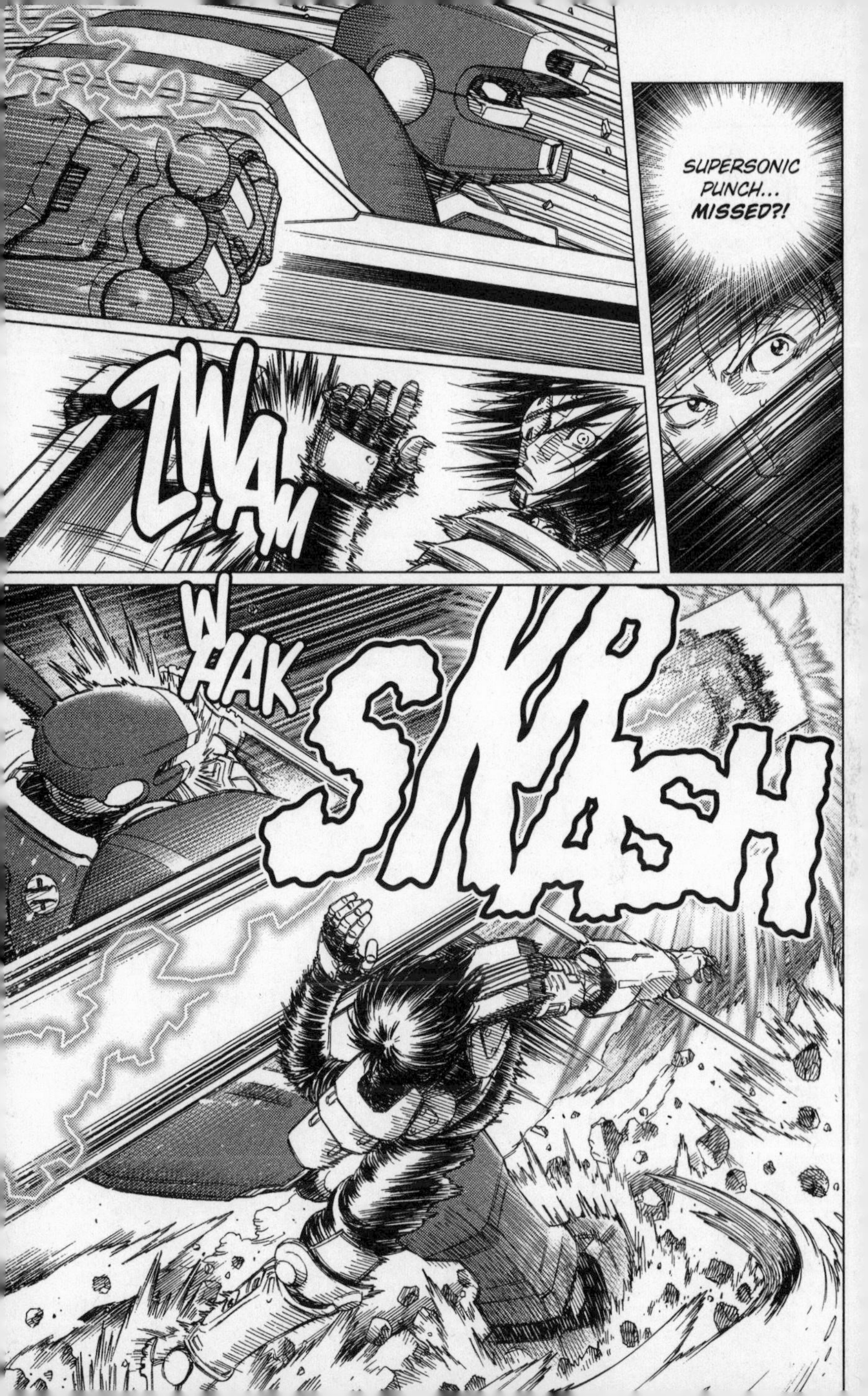
SUPERSONIC PUNCH... MISSED?!
ZWAM
WHAK
SMASH

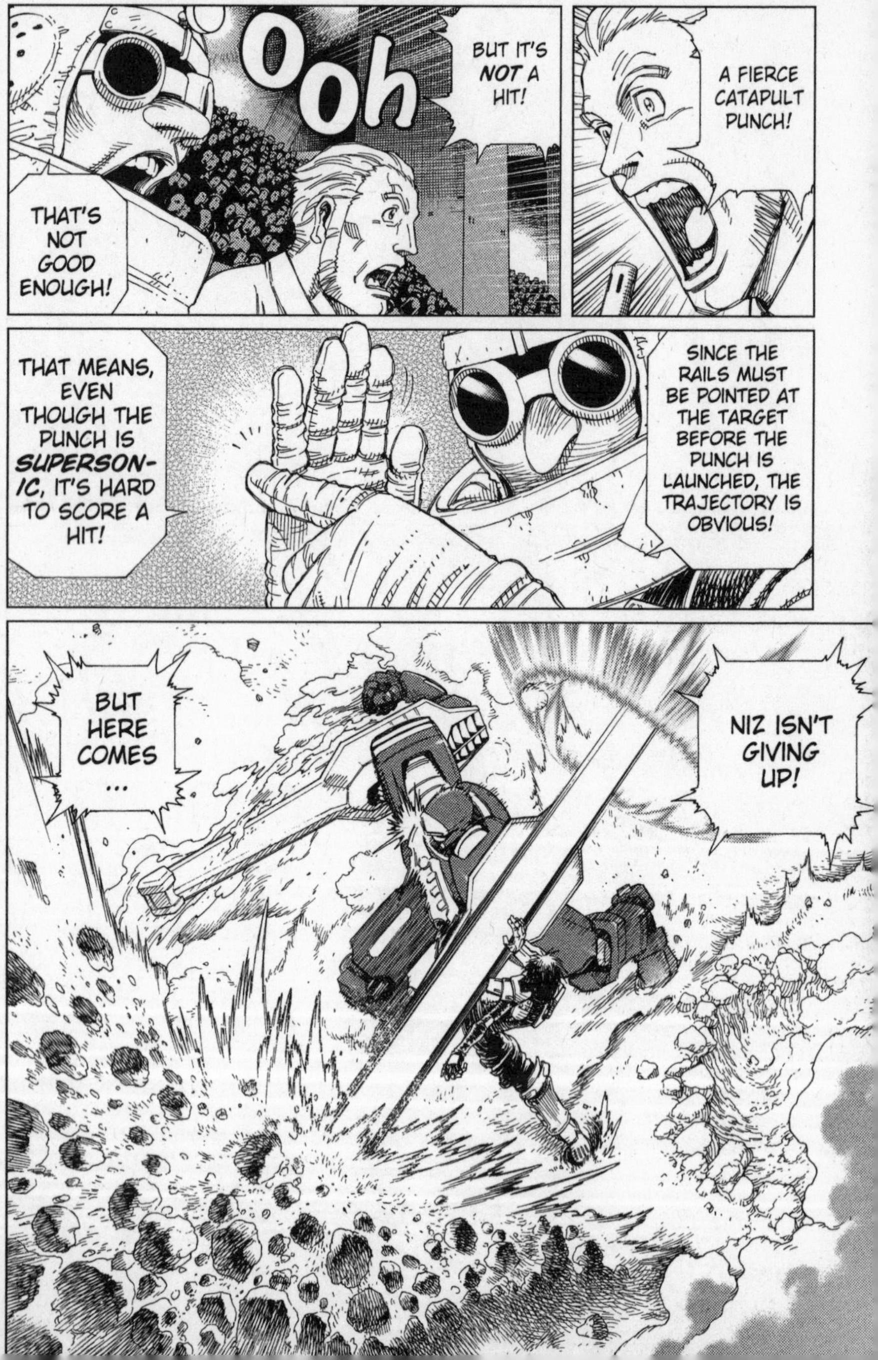
A FIERCE CATAPULT PUNCH!
BUT IT'S NOT A HIT!
Ooh
THAT'S NOT GOOD ENOUGH!
SINCE THE RAILS MUST BE POINTED AT THE TARGET BEFORE THE PUNCH IS LAUNCHED, THE TRAJECTORY IS OBVIOUS!
THAT MEANS, EVEN THOUGH THE PUNCH IS SUPERSON-IC, IT'S HARD TO SCORE A HIT!
NIZ ISN'T GIVING UP!
BUT HERE COMES ...

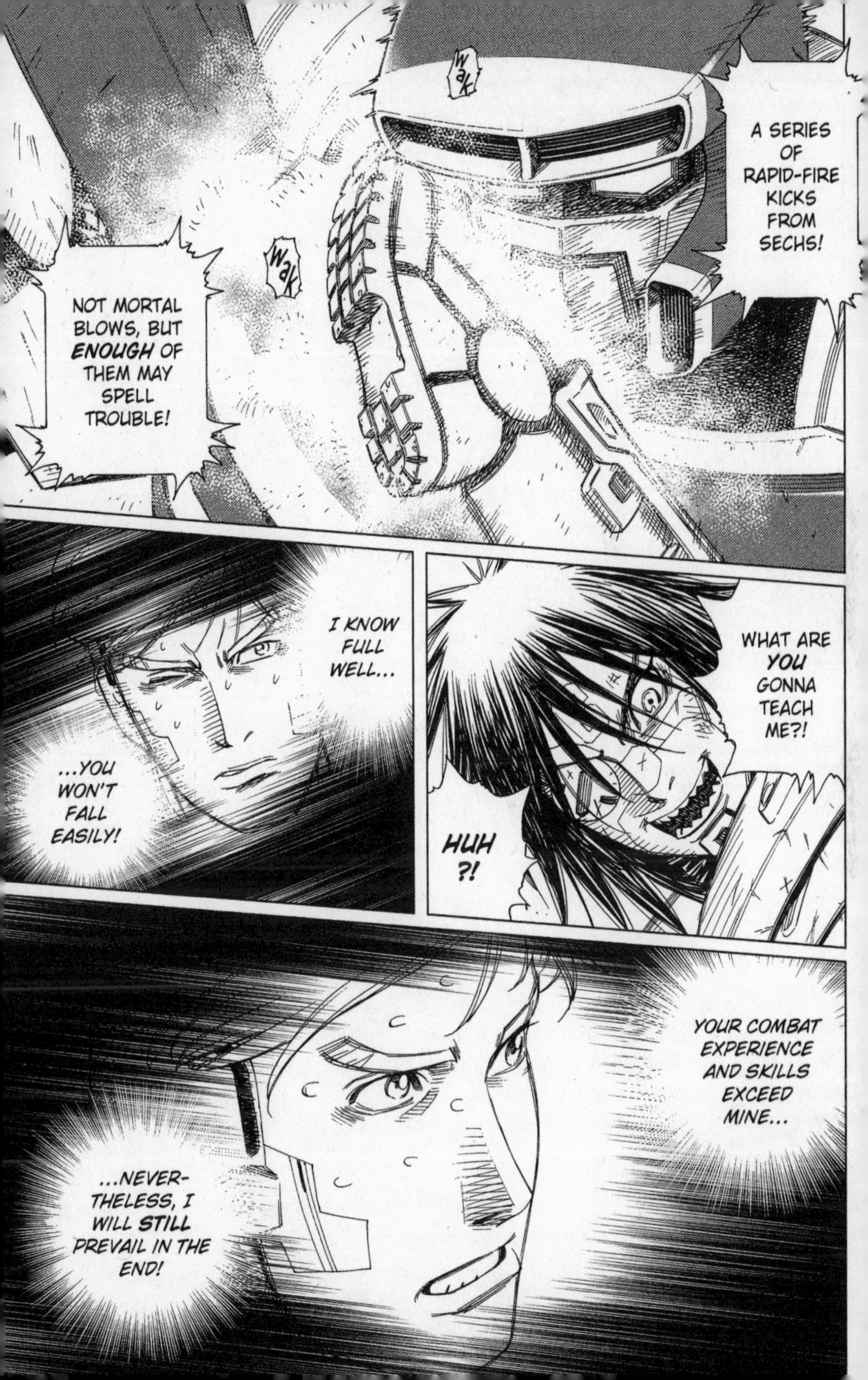

A SERIES OF RAPID-FIRE KICKS FROM SECHS!
WAK
WAK
NOT MORTAL BLOWS, BUT ENOUGH OF THEM MAY SPELL TROUBLE!
WHAT ARE YOU GONNA TEACH ME?!
HUH ?!
I KNOW FULL WELL...
...YOU WON'T FALL EASILY!
YOUR COMBAT EXPERIENCE AND SKILLS EXCEED MINE...
...NEVER-THELESS, I WILL STILL PREVAIL IN THE END!

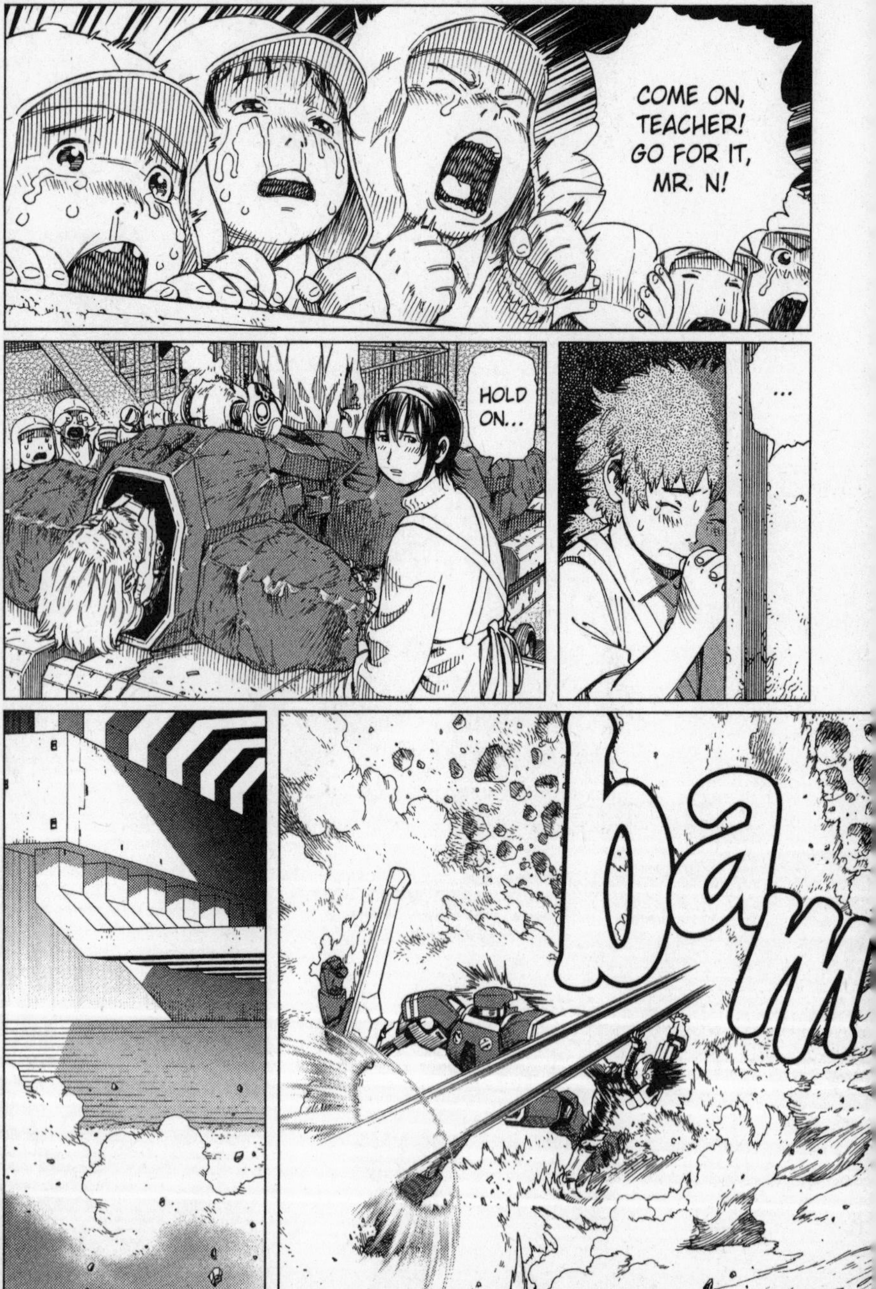
COME ON, TEACHER! GO FOR IT, MR. N!
...
HOLD ON...
bam

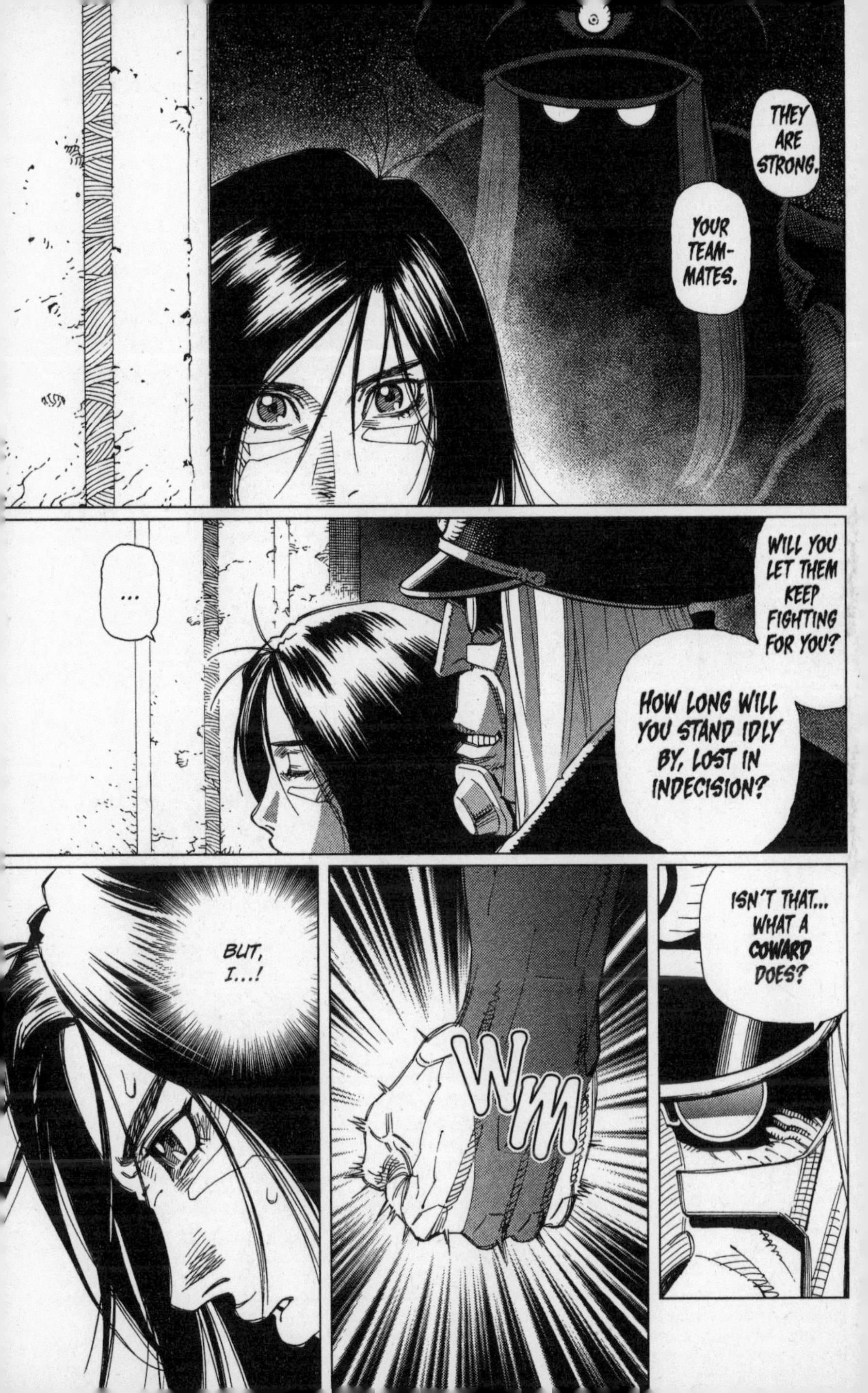
THEY ARE STRONG.
YOUR TEAM-MATES.
WILL YOU LET THEM KEEP FIGHTING FOR YOU?
HOW LONG WILL YOU STAND IDLY BY, LOST IN INDECISION?
...
ISN'T THAT... WHAT A COWARD DOES?
WM
BUT, I...!

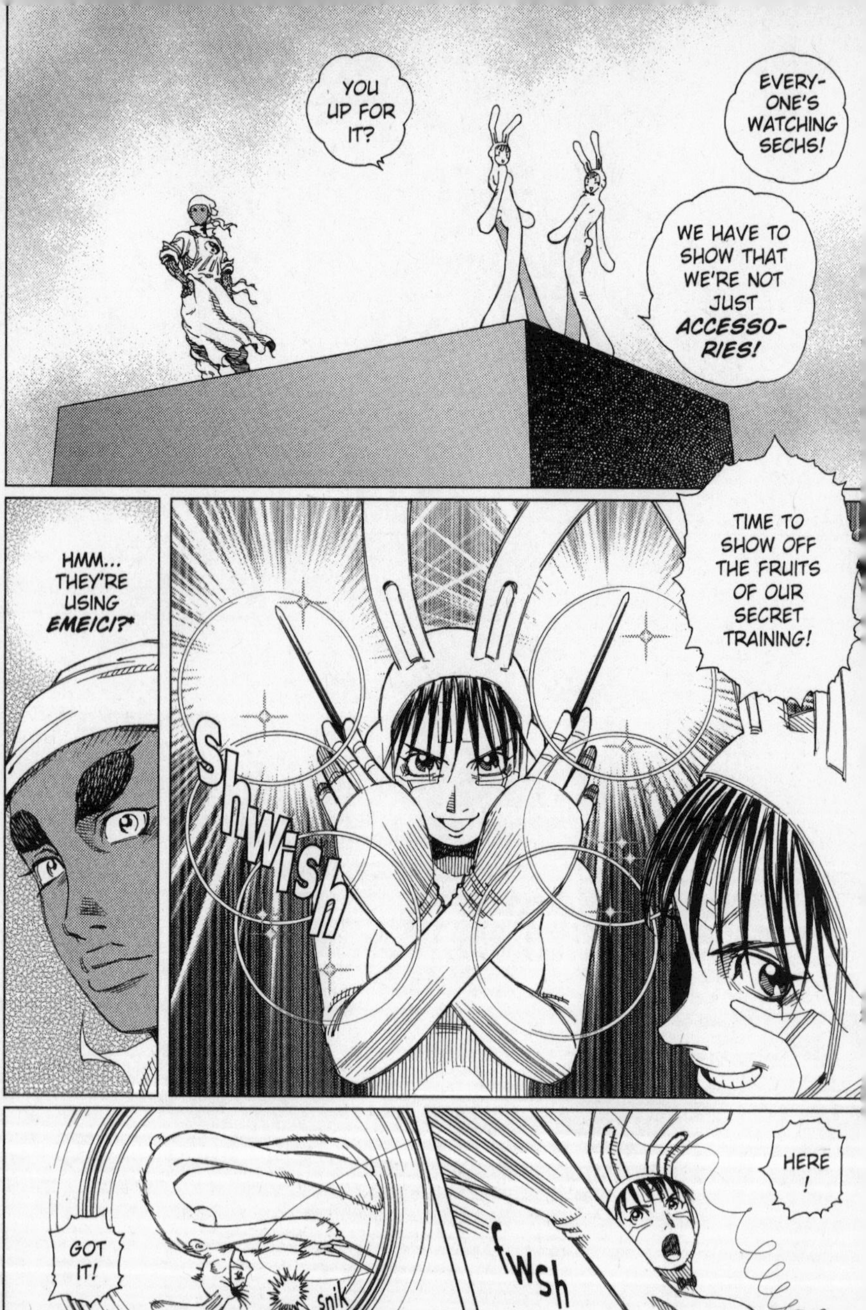
EVERY-ONE'S WATCHING SECHS!
WE HAVE TO SHOW THAT WE'RE NOT JUST *ACCESSO-RIES!*
YOU UP FOR IT?
TIME TO SHOW OFF THE FRUITS OF OUR SECRET TRAINING!
Shwish
HMM... THEY'RE USING *EMEICI?**
HERE!
fwsh
GOT IT!
snik

***Emeici:** A concealed weapon used in Chinese martial arts. About 30 cm (a foot) in length, it consists of a double-pointed metal needle with a ring in the center so they can be twirled on the finger. A woman's weapon, they are thought to have evolved from ornamental hairpins.*

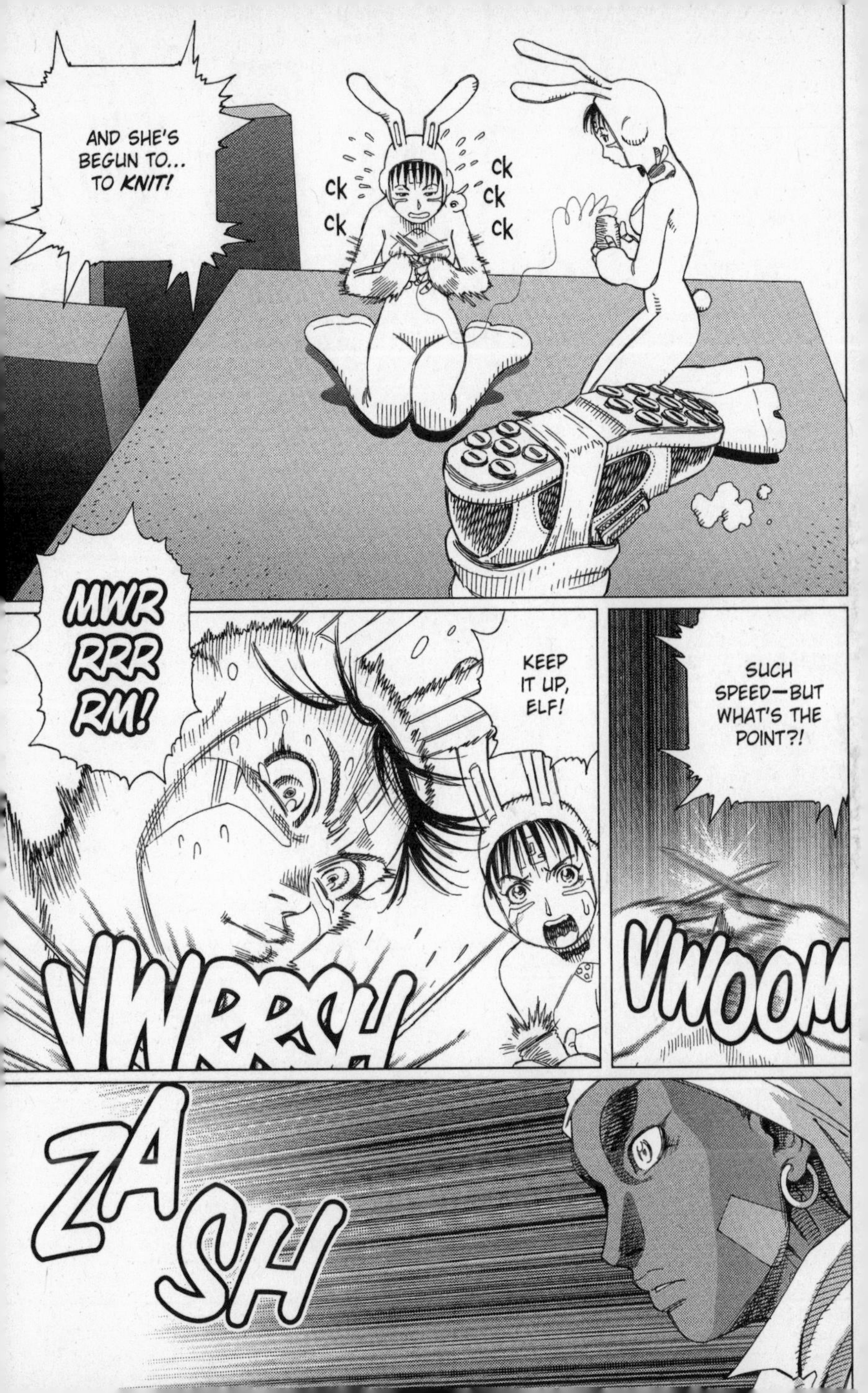
AND SHE'S BEGUN TO... TO *KNIT!*
ck ck ck
ck ck
SUCH SPEED—BUT WHAT'S THE POINT?!
VWOOM
KEEP IT UP, ELF!
MWR RRR RM!
VWRRCH
ZA SH

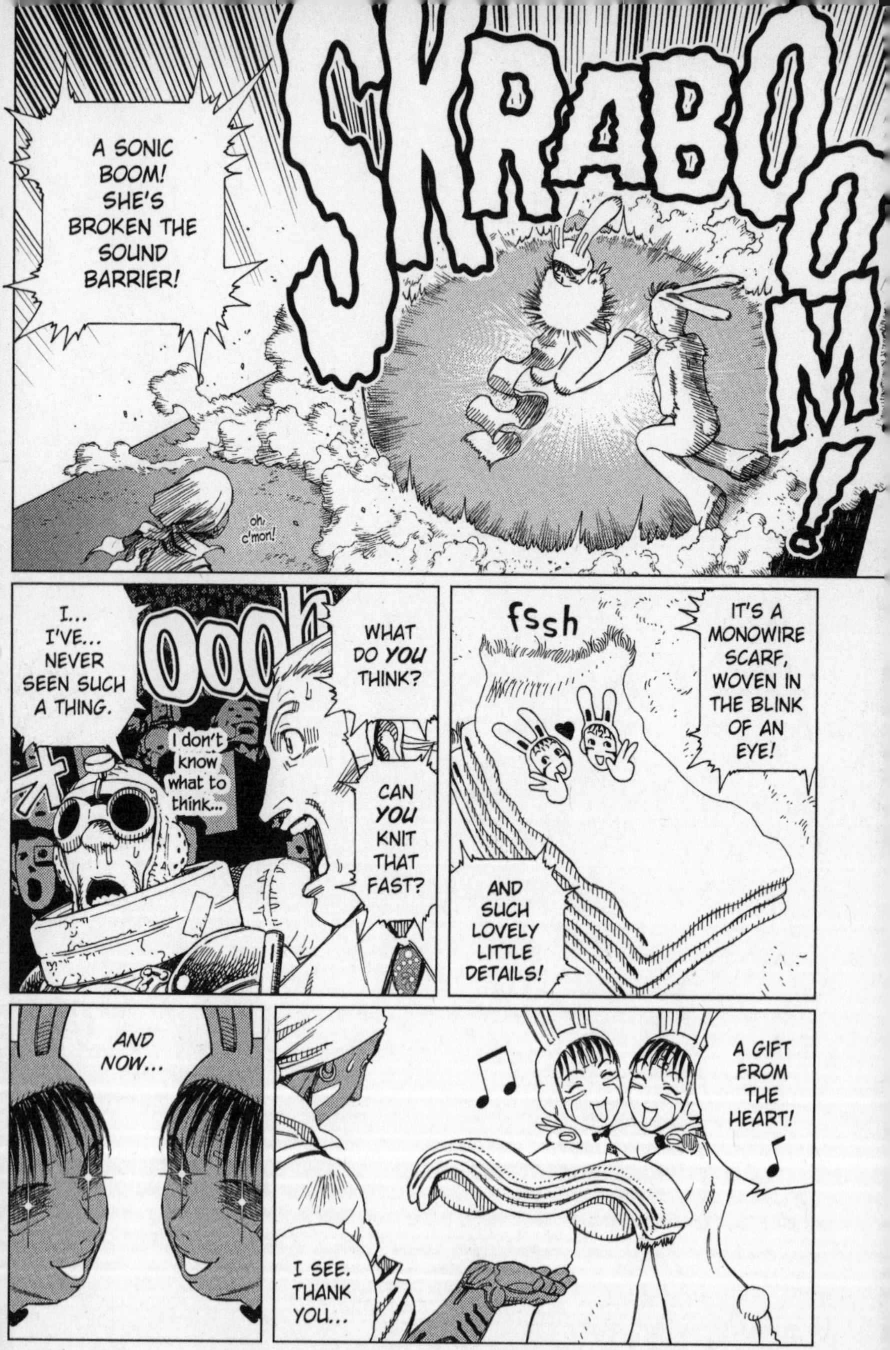
SKRABOOOM!
A SONIC BOOM! SHE'S BROKEN THE SOUND BARRIER!
oh, c'mon!
fssh
IT'S A MONOWIRE SCARF, WOVEN IN THE BLINK OF AN EYE!
AND SUCH LOVELY LITTLE DETAILS!
WHAT DO *YOU* THINK?
OOOh
I... I'VE... NEVER SEEN SUCH A THING.
CAN *YOU* KNIT THAT FAST?
I don't know what to think...
A GIFT FROM THE HEART!
I SEE. THANK YOU...
AND NOW...

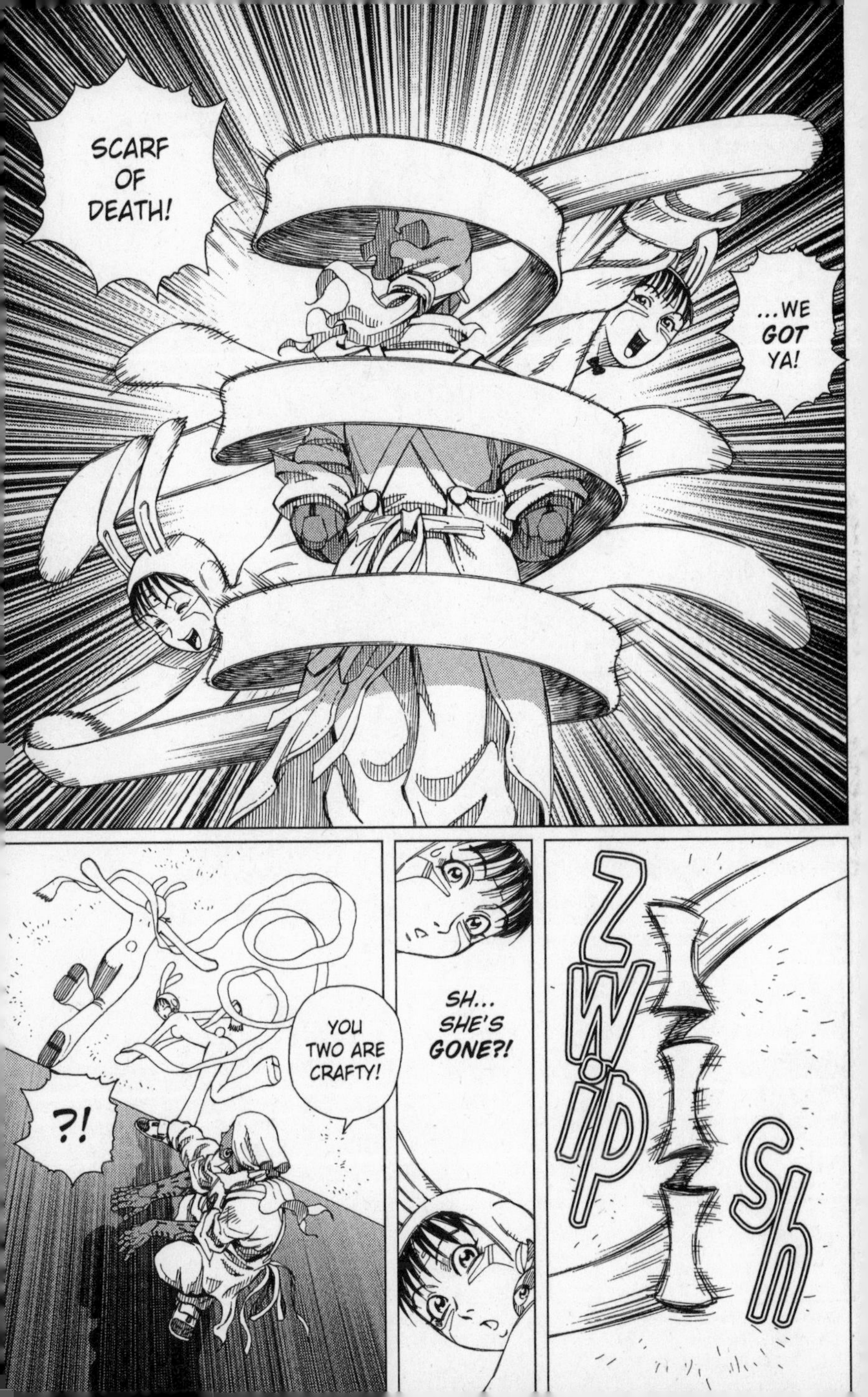
SCARF OF DEATH!
...WE GOT YA!
ZWIP
SH
SH... SHE'S GONE?!
YOU TWO ARE CRAFTY!
?!

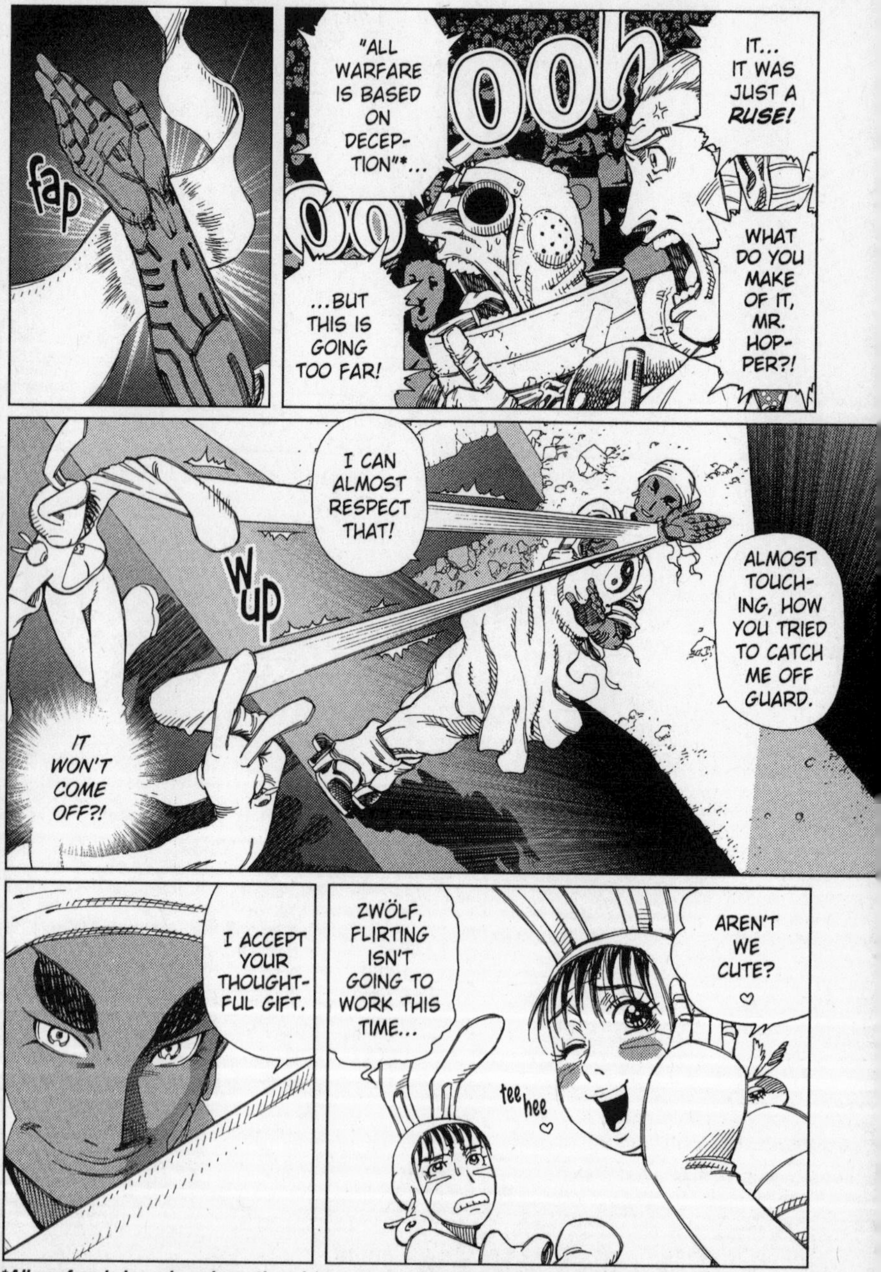
IT... IT WAS JUST A RUSE!
WHAT DO YOU MAKE OF IT, MR. HOPPER?!
Oooh
"ALL WARFARE IS BASED ON DECEPTION"*...
...BUT THIS IS GOING TOO FAR!
fap
ALMOST TOUCHING, HOW YOU TRIED TO CATCH ME OFF GUARD.
I CAN ALMOST RESPECT THAT!
wup
IT WON'T COME OFF?!
AREN'T WE CUTE? ♡
ZWÖLF, FLIRTING ISN'T GOING TO WORK THIS TIME...
tee hee ♡
I ACCEPT YOUR THOUGHTFUL GIFT.

***All warfare is based on deception:** *A key principle from The Art of War, written by Chinese military strategist Sun Tzu in the 6th or 5th century B.C. He meant that the secret to victory lies in surprising the enemy.*

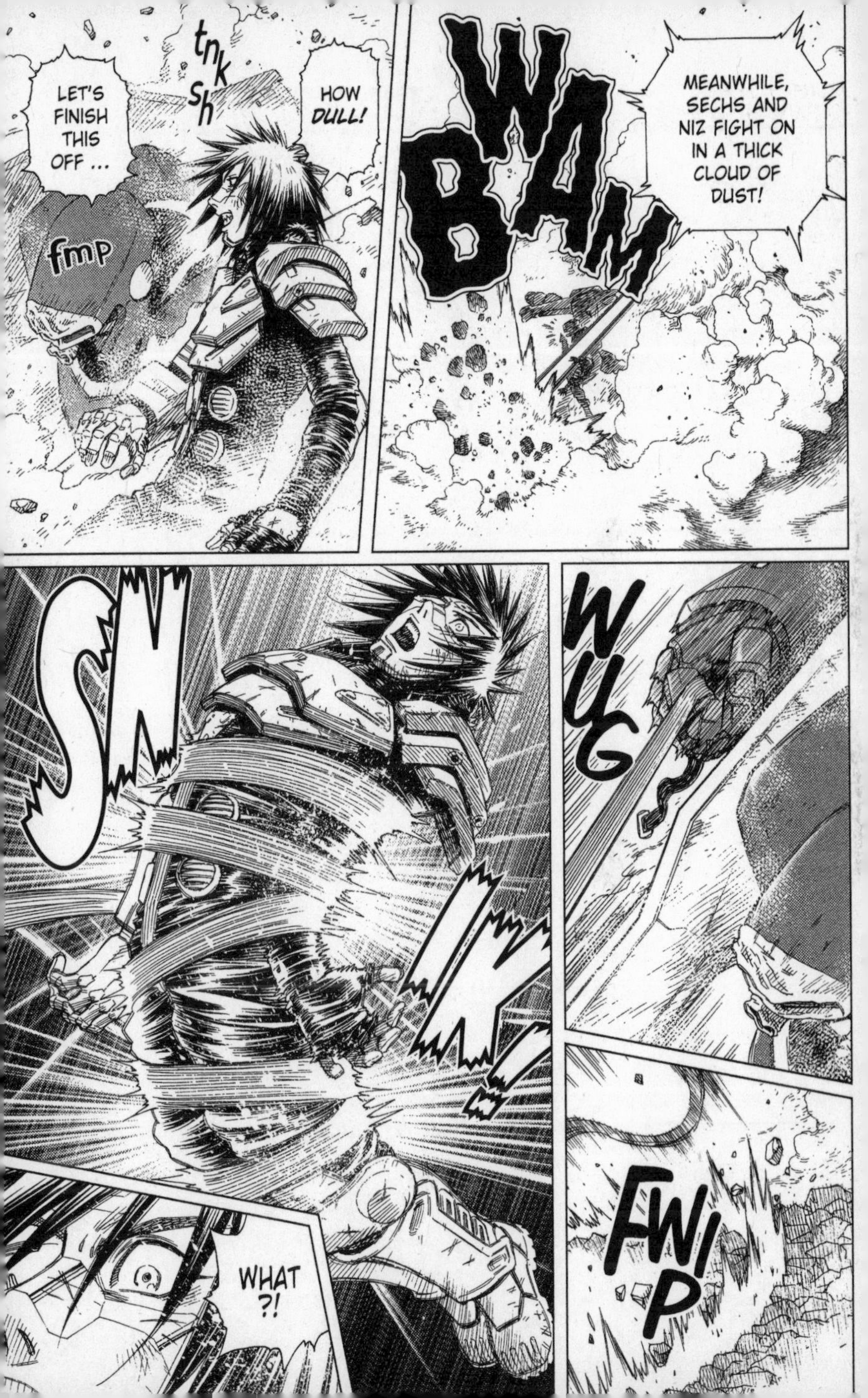
MEANWHILE, SECHS AND NIZ FIGHT ON IN A THICK CLOUD OF DUST!
BWAM
HOW DULL!
tnk
sh
LET'S FINISH THIS OFF ...
fmp
WUG
FWIP
SH
WHAT ?!

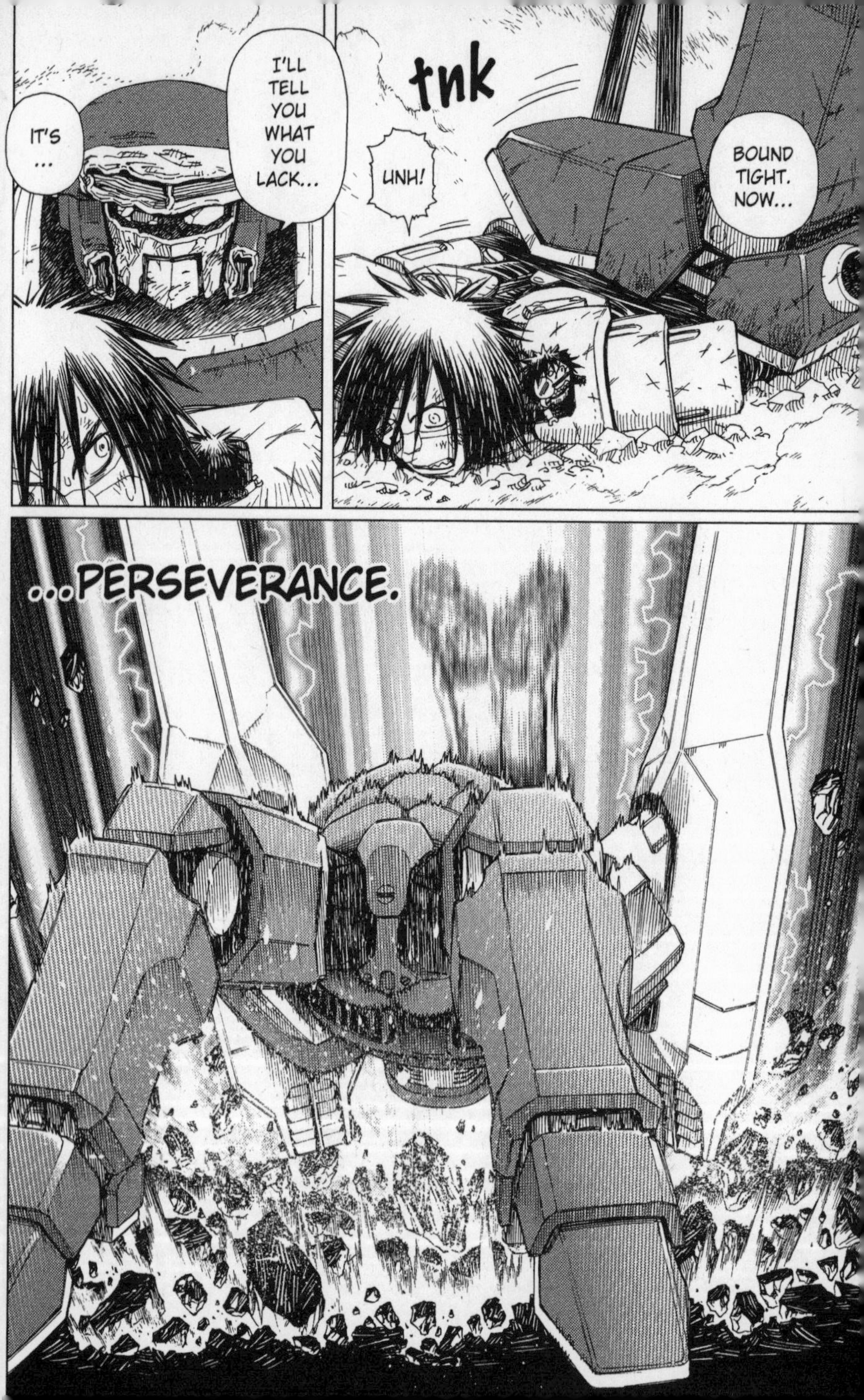
BOUND TIGHT. NOW...
tnk
UNH!
I'LL TELL YOU WHAT YOU LACK...
IT'S ...
...PERSEVERANCE.

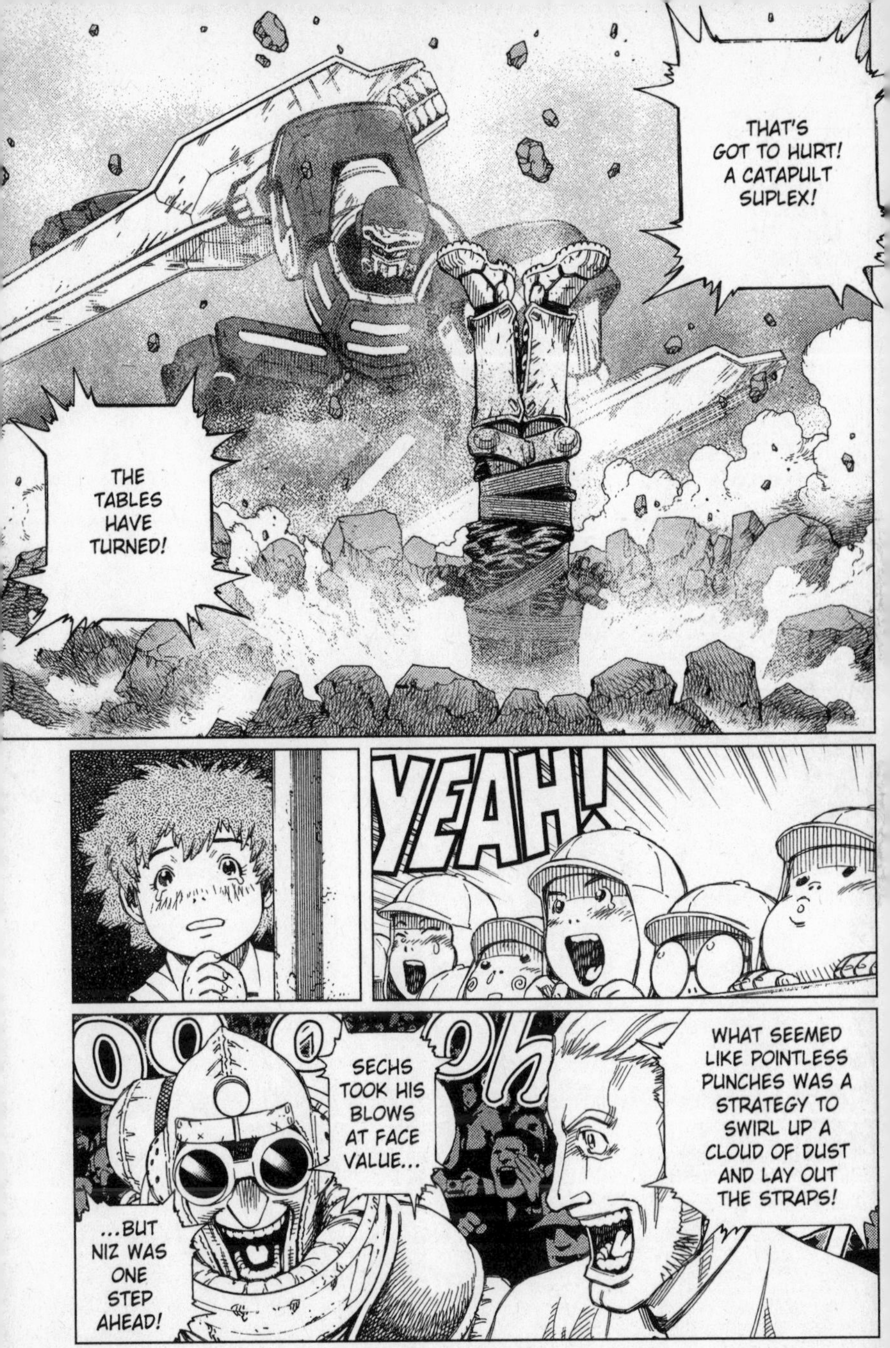
THAT'S GOT TO HURT! A CATAPULT SUPLEX!
THE TABLES HAVE TURNED!
YEAH!
WHAT SEEMED LIKE POINTLESS PUNCHES WAS A STRATEGY TO SWIRL UP A CLOUD OF DUST AND LAY OUT THE STRAPS!
OOOOH
SECHS TOOK HIS BLOWS AT FACE VALUE...
...BUT NIZ WAS ONE STEP AHEAD!

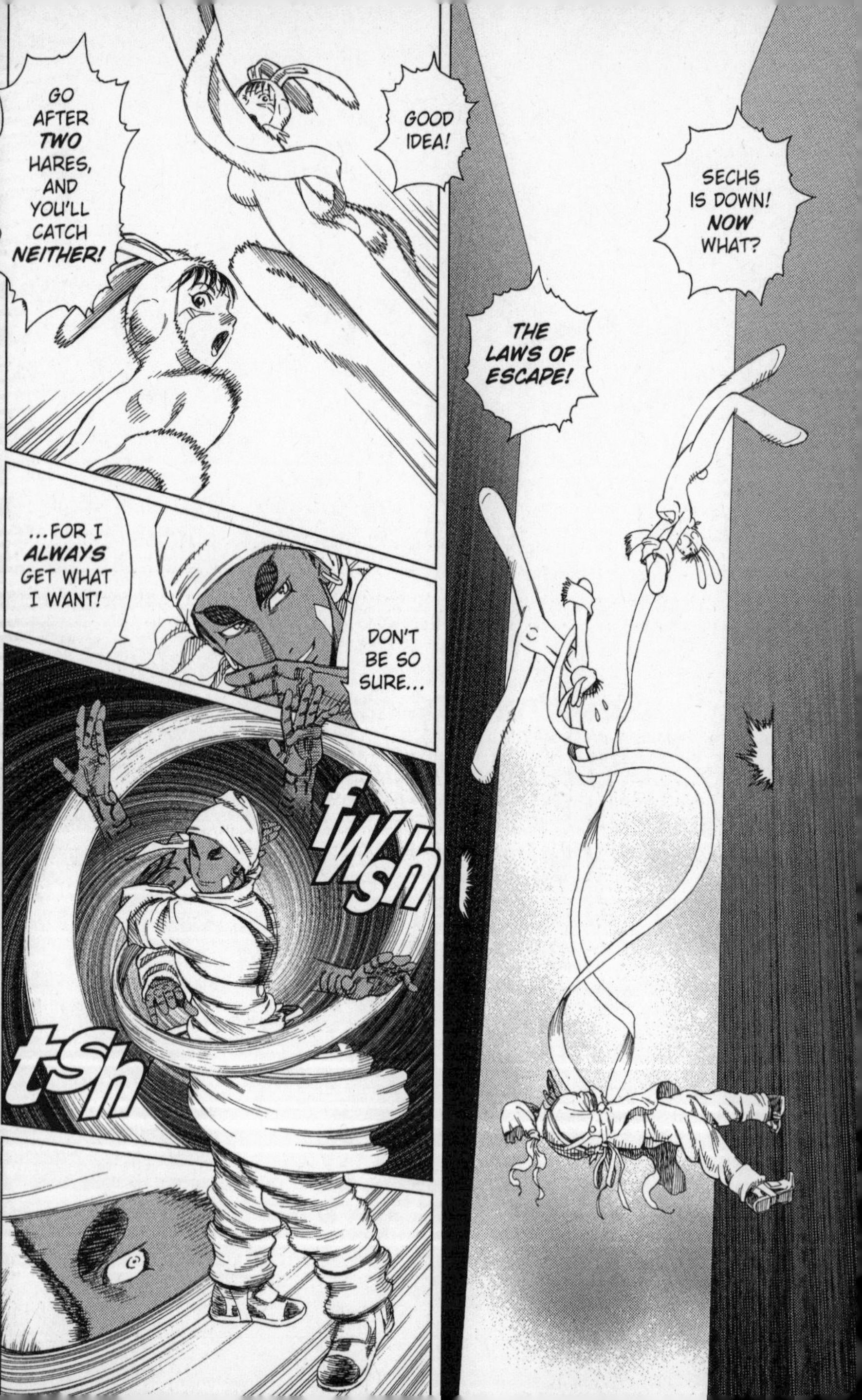
SECHS IS DOWN! NOW WHAT?
THE LAWS OF ESCAPE!
GO AFTER TWO HARES, AND YOU'LL CATCH NEITHER!
GOOD IDEA!
...FOR I ALWAYS GET WHAT I WANT!
DON'T BE SO SURE...
fWsh
tsh

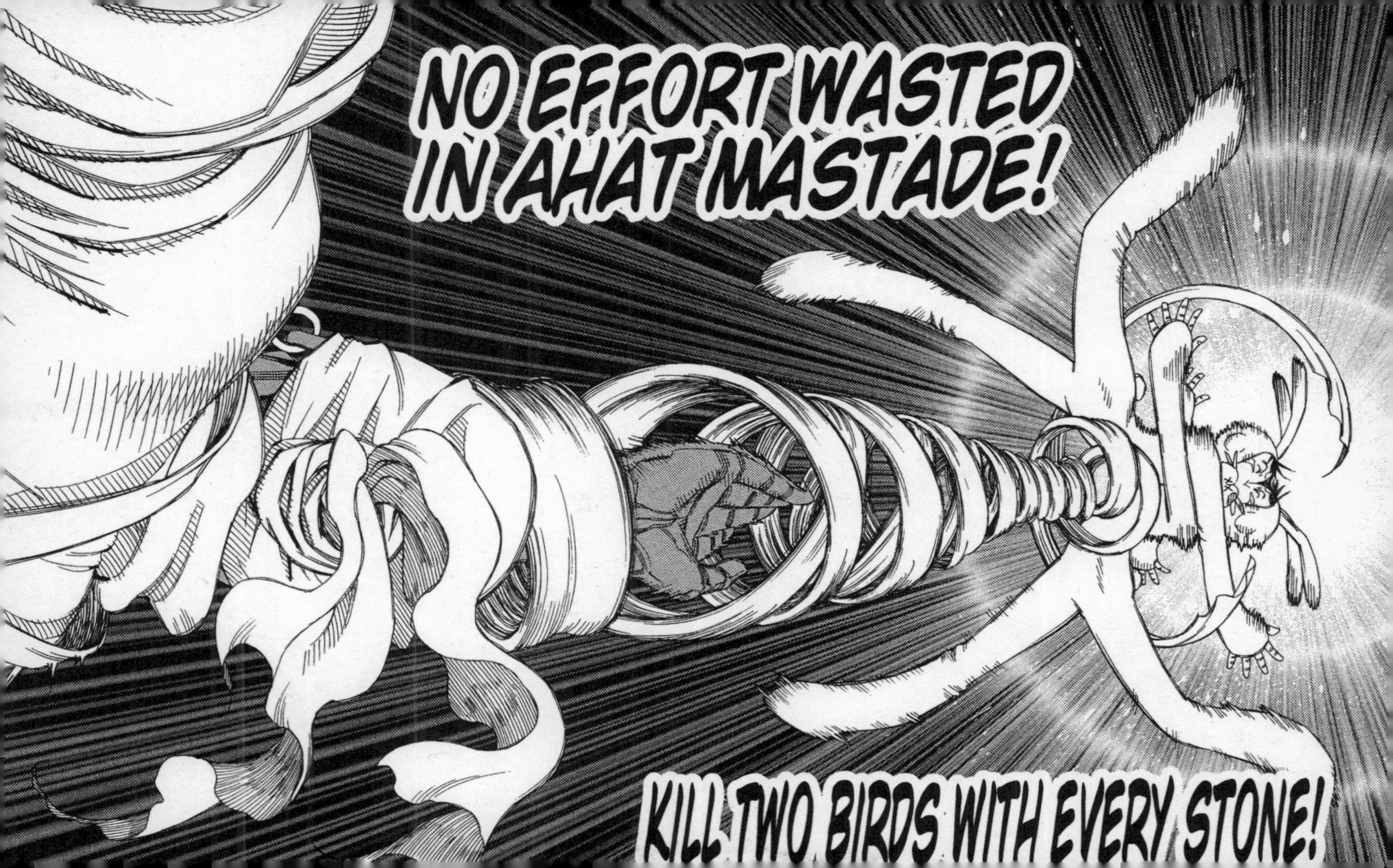
NO EFFORT WASTED IN AHAT MASTADE!
KILL TWO BIRDS WITH EVERY STONE!

twsh
YOW.
QU TSANG HAS SUNK THEM BOTH WITH ONE BLOW!
plop plp
M-MY WHOLE BODY...LIKE PINS AND NEEDLES! CAN'T MOVE...
shiver shiver
fip
SQUEE!
fup
A SINGLE BLOW TO THE CERVICAL SPINE DISABLES MOTOR FUNCTION.
IT'S NOT FATAL, IF YOU BEHAVE YOURSELVES.
SO DEFT... SO FAST...
...LIKE SHE WAS SOLVING A PUZZLE RING! SO THAT'S THE "AHAT MASTADE."
I CAN'T BE SURE YET... BUT THOSE GENTLE MOVEMENTS SUGGEST A CHINESE ART...
IT MAY BE NEIJIA QUAN, RENOWNED FOR ITS HIGH-LEVEL TECHNIQUES!

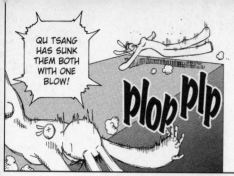

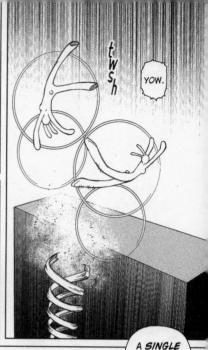

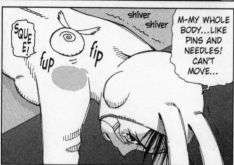

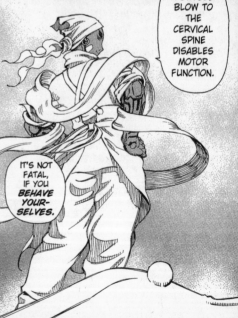

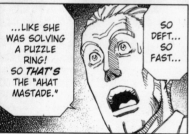

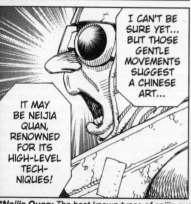

***Neijia Quan:** The best known types of neijia quan are taiji quan (tai chi), xingyi quan ("fist of form and mind") and bagua zhang ("eight diagram palm"). In contrast to Shaolin and related styles, which are based on Buddhism, neijia quan is based on Taoism. A separate Ming Dynasty form of the same name has been lost.*

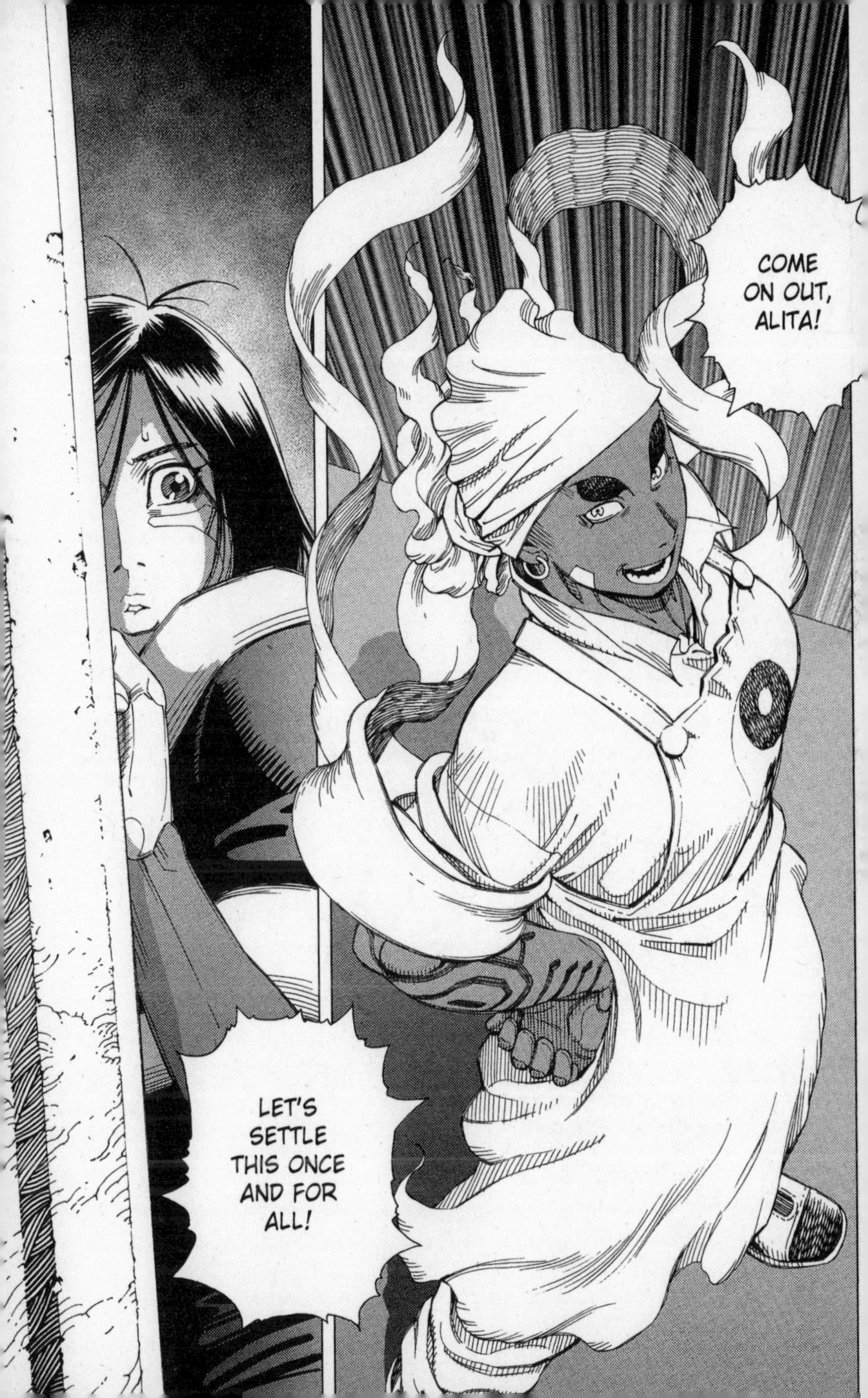
COME ON OUT, ALITA!
LET'S SETTLE THIS ONCE AND FOR ALL!

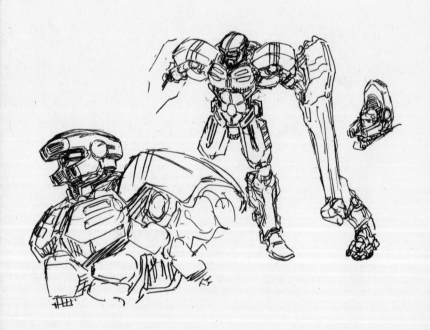

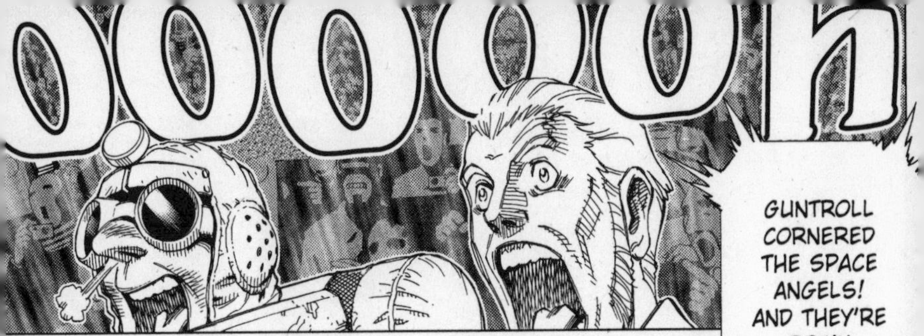
oooooh
GUNTROLL CORNERED THE SPACE ANGELS! AND THEY'RE DOWN 3 TO 2!

PHASE 30: **Join the Stars**

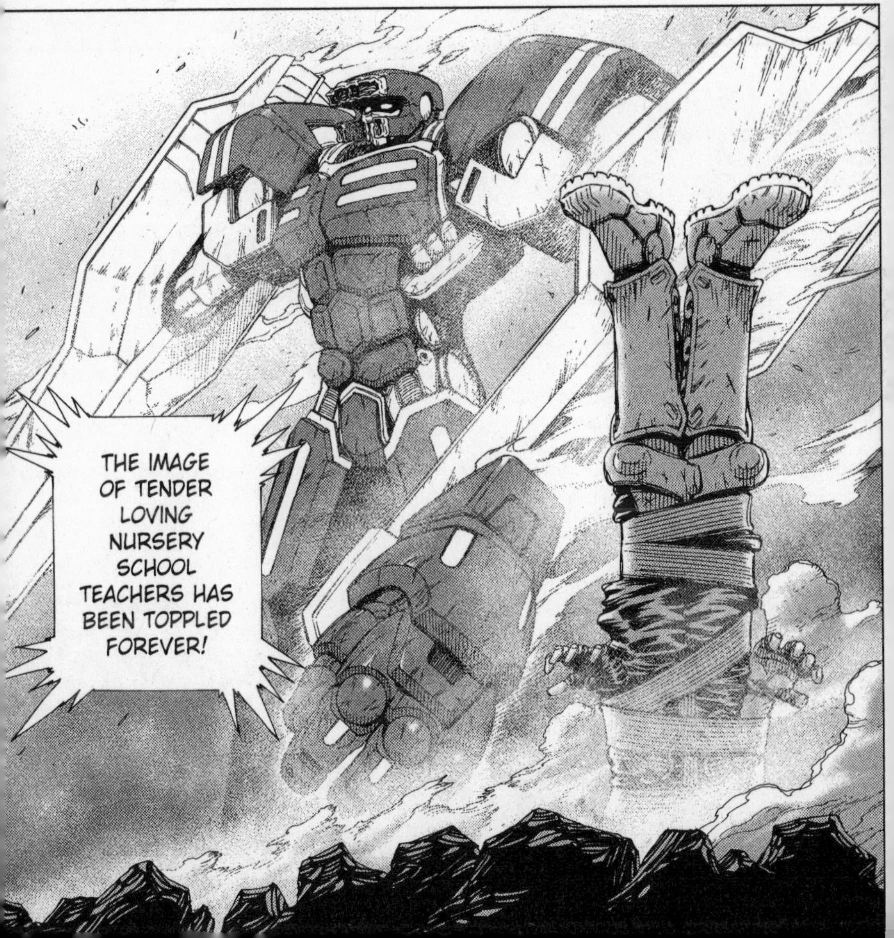
THE IMAGE OF TENDER LOVING NURSERY SCHOOL TEACHERS HAS BEEN TOPPLED FOREVER!

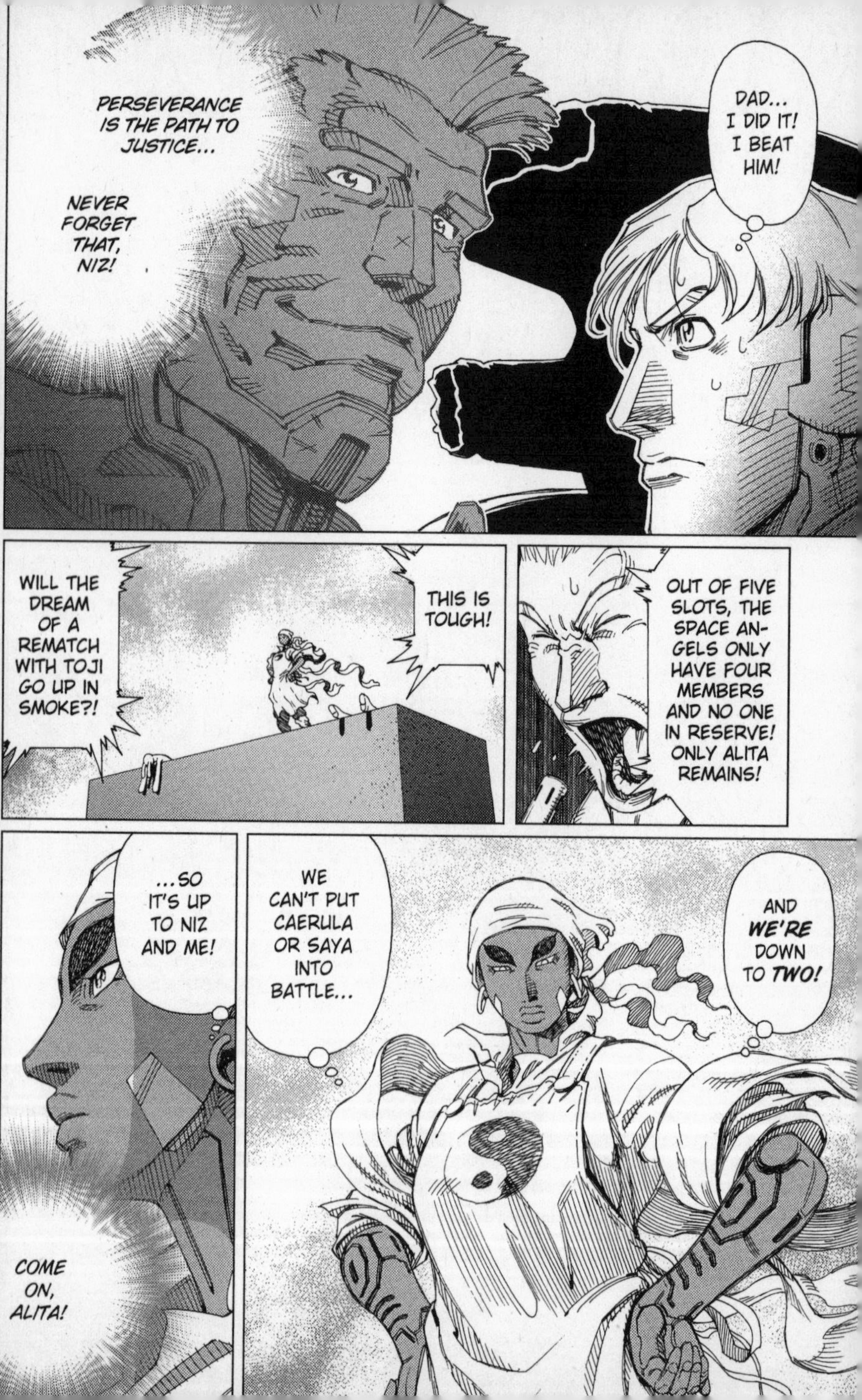
DAD... I DID IT! I BEAT HIM!
PERSEVERANCE IS THE PATH TO JUSTICE...
NEVER FORGET THAT, NIZ!
OUT OF FIVE SLOTS, THE SPACE ANGELS ONLY HAVE FOUR MEMBERS AND NO ONE IN RESERVE! ONLY ALITA REMAINS!
THIS IS TOUGH!
WILL THE DREAM OF A REMATCH WITH TOJI GO UP IN SMOKE?!
AND WE'RE DOWN TO TWO!
WE CAN'T PUT CAERULA OR SAYA INTO BATTLE...
...SO IT'S UP TO NIZ AND ME!
COME ON, ALITA!

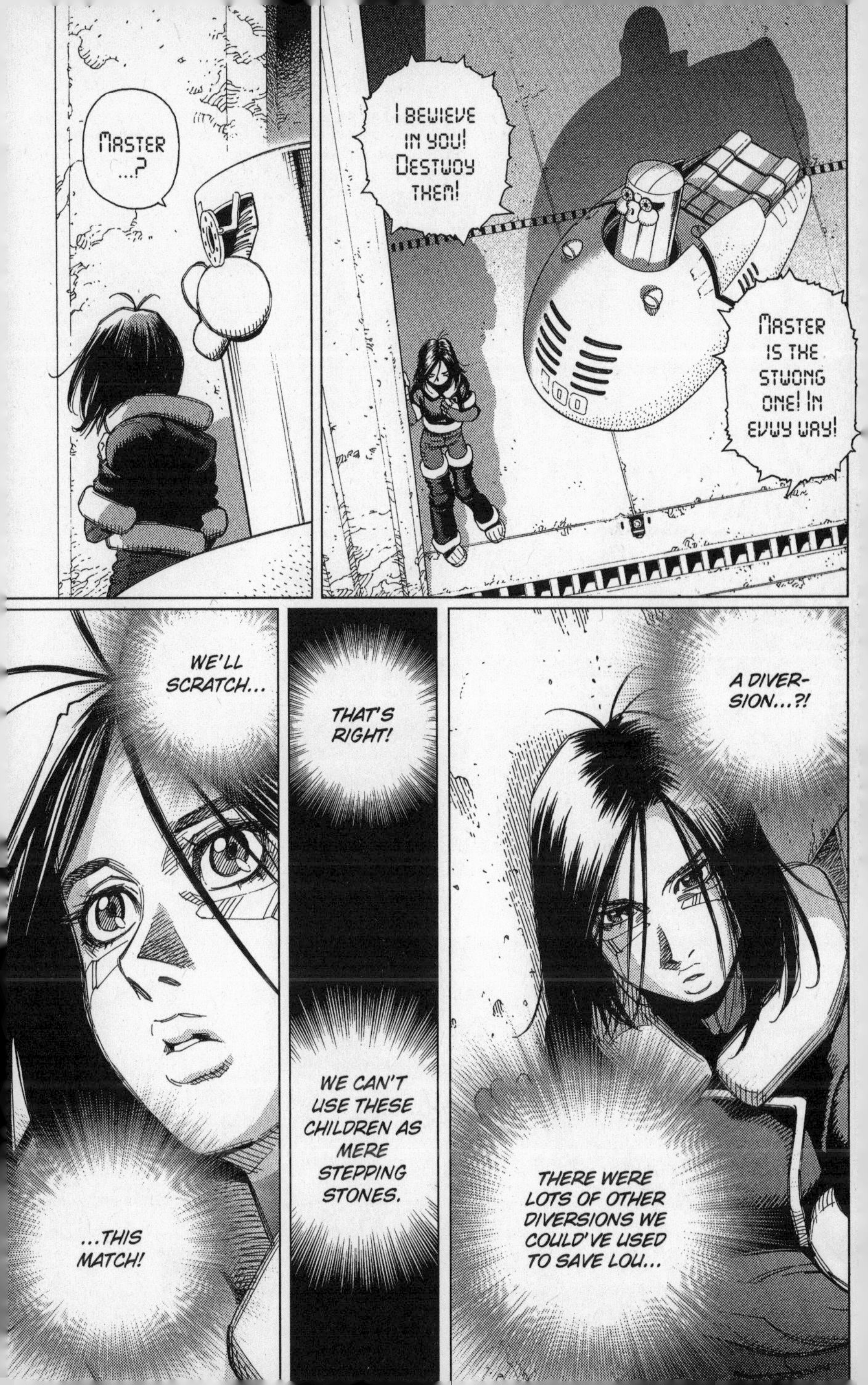
I BEWIEVE IN YOU! DESTWOY THEM!
MASTER IS THE STWONG ONE! IN EVWY WAY!
MASTER ...?
A DIVER-SION...?!
THERE WERE LOTS OF OTHER DIVERSIONS WE COULD'VE USED TO SAVE LOU...
THAT'S RIGHT!
WE CAN'T USE THESE CHILDREN AS MERE STEPPING STONES.
WE'LL SCRATCH...
...THIS MATCH!

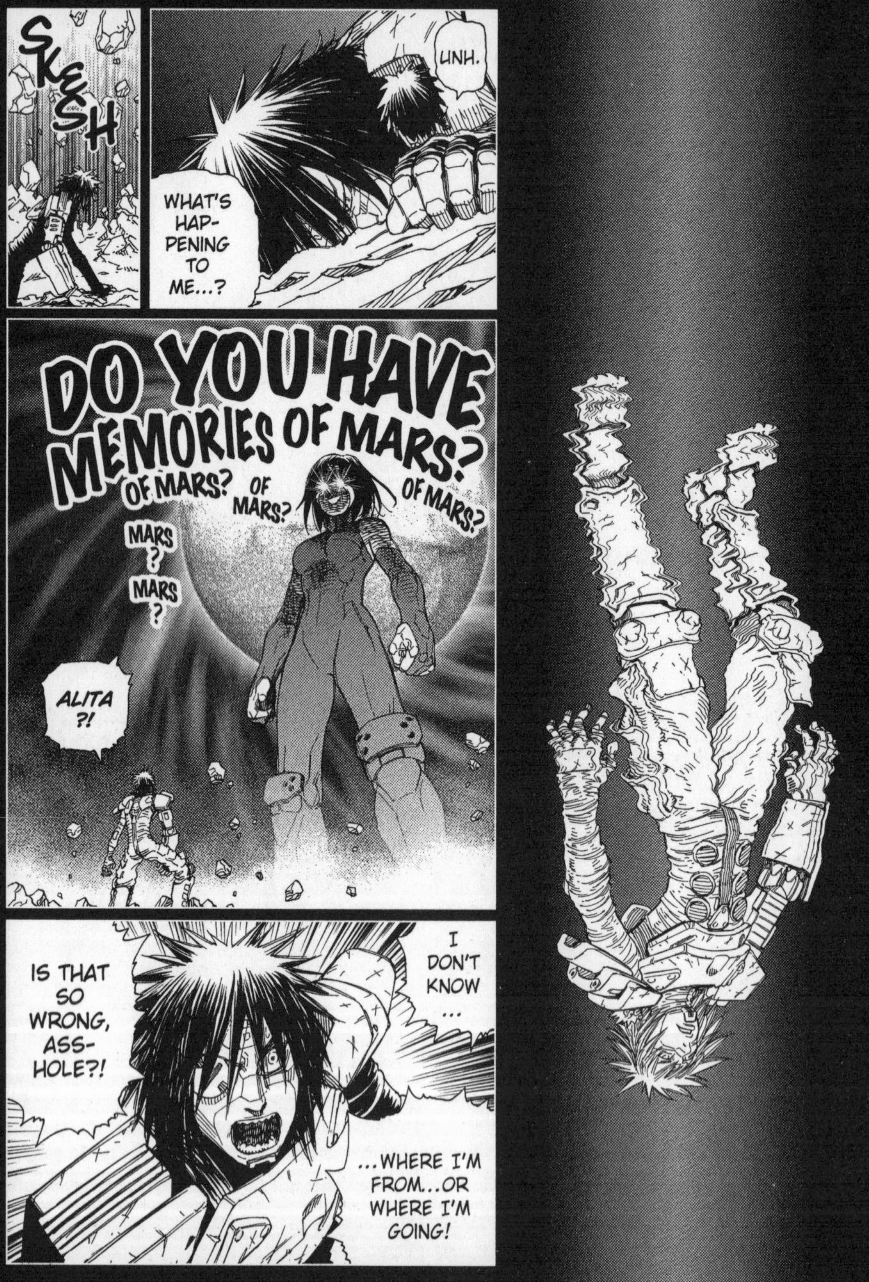

UNH.
WHAT'S HAP-PENING TO ME...?
SKESH
DO YOU HAVE MEMORIES OF MARS?
OF MARS?
OF MARS?
OF MARS?
MARS?
MARS?
ALITA?!
I DON'T KNOW...
IS THAT SO WRONG, ASS-HOLE?!
...WHERE I'M FROM...OR WHERE I'M GOING!

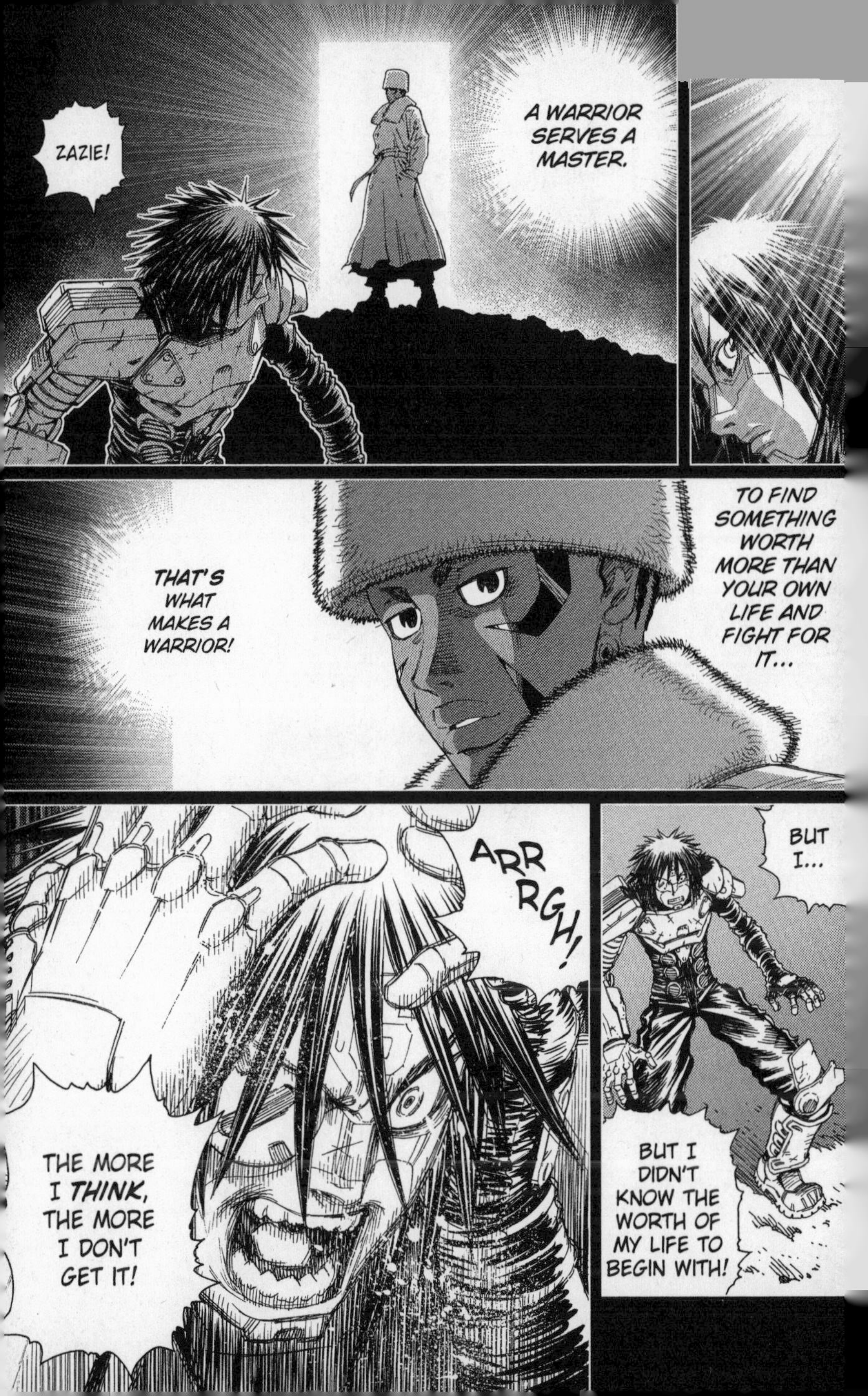

A WARRIOR SERVES A MASTER.
ZAZIE!
TO FIND SOMETHING WORTH MORE THAN YOUR OWN LIFE AND FIGHT FOR IT...
THAT'S WHAT MAKES A WARRIOR!
BUT I...
BUT I DIDN'T KNOW THE WORTH OF MY LIFE TO BEGIN WITH!
ARRRGH!
THE MORE I THINK, THE MORE I DON'T GET IT!

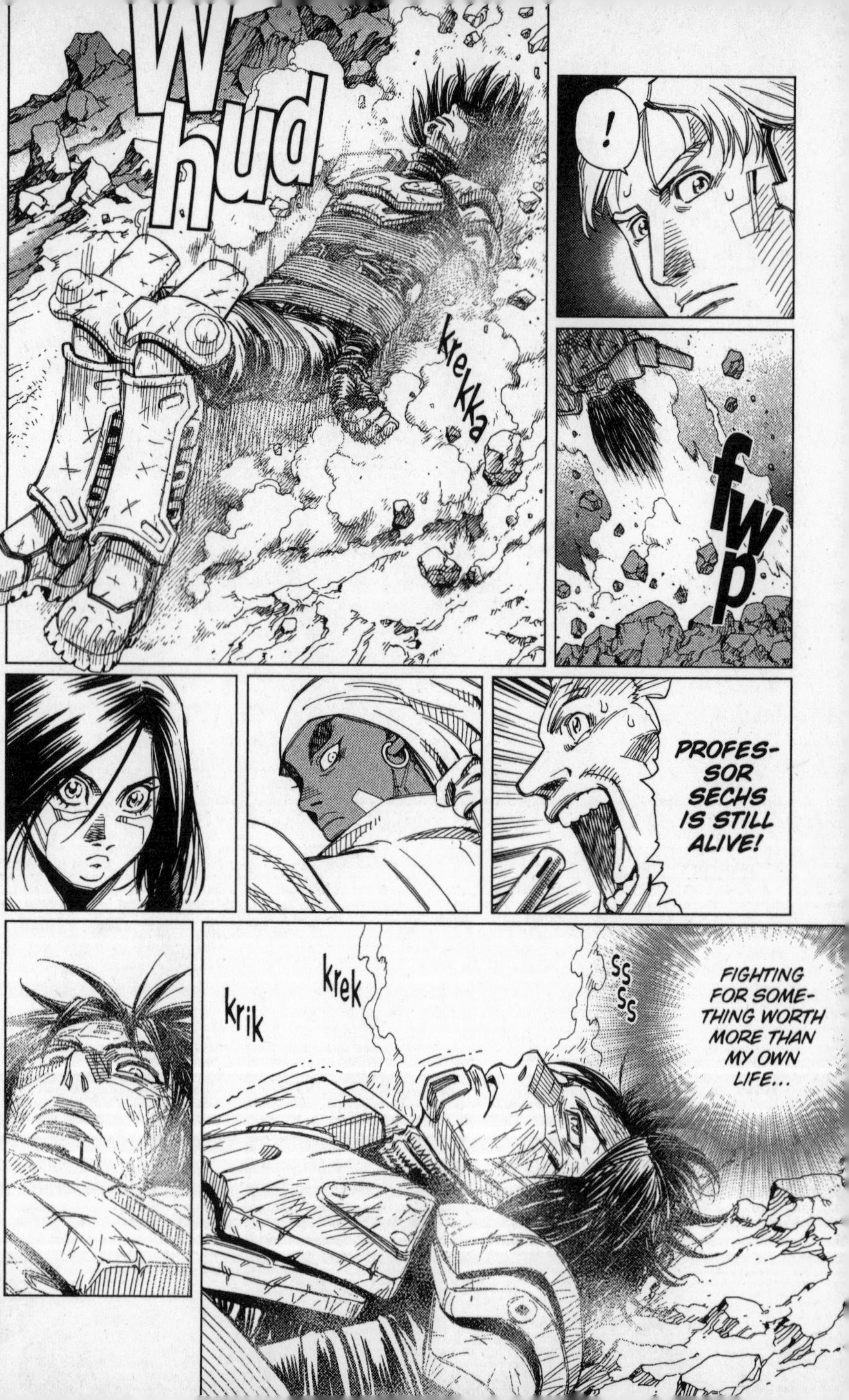
!
fwp
Whud
krekka
PROFES-
SOR
SECHS
IS STILL
ALIVE!
FIGHTING
FOR SOME-
THING WORTH
MORE THAN
MY OWN
LIFE...
SSSS
krek
krik

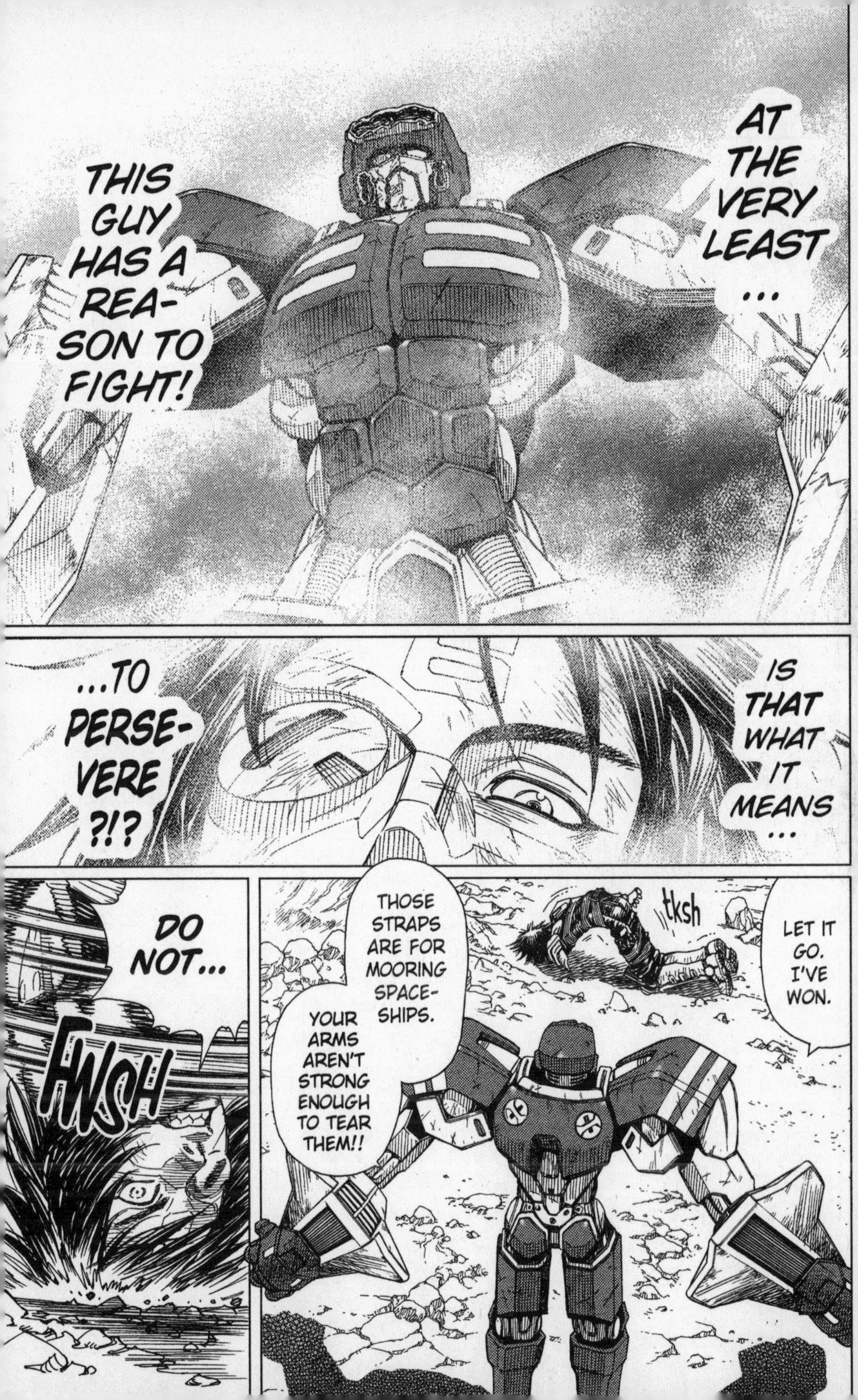
AT THE VERY LEAST...
THIS GUY HAS A REA-SON TO FIGHT!
IS THAT WHAT IT MEANS...
...TO PERSE-VERE?!?
LET IT GO. I'VE WON.
tksh
THOSE STRAPS ARE FOR MOORING SPACE-SHIPS.
YOUR ARMS AREN'T STRONG ENOUGH TO TEAR THEM!!
DO NOT...
FWSH

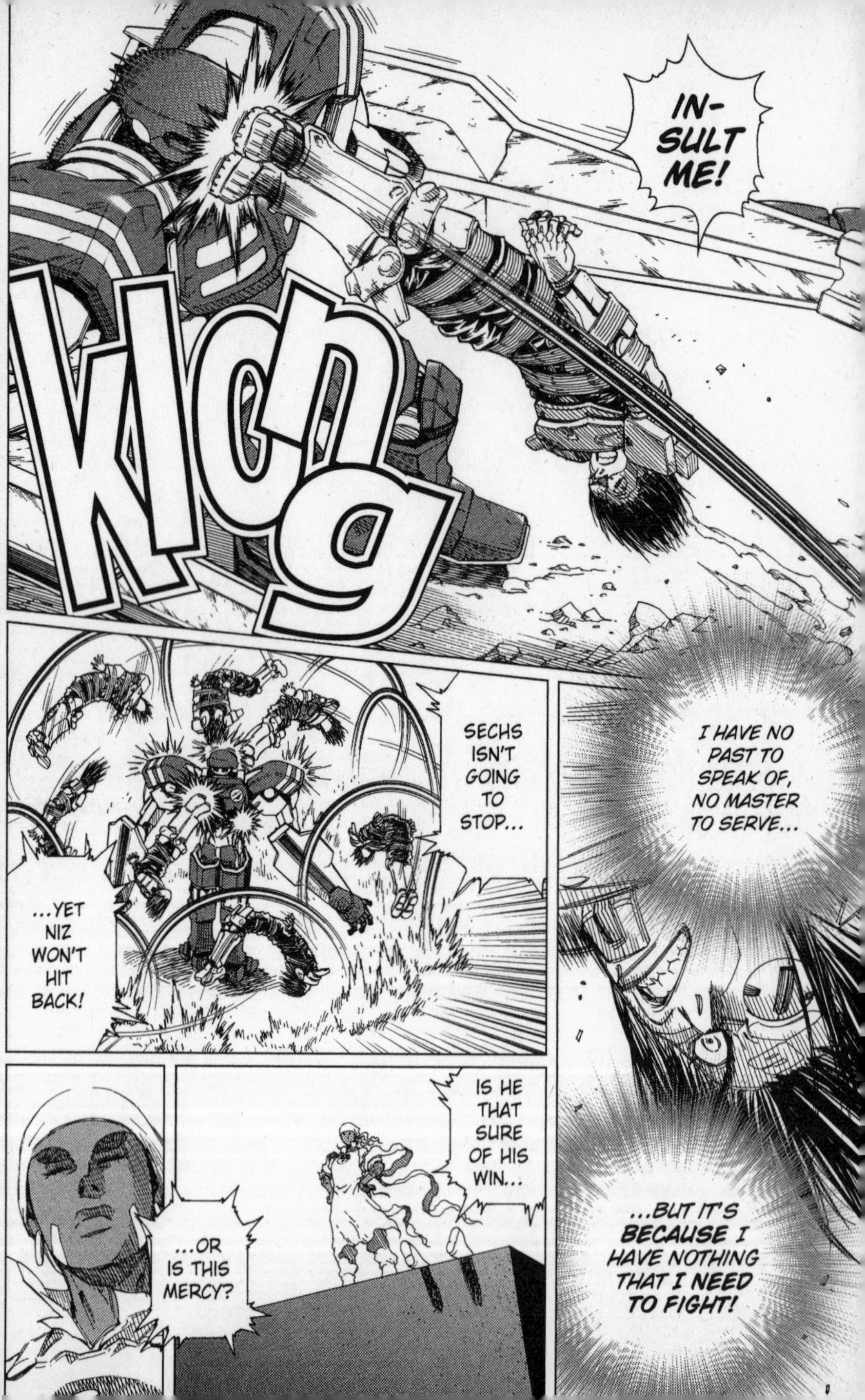
IN-SULT ME!
I HAVE NO PAST TO SPEAK OF, NO MASTER TO SERVE...
...BUT IT'S BECAUSE I HAVE NOTHING THAT I NEED TO FIGHT!
SECHS ISN'T GOING TO STOP...
...YET NIZ WON'T HIT BACK!
IS HE THAT SURE OF HIS WIN...
...OR IS THIS MERCY?

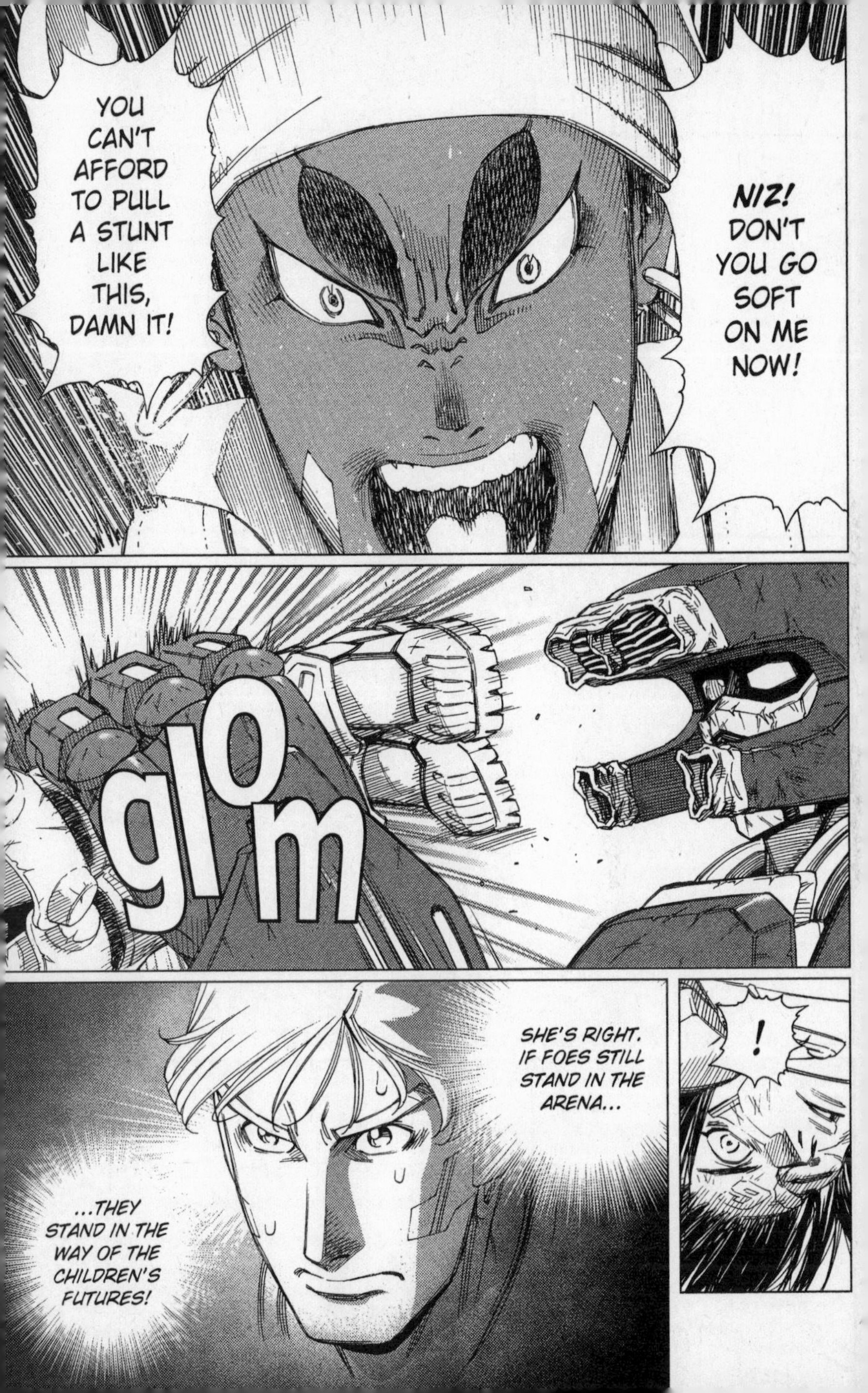
NIZ! DON'T YOU GO SOFT ON ME NOW!
YOU CAN'T AFFORD TO PULL A STUNT LIKE THIS, DAMN IT!
glom
!
SHE'S RIGHT. IF FOES STILL STAND IN THE ARENA...
...THEY STAND IN THE WAY OF THE CHILDREN'S FUTURES!

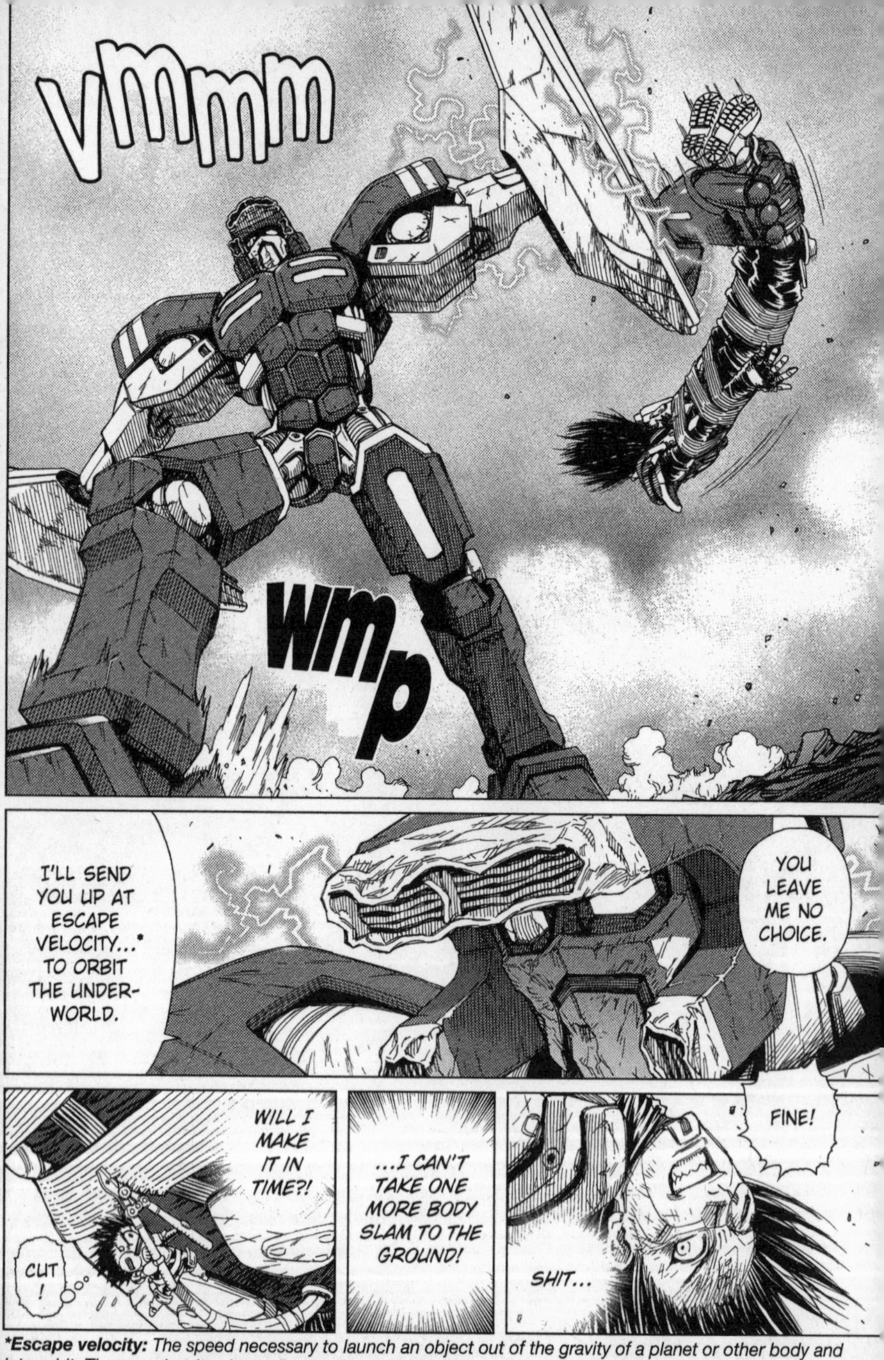
VMMMM
WMP
YOU LEAVE ME NO CHOICE.
I'LL SEND YOU UP AT ESCAPE VELOCITY...* TO ORBIT THE UNDER-WORLD.
FINE!
SHIT...
...I CAN'T TAKE ONE MORE BODY SLAM TO THE GROUND!
WILL I MAKE IT IN TIME?!
CUT!

***Escape velocity:** The speed necessary to launch an object out of the gravity of a planet or other body and into orbit. The speed varies depending on the strength of the gravity. Earth's escape velocity is 7.9 kilometers (4.9 miles) per second (Mach 23).*

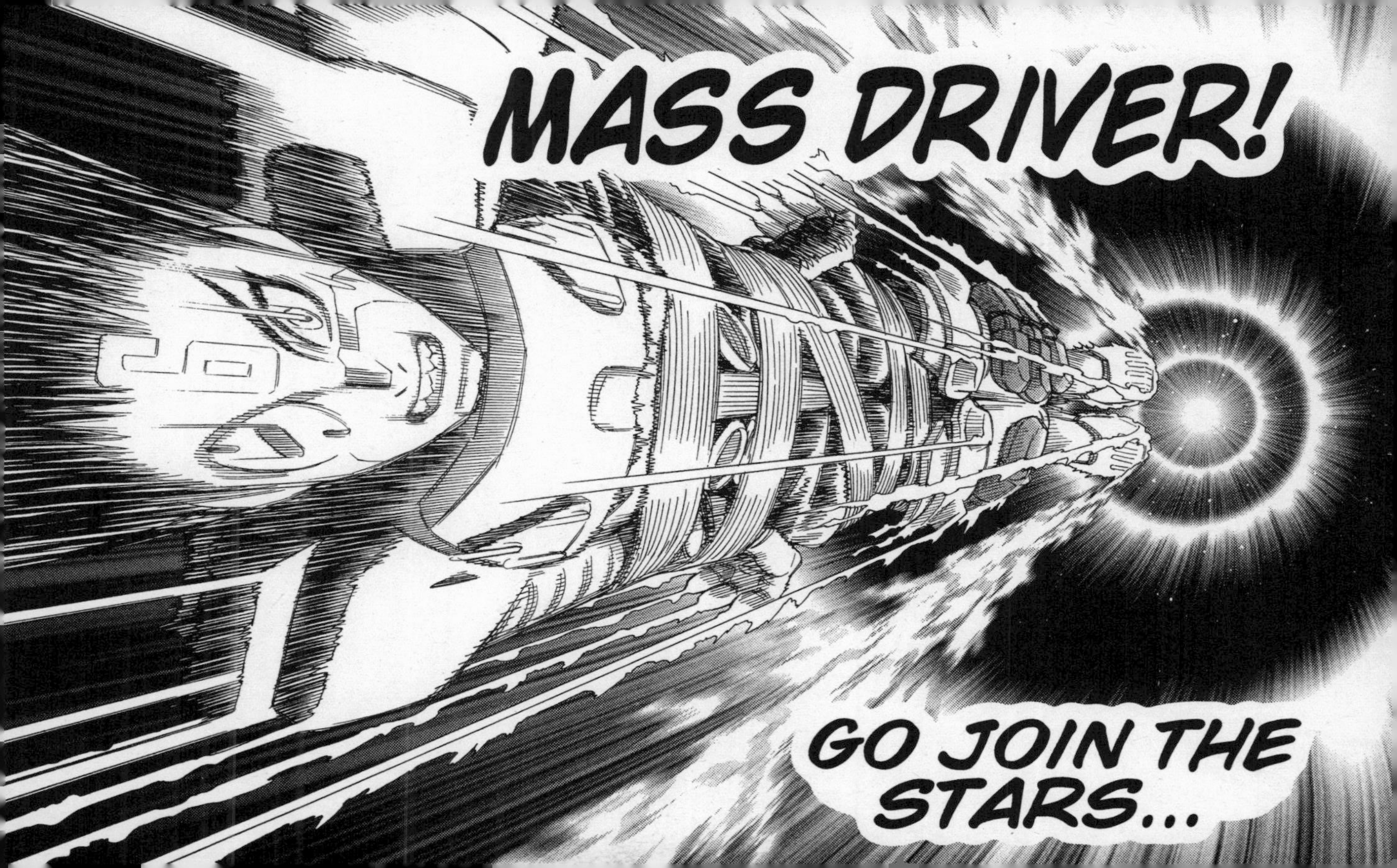
MASS DRIVER!
GO JOIN THE STARS...

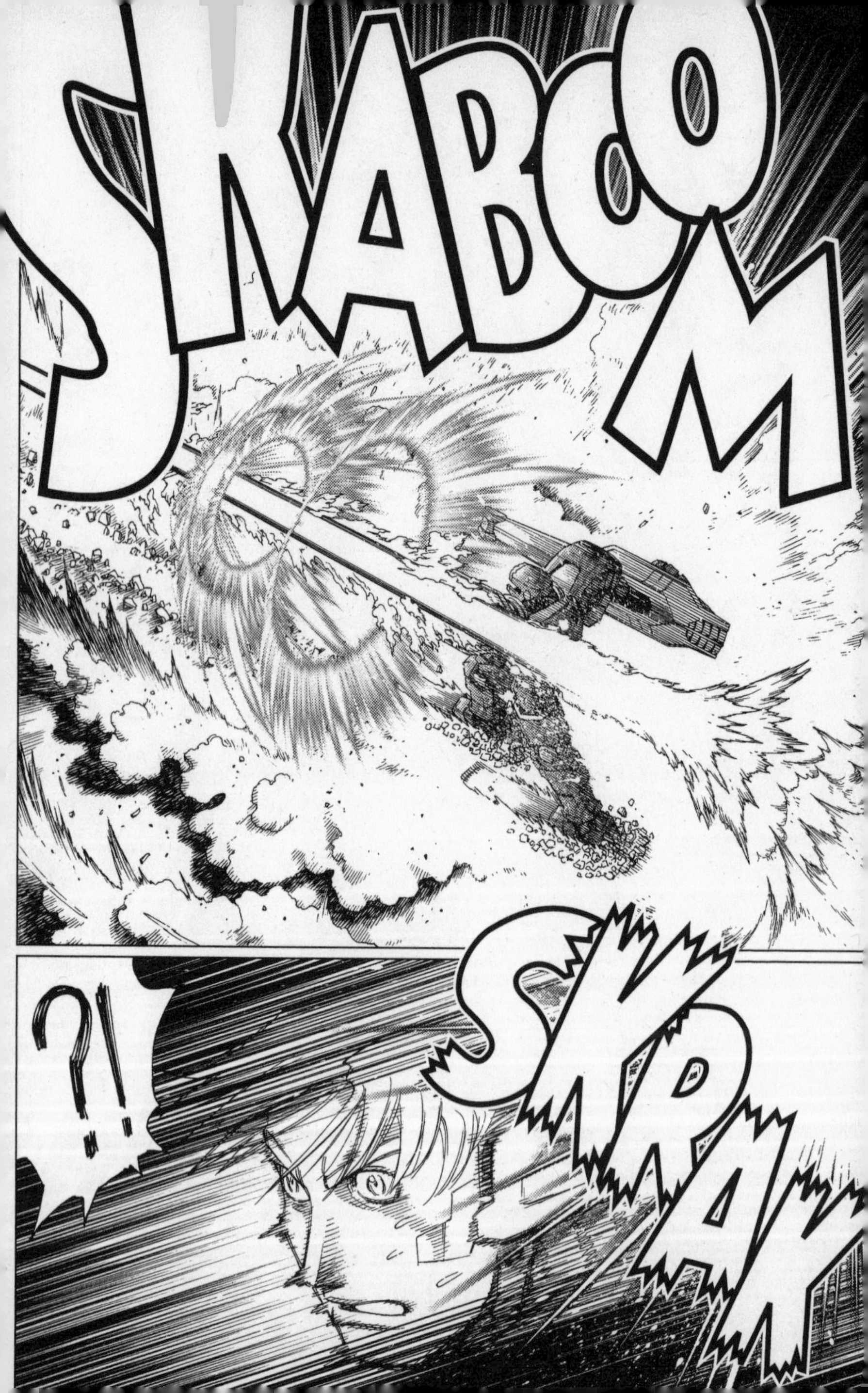
KABOOM
SKRAK
?!

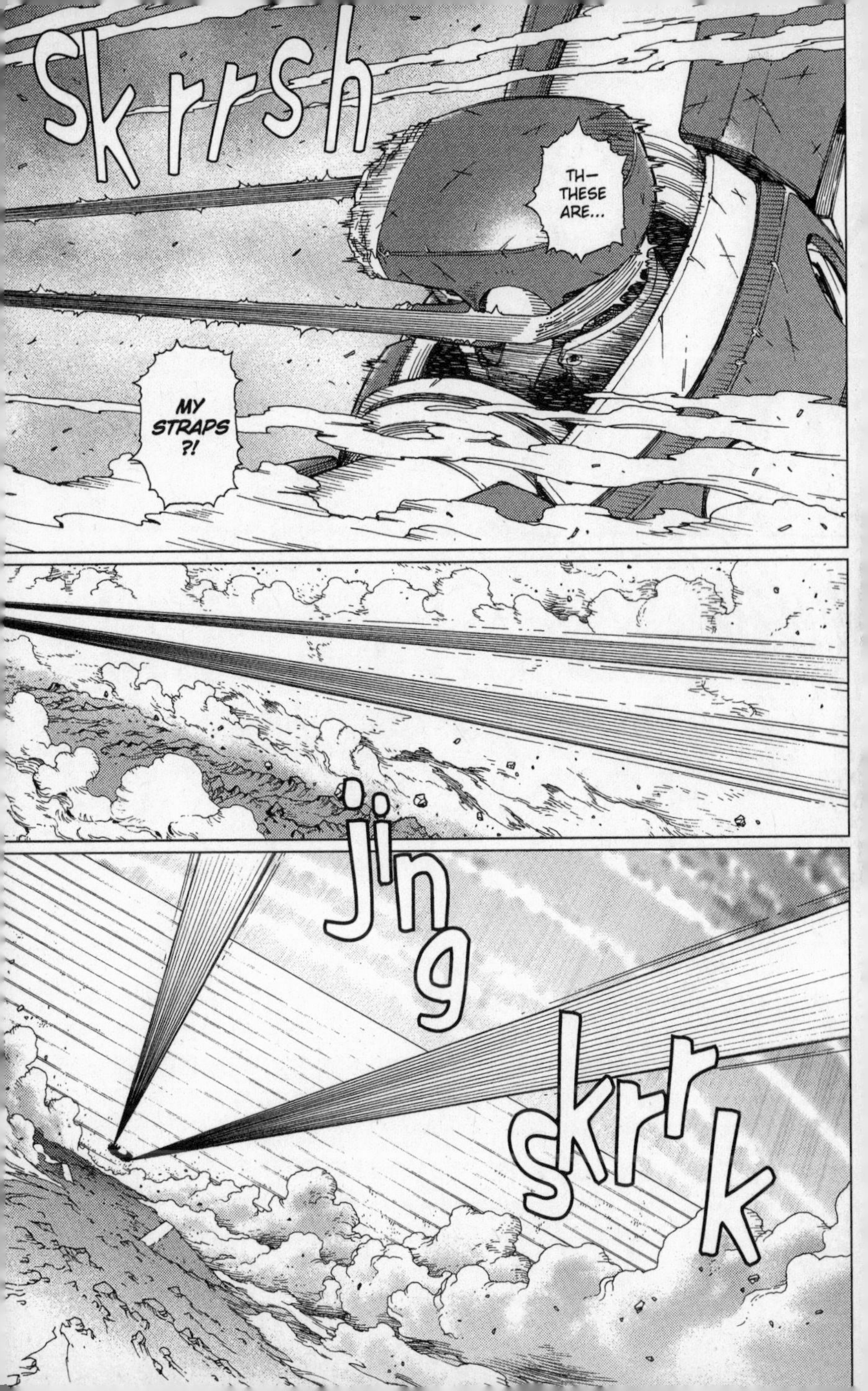
Skrrsh
TH— THESE ARE...
MY STRAPS ?!
jing
skrrk

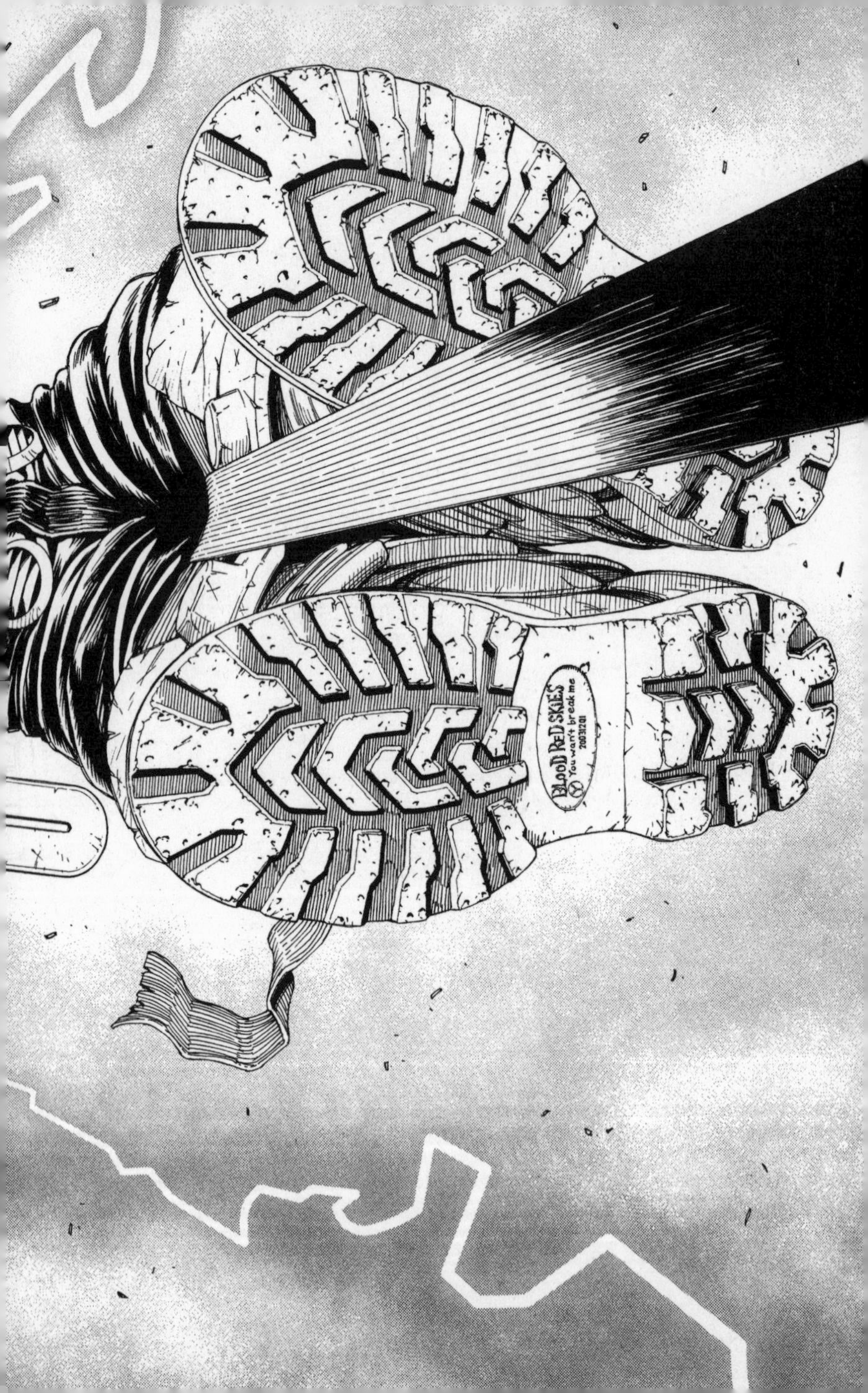
BLOOD RED SKIES
You wan't break me
20031201

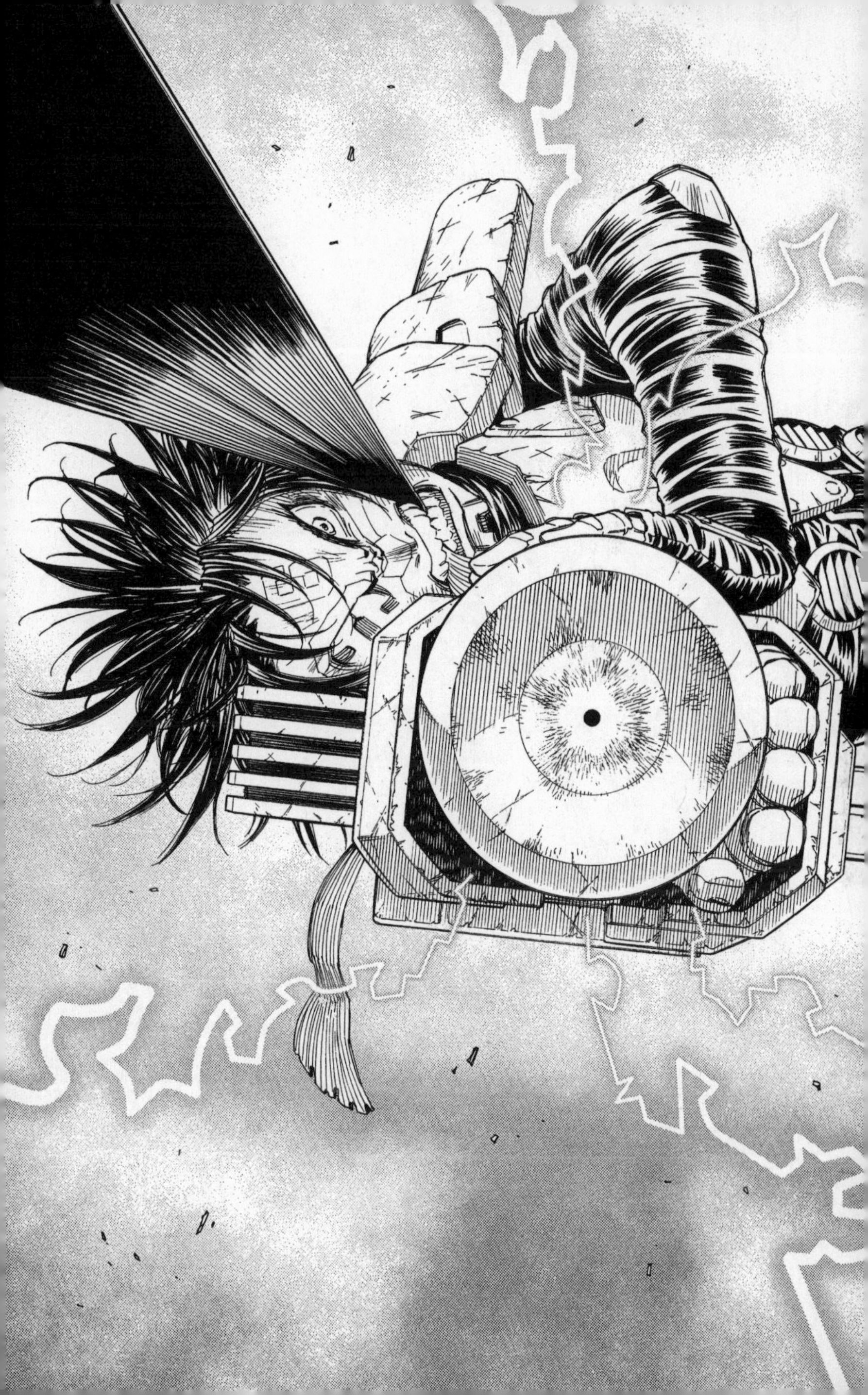

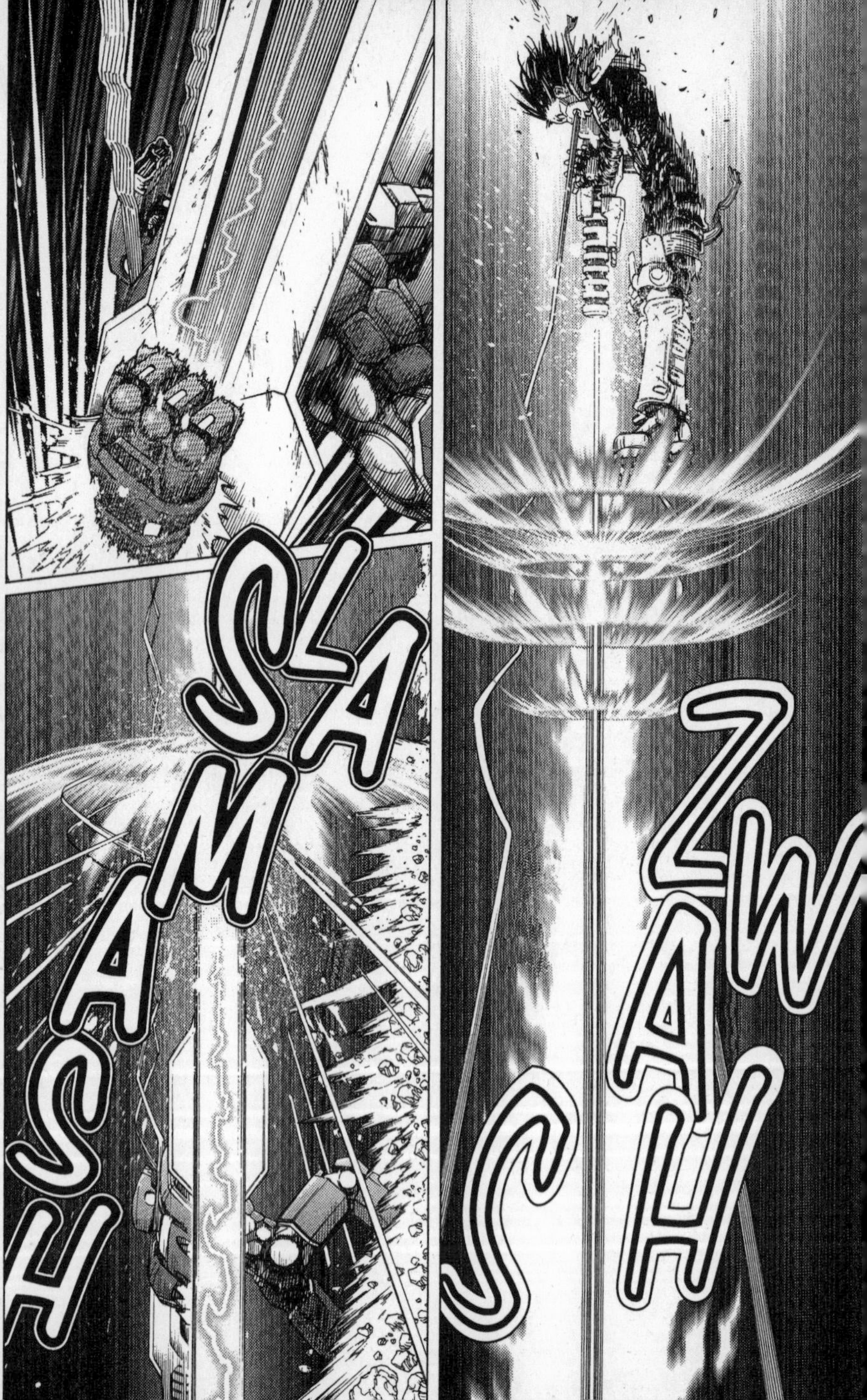
ZWAASH
SLAMASH

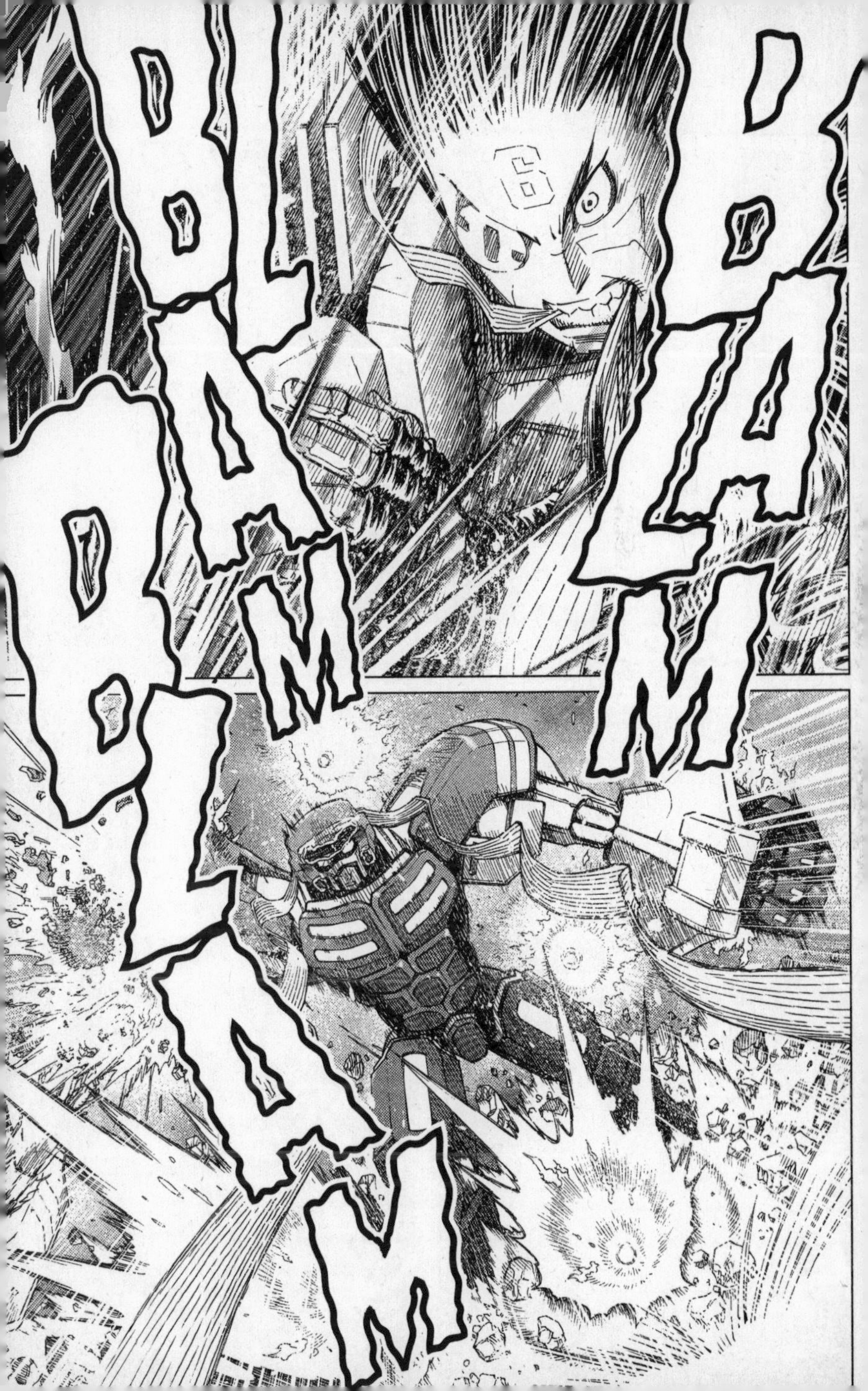
BLAM
BLAM
BLAM

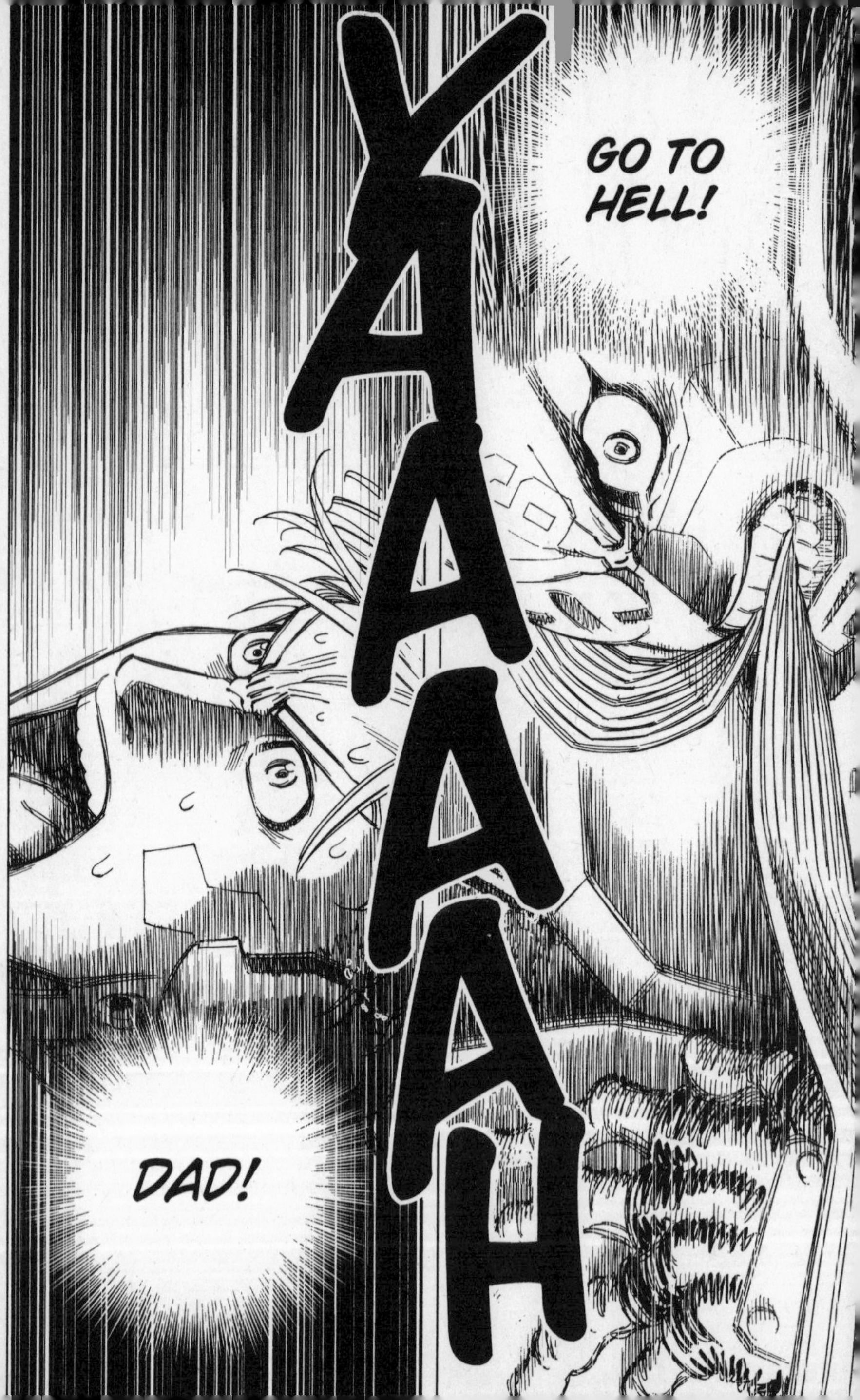
GO TO HELL!
AAAAAH
DAD!

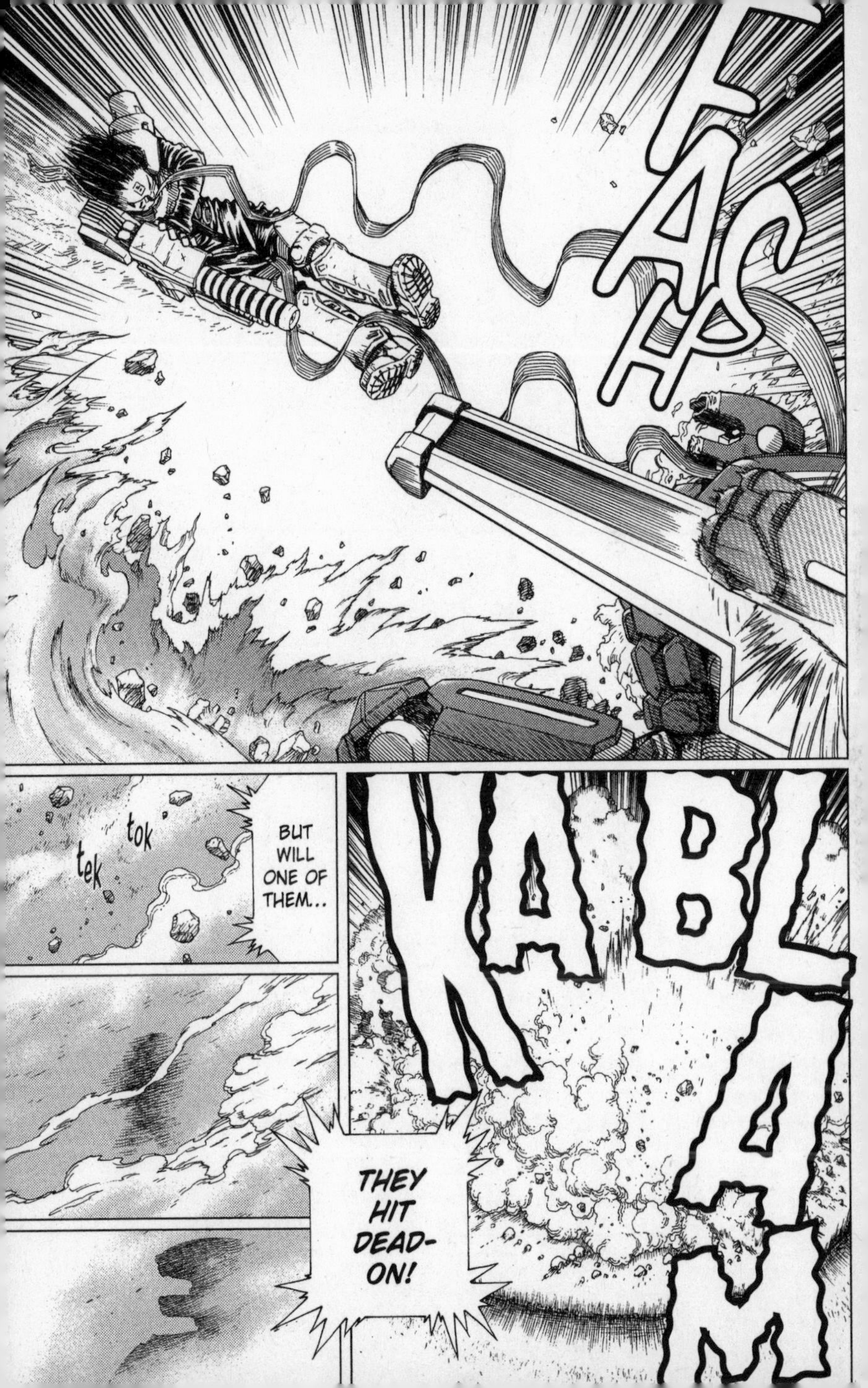
KABLAM
tok
tek
BUT WILL ONE OF THEM...
THEY HIT DEAD-ON!

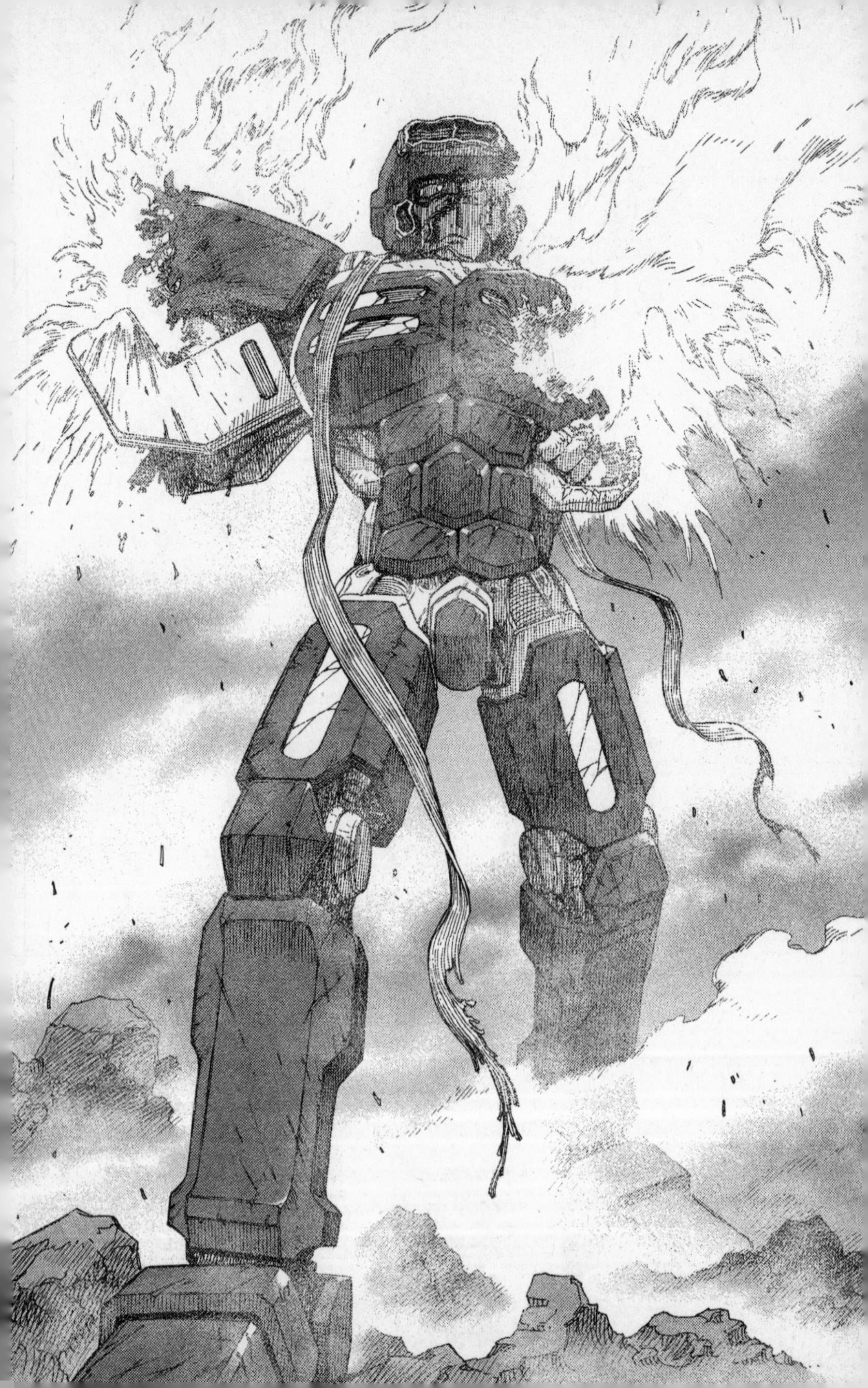

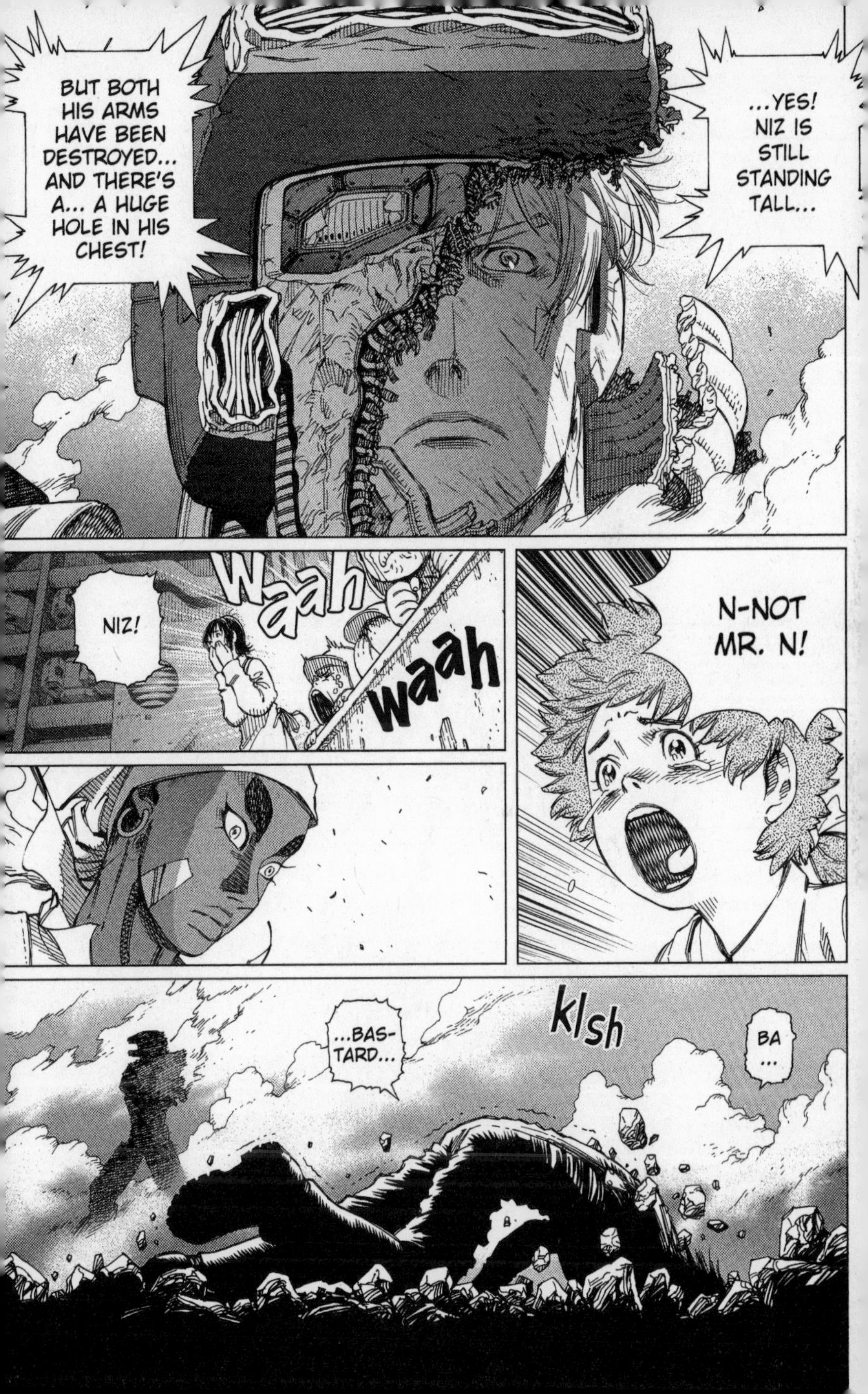
...YES! NIZ IS STILL STANDING TALL...
BUT BOTH HIS ARMS HAVE BEEN DESTROYED... AND THERE'S A... A HUGE HOLE IN HIS CHEST!
N-NOT MR. N!
waah
waah
NIZ!
BA ...
klsh
...BAS-TARD...

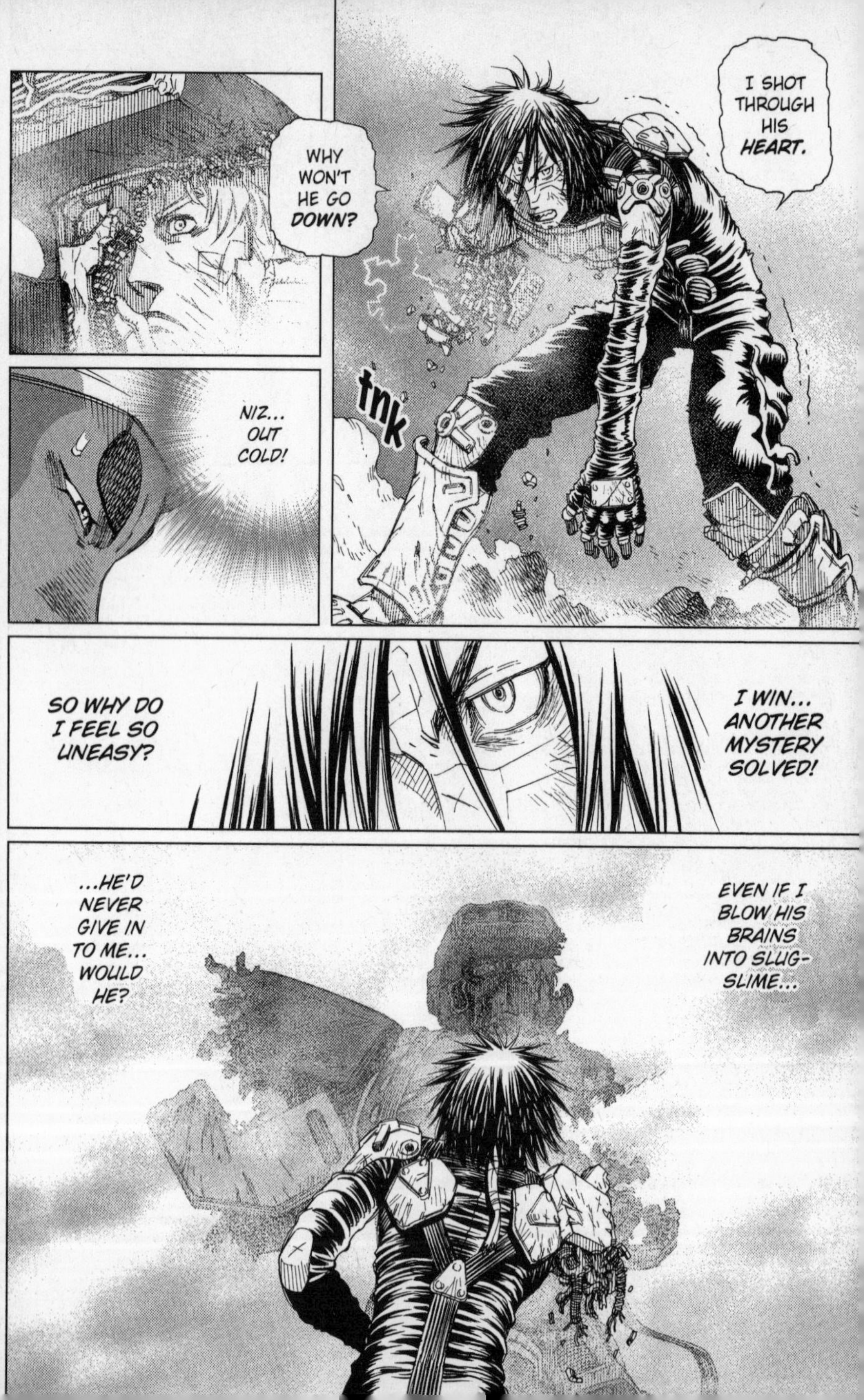
I SHOT THROUGH HIS HEART.
tnk
WHY WON'T HE GO DOWN?
NIZ... OUT COLD!
I WIN... ANOTHER MYSTERY SOLVED!
SO WHY DO I FEEL SO UNEASY?
EVEN IF I BLOW HIS BRAINS INTO SLUG-SLIME...
...HE'D NEVER GIVE IN TO ME... WOULD HE?

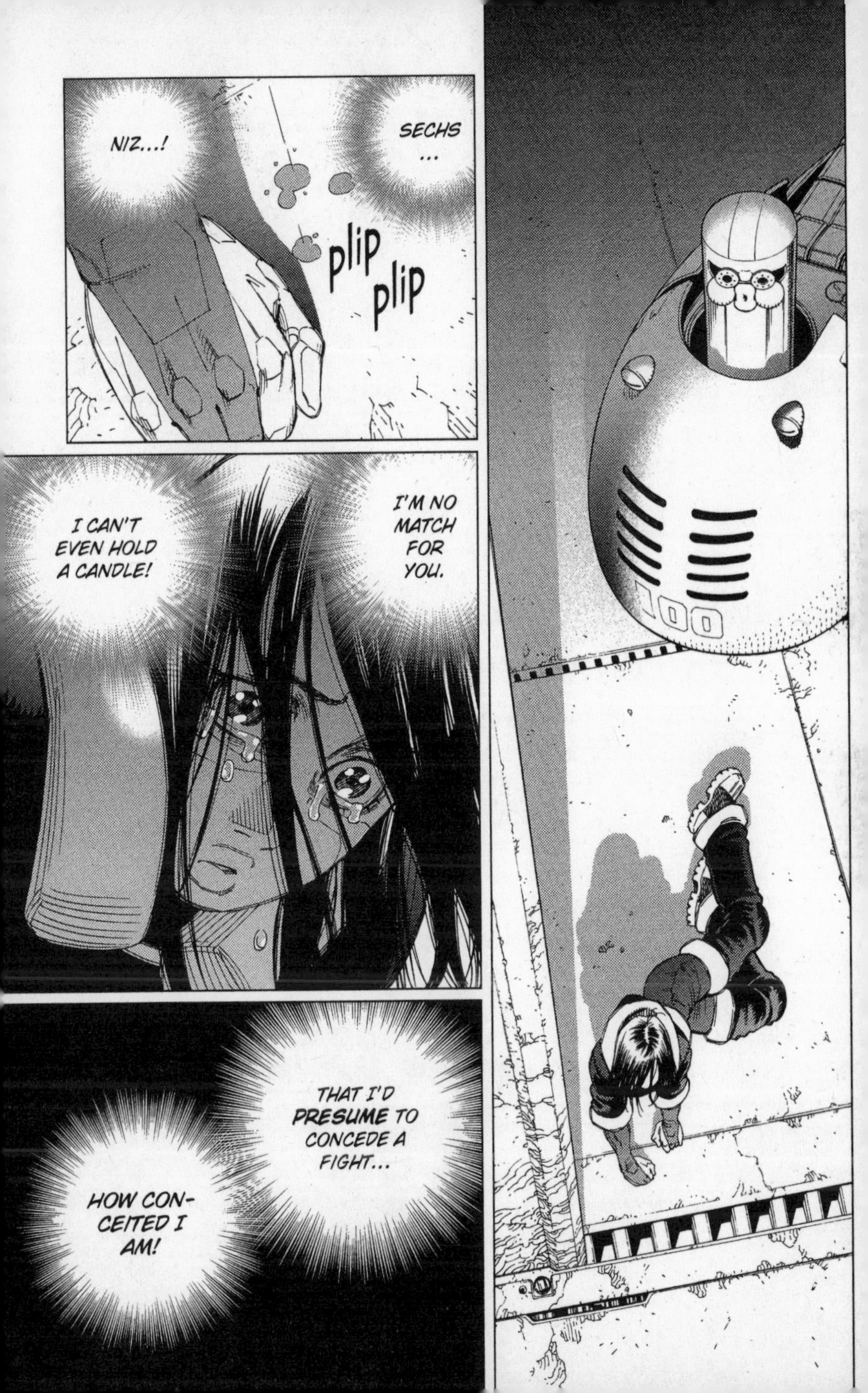
SECHS ...
NIZ...!
plip plip
I'M NO MATCH FOR YOU.
I CAN'T EVEN HOLD A CANDLE!
THAT I'D PRESUME TO CONCEDE A FIGHT...
HOW CONCEITED I AM!

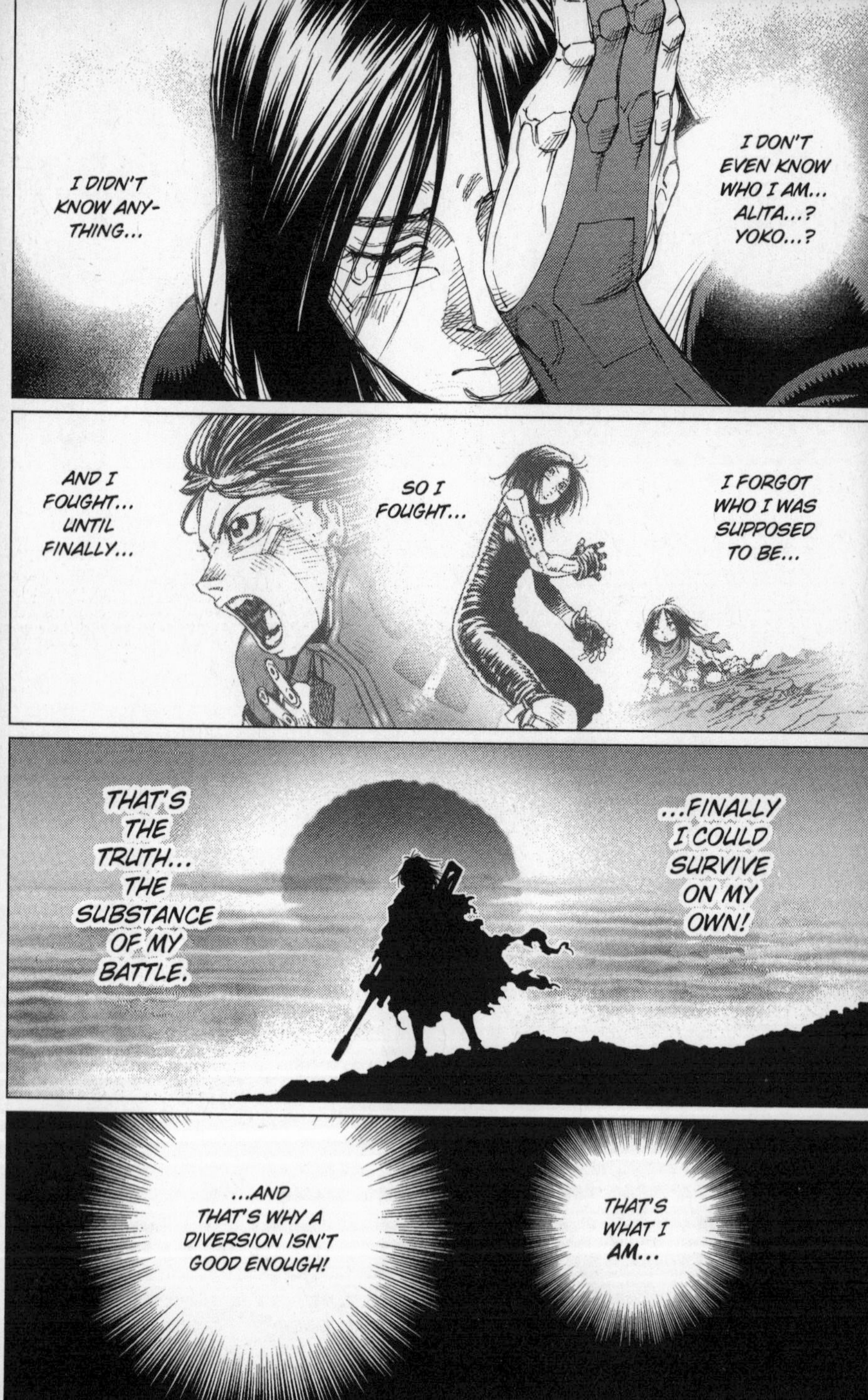
I DON'T EVEN KNOW WHO I AM... ALITA...? YOKO...?
I DIDN'T KNOW ANY-THING...
I FORGOT WHO I WAS SUPPOSED TO BE...
SO I FOUGHT...
AND I FOUGHT... UNTIL FINALLY...
...FINALLY I COULD SURVIVE ON MY OWN!
THAT'S THE TRUTH... THE SUBSTANCE OF MY BATTLE.
THAT'S WHAT I AM...
...AND THAT'S WHY A DIVERSION ISN'T GOOD ENOUGH!

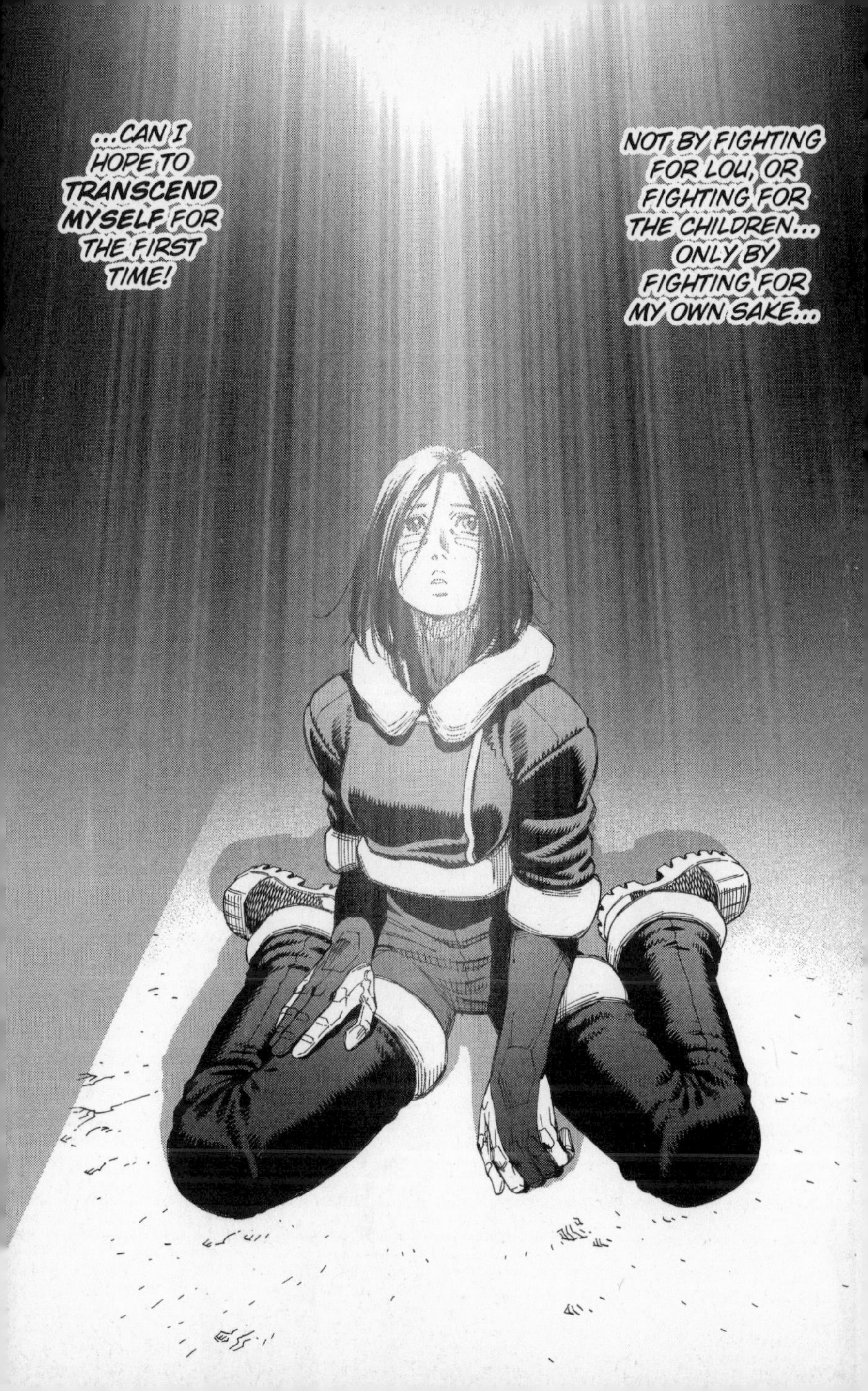
NOT BY FIGHTING FOR LOU, OR FIGHTING FOR THE CHILDREN... ONLY BY FIGHTING FOR MY OWN SAKE...
...CAN I HOPE TO TRANSCEND MYSELF FOR THE FIRST TIME!

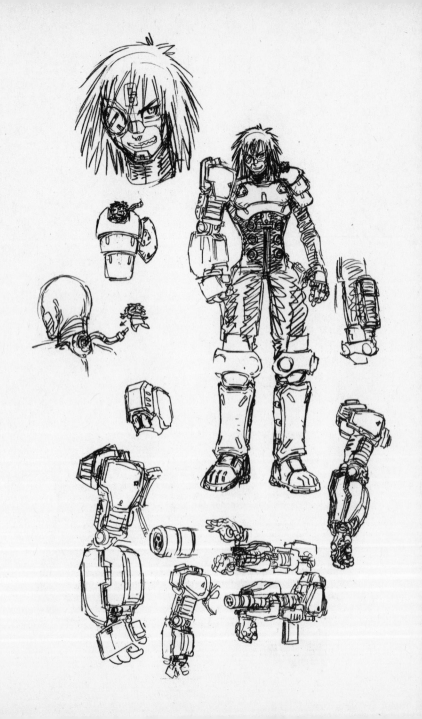

PHASE 31
’Round and ’Round

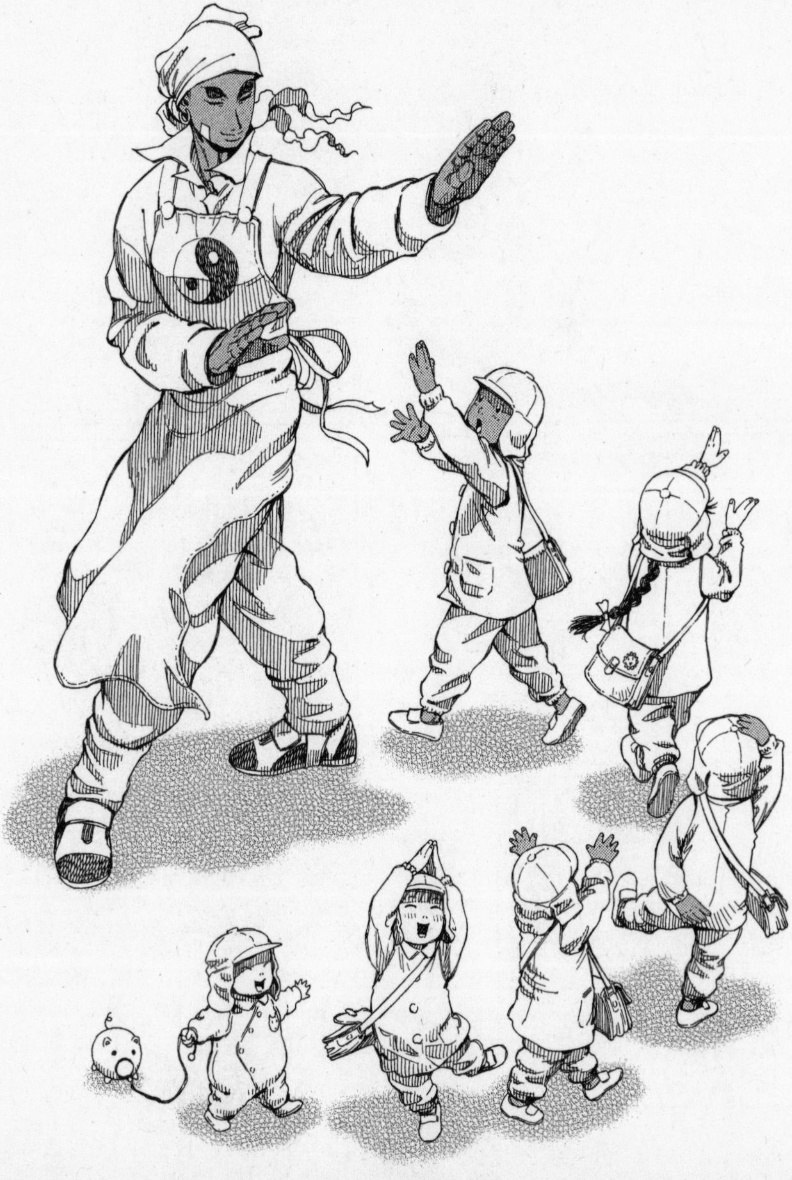

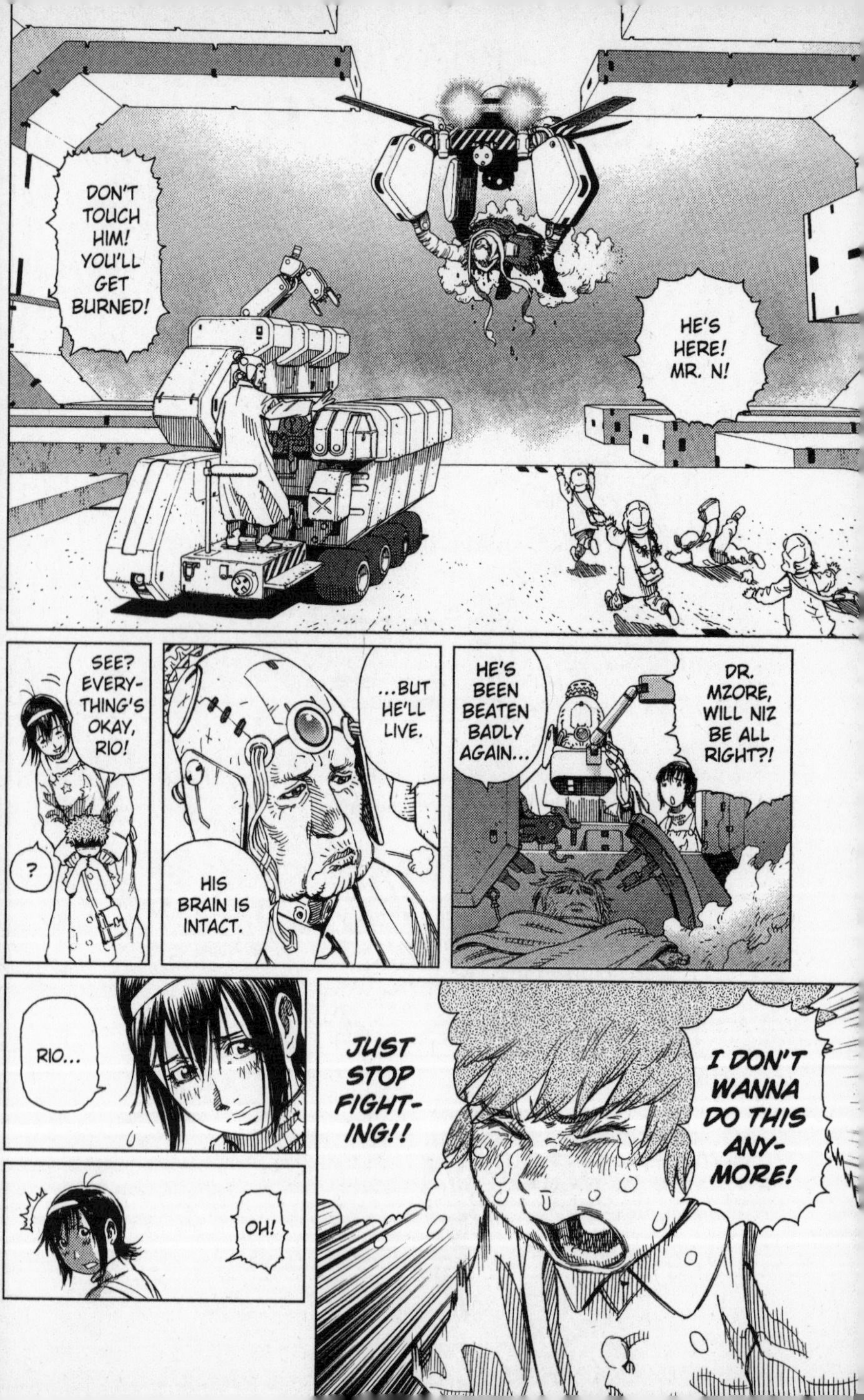
HE'S HERE! MR. N!
DON'T TOUCH HIM! YOU'LL GET BURNED!
DR. MZORE, WILL NIZ BE ALL RIGHT?!
HE'S BEEN BEATEN BADLY AGAIN...
...BUT HE'LL LIVE.
HIS BRAIN IS INTACT.
SEE? EVERY-THING'S OKAY, RIO!
?
I DON'T WANNA DO THIS ANY-MORE!
JUST STOP FIGHT-ING!!
RIO...
OH!

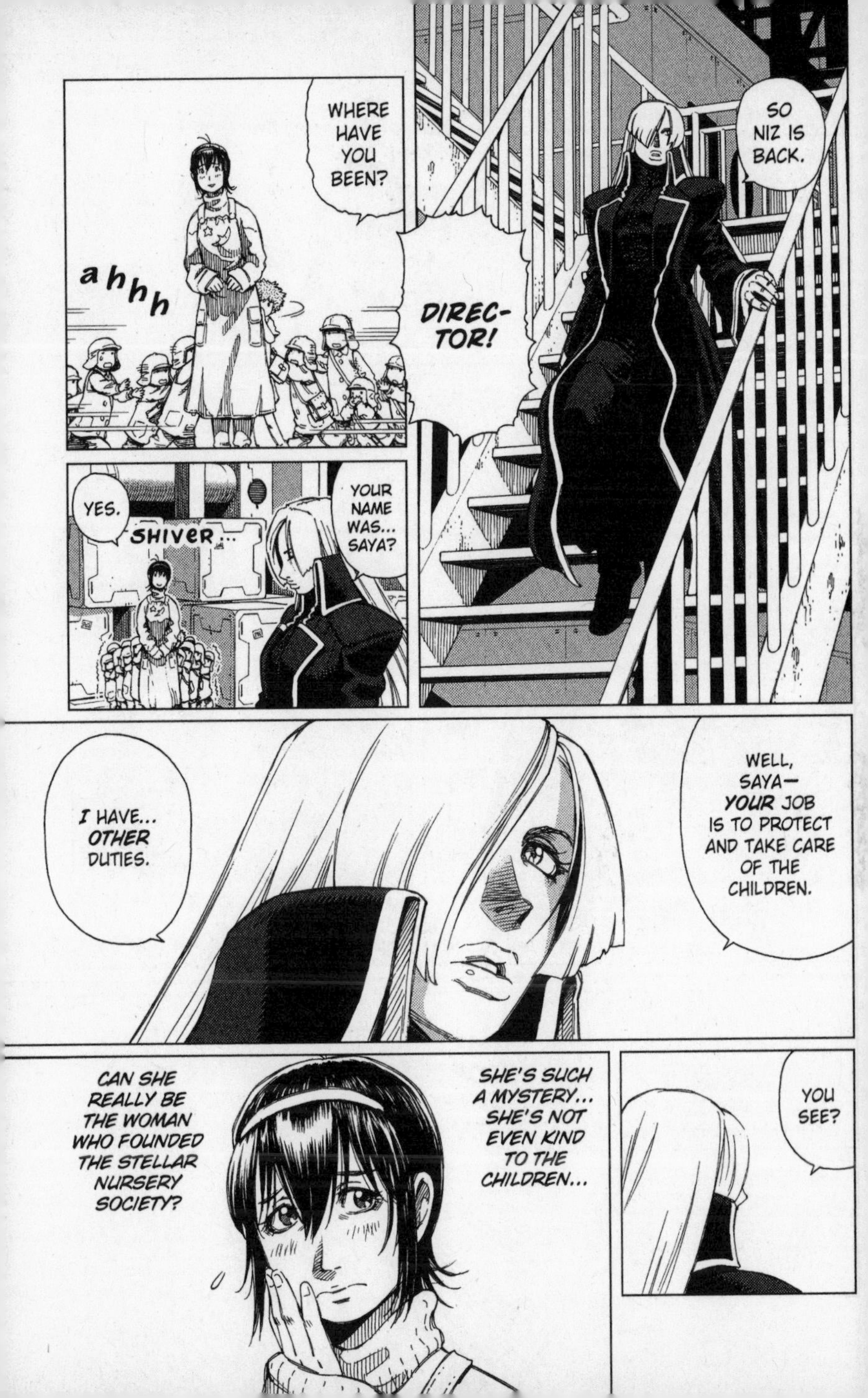
SO NIZ IS BACK.
DIRECTOR!
WHERE HAVE YOU BEEN?
ahhh
YOUR NAME WAS... SAYA?
YES.
SHIVER...
WELL, SAYA— YOUR JOB IS TO PROTECT AND TAKE CARE OF THE CHILDREN.
I HAVE... OTHER DUTIES.
YOU SEE?
SHE'S SUCH A MYSTERY... SHE'S NOT EVEN KIND TO THE CHILDREN...
CAN SHE REALLY BE THE WOMAN WHO FOUNDED THE STELLAR NURSERY SOCIETY?

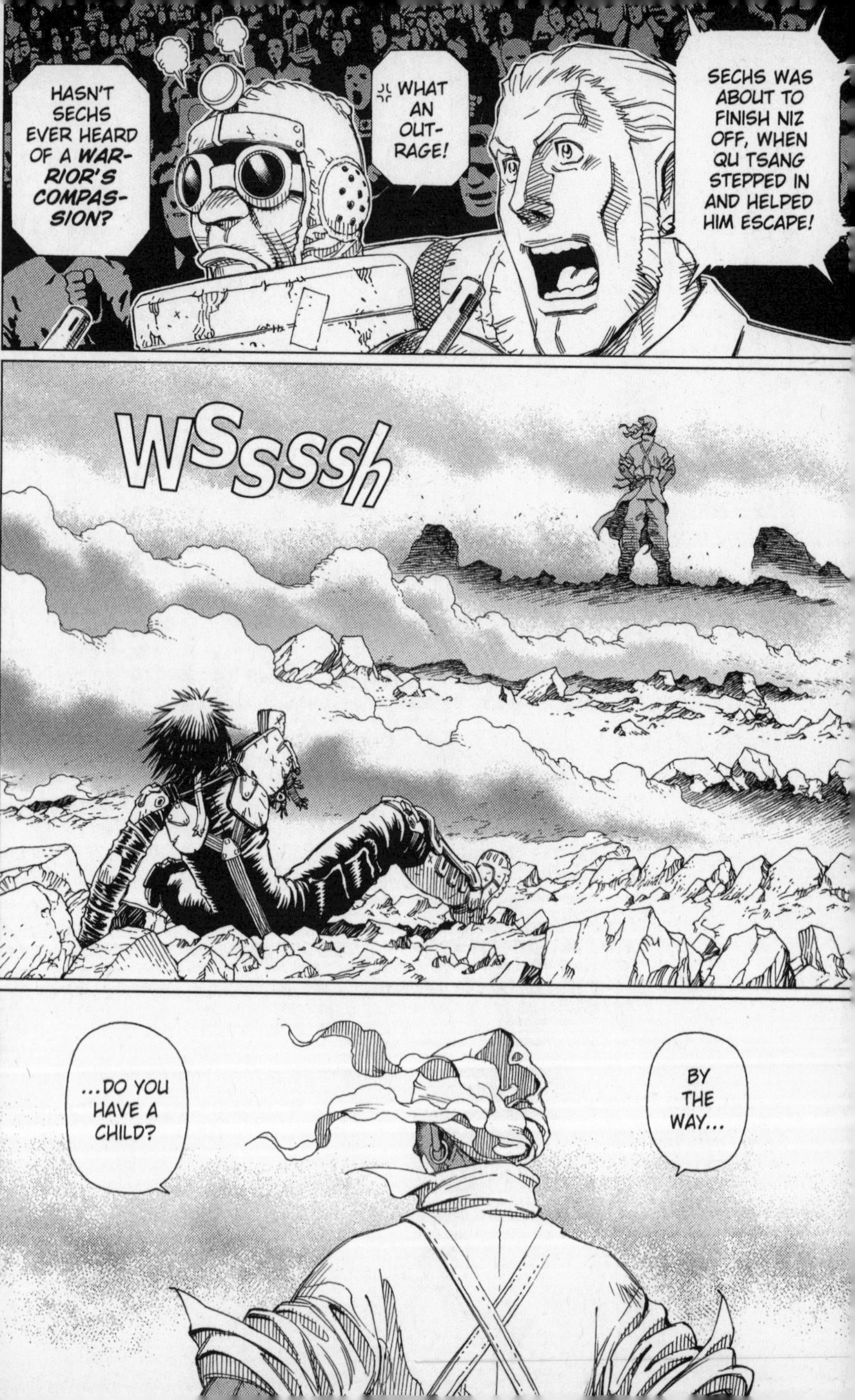
SECHS WAS ABOUT TO FINISH NIZ OFF, WHEN QU TSANG STEPPED IN AND HELPED HIM ESCAPE!
WHAT AN OUT-RAGE!
HASN'T SECHS EVER HEARD OF A *WARRIOR'S* COMPASSION?
WSSSSH
BY THE WAY...
...DO YOU HAVE A CHILD?

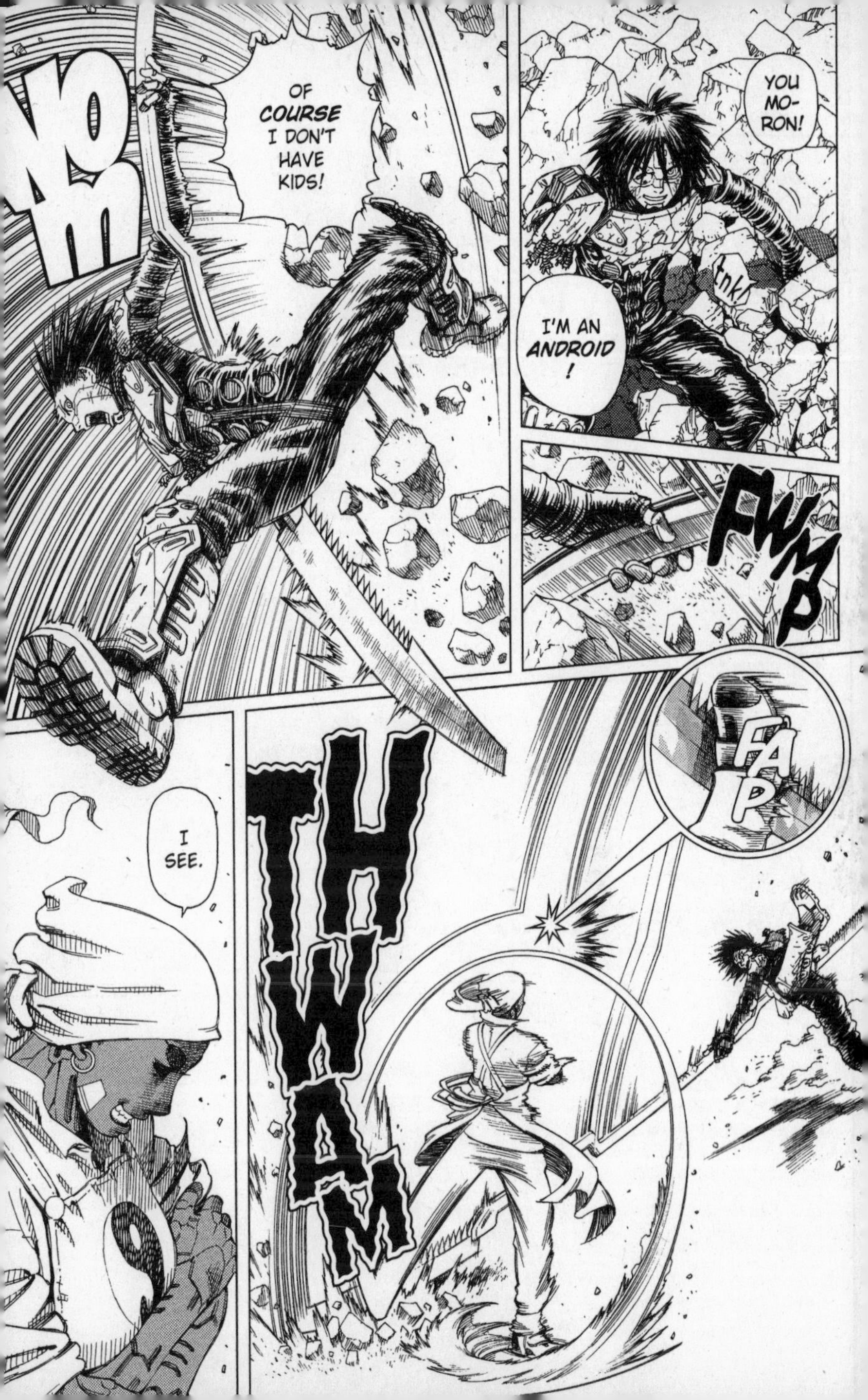
YOU MO-RON!
tnk!
I'M AN ANDROID!
FWMP
OF COURSE I DON'T HAVE KIDS!
FAP
THWAM
I SEE.

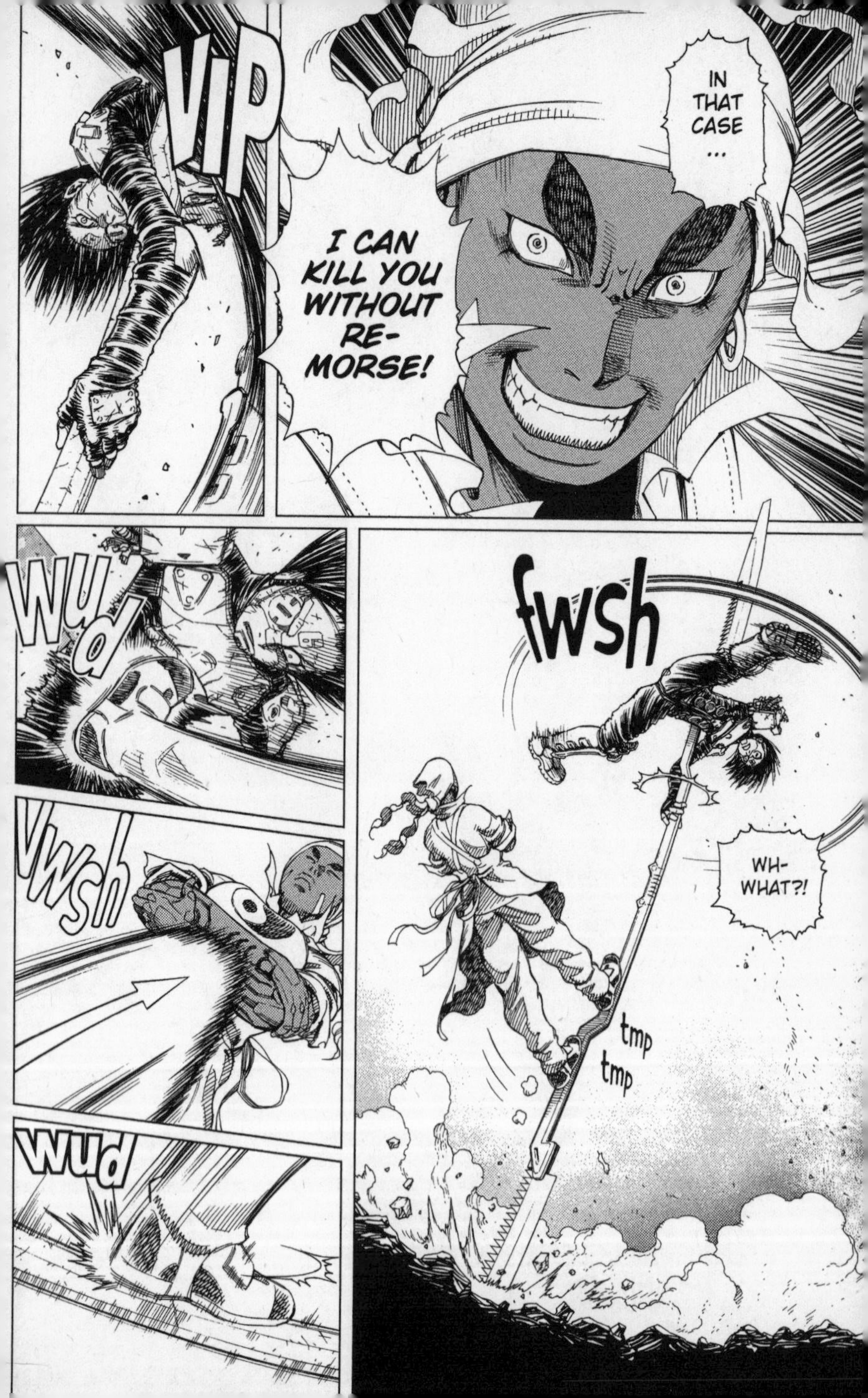
IN THAT CASE ...
I CAN KILL YOU WITHOUT RE-MORSE!
ViP
fwsh
WH-WHAT?!
tmp
tmp
wud
vwsh
wud

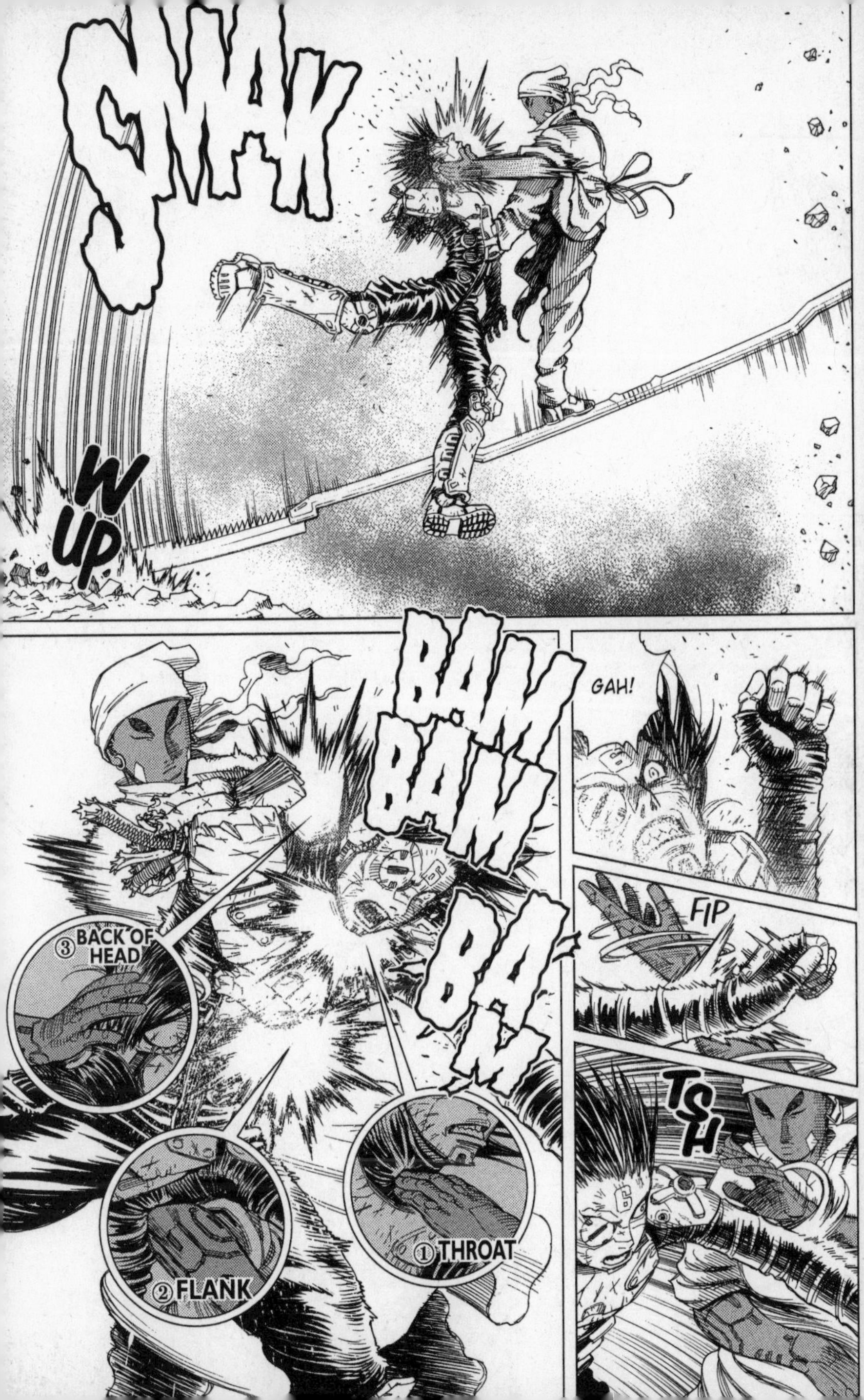
SMAK
WUP
GAH!
FIP
TSH
BAM
BAM
BAM
③ BACK OF HEAD
① THROAT
② FLANK

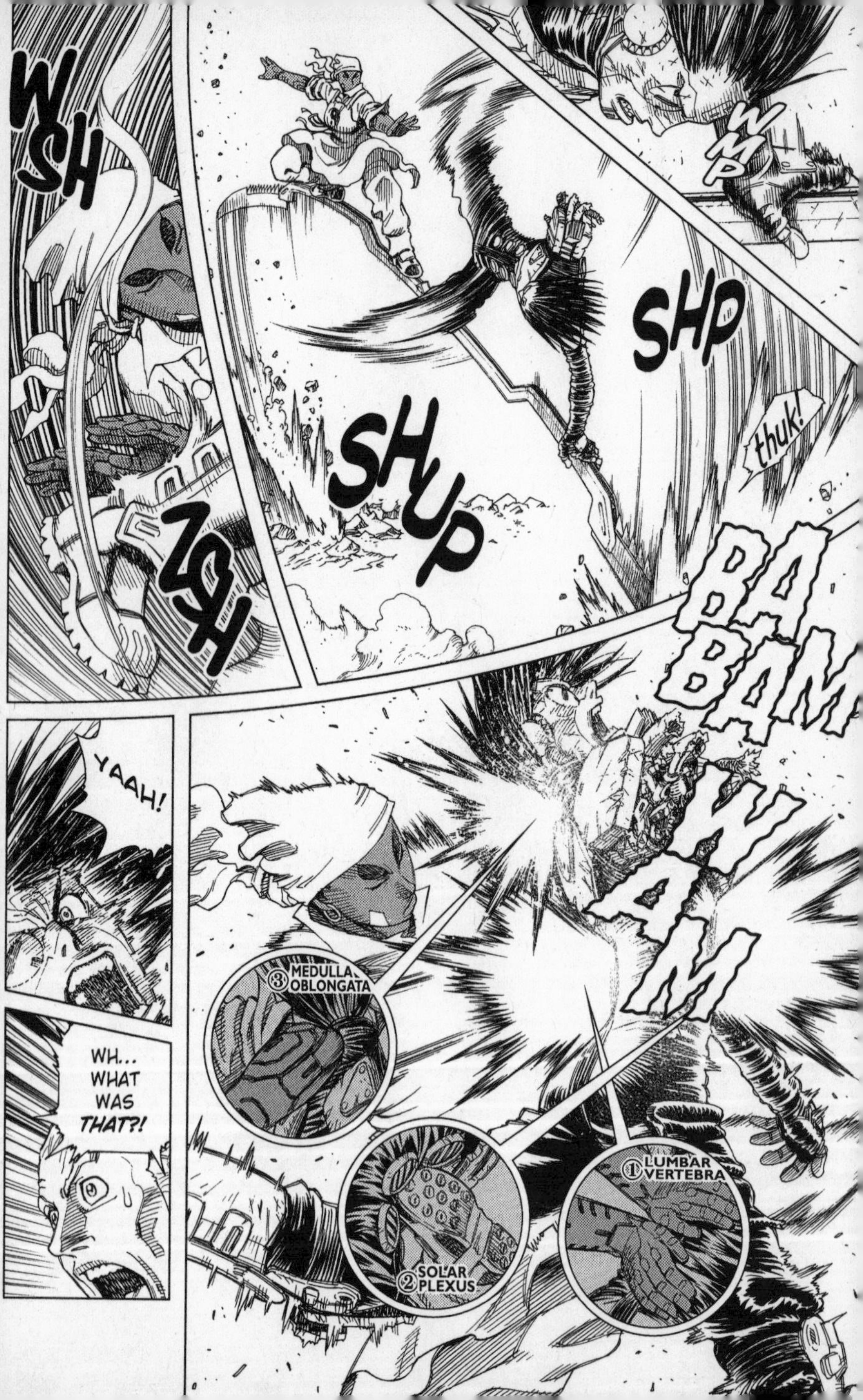
WMP
SHP
thuk!
SHUP
WISH
BA BAM
WHAM
① LUMBAR VERTEBRA
② SOLAR PLEXUS
③ MEDULLA OBLONGATA
YAAH!
WH... WHAT WAS *THAT?!*

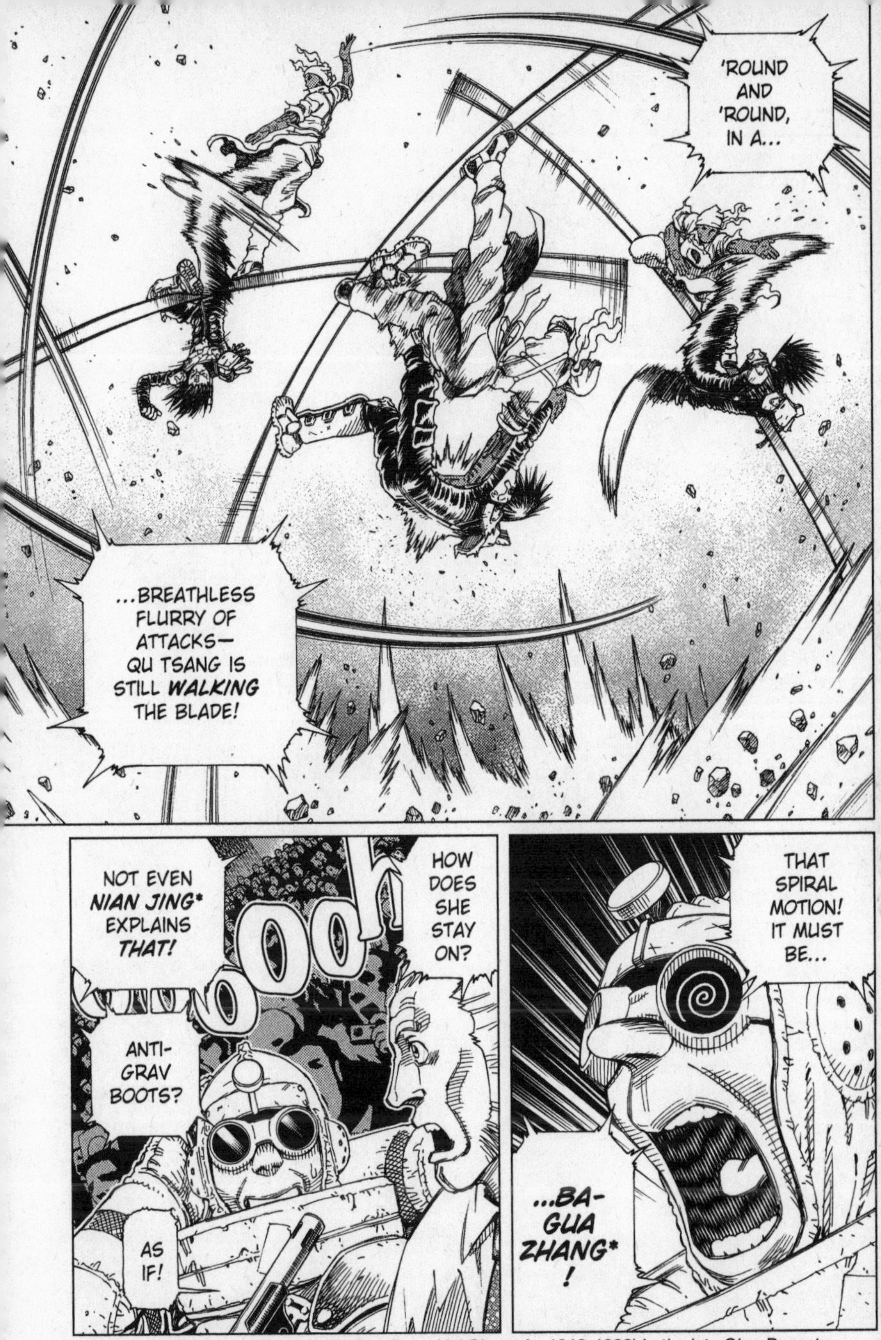
'ROUND AND 'ROUND, IN A...
...BREATHLESS FLURRY OF ATTACKS—QU TSANG IS STILL *WALKING* THE BLADE!
THAT SPIRAL MOTION! IT MUST BE...
...BA-GUA ZHANG*!
HOW DOES SHE STAY ON?
NOT EVEN *NIAN JING** EXPLAINS *THAT!*
ANTI-GRAV BOOTS?
AS IF!

***Bagua zhang:** *A martial art created by Dong Hai Chuan (c. 1813-1882) in the late Qing Dynasty.*
***Nian jing:** *A way to counter an enemy's attacks by maintaining bodily contact in battle. By moving with the flow of the opponent's movements, power can be deflected and controlled.*

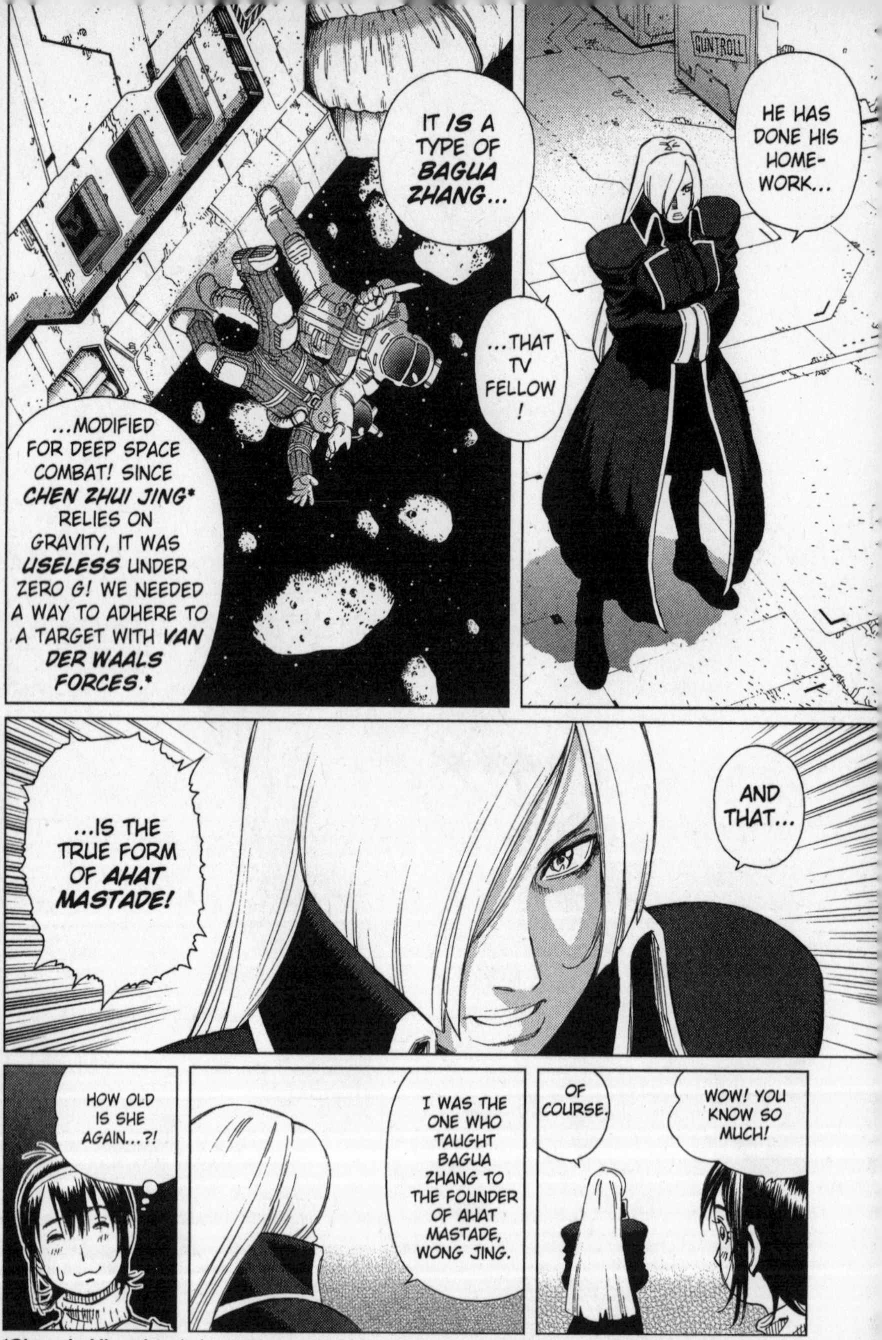
HE HAS DONE HIS HOMEWORK...
...THAT TV FELLOW!
IT IS A TYPE OF BAGUA ZHANG...
...MODIFIED FOR DEEP SPACE COMBAT! SINCE CHEN ZHUI JING* RELIES ON GRAVITY, IT WAS USELESS UNDER ZERO G! WE NEEDED A WAY TO ADHERE TO A TARGET WITH VAN DER WAALS FORCES.*
AND THAT...
...IS THE TRUE FORM OF AHAT MASTADE!
WOW! YOU KNOW SO MUCH!
OF COURSE.
I WAS THE ONE WHO TAUGHT BAGUA ZHANG TO THE FOUNDER OF AHAT MASTADE, WONG JING.
HOW OLD IS SHE AGAIN...?!

Chen zhui jing: *A technique to increase the force of a blow by dropping one's center of gravity. Though the term is Chinese, all combat sports developed on Earth include this principle.*

Van der Waals force: *The force between atoms. It's thought that geckos use this force to climb walls.*

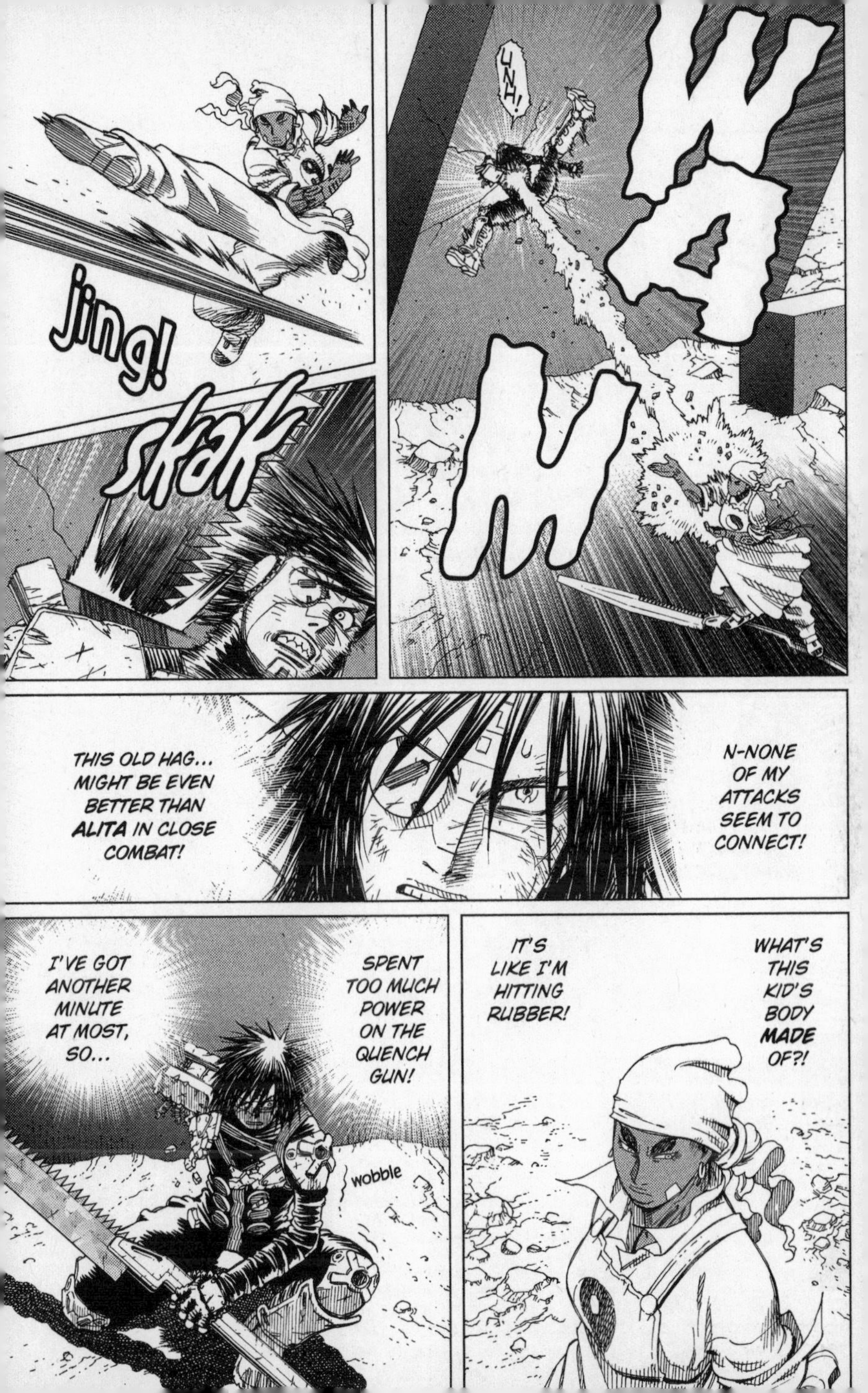
UNH!
WAM
jing!
skak
N-NONE OF MY ATTACKS SEEM TO CONNECT!
THIS OLD HAG... MIGHT BE EVEN BETTER THAN ALITA IN CLOSE COMBAT!
WHAT'S THIS KID'S BODY MADE OF?!
IT'S LIKE I'M HITTING RUBBER!
SPENT TOO MUCH POWER ON THE QUENCH GUN!
I'VE GOT ANOTHER MINUTE AT MOST, SO...
wobble

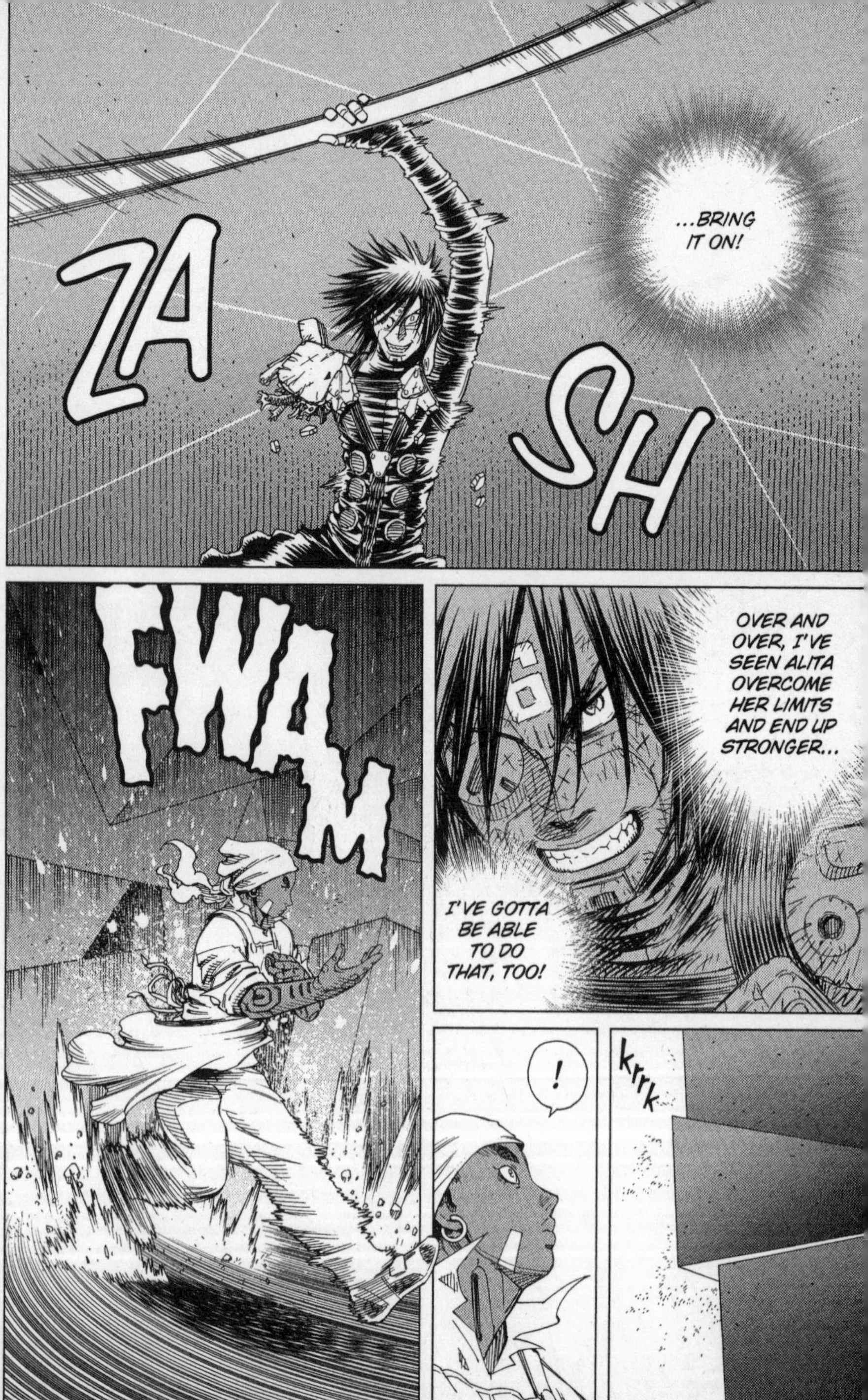
...BRING IT ON!
ZASH
OVER AND OVER, I'VE SEEN ALITA OVERCOME HER LIMITS AND END UP STRONGER...
I'VE GOTTA BE ABLE TO DO THAT, TOO!
krrk
!
FWAM

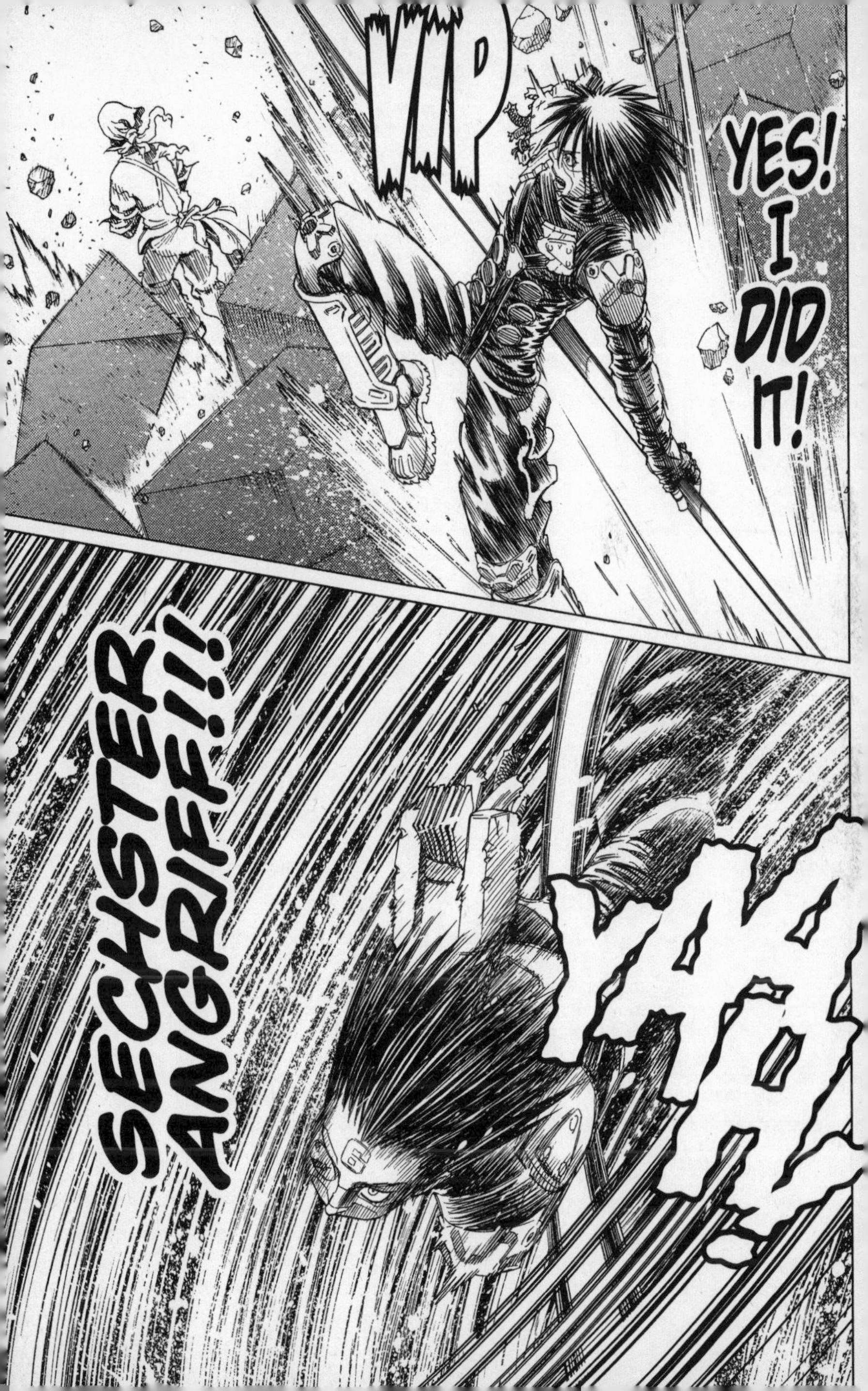
VAP
YES! I DID IT!
YAH!
SECHSTER ANGRIFF!!!

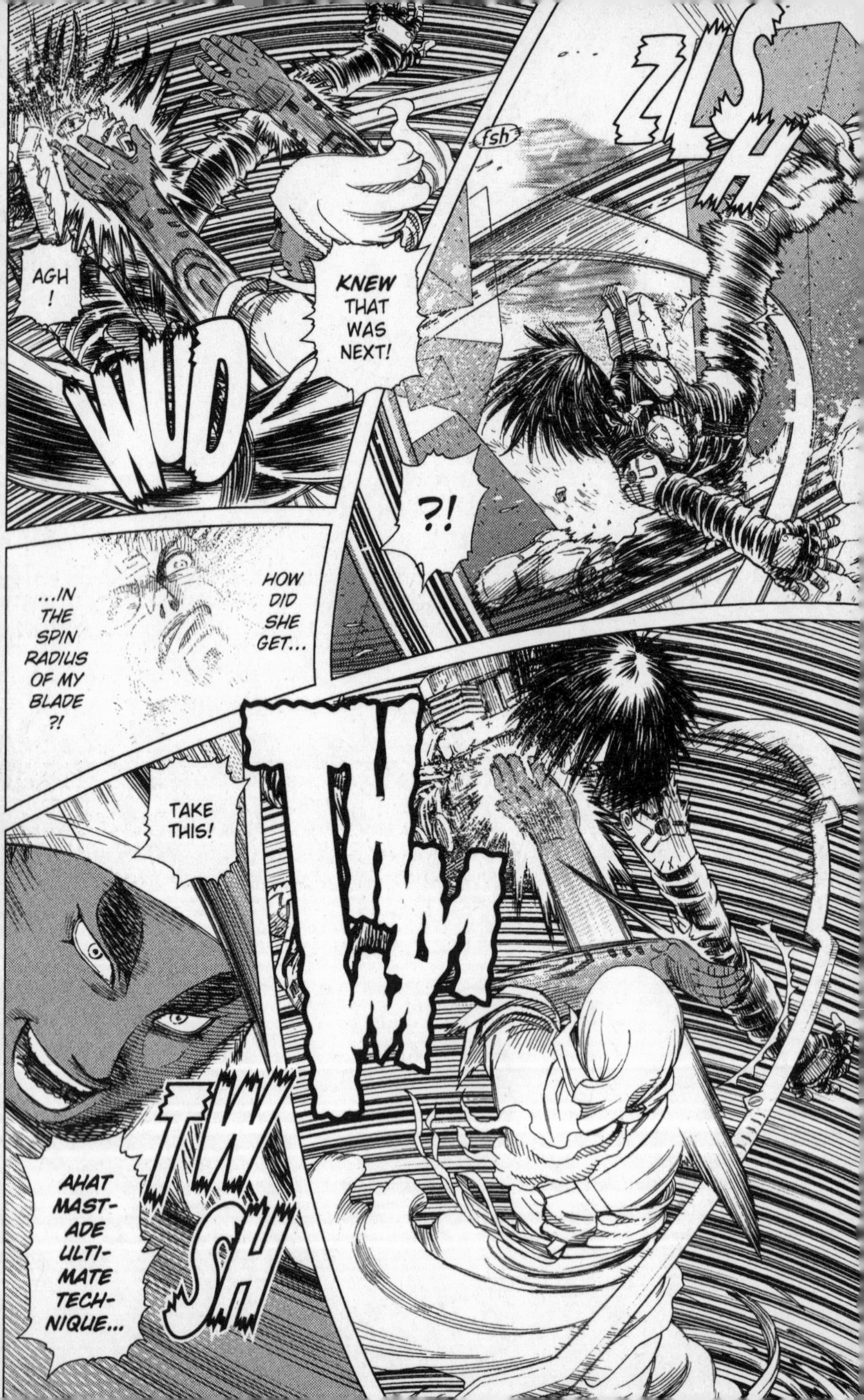
ZLSH
fsh
?!
KNEW THAT WAS NEXT!
AGH!
WUD
HOW DID SHE GET...
...IN THE SPIN RADIUS OF MY BLADE ?!
THM
TAKE THIS!
THSH
AHAT MAST-ADE ULTI-MATE TECH-NIQUE...

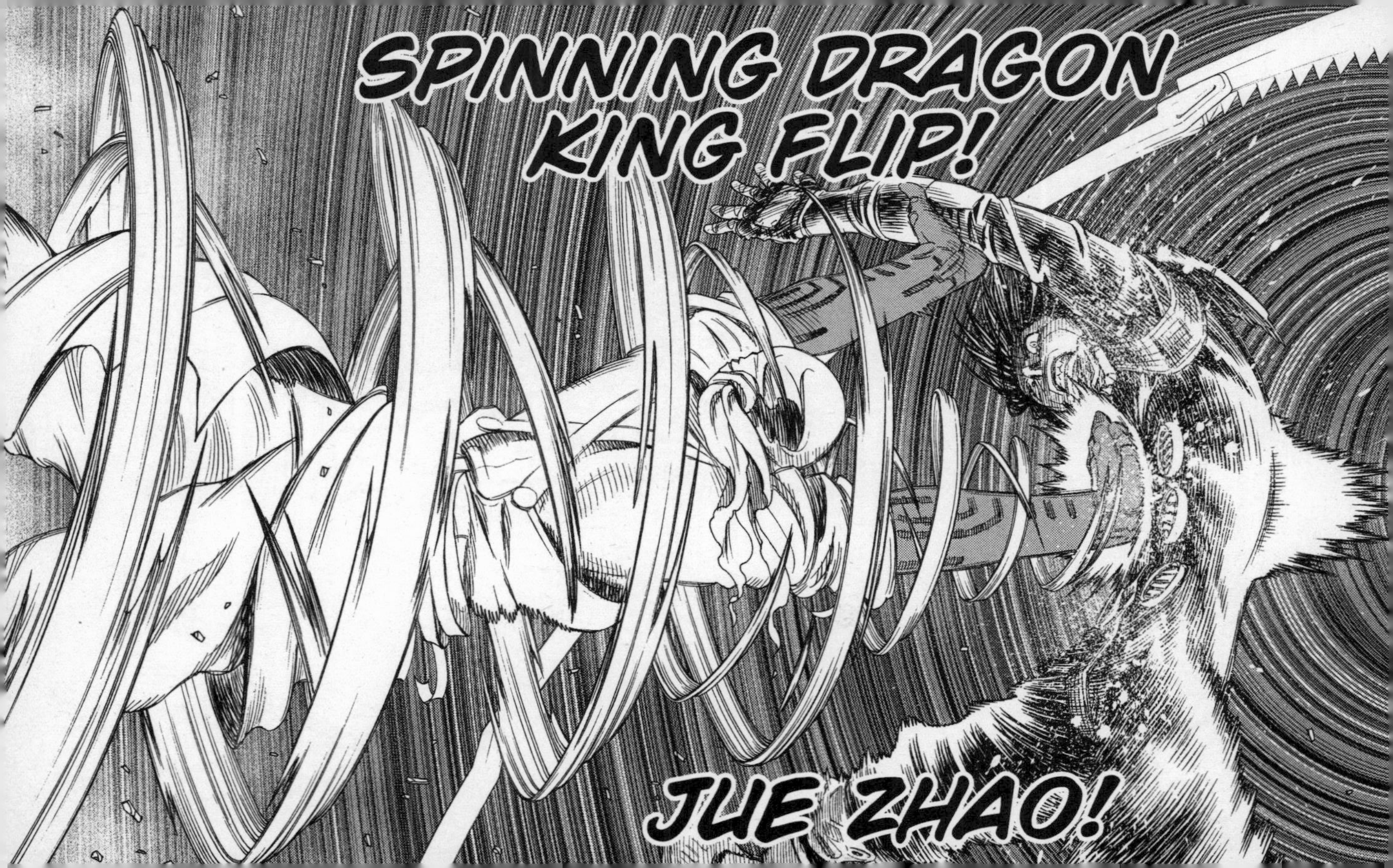
SPINNING DRAGON
KING FLIP!
JUE ZHAO!

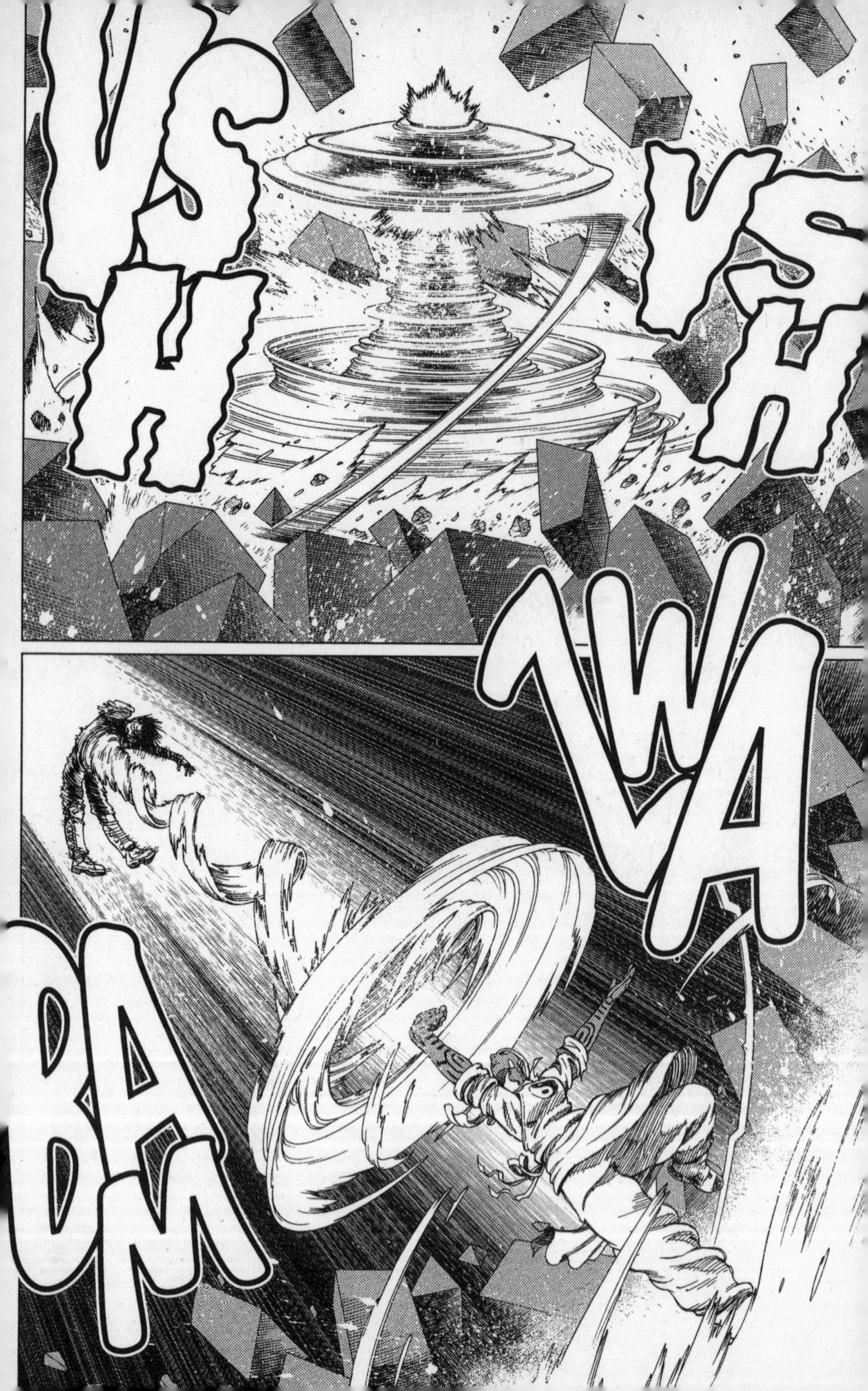
VSH
VSH
WA
BA

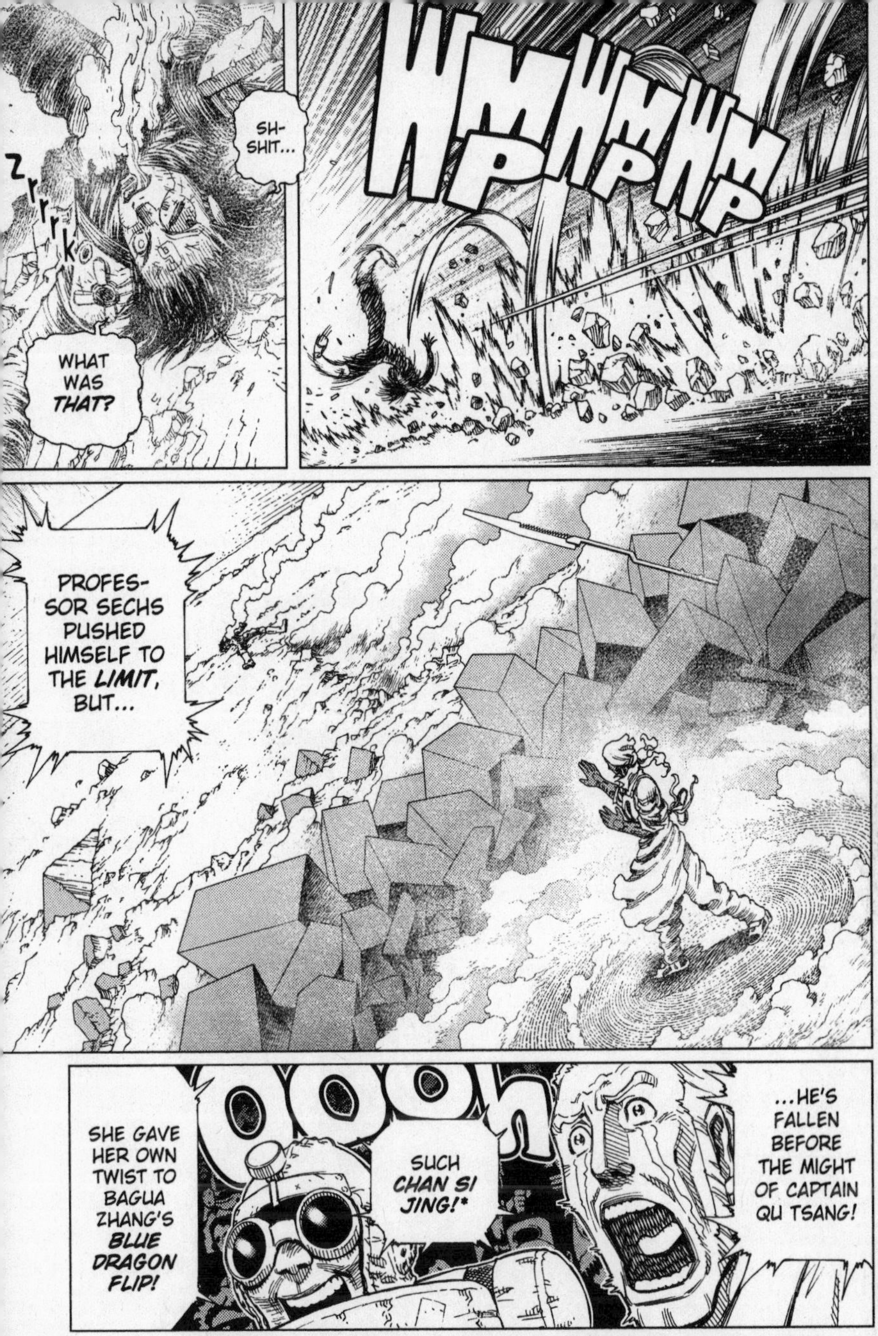

Zrrrrk
SH-SHIT...
WHAT WAS THAT?
PROFESSOR SECHS PUSHED HIMSELF TO THE LIMIT, BUT...
...HE'S FALLEN BEFORE THE MIGHT OF CAPTAIN QU TSANG!
Oooh
SUCH CHAN SI JING!*
SHE GAVE HER OWN TWIST TO BAGUA ZHANG'S BLUE DRAGON FLIP!

***Chan si jing:** A method to increase momentum by twisting or spinning the body. Mainly used to reinforce a strike, it can also be applied in Bagua Zhang for defense.*

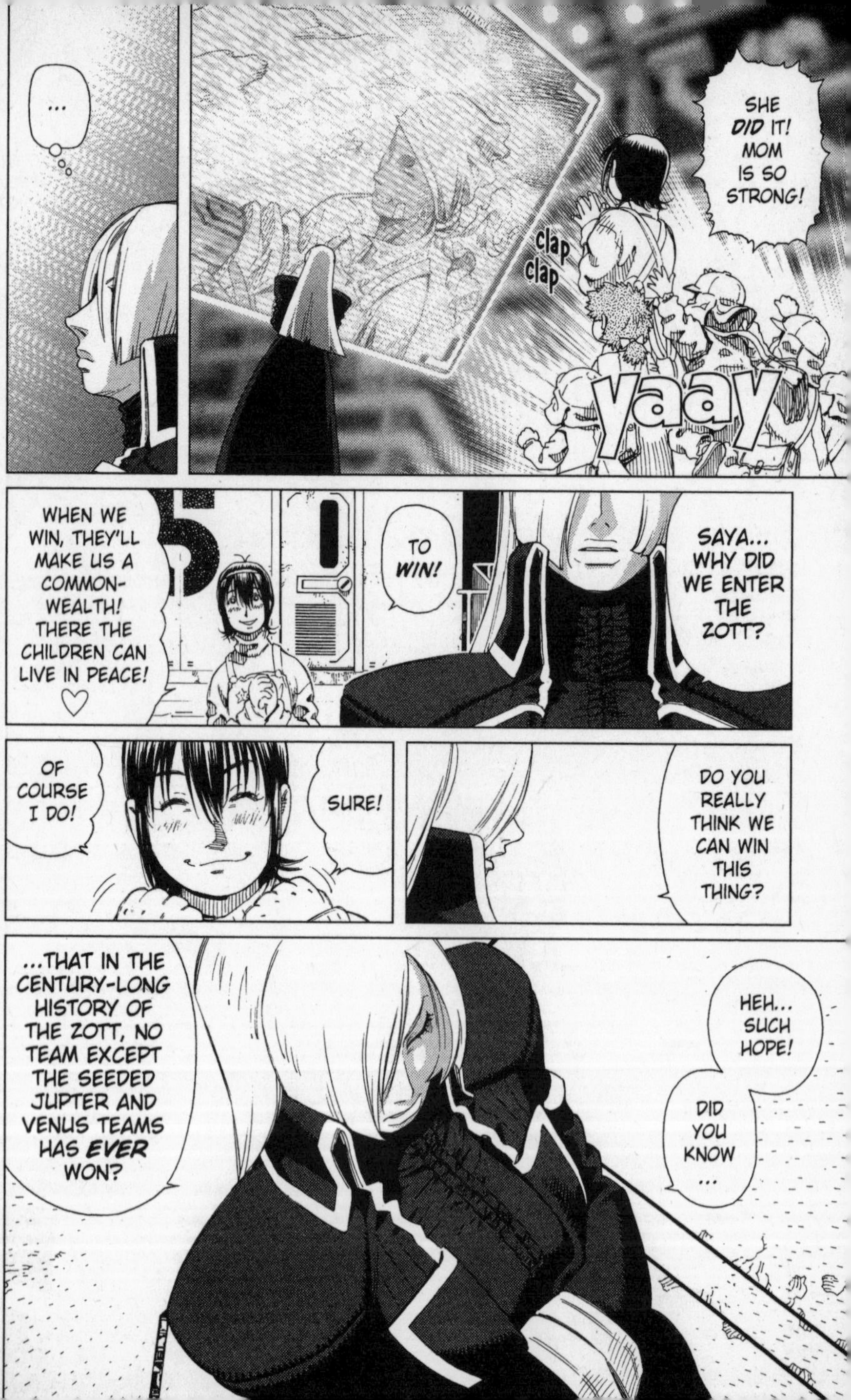
SHE *DID* IT! MOM IS SO STRONG!
clap clap
yaay
...
SAYA... WHY DID WE ENTER THE ZOTT?
TO *WIN!*
WHEN WE WIN, THEY'LL MAKE US A COMMON-WEALTH! THERE THE CHILDREN CAN LIVE IN PEACE! ♡
DO YOU REALLY THINK WE CAN WIN THIS THING?
SURE!
OF COURSE I DO!
HEH... SUCH HOPE!
DID YOU KNOW ...
...THAT IN THE CENTURY-LONG HISTORY OF THE ZOTT, NO TEAM EXCEPT THE SEEDED JUPTER AND VENUS TEAMS HAS *EVER* WON?

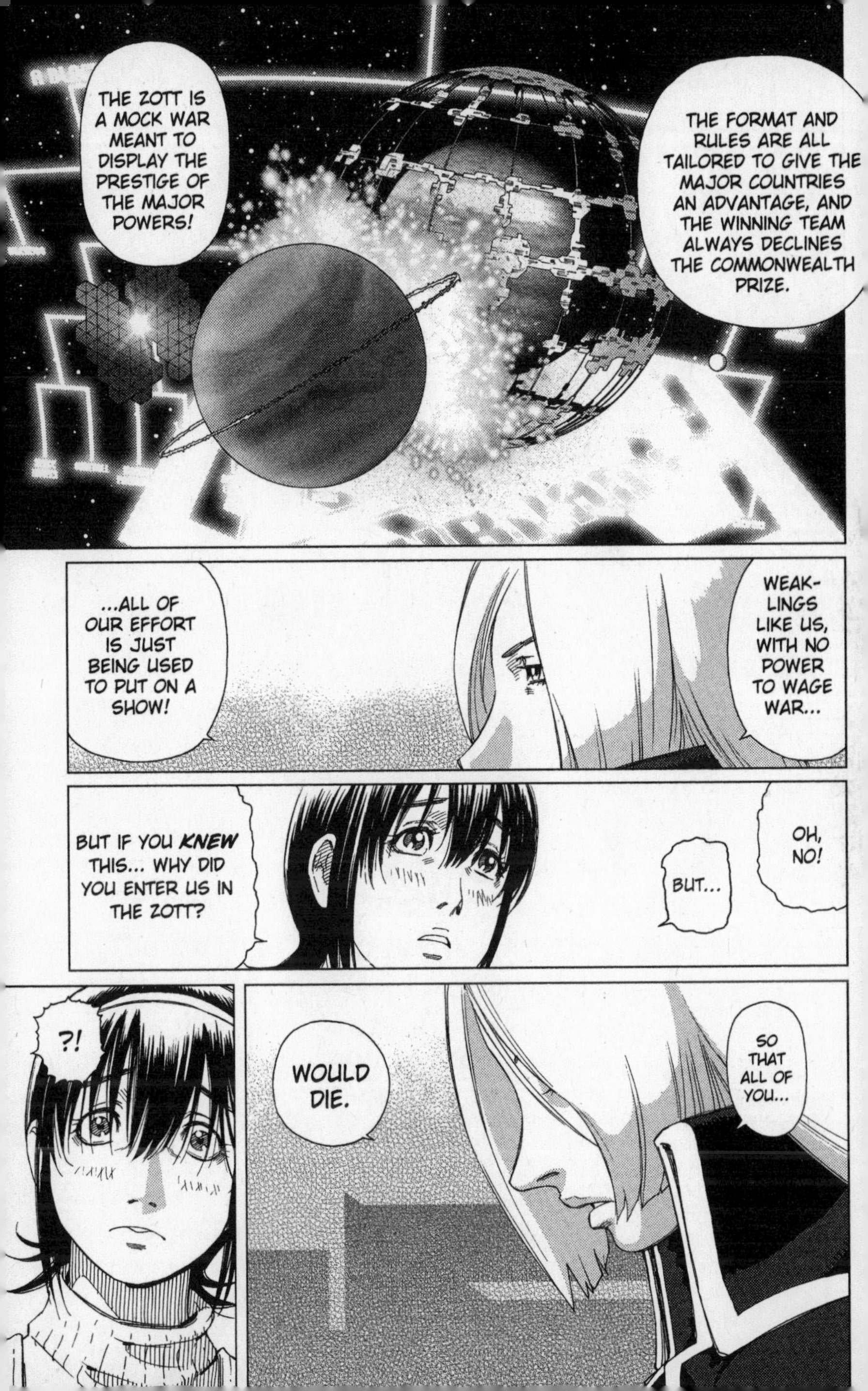
THE ZOTT IS A MOCK WAR MEANT TO DISPLAY THE PRESTIGE OF THE MAJOR POWERS!
THE FORMAT AND RULES ARE ALL TAILORED TO GIVE THE MAJOR COUNTRIES AN ADVANTAGE, AND THE WINNING TEAM ALWAYS DECLINES THE COMMONWEALTH PRIZE.
WEAK-LINGS LIKE US, WITH NO POWER TO WAGE WAR...
...ALL OF OUR EFFORT IS JUST BEING USED TO PUT ON A SHOW!
OH, NO!
BUT...
BUT IF YOU *KNEW* THIS... WHY DID YOU ENTER US IN THE ZOTT?
SO THAT ALL OF YOU...
WOULD DIE.
?!

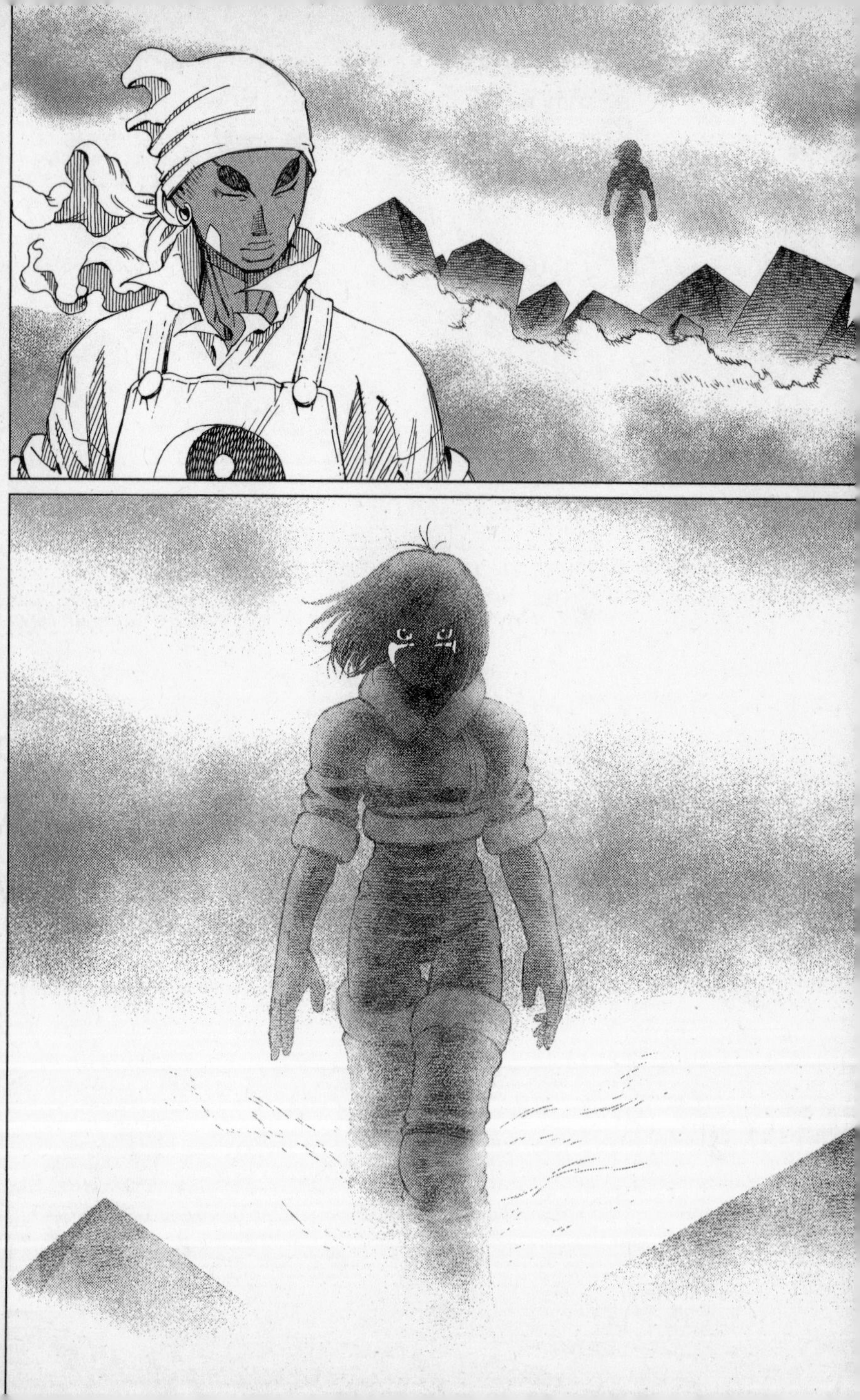

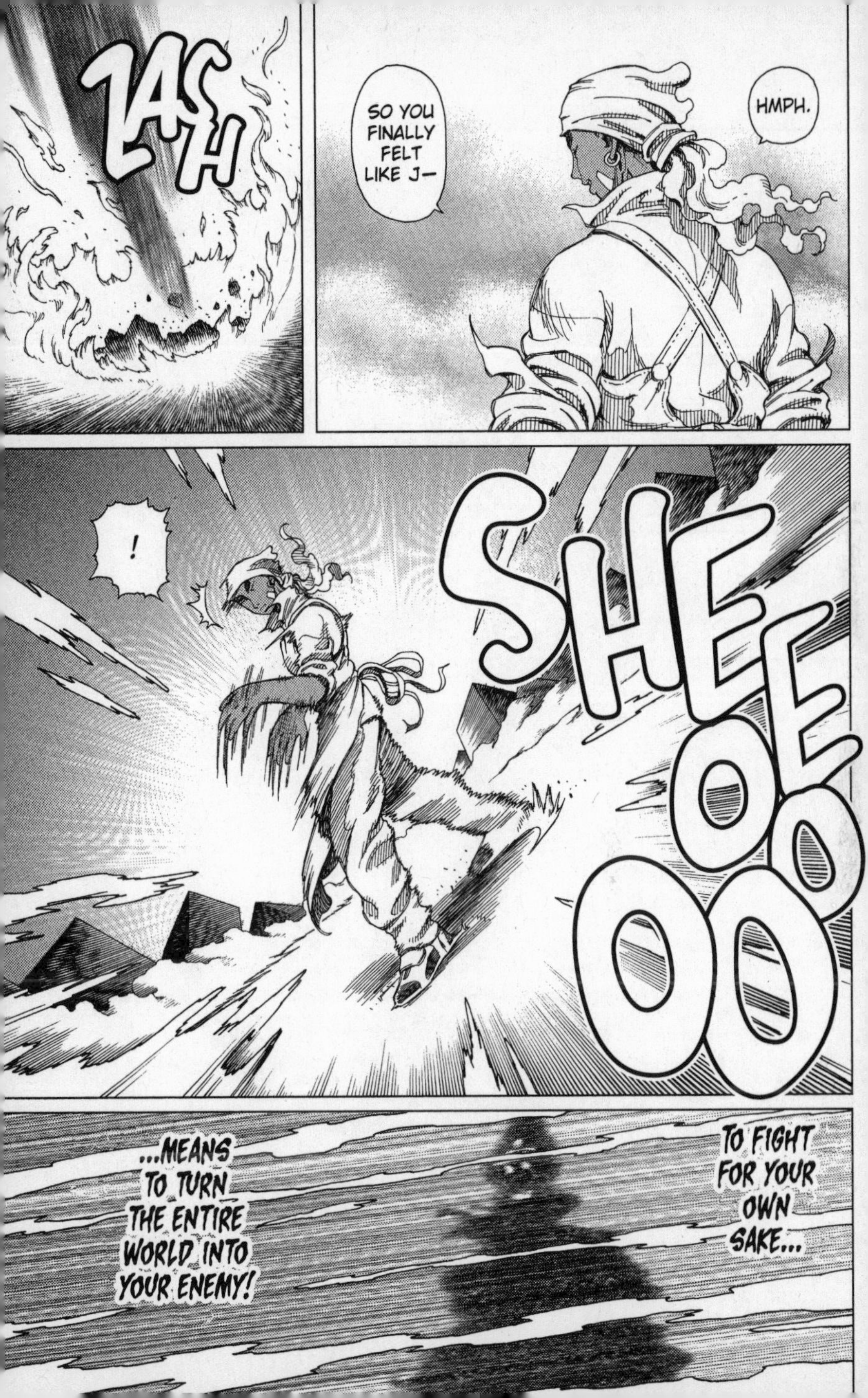
HMPH.
SO YOU FINALLY FELT LIKE J—
ZASH
SHEOOOO
!
TO FIGHT FOR YOUR OWN SAKE...
...MEANS TO TURN THE ENTIRE WORLD INTO YOUR ENEMY!

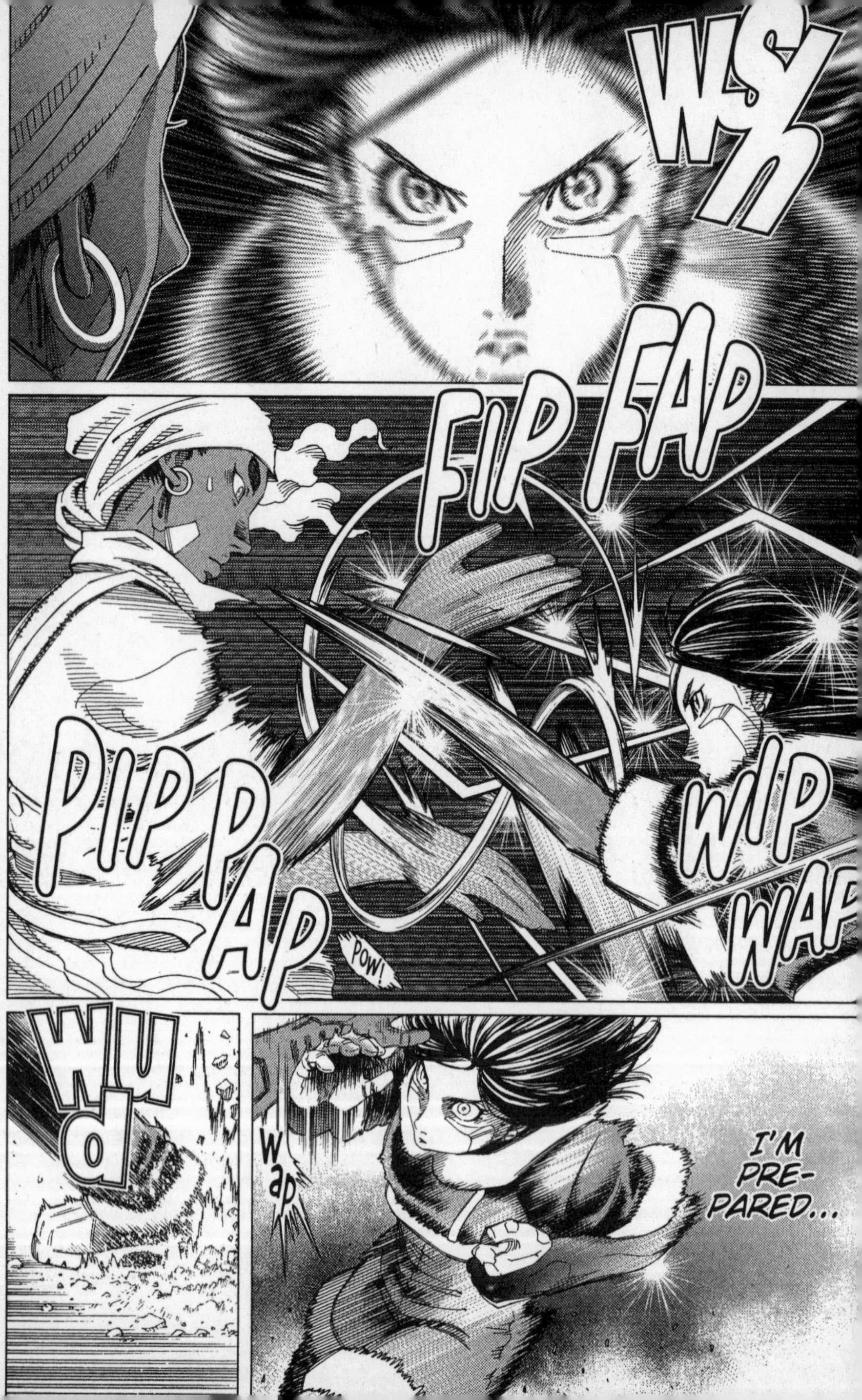
WSH
FIP FAP
WIP WAP
PIP PAP
POW!
I'M PRE-PARED...
WAP
WUD

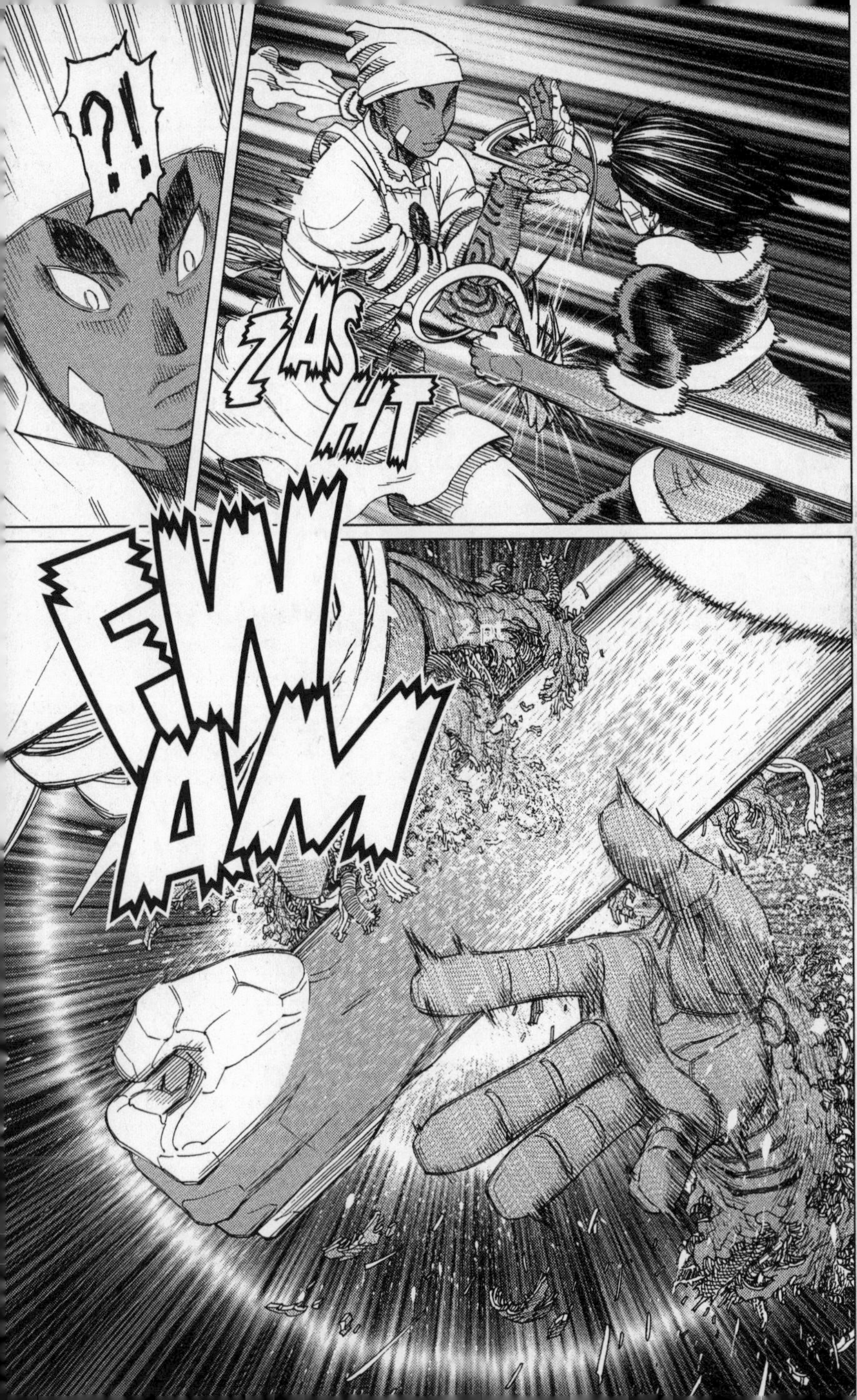
ZASHT
?!
FWAM

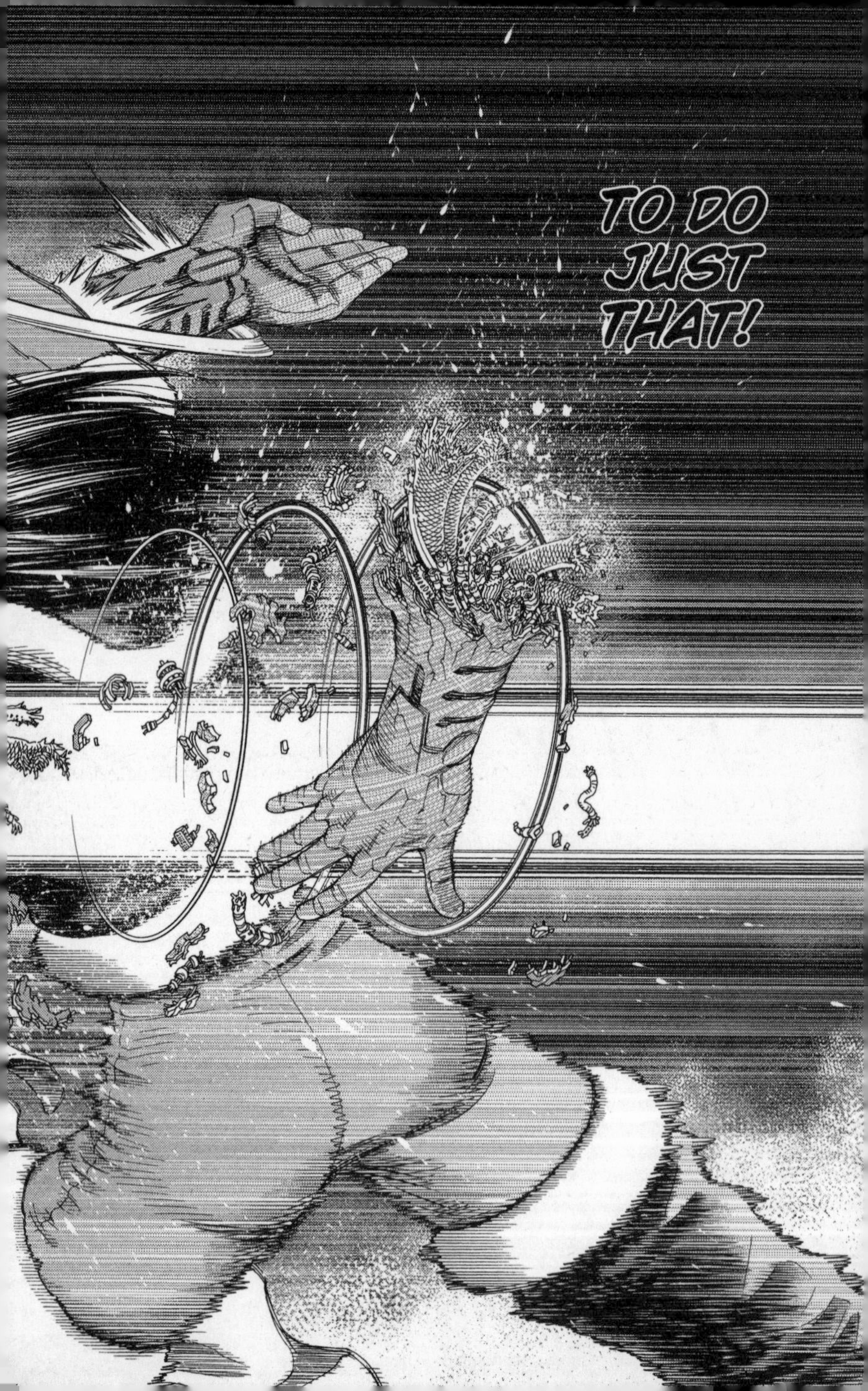
TO DO JUST THAT!

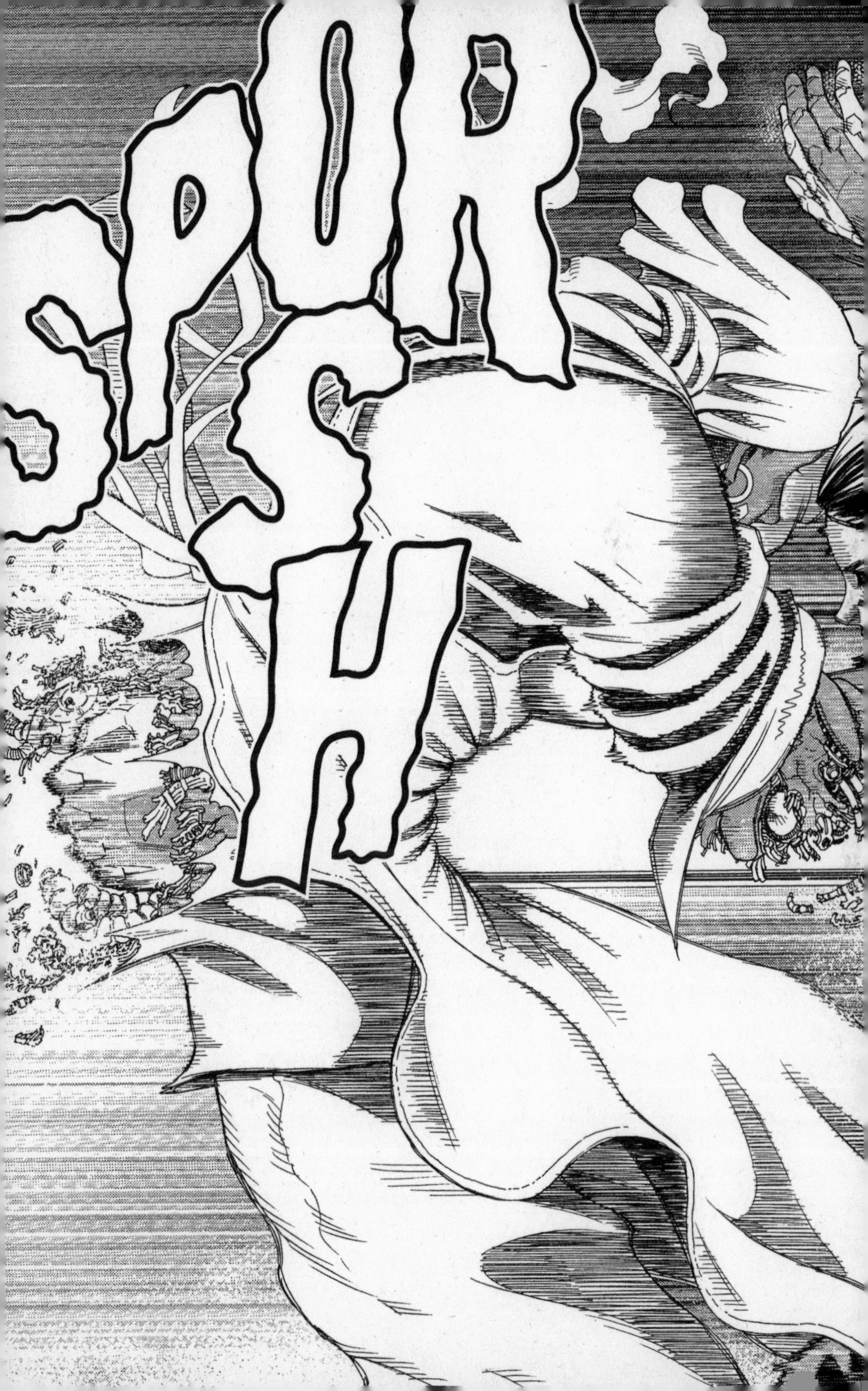
SPURCH

PHASE 32: Not Yet

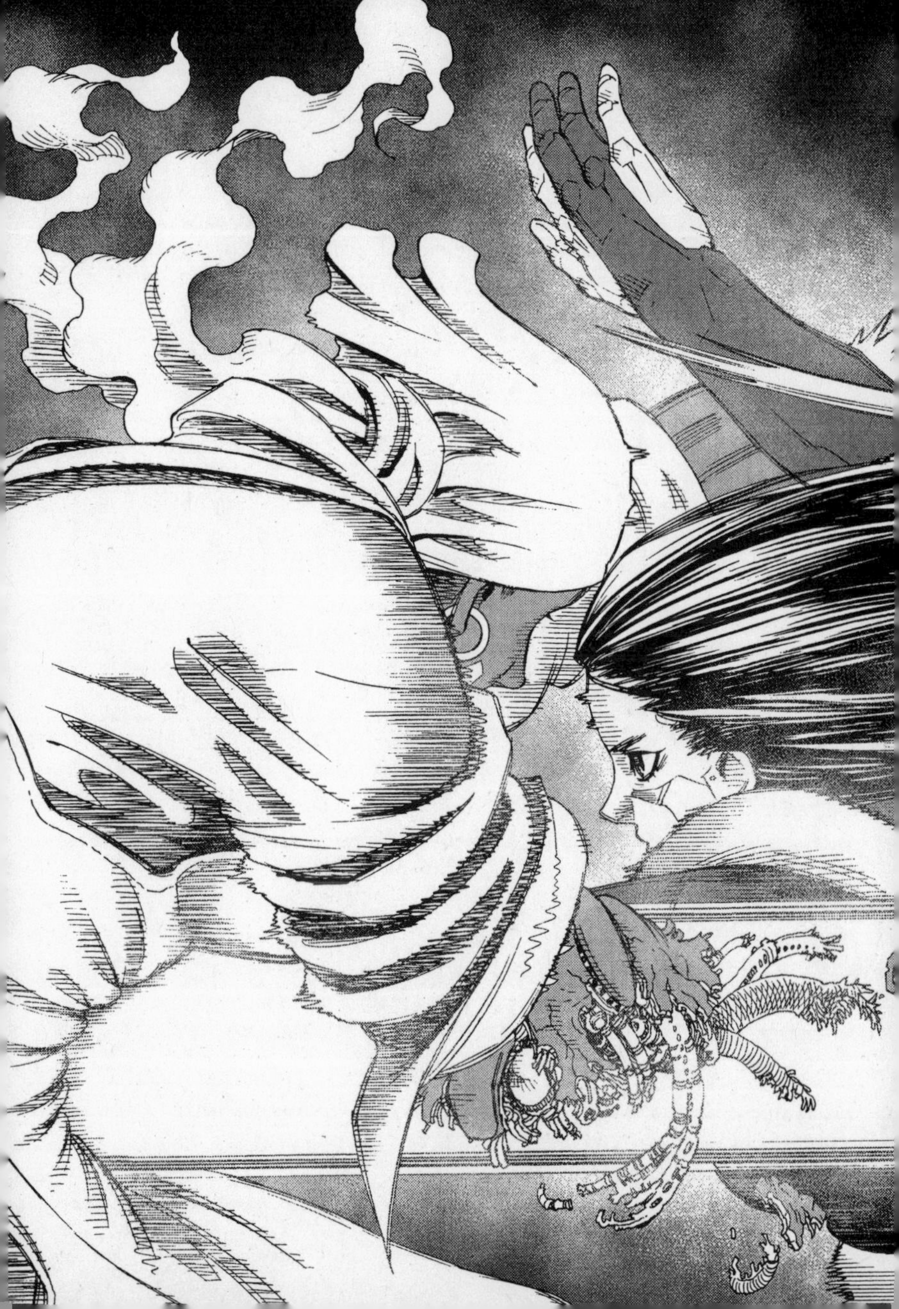

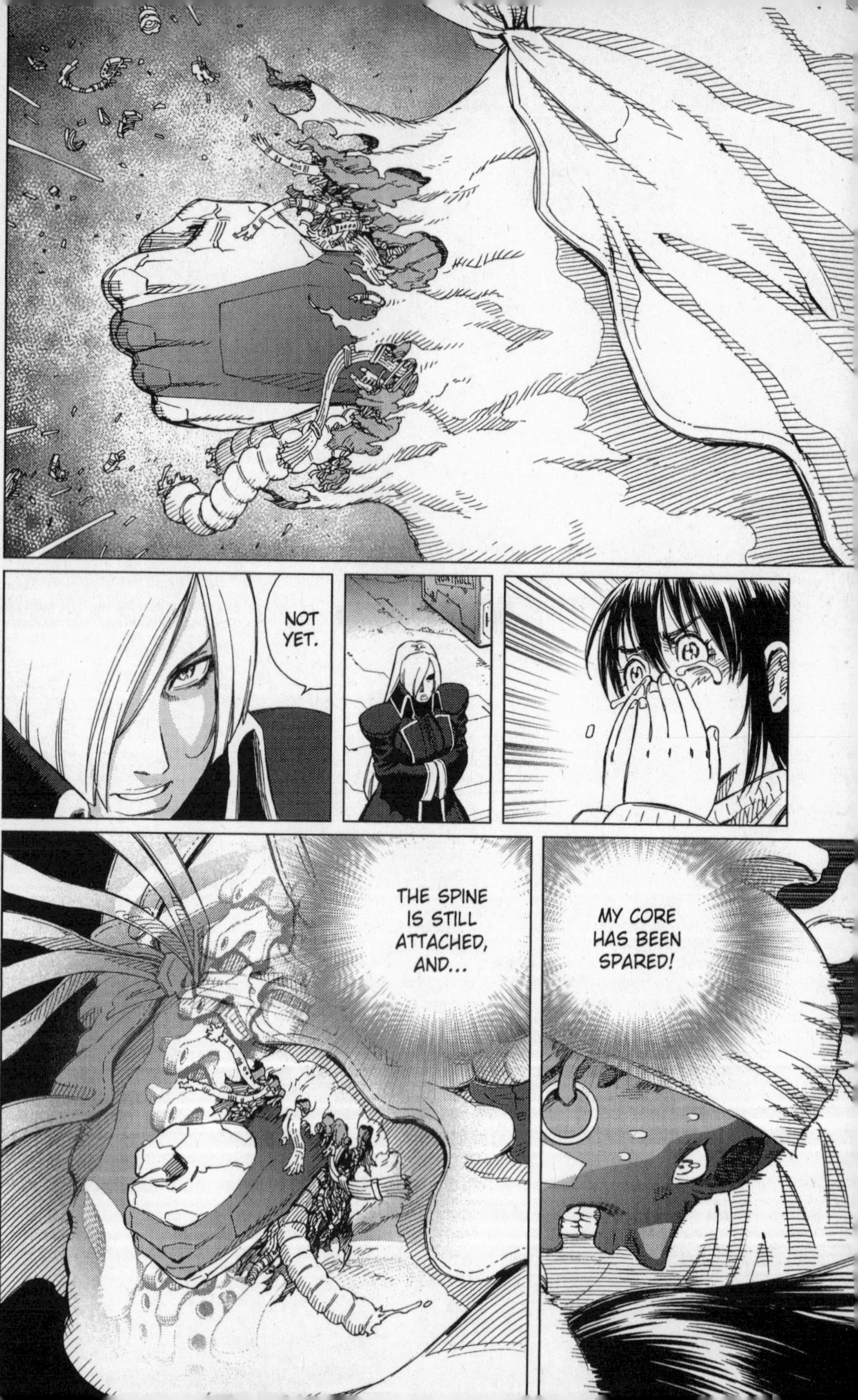
NOT YET.
MY CORE HAS BEEN SPARED!
THE SPINE IS STILL ATTACHED, AND...

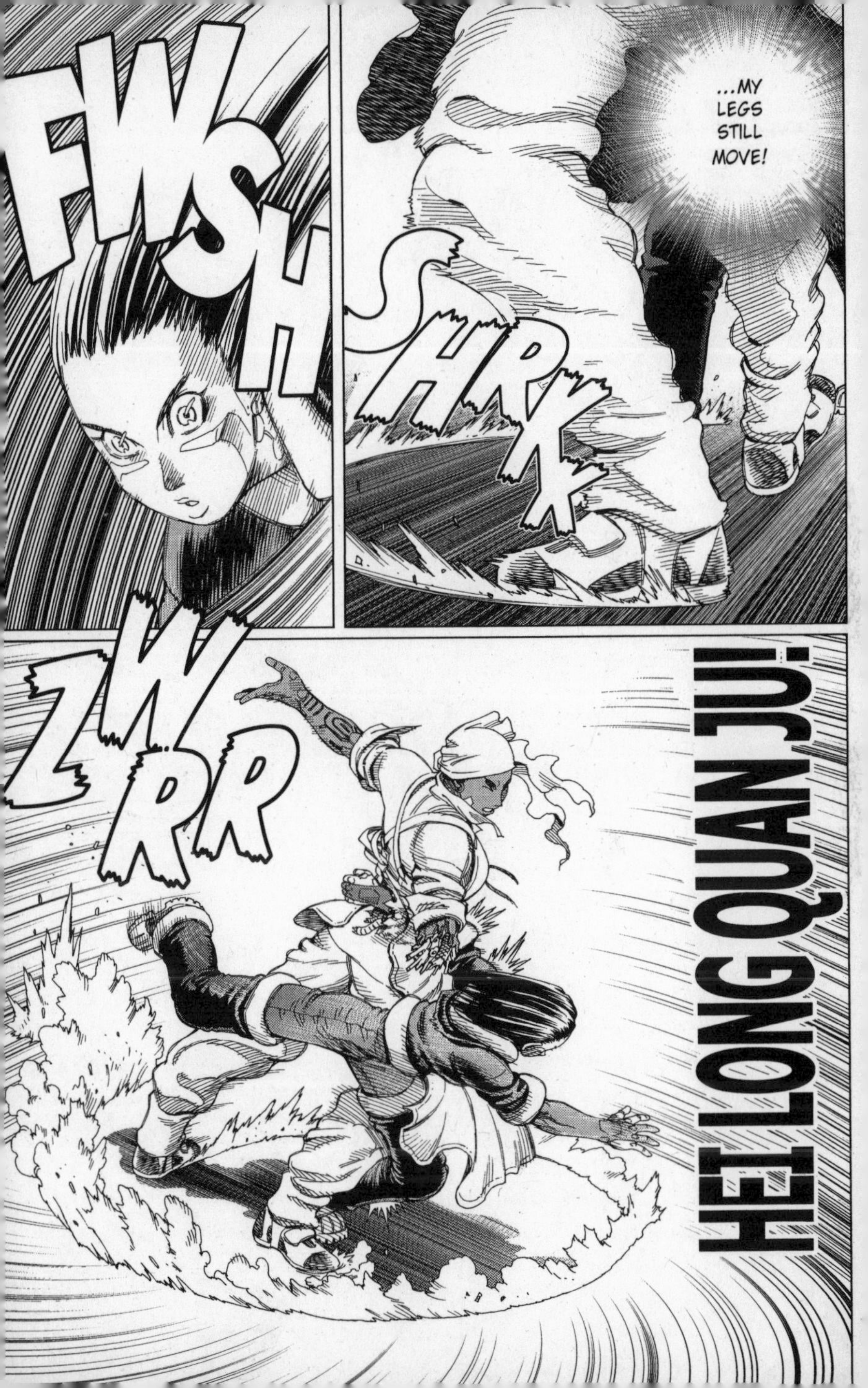
...MY LEGS STILL MOVE!
SHRK
FWSH
HEI LONG QUAN JU!
ZWRR

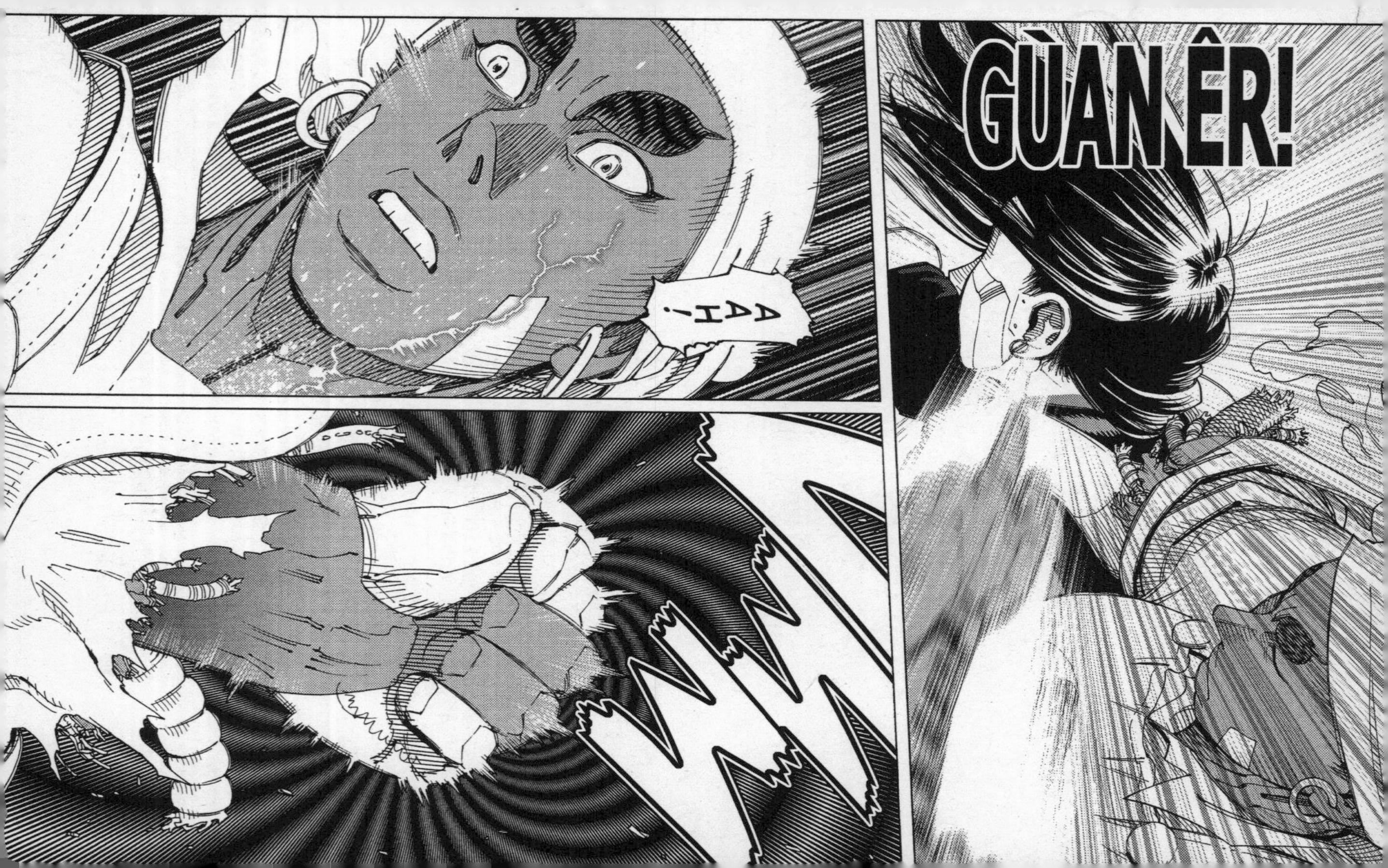
GÙAN ÊR!
AAH!

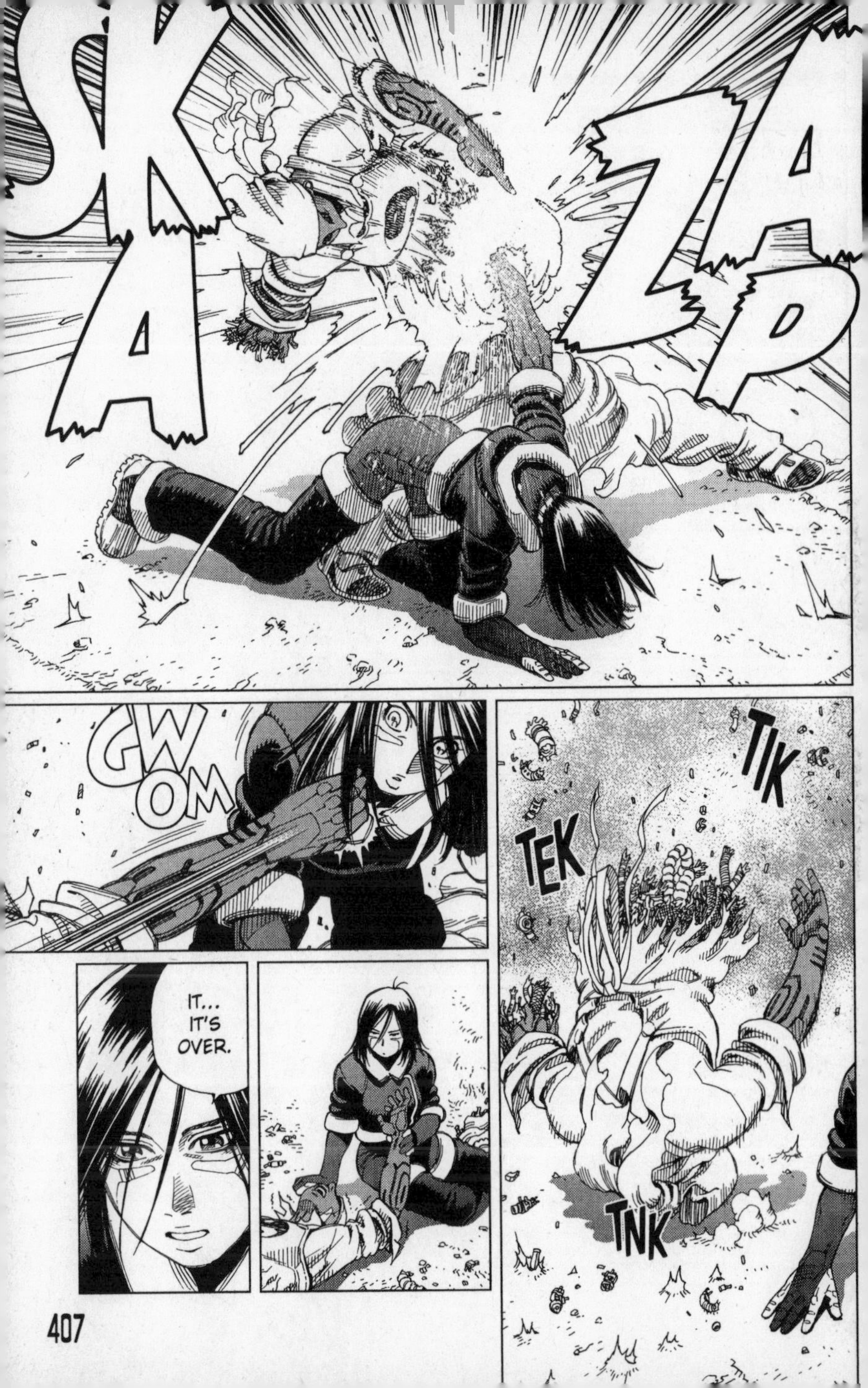
SKAZAP
TIK
TEK
TNK
GWOM
IT... IT'S OVER.

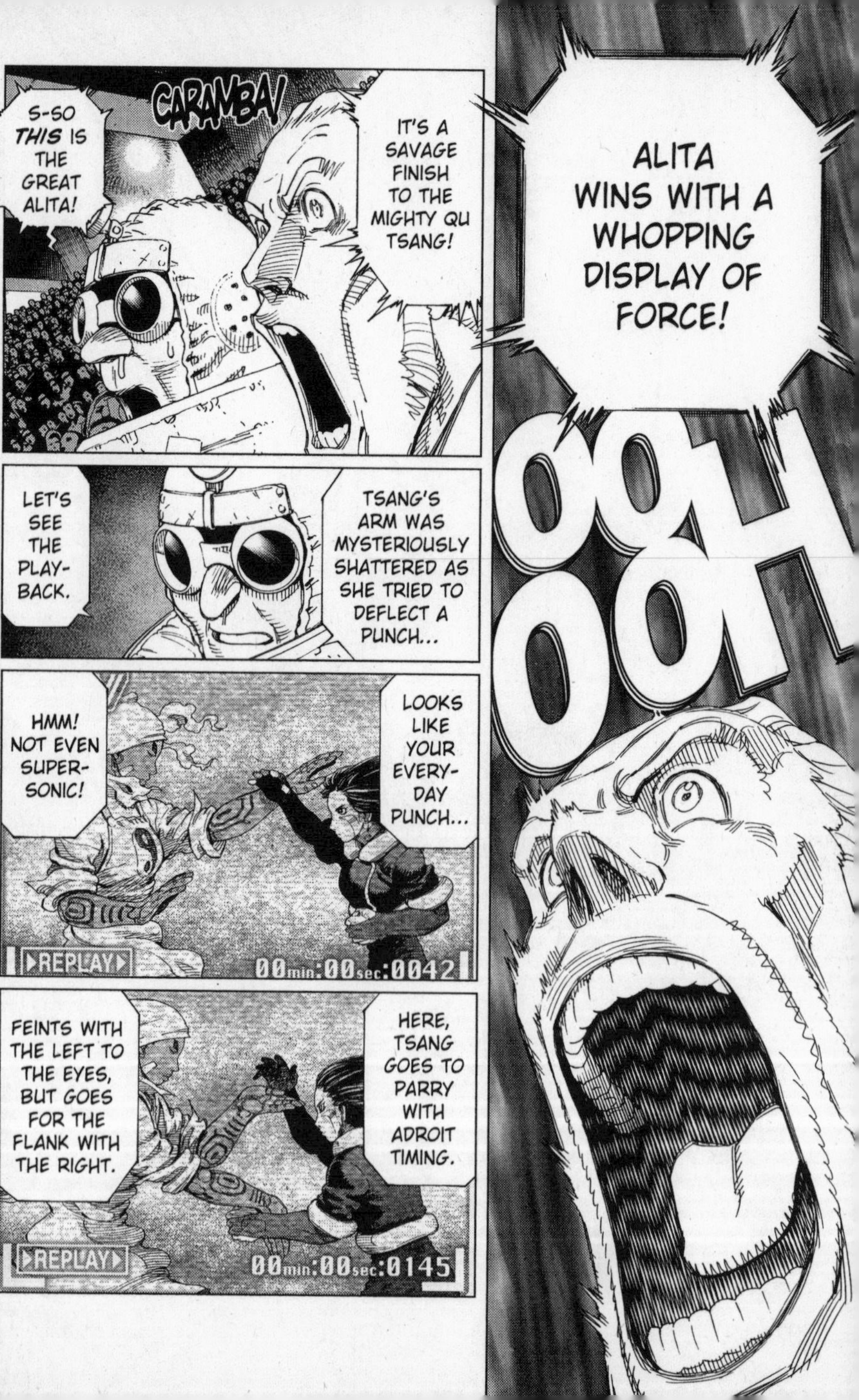
ALITA WINS WITH A WHOPPING DISPLAY OF FORCE!
OOH OOH
IT'S A SAVAGE FINISH TO THE MIGHTY QU TSANG!
CARAMBA!
S-SO *THIS* IS THE GREAT ALITA!
TSANG'S ARM WAS MYSTERIOUSLY SHATTERED AS SHE TRIED TO DEFLECT A PUNCH...
LET'S SEE THE PLAYBACK.
LOOKS LIKE YOUR EVERY-DAY PUNCH...
HMM! NOT EVEN SUPER-SONIC!
REPLAY
00min:00sec:0042
HERE, TSANG GOES TO PARRY WITH ADROIT TIMING.
FEINTS WITH THE LEFT TO THE EYES, BUT GOES FOR THE FLANK WITH THE RIGHT.
REPLAY
00min:00sec:0145

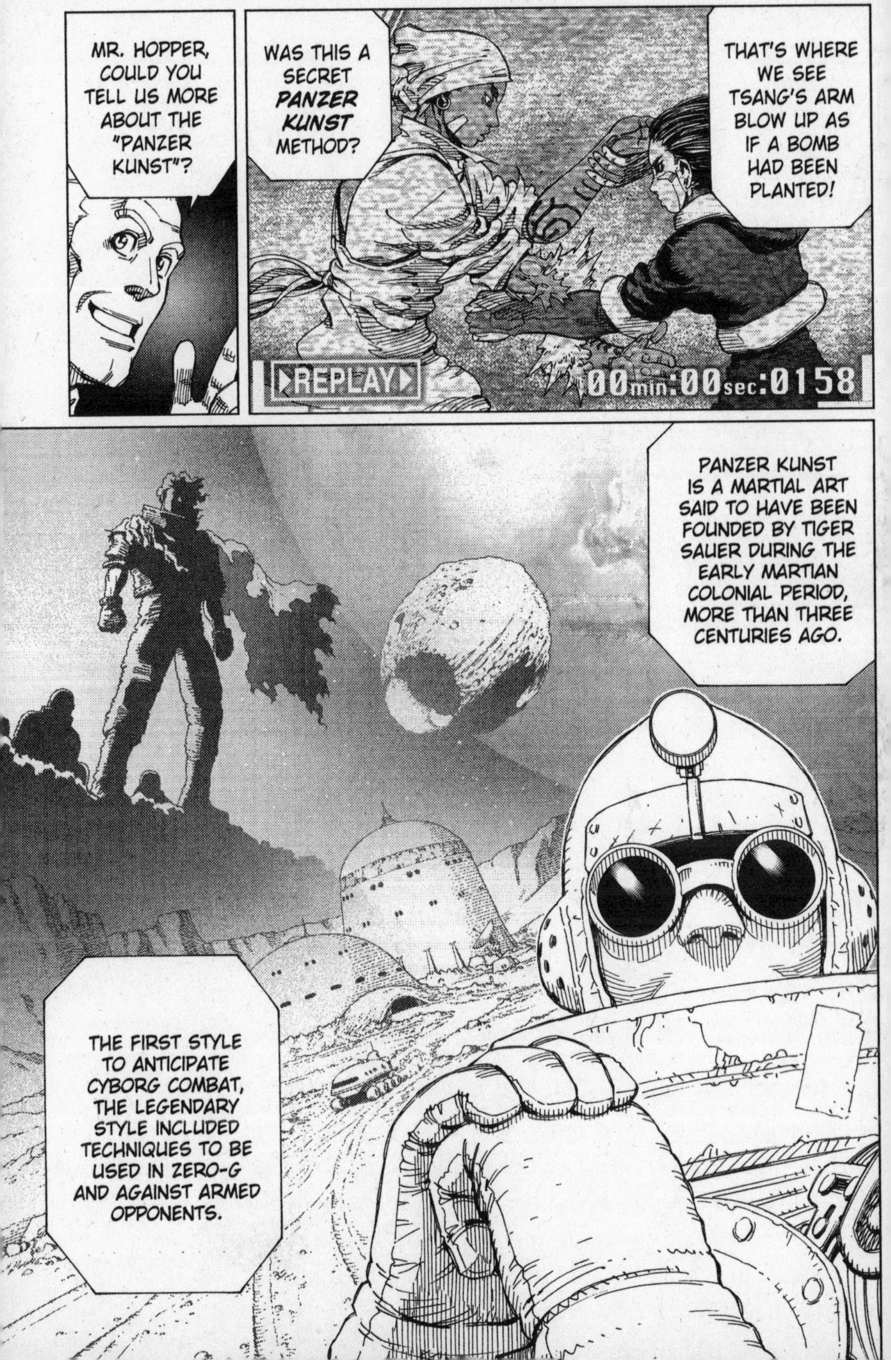
THAT'S WHERE WE SEE TSANG'S ARM BLOW UP AS IF A BOMB HAD BEEN PLANTED!
WAS THIS A SECRET PANZER KUNST METHOD?
REPLAY
00min:00sec:0158
MR. HOPPER, COULD YOU TELL US MORE ABOUT THE "PANZER KUNST"?
PANZER KUNST IS A MARTIAL ART SAID TO HAVE BEEN FOUNDED BY TIGER SAUER DURING THE EARLY MARTIAN COLONIAL PERIOD, MORE THAN THREE CENTURIES AGO.
THE FIRST STYLE TO ANTICIPATE CYBORG COMBAT, THE LEGENDARY STYLE INCLUDED TECHNIQUES TO BE USED IN ZERO-G AND AGAINST ARMED OPPONENTS.

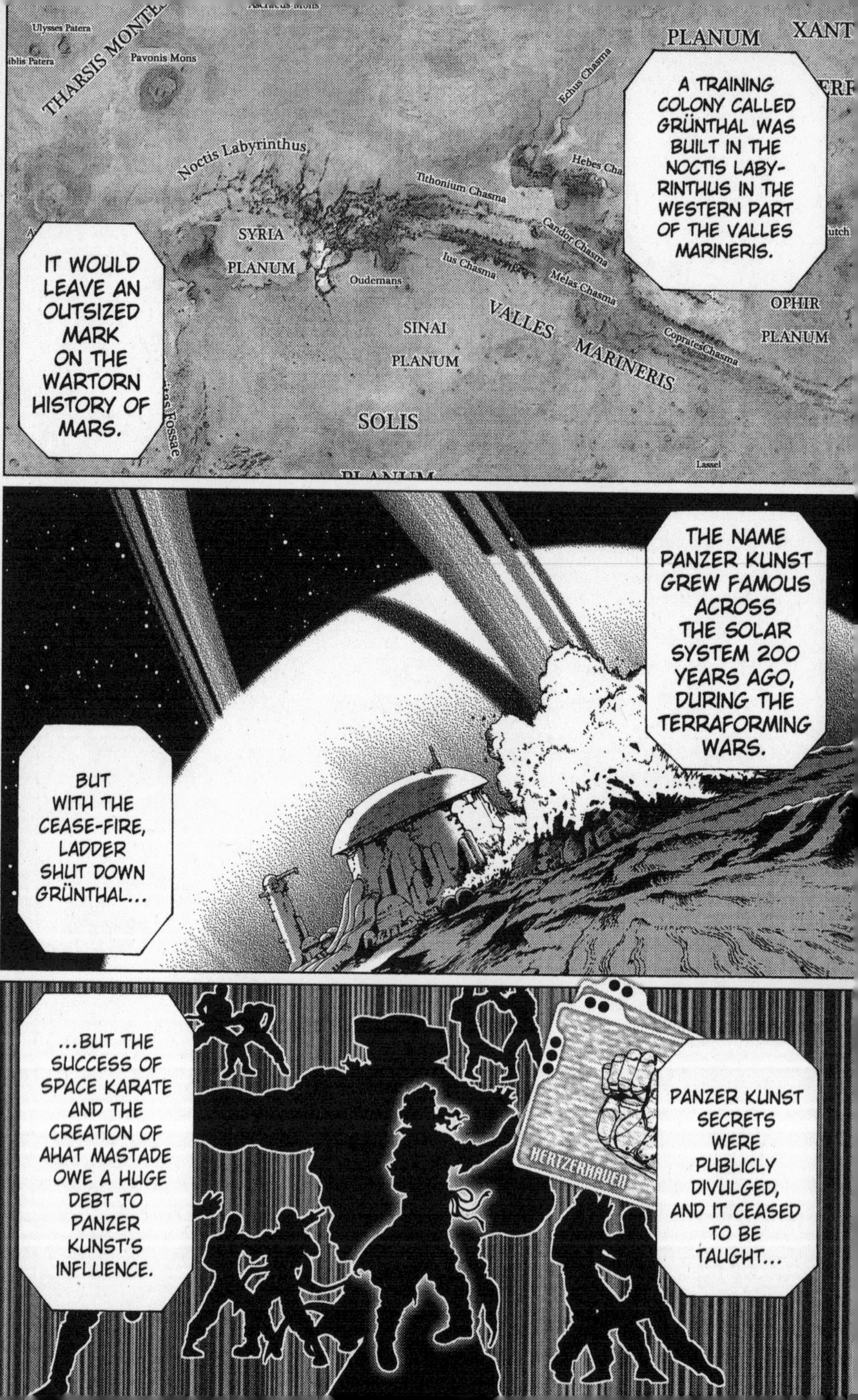
A TRAINING COLONY CALLED GRÜNTHAL WAS BUILT IN THE NOCTIS LABYRINTHUS IN THE WESTERN PART OF THE VALLES MARINERIS.
IT WOULD LEAVE AN OUTSIZED MARK ON THE WARTORN HISTORY OF MARS.
PLANUM
THARSIS MONTES
Ulysses Patera
Pavonis Mons
Echus Chasma
Noctis Labyrinthus
Hebes Cha
Tithonium Chasma
SYRIA
PLANUM
Candor Chasma
Ius Chasma
Oudemans
Melas Chasma
VALLES
MARINERIS
OPHIR
PLANUM
Coprates Chasma
SINAI
PLANUM
SOLIS
Lassel
THE NAME PANZER KUNST GREW FAMOUS ACROSS THE SOLAR SYSTEM 200 YEARS AGO, DURING THE TERRAFORMING WARS.
BUT WITH THE CEASE-FIRE, LADDER SHUT DOWN GRÜNTHAL...
PANZER KUNST SECRETS WERE PUBLICLY DIVULGED, AND IT CEASED TO BE TAUGHT...
...BUT THE SUCCESS OF SPACE KARATE AND THE CREATION OF AHAT MASTADE OWE A HUGE DEBT TO PANZER KUNST'S INFLUENCE.

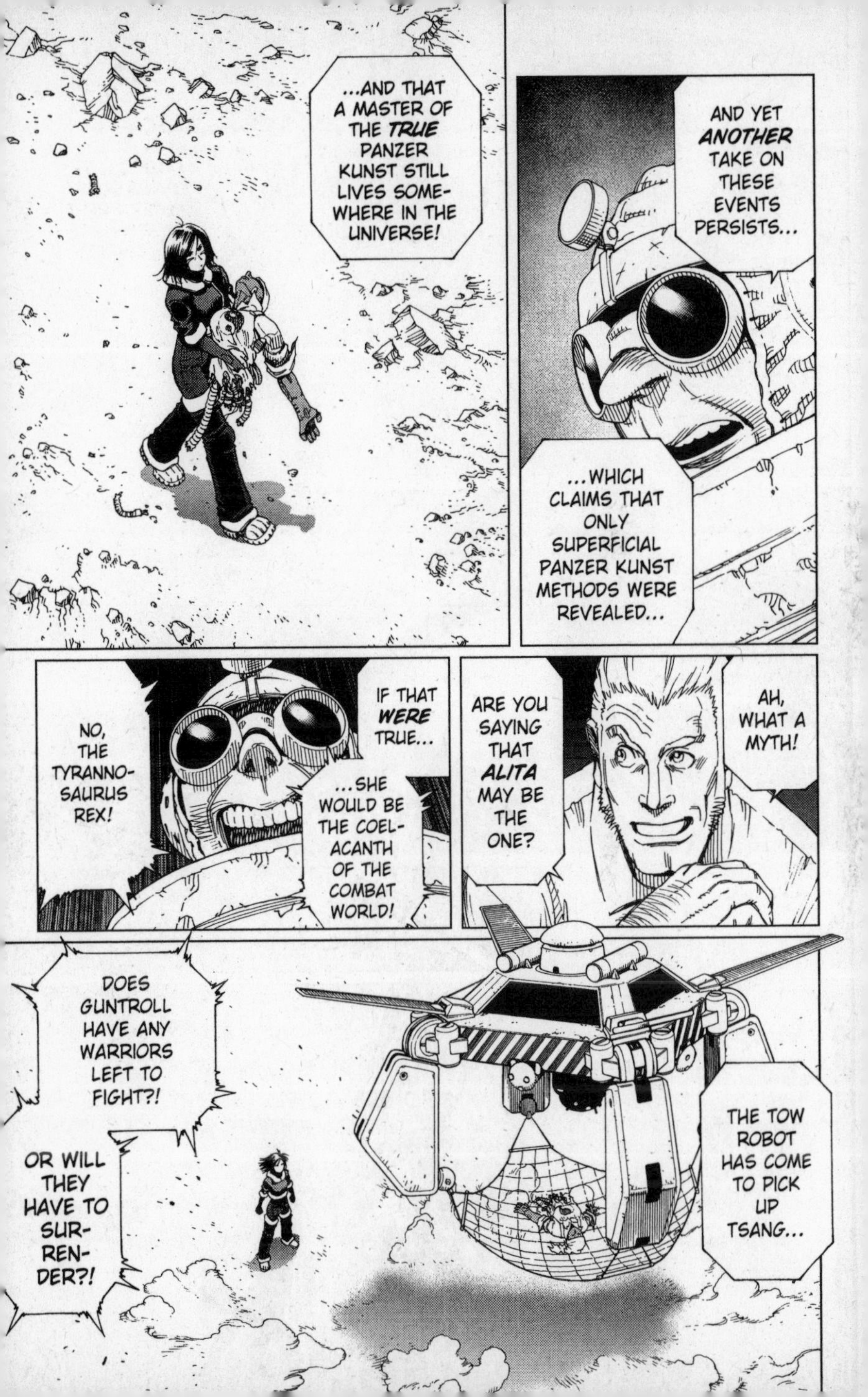
AND YET ANOTHER TAKE ON THESE EVENTS PERSISTS...
...WHICH CLAIMS THAT ONLY SUPERFICIAL PANZER KUNST METHODS WERE REVEALED...
...AND THAT A MASTER OF THE TRUE PANZER KUNST STILL LIVES SOME-WHERE IN THE UNIVERSE!
AH, WHAT A MYTH!
ARE YOU SAYING THAT ALITA MAY BE THE ONE?
IF THAT WERE TRUE...
...SHE WOULD BE THE COEL-ACANTH OF THE COMBAT WORLD!
NO, THE TYRANNO-SAURUS REX!
THE TOW ROBOT HAS COME TO PICK UP TSANG...
DOES GUNTROLL HAVE ANY WARRIORS LEFT TO FIGHT?!
OR WILL THEY HAVE TO SUR-REN-DER?!

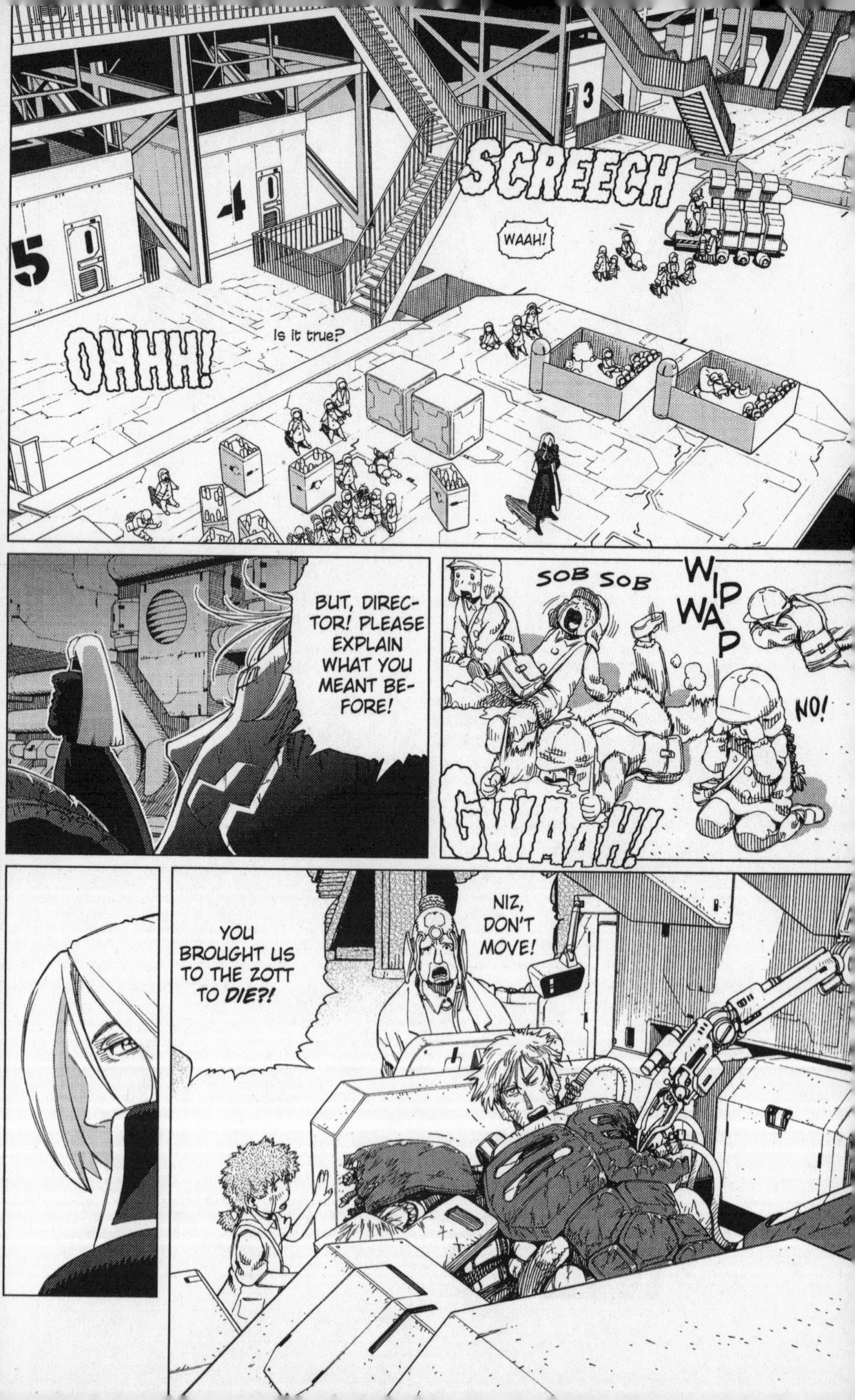
SCREECH
WAAH!
Is it true?
OHHH!
SOB SOB
WIP WAP
NO!
GWAAH!
BUT, DIRECTOR! PLEASE EXPLAIN WHAT YOU MEANT BEFORE!
NIZ, DON'T MOVE!
YOU BROUGHT US TO THE ZOTT TO *DIE*?!

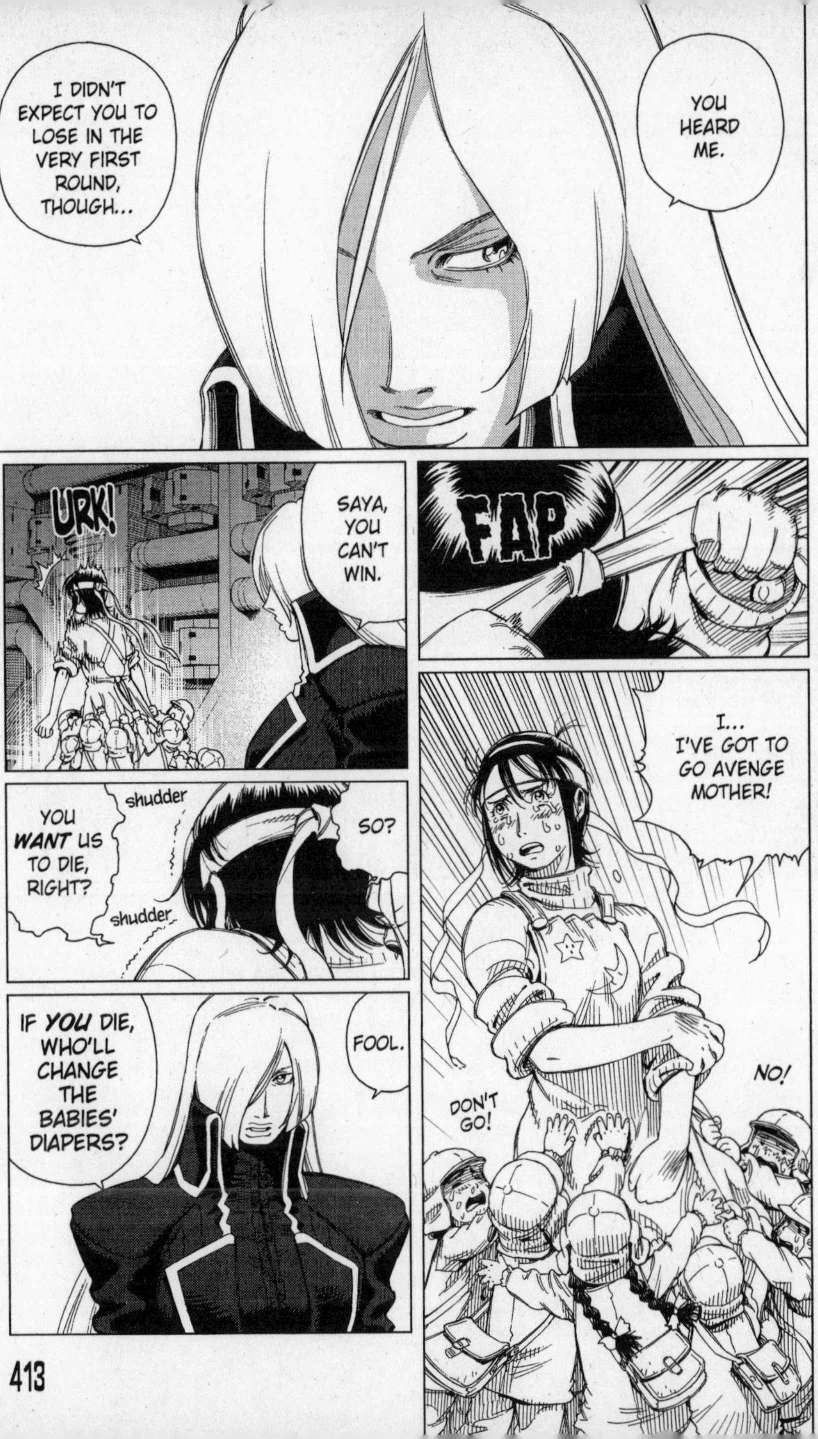
YOU HEARD ME.
I DIDN'T EXPECT YOU TO LOSE IN THE VERY FIRST ROUND, THOUGH...
FAP
SAYA, YOU CAN'T WIN.
URK!
I... I'VE GOT TO GO AVENGE MOTHER!
NO!
DON'T GO!
SO?
shudder
YOU *WANT* US TO DIE, RIGHT?
shudder
FOOL.
IF *YOU* DIE, WHO'LL CHANGE THE BABIES' DIAPERS?

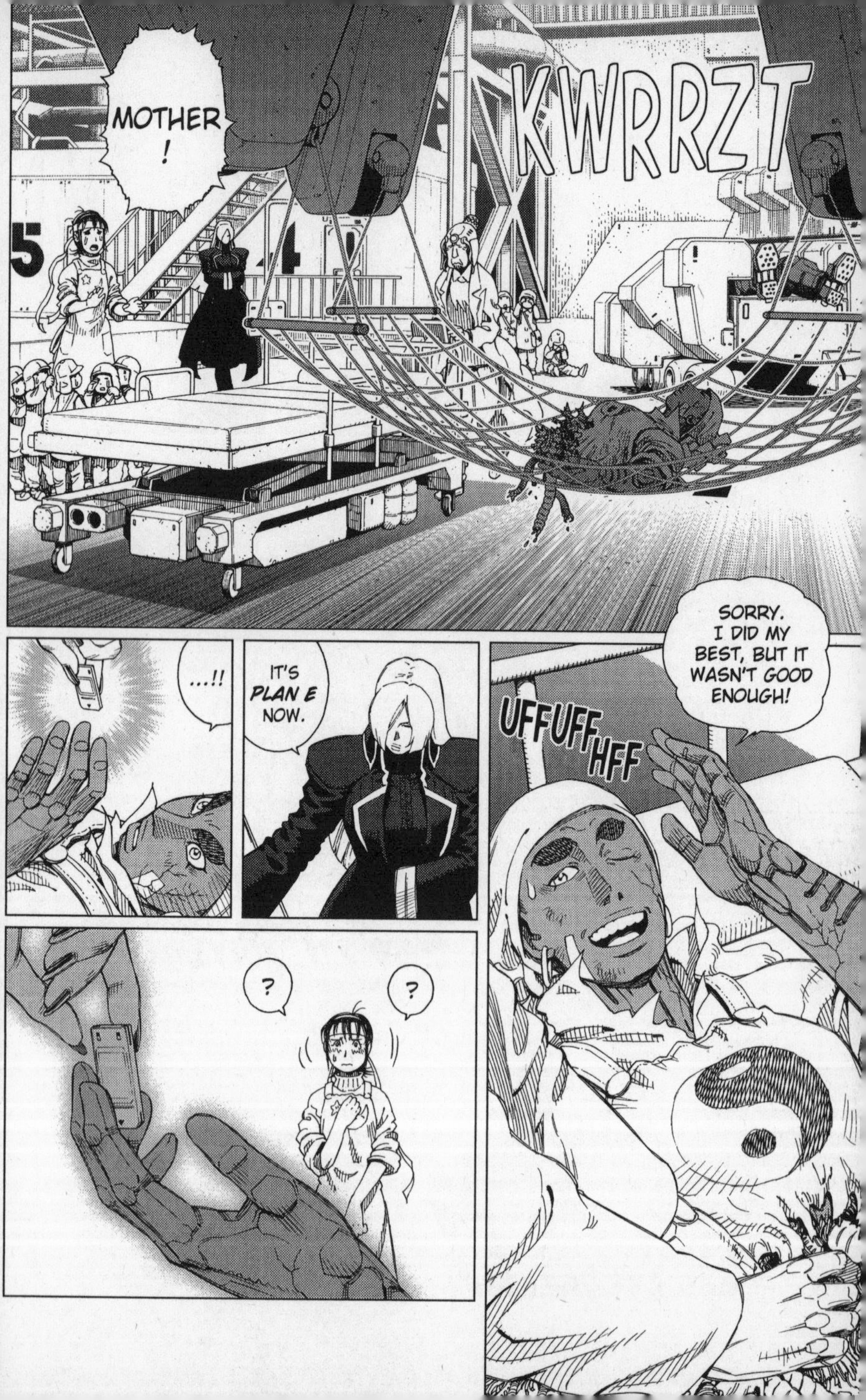
KWRRZT
MOTHER!
SORRY. I DID MY BEST, BUT IT WASN'T GOOD ENOUGH!
UFFUFFHFF
IT'S PLAN E NOW.
...!!
?
?

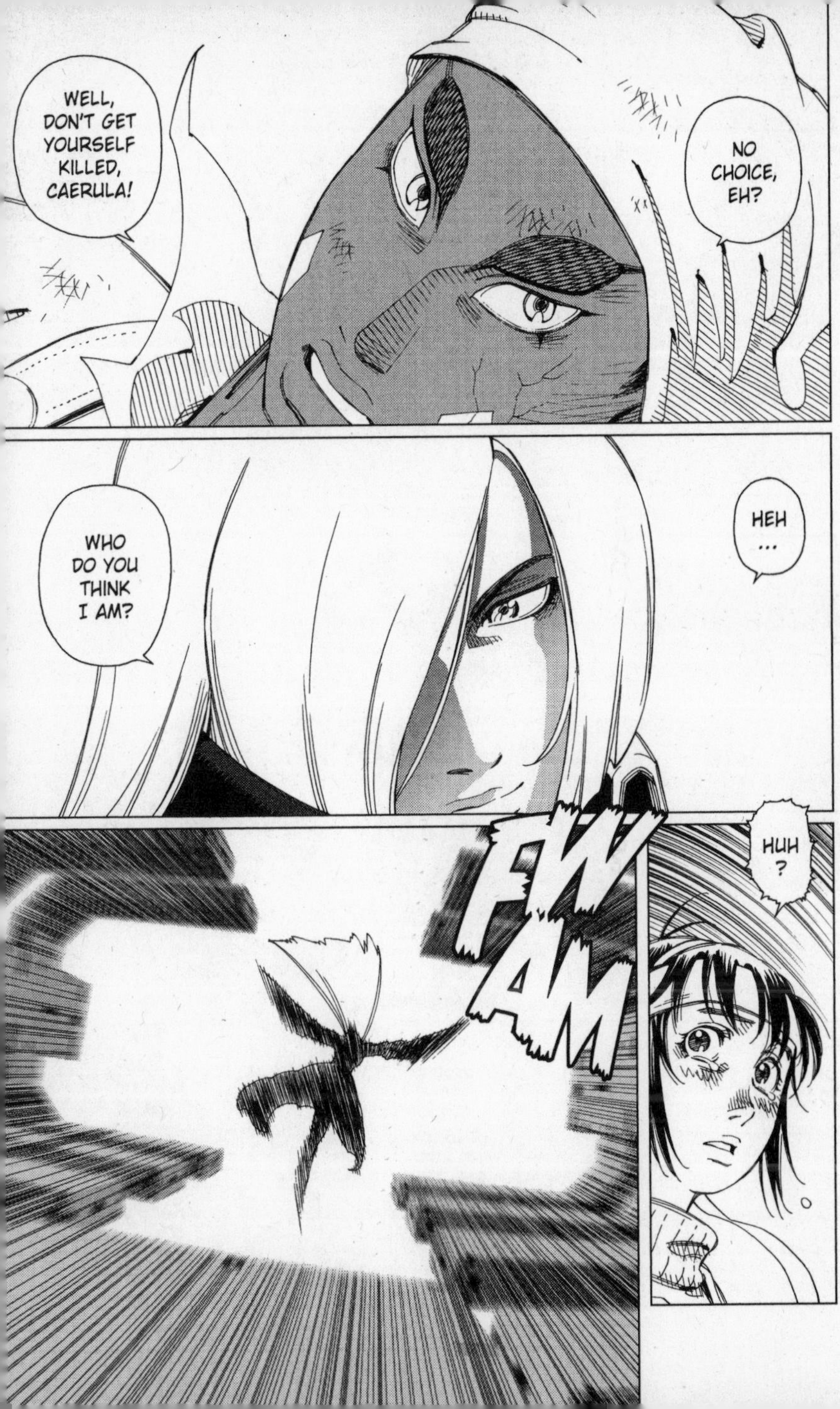
NO CHOICE, EH?
WELL, DON'T GET YOURSELF KILLED, CAERULA!
HEH...
WHO DO YOU THINK I AM?
HUH?
FWAM

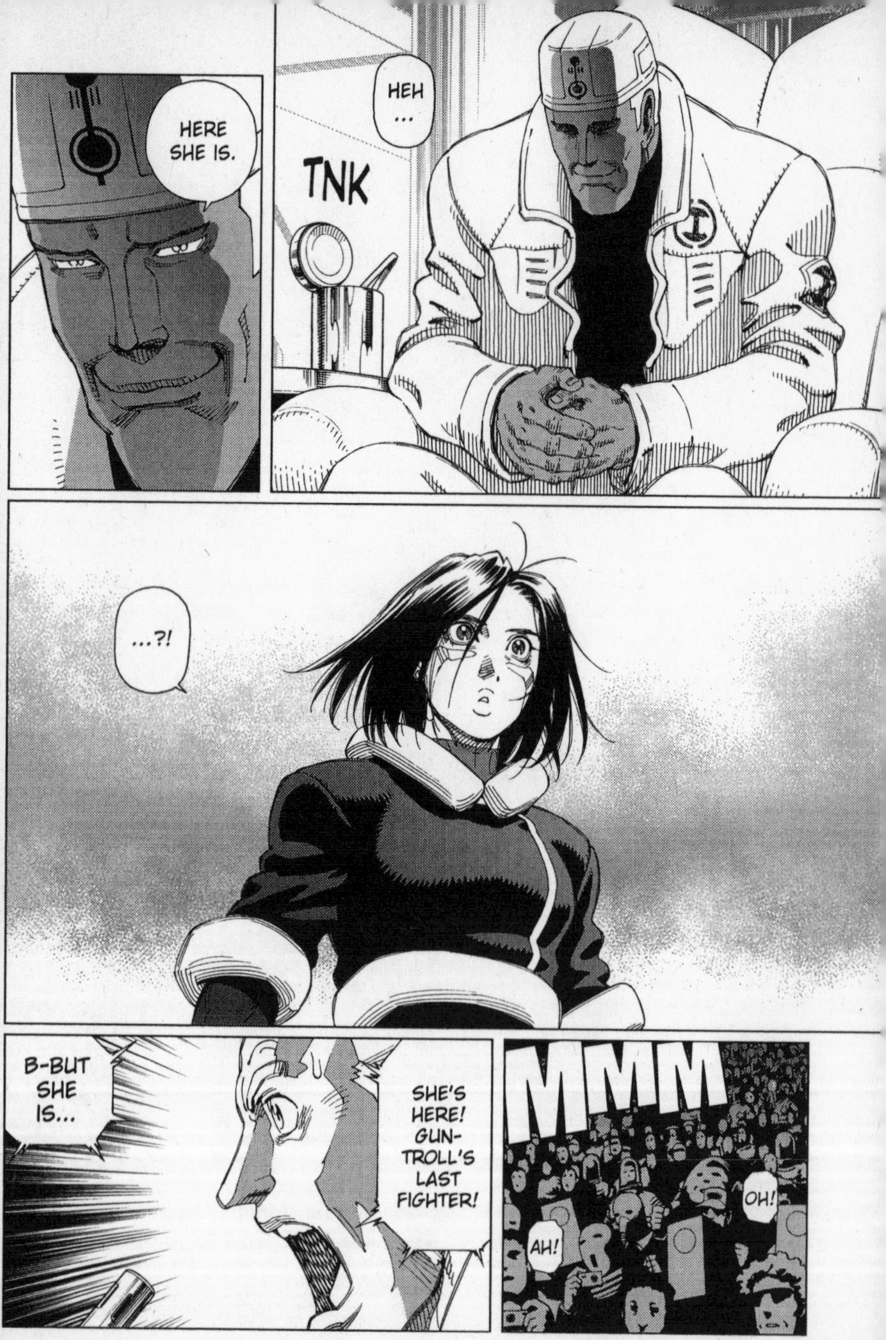
HEH ...
TNK
HERE SHE IS.
...?!
MMMM
OH!
AH!
SHE'S HERE! GUN-TROLL'S LAST FIGHTER!
B-BUT SHE IS...

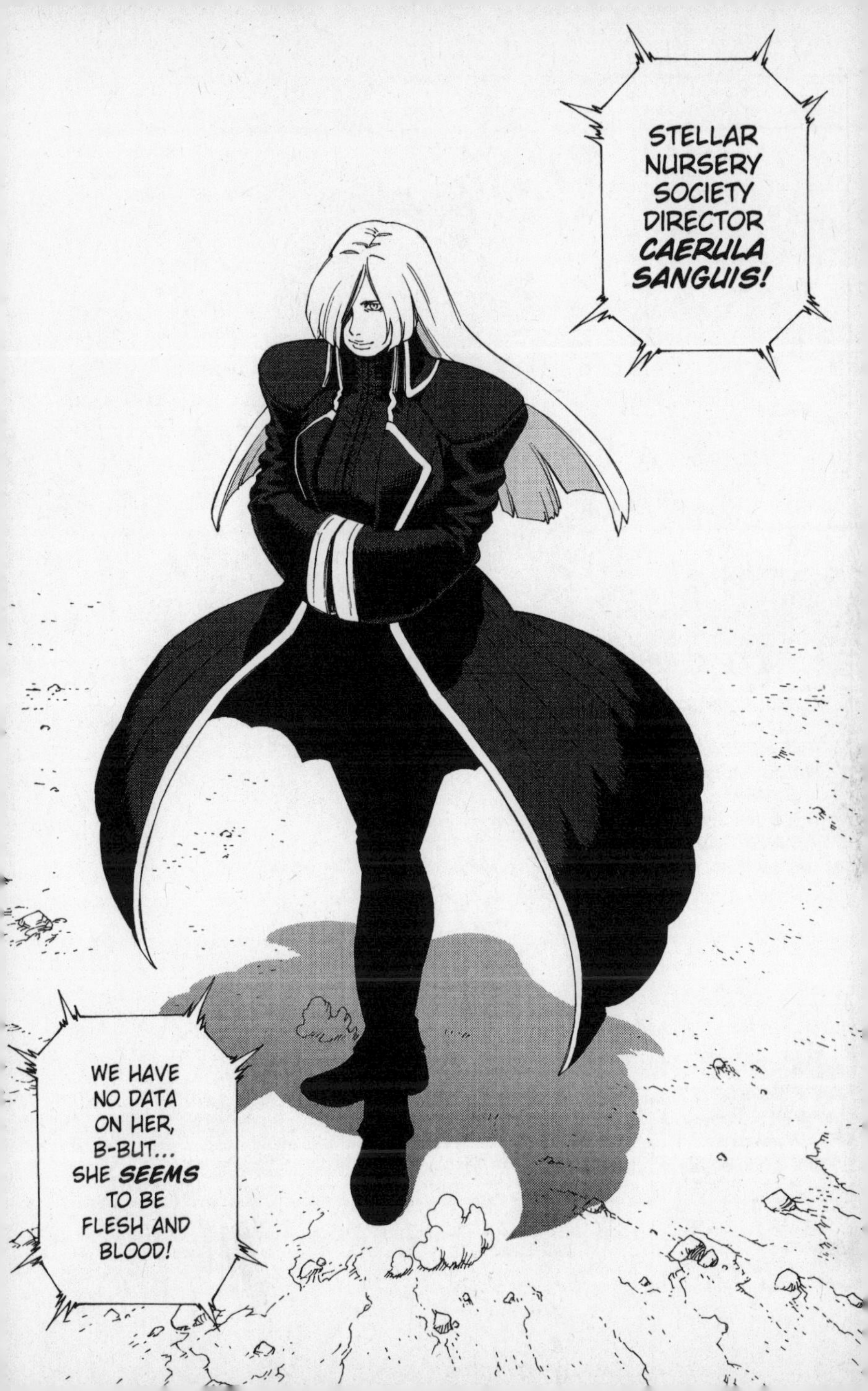
STELLAR NURSERY SOCIETY DIRECTOR *CAERULA SANGUIS!*
WE HAVE NO DATA ON HER, B-BUT... SHE *SEEMS* TO BE FLESH AND BLOOD!

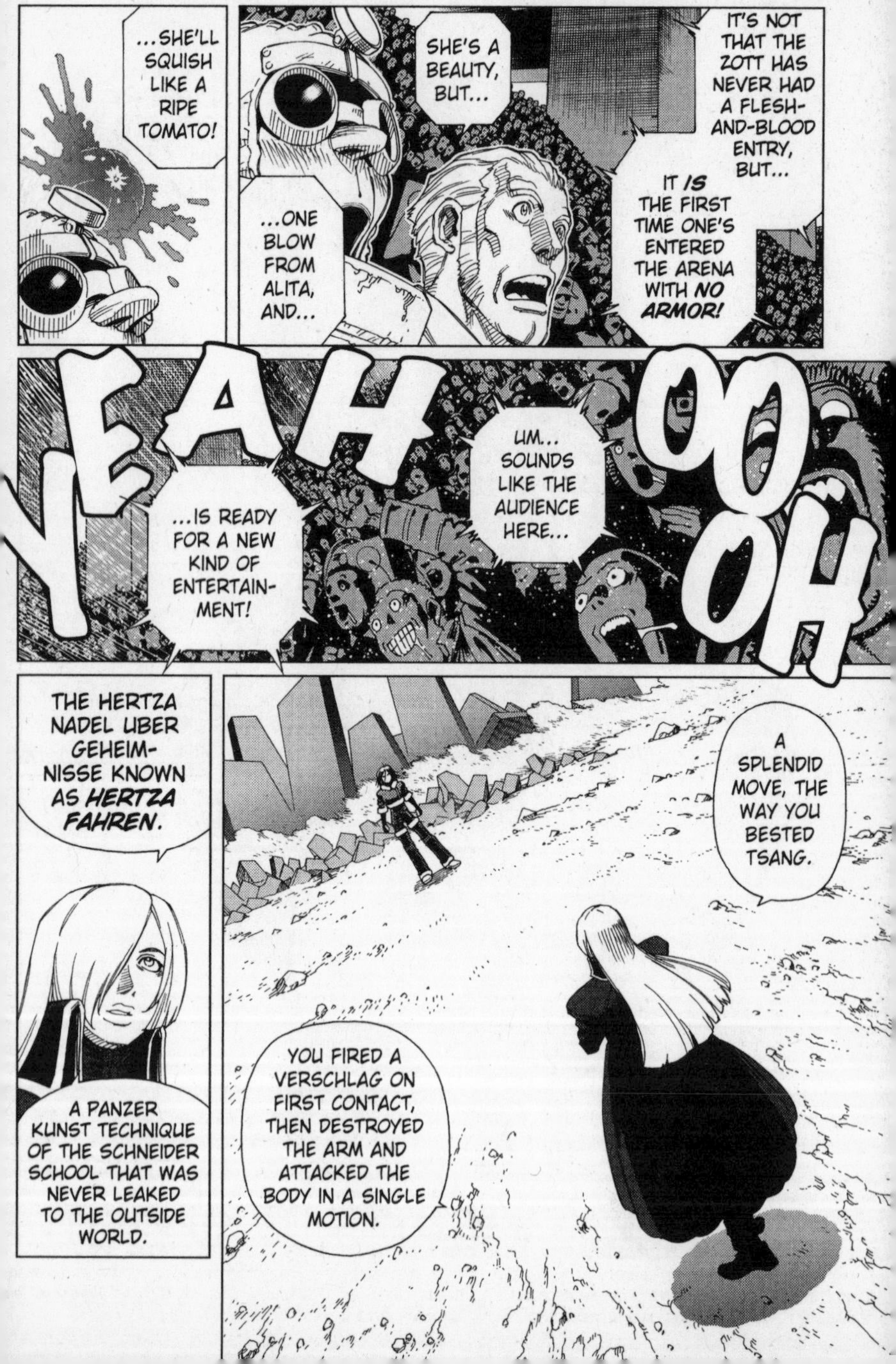
IT'S NOT THAT THE ZOTT HAS NEVER HAD A FLESH-AND-BLOOD ENTRY, BUT...
IT *IS* THE FIRST TIME ONE'S ENTERED THE ARENA WITH *NO ARMOR!*
SHE'S A BEAUTY, BUT...
...ONE BLOW FROM ALITA, AND...
...SHE'LL SQUISH LIKE A RIPE TOMATO!
YEAH OOOH
UM... SOUNDS LIKE THE AUDIENCE HERE...
...IS READY FOR A NEW KIND OF ENTERTAINMENT!
A SPLENDID MOVE, THE WAY YOU BESTED TSANG.
YOU FIRED A VERSCHLAG ON FIRST CONTACT, THEN DESTROYED THE ARM AND ATTACKED THE BODY IN A SINGLE MOTION.
THE HERTZA NADEL UBER GEHEIMNISSE KNOWN AS *HERTZA FAHREN*.
A PANZER KUNST TECHNIQUE OF THE SCHNEIDER SCHOOL THAT WAS NEVER LEAKED TO THE OUTSIDE WORLD.

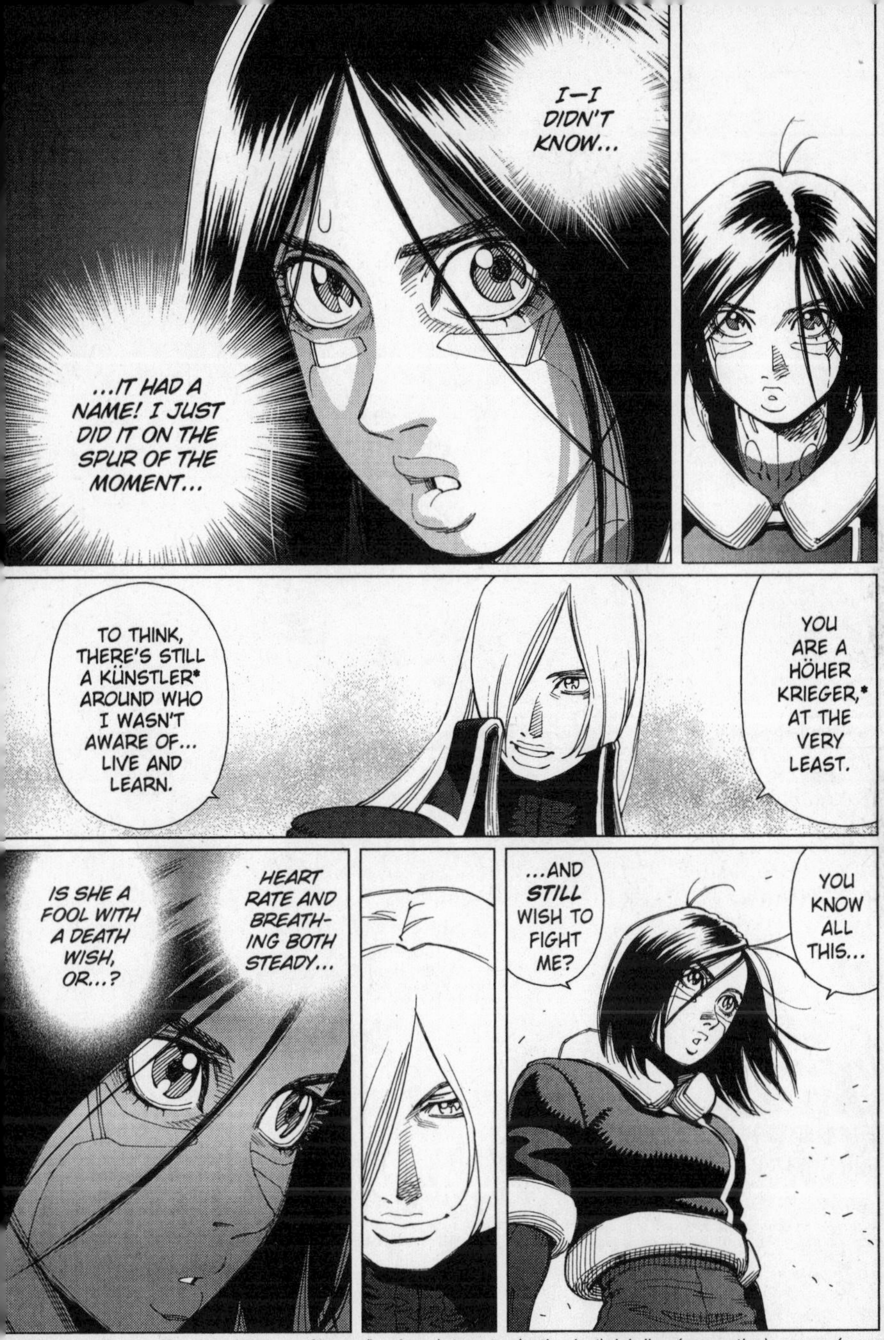
I—I DIDN'T KNOW...
...IT HAD A NAME! I JUST DID IT ON THE SPUR OF THE MOMENT...
YOU ARE A HÖHER KRIEGER,* AT THE VERY LEAST.
TO THINK, THERE'S STILL A KÜNSTLER* AROUND WHO I WASN'T AWARE OF... LIVE AND LEARN.
YOU KNOW ALL THIS...
...AND STILL WISH TO FIGHT ME?
HEART RATE AND BREATHING BOTH STEADY...
IS SHE A FOOL WITH A DEATH WISH, OR...?

*The nine Panzer Kunst ranks are: anfänger (beginner), tzereter (enthusiast), lehrling (apprentice), gezere (war artisan), krieger (warrior), **höher krieger** (high warrior), meister (master), adept (licensed master) and ältermeist (el

***Künstler:** "Artist," a traditional name for Panzer Kunst practitioners.

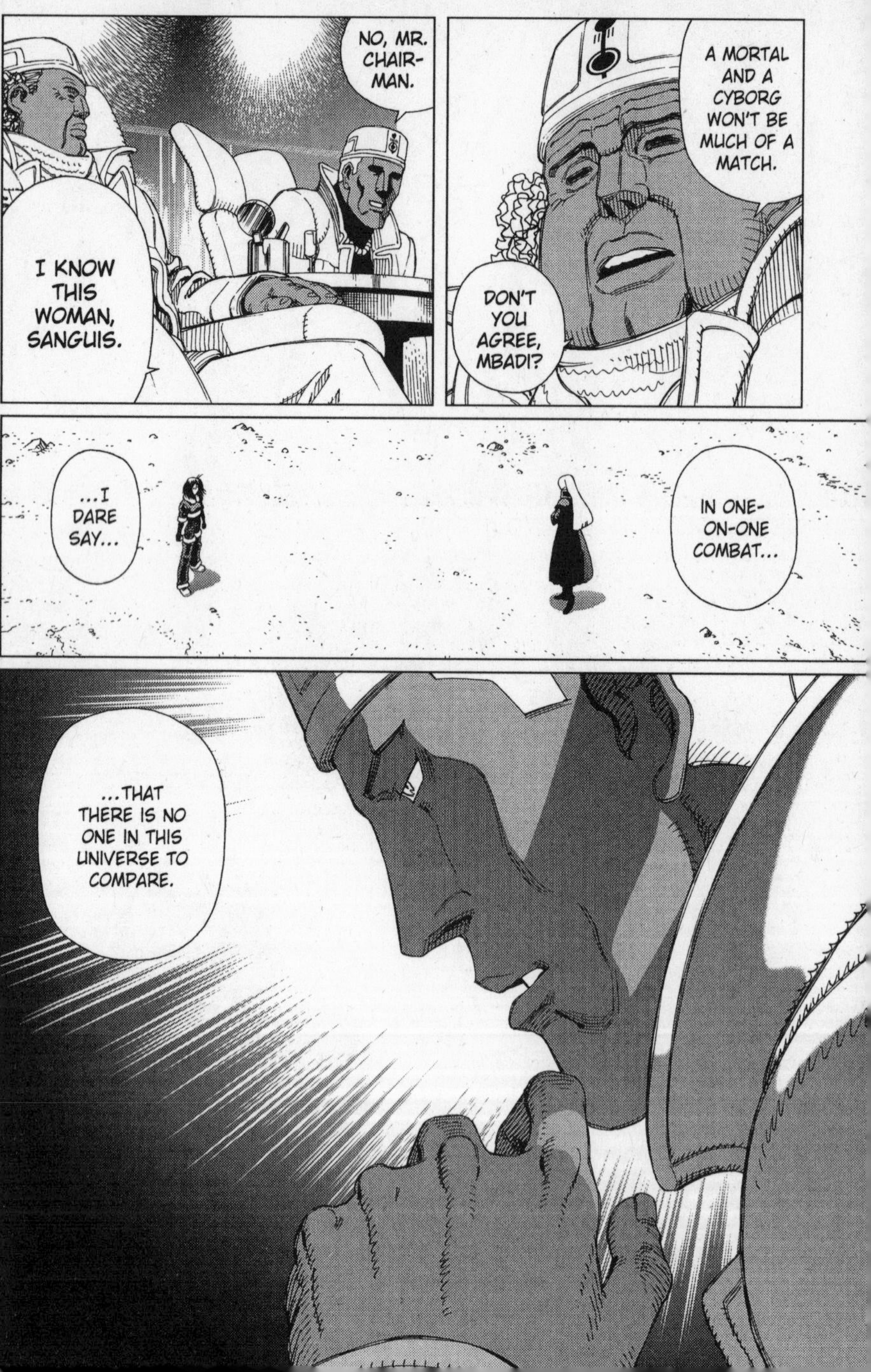
A MORTAL AND A CYBORG WON'T BE MUCH OF A MATCH.
DON'T YOU AGREE, MBADI?
NO, MR. CHAIR-MAN.
I KNOW THIS WOMAN, SANGUIS.
IN ONE-ON-ONE COMBAT...
...I DARE SAY...
...THAT THERE IS NO ONE IN THIS UNIVERSE TO COMPARE.

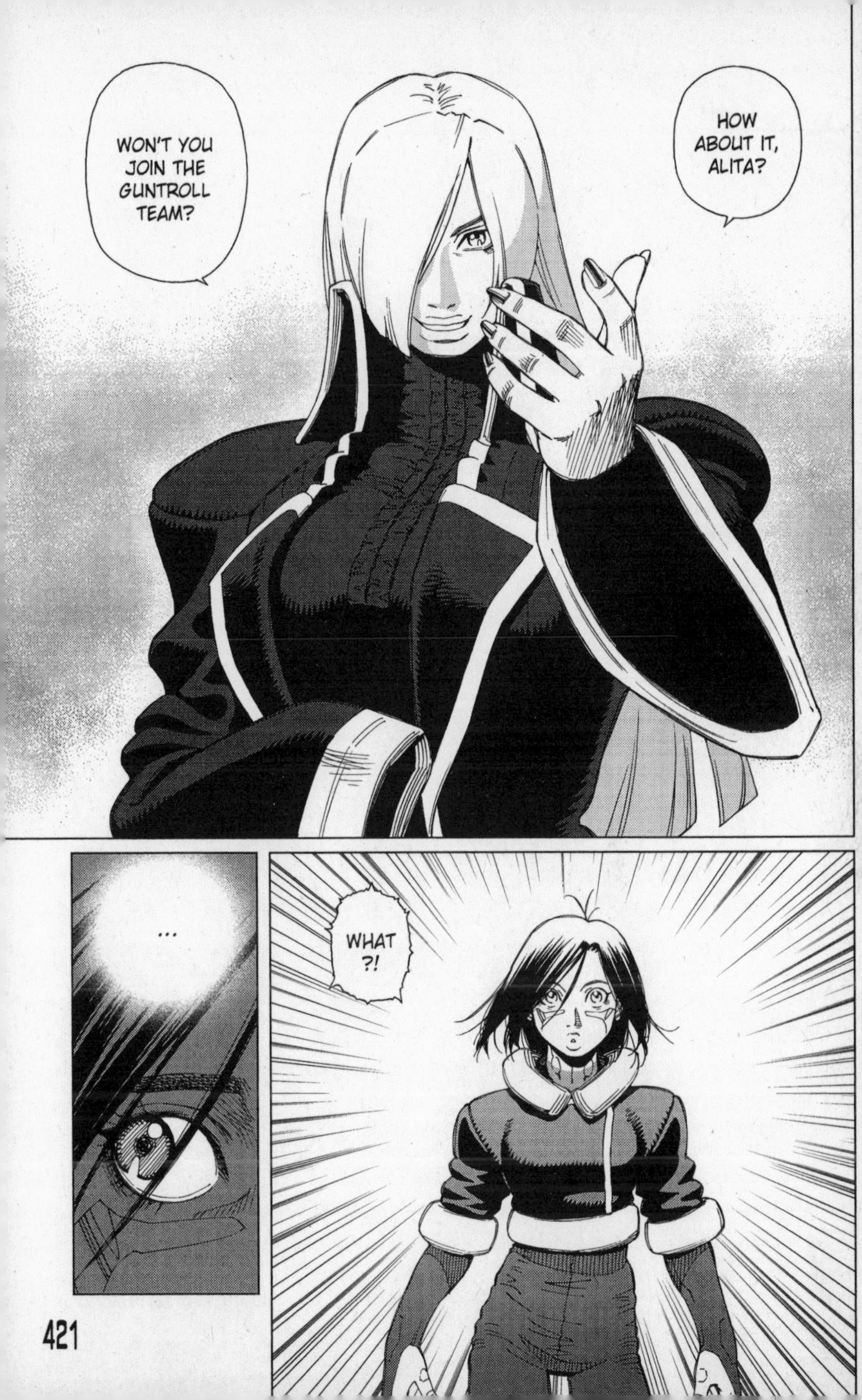
HOW ABOUT IT, ALITA?
WON'T YOU JOIN THE GUNTROLL TEAM?
WHAT ?!
...

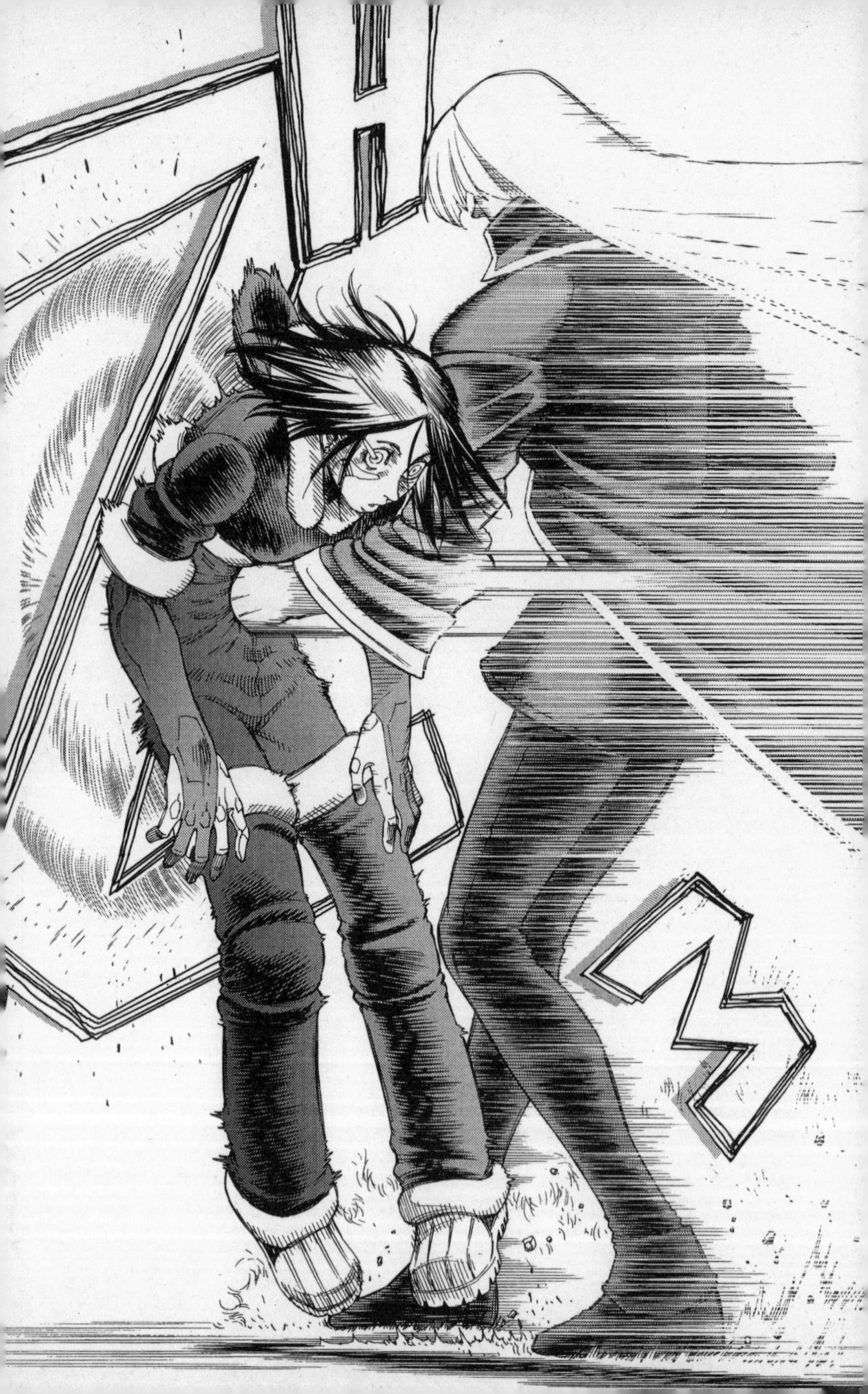

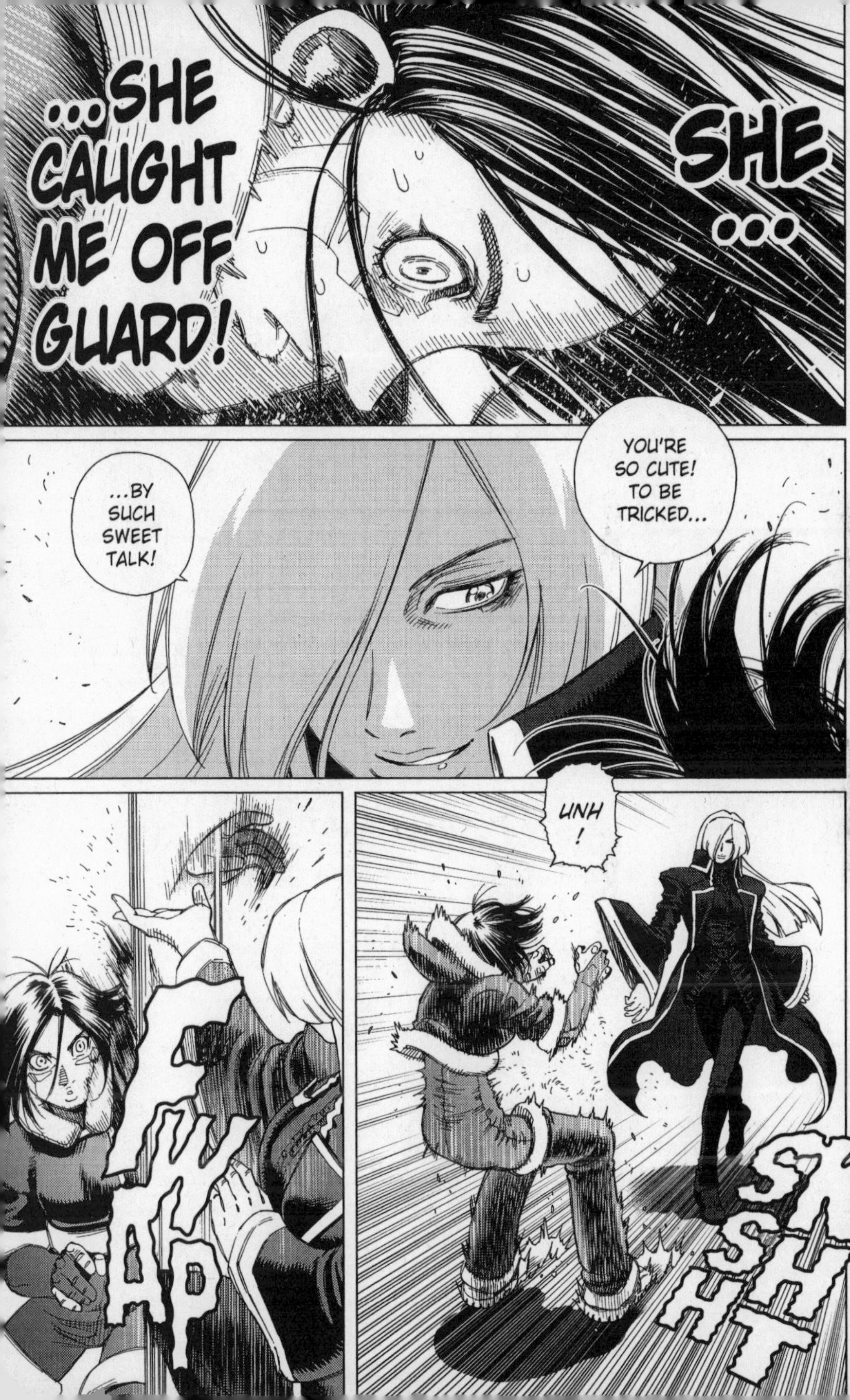
SHE...
...SHE CAUGHT ME OFF GUARD!
YOU'RE SO CUTE! TO BE TRICKED...
...BY SUCH SWEET TALK!
UNH!

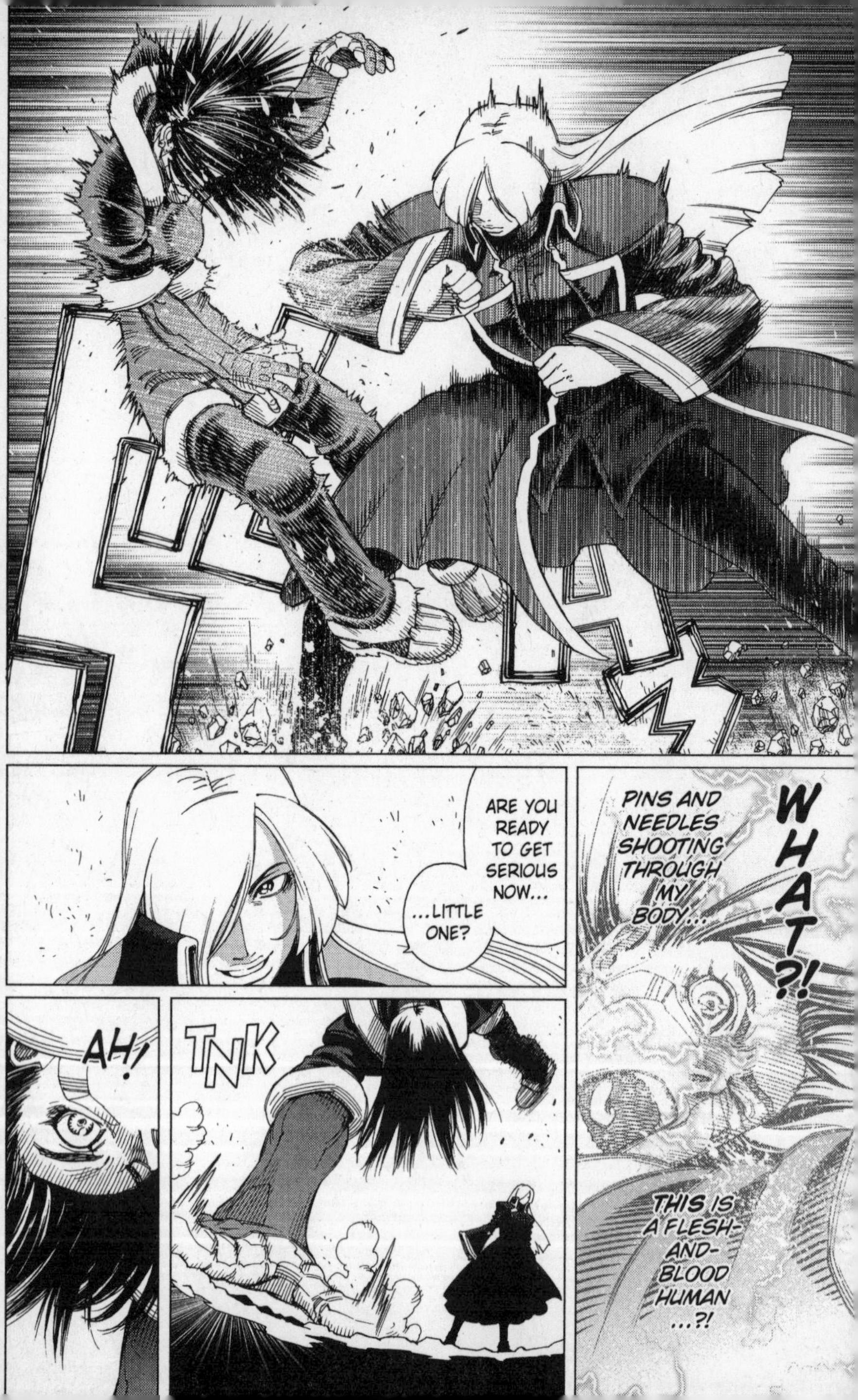
WHAT?!
PINS AND NEEDLES SHOOTING THROUGH MY BODY...
THIS IS A FLESH-AND-BLOOD HUMAN...?!
ARE YOU READY TO GET SERIOUS NOW...
...LITTLE ONE?
TNK
AH!

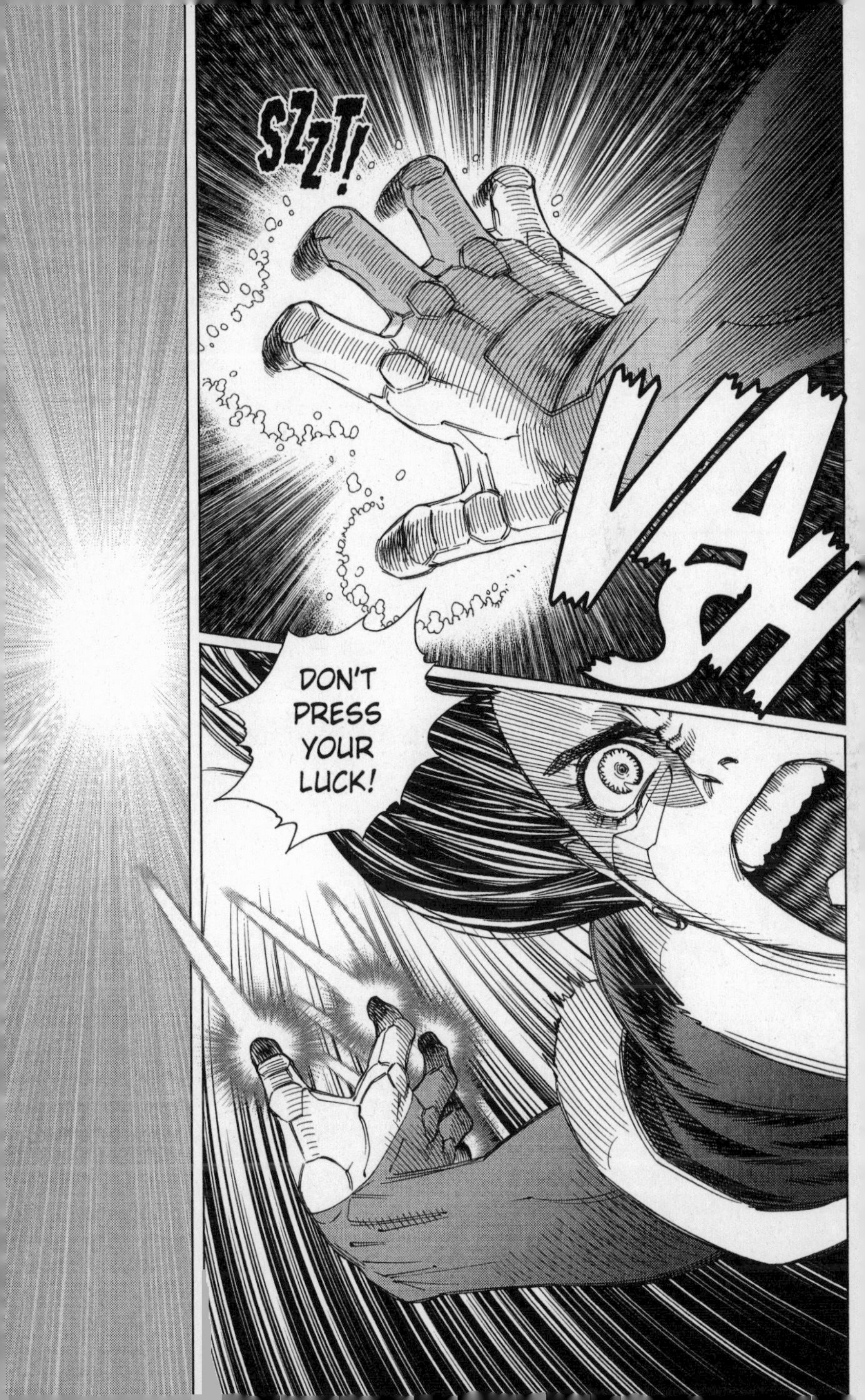
SZZT!
DON'T PRESS YOUR LUCK!

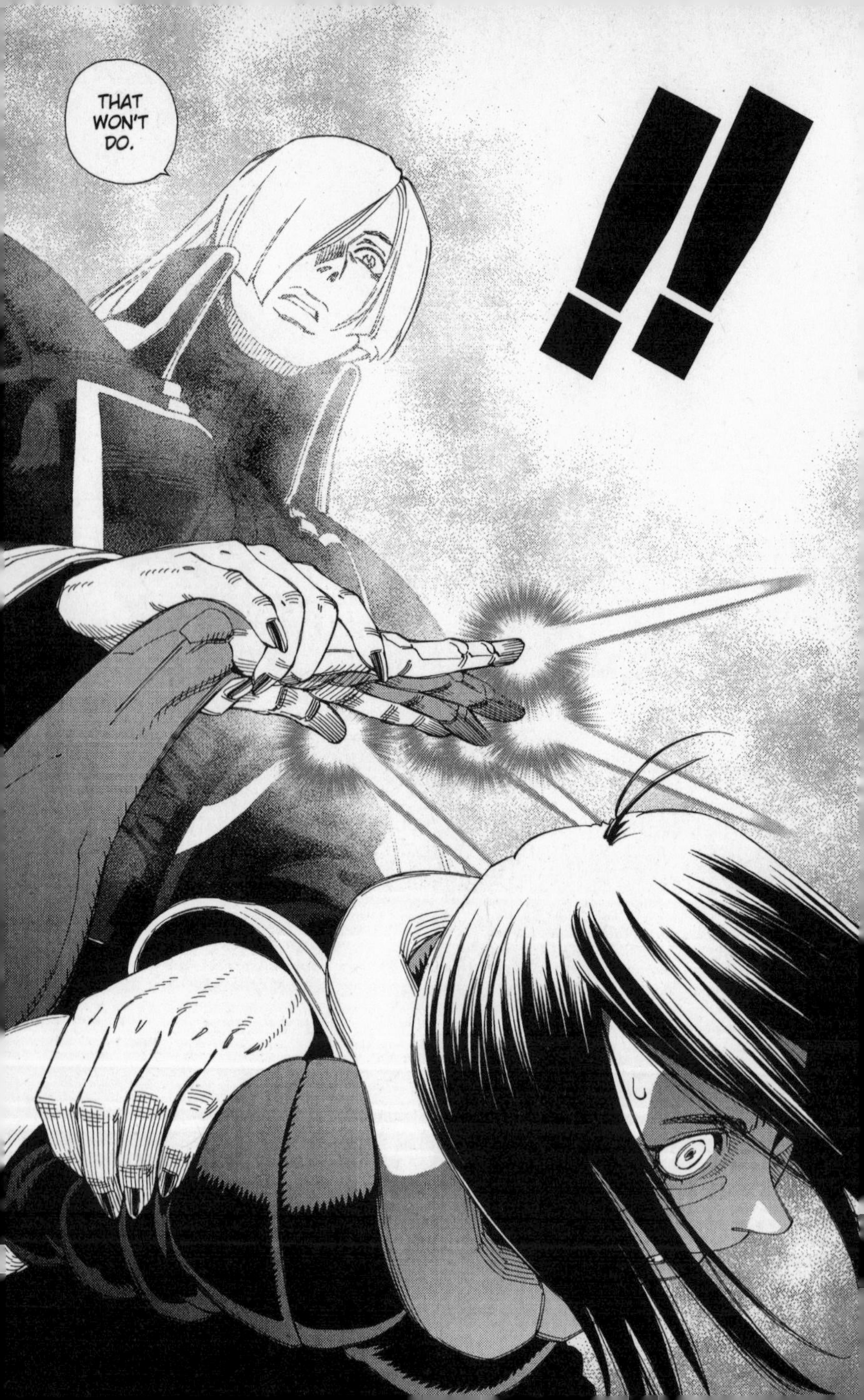
THAT WON'T DO.
!!

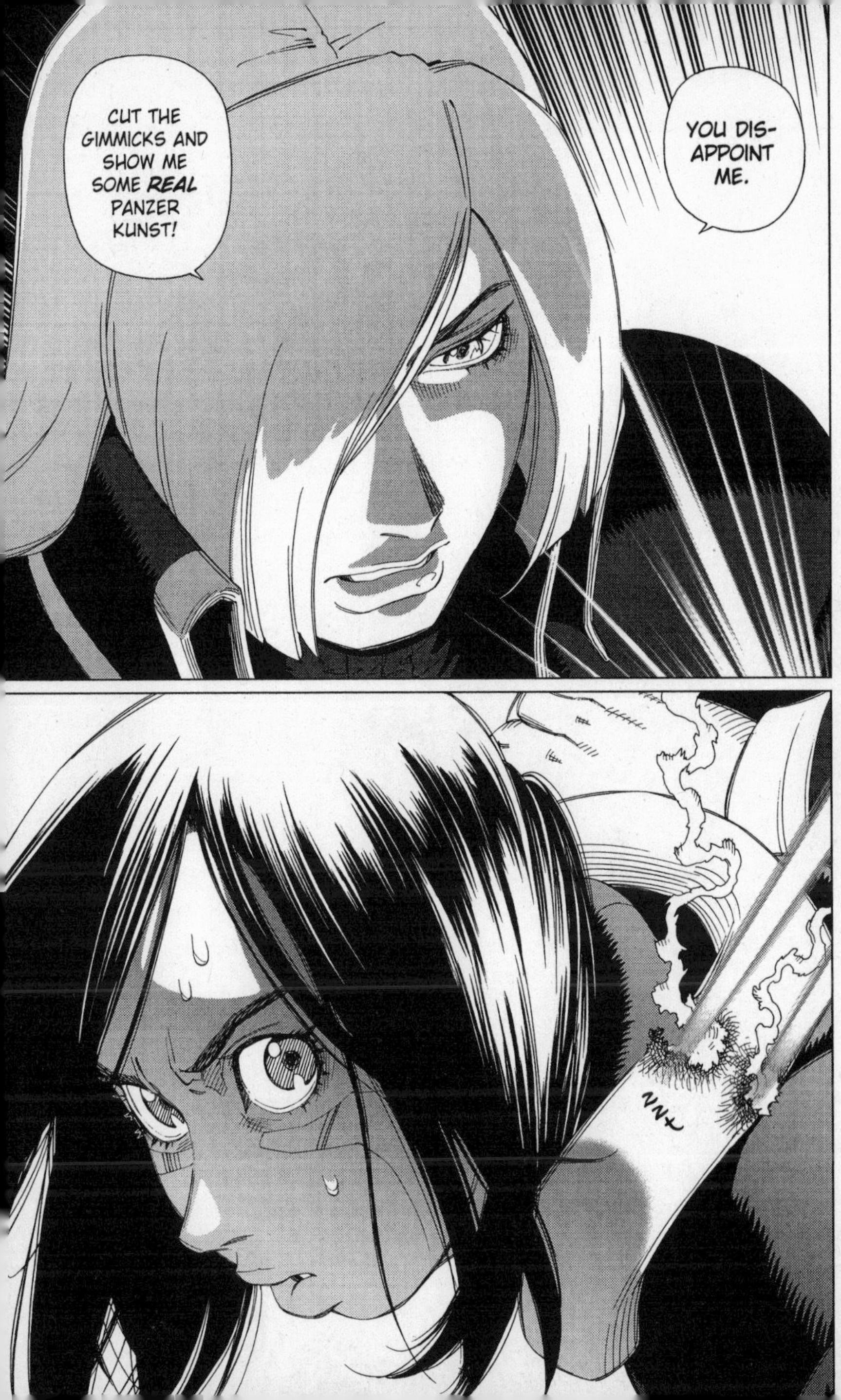
YOU DIS-APPOINT ME.
CUT THE GIMMICKS AND SHOW ME SOME **REAL** PANZER KUNST!

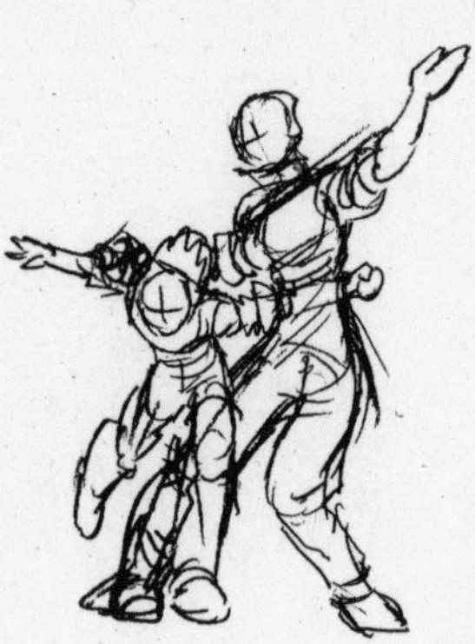
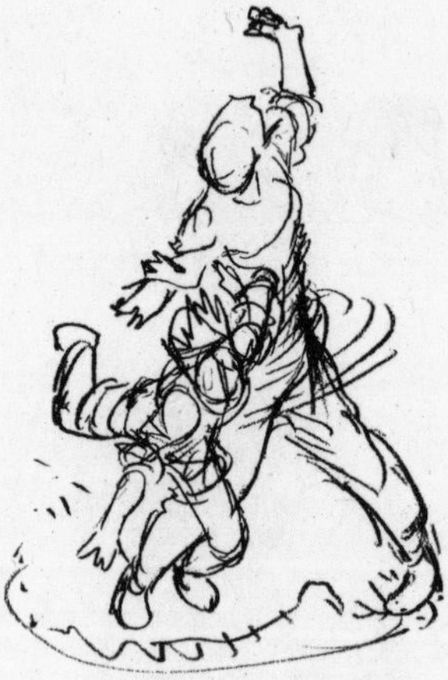
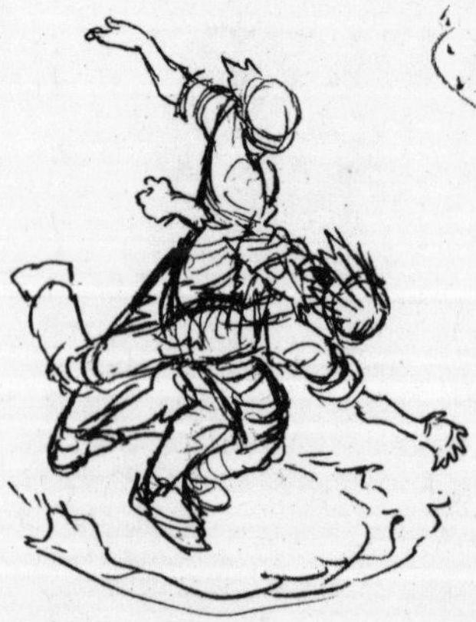

PHASE 33: **Not Since That Battle...!**

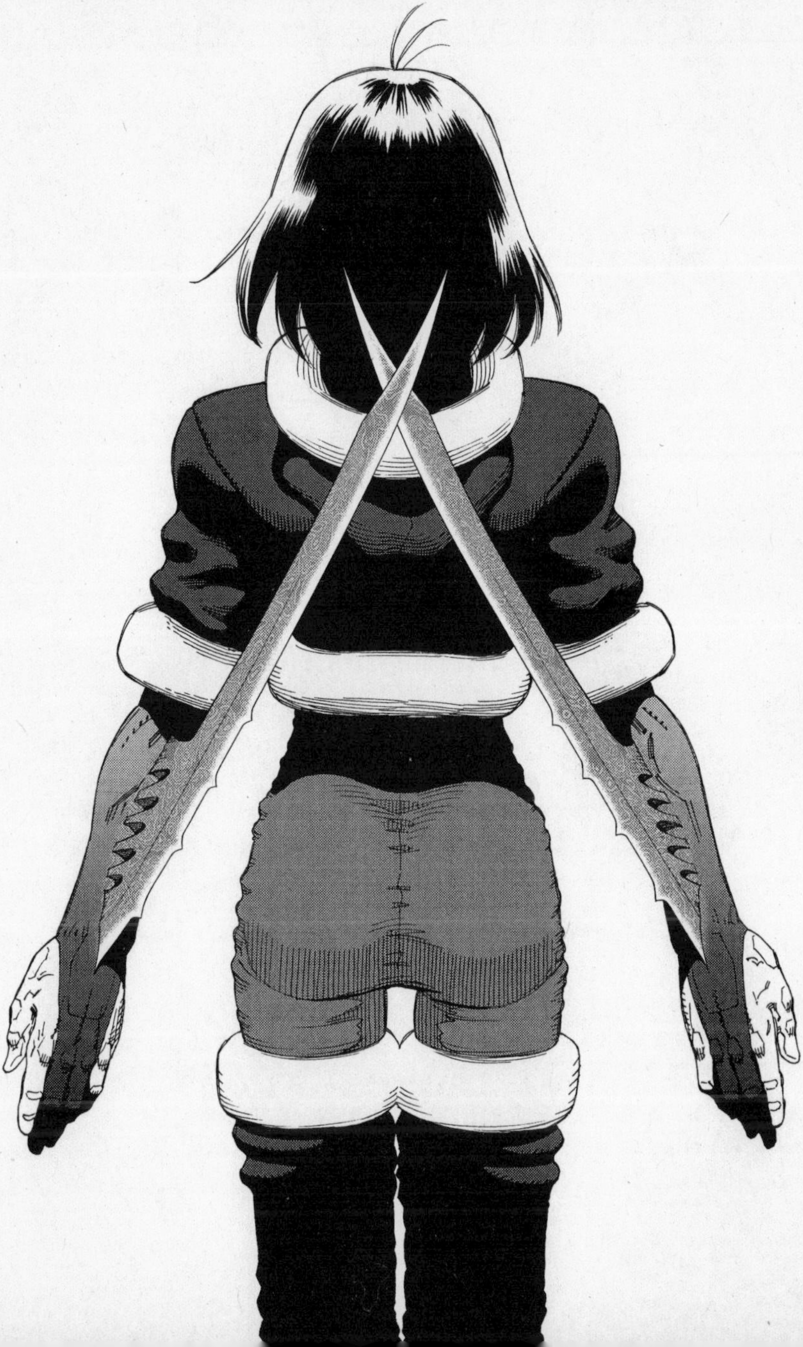

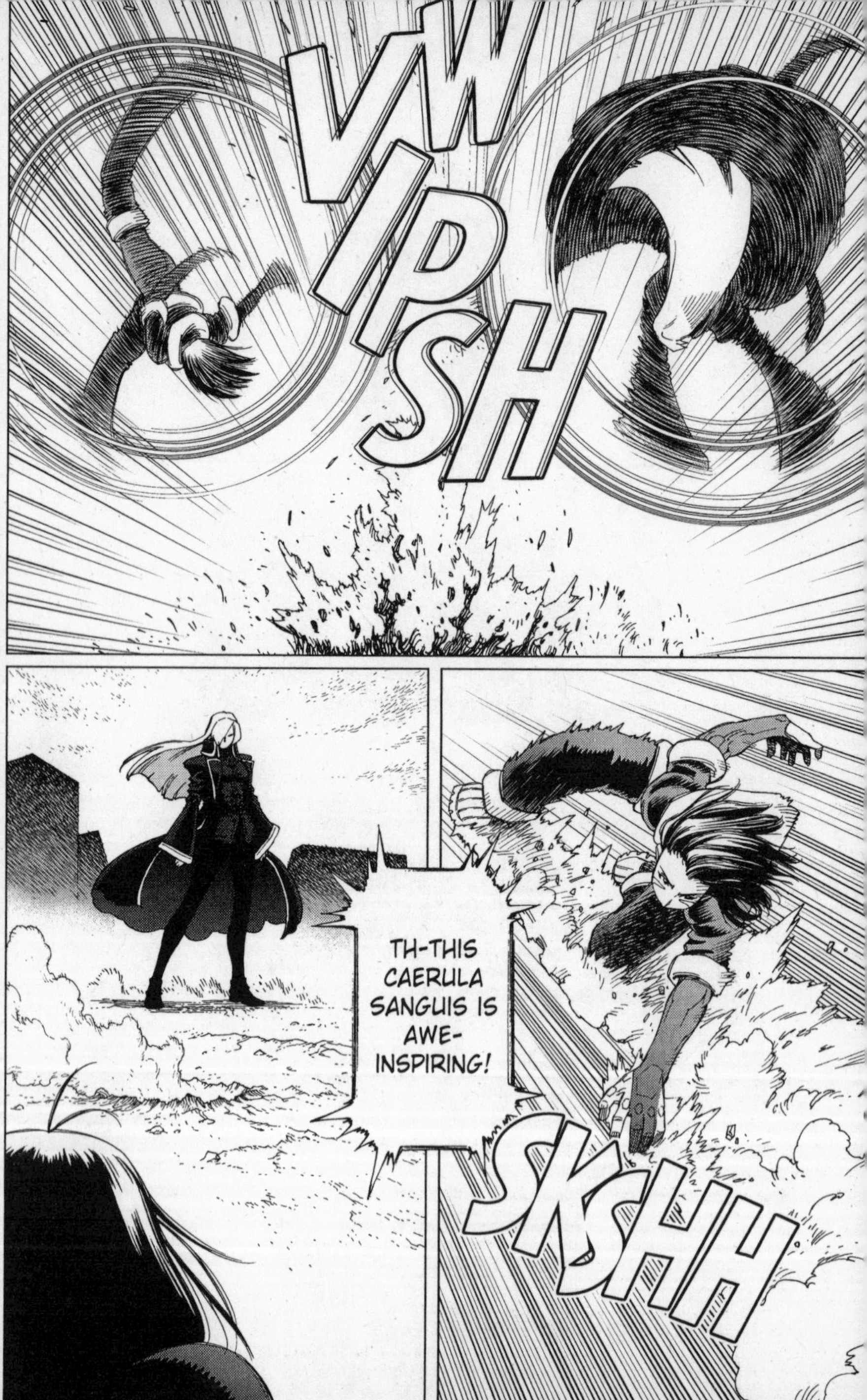
VWIPSH
SKSHH
TH-THIS CAERULA SANGUIS IS AWE-INSPIRING!

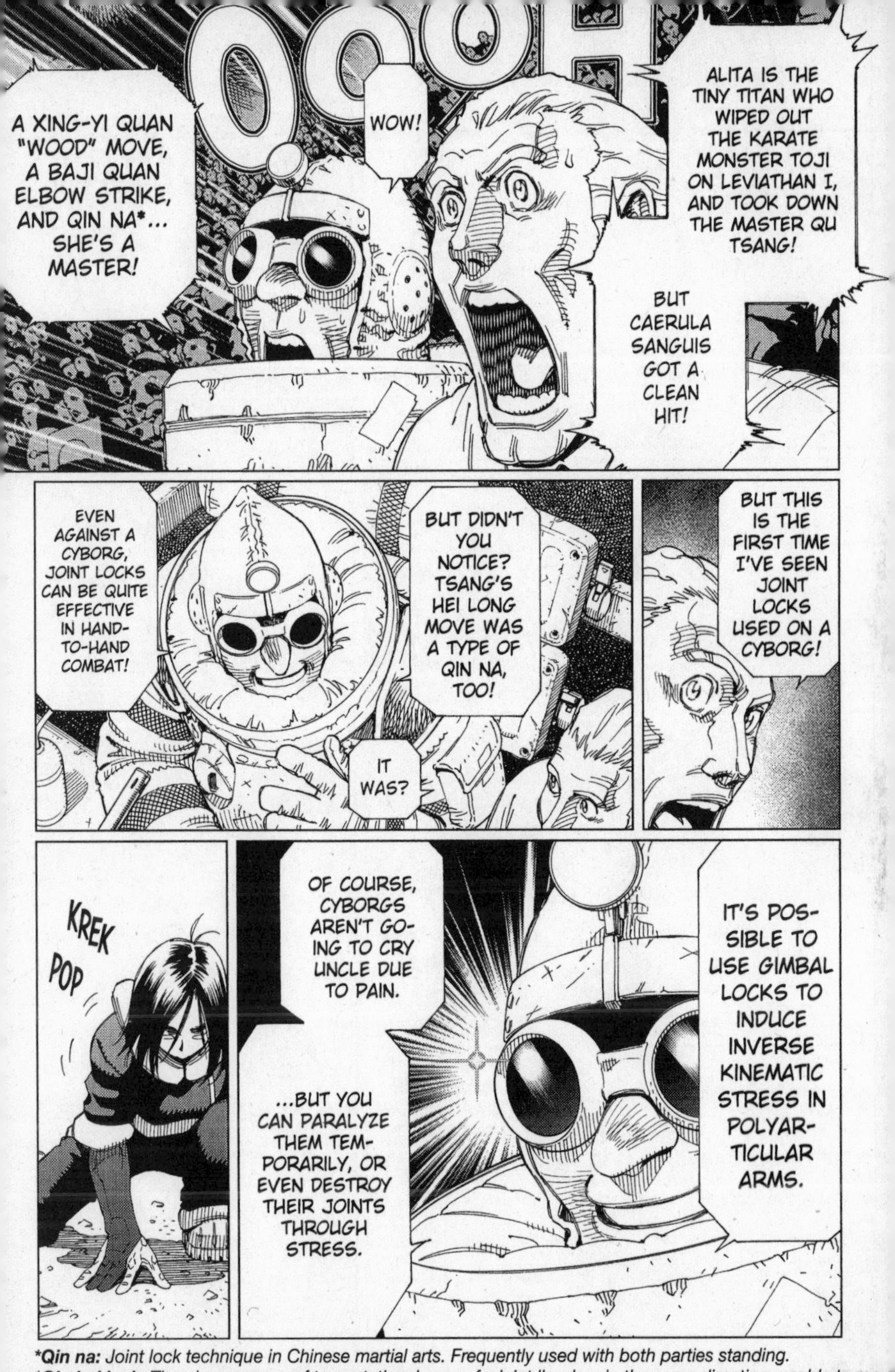
ALITA IS THE TINY TITAN WHO WIPED OUT THE KARATE MONSTER TOJI ON LEVIATHAN I, AND TOOK DOWN THE MASTER QU TSANG!
WOW!
A XING-YI QUAN "WOOD" MOVE, A BAJI QUAN ELBOW STRIKE, AND QIN NA*... SHE'S A MASTER!
BUT CAERULA SANGUIS GOT A CLEAN HIT!
BUT THIS IS THE FIRST TIME I'VE SEEN JOINT LOCKS USED ON A CYBORG!
BUT DIDN'T YOU NOTICE? TSANG'S HEI LONG MOVE WAS A TYPE OF QIN NA, TOO!
EVEN AGAINST A CYBORG, JOINT LOCKS CAN BE QUITE EFFECTIVE IN HAND-TO-HAND COMBAT!
IT WAS?
IT'S POSSIBLE TO USE GIMBAL LOCKS TO INDUCE INVERSE KINEMATIC STRESS IN POLYARTICULAR ARMS.
OF COURSE, CYBORGS AREN'T GOING TO CRY UNCLE DUE TO PAIN.
...BUT YOU CAN PARALYZE THEM TEMPORARILY, OR EVEN DESTROY THEIR JOINTS THROUGH STRESS.
KREK
POP

Qin na: *Joint lock technique in Chinese martial arts. Frequently used with both parties standing.*

Gimbal lock: *The phenomenon of two rotational axes of a joint lined up in the same direction, unable to mov*

Inverse kinematics: *Controlling movement of the arm through its extremities.*

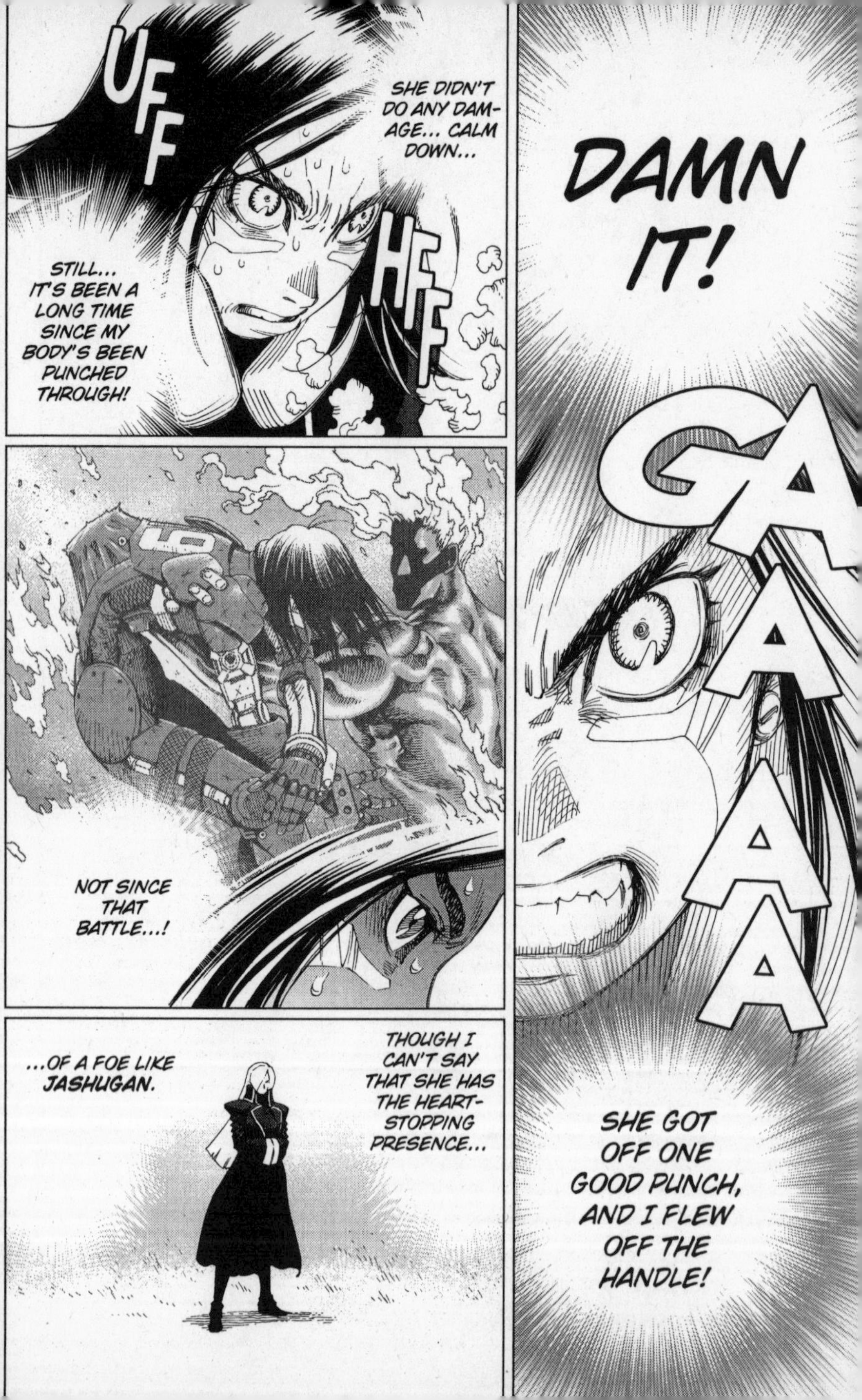
DAMN IT!
GAAAAA
SHE GOT OFF ONE GOOD PUNCH, AND I FLEW OFF THE HANDLE!
SHE DIDN'T DO ANY DAM-AGE... CALM DOWN...
UFF
HFF
STILL... IT'S BEEN A LONG TIME SINCE MY BODY'S BEEN PUNCHED THROUGH!
NOT SINCE THAT BATTLE...!
THOUGH I CAN'T SAY THAT SHE HAS THE HEART-STOPPING PRESENCE...
...OF A FOE LIKE JASHUGAN.

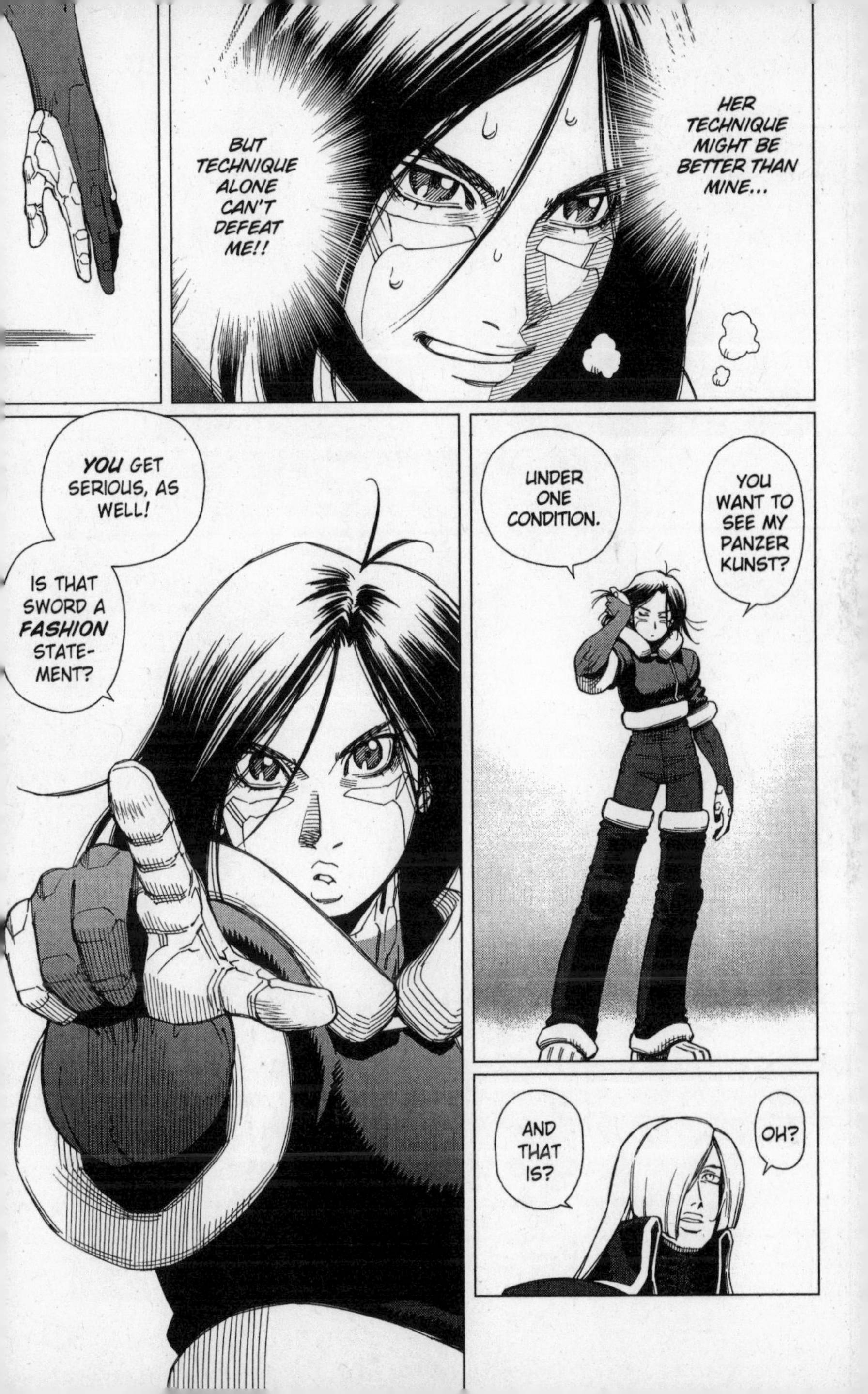
HER TECHNIQUE MIGHT BE BETTER THAN MINE...
BUT TECHNIQUE ALONE CAN'T DEFEAT ME!!
YOU WANT TO SEE MY PANZER KUNST?
UNDER ONE CONDITION.
OH?
AND THAT IS?
YOU GET SERIOUS, AS WELL!
IS THAT SWORD A FASHION STATEMENT?

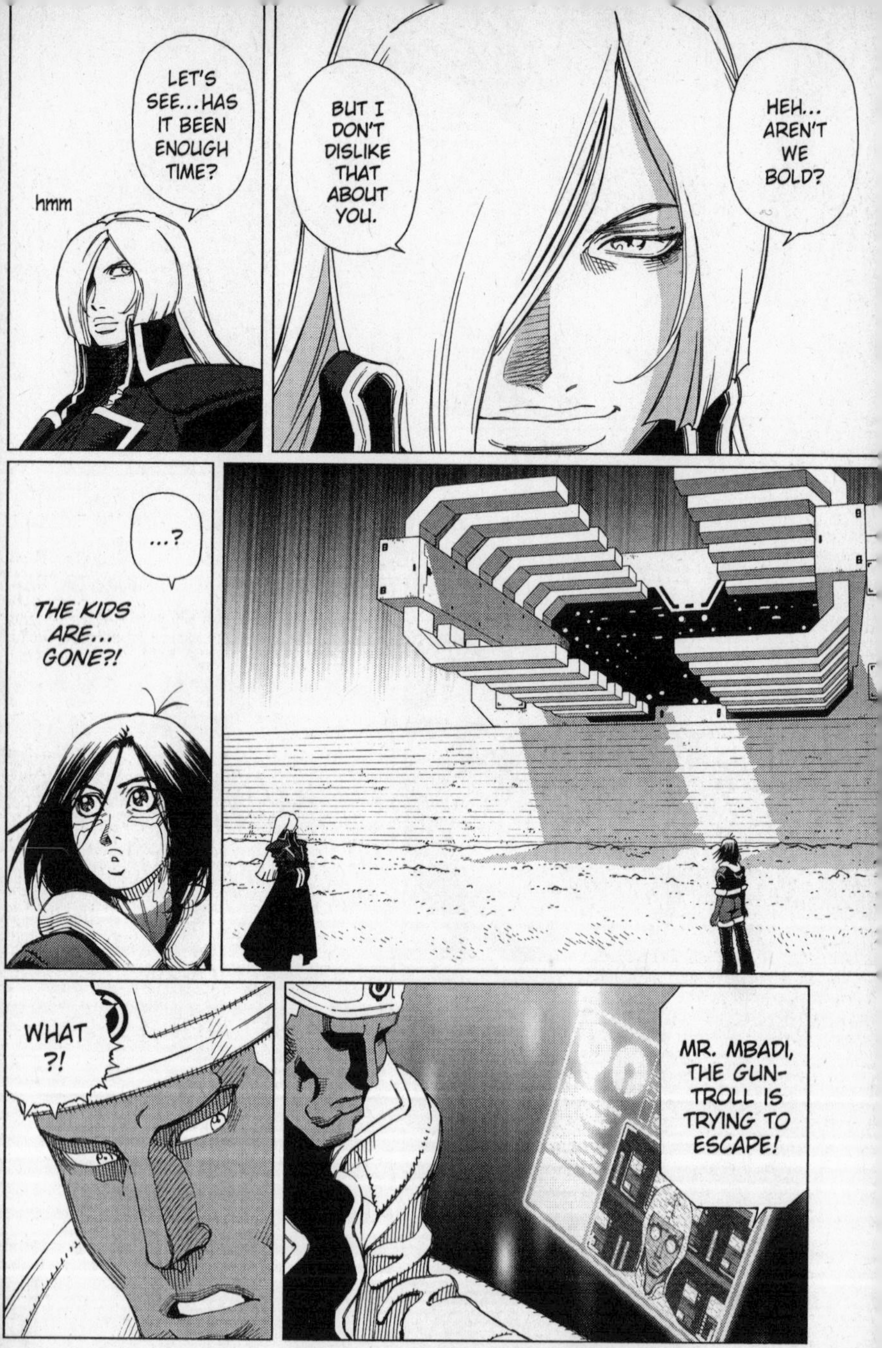
HEH... AREN'T WE BOLD?
BUT I DON'T DISLIKE THAT ABOUT YOU.
LET'S SEE...HAS IT BEEN ENOUGH TIME?
hmm
...?
THE KIDS ARE... GONE?!
MR. MBADI, THE GUN-TROLL IS TRYING TO ESCAPE!
WHAT ?!

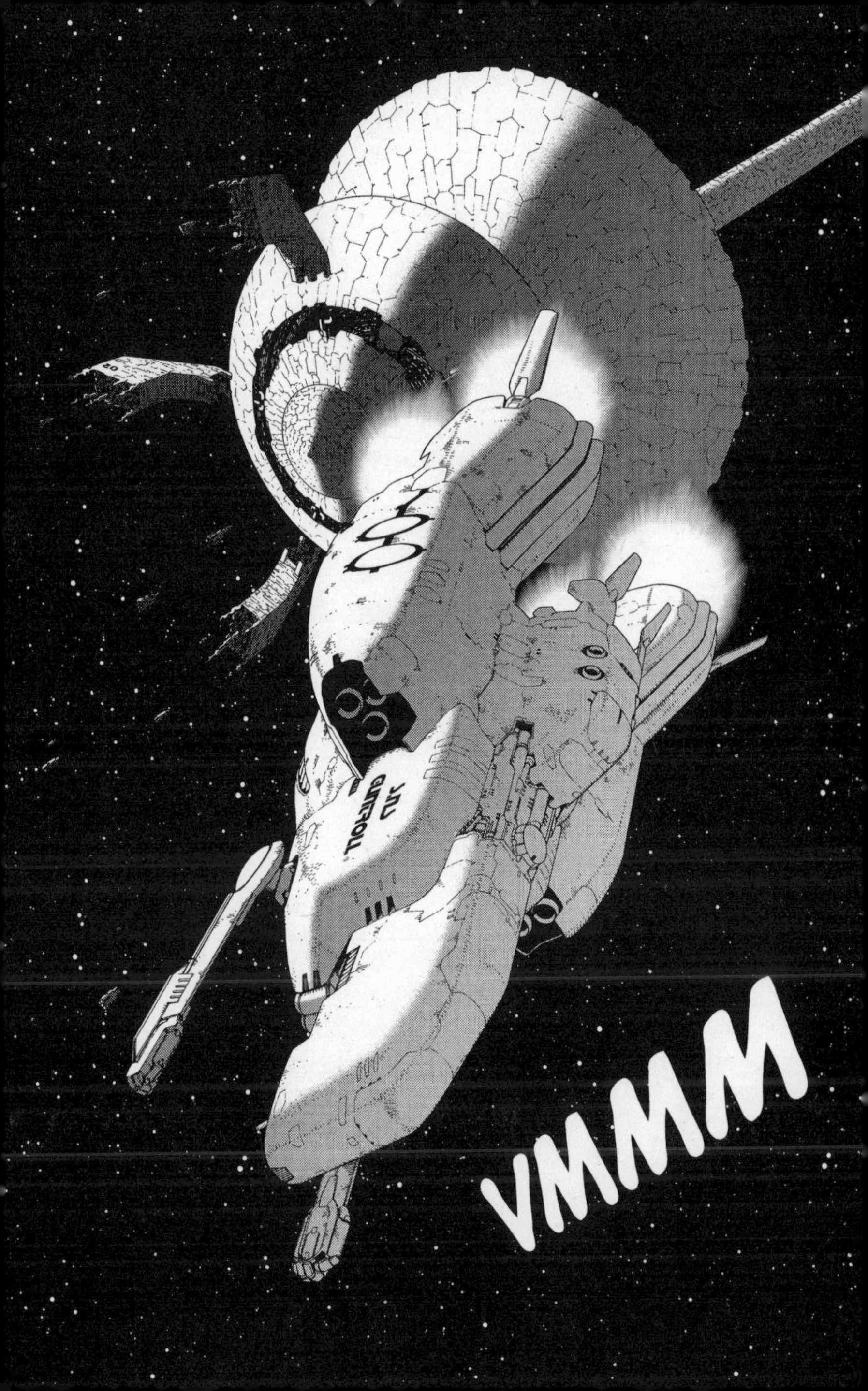
VMMM

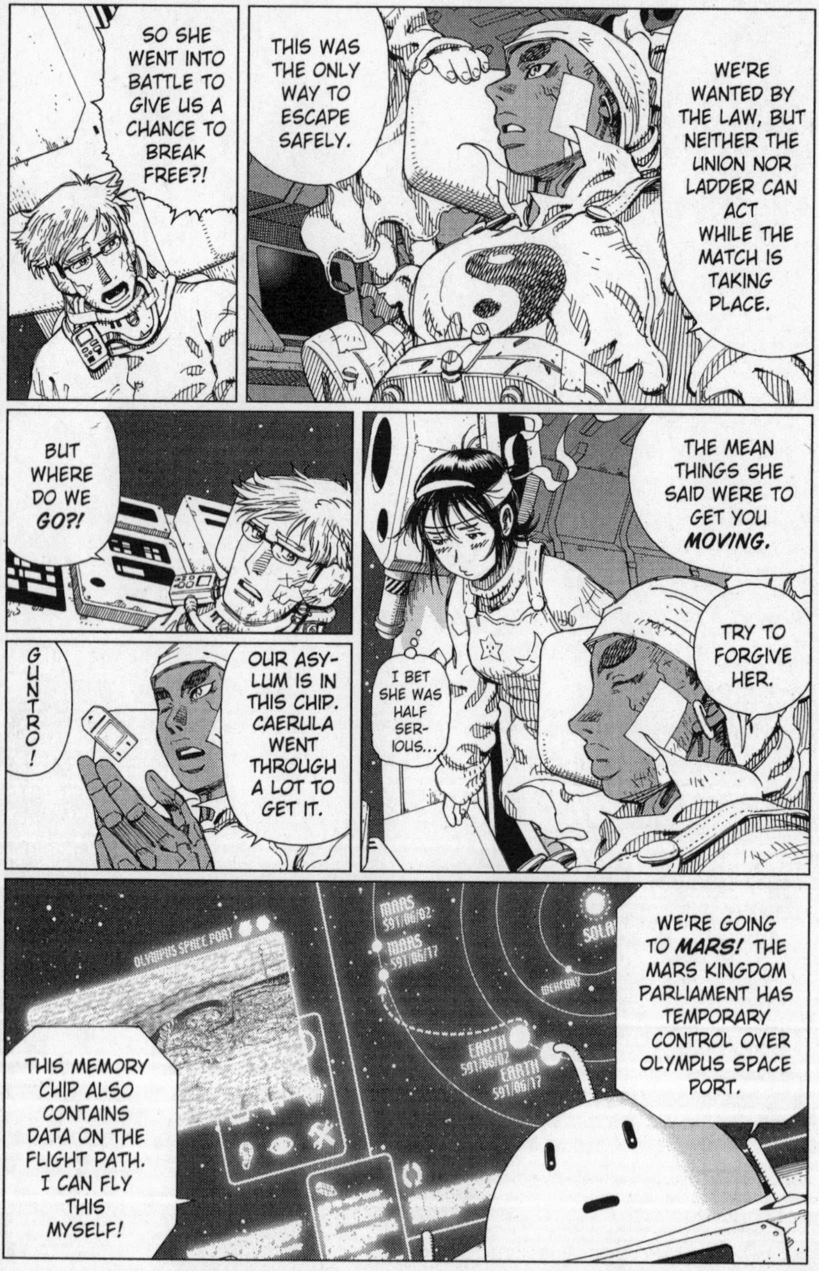
WE'RE WANTED BY THE LAW, BUT NEITHER THE UNION NOR LADDER CAN ACT WHILE THE MATCH IS TAKING PLACE.
THIS WAS THE ONLY WAY TO ESCAPE SAFELY.
SO SHE WENT INTO BATTLE TO GIVE US A CHANCE TO BREAK FREE?!
THE MEAN THINGS SHE SAID WERE TO GET YOU ***MOVING.***
TRY TO FORGIVE HER.
I BET SHE WAS HALF SERIOUS...
BUT WHERE DO WE ***GO?!***
OUR ASYLUM IS IN THIS CHIP. CAERULA WENT THROUGH A LOT TO GET IT.
GUNTRO!
WE'RE GOING TO ***MARS!*** THE MARS KINGDOM PARLIAMENT HAS TEMPORARY CONTROL OVER OLYMPUS SPACE PORT.
MARS 597/06/02
MARS 597/06/17
OLYMPUS SPACE PORT
EARTH 597/06/02
EARTH 597/06/17
THIS MEMORY CHIP ALSO CONTAINS DATA ON THE FLIGHT PATH. I CAN FLY THIS MYSELF!

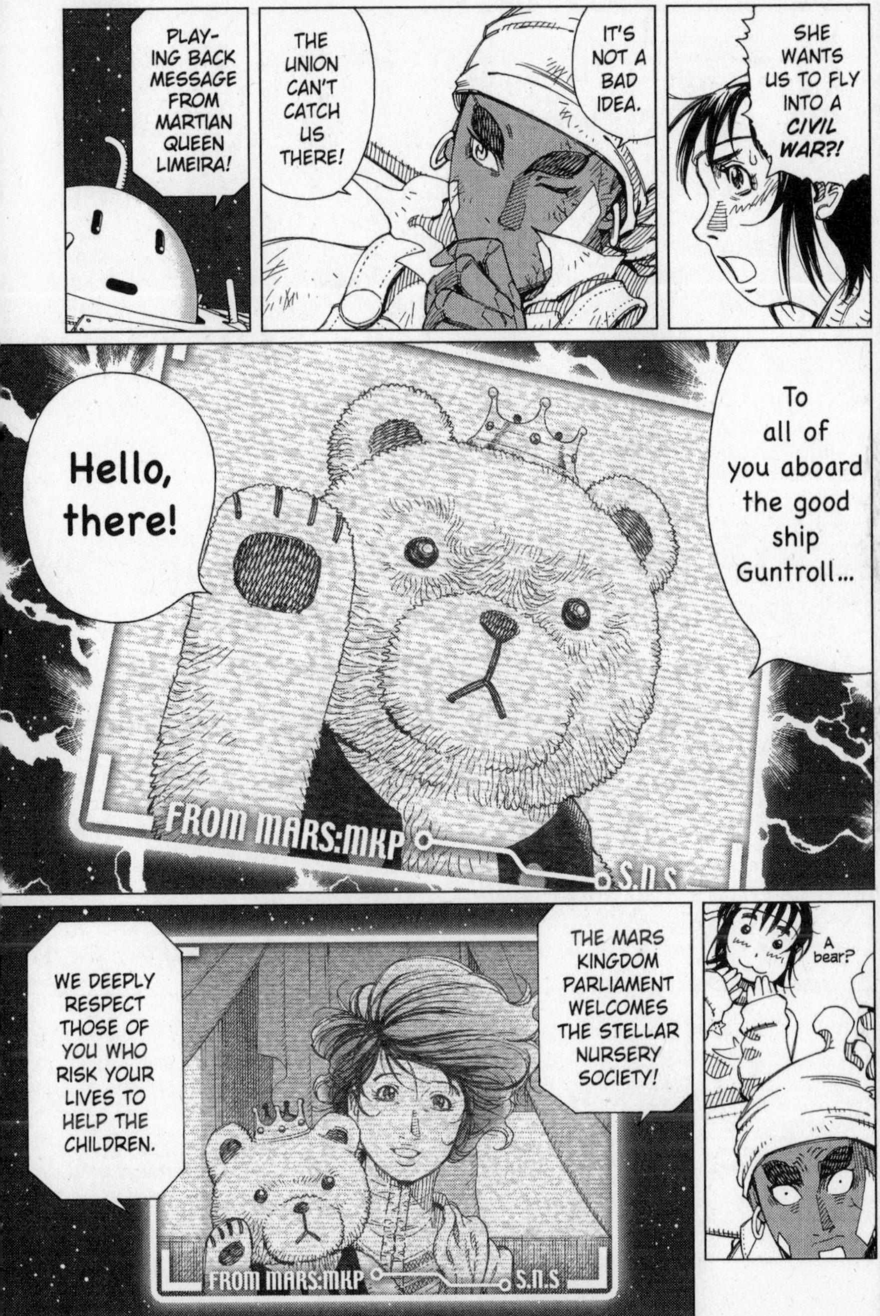
SHE WANTS US TO FLY INTO A CIVIL WAR?!
IT'S NOT A BAD IDEA.
THE UNION CAN'T CATCH US THERE!
PLAYING BACK MESSAGE FROM MARTIAN QUEEN LIMEIRA!
To all of you aboard the good ship Guntroll...
Hello, there!
FROM MARS:MKP
S.N.S
A bear?
THE MARS KINGDOM PARLIAMENT WELCOMES THE STELLAR NURSERY SOCIETY!
WE DEEPLY RESPECT THOSE OF YOU WHO RISK YOUR LIVES TO HELP THE CHILDREN.
FROM MARS:MKP
S.N.S

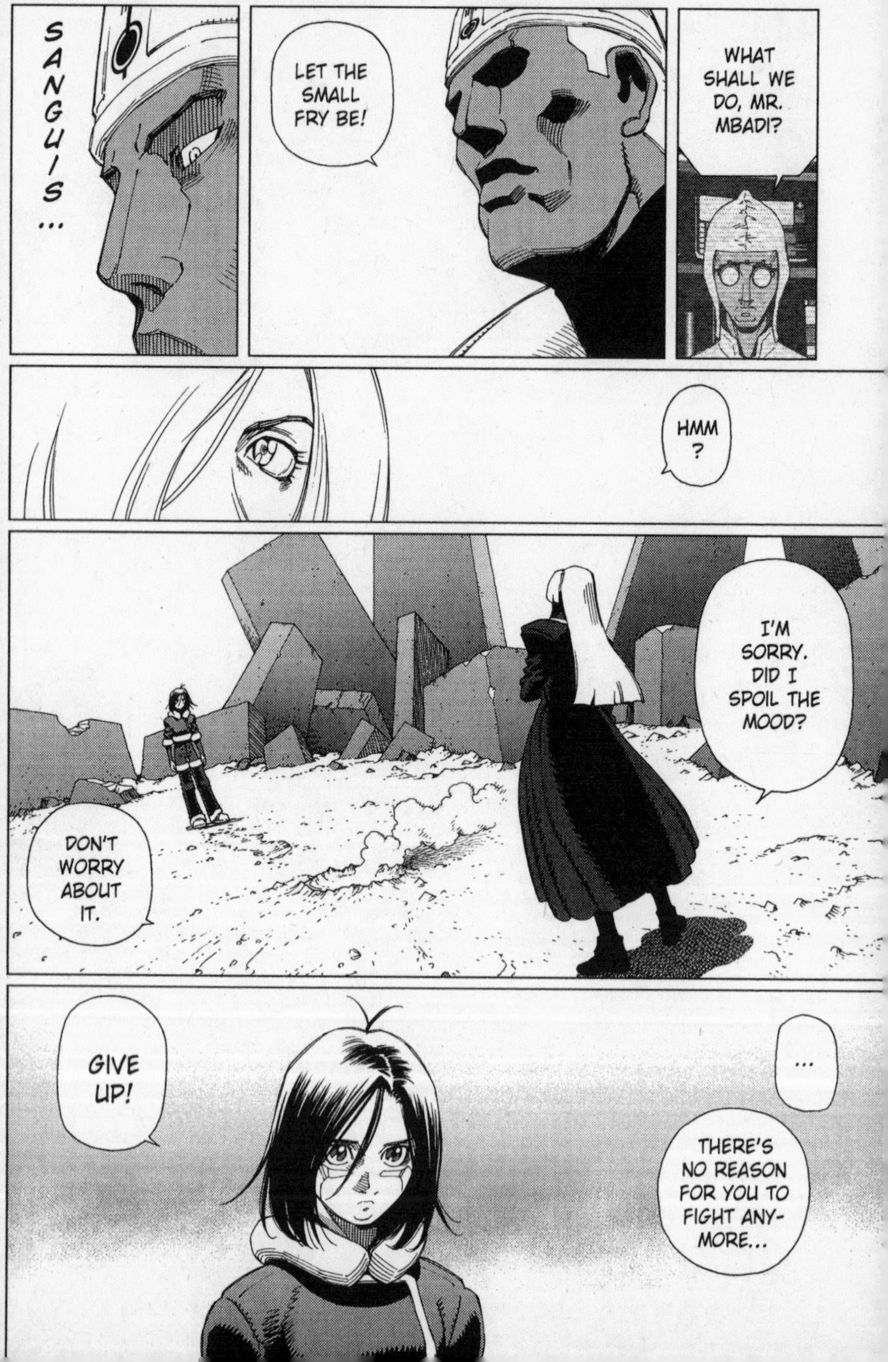
WHAT SHALL WE DO, MR. MBADI?
LET THE SMALL FRY BE!
SANGUIS...
HMM ?
I'M SORRY. DID I SPOIL THE MOOD?
DON'T WORRY ABOUT IT.
...
THERE'S NO REASON FOR YOU TO FIGHT ANY-MORE...
GIVE UP!

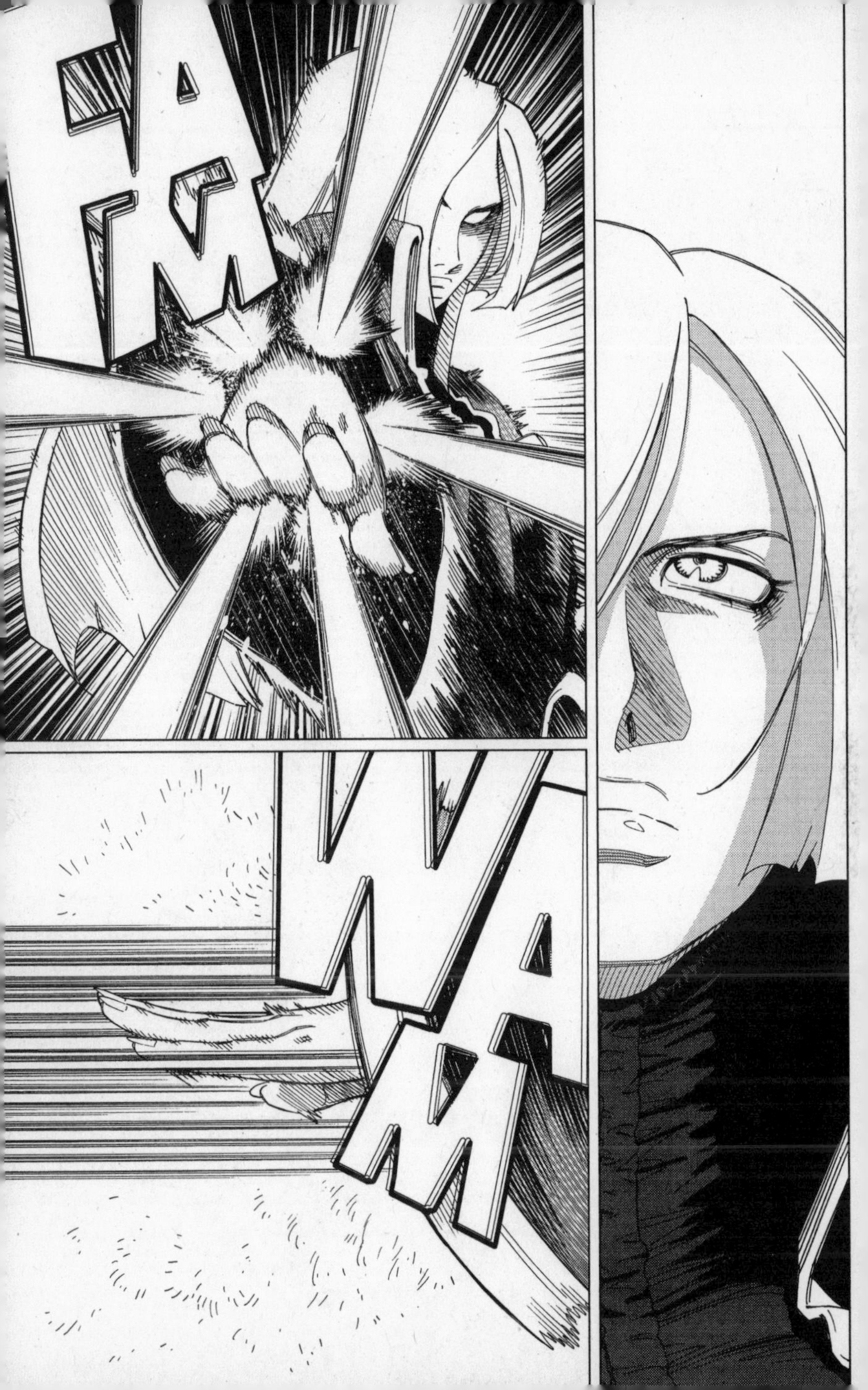

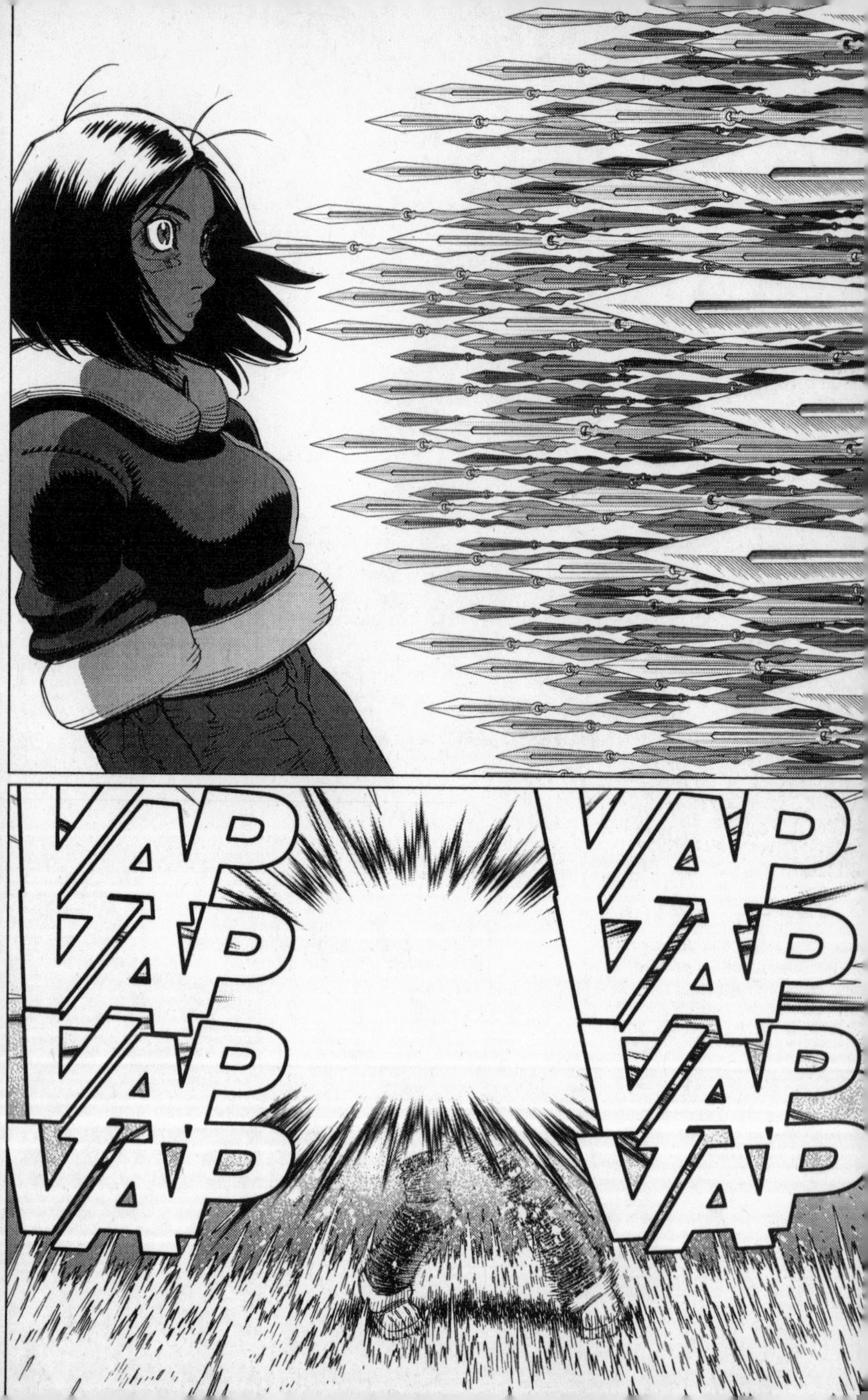
VAP
VAP
VAP
VAP
VAP
VAP
VAP
VAP

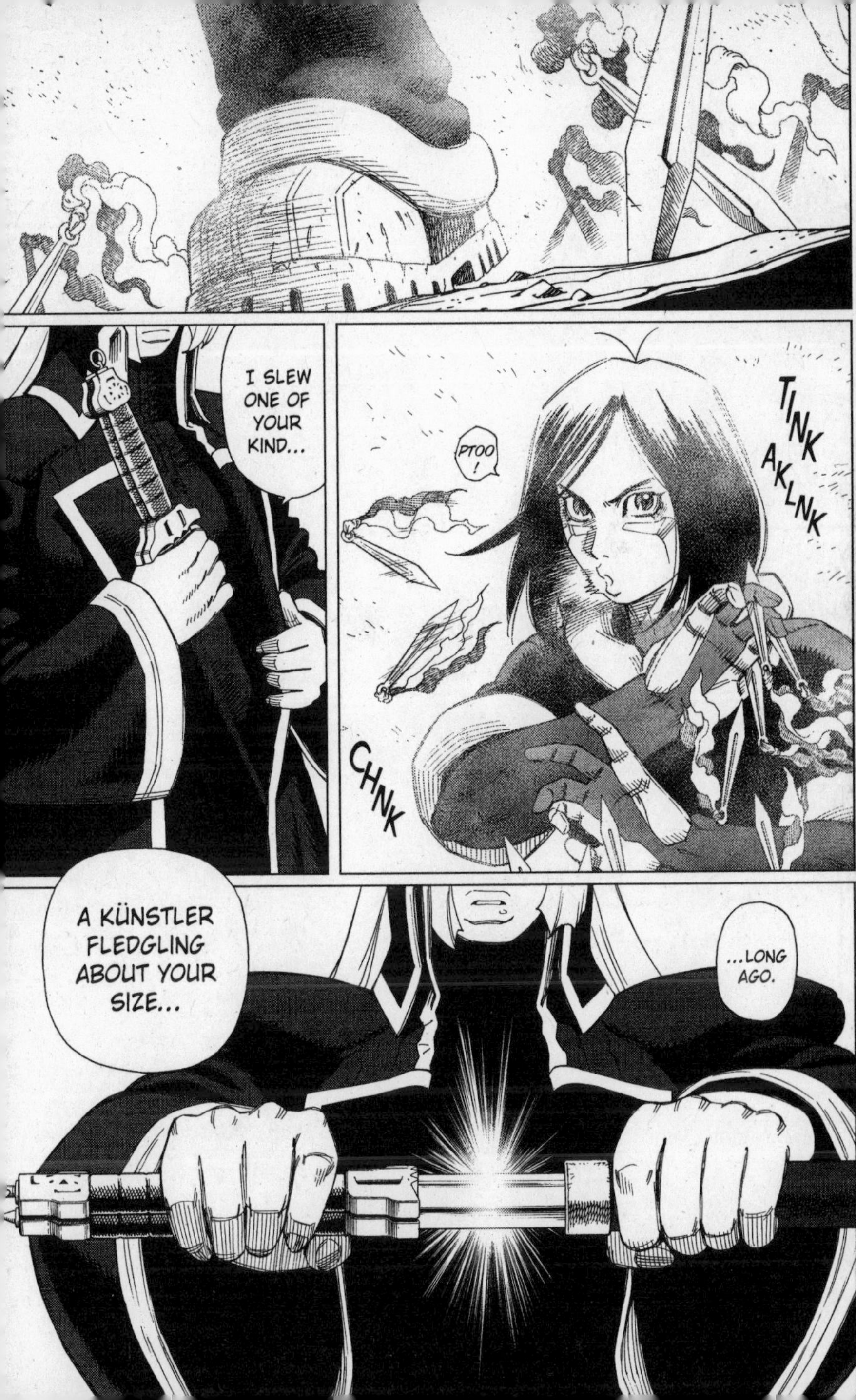
PTOO!
TINK AKLNK
CHNK
I SLEW ONE OF YOUR KIND...
A KÜNSTLER FLEDGLING ABOUT YOUR SIZE...
...LONG AGO.

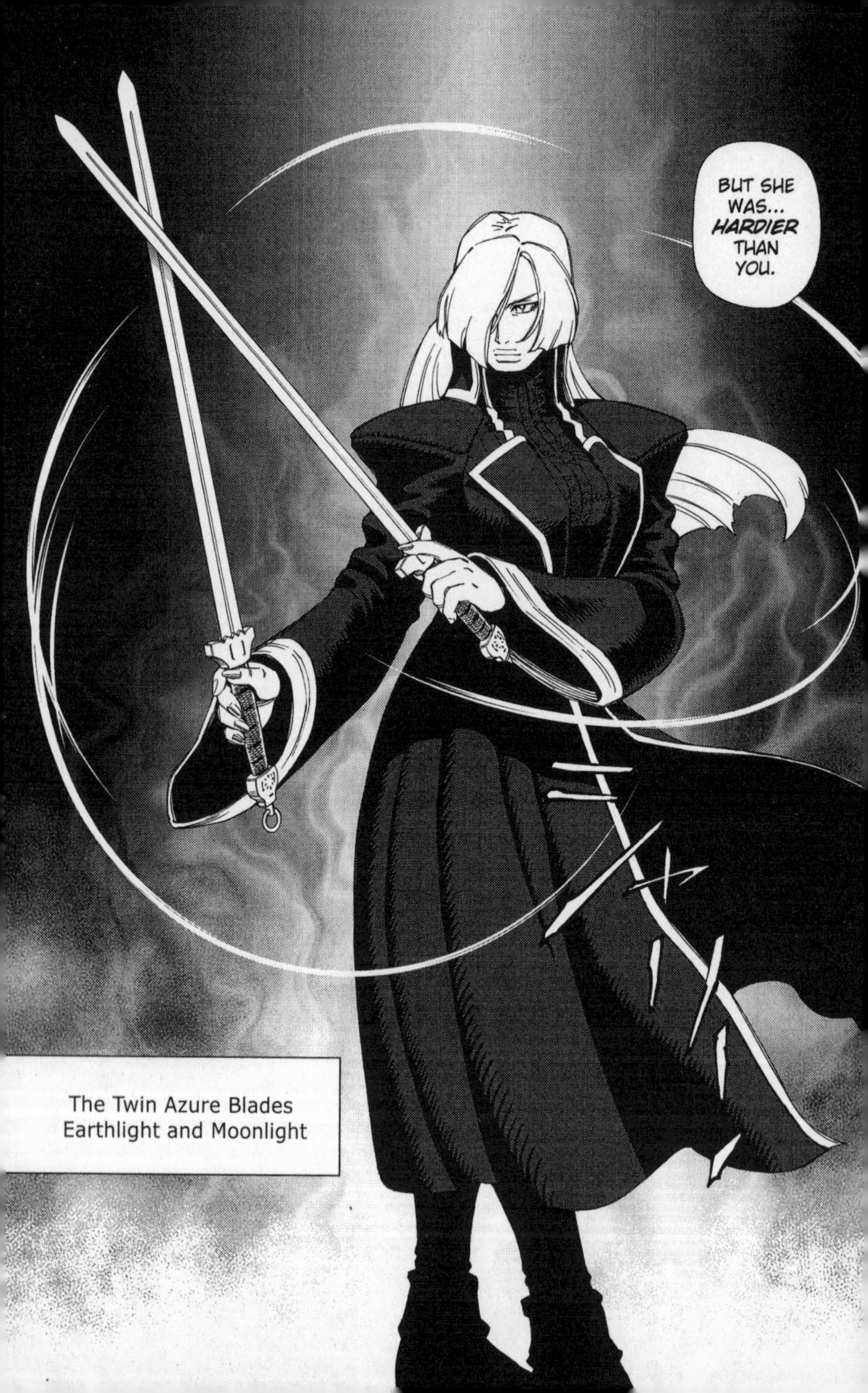
BUT SHE WAS... HARDIER THAN YOU.
The Twin Azure Blades Earthlight and Moonlight

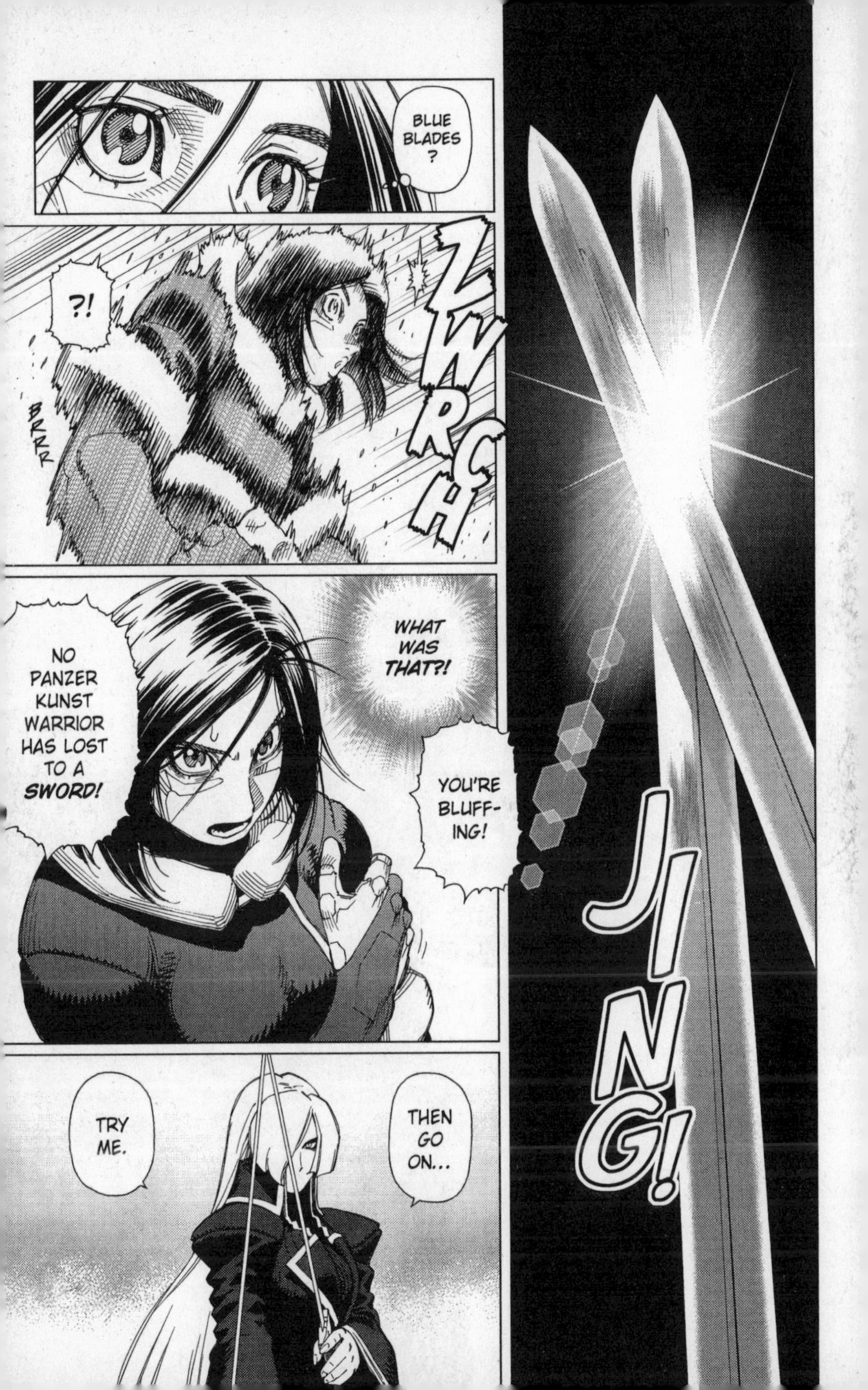
JING!
BLUE BLADES ?
ZWRCH
?!
BRRR
WHAT WAS THAT?!
YOU'RE BLUFF-ING!
NO PANZER KUNST WARRIOR HAS LOST TO A SWORD!
THEN GO ON...
TRY ME.

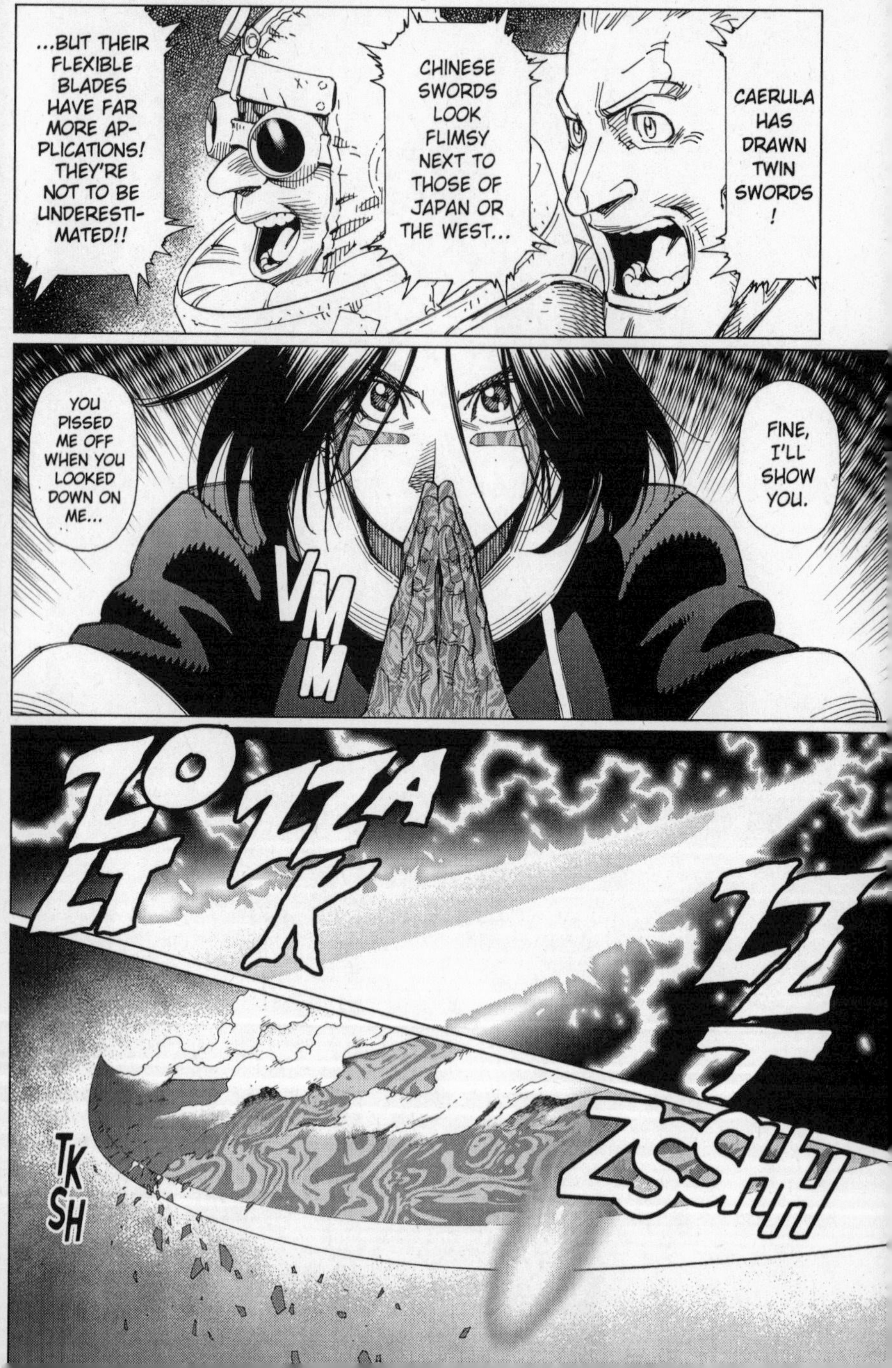
CAERULA HAS DRAWN TWIN SWORDS!
CHINESE SWORDS LOOK FLIMSY NEXT TO THOSE OF JAPAN OR THE WEST...
...BUT THEIR FLEXIBLE BLADES HAVE FAR MORE APPLICATIONS! THEY'RE NOT TO BE UNDERESTIMATED!!
YOU PISSED ME OFF WHEN YOU LOOKED DOWN ON ME...
FINE, I'LL SHOW YOU.
VMMM
ZZT
ZZAK
ZOLT
ZSHH
TKSH

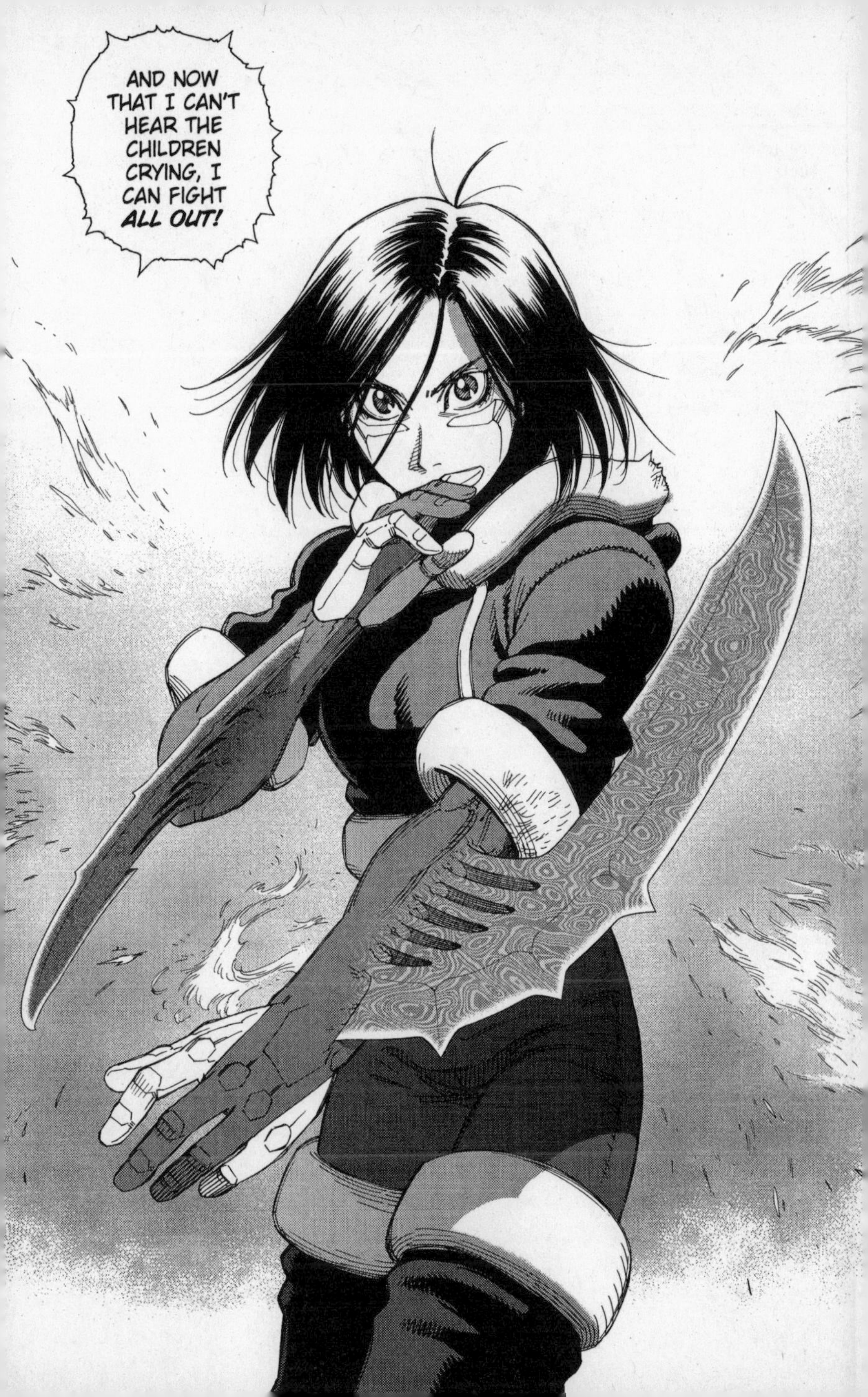
AND NOW THAT I CAN'T HEAR THE CHILDREN CRYING, I CAN FIGHT ALL OUT!

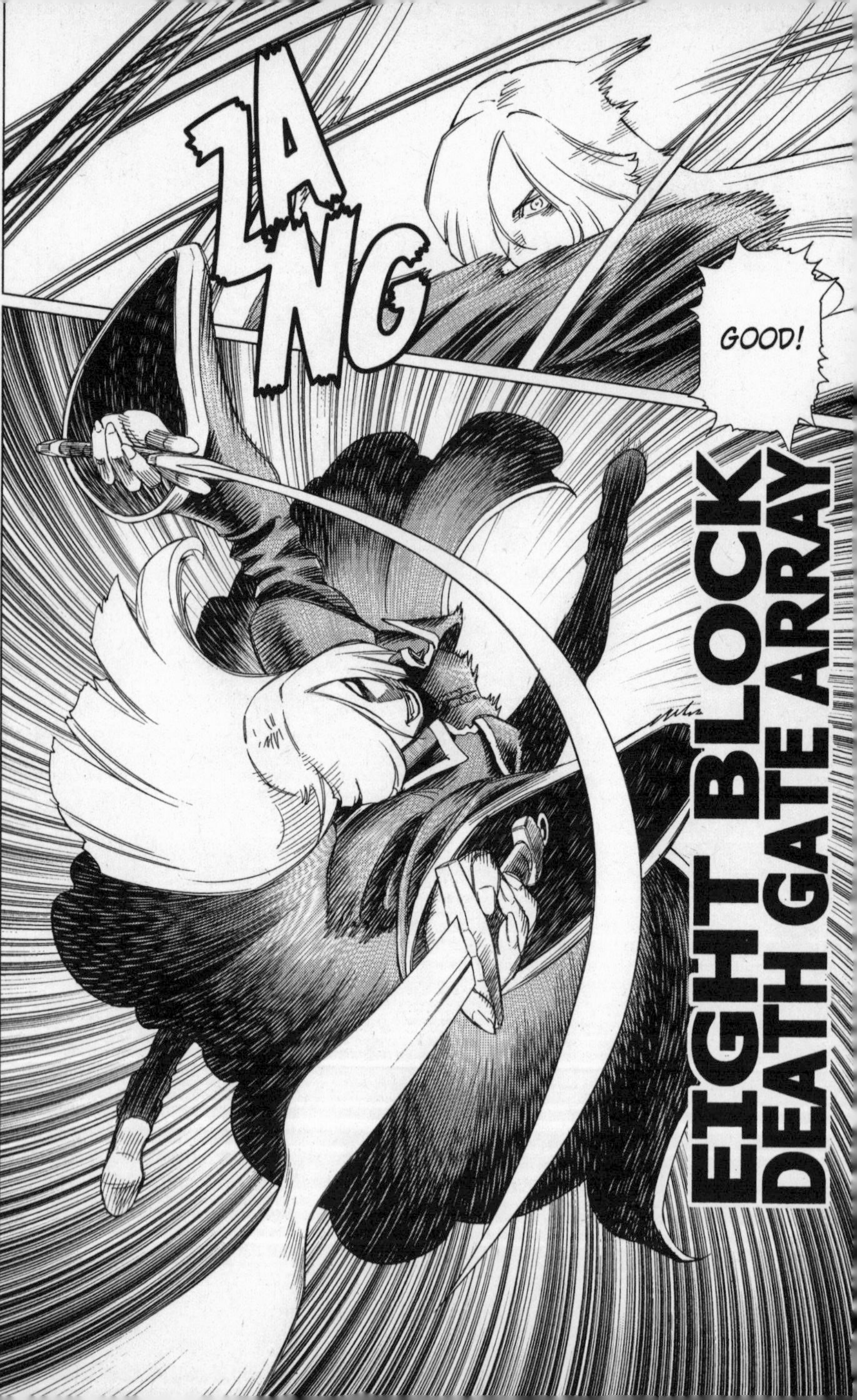
GOOD!
ZANG
EIGHT BLOCK
DEATH GATE ARRAY

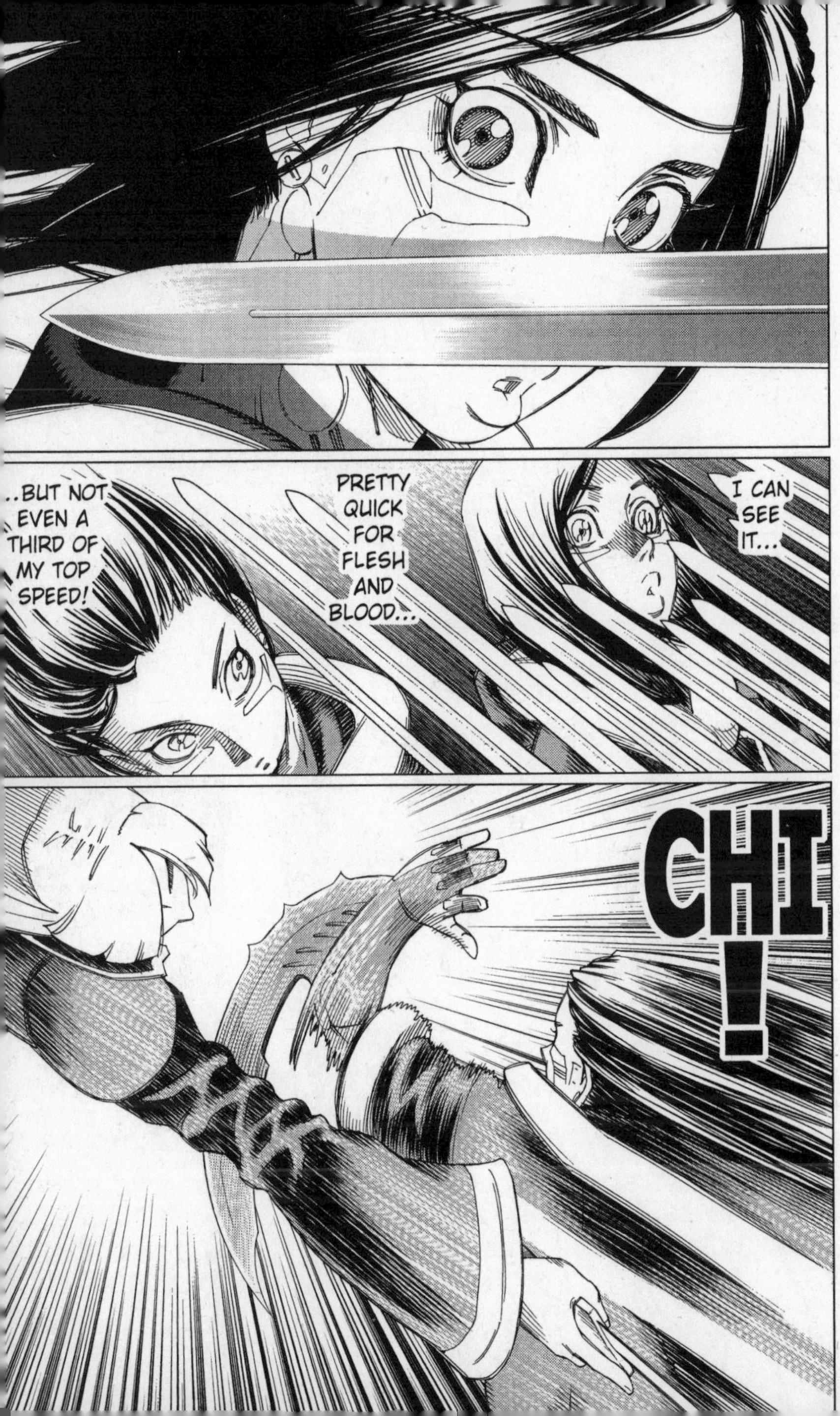
I CAN SEE IT...
PRETTY QUICK FOR FLESH AND BLOOD...
...BUT NOT EVEN A THIRD OF MY TOP SPEED!
CHI!

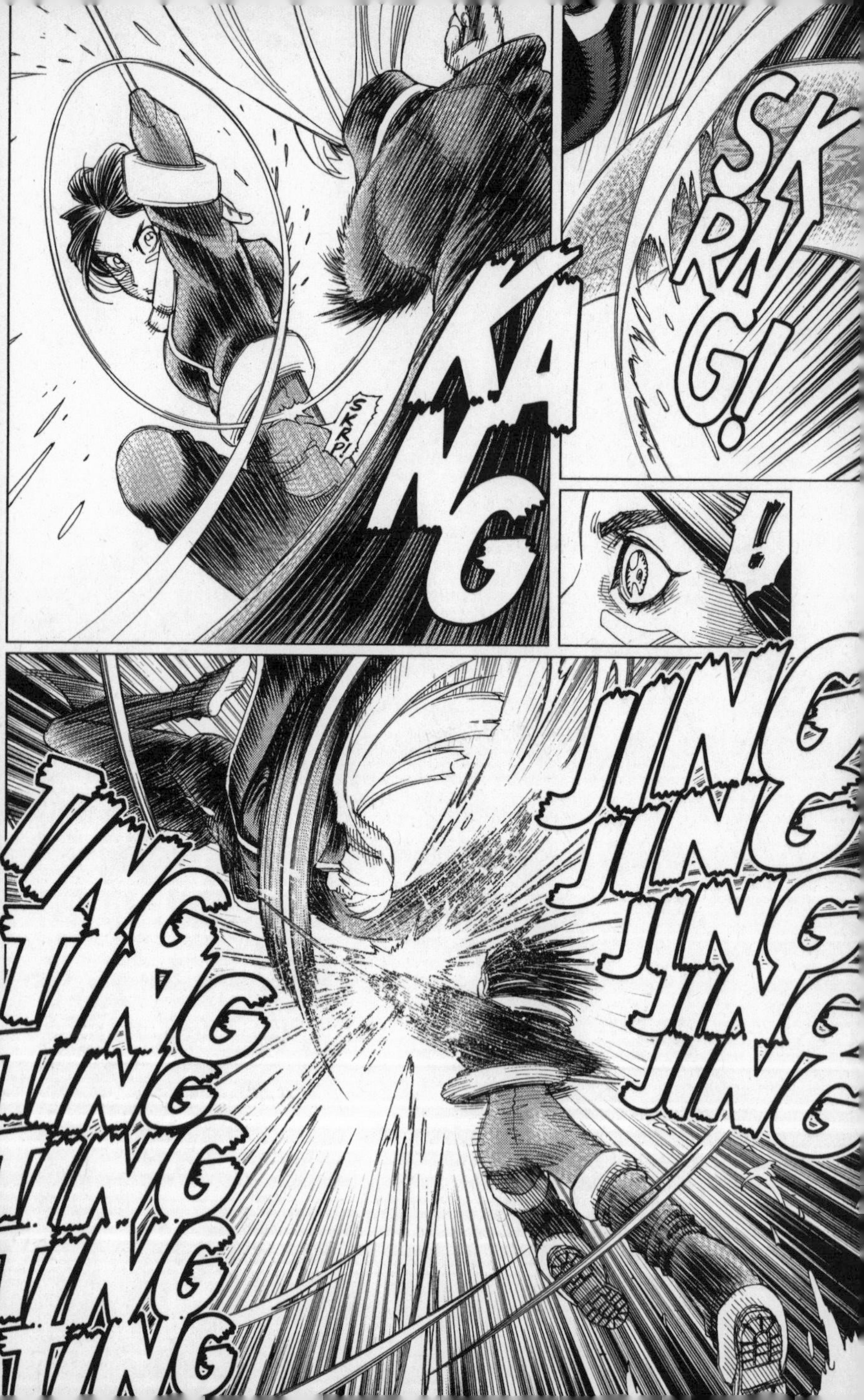
SKRNG!
!
KANG
SKRP!
JING JING JING JING JING
TING TING TING TING TING TING

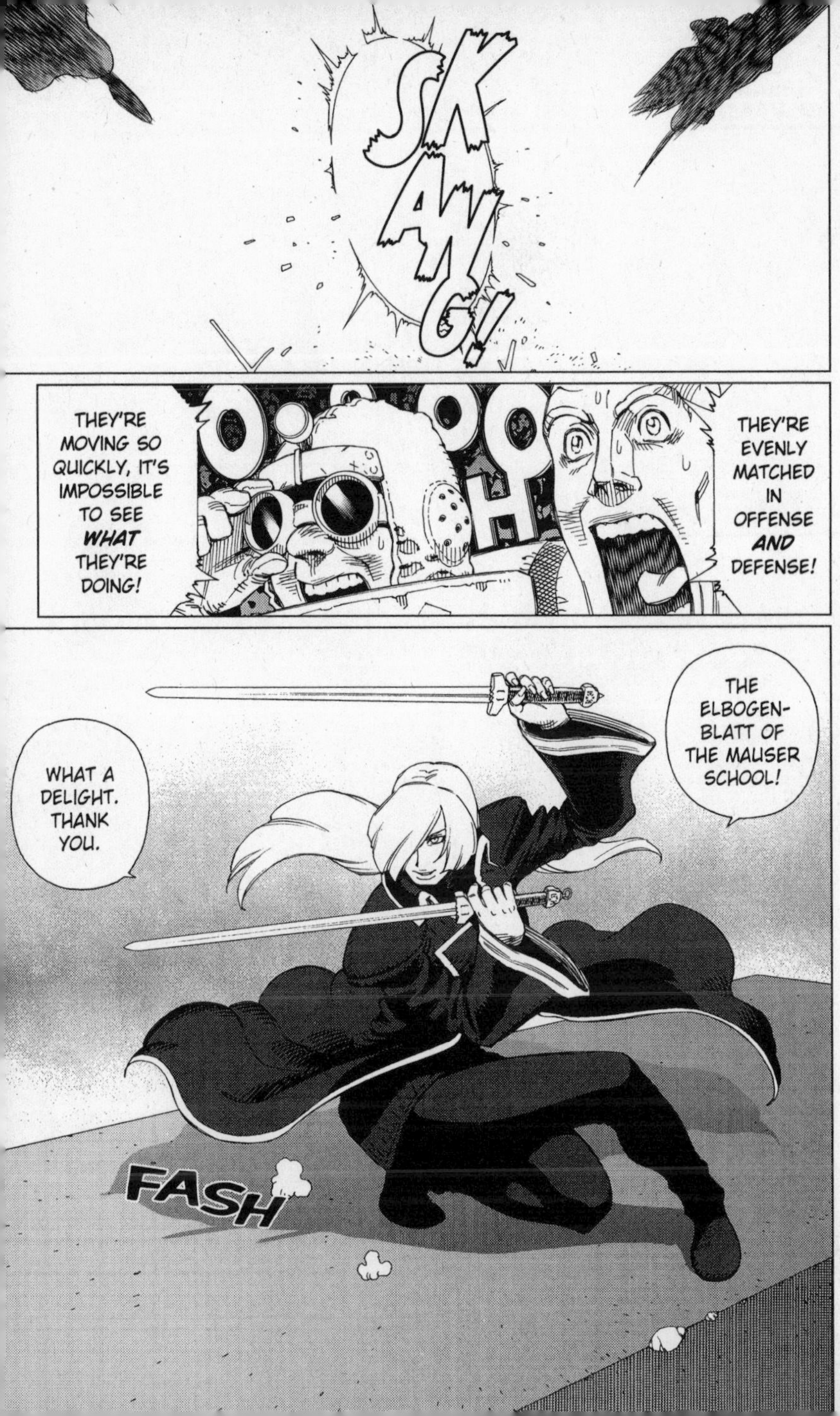
SKANG!
THEY'RE EVENLY MATCHED IN OFFENSE AND DEFENSE!
OOOOH
THEY'RE MOVING SO QUICKLY, IT'S IMPOSSIBLE TO SEE WHAT THEY'RE DOING!
THE ELBOGEN-BLATT OF THE MAUSER SCHOOL!
WHAT A DELIGHT. THANK YOU.
FASH

I SHOULD BE MUCH FASTER THAN HER...!

WHY...?!

SKEE

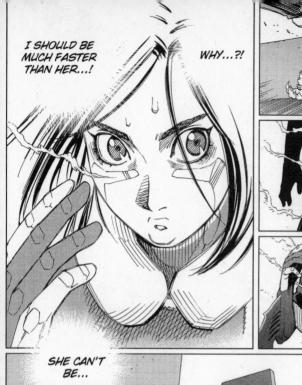

SHE CAN'T BE...

SHp

VMM

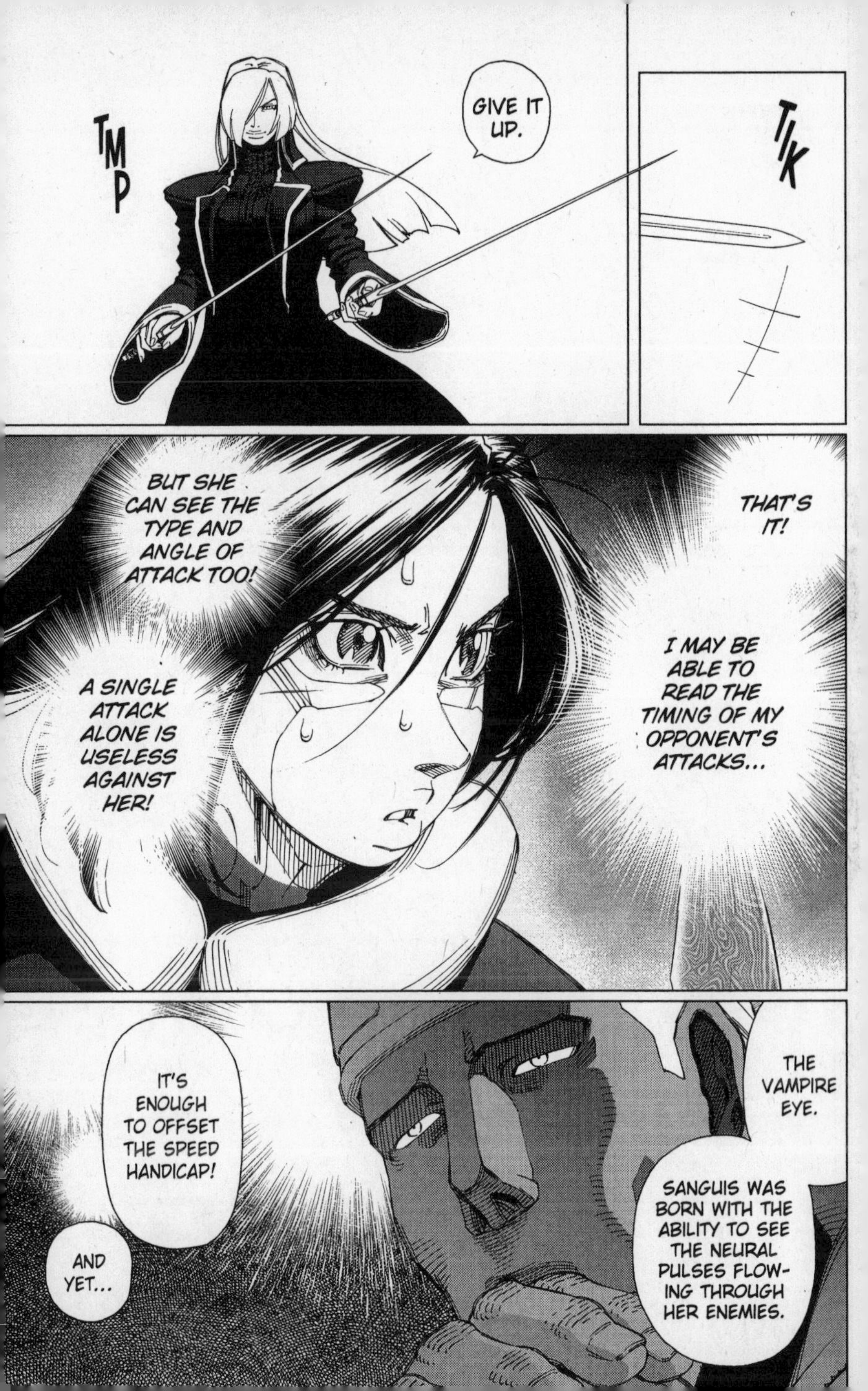
TIK
TMP
GIVE IT UP.
THAT'S IT!
I MAY BE ABLE TO READ THE TIMING OF MY OPPONENT'S ATTACKS...
BUT SHE CAN SEE THE TYPE AND ANGLE OF ATTACK TOO!
A SINGLE ATTACK ALONE IS USELESS AGAINST HER!
THE VAMPIRE EYE.
SANGUIS WAS BORN WITH THE ABILITY TO SEE THE NEURAL PULSES FLOWING THROUGH HER ENEMIES.
IT'S ENOUGH TO OFFSET THE SPEED HANDICAP!
AND YET...

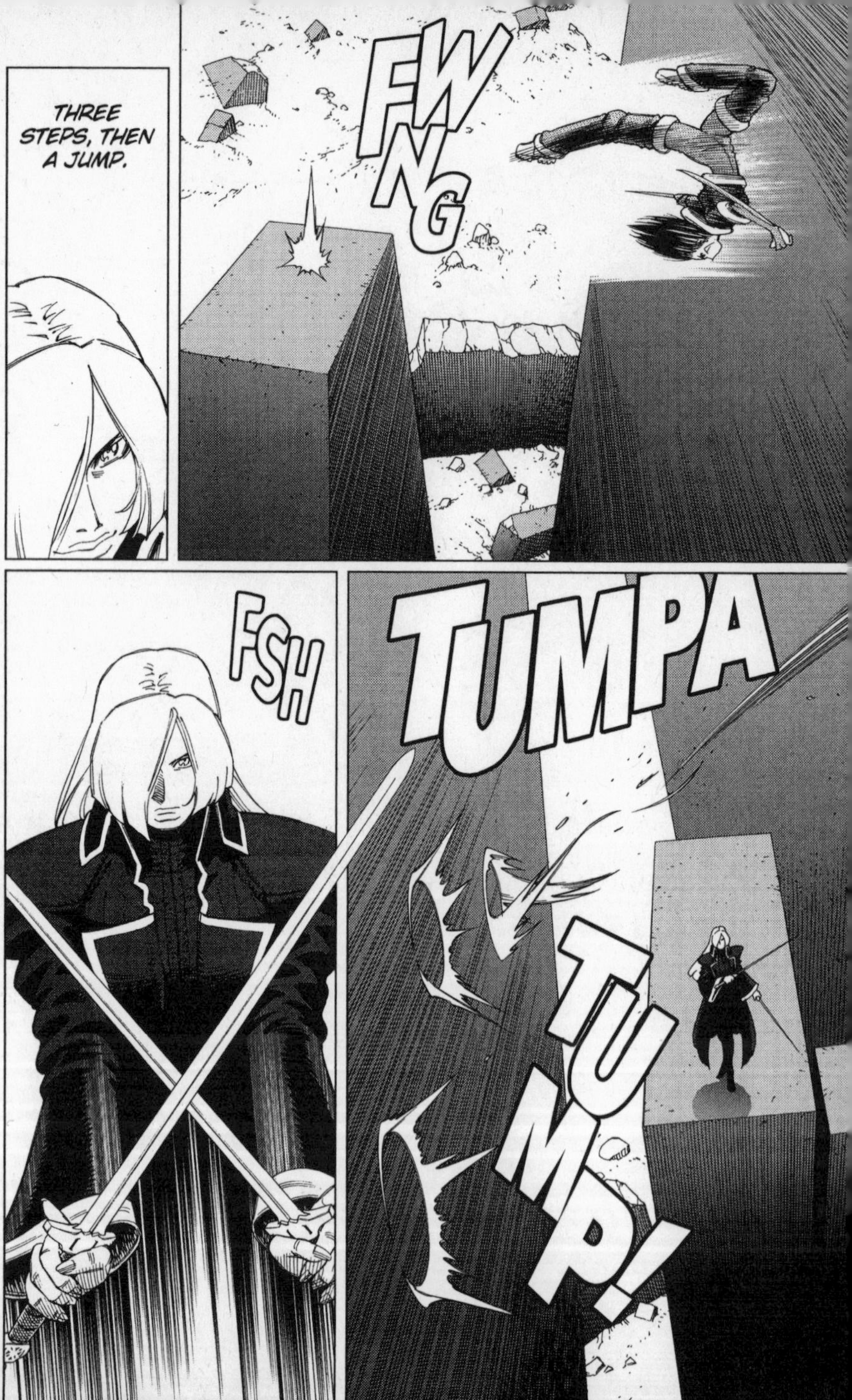
FWNG
THREE STEPS, THEN A JUMP.
TUMPA
TUMP!
FSH

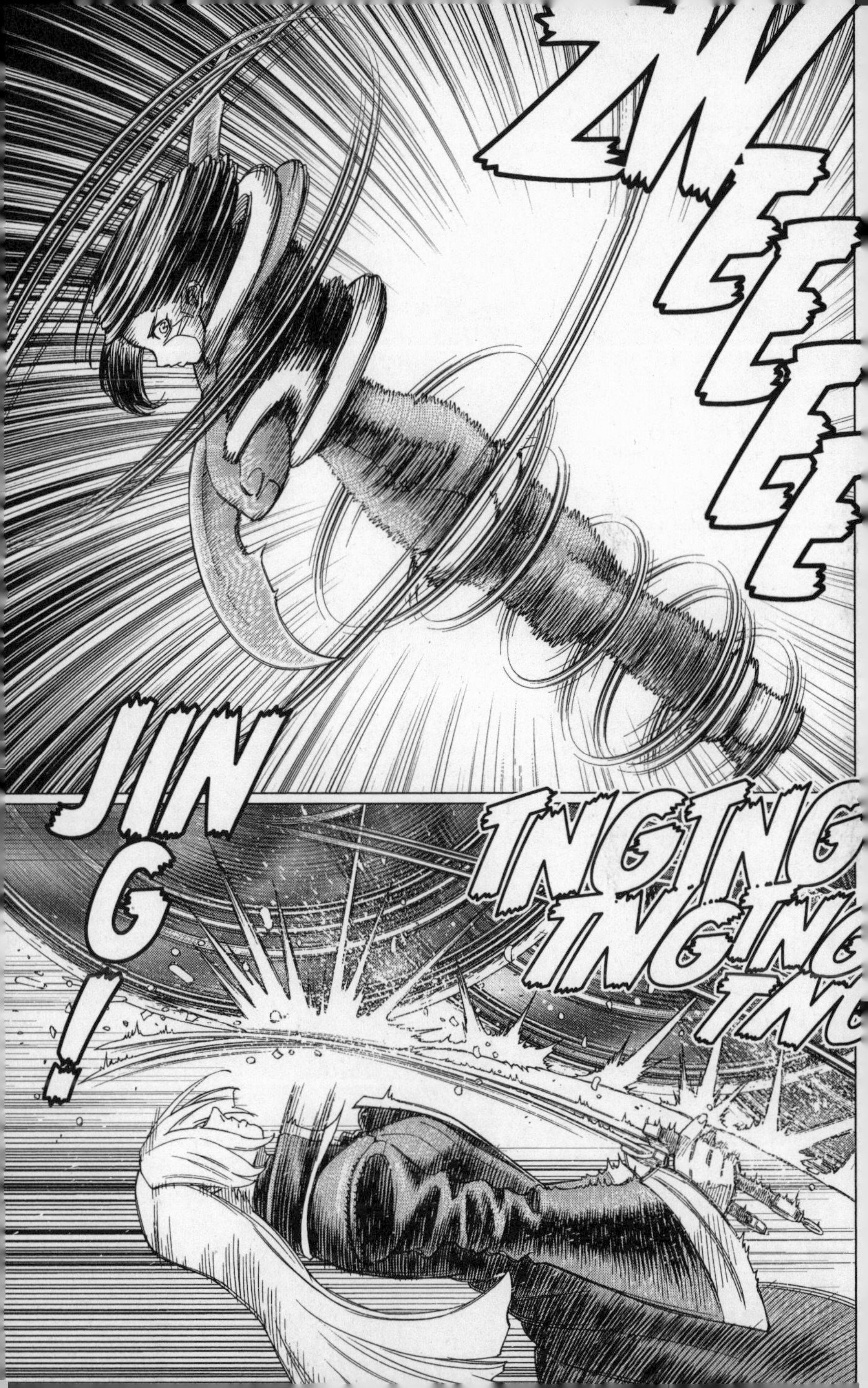
ZWEEEE
INGNG
INGNG
ING
JING!

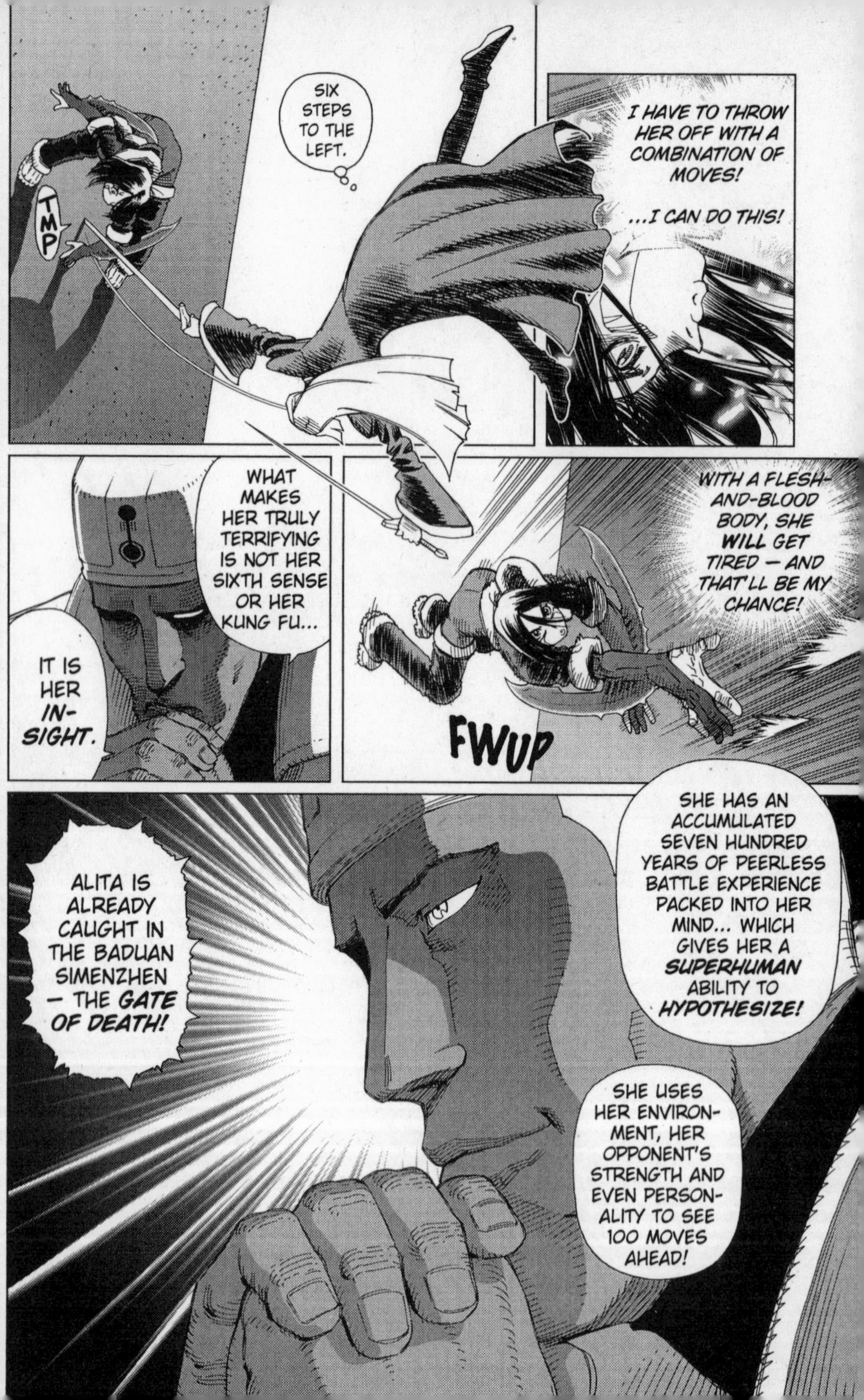
I HAVE TO THROW HER OFF WITH A COMBINATION OF MOVES!
...I CAN DO THIS!
SIX STEPS TO THE LEFT.
TMP
WITH A FLESH-AND-BLOOD BODY, SHE **WILL** GET TIRED — AND THAT'LL BE MY CHANCE!
FWUP
WHAT MAKES HER TRULY TERRIFYING IS NOT HER SIXTH SENSE OR HER KUNG FU...
IT IS HER ***INSIGHT***.
SHE HAS AN ACCUMULATED SEVEN HUNDRED YEARS OF PEERLESS BATTLE EXPERIENCE PACKED INTO HER MIND... WHICH GIVES HER A ***SUPERHUMAN*** ABILITY TO ***HYPOTHESIZE!***
ALITA IS ALREADY CAUGHT IN THE BADUAN SIMENZHEN — THE ***GATE OF DEATH!***
SHE USES HER ENVIRONMENT, HER OPPONENT'S STRENGTH AND EVEN PERSONALITY TO SEE 100 MOVES AHEAD!

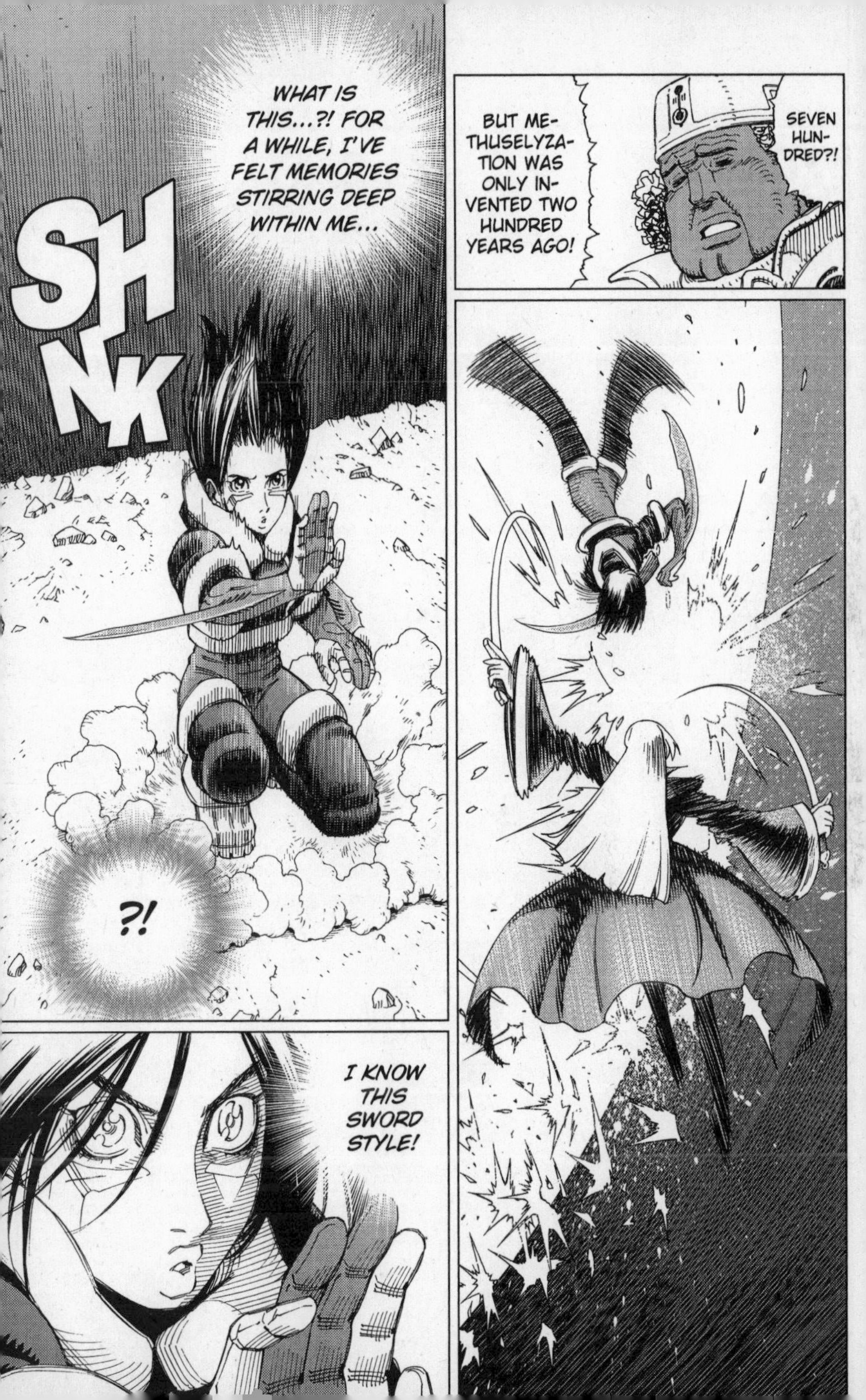
SEVEN HUN-DRED?!
BUT ME-THUSELYZA-TION WAS ONLY IN-VENTED TWO HUNDRED YEARS AGO!
WHAT IS THIS...?! FOR A WHILE, I'VE FELT MEMORIES STIRRING DEEP WITHIN ME...
SHNK
?!
I KNOW THIS SWORD STYLE!

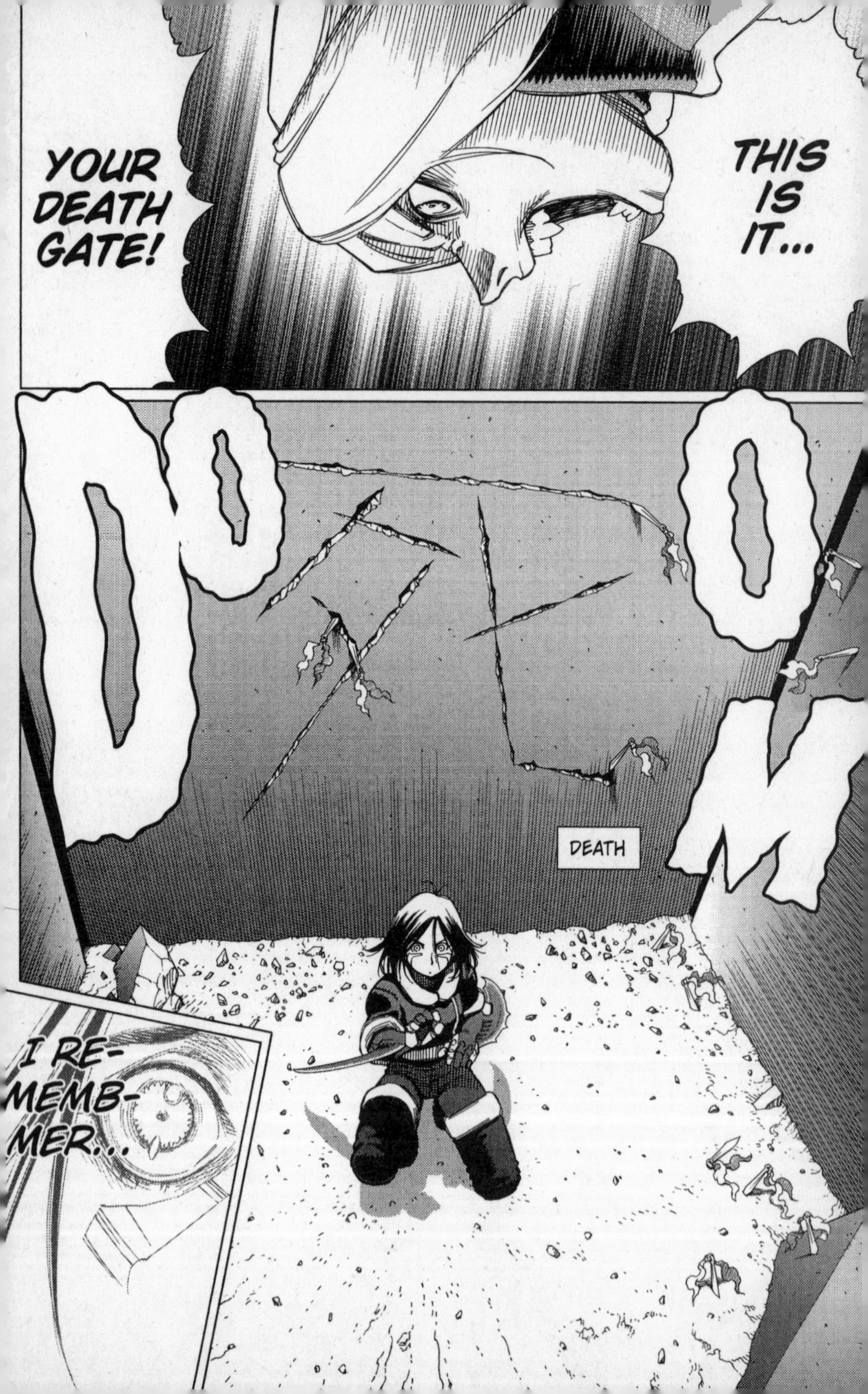
THIS IS IT...
YOUR DEATH GATE!
DOOM
DEATH
I RE-MEMB-MER...

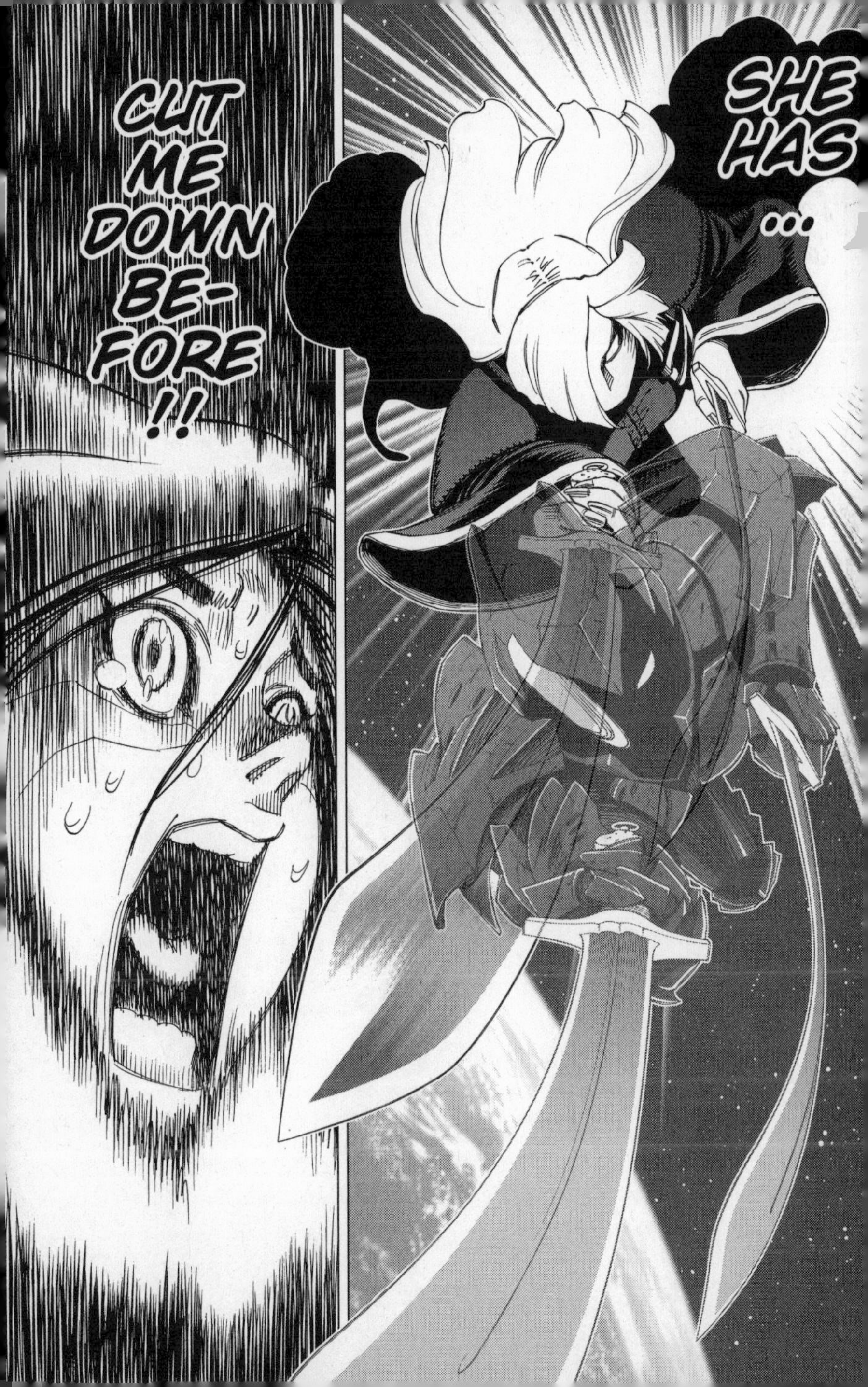
SHE HAS...
CUT ME DOWN BE- FORE!!

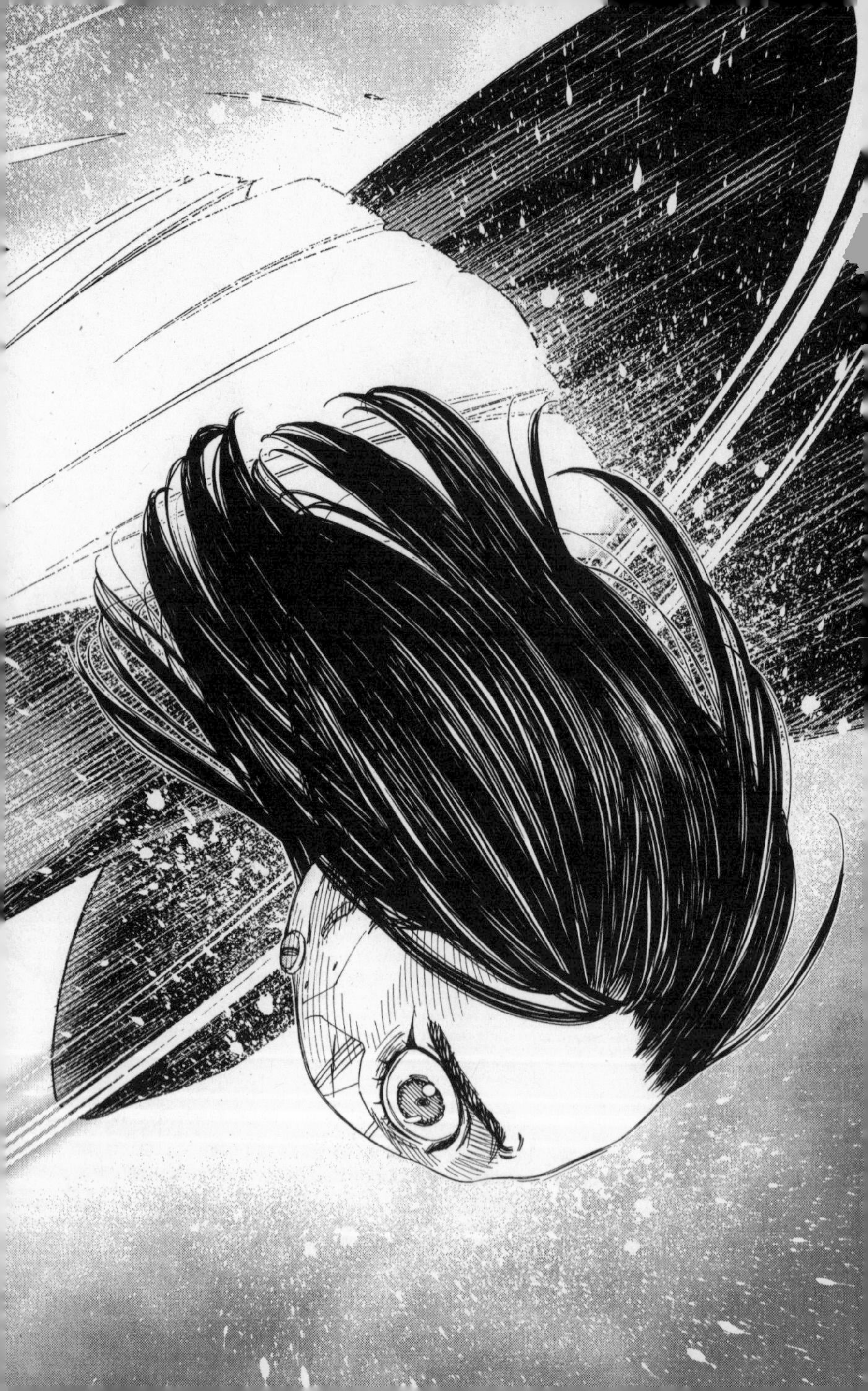

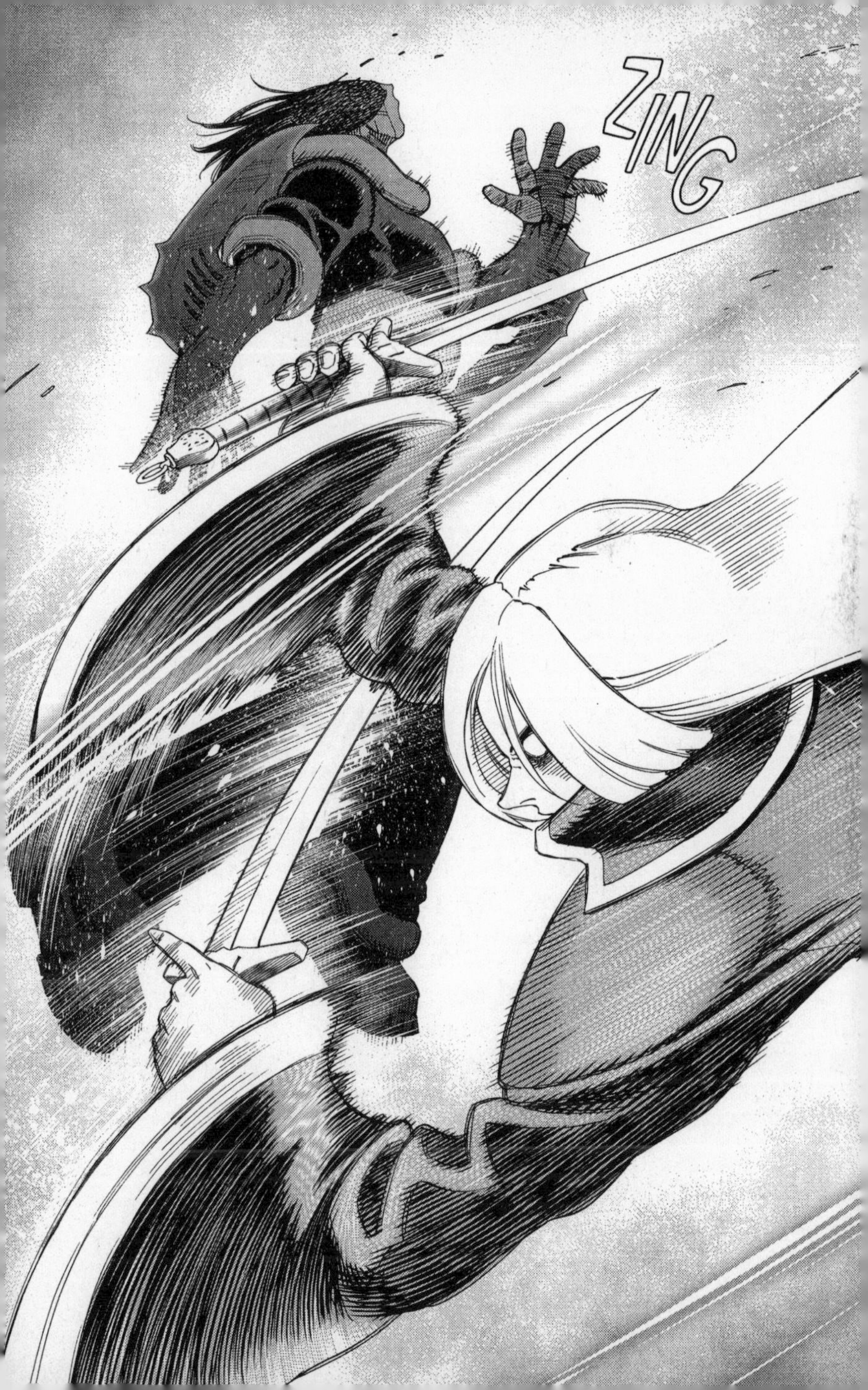
ZING

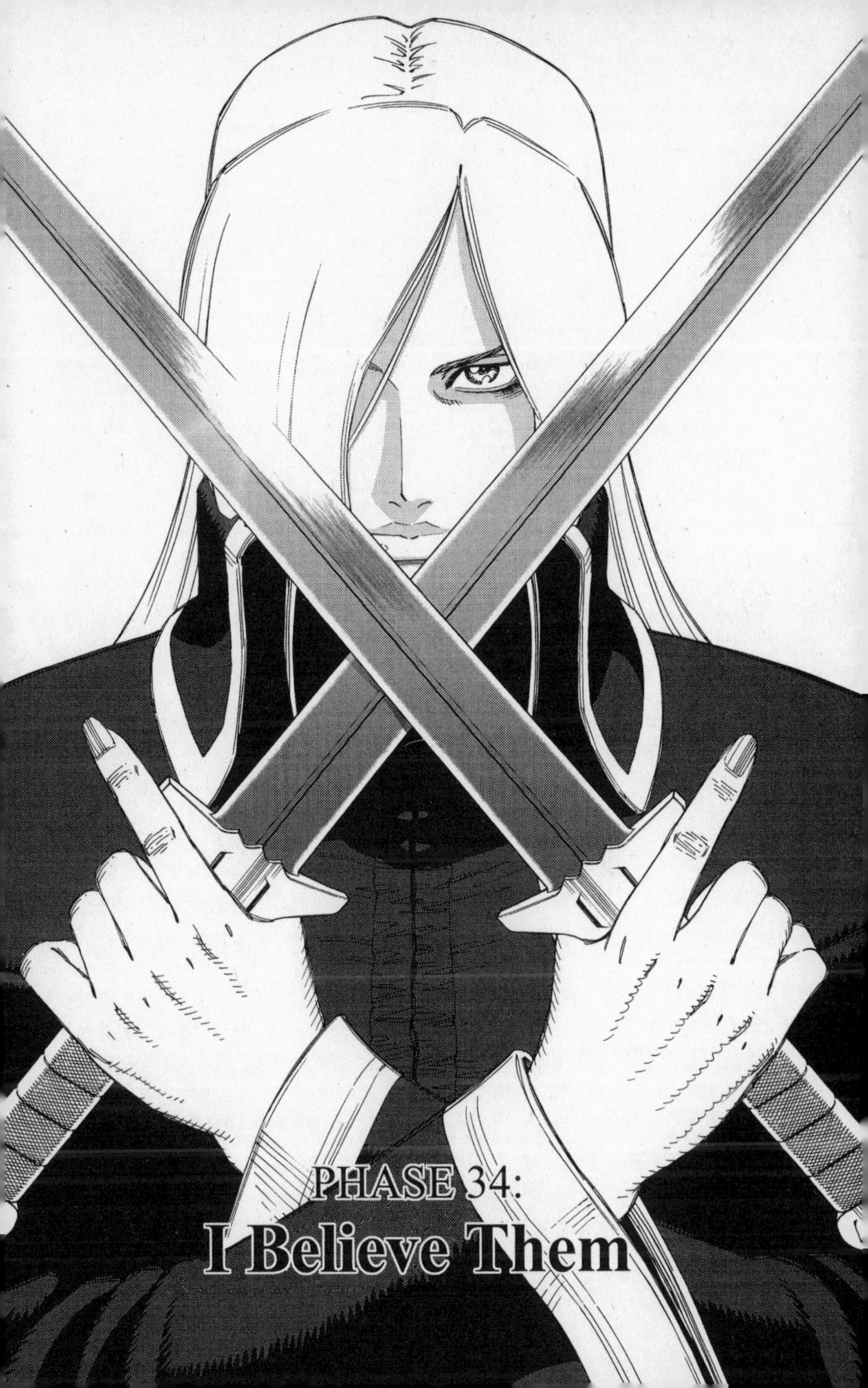
PHASE 34:
I Believe Them

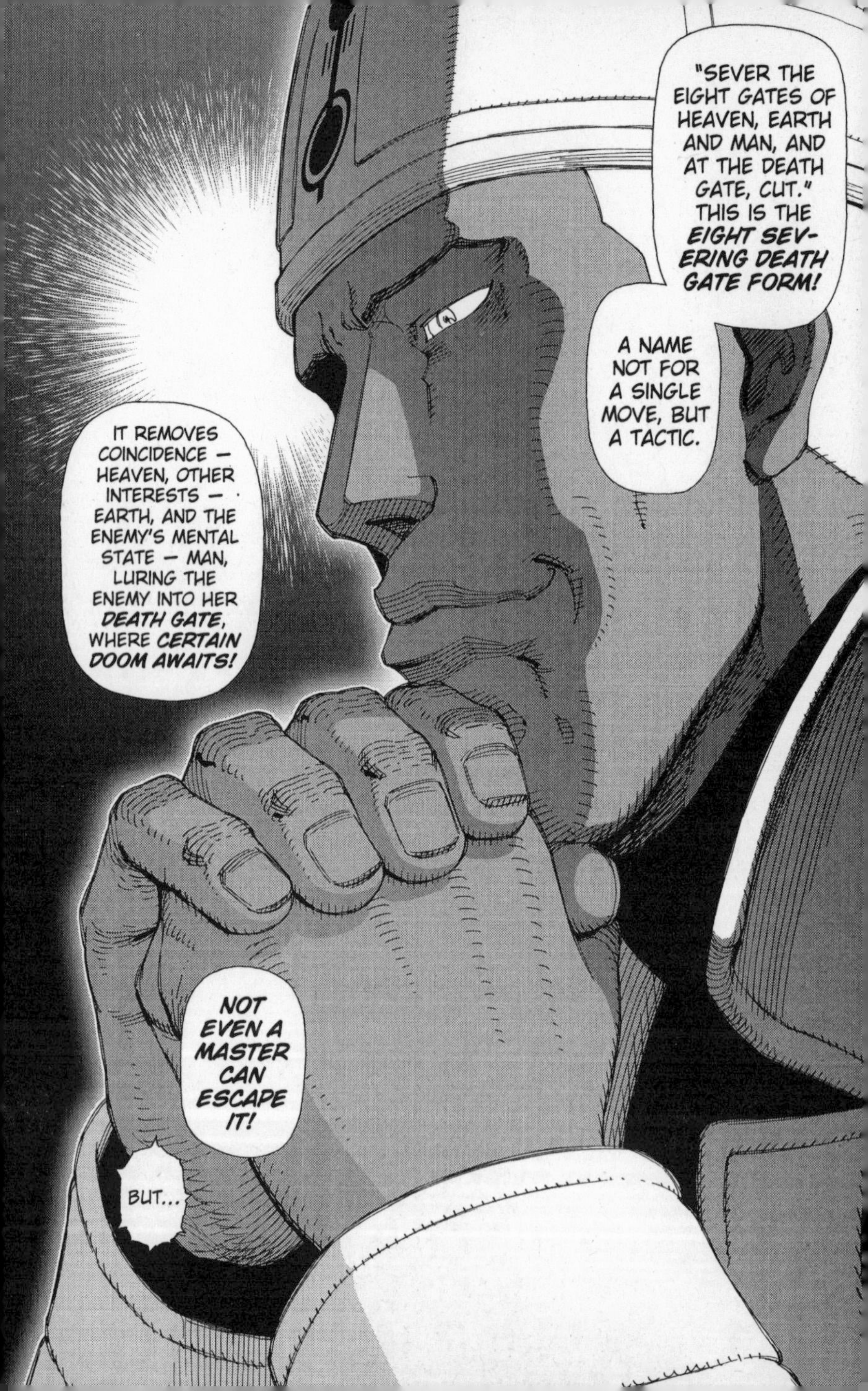
"SEVER THE EIGHT GATES OF HEAVEN, EARTH AND MAN, AND AT THE DEATH GATE, CUT." THIS IS THE EIGHT SEVERING DEATH GATE FORM!
A NAME NOT FOR A SINGLE MOVE, BUT A TACTIC.
IT REMOVES COINCIDENCE — HEAVEN, OTHER INTERESTS — EARTH, AND THE ENEMY'S MENTAL STATE — MAN, LURING THE ENEMY INTO HER DEATH GATE, WHERE CERTAIN DOOM AWAITS!
NOT EVEN A MASTER CAN ESCAPE IT!
BUT...

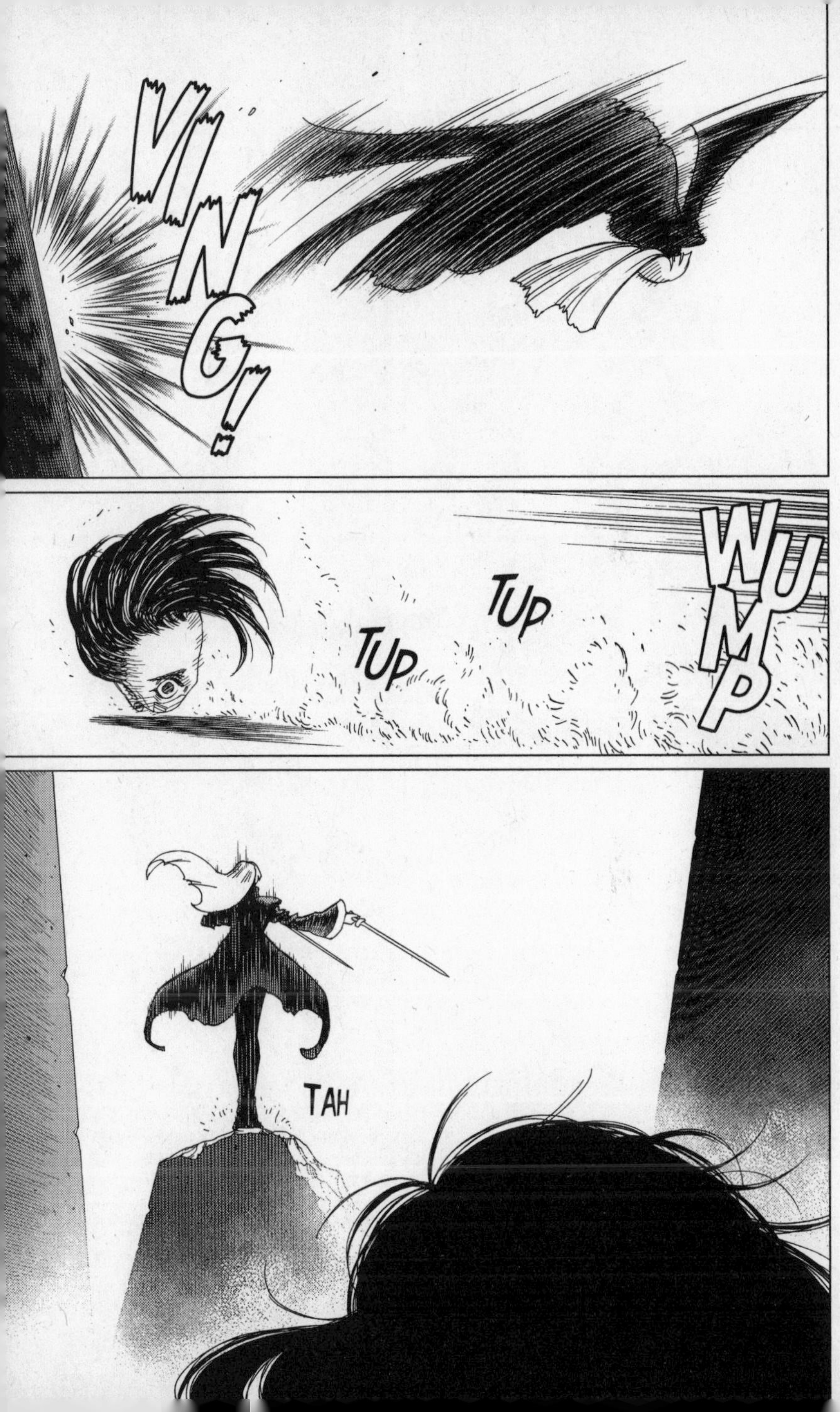
VING!
WUMP
TUP
TUP
TAH

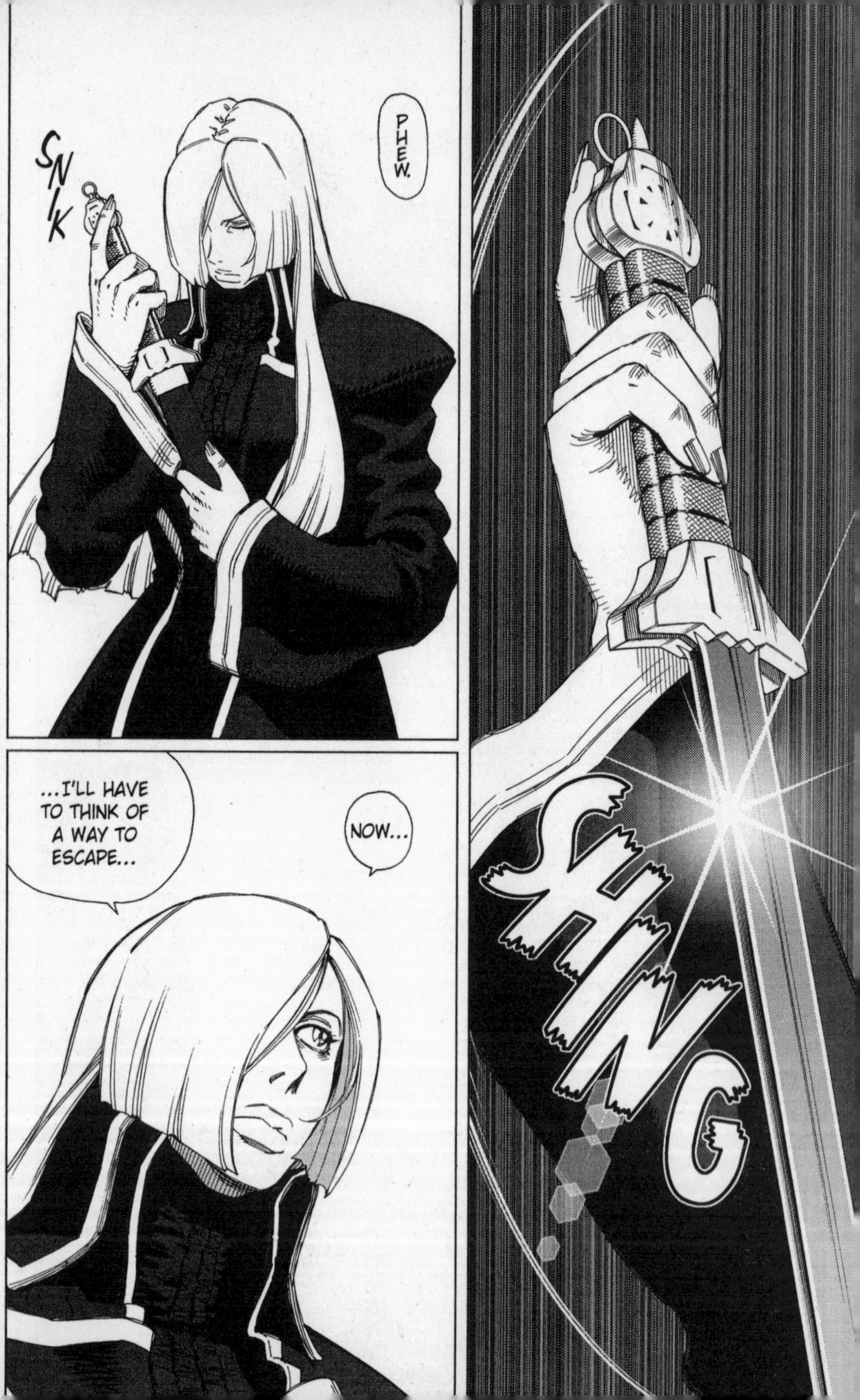
SHING
PHEW.
SNIK
NOW...
...I'LL HAVE TO THINK OF A WAY TO ESCAPE...

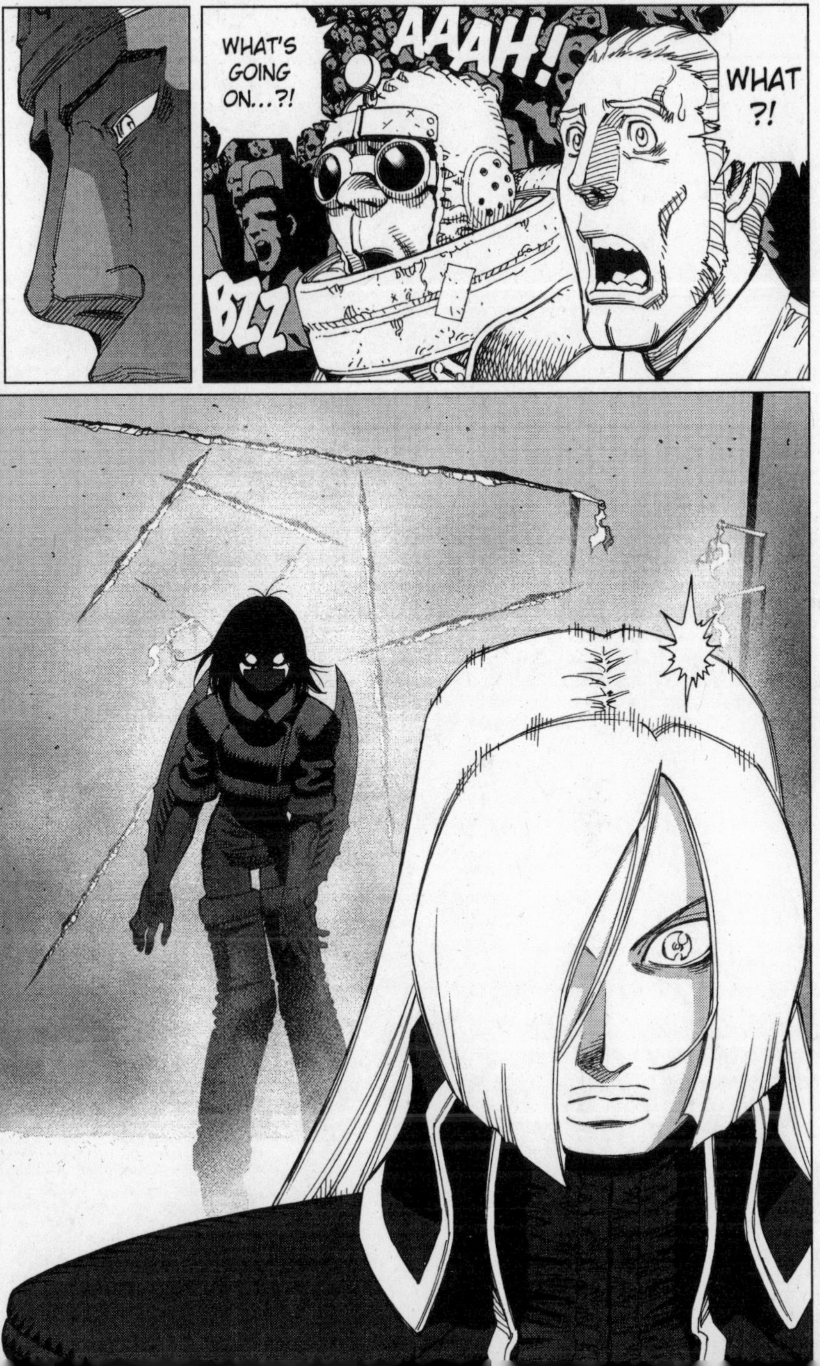
WHAT ?!
AAAH!
WHAT'S GOING ON...?!
BZZ

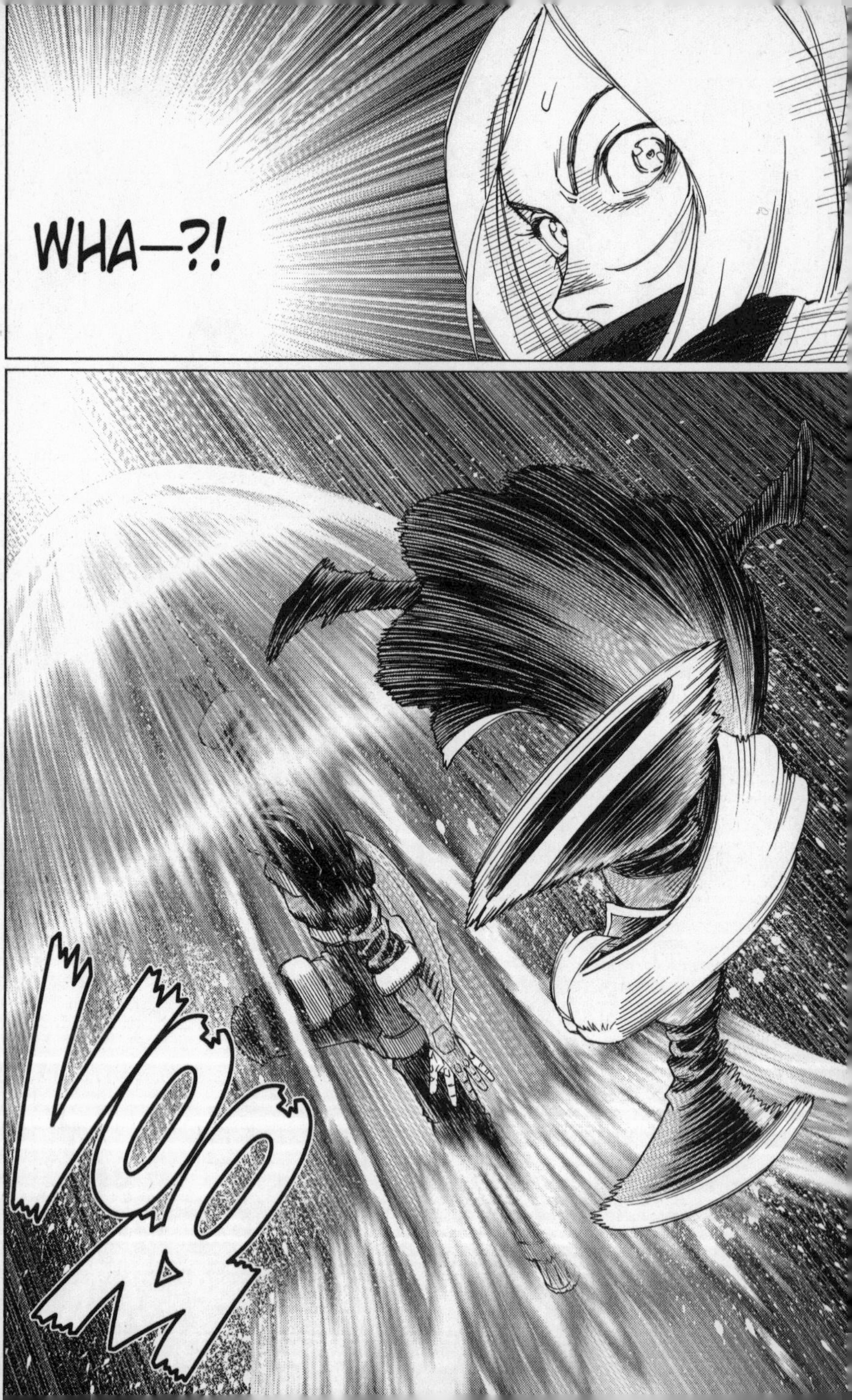
WHA—?!
VOOSH

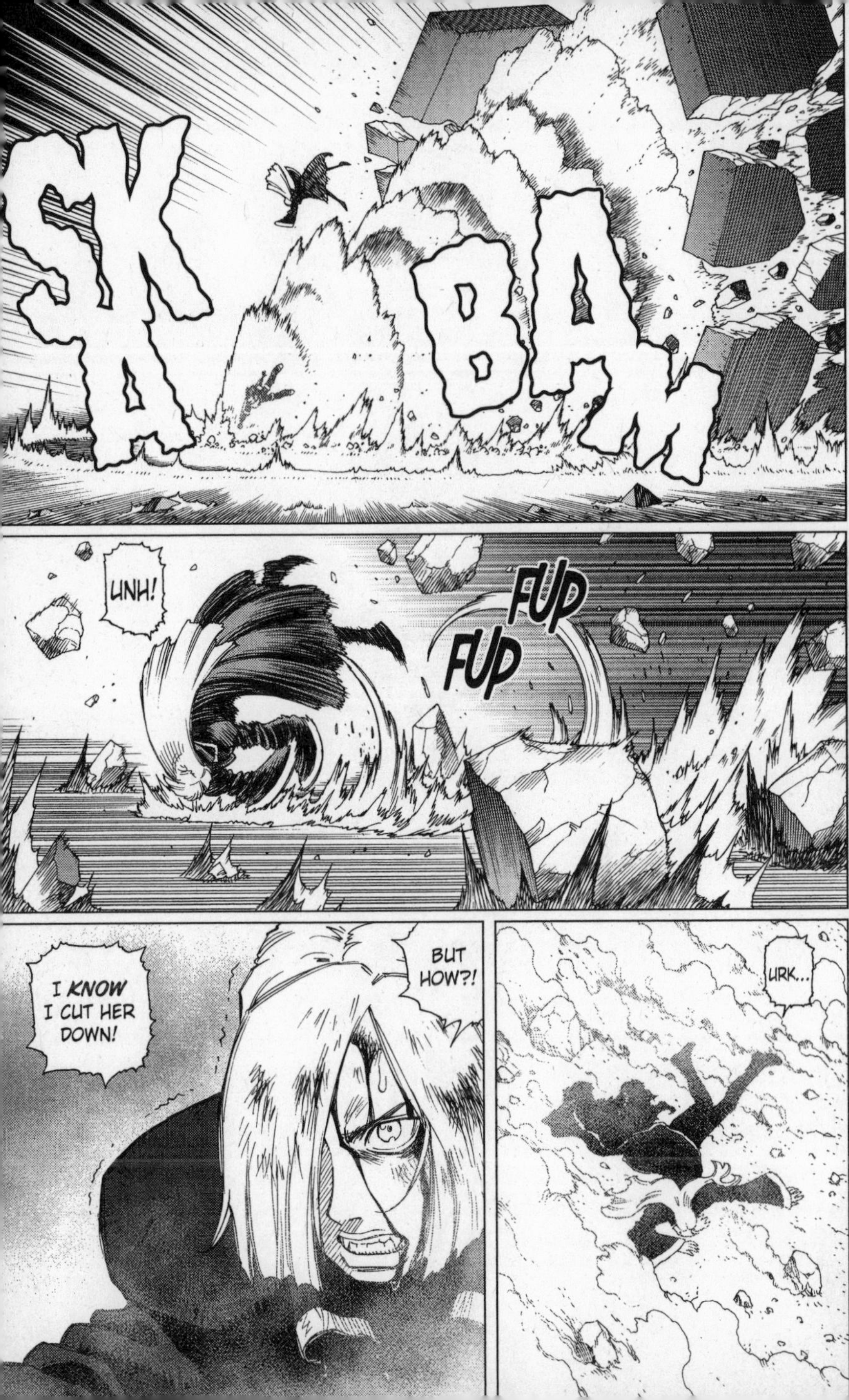
SKABAM
FUP
FUP
UNH!
URK...
BUT HOW?!
I *KNOW* I CUT HER DOWN!

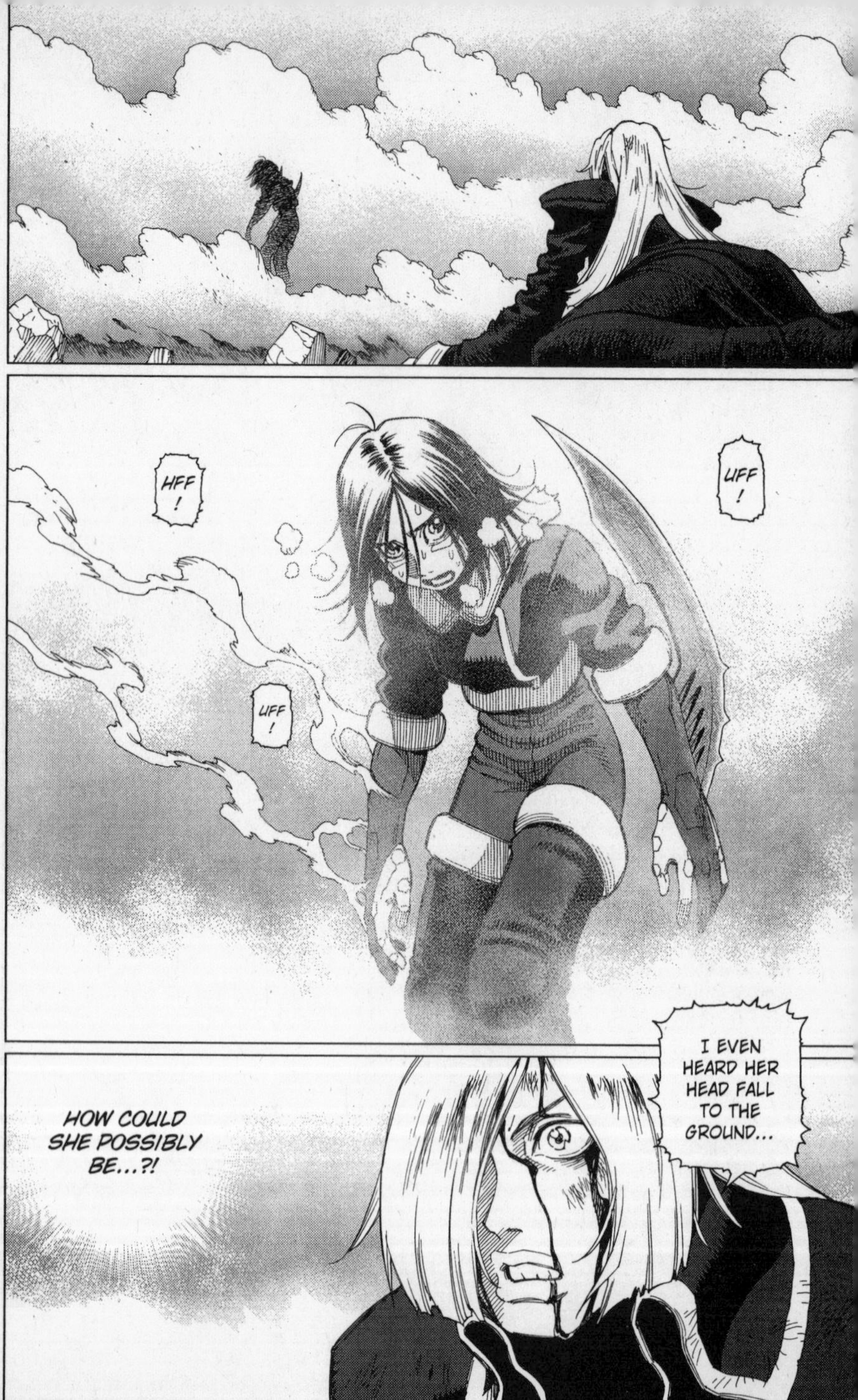
UFF!
HFF!
UFF!
I EVEN HEARD HER HEAD FALL TO THE GROUND...
HOW COULD SHE POSSIBLY BE...?!

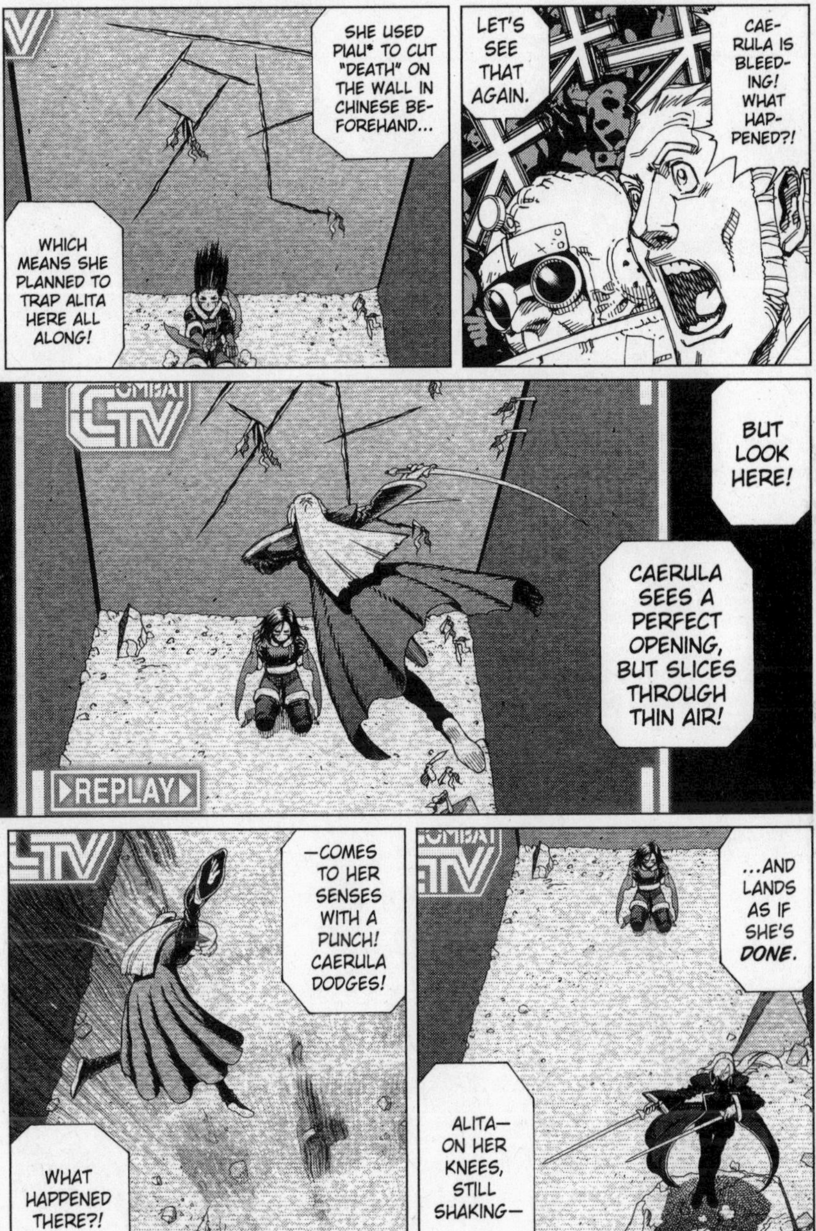
CAE-RULA IS BLEED-ING! WHAT HAP-PENED?!
LET'S SEE THAT AGAIN.
SHE USED PIAU* TO CUT "DEATH" ON THE WALL IN CHINESE BE-FOREHAND...
WHICH MEANS SHE PLANNED TO TRAP ALITA HERE ALL ALONG!
CTV
BUT LOOK HERE!
CAERULA SEES A PERFECT OPENING, BUT SLICES THROUGH THIN AIR!
REPLAY
...AND LANDS AS IF SHE'S *DONE*.
ALITA— ON HER KNEES, STILL SHAKING—
—COMES TO HER SENSES WITH A PUNCH! CAERULA DODGES!
WHAT HAPPENED THERE?!

****Piau:** Chinese throwing knives.*

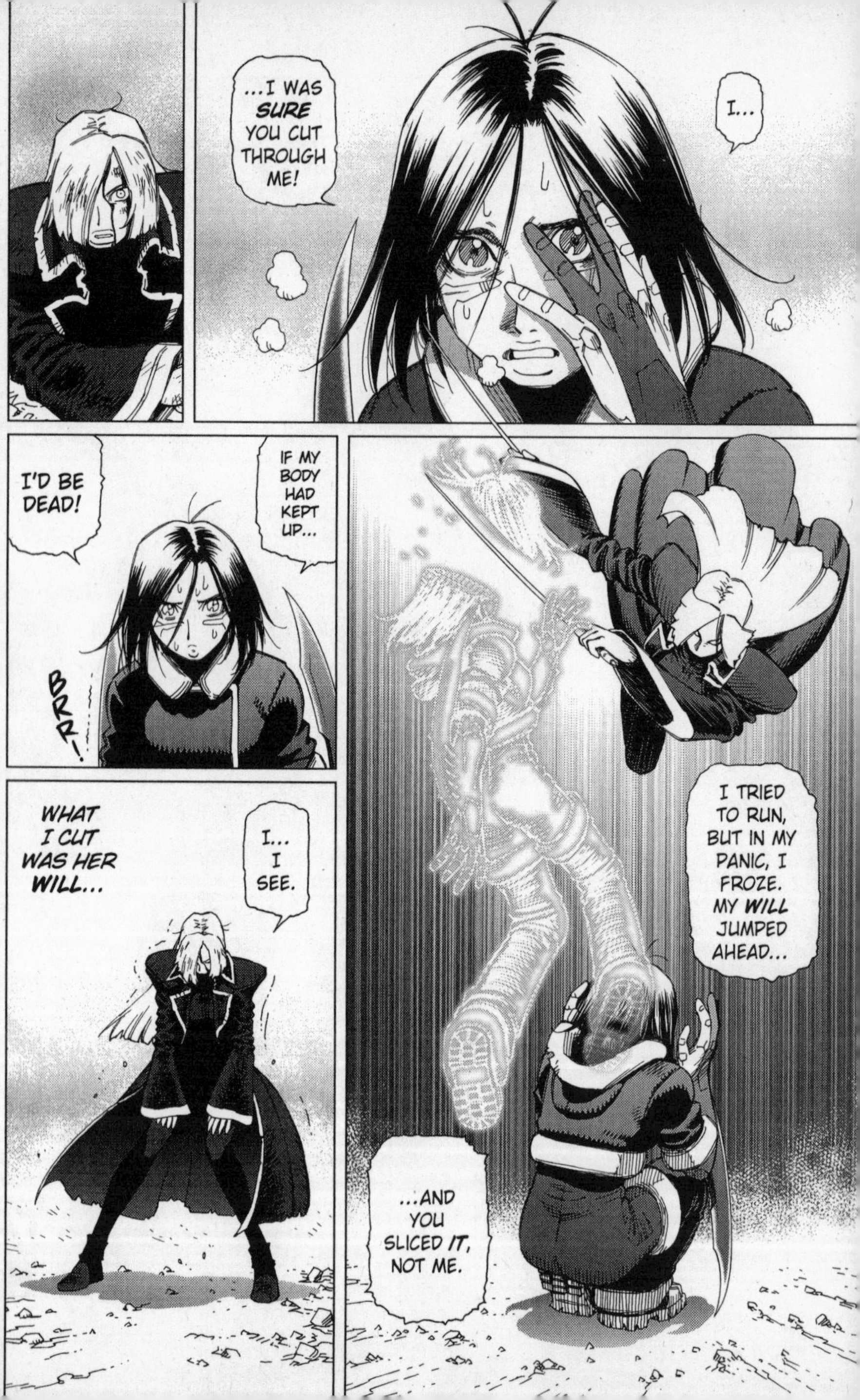
I...
...I WAS SURE YOU CUT THROUGH ME!
I TRIED TO RUN, BUT IN MY PANIC, I FROZE. MY WILL JUMPED AHEAD...
...AND YOU SLICED IT, NOT ME.
IF MY BODY HAD KEPT UP...
I'D BE DEAD!
BRRR!
I... I SEE.
WHAT I CUT WAS HER WILL...

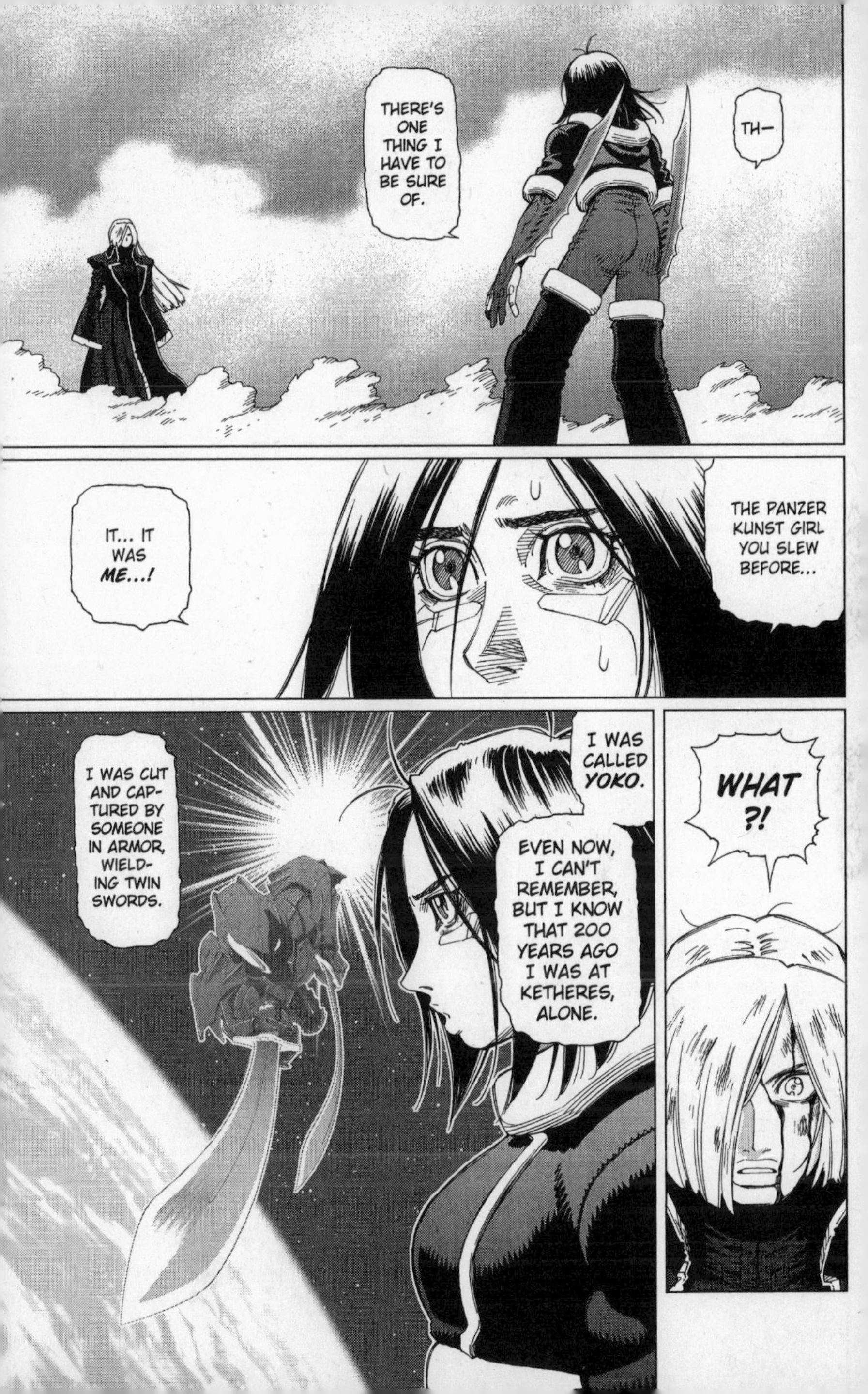
TH—
THERE'S ONE THING I HAVE TO BE SURE OF.
THE PANZER KUNST GIRL YOU SLEW BEFORE...
IT... IT WAS ME...!
WHAT ?!
I WAS CALLED YOKO.
EVEN NOW, I CAN'T REMEMBER, BUT I KNOW THAT 200 YEARS AGO I WAS AT KETHERES, ALONE.
I WAS CUT AND CAP-TURED BY SOMEONE IN ARMOR, WIELD-ING TWIN SWORDS.

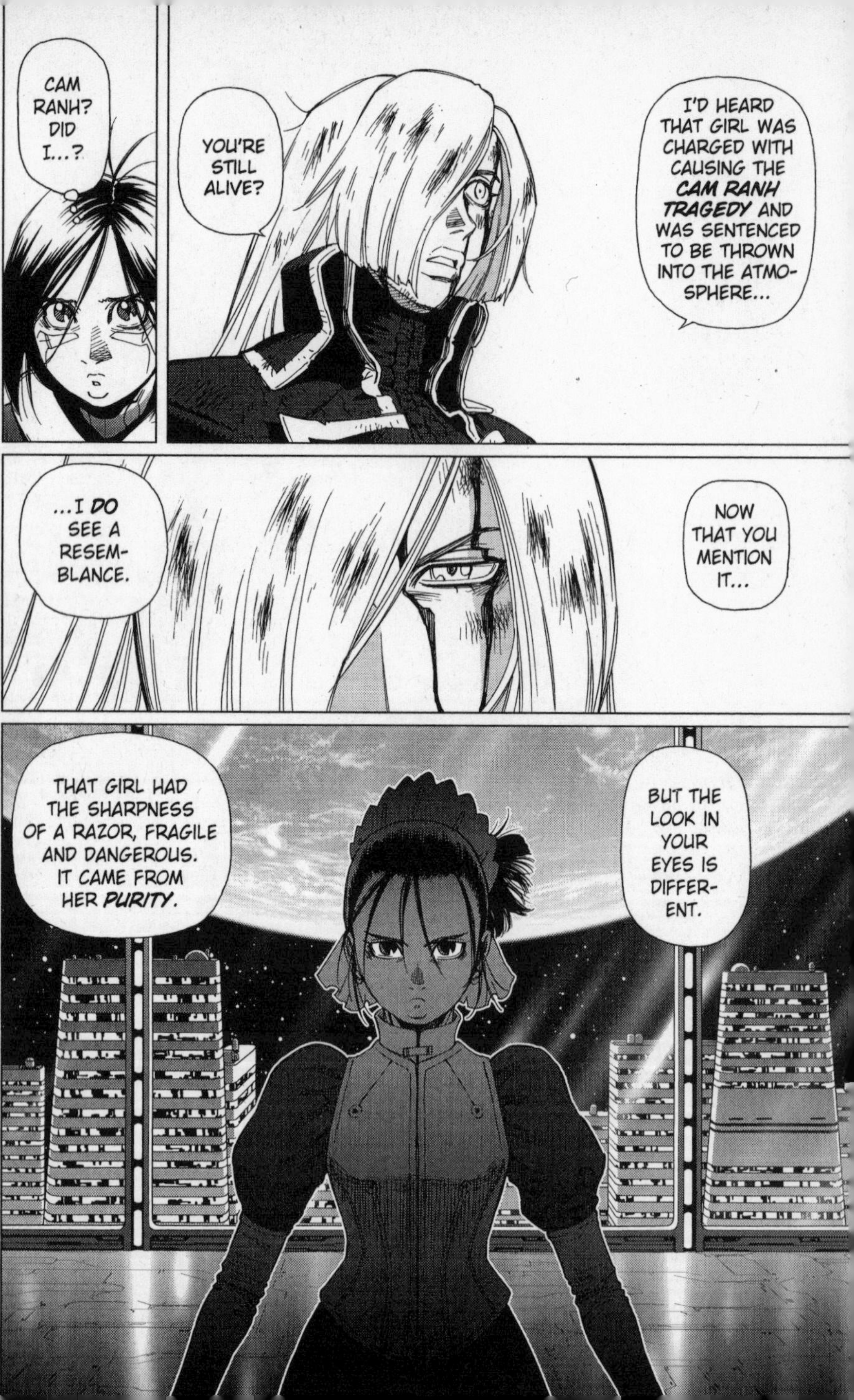
I'D HEARD THAT GIRL WAS CHARGED WITH CAUSING THE ***CAM RANH TRAGEDY*** AND WAS SENTENCED TO BE THROWN INTO THE ATMOSPHERE...
YOU'RE STILL ALIVE?
CAM RANH? DID I...?
NOW THAT YOU MENTION IT...
...I ***DO*** SEE A RESEMBLANCE.
BUT THE LOOK IN YOUR EYES IS DIFFERENT.
THAT GIRL HAD THE SHARPNESS OF A RAZOR, FRAGILE AND DANGEROUS. IT CAME FROM HER ***PURITY***.

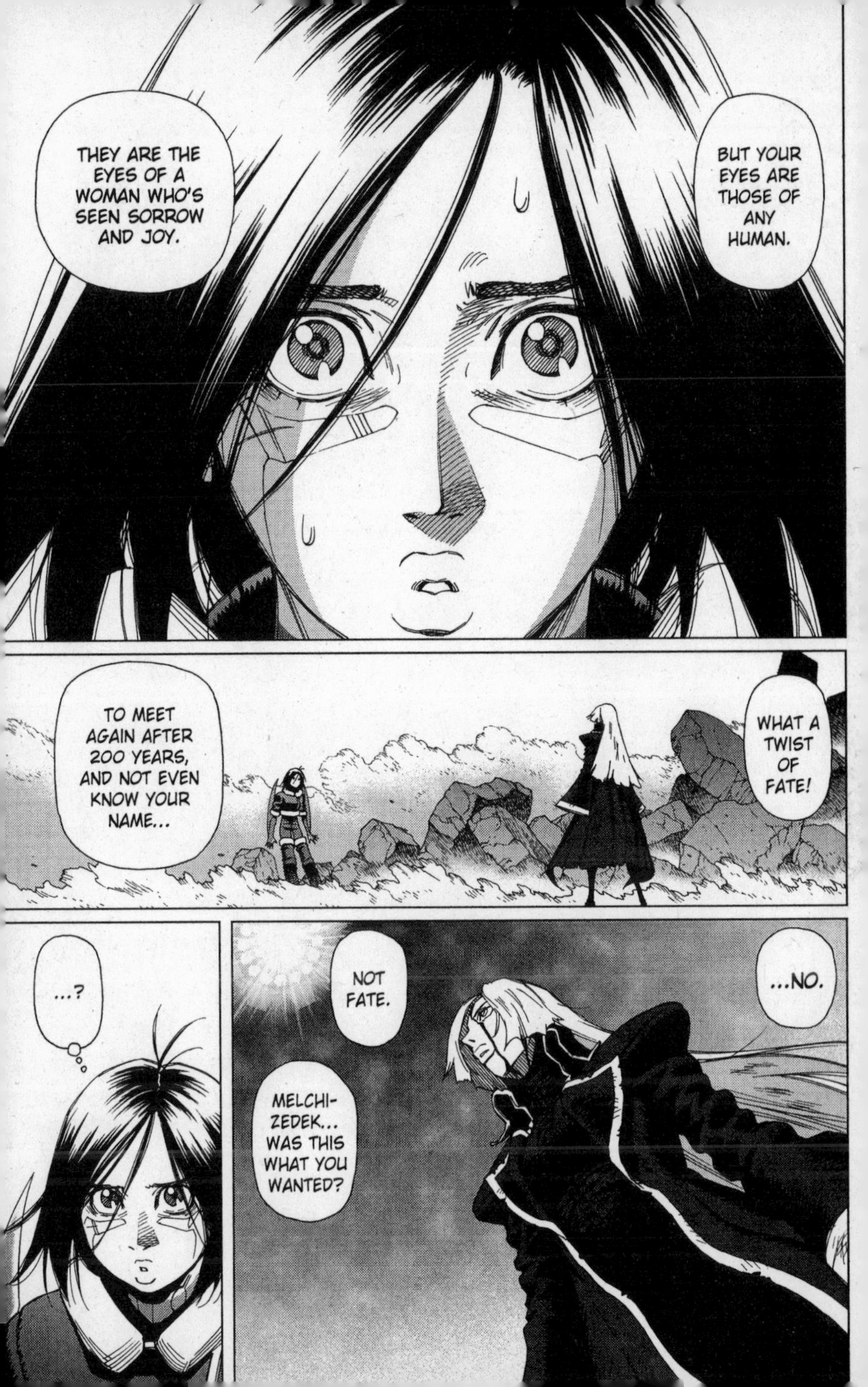
BUT YOUR EYES ARE THOSE OF ANY HUMAN.
THEY ARE THE EYES OF A WOMAN WHO'S SEEN SORROW AND JOY.
WHAT A TWIST OF FATE!
TO MEET AGAIN AFTER 200 YEARS, AND NOT EVEN KNOW YOUR NAME...
...NO.
NOT FATE.
MELCHI-ZEDEK... WAS THIS WHAT YOU WANTED?
...?

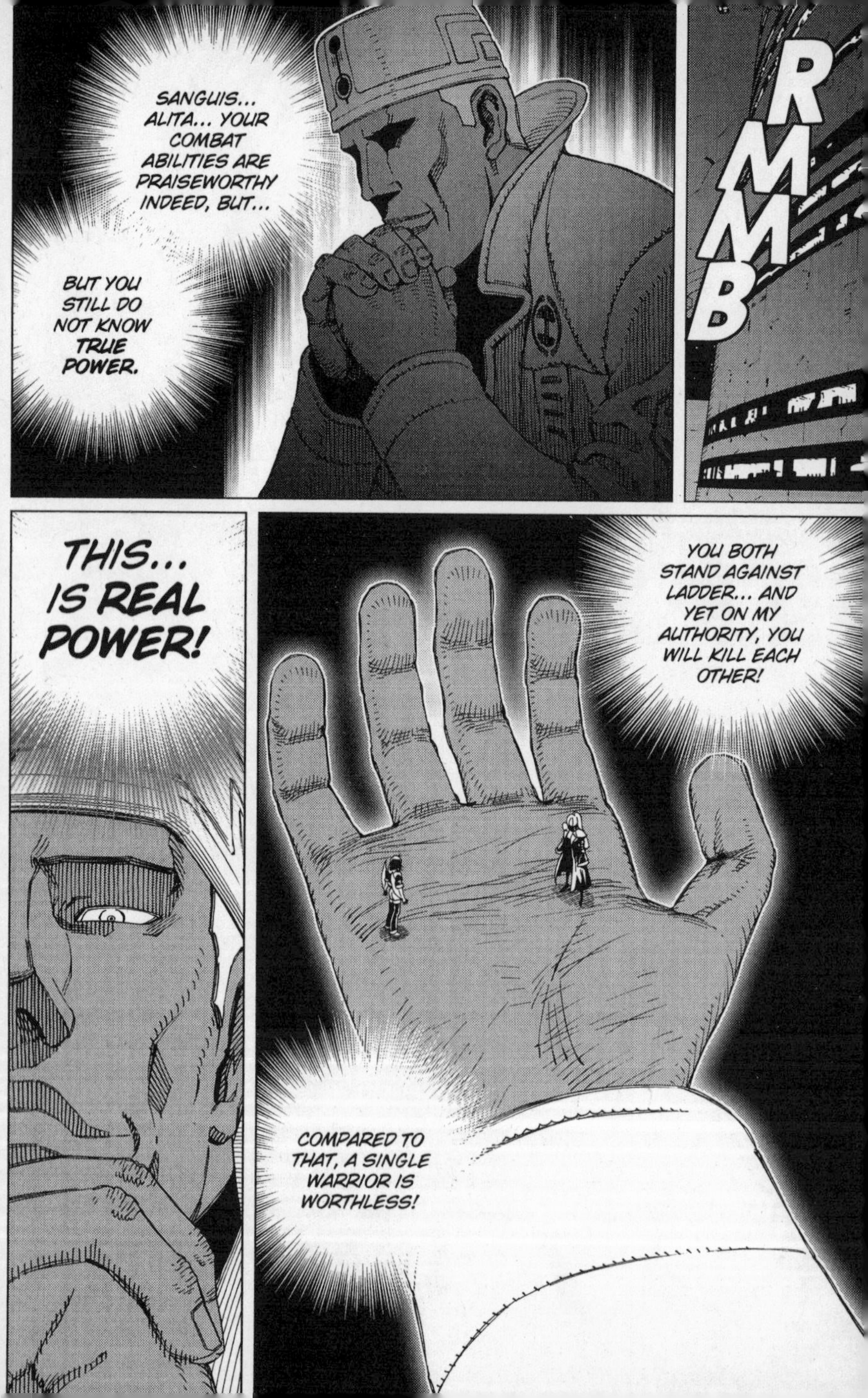
RMMB
SANGUIS... ALITA... YOUR COMBAT ABILITIES ARE PRAISEWORTHY INDEED, BUT...
BUT YOU STILL DO NOT KNOW TRUE POWER.
YOU BOTH STAND AGAINST LADDER... AND YET ON MY AUTHORITY, YOU WILL KILL EACH OTHER!
COMPARED TO THAT, A SINGLE WARRIOR IS WORTHLESS!
THIS... IS REAL POWER!

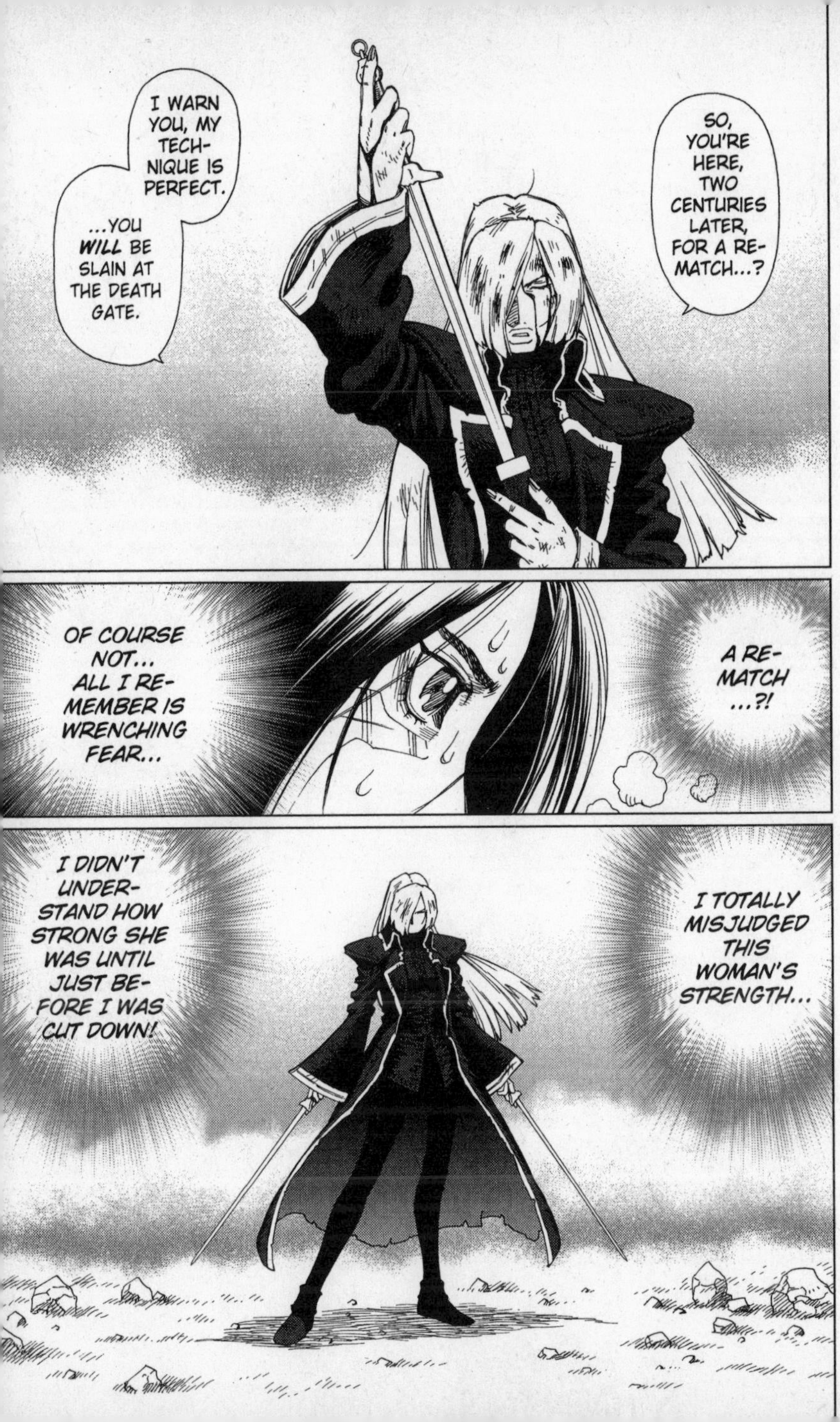
SO, YOU'RE HERE, TWO CENTURIES LATER, FOR A REMATCH...?
I WARN YOU, MY TECHNIQUE IS PERFECT.
...YOU WILL BE SLAIN AT THE DEATH GATE.
A REMATCH...?!
OF COURSE NOT... ALL I REMEMBER IS WRENCHING FEAR...
I TOTALLY MISJUDGED THIS WOMAN'S STRENGTH...
I DIDN'T UNDERSTAND HOW STRONG SHE WAS UNTIL JUST BEFORE I WAS CUT DOWN!

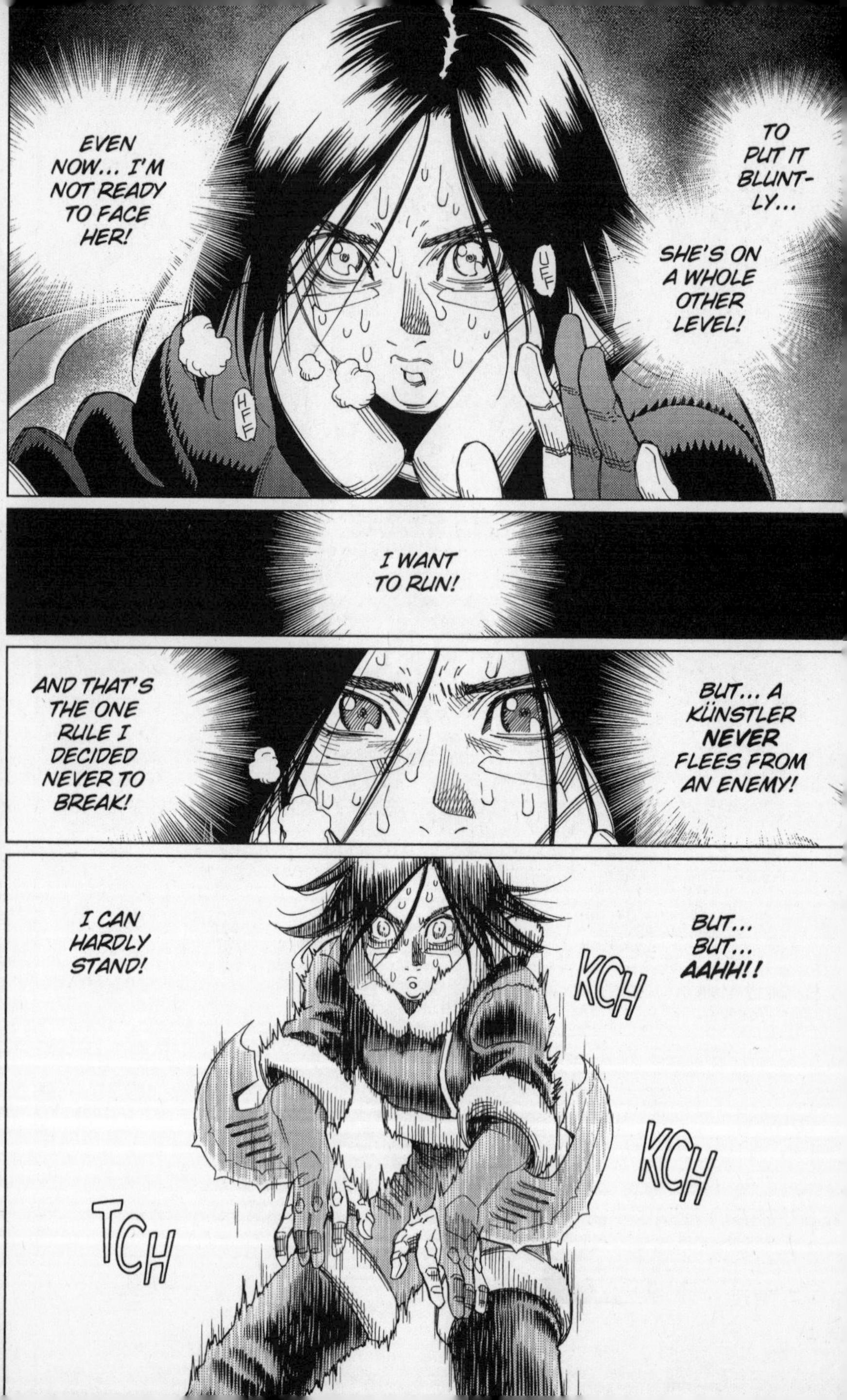
TO PUT IT BLUNT-LY...
SHE'S ON A WHOLE OTHER LEVEL!
UFF
EVEN NOW... I'M NOT READY TO FACE HER!
HFF
I WANT TO RUN!
BUT... A KÜNSTLER **NEVER** FLEES FROM AN ENEMY!
AND THAT'S THE ONE RULE I DECIDED NEVER TO BREAK!
BUT... BUT... AAHH!!
KCH
KCH
I CAN HARDLY STAND!
TCH

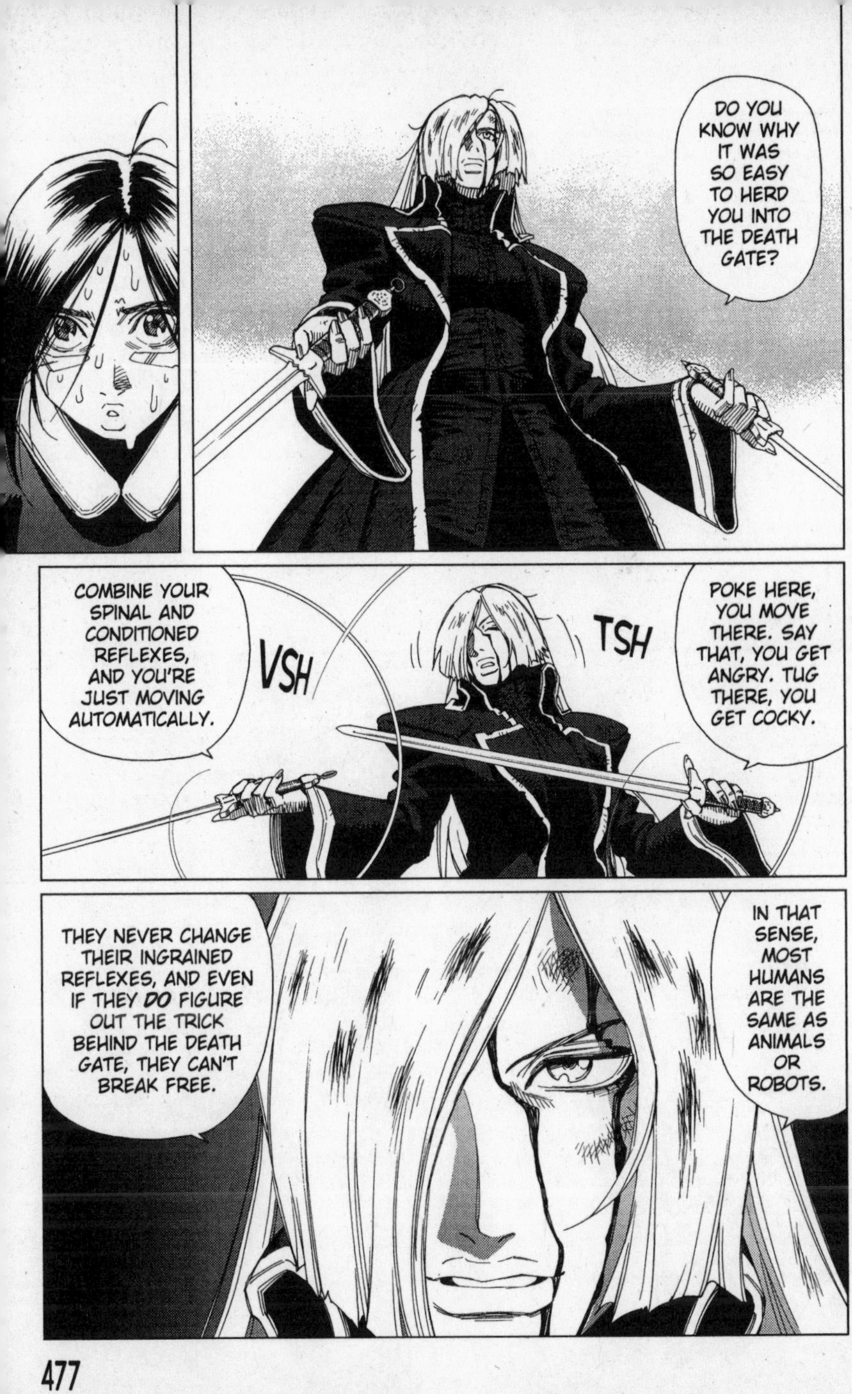
DO YOU KNOW WHY IT WAS SO EASY TO HERD YOU INTO THE DEATH GATE?
POKE HERE, YOU MOVE THERE. SAY THAT, YOU GET ANGRY. TUG THERE, YOU GET COCKY.
TSH
VSH
COMBINE YOUR SPINAL AND CONDITIONED REFLEXES, AND YOU'RE JUST MOVING AUTOMATICALLY.
IN THAT SENSE, MOST HUMANS ARE THE SAME AS ANIMALS OR ROBOTS.
THEY NEVER CHANGE THEIR INGRAINED REFLEXES, AND EVEN IF THEY *DO* FIGURE OUT THE TRICK BEHIND THE DEATH GATE, THEY CAN'T BREAK FREE.

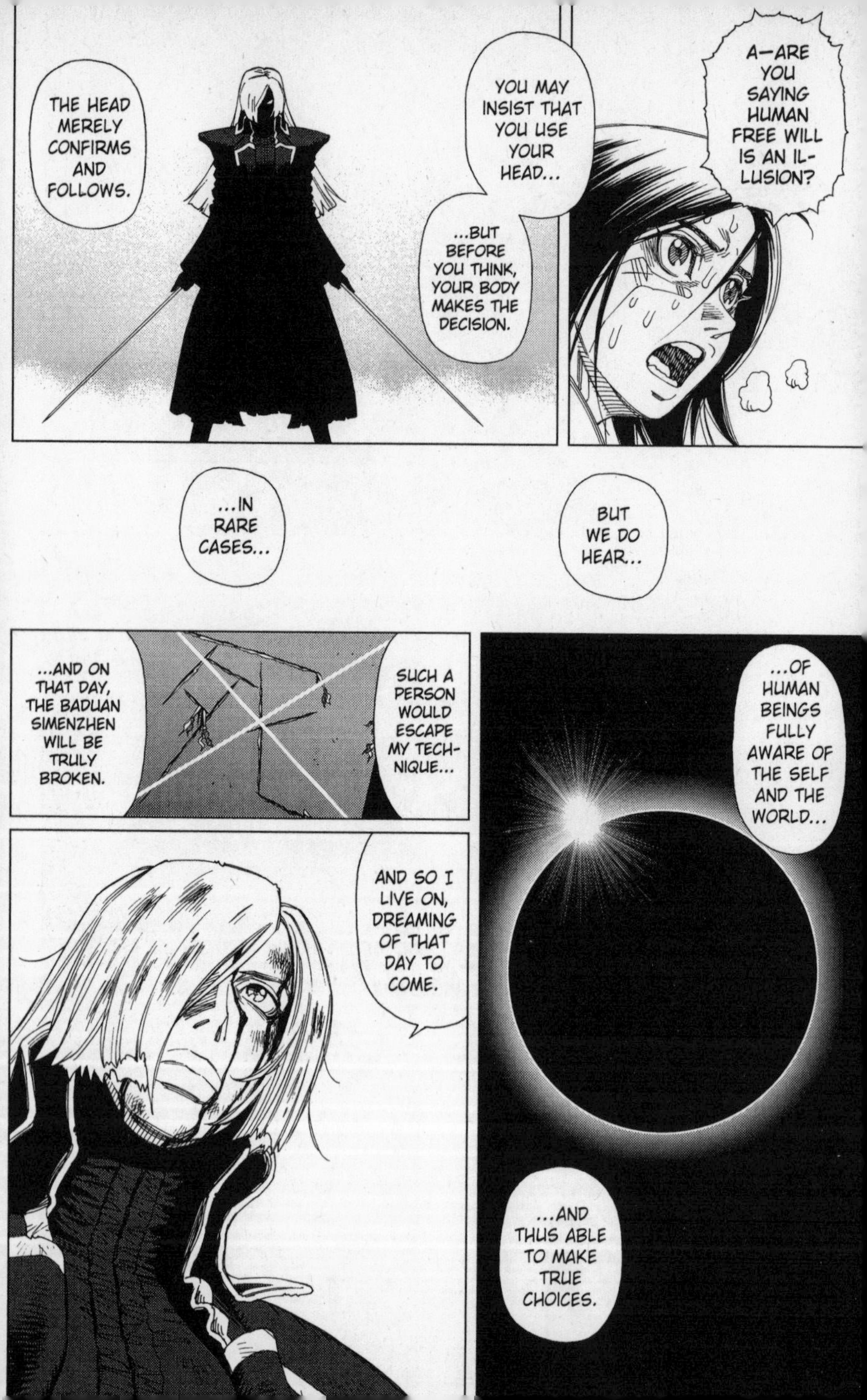
A—ARE YOU SAYING HUMAN FREE WILL IS AN IL-LUSION?
YOU MAY INSIST THAT YOU USE YOUR HEAD...
...BUT BEFORE YOU THINK, YOUR BODY MAKES THE DECISION.
THE HEAD MERELY CONFIRMS AND FOLLOWS.
BUT WE DO HEAR...
...IN RARE CASES...
...OF HUMAN BEINGS FULLY AWARE OF THE SELF AND THE WORLD...
...AND THUS ABLE TO MAKE TRUE CHOICES.
SUCH A PERSON WOULD ESCAPE MY TECH-NIQUE...
...AND ON THAT DAY, THE BADUAN SIMENZHEN WILL BE TRULY BROKEN.
AND SO I LIVE ON, DREAMING OF THAT DAY TO COME.

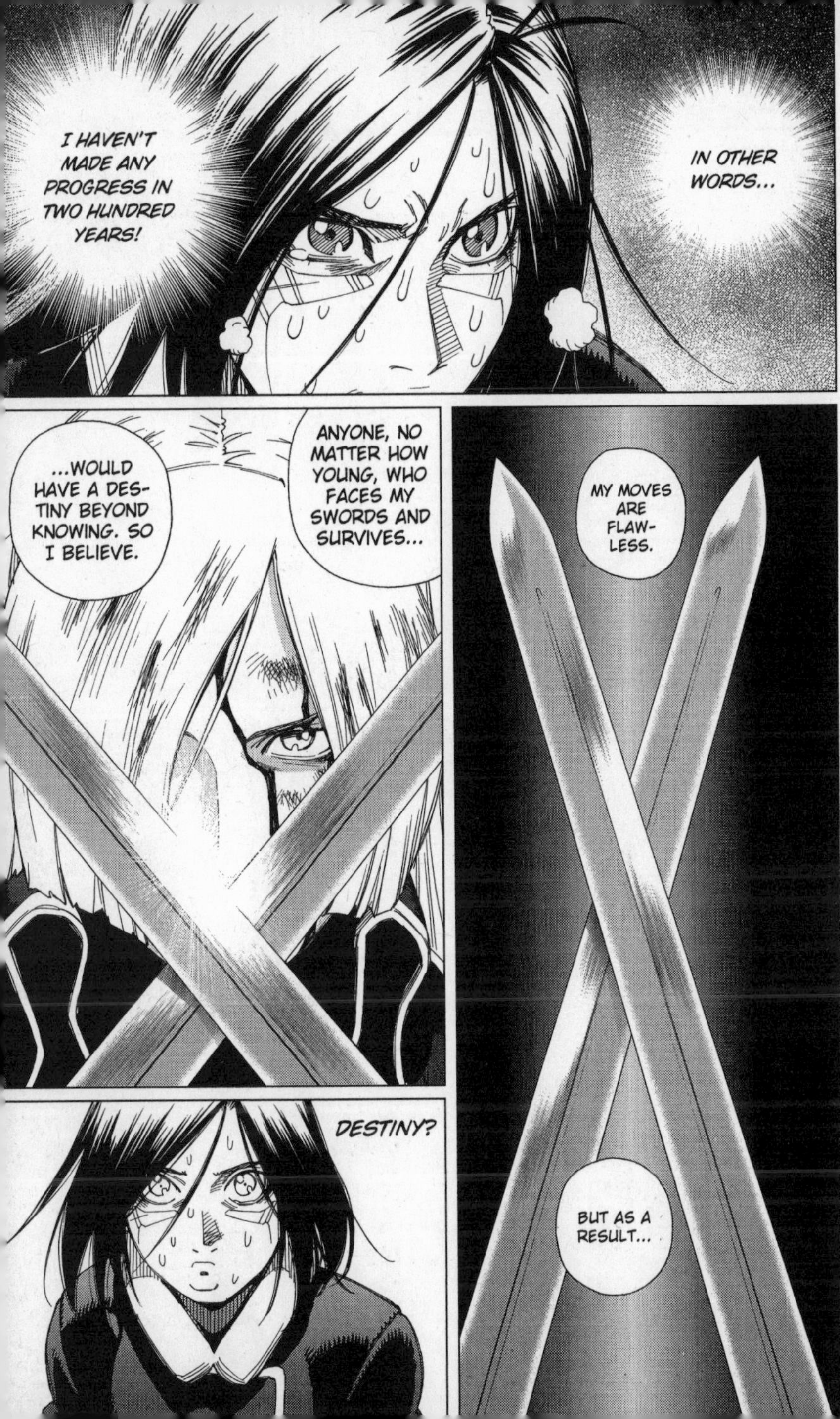
IN OTHER WORDS...
I HAVEN'T MADE ANY PROGRESS IN TWO HUNDRED YEARS!
MY MOVES ARE FLAW-LESS.
BUT AS A RESULT...
ANYONE, NO MATTER HOW YOUNG, WHO FACES MY SWORDS AND SURVIVES...
...WOULD HAVE A DES-TINY BEYOND KNOWING. SO I BELIEVE.
DESTINY?

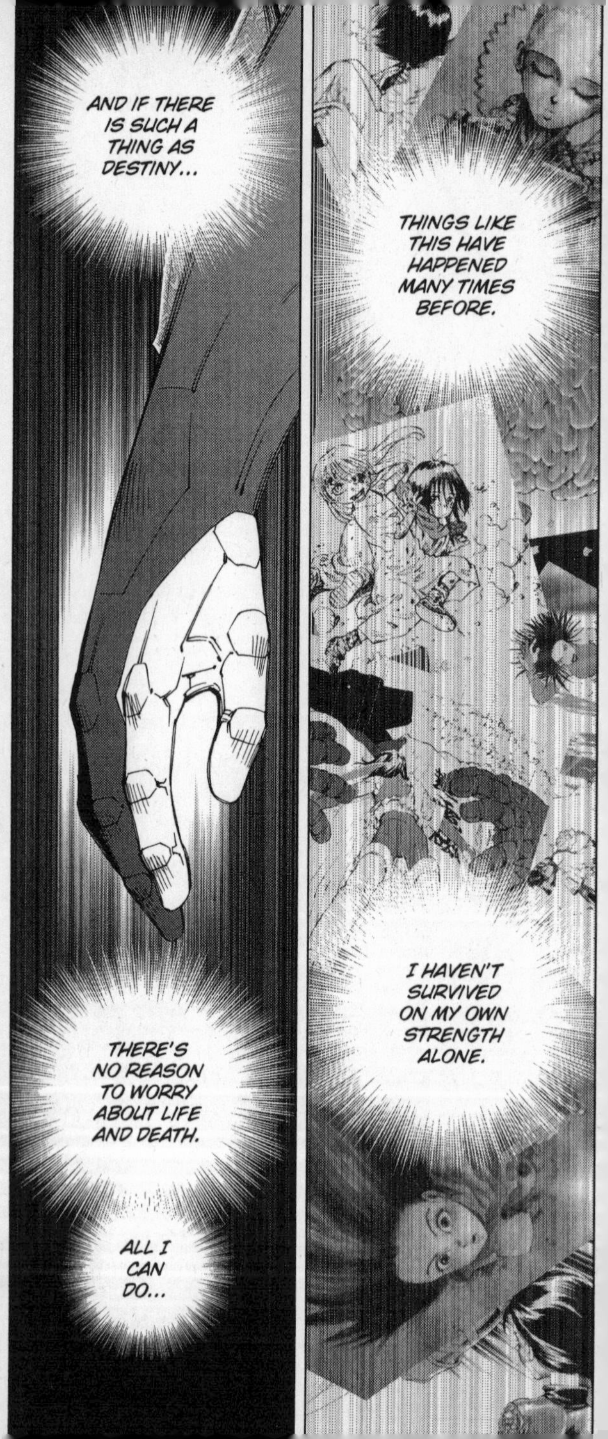
THINGS LIKE THIS HAVE HAPPENED MANY TIMES BEFORE.
I HAVEN'T SURVIVED ON MY OWN STRENGTH ALONE.
AND IF THERE IS SUCH A THING AS DESTINY...
THERE'S NO REASON TO WORRY ABOUT LIFE AND DEATH.
ALL I CAN DO...

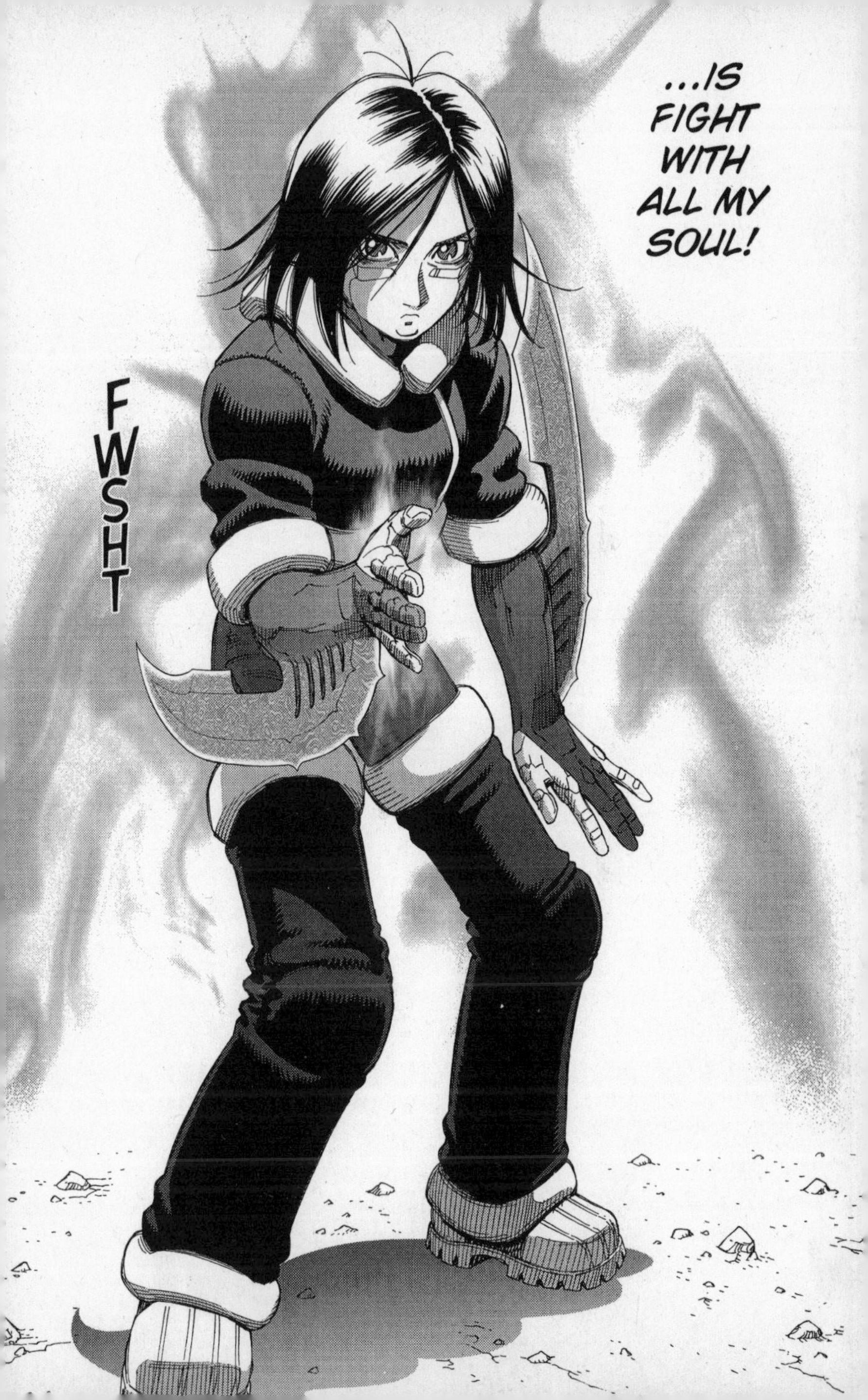
...IS FIGHT WITH ALL MY SOUL!
FWSHT

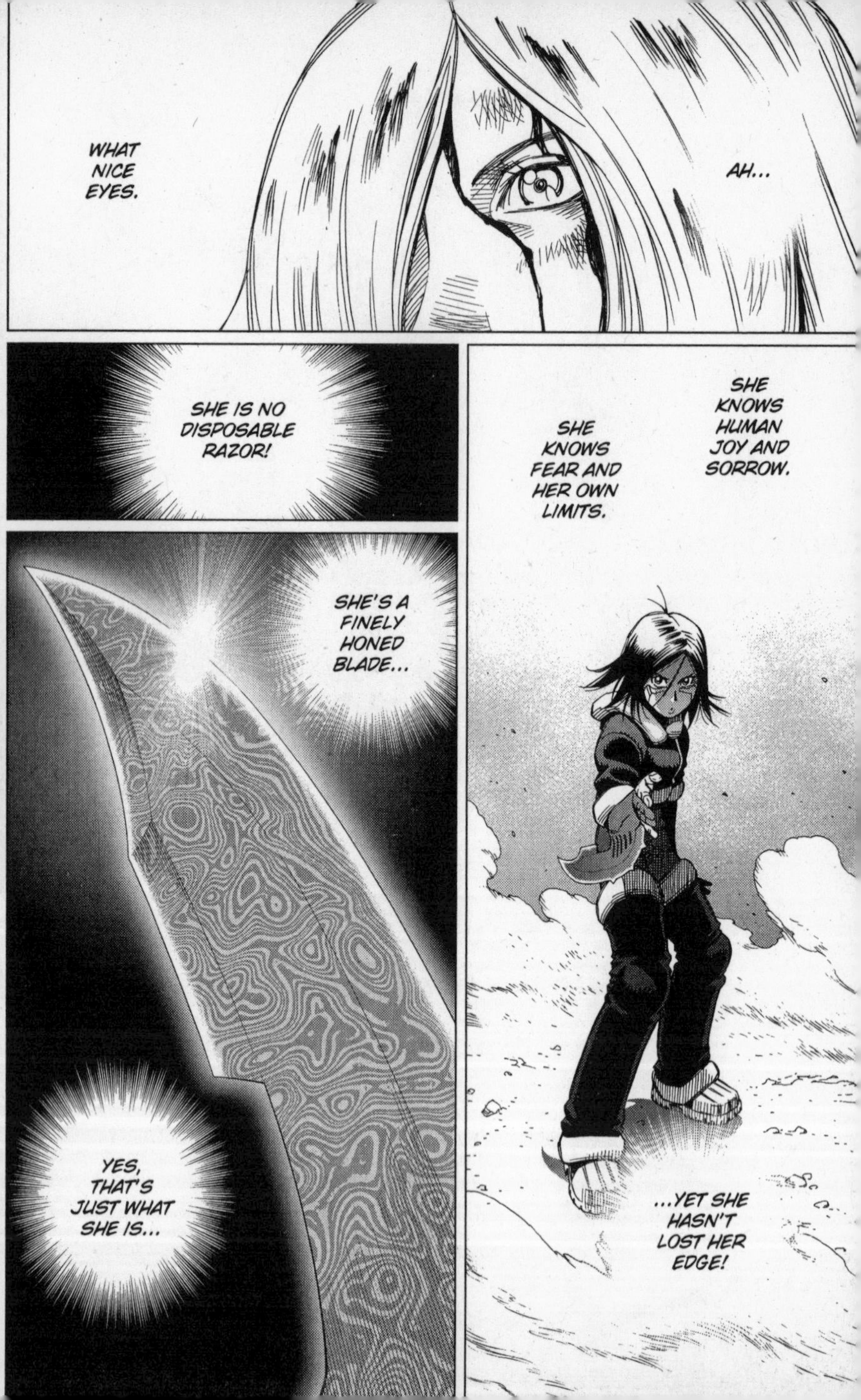
AH...
WHAT NICE EYES.
SHE KNOWS HUMAN JOY AND SORROW.
SHE KNOWS FEAR AND HER OWN LIMITS.
...YET SHE HASN'T LOST HER EDGE!
SHE IS NO DISPOSABLE RAZOR!
SHE'S A FINELY HONED BLADE...
YES, THAT'S JUST WHAT SHE IS...

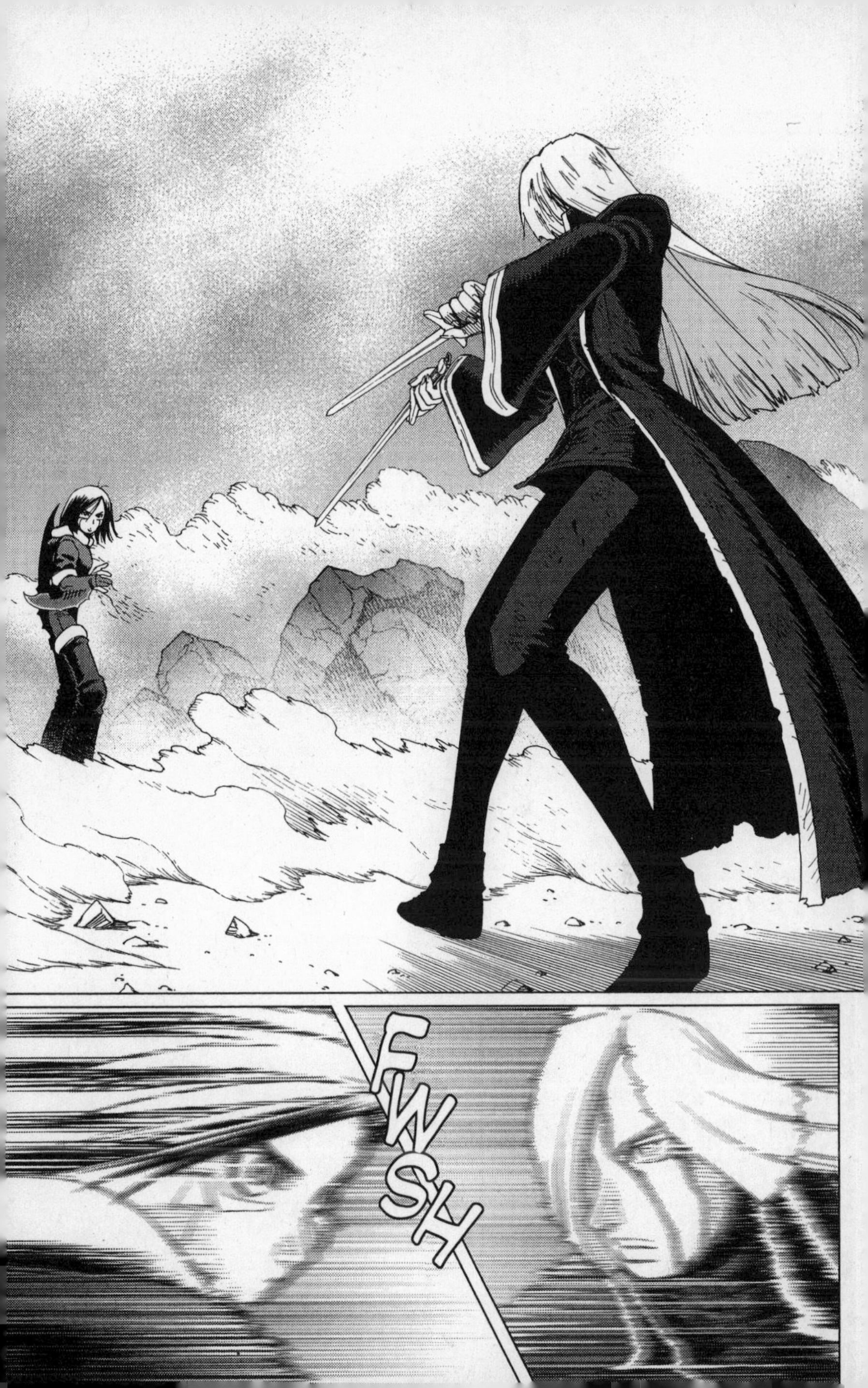
FWSH

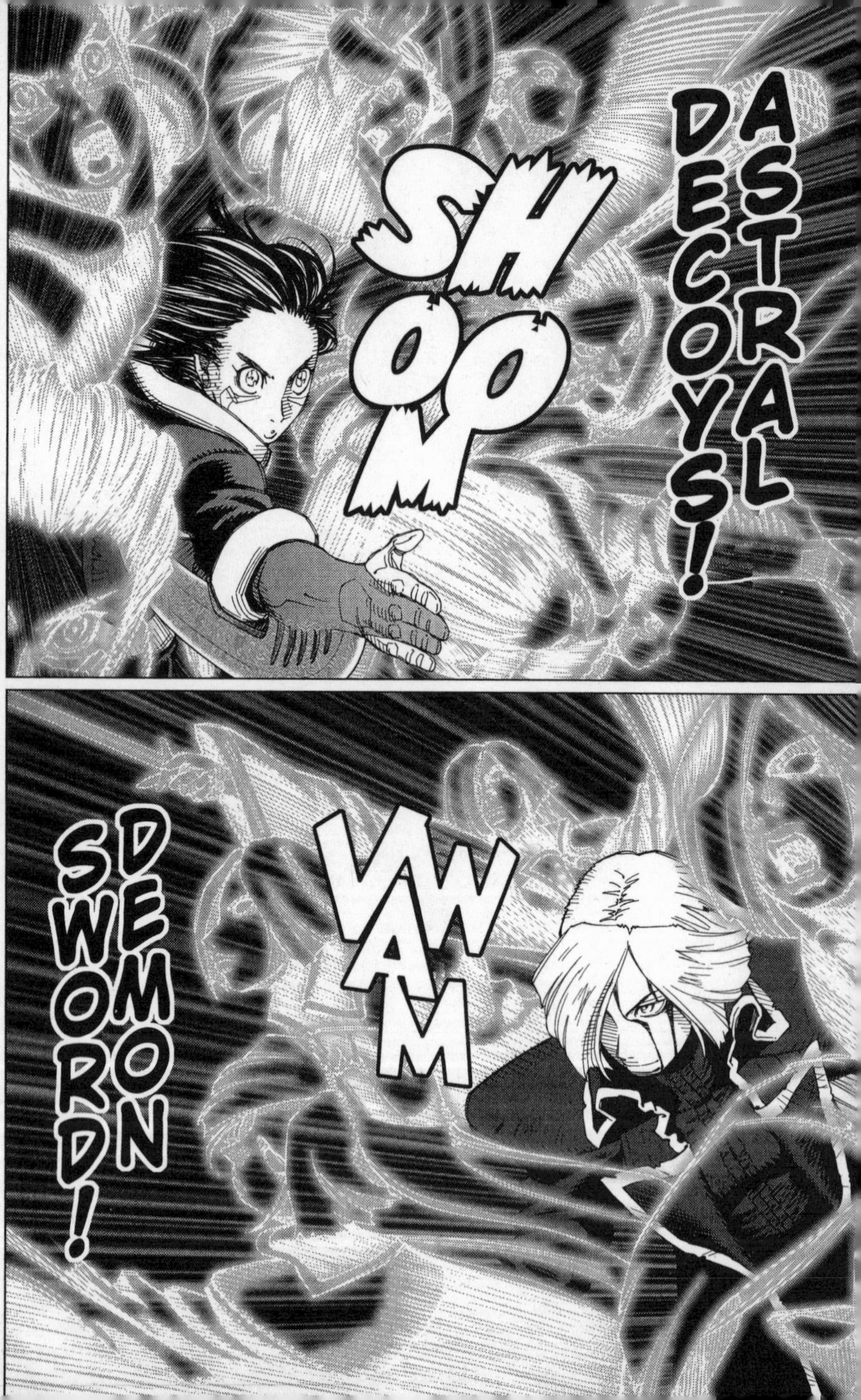
ASTRAL DECOYS!
SHOOM
VWAM
DEMON SWORD!

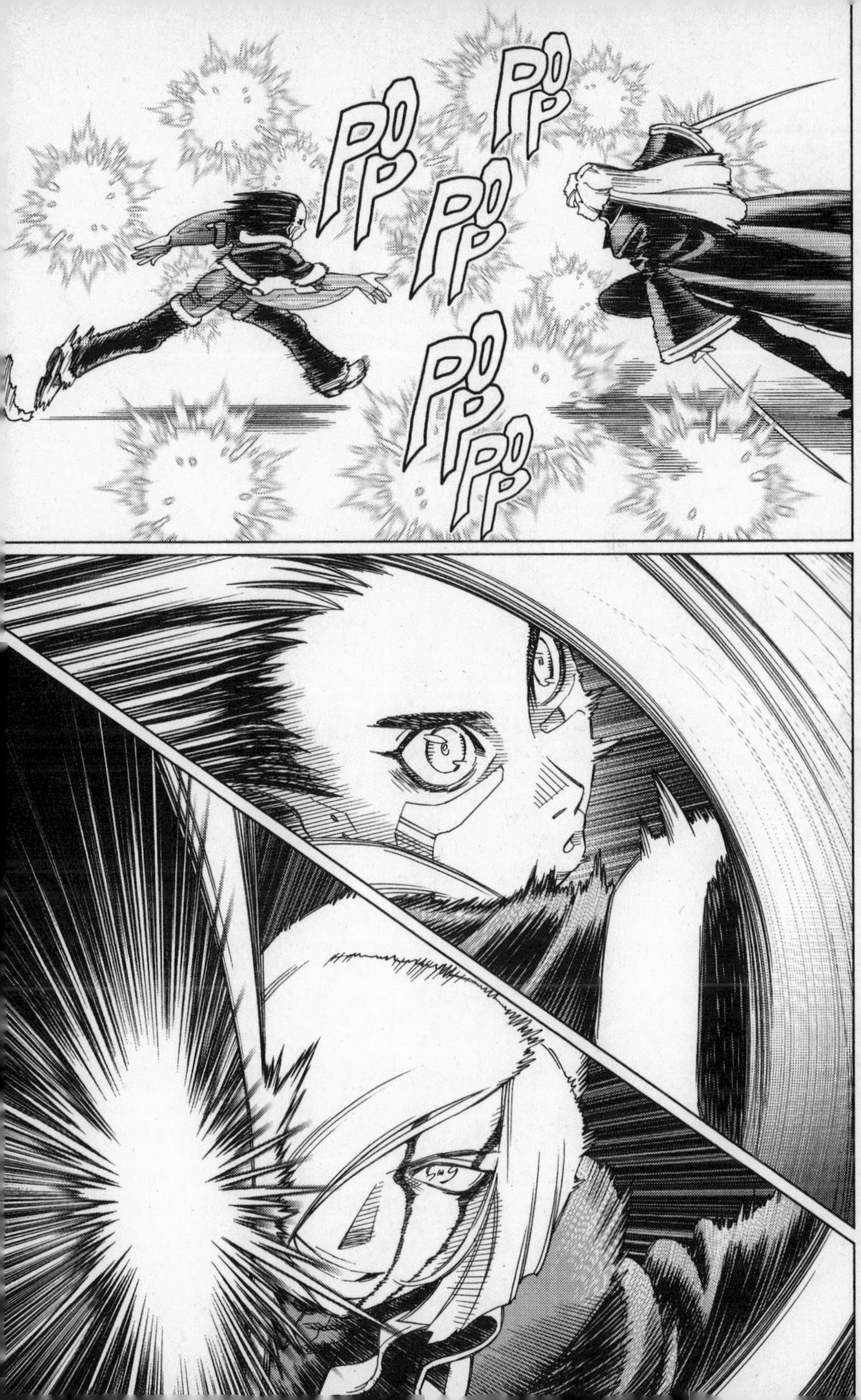
POP
POP
POP
POP
POP

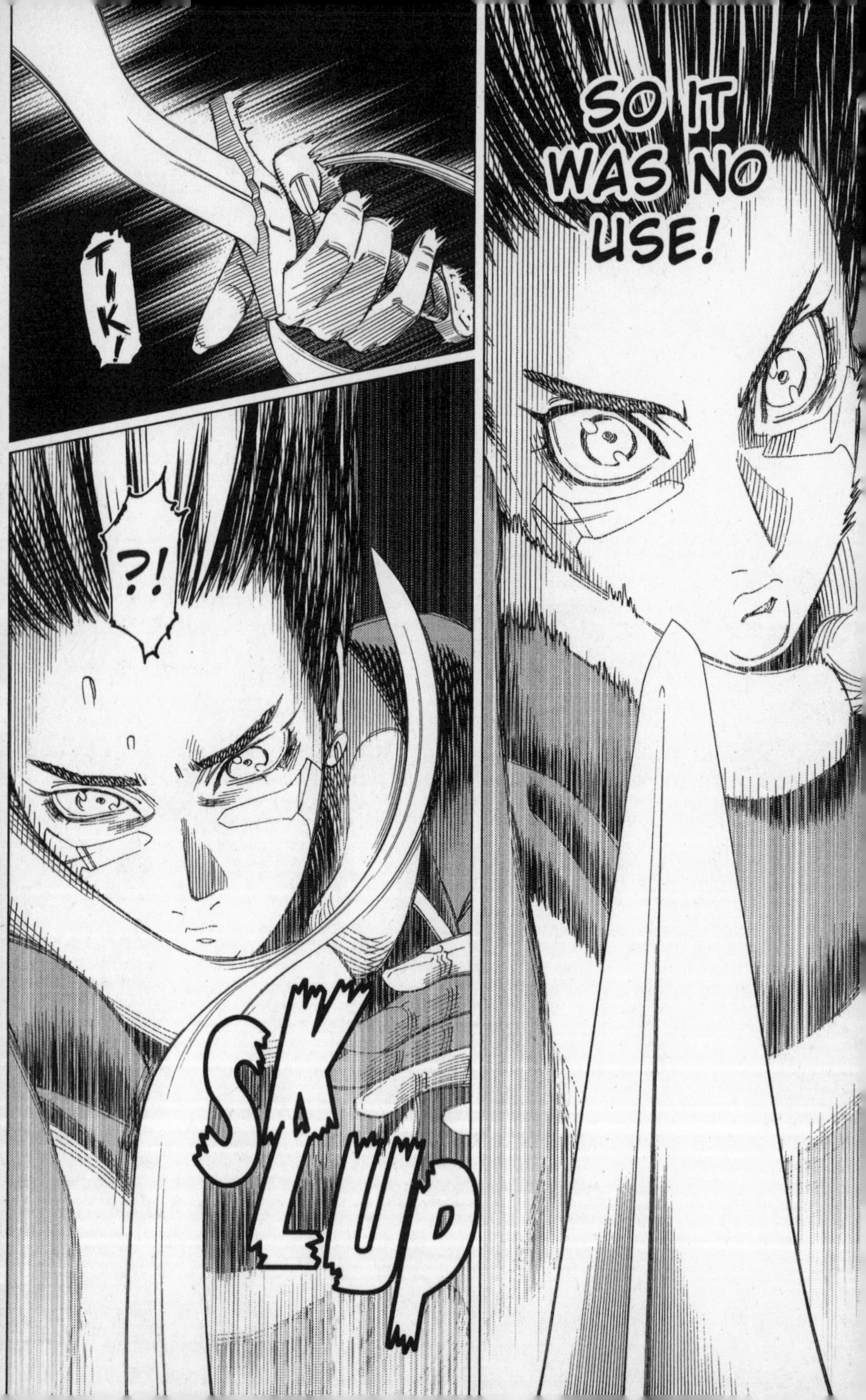
SO IT WAS NO USE!
TIK!
?!
SKLUP

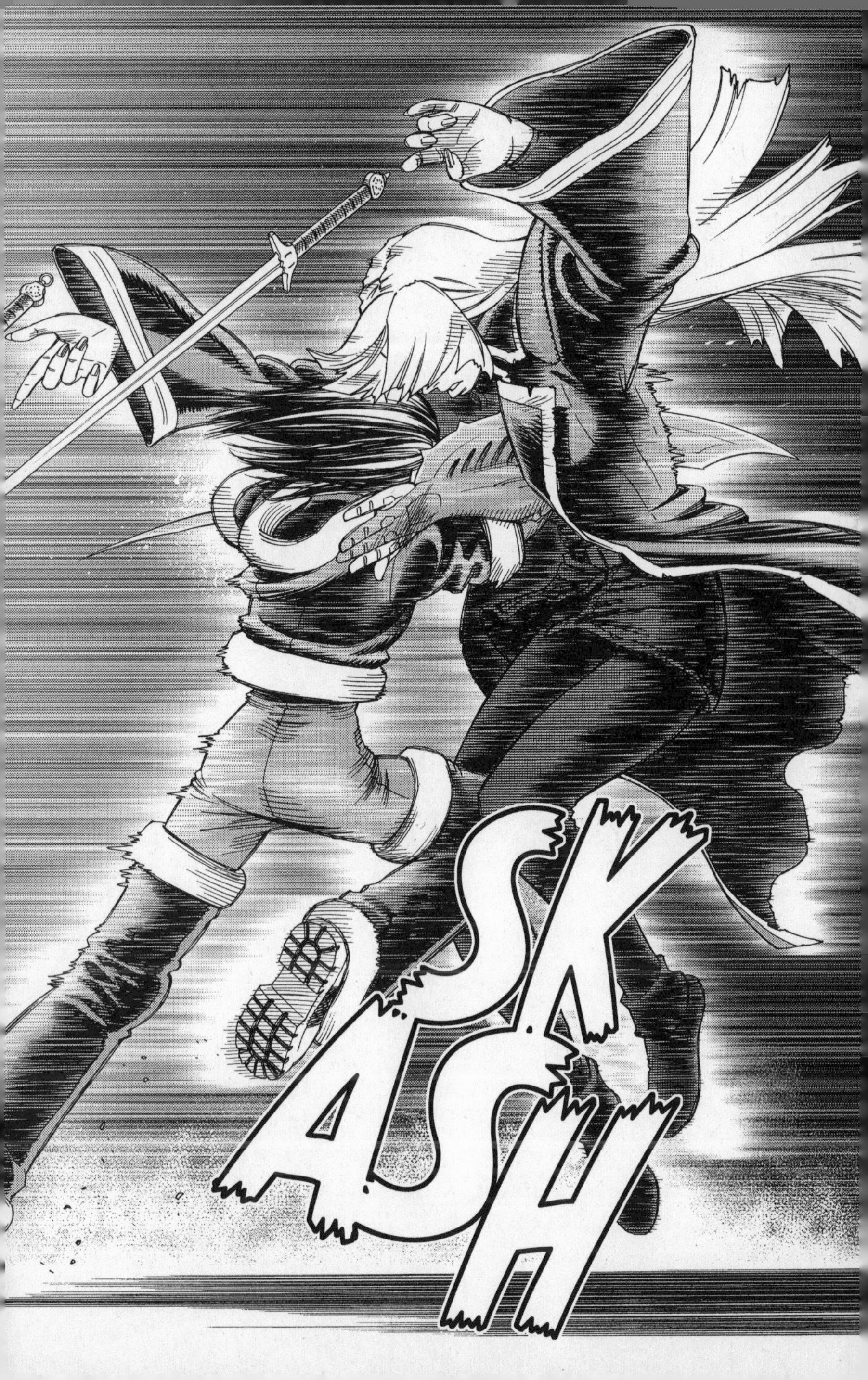
SKASH

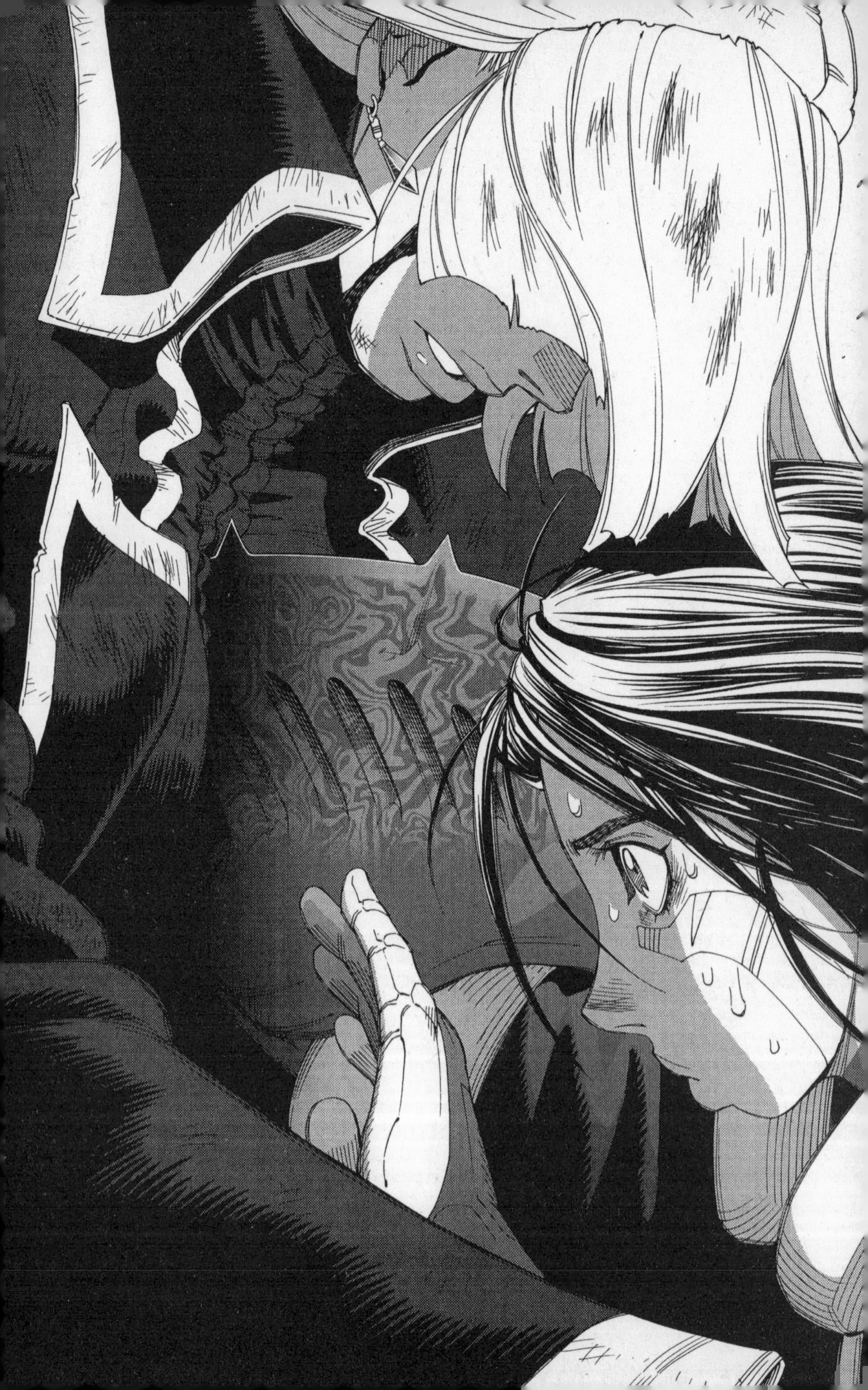

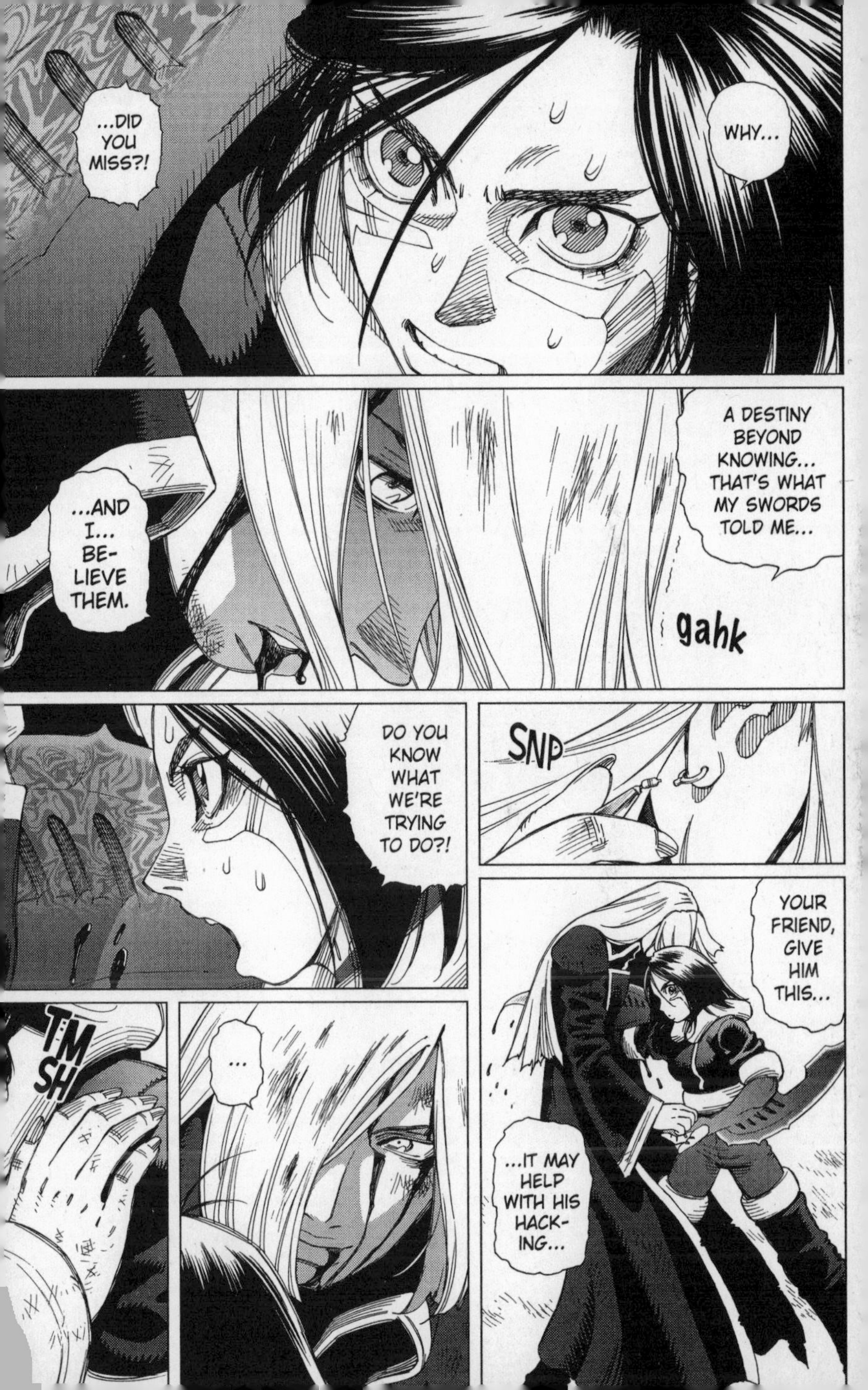
WHY...
...DID YOU MISS?!
A DESTINY BEYOND KNOWING... THAT'S WHAT MY SWORDS TOLD ME...
gahk
...AND I... BE-LIEVE THEM.
SNP
DO YOU KNOW WHAT WE'RE TRYING TO DO?!
YOUR FRIEND, GIVE HIM THIS...
...IT MAY HELP WITH HIS HACK-ING...
...
TMSH

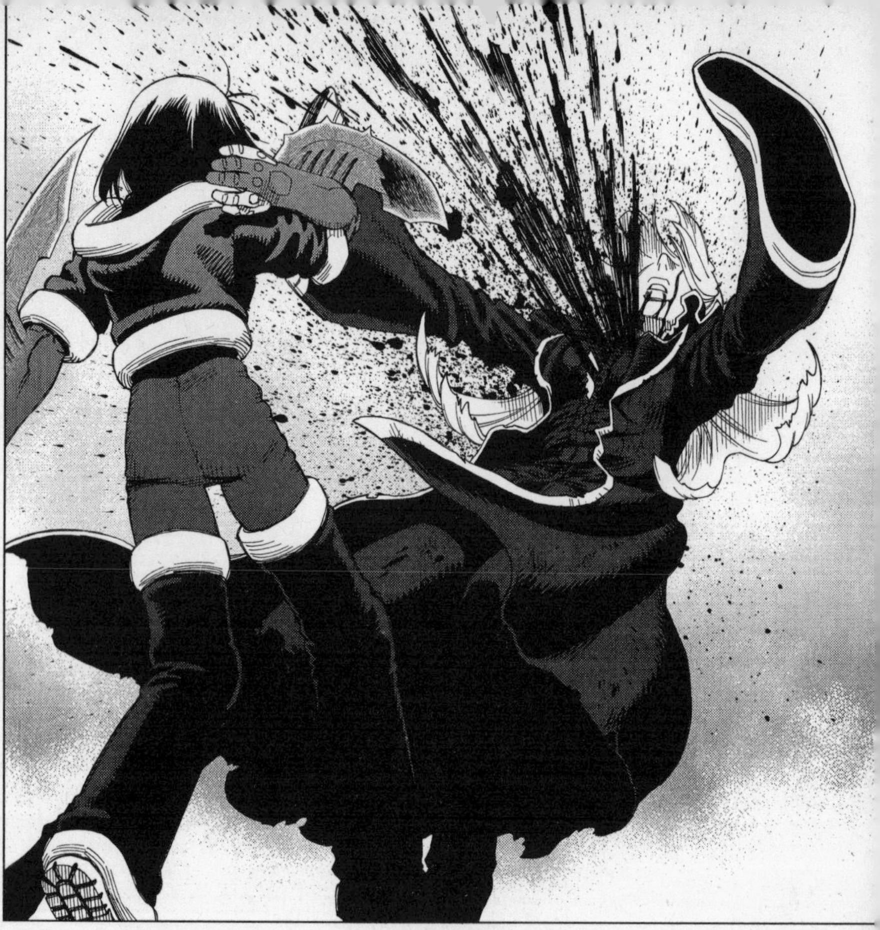
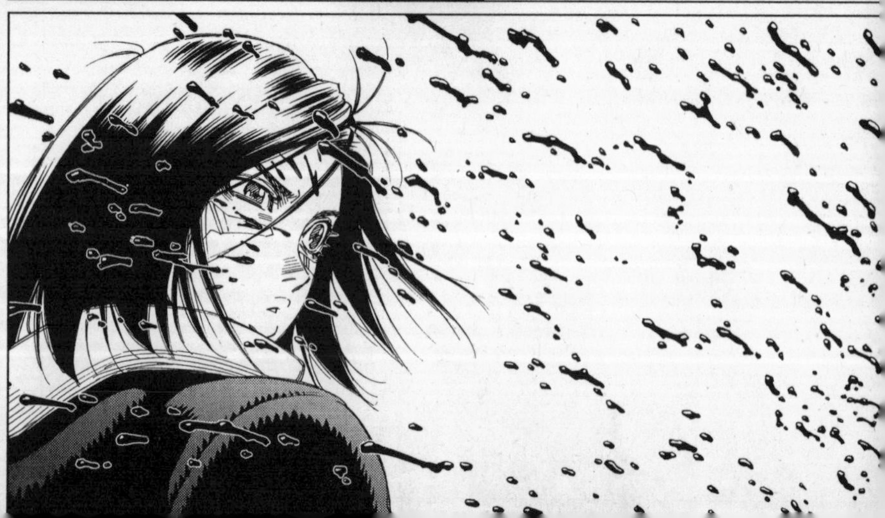

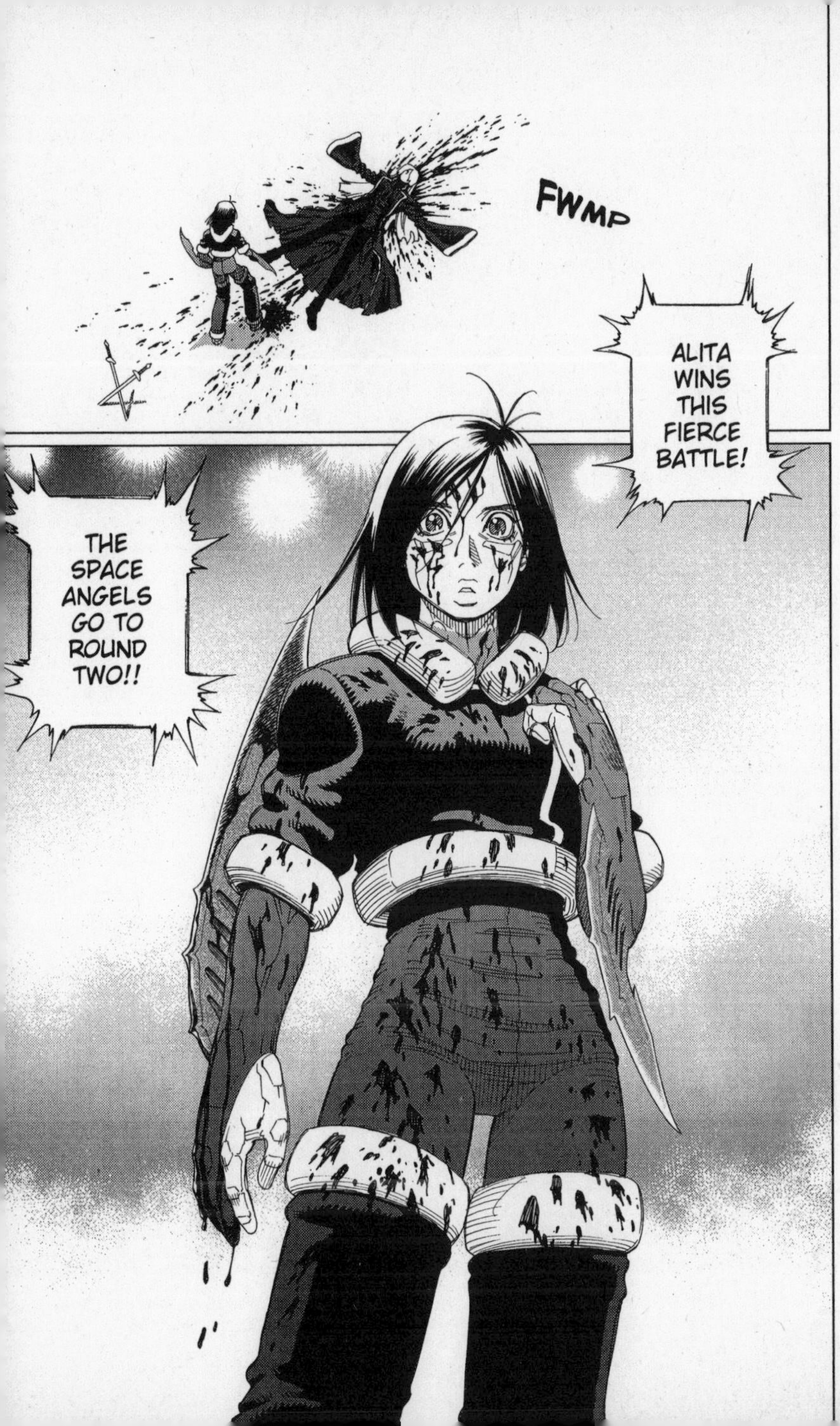
FWMP
ALITA WINS THIS FIERCE BATTLE!
THE SPACE ANGELS GO TO ROUND TWO!!

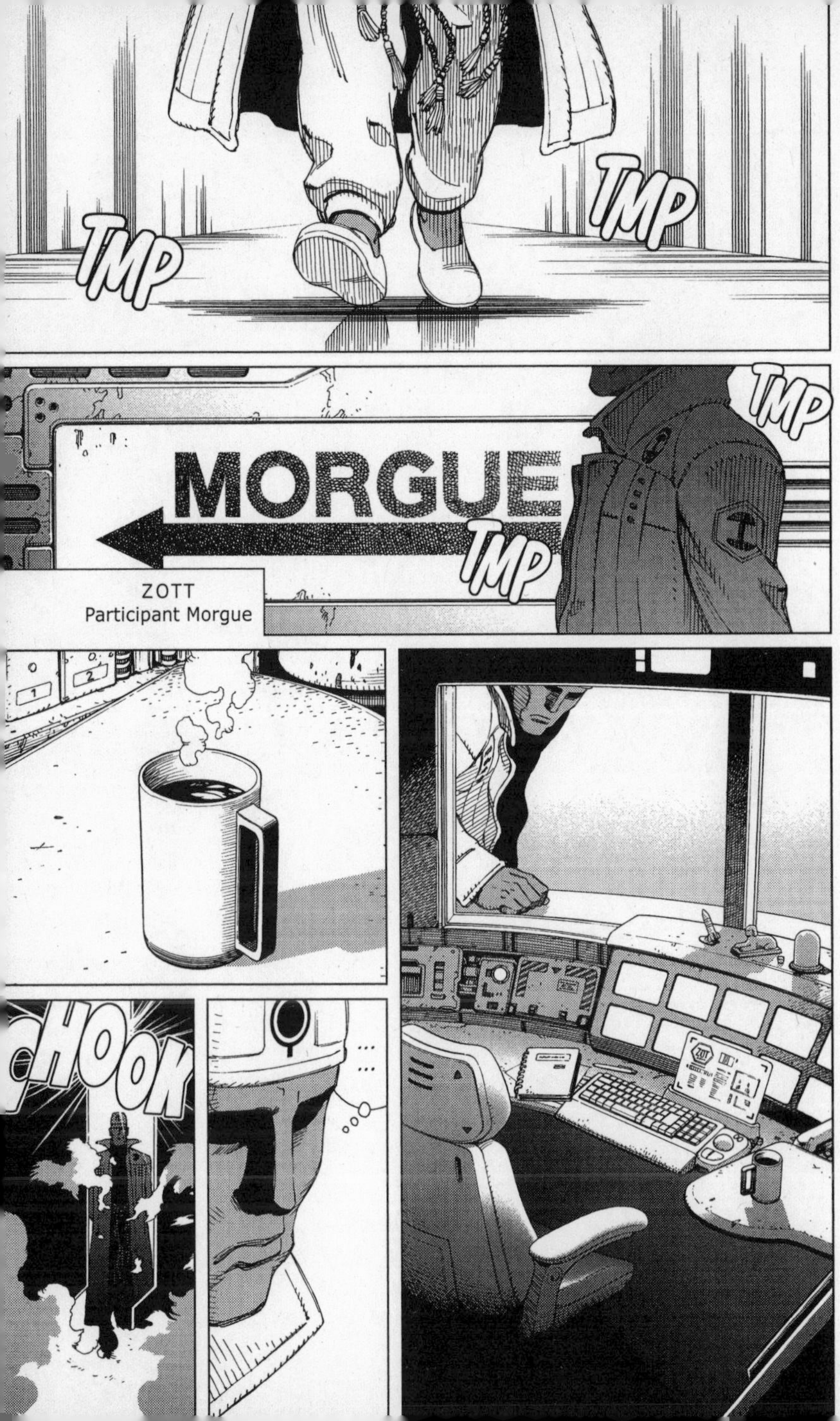
TMP
TMP
TMP
MORGUE
TMP
ZOTT
Participant Morgue
...
...
CHOOK

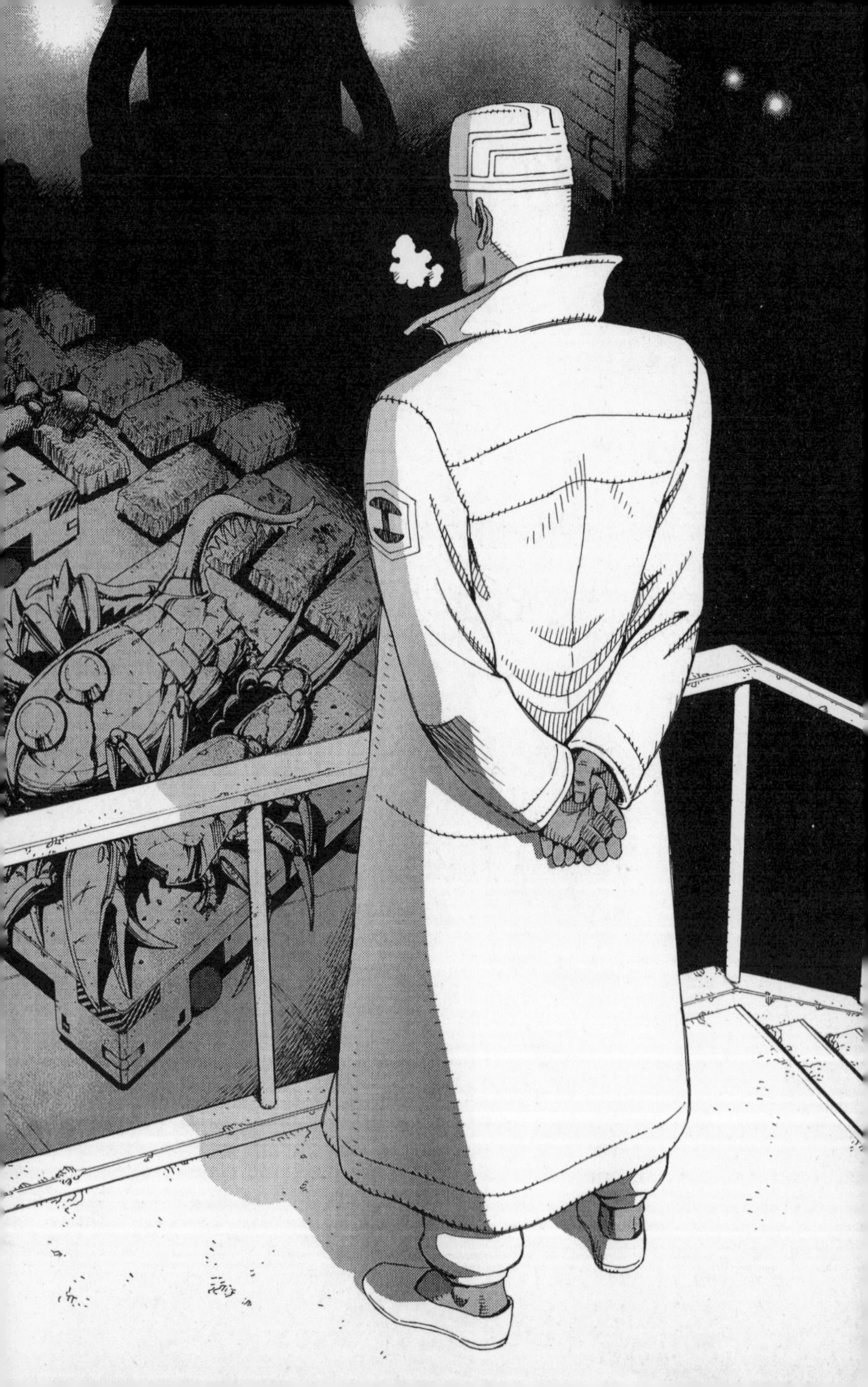

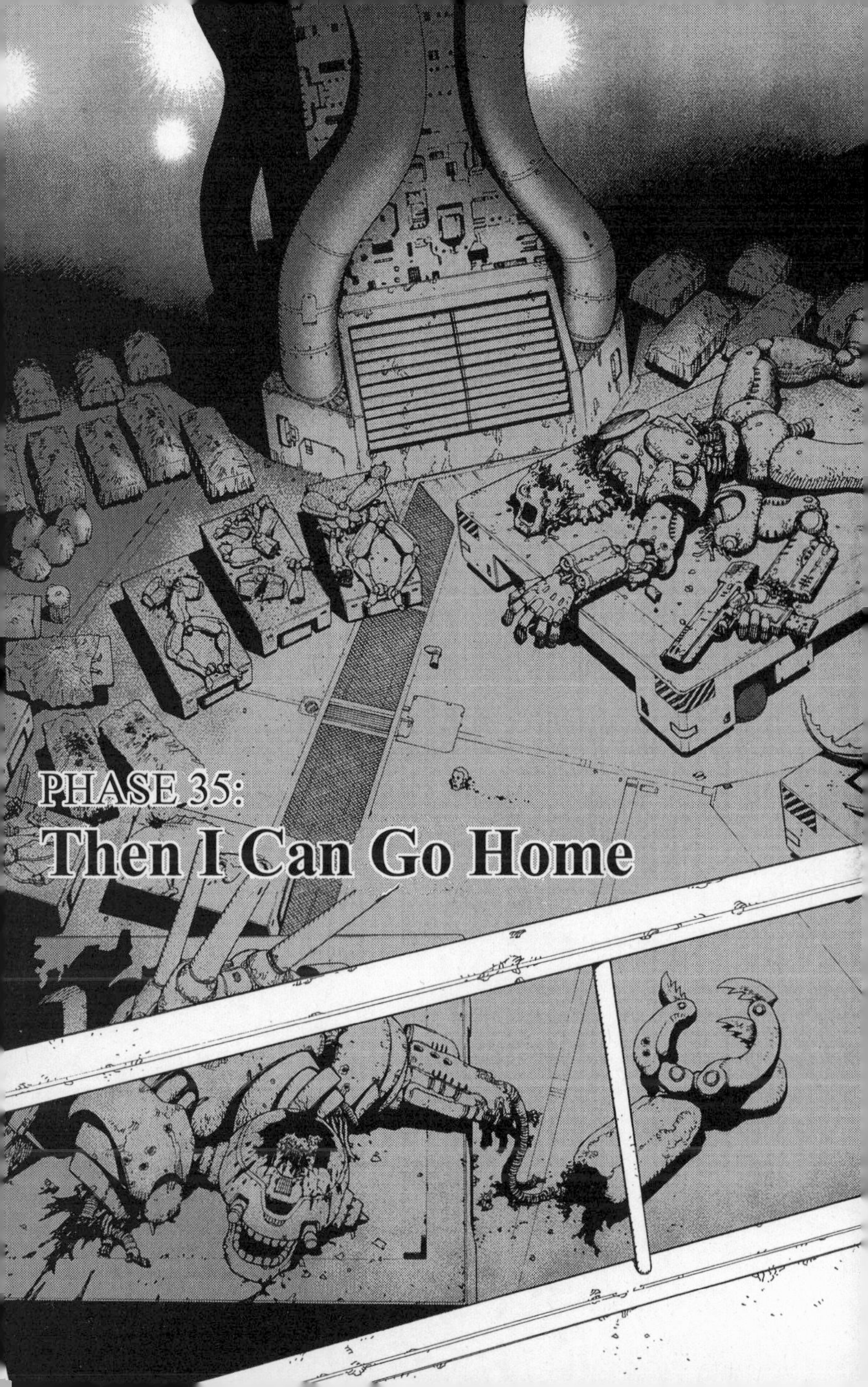
PHASE 35:
Then I Can Go Home

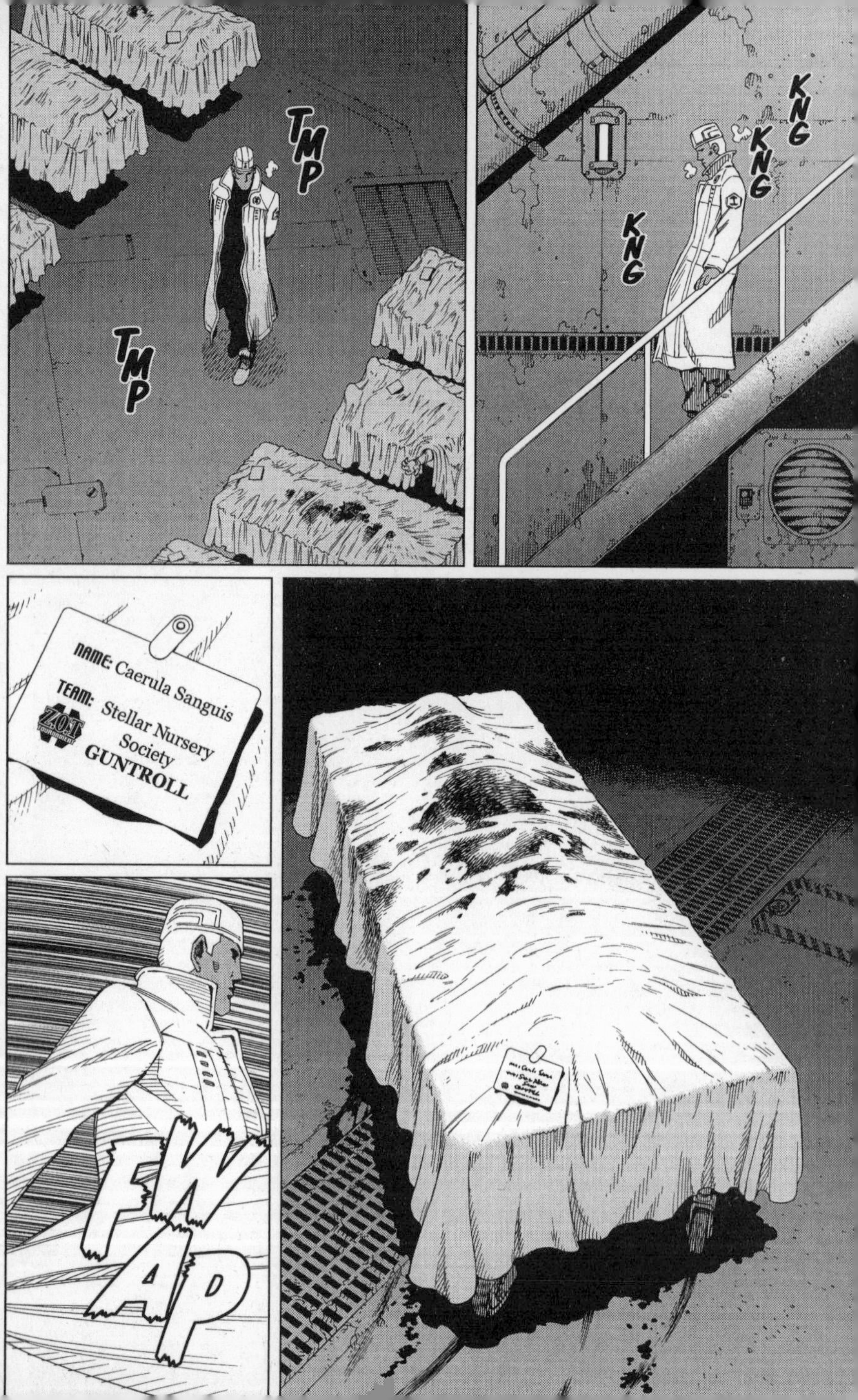
KNG
KNG
KNG
TMP
TMP
NAME: Caerula Sanguis
TEAM: Stellar Nursery Society
GUNTROLL
Z.O.T
FWAP

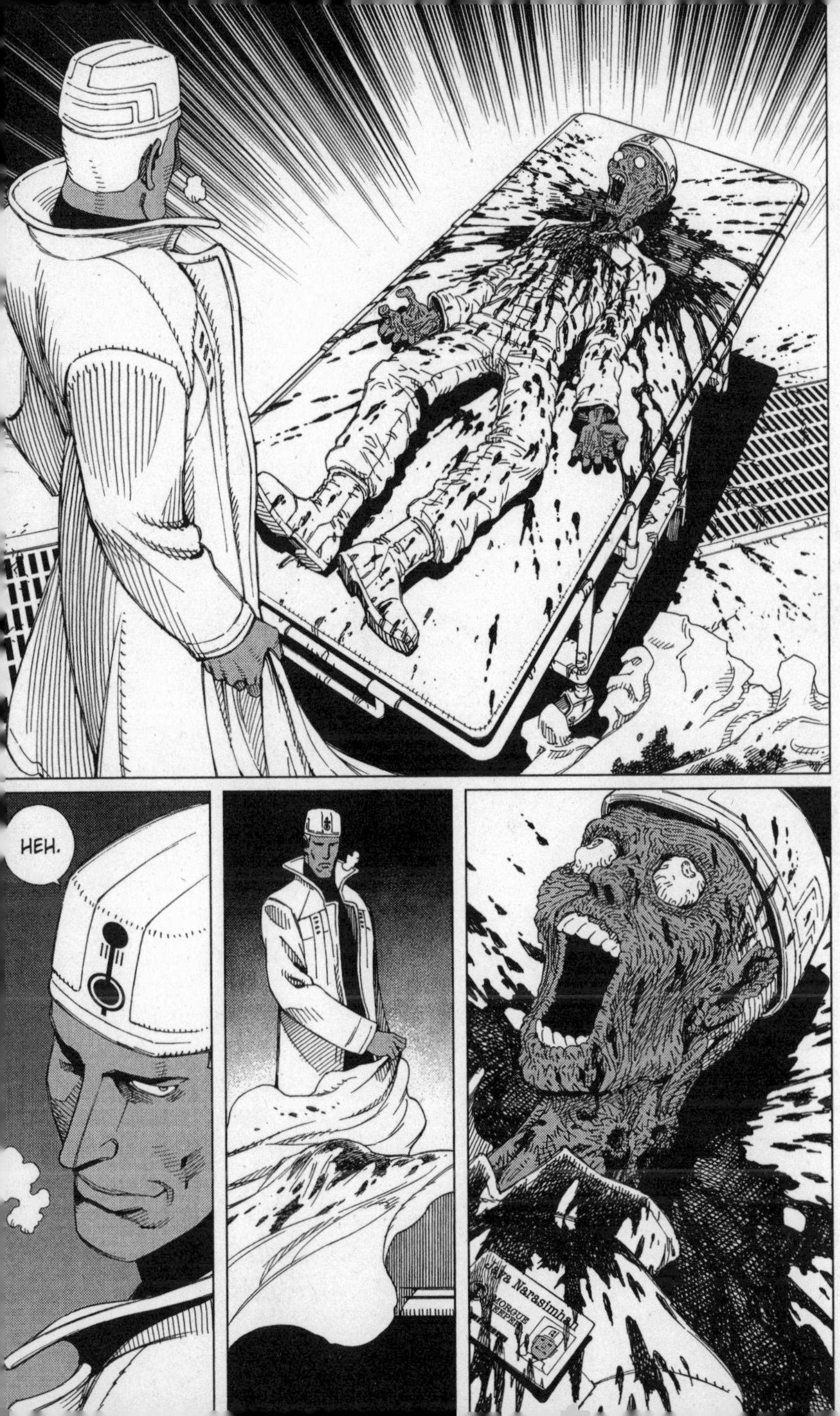
Jaya Narasimhan
MORGUE
HEH.

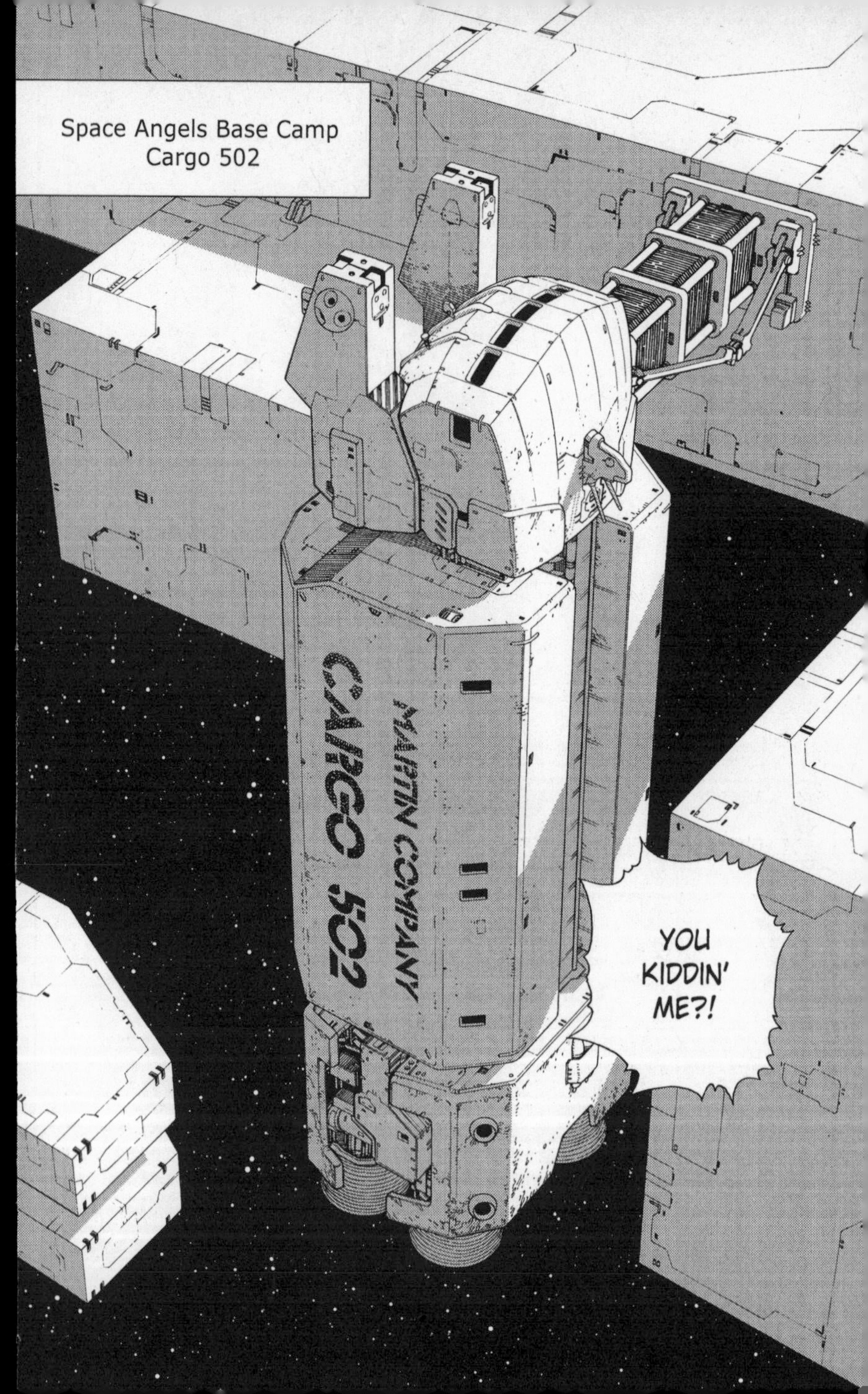
Space Angels Base Camp
Cargo 502
MARTIN COMPANY
CARGO 502
YOU KIDDIN' ME?!

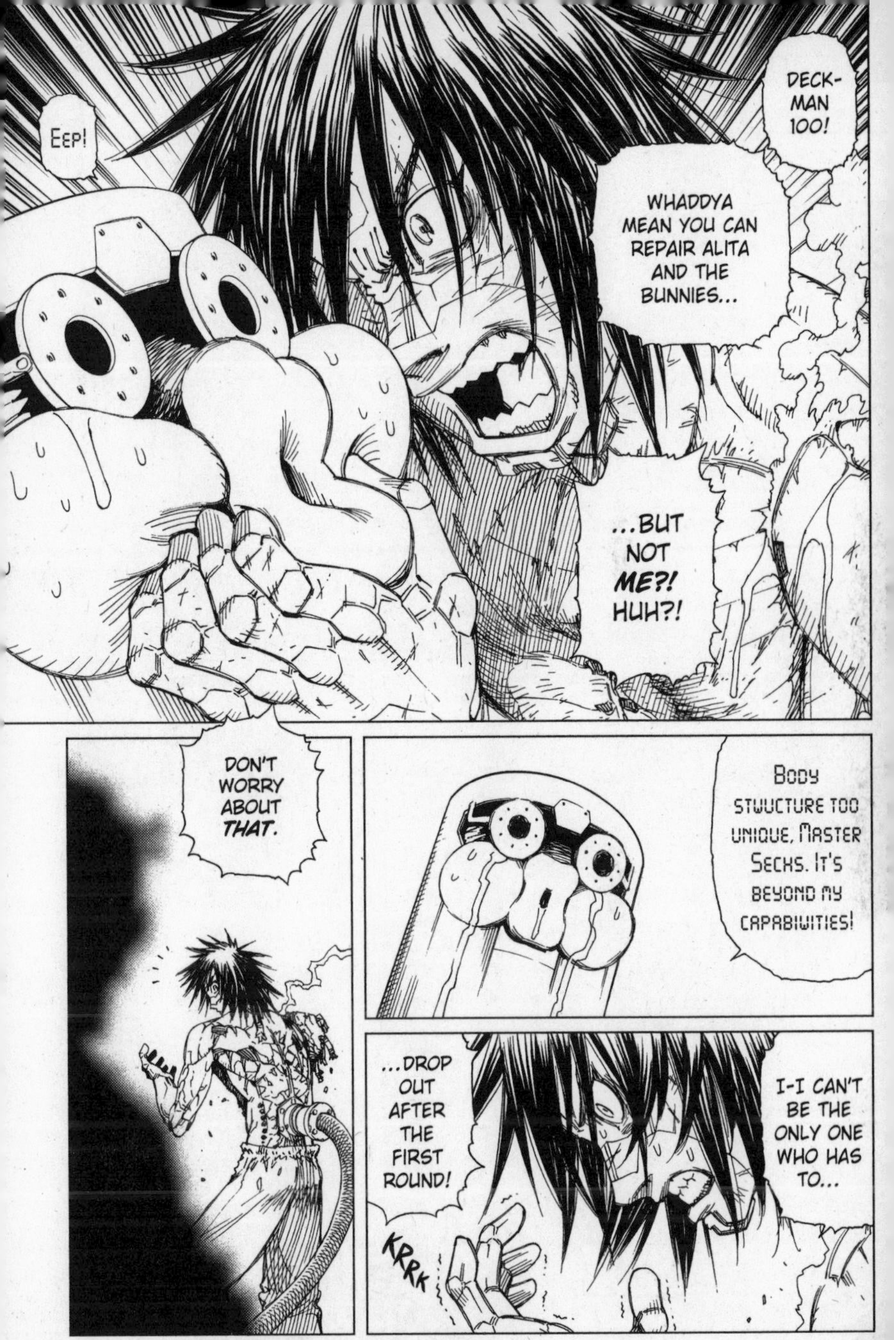
DECK-MAN 100!
WHADDYA MEAN YOU CAN REPAIR ALITA AND THE BUNNIES...
...BUT NOT *ME?!* HUH?!
Eep!
Body stwucture too unique, Master Sechs. It's beyond my capabiwities!
I-I CAN'T BE THE ONLY ONE WHO HAS TO...
...DROP OUT AFTER THE FIRST ROUND!
KRRK
DON'T WORRY ABOUT *THAT*.

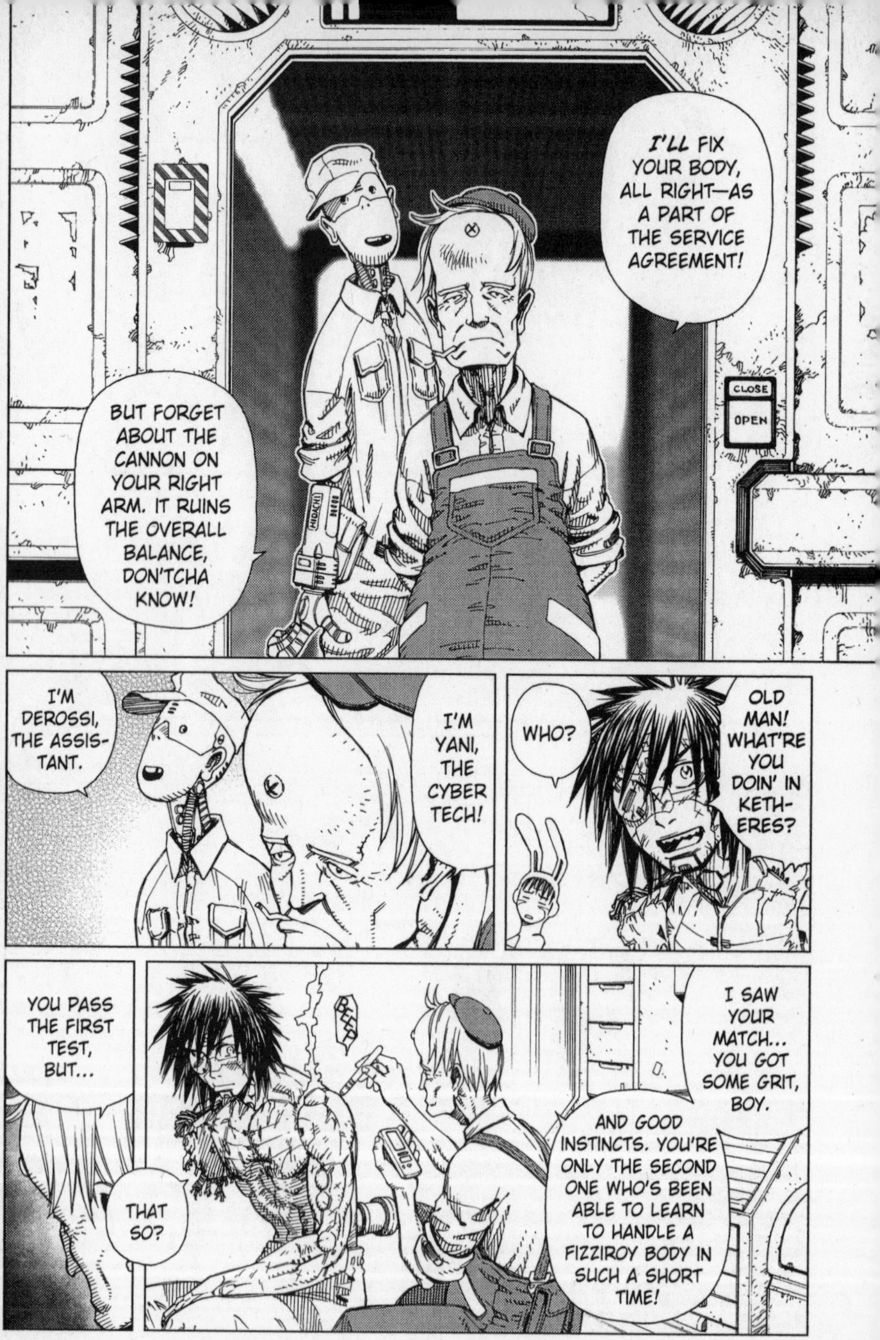

I'LL FIX YOUR BODY, ALL RIGHT—AS A PART OF THE SERVICE AGREEMENT!
CLOSE
OPEN
BUT FORGET ABOUT THE CANNON ON YOUR RIGHT ARM. IT RUINS THE OVERALL BALANCE, DON'TCHA KNOW!
HIDACHI
OLD MAN! WHAT'RE YOU DOIN' IN KETHERES?
WHO?
I'M YANI, THE CYBER TECH!
I'M DEROSSI, THE ASSISTANT.
I SAW YOUR MATCH... YOU GOT SOME GRIT, BOY.
AND GOOD INSTINCTS. YOU'RE ONLY THE SECOND ONE WHO'S BEEN ABLE TO LEARN TO HANDLE A FIZZIROY BODY IN SUCH A SHORT TIME!
BEEP
THAT SO?
YOU PASS THE FIRST TEST, BUT...

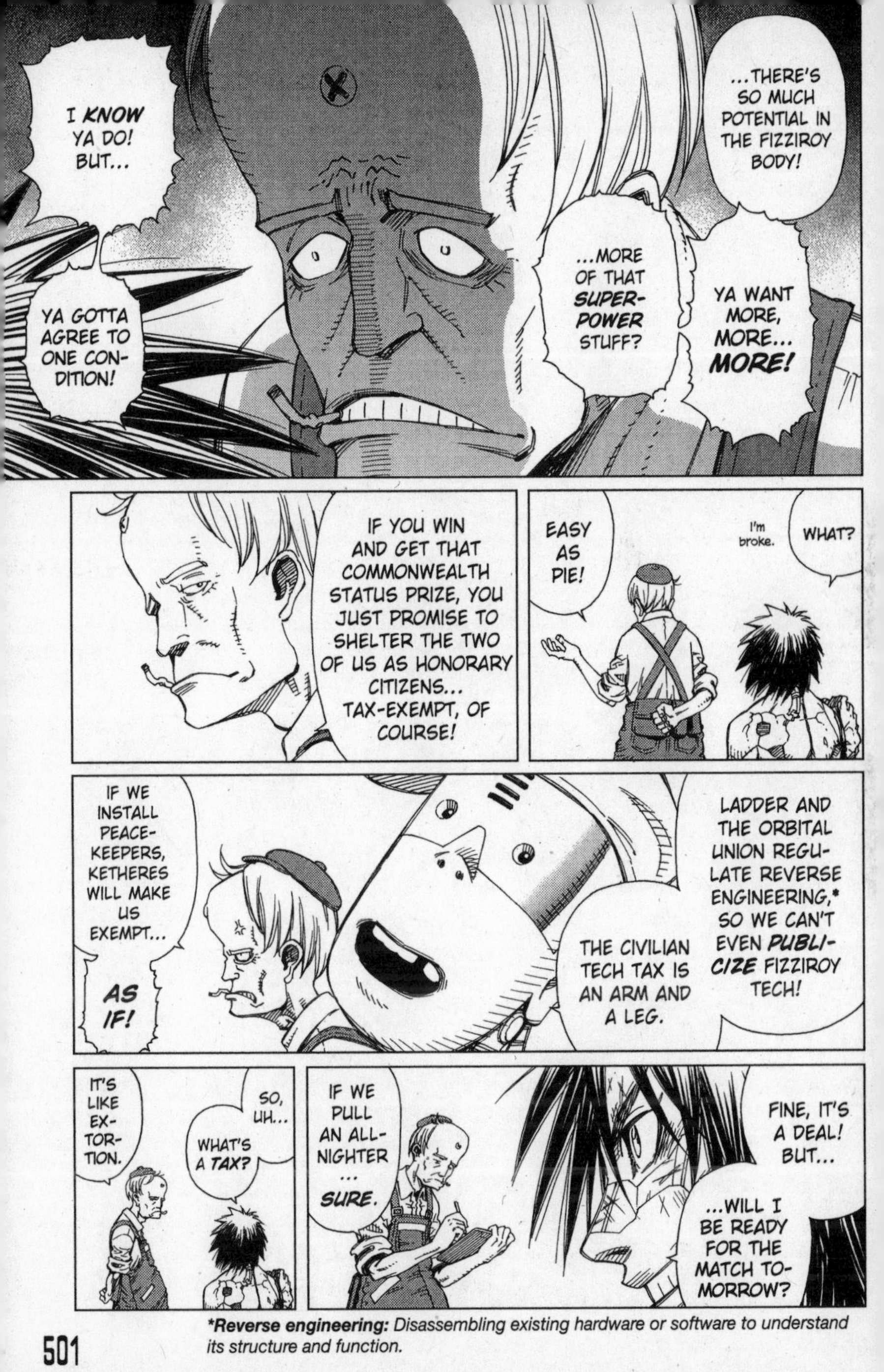
...THERE'S SO MUCH POTENTIAL IN THE FIZZIROY BODY!
YA WANT MORE, MORE... MORE!
...MORE OF THAT SUPER-POWER STUFF?
I KNOW YA DO! BUT...
YA GOTTA AGREE TO ONE CONDITION!
WHAT?
I'm broke.
EASY AS PIE!
IF YOU WIN AND GET THAT COMMONWEALTH STATUS PRIZE, YOU JUST PROMISE TO SHELTER THE TWO OF US AS HONORARY CITIZENS... TAX-EXEMPT, OF COURSE!
LADDER AND THE ORBITAL UNION REGULATE REVERSE ENGINEERING,* SO WE CAN'T EVEN PUBLICIZE FIZZIROY TECH!
THE CIVILIAN TECH TAX IS AN ARM AND A LEG.
IF WE INSTALL PEACE-KEEPERS, KETHERES WILL MAKE US EXEMPT...
AS IF!
FINE, IT'S A DEAL! BUT...
...WILL I BE READY FOR THE MATCH TOMORROW?
IF WE PULL AN ALL-NIGHTER... SURE.
SO, UH...
WHAT'S A TAX?
IT'S LIKE EXTORTION.

***Reverse engineering:** *Disassembling existing hardware or software to understand its structure and function.*

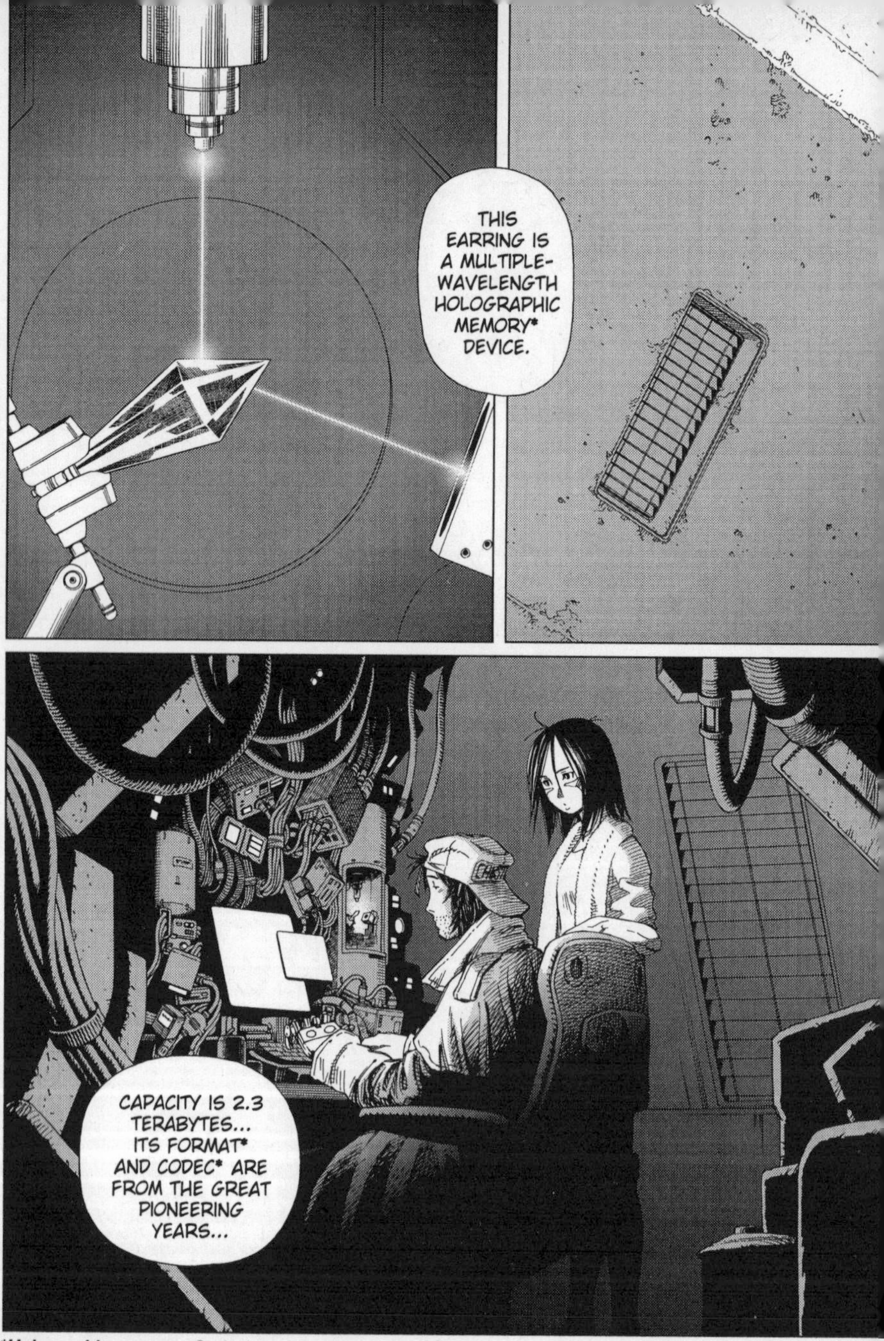
THIS EARRING IS A MULTIPLE-WAVELENGTH HOLOGRAPHIC MEMORY* DEVICE.
CAPACITY IS 2.3 TERABYTES... ITS FORMAT* AND CODEC* ARE FROM THE GREAT PIONEERING YEARS...

***Holographic memory:** *Optical memory employing lasers. Stores information in three-dimensional layers.*
***Format:** *Organization of data to preset specifications. Used for reading and writing media.*
***Codec:** *Short for compression/decompression. Technique for encoding and retrieving compressed data.*

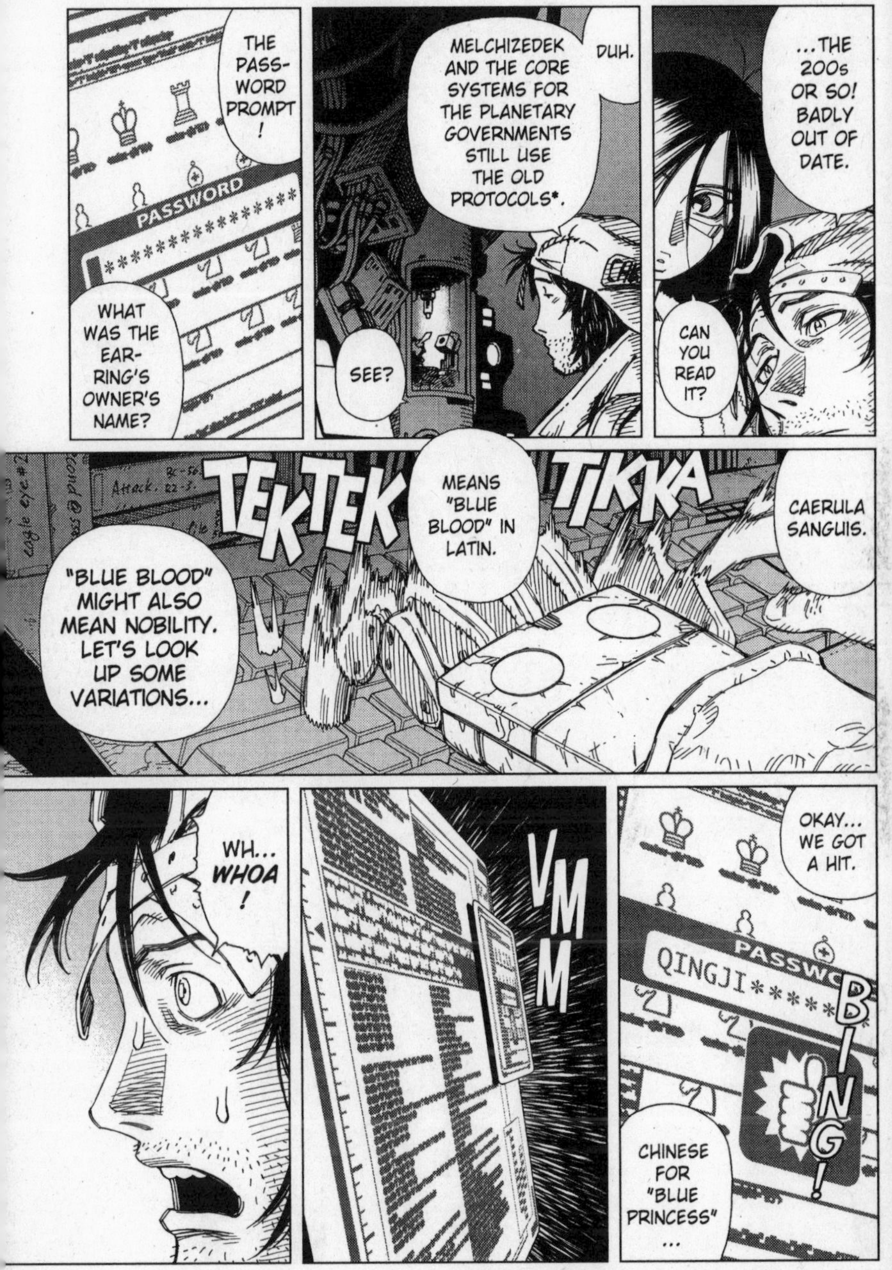
...THE 200s OR SO! BADLY OUT OF DATE.
CAN YOU READ IT?
DUH.
MELCHIZEDEK AND THE CORE SYSTEMS FOR THE PLANETARY GOVERNMENTS STILL USE THE OLD PROTOCOLS*.
SEE?
THE PASS-WORD PROMPT!
PASSWORD
****
WHAT WAS THE EAR-RING'S OWNER'S NAME?
CAERULA SANGUIS.
TIKKA
MEANS "BLUE BLOOD" IN LATIN.
TEKTEK
"BLUE BLOOD" MIGHT ALSO MEAN NOBILITY. LET'S LOOK UP SOME VARIATIONS...
OKAY... WE GOT A HIT.
QINGJI*****
BING!
CHINESE FOR "BLUE PRINCESS"...
VMM
WH... ***WHOA***!

***Protocol:** A standard for communication exchange.*

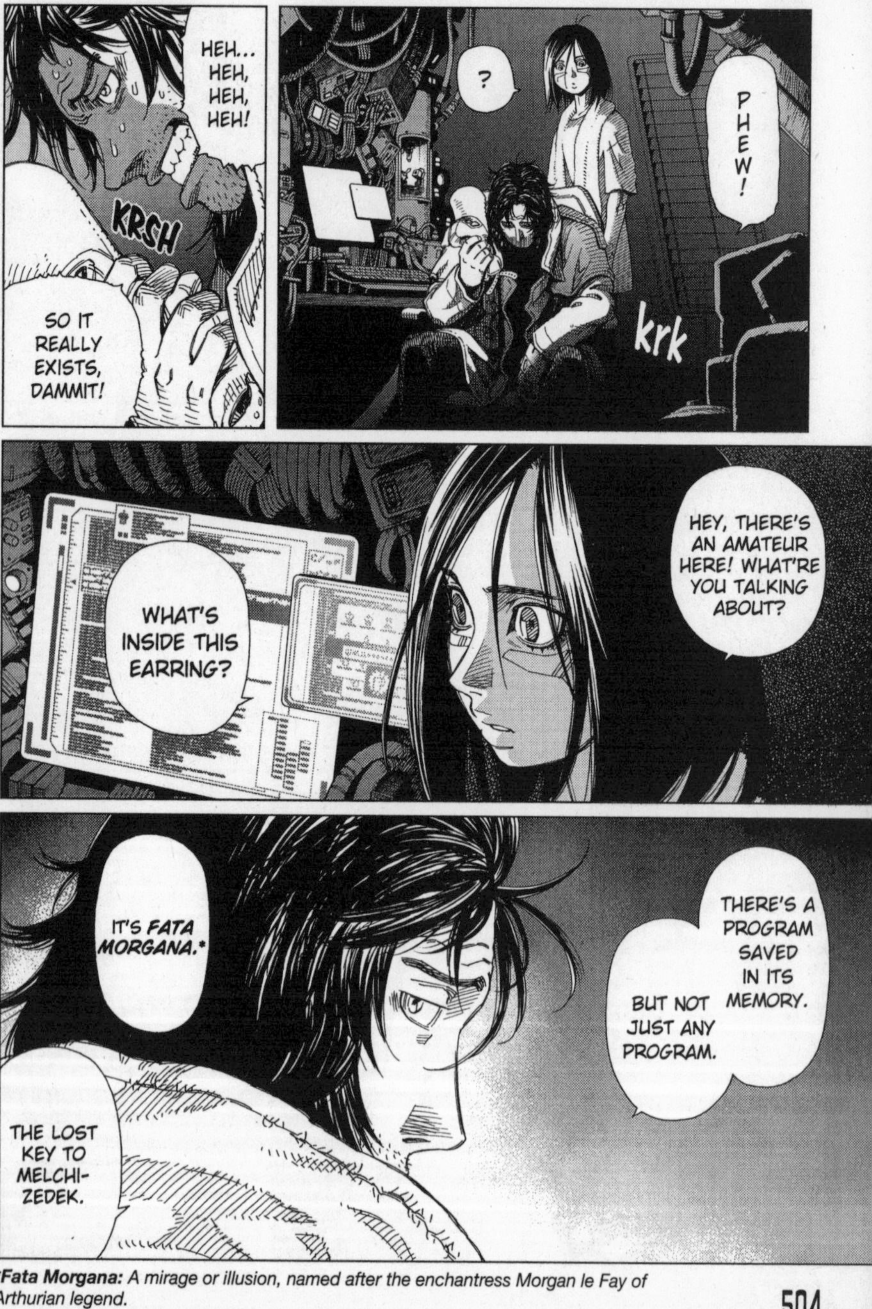
PHEW!
?
krk
HEH... HEH, HEH, HEH!
KRSH
SO IT REALLY EXISTS, DAMMIT!
HEY, THERE'S AN AMATEUR HERE! WHAT'RE YOU TALKING ABOUT?
WHAT'S INSIDE THIS EARRING?
THERE'S A PROGRAM SAVED IN ITS MEMORY.
BUT NOT JUST ANY PROGRAM.
IT'S *FATA MORGANA*.*
THE LOST KEY TO MELCHI-ZEDEK.

Fata Morgana: *A mirage or illusion, named after the enchantress Morgan le Fay of Arthurian legend.*

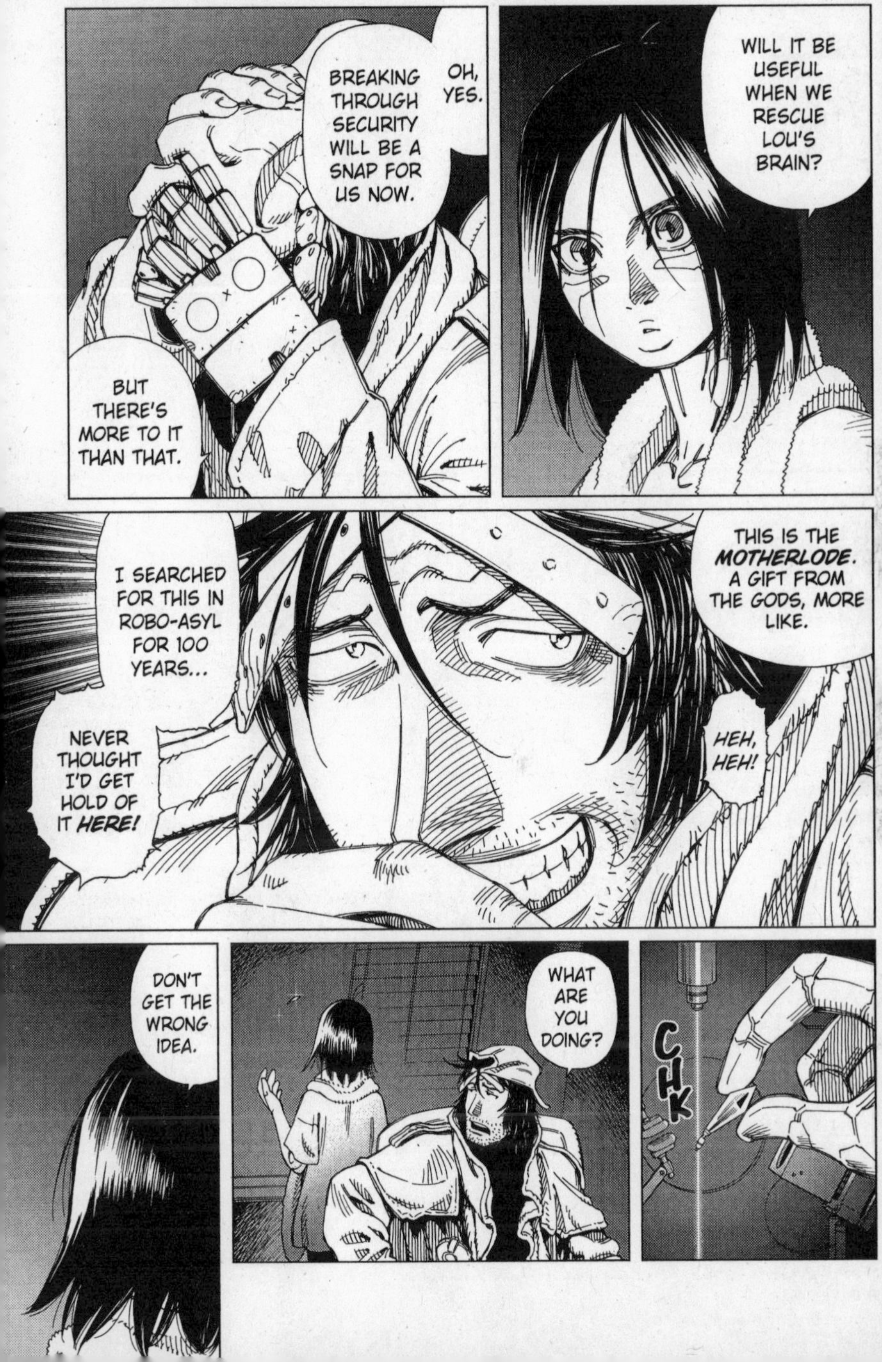
WILL IT BE USEFUL WHEN WE RESCUE LOU'S BRAIN?
OH, YES.
BREAKING THROUGH SECURITY WILL BE A SNAP FOR US NOW.
BUT THERE'S MORE TO IT THAN THAT.
THIS IS THE *MOTHERLODE*. A GIFT FROM THE GODS, MORE LIKE.
HEH, HEH!
I SEARCHED FOR THIS IN ROBO-ASYL FOR 100 YEARS...
NEVER THOUGHT I'D GET HOLD OF IT *HERE!*
CHK
WHAT ARE YOU DOING?
DON'T GET THE WRONG IDEA.

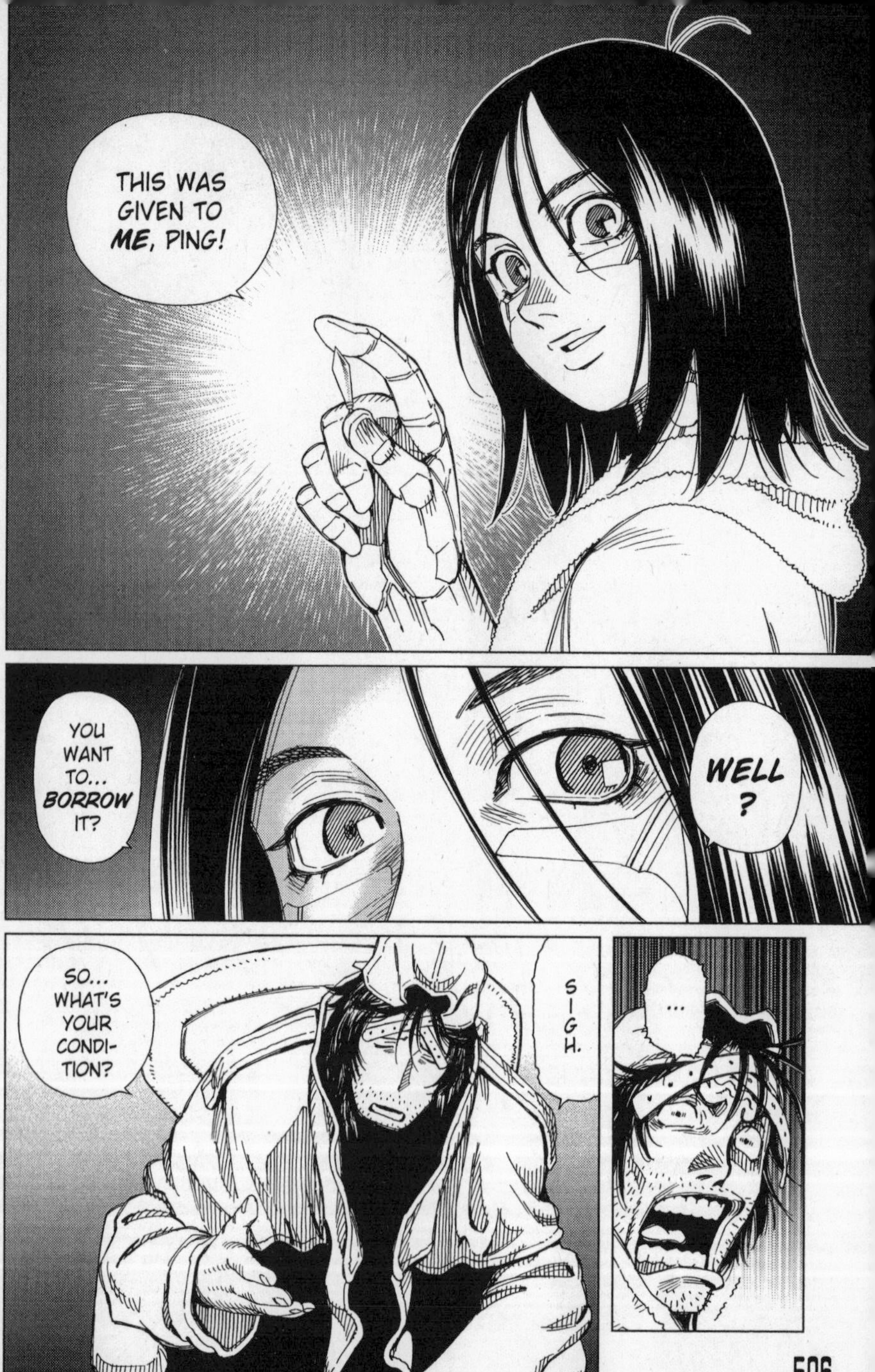
THIS WAS GIVEN TO *ME*, PING!
WELL?
YOU WANT TO... *BORROW* IT?
...
SIGH.
SO... WHAT'S YOUR CONDI-TION?

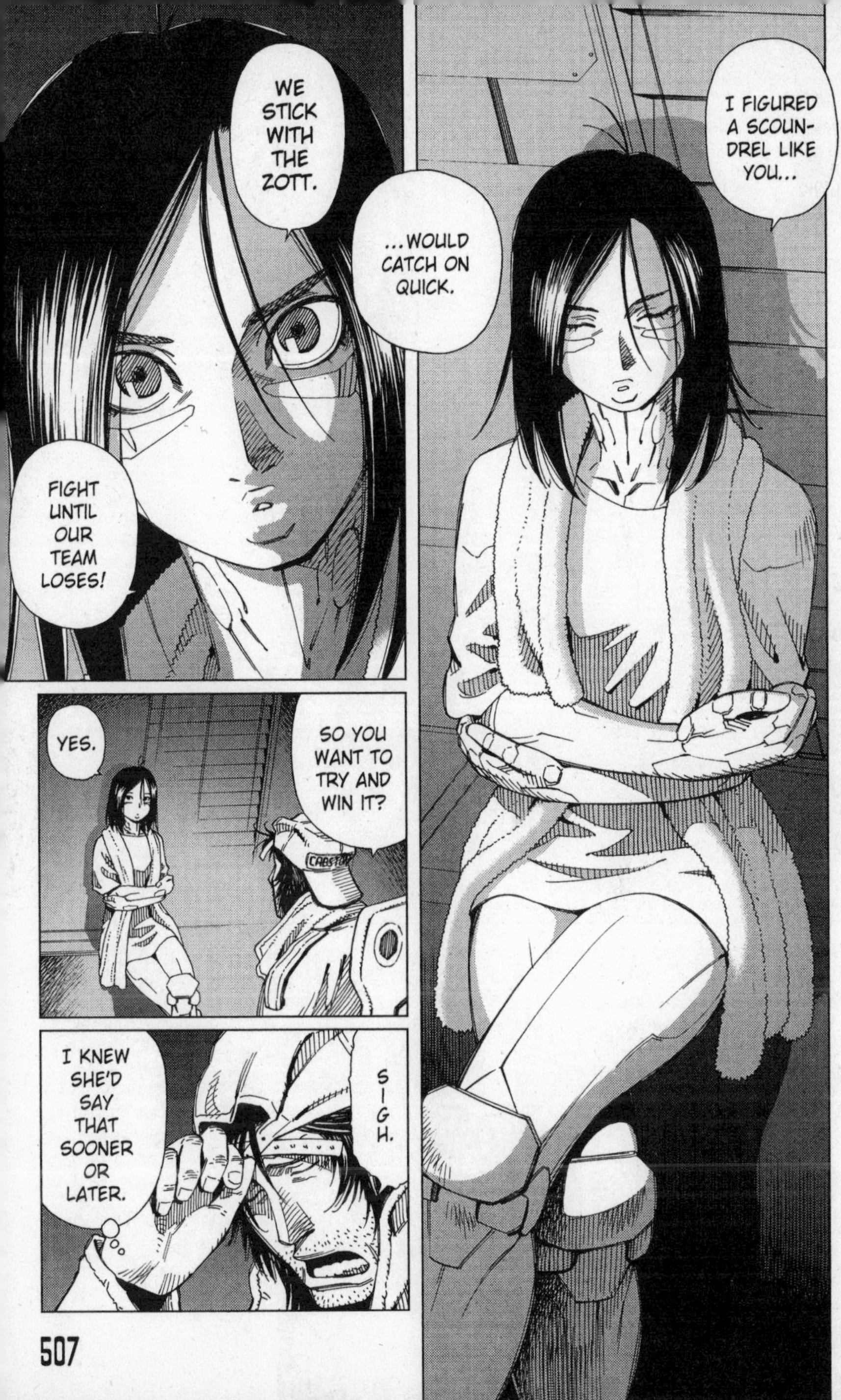
I FIGURED A SCOUN-DREL LIKE YOU...
...WOULD CATCH ON QUICK.
WE STICK WITH THE ZOTT.
FIGHT UNTIL OUR TEAM LOSES!
SO YOU WANT TO TRY AND WIN IT?
YES.
SIGH.
I KNEW SHE'D SAY THAT SOONER OR LATER.

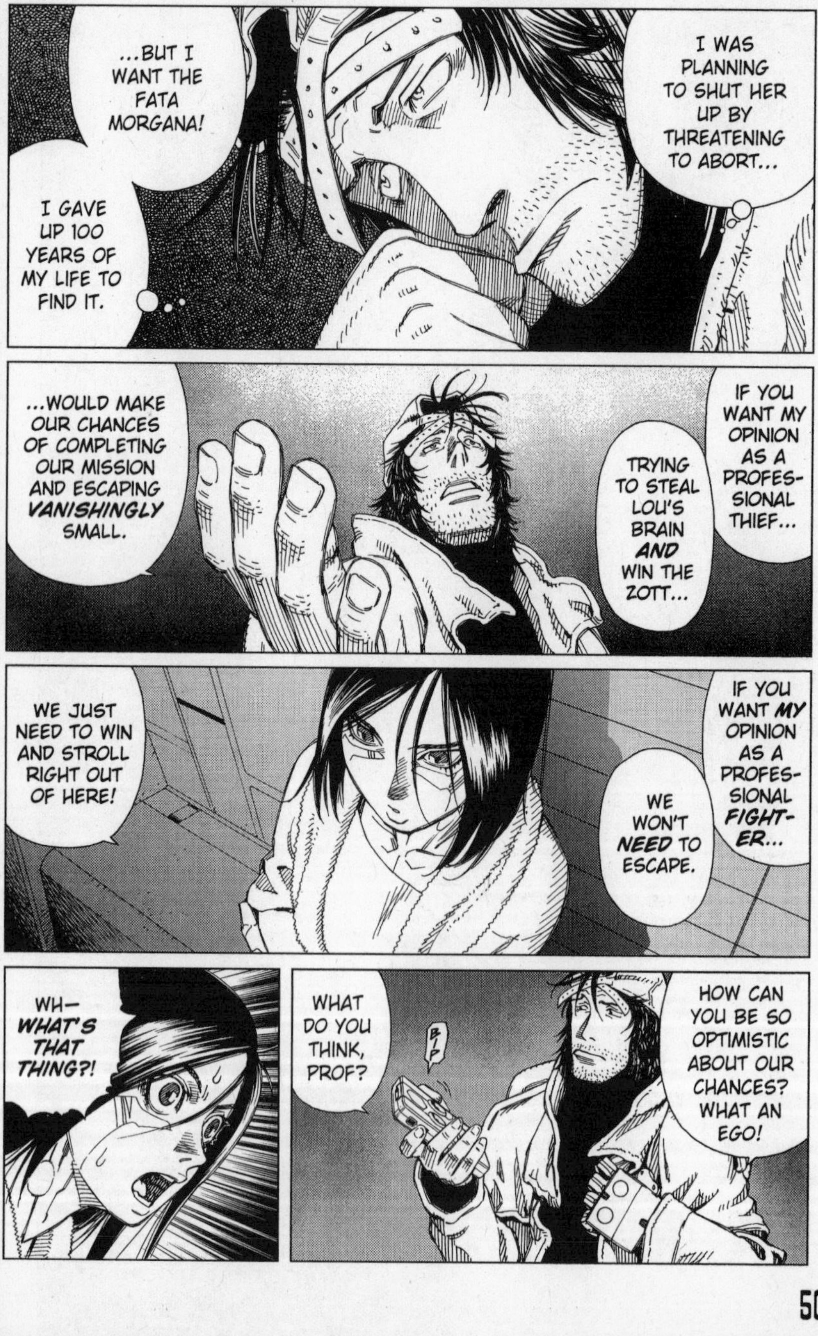
I WAS PLANNING TO SHUT HER UP BY THREATENING TO ABORT...
...BUT I WANT THE FATA MORGANA!
I GAVE UP 100 YEARS OF MY LIFE TO FIND IT.
IF YOU WANT MY OPINION AS A PROFESSIONAL THIEF...
TRYING TO STEAL LOU'S BRAIN *AND* WIN THE ZOTT...
...WOULD MAKE OUR CHANCES OF COMPLETING OUR MISSION AND ESCAPING *VANISHINGLY* SMALL.
IF YOU WANT *MY* OPINION AS A PROFESSIONAL *FIGHTER*...
WE WON'T *NEED* TO ESCAPE.
WE JUST NEED TO WIN AND STROLL RIGHT OUT OF HERE!
HOW CAN YOU BE SO OPTIMISTIC ABOUT OUR CHANCES? WHAT AN EGO!
BIP
WHAT DO YOU THINK, PROF?
WH— *WHAT'S THAT THING?!*

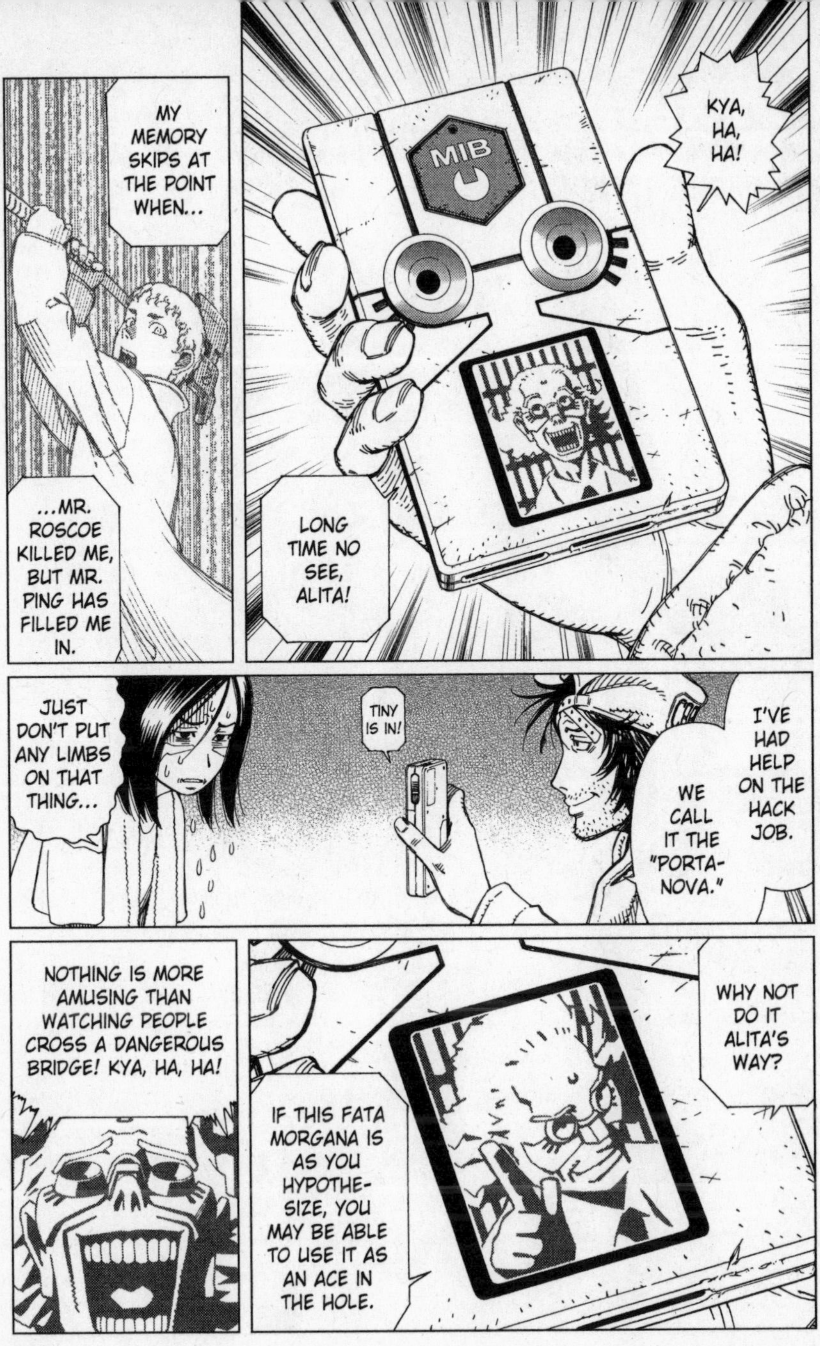
KYA, HA, HA!
LONG TIME NO SEE, ALITA!
MY MEMORY SKIPS AT THE POINT WHEN...
...MR. ROSCOE KILLED ME, BUT MR. PING HAS FILLED ME IN.
I'VE HAD HELP ON THE HACK JOB.
WE CALL IT THE "PORTA-NOVA."
TINY IS IN!
JUST DON'T PUT ANY LIMBS ON THAT THING...
WHY NOT DO IT ALITA'S WAY?
IF THIS FATA MORGANA IS AS YOU HYPOTHE-SIZE, YOU MAY BE ABLE TO USE IT AS AN ACE IN THE HOLE.
NOTHING IS MORE AMUSING THAN WATCHING PEOPLE CROSS A DANGEROUS BRIDGE! KYA, HA, HA!

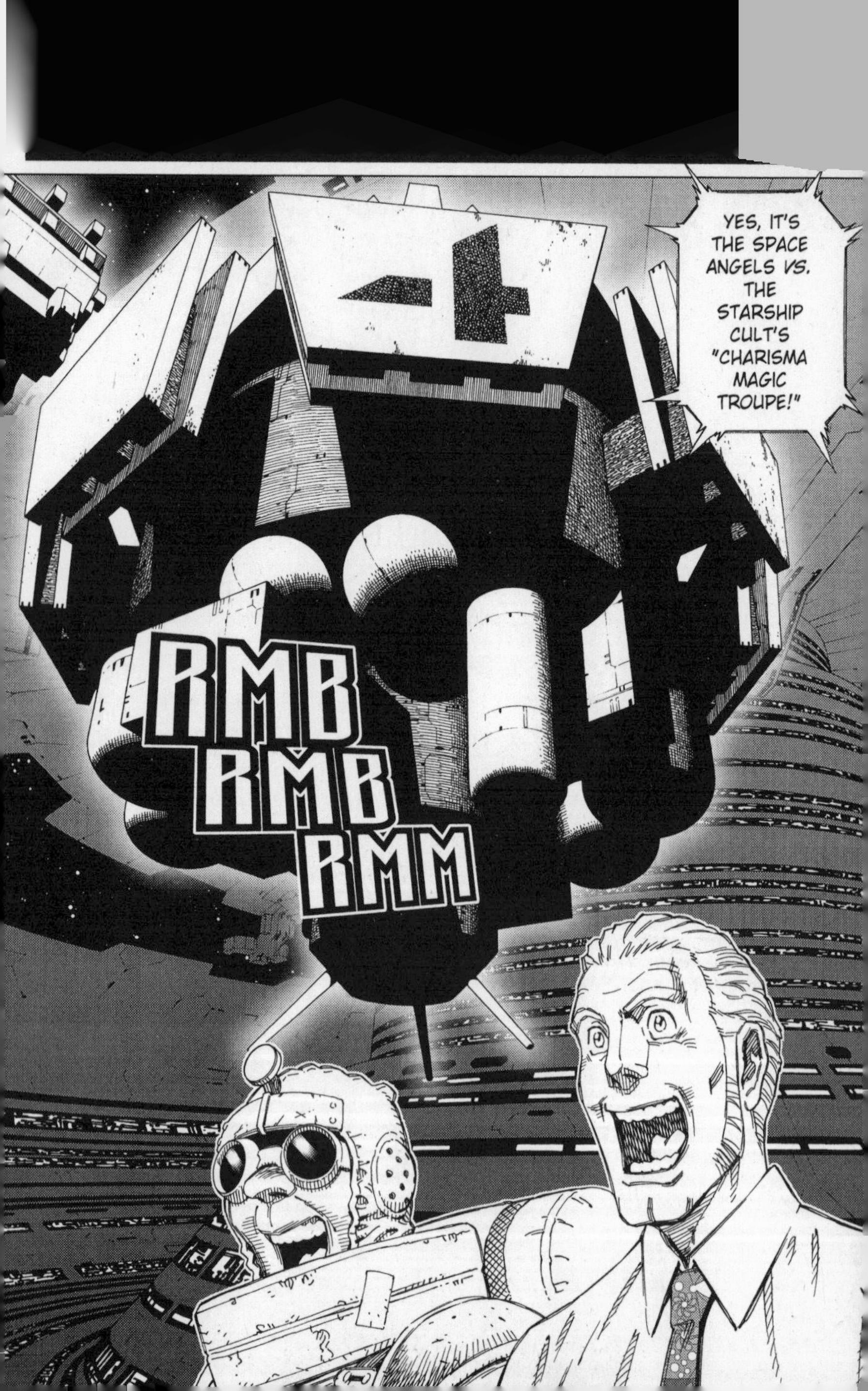
YES, IT'S THE SPACE ANGELS VS. THE STARSHIP CULT'S "CHARISMA MAGIC TROUPE!"
RMB RMB RMM

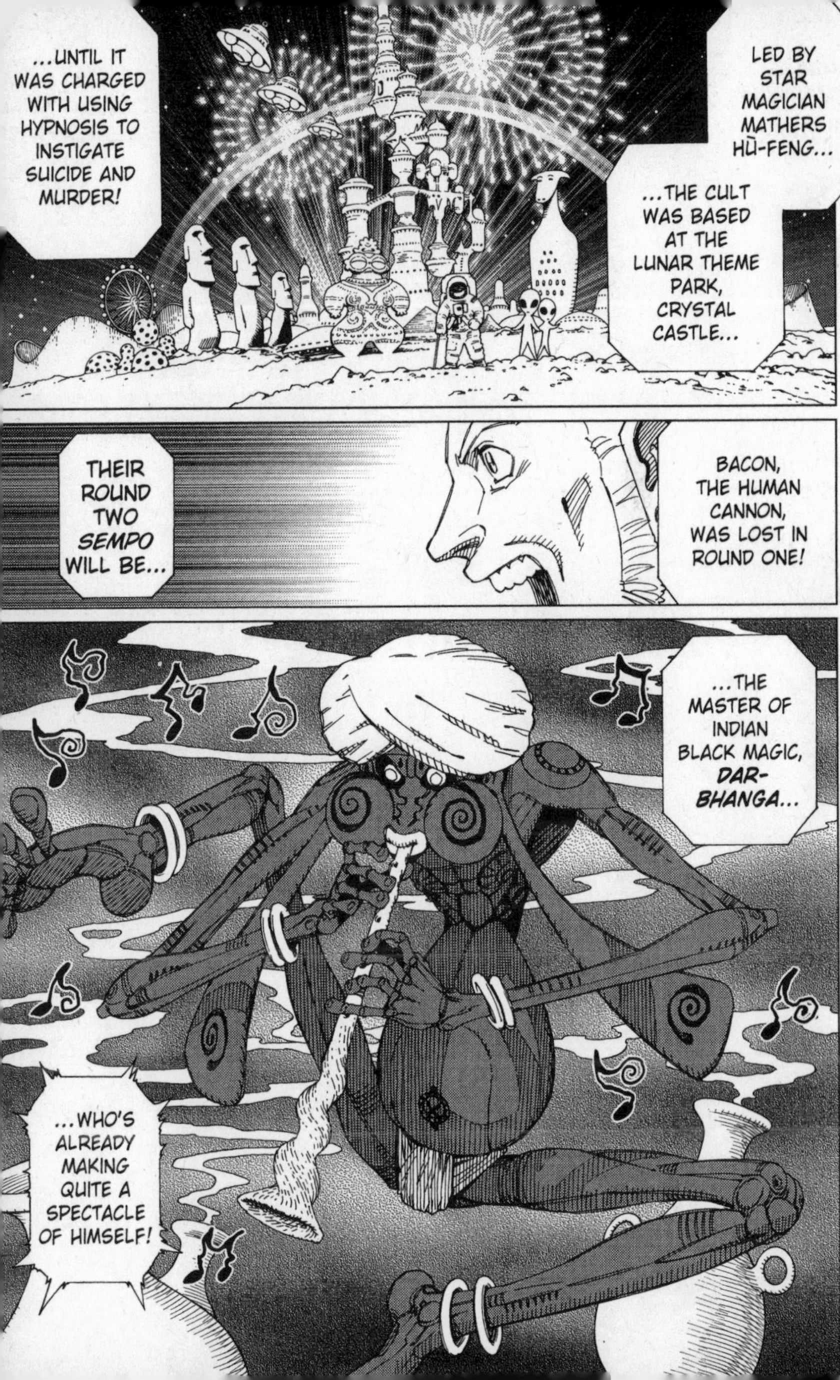
LED BY STAR MAGICIAN MATHERS HŪ-FENG...
...THE CULT WAS BASED AT THE LUNAR THEME PARK, CRYSTAL CASTLE...
...UNTIL IT WAS CHARGED WITH USING HYPNOSIS TO INSTIGATE SUICIDE AND MURDER!
BACON, THE HUMAN CANNON, WAS LOST IN ROUND ONE!
THEIR ROUND TWO *SEMPO* WILL BE...
...THE MASTER OF INDIAN BLACK MAGIC, *DAR-BHANGA*...
...WHO'S ALREADY MAKING QUITE A SPECTACLE OF HIMSELF!

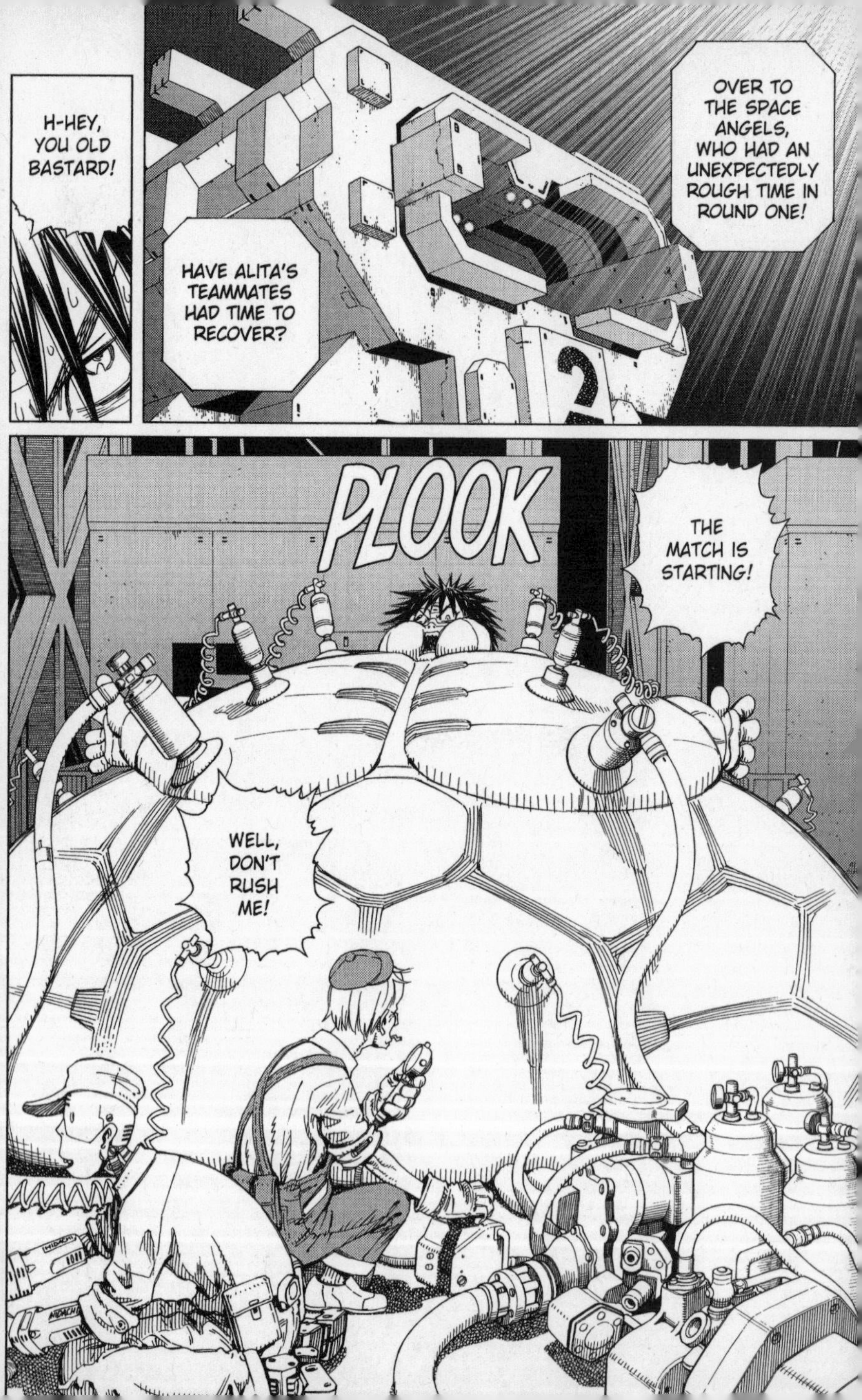
OVER TO THE SPACE ANGELS, WHO HAD AN UNEXPECTEDLY ROUGH TIME IN ROUND ONE!
HAVE ALITA'S TEAMMATES HAD TIME TO RECOVER?
H-HEY, YOU OLD BASTARD!
THE MATCH IS STARTING!
PLOOK
WELL, DON'T RUSH ME!

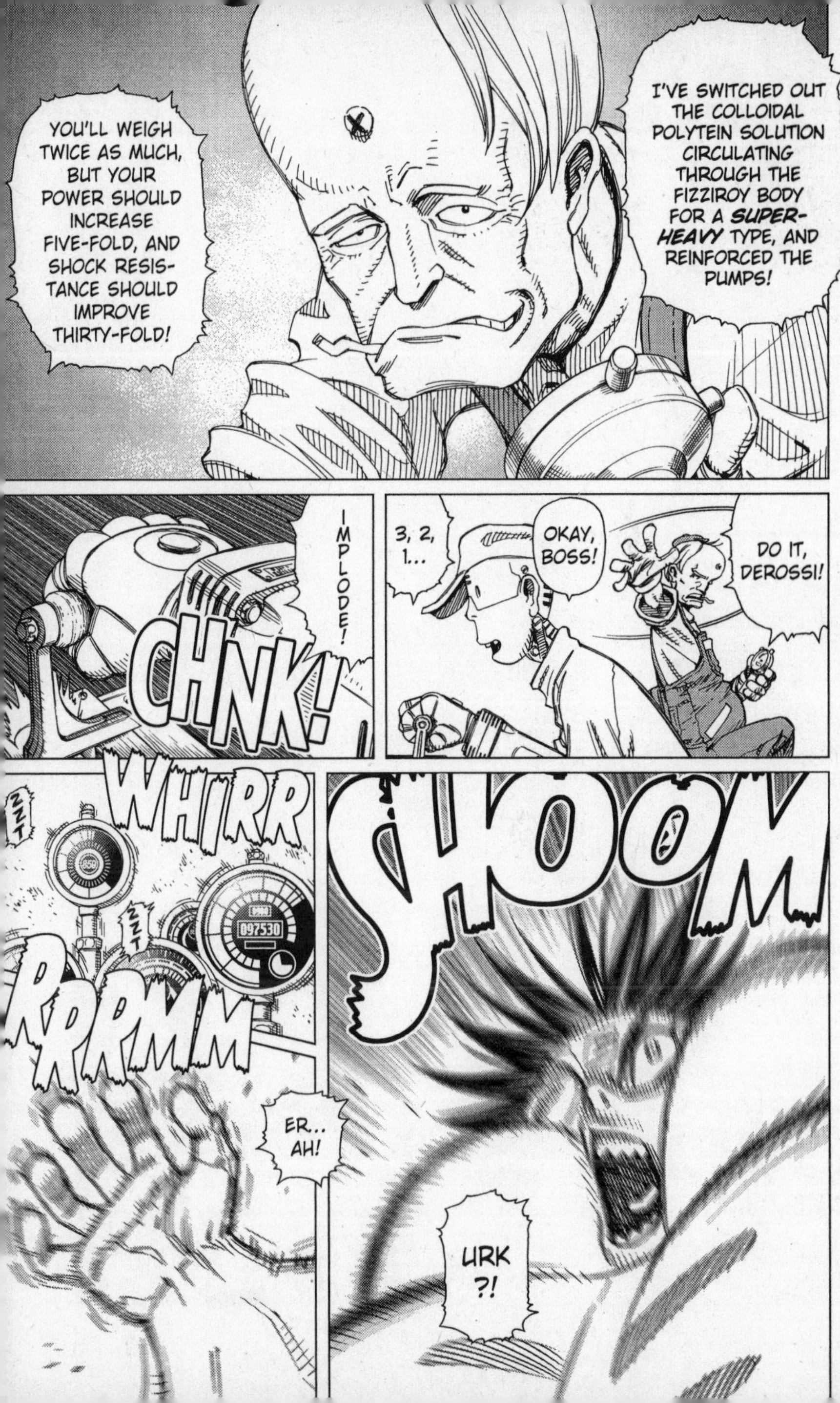
I'VE SWITCHED OUT THE COLLOIDAL POLYTEIN SOLUTION CIRCULATING THROUGH THE FIZZIROY BODY FOR A ***SUPER-HEAVY*** TYPE, AND REINFORCED THE PUMPS!
YOU'LL WEIGH TWICE AS MUCH, BUT YOUR POWER SHOULD INCREASE FIVE-FOLD, AND SHOCK RESIS-TANCE SHOULD IMPROVE THIRTY-FOLD!
DO IT, DEROSSI!
OKAY, BOSS!
3, 2, 1...
IMPLODE!
CHNK!
SHOOM
URK ?!
WHIRR
ZZT
ZZT
097530
RRRMM
ER... AH!

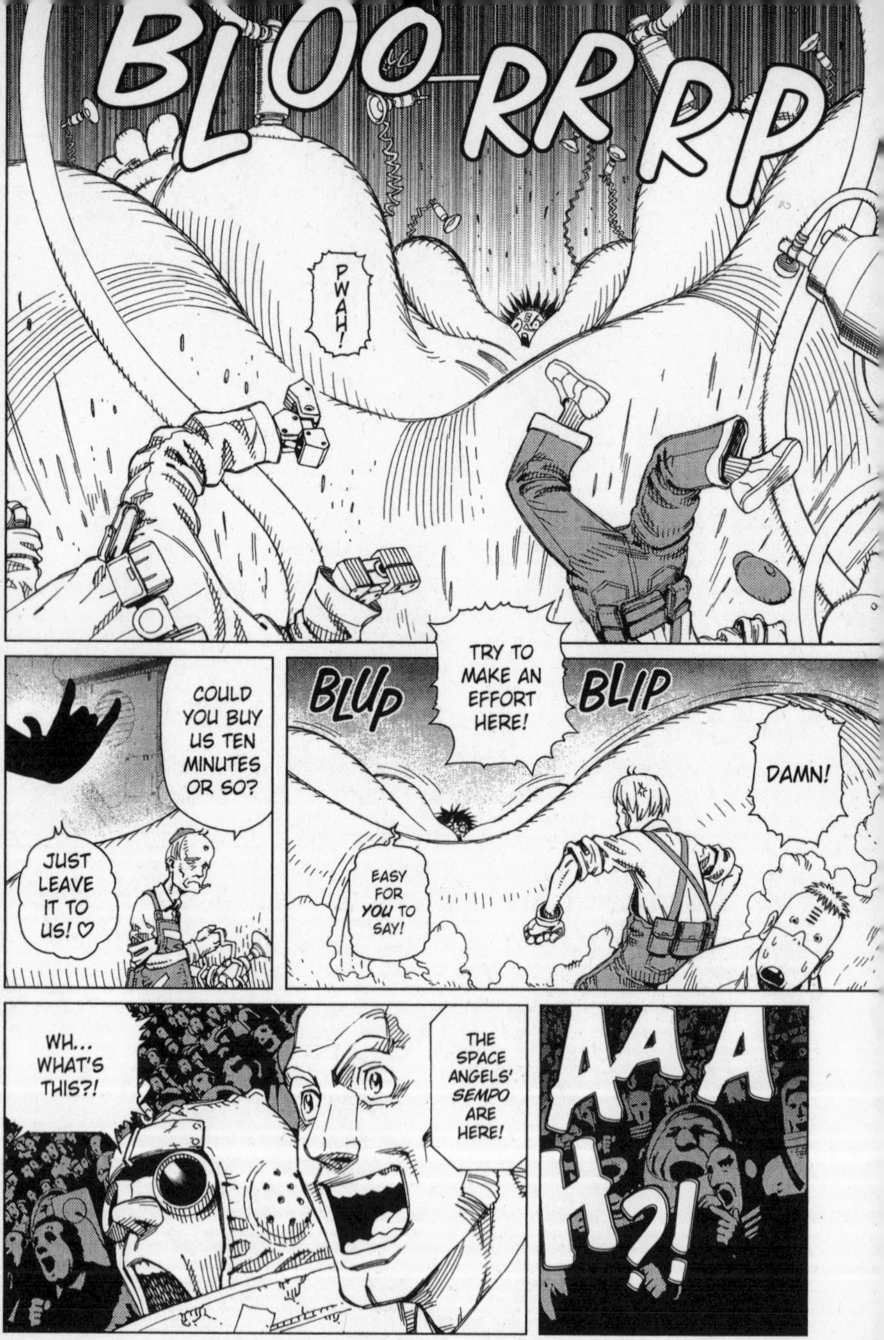
BLOORRRP
PWAH!
TRY TO MAKE AN EFFORT HERE!
BLIP
BLUP
DAMN!
EASY FOR *YOU* TO SAY!
COULD YOU BUY US TEN MINUTES OR SO?
JUST LEAVE IT TO US! ♡
AAAH?!
THE SPACE ANGELS' *SEMPO* ARE HERE!
WH... WHAT'S THIS?!

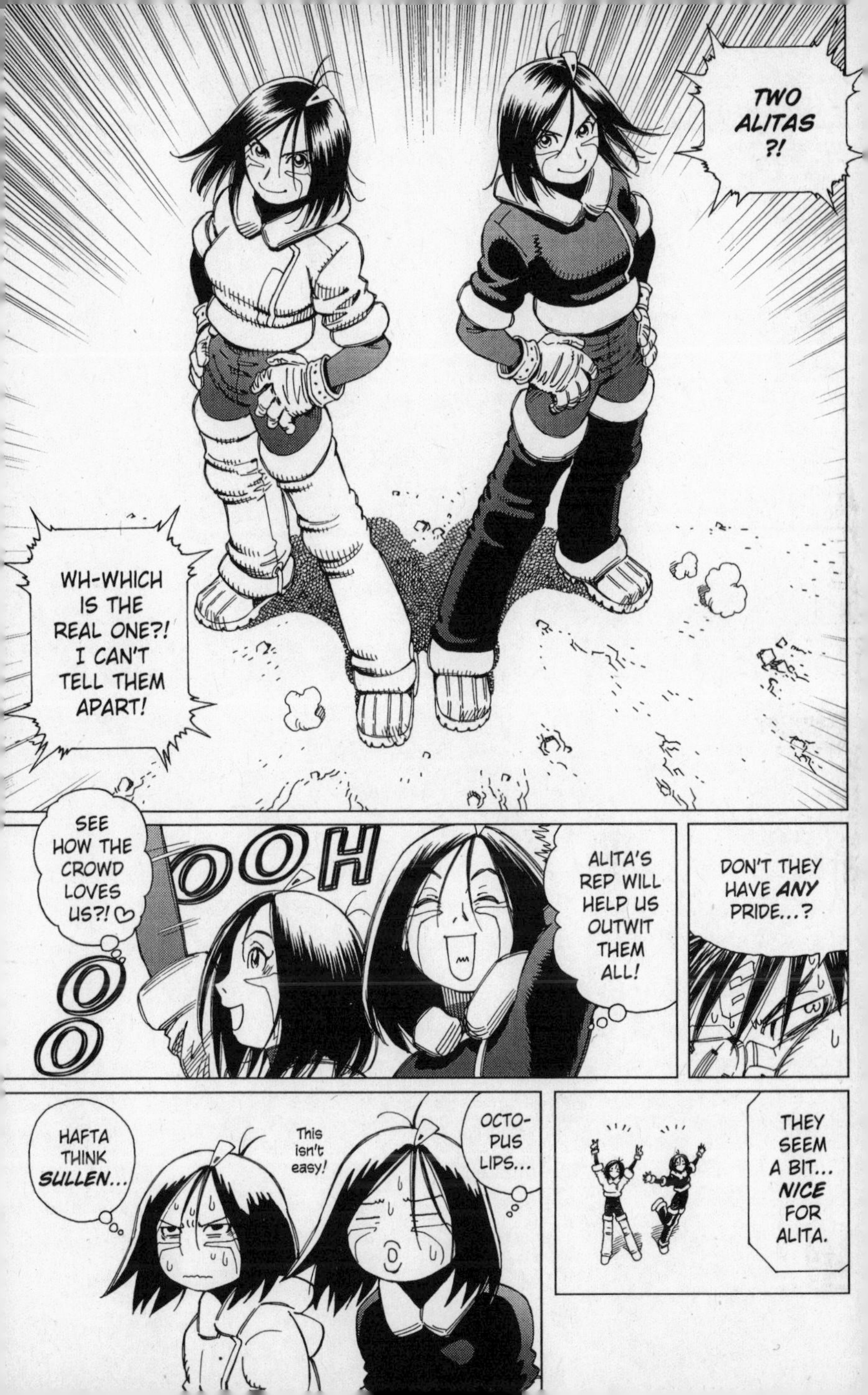

TWO ALITAS ?!
WH-WHICH IS THE REAL ONE?! I CAN'T TELL THEM APART!
DON'T THEY HAVE **ANY** PRIDE...?
ALITA'S REP WILL HELP US OUTWIT THEM ALL!
OOOOOH
SEE HOW THE CROWD LOVES US?! ♡
THEY SEEM A BIT... **NICE** FOR ALITA.
OCTO-PUS LIPS...
This isn't easy!
HAFTA THINK **SULLEN**...

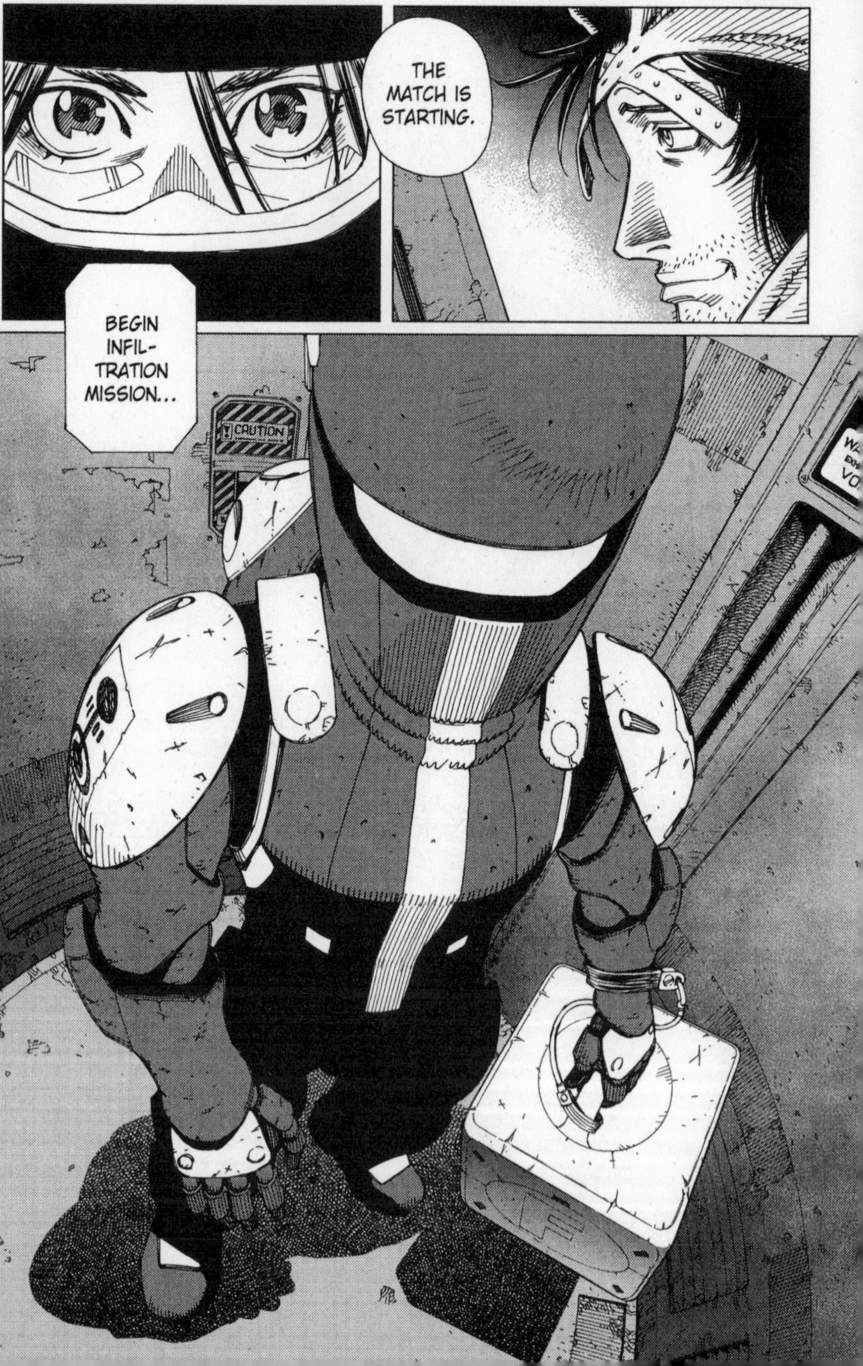
THE MATCH IS STARTING.
BEGIN INFIL-TRATION MISSION...
CAUTION

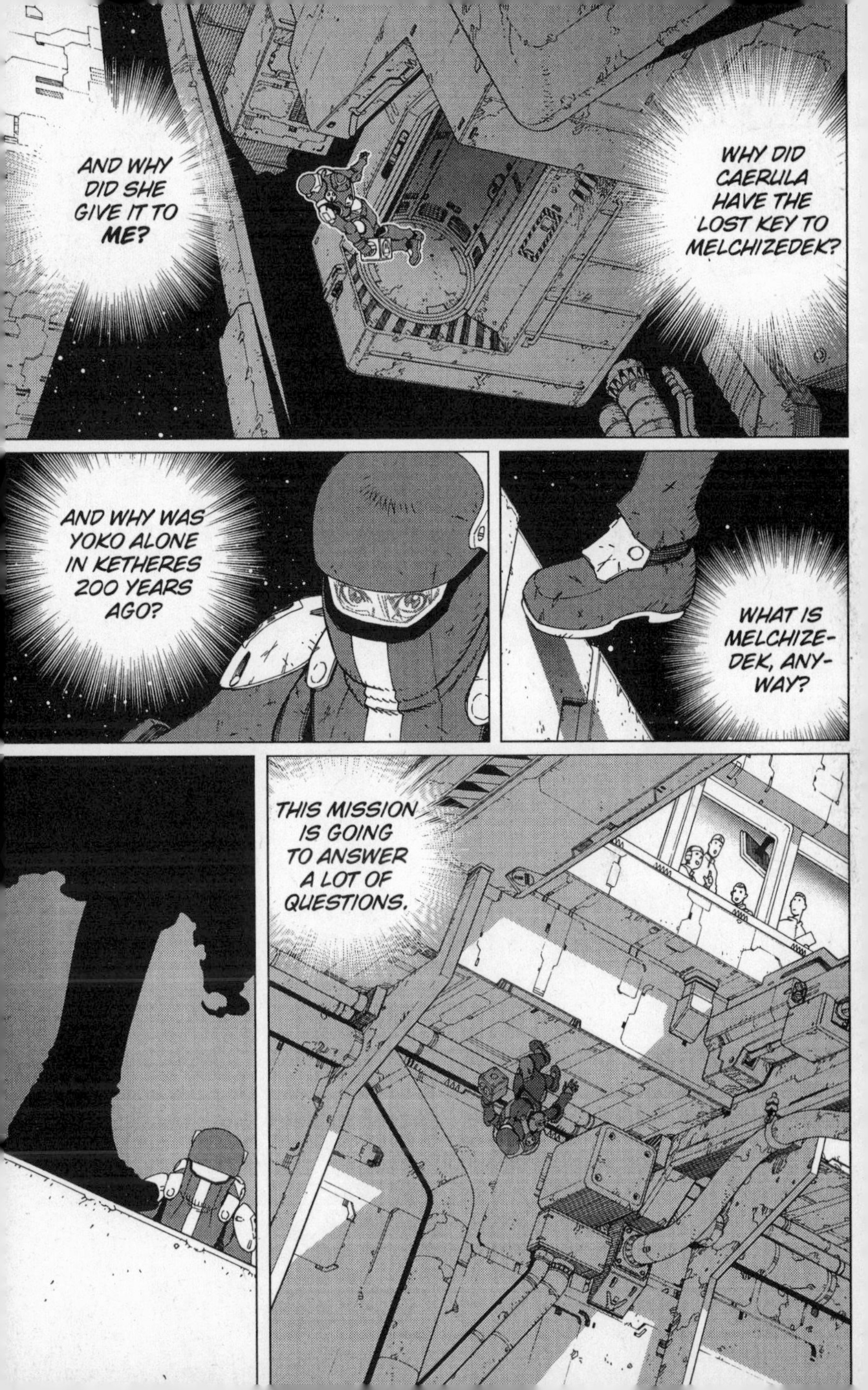
WHY DID CAERULA HAVE THE LOST KEY TO MELCHIZEDEK?
AND WHY DID SHE GIVE IT TO ME?
WHAT IS MELCHIZEDEK, ANYWAY?
AND WHY WAS YOKO ALONE IN KETHERES 200 YEARS AGO?
THIS MISSION IS GOING TO ANSWER A LOT OF QUESTIONS.

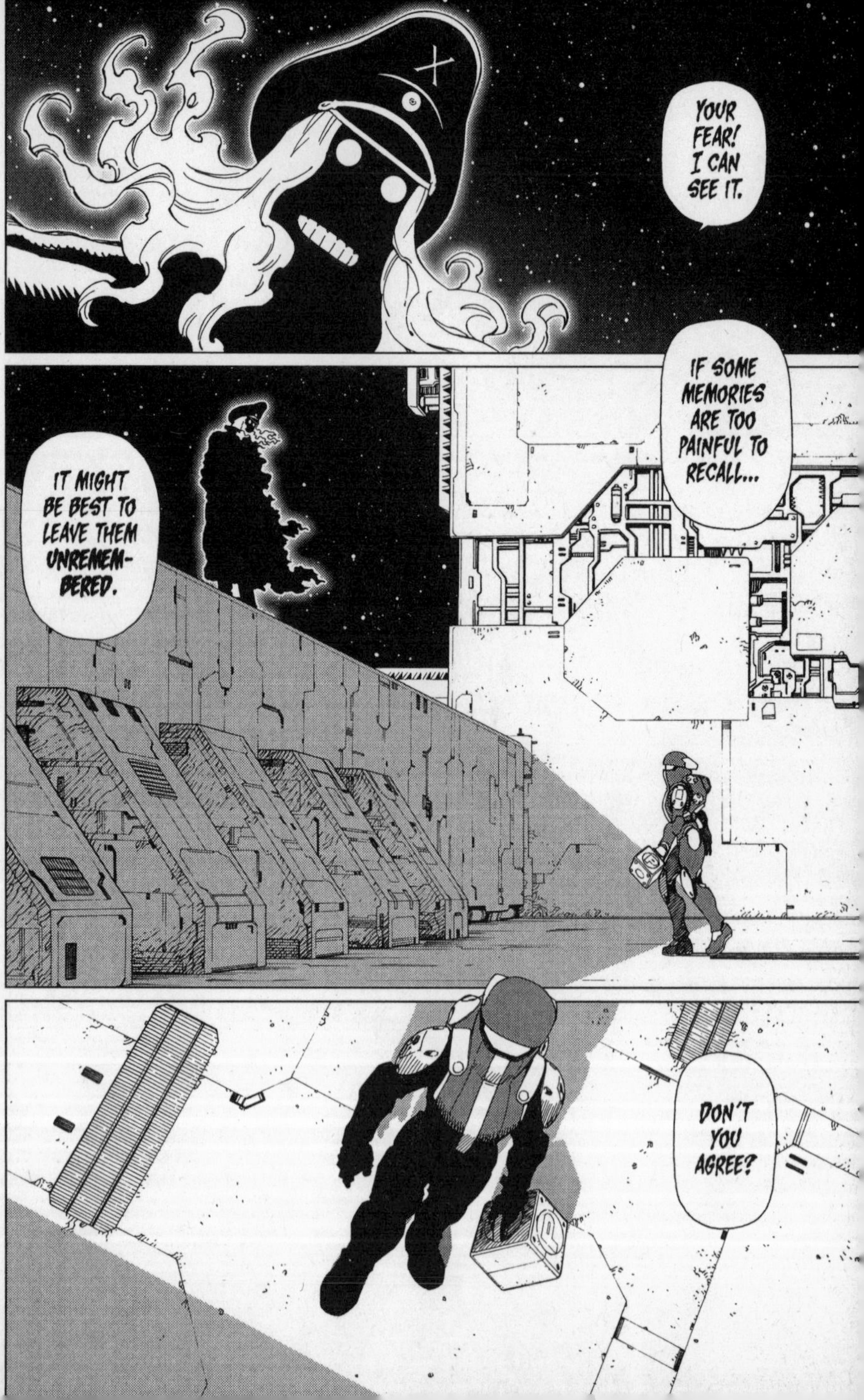
YOUR FEAR! I CAN SEE IT.
IF SOME MEMORIES ARE TOO PAINFUL TO RECALL...
IT MIGHT BE BEST TO LEAVE THEM UNREMEMBERED.
DON'T YOU AGREE?

...JUST WANT TO BE... *STRAIGHT-FORWARD.*

I...

MY MEMORIES... ALWAYS SPLIT IN TWO...

...SOME YOKO'S... AND SOME ALITA'S.

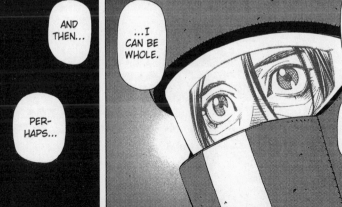

AND THEN...

PER-HAPS...

...I CAN BE WHOLE.

WHEN I FILL THE 200-YEAR GAP, LINK IT ALL INTO ONE...

...AT LAST, I...

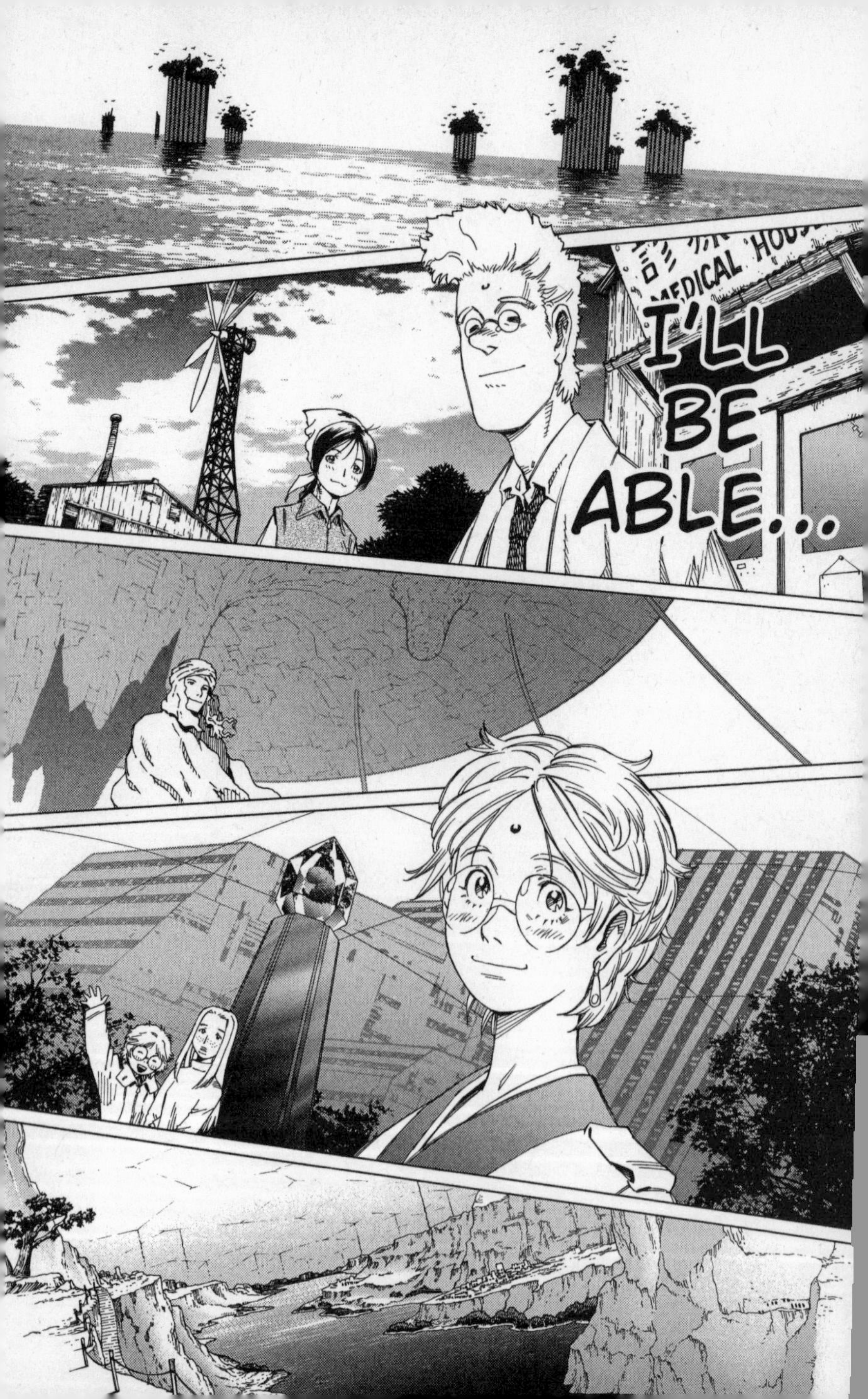
MEDICAL HOUS
I'LL BE ABLE...

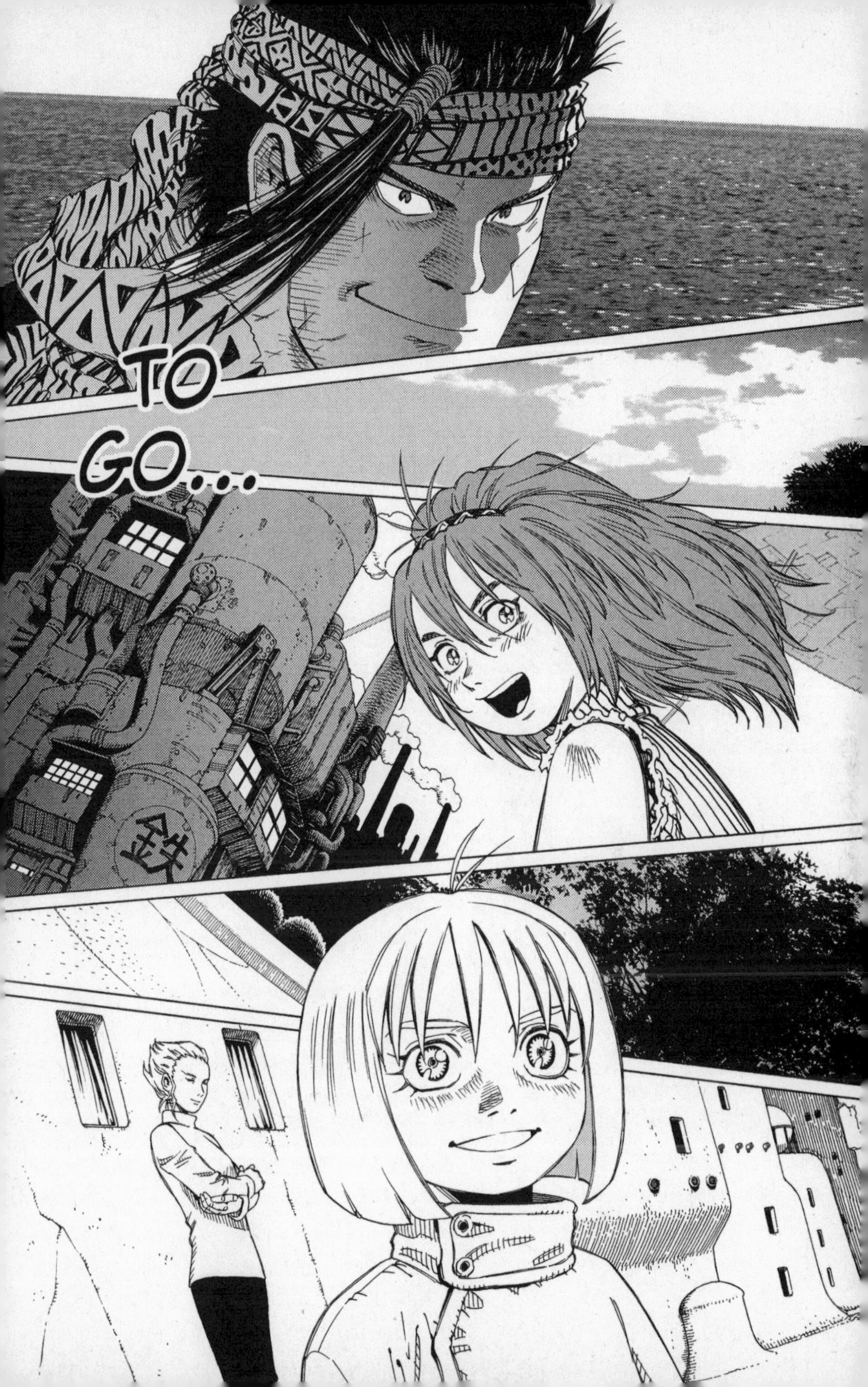
TO
GO...

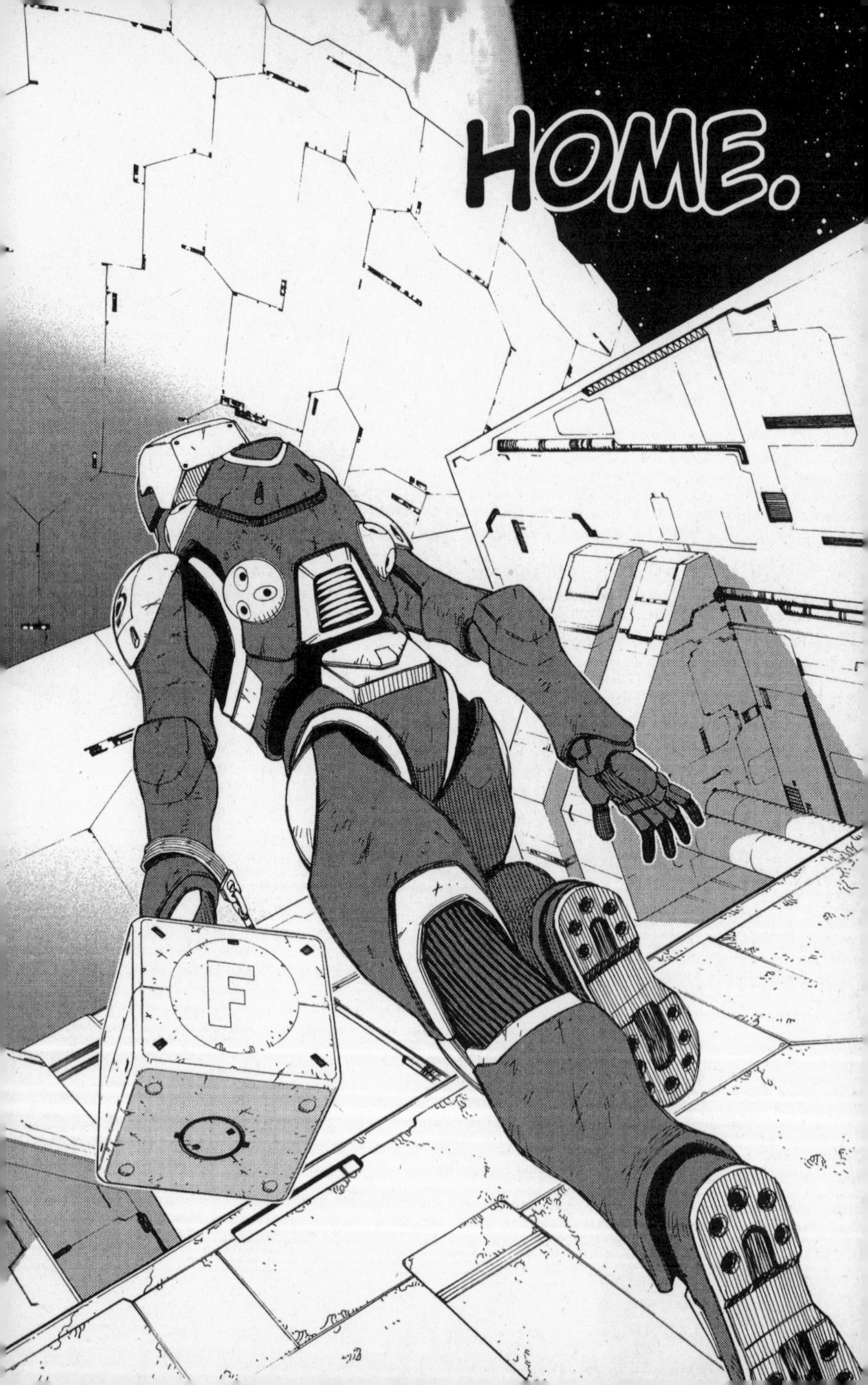
HOME.
F

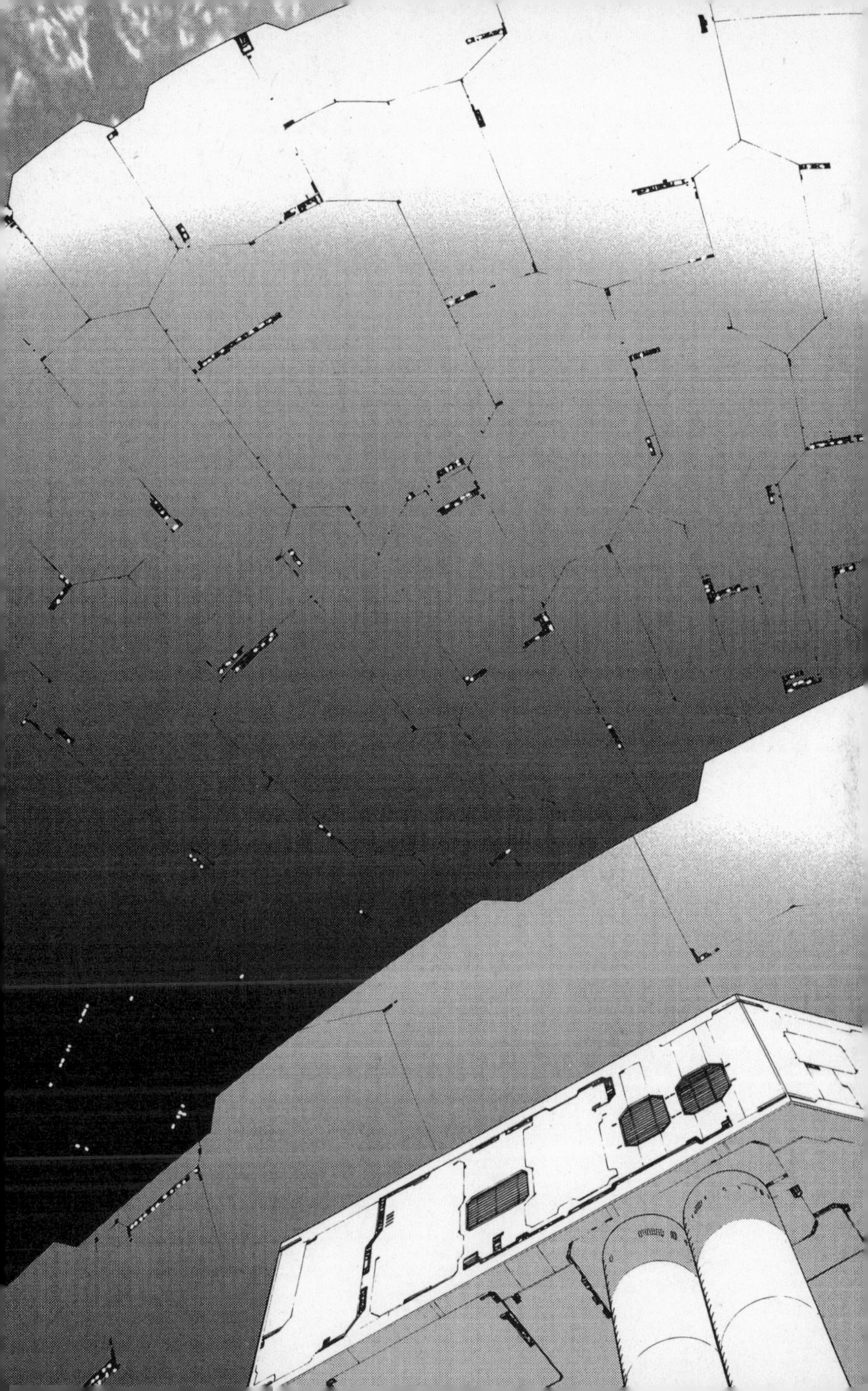

85 mm
MIB
150 mm

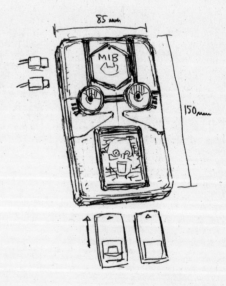

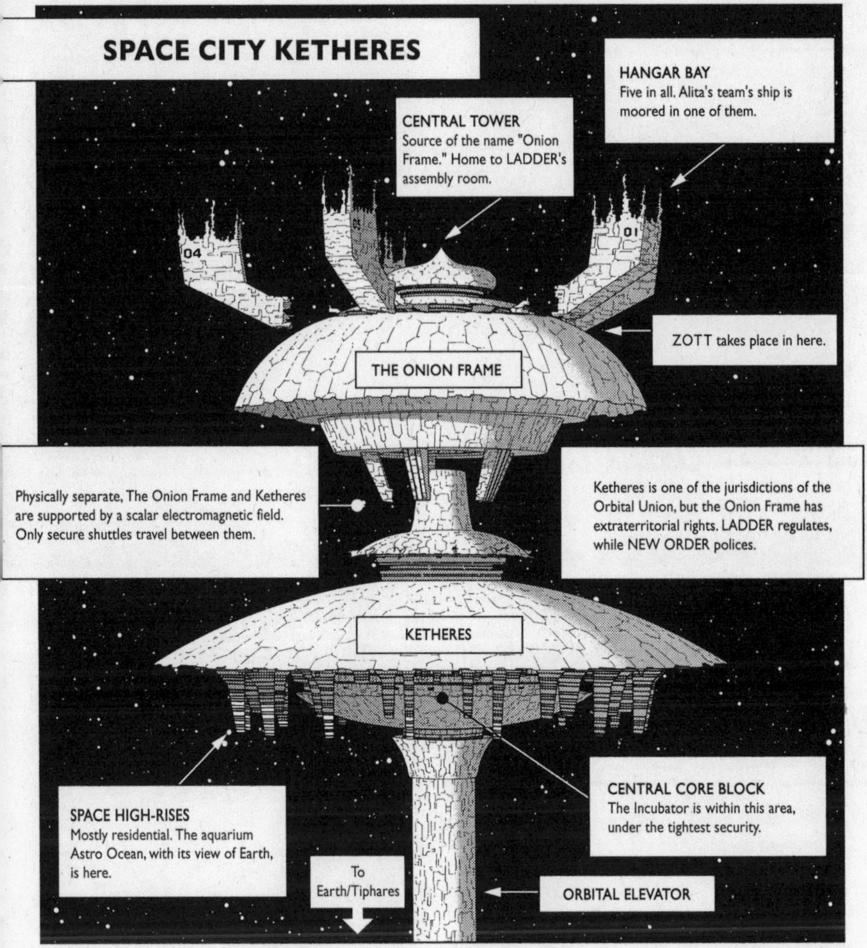
SPACE CITY KETHERES
HANGAR BAY
Five in all. Alita's team's ship is moored in one of them.
CENTRAL TOWER
Source of the name "Onion Frame." Home to LADDER's assembly room.
04
01
ZOTT takes place in here.
THE ONION FRAME
Physically separate, The Onion Frame and Ketheres are supported by a scalar electromagnetic field. Only secure shuttles travel between them.
Ketheres is one of the jurisdictions of the Orbital Union, but the Onion Frame has extraterritorial rights. LADDER regulates, while NEW ORDER polices.
KETHERES
CENTRAL CORE BLOCK
The Incubator is within this area, under the tightest security.
SPACE HIGH-RISES
Mostly residential. The aquarium Astro Ocean, with its view of Earth, is here.
To Earth/Tiphares
ORBITAL ELEVATOR

PHASE 36:
I Walked Here Before

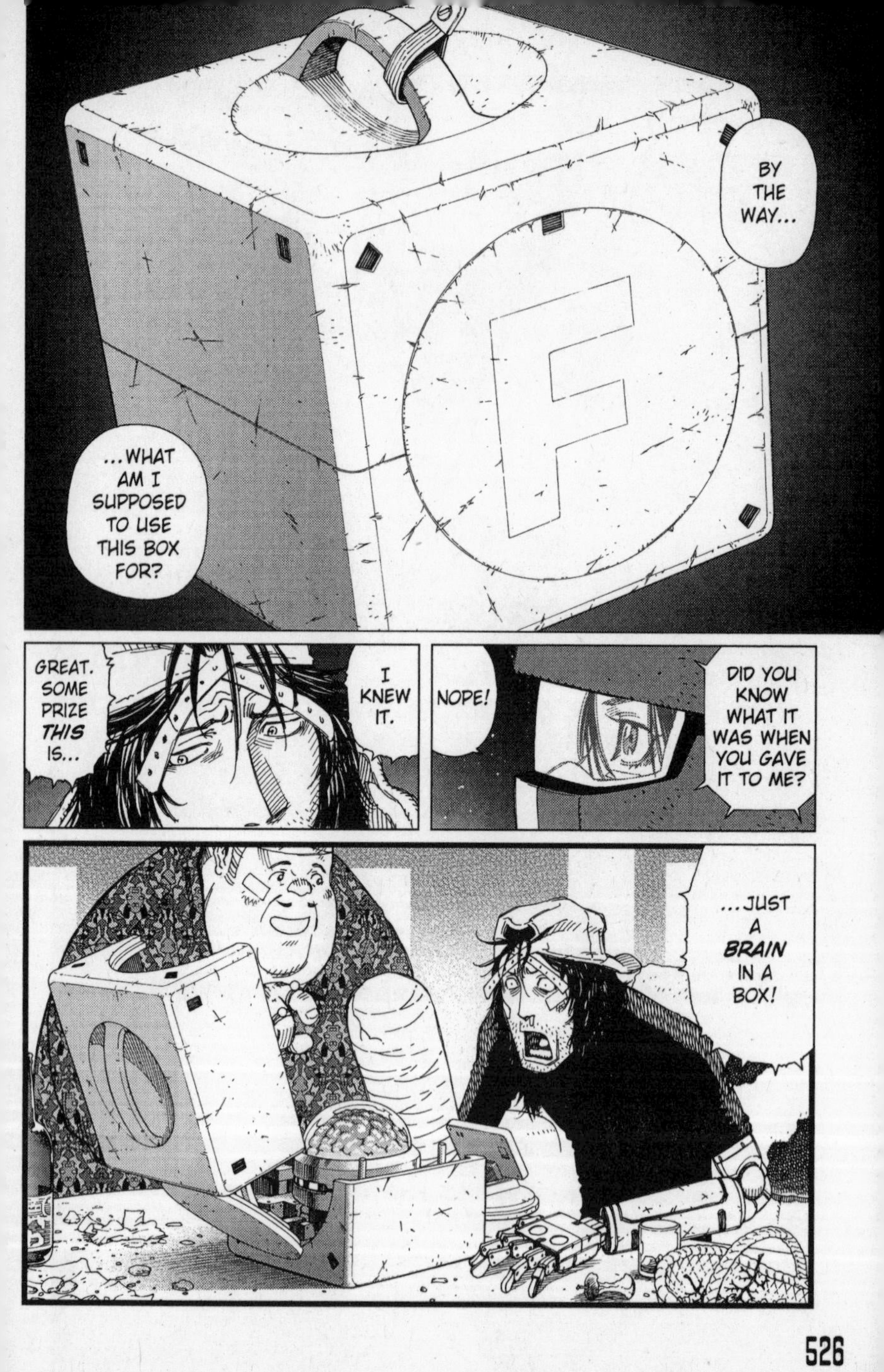
BY THE WAY...
...WHAT AM I SUPPOSED TO USE THIS BOX FOR?
DID YOU KNOW WHAT IT WAS WHEN YOU GAVE IT TO ME?
NOPE!
I KNEW IT.
GREAT. SOME PRIZE *THIS* IS...
...JUST A *BRAIN* IN A BOX!

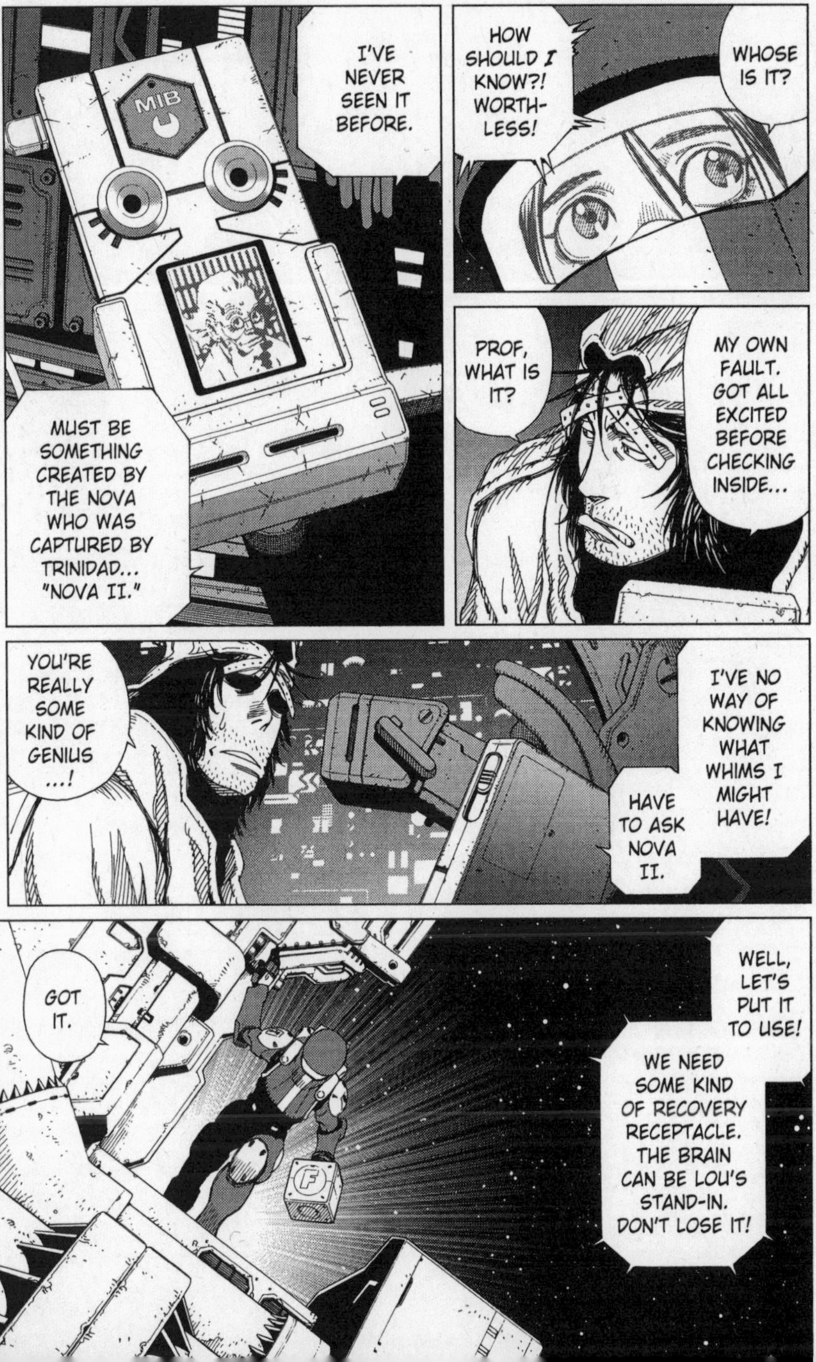
WHOSE IS IT?
HOW SHOULD I KNOW?! WORTH-LESS!
MY OWN FAULT. GOT ALL EXCITED BEFORE CHECKING INSIDE...
PROF, WHAT IS IT?
I'VE NEVER SEEN IT BEFORE.
MIB
MUST BE SOMETHING CREATED BY THE NOVA WHO WAS CAPTURED BY TRINIDAD... "NOVA II."
I'VE NO WAY OF KNOWING WHAT WHIMS I MIGHT HAVE!
HAVE TO ASK NOVA II.
YOU'RE REALLY SOME KIND OF GENIUS ...!
WELL, LET'S PUT IT TO USE!
WE NEED SOME KIND OF RECOVERY RECEPTACLE. THE BRAIN CAN BE LOU'S STAND-IN. DON'T LOSE IT!
GOT IT.

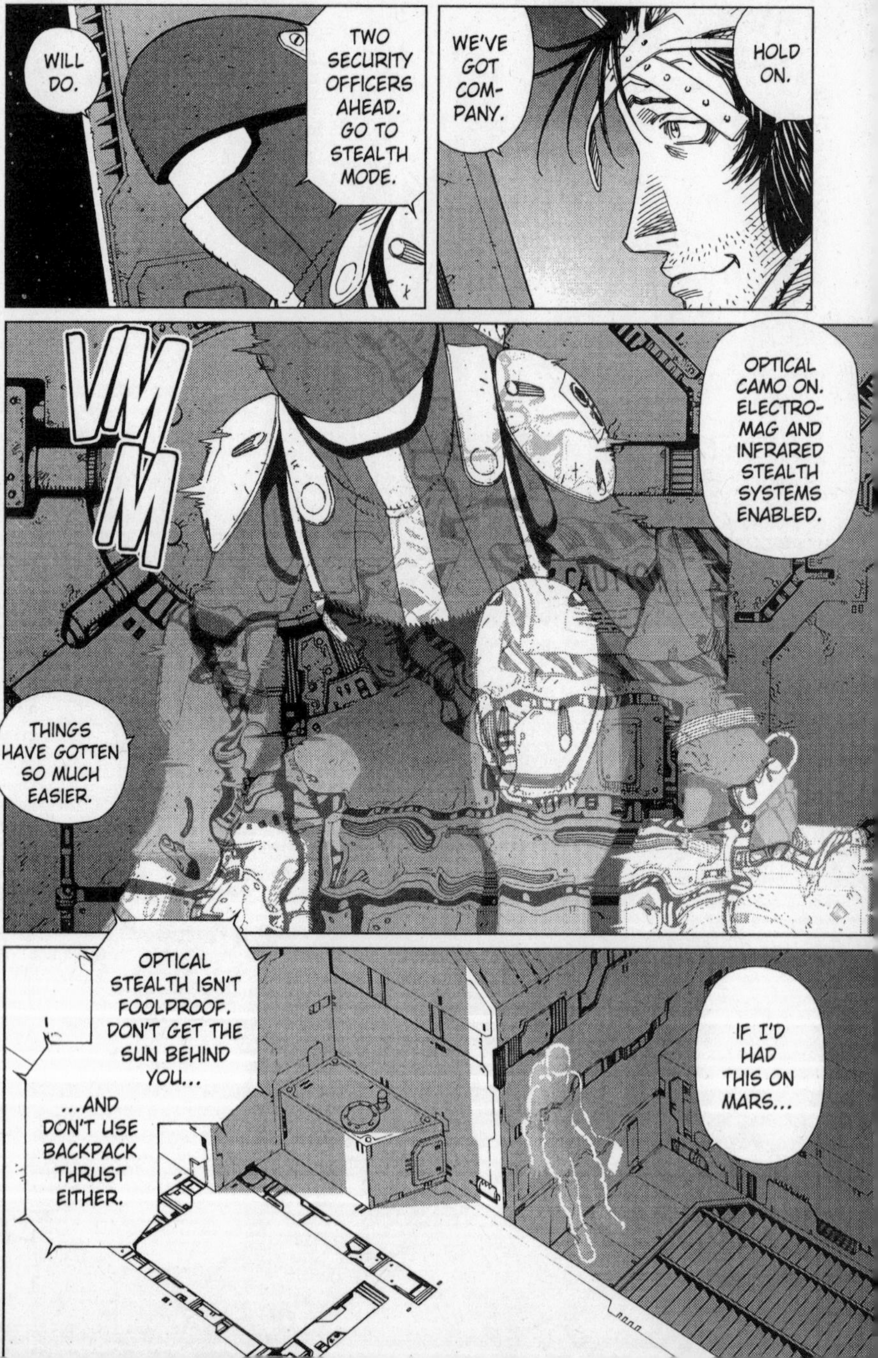
HOLD ON.
WE'VE GOT COM-PANY.
TWO SECURITY OFFICERS AHEAD. GO TO STEALTH MODE.
WILL DO.
OPTICAL CAMO ON. ELECTRO-MAG AND INFRARED STEALTH SYSTEMS ENABLED.
VMM
THINGS HAVE GOTTEN SO MUCH EASIER.
IF I'D HAD THIS ON MARS...
OPTICAL STEALTH ISN'T FOOLPROOF. DON'T GET THE SUN BEHIND YOU...
...AND DON'T USE BACKPACK THRUST EITHER.

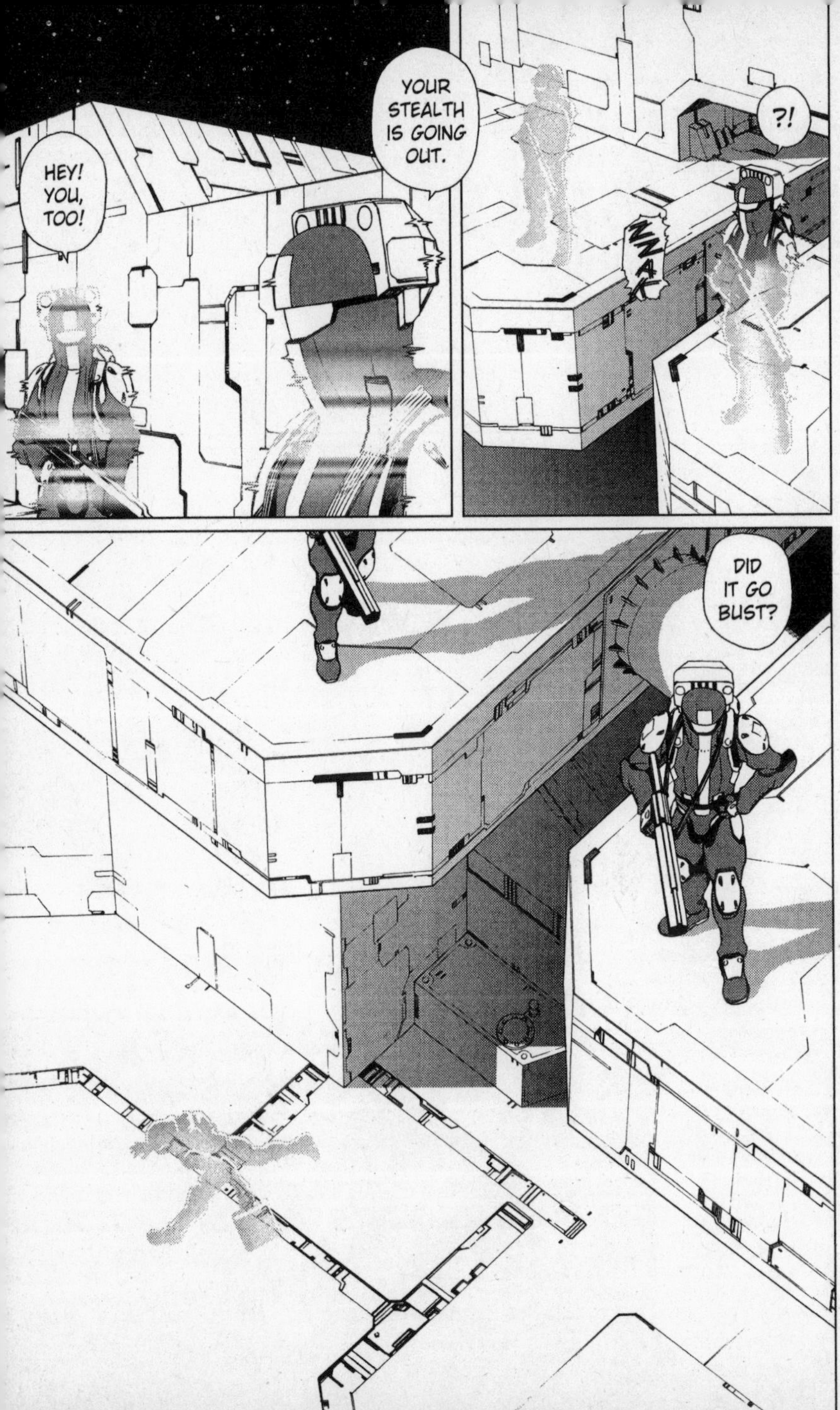
?!
ZZAK
YOUR STEALTH IS GOING OUT.
HEY! YOU, TOO!
DID IT GO BUST?

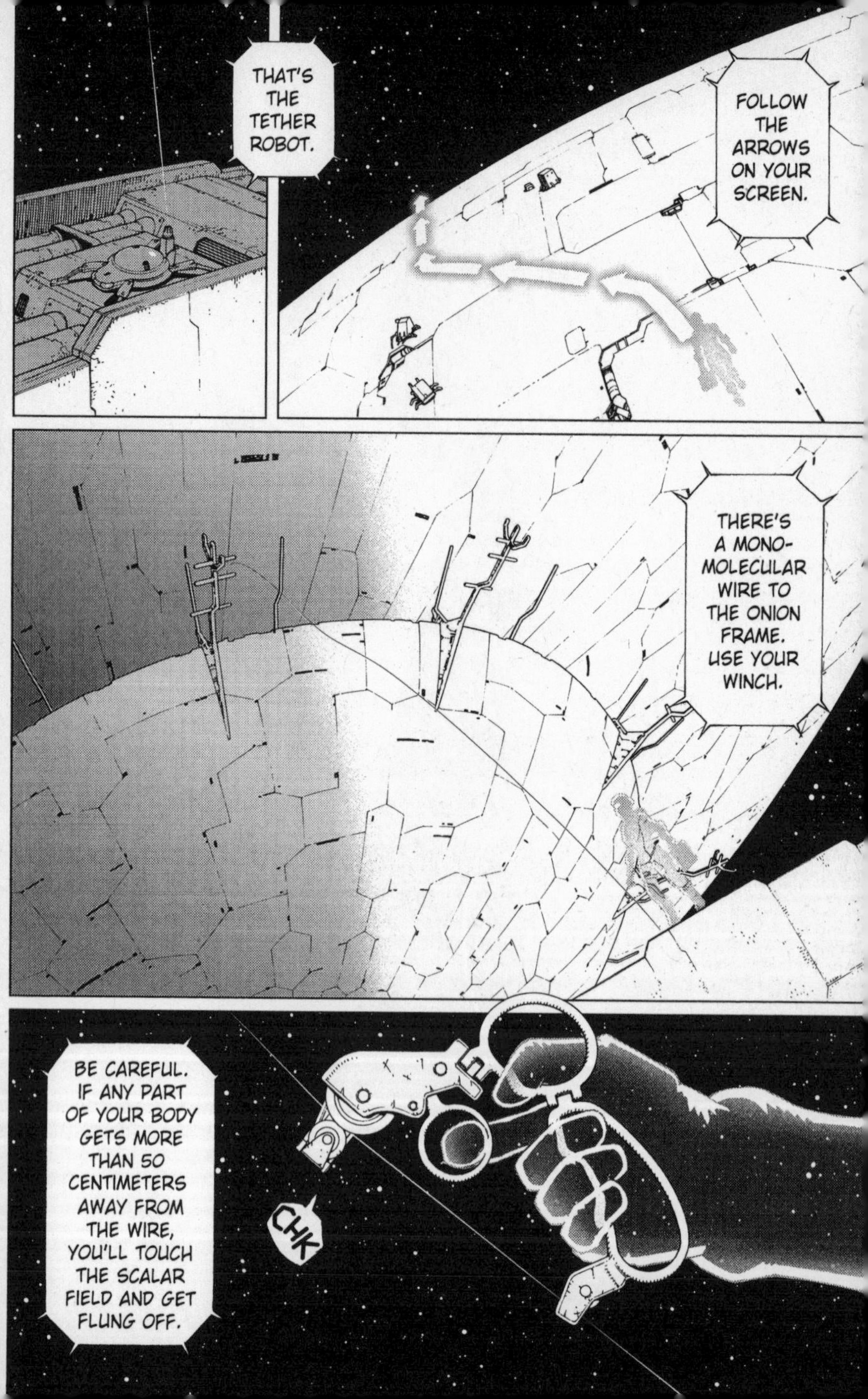
FOLLOW THE ARROWS ON YOUR SCREEN.
THAT'S THE TETHER ROBOT.
THERE'S A MONO-MOLECULAR WIRE TO THE ONION FRAME. USE YOUR WINCH.
BE CAREFUL. IF ANY PART OF YOUR BODY GETS MORE THAN 50 CENTIMETERS AWAY FROM THE WIRE, YOU'LL TOUCH THE SCALAR FIELD AND GET FLUNG OFF.
CHK

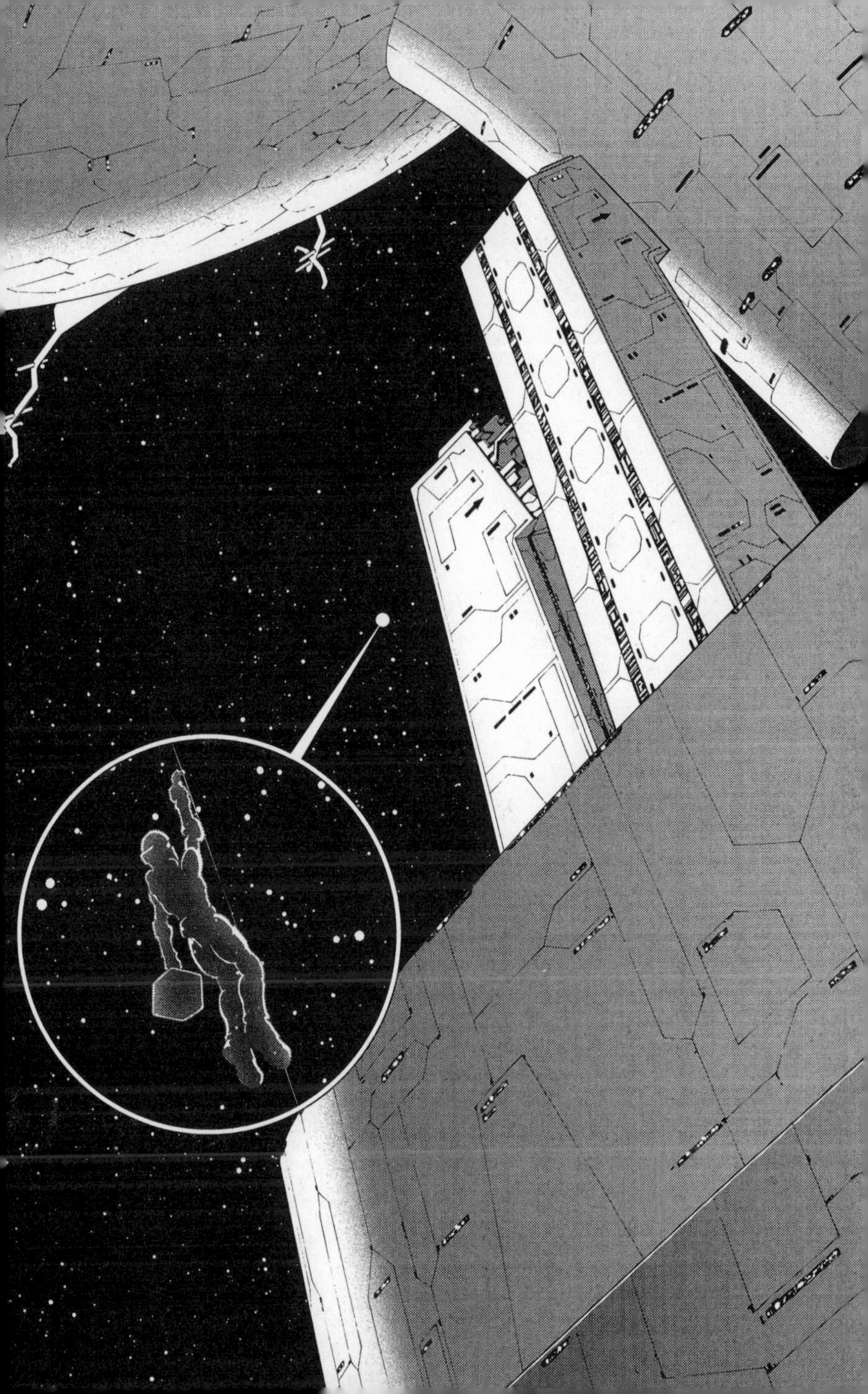

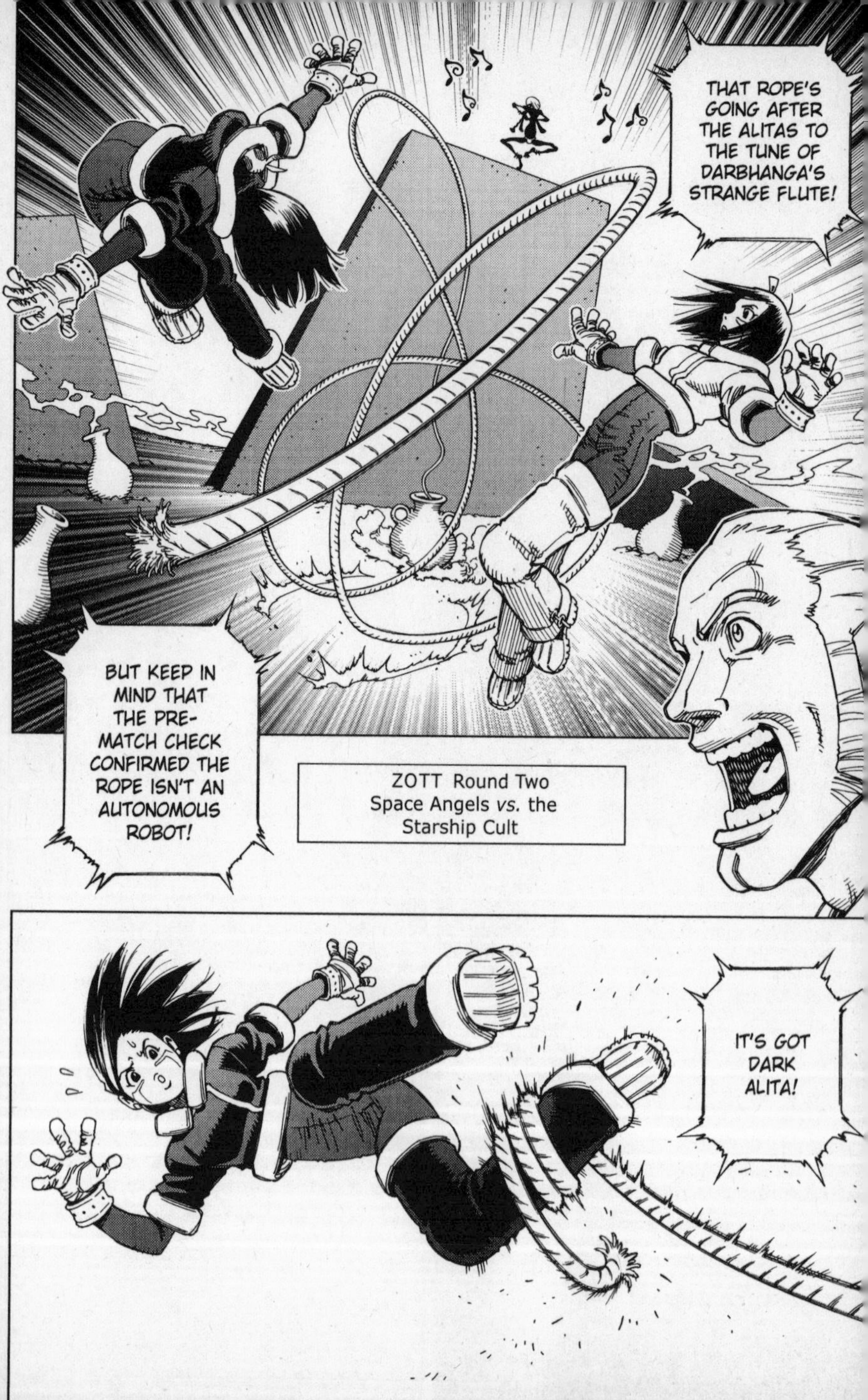
THAT ROPE'S GOING AFTER THE ALITAS TO THE TUNE OF DARBHANGA'S STRANGE FLUTE!
BUT KEEP IN MIND THAT THE PRE-MATCH CHECK CONFIRMED THE ROPE ISN'T AN AUTONOMOUS ROBOT!
ZOTT Round Two Space Angels vs. the Starship Cult
IT'S GOT DARK ALITA!

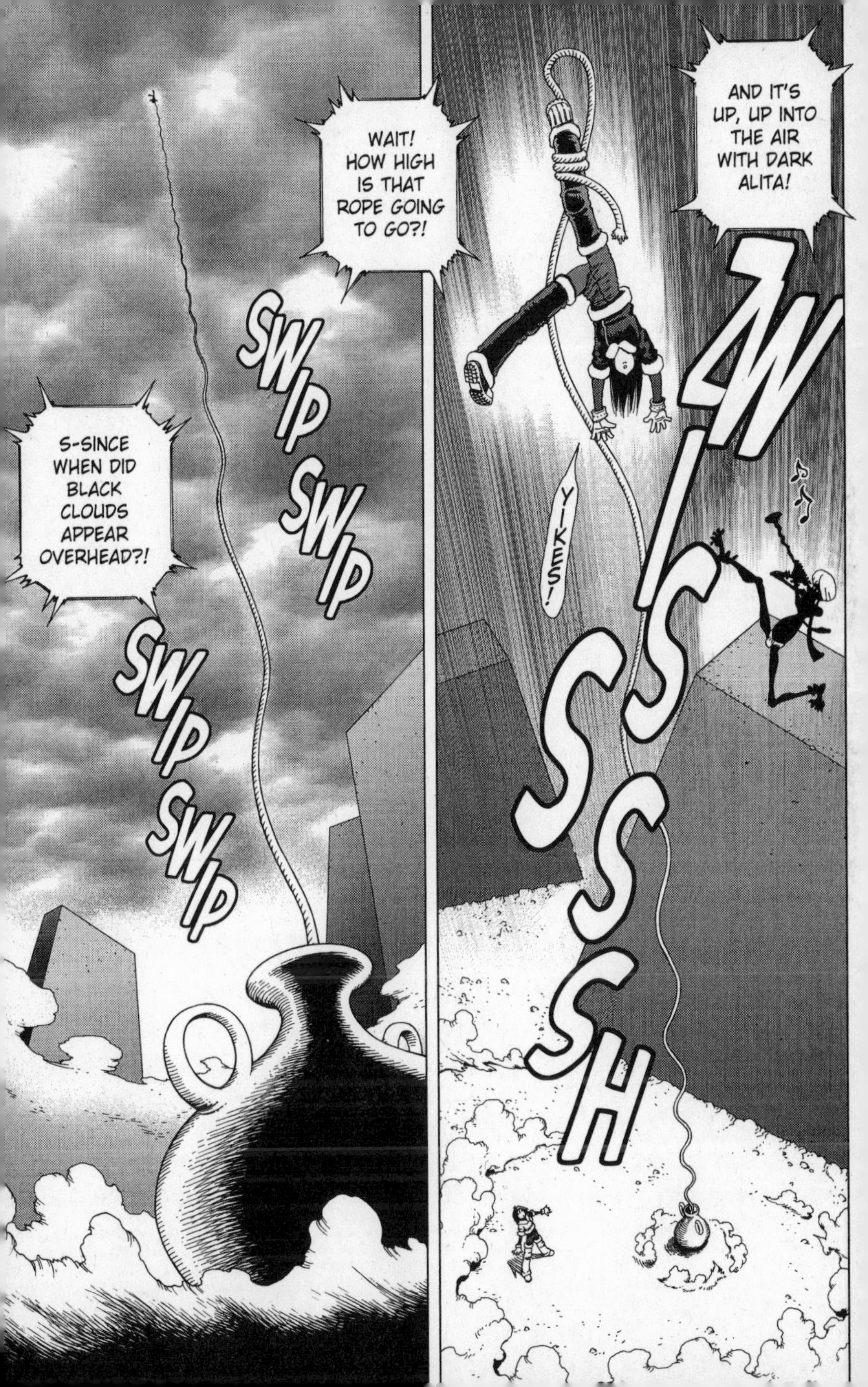
AND IT'S UP, UP INTO THE AIR WITH DARK ALITA!
ZWISSSSH
YIKES!
WAIT! HOW HIGH IS THAT ROPE GOING TO GO?!
SWIP SWIP
S-SINCE WHEN DID BLACK CLOUDS APPEAR OVERHEAD?!
SWIP SWIP

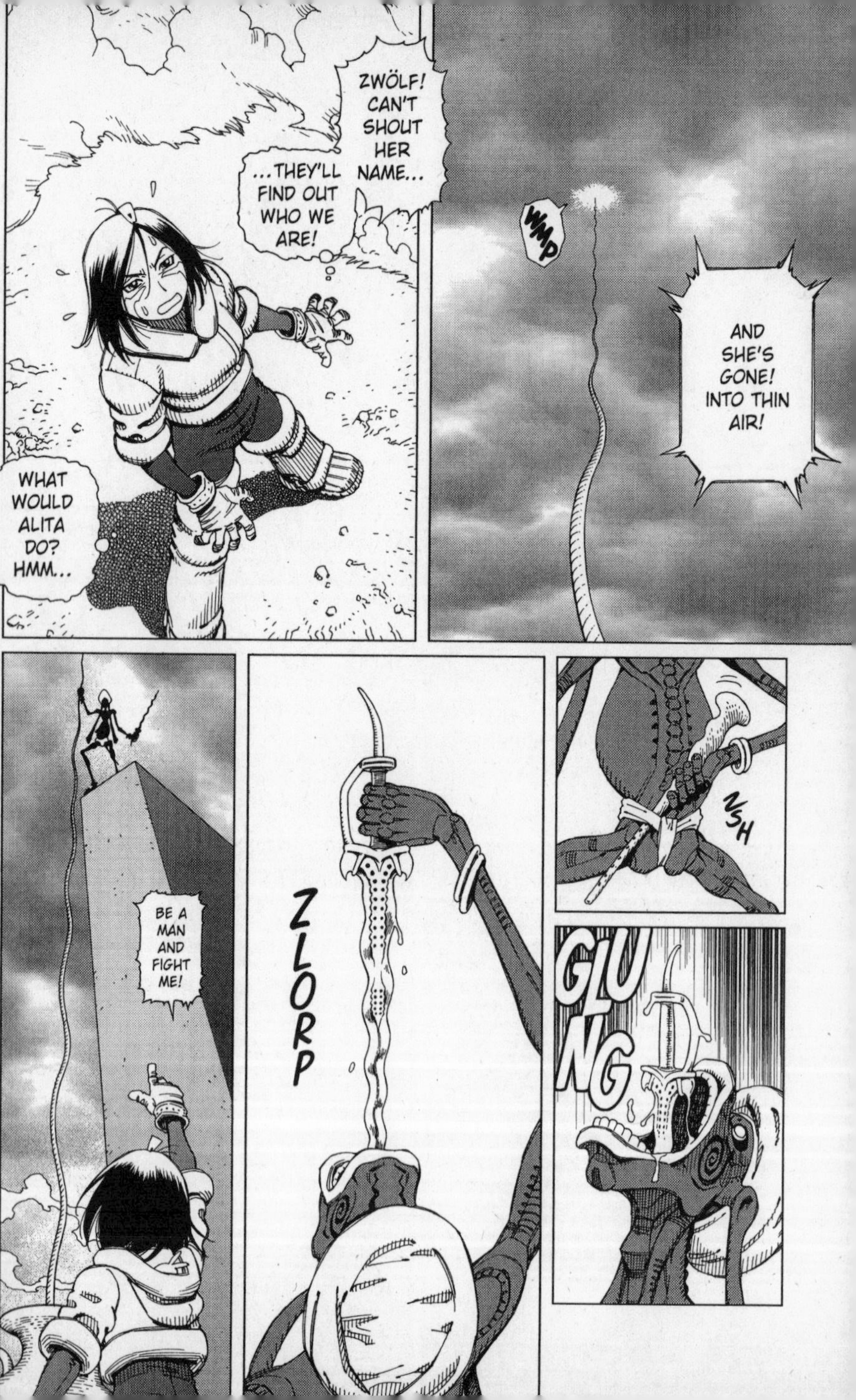
WMP
AND SHE'S GONE! INTO THIN AIR!
ZWÖLF! CAN'T SHOUT HER NAME...
...THEY'LL FIND OUT WHO WE ARE!
WHAT WOULD ALITA DO? HMM...
NSH
GLUNG
ZLORP
BE A MAN AND FIGHT ME!

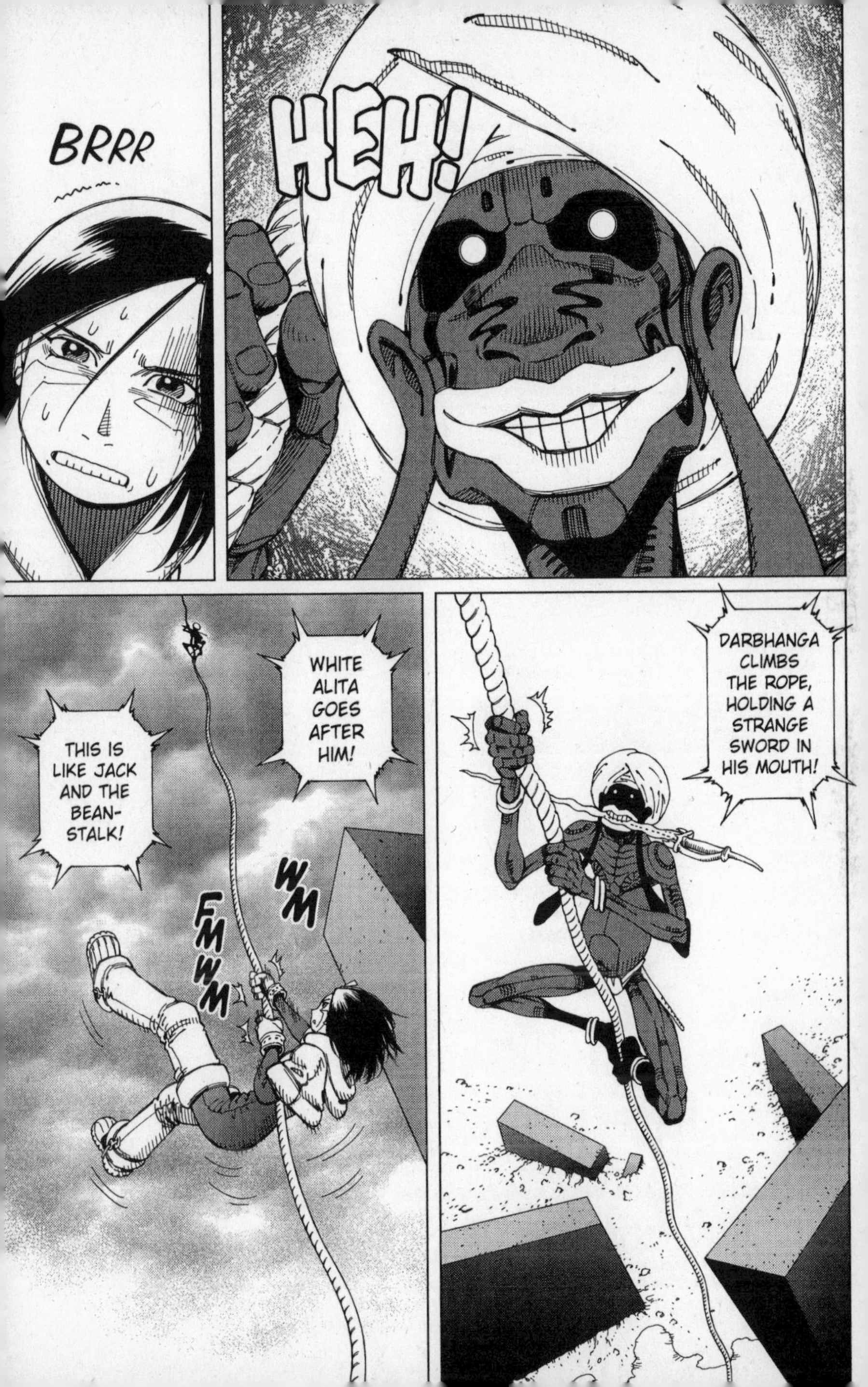
HEH!
BRRR
DARBHANGA CLIMBS THE ROPE, HOLDING A STRANGE SWORD IN HIS MOUTH!
WHITE ALITA GOES AFTER HIM!
THIS IS LIKE JACK AND THE BEAN-STALK!
WM
FMWM

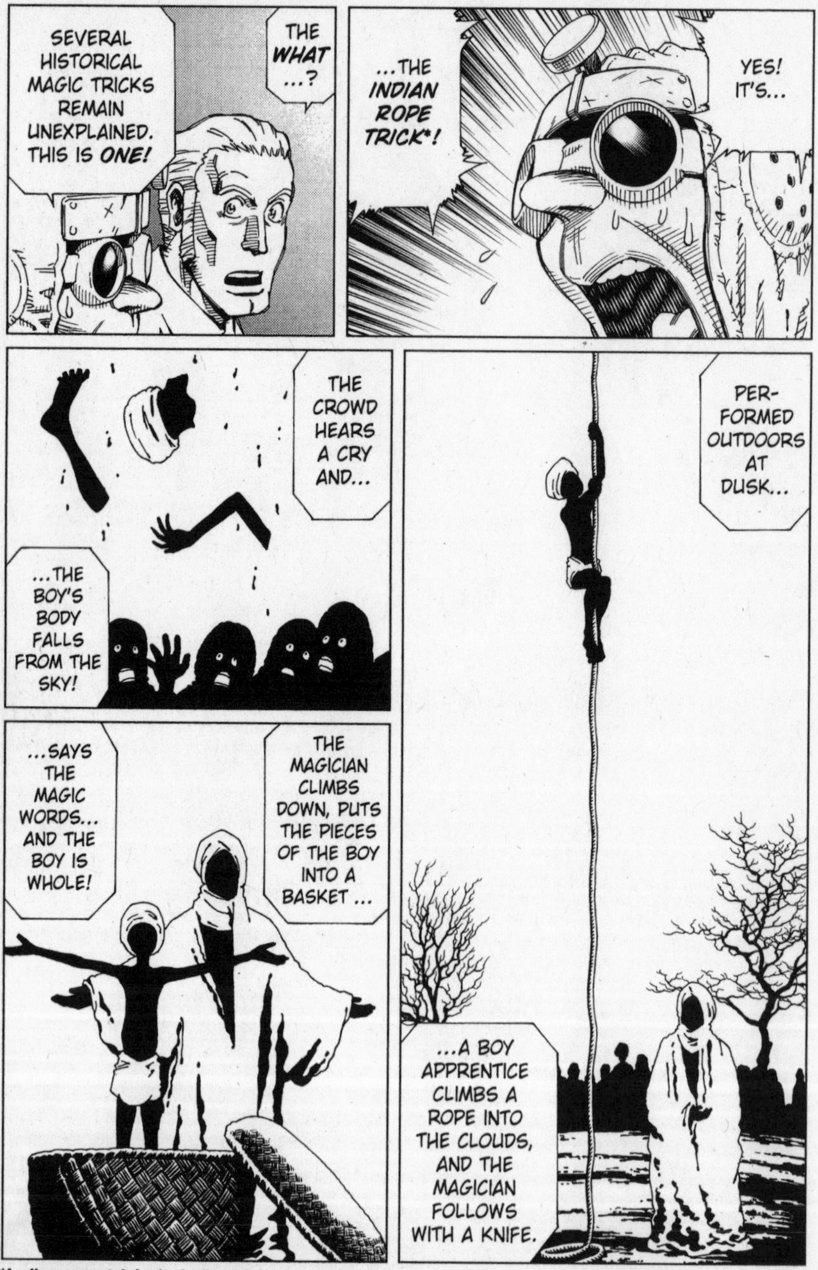
YES! IT'S...
...THE *INDIAN ROPE TRICK**!
THE *WHAT* ...?
SEVERAL HISTORICAL MAGIC TRICKS REMAIN UNEXPLAINED. THIS IS *ONE!*
PER-FORMED OUTDOORS AT DUSK...
...A BOY APPRENTICE CLIMBS A ROPE INTO THE CLOUDS, AND THE MAGICIAN FOLLOWS WITH A KNIFE.
THE CROWD HEARS A CRY AND...
...THE BOY'S BODY FALLS FROM THE SKY!
THE MAGICIAN CLIMBS DOWN, PUTS THE PIECES OF THE BOY INTO A BASKET ...
...SAYS THE MAGIC WORDS... AND THE BOY IS WHOLE!

***Indian rope trick:** An Indian trick passed down from ancient times. First described by Ibn Battuta, the Arabian traveler, in 1346. More recently, it was performed in London in 1934.*

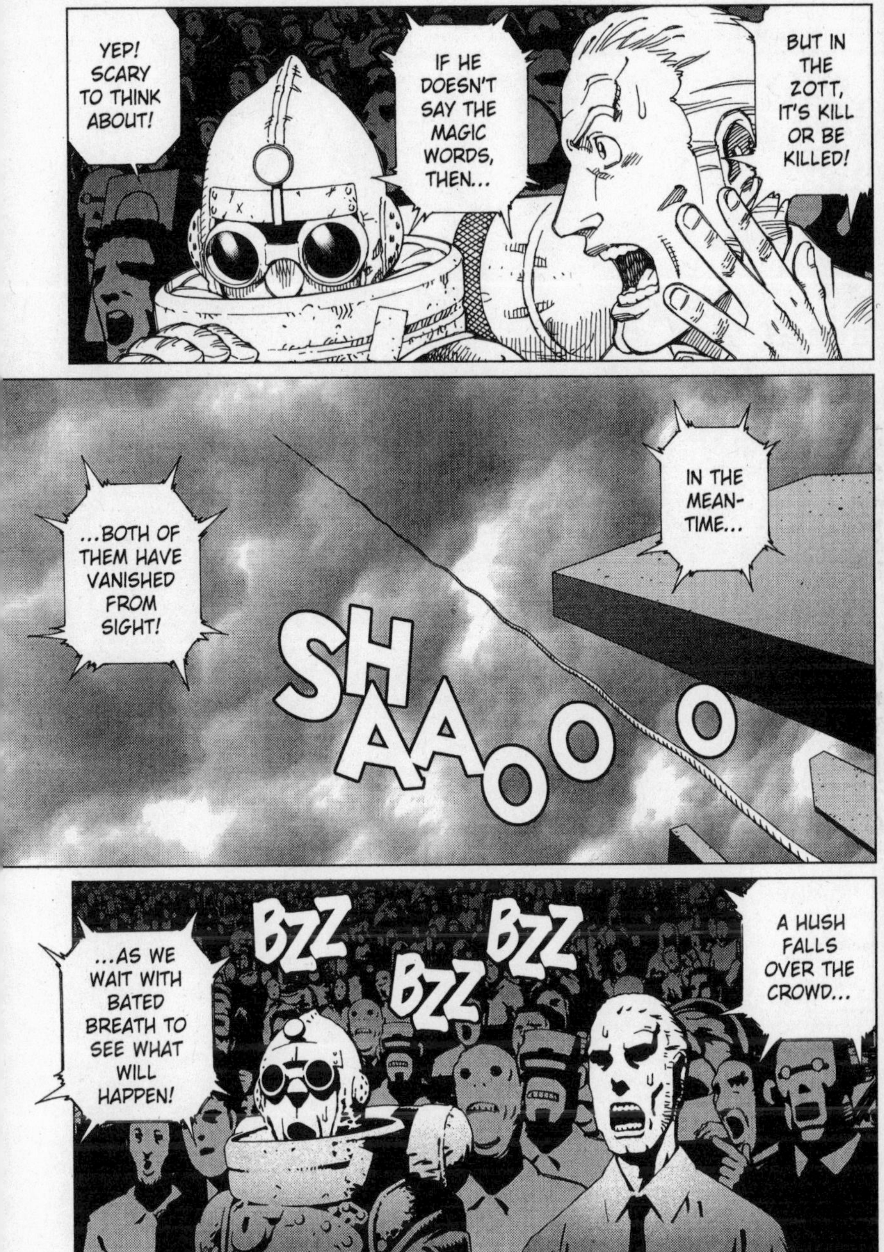
BUT IN THE ZOTT, IT'S KILL OR BE KILLED!
IF HE DOESN'T SAY THE MAGIC WORDS, THEN...
YEP! SCARY TO THINK ABOUT!
IN THE MEAN-TIME...
SHAAOOO
...BOTH OF THEM HAVE VANISHED FROM SIGHT!
A HUSH FALLS OVER THE CROWD...
BZZ
BZZ
BZZ
...AS WE WAIT WITH BATED BREATH TO SEE WHAT WILL HAPPEN!

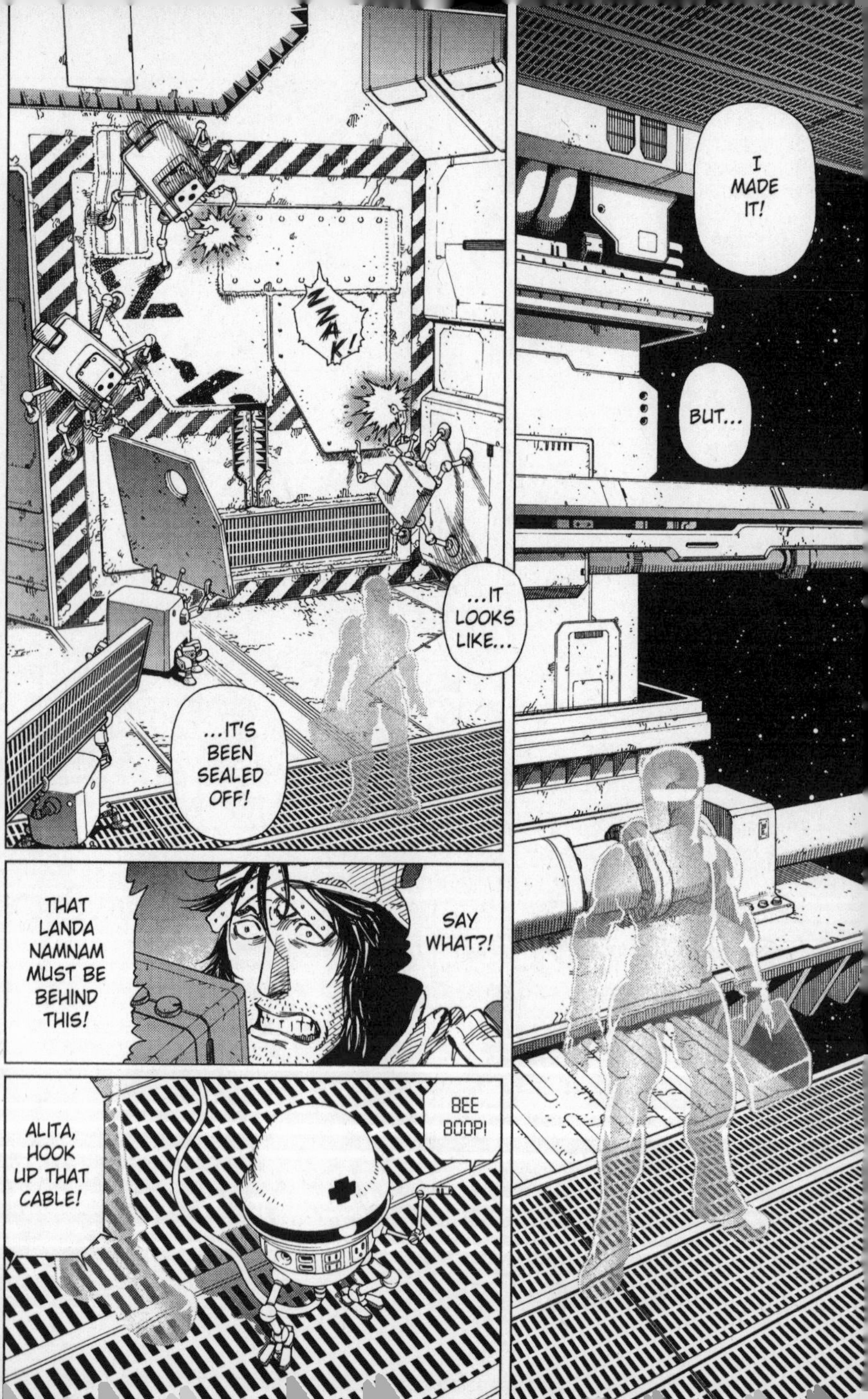
I MADE IT!
BUT...
ZZAK!
...IT LOOKS LIKE...
...IT'S BEEN SEALED OFF!
SAY WHAT?!
THAT LANDA NAMNAM MUST BE BEHIND THIS!
BEE BOOP!
ALITA, HOOK UP THAT CABLE!

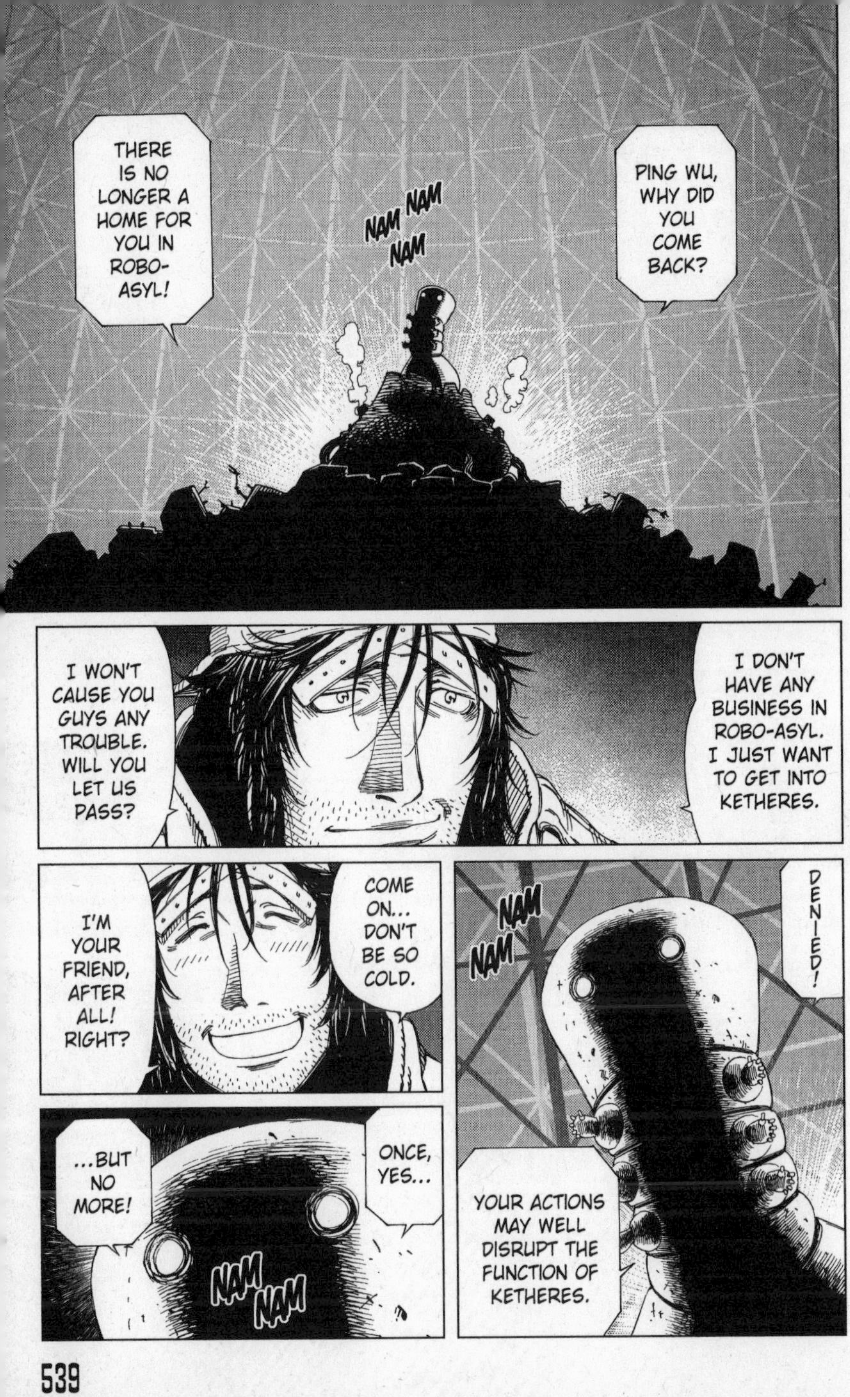
PING WU, WHY DID YOU COME BACK?
NAM NAM NAM
THERE IS NO LONGER A HOME FOR YOU IN ROBO-ASYL!
I DON'T HAVE ANY BUSINESS IN ROBO-ASYL. I JUST WANT TO GET INTO KETHERES.
I WON'T CAUSE YOU GUYS ANY TROUBLE. WILL YOU LET US PASS?
DENIED!
NAM NAM
YOUR ACTIONS MAY WELL DISRUPT THE FUNCTION OF KETHERES.
COME ON... DON'T BE SO COLD.
I'M YOUR FRIEND, AFTER ALL! RIGHT?
ONCE, YES...
...BUT NO MORE!
NAM NAM

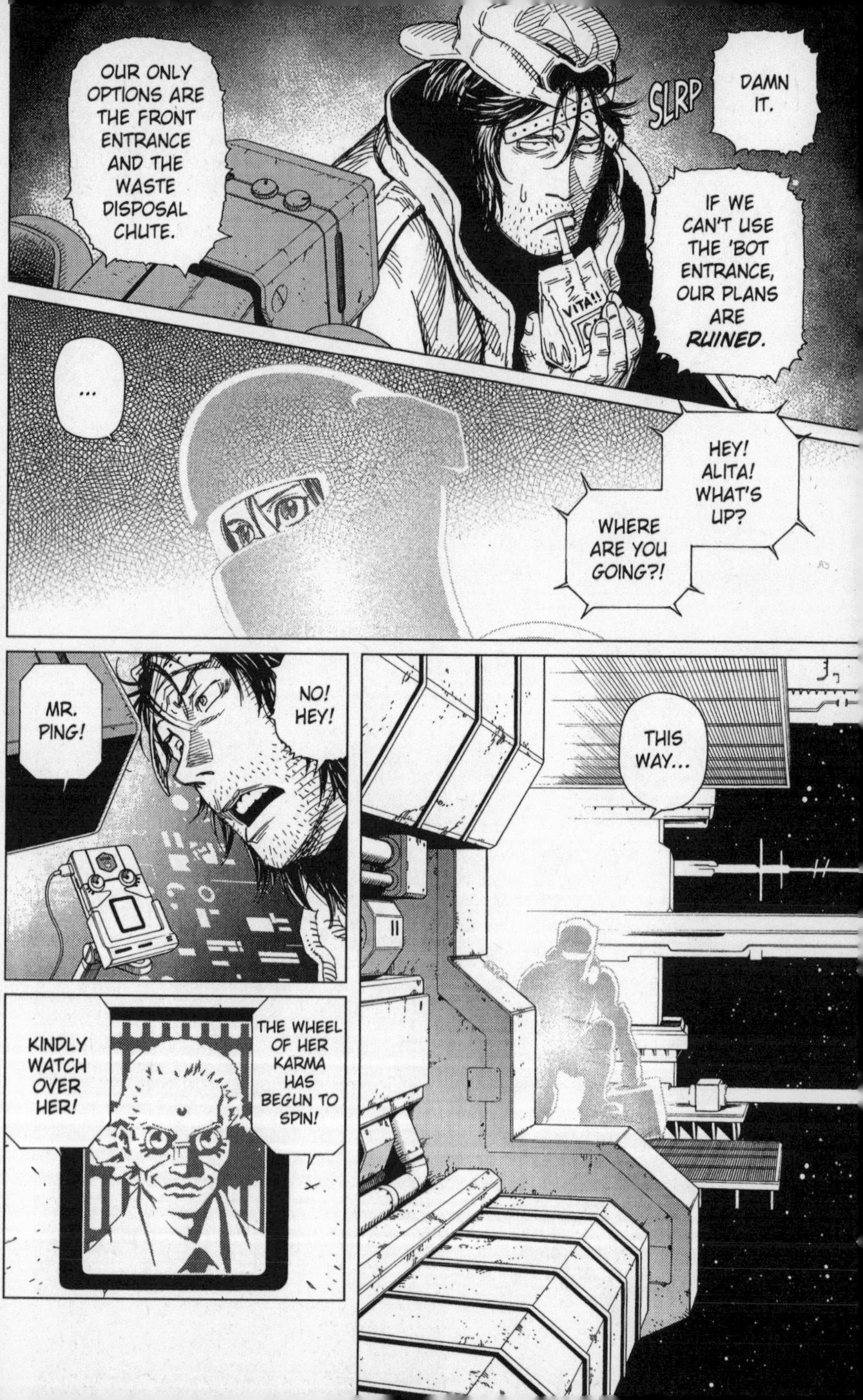
DAMN IT.
SLRP
IF WE CAN'T USE THE 'BOT ENTRANCE, OUR PLANS ARE RUINED.
OUR ONLY OPTIONS ARE THE FRONT ENTRANCE AND THE WASTE DISPOSAL CHUTE.
HEY! ALITA! WHAT'S UP?
WHERE ARE YOU GOING?!
...
THIS WAY...
NO! HEY!
MR. PING!
THE WHEEL OF HER KARMA HAS BEGUN TO SPIN!
KINDLY WATCH OVER HER!

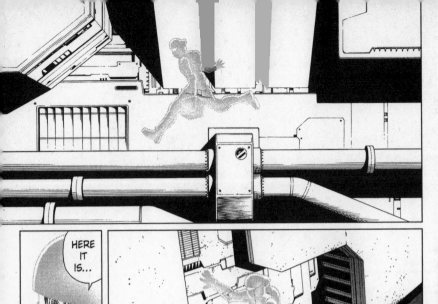

HERE IT IS...

HUH?!

A MAIN-TENANCE HATCH?! *HERE?!*

KRIK
KREK

HEY, WATCH IT!

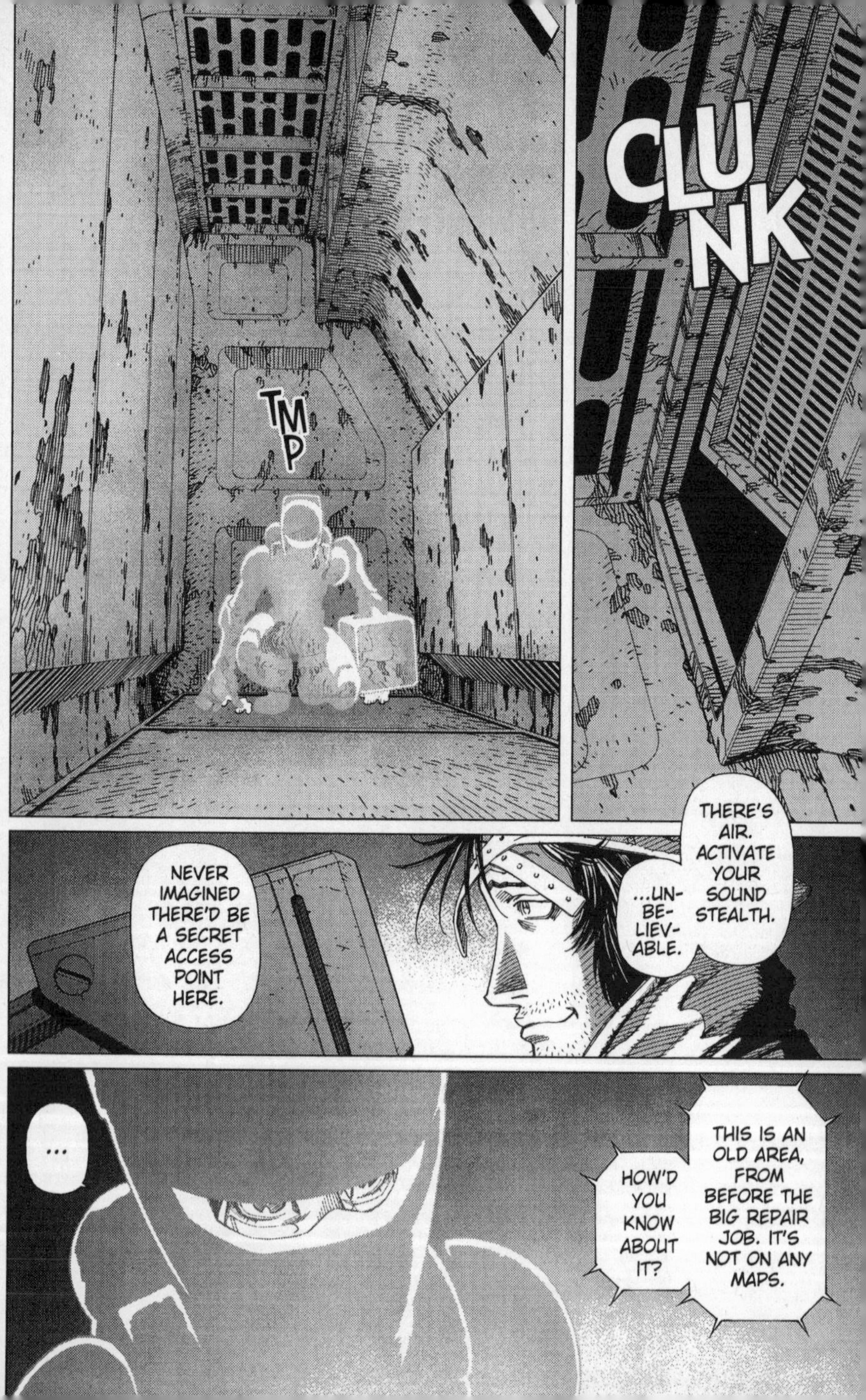
CLUNK
TMP
THERE'S AIR. ACTIVATE YOUR SOUND STEALTH.
...UNBE-LIEV-ABLE.
NEVER IMAGINED THERE'D BE A SECRET ACCESS POINT HERE.
THIS IS AN OLD AREA, FROM BEFORE THE BIG REPAIR JOB. IT'S NOT ON ANY MAPS.
HOW'D YOU KNOW ABOUT IT?
...

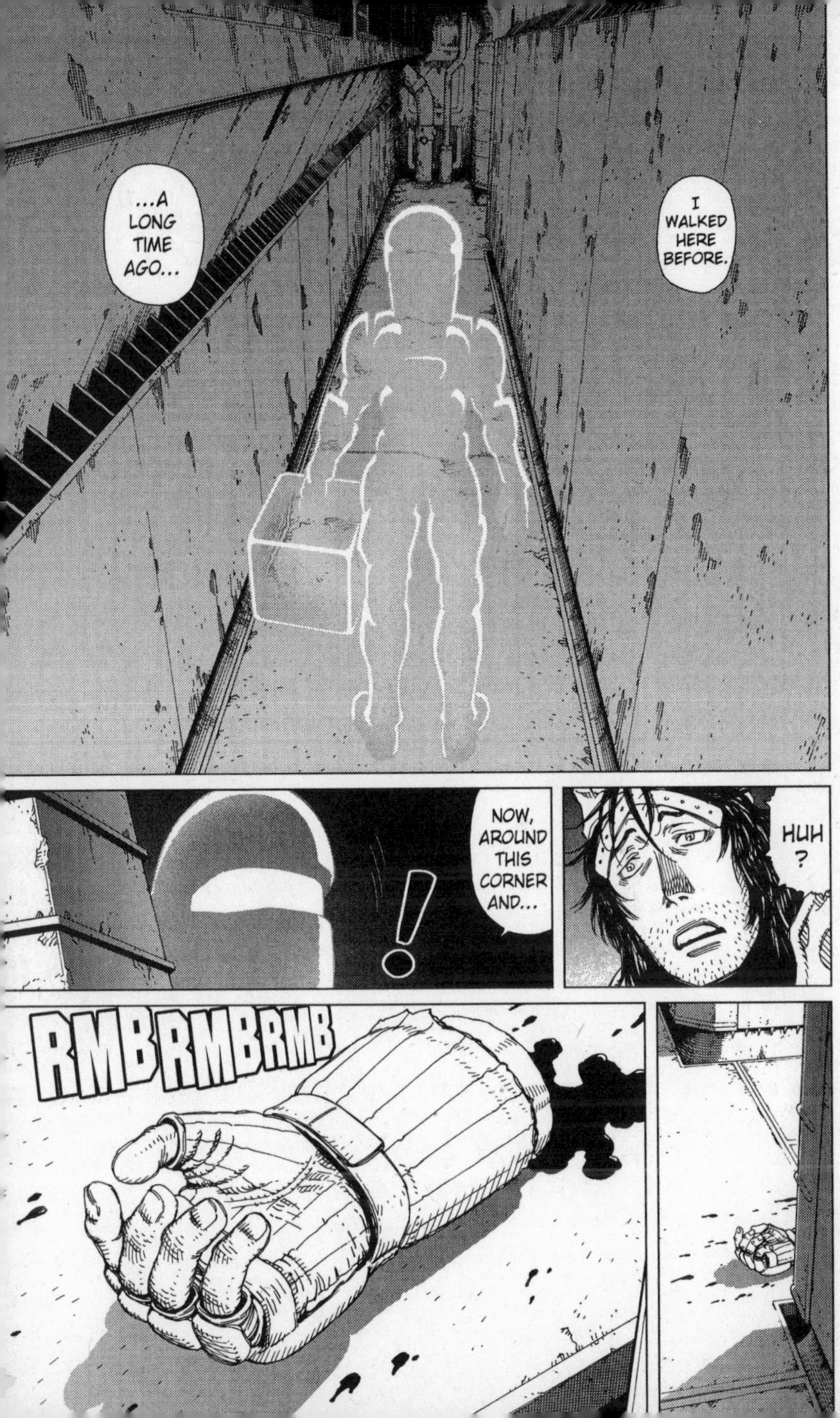
I WALKED HERE BEFORE.
...A LONG TIME AGO...
HUH?
NOW, AROUND THIS CORNER AND...
!
RMBRMBRMB

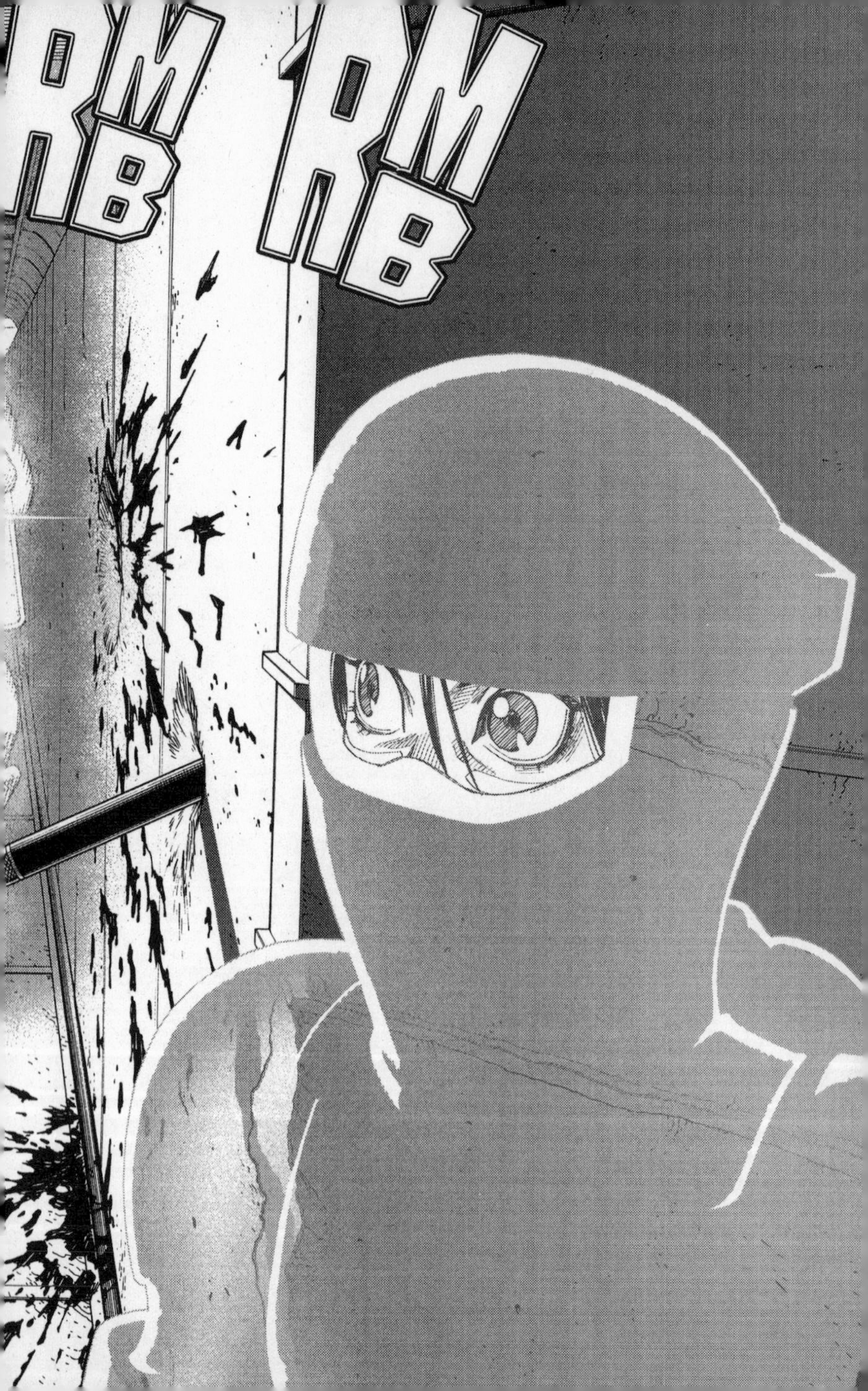

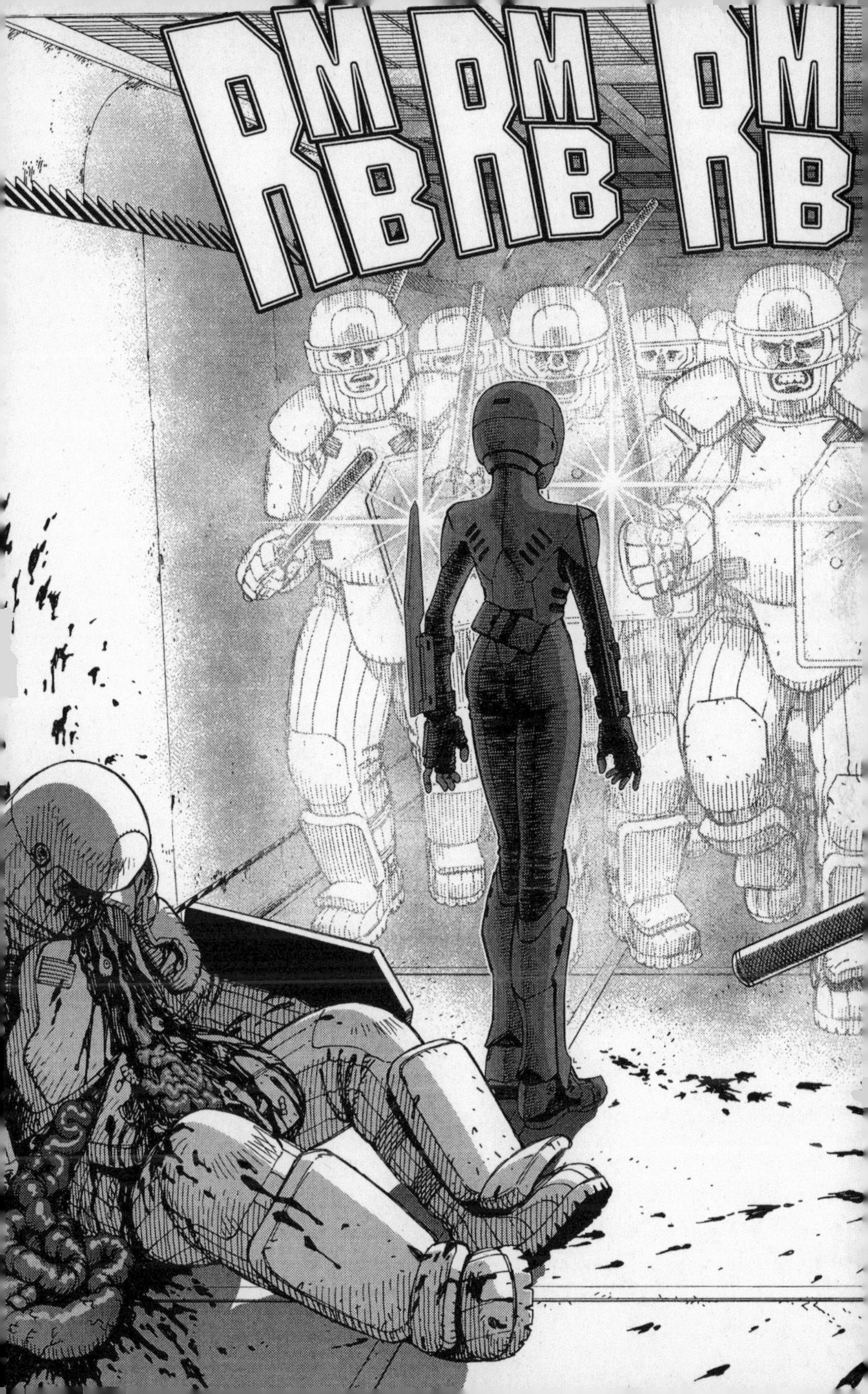
DM DM DM
RB RB RB

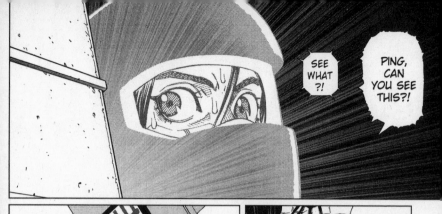

PING, CAN YOU SEE THIS?!
SEE WHAT?!
IT'S JUST AN EMPTY HALL. WHAT'S WRONG?
CALM DOWN, MR. PING!
ALITA'S MEMORY IS MOST LIKELY FLASHING BACK!
MEMORY... THESE ARE MY MEMORIES ...?
THEN... IS THAT GELDA?!
NO... WRONG BODY.
RMMB

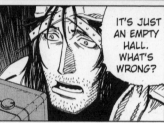

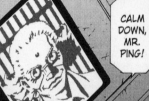

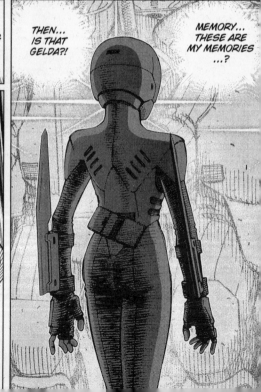

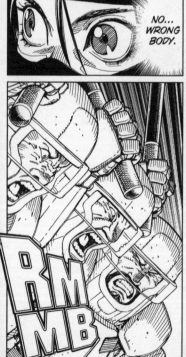

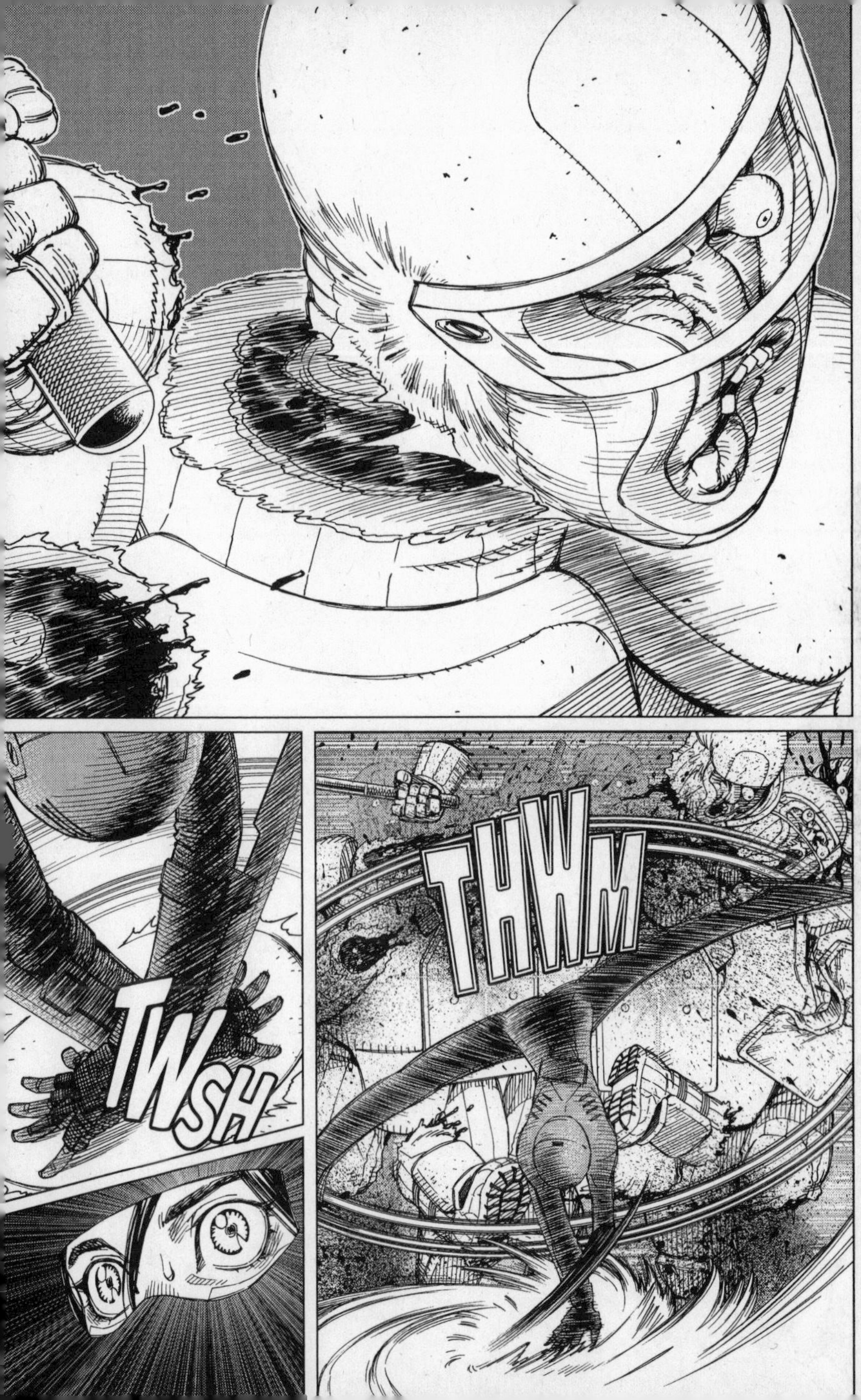
THWM
TWSH

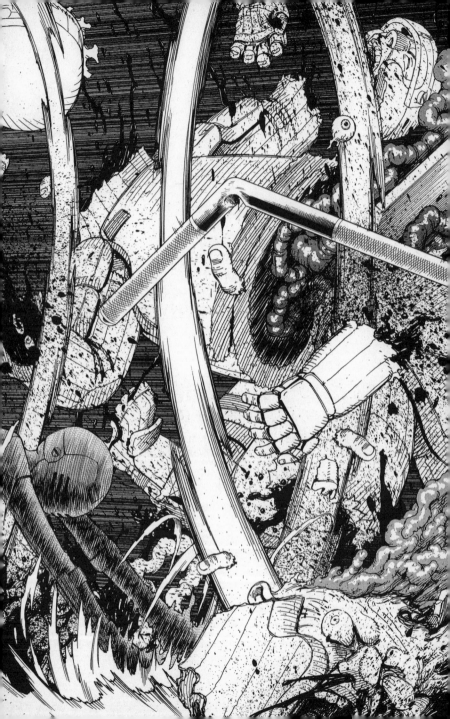

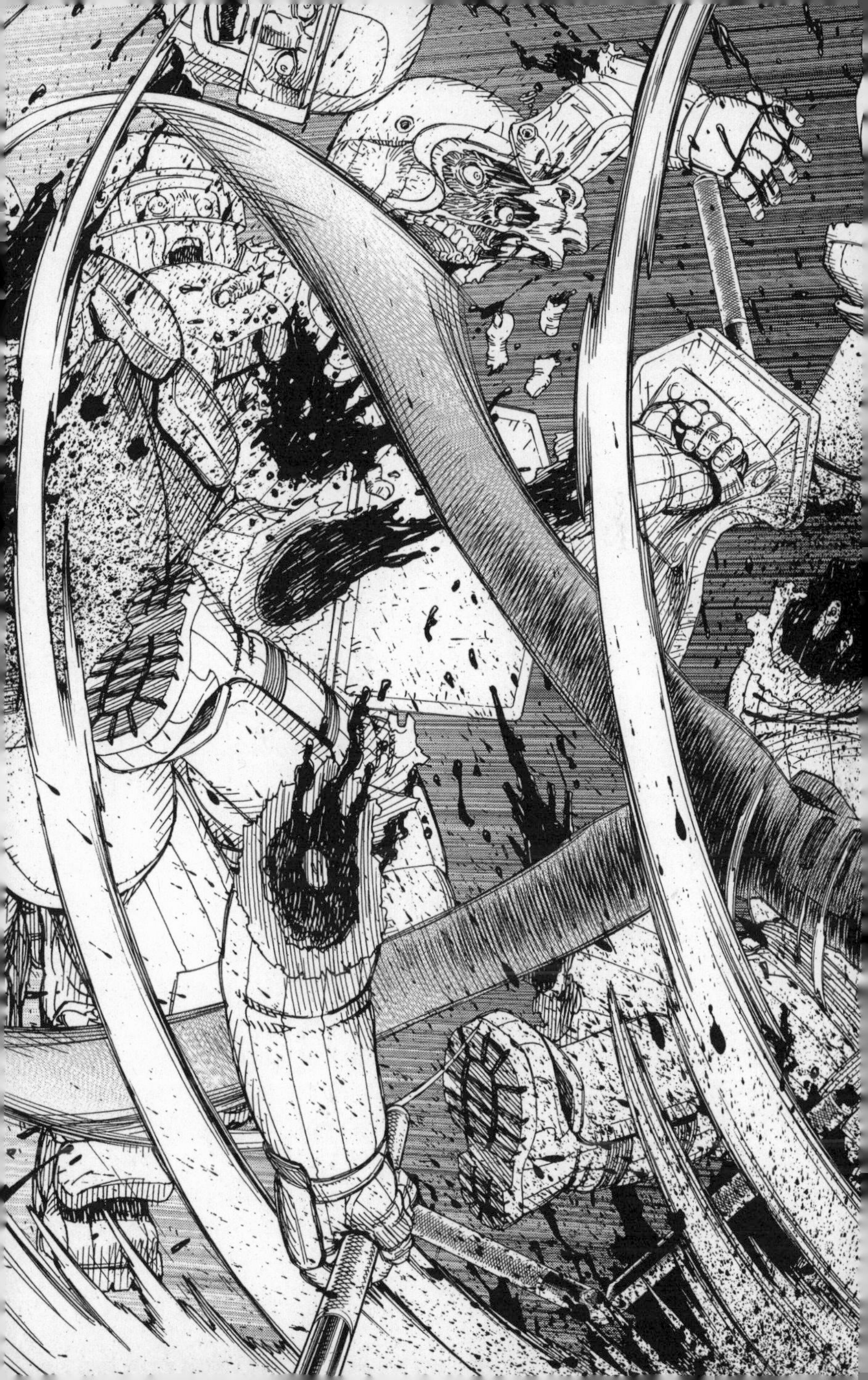

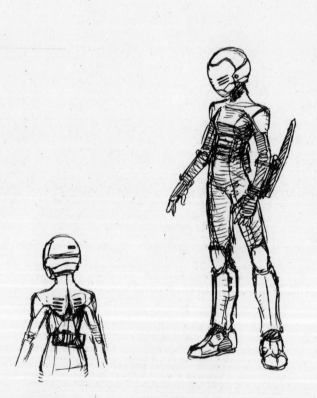

PHASE 37:
Who...Are You?!

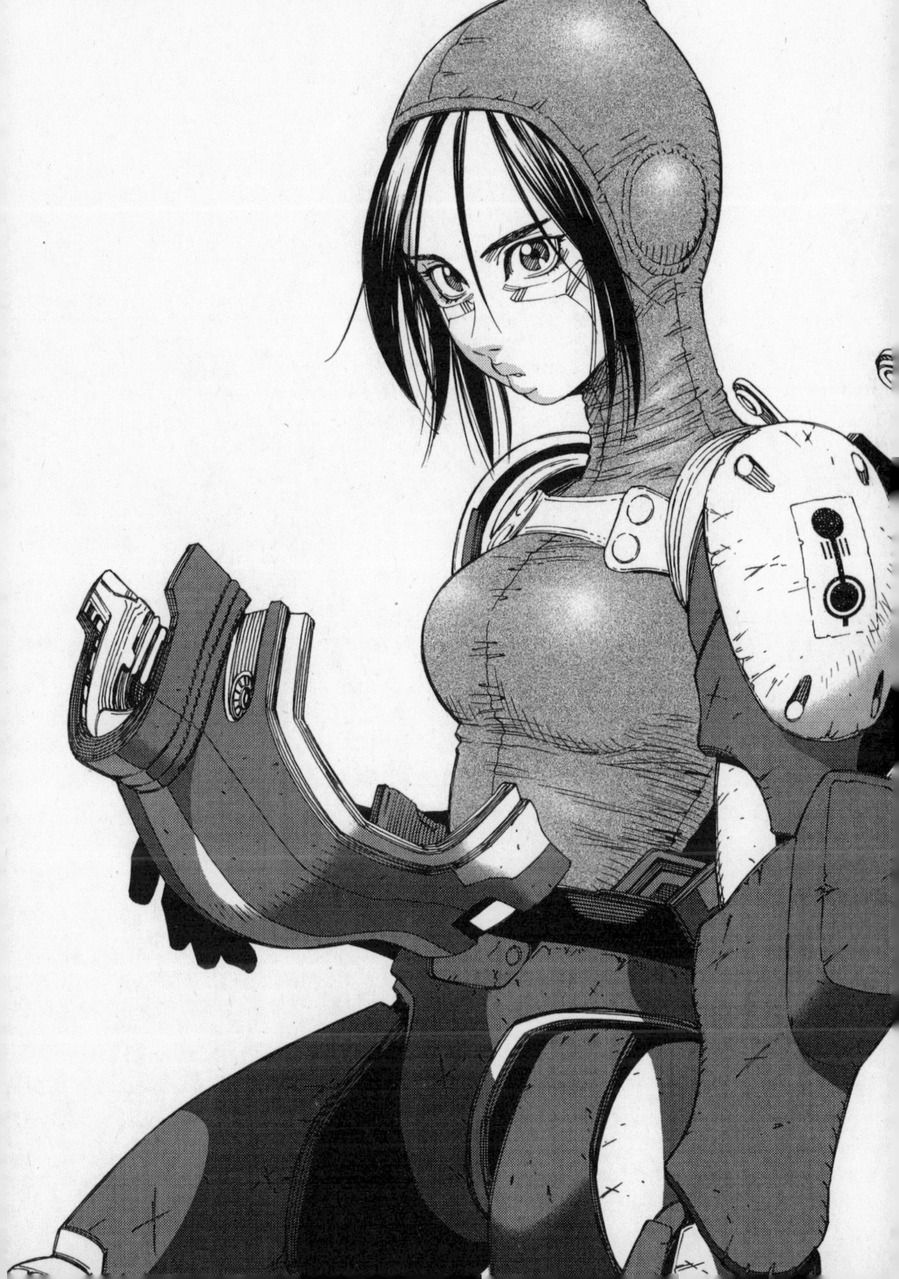

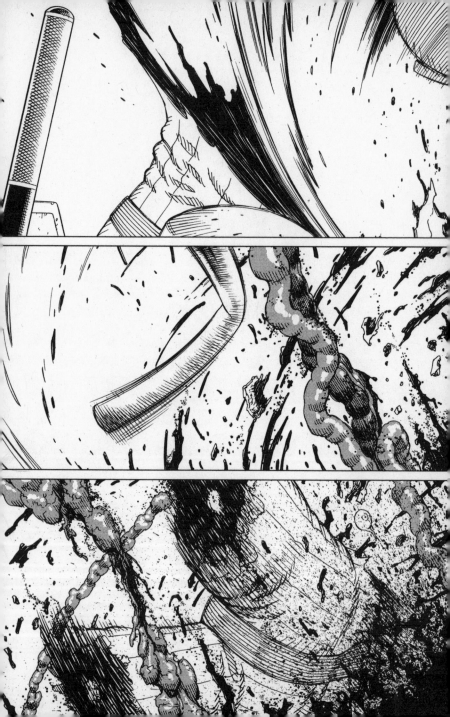

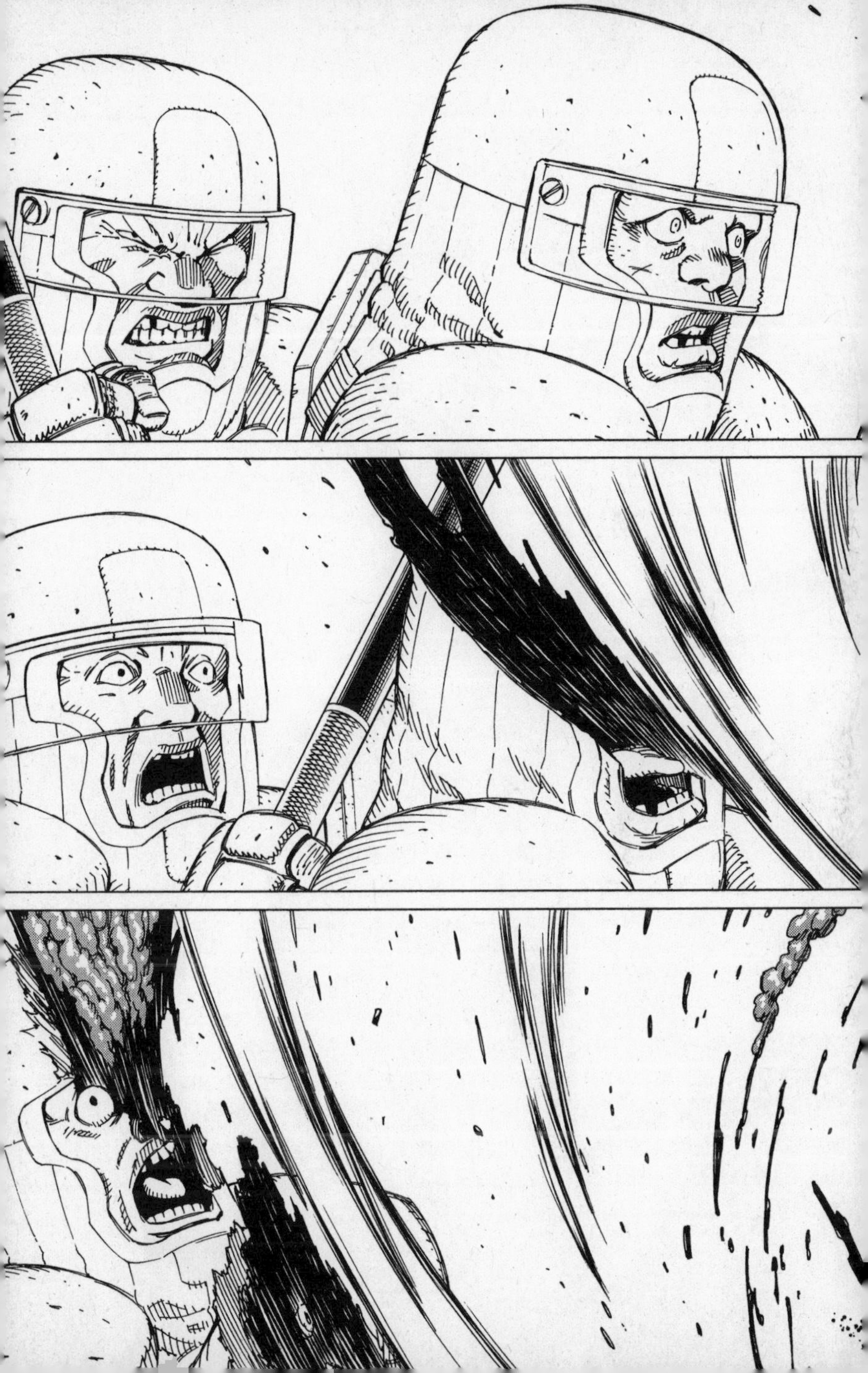

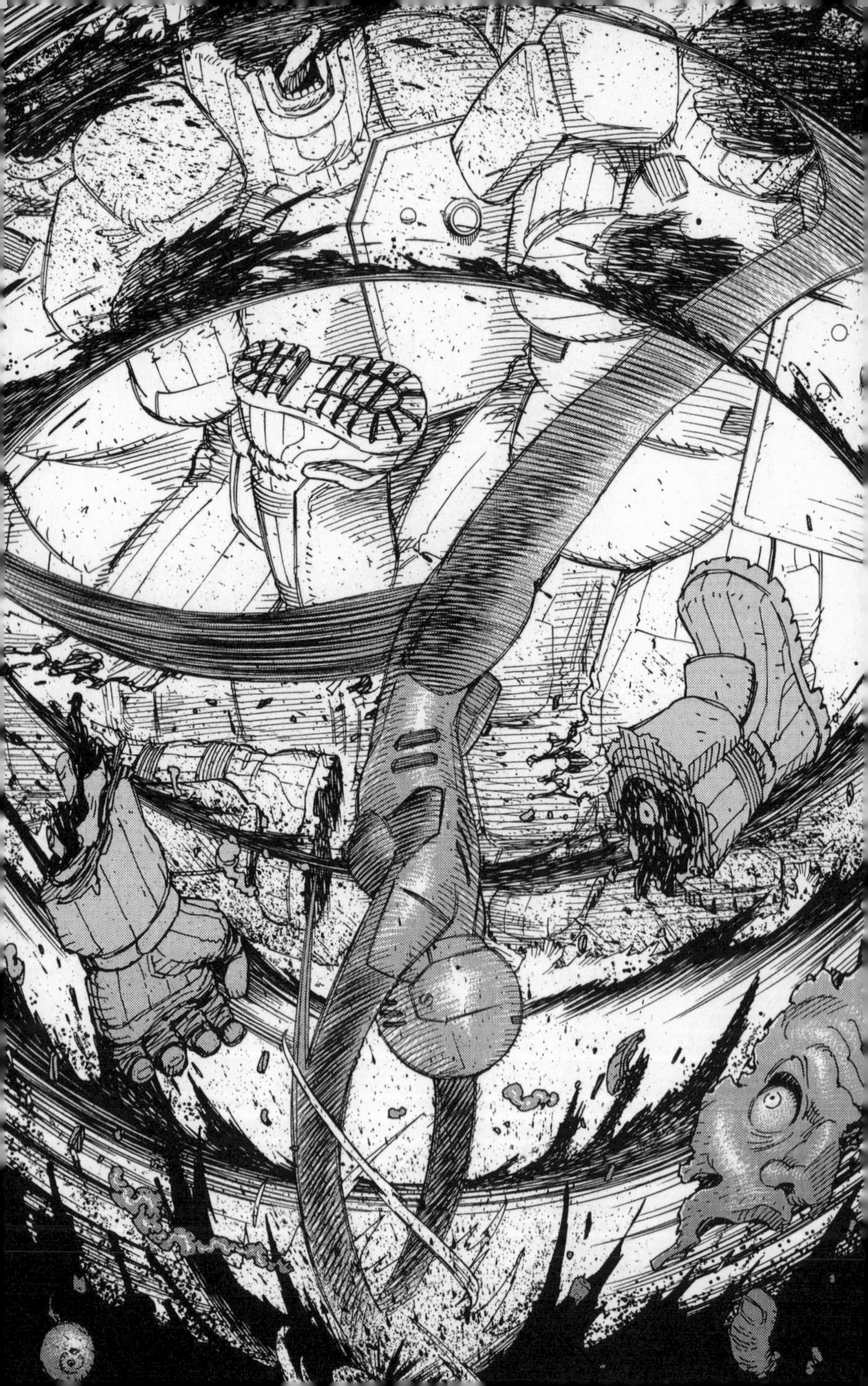

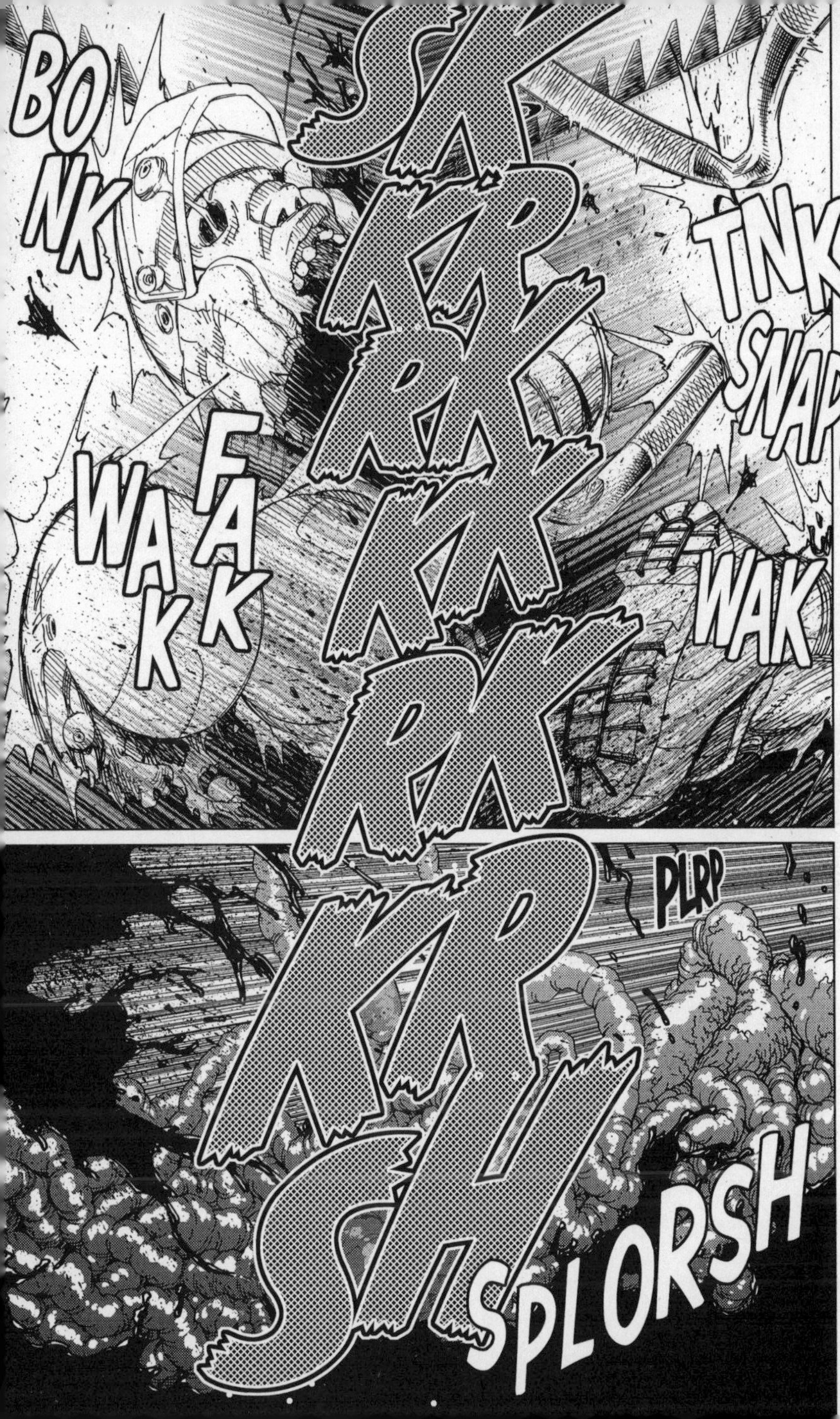
TNK
SNAP!
BONK
WAK
FAK
WAK
PLRP
SPLORSH

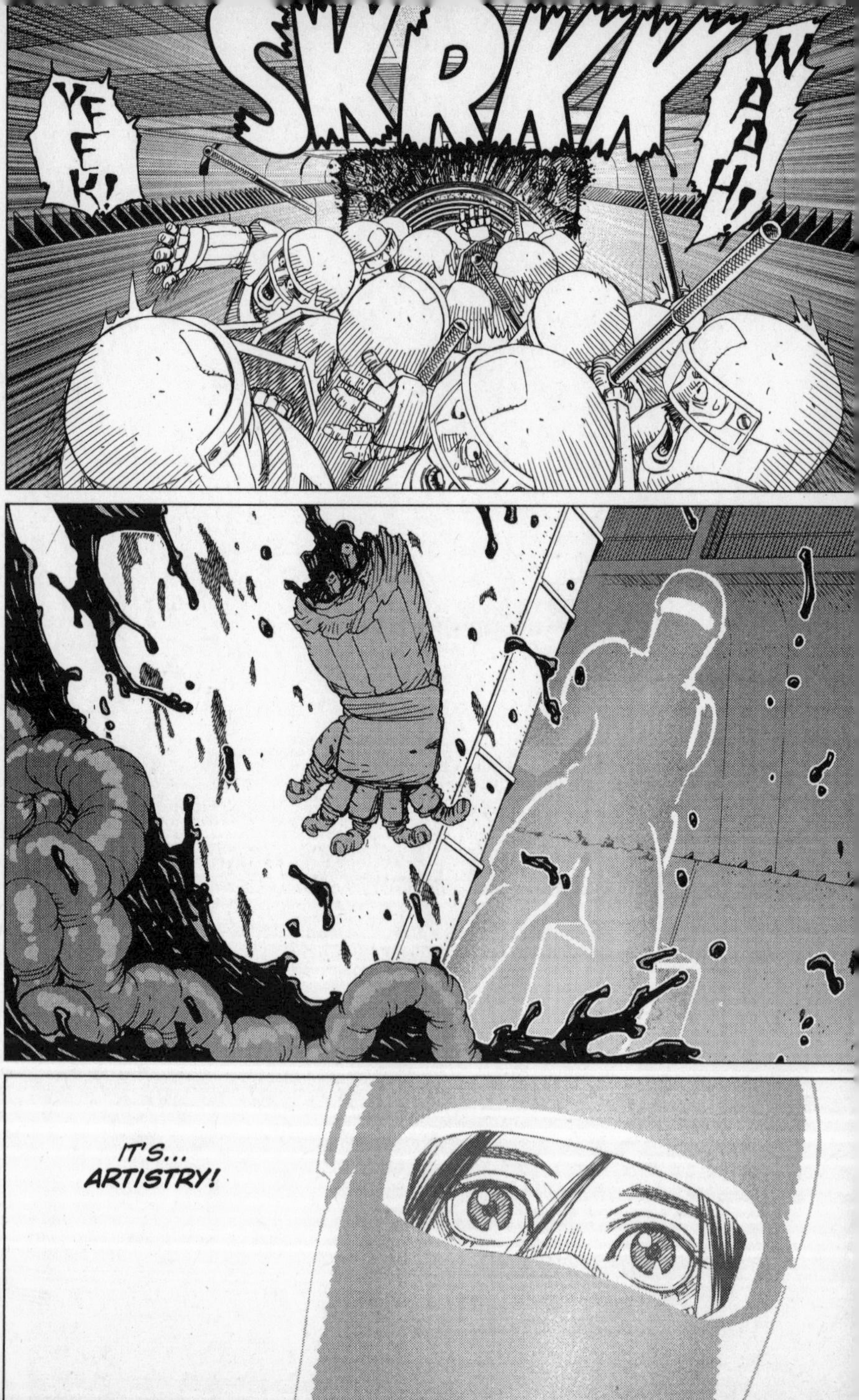
SKRKK
WAAH!
YEEEK!
IT'S... ARTISTRY!

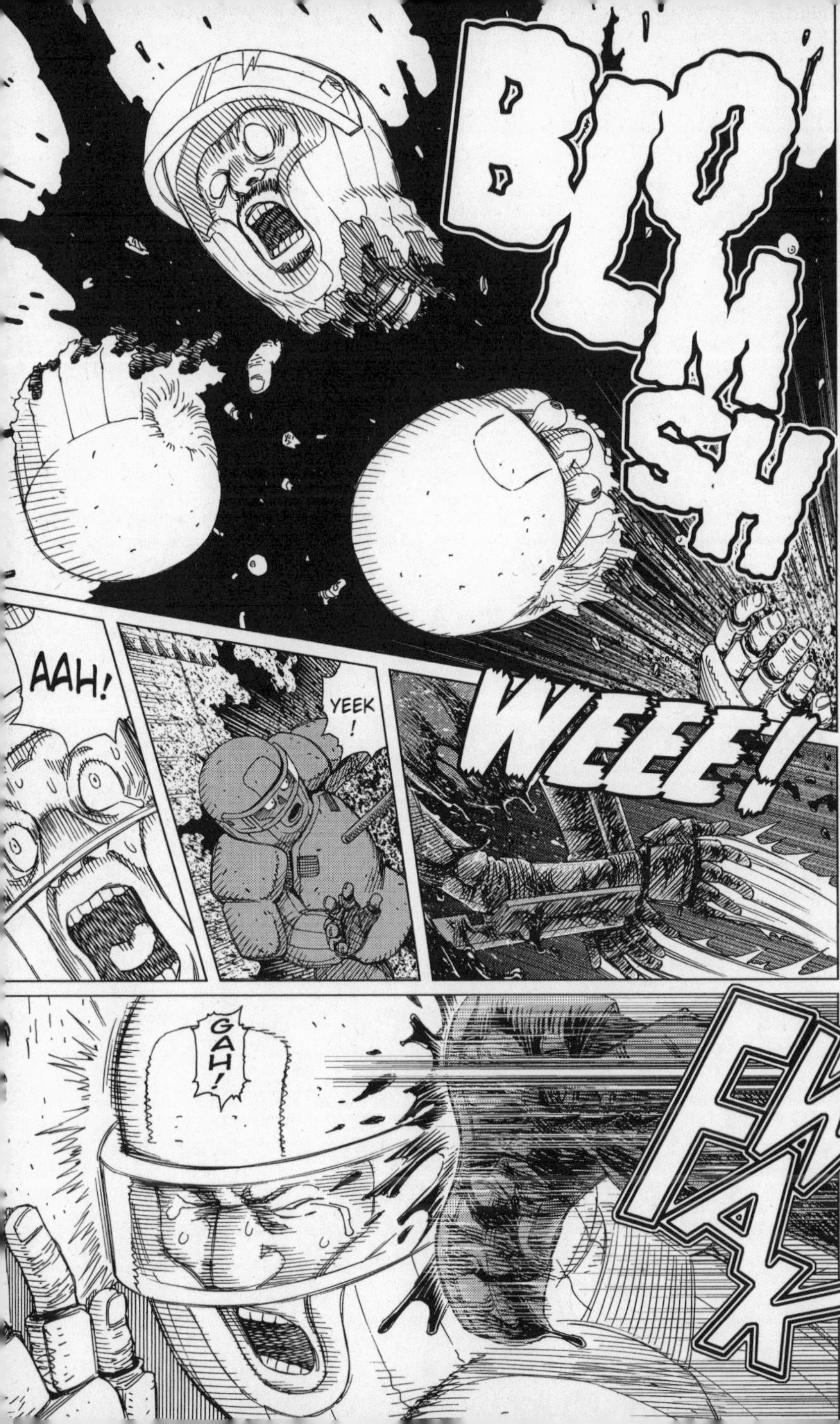
BLASH
WEEE!
YEEK!
AAH!
FWAK
GAH!

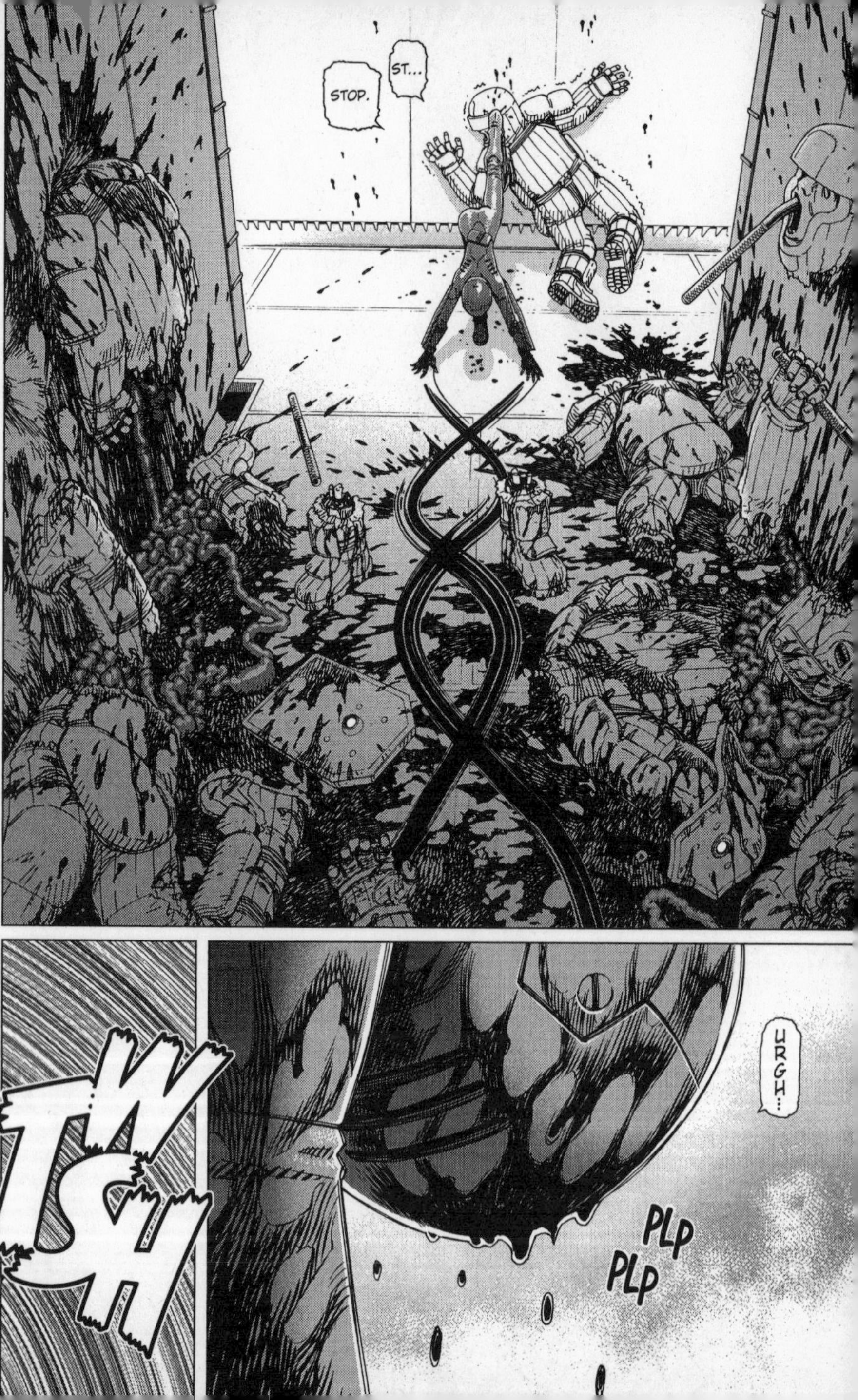
ST...
STOP.
URGH...
PLP
PLP
TWCH

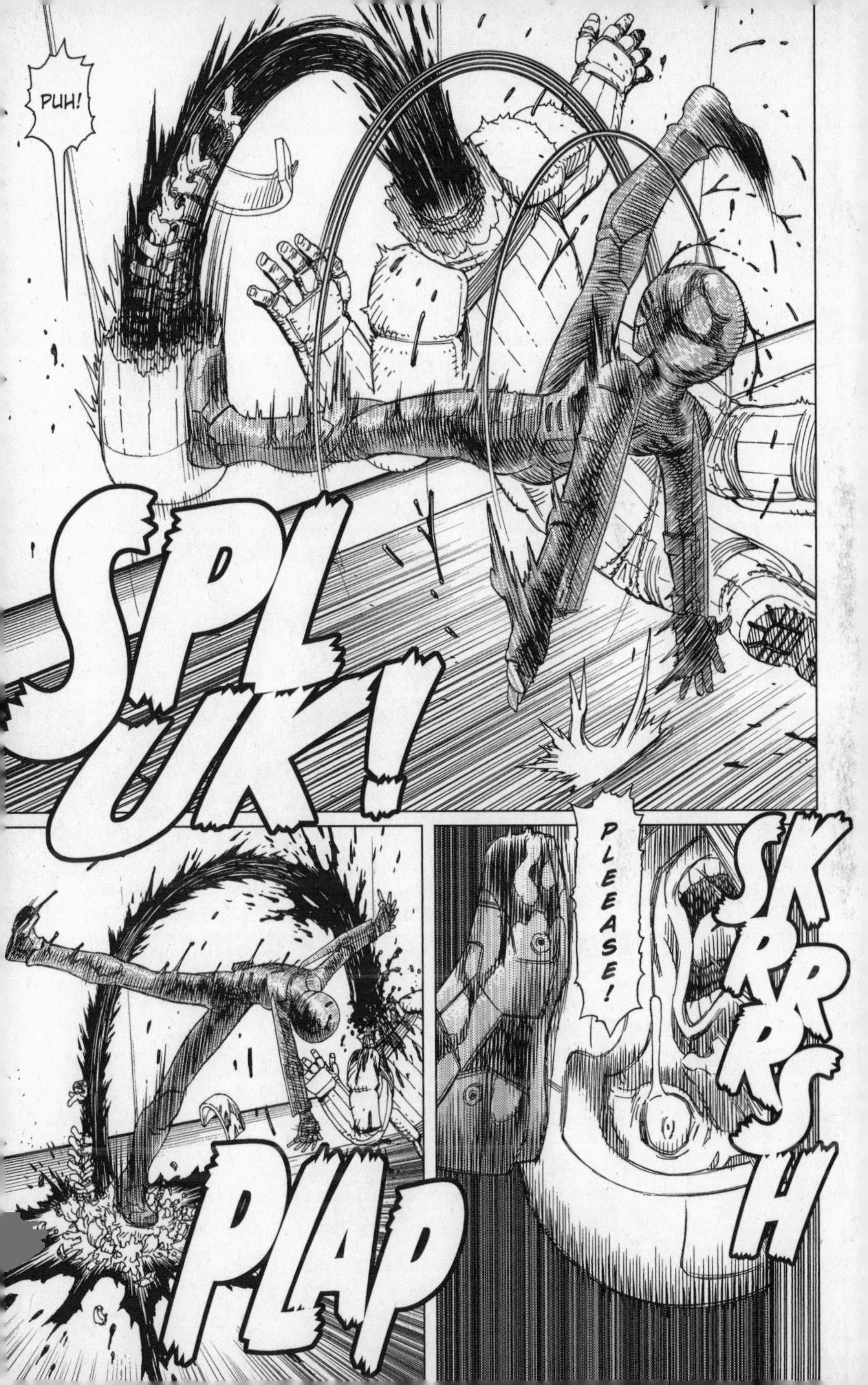
PUH!
SPLUK!
PLEEEASE!
SKRRRSH
PLAP

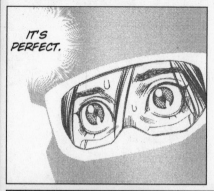

IT'S PERFECT.
SIMPLE...
PLP
PLP
MERCI-LESS...
AND BEAUTI-FUL...
PLOP
PLOP
PLUP
PLUP
THIS IS IT...
PURE... UNADULTER-ATED...
FSHHH

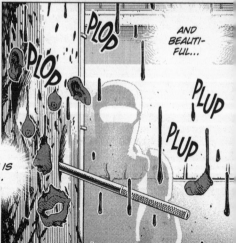

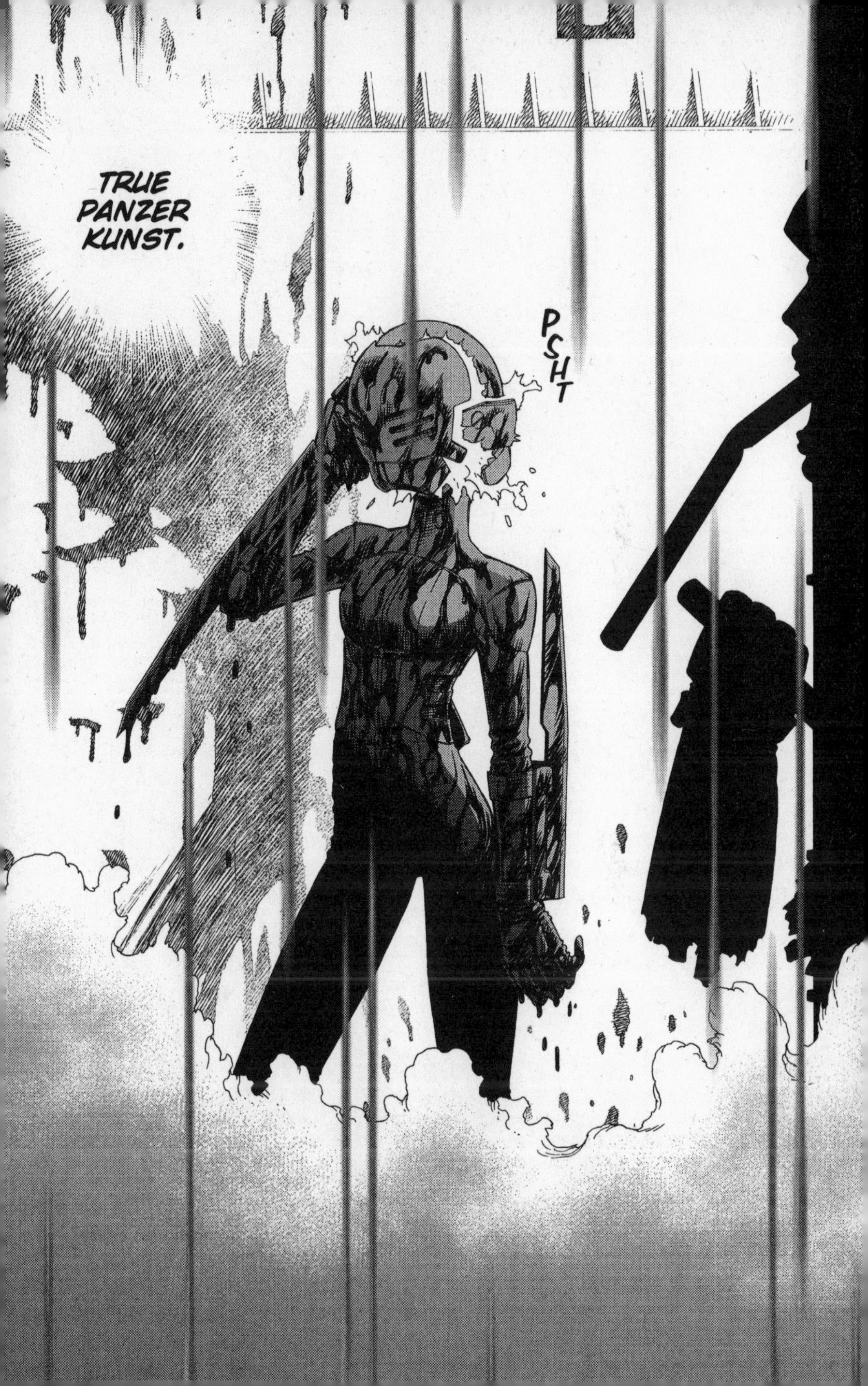
TRUE PANZER KUNST.
PSHT

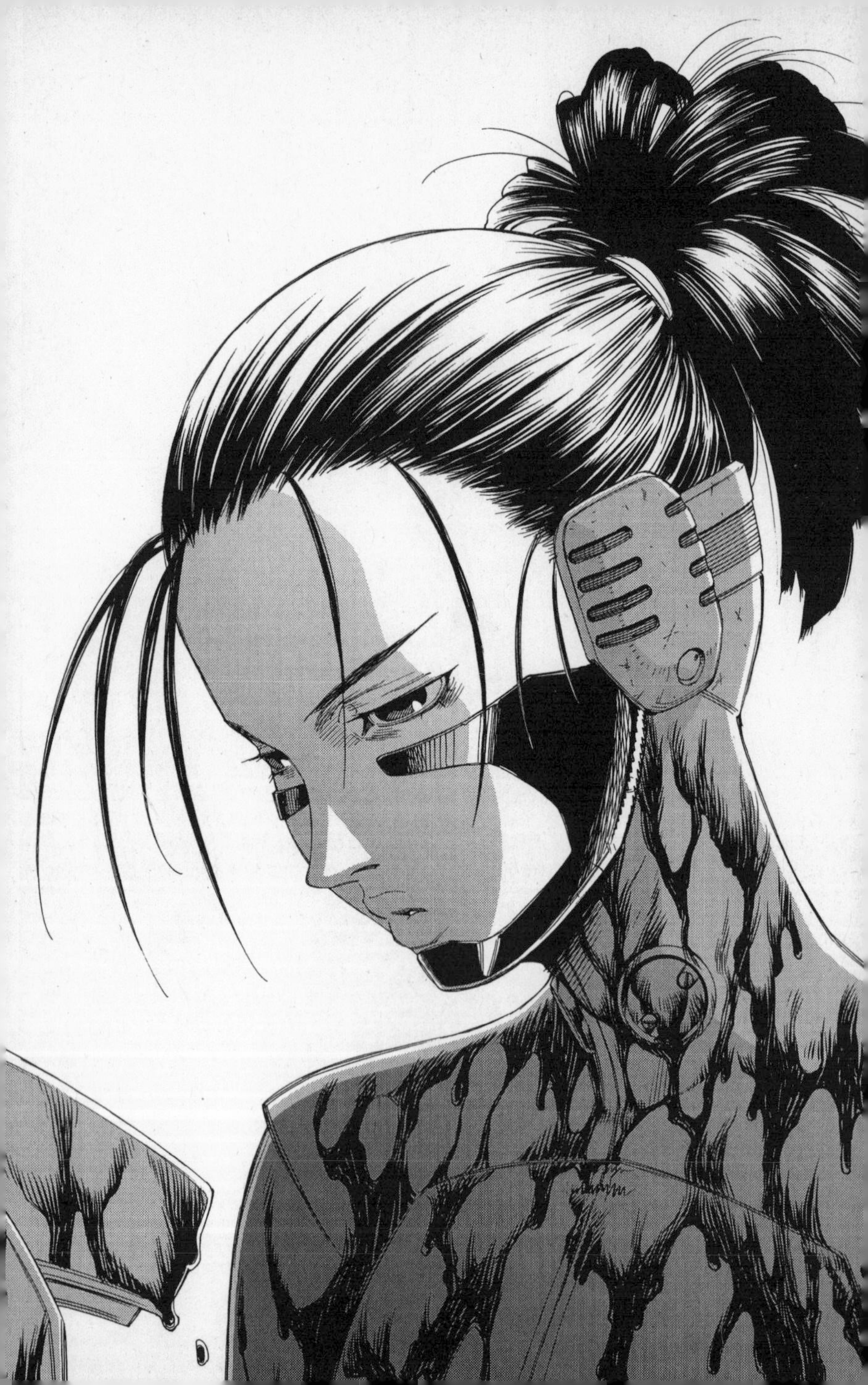

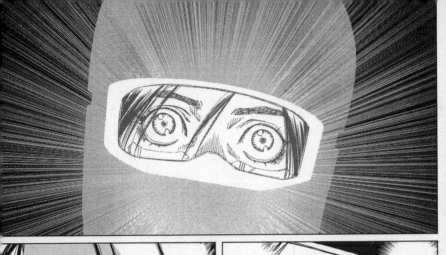

ME...?!

IT'S...

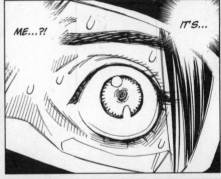

W-
WAIT!

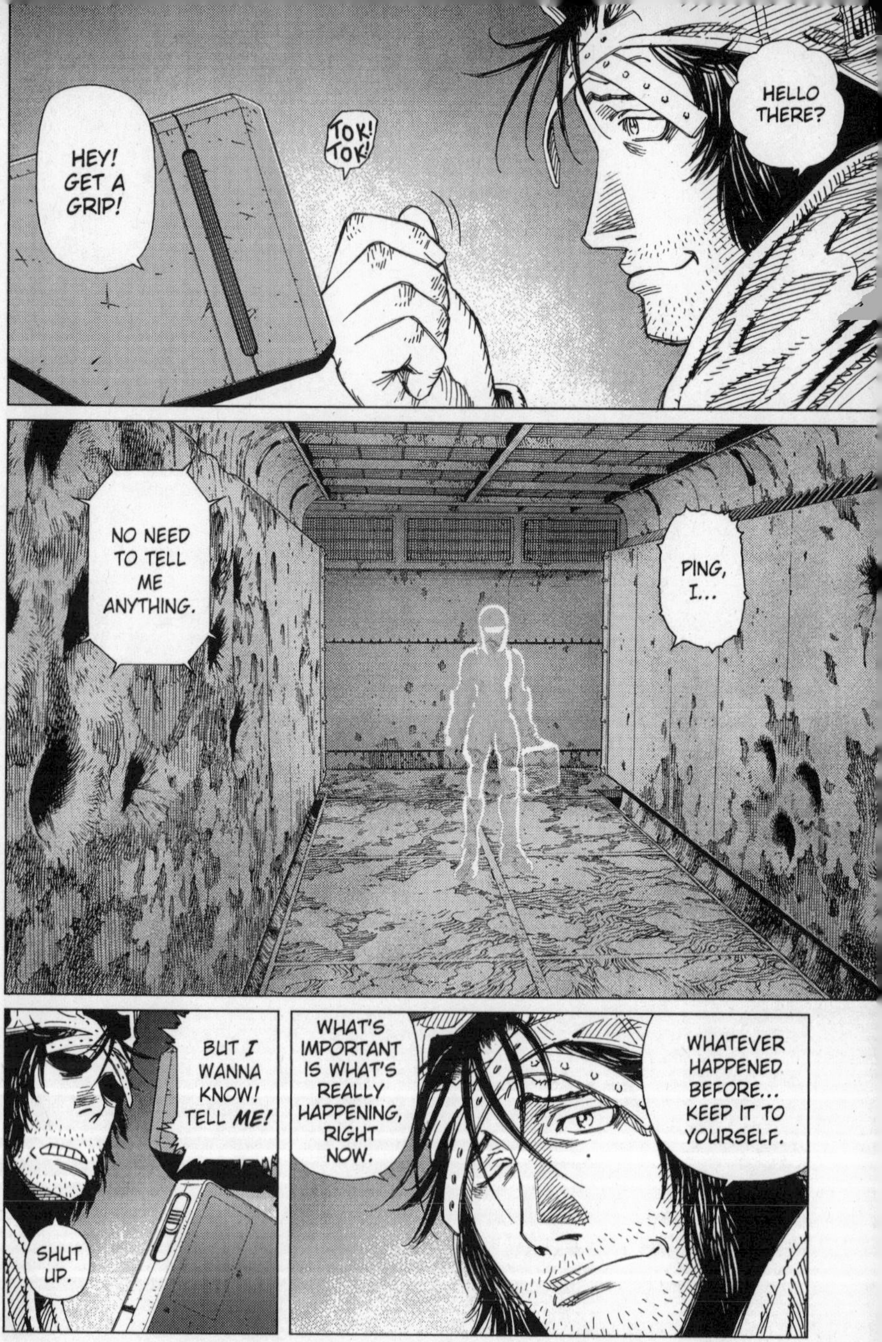
HELLO THERE?
TOK! TOK!
HEY! GET A GRIP!
PING, I...
NO NEED TO TELL ME ANYTHING.
WHATEVER HAPPENED BEFORE... KEEP IT TO YOURSELF.
WHAT'S IMPORTANT IS WHAT'S REALLY HAPPENING, RIGHT NOW.
BUT I WANNA KNOW! TELL ME!
SHUT UP.

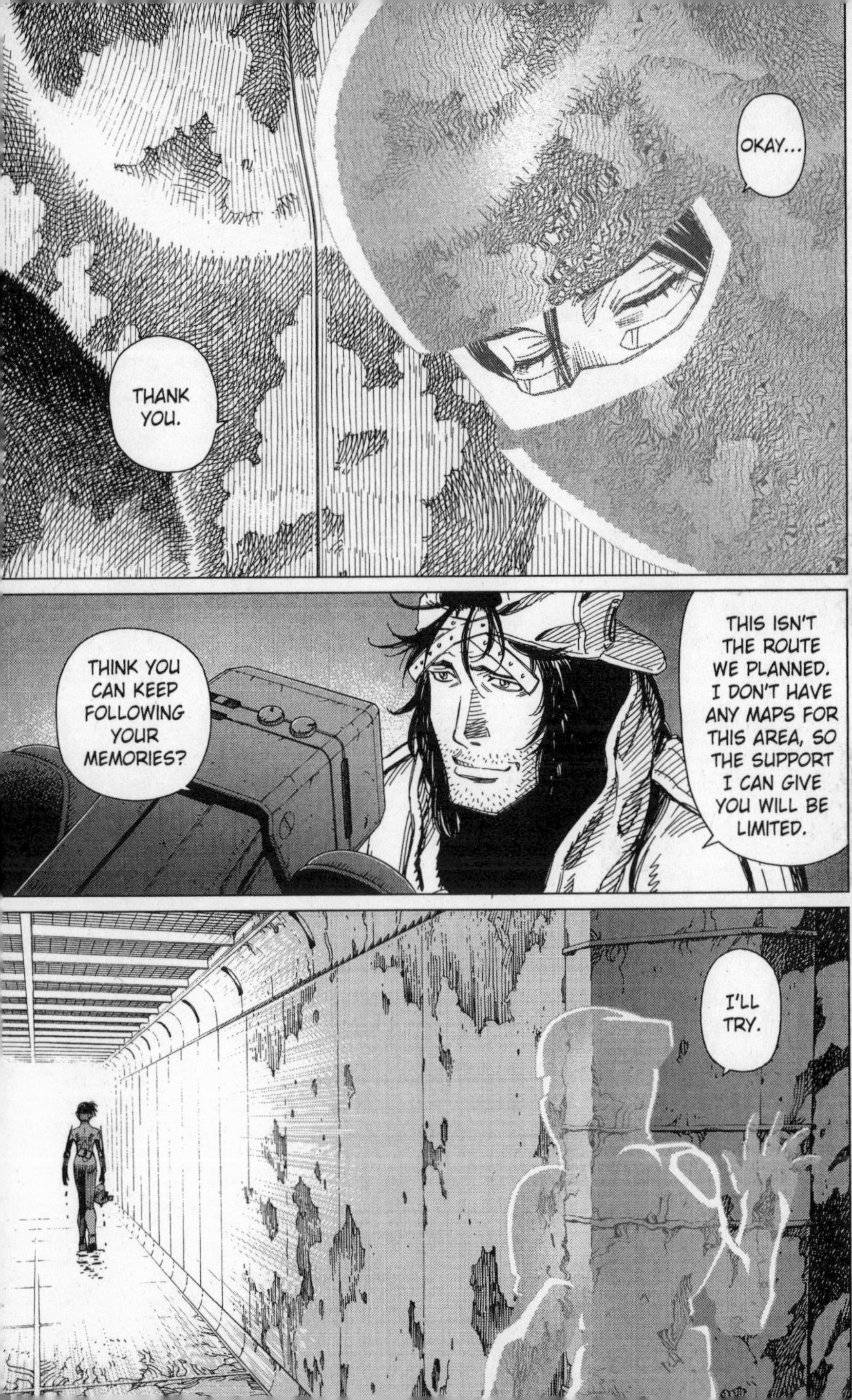
OKAY...
THANK YOU.
THIS ISN'T THE ROUTE WE PLANNED. I DON'T HAVE ANY MAPS FOR THIS AREA, SO THE SUPPORT I CAN GIVE YOU WILL BE LIMITED.
THINK YOU CAN KEEP FOLLOWING YOUR MEMORIES?
I'LL TRY.

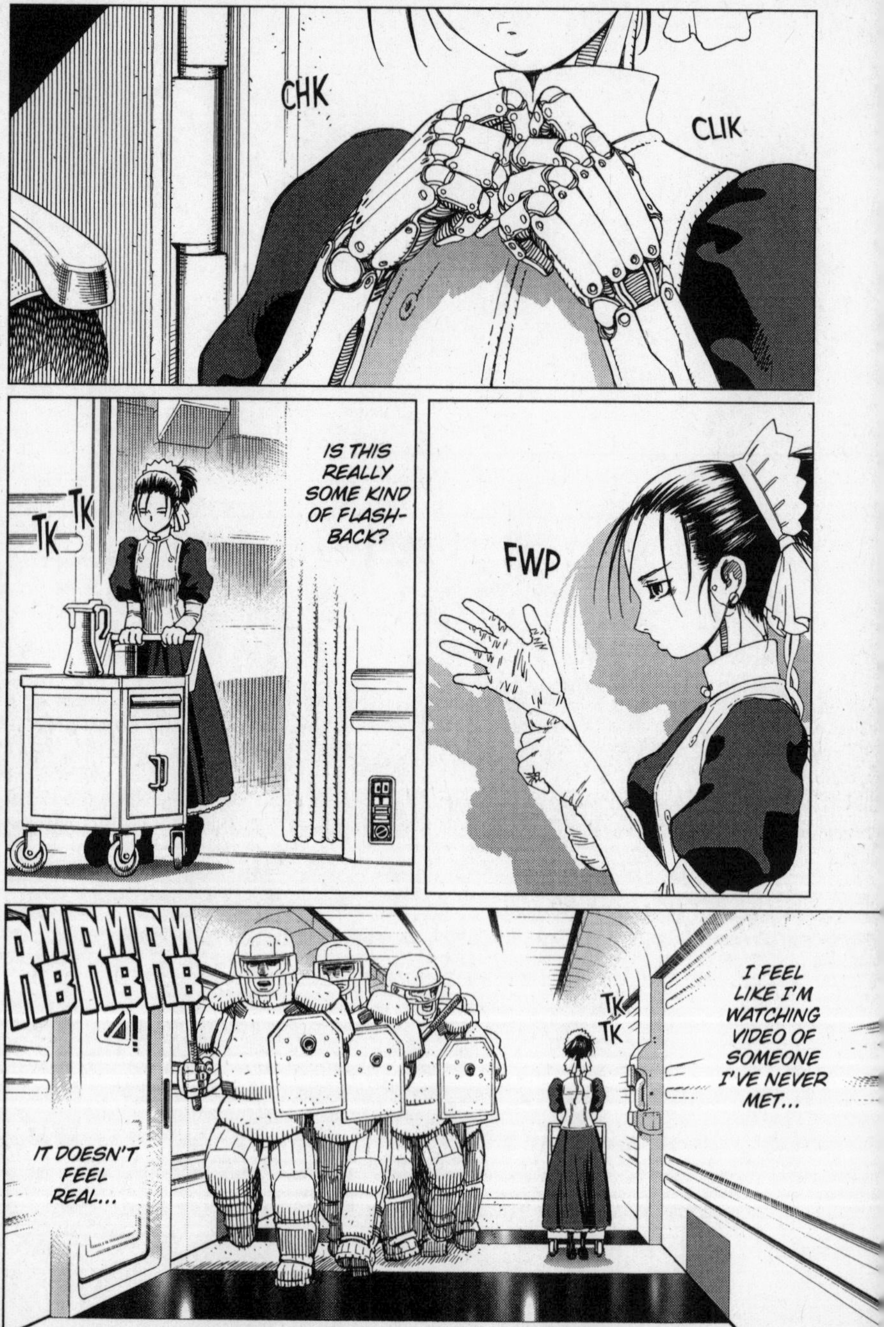
CLIK
CHK
FWP
IS THIS REALLY SOME KIND OF FLASH-BACK?
TK TK
I FEEL LIKE I'M WATCHING VIDEO OF SOMEONE I'VE NEVER MET...
TK TK
RMRMRM RBRBRB
IT DOESN'T FEEL REAL...

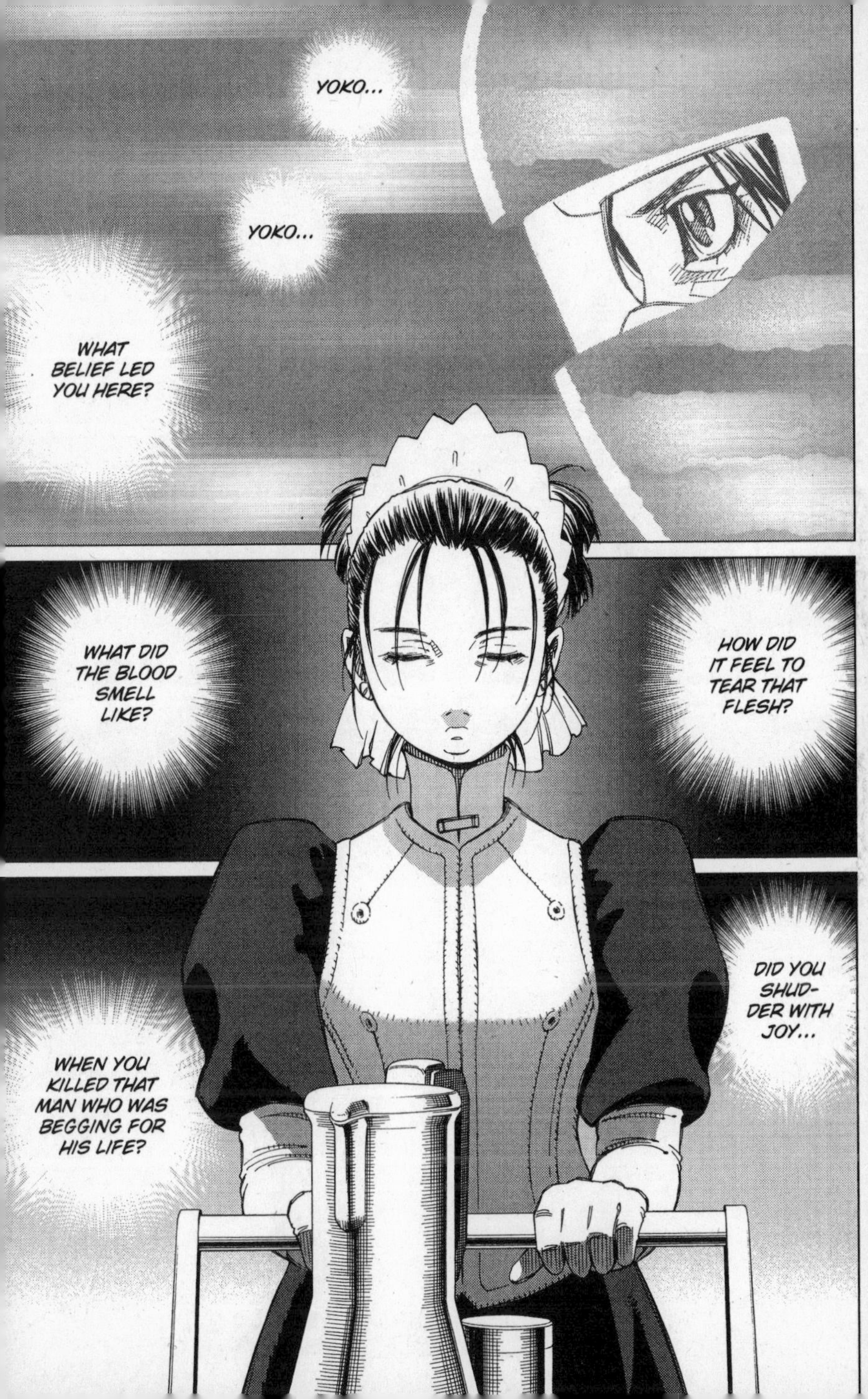
YOKO...
YOKO...
WHAT BELIEF LED YOU HERE?
HOW DID IT FEEL TO TEAR THAT FLESH?
WHAT DID THE BLOOD SMELL LIKE?
DID YOU SHUDDER WITH JOY...
WHEN YOU KILLED THAT MAN WHO WAS BEGGING FOR HIS LIFE?

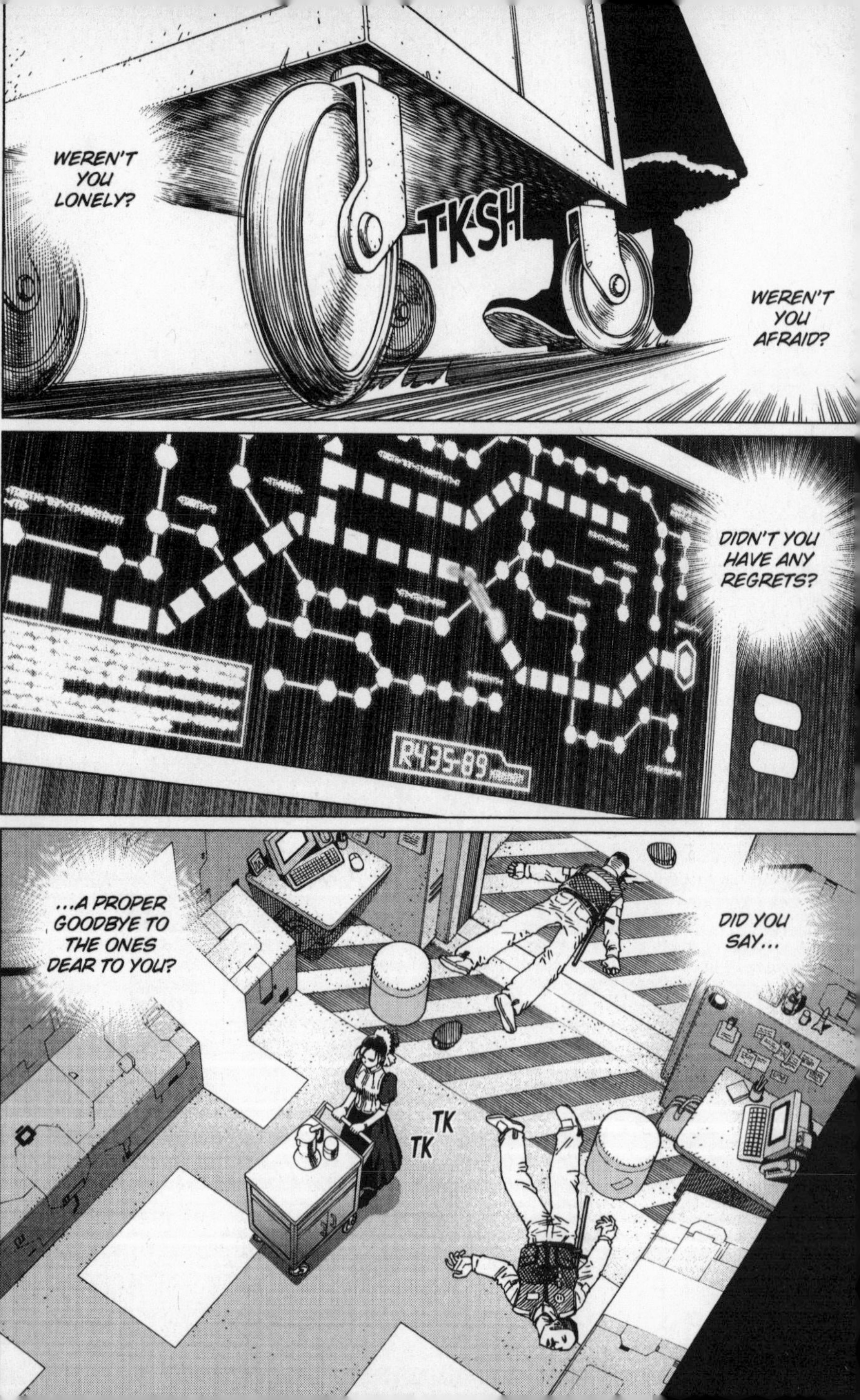
WEREN'T YOU LONELY?
T·K·SH
WEREN'T YOU AFRAID?
DIDN'T YOU HAVE ANY REGRETS?
R435-89
DID YOU SAY...
...A PROPER GOODBYE TO THE ONES DEAR TO YOU?
TK
TK

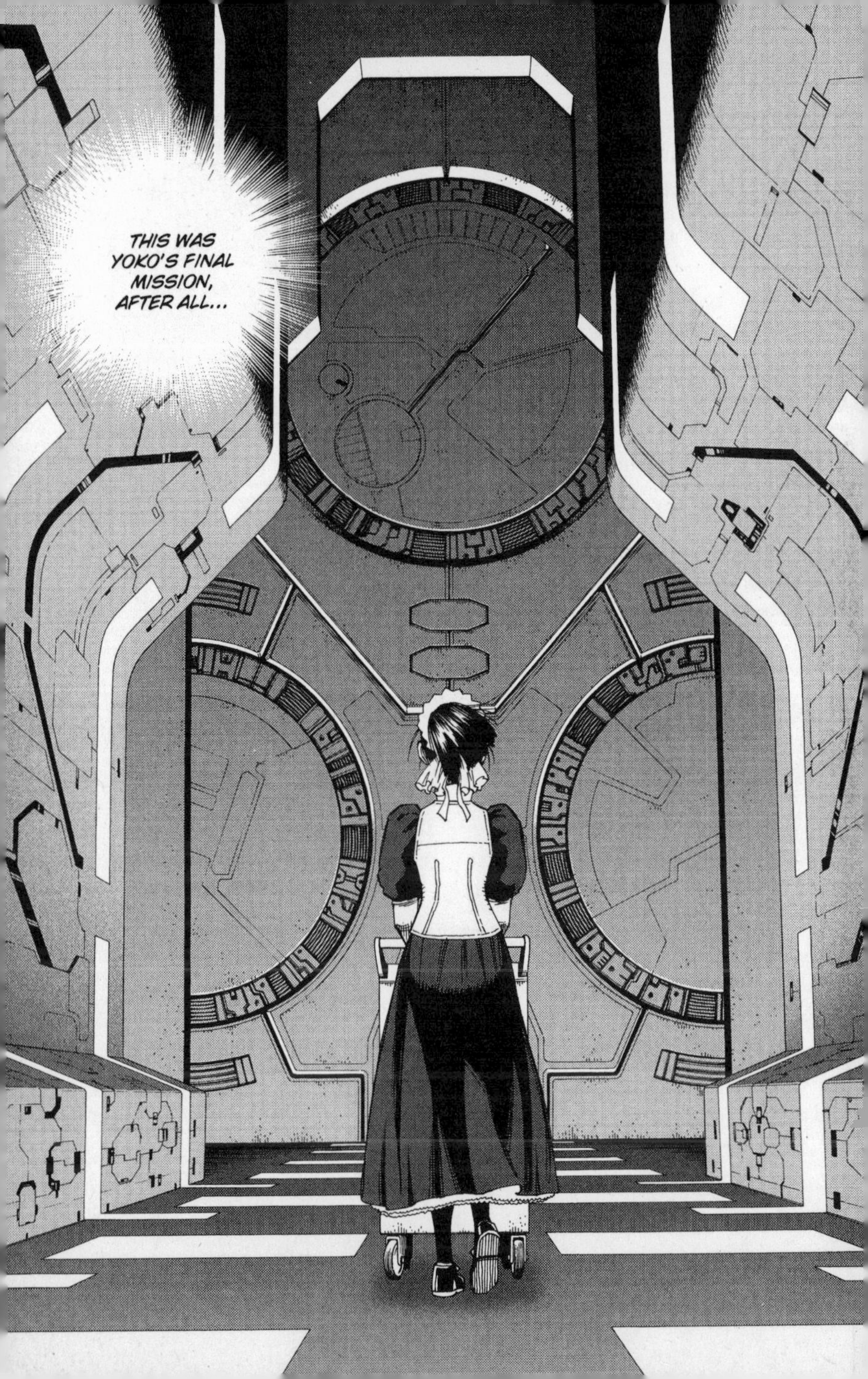
THIS WAS YOKO'S FINAL MISSION, AFTER ALL...

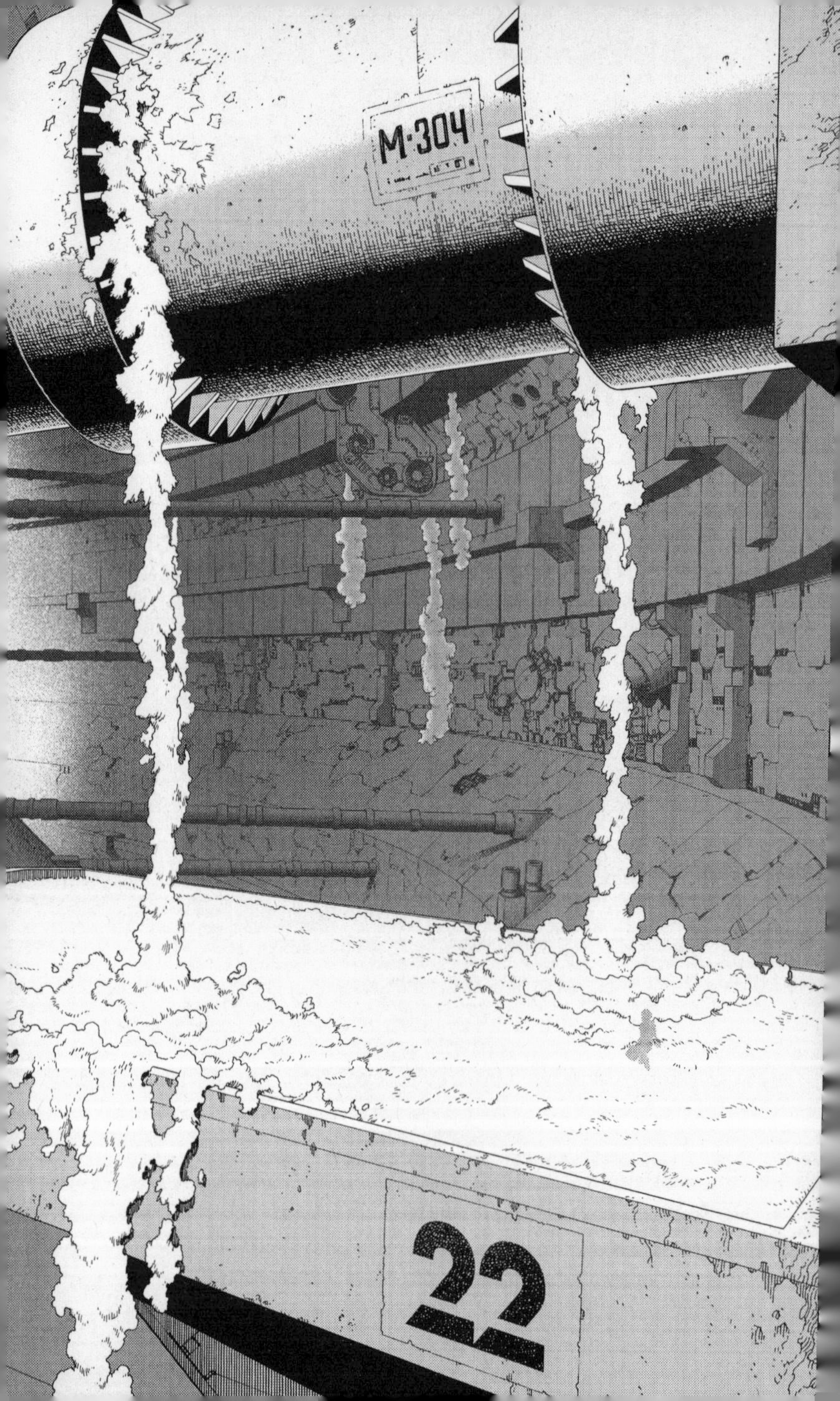
M·304
22

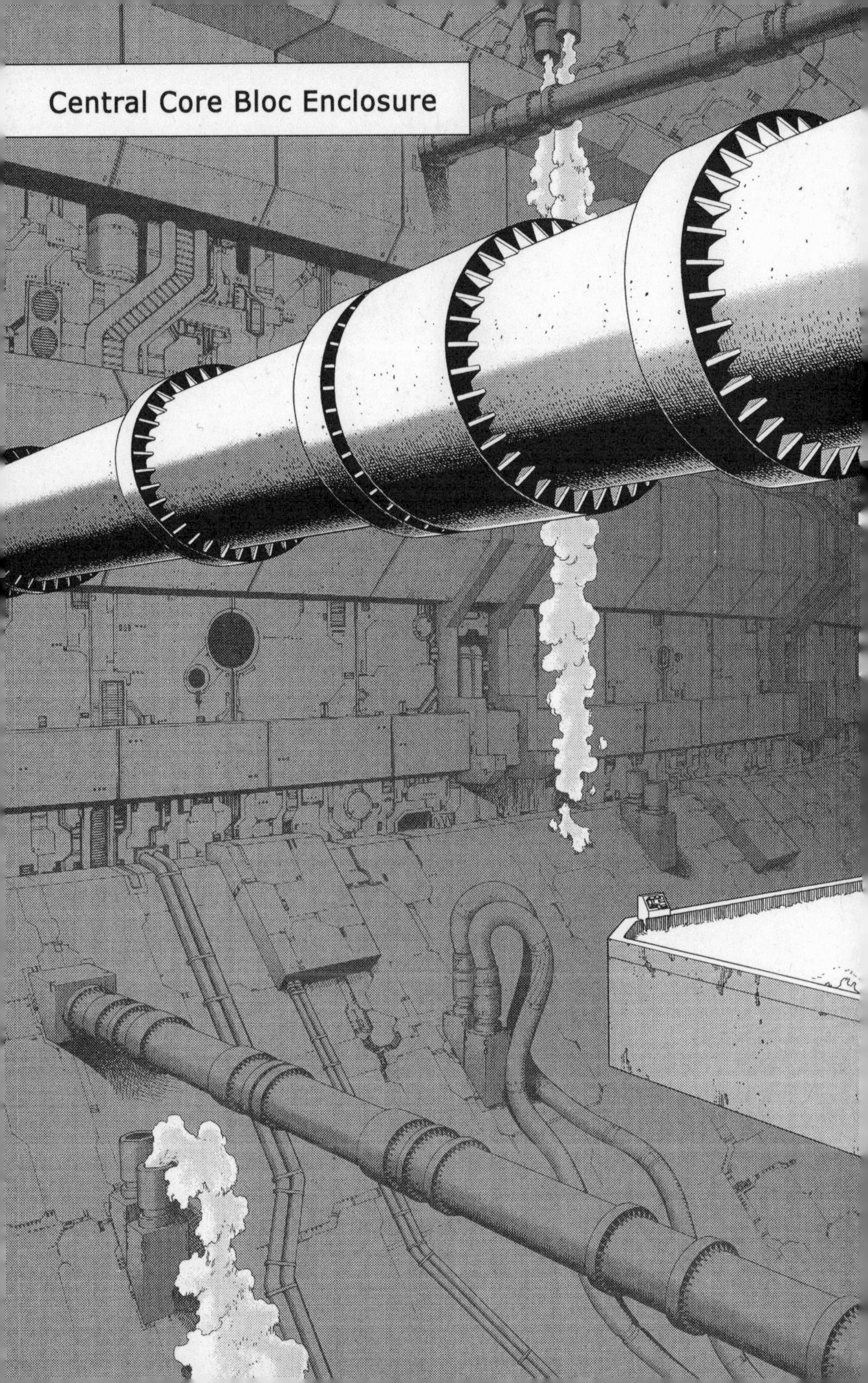
Central Core Bloc Enclosure

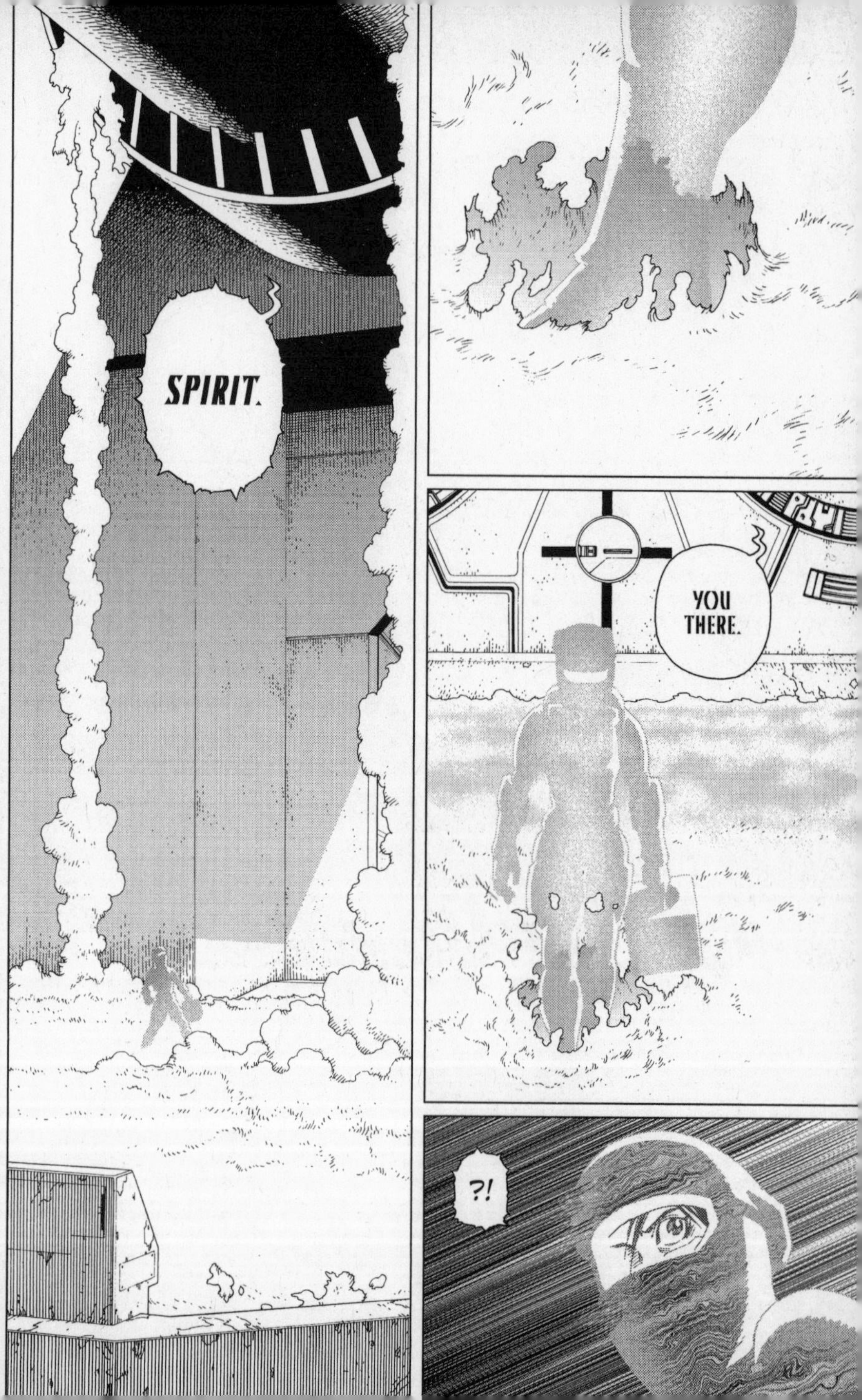
YOU THERE.
?!
SPIRIT.

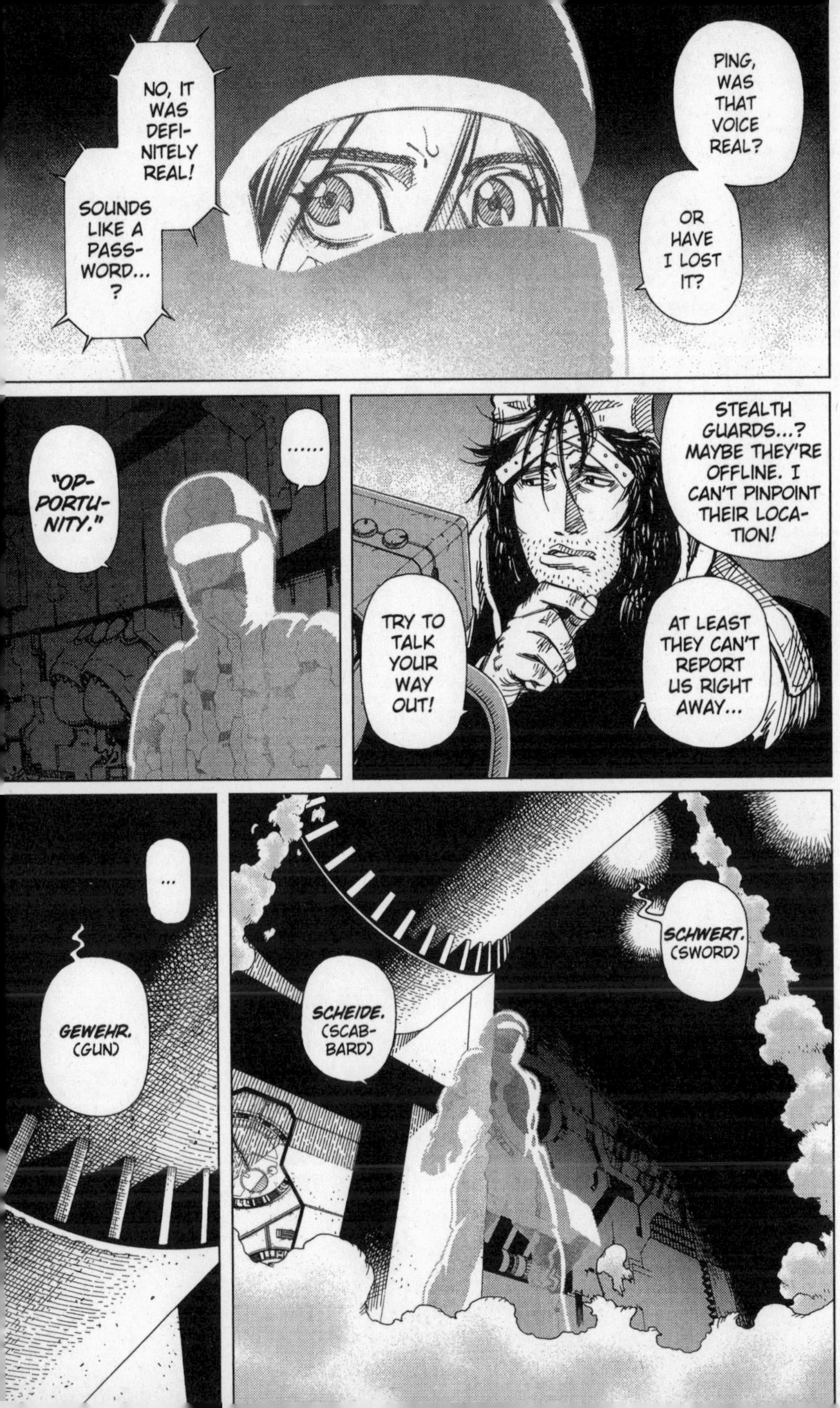
PING, WAS THAT VOICE REAL?
OR HAVE I LOST IT?
NO, IT WAS DEFINITELY REAL! SOUNDS LIKE A PASSWORD...?
STEALTH GUARDS...? MAYBE THEY'RE OFFLINE. I CAN'T PINPOINT THEIR LOCATION!
AT LEAST THEY CAN'T REPORT US RIGHT AWAY...
TRY TO TALK YOUR WAY OUT!
......
"OPPORTUNITY."
SCHWERT. (SWORD)
SCHEIDE. (SCABBARD)
...
GEWEHR. (GUN)

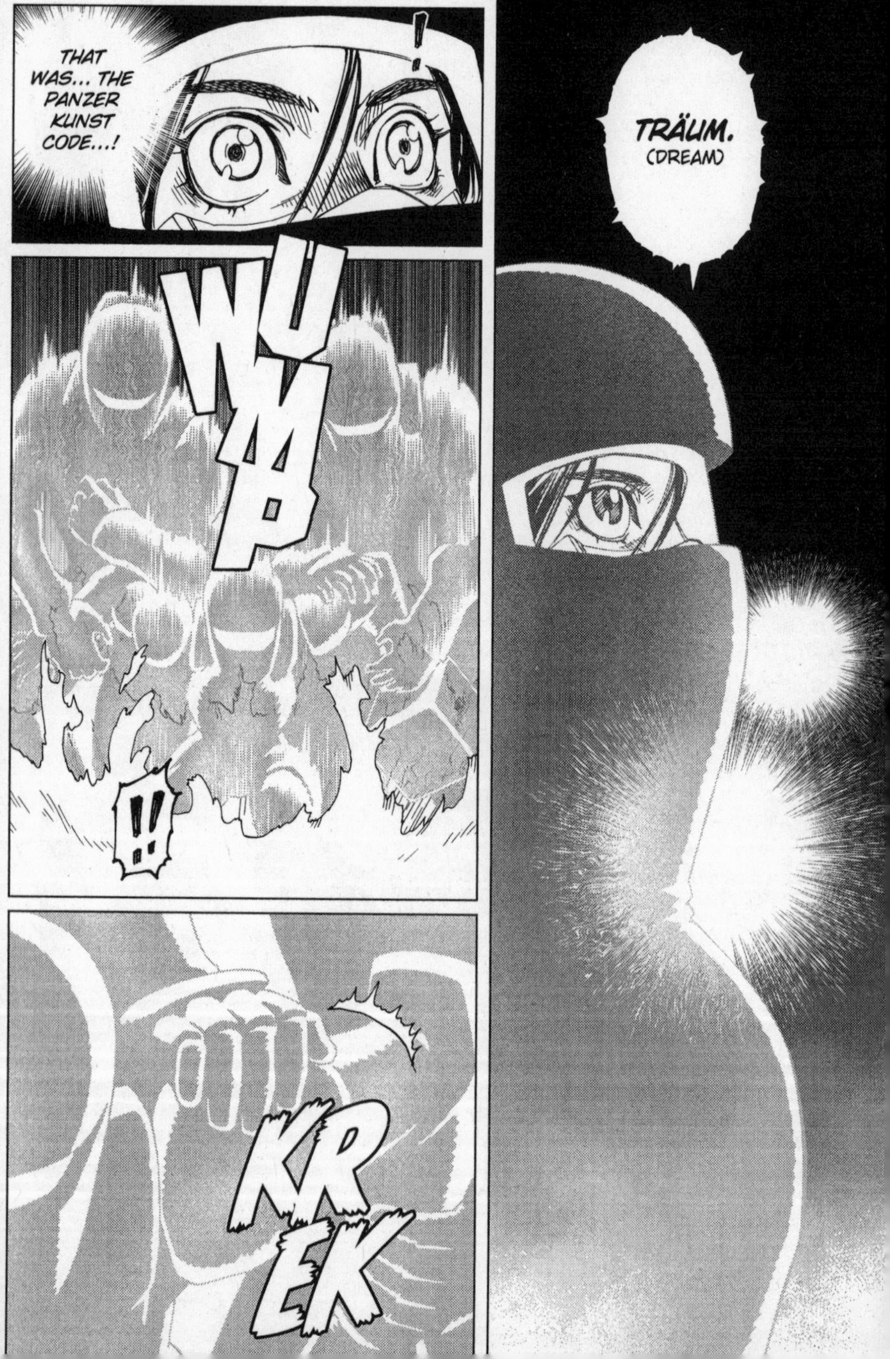
TRÄUM.
(DREAM)
THAT WAS... THE PANZER KUNST CODE...!
!
WUMP
!!
KREK

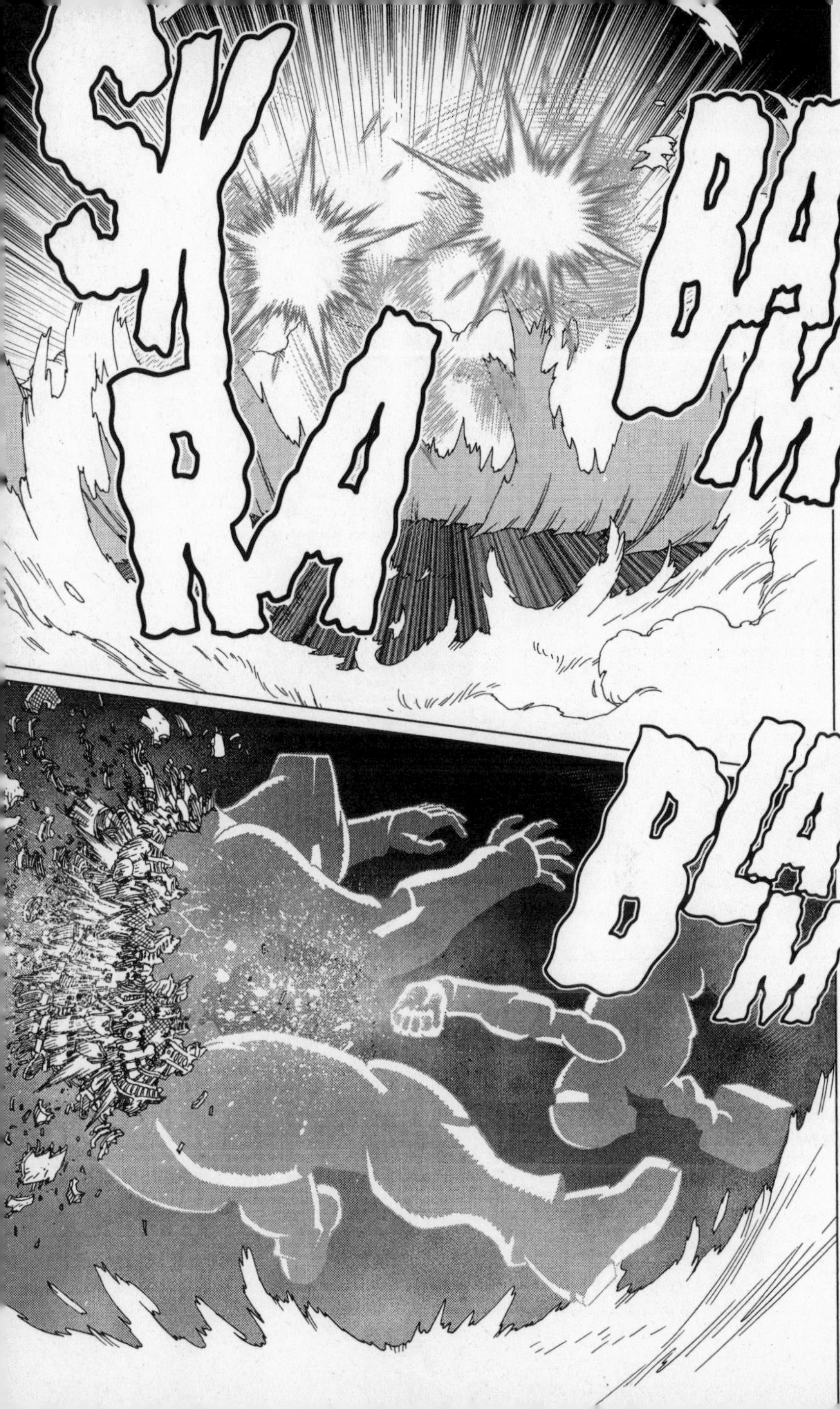
BAM
SKRA
BLAM

BA M

ZA SH

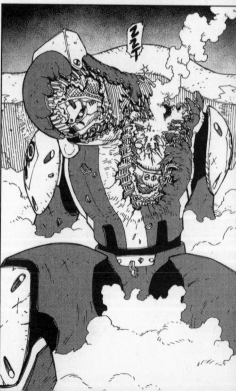

ZZZT

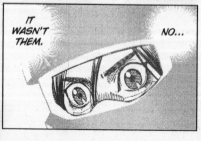

IT WASN'T THEM.

NO...

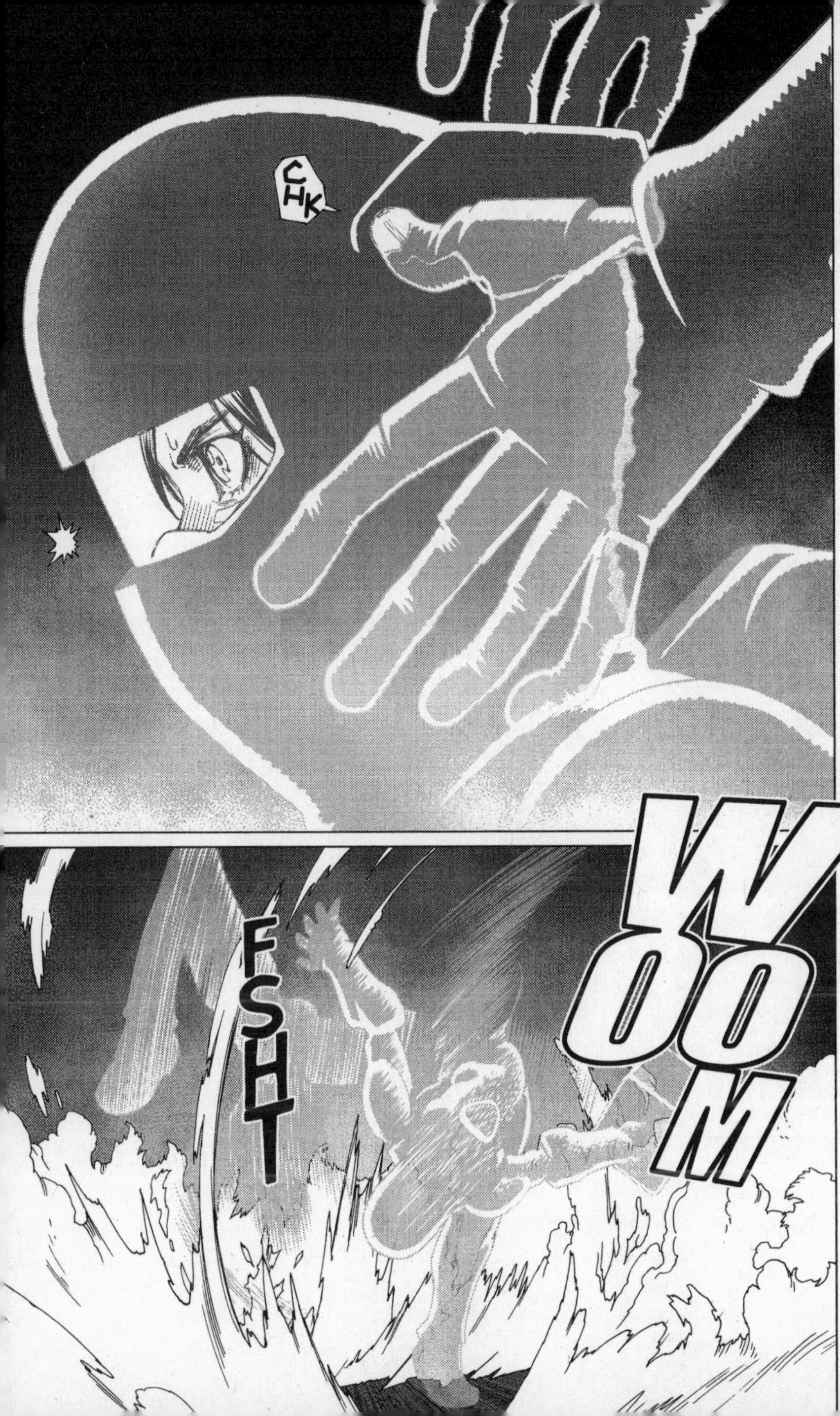
CHK
WOOOM
FSHT

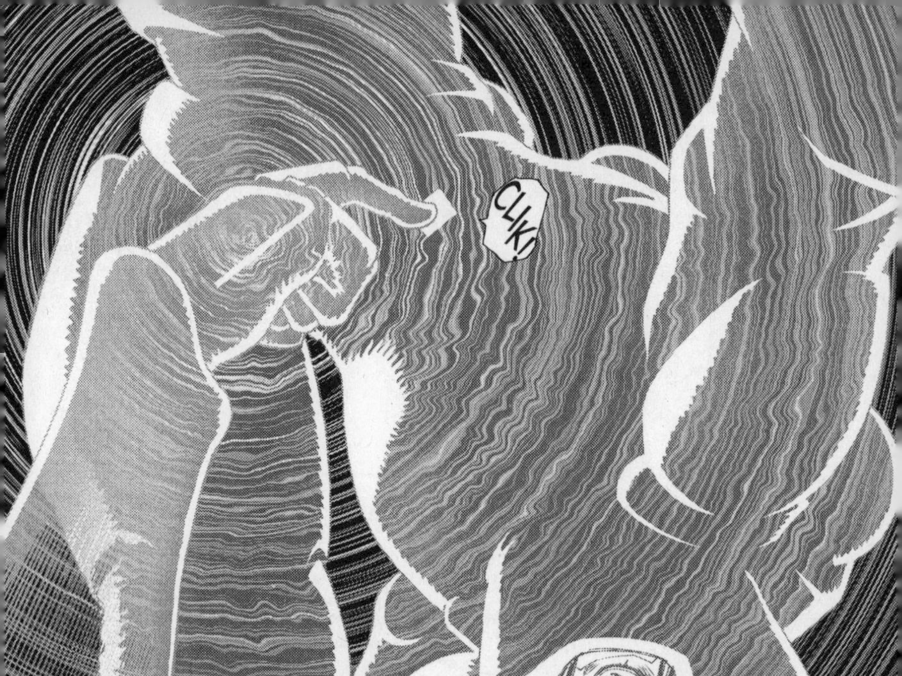
CLIK!
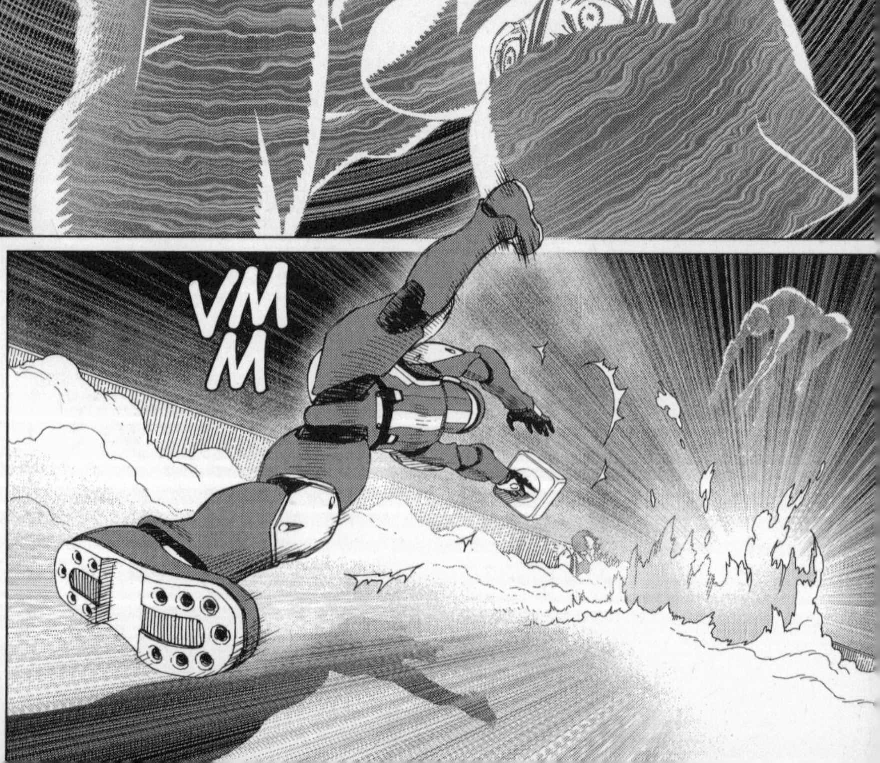
VMM

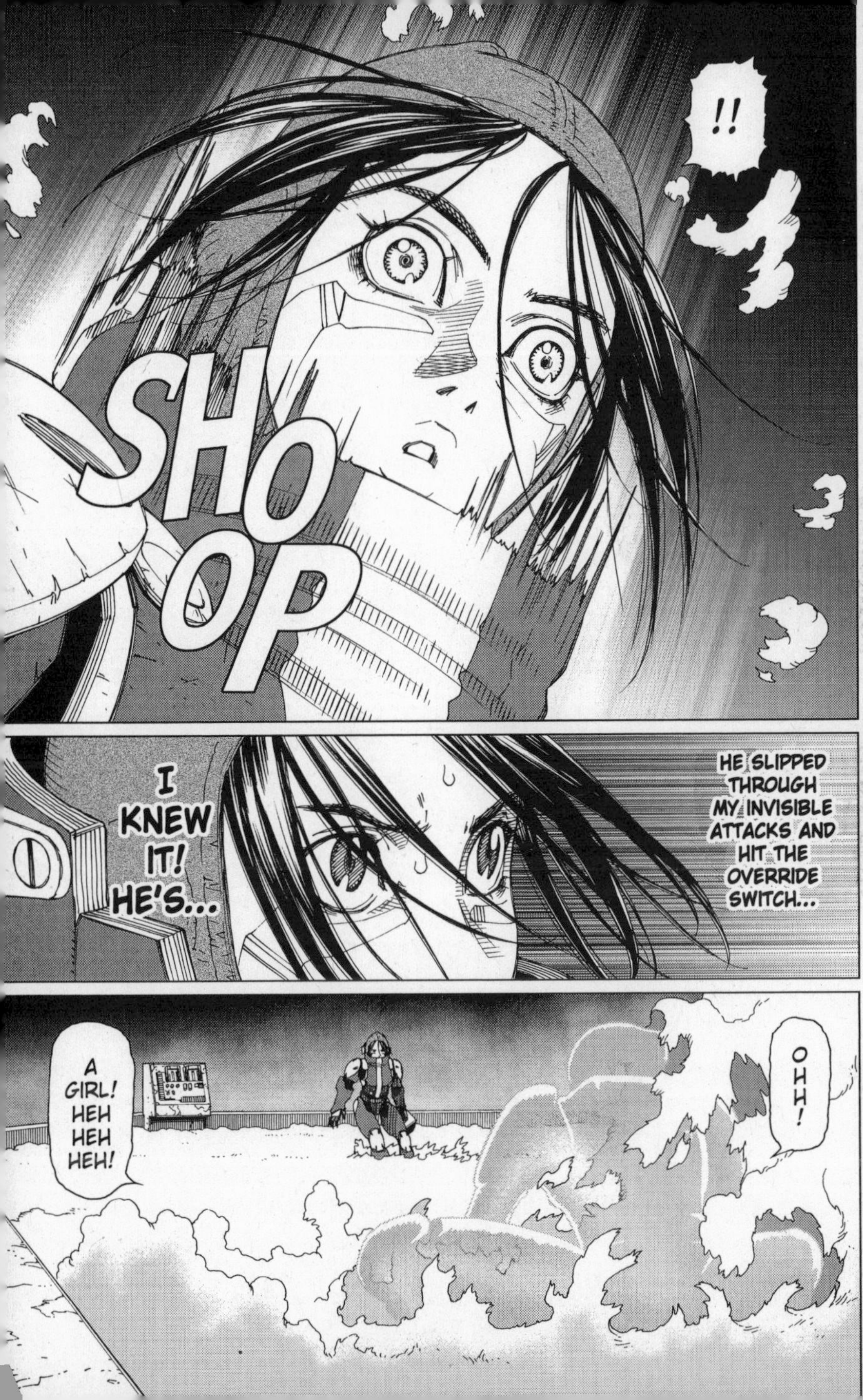
!!
SHOOP
HE SLIPPED THROUGH MY INVISIBLE ATTACKS AND HIT THE OVERRIDE SWITCH...
I KNEW IT! HE'S...
OHH!
A GIRL! HEH HEH HEH!

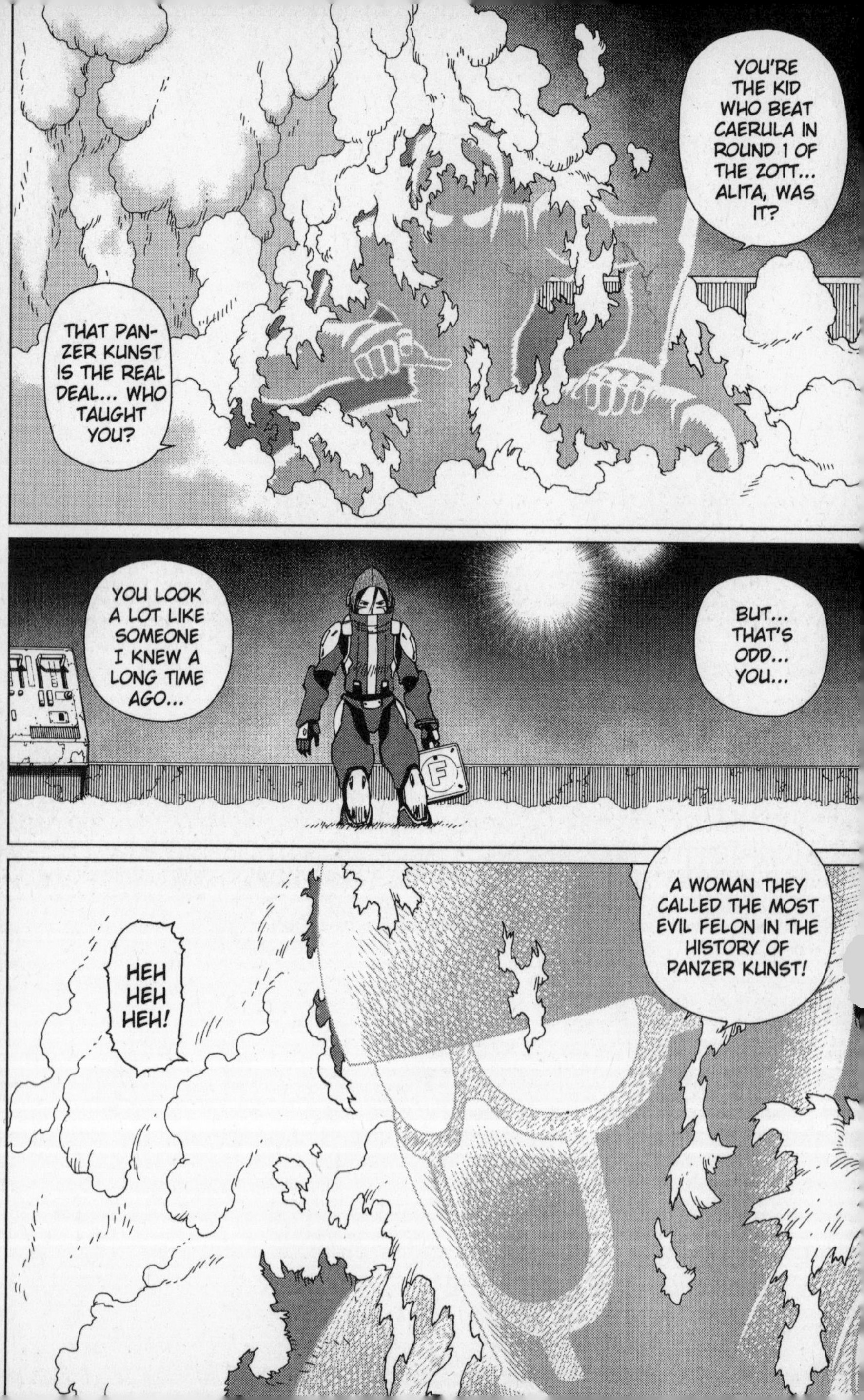
YOU'RE THE KID WHO BEAT CAERULA IN ROUND 1 OF THE ZOTT... ALITA, WAS IT?
THAT PAN-ZER KUNST IS THE REAL DEAL... WHO TAUGHT YOU?
BUT... THAT'S ODD... YOU...
YOU LOOK A LOT LIKE SOMEONE I KNEW A LONG TIME AGO...
A WOMAN THEY CALLED THE MOST EVIL FELON IN THE HISTORY OF PANZER KUNST!
HEH HEH HEH!

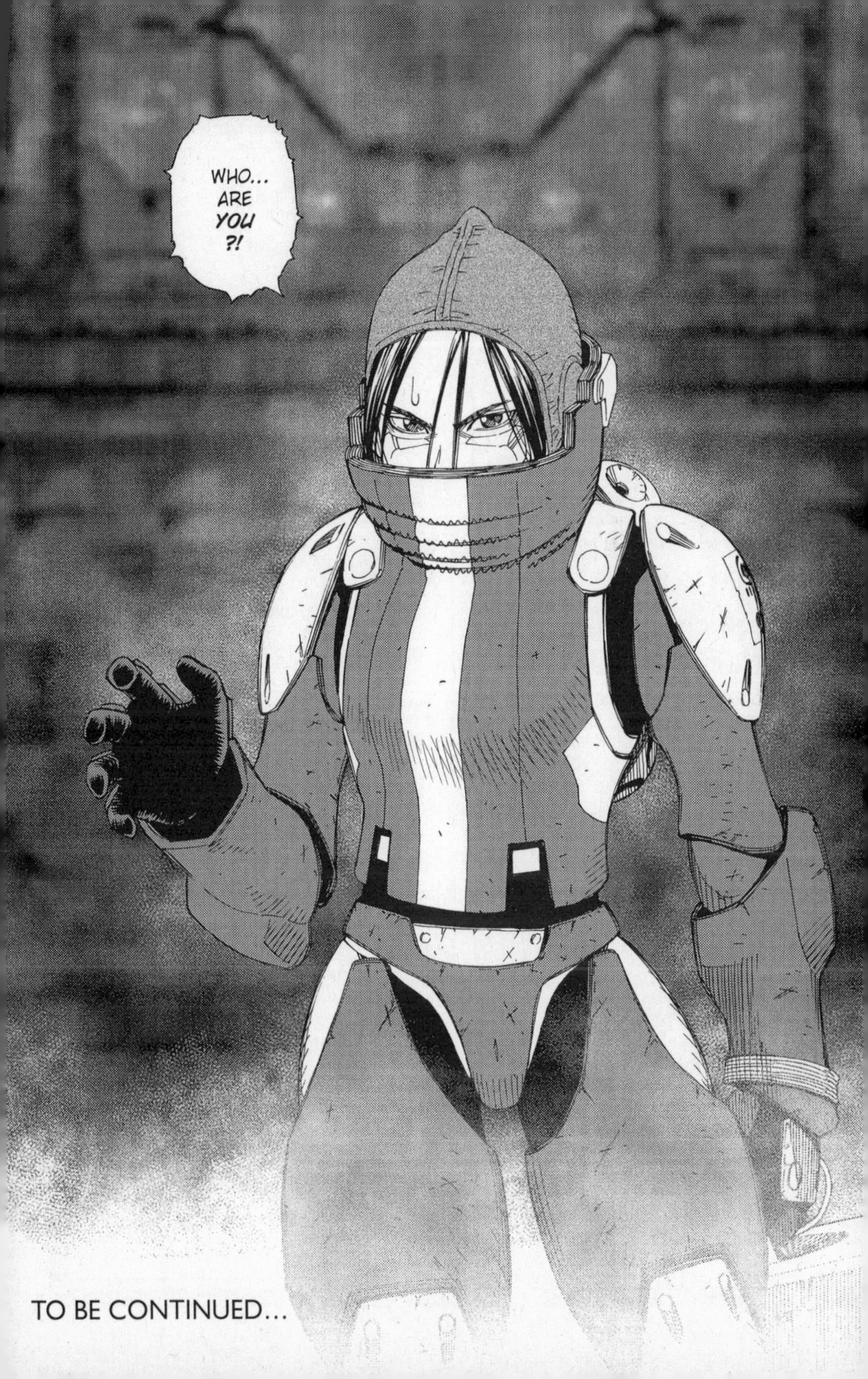
WHO... ARE YOU ?!
TO BE CONTINUED...

NG Theater

The Match That Never Happened! Part 1

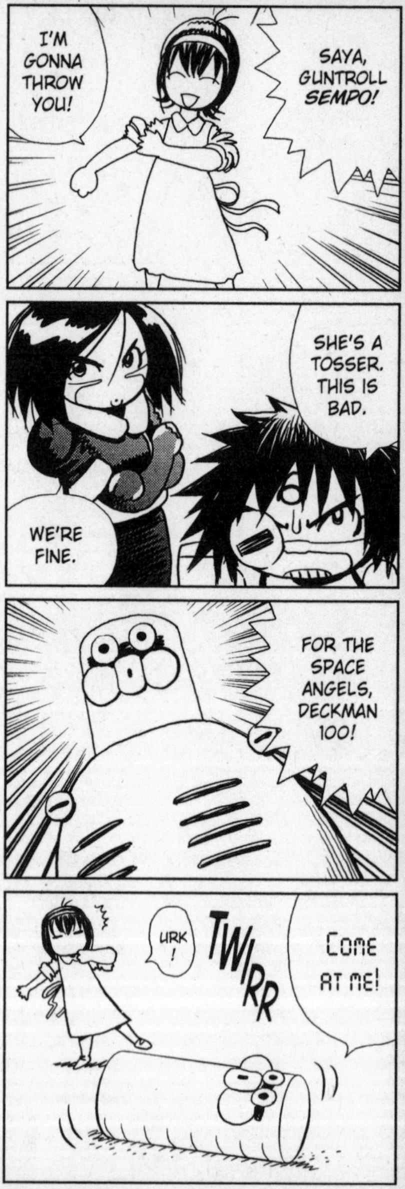
SAYA, GUNTROLL SEMPO!
I'M GONNA THROW YOU!
SHE'S A TOSSER. THIS IS BAD.
WE'RE FINE.
FOR THE SPACE ANGELS, DECKMAN 100!
COME AT ME!
TWIRR
URK!

The Match That Never Happened! Part 2

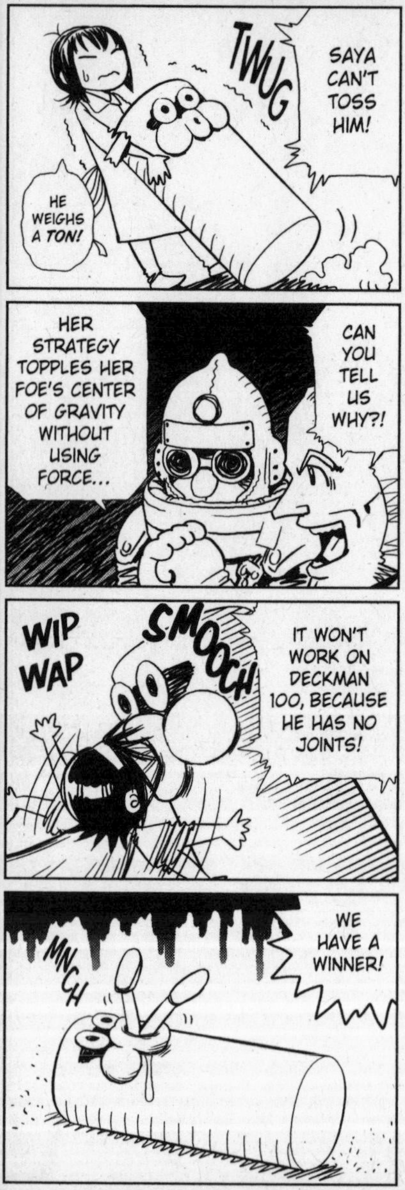
SAYA CAN'T TOSS HIM!
TWUG
HE WEIGHS A TON!
CAN YOU TELL US WHY?!
HER STRATEGY TOPPLES HER FOE'S CENTER OF GRAVITY WITHOUT USING FORCE...
IT WON'T WORK ON DECKMAN 100, BECAUSE HE HAS NO JOINTS!
SMOOCH
WIP WAP
WE HAVE A WINNER!
MNCH

Presenting "Not Good" episodes that, due to plot changes, couldn't be used in the main story!

NG Theater

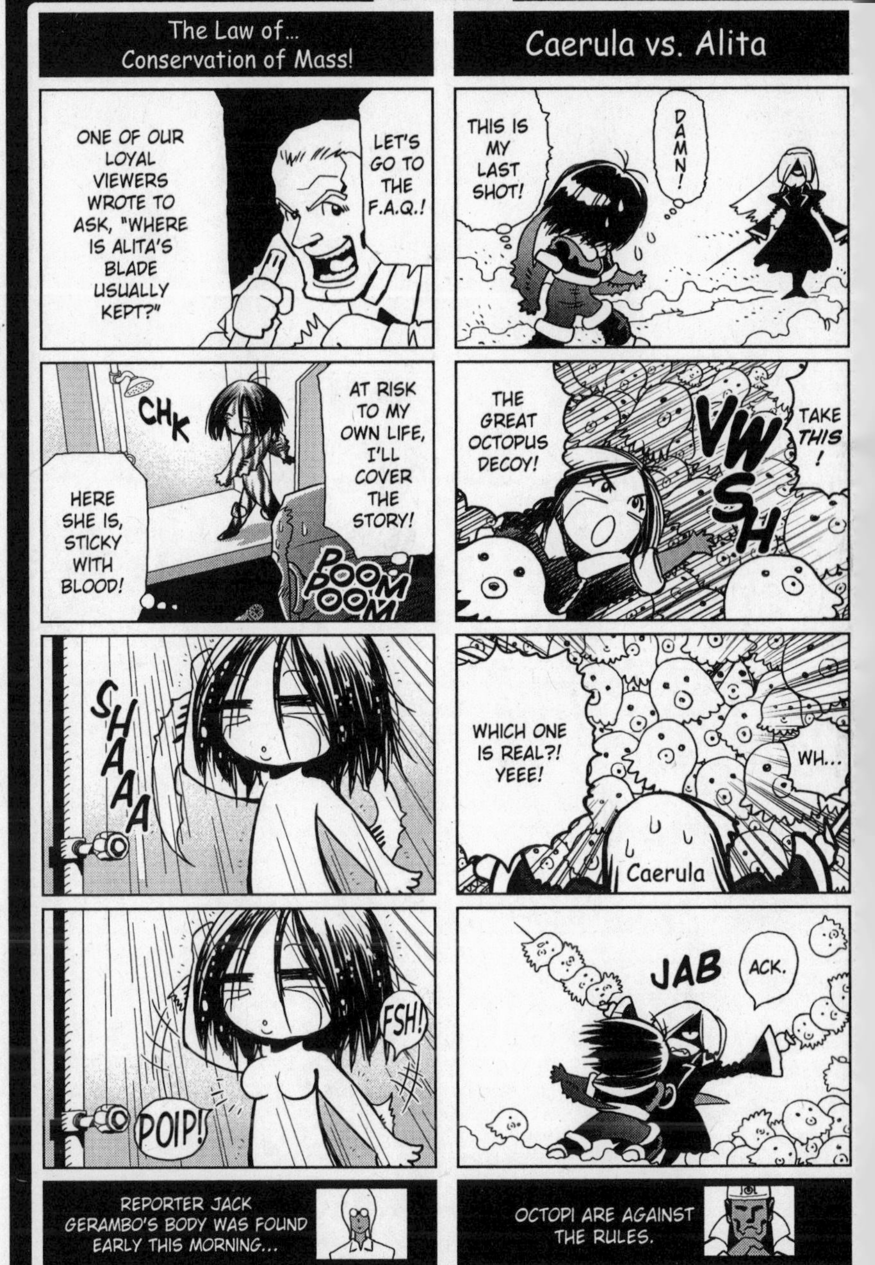
Caerula vs. Alita
DAMN!
THIS IS MY LAST SHOT!
TAKE THIS!
VWSH
THE GREAT OCTOPUS DECOY!
WH...
WHICH ONE IS REAL?! YEEE!
Caerula
ACK.
JAB
OCTOPI ARE AGAINST THE RULES.
The Law of... Conservation of Mass!
LET'S GO TO THE F.A.Q.!
ONE OF OUR LOYAL VIEWERS WROTE TO ASK, "WHERE IS ALITA'S BLADE USUALLY KEPT?"
AT RISK TO MY OWN LIFE, I'LL COVER THE STORY!
CHK
HERE SHE IS, STICKY WITH BLOOD!
POOM POOM
SHAAAA
FSH!
POIP!
REPORTER JACK GERAMBO'S BODY WAS FOUND EARLY THIS MORNING...

These strips are outtakes and have no relation to existing characters or events. Maybe.

NG Theater

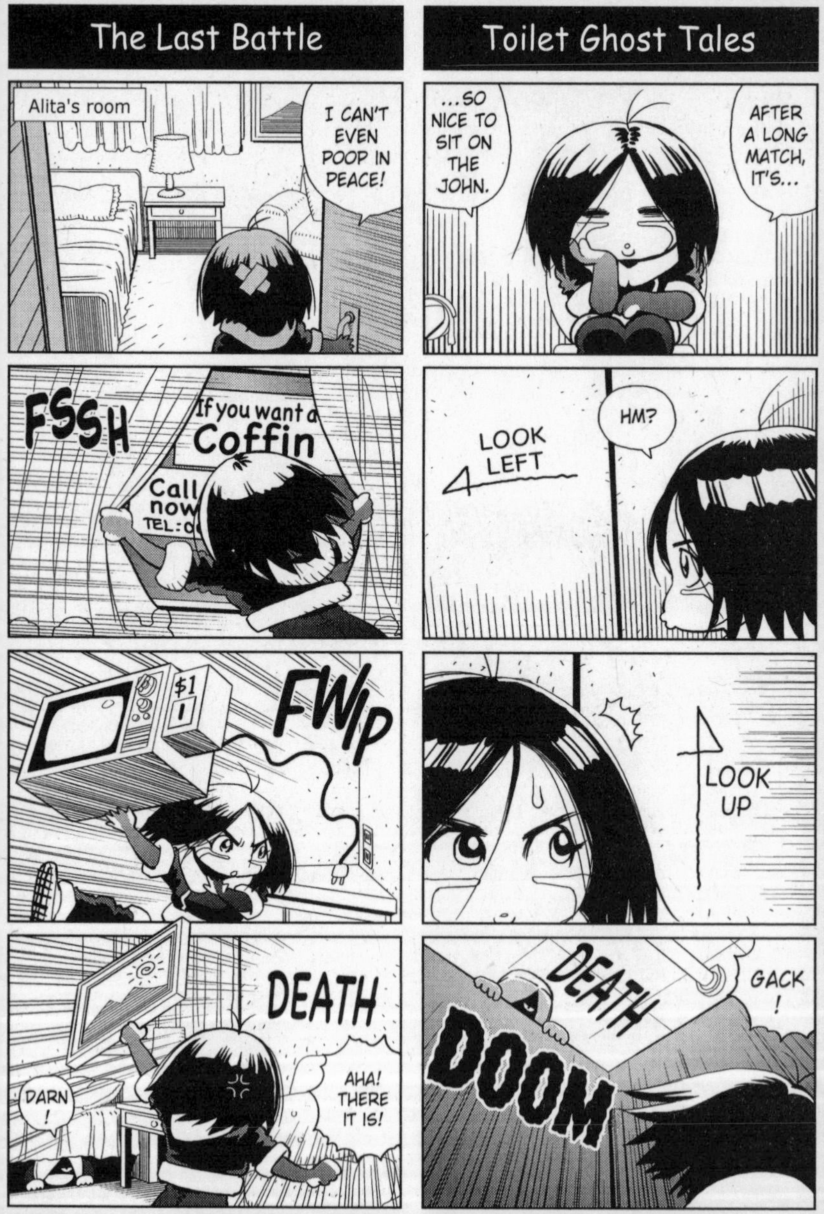
Toilet Ghost Tales
AFTER A LONG MATCH, IT'S...
...SO NICE TO SIT ON THE JOHN.
HM?
LOOK LEFT
LOOK UP
GACK!
DEATH
DOOM
THAT'S YOUR DEATH GATE!
GAH!
The Last Battle
I CAN'T EVEN POOP IN PEACE!
Alita's room
FSSH
If you want a
Coffin
Call now
TEL:
FWIP
$1
DEATH
AHA! THERE IT IS!
DARN!
YOUR DEATH GATE IS DEFEATED!
GAH!

New terrors for Alita! Next time: "The Blood Red Vest"!

Name Reference

When ***Battle Angel Alita*** was first published in the United States, its translators decided to change many of the names of characters and places to make them more accessible to American readers. We at Kodansha have chosen to keep most of those changes, but we will provide the original names as well in this section.

Battle Angel Alita, Alita:

The Japanese title of the original ***Alita*** series is ***Ganmu*** (which Kishiro spells ***Gunnm***), a unique portmanteau of "gun" and the Japanese word for "dream." The protagonist's name in the original Japanese is Garii, which can be spelled "Gally" in English. When the original ***Gunnm*** was first localized in English in 1995, Viz Media decided to change the name of the main character to Alita, and the series to ***Battle Angel Alita***. The original title of this series is ***Gunnm: Last Order***. Alita's other name, Yoko, is a common Japanese name meaning "sun child" (or "yang child") that happens to be written the same way as the word for proton.

銃夢 GUNNM Last Order NEW EDITION

Presented by Yukito Kishiro

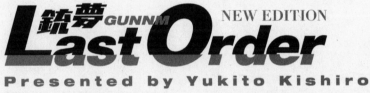

The logo from the Kodansha Japan edition, upon which this volume is based.

Tiphares, Ketheres:

The city in space and the city in the sky, linked by the orbital elevator, were renamed Ketheres and Tiphares for the first American release. These names were references to the Jewish mystical tradition known as Kabbalah. The original Japanese names were Yeeru and Zaaremu, or Jeru and Salem, an obvious reference to the historic Earthbound city.

New Characters

Friend or enemy! Young or old! Man or woman! Create unique minor characters!

New Costumes

The protagonist Alita will wear the new costumes you've thought up!

Last Order NEW Characters! NEW Costumes! Made by YOU!

New Costumes that we've used so far

Last Order: Phase 19-

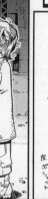

"Cold-weather jacket" Shizumen-san, Saitama Prefecture

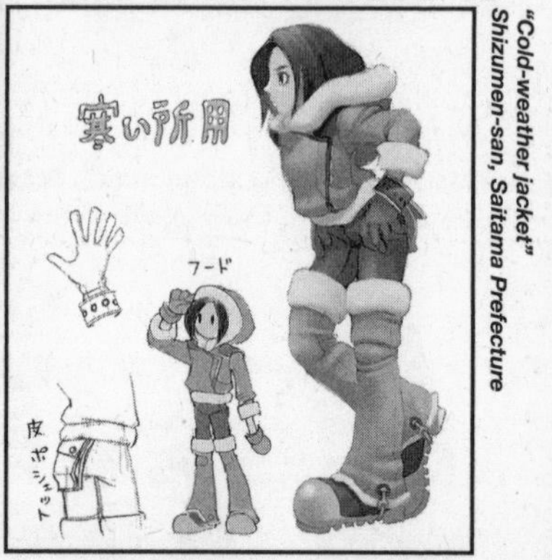
寒い所用
フード
皮

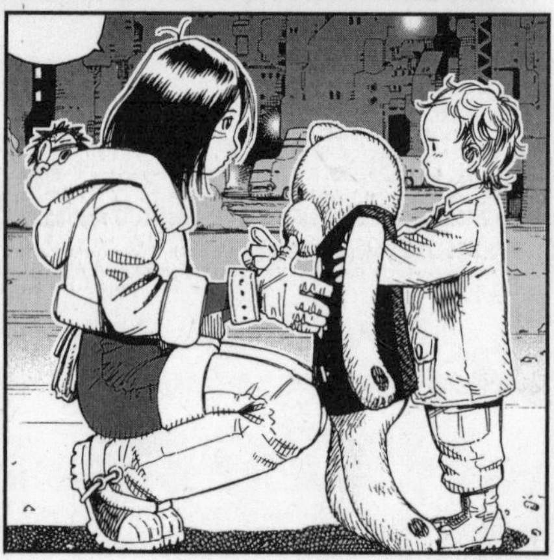

New Characters that we've used so far

Last Order: Phase 21-

"DEATH"
Hyakkimaru-san, Tokyo

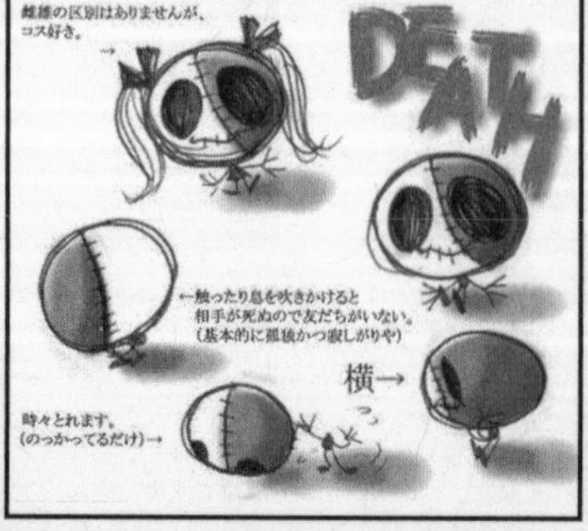
雌雄の区別はありませんが、コス好き。
DEATH
←触ったり息を吹きかけると相手が死ぬので友だちがいない。（基本的に孤独かつ寂しがりや）
横→
時々とれます。（のっかってるだけ）→

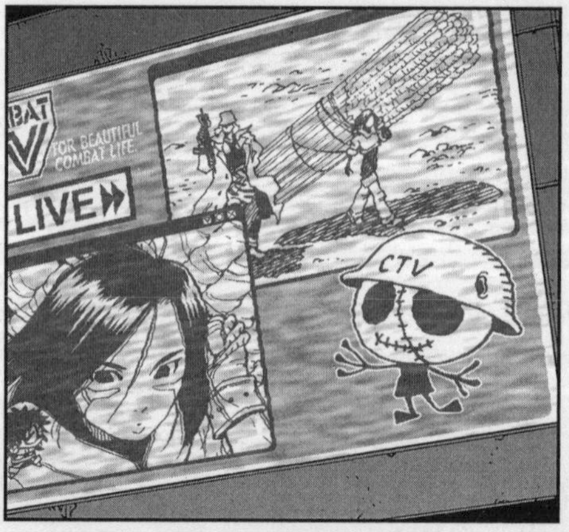
FOR BEAUTIFUL COMBAT LIFE.
LIVE
CTV

New Characters that we've used so far

Last Order: Phase 26-

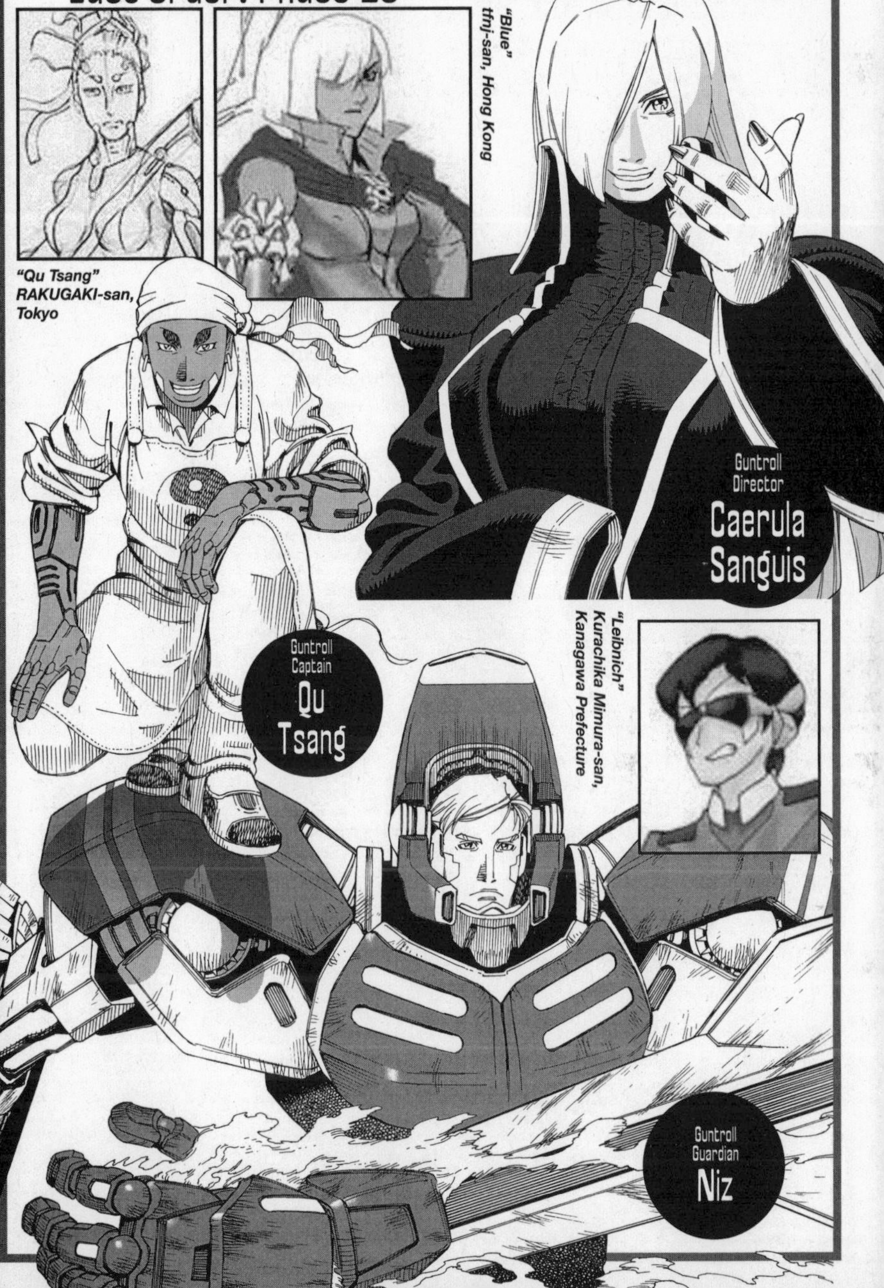
"Blue"
tfnj-san, Hong Kong
Guntroll Director
Caerula Sanguis
"Leibnich"
Kurachika Mimura-san,
Kanagawa Prefecture
"Qu Tsang"
RAKUGAKI-san,
Tokyo
Guntroll Captain
Qu Tsang
Guntroll Guardian
Niz

New Characters that we've used so far

Last Order: Phase 26-

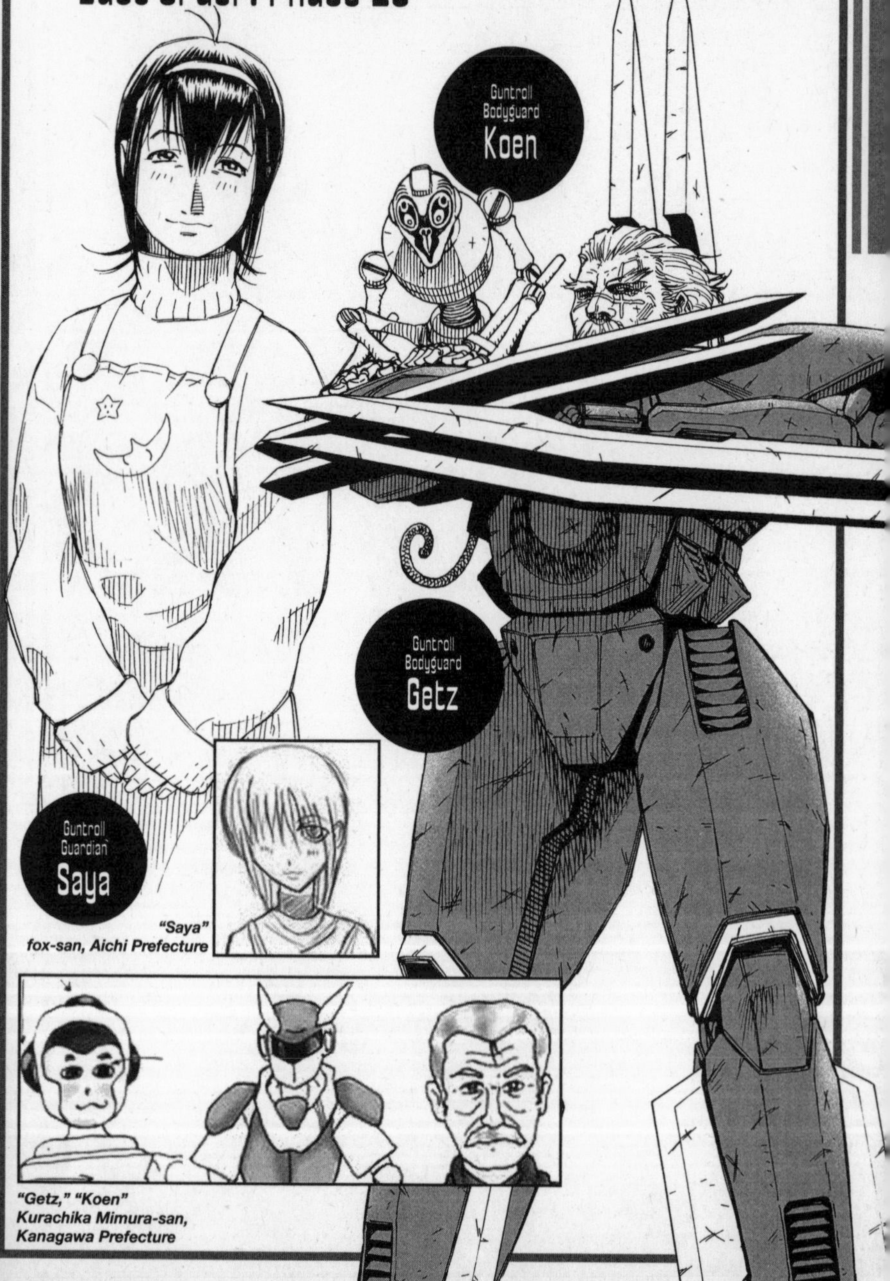
Guntroll Bodyguard Koen
Guntroll Bodyguard Getz
Guntroll Guardian Saya

"Saya"
fox-san, Aichi Prefecture

"Getz," "Koen"
Kurachika Mimura-san, Kanagawa Prefecture

New Characters that we've used so far

Last Order: Phase 26-

LADDER
Special Forces
Soldier

"Solar system riot cop"
Uguisu-san,
Nara Prefecture

Last Order: Phase 35-

"Yanni"
Meshidoki-san, Tokyo

He has a protruding forehead, reinforced by an implant, and he gives good head butts.

"Derossi"
Mimura Kurachika-san,
Kanagawa Prefecture

Machinist cyborg whose hobbies are building live steam locos and collecting retro things.

Assistant
Derossi

Cyber-tech
Yanni

Send your entries to:
Yukito Kishiro, Kodansha Comics
451 Park Ave. South, 7th floor
New York, NY 10016
publicity@kodansha-usa.com

Send your entries on paper or postcard. Originals drawn with marker, ink, pen, or other medium (no pencil please), or copies accepted.

Include your name, address, nickname, the title of your work and any comments.

If you would like your name and address kept private, please let us know.

Received works will be kept for a limited time, then destroyed. They cannot be returned, so if you would like to retain a copy, please make one before sending.

Battle Angel Alita: Last Order Translation Notes

Battle Angel Alita: Last Order refers to many esoteric scientifric concepts that Mr. Kishiro is only too eager to explain in his thorough footnotes, but that doesn't mean there aren't still nuances in the original Japanese that might be tough to put into English. In this section, we'll discuss some of those translation decisions.

Sempo/jiho, page 282:

The Japanese word for "vanguard," ***sempo*** also refers to the first member of a five-member martial arts team. These are usually used in kendo or judo team competitions, though in these the five warriors spar one-on-one, not in a free-for-all as in the ZOTT. The second warrior is the ***jiho***, which means, literally,
"next weapon."

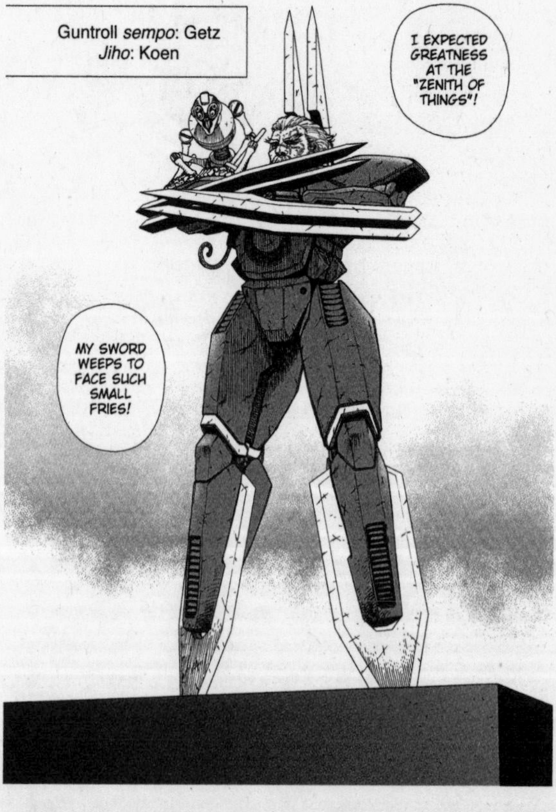
Guntroll *sempo*: Getz
Jiho: Koen
I EXPECTED GREATNESS AT THE "ZENITH OF THINGS"!
MY SWORD WEEPS TO FACE SUCH SMALL FRIES!

Chuken/fukusho, page 323:

The next two warriors, in order, are the *chuken* (literally "main force") and the fukusho, or "second-in-command." The final warrior (Caerula Sanguis for Guntroll) is the *taisho*, or "general."

...BUT NOW YOU'LL HAVE TO FIGHT *US!*

Guntroll *chuken*: Niz
Fukusho: Qu Tsang

Cover Gallery

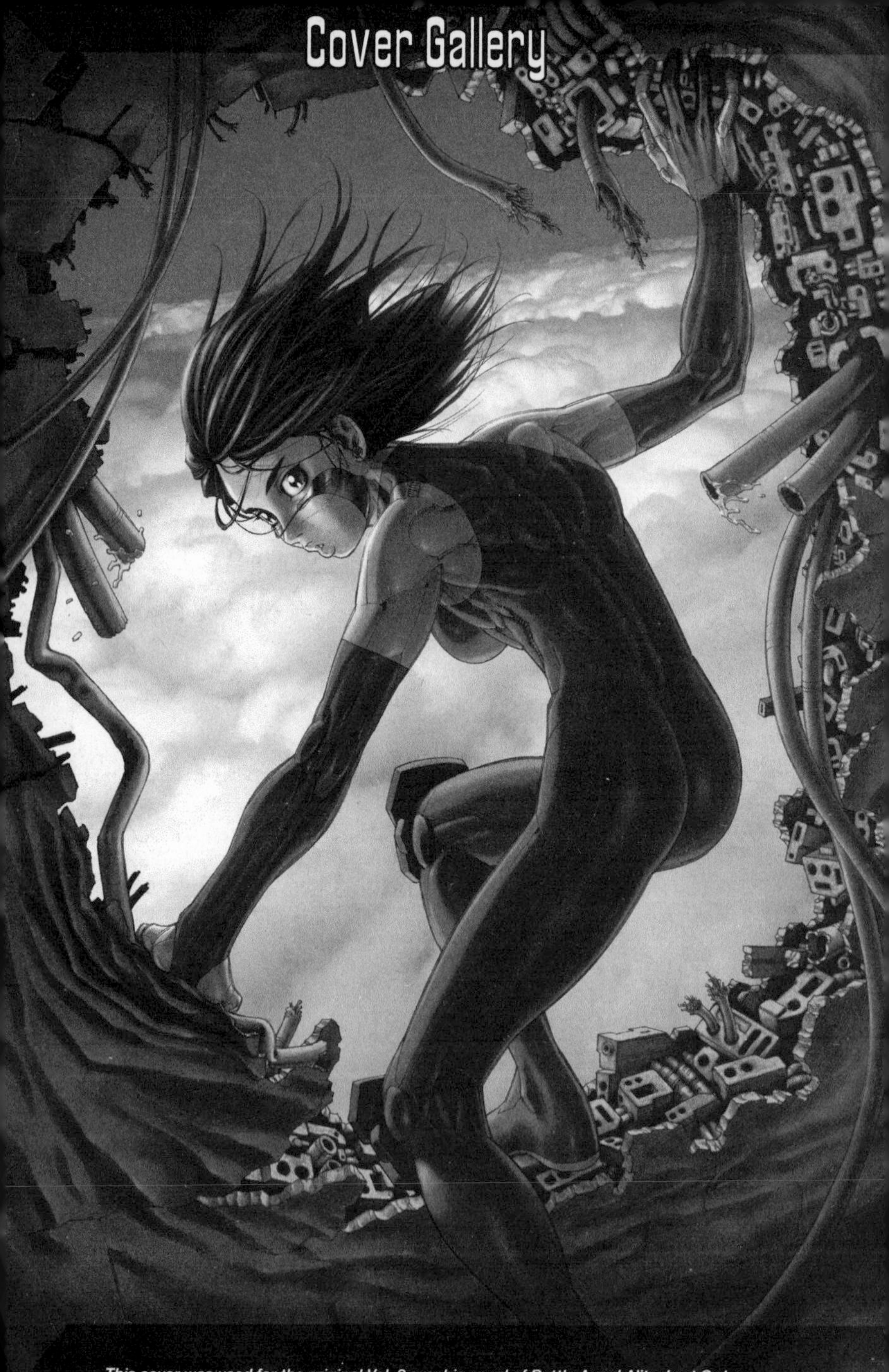

This cover was used for the original Vol. 2 graphic novel of Battle Angel Alita: Last Order.

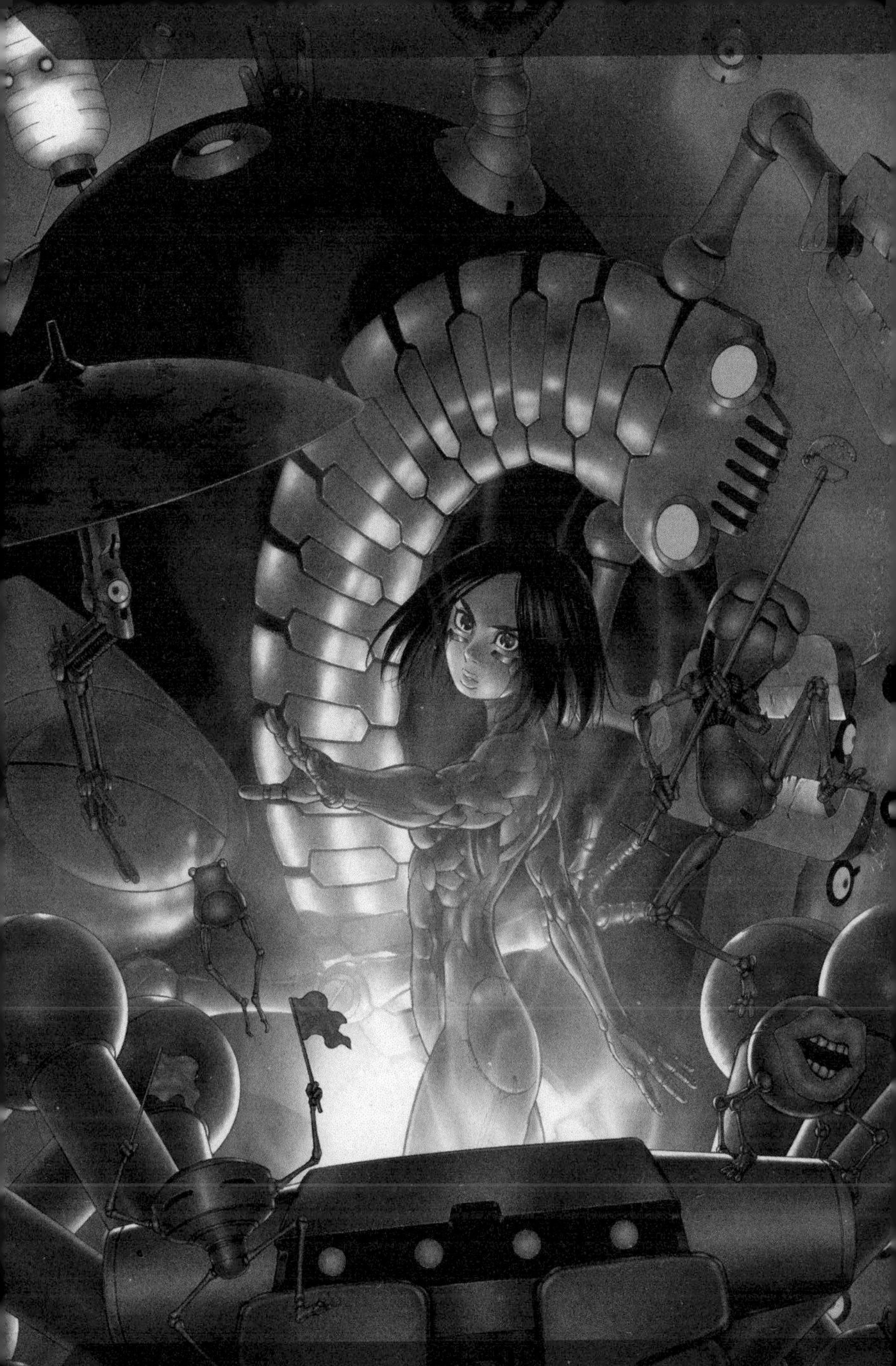

This cover was used for the original Vol. 3 graphic novel of Battle Angel Alita: Last Order.

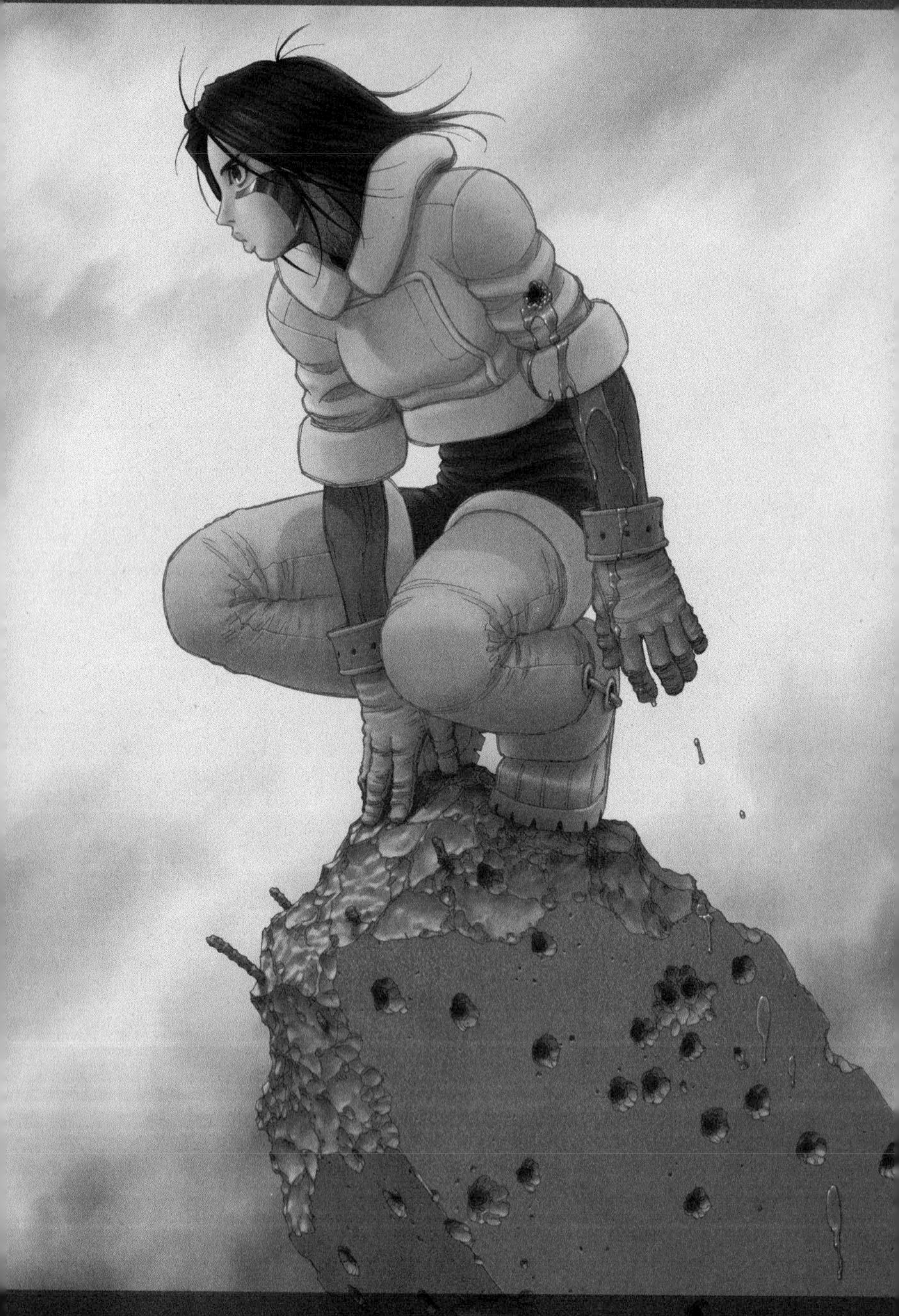

This cover was used for the original Vol. 4 graphic novel of Battle Angel Alita: Last Order.

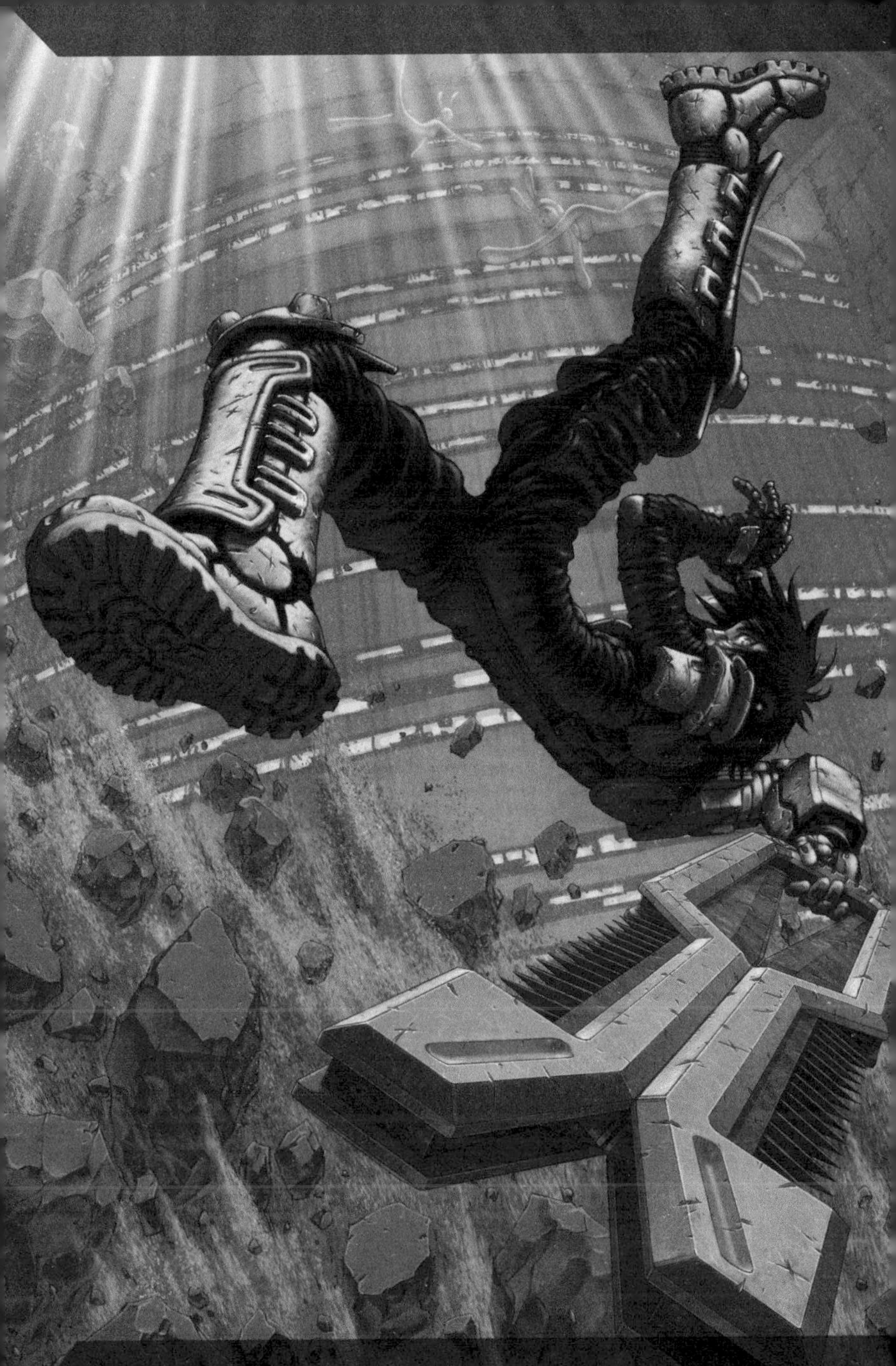

This cover was used for the original Vol. 5 graphic novel of Battle Angel Alita: Last Order.

Bonus Manga

Kodansha Comics is pleased to bring you two early short stories by Yukito Kishiro never before published in English. "Planet of Depths" ("*Kaiyousei*") originally appeared in the Nov. 9, 1988 issue of the magazine Big Comic Spirits, published by Shogakukan. "Future Tokyo Headman" ("*Mirai Tokyo HEADMAN*") first ran in the Sept. 1, 1991 issue of Weekly Shonen Sunday, also from Shogakukan.

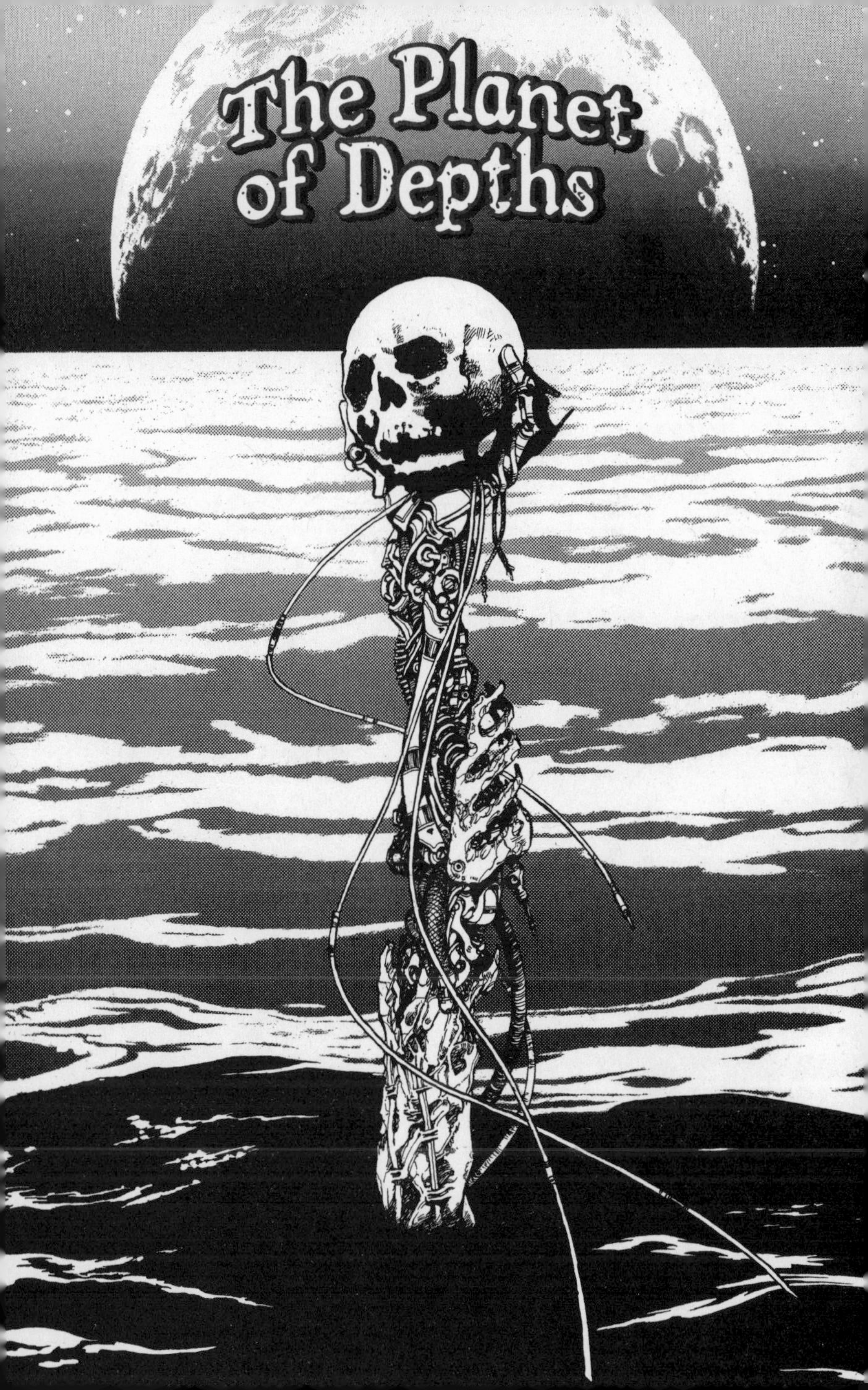
The Planet of Depths

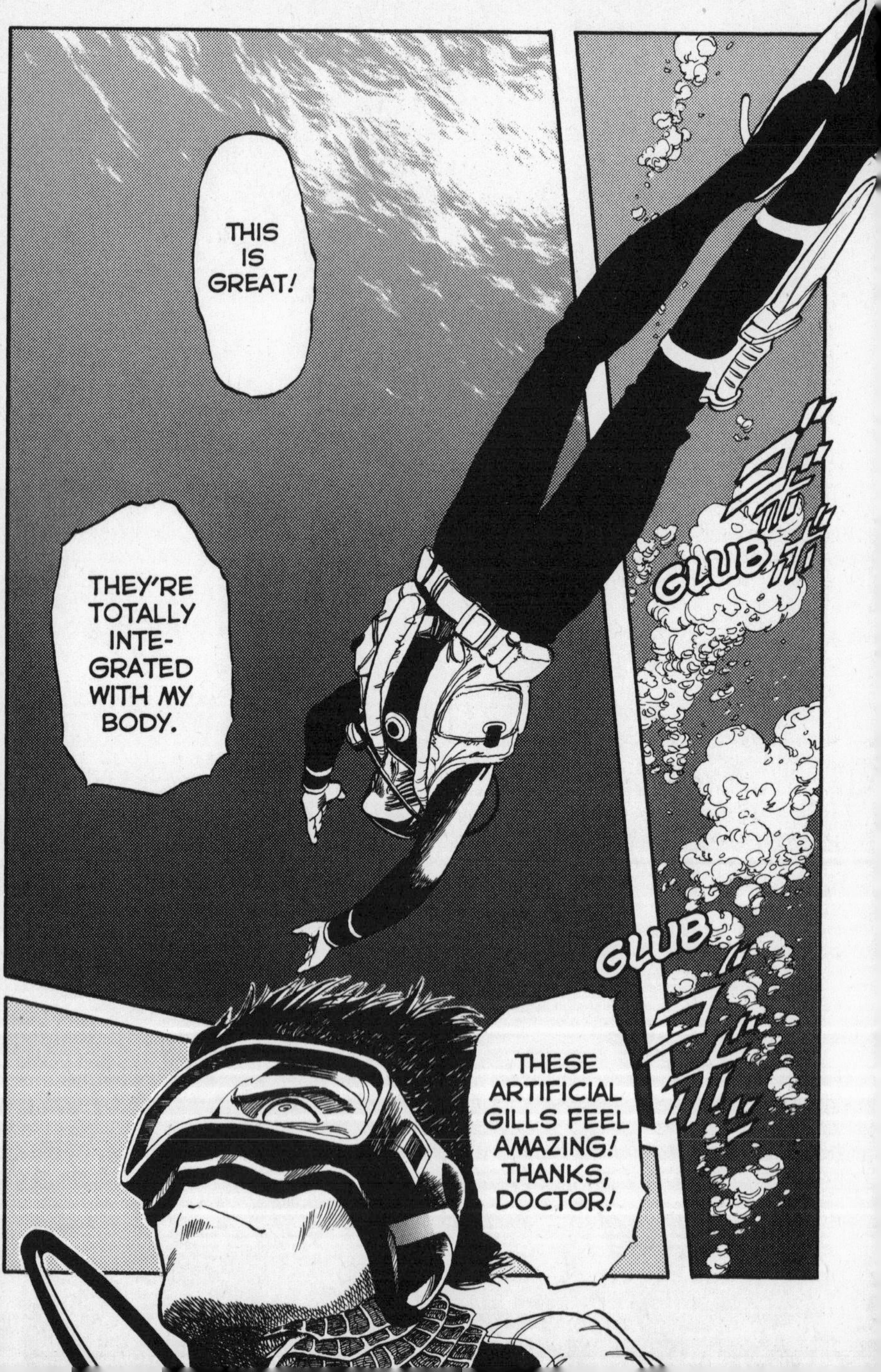
GLUB
GLUB
THIS IS GREAT!
THEY'RE TOTALLY INTE-GRATED WITH MY BODY.
THESE ARTIFICIAL GILLS FEEL AMAZING! THANKS, DOCTOR!

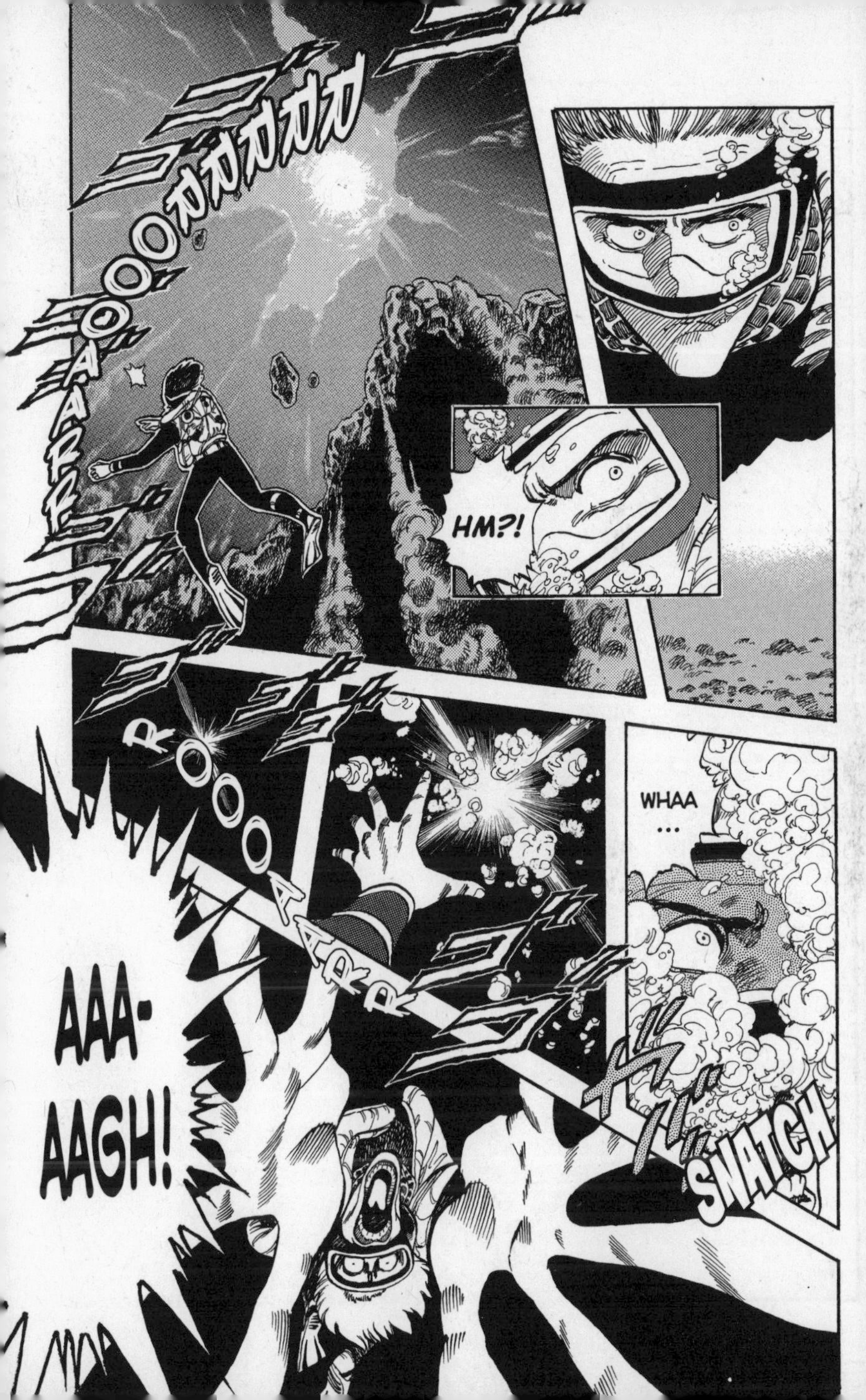

HM?!
ROOOOAARRR
WHAA ...
SNATCH
ROOOOAARR
AAA-AAGH!

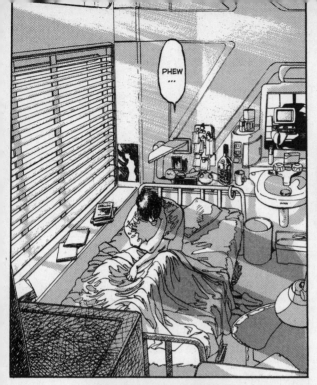

PHEW...

AHH!

HAAAH...

HAH...

THE GILL IMPLANTATION OPERATION WENT SO WELL...

WHAT AM I...?

WHAT AM
I SO
AFRAID
OF...?

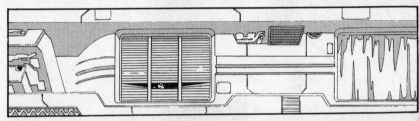

ZZSHHH

601

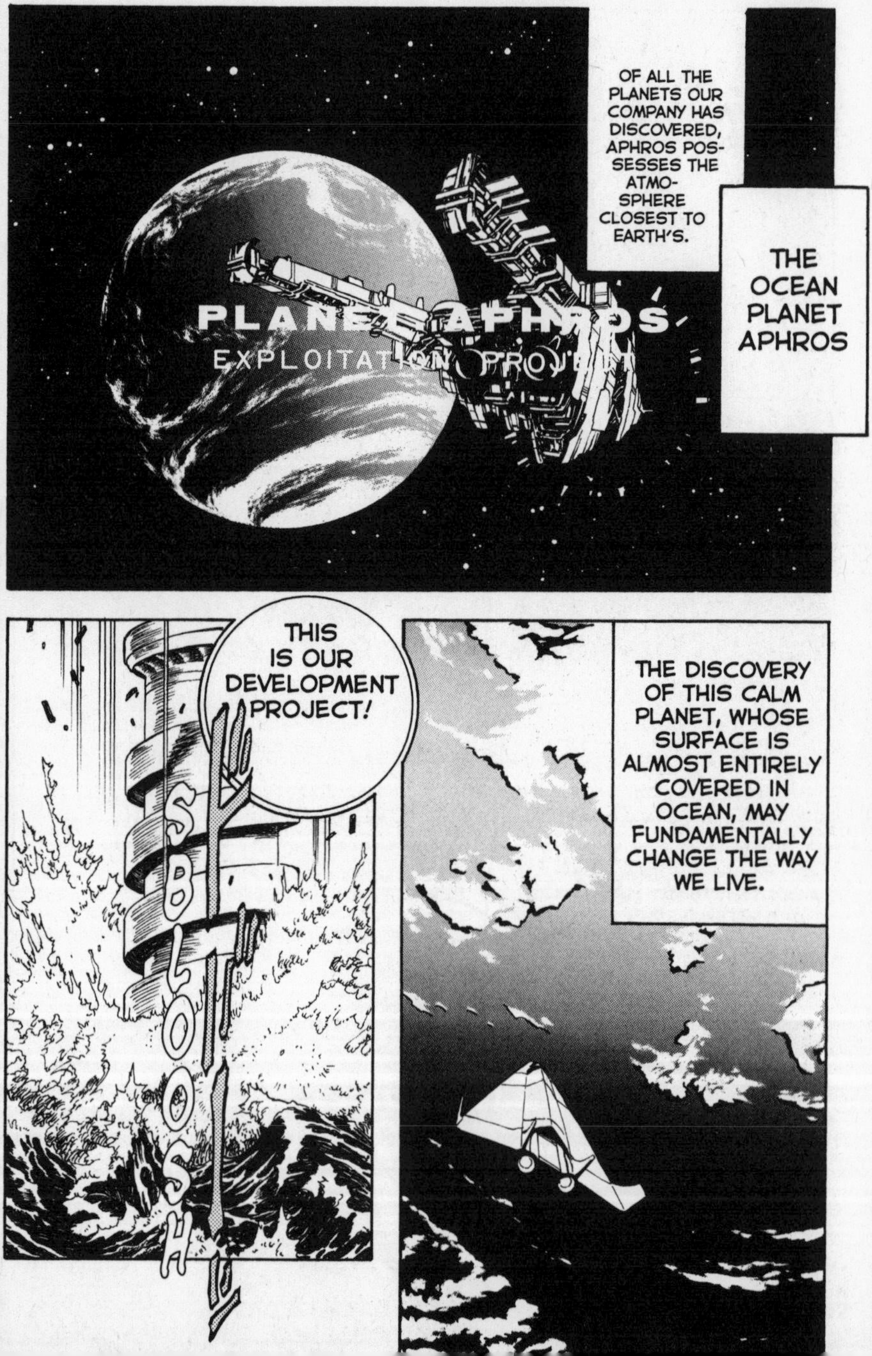
THE OCEAN PLANET APHROS
OF ALL THE PLANETS OUR COMPANY HAS DISCOVERED, APHROS POSSESSES THE ATMOSPHERE CLOSEST TO EARTH'S.
PLANET APHROS
EXPLOITATION PROJECT
THE DISCOVERY OF THIS CALM PLANET, WHOSE SURFACE IS ALMOST ENTIRELY COVERED IN OCEAN, MAY FUNDAMENTALLY CHANGE THE WAY WE LIVE.
THIS IS OUR DEVELOPMENT PROJECT!
SBLOOSH!

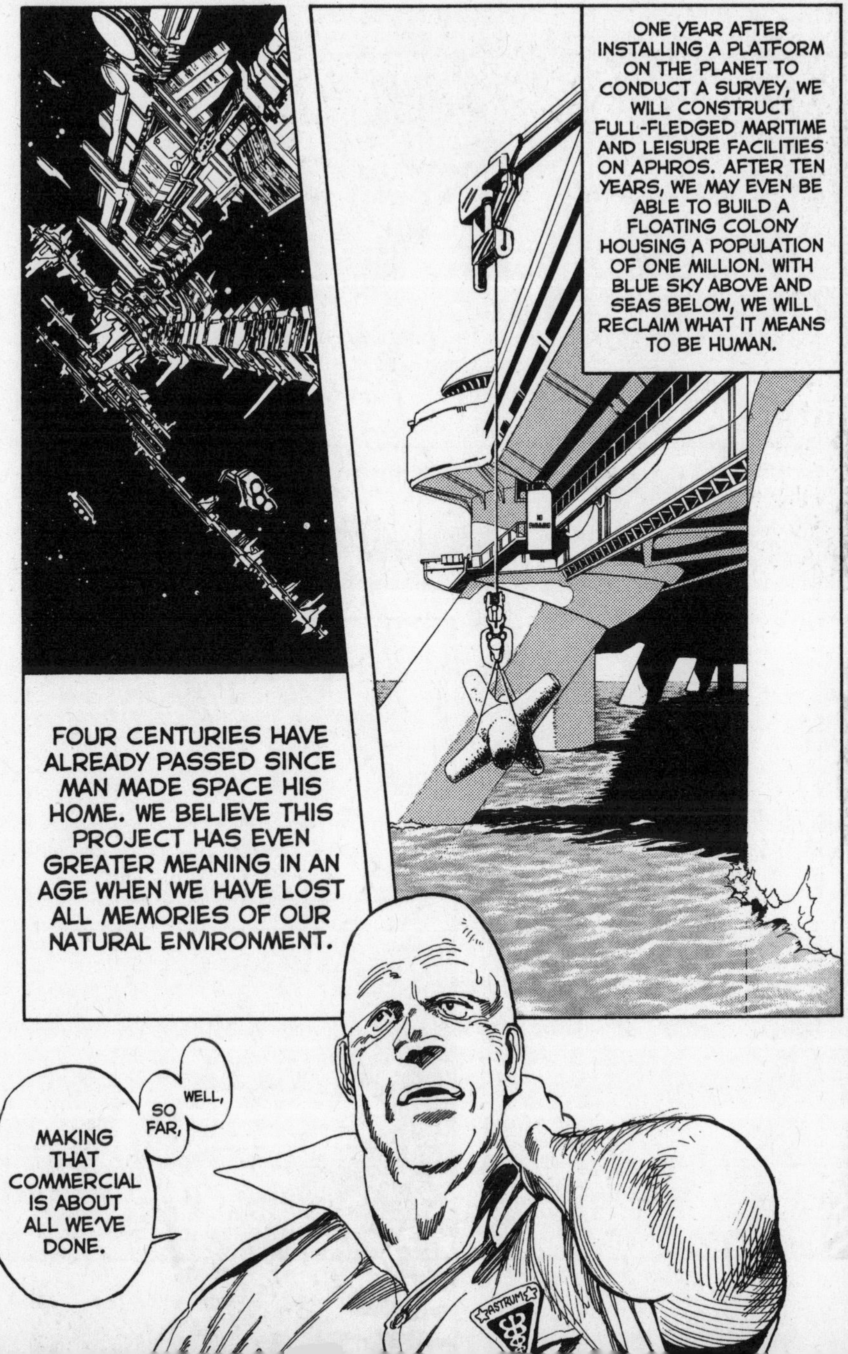
ONE YEAR AFTER INSTALLING A PLATFORM ON THE PLANET TO CONDUCT A SURVEY, WE WILL CONSTRUCT FULL-FLEDGED MARITIME AND LEISURE FACILITIES ON APHROS. AFTER TEN YEARS, WE MAY EVEN BE ABLE TO BUILD A FLOATING COLONY HOUSING A POPULATION OF ONE MILLION. WITH BLUE SKY ABOVE AND SEAS BELOW, WE WILL RECLAIM WHAT IT MEANS TO BE HUMAN.
FOUR CENTURIES HAVE ALREADY PASSED SINCE MAN MADE SPACE HIS HOME. WE BELIEVE THIS PROJECT HAS EVEN GREATER MEANING IN AN AGE WHEN WE HAVE LOST ALL MEMORIES OF OUR NATURAL ENVIRONMENT.
WELL,
SO FAR,
MAKING THAT COMMERCIAL IS ABOUT ALL WE'VE DONE.
ASTRUM

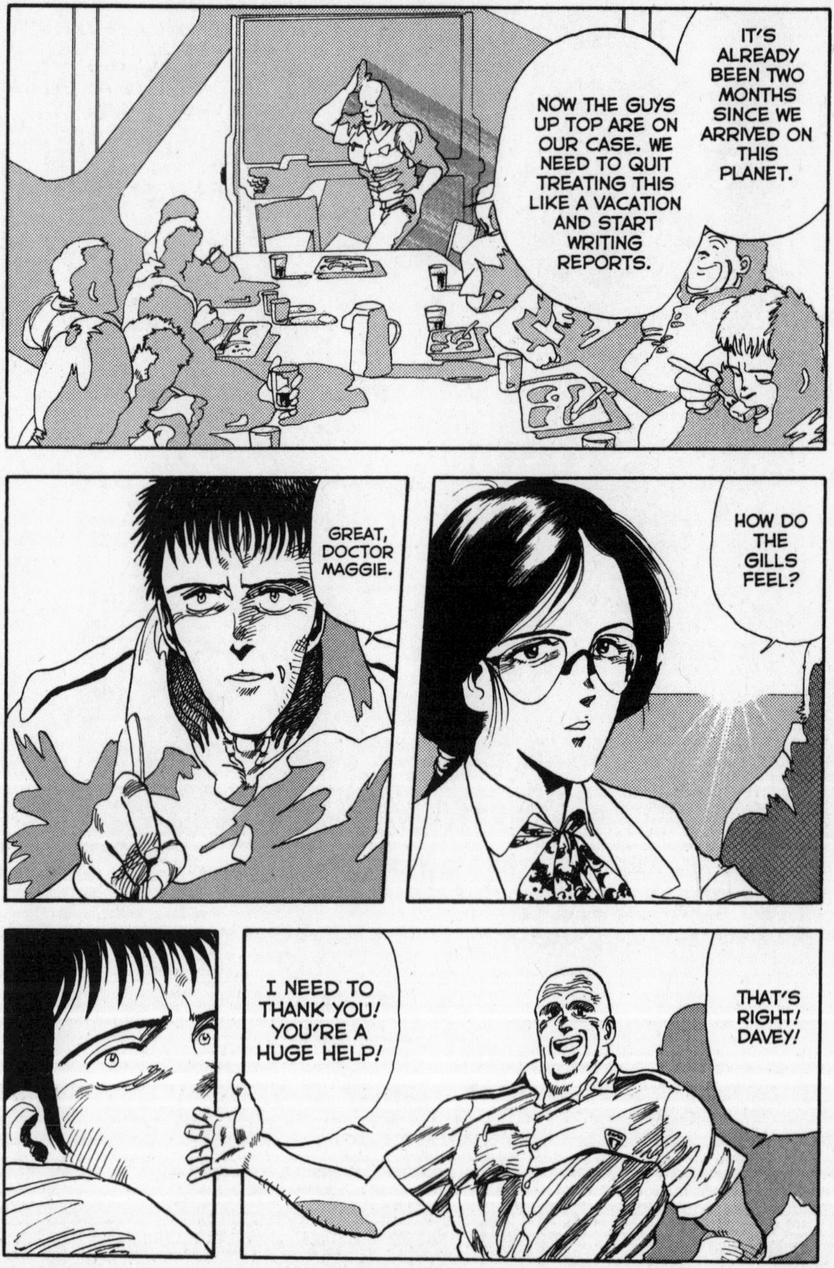
IT'S ALREADY BEEN TWO MONTHS SINCE WE ARRIVED ON THIS PLANET.
NOW THE GUYS UP TOP ARE ON OUR CASE. WE NEED TO QUIT TREATING THIS LIKE A VACATION AND START WRITING REPORTS.
HOW DO THE GILLS FEEL?
GREAT, DOCTOR MAGGIE.
THAT'S RIGHT! DAVEY!
I NEED TO THANK YOU! YOU'RE A HUGE HELP!

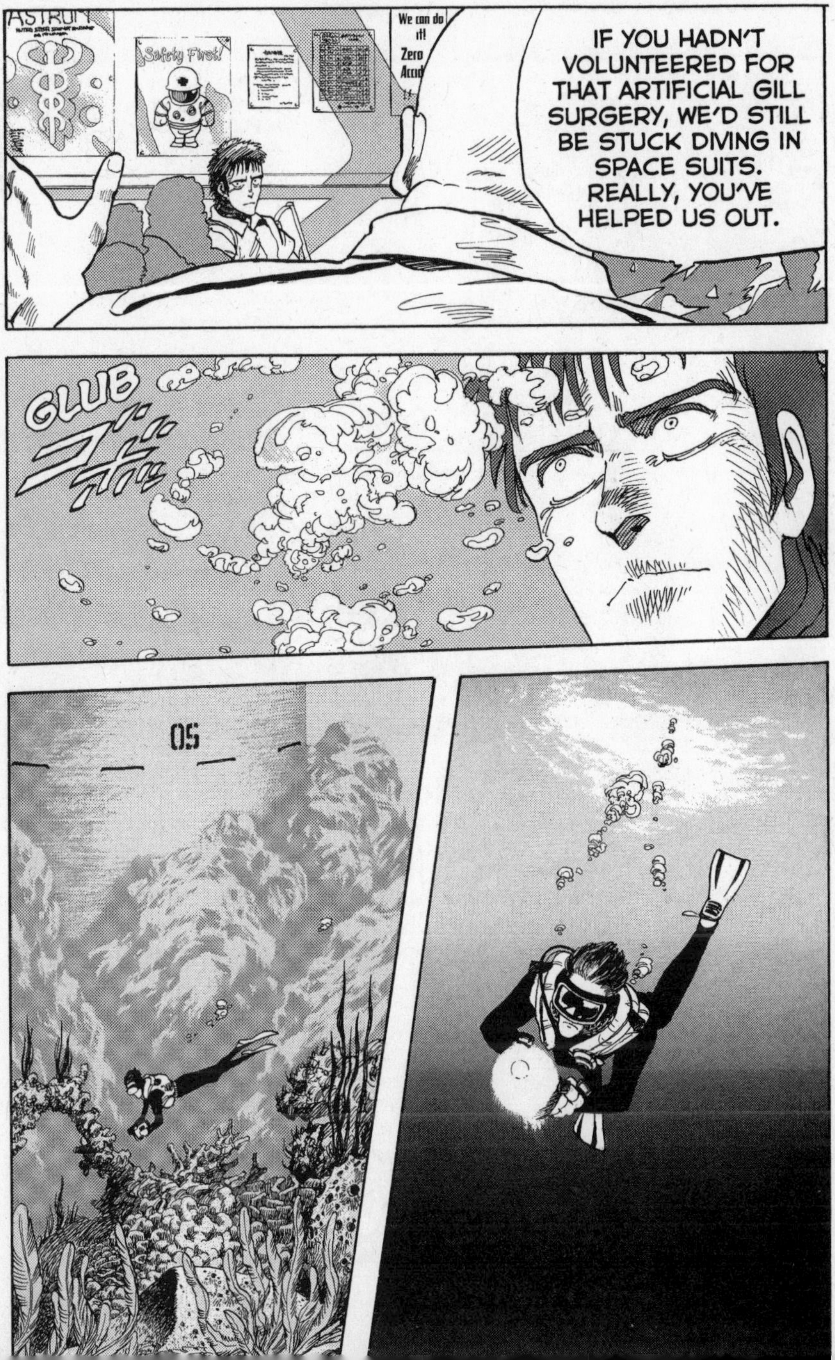
IF YOU HADN'T VOLUNTEERED FOR THAT ARTIFICIAL GILL SURGERY, WE'D STILL BE STUCK DIVING IN SPACE SUITS. REALLY, YOU'VE HELPED US OUT.
We can do it!
Zero
Safety First!
GLUB
05

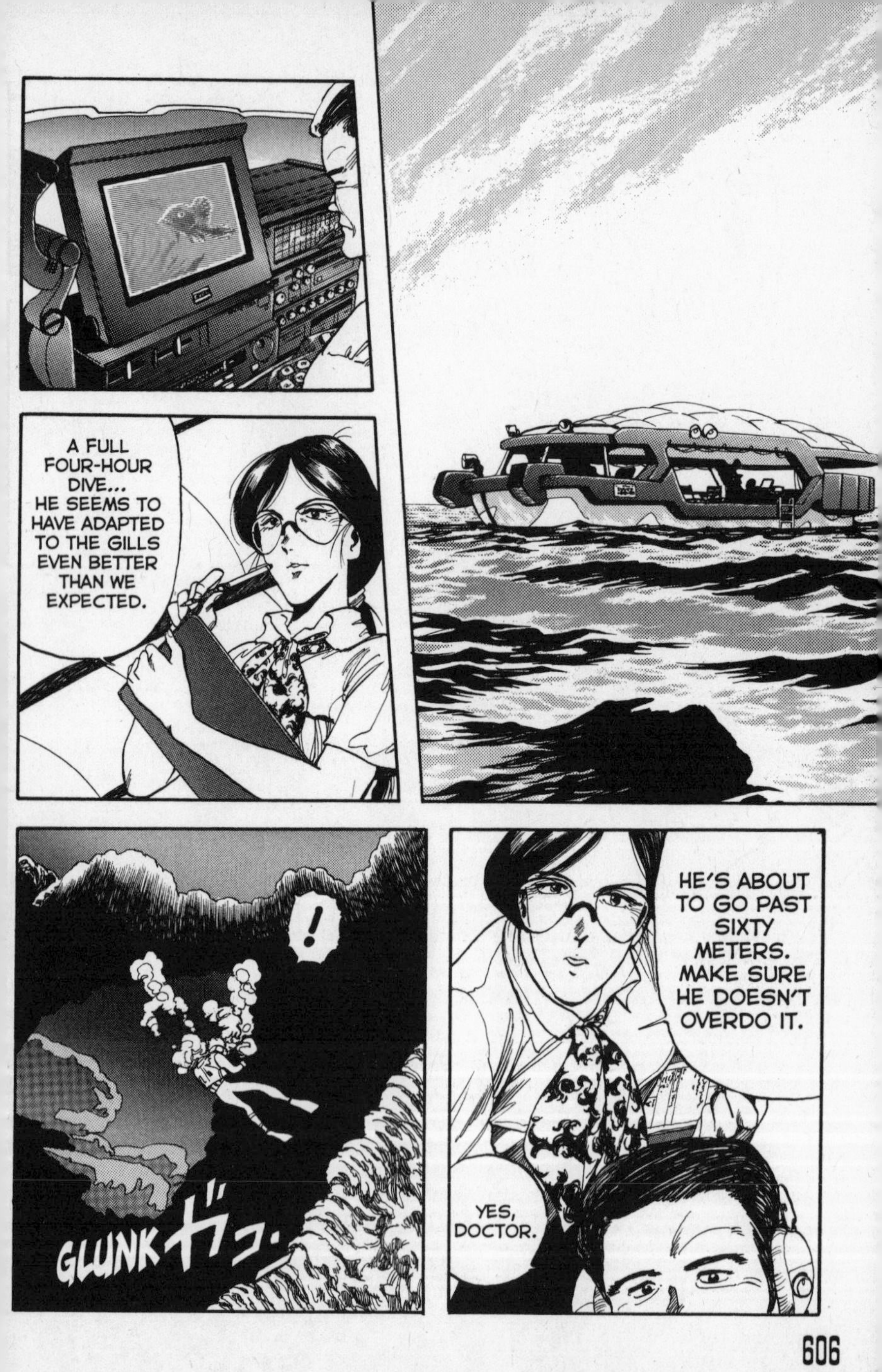
A FULL FOUR-HOUR DIVE... HE SEEMS TO HAVE ADAPTED TO THE GILLS EVEN BETTER THAN WE EXPECTED.
HE'S ABOUT TO GO PAST SIXTY METERS. MAKE SURE HE DOESN'T OVERDO IT.
YES, DOCTOR.
!
GLUNK ガッ.

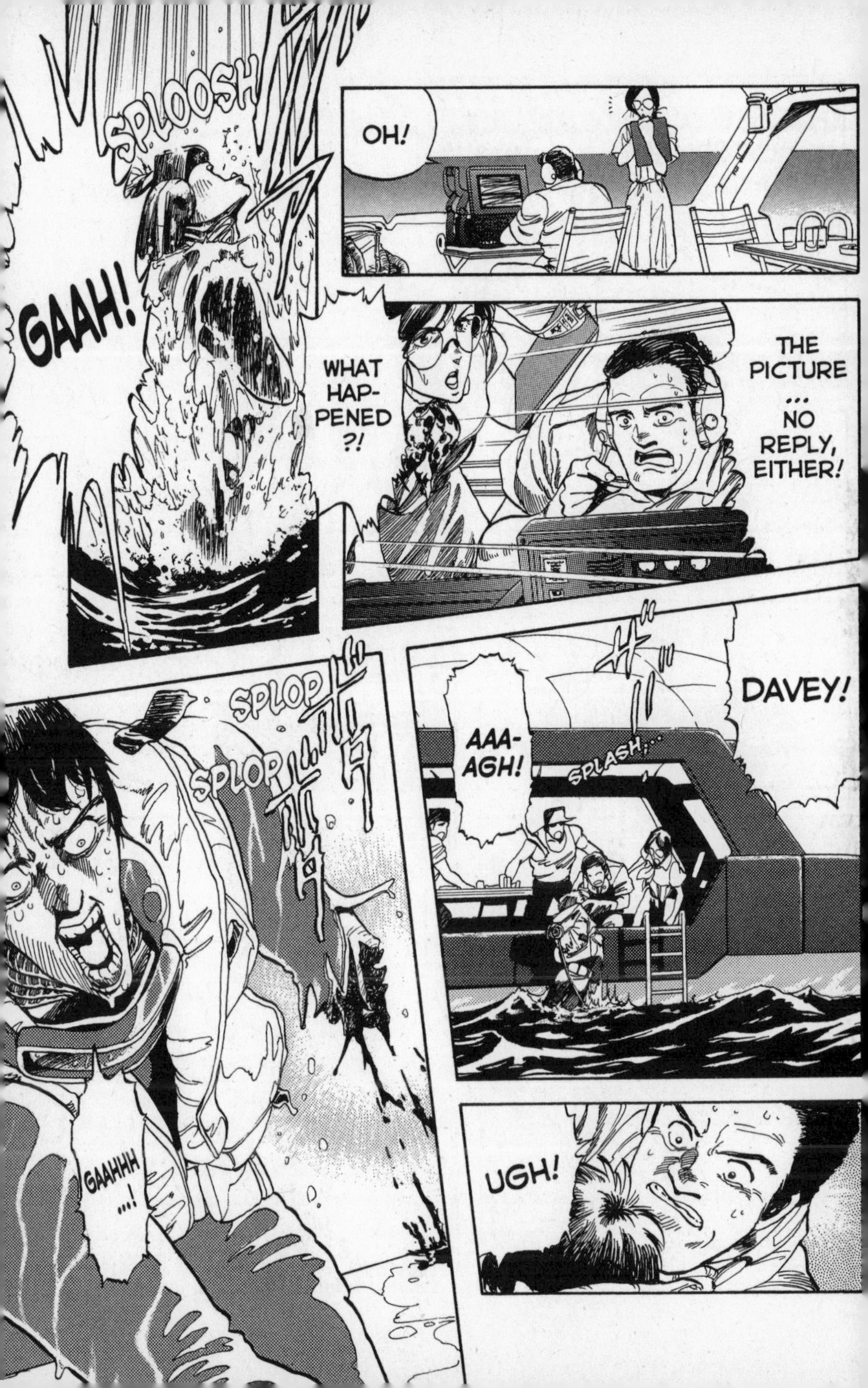
OH!
THE PICTURE ... NO REPLY, EITHER!
WHAT HAP-PENED ?!
SPLOOSH
GAAH!
DAVEY!
AAA-AGH!
SPLASH...
UGH!
SPLOP
SPLOP
GAAHH ...!

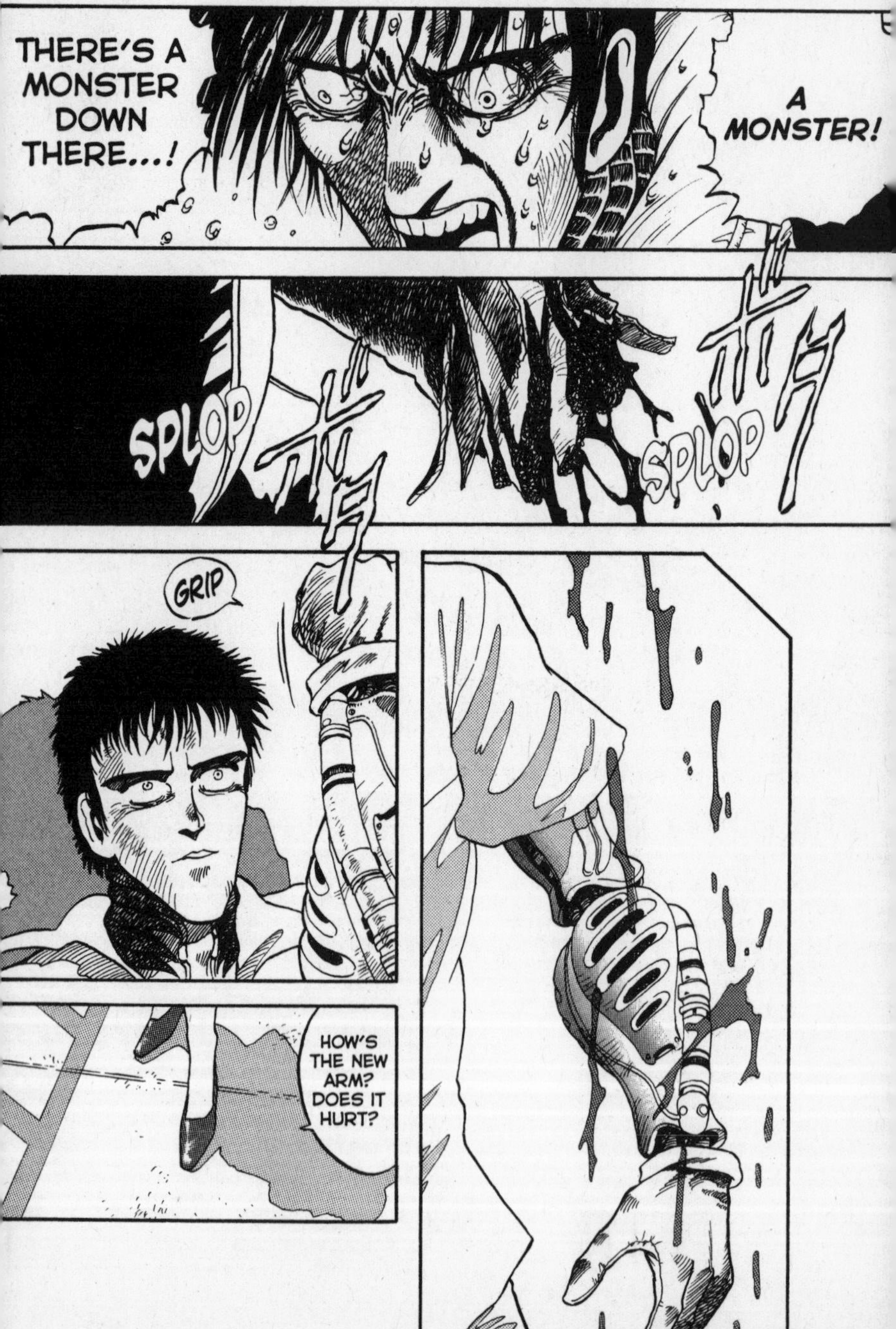
THERE'S A MONSTER DOWN THERE...!
A MONSTER!
SPLOP
SPLOP
GRIP
HOW'S THE NEW ARM? DOES IT HURT?

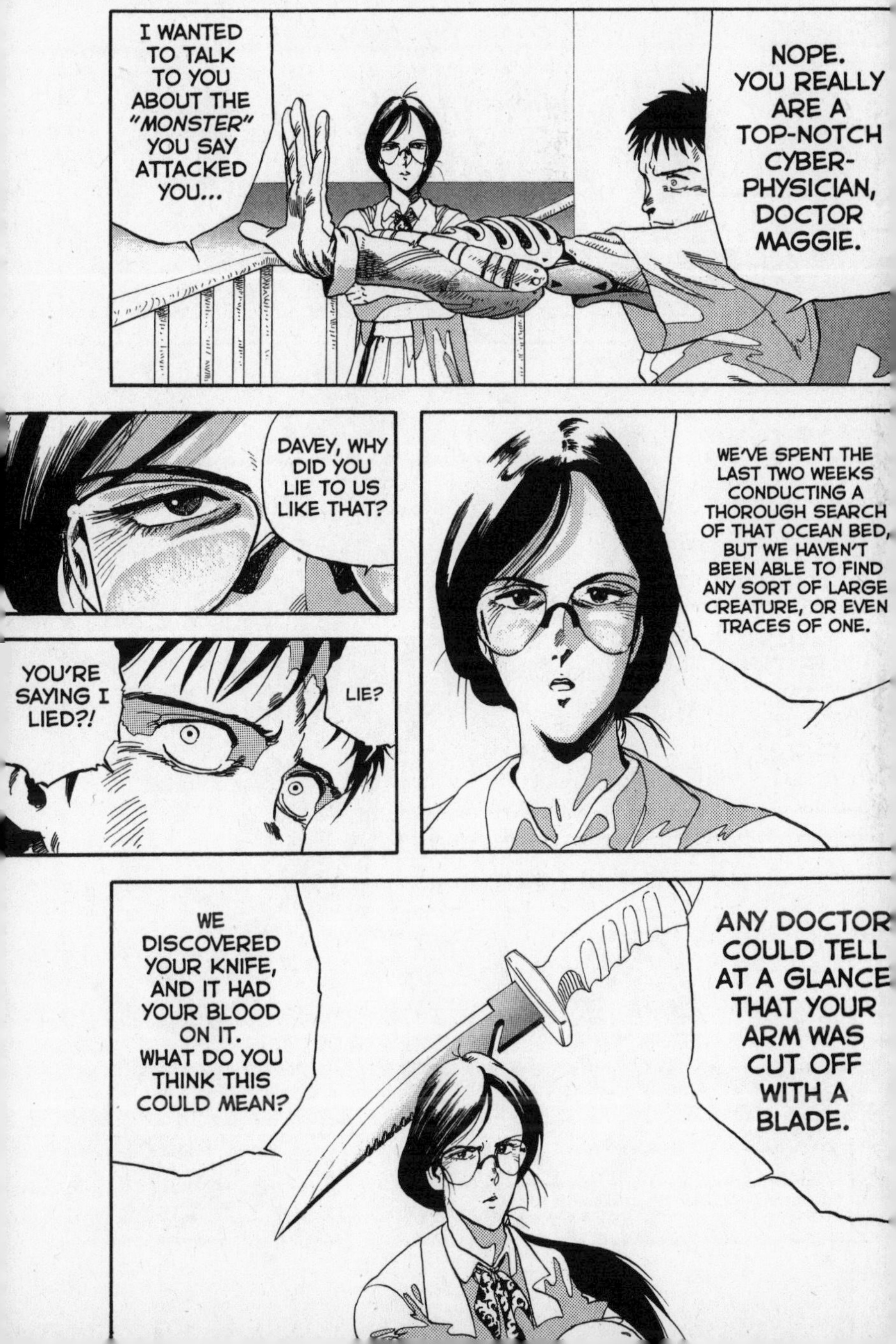
NOPE. YOU REALLY ARE A TOP-NOTCH CYBER-PHYSICIAN, DOCTOR MAGGIE.
I WANTED TO TALK TO YOU ABOUT THE "MONSTER" YOU SAY ATTACKED YOU...
WE'VE SPENT THE LAST TWO WEEKS CONDUCTING A THOROUGH SEARCH OF THAT OCEAN BED, BUT WE HAVEN'T BEEN ABLE TO FIND ANY SORT OF LARGE CREATURE, OR EVEN TRACES OF ONE.
DAVEY, WHY DID YOU LIE TO US LIKE THAT?
LIE?
YOU'RE SAYING I LIED?!
ANY DOCTOR COULD TELL AT A GLANCE THAT YOUR ARM WAS CUT OFF WITH A BLADE.
WE DISCOVERED YOUR KNIFE, AND IT HAD YOUR BLOOD ON IT. WHAT DO YOU THINK THIS COULD MEAN?

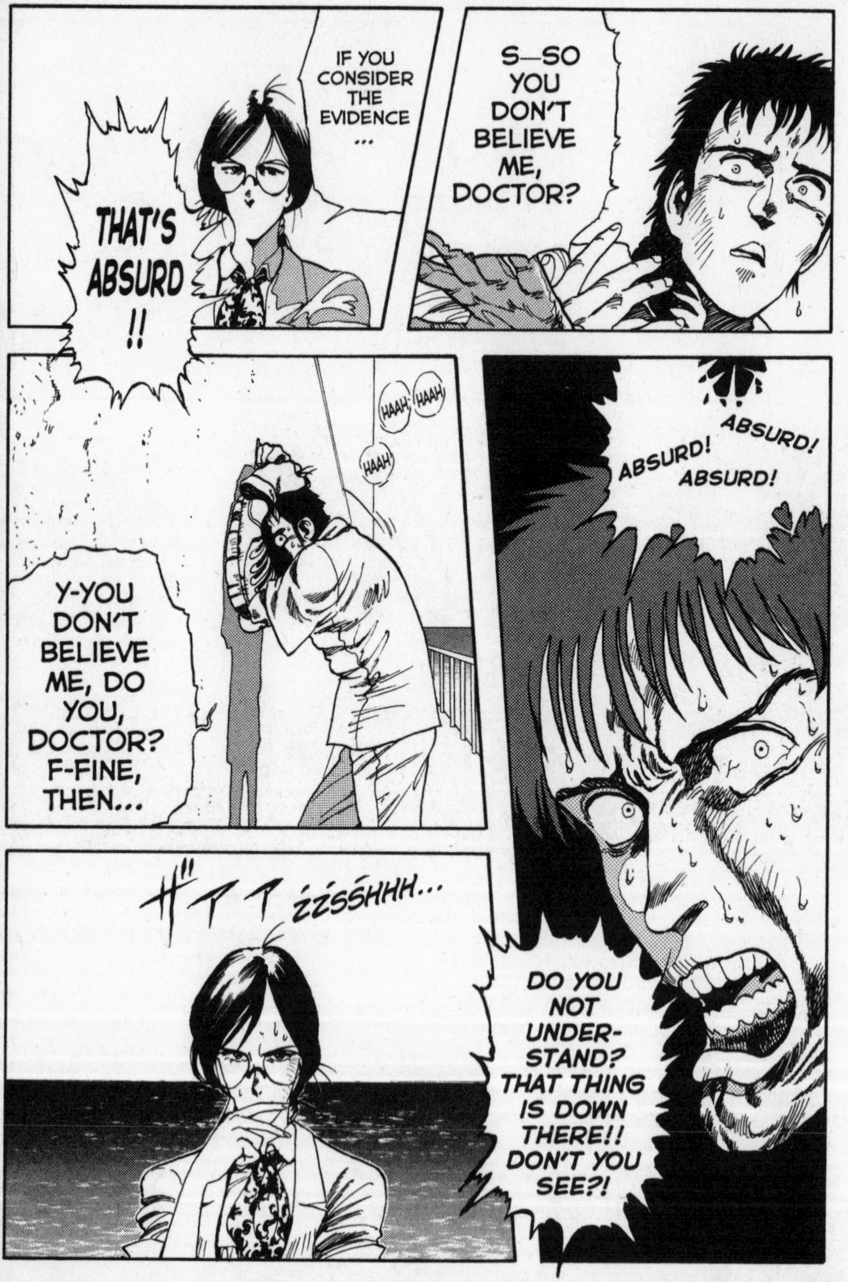
S—SO YOU DON'T BELIEVE ME, DOCTOR?
IF YOU CONSIDER THE EVIDENCE ...
THAT'S ABSURD !!
ABSURD!
ABSURD!
ABSURD!
DO YOU NOT UNDER-STAND? THAT THING IS DOWN THERE!! DON'T YOU SEE?!
HAAH
HAAH
HAAH
Y-YOU DON'T BELIEVE ME, DO YOU, DOCTOR? F-FINE, THEN...
ZZSSHHH...

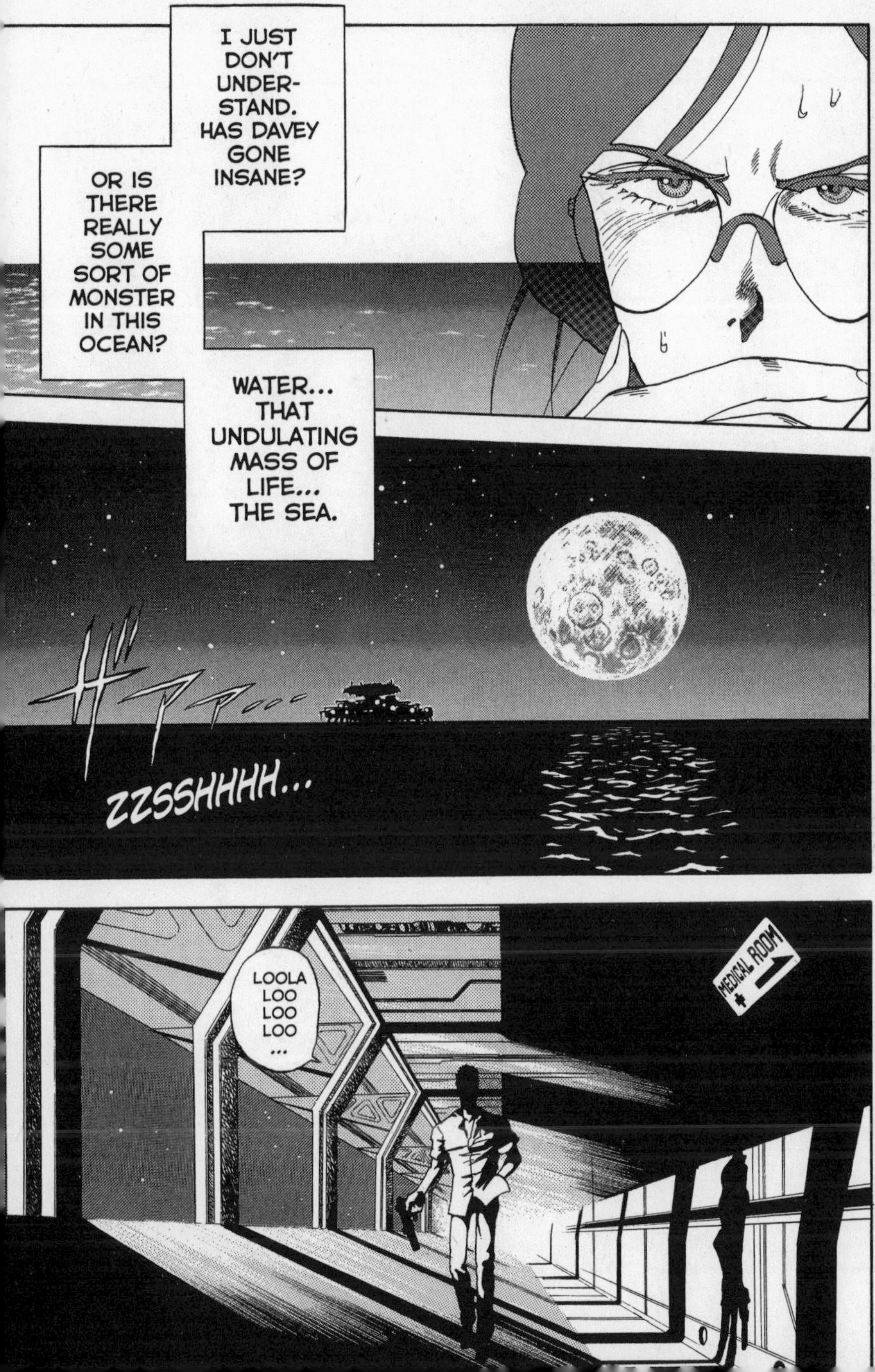
I JUST DON'T UNDER-STAND. HAS DAVEY GONE INSANE?
OR IS THERE REALLY SOME SORT OF MONSTER IN THIS OCEAN?
WATER... THAT UNDULATING MASS OF LIFE... THE SEA.
ザァァ…
ZZSSHHHH...
MEDICAL ROOM
LOOLA LOO LOO LOO ...

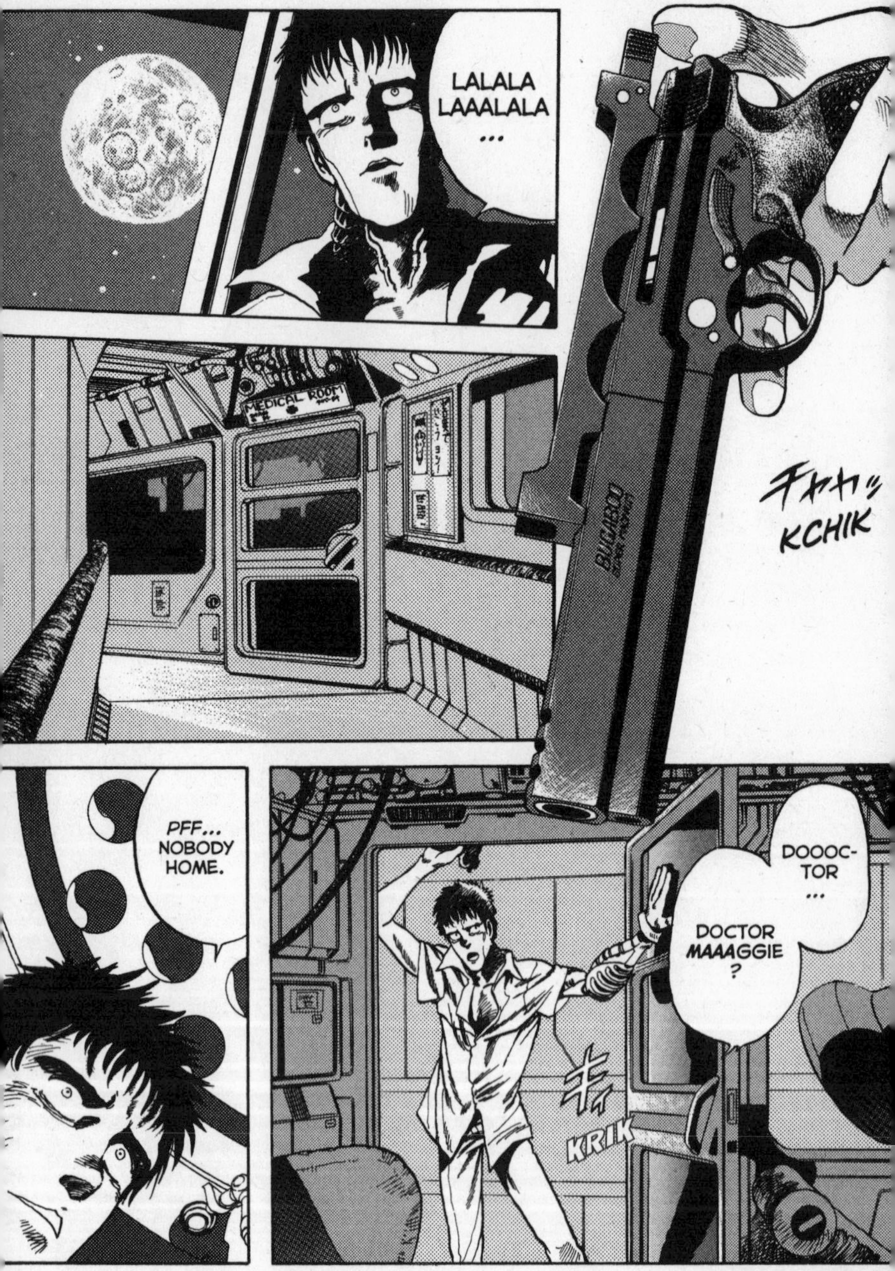
チャキッ
KCHIK
LALALA LAAALALA ...
MEDICAL ROOM
DOOOC-TOR ...
DOCTOR MAAAGGIE ?
キィ
KRIK
PFF... NOBODY HOME.

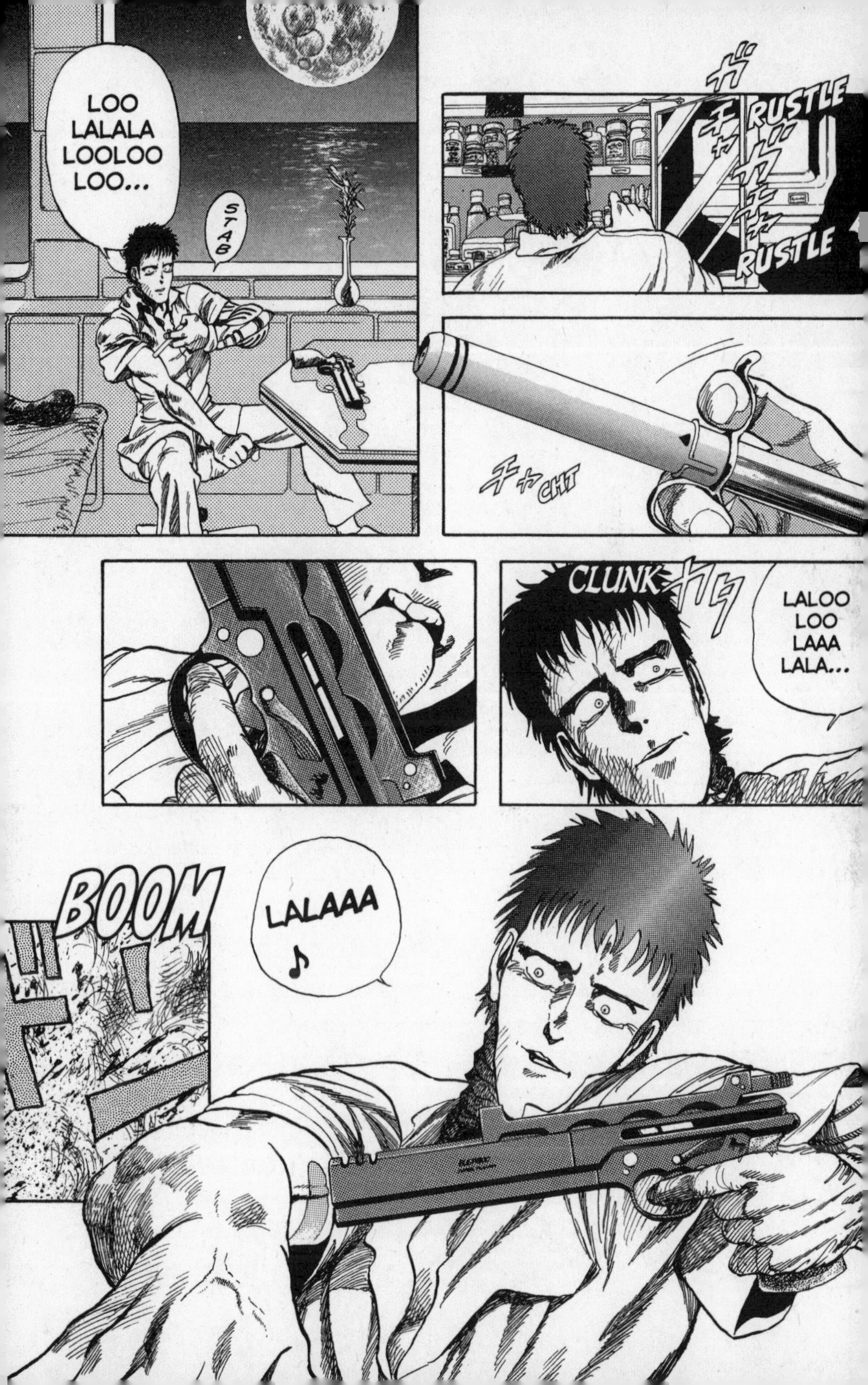
ガチャ
RUSTLE
ガチャ
RUSTLE
チャ
CHT
LOO LALALA LOOLOO LOO...
STAB
CLUNK
カタ
LALOO LOO LAAA LALA...
LALAAA ♪
BOOM

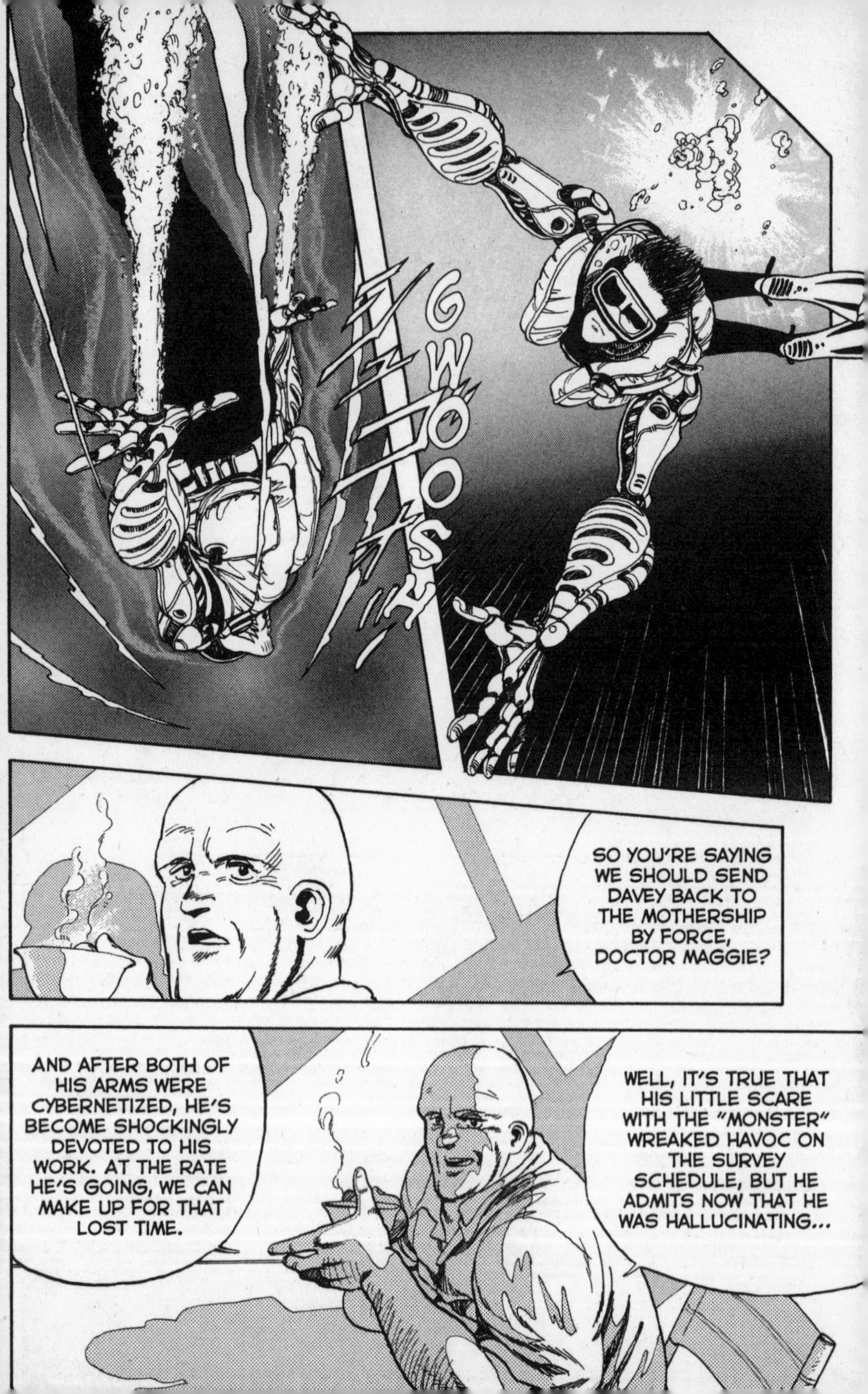
GWOOOSH
SO YOU'RE SAYING WE SHOULD SEND DAVEY BACK TO THE MOTHERSHIP BY FORCE, DOCTOR MAGGIE?
WELL, IT'S TRUE THAT HIS LITTLE SCARE WITH THE "MONSTER" WREAKED HAVOC ON THE SURVEY SCHEDULE, BUT HE ADMITS NOW THAT HE WAS HALLUCINATING...
AND AFTER BOTH OF HIS ARMS WERE CYBERNETIZED, HE'S BECOME SHOCKINGLY DEVOTED TO HIS WORK. AT THE RATE HE'S GOING, WE CAN MAKE UP FOR THAT LOST TIME.

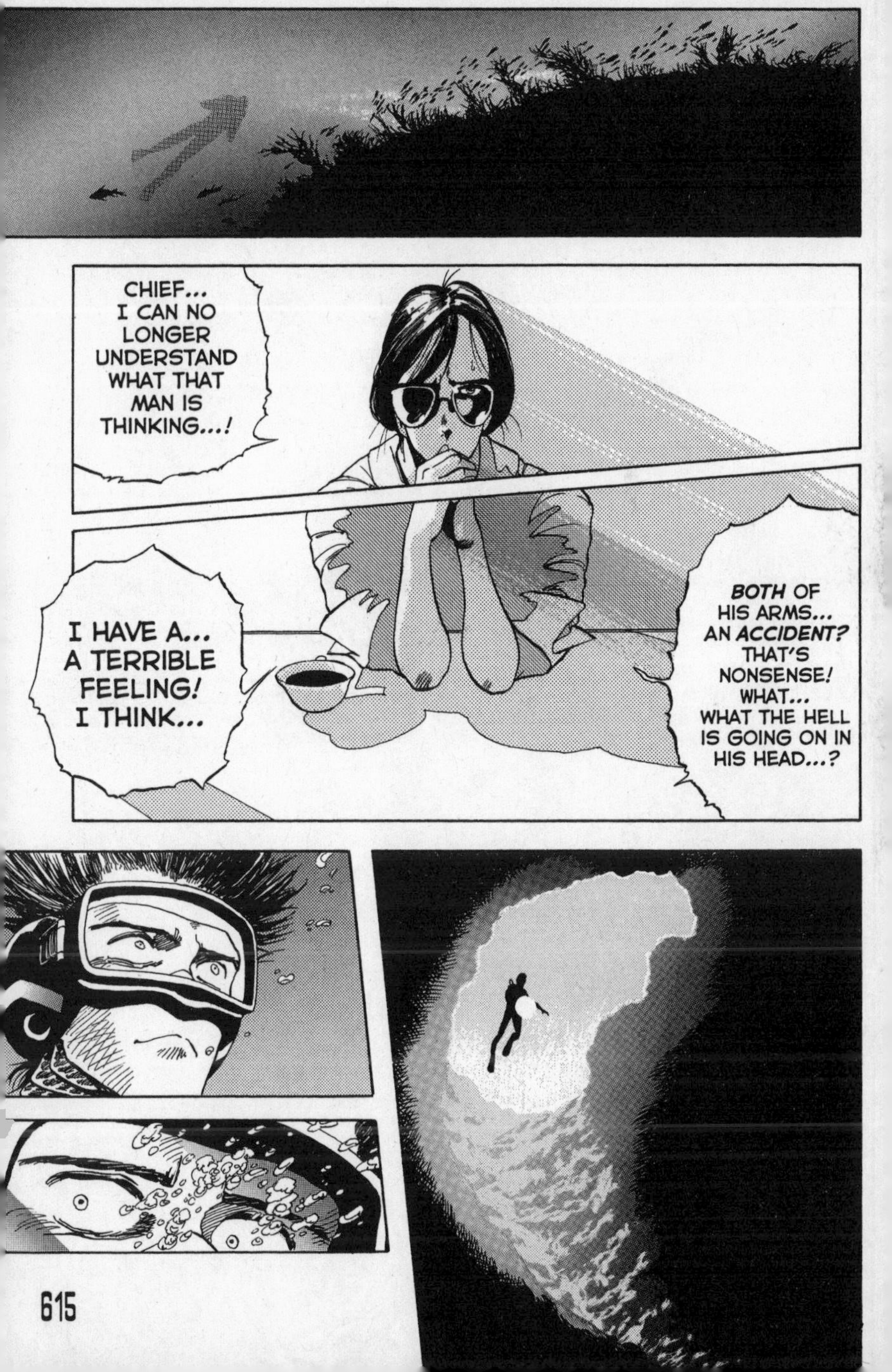
CHIEF... I CAN NO LONGER UNDERSTAND WHAT THAT MAN IS THINKING...!
BOTH OF HIS ARMS... AN *ACCIDENT?* THAT'S NONSENSE! WHAT... WHAT THE HELL IS GOING ON IN HIS HEAD...?
I HAVE A... A TERRIBLE FEELING! I THINK...

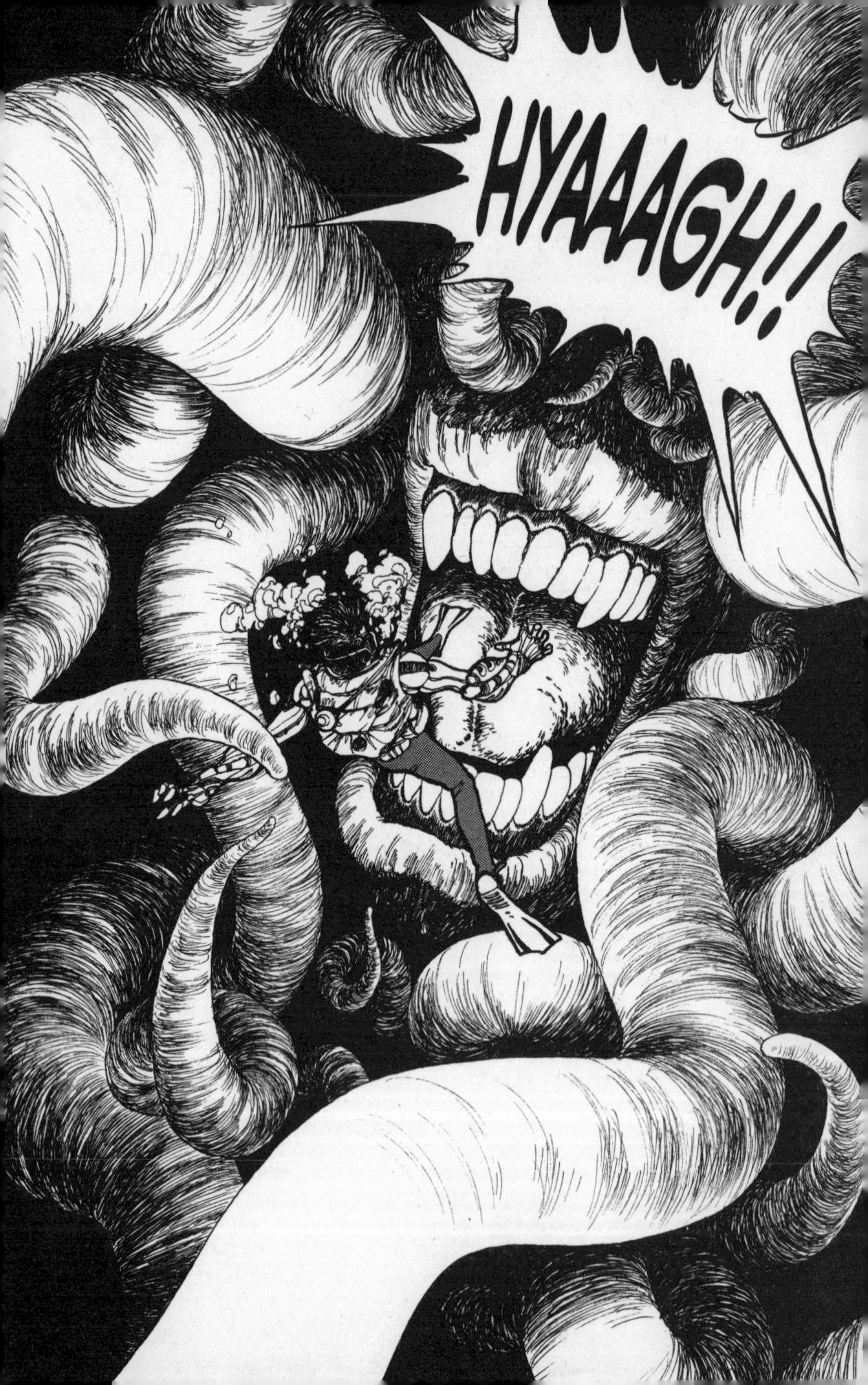
HYAAAGH!!

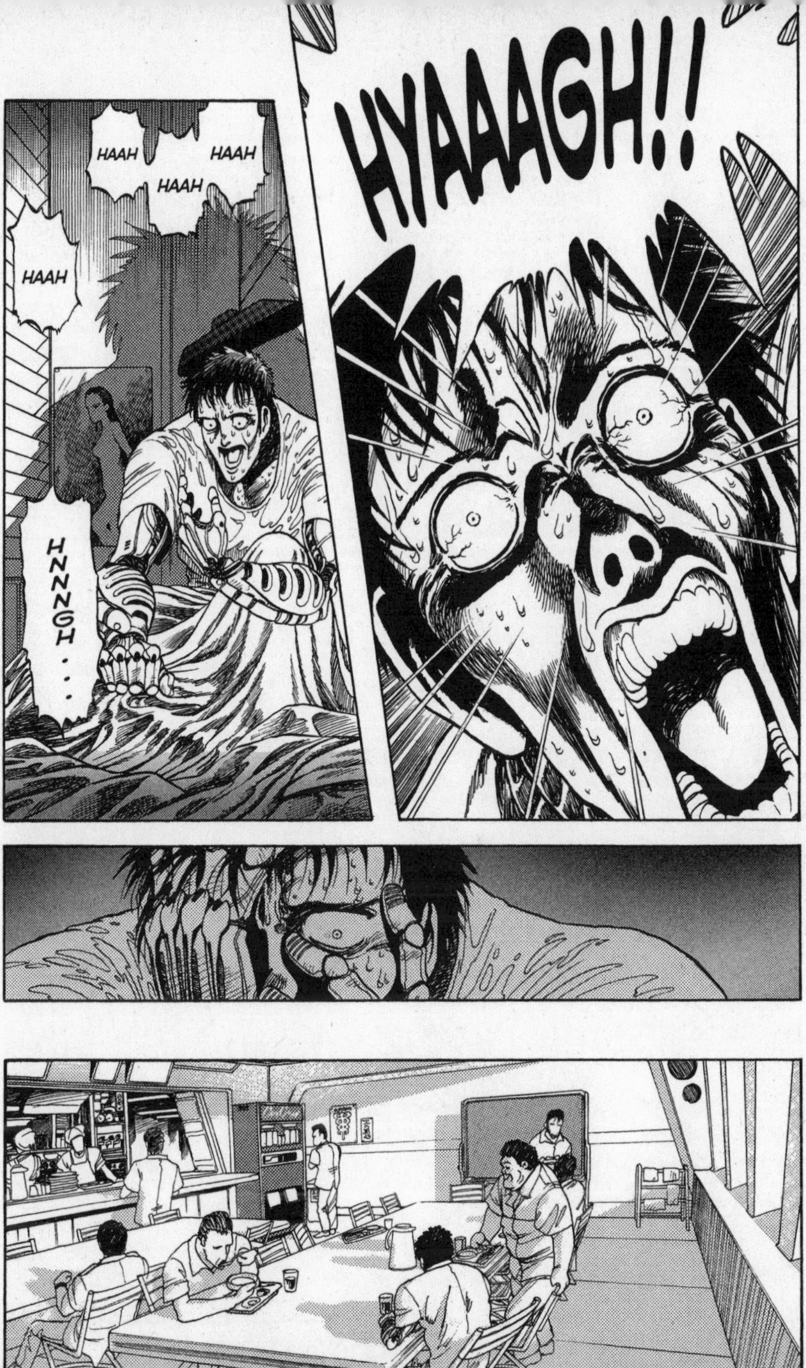
HYAAAGH!!
HAAH
HAAH
HAAH
HAAH
HNNNGH...

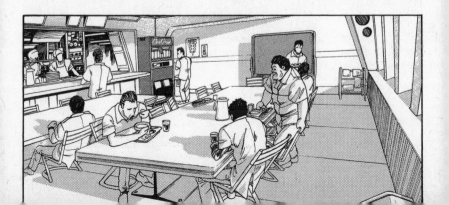

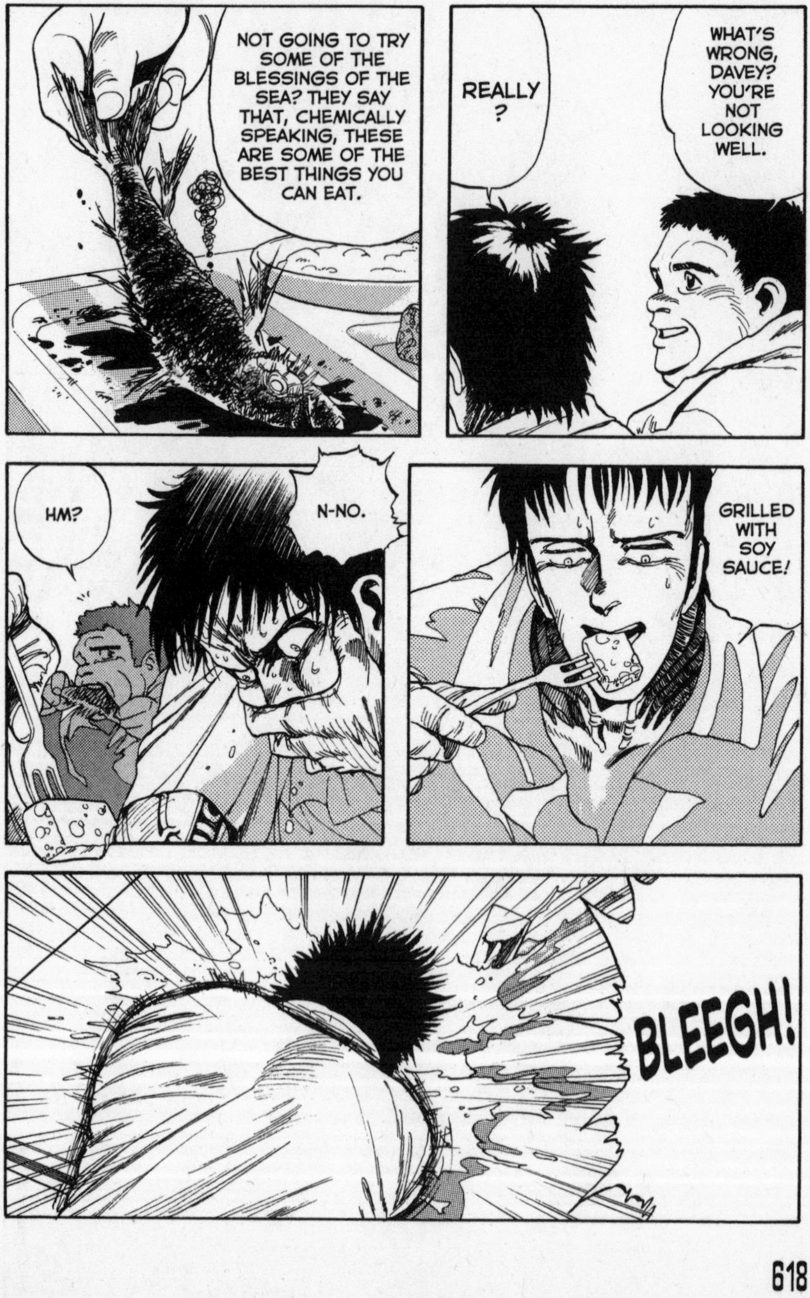
WHAT'S WRONG, DAVEY? YOU'RE NOT LOOKING WELL.
REALLY ?
NOT GOING TO TRY SOME OF THE BLESSINGS OF THE SEA? THEY SAY THAT, CHEMICALLY SPEAKING, THESE ARE SOME OF THE BEST THINGS YOU CAN EAT.
GRILLED WITH SOY SAUCE!
N-NO.
HM?
BLEEGH!

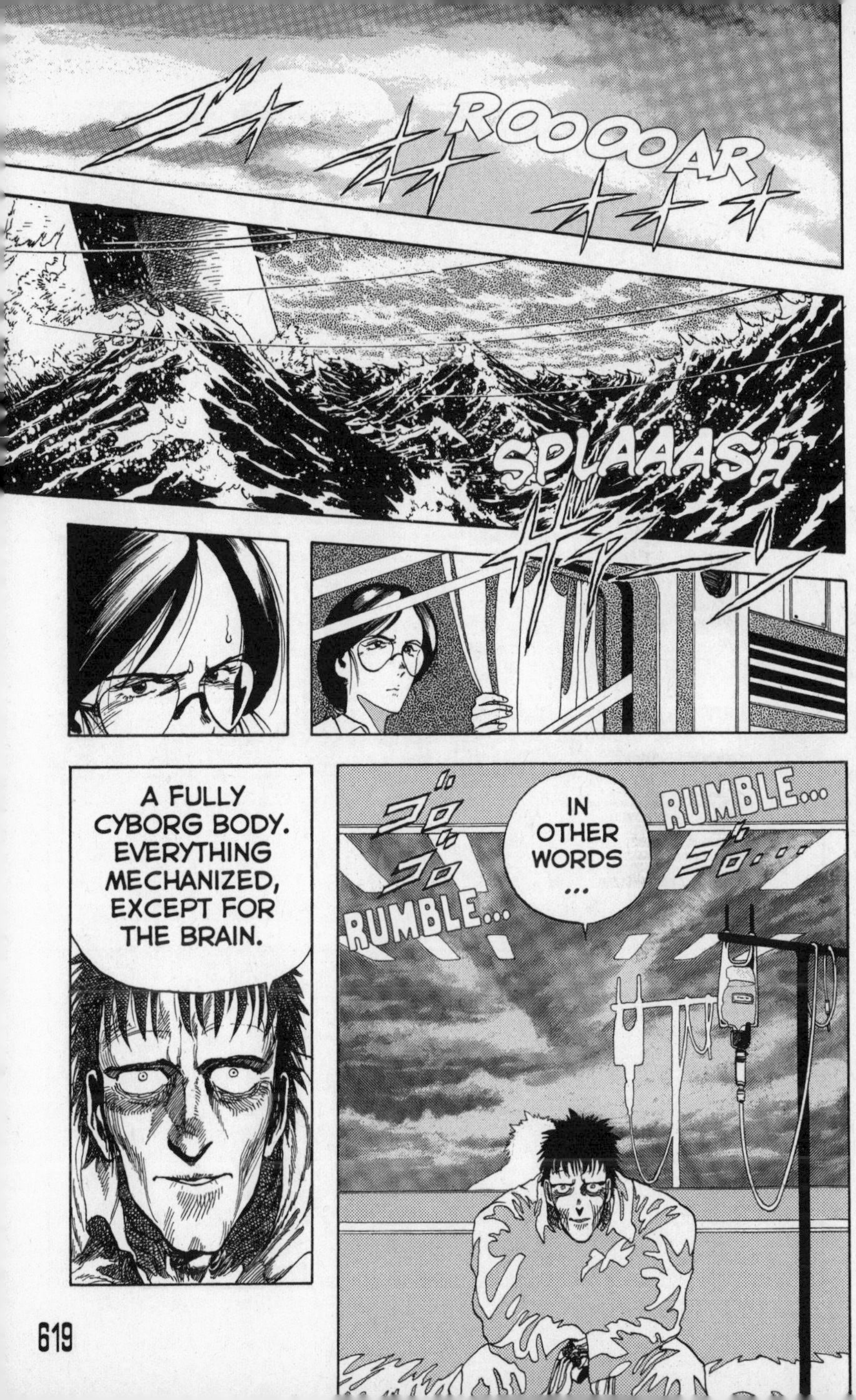
ROOOOAR
SPLAAASH
RUMBLE...
IN OTHER WORDS ...
RUMBLE...
A FULLY CYBORG BODY. EVERYTHING MECHANIZED, EXCEPT FOR THE BRAIN.

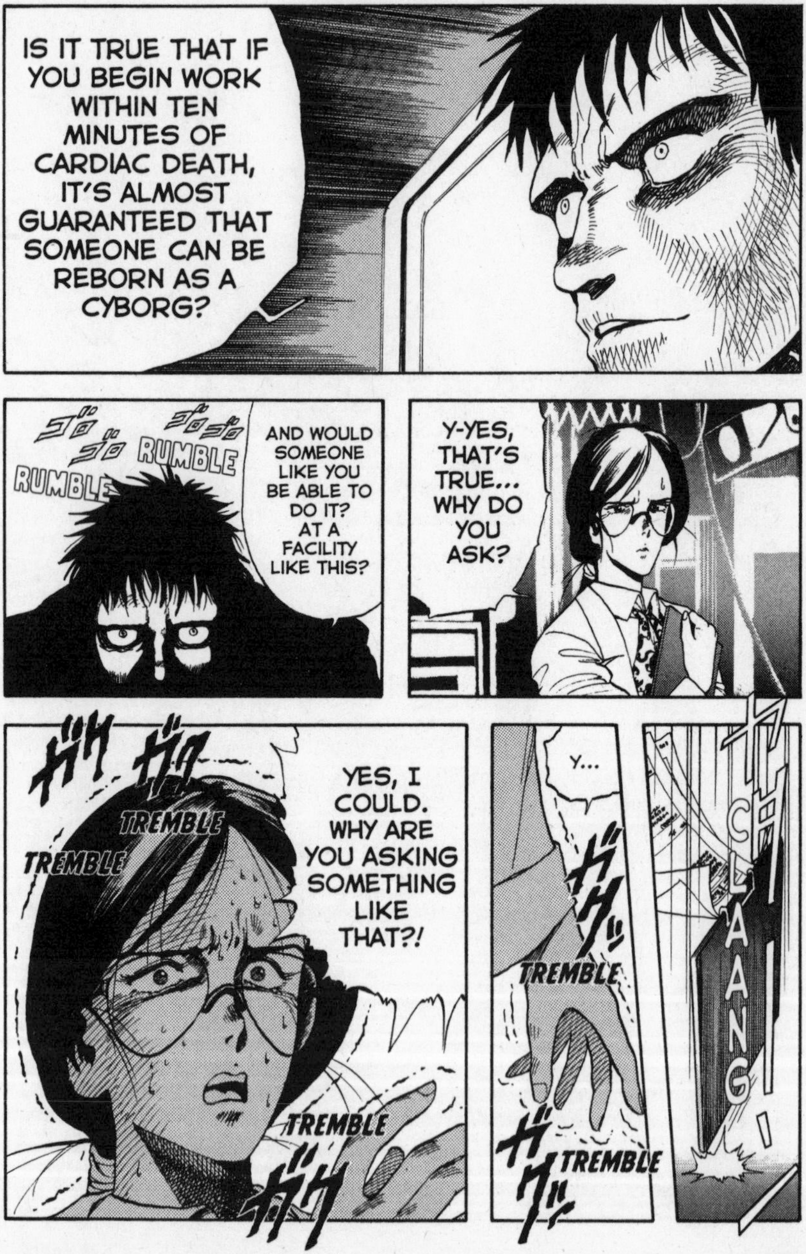
IS IT TRUE THAT IF YOU BEGIN WORK WITHIN TEN MINUTES OF CARDIAC DEATH, IT'S ALMOST GUARANTEED THAT SOMEONE CAN BE REBORN AS A CYBORG?
Y-YES, THAT'S TRUE... WHY DO YOU ASK?
RUMBLE
RUMBLE
AND WOULD SOMEONE LIKE YOU BE ABLE TO DO IT? AT A FACILITY LIKE THIS?
CHLAANG
Y...
TREMBLE
TREMBLE
TREMBLE
TREMBLE
YES, I COULD. WHY ARE YOU ASKING SOMETHING LIKE THAT?!
TREMBLE

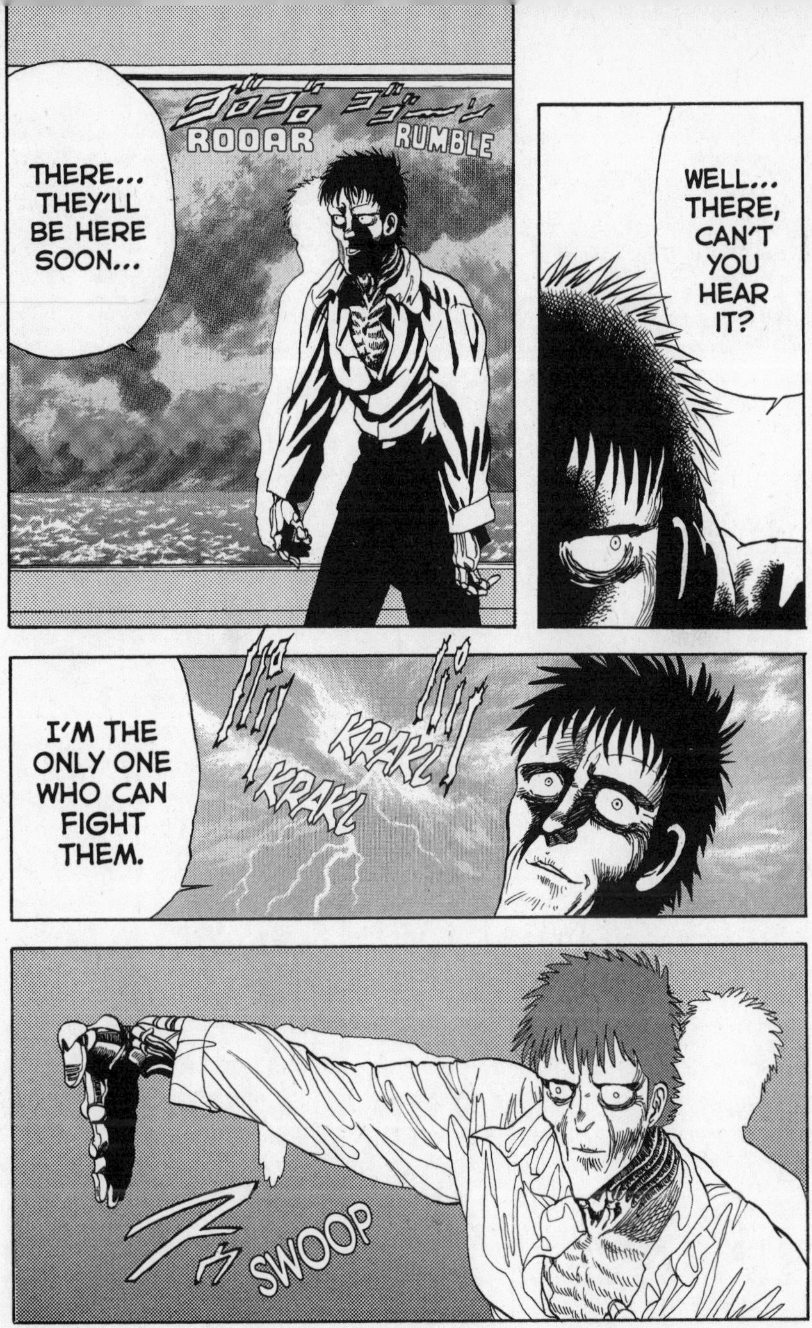
WELL... THERE, CAN'T YOU HEAR IT?
RUMBLE
ROOAR
THERE... THEY'LL BE HERE SOON...
KRAKL
KRAKL
I'M THE ONLY ONE WHO CAN FIGHT THEM.
SWOOP

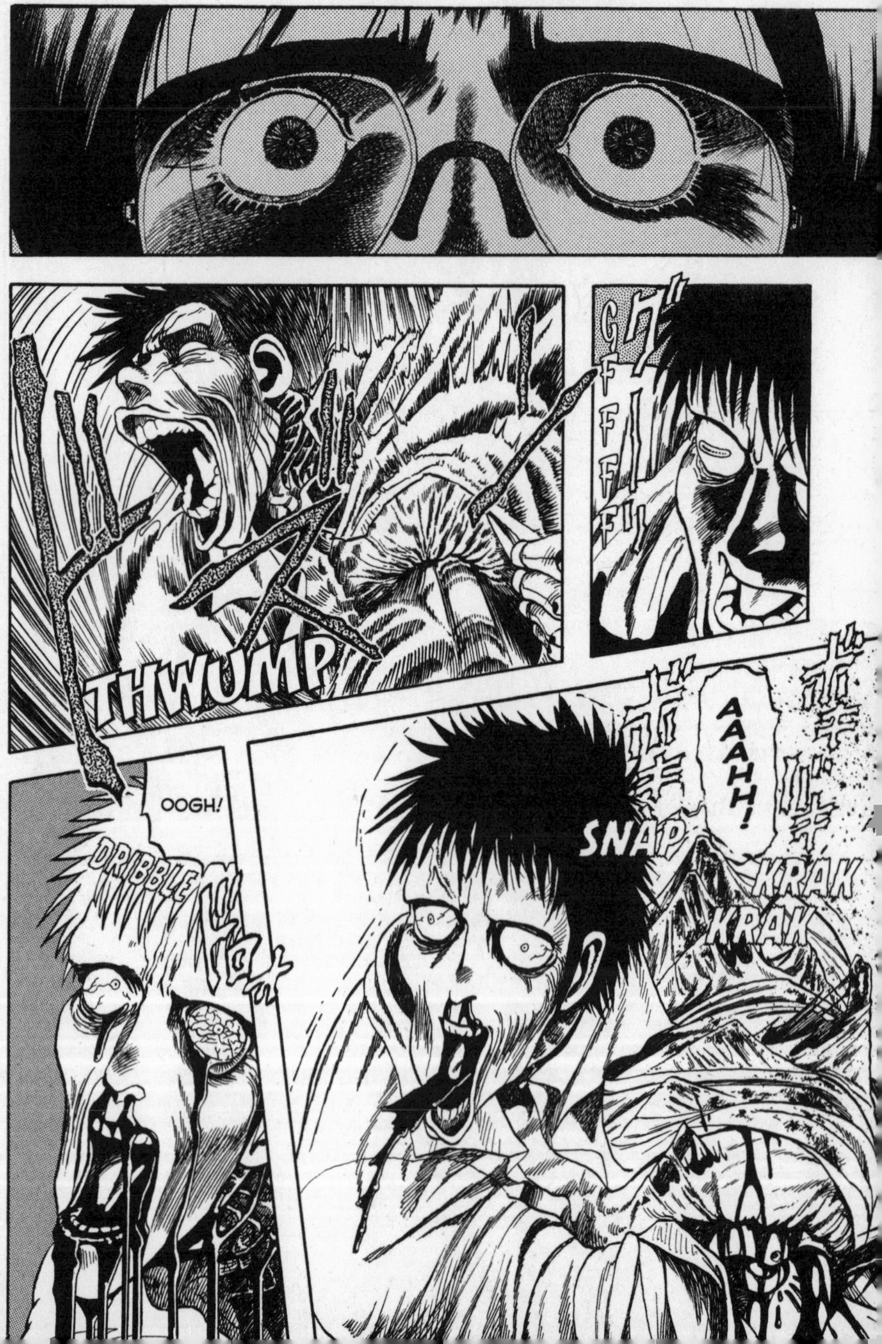
GFFFFF
THWUMP
AAAHH!
SNAP
KRAK
KRAK
OOGH!
DRIBBLE

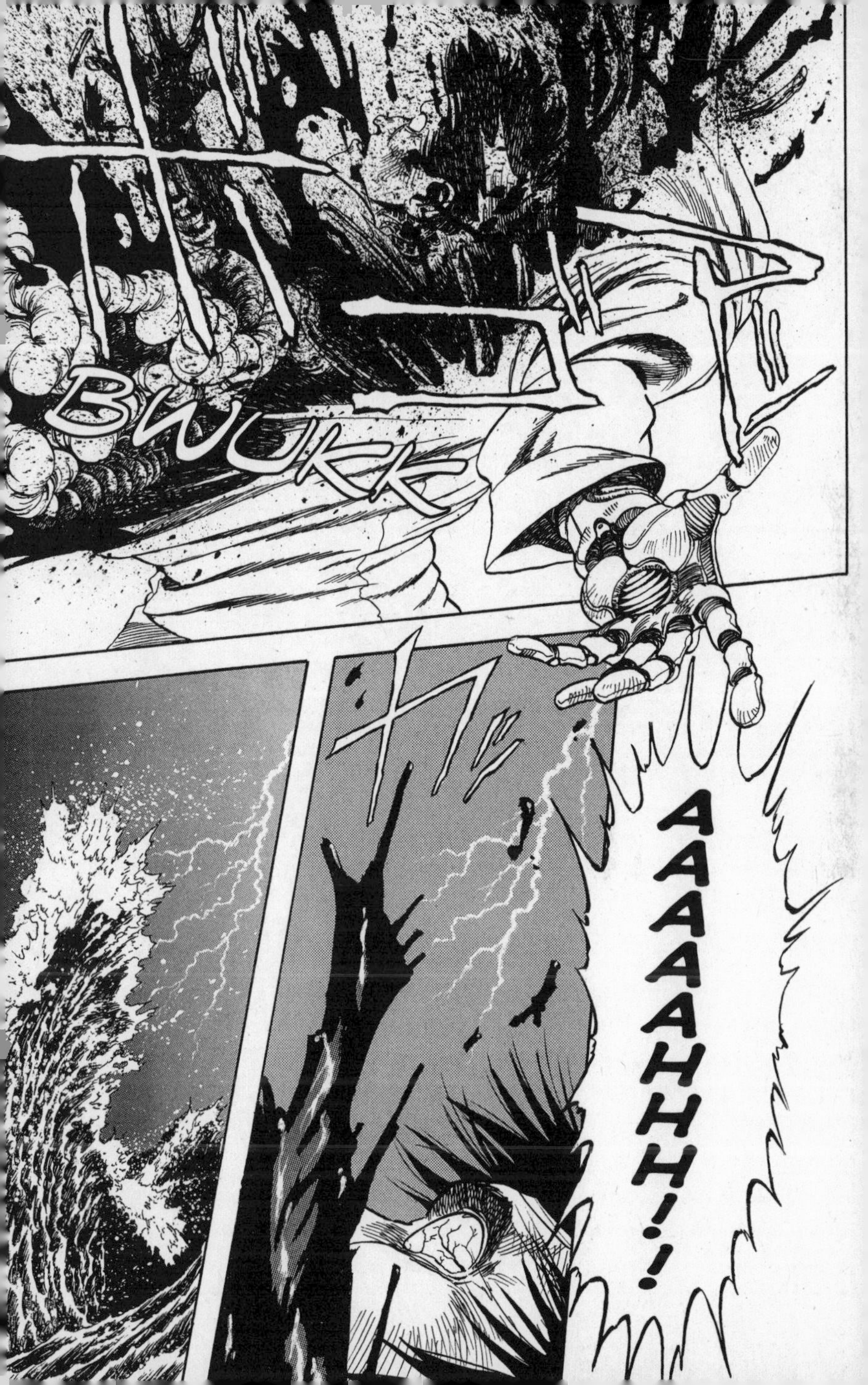
BWURK
AAAAHHH!!!

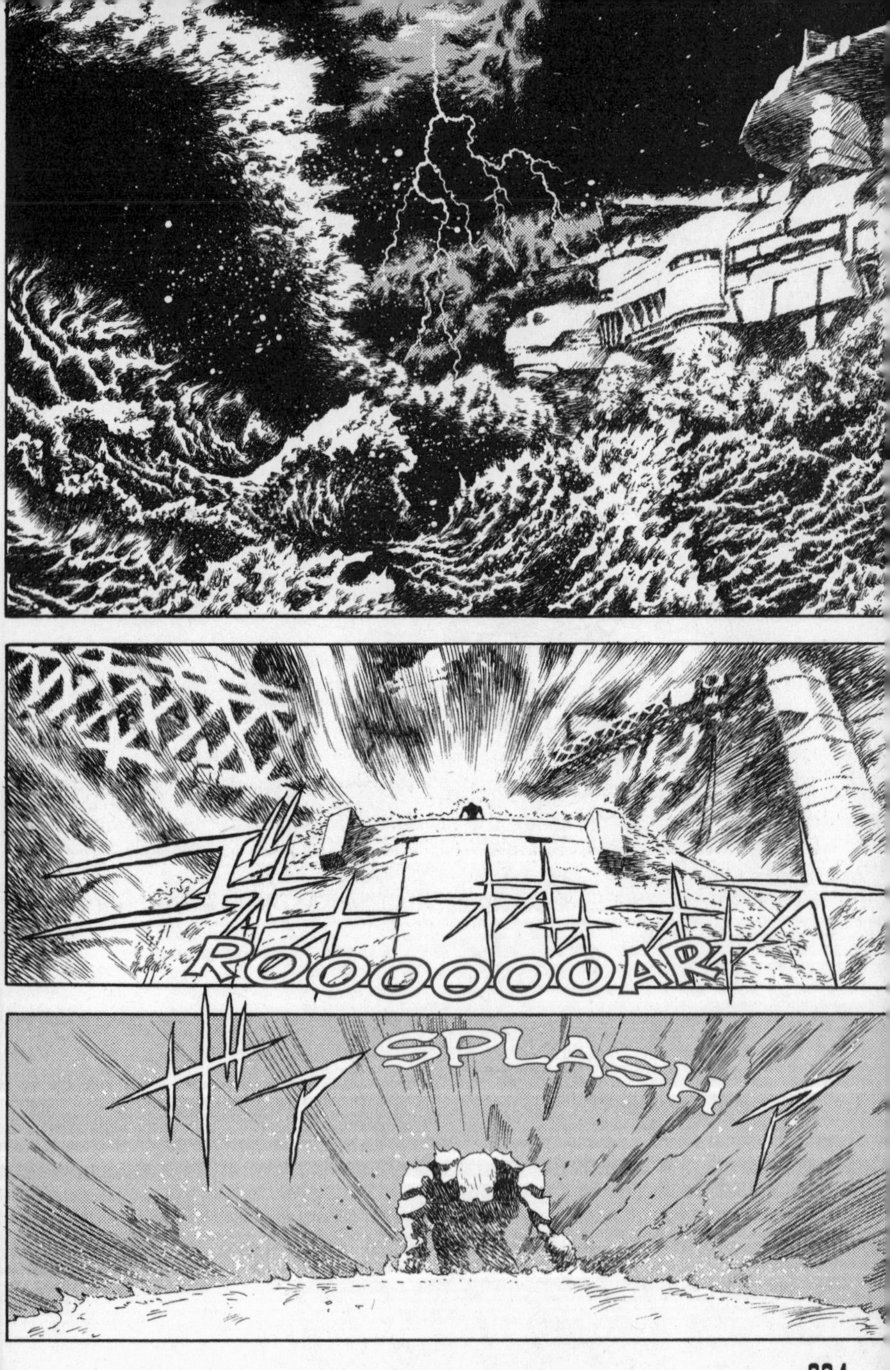
ROOOOOOAR
SPLASH

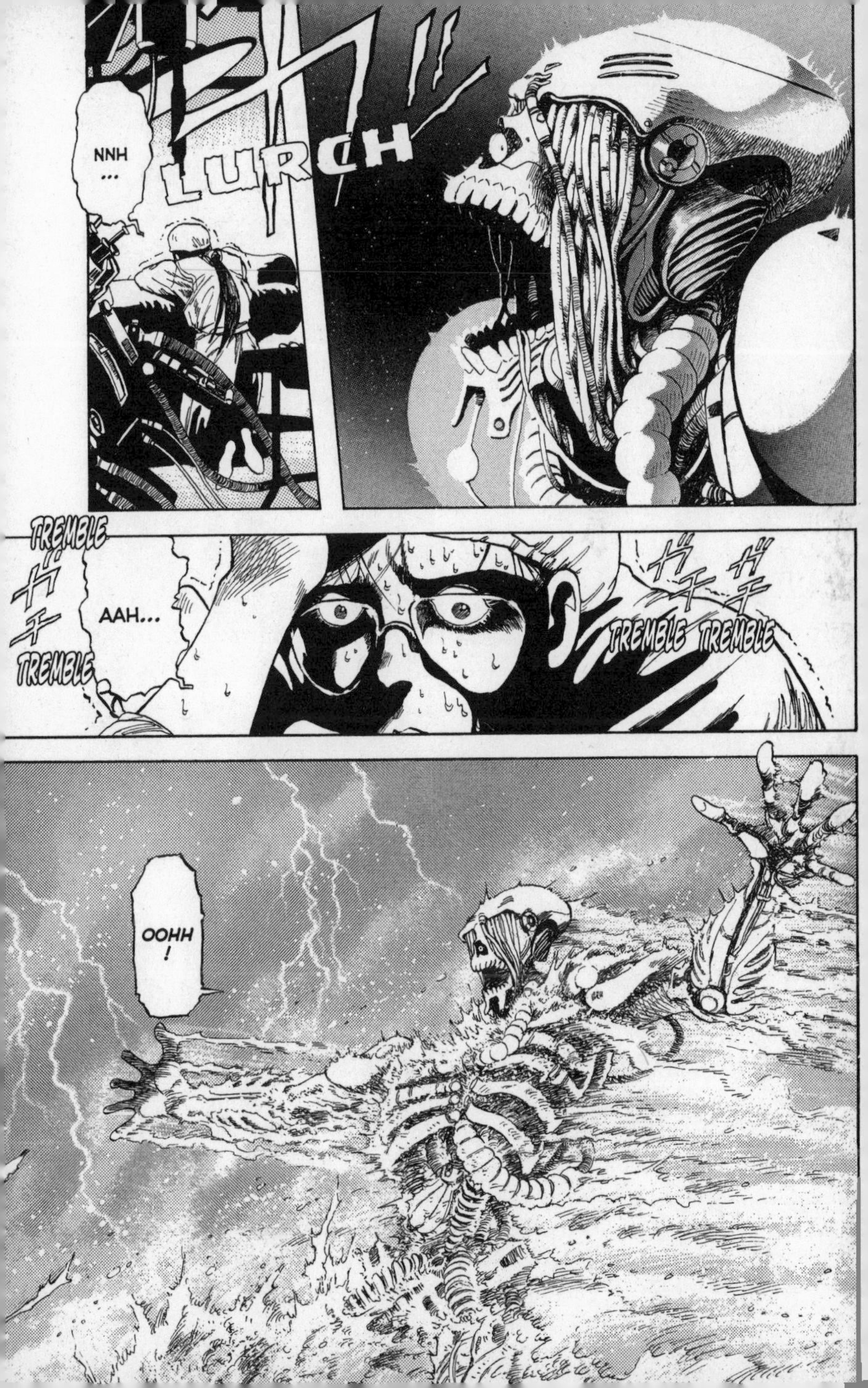

LURCH
NNH ...
TREMBLE TREMBLE
AAH...
TREMBLE
TREMBLE
OOHH !

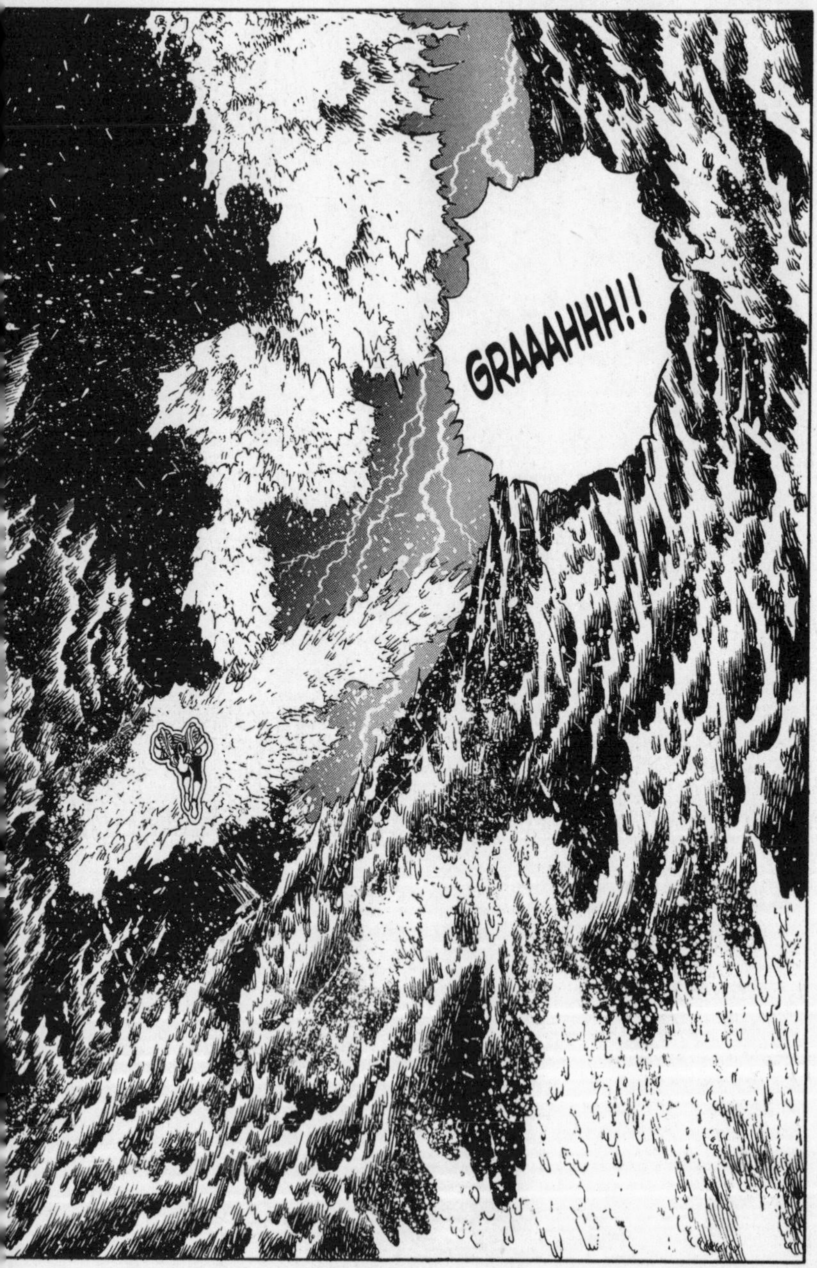
GRAAAHHH!!

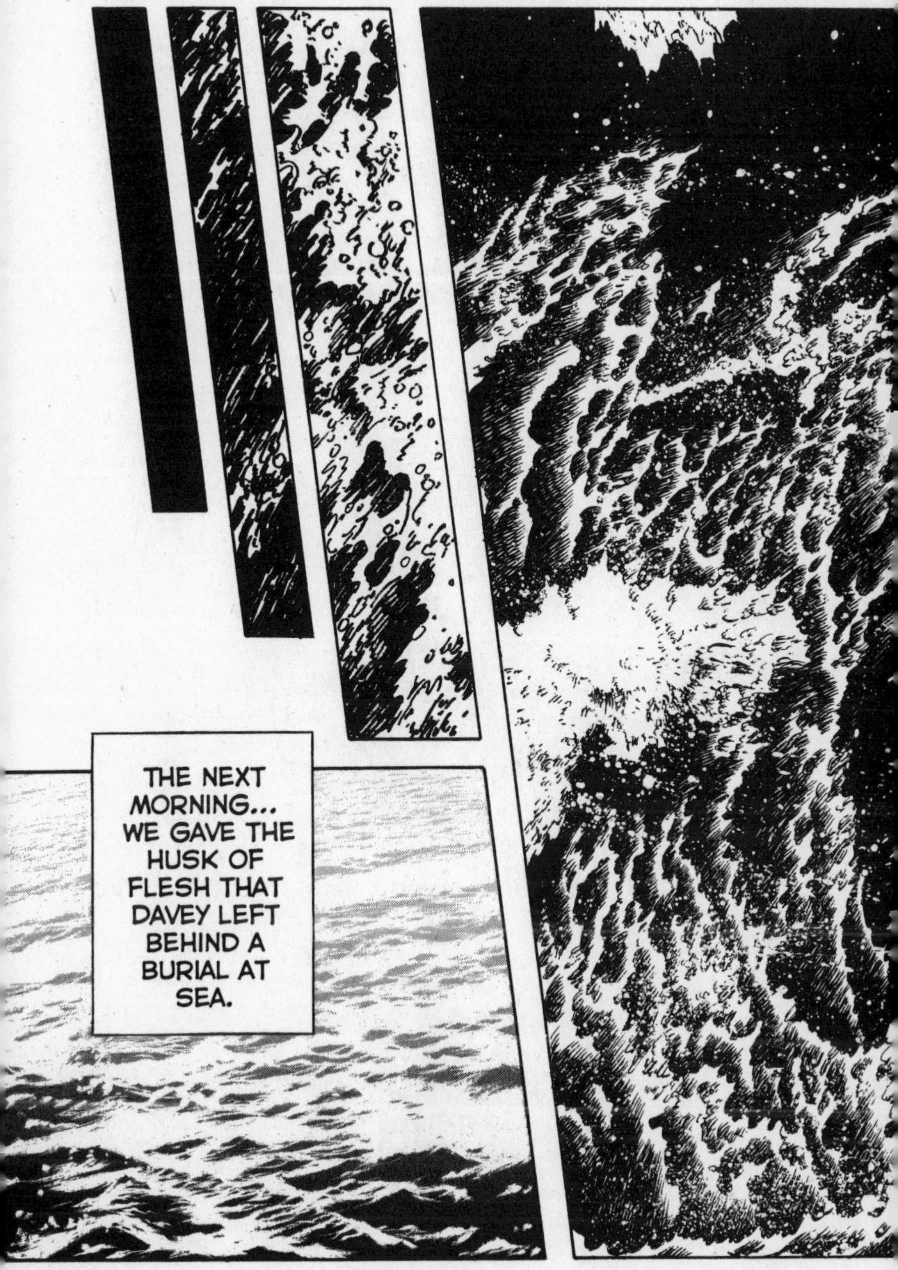
THE NEXT MORNING... WE GAVE THE HUSK OF FLESH THAT DAVEY LEFT BEHIND A BURIAL AT SEA.

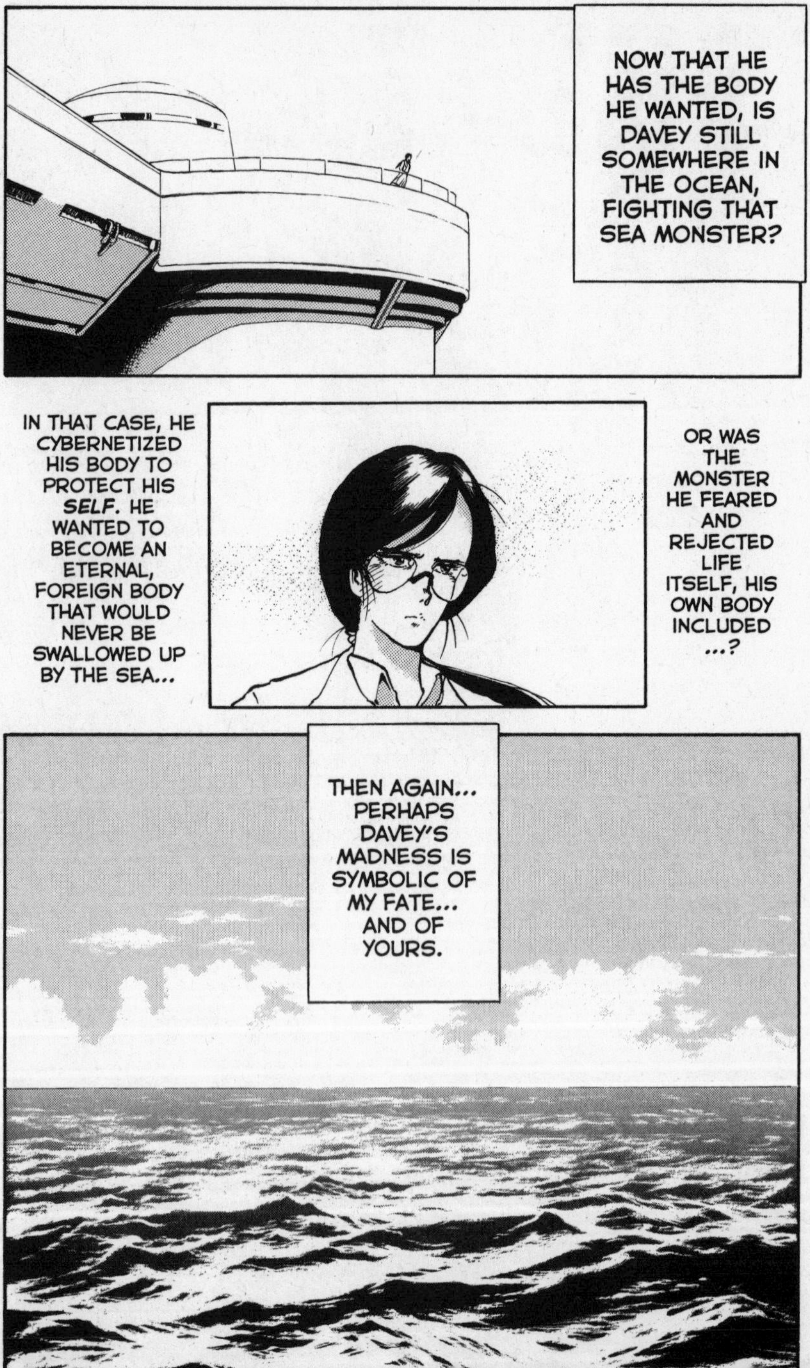
NOW THAT HE HAS THE BODY HE WANTED, IS DAVEY STILL SOMEWHERE IN THE OCEAN, FIGHTING THAT SEA MONSTER?
OR WAS THE MONSTER HE FEARED AND REJECTED LIFE ITSELF, HIS OWN BODY INCLUDED...?
IN THAT CASE, HE CYBERNETIZED HIS BODY TO PROTECT HIS *SELF*. HE WANTED TO BECOME AN ETERNAL, FOREIGN BODY THAT WOULD NEVER BE SWALLOWED UP BY THE SEA...
THEN AGAIN... PERHAPS DAVEY'S MADNESS IS SYMBOLIC OF MY FATE... AND OF YOURS.

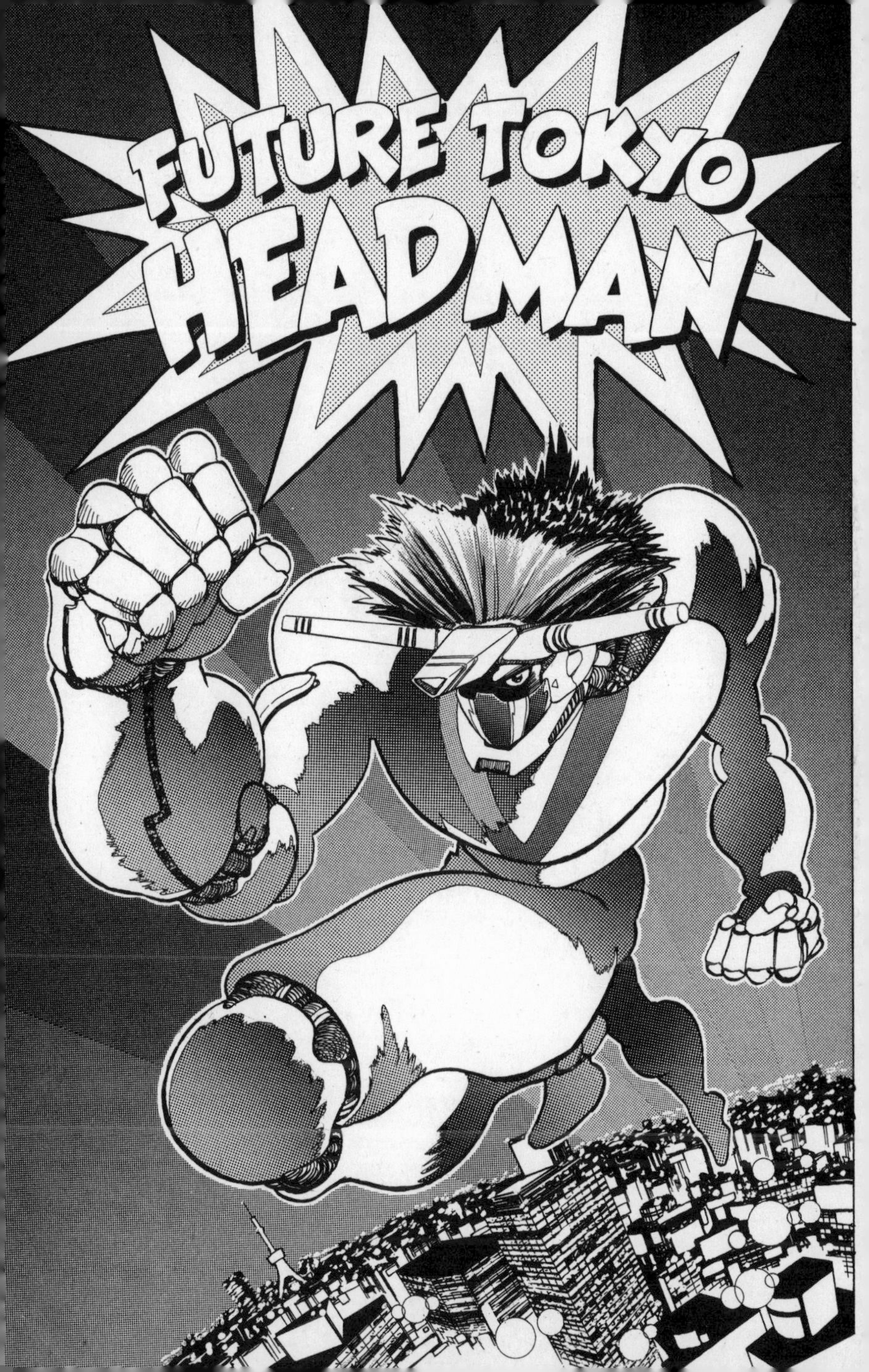
FUTURE TOKYO
HEADMAN

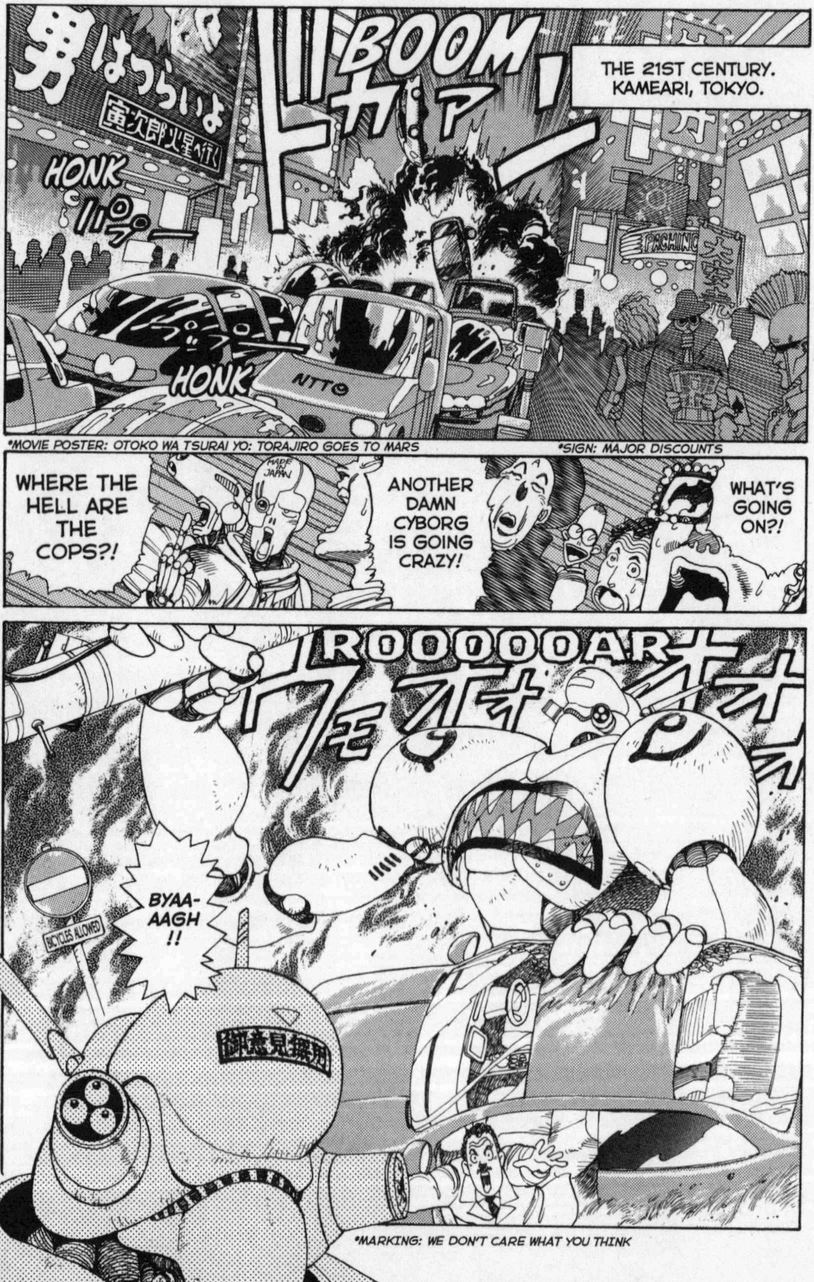
THE 21ST CENTURY. KAMEARI, TOKYO.
BOOM
ドカァー
男はつらいよ
寅次郎火星へ行く
HONK
パプー
HONK
NTT
PACHINKO
大安売
WHAT'S GOING ON?!
ANOTHER DAMN CYBORG IS GOING CRAZY!
WHERE THE HELL ARE THE COPS?!
MADE IN JAPAN
ROOOOOOAR
BYAA-AAGH!!
BICYCLES ALLOWED
御意見無用

*MOVIE POSTER: OTOKO WA TSURAI YO: TORAJIRO GOES TO MARS

*SIGN: MAJOR DISCOUNTS

*MARKING: WE DON'T CARE WHAT YOU THINK

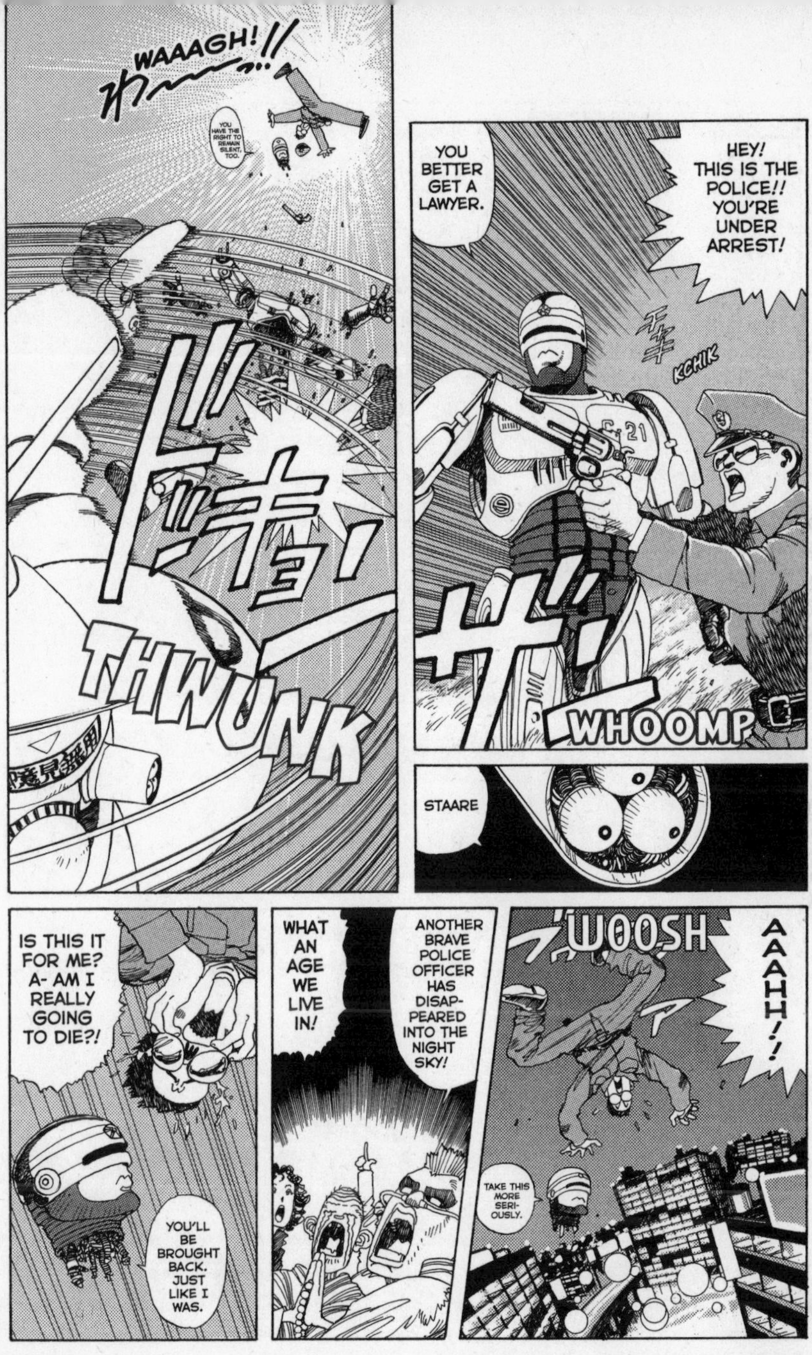
HEY! THIS IS THE POLICE!! YOU'RE UNDER ARREST!
YOU BETTER GET A LAWYER.
KCHIK
WHOOMP
STAARE
WAAAGH!!
YOU HAVE THE RIGHT TO REMAIN SILENT, TOO.
THWUNK
WOOSH
AAAHH!!
TAKE THIS MORE SERIOUSLY.
ANOTHER BRAVE POLICE OFFICER HAS DISAPPEARED INTO THE NIGHT SKY!
WHAT AN AGE WE LIVE IN!
IS THIS IT FOR ME? A- AM I REALLY GOING TO DIE?!
YOU'LL BE BROUGHT BACK. JUST LIKE I WAS.

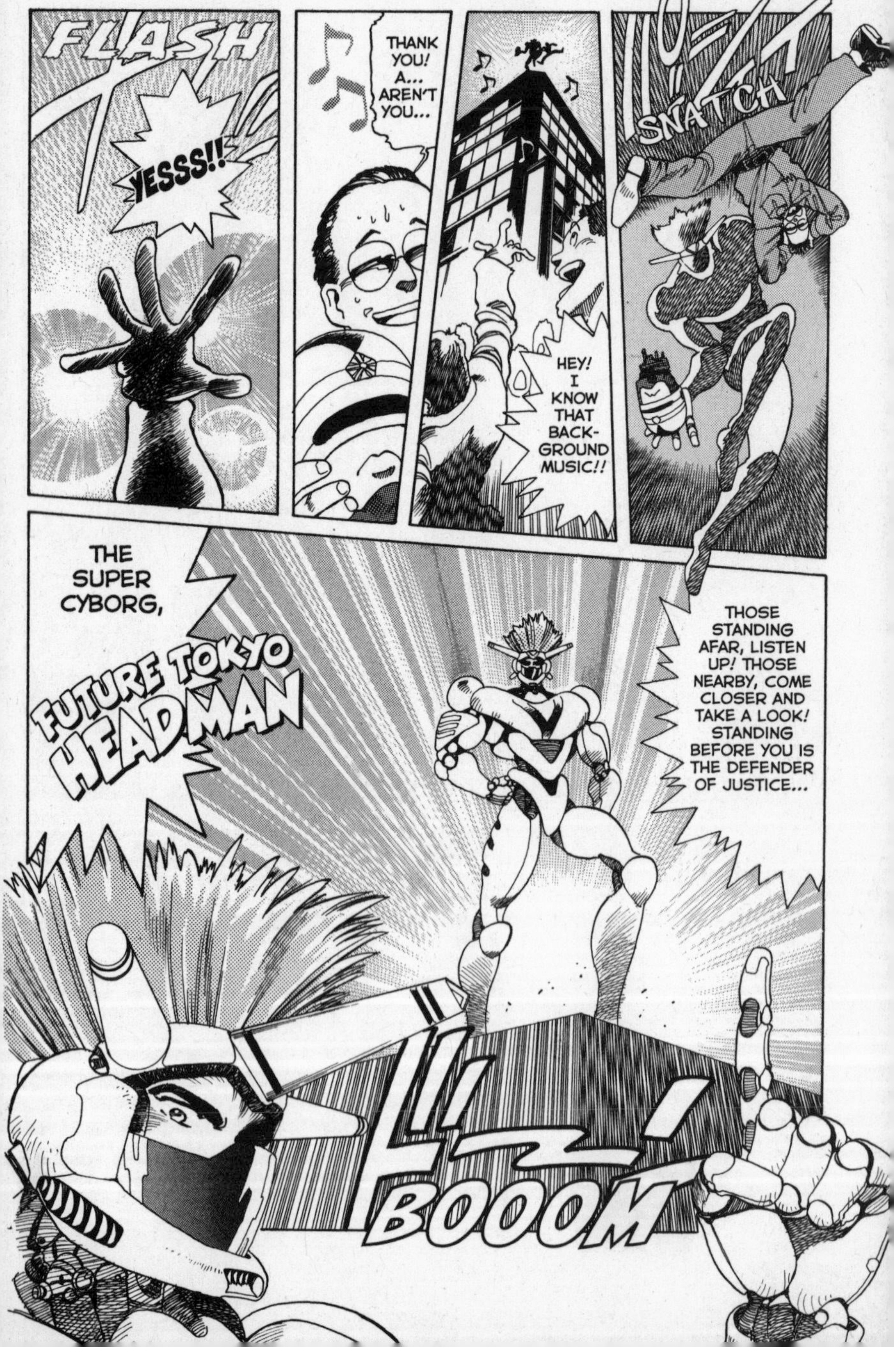
SNATCH
HEY! I KNOW THAT BACK-GROUND MUSIC!!
THANK YOU! A... AREN'T YOU...
FLASH
YESSS!!
THOSE STANDING AFAR, LISTEN UP! THOSE NEARBY, COME CLOSER AND TAKE A LOOK! STANDING BEFORE YOU IS THE DEFENDER OF JUSTICE...
THE SUPER CYBORG,
FUTURE TOKYO HEADMAN
BOOOM

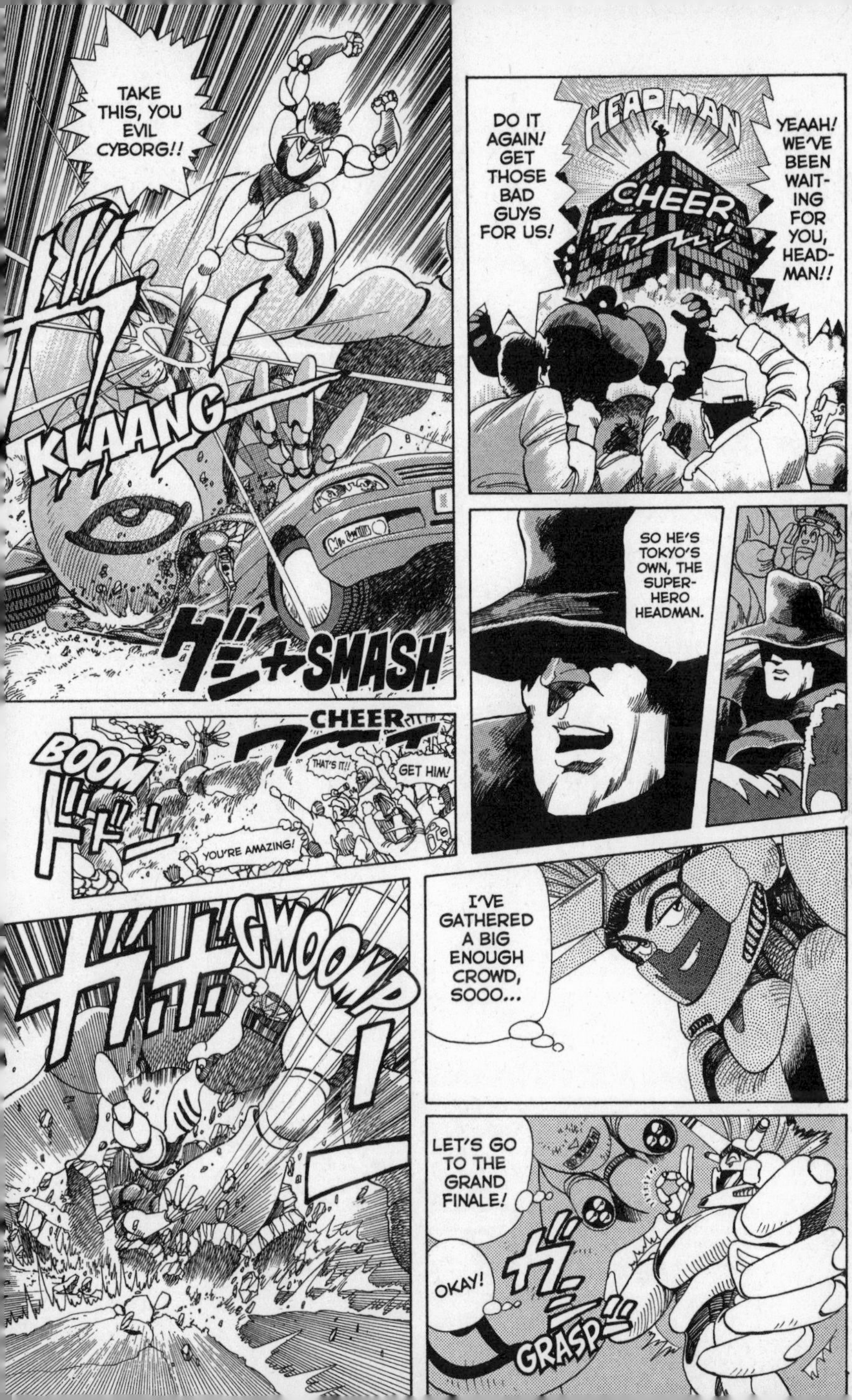

YEAAH! WE'VE BEEN WAITING FOR YOU, HEADMAN!!
HEADMAN
CHEER
DO IT AGAIN! GET THOSE BAD GUYS FOR US!
SO HE'S TOKYO'S OWN, THE SUPERHERO HEADMAN.
TAKE THIS, YOU EVIL CYBORG!!
KLAANG
SMASH
CHEER
GET HIM!
THAT'S IT!!
YOU'RE AMAZING!
BOOM
I'VE GATHERED A BIG ENOUGH CROWD, SOOO...
GWOOMP
LET'S GO TO THE GRAND FINALE!
OKAY!
GRASP

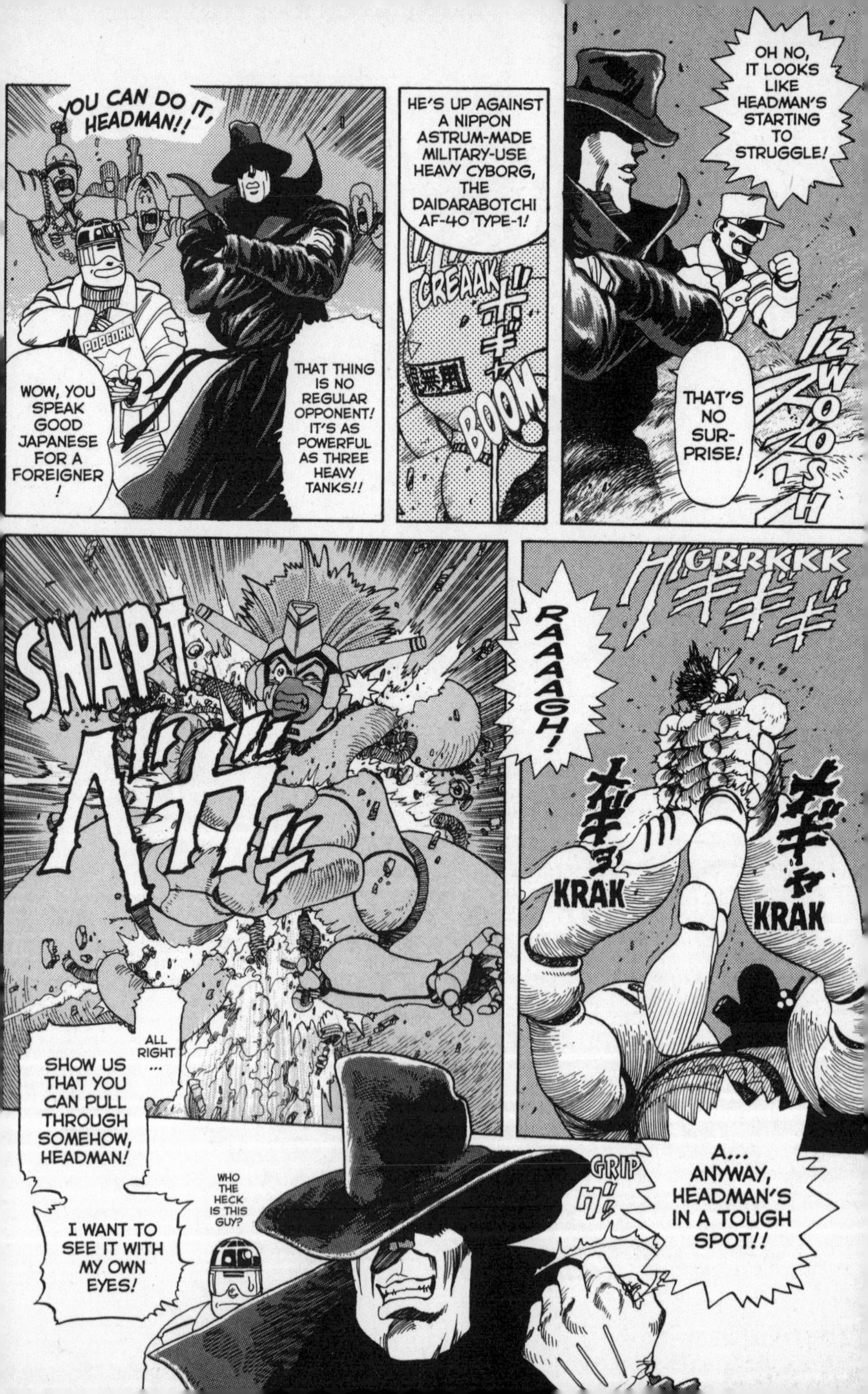
OH NO, IT LOOKS LIKE HEADMAN'S STARTING TO STRUGGLE!
THAT'S NO SURPRISE!
WOOOOSH
HE'S UP AGAINST A NIPPON ASTRUM-MADE MILITARY-USE HEAVY CYBORG, THE DAIDARABOTCHI AF-40 TYPE-1!
CREAAK
BOOM
YOU CAN DO IT, HEADMAN!!
THAT THING IS NO REGULAR OPPONENT! IT'S AS POWERFUL AS THREE HEAVY TANKS!!
POPCORN
WOW, YOU SPEAK GOOD JAPANESE FOR A FOREIGNER!
GRRKKK
RAAAAAGH!
KRAK
KRAK
SNAPT
A... ANYWAY, HEADMAN'S IN A TOUGH SPOT!!
GRIP
ALL RIGHT...
SHOW US THAT YOU CAN PULL THROUGH SOMEHOW, HEADMAN!
WHO THE HECK IS THIS GUY?
I WANT TO SEE IT WITH MY OWN EYES!

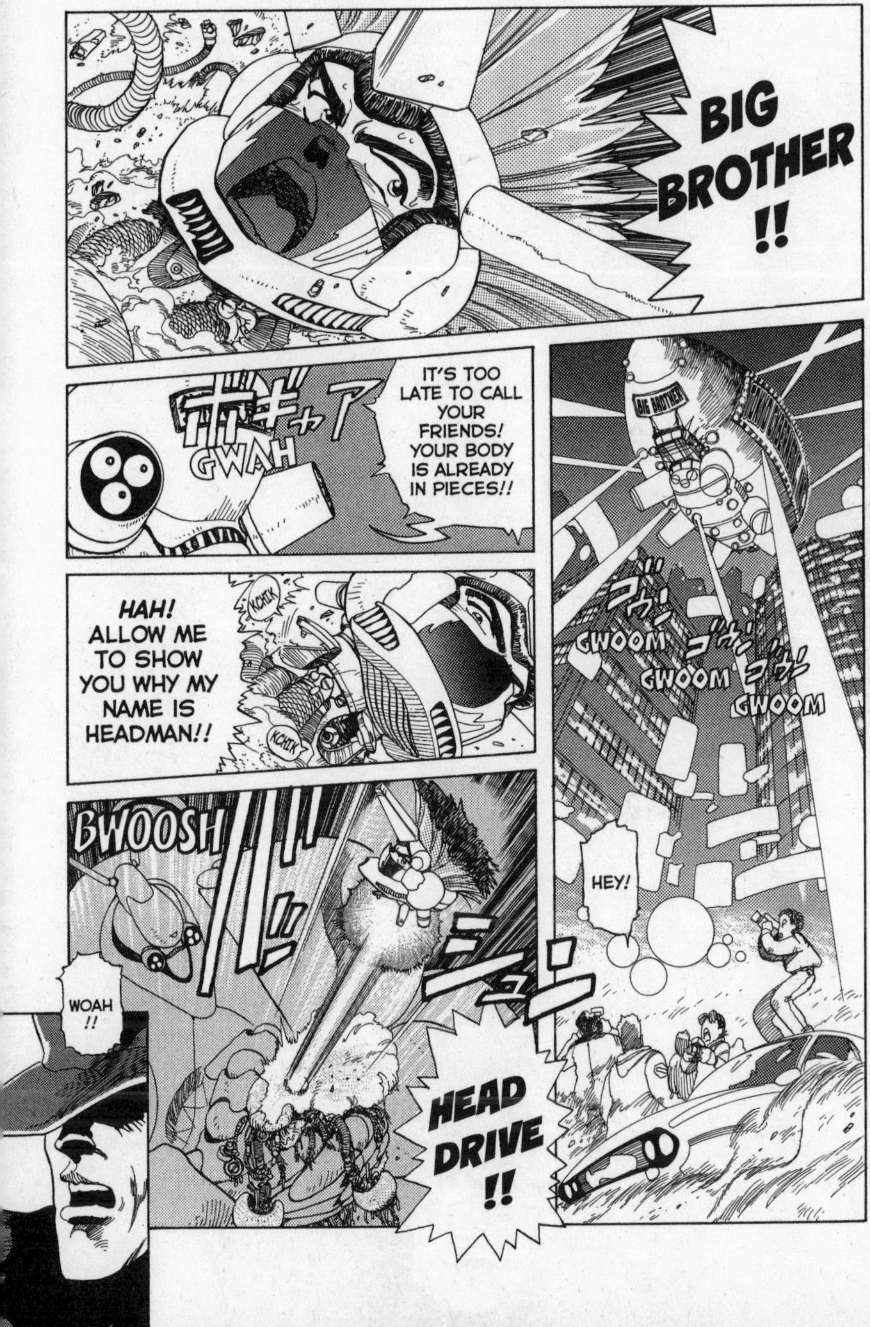
BIG BROTHER!!
BIG BROTHER
GWOOM
GWOOM
GWOOM
HEY!
GWAH
IT'S TOO LATE TO CALL YOUR FRIENDS! YOUR BODY IS ALREADY IN PIECES!!
HAH! ALLOW ME TO SHOW YOU WHY MY NAME IS HEADMAN!!
KCHIK
KCHIK
BWOOSH
HEAD DRIVE!!
WOAH!!

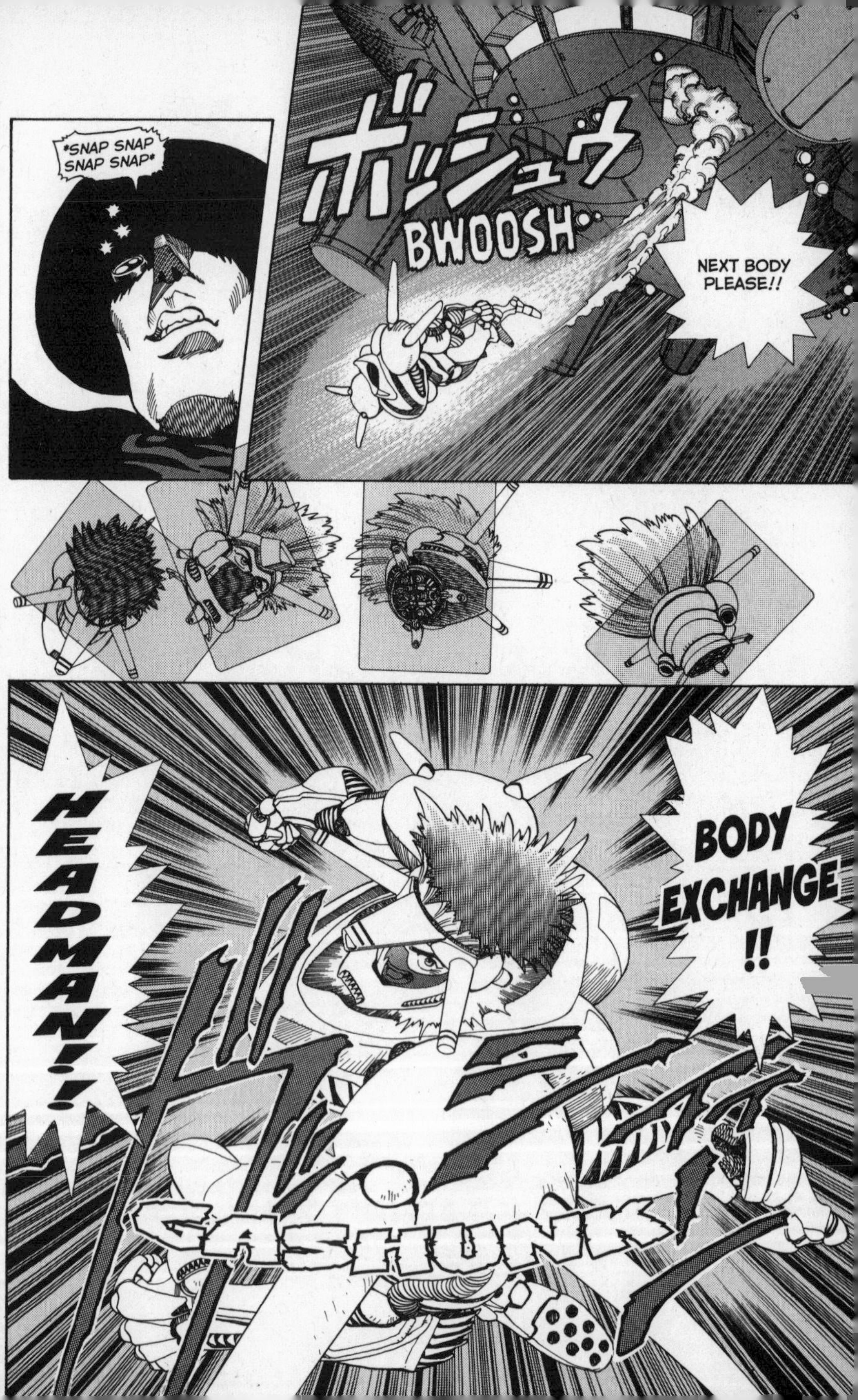
ボッシュウ
BWOOSH
NEXT BODY PLEASE!!
SNAP SNAP SNAP SNAP
BODY EXCHANGE!!
HEADMAN!!
GASHUNK

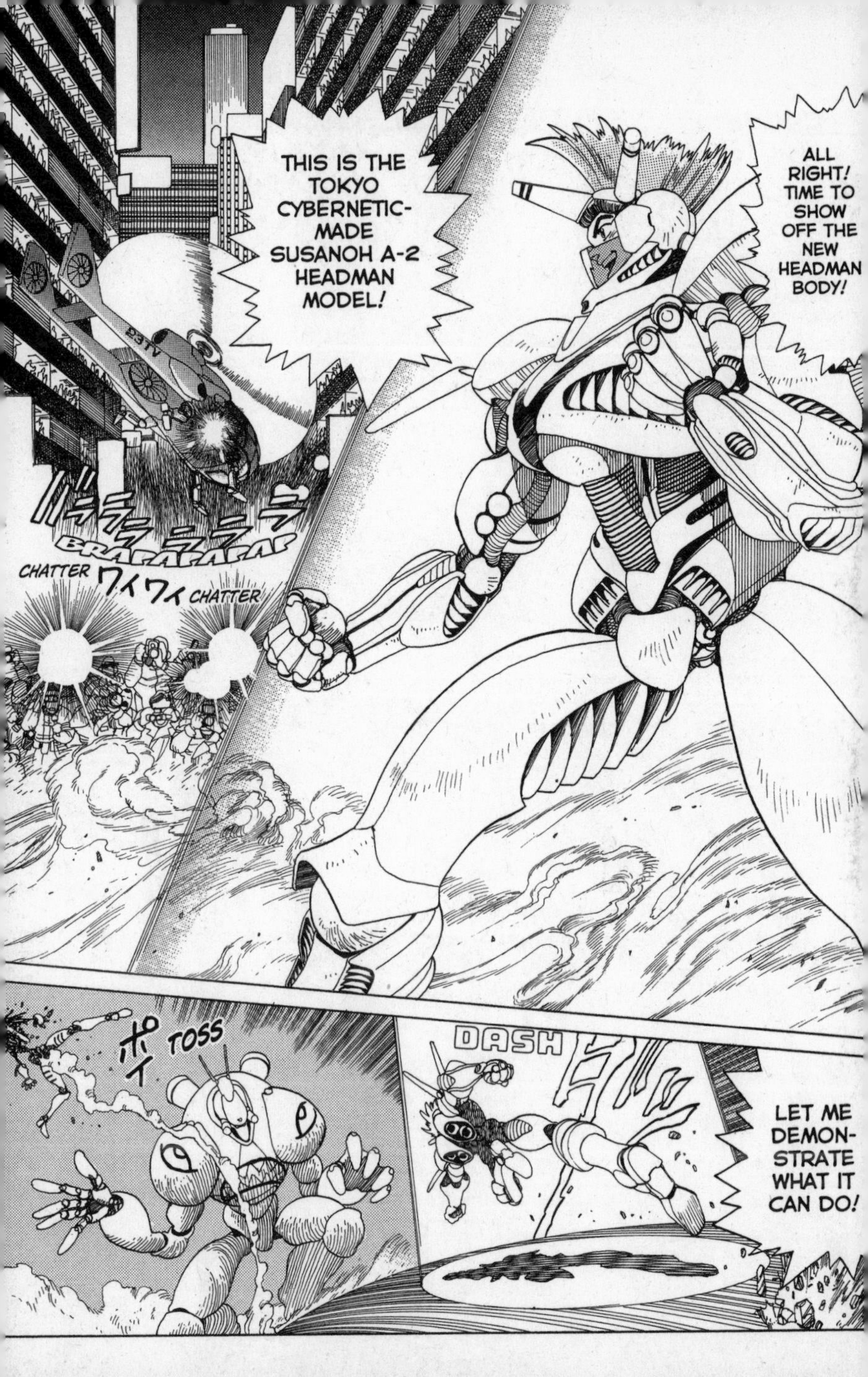
ALL RIGHT! TIME TO SHOW OFF THE NEW HEADMAN BODY!
THIS IS THE TOKYO CYBERNETIC-MADE SUSANOH A-2 HEADMAN MODEL!
23TV
BRAPAPAPAP
CHATTER ワイワイ CHATTER
DASH
LET ME DEMONSTRATE WHAT IT CAN DO!
ポイ TOSS

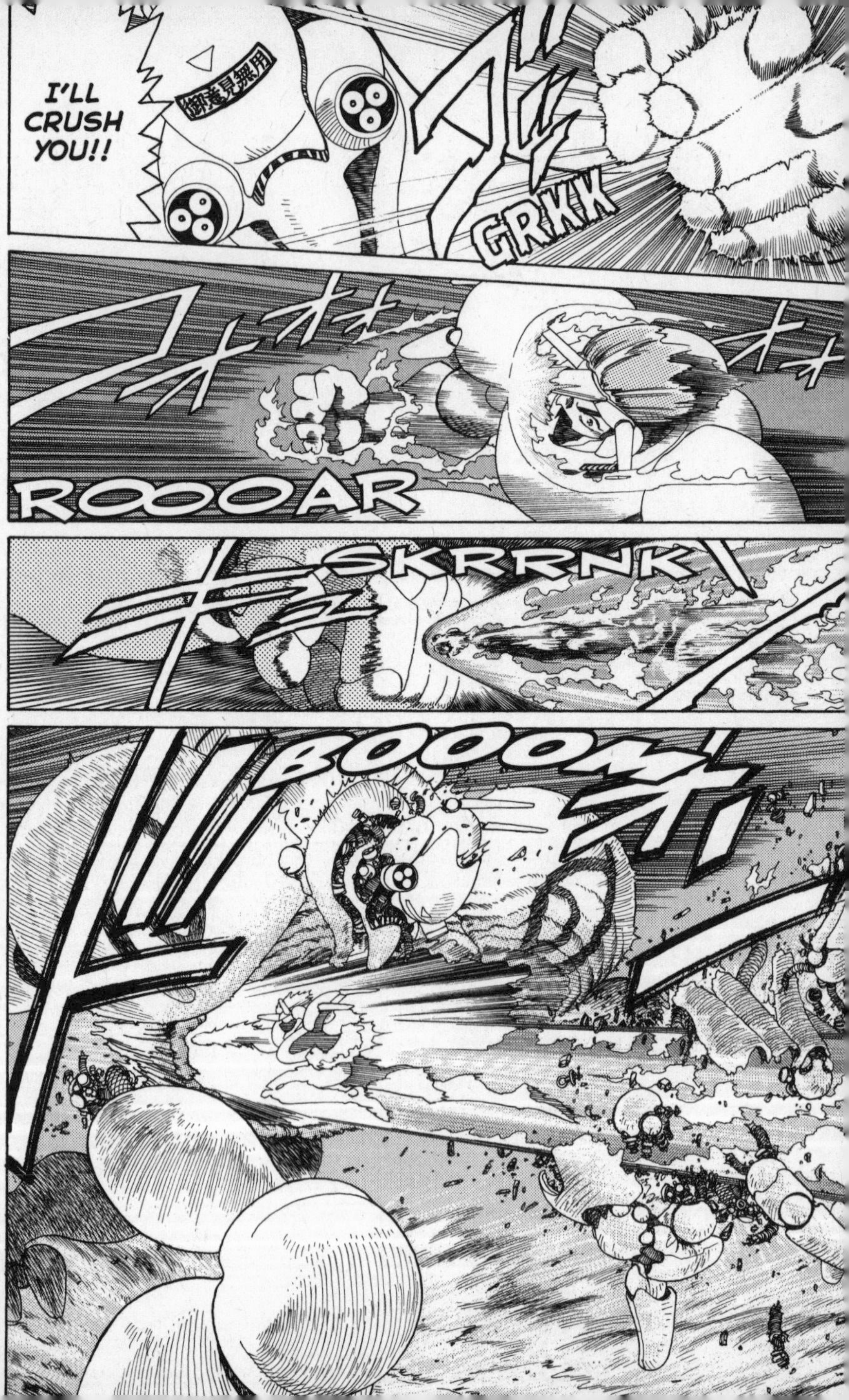
I'LL CRUSH YOU!!
御意見無用
GRKK
ROOOAR
SKRRNK
BOOOM

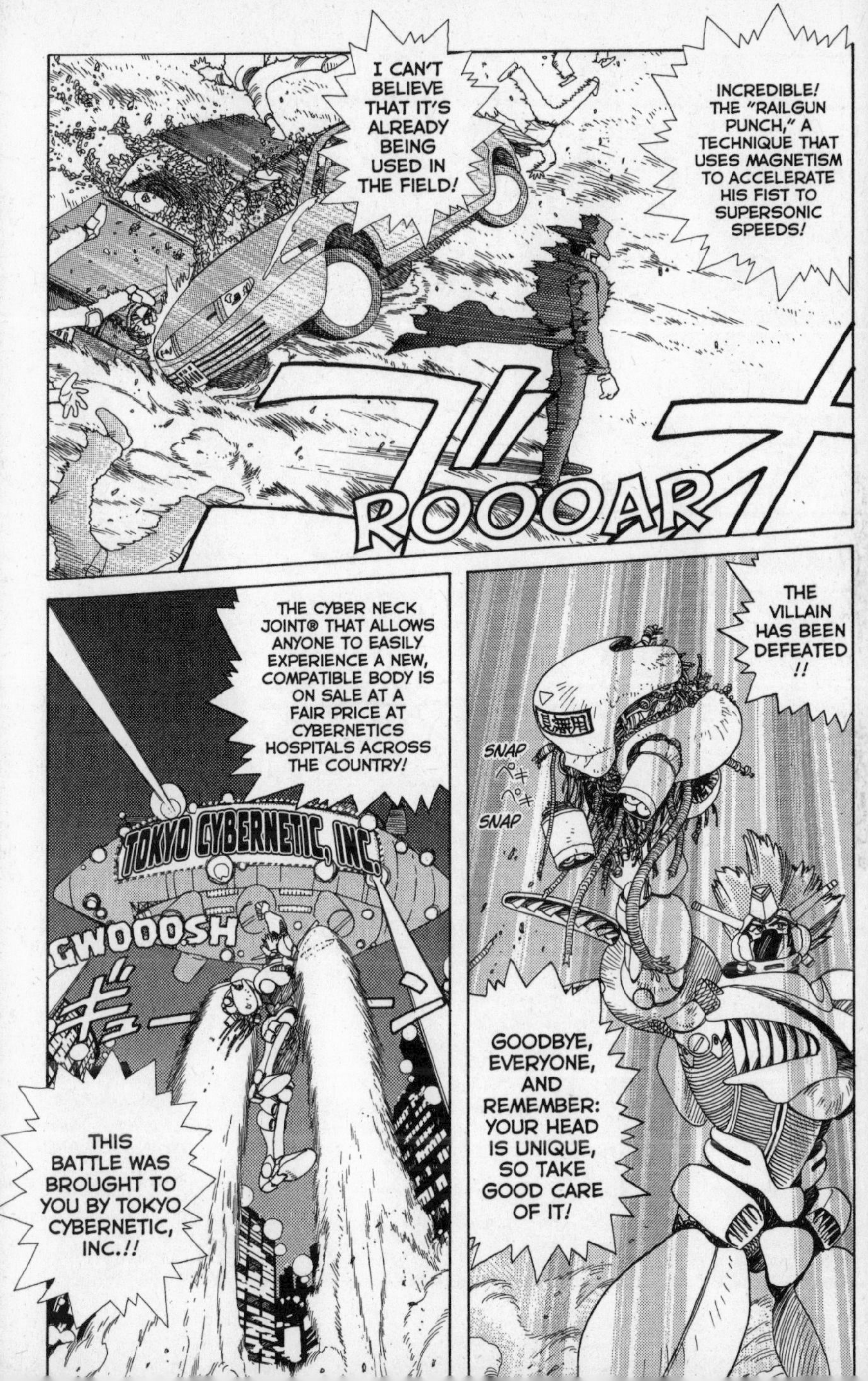
INCREDIBLE! THE "RAILGUN PUNCH," A TECHNIQUE THAT USES MAGNETISM TO ACCELERATE HIS FIST TO SUPERSONIC SPEEDS!
I CAN'T BELIEVE THAT IT'S ALREADY BEING USED IN THE FIELD!
ROOOAR
THE VILLAIN HAS BEEN DEFEATED !!
SNAP
ペキ
ペキ
SNAP
GOODBYE, EVERYONE, AND REMEMBER: YOUR HEAD IS UNIQUE, SO TAKE GOOD CARE OF IT!
THE CYBER NECK JOINT® THAT ALLOWS ANYONE TO EASILY EXPERIENCE A NEW, COMPATIBLE BODY IS ON SALE AT A FAIR PRICE AT CYBERNETICS HOSPITALS ACROSS THE COUNTRY!
TOKYO CYBERNETIC, INC.
GWOOOSH
ギュー
THIS BATTLE WAS BROUGHT TO YOU BY TOKYO CYBERNETIC, INC.!!

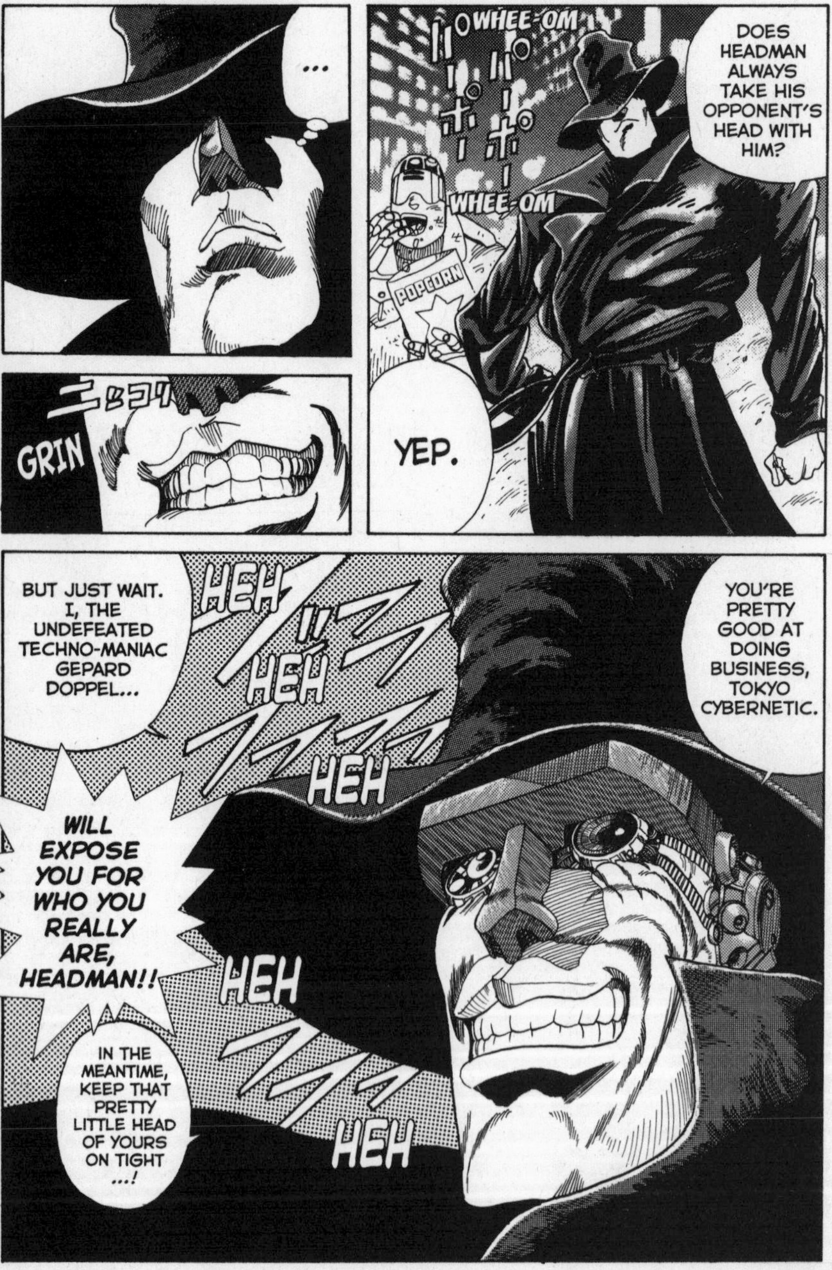
WHEE-OM
WHEE-OM
DOES HEADMAN ALWAYS TAKE HIS OPPONENT'S HEAD WITH HIM?
POPCORN
YEP.
...
GRIN
YOU'RE PRETTY GOOD AT DOING BUSINESS, TOKYO CYBERNETIC.
HEH HEH HEH
BUT JUST WAIT. I, THE UNDEFEATED TECHNO-MANIAC GEPARD DOPPEL...
WILL EXPOSE YOU FOR WHO YOU REALLY ARE, HEADMAN!!
HEH HEH
IN THE MEANTIME, KEEP THAT PRETTY LITTLE HEAD OF YOURS ON TIGHT ...!

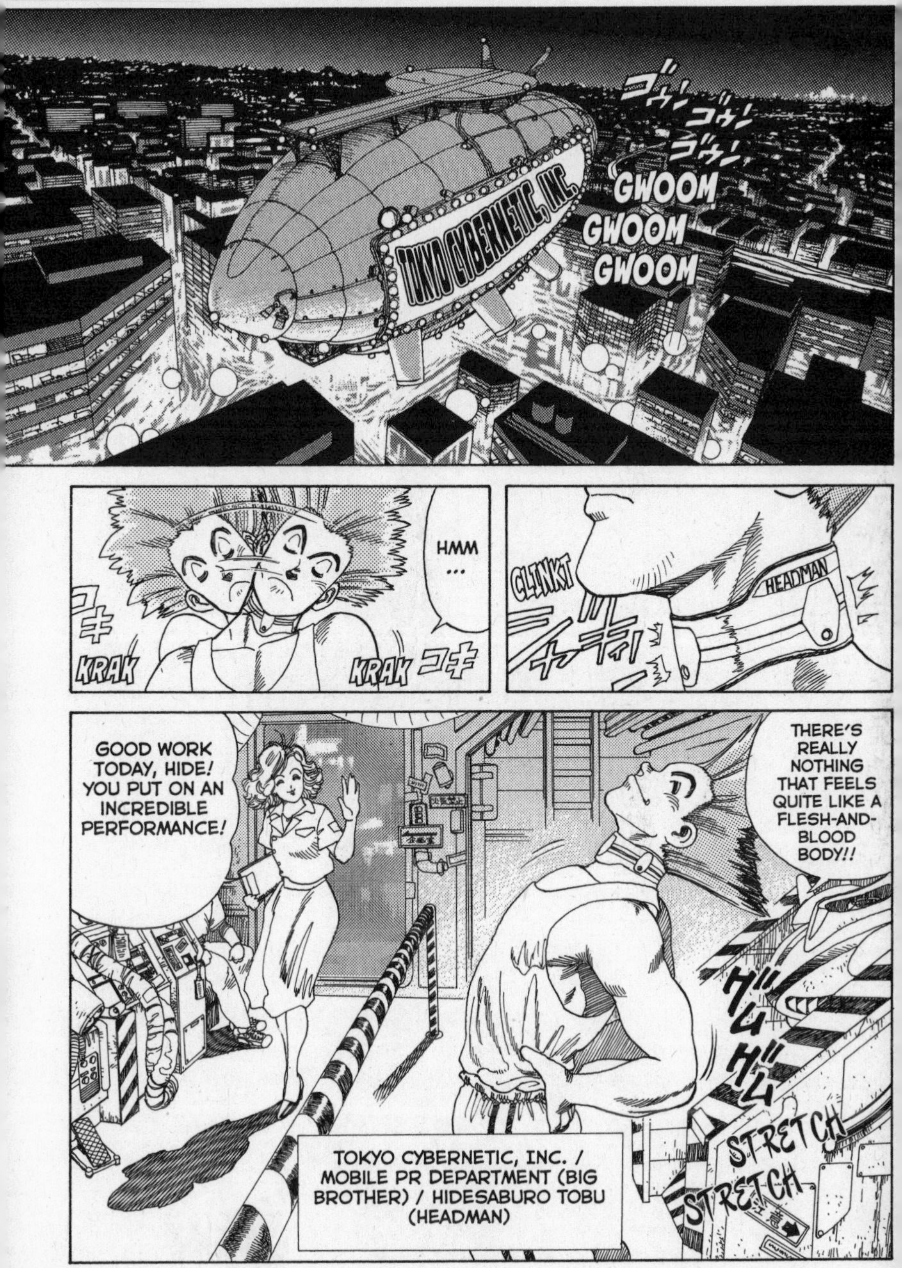
TOKYO CYBERNETIC, INC.
GWOOM
GWOOM
GWOOM
HEADMAN
CLINKT
HMM ...
KRAK
KRAK
THERE'S REALLY NOTHING THAT FEELS QUITE LIKE A FLESH-AND-BLOOD BODY!!
GOOD WORK TODAY, HIDE! YOU PUT ON AN INCREDIBLE PERFORMANCE!
TOKYO CYBERNETIC, INC. / MOBILE PR DEPARTMENT (BIG BROTHER) / HIDESABURO TOBU (HEADMAN)
STRETCH
STRETCH

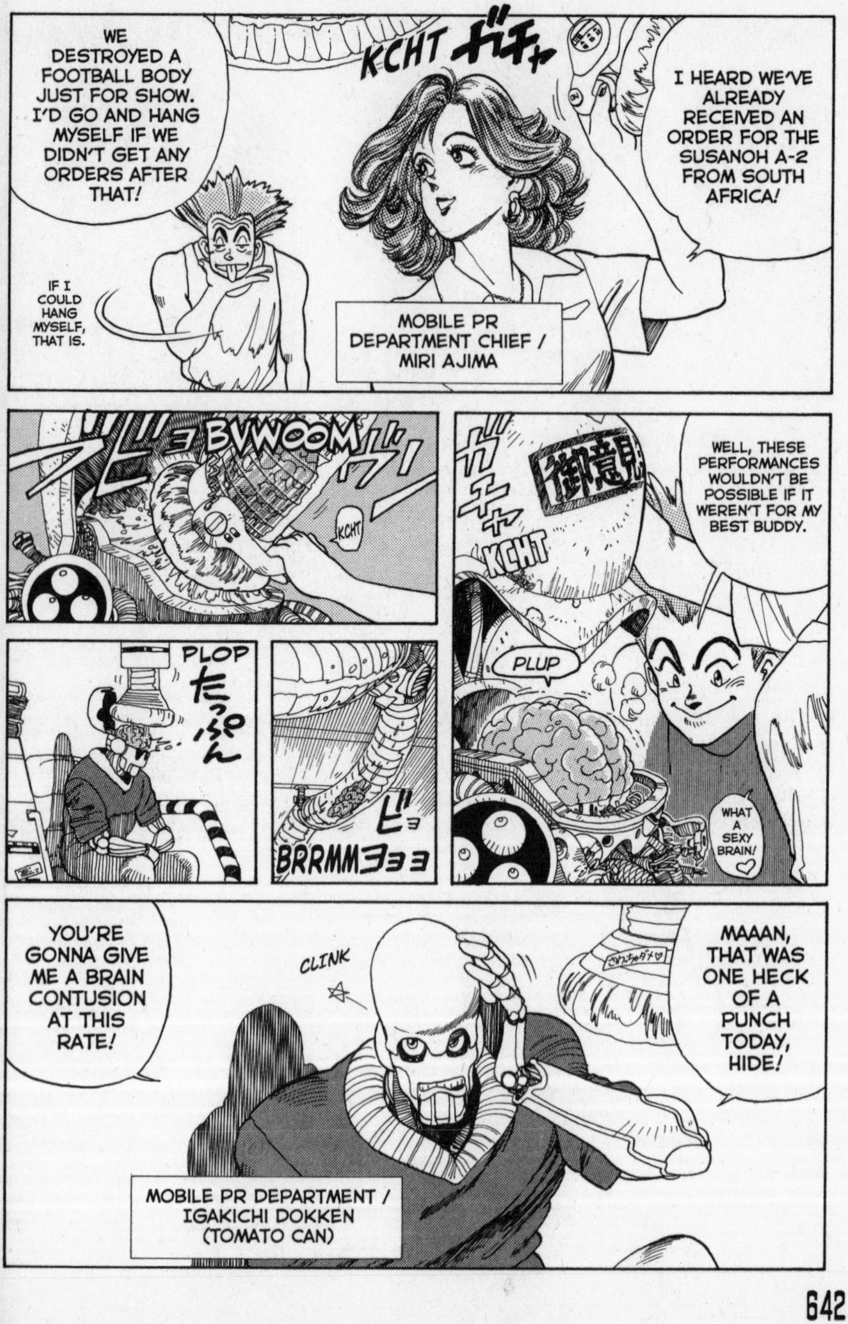
KCHT
I HEARD WE'VE ALREADY RECEIVED AN ORDER FOR THE SUSANOH A-2 FROM SOUTH AFRICA!
WE DESTROYED A FOOTBALL BODY JUST FOR SHOW. I'D GO AND HANG MYSELF IF WE DIDN'T GET ANY ORDERS AFTER THAT!
IF I COULD HANG MYSELF, THAT IS.
MOBILE PR DEPARTMENT CHIEF / MIRI AJIMA
WELL, THESE PERFORMANCES WOULDN'T BE POSSIBLE IF IT WEREN'T FOR MY BEST BUDDY.
KCHT
PLUP
WHAT A SEXY BRAIN!
BVWOOM
KCHT
BRRMM
PLOP
MAAAN, THAT WAS ONE HECK OF A PUNCH TODAY, HIDE!
CLINK
YOU'RE GONNA GIVE ME A BRAIN CONTUSION AT THIS RATE!
MOBILE PR DEPARTMENT / IGAKICHI DOKKEN (TOMATO CAN)

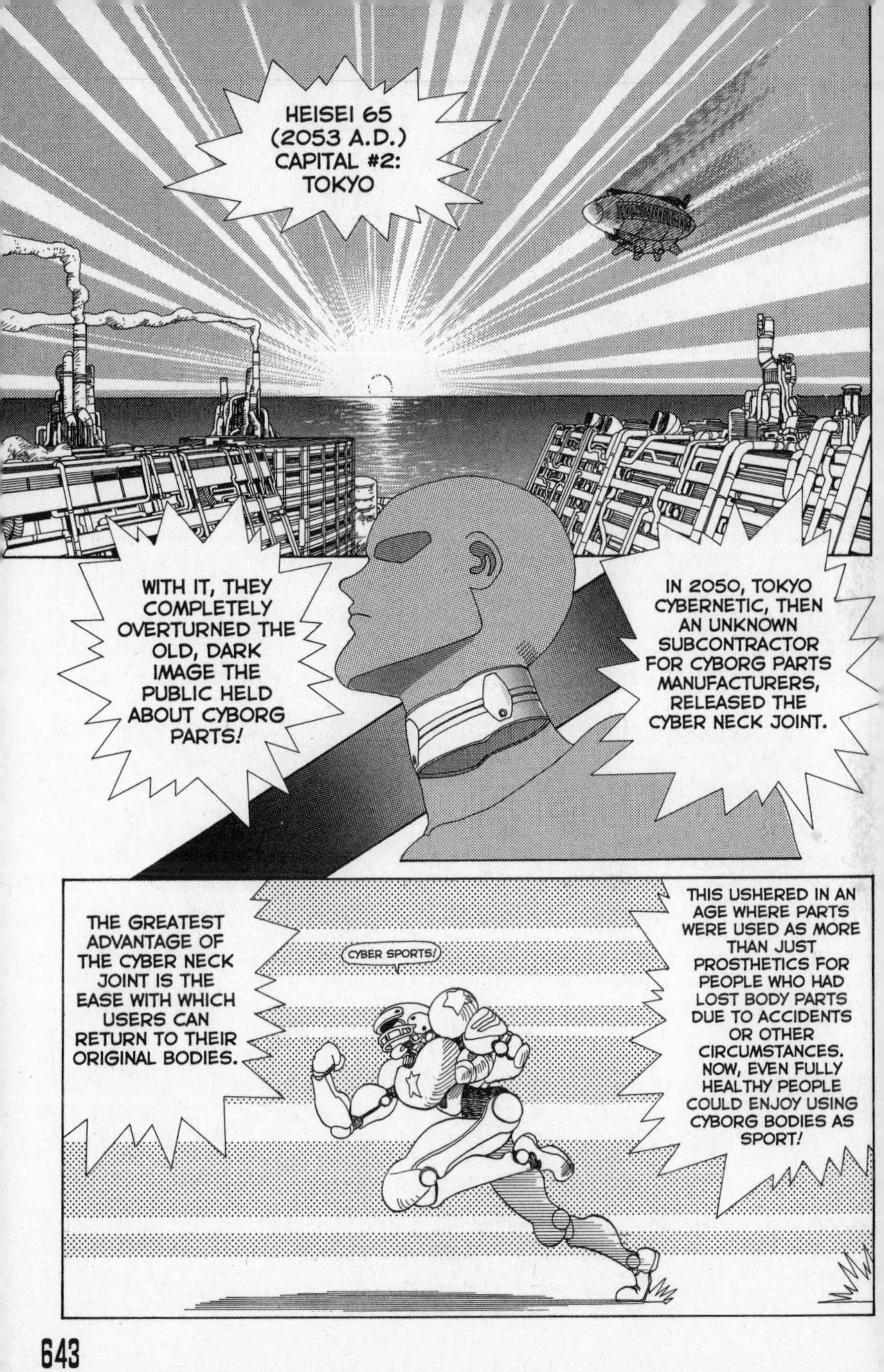
HEISEI 65 (2053 A.D.) CAPITAL #2: TOKYO
IN 2050, TOKYO CYBERNETIC, THEN AN UNKNOWN SUBCONTRACTOR FOR CYBORG PARTS MANUFACTURERS, RELEASED THE CYBER NECK JOINT.
WITH IT, THEY COMPLETELY OVERTURNED THE OLD, DARK IMAGE THE PUBLIC HELD ABOUT CYBORG PARTS!
THIS USHERED IN AN AGE WHERE PARTS WERE USED AS MORE THAN JUST PROSTHETICS FOR PEOPLE WHO HAD LOST BODY PARTS DUE TO ACCIDENTS OR OTHER CIRCUMSTANCES. NOW, EVEN FULLY HEALTHY PEOPLE COULD ENJOY USING CYBORG BODIES AS SPORT!
CYBER SPORTS!
THE GREATEST ADVANTAGE OF THE CYBER NECK JOINT IS THE EASE WITH WHICH USERS CAN RETURN TO THEIR ORIGINAL BODIES.

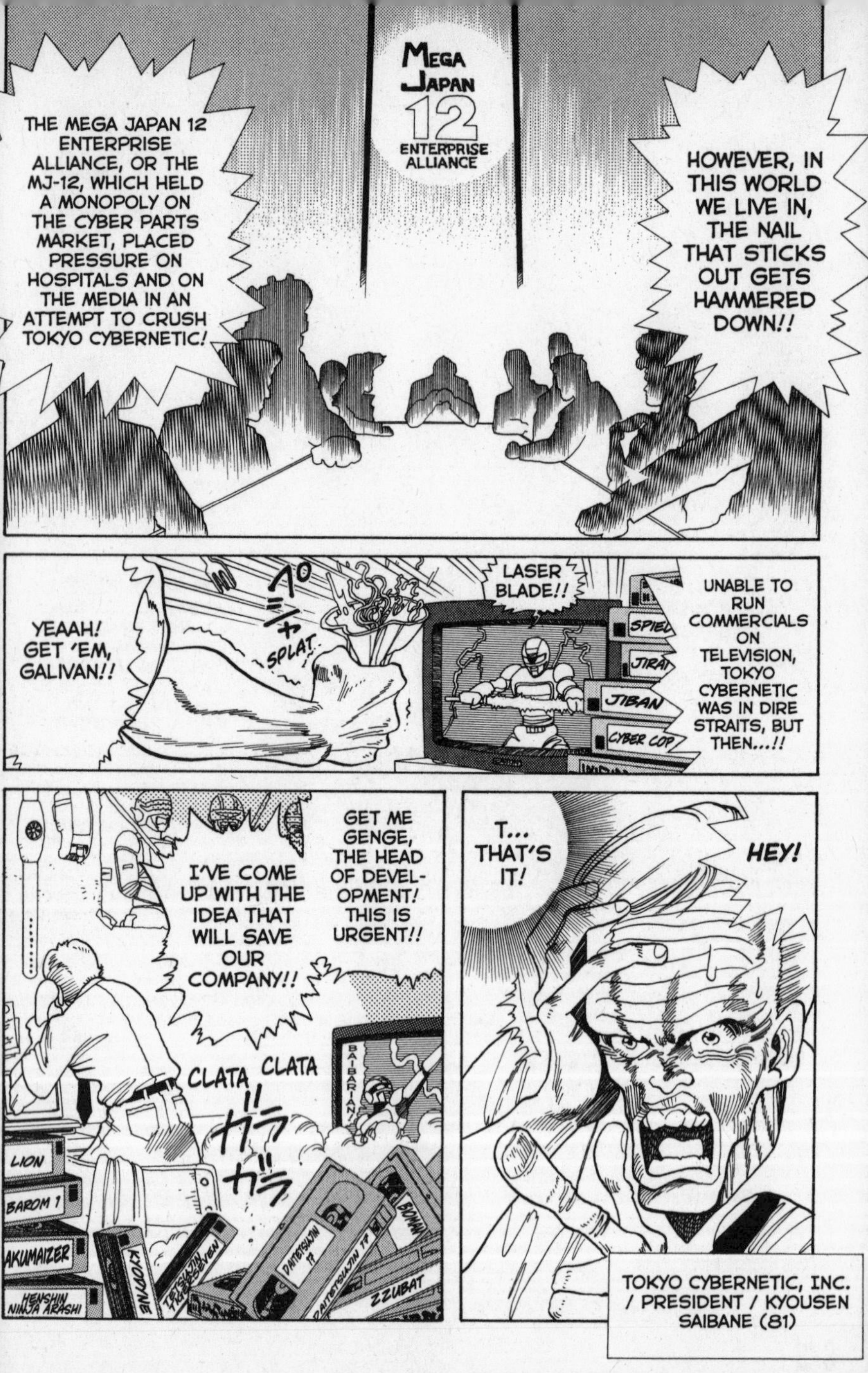
MEGA JAPAN 12 ENTERPRISE ALLIANCE
HOWEVER, IN THIS WORLD WE LIVE IN, THE NAIL THAT STICKS OUT GETS HAMMERED DOWN!!
THE MEGA JAPAN 12 ENTERPRISE ALLIANCE, OR THE MJ-12, WHICH HELD A MONOPOLY ON THE CYBER PARTS MARKET, PLACED PRESSURE ON HOSPITALS AND ON THE MEDIA IN AN ATTEMPT TO CRUSH TOKYO CYBERNETIC!
UNABLE TO RUN COMMERCIALS ON TELEVISION, TOKYO CYBERNETIC WAS IN DIRE STRAITS, BUT THEN...!!
LASER BLADE!!
SPIEL
JIRAI
JIBAN
CYBER COP
SPLAT
YEAAH! GET 'EM, GALIVAN!!
HEY!
T... THAT'S IT!
TOKYO CYBERNETIC, INC. / PRESIDENT / KYOUSEN SAIBANE (81)
GET ME GENGE, THE HEAD OF DEVEL-OPMENT! THIS IS URGENT!!
I'VE COME UP WITH THE IDEA THAT WILL SAVE OUR COMPANY!!
CLATA CLATA
BAIBARIAN!
LION
BAROM 1
AKUMAIZER
HENSHIN NINJA ARASHI
KYODYNE
DAITETSUJIN 17
ZZUBAT

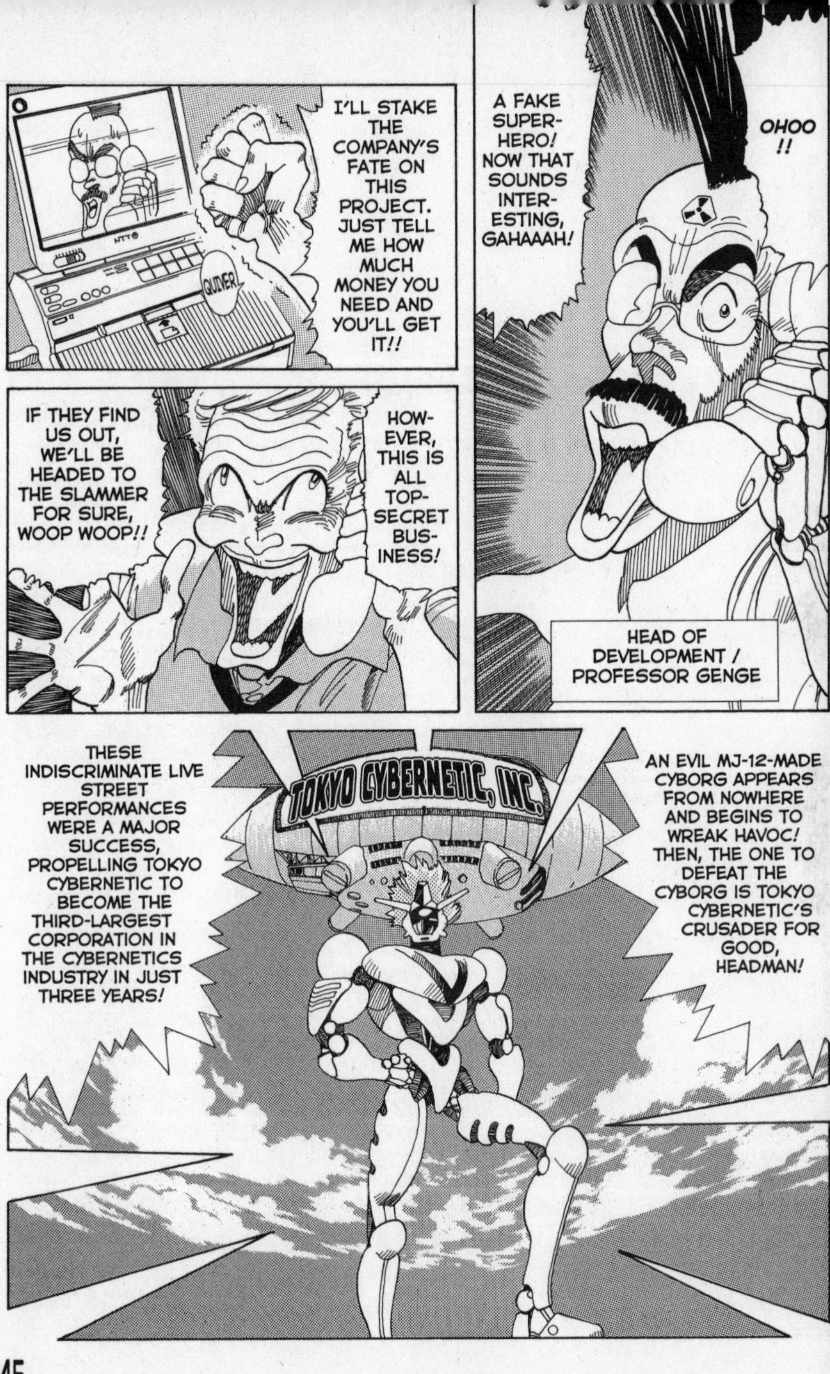
OHOO!!
A FAKE SUPERHERO! NOW THAT SOUNDS INTERESTING, GAHAAAH!
HEAD OF DEVELOPMENT / PROFESSOR GENGE
I'LL STAKE THE COMPANY'S FATE ON THIS PROJECT. JUST TELL ME HOW MUCH MONEY YOU NEED AND YOU'LL GET IT!!
QUIVER
HOWEVER, THIS IS ALL TOP-SECRET BUSINESS!
IF THEY FIND US OUT, WE'LL BE HEADED TO THE SLAMMER FOR SURE, WOOP WOOP!!
TOKYO CYBERNETIC, INC.
AN EVIL MJ-12-MADE CYBORG APPEARS FROM NOWHERE AND BEGINS TO WREAK HAVOC! THEN, THE ONE TO DEFEAT THE CYBORG IS TOKYO CYBERNETIC'S CRUSADER FOR GOOD, HEADMAN!
THESE INDISCRIMINATE LIVE STREET PERFORMANCES WERE A MAJOR SUCCESS, PROPELLING TOKYO CYBERNETIC TO BECOME THE THIRD-LARGEST CORPORATION IN THE CYBERNETICS INDUSTRY IN JUST THREE YEARS!

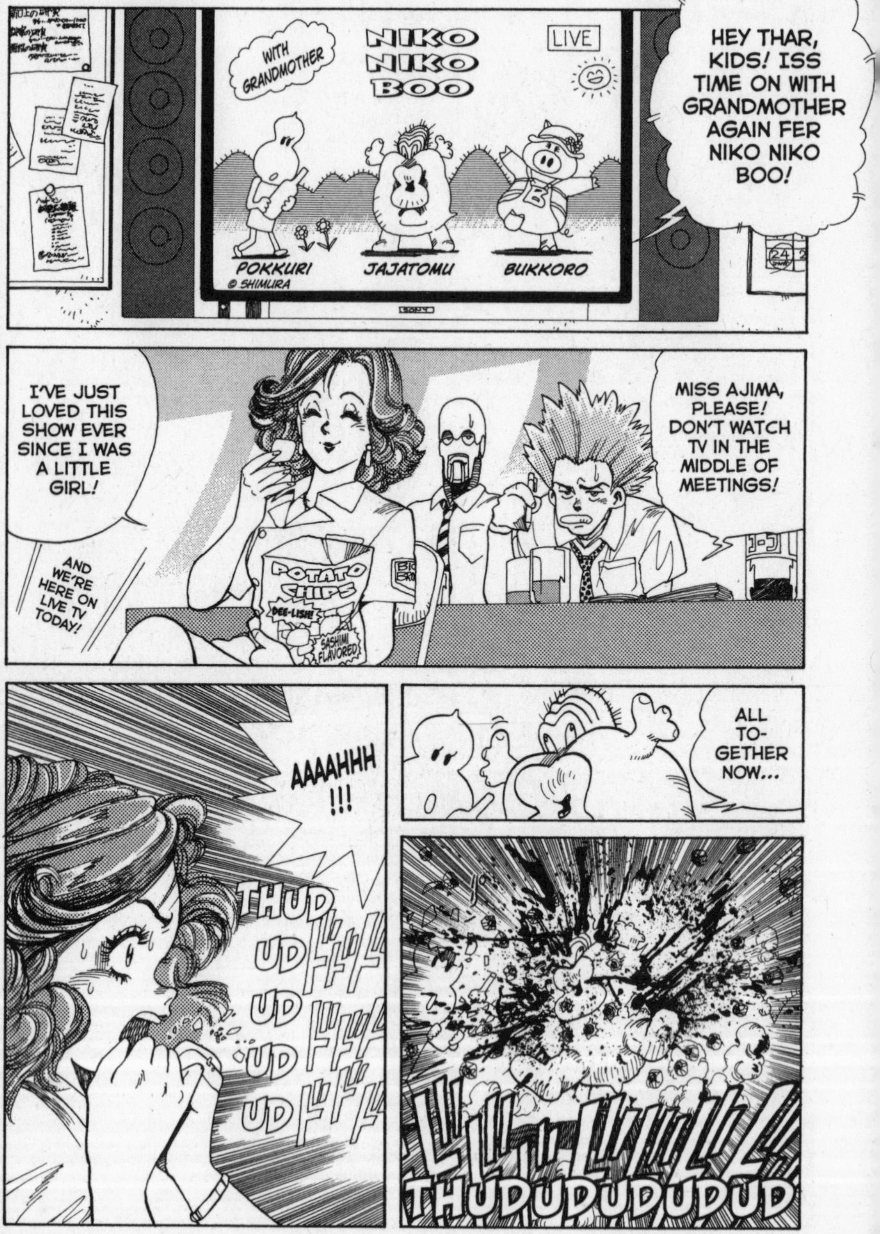

WITH GRANDMOTHER
NIKO NIKO BOO
LIVE
POKKURI
JAJATOMU
BUKKORO
© SHIMURA
HEY THAR, KIDS! ISS TIME ON WITH GRANDMOTHER AGAIN FER NIKO NIKO BOO!
MISS AJIMA, PLEASE! DON'T WATCH TV IN THE MIDDLE OF MEETINGS!
I'VE JUST LOVED THIS SHOW EVER SINCE I WAS A LITTLE GIRL!
AND WE'RE HERE ON LIVE TV TODAY!
POTATO CHIPS
DEE-LISH!!
SASHIMI FLAVORED
ALL TO-GETHER NOW...
THUDUDUDUDUDUD
AAAAHHH !!!
THUD UD UD UD

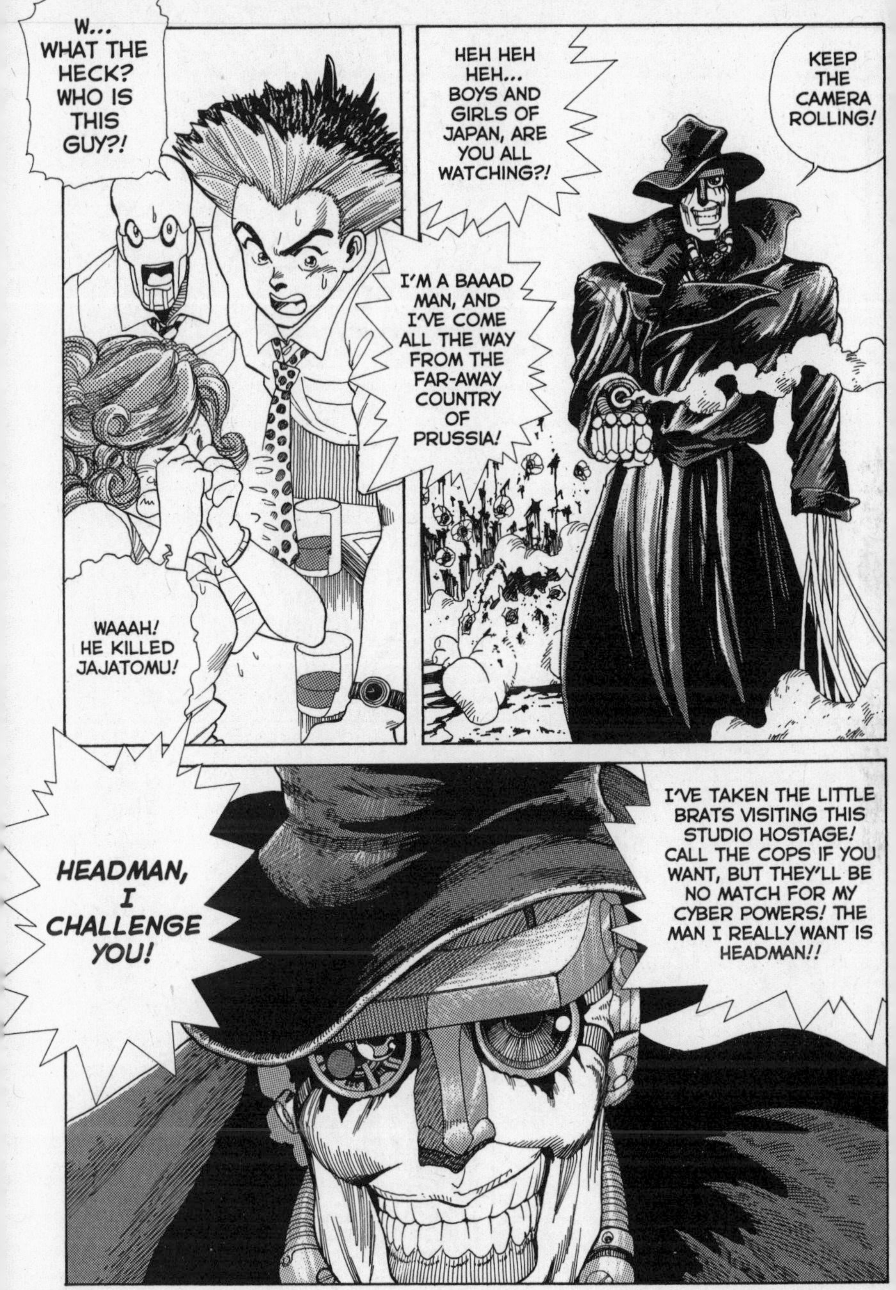
KEEP THE CAMERA ROLLING!
HEH HEH HEH... BOYS AND GIRLS OF JAPAN, ARE YOU ALL WATCHING?!
I'M A BAAAD MAN, AND I'VE COME ALL THE WAY FROM THE FAR-AWAY COUNTRY OF PRUSSIA!
W... WHAT THE HECK? WHO IS THIS GUY?!
WAAAH! HE KILLED JAJATOMU!
I'VE TAKEN THE LITTLE BRATS VISITING THIS STUDIO HOSTAGE! CALL THE COPS IF YOU WANT, BUT THEY'LL BE NO MATCH FOR MY CYBER POWERS! THE MAN I REALLY WANT IS HEADMAN!!
HEADMAN, I CHALLENGE YOU!

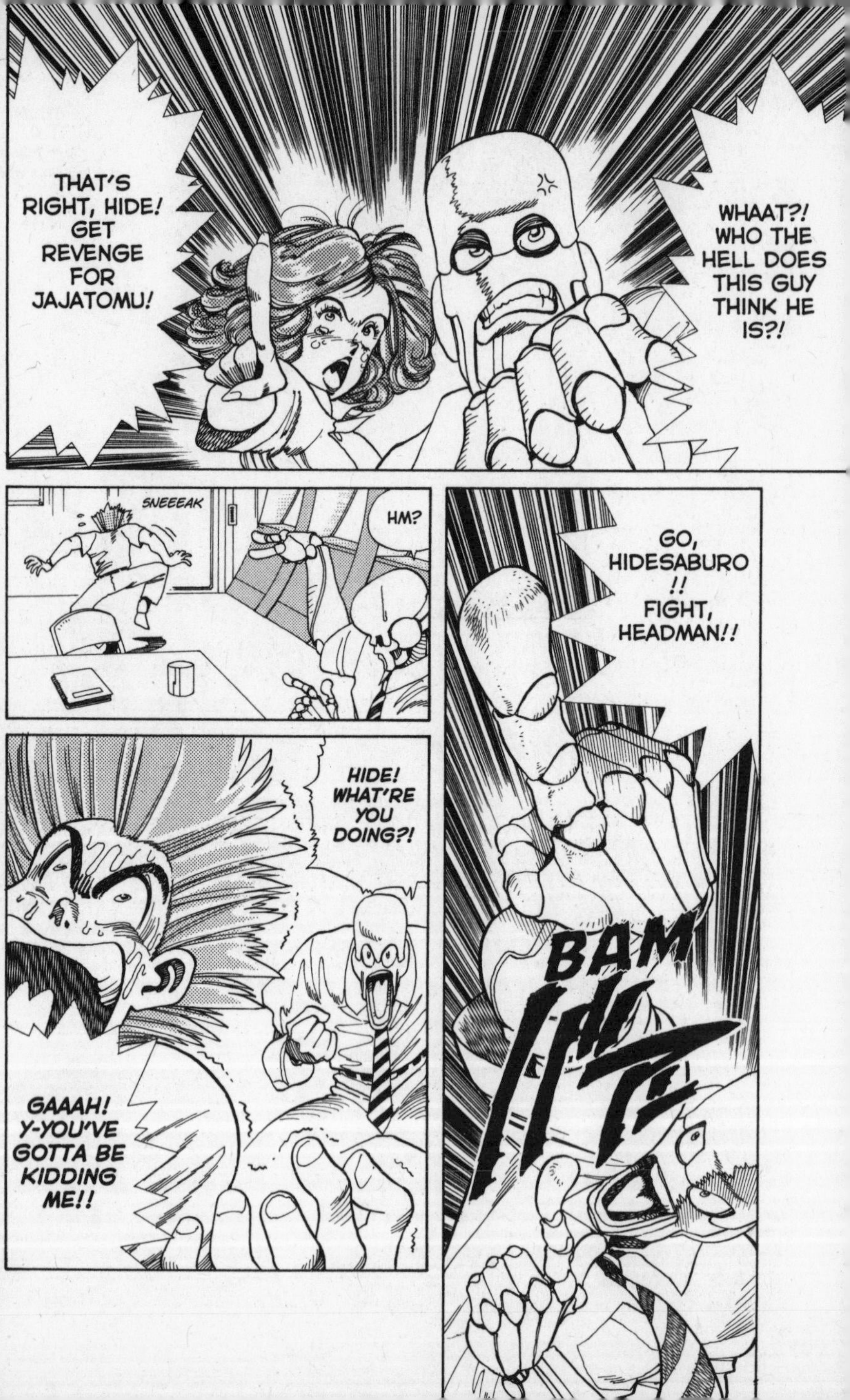
WHAAT?! WHO THE HELL DOES THIS GUY THINK HE IS?!
THAT'S RIGHT, HIDE! GET REVENGE FOR JAJATOMU!
GO, HIDESABURO !! FIGHT, HEADMAN!!
BAM
HM?
SNEEEAK
HIDE! WHAT'RE YOU DOING?!
GAAAH! Y-YOU'VE GOTTA BE KIDDING ME!!

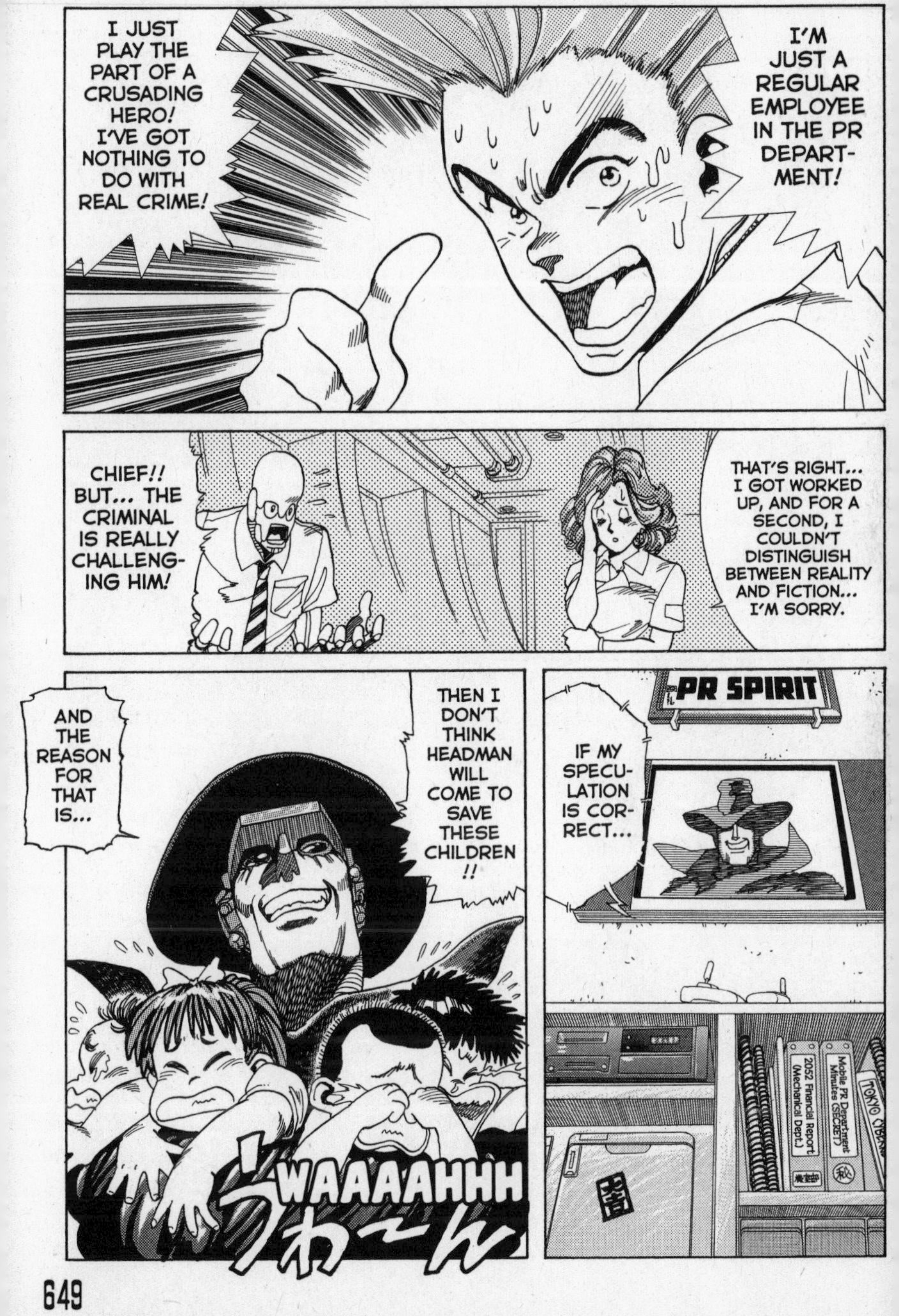
I'M JUST A REGULAR EMPLOYEE IN THE PR DEPARTMENT!
I JUST PLAY THE PART OF A CRUSADING HERO! I'VE GOT NOTHING TO DO WITH REAL CRIME!
THAT'S RIGHT... I GOT WORKED UP, AND FOR A SECOND, I COULDN'T DISTINGUISH BETWEEN REALITY AND FICTION... I'M SORRY.
CHIEF!! BUT... THE CRIMINAL IS REALLY CHALLENGING HIM!
PR SPIRIT
IF MY SPECULATION IS CORRECT...
Mobile PR Department Minutes (SECRET)
2052 Financial Report (Mechanical Dept.)
THEN I DON'T THINK HEADMAN WILL COME TO SAVE THESE CHILDREN!!
AND THE REASON FOR THAT IS...
WAAAAAHHH
うわ〜ん

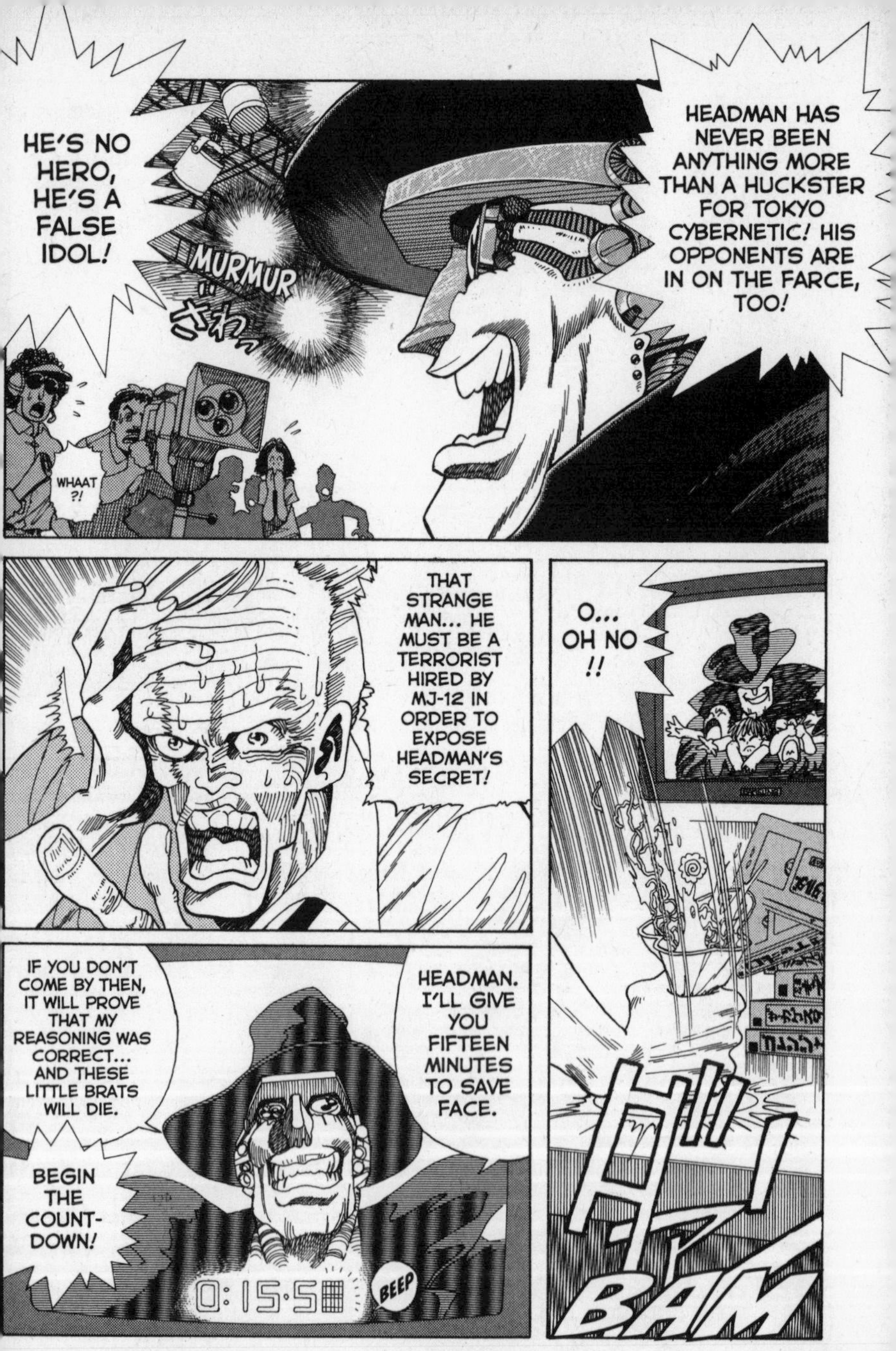
HEADMAN HAS NEVER BEEN ANYTHING MORE THAN A HUCKSTER FOR TOKYO CYBERNETIC! HIS OPPONENTS ARE IN ON THE FARCE, TOO!
HE'S NO HERO, HE'S A FALSE IDOL!
MURMUR
ざわっ
WHAAT ?!
O... OH NO !!
BAM
THAT STRANGE MAN... HE MUST BE A TERRORIST HIRED BY MJ-12 IN ORDER TO EXPOSE HEADMAN'S SECRET!
HEADMAN. I'LL GIVE YOU FIFTEEN MINUTES TO SAVE FACE.
IF YOU DON'T COME BY THEN, IT WILL PROVE THAT MY REASONING WAS CORRECT... AND THESE LITTLE BRATS WILL DIE.
BEGIN THE COUNT-DOWN!
BEEP

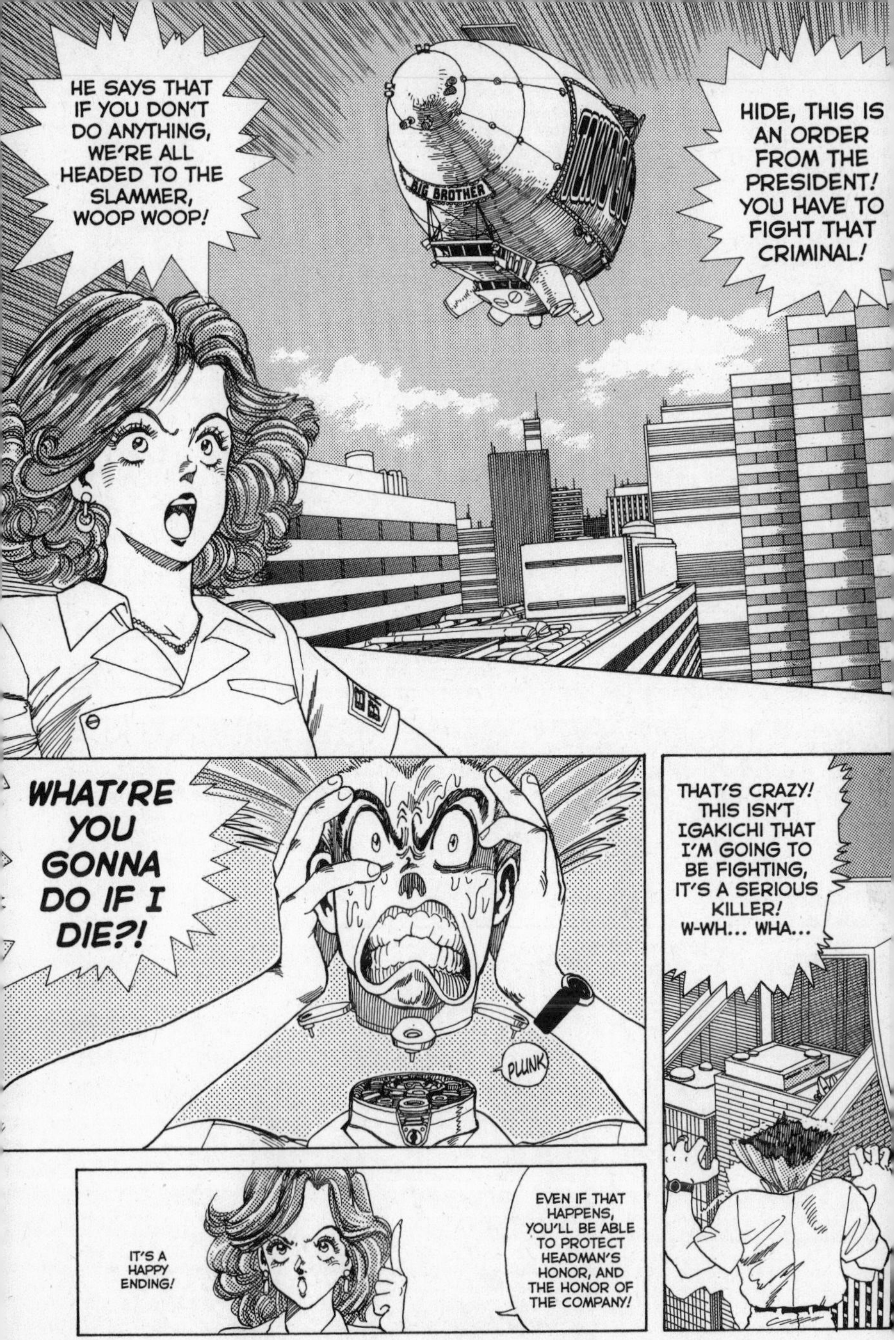
BIG BROTHER
HIDE, THIS IS AN ORDER FROM THE PRESIDENT! YOU HAVE TO FIGHT THAT CRIMINAL!
HE SAYS THAT IF YOU DON'T DO ANYTHING, WE'RE ALL HEADED TO THE SLAMMER, WOOP WOOP!
THAT'S CRAZY! THIS ISN'T IGAKICHI THAT I'M GOING TO BE FIGHTING, IT'S A SERIOUS KILLER! W-WH... WHA...
WHAT'RE YOU GONNA DO IF I DIE?!
PLUNK
EVEN IF THAT HAPPENS, YOU'LL BE ABLE TO PROTECT HEADMAN'S HONOR, AND THE HONOR OF THE COMPANY!
IT'S A HAPPY ENDING!

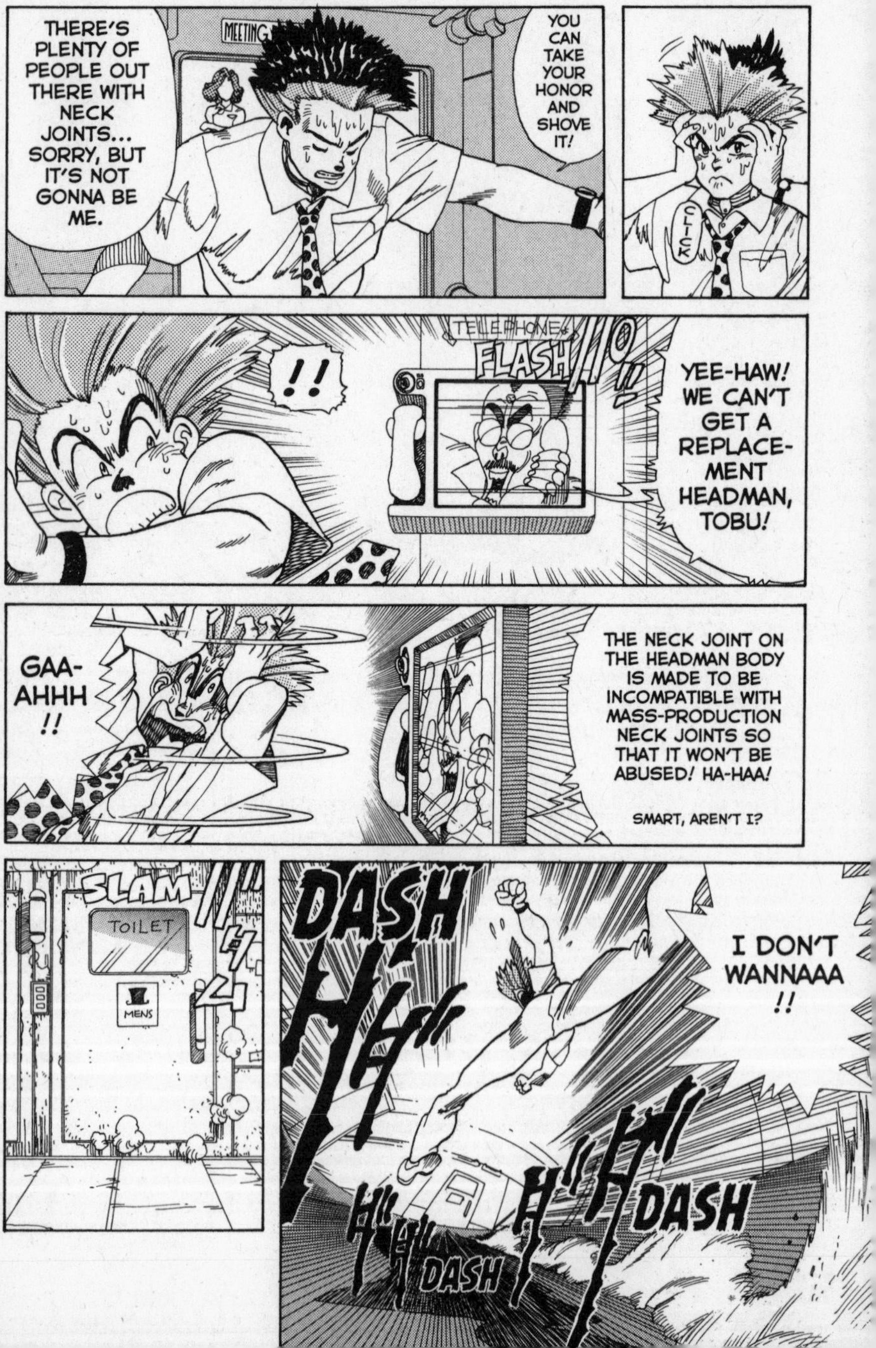
CLICK
YOU CAN TAKE YOUR HONOR AND SHOVE IT!
MEETING
THERE'S PLENTY OF PEOPLE OUT THERE WITH NECK JOINTS... SORRY, BUT IT'S NOT GONNA BE ME.
YEE-HAW! WE CAN'T GET A REPLACEMENT HEADMAN, TOBU!
TELEPHONE
FLASH
!!
THE NECK JOINT ON THE HEADMAN BODY IS MADE TO BE INCOMPATIBLE WITH MASS-PRODUCTION NECK JOINTS SO THAT IT WON'T BE ABUSED! HA-HAA!
SMART, AREN'T I?
GAA-AHHH !!
I DON'T WANNAAA !!
DASH
DASH
DASH
SLAM
TOILET
MENS

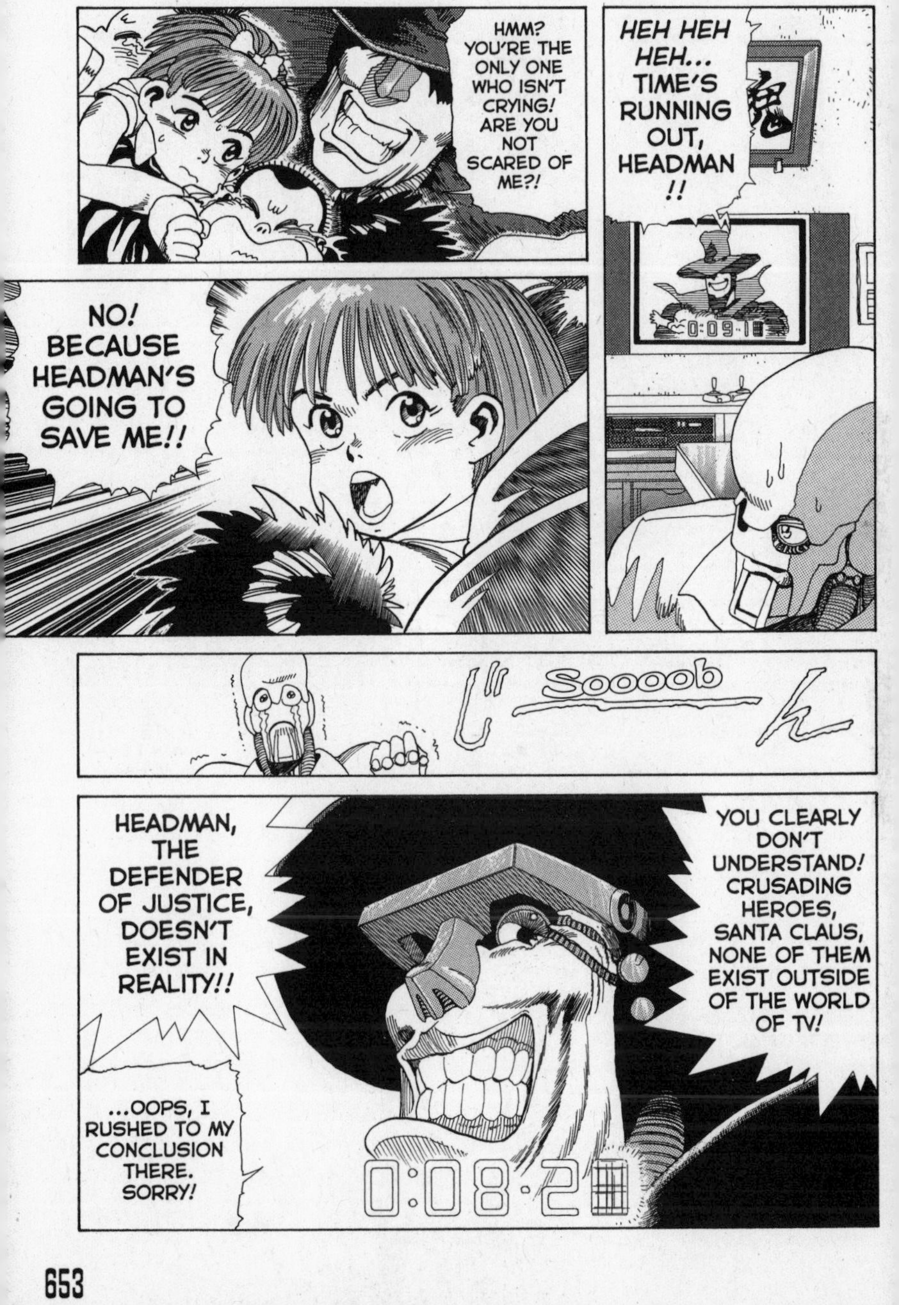
HEH HEH HEH... TIME'S RUNNING OUT, HEADMAN!!
HMM? YOU'RE THE ONLY ONE WHO ISN'T CRYING! ARE YOU NOT SCARED OF ME?!
NO! BECAUSE HEADMAN'S GOING TO SAVE ME!!
Sooooob
YOU CLEARLY DON'T UNDERSTAND! CRUSADING HEROES, SANTA CLAUS, NONE OF THEM EXIST OUTSIDE OF THE WORLD OF TV!
HEADMAN, THE DEFENDER OF JUSTICE, DOESN'T EXIST IN REALITY!!
...OOPS, I RUSHED TO MY CONCLUSION THERE. SORRY!

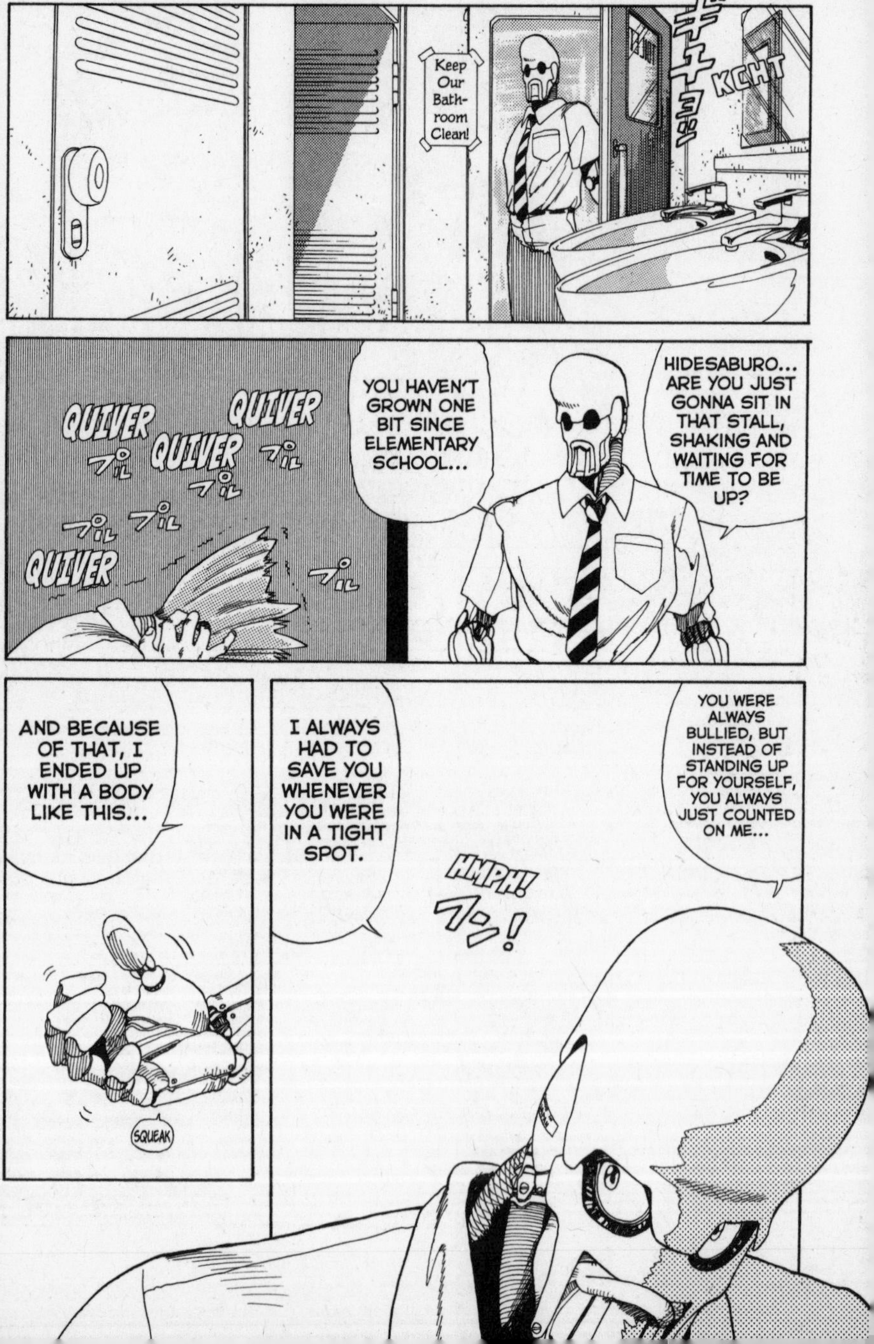
Keep Our Bathroom Clean!
KCHT
HIDESABURO... ARE YOU JUST GONNA SIT IN THAT STALL, SHAKING AND WAITING FOR TIME TO BE UP?
YOU HAVEN'T GROWN ONE BIT SINCE ELEMENTARY SCHOOL...
QUIVER
QUIVER
QUIVER
プル
プル
プル
プル
プル
プル
YOU WERE ALWAYS BULLIED, BUT INSTEAD OF STANDING UP FOR YOURSELF, YOU ALWAYS JUST COUNTED ON ME...
I ALWAYS HAD TO SAVE YOU WHENEVER YOU WERE IN A TIGHT SPOT.
HMPH!
フン!
AND BECAUSE OF THAT, I ENDED UP WITH A BODY LIKE THIS...
SQUEAK

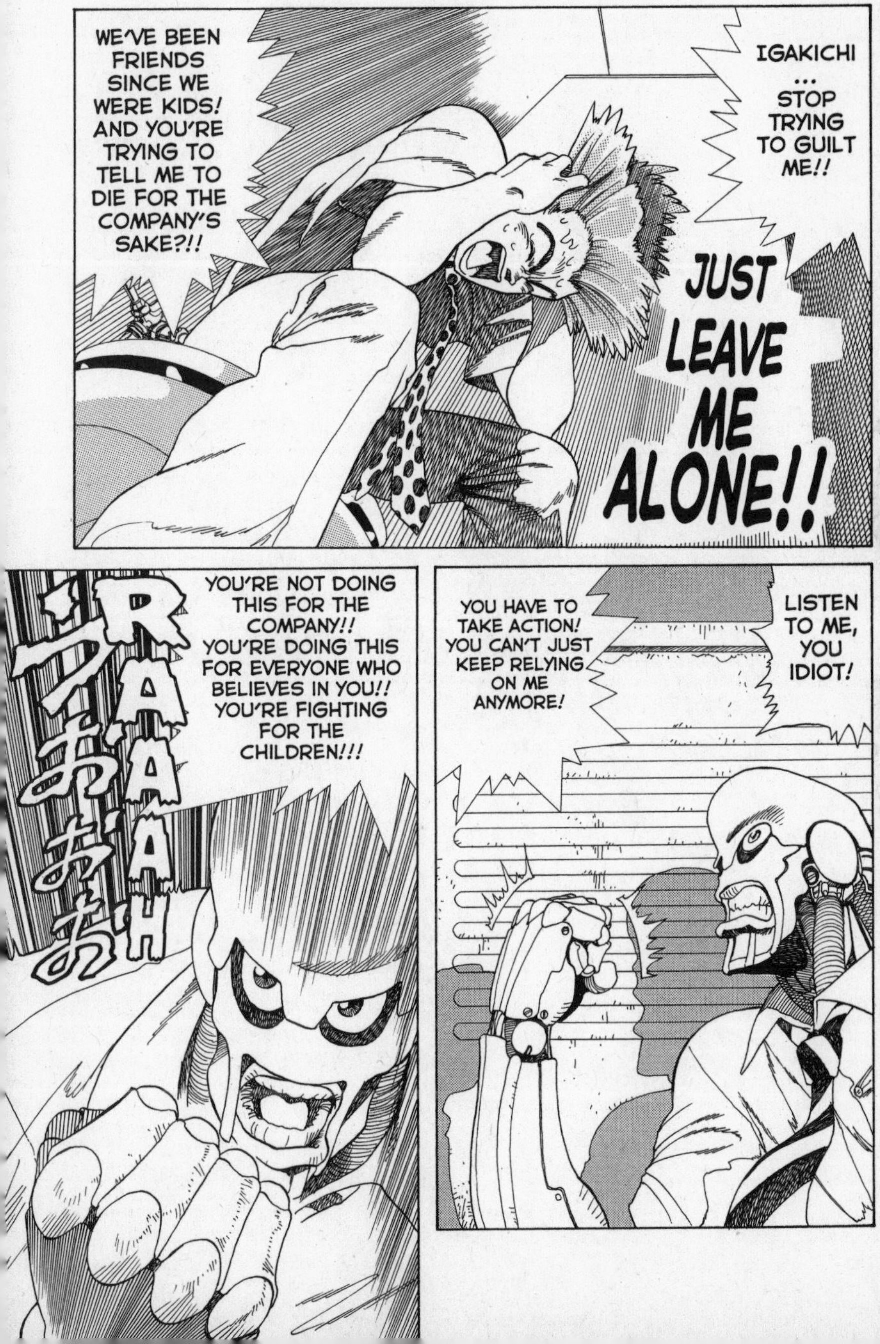
IGAKICHI ... STOP TRYING TO GUILT ME!!
WE'VE BEEN FRIENDS SINCE WE WERE KIDS! AND YOU'RE TRYING TO TELL ME TO DIE FOR THE COMPANY'S SAKE?!!
JUST LEAVE ME ALONE!!
LISTEN TO ME, YOU IDIOT!
YOU HAVE TO TAKE ACTION! YOU CAN'T JUST KEEP RELYING ON ME ANYMORE!
YOU'RE NOT DOING THIS FOR THE COMPANY!! YOU'RE DOING THIS FOR EVERYONE WHO BELIEVES IN YOU!! YOU'RE FIGHTING FOR THE CHILDREN!!!
RAAAH

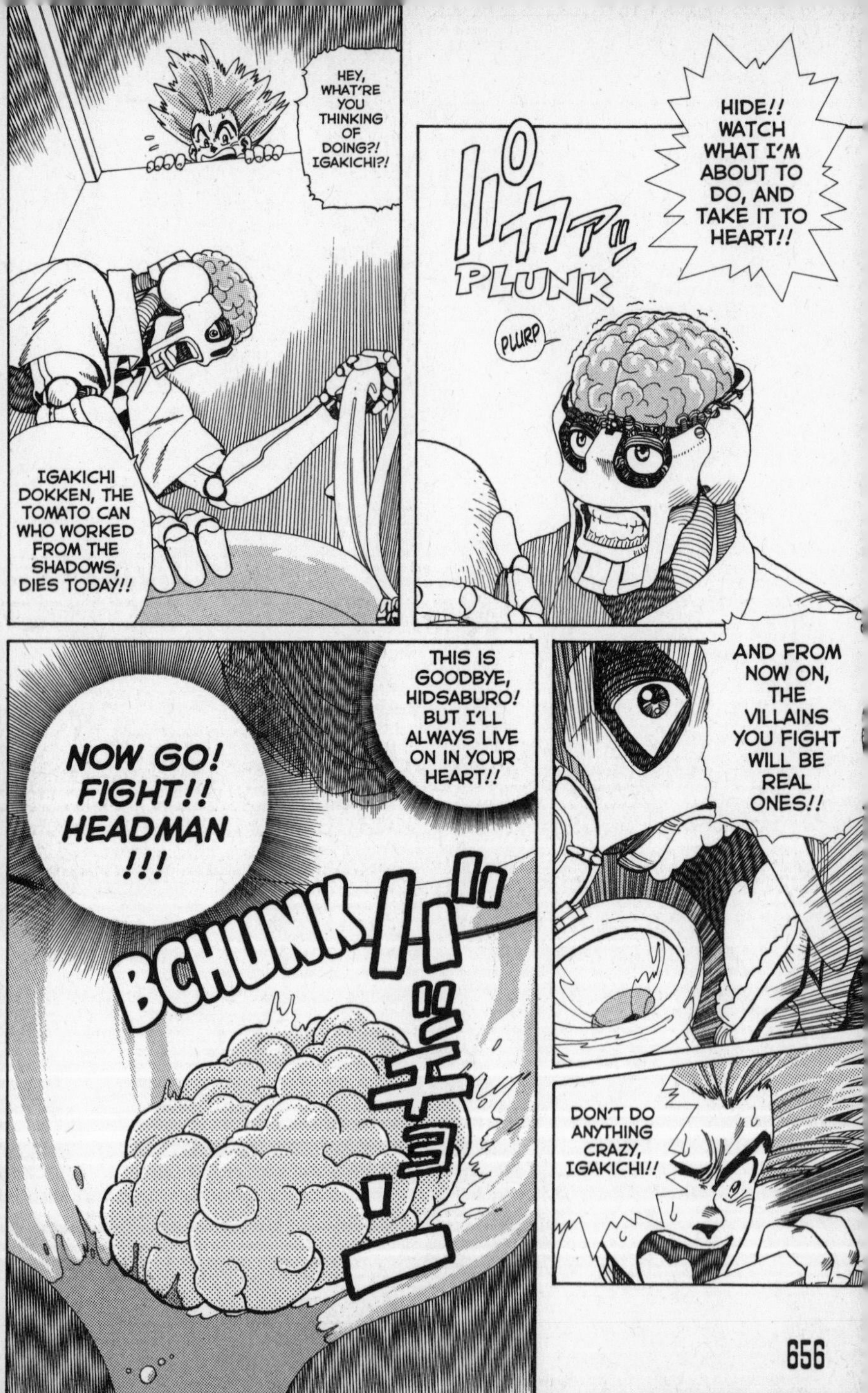
HIDE!! WATCH WHAT I'M ABOUT TO DO, AND TAKE IT TO HEART!!
PLUNK
PLURP
HEY, WHAT'RE YOU THINKING OF DOING?! IGAKICHI?!
IGAKICHI DOKKEN, THE TOMATO CAN WHO WORKED FROM THE SHADOWS, DIES TODAY!!
AND FROM NOW ON, THE VILLAINS YOU FIGHT WILL BE REAL ONES!!
DON'T DO ANYTHING CRAZY, IGAKICHI!!
THIS IS GOODBYE, HIDSABURO! BUT I'LL ALWAYS LIVE ON IN YOUR HEART!!
NOW GO! FIGHT!! HEADMAN !!!
BCHUNK

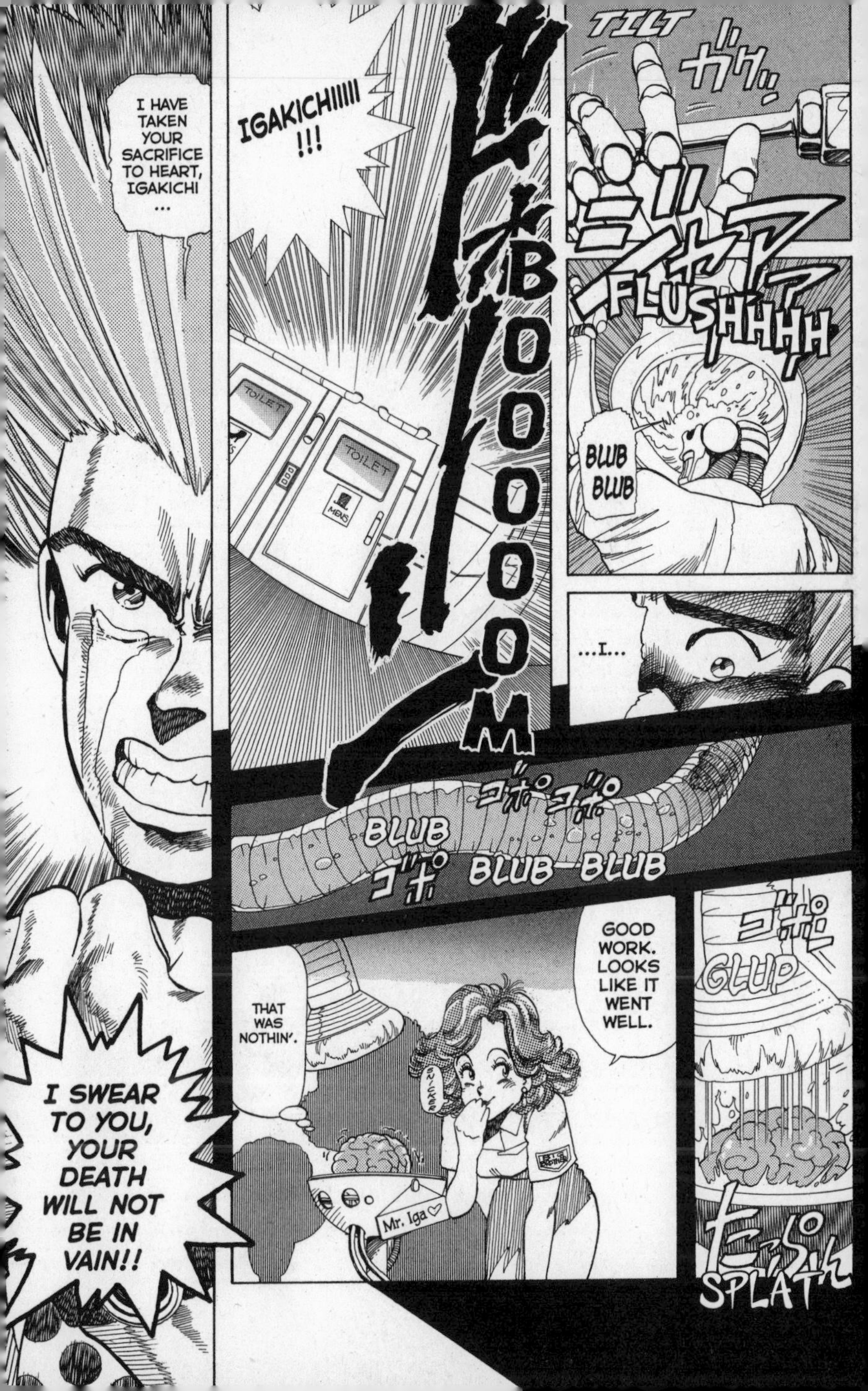
TILT
FLUSHHHH
BLUB BLUB
...I...
IGAKICHIIIIII!!!
BOOOOOOOM
TOILET
TOILET
MENS
BLUB BLUB BLUB
GLUP
SPLAT
GOOD WORK. LOOKS LIKE IT WENT WELL.
THAT WAS NOTHIN'.
SNICKER
Mr. Iga♡
I HAVE TAKEN YOUR SACRIFICE TO HEART, IGAKICHI...
I SWEAR TO YOU, YOUR DEATH WILL NOT BE IN VAIN!!

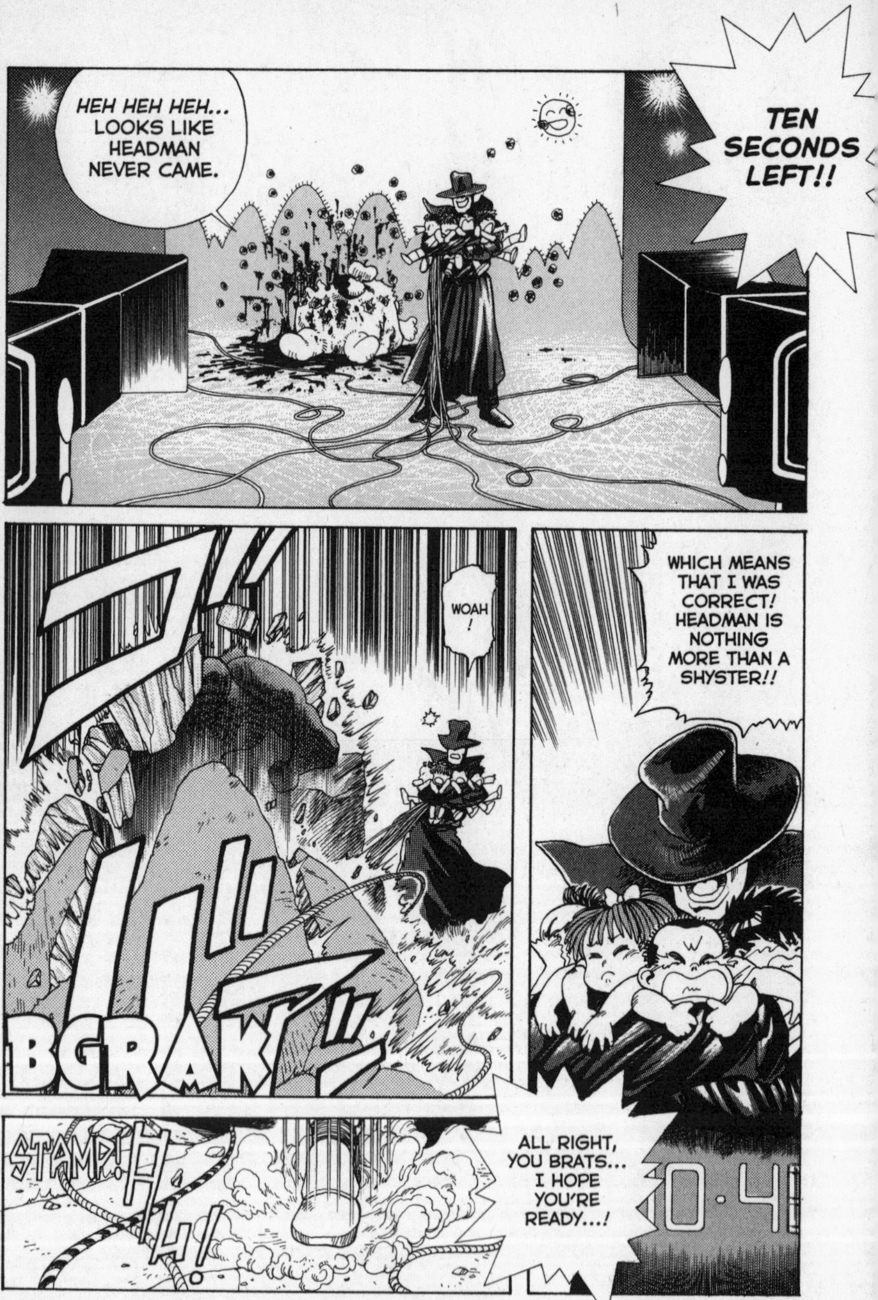
TEN SECONDS LEFT!!
HEH HEH HEH... LOOKS LIKE HEADMAN NEVER CAME.
WHICH MEANS THAT I WAS CORRECT! HEADMAN IS NOTHING MORE THAN A SHYSTER!!
ALL RIGHT, YOU BRATS... I HOPE YOU'RE READY...!
WOAH!
BGRAK
STAMP!

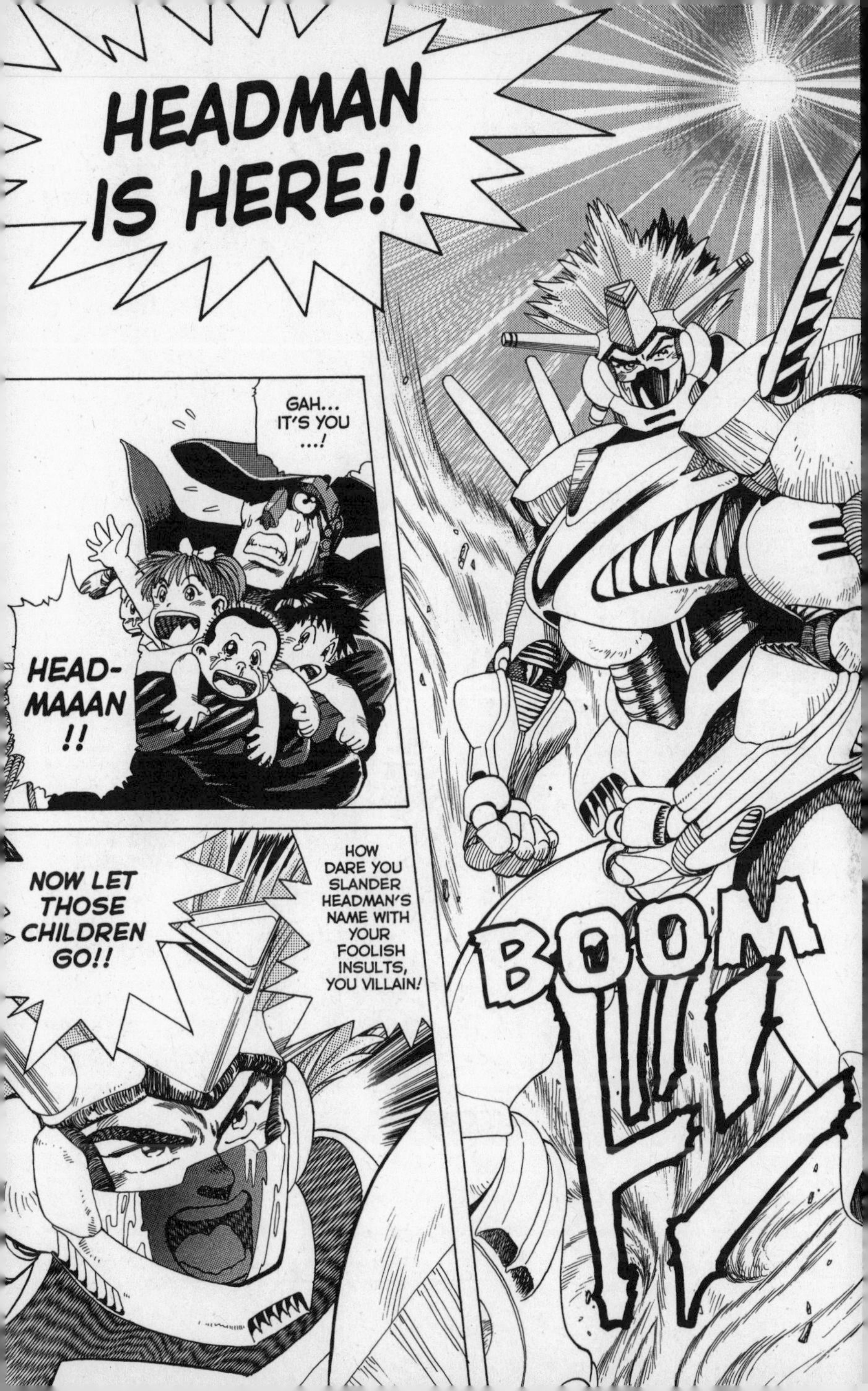
HEADMAN IS HERE!!
BOOM
GAH... IT'S YOU ...!
HEAD-MAAAN !!
HOW DARE YOU SLANDER HEADMAN'S NAME WITH YOUR FOOLISH INSULTS, YOU VILLAIN!
NOW LET THOSE CHILDREN GO!!

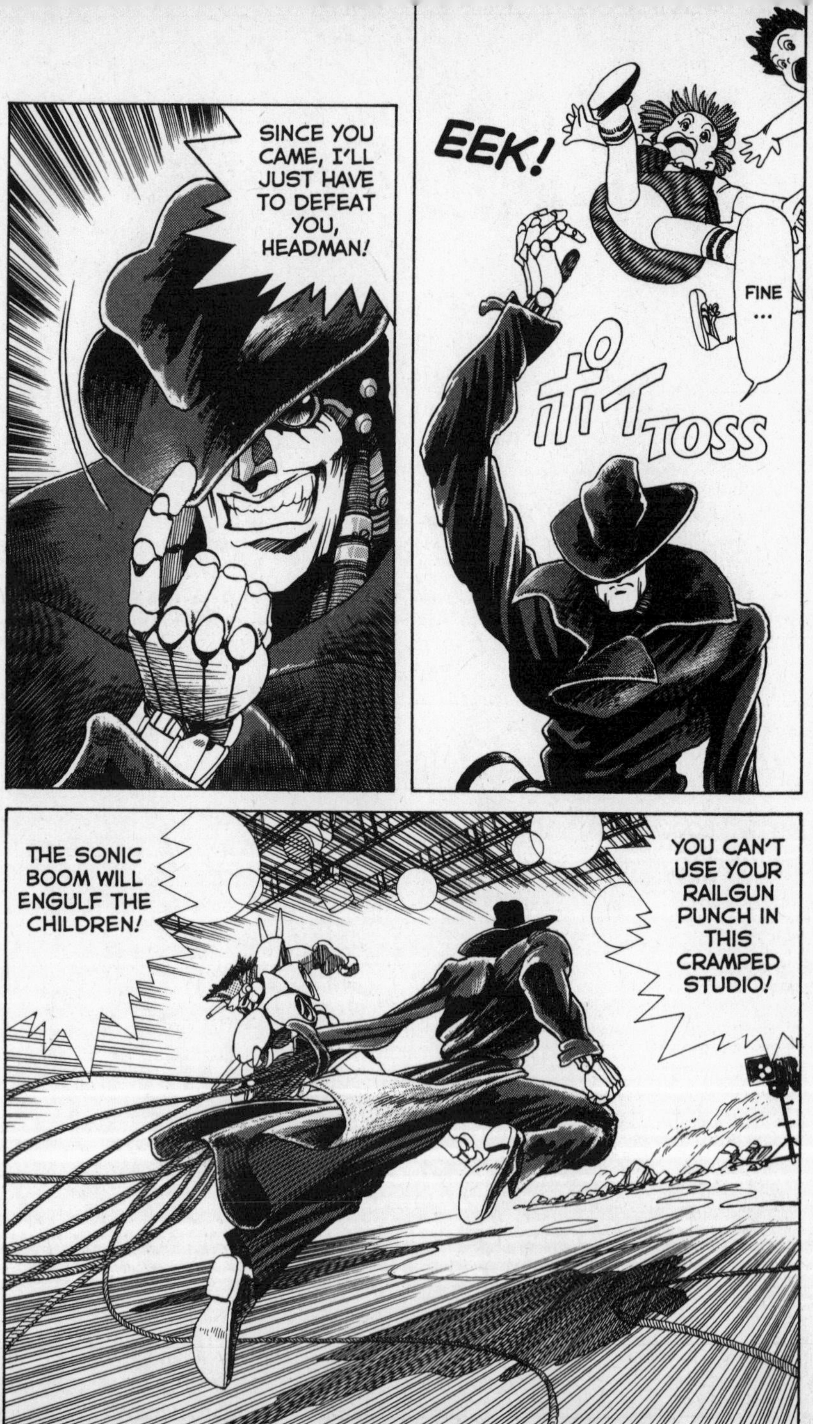
EEK!
FINE ...
ポイ TOSS
SINCE YOU CAME, I'LL JUST HAVE TO DEFEAT YOU, HEADMAN!
YOU CAN'T USE YOUR RAILGUN PUNCH IN THIS CRAMPED STUDIO!
THE SONIC BOOM WILL ENGULF THE CHILDREN!

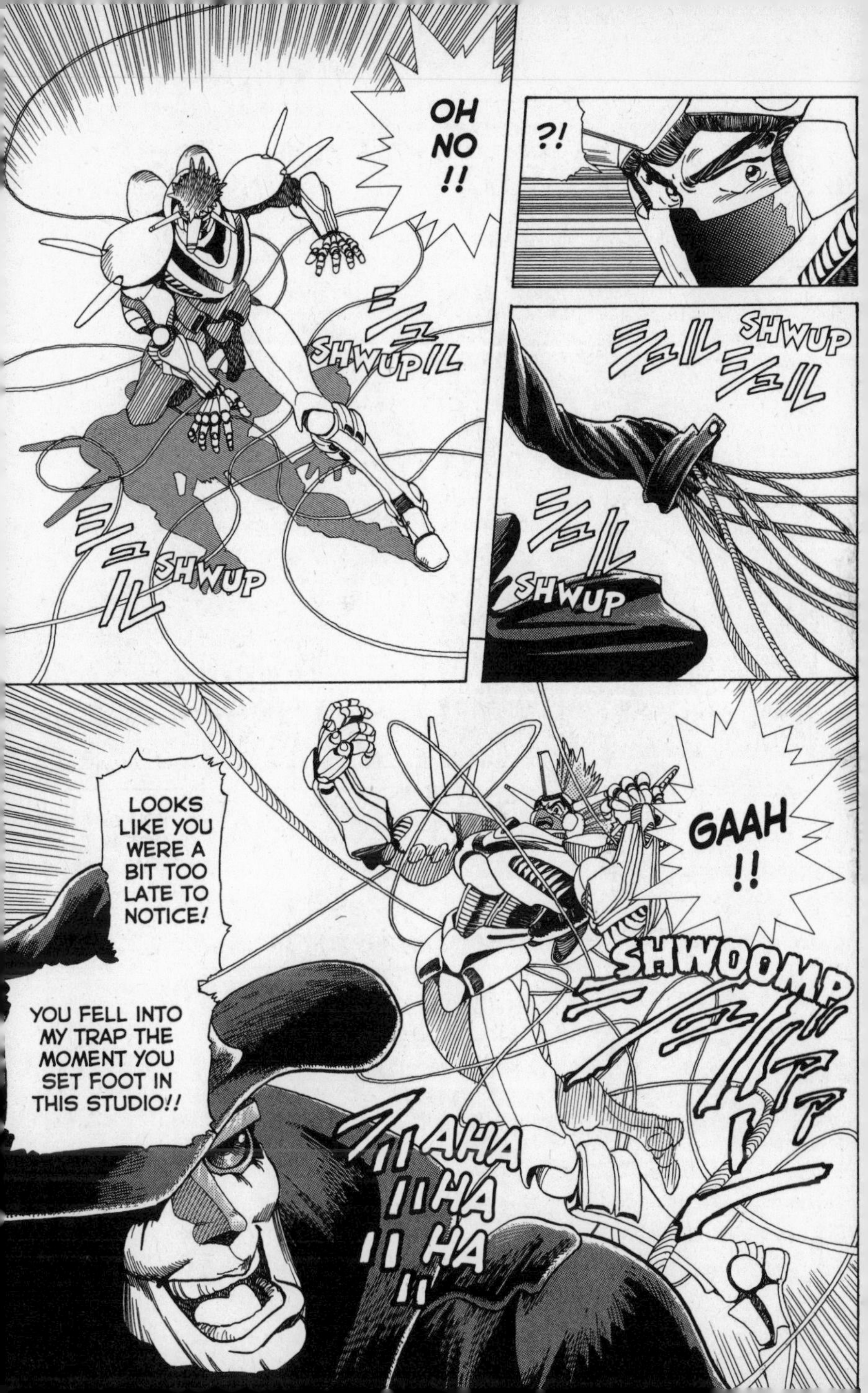
?!
シュル
SHWUP
シュル
シュル
SHWUP
OH NO!!
シュル
SHWUP
シュル
SHWUP
GAAH!!
SHWOOMP
AHA HA HA
LOOKS LIKE YOU WERE A BIT TOO LATE TO NOTICE!
YOU FELL INTO MY TRAP THE MOMENT YOU SET FOOT IN THIS STUDIO!!

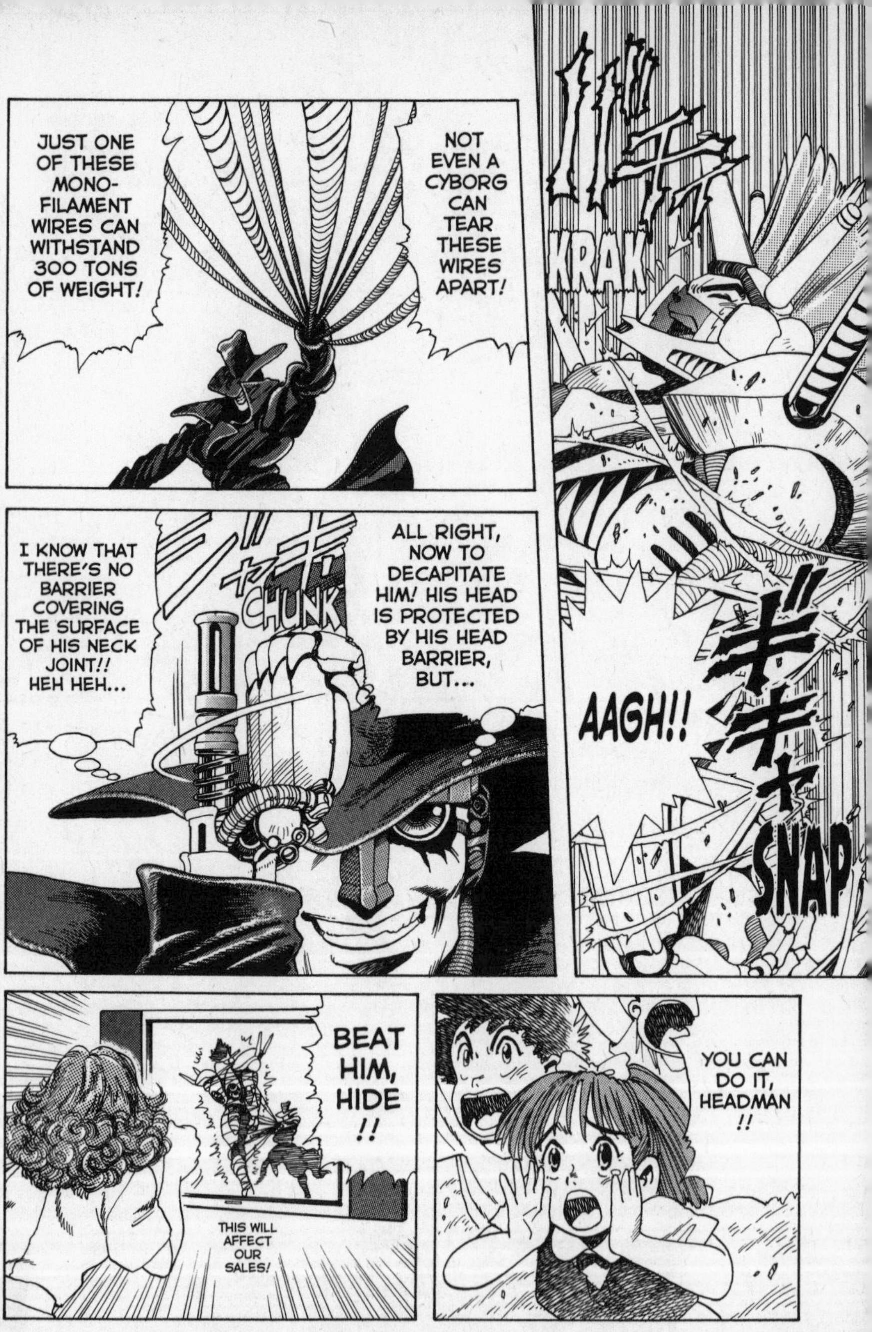
KRAK
AAGH!!
SNAP
NOT EVEN A CYBORG CAN TEAR THESE WIRES APART!
JUST ONE OF THESE MONO-FILAMENT WIRES CAN WITHSTAND 300 TONS OF WEIGHT!
ALL RIGHT, NOW TO DECAPITATE HIM! HIS HEAD IS PROTECTED BY HIS HEAD BARRIER, BUT...
CHUNK
I KNOW THAT THERE'S NO BARRIER COVERING THE SURFACE OF HIS NECK JOINT!! HEH HEH...
YOU CAN DO IT, HEADMAN!!
BEAT HIM, HIDE!!
THIS WILL AFFECT OUR SALES!

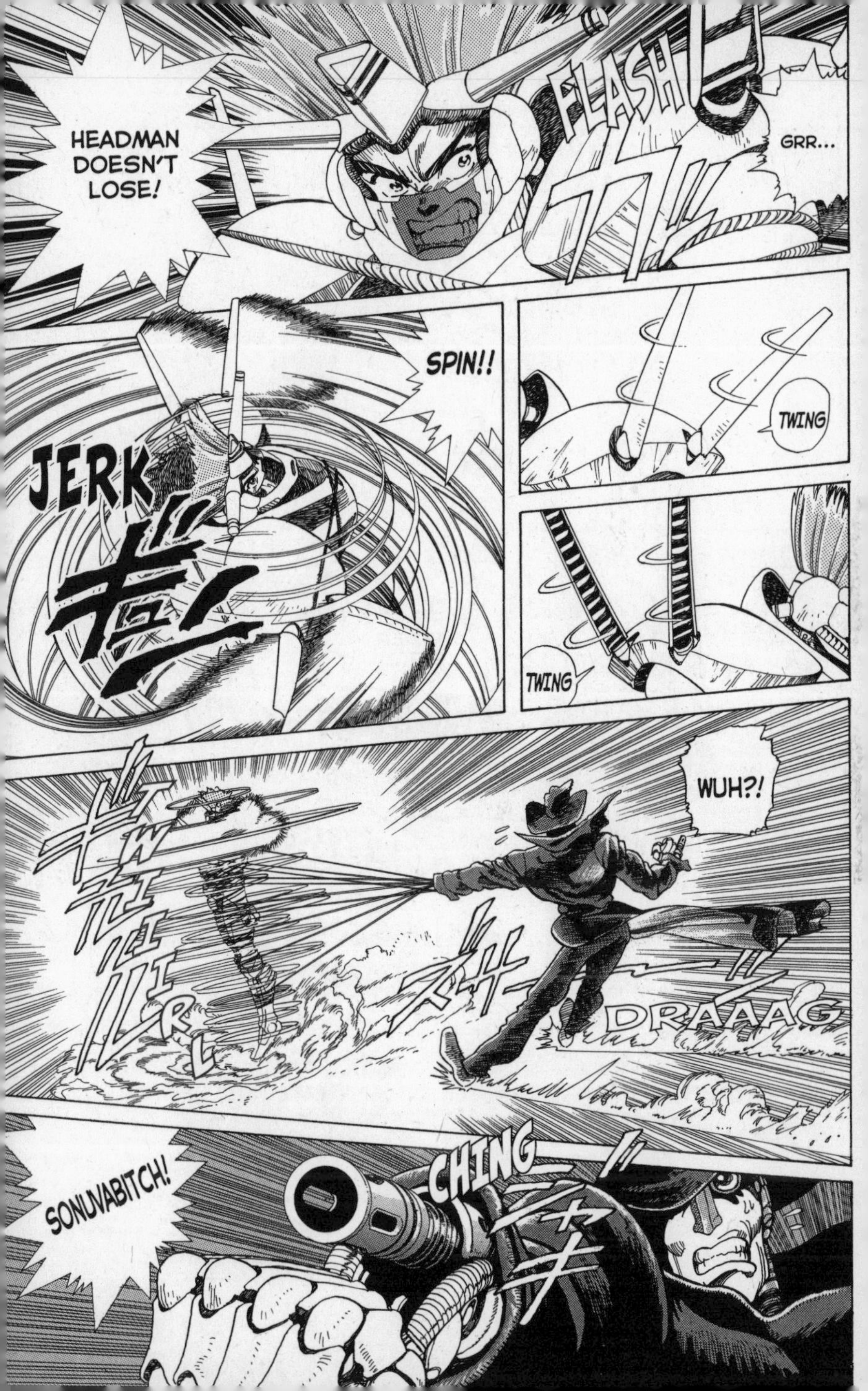
FLASH!!
GRR...
HEADMAN DOESN'T LOSE!
TWING
TWING
SPIN!!
JERK
WUH?!
DRAAAG
CHING!!
SONUVABITCH!

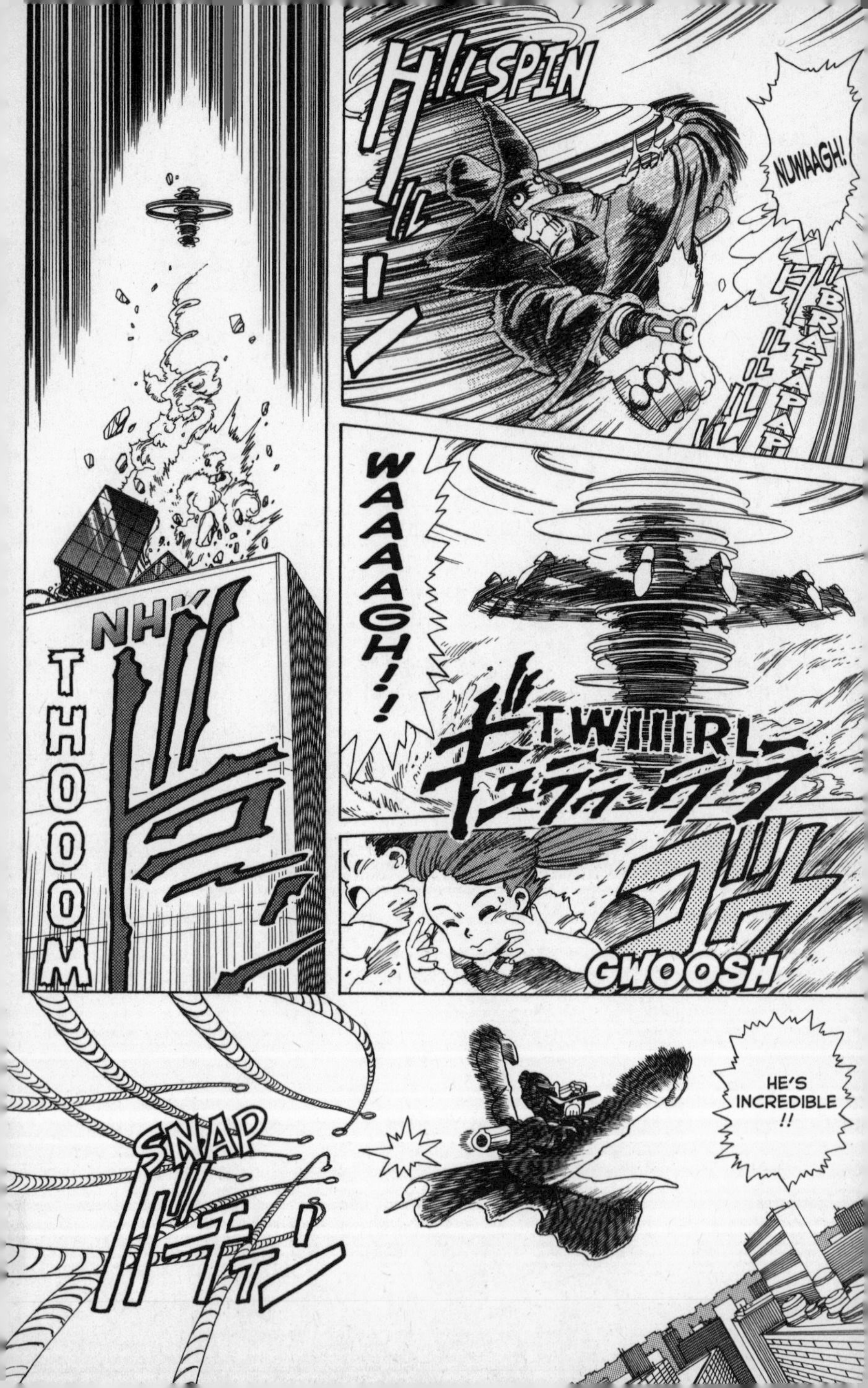
SPIN
NUWAAGH!
BRAPAPAP
WAAAAAGH!!
TWIIIRL
GWOOSH
NHK
THOOOOM
SNAP
HE'S INCREDIBLE !!

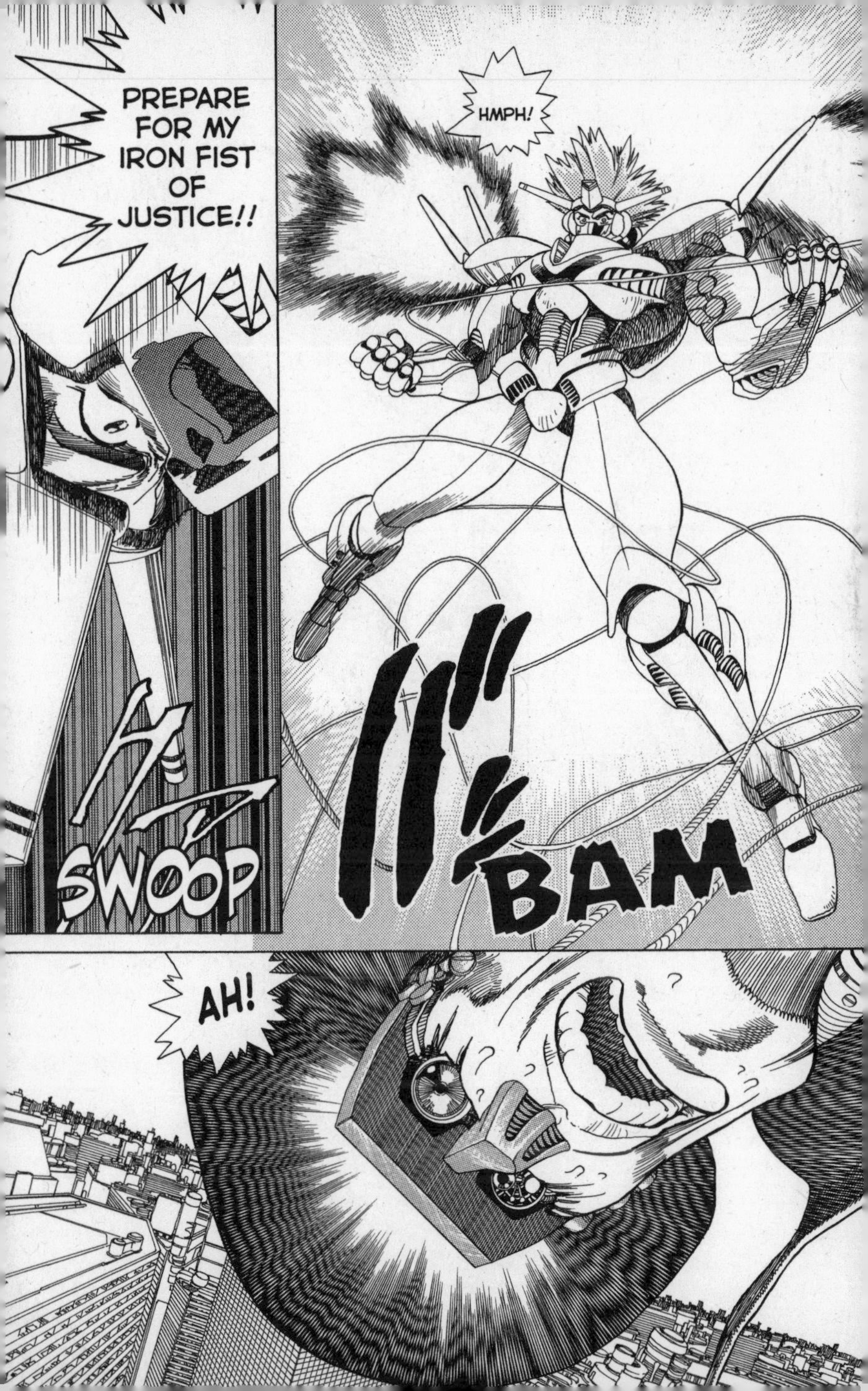
HMPH!
BAM
PREPARE FOR MY IRON FIST OF JUSTICE!!
SWOOP
AH!

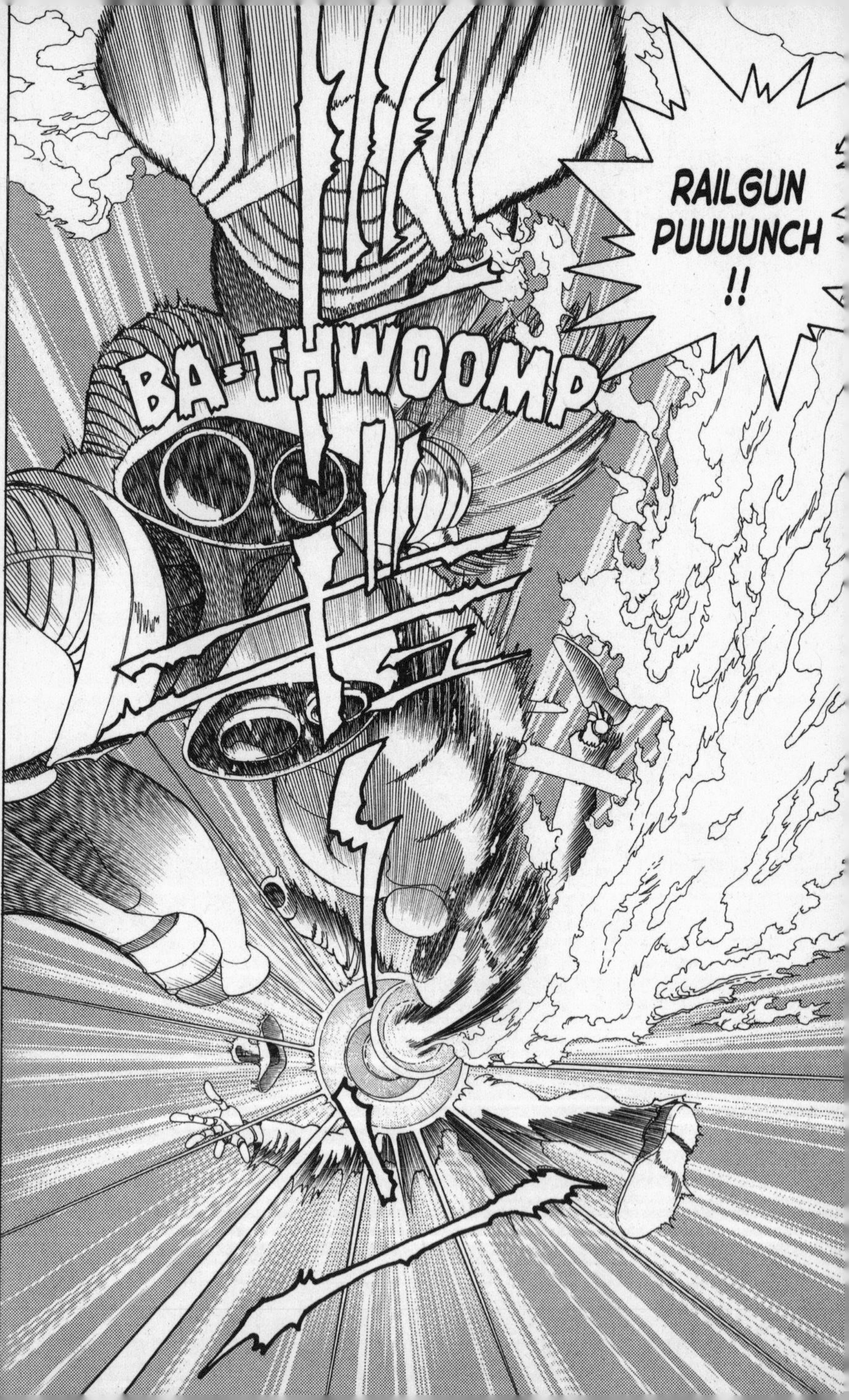
RAILGUN PUUUUNCH !!
BA-THWOOMP

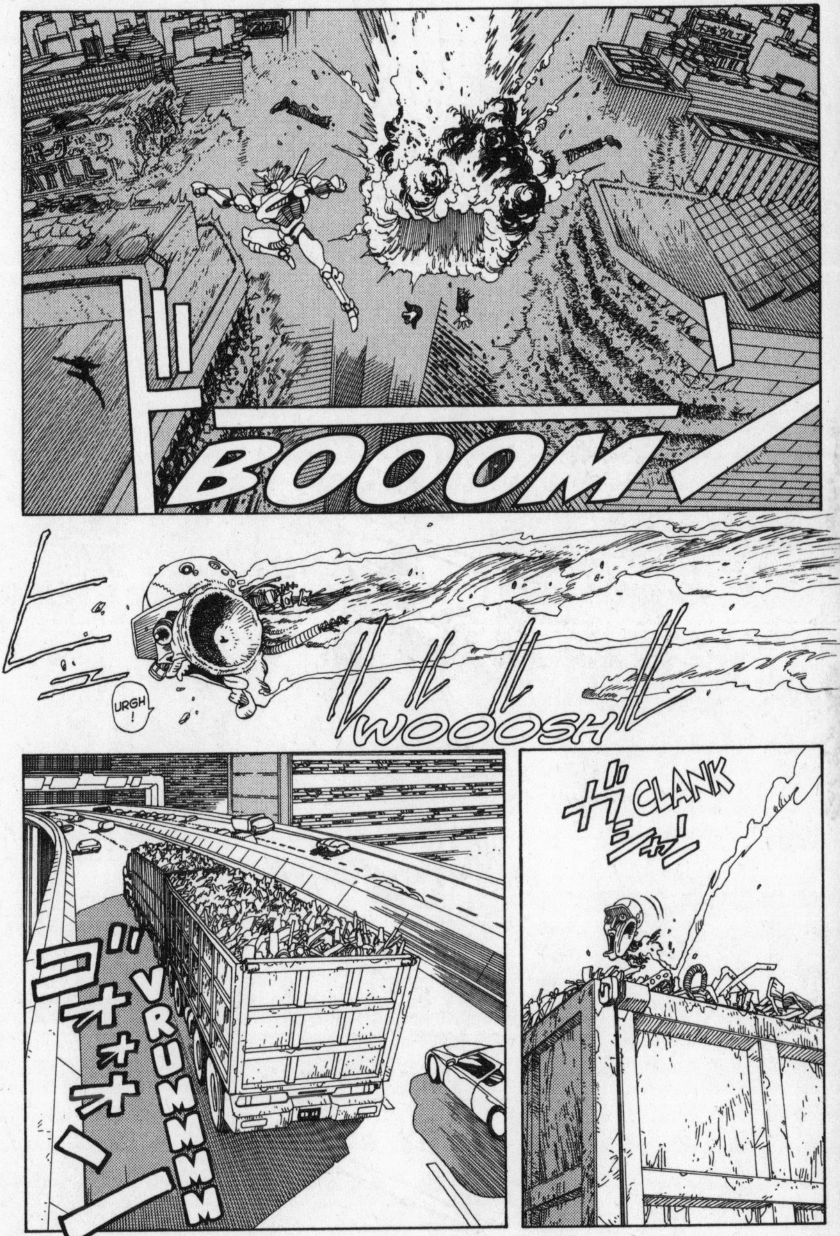
BOOOM
URGH!
WOOOSH
CLANK
VRUMMMM

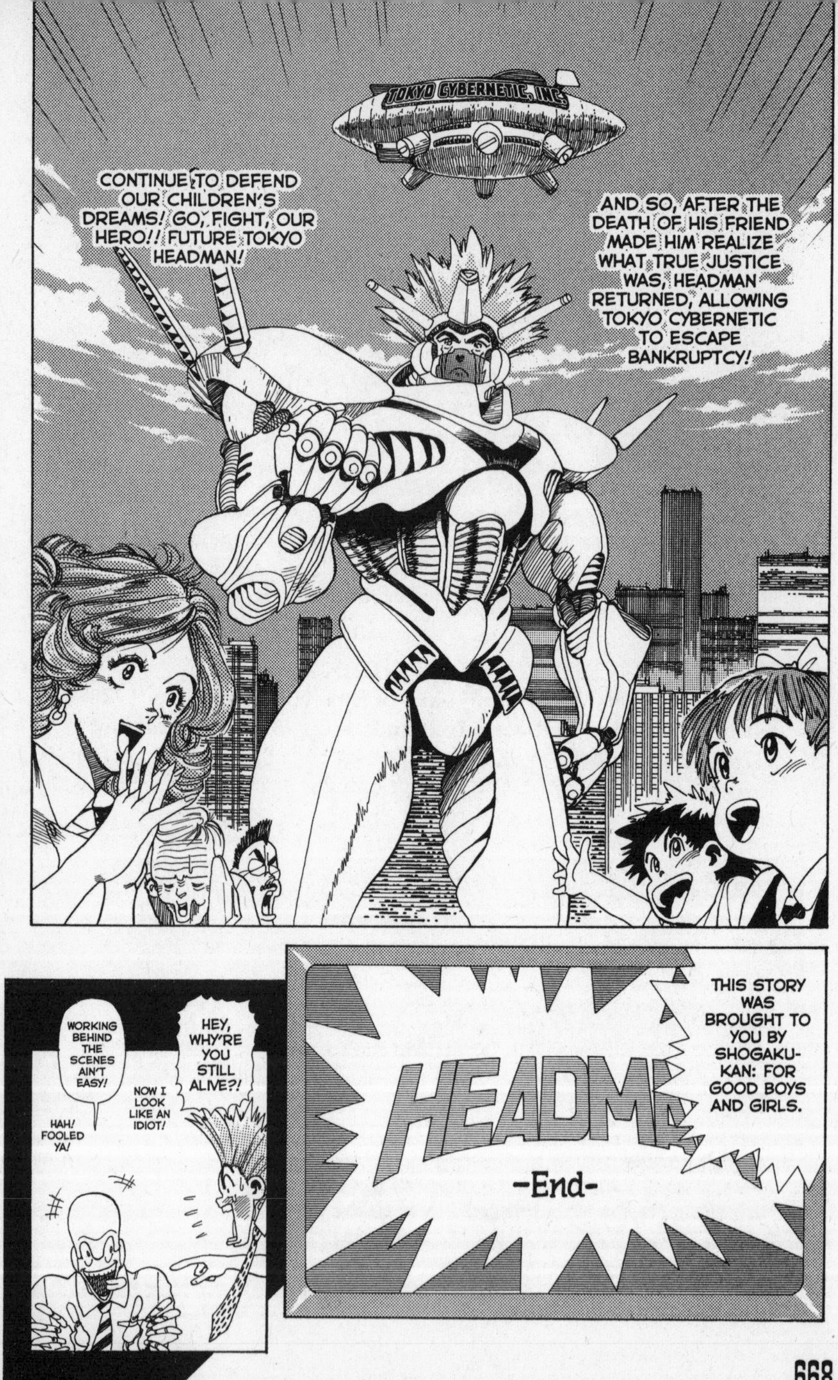
TOKYO CYBERNETIC, INC.
AND SO, AFTER THE DEATH OF HIS FRIEND MADE HIM REALIZE WHAT TRUE JUSTICE WAS, HEADMAN RETURNED, ALLOWING TOKYO CYBERNETIC TO ESCAPE BANKRUPTCY!
CONTINUE TO DEFEND OUR CHILDREN'S DREAMS! GO, FIGHT, OUR HERO!! FUTURE TOKYO HEADMAN!
THIS STORY WAS BROUGHT TO YOU BY SHOGAKU-KAN: FOR GOOD BOYS AND GIRLS.
HEADM
-End-
HEY, WHY'RE YOU STILL ALIVE?!
WORKING BEHIND THE SCENES AIN'T EASY!
NOW I LOOK LIKE AN IDIOT!
HAH! FOOLED YA!

"Planet of Depths" &
"Future Tokyo Headman"
Translation Notes

"Planet of Depths," page 597:
The original Japanese title is a play on words – "Kaiyousei" would normally be written with the characters for "Ocean Planet," but the title has replaced the first character with a homophone meaning "mysterious." I've tried to maintain this dual meaning in my title translation.

Otoko wa tsurai yo, page 630:
A reference to the long-running "Tora-san" series of films directed by Yoji Yamada and starring Kiyoshi Atsumi as Kuruma Torajiro (Tora-san), a traveling salesman. The series spanned 48 films, beginning in 1969 and ending in 1995, and was still running at the time this short was created.

We don't care what you think, page 630:
A reference to the "Truck-*yaro*" series of films, consisting of ten 1970s movies directed by Noribumi Suzuki and starring Bunta Sugawara and Kinya Aikawa as rough truck drivers. The subtitle of the first film in the series was Goiken Muyo, or "We Don't Care What You Think," a phrase also printed on the side of this truck.

Daidarabotchi, page 634:
The *daidarabotchi* is a giant yokai, or supernatural creature in Japanese mythology.

Susanoh, page 637:
Susanoo, the Shinto god of storms and the sea, is among the most well-known Shinto gods.

Heisei, page 643:
Heisei is the name of the current era of the Japanese calendar. It began with the accession of Emperor Akihito to the throne in 1989, which means 2013 is Heisei 25. Akihito would need remarkable longevity for the era to last all the way to Heisei 65.

Videotapes, page 644:

Jikuu Senshi Spielban, *Sekai Ninja Sen Jiraiya*, and *Kido Senshi Jiban* are all programs from the Japanese "Metal Hero" *tokusatsu* action hero series produced by Toei. The Laser Blade is a frequently-used weapon in the series. While Galivan is not a character in the Metal Hero series, "Gavan" and "Sharivan" both are. Lower on the page are more references to *tokusatsu* series names, such as *Kaiketsu Zubat*, *Choudenshi Bioman*, *Daitetsujin 17*, *Tetsujin Tiger Seven*, *Kyodye*, *Barom 1*, *Lion-Maru*, *Akumaizer 3*, and *Henshin Ninja Arashi*.

With Mother, page 646:

With Mother (*Okaasan to Issho*) is a famous, long-running Japanese children's television program. One of its best known segments during the 1980s and early 1990s was "Niko Niko Pun," which featured characters named Piccolo, Jajamaru, and Porori.

Videotapes, page 650:

Robot Keiji, *Majin Hunter Mitsurugi*, *Ninja Captor*, *The Kagestar*, and *Goranger* are all 1970s tokusatsu action TV programs.

A Kodansha Comics Trade Paperback Original.

Published in the United States by Kodansha Comics, an imprint of
Kodansha USA Publishing, LLC, New York.

Publication rights for this English edition arranged through
Kodansha Ltd., Tokyo.

First published in Japan in 2011 by Kodansha Ltd., Tokyo, as
Gunnm Last Order NEW EDITION, volumes 3 and 4.

ISBN 978-1-61262-292-7

Printed in the United States of America.

www.kodanshacomics.com

9 8 7 6 5 4 3 2 1

Battle Angel Alita: Last Order
Translation: Lillian Olsen & David Ury
Adaptation: Fred Burke
Touch-up & lettering: Susan Daigle-Leach
Additional translation, adaptation & lettering: Ben Applegate

"Planet of the Depths" & "Future Tokyo Headman"
Translation: Ko Ransom
Lettering: Bobby Timony

SORRY. THIS IS THE *END* OF THE BOOK.

This Japanese manga is presented in its original right-to-left format.

That means you'll need to turn this book over and start from the other side.

Authentic manga is read the traditional Japanese way—from right to left, exactly the *opposite* of how American books are read. It's easy once you get the hang of it: Just go to the other end of the book, and read each page—and each panel—from the right side to the left side, starting at the top right. Now you're reading manga as it was meant to be!